Step 2 - Practice

Making it easy to learn new things!

ORION gives you feedback on your performance, and you pick where to practice or study.

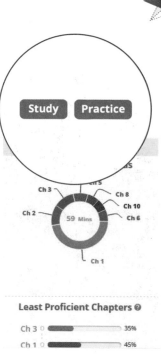

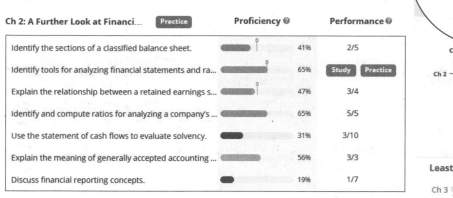

Ch 2: A Further Look at Financi... [Practice]	Proficiency	Performance
Identify the sections of a classified balance sheet.	41%	2/5
Identify tools for analyzing financial statements and ra...	65%	[Study] [Practice]
Explain the relationship between a retained earnings s...	47%	3/4
Identify and compute ratios for analyzing a company's ...	65%	5/5
Use the statement of cash flows to evaluate solvency.	31%	3/10
Explain the meaning of generally accepted accounting ...	56%	3/3
Discuss financial reporting concepts.	19%	1/7

Least Proficient Chapters

| Ch 3 | 35% |
| Ch 1 | 45% |

Step 3 - Maintain

Making it easy to remember everything you learn!

ORION provides a number of views into your overall proficiency so you can quickly review the things you might have forgotten before a quiz or exam.

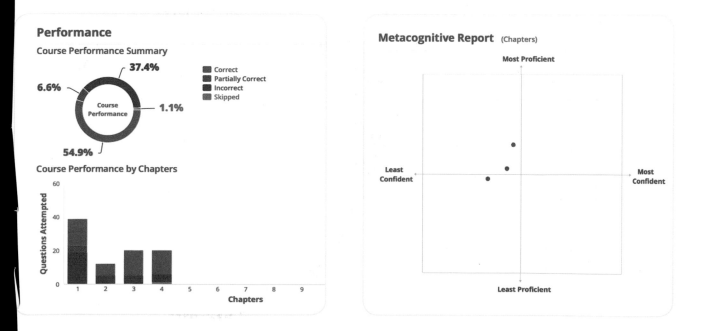

Performance

Course Performance Summary

- 37.4%
- 6.6%
- 1.1%
- 54.9%

Course Performance

■ Correct
■ Partially Correct
■ Incorrect
■ Skipped

Course Performance by Chapters

Metacognitive Report (Chapters)

Most Proficient

Least Confident — Most Confident

Least Proficient

MANAGERIAL ACCOUNTING

TOOLS FOR BUSINESS DECISION-MAKING

Fourth Canadian Edition

Jerry J. Weygandt Ph.D., CPA
Arthur Andersen Alumni Emeritus Professor of Accounting
University of Wisconsin—Madison
Madison, Wisconsin

Paul D. Kimmel Ph.D., CPA
Associate Professor of Accounting
University of Wisconsin—Milwaukee
Milwaukee, Wisconsin

Donald E. Kieso Ph.D., CPA
KPMG Emeritus Professor of Accounting
Northern Illinois University
DeKalb, Illinois

Ibrahim M. Aly Ph.D.
Professor of Accounting
John Molson School of Business
Concordia University
Montreal, Quebec

Library and Archives Canada Cataloguing in Publication

Weygandt, Jerry J., author
    Managerial accounting : tools for business decision-making / Jerry J. Weygandt, Ph.D., CPA, Paul D. Kimmel, Ph.D., CPA, Donald E. Kieso, Ph.D., CPA, Ibrahim M. Aly, Ph.D. — Fourth Canadian edition.

Issued in print and electronic formats.
ISBN 978-1-118-85699-4 (bound).—ISBN 978-1-119-04807-7 (loose-leaf).--
ISBN 978-1-119-04808-4 (pdf)

    1. Managerial accounting—Textbooks. I. Kieso, Donald E., author II. Kimmel, Paul D., author III. Aly, Ibrahim M., author IV. Title.

HF5657.4.W49 2014   658.15'11   C2014-906823-9
                                                       C2014-906824-7

Production Credits
Acquisitions Editor: Zoë Craig
Vice President and Publisher: Veronica Visentin
Director of Marketing: Joan Lewis-Milne
Marketing Manager: Anita Osborne
Editorial Manager: Karen Staudinger
Developmental Editor: Daleara Jamasji Hirjikaka
Editorial Assistant: Maureen Lau
Cover and Interior Design: Joanna Vieira
Cover Image: Ralph Lee Hopkins, Lonely Planet Images, Getty
Production: Denise Showers, Senior Project Manager, Aptara Inc.
Typesetting: Aptara Inc.
Printing & Binding: Quad/Graphics

Printed and bound in the United States of America
2 3 4 5 QG 19 18 17 16

John Wiley & Sons Canada, Ltd.
5353 Dundas Street West, Suite 400
Toronto, ON, M9B 6H8 Canada

Visit our website at : www.wiley.ca

Your TEAM *FOR* SUCCESS in Accounting

Wiley is your partner in accounting education. We want to be the publisher you think of first when it comes to quality content, reliable technology, innovative resources, professional training, and unparalleled support for your accounting classroom.

Your Wiley Accounting Team for Success has three distinctive advantages that you won't find with any other publisher:

- Author commitment
- WileyPLUS
- Wiley Faculty Network

AUTHOR COMMITMENT
A Proven Author Team of Inspired Teachers

The Team for Success authors bring years of practical and academic experience, as well as their passion for teaching, to the development of each textbook that relates accounting concepts to real-world experiences.

The authors understand the mindset and time limitations of today's student. They demonstrate an ability to effectively deliver complex information so that it is clear and understandable while staying one step ahead of emerging global trends in business.

COLLABORATION. INNOVATION. EXPERIENCE.

After decades of success as outstanding educators, the authors of this book, who are part of the Wiley Accounting Team for Success, understand that teaching accounting goes beyond simply presenting data. The authors are truly effective because they know that teaching is about telling compelling stories in ways that make each concept come to life.

Through their textbooks, supplements, on-line learning tools, and classrooms, these authors have developed a comprehensive pedagogy that engages students in learning and faculty in teaching.

Many Ways in One Direction

Our **Team for Success** has developed a learning system that addresses every learning style. Each year brings new insights, feedback, ideas, and improvements on how to deliver the material to every student with a passion for the subject in a format that gives them the best chance to succeed. The key to the team's approach is in understanding that, just as there are many different ways to learn, there are also many different ways to teach.

WileyPLUS
WILEYPLUS
An Experienced Team of Support Professionals

The *WileyPLUS* account managers understand the time constraints of busy faculty who want to provide the best resources available to their students with minimal frustrations and planning time. They know how intimidating a new version of software can sometimes be, so they are sure to make the transition easy and painless. Account managers act as your personal contact and expert resource for training, course set-up, and shortcuts throughout the *WileyPLUS* experience. Your success as an educator directly correlates with student success, and that's our goal. The Wiley Accounting Team for Success truly strives for YOUR success! Partner with us today!

WILEY FACULTY NETWORK
A Team of Educators Dedicated to Your Professional Development

The Wiley Faculty Network (WFN) is a global group of seasoned accounting professionals who share best practices in teaching with their peers. Our Virtual Guest Lecture Series provides the opportunity you need for professional development in an on-line environment that is relevant, convenient, and collaborative. The quality of these seminars and workshops meets the strictest standards, so we are proud to offer valuable professional development credits to attendees who require these. With a number of faculty mentors in accounting, it's easy to find help with your most challenging curriculum questions—just ask our experts!

U.S. Edition

Jerry J. Weygandt, Ph.D., CPA, is the Arthur Andersen Alumni Emeritus Professor of Accounting at the University of Wisconsin—Madison. He holds a Ph.D. in accounting from the University of Illinois. Articles by Professor Weygandt have appeared in *Accounting Review, Journal of Accounting Research, Accounting Horizons, Journal of Accountancy*, and other academic and professional journals. Professor Weygandt is author of other accounting and financial reporting books and is a member of the American Accounting Association, the American Institute of Certified Public Accountants, and the Wisconsin Society of Certified Public Accountants. He has served on numerous committees of the American Accounting Association and as a member of the editorial board of *Accounting Review*; he has also served as President and Secretary-Treasurer of the American Accounting Association. In addition, he has been actively involved with the American Institute of Certified Public Accountants and has been a member of the Accounting Standards Executive Committee of that organization. He served on the FASB task force that examined the reporting issues related to accounting for income taxes and as a trustee of the Financial Accounting Foundation. Professor Weygandt has received the Chancellor's Award for Excellence in Teaching and the Beta Gamma Sigma Dean's Teaching Award. He is on the board of directors of M&I Bank of Southern Wisconsin. He is the recipient of the Wisconsin Institute of CPAs' Outstanding Educator's Award and the Lifetime Achievement Award. In 2001, he received the American Accounting Association's Outstanding Accounting Educator Award.

Paul D. Kimmel, Ph.D., CPA, received his bachelor's degree from the University of Minnesota and his doctorate in accounting from the University of Wisconsin. He is an Associate Professor at the University of Wisconsin—Milwaukee, and has public accounting experience with Deloitte & Touche. He was the recipient of the UWM School of Business Advisory Council Teaching Award, the Reggie Taite Excellence in Teaching Award, and a three-time winner of the Outstanding Teaching Assistant Award at the University of Wisconsin. He is also a recipient of the Elijah Watts Sells Award for Honorary Distinction for his results on the CPA exam. He is a member of the American Accounting Association and the Institute of Management Accountants and has published articles in *Accounting Review, Accounting Horizons, Advances in Management Accounting, Managerial Finance, Issues in Accounting Education*, and *Journal of Accounting Education*, as well as other journals. His research interests include accounting for financial instruments and innovation in accounting education. He has published papers and given numerous talks on incorporating critical thinking into accounting education, and helped prepare a catalogue of critical thinking resources for the Federated Schools of Accountancy.

Donald E. Kieso, Ph.D., CPA, received his bachelor's degree from Aurora University and his doctorate in accounting from the University of Illinois. He has served as chairman of the Department of Accountancy and is currently the KPMG Emeritus Professor of Accounting at Northern Illinois University. He has public accounting experience with Price Waterhouse & Co. and Arthur Andersen & Co. and research experience with the Research Division of the American Institute of Certified Public Accountants. He is a recipient of NIU's Teaching Excellence Award and four Golden Apple Teaching Awards. Professor Kieso is a member of the American Accounting Association, the American Institute of Certified Public Accountants, and the Illinois CPA Society. He has served as a member of the Board of Directors of the Illinois CPA Society, the AACSB's Accounting Accreditation Committees, the State of Illinois Comptroller's Commission, as Secretary-Treasurer of the Federation of Schools of Accountancy, and as Secretary-Treasurer of the American Accounting Association. Professor Kieso is currently serving on the Board of Trustees and Executive Committee of Aurora University, and is a member of various other boards. From 1989 to 1993, he served as a charter member of the national Accounting Education Change Commission. He is the recipient of the Outstanding Accounting Educator Award from the Illinois CPA Society, the FSA's Joseph A. Silvoso Award of Merit, the NIU Foundation's Humanitarian Award for Service to Higher Education, the Distinguished Service Award from the Illinois CPA Society, and in 2003 an honorary doctorate from Aurora University.

Canadian Edition

Ibrahim M. Aly, Ph.D., is a professor in the Department of Accountancy at the John Molson School of Business, Concordia University, where he has been on faculty since 1989. Professor Aly holds a Ph.D. and MBA (with distinction) in accounting from the University of North Texas, as well as an M.S. and B.Comm. in accounting with distinction from Cairo University, Egypt. Professor Aly has taught at a variety of universities in Egypt, Saudi Arabia, the United States, and Canada and he has developed and coordinated many accounting courses at both the undergraduate and graduate levels. He participated in the Symposium on Models of Accounting Education, sponsored by the Accounting Education Change Commission of the American Accounting Association. Throughout his many years of teaching, Professor Aly's method of instruction has consistently been met with high praise from his students. He won the College of Business Teaching Innovation Award for two consecutive years. Professor Aly has published in reputable refereed journals in the fields of managerial accounting, financial accounting, behavioural accounting, and accounting education. In addition, he has previously published a book on management accounting entitled *Readings in Management Accounting: New Rules for New Games in Manufacturing and Service Organizations*. He has presented his work at over 35 scholarly national and international conferences, and been chosen as the Department of Accountancy Research Professor. He has organized the department's luncheon presentations series and the Ph.D. visiting speaker series, both of which provide an indispensable academic service to graduate students and professors. Professor Aly has given numerous workshops and seminars on financial and managerial accounting.

ACKNOWLEDGEMENTS

I would like to express my appreciation to the many people who have contributed to the development of this textbook. I gratefully acknowledge the valuable suggestions that I received from instructors of managerial accounting, including users of the previous editions of the text. Their contribution significantly improved the content and pedagogy of the final product.

Reviewers

Margo Burtch, Seneca College

Leelah Dawson, Camosun College

Kathy Faber, Conestoga College

Rosalie Harms, University of Winnipeg

Margery Heuser, Okanagan College

David Hoffman, Seneca College

Winston Marcellin, George Brown College

Geoffrey Prince, Centennial College

Philip Thomas, Niagara College

Ancillary Authors and Contributors

Margo Burtch, Seneca College

Angela Davis, Booth University College

Robert Ducharme, University of Waterloo

Ilene Gilborn, Mount Royal University

Sandy Kizan, Athabasca University

Richard Michalski, McMaster University

Mary Oxner, St. Francis Xavier University

Laurie Sinclair, Mount Saint Vincent University

I would like to extend my sincere appreciation to the U.S. authors of this textbook for their willingness to share their work with me. They have advanced the discussion of management accounting from that established in traditional textbooks, which focused on "number-crunchers," to a more modern view of accountants as critical participants in the business decision-making process. The features of this book will help accounting students discover a reasonable balance between learning managerial accounting techniques and gaining essential skills and how to apply them when they enter the workforce.

My appreciation is also extended to CPA Canada for permission to use or adapt problems from past examinations.

I express my gratitude to the many fine people at John Wiley & Sons Canada who have professionally guided this text through the development and publication process. In particular, I acknowledge the publisher, Veronica Visentin, for her interest in and support of this fourth Canadian edition of the textbook. In addition, I extend my appreciation to Wiley Canada's editorial staff, who were terrific in guiding me through this challenging process, especially Zoë Craig, Acquisitions Editor; Deanna Durnford, Supplements Coordinator; Daleara Hirjikaka, Developmental Editor; Anita Osborne, Marketing Manager; Karen Staudinger, Editorial Manager; and Carolyn Wells, Vice-President, Digital & Business Solutions. I also extend my appreciation to all other members of the publishing team at John Wiley & Sons Canada who worked together to complete this project. The editorial expertise of Laurel Hyatt, Zofia Laubitz, Denise Showers, and Belle Wong is also very much appreciated.

Finally, special thanks and gratitude are extended to my family for their support and encouragement.

Suggestions and comments from users—instructors and students alike—will be appreciated.

Ibrahim Aly
Montreal, Quebec

What's New?

WileyPLUS with ORION

Available in WileyPLUS with Orion, an adaptive study and practice tool that helps students build proficiency in course topics. Up to 400 new, multiple-choice questions were written for each chapter.

Updated Content and Design

We scrutinized all chapter material to find new ways to engage students and help them learn accounting concepts. Up-to-date coverage and new discussions of important managerial accounting topics include Chapter 1, **sustainable business**, Chapter 7 **retain or replace equipment**, and Chapter 9, **total cost pricing**. Homework problems were updated in all chapters.

New learning objective modules join practice and textbook concepts. Most learning objectives now close with a DO IT! exercise and solution. The new learning objective modules help students practise their understanding before they move on to different topics in other learning objectives. The new learning objective approach motivates students and helps them make the best use of their time.

WileyPLUS Videos

Over 100 videos are available in WileyPLUS. The videos walk students through relevant homework problems and solutions, review important concepts, and explore topics in a real-world context.

Student Practice and Solutions

New practice opportunities with solutions are integrated throughout the textbook and WileyPLUS course. Each textbook chapter provides students with learning objective summaries, multiple-choice questions with answers, and both Comprehensive Do It! and Using the Decision Toolkit problems with solutions. Also, learning objectives in the textbook are followed by a Do It! exercise with an accompanying solution.

In WileyPLUS, selected brief exercises, Do It! exercises, and exercises are available for practice with each chapter. Where possible, questions are algorithmic, providing students with multiple opportunities for advanced practice.

Real World Context: Feature Stories and Comprehensive Problems

New feature stories apply chapter topics to new real-world company examples. Beginning in Chapter 1, we introduce **Current Designs**, a US-based kayak-making company with Canadian origins. We then follow up with a new decision-making problem in every chapter based on this real-world company. Each problem presents realistic managerial accounting situations that students must analyze to determine the best course of action. This problem is accompanied by a continuing Excel tutorial in each chapter. Throughout the chapters, the real-world insight boxes show how people in actual companies make decisions using accounting information. Answers to the critical thinking questions that follow each box are provided in the instructor's manual.

Comprehensive Homework Material with Excel

Each chapter concludes with revised Self-Test Questions, Brief Exercises, Do It! Review, Exercises, and Problems. Exercises and problems marked with a pencil icon help students practice business writing skills. Items marked with a handshake icon focus on accounting situations faced by service companies. An icon identifies Exercises and Problems that can be solved using Excel templates on the book's companion website and in WileyPLUS. The Waterways Continuing Problem uses the business activities of a fictional company, to help students apply managerial accounting topics to a realistic entrepreneurial situation. A continuing Excel tutorial is available at the end of each chapter with the Decision-Making at Current Designs problem.

More information about the fourth edition is available on the book's website at **www.wiley.com/go/managerialcanada**.

passion success
teaching
**collaboration
expertise**
collaboration
teamteaching
passion for teaching
success expertise
collaboration passion

team *for* success

Practice Made Simple

The Team for Success is focused on helping students get the most out of their accounting course by **making practice simple**. Both in the printed text and the online environment of *WileyPLUS*, new opportunities for self-guided practice allow students to check their knowledge of accounting concepts, skills, and problem-solving techniques as they receive individual feedback at the question, learning objective, and course level.

Personalized Practice

Based on cognitive science, **WileyPLUS with ORION** is a personalized, adaptive learning experience that gives students the practice they need to build proficiency on topics while using their study time most effectively. The adaptive engine is powered by hundreds of unique questions per chapter, giving students endless opportunities for practice throughout the course.

Streamlined Learning Objectives

Newly streamlined learning objectives help students make the best use of their time outside of class. Each learning objective contains a variety of practice and assessment questions, review material, and educational videos, so that no matter where students begin their work, the relevant resources and practice are readily accessible.

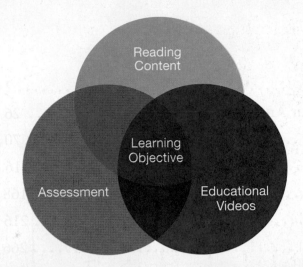

Review and Practice

Students have more opportunities for self-guided practice in the text and in WileyPLUS.

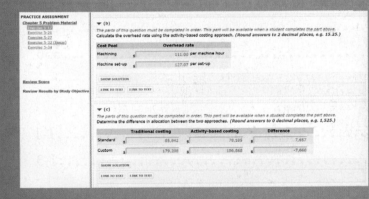

The text includes worked out solutions to select questions, exercises, and problems, plus:

- Learning Objectives Review
- Glossary Review
- Practice Multiple-Choice Questions
- Do It! Exercises and Solutions
- Comprehensive Do It! Problem and Solutions
- Using the Decision Toolkit Problems and Solutions

WileyPLUS includes updated practice assignments featuring several Do ITs, Brief Exercises, and Exercises, giving students the opportunity to check their work or see the answer and solution after their final attempt.

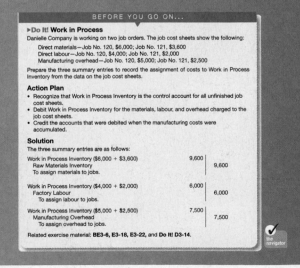

BRIEF CONTENTS

CONTENTS

Managerial Accounting

The Navigator is a learning system that prompts you to use the learning aids in the chapter and helps you set priorities as you study.

The Navigator
Chapter 1

- [ ] Scan *Study Objectives*
- [ ] Read *Feature Story*
- [ ] Read *Chapter Preview*
- [ ] Read text and answer *Before You Go On* p. 5, p. 8, p. 12, p. 18
- [ ] Review *Summary of Study Objectives*
- [ ] Answer *Self-Study Questions*
- [ ] Complete assignments

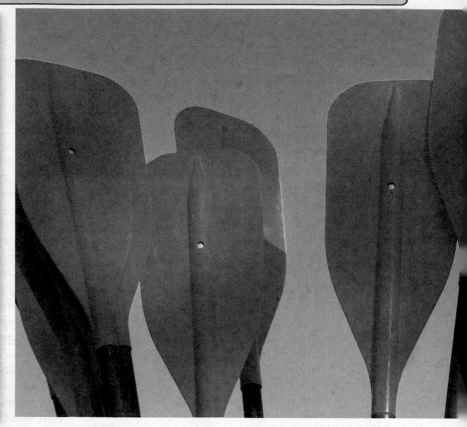

study objectives

Study Objectives give you a framework for learning the specific concepts covered in the chapter.

After studying this chapter, you should be able to do the following:

1. Explain the distinguishing features of managerial accounting.
2. Identify the three broad functions of management and the role of management accountants in an organizational structure.
3. Explain the importance of business ethics.
4. Identify changes and trends in managerial accounting.

ACCOUNTING KEEPS BUSINESSES AFLOAT

Growing up on Vancouver Island, Brian Henry explored the beautiful coastline by kayak. Feeling the need to have better equipment that was suited to the rugged environment, Mr. Henry began building sea kayaks for himself and his friends. In the late 1970s, that turned into a business, Current Designs, which expanded to design and build kayaks out of increasingly sophisticated materials. Over the years, Current Designs teamed up with world-famous kayakers to design models sold all over the world.

Meanwhile, on the inland waterways of Minnesota, Mike Cichanowski grew up paddling a canoe to explore the Mississippi River. He, too, started designing and building his own boats—in this case, canoes—and eventually took out a bank loan and built his own small shop, giving birth to the company Wenonah Canoe.

In 1991, as kayaking became more popular, Wenonah Canoe became the U.S. distributor of Current Designs kayaks. By 1999, Mr. Cichanowski made another critical business decision when Wenonah Canoe purchased majority ownership of Current Designs. In 2004, Mr. Cichanowski moved Current Designs' operations in Victoria to Minnesota, saying that 70% of boats made in Victoria were shipped to the United States. "The logistics of invoicing, shipping and handling those boats multiple times has led the company to look at a strategy of consolidating manufacturing and shipping at a single U.S. location," Wenonah said in a news release.

Today, Wenonah Canoe's 90 employees produce and sell about 12,000 canoes and kayaks per year through 500 retailers around the world.

Entrepreneurs like Mr. Cichanowski and Mr. Henry will tell you that business success is "a three-legged stool." The first leg is the knowledge and commitment to make a great product. Wenonah's canoes and Current Designs' kayaks are widely regarded as among the very best. The second leg is the ability to sell your product. Both companies started off making great boats, but it took a little longer to figure out how to sell them.

The third leg is not something that you would immediately associate with entrepreneurial success. It is what goes on behind the scenes—accounting. Good accounting information is absolutely critical to the countless decisions, big and small, that ensure the survival and growth of companies. Good accounting information allowed Mr. Henry to decide to sell to Wenonah and Mr. Cichanowski to decide to buy Current Designs and later move its production to Minnesota.

Bottom line: No matter how good your product is, and no matter how many units you sell, if you don't have a firm grip on your numbers, you are up a creek without a paddle.

Sources: Darrell Ehrlick, "Wenonah Canoe Buys Kayak Firm; Move Will Bring Jobs to Winona," WinonaDailyNews.com, April 19, 2011; Sea Stachura, "Wenonah Canoe Steers Straight in the Recession," Minnesota Public Radio, www.mprnews.org, March 20, 2009; Norman Gidney, "Kayak Maker to Shut Down," *Victoria Times Colonist*, April 30, 2004, p. B4; Current Designs corporate website, www.cdkayak.com; Wenonah Canoe corporate website, www.wenonah.com.

Preview of Chapter 1

This chapter focuses on issues dealing with the field and substance of managerial accounting. In a previous financial accounting course, you learned about the form and content of **financial statements for external users** of financial information, such as shareholders and creditors. These financial statements are the main product of financial accounting. Managerial accounting focuses primarily on the preparation of **reports for internal users** of financial information, such as the managers and officers of a company. Managers are evaluated on the results of their decisions. In today's rapidly changing global environment, managers must often make decisions that determine their company's fate—and their own. Managerial accounting provides tools that help management make decisions and evaluate the effectiveness of those decisions.

The chapter is organized as follows:

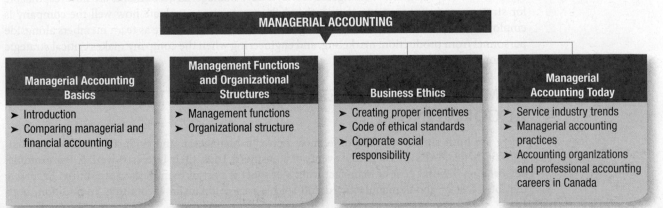

MANAGERIAL ACCOUNTING			
Managerial Accounting Basics	**Management Functions and Organizational Structures**	**Business Ethics**	**Managerial Accounting Today**
➤ Introduction ➤ Comparing managerial and financial accounting	➤ Management functions ➤ Organizational structure	➤ Creating proper incentives ➤ Code of ethical standards ➤ Corporate social responsibility	➤ Service industry trends ➤ Managerial accounting practices ➤ Accounting organizations and professional accounting careers in Canada

Managerial Accounting Basics

INTRODUCTION

Managerial accounting, also called management accounting, is a field of accounting that provides economic and financial information for managers and other internal users.

The skills that you will learn in this course will be vital to your future success in business. You don't believe us? Let's look at some examples of some of the crucial activities of employees at Current Designs, and where those activities are addressed in this textbook.

In order to know whether it is making a profit, Current Designs needs accurate information about the cost of each kayak. But first, we explain the field and substance of managerial accounting (Chapter 1). Chapter 2 explains various managerial cost concepts that are useful in planning, directing, and controlling. We also present cost flows and the process of cost accumulation in a manufacturing environment and costs and how they are reported in the financial statements. Chapters 3, 4, and 5 calculate the cost of providing a service or manufacturing a product. And to stay profitable, Current Designs must adjust the number of kayaks it produces in light of changes in economic conditions and consumer tastes. It then needs to understand how changes in the number of kayaks it produces impact its production costs and profitability (Chapter 6). Further, Current Designs' managers must often consider alternative courses of action. For example, should the company accept a special order from a customer, produce a particular kayak component internally or outsource it, or continue or discontinue a particular product line (Chapter 7)? Chapter 8 evaluates the impact on decision-making of alternative approaches for costing inventory. Finally, one of the most important, and most difficult, decisions is what price to charge for the kayaks (Chapter 9). In order to plan for the future, Current Designs prepares budgets (Chapter 10), and it then compares its budgeted numbers with its actual results to evaluate performance and identify areas that need to change (Chapters 11 and 12). Finally, it sometimes needs to make substantial investment decisions, such as the building of a new plant or the purchase of new equipment (Chapter 13).

Someday, you are going to face decisions just like these. You may end up in sales, marketing, management, production, or finance. You may work for a company that provides medical care, produces software, or serves up mouth-watering meals. No matter what your position is, and no matter what your product, the skills you acquire in this class will increase your chances of business success. Put another way, in business you can either guess, or you can make an informed decision. As the CEO of Microsoft once noted: "If you're supposed to be making money in business and supposed to be satisfying customers and building market share, there are numbers that characterize those things. And if somebody can't speak to me quantitatively about it, then I'm nervous." This course gives you the skills you need to quantify information so you can make informed business decisions.

Managerial accounting applies to all types of businesses—service, merchandising, and manufacturing. It also applies to all forms of business organizations—proprietorships, partnerships, and corporations. Managerial accounting is needed in not-for-profit entities, including governments, as well as in profit-oriented enterprises.

In the past, managerial accountants were primarily engaged in cost accounting: collecting and reporting costs to management. Recently, that role has changed significantly. First, as the manufacturing environment has become more automated, methods used to determine the amount and type of cost in a product have changed. Second, today's managerial accountants are now responsible for strategic cost management; that is, they help management evaluate how well the company is employing its resources. As a result, managerial accountants now serve as team members alongside personnel from production, marketing, and engineering when the company makes critical strategic decisions.

COMPARING MANAGERIAL AND FINANCIAL ACCOUNTING

There are both similarities and differences between managerial and financial accounting. First, both fields deal with the economic events of a business. Thus, their interests overlap. For example, *determining* the unit cost of manufacturing a product is part of managerial accounting. *Reporting* the total cost of goods manufactured and sold is part of financial accounting. In addition, both managerial and financial accounting require that a company's economic events be quantified and communicated to interested parties.

Illustration 1-1 summarizes the principal differences between financial accounting and managerial accounting. The varied needs for economic data among interested parties are the reason for many of the differences.

►Illustration 1-1

Differences between financial and managerial accounting

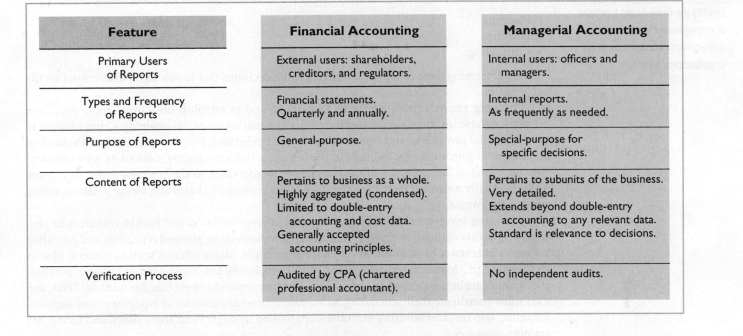

Feature	Financial Accounting	Managerial Accounting
Primary Users of Reports	External users: shareholders, creditors, and regulators.	Internal users: officers and managers.
Types and Frequency of Reports	Financial statements. Quarterly and annually.	Internal reports. As frequently as needed.
Purpose of Reports	General-purpose.	Special-purpose for specific decisions.
Content of Reports	Pertains to business as a whole. Highly aggregated (condensed). Limited to double-entry accounting and cost data. Generally accepted accounting principles.	Pertains to subunits of the business. Very detailed. Extends beyond double-entry accounting to any relevant data. Standard is relevance to decisions.
Verification Process	Audited by CPA (chartered professional accountant).	No independent audits.

BEFORE YOU GO ON...

►Do It! Managerial Accounting Concepts

Indicate whether the following statements are true or false.

1. Managerial accountants have a single role within an organization: collecting and reporting costs to management.

2. Financial accounting reports are general-purpose and intended for external users.

3. Managerial accounting reports are special-purpose and issued as frequently as needed.

Action Plan

• Understand that managerial accounting is a field of accounting that provides economic and financial information for managers and other internal users.
• Understand that financial accounting provides information for external users.

Solution

1. False. Managerial accountants determine product costs. In addition, managerial accountants are now held responsible for evaluating how well the company is employing its resources. As a result, when the company makes critical strategic decisions, managerial accountants serve as team members alongside personnel from production, marketing, and engineering.

2. True.

3. True.

Related exercise material: **E1-3, E1-7,** and **E1-8,** and **Do It! D1-1.**

The Do It! Exercises ask you to put newly acquired knowledge to work. They outline the Action Plan necessary to complete the exercise, and they show a Solution.

the navigator

Management Functions and Organizational Structures

MANAGEMENT FUNCTIONS

Managers' activities and responsibilities can be classified into three broad functions:

1. Planning
2. Directing
3. Controlling

In performing these functions, managers make decisions that have a significant impact on the organization.

Planning requires management to look ahead and to establish objectives. These objectives are often diverse: maximizing short-term profits and market share, maintaining a commitment to environmental protection, and contributing to social programs. For example, Hewlett-Packard, in an attempt to gain a stronger foothold in the computer industry, greatly reduced its prices to compete with Dell. A key objective of management is to add **value** to the business under its control. Value is usually measured by the trading price of the company's shares and by the potential selling price of the company.

Directing involves coordinating a company's diverse activities and human resources to produce a smoothly running operation. This includes implementing planned objectives and providing necessary incentives to motivate employees. For example, manufacturers such as General Motors of Canada Ltd., Magna International Inc., and Dare Foods Ltd. must coordinate their purchasing, manufacturing, warehousing, and selling. Service corporations such as Air Canada, Telus, and CGI must coordinate their scheduling, sales, service, and acquisitions of equipment and supplies. Directing also involves selecting executives, appointing managers and supervisors, and hiring and training employees.

The third management function, **controlling**, is the process of keeping the company's activities on track. In controlling operations, managers determine whether planned goals are being achieved. When there are deviations from target objectives, managers must decide what changes are needed to get back on track. Scandals at companies like Nortel Networks and Hollinger Inc. attest to the fact that companies must have adequate controls to ensure that the company develops and distributes accurate information.

How do managers achieve control? A smart manager in a small operation can make personal observations, ask good questions, and know how to evaluate the answers. But using this approach in a large organization would result in chaos. Imagine the president of Current Designs trying to determine whether planned objectives are being met without some record of what has happened and what is expected to occur. Thus, large businesses typically use a formal system of evaluation. These systems include such features as budgets, responsibility centres, and performance evaluation reports—all of which are features of managerial accounting.

Decision-making is not a separate management function. Rather, it is the outcome of the exercise of good judgement in planning, directing, and controlling.

BUSINESS INSIGHT   *"Lean" Luxury*

Louis Vuitton is a French manufacturer of high-end handbags, luggage, and shoes. Its reputation for quality and style allows it to charge up to several thousand dollars for an item. But often in the past, when demand was hot, supply was nonexistent—shelves were empty, and would-be buyers left empty-handed.

Luxury-goods manufacturers used to consider stock-outs to be a good thing, but Louis Vuitton changed its attitude. The company adopted "lean" processes used by car manufacturers and electronics companies to speed up production. Work is done by flexible teams, with jobs organized based on how long a task takes. Team members were reconfigured into U-shaped workspaces to save time and floor space, and robots are used in some factories to save workers from walking to get more materials. By reducing wasted time and eliminating bottlenecks, what used to take 20 to 30 workers eight days to do now takes 6 to 12 workers one day. Also, production employees who used to specialize on a single task on a single product are now multiskilled. This allows them to quickly switch products to meet demand.

To make sure that the factory is making the right products, within a week of a product launch, Louis Vuitton stores around the world feed sales information to the headquarters in France, and production is adjusted accordingly. Finally, the new production processes have also improved quality. Returns of some products are down by two thirds, which makes quite a difference to the bottom line when the products are pricey.

Sources: Hugues Pichon, "Lean à la Mode," *Lean Management Journal*, November 2012, p. 29; "Louis Vuitton, l'industriel," *L'Usine Nouvelle*, July 7, 2011; Christina Passariello, "At Vuitton, Growth in Small Batches," *Wall Street Journal*, June 27, 2011; Christina Passariello, "Louis Vuitton Tries Modern Methods on Factory Lines," *Wall Street Journal*, October 9, 2006.

What are some of the steps that this company has taken in order to ensure that production meets demand?

ORGANIZATIONAL STRUCTURES

In order to assist in carrying out management functions, most companies prepare **organization charts** that show the interrelationships of activities and the delegation of authority and responsibility within the company. Illustration 1-2 provides a typical organization chart showing the delegation of responsibility.

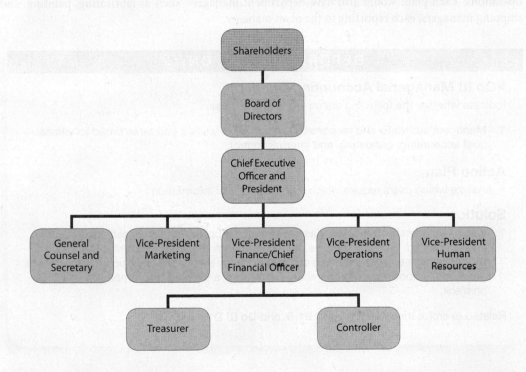

►Illustration 1-2
Corporation organization chart

Shareholders own the corporation, but they manage it indirectly through a **board of directors**, which they elect. Even not-for-profit organizations have boards of directors. The board formulates the operating policies for the company or organization. The board also selects officers, such as a president and one or more vice-presidents, to execute policy and perform daily management functions.

The **chief executive officer (CEO)** has overall responsibility for managing the business. Obviously, even in a small business, in order to accomplish organizational objectives, the company relies on the delegation of responsibilities. As the organization chart in Illustration 1-2 shows, the CEO delegates responsibility to other officers. Each member of the organization has a clearly defined role to play.

Responsibilities within the company are frequently classified as either line or staff positions. Employees with **line positions** are directly involved in the company's main revenue-generating operating activities. Examples of line positions would be the vice-president of operations, vice-president of marketing, plant managers, supervisors, and production personnel. Employees with **staff positions** are involved in activities that support the efforts of the line employees. In firms like General Motors or Petro-Canada, employees in the finance, legal, and human resources departments have staff positions. While the activities of staff employees are vital to the company, these employees are really there only to serve the line employees involved in the company's main operations.

The **chief financial officer (CFO)** is responsible for all of the accounting and finance issues the company faces. The CFO is supported by the **controller** and the **treasurer**. The controller's responsibilities include (1) maintaining the accounting records; (2) maintaining an adequate system of internal control; and (3) preparing financial statements, tax returns, and internal reports. The treasurer has custody of the corporation's funds and is responsible for maintaining the company's cash position.

Also serving the CFO are the **internal audit staff**. The audit staff's responsibilities include reviewing the reliability and integrity of financial information provided by the controller and treasurer. Audit staff members also ensure that internal control systems are functioning properly to safeguard corporate assets. In addition, they investigate compliance with policies and regulations and, in many companies, they determine whether resources are being used in the most economical and efficient fashion.

The vice-president of operations oversees employees with line positions. For example, the company might have multiple plant managers, and each one would report to the vice-president of operations. Each plant would also have department managers, such as fabricating, painting, and shipping managers, each reporting to the plant manager.

BEFORE YOU GO ON...

▶Do It! Managerial Accounting Concepts

Indicate whether the following statement is true or false.

1. Managers' activities and responsibilities can be classified into three broad functions: cost accounting, budgeting, and internal control.

Action Plan

- Analyze which users require which different types of information.

Solution

1. False. Managers' activities are classified into three broad functions: planning, directing, and controlling. Planning requires managers to look ahead to establish objectives. Directing involves coordinating a company's diverse activities and human resources to produce a smooth-running operation. Controlling is keeping the company's activities on track.

Related exercise material: **E1-5** and **E1-6,** and **Do It! D1-1.**

the navigator

Business Ethics

STUDY OBJECTIVE 3

Explain the importance of business ethics.

All employees in an organization are expected to act ethically in their business activities. Given the importance of ethical behaviour to corporations and their owners (shareholders), an increasing number of organizations provide codes of business ethics for their employees.

Despite these efforts, recent business scandals have resulted in massive investment losses and large employee layoffs. A recent survey of fraud by international accounting firm KPMG reported a 13% increase in instances of corporate fraud compared with five years earlier. It noted that while employee fraud (such things as expense account abuse, payroll fraud, and theft of assets) represented 60% of all instances of fraud, financial reporting fraud (the intentional misstatement of financial reports) was the most costly to companies. That should not be surprising given the long list of companies, such as Nortel, Enron, Global Crossing, and WorldCom, that have engaged in or been accused of engaging in massive financial frauds, which have led to huge financial losses and thousands of lost jobs.

CREATING PROPER INCENTIVES

Companies like BCE, CGI, Motorola, IBM, and Nike use complex systems to control and evaluate the actions of managers. They dedicate substantial resources to monitor and effectively evaluate the actions of employees. Unfortunately, these systems and controls sometimes unwittingly create incentives for managers to take unethical actions. For example, companies prepare budgets to provide direction. Because the budget is also used as an evaluation tool, some managers try to play a "game" by using budgetary slack; that is, they build some slack into the budget by underestimating their division's predicted performance so that it will be easier to meet their performance targets. On the other hand, if the budget is set at unattainable levels, managers sometimes take unethical actions to meet the targets in order to receive higher compensation or, in some cases, keep their jobs.

BUSINESS INSIGHT *Ethics Breach at Nortel*

Canadian-based Nortel Networks Corp. was once the largest supplier of telecommunications equipment in the world. In 2004, Nortel fired CEO Frank Dunn and two other senior executives in connection with an internal probe of the company's financial practices. Later that year, Nortel fired seven more financial managers as it continued to sort out the accounting scandal that led to the dismissal of its president. The financial shenanigans drew the attention of federal prosecutors from the U.S. Attorney's office in Dallas, and from the RCMP. Dunn and two other former senior executives were charged with fraud, but found not guilty in 2013 as the judge said the accounting decisions that led to the charges were either not fraudulent or were immaterial for such a large company as Nortel. Securities regulators in both countries were also looking into the accounting irregularities that caused Nortel to restate its results for several years. Among other things, the company said it actually lost money in the first half of 2003, whereas it had previously reported a net profit of $40 million. In 2006, Nortel reached an agreement in principle for proposed global settlement of class action litigation launched by shareholders who suffered huge losses as Nortel's stock price plummeted. The company agreed to pay U.S. $575 million cash and issue common shares representing 14.5% of current equity. In 2009, Nortel declared bankruptcy and liquidated, auctioning off its patents for $4.5 billion.

Sources: Janet McFarland and Richard Blackwell, "Three Former Nortel Executives Found Not Guilty of Fraud," *The Globe and Mail*, January 14, 2013; Charles Arthur, "Nortel Patents Sold for $4.5bn," *The Guardian*, July 1, 2011; James Bagnall, "The Beginning of the End: How an Accounting Scandal Permanently Weakened Nortel," *The Ottawa Citizen*, November 2, 2009; "Nortel Cheques in the Mail," *The Gazette*, May 16, 2008, B-1; Jeffry Bartash, "U.S. Investigators Target Nortel," www.cbs.marketwatch.com, May 14, 2004.

What can companies do to create disincentives for managers to act unethically?

Unethical actions similar to those committed at Nortel have also taken place in the United States. For example, in recent years, airline manufacturer Boeing has been plagued by a series of scandals, including charges of overbilling, corporate espionage, and illegal conflicts of interest. Some long-time employees of Boeing blame the decline in ethics on a change in the corporate culture that took place after Boeing merged with McDonnell Douglas. They suggest that evaluation systems that were implemented after the merger to monitor results and evaluate employee performance made employees believe they needed to succeed no matter what.

Although manufacturing companies need to establish production goals for their processes, if controls are not effective and realistic, problems develop. To illustrate, Schering-Plough, a pharmaceutical manufacturer, found that employees were so concerned with meeting production standards that they failed to monitor the quality of the product, and as a result the dosages were often wrong.

CODE OF ETHICAL STANDARDS

In response to corporate scandals in 2000 and 2001, the U.S. Congress enacted legislation to help prevent lapses in internal control. This legislation, referred to as the Sarbanes-Oxley Act of 2002 (SOX), had important implications for the financial community. One result of SOX was the clarification of top management's responsibility for the company's financial statements. CEOs and CFOs must now certify that financial statements give a fair presentation of the company's operating results and its financial condition. In addition, top managers must certify that the company maintains an adequate system of internal controls to safeguard the company's assets and ensure accurate financial reports.

Another result of Sarbanes-Oxley is that companies now pay more attention to the composition of the board of directors. In particular, members of the audit committee of the board of directors must all be entirely independent (that is, non-employees) and at least one must be a financial expert.

Finally, to increase the likelihood of compliance with the rules that are part of the new legislation, the law substantially increases the penalties for misconduct.

In Canada, as discussed in the December 2003 issue of *CA Magazine*, "after the Bre-X Minerals Ltd., Cinar, and Livent Inc. scandals, steps were also taken to remedy market and financial manipulations . . . the Canadian Securities Administrators, federal and provincial securities regulators, the Office of the Superintendent of Financial Institutions (OSFI) and the accounting profession set up the Canadian Public Accountability Board (CPAB), which is charged with overseeing the independence and transparency of the Canadian accounting system. According to the OSFI, 'The mission of the CPAB is to contribute to public confidence in the integrity of financial reporting of Canadian public companies by promoting high quality, independent auditing . . .'"

In January 2004, the Ontario Securities Commission (OSC), in conjunction with the Canadian Securities Administrators, introduced regulations governing the composition and duties of audit committees, as well as their members' behaviour. The new regulations were also adopted by all provincial and territorial securities regulators, except for British Columbia's. "'The rules are as robust as parallel rules required by the U.S. Sarbanes-Oxley legislation, but address unique Canadian concerns,' said OSC chair David Brown in a release announcing the proposed rules."[1]

Canadian corporate governance regulation was established in 2005. National Policy 58-201 Corporate Governance Guidelines provides guidance on corporate governance practices for various reasons including the need to achieve a balance between protecting investors and encouraging fair and efficient capital markets.

To provide guidance for managerial accountants, the U.S. Institute of Management Accountants (IMA) has developed a code of ethical standards entitled IMA Standards of Ethical Conduct for Practitioners of Management Accounting and Financial Management. The code states that management accountants should not commit acts in violation of these standards, nor should they condone such acts by others within their organizations. In Canada, each province has its own code of ethics and rules and guidelines of professional conduct.

In Canada, the professional accounting organization plays an important role in promoting high standards of ethics in the accounting profession. These standards of ethics can be used as guidelines in dealing with the public and the association's members. The IMA's **Statement of Ethical Professional Practice** provides the following codes of conduct regarding **competence, confidentiality, integrity, and credibility**:

Competence

Management accountants have a responsibility to

- maintain professional competence.
- perform professional duties in accordance with relevant laws, regulations, and technical standards.
- prepare complete and clear reports and recommendations.

---

[1]Gilles des Roberts, "On the hot seat," *CA Magazine* (December 2003).

- communicate professional limitations that would preclude responsible judgement or successful performance of an activity.

Confidentiality

Management accountants have a responsibility to

- refrain from disclosing confidential information.
- inform subordinates as to how to handle confidential information.
- refrain from using confidential information for unethical or illegal advantage.

Integrity

Management accountants have a responsibility to

- avoid conflicts of interest.
- refrain from activity that would prejudice their ability to carry out their duties ethically.
- refrain from engaging in or supporting any activity that would discredit the accounting profession.

Credibility

Management accountants have a responsibility to

- communicate information fairly and objectively.
- disclose fully all relevant information that could reasonably be expected to influence a user's understanding of the reports, comments, and recommendations presented.

CORPORATE SOCIAL RESPONSIBILITY

Another aspect of business ethics is the growing trend toward **corporate social responsibility**. Many companies have begun to evaluate not just corporate profitability but also corporate social responsibility. In addition to profitability, corporate social responsibility considers a company's efforts to employ sustainable business practices with regard to its employees and the environment. This is sometimes referred to as the **triple bottom line** because it evaluates a company's performance with regard to people, planet, and profit. These companies are still striving to maximize profits—in a competitive world, they won't survive long if they don't. In fact, you might recognize a few of the names on the Forbes.com list of the 100 most sustainable companies in the world, such as General Electric, adidas, Toyota, Coca-Cola, or Starbucks. These companies have learned that with a long-term, sustainable approach, they can maximize profits while also acting in the best interest of their employees, their communities, and the environment. At various points within this textbook, we will discuss situations where real companies use the very skills that you are learning to evaluate decisions from a sustainable perspective.

Sustainable business practices present numerous issues for management and managerial accountants. First, companies must decide what items need to be measured, generally those that are of utmost importance to its stakeholders. For example, a particular company might be most concerned with minimizing water pollution or maximizing employee safety. Then, for each item identified, the company must determine measurable attributes that provide relevant information about the company's performance with regard to that item, such as amount of waste released into public waterways or number of accidents per 1,000 hours worked. Finally, the company needs to consider the materiality of the item, the cost of measuring these attributes, and the reliability of the measurements. If the company uses this information to make decisions, then accuracy is critical. Of particular concern is whether the measurements can be verified by an outside third party. Unlike financial reporting, the reporting of sustainable business practices currently has no agreed-upon standard-setter. A number of organizations have, however, published sustainability reporting guidelines. Illustration 1-3 provides a list of major categories in guidelines from the Global Reporting Initiative and from the International Organization for Standardization (ISO), and a sample of topics or "aspects" that companies might consider within each category.

| | Economic | Environmental | Social | | | | |
			Labour Practices and Decent Work	Human Rights	Society	Product Responsibility
Global Reporting Initiative aspects	Economic performance	Energy	Occupational health and safety	Child labour	Anti-corruption	Customer health and safety
	Procurement practices	Effluents and waste	Training and education	Indigenous rights	Anti-competitive behaviour	Product and service labelling
ISO 26000:2010 aspects	Social investment	Sustainable resource use	Conditions of work and social protection	Discrimination and vulnerable groups	Fair operating practices	Protecting consumers' health and safety
	Wealth and income creation	Climate change mitigation and adaptation	Human development and training in the workplace	Civil and political rights	Responsible political involvement	Fair marketing, factual and unbiased information and fair contractual practices

Sources: Global Reporting Initiative, *G4 Sustainability Reporting Guidelines*; Global Reporting Initiative and International Organization for Standardization, "IGRI G4 Guidelines and ISO 26000:2010: How to Use the GRI G4 Guidelines and ISO 26000 in Conjunction"; James Margolis, "The Global Reporting Initiative (GRI) Issues New Guidelines—What Will These Mean for Business?," ERM Group Inc., July 23, 2013.

▶Illustration 1-3

Categories and sample aspects in Global Reporting Initiative and ISO 26000:2010 guidelines

BEFORE YOU GO ON...

▶Do It! Managerial Accounting Concepts

Indicate whether the following statements are true or false.

1. As a result of the Sarbanes-Oxley Act of 2002, managerial accounting reports must now comply with accounting principles accepted by the accounting profession.

2. Top managers must certify that a company maintains an adequate system of internal controls.

3. A company's efforts to employ sustainable business practices with regard to its employees, society, and the environment is referred to as corporate social responsibility.

Action Plan

• Understand the importance of espousing and promoting high standards of ethics in the accounting profession.

Solution

1. False. SOX clarifies top management's responsibility for the company's financial statements. In addition, top managers must certify that the company maintains an adequate system of internal control to safeguard the company's assets and ensure accurate financial reports.

2. True.

3. True.

Related exercise material: **E1-4** and **Do It! D1-1**.

the navigator

Managerial Accounting Today

STUDY OBJECTIVE 4

Identify changes and trends in managerial accounting.

To compete successfully in today's deregulated global environment, many Canadian and American manufacturing and service industries have begun implementing strategic management programs. These are designed to improve quality, reduce costs, and regain the competitive position the companies once held in the world marketplace. This approach focuses on the long-term goals and objectives of the organization, as well as a full analysis of the environment in which the business is operating. The analysis covers all the internal operations and resources of the organization, as well as the external aspects of its environment. It includes competitors, suppliers, customers, and legal and regulatory changes, as well as the economy as a whole.

This new approach requires changes to traditional management accounting, which has been widely criticized for being too narrow, highly quantitative, and aimed at the needs of financial reporting, and for contributing little to the overall policy and direction of the organization. In this regard, as one author says, management accounting needs to be released from the factory floor so that it can meet market challenges directly.[2] The result is a new variety of management accounting that expands the information provided to decision makers. The following section explains the expanding role of management accounting in the twenty-first century.

SERVICE INDUSTRY TRENDS

In recent decades, the Canadian and U.S. economies in general have shifted toward an emphasis on providing services, rather than goods. Today over 50% of Canadian and U.S. workers are employed by service companies, and that percentage is expected to increase in coming years. Most of the techniques that you will learn in this course are equally applicable to service and manufacturing entities.

Managers of service companies look to managerial accounting to answer many questions. Illustration 1-4 presents examples of such questions. In some instances, the managerial accountant may need to develop new systems for measuring the cost of serving individual customers. In others, he or she may need new operating controls to improve the quality and efficiency of specific services. Many of the examples we present in subsequent chapters will relate to service companies. To highlight the relevance of the techniques used in this course for service companies, we have placed a service company icon next to those items in the end-of-chapter materials that relate to non-manufacturing companies.

Industry/Company	Questions Faced by Service-Company Managers
Transportation (WestJet Airlines)	• whether to buy new or used planes • whether to service a new route
Package delivery services (Purolator, FedEx)	• what fee structure to use • what mode of transportation to use
Telecommunications (BCE Inc.)	• what fee structure to use • whether to service a new community • how many households it will take to break even • whether to invest in a new satellite or lay new cable
Professional services (lawyers, accountants, dentists)	• how much to charge for particular services • how much office overhead to allocate to particular jobs • how efficient and productive individual staff members are
Financial institutions (Bank of Montreal, TD Waterhouse)	• which services to charge for, and which to provide for free • whether to build a new branch office or to install a new ATM • whether fees should vary depending on the size of the customers' accounts
Health care (TLC The Laser Center Inc.)	• whether to invest in new equipment • how much to charge for various services • how to measure the quality of the services provided

▶Illustration 1-4

Service industries and companies and the managerial accounting questions they face

---

[2]M. Bromwich, "The Case for Strategic Management Accounting: The Role of Accounting Information for Strategy in Competitive Markets," *Accounting, Organizations and Society*, 25 (2) (1990): 221.

MANAGERIAL ACCOUNTING PRACTICES

As discussed earlier, the practice of managerial accounting has changed significantly in recent years to better meet the needs of managers. The following sections explain some well-established managerial accounting practices.

Focus on the Value Chain

The **value chain** refers to all activities associated with providing a product or service. For a manufacturer, these include research and development, product design, the acquisition of raw materials, production, sales and marketing, delivery, customer relations, and subsequent service. Illustration 1-5 shows the value chain for a manufacturer. In recent years, companies have made huge advances in analyzing all stages of the value chain in an effort to improve productivity and eliminate waste, all while continually trying to improve quality. Japanese automobile manufacturer Toyota pioneered many of these innovations.

Research and development and product design

Acquisition of raw materials

Production

Sales and marketing

Delivery

Customer relations and subsequent service

▶Illustration 1-5
A manufacturer's value chain

In the 1980s, many companies purchased giant machines to replace humans in the manufacturing process. These machines were designed to produce large batches of products. In recent years, these manufacturing processes have been recognized as being very wasteful. They require vast amounts of inventory storage capacity and a lot of movement of materials. Consequently, many companies have re-engineered their manufacturing processes. For example, the manufacturing company Pratt and Whitney has replaced many of its large machines with smaller, more flexible ones, and has begun reorganizing its plants for a more efficient flow of goods. With these changes, Pratt and Whitney was able to reduce the time that its turbine engine blades spend in the grinding section from 10 days to two hours. It also cut the total amount of time spent making a blade from 22 days to 7 days. The improvements that have resulted from analyses of the value chain have made companies far more responsive to customer needs, and have improved profitability.

Technological Change

Technology has played a large role in the value chain. Computerization and automation have permitted companies to be more effective in streamlining production, thus enhancing the value chain. For example, many companies now employ **enterprise resource planning (ERP) software systems**, such as those provided by SAP, which provide a comprehensive, centralized, and integrated source of information that is used to manage all major business processes, from purchasing to manufacturing to recording human resources.

In large companies, an ERP system might replace as many as 200 individual software packages. For example, an ERP system can eliminate the need for individual software packages for personnel, inventory management, receivables, and payroll. Because the value chain goes beyond the walls of the company, ERP systems also collect information from and provide it to the company's major suppliers, customers, and business partners. The largest ERP provider, the German corporation SAP, has more than 36,000 customers worldwide.

Another example of technological change is **computer-integrated manufacturing (CIM)**. Using CIM, many companies can now manufacture products that are untouched by human hands. An example is the use of robotic equipment in the steel and automobile industries. Workers monitor the manufacturing process by watching instrument panels. Automation significantly reduces direct labour costs in many cases.

Also, the widespread use of computers has greatly reduced the cost of accumulating, storing, and reporting managerial accounting information. Computers now make it possible to do more detailed costing of products, processes, and services than was possible under manual processing.

Technology is also affecting the value chain through business-to-business (B2B) e-commerce on the Internet. The Internet has dramatically changed the way corporations do business with one another. Inter-organizational information systems connected over the Internet enable customers and suppliers to share information nearly instantaneously. In addition, the Internet has changed the marketplace, often cutting out intermediaries (the "middlemen"). The automobile, airline, hotel, and electronics industries have made commitments to purchase some or all of their supplies and raw materials in the huge B2B electronic marketplaces. For example, Hilton Hotels recently committed itself to purchasing as much as $1.5 billion of bedsheets, pest control services, and other items from an on-line supplier, PurchasePro.com.

Just-in-Time Inventory Methods

Many companies have significantly lowered their inventory levels and costs by using **just-in-time (JIT) inventory** methods, which is an innovation that resulted from the focus on the value chain. Under a just-in-time method, goods are manufactured or purchased just in time for use. Alcoa Canada is famous for having developed a system for making products in response to individual customer requests, with each product custom made to meet each customer's particular specifications. Another example is Dell Corporation, which takes less than 48 hours to assemble a computer to customer specifications and put it on a truck. By integrating its information systems with those of its suppliers, Dell reduced its inventories to nearly zero. This is a huge advantage in an industry where products become obsolete nearly overnight. No wonder that JIT is sometimes also called "lean production."

Quality

JIT inventory systems also require an increased emphasis on product quality. If products are produced only as they are needed, it is very costly for the company to have to stop production because of defects or machine breakdowns. Many companies have installed **total quality management (TQM)** systems to reduce defects in finished products. The goal is to achieve zero defects. These systems require timely data on defective products, rework costs, and the cost of honouring warranty contracts. Often this information is used to help redesign the product in a way that makes it less likely to have a defect. Or it may be used to re-engineer the production process to reduce set-up time and decrease the potential for error. TQM systems also provide information on non-financial measures, such as customer satisfaction, the number of service calls, and the time needed to generate reports. Attention to these measures, which employees can control, leads to increased profitability and improves all aspects of the value chain.

Activity-Based Costing

Overhead costs have become an increasingly large component of product and service costs. By definition, overhead costs cannot be directly traced to individual products. But to determine each product's cost, overhead must be allocated to the various products. In order to obtain more accurate product costs, many companies now allocate overhead using **activity-based costing (ABC)**. Under ABC, overhead is allocated based on each product's use of economic resources as it undergoes various activities. For example, the company can keep track of the cost of setting up machines for each batch of a production process. Then a particular product can be allocated part of the total set-up cost based on the number of set-ups that product required.

Activity-based costing is beneficial because it results in more accurate product costing and in more careful scrutiny of all activities in the **supply chain**. For example, if a product's cost is high because it requires a high number of set-ups, management will be motivated to determine how to produce the product using as few machine set-ups as possible. ABC is now widely used by both manufacturing and service companies. Chapter 5 discusses ABC further.

Theory of Constraints

All companies have certain aspects of their business that create "bottlenecks"—constraints that limit the company's potential profitability. An important aspect of managing the value chain is identifying these constraints. The **theory of constraints** is a specific approach used to identify and manage constraints in order to achieve the company's goals. Automobile manufacturer General Motors is using the theory of constraints in all of its North American plants. The company has found that it is most profitable when it focuses on fixing bottlenecks, rather than worrying about whether all aspects of the company are functioning at full capacity. It has greatly improved the company's ability to effectively use overtime labour while meeting customer demand. Chapter 7 discusses applications of the theory of constraints.

Lean Manufacturing

Lean manufacturing is a process increasingly used by many firms to manage their operations more efficiently and with more control. It sets out to eliminate waste and to concentrate more accurately on the needs of the customer. The process is in contrast to traditional mass-production operations, which maximize profits through efficiency of machine utilization and economies of scale and require large amounts of direct labour to complete most products. Today most products require little direct labour to complete, due in large part to advancements in automation. Customers now dictate requirements to suppliers and often look for smaller quantities of individualized products. Lean manufacturing was developed in response to this changing manufacturing environment.

Researchers have highlighted five basic principles that are crucial to the lean thinking process: specify value, identify the value stream, create flow, respond to customer pull or demands, and aim for perfection.

Step one, value, is the process of "target costing," which is the acceptable cost customers are willing to pay for a specific product. The key is to achieve the optimal price for customers while realizing the greatest profit potential for the company. Step two, the value stream, is the entire flow of a product's life cycle through each stage of production. It is the central element in understanding how a company can evaluate what is value-added and what is waste. Step three, the flow, refers to the need for the production process to have a continuous flow. Any disruptions in the value stream can have detrimental effects on the functioning of a company and on its customer satisfaction. Step four, the pull principle, states that a product should not be made until a customer orders it. To achieve this pull approach, the company's production capacity is flexible and each stage of the value chain is well designed and defined. The final principle, perfection, deals with the target quality that management seeks to obtain via its customers' needs.

Changing traditional mass-production thinking to lean thinking requires changes in the ways companies control, measure, and account for their processes. Chapters 8 and 9 discuss some applications of lean manufacturing.

BUSINESS INSIGHT   *"Lean" Labour*

Manufacturing employment has been steadily falling in Canada, shedding 278,000 jobs from 2000 to 2007 and another 188,000 jobs shortly after the 2008–09 recession. One reason for that is that many factories have adopted lean manufacturing practices. This means that production relies less on large numbers of low-skilled workers, and more on machines and a few highly skilled workers. But these highly skilled workers tend to have more job security. With lean manufacturing, a single employee can support far more dollars in sales. Thus, it requires a larger decline in sales before an employee would need to be laid off in order to continue to break even. Also, because the employees are highly skilled, employers are reluctant to lose the investment in training them. Instead of layoffs, many manufacturers have resorted to cutting employee hours.

Sources: Statistics Canada, *Canada Year Book* 2011, Catalogue number 11-402-X; Timothy Aeppel and Justin Lahart, "Lean Factories Find It Hard to Cut Jobs Even in a Slump," *Wall Street Journal Online*, March 9, 2009; Kronos, "The Lean Workforce: Applying Lean Principles to Improve Workforce Management," 2009.

Would you characterize labour costs as being a fixed cost, a variable cost, or something else in this situation?

Balanced Scorecard

As companies implement various business practice innovations, managers have sometimes focused too enthusiastically on the latest innovation and paid less attention to other areas of the business. For example, in focusing on improving quality, companies sometimes lose sight of cost/benefit considerations. Similarly, in focusing on reducing inventory levels through just-in-time inventory, companies sometimes lose sales due to inventory shortages. The **balanced scorecard** is a performance-measurement approach that uses both financial and non-financial measures to evaluate all aspects of a company's operations in an *integrated* way. As shown in the figure in the margin, the performance measures are linked by cause and effect to ensure that they all connect to the company's overall objectives.

For example, the company may want to increase its return on assets, a common financial performance measure (calculated as net income divided by average total assets). It will then identify a series of linked goals that, if each one is accomplished, will ultimately result in an increase in return on assets. For example, in order to increase return on assets, sales must increase. In order to increase sales, customer satisfaction must be increased. In order to increase customer satisfaction, product defects must be reduced. In order to reduce product defects, employee training must be increased. Note the linkage, which starts with employee training and ends with return on assets. Each objective will have associated performance measures.

The use of the balanced scorecard is widespread among some well-known and respected companies. For example, Hilton Hotels Corporation uses the balanced scorecard to evaluate the performance of employees at all of its hotel chains. Walmart employs the balanced scorecard, and actually extends its use to evaluation of its suppliers. For example, Walmart recently awarded Welch Company the "Dry Grocery Division Supplier of the Year Award" for its balanced scorecard results. The Palladium Group, a U.S. management consulting firm, even has awards for effective use of the balanced scorecard. Among the recent recipients of the Balanced Scorecard Hall of Fame Award is the Canadian Blood Services, for "achieving breakthrough performance results using the Balanced Scorecard."[3] The balanced scorecard is discussed further in Chapter 12.

Reprinted by permission of Harvard Business School Press. From R. Kaplan and D. Norton, *The Balanced Scorecard* (Boston, MA, 1996), page 9. Copyright © 1996 by the Harvard Business School Publishing Corporation; all rights reserved.

ACCOUNTING ORGANIZATIONS AND PROFESSIONAL ACCOUNTING CAREERS IN CANADA

In Canada the accounting profession has recently been reorganized by the founding of CPA Canada (Chartered Professional Accountants) in 2013, into which the three legacy accounting bodies (Chartered Accountants (CA), Certified Management Accountants (CMA), and Certified General Accountants (CGA) were merged. At the time of writing, all provincial/territorial CA and CMA Orders had chosen to belong to CPA Canada as had most CGA provincial bodies with the exception of CGA Ontario and Manitoba.

Because of the risks and opportunities facing the accounting profession in Canada and worldwide, CPA Canada was founded to create a larger unified profession that would mean a more prominent and cohesive Canadian presence internationally. For instance, the AICPA (American Institute of Certified Public Accountants) is aggressively seeking to expand its global footprint by opening exam centres for the U.S. CPA exam outside of the United States. In conjunction with the CIMA (Chartered Institute of Management Accountants-U.K.) the AICPA jointly developed a new global management accounting designation (CGMA).

Further it was thought that CPA Canada could provide enhanced professional development and training opportunities as well as improved services and benefits to its members by eliminating duplication and competition among the former accounting bodies. Lifelong learning is an important part of the profession and as a CPA, member professional development continues through taking courses, some leading to specializations such as tax, forensic accounting, strategic management, and public sector accounting.

---

[3]Palladium Group news release, "Palladium Group Honors Canadian Blood Services and the Republic of Korea's Ministry of Government Administration and Home Affairs with Prestigious BSC Hall of Fame Award" (October 10, 2007); www.thepalladiumgroup.com.

BEFORE YOU GO ON...

▶Do It! Trends in Managerial Accounting

Match the descriptions that follow with the corresponding terms.

Descriptions:
1. _____ All activities associated with providing a product or service.
2. _____ A method of allocating overhead based on each product's use of activities in making the product.
3. _____ Systems implemented to reduce defects in finished products with the goal of achieving zero defects.
4. _____ A performance-measurement approach that uses both financial and non-financial measures, tied to company objectives, to evaluate a company's operations in an integrated fashion.
5. _____ Inventory system in which goods are manufactured or purchased just as they are needed for use.

Terms:
(a) Activity-based costing
(b) Balanced scorecard
(c) Just-in-time (JIT) inventory
(d) Total quality management (TQM)
(e) Value chain

Action Plan

- Develop a forward-looking view, in order to advise and provide information to various members of the organization.
- Understand current business trends and issues.

Solution

1. e   2. a   3. d   4. b   5. c

Related exercise material: **E1-9** and **Do it! D1-2**.

ALL ABOUT YOU   *How Sharp Are Your Decision-Making Skills?*

As you will see in this text, good financial information is crucial for management decision-making. You've already made important decisions in choosing a university, a program, and courses. What factors went into your decision—how much was factual and how much was intuitive? Do you feel you made the right decisions? A 2013 survey of first-year students at 35 Canadian universities found that more than 9 in 10 said they were satisfied with their decision to attend their university. This is good news for them, because the average university undergraduate tuition in Canada for the 2013–14 year was $5,772, so a lot of money is at stake.

What Do You Think?

Suppose you haven't chosen a major yet. You research information on expected salaries for graduates in various fields. Should you choose your major based on potential earnings?

YES—University is costly and hard work so I want to see a good return on my money and time invested.

NO—I want to study and work in a field that I love; the money will follow.

Sources: Statistics Canada, "University Tuition Fees, 2013/2014," *The Daily*, September 12, 2013; Canadian University Survey Consortium, "2013 First-Year University Student Survey Master Report," June 2013; Business Development Bank of Canada, "Top 7 Decision-Making Tips for Managers," June 13, 2010.

Summary of Study Objectives

> The **Summary of Study Objectives** repeats the main points related to the Study Objectives. It gives you an opportunity to review what you have learned.

1. *Explain the distinguishing features of managerial accounting.* Managerial accounting is needed in all types of businesses—service, merchandising, and manufacturing. It also applies to all forms of business organization—proprietorships, partnerships, and corporations. Managerial accounting is needed in not-for-profit entities, as well as in profit-oriented enterprises. Managerial accounting provides tools that help management make decisions and evaluate the effectiveness of those decisions.

   The distinguishing features of managerial accounting are

   - the primary users of reports—internal users, who are officers, department heads, managers, and supervisors in the company;
   - the type and frequency of reports—internal reports that are issued as frequently as needed;
   - the purpose of reports—to provide special-purpose information for a particular user for a specific decision;
   - the content of reports—pertains to subunits of the business and may be very detailed and may extend beyond the double-entry accounting system; the reporting standard is relevant to the decision being made; and
   - the verification of reports—no independent audits.

2. *Identify the three broad functions of management and the role of management accountants in an organizational structure.* The three functions are planning, directing, and controlling. Planning requires management to look ahead and to establish objectives. Directing involves coordinating a company's diverse activities and human resources to produce a smoothly running operation. Controlling is the process of keeping the activities on track.

   Management accountants serve as staff members in an organization and play an important role in providing the required information for decision-making.

3. *Explain the importance of business ethics.* All employees in an organization are expected to act ethically in their business activities. In Canada, the professional accounting organization promotes high standards of ethics in the accounting profession. These standards of ethics can be used as guidelines in dealing with the public and the organizations' members. In the United States, the Institute of Management Accountants' Statement of Ethical Professional Practice provides the codes of conduct regarding competence, confidentiality, integrity, and credibility. Moreover, companies are now evaluating their performance with regard to their corporate social responsibility.

4. *Identify changes and trends in managerial accounting.* Managerial accounting has experienced many changes in recent years. Among these are a shift toward meeting the needs of service companies and improving practices to better meet the needs of managers. Improved practices include a focus on managing the value chain through techniques such as just-in-time inventory, and technological applications such as enterprise resource planning (ERP). In addition, techniques have been developed to improve decision-making, such as the theory of constraints and activity-based costing (ABC). Finally, many companies now use the balanced scorecard in order to have a more comprehensive view of the company's operations.

   In Canada, the accounting profession has recently been reorganized by the founding of CPA Canada (Chartered Professional Accountants) in 2013, and into which the three legacy accounting bodies—Chartered Accountants (CA), Certified Management Accountants (CMA), and Certified General Accountants (CGA)—were merged.

Glossary

Activity-based costing (ABC) A method of allocating overhead based on each product's use of activities. (p. 15)

Balanced scorecard A performance-measurement approach that uses both financial and non-financial measures that are tied to company objectives to evaluate a company's operations in an integrated way. (p. 17)

Board of directors The group of officials elected by the shareholders of a corporation or non-profit organization to formulate operating policies, select officers, and otherwise manage the company. (p. 7)

Chief executive officer (CEO) The corporate officer who has overall responsibility for managing the business; he or she delegates parts of that responsibility to other corporate officers. (p. 7)

Chief financial officer (CFO) The corporate officer who is responsible for all of a company's accounting and finance issues. (p. 8)

Controller The financial officer who is responsible for a company's accounting records, system of internal control, and preparation of financial statements, tax returns, and internal reports. (p. 8)

Corporate social responsibility The efforts of a company to employ sustainable business practices with regard to its employees and the environment. (p. 11).

Enterprise resource planning (ERP) software system Software that provides a comprehensive, centralized, integrated source of information that is used to manage all major business processes. (p. 14)

Just-in-time (JIT) inventory An inventory system in which goods are manufactured or purchased just in time for use. (p. 15)

Line positions Jobs that are directly involved in a company's main revenue-generating operating activities. (p. 8)

Managerial accounting A field of accounting that provides economic and financial information for managers and other internal users. (p. 4)

Staff positions Jobs that support the efforts of line employees. (p. 8)

Supply chain All activities from the receipt of an order to the delivery of a product or service. (p. 15)

Theory of constraints The practice of identifying constraints that impede a company's ability to provide a good or service, and dealing with the constraints to maximize profitability. (p. 16)

Total quality management (TQM) Systems implemented to reduce defects in finished products with the goal of achieving zero defects. (p. 15)

Treasurer The financial officer who is responsible for the custody of a company's funds and for maintaining its cash position. (p. 8)

Triple bottom line The evaluation of a company's social responsibility performance with regard to people, planet, and profit. (p. 11)

Value chain All activities associated with providing a product or service. (p. 14)

WileyPLUS   Self-Test, Exercises, and many more components are available for practice in WileyPlus.

Self-Study Questions

Answers are at the end of the chapter.

(SO 1)   1. Managerial accounting
   (a) is governed by generally accepted accounting principles.
   (b) emphasizes special-purpose information.
   (c) pertains to the entity as a whole and is highly aggregated.
   (d) is limited to cost data.

(SO 3)   2. Which of the following is not one of the categories in the *Statement of Ethical Professional Practice*?
   (a) Confidentiality
   (b) Competence
   (c) Integrity
   (d) Independence

(SO 2)   3. The management of an organization performs several broad functions. They are
   (a) planning, directing, and selling.
   (b) planning, directing, and controlling.
   (c) planning, manufacturing, and controlling.
   (d) directing, manufacturing, and controlling.

(SO 4)   4. Which one of the following is **not** a main component of the value chain sequence?
   (a) ERP
   (b) Sales and marketing
   (c) Production
   (d) Customer relations

(SO 4)   5. What is "balanced" in the balanced scorecard approach?
   (a) The number of products produced
   (b) The emphasis on financial and non-financial performance measurements
   (c) The amount of costs allocated to products
   (d) The number of defects found on each product

(SO 1)   6. Managerial accounting information is generally prepared for
   (a) shareholders.
   (b) managers.

   (c) regulatory agencies.
   (d) investors.

(SO 1)   7. Managerial accounting information
   (a) pertains to the entity as a whole and is highly aggregated.
   (b) must be prepared according to generally accepted accounting principles.
   (c) pertains to subunits of the entity and may be very detailed.
   (d) is prepared only once a year.

(SO 1)   8. The major reporting standard for management accountants is
   (a) the *Statement of Ethical Professional Practice*.
   (b) the Sarbanes-Oxley Act of 2002.
   (c) relevance to decisions.
   (d) generally accepted accounting principles.

(SO 4)   9. Which of the following managerial accounting techniques attempts to allocate manufacturing overhead in a more meaningful fashion?
   (a) Just-in-time inventory
   (b) Total quality management
   (c) Balanced scorecard
   (d) Activity-based costing

(SO 3) 10. Corporate social responsibility refers to:
   (a) the practice by management of reviewing all business processes in an effort to increase productivity and eliminate waste.
   (b) an approach used to allocate overhead based on each product's use of activities.
   (c) the attempt by management to identify and eliminate constraints within the value chain.
   (d) efforts by companies to employ sustainable business practices with regard to employees and the environment.

Do It! Review

D1-1　Indicate whether the following statements are true or false.

1. Managerial accountants explain and report manufacturing and nonmanufacturing costs, determine cost behaviours, and perform cost-volume-profit analysis, but are not involved in the budget process.
2. Financial accounting reports pertain to subunits of the business and are very detailed.
3. Managerial accounting reports must follow generally accepted accounting principles and are audited by chartered accountants.
4. Managers' activities and responsibilities can be classified into three broad functions: planning, directing, and controlling.
5. As a result of the Sarbanes-Oxley Act of 2002, top managers must certify that the company maintains an adequate system of internal control.
6. Management accountants follow a code of ethics developed by the U.S. Institute of Management Accountants.

(SO 1, 2, 3)
Identify managerial accounting concepts.

D1-2　Match the descriptions that follow with the corresponding terms.

Descriptions:

1. _____ Inventory system in which goods are manufactured or purchased just as they are needed for sale
2. _____ A method of allocating overhead based on each product's use of activities in making the product
3. _____ Systems that are especially important to firms adopting just-in-time inventory methods
4. _____ One part of the value chain for a manufacturing company
5. _____ The North American economy is trending toward this
6. _____ A performance-measurement approach that uses both financial and nonfinancial measures, tied to company objectives, to evaluate a company's operations in an integrated fashion

(SO 4)
Identify trends in managerial accounting.

Terms:
(a) Activity-based costing
(b) Balanced scorecard
(c) Total quality management (TQM)

(d) Research and development, and product design
(e) Service industries
(f) Just-in-time (JIT) inventory

Exercises

E1-3　The following table compares various features between managerial and financial accounting:

	Financial Accounting	Managerial Accounting
Primary users		
Type of reports		
Frequency of reports		
Purpose of reports		
Content of reports		
Verification		

(SO 1)
Explain the distinguishing features of managerial accounting.

Instructions
Complete the table above.

E1-4　The U.S. Institute of Management Accountants has promulgated ethical standards for managerial accountants.

Instructions
Identify the four specific standards.

(SO 3)
Explain the importance of business ethics.

E1-5　Listed below are the three functions of the management of an organization.

1. Planning　　2. Directing　　3. Controlling

(SO 2)
Identify the three broad functions of management.

Instructions
Identify which of the following statements best describes each of the above functions:
(a) _____ requires management to look ahead and to establish objectives. A key objective of management is to add value to the business.
(b) _____ involves coordinating a company's diverse activities and human resources to produce a smoothly running operation. This function relates to the implementation of planned objectives.

(c) _____ is the process of keeping the activities on track. Management must determine whether goals are being met and what changes are necessary when there are deviations.

(SO 2)
Identify the role of management accountants in an organizational structure.

E1-6   The following is a list of terms related to a company's organizational structure:

1. _____ Board of directors
2. _____ Chief financial officer
3. _____ Treasurer
4. _____ Controller
5. _____ Line position
6. _____ Chief executive officer
7. _____ Staff position

Instructions
Match each of the above terms with the appropriate statement below.
(a) Employee who has overall responsibility for managing the business
(b) Employees who are directly involved in the company's primary revenue-generating activities
(c) Employee with overall responsibility for all accounting and finance issues
(d) Group of people elected by the shareholders that selects and oversees company officers and formulates operating policies
(e) Employee who provides support services to those employees who are directly involved in the company's primary revenue-generating activities
(f) Employee who maintains accounting records and the system of internal controls, and prepares financial statements, tax returns, and internal reports
(g) Employee who has custody of the company's funds and maintains the company's cash position

(SO 1)
Explain the distinguishing features of managerial accounting.

E1-7   Financial accounting information and managerial accounting information have a number of distinguishing characteristics, which are listed below.

_____ 1. General-purpose reports
_____ 2. Reports are used internally
_____ 3. Prepared in accordance with generally accepted accounting principles
_____ 4. Special-purpose reports
_____ 5. Limited to historical cost data
_____ 6. Reporting standard is relevant to the decision to be made
_____ 7. Financial statements
_____ 8. Reports generally pertain to the business as a whole
_____ 9. Reports generally pertain to subunits
_____ 10. Reports issued quarterly or annually

Instructions
For each of the characteristics listed above, indicate which characteristics are more closely related to financial accounting by placing the letter "F" in the space to the left of the item and indicate those characteristics that are more closely associated with managerial accounting by placing the letter "M" to the left of the item.

(SO 1)
Explain the distinguishing features of managerial accounting.

E1-8   Chris Koplinski has prepared the following list of statements about managerial accounting and financial accounting.

1. Financial accounting focuses on providing information to internal users.
2. Analyzing cost-volume-profit relationships is part of managerial accounting.
3. Preparation of budgets is part of financial accounting.
4. Managerial accounting applies only to merchandising and manufacturing companies.
5. Both managerial accounting and financial accounting deal with many of the same economic events.
6. Managerial accounting reports are prepared only quarterly and annually.
7. Financial accounting reports are general-purpose reports.
8. Managerial accounting reports pertain to subunits of the business.
9. Managerial accounting reports must comply with generally accepted accounting principles.
10. Although managerial accountants are expected to behave ethically, there is no code of ethical standards for managerial accountants.

Instructions
Identify each statement as true or false. If false, indicate how to correct the statement.

E1-9 The following is a list of terms related to managerial accounting practices.

(SO 4)
Identify various managerial accounting practices.

1. Activity-based costing
2. Just-in-time inventory
3. Balanced scorecard
4. Value chain

Instructions

Match each of the terms with the statement below that best describes the term.

(a) _____ A performance-measurement technique that attempts to consider and evaluate all aspects of performance using financial and nonfinancial measures in an integrated fashion

(b) _____ The group of activities associated with providing a product or service

(c) _____ An approach used to reduce the cost associated with handling and holding inventory by reducing the amount of inventory on hand

(d) _____ A method used to allocate overhead to products based on each product's use of the activities that cause the incurrence of the overhead cost

Cases

C1-10 Love All is a fairly large manufacturing company of hockey equipment, located in Toronto. The company manufactures hockey sticks, pucks, clothing, and skates, all bearing the company's distinctive logo, a large green question mark on a white flocked hockey puck. The company's sales have been increasing over the past 10 years.

The hockey sticks division has recently implemented several advanced manufacturing techniques. Robot arms hold the hockey sticks in place while glue dries, and machine vision systems check for defects. The engineering and design team uses computerized drafting and testing of new products. The following managers work in the hockey sticks division:

Hayley Geagea, sales manager (supervises all sales representatives)
Luc Lemieux, technical specialist (supervises computer programmers)

Gary Richardson, cost accounting manager (supervises cost accountants)
Manny Cordoza, production supervisor (supervises all manufacturing employees)
Patrick Dumoulin, engineer (supervises all new-product design teams)

Instructions

(a) What are the primary information needs of each manager?
(b) Which, if any, financial accounting report(s) is each likely to use?
(c) Name one special-purpose management accounting report that could be designed for each manager. Include the name of the report, the information it would contain, and how frequently it should be issued.

C1-11 Million Dollar Mills is a manufacturing firm. The company carefully prepares all financial statements in accordance with Accounting Standards for Private Enterprises (ASPE), and gives a copy of all financial statements to each department. In addition, the company keeps records on quality control, safety, and its environmental pollution. It then prepares "scorecards" for each department indicating their performance. Recently, the financial impact of the second set of information was added, and the information has been used in the evaluation of employees for merit pay and promotions.

At the most recent employee meeting, Thanh Nguyen, marketing manager, expressed his discomfort with the system. He said there was

no guarantee that the second set of information was fair, since there were no generally accepted principles for this kind of information. He also said that it was kind of like keeping two sets of books—one following all legal requirements, and the other one actually used by the company.

Instructions

(a) Is it ethical to evaluate managers in the way described? Explain briefly.
(b) Name at least two safeguards the company could build into its system to ensure the ethical treatment of employees.

Ethics cases ask you to reflect on typical ethical dilemmas, analyze the stakeholders and the issues involved, and decide on an appropriate course of action.

"All About You" Activity

C1-12 The primary purpose of managerial accounting is to provide information useful for management decisions. Many of the managerial accounting techniques that you learn in this course will be useful for decisions you make in your everyday life. After you graduate, one of the next important decisions you'll have to make is where to work.

Instructions
Suppose that you go for job interviews and are given an offer of employment by two competing firms for the same entry-level position. They are offering the same salary and benefits. Their offices are in different cities. They are both public companies, so their annual reports containing financial and other information are available to you for free on their websites. For each of the following factors, provide an example of the numerical information you would need to help decide which firm to work for.
(a) Which company is currently more profitable
(b) Which city is more economical to live in
(c) Which company has better long-term prospects
(d) Which company might have more opportunities for advancement

Decision-Making at Current Designs

Each chapter contains an exercise based on Current Designs, the company that was featured at the beginning of this chapter. We are excited to present hypothetical managerial accounting situations that are based on the operations of a real company. However, to protect the proprietary nature of this information, the amounts in these exercises are realistic but not the actual data that would be found in Current Designs' accounting records. Students can also work through this exercise following an Excel tutorial available in WileyPLUS and the book's companion website. Each chapter's tutorial focuses on a different Excel function or feature.

DM1-1 Mike Cichanowski founded Wenonah Canoe and later purchased Current Designs, a company that designs and manufactures kayaks. The kayak-manufacturing facility is located just a few minutes from the canoe company's headquarters in Winona, Minnesota.

Current Designs makes kayaks using two different processes. The rotational moulding process uses high temperature to melt polyethylene powder in a closed rotating metal mould to produce a complete kayak hull and deck in a single piece. These kayaks are less labour-intensive and less expensive for the company to produce and sell.

Its other kayaks use the vacuum-bagged composite lamination process (which we will refer to as the composite process). Layers of fibreglass or Kevlar® are carefully placed by hand in a mould and are bonded with resin. Then, a high-pressure vacuum is used to eliminate any excess resin that would otherwise add weight and reduce strength of the finished kayak. These kayaks require a great deal of skilled labour as each boat is individually finished. The exquisite finish of the vacuum bagged composite kayaks gave rise to Current Designs' tag line, "A work of art, made for life."

Current Designs has the following managers:
Mike Cichanowski, CEO
Diane Buswell, Controller
Deb Welch, Purchasing Manager
Bill Johnson, Sales Manager
Dave Thill, Kayak Plant Manager
Rick Thrune, Production Manager for Composite Kayaks

Instructions
(a) What are the primary information needs of each manager?
(b) Name one special-purpose management accounting report that could be designed for each manager. Include the name of the report, the information it would contain, and how frequently it should be issued.

Waterways Continuing Problem

WCP-1 Waterways Corporation is a private company providing irrigation and drainage products and services for residential, commercial, and public sector projects, including farms, parks, and sports fields. It has a plant located in a small city north of Toronto that manufactures the products it markets to retail outlets across Canada. It also maintains a division that provides installation and warranty servicing in the Greater Toronto Area.

The mission of Waterways is to manufacture quality parts that can be used for effective water management, be it drainage or irrigation. The company hopes to satisfy its customers with its products, provide rapid and responsible service, and serve the community and the employees who represent it in each community.

The company has been growing rapidly, so management is considering new ideas to help the company continue its growth and maintain the high quality of its products. Waterways was founded by Phil Clark Sr., who has since retired. He continues to own a majority of the company shares. Now his son, Phil Clark Jr., is the company president and chief executive officer (CEO). Working with Phil from the company's inception is his brother, Ben, whose sprinkler designs and ideas about the installation of proper systems have been a major reason for the company's success. Ben is the vice-president of operations who oversees all aspects of design and production in the company.

The plant itself is managed by Ryan Smith, who reports to Ben. First-line supervisors reporting to Ryan are responsible for the plant employees. The plant makes all of the parts for the irrigation and drainage systems. The purchasing department is managed by Jo Chan, who also reports to Ryan.

The installation and training division is overseen by service vice-president Lee Williams, who supervises the managers of the six local installation operations. Each of these local managers hires his or her own local service people. These service employees are trained at headquarters under Lee's direction because of the uniqueness of the company's products.

Kim Martin acts as vice-president of human resources. Kim manages a small team that is responsible for human resource devel-opment, salary administration, and group benefits. Each department does its own hiring. Madison Tremblay is the sales and marketing vice-president, with a sales force of 10 experienced professionals.

The accounting and finance division of the company is headed by Jordan Leigh, CA, as vice-president of finance and chief financial officer (CFO). There is a small staff of professionally designated accountants, including a controller and a treasurer, and a clerical staff who maintain the financial records.

Instructions

Based on the information provided, construct an organizational chart for Waterways Corporation.

Answers to Self-Study Questions

1. b   **2.** d   **3.** b   **4.** a   **5.** b   **6.** b   **7.** c   **8.** c   **9.** d   **10.** d

Remember to go back to the beginning of the chapter to check off your completed work!

←

Managerial Cost Concepts and Cost Behaviour Analysis

The Navigator
Chapter 2

- [ ] Scan *Study Objectives*
- [ ] Read *Feature Story*
- [ ] Read *Chapter Preview*
- [ ] Read text and answer *Before You Go On* p. 32, p. 36, p. 39, p. 43
- [ ] Work *Using the Decision Toolkit*
- [ ] Review *Summary of Study Objectives*
- [ ] Review *Decision Toolkit—A Summary*
- [ ] Work *Comprehensive Do It!*
- [ ] Answer *Self-Study Questions*
- [ ] Complete assignments

study objectives

the navigator

After studying this chapter, you should be able to do the following:

1. Define the three classes of manufacturing costs and differentiate between product costs and period costs.

2. Explain variable, fixed, and mixed costs and the relevant range.

3. Apply the high-low method to determine the components of mixed costs.

4. Demonstrate how to calculate cost of goods manufactured and prepare financial statements for a manufacturer.

MINING COST-CUTTING POTENTIAL

The Potash Corporation of Saskatchewan Inc. is the world's largest fertilizer company by capacity. Because fertilizer is a commodity—in other words, the market determines the price, which can fluctuate widely based on supply and demand—PotashCorp must control its costs in order to make a profit.

PotashCorp's primary products are potash, phosphate, and nitrogen, used to make fertilizer and also livestock feed and industrial goods, including soap, water softeners, and plastics. The corporation operates in seven countries. Potash is mined from evaporated sea deposits, mainly found in PotashCorp's mines across Saskatchewan. Phosphate comes from rocks made from marine fossils, and nitrogen is found in air but must be converted into other products, such as ammonia and urea, to help plants grow. All of these products require machinery- and labour-intensive processes. In 2013, on sales of U.S. $7.3 billion, PotashCorp's major expenses—cost of goods sold and cost of freight, transportation, and distribution—added up to $4.5 billion.

In order to reduce costs, the corporation in 2013 announced that it would reduce its workforce in Canada, the United States, and Trinidad by about 18%. "This was not an easy decision but it is a necessary one," said then-President and Chief Executive Officer Bill Doyle. PotashCorp planned to close higher-cost facilities and increase production at its lowest-cost operations. The corporation expected that it could reduce the cost of producing one tonne of potash by $15 to $20 in 2014, and by $20 to $30 per tonne in 2016.

In another cost-cutting move, the corporation launched a project to start recovering and using some of the coarse phosphate that usually becomes waste at its phosphate mine in North Carolina. PotashCorp says the project increased the mine's production and lowered the mine's costs.

PotashCorp recently added 2,000 custom-built, high-capacity rail cars to its owned and leased fleet that ships products to the United States in order to increase volumes per train load, which reduces transportation costs per load.

While high costs are usually a challenge for businesses, they can sometimes work to their advantage. In the case of PotashCorp, it notes that the high cost of developing new potash mines is a barrier to more competitors entering the business. The corporation estimates it would cost at least $4.2 billion and take more than seven years to build a new 2-million-tonne potash mine in Saskatchewan, home to half the world's potash deposits. While these staggering capital costs keep competitors at bay, it also means that PotashCorp has been expanding all of its existing mines rather than building new ones.

Sources: PotashCorp, 2013 Annual Integrated Report; "PotashCorp Announces Operating and Workforce Changes," PotashCorp news release and accompanying video statement from William Doyle, December 3, 2013; Brent Jang, "In Aftermath of Cartel Breakup, Potash Prices Slide," *The Globe and Mail*, August 22, 2013; "5 Ws and an H about P," PotashCorp, n.d.

the navigator

Preview of Chapter 2

This chapter focuses on issues illustrated in the feature story about Potash Corporation of Saskatchewan Inc. These include determining and controlling the costs of materials, labour, and overhead and the relationship between costs and profits. Managers use cost information to make various decisions. They need to understand a variety of cost concepts and how changes in the level of business activity affect these costs. In this chapter, we explain various managerial cost concepts that are useful in planning, directing, and controlling. We also present cost flows and the process of cost accumulation in a manufacturing environment.

The chapter is organized as follows:

the navigator

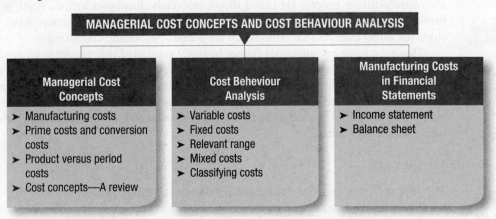

MANAGERIAL COST CONCEPTS AND COST BEHAVIOUR ANALYSIS

Managerial Cost Concepts	Cost Behaviour Analysis	Manufacturing Costs in Financial Statements
➤ Manufacturing costs	➤ Variable costs	➤ Income statement
➤ Prime costs and conversion costs	➤ Fixed costs	➤ Balance sheet
➤ Product versus period costs	➤ Relevant range	
➤ Cost concepts—A review	➤ Mixed costs	
	➤ Classifying costs	

Managerial Cost Concepts

In order for managers at companies like PotashCorp to plan, direct, and control operations effectively, they need good information. One very important type of information is related to costs. Managers should ask questions such as the following:

1. What costs are involved in making a product or providing a service?
2. If we decrease production volume, will costs decrease?
3. What impact will automation have on total costs?
4. How can we best control costs?

To answer these questions, managers need reliable and relevant cost information. We now explain and illustrate the various cost categories that management uses. But first, **what does cost mean?** Accountants define cost as an economic resource given up or foregone to accomplish a particular objective. **What does cost object mean?** A cost object is anything for which we want to calculate a cost, such as a product (soft drink), a product line, or service, or a process for which cost information is measured and accumulated. Management accountants use different systems, or classifications, to develop cost information.

MANUFACTURING COSTS

Manufacturing consists of activities and processes that convert raw materials into finished goods. In contrast, merchandising sells goods in the same form in which they are purchased. Manufacturing costs are typically classified as shown in Illustration 2-1.

▶Illustration 2-1

Classifications of manufacturing costs

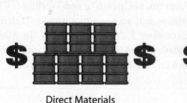  

Direct Materials   Direct Labour   Manufacturing Overhead

Direct Materials

Direct Materials

To obtain the materials that will be converted into the finished product, the manufacturer purchases raw materials. **Raw materials** are the basic materials and parts used in the manufacturing process. For example, auto manufacturers such as General Motors of Canada, Honda Canada, and Ford Motor Co. of Canada, use steel, plastics, and tires as raw materials in making cars.

Raw materials that can be physically and directly associated with the finished product during the manufacturing process are called **direct materials**. Examples include flour in the baking of bread, syrup in the bottling of soft drinks, and steel in the making of automobiles. In the feature story, the direct materials for PotashCorp are potash, phosphate, and nitrogen.

However, some raw materials cannot be easily associated with the finished product. These are called indirect materials. **Indirect materials** have one of two characteristics: (1) they do not physically become part of the finished product, such as lubricants and polishing compounds, or (2) they cannot be easily traced because their physical association with the finished product is too small in terms of cost, such as sandpaper and glue. Companies account for indirect materials as part of the **manufacturing overhead**.

Direct Labour

Direct Labour

The work of factory employees that can be physically and directly associated with converting raw materials into finished goods is called **direct labour**. Bottlers at Cott Corporation and bakers at McCain Foods are employees whose activities are usually classified as direct labour. But some work of factory employees cannot be easily associated with the finished product. This work is called indirect labour. **Indirect labour** has one of two characteristics: (1) it is the work of factory employees that has no physical association with the finished product, or (2) it is work for which it is impractical to trace costs to the goods produced. Examples include wages of maintenance people, timekeepers, and supervisors. Like indirect materials, indirect labour is classified as **manufacturing overhead**.

Manufacturing Overhead

Manufacturing overhead consists of costs that are indirectly associated with the manufacture of the finished product. These costs may also be manufacturing costs that cannot be classified as direct materials or direct labour. Manufacturing overhead includes indirect materials, indirect labour, depreciation on factory buildings and machines, and insurance, taxes, and maintenance on factory facilities.

One study found the following magnitudes of the three different product costs as a percentage of the total product cost: direct materials 54%, direct labour 13%, and manufacturing overhead 33%. Note that the direct labour component is the smallest. This component of product cost is dropping substantially because of automation. Companies are working hard to increase productivity by decreasing labour. In some companies, direct labour has become as little as 5% of the total cost.

Allocating materials and labour costs to specific products is fairly straightforward. Good record keeping can tell a company how much plastic is used in making each type of gear, or how many hours of factory labour are used to assemble a part. But allocating overhead costs to specific products presents problems. How much of the purchasing agent's salary is attributable to the hundreds of different products made in the same plant? What about the grease that keeps the machines humming, or the computers that make sure employees get paid on time? Boiled down to its simplest form, the question becomes: Which products involve which costs? In subsequent chapters, we show various methods of allocating overhead to products.

PRIME COSTS AND CONVERSION COSTS

Prime costs and conversion costs are two other terms that managers and accountants use in manufacturing accounting systems. As shown in Illustration 2-2, **prime costs** are the sum of all direct materials costs and direct labour costs. These are all direct manufacturing costs. **Conversion costs** are the sum of all direct labour costs and manufacturing overhead costs, which together are the costs of converting raw materials into a final product.

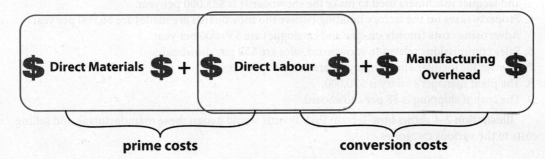

▶Illustration 2-2
Prime costs and conversion costs

PRODUCT VERSUS PERIOD COSTS

Each of the manufacturing cost components (direct materials, direct labour, and manufacturing overhead) are product costs. As the term suggests, **product costs** are costs that are a necessary and integral part of producing the finished product. Companies record product costs, when incurred, as inventory. Under the matching principle, these costs do not become expenses until the company sells the finished goods inventory. At that point, the company records the expense as cost of goods sold.

Period costs are costs that are matched with the revenue of a specific time period rather than included as part of the cost of a saleable product. These are non-manufacturing costs. Period costs include selling and administrative expenses. They are deducted from revenues in the period in which they are incurred, in order to determine net income. Illustration 2-3 shows the difference between product costs and period costs.

Manufacturing Overhead

Alternative Terminology
Terms such as *factory overhead, indirect manufacturing costs,* and *burden* are sometimes used instead of *manufacturing overhead.*

Alternative Terminology notes present synonymous terms that are used in practice.

Helpful Hint
An unethical manager may choose to inflate the company's earnings by improperly including period costs (such as selling and administrative expenses not related to production) in the ending inventory balances.

Alternative Terminology
Product costs are also called *inventoriable costs.*

▶Illustration 2-3
Product versus period costs

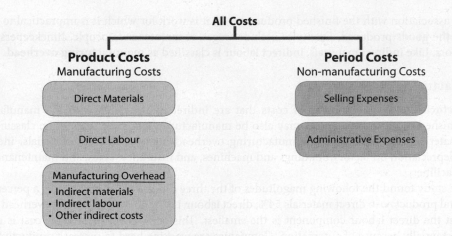

▶Illustration 2-3
Product versus period costs

COST CONCEPTS—A REVIEW

Product Costing for Manufacturing Companies

You will learn a number of cost concepts in this chapter. Because many of these concepts are new, we provide here an extended example for review. Suppose you started your own snowboard factory, Terrain Park Boards. Think that's impossible? Burton Snowboards was started by Jake Burton Carpenter when he was only 23 years old. Jake initially experimented with 100 different prototype designs before settling on a final design. Then Jake, along with two relatives and a friend, started making 50 boards per day in Collingwood, Ontario. Unfortunately, while they made a lot of boards in their first year, they were only able to sell 300 of them. To get by during those early years, Jake taught tennis and tended bar to pay the bills.

Here are some of the costs that your snowboard factory would incur.

1. The materials cost of each snowboard (wood cores, fibreglass, resins, metal screw holes, metal edges, and ink) is $30.
2. The labour costs (for example, to trim and shape each board using jigsaws and band saws) are $40.
3. Depreciation on the factory building and equipment (for example, presses, grinding machines, and lacquer machines) used to make the snowboards is $25,000 per year.
4. Property taxes on the factory building (where the snowboards are made) are $6,000 per year.
5. Advertising costs (mostly on-line and catalogue) are $30,000 per year.
6. Sales commissions related to snowboard sales are $20 per snowboard.
7. Salaries for maintenance employees are $45,000 per year.
8. The plant manager's salary is $70,000.
9. The cost of shipping is $8 per snowboard.

Illustration 2-4 shows how Terrain Park Boards would assign these manufacturing and selling costs to the various categories.

▶Illustration 2-4

Assignment of costs to cost categories

Cost Item	Product Costs			Period Costs
	Direct Materials	Direct Labour	Manufacturing Overhead	
1. Material cost ($30) per board	X			
2. Labour costs ($40) per board		X		
3. Depreciation on factory equipment ($25,000 per year)			X	
4. Property taxes on factory building ($6,000 per year)			X	
5. Advertising costs ($30,000 per year)				X
6. Sales commissions ($20 per board)				X
7. Maintenance salaries (factory facilities) ($45,000 per year)			X	
8. Salary of plant manager ($70,000)			X	
9. Cost of shipping boards ($8 per board)				X

Remember that total manufacturing costs are the sum of the **product costs**—direct materials, direct labour, and manufacturing overhead. If Terrain Park Boards produces 10,000 snowboards the first year, the total manufacturing costs would be $846,000, as shown in Illustration 2-5.

Cost Number and Item	Manufacturing Cost
1. Material cost ($30 × 10,000)	$300,000
2. Labour cost ($40 × 10,000)	400,000
3. Depreciation on factory equipment	25,000
4. Property taxes on factory building	6,000
5. Advertising costs ($30,000/year)*	X
6. Sales commissions ($20/door)*	X
7. Maintenance salaries (factory facilities)	45,000
8. Salary of plant manager	70,000
9. Cost of shipping boards ($8 per board)*	X
Total manufacturing costs	$846,000

*Period costs or selling expenses

Knowing the total manufacturing costs, Terrain Park Boards can calculate the manufacturing cost per unit. Assuming 10,000 units, the cost to produce one snowboard is $84.60 ($846,000 ÷ 10,000 units).

In subsequent chapters, we will use extensively the cost concepts discussed in this chapter. Study Illustration 2-4 carefully. If you do not understand any of these classifications of manufacturing costs, go back and reread the appropriate section in this chapter.

Product Costing for Service Industries

This chapter focuses on product costs for manufacturers. But as stated in Chapter 1, the Canadian and U.S. economies in general have shifted toward an emphasis on providing services, rather than on producing goods. Today more than 50% of North American workers are employed by service companies. Airlines, marketing agencies, cable television companies, and restaurants are just a few examples of service companies. How do service companies differ from manufacturing companies when it comes to product costing? One good way to differentiate these two types of companies is by how quickly the product is used or consumed by the customer—services are consumed immediately. For example, when a restaurant produces a meal, that meal is not put in inventory, but it is instead consumed immediately. An airline uses special equipment to provide its product, but again, the output of that equipment is consumed immediately by the customer in the form of a flight. And a marketing agency performs services for its clients that are immediately consumed by the customer in the form of a marketing plan. For a manufacturing company, such as Bombardier Inc., there is often a long lead time before its product (such as an airplane) is used or consumed by the customer.

In presenting our initial examples, we used manufacturing companies because accounting for the manufacturing environment requires the use of the broadest range of accounts. That is, the accounts used by service companies represent a subset of those used by manufacturers because service companies are not producing inventory. Neither the restaurant, the airline, nor the marketing agency discussed above produces an inventoriable product. However, just like a manufacturer, each needs to keep track of the costs of its services in order to know whether it is generating a profit. A successful restaurateur needs to know the cost of each offering on the menu, an airline needs to know the cost of flight service to each destination, and a marketing agency needs to know the cost to develop a marketing plan. Thus, the techniques shown in this chapter to accumulate manufacturing costs to determine manufacturing inventory are equally useful for determining the costs of providing services.

For example, let's consider the costs that Hewlett-Packard (HP) might incur on a consulting engagement. A significant portion of its costs would be salaries of consulting personnel. It might also incur travel costs, materials, software costs, and depreciation charges on equipment used by the employees to provide the consulting service. In the same way that it needs to keep track of the cost of manufacturing its computers and printers, HP needs to know what its costs are on each consulting job. It could prepare a cost of services provided schedule similar to the cost of goods manufactured schedule in Illustration 2-17 later in the chapter. The structure would be essentially the same as the cost of goods manufactured schedule, but section headings would be reflective of the costs of the particular service organization.

BUSINESS INSIGHT   *Grounded in Cost Control*

Calgary-based WestJet Airlines has competed on price with full-service competitor Air Canada since the budget airline first took to the skies. How does it keep its fares lower? By keeping costs under control. For example, it has one centralized ground operations office, instead of one in every airport, and its pilots all work from Calgary headquarters instead of regional bases. WestJet and its regional service Encore use just two types of plane—the Boeing 737 and Bombardier Q400—to lower maintenance bills. It's managed to rein in its costs at an estimated one-third lower than those of Air Canada. As a result, WestJet was able to add value for shareholders by paying its first-ever dividend in early 2011, becoming one of the few airlines in the world to do so.

Sources: Ross Marowits, The Canadian Press, "WestJet Unveils Launch of Encore Eastern Expansion with First Service in Toronto," *The Globe and Mail*, January 20, 2014; Brent Jang, "WestJet Shares Appear Ready for Takeoff," *The Globe and Mail*, January 19, 2011; Scott Deveau, "WestJet Initiates Dividend, Share Buyback," *Financial Post*, November 3, 2010; James Careless, "Today's Efficient Flight Departments," *Wings Magazine*, May-June 2010.

What are some other ways that airlines can keep costs down?

BEFORE YOU GO ON...

▶Do It! Managerial Cost Concepts

A bicycle company has these costs: tires, salaries of employees who put tires on the wheels, factory building depreciation, lubricants, spokes, salary of factory manager, handlebars, and salaries of factory maintenance employees. Classify each cost as direct materials, direct labour, or overhead.

Action Plan

- Classify as direct materials any raw materials that can be physically and directly associated with the finished product.
- Classify as direct labour the work of factory employees that can be physically and directly associated with the finished product.
- Classify as manufacturing overhead any costs that are indirectly associated with the finished product.

Solution

Tires, spokes, and handlebars are direct materials. Salaries of employees who put tires on the wheels are direct labour. All of the other costs are manufacturing overhead.

Related exercise material: **BE2–1, BE2–2, BE2–3, BE2–9, E2-18, E2-19, E2-20, E2–21, E2-22, E2-29,** and **Do It! D2-14.**

the navigator

Cost Behaviour Analysis

STUDY OBJECTIVE 2
Explain variable, fixed, and mixed costs and the relevant range.

Cost behaviour analysis is the study of how specific costs respond to changes in the level of business activity. As you might expect, some costs change and others remain the same. For example, for an airline company such as Air Canada or WestJet, the longer the flight, the higher the fuel costs. On the other hand, Montreal General Hospital's employee costs to run the emergency room on any particular night are relatively constant regardless of the number of patients treated. Knowledge of cost behaviour helps management plan activities and decide between alternative courses of action.

The starting point in cost behaviour analysis is measuring the key business activities. Activity levels may be expressed in terms of sales dollars (in a retail company), kilometres driven (in a trucking company), room occupancy (in a hotel), or dance classes taught (by a dance studio). Many companies use more than one measurement base. A manufacturer, for example, may use direct labour hours or units of output for manufacturing costs, and sales revenue or units sold for selling expenses.

For an activity level to be useful in cost behaviour analysis, changes in the level or volume of activity should be correlated with changes in costs. The activity level selected is referred to as the activity (or volume) index. The **activity index** identifies the activity that causes changes in the behaviour of costs. With an appropriate activity index, it is possible to classify the behaviour of costs in response to changes in activity levels into three categories: variable, fixed, or mixed.

VARIABLE COSTS

Variable costs are costs that vary **in total** directly and proportionally with changes in the activity level. If the level increases by 10%, total variable costs will increase by 10%. If the level of activity decreases by 25%, variable costs will decrease by 25%. Examples of variable costs include direct materials and direct labour for a manufacturer; cost of goods sold, sales commissions, and freight out for a merchandiser; and gasoline for an airline or trucking company. A variable cost may also be defined as a cost that **remains the same *per unit* at every level of activity**.

To illustrate the behaviour of a variable cost, assume that Damon Company manufactures tablet computers that contain a $10 camera. The activity index is the number of tablets produced. As each tablet is manufactured, the total cost of the cameras increases by $10. As shown in part (a) of Illustration 2-6, the total cost of the cameras will be $20,000 if 2,000 tablets are produced, and $100,000 if 10,000 tablets are produced. We can also see that the variable cost remains the same per unit as the level of activity changes. As shown in part (b) of Illustration 2-6, the unit cost of $10 for the cameras is the same whether 2,000 or 10,000 tablets are produced.

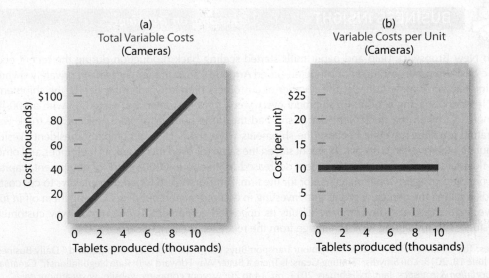

▶Illustration 2-6
Behaviour of total and unit variable costs

Companies that rely heavily on labour to manufacture a product, such as Nike or Reebok, or to provide a service, such as the public accounting firm KPMG, are likely to have many variable costs. In contrast, companies that use a lot of capital assets to generate revenue, such as BCE or Encana, may have few variable costs.

FIXED COSTS

Fixed costs are costs that **remain the same in total within the relevant range** regardless of changes in the activity level. Examples include property taxes, insurance, rent, supervisory salaries, and depreciation on buildings and equipment. Because total fixed costs remain constant as activity changes, it follows that **fixed costs per unit vary inversely with activity**. In other words, **as volume increases, unit cost declines, and vice versa**.

Helpful Hint
True or false: The variable cost per unit changes directly and proportionately with changes in activity. Answer: False. The cost per unit remains constant at all levels of activity.

To illustrate the behaviour of fixed costs, assume that Damon Company leases its production facilities at a cost of $10,000 per month. The total fixed costs of the facilities will remain constant at every level of activity, as shown in part (a) of Illustration 2-7. But, on a per-unit basis, the cost of rent will decline as activity increases, as shown in part (b) of Illustration 2-7. At 2,000 units, the unit cost is $5 ($10,000 ÷ 2,000). When 10,000 tablets are produced, the unit cost is only $1 ($10,000 ÷ 10,000).

The trend for many manufacturers is to have more fixed costs and fewer variable costs. This trend is the result of an increased use of automation and less use of employee labour. As a result, depreciation and lease charges (fixed costs) increase, whereas direct labour costs (variable costs) decrease.

▶Illustration 2-7

Behaviour of total and unit fixed costs

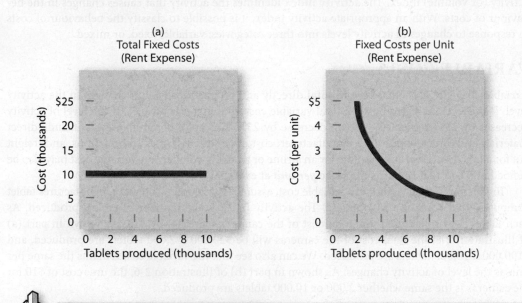

When New Brunswick pulp and paper mills started scaling back production during the recent economic crisis, that hurt business for Moncton-based Armour Transportation Systems, a privately owned trucking firm in Atlantic Canada. The number of customers didn't dwindle; the size of the shipments did. "Instead of having a 1,000-lb. shipment every week for a customer, you ended up with a 600-lb. shipment. So when the truck went out, it still had the same number of stops, except the truck was generating a lot less revenue because the shipments were smaller," said company president Wesley Armour. In other words, costs per shipment stayed the same (or even increased, as fuel prices and other costs fluctuated) but revenue per shipment decreased. With about 4,000 pieces of equipment, capital and operating costs are a significant factor for the firm. Armour looked for additional ways to cut costs, including taking the company profits and investing in equipment and buildings, paying them off in full to save financing costs. The company credits its upgraded equipment as one reason why customers have stuck with it, helping Armour emerge from the recession a stronger carrier.

Sources: The Canadian Press, "NB & NL: Armour Transport Buys Way's Transport of Newfoundland," Daily Business Buzz, June 18, 2013; Lou Smyrlis, "Shifting Gears: Is There a Better Way Forward with Rate Negotiations?," *Canadian Transportation & Logistics*, January/February 2013, pp. 14 to 20; Armour company website, www.armour.ca.

How could a trucking firm control costs if the size and number of shipments increased?

BUSINESS INSIGHT   *Keeping on Trucking*

RELEVANT RANGE

In Illustration 2-6, a straight line was drawn throughout the entire range of the activity index for total variable costs. Basically, the assumption was that the costs were **linear**. If a relationship is linear (that is, straight-line), then changes in the activity index will result in a direct, proportional change in the variable cost. For example, if the activity level doubles, the cost doubles.

It is now necessary to ask: Is the straight-line relationship realistic? In most business situations, a straight-line relationship **does not exist** for variable costs throughout the entire range of possible activity. At abnormally low levels of activity, it may be impossible to be cost-efficient. Small-scale operations may not allow the company to obtain quantity discounts for raw materials or to use specialized labour. In contrast, at abnormally high levels of activity, labour costs may increase sharply because of overtime pay. Also, at high activity levels, materials costs may jump significantly because of excess spoilage caused by worker fatigue. As a result, in the real world, the relationship between the behaviour of a variable cost and changes in the activity level is often **curvilinear**, as shown in part (a) of Illustration 2-8. In the curved sections of the line, a change in the activity index will not result in a direct, proportional change in the variable cost. That is, a doubling of the activity index will not result in an exact doubling of the variable cost. The variable cost may be more than double, or it may be less than double.

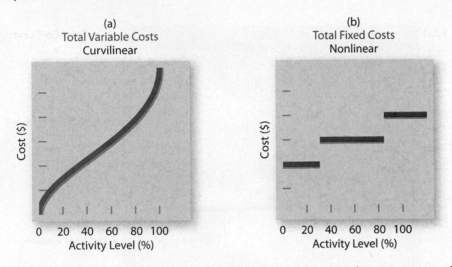

►Illustration 2-8
Nonlinear behaviour of variable and fixed costs

Total fixed costs also do not have a straight-line relationship over the entire range of activity. Some fixed costs will not change. But it is possible for management to change other fixed costs. For example, a dance studio's rent might start out variable and then become fixed at a certain amount. It could then increase to a new fixed amount when the size of the studio increases beyond a certain point. An example of the behaviour of total fixed costs through all potential levels of activity is shown in part (b) of Illustration 2-8.

For most companies, operating at almost zero or at 100% capacity is the exception rather than the rule. Instead, companies often operate over a narrower range, such as 40 to 80% of capacity. The range that a company expects to operate in during a year is called the **relevant range** of the activity index. Within the relevant range, as shown in both diagrams in Illustration 2-9, there is usually a straight-line relationship for both variable and fixed costs.

Helpful Hint
Fixed costs that may be changeable include research, such as new product development, and management training programs.

Alternative Terminology
The *relevant range* is also called the *normal* or *practical range*.

►Illustration 2-9
Linear behaviour within relevant range

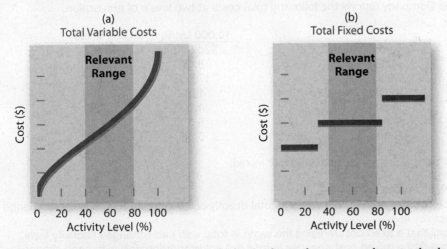

As you can see, although the linear (straight-line) relationship may not be completely realistic, **the linear assumption produces useful data for cost behaviour analysis as long as the level of activity stays in the relevant range.**

MIXED COSTS

Mixed costs are costs that have both a variable element and a fixed element. They are sometimes called semi-variable costs. **Mixed costs change in total but not proportionally with changes in the activity level.**

The rental of a U-Haul truck is a good example of a mixed cost. Assume that local rental terms for a five-metre truck, including insurance, are $50 per day plus 25 cents per kilometre. When the cost of a one-day rental is being determined, the charge per day is a fixed cost (with respect to $50 rent, including insurance), whereas the kilometre charge is a variable cost. Illustration 2-10 shows the rental cost for a one-day rental.

▶Illustration 2-10
Behaviour of mixed costs

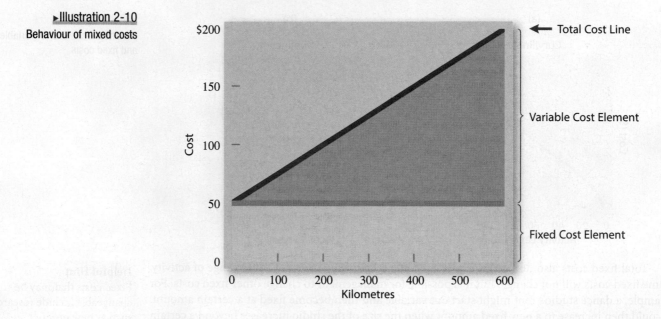

In this case, the fixed cost element is the cost of having the service available. The variable cost element is the cost of actually using the service. Another example of a mixed cost is utility costs (electricity, telephone, and so on), where there is a flat service fee plus a usage charge.

BEFORE YOU GO ON...

▶Do It! Types of Costs

Helena Company reports the following total costs at two levels of production.

	10,000 Units	20,000 Units
Direct materials	$20,000	$40,000
Maintenance	8,000	10,000
Direct labour	17,000	34,000
Indirect materials	1,000	2,000
Depreciation	4,000	4,000
Utilities	3,000	5,000
Rent	6,000	6,000

Classify each cost as variable, fixed, or mixed.

Action Plan

- Recall that a variable cost varies in total directly and proportionately with each change in activity level.
- Recall that a fixed cost remains the same in total with each change in activity level.
- Recall that a mixed cost changes in total but not proportionately with each change in activity level.

Solution

Direct materials, direct labour, and indirect materials are variable costs.
Depreciation and rent are fixed costs.
Maintenance and utilities are mixed costs.

Related exercise material: **BE2-5, E2-23, E2-26, E2-28,** and **Do It! D2-15.**

the navigator

CLASSIFYING COSTS

For cost behaviour analysis, **mixed costs must be classified into their fixed and variable elements**. How does management make the classification? One possibility is to determine the variable and fixed components each time a mixed cost is incurred. However, because of time and cost constraints, this approach is rarely used. Instead, the usual approach is to determine the variable and fixed cost components of the total cost **at the end of a period of time**. The company does this by using its past experience with the behaviour of the mixed cost at various levels of activity. Management may use any of several methods in making the determination. We will explain the **high-low method** here. Other methods include the scatter diagram method and least squares regression analysis. These other methods are explained in cost accounting courses.

High-Low Method

The **high-low method** uses the total costs incurred at the high and low levels of *activity*. The difference in costs between the high and low levels represents variable costs, since only the variable cost element can change as activity levels change. The steps in calculating fixed and variable costs under this method are as follows:

1. Determine the variable cost per unit by using the formula in Illustration 2-11.

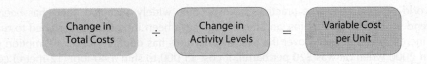

STUDY OBJECTIVE 3

Apply the high-low method to determine the components of mixed costs.

▶Illustration 2-11
Formula for variable cost per unit using the high-low method

To illustrate, assume that Metro Transit Company has the maintenance costs and kilometres driven data for its fleet of buses over a four-month period, as shown in Illustration 2-12:

▶Illustration 2-12
Assumed maintenance costs and kilometres driven data

Month	Kilometres Driven	Total Cost	Month	Kilometres Driven	Total Cost
January	40,000	$30,000	March	70,000	$49,000
February	80,000	48,000	April	100,000	63,000

The high and low levels of activity are 100,000 kilometres in April and 40,000 kilometres in January. The maintenance costs at these two levels are $63,000 and $30,000, respectively. The difference in maintenance costs is $33,000 ($63,000 − $30,000) and the difference in kilometres is 60,000 (100,000 − 40,000). Therefore, for Metro Transit, the variable cost per unit is $0.55, calculated as follows:

$$\$33,000 \div 60,000 = \$0.55$$

2. Determine the fixed cost by subtracting the total variable cost at either the high or the low activity level from the total cost at that activity level.

For Metro Transit, the calculations are shown in Illustration 2-13.

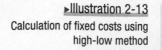

►Illustration 2-13
Calculation of fixed costs using high-low method

| | Activity Level | |
	High	Low
Total cost	$63,000	$30,000
Less: Variable costs		
100,000 × $0.55	55,000	
40,000 × $0.55		22,000
Total fixed costs	$ 8,000	$ 8,000

Maintenance costs are therefore $8,000 per month plus $0.55 per kilometre. This is represented by the following formula:

$$\text{Maintenance costs} = 8,000 + \$0.55 \text{ (kilometres driven)}$$

For example, at 90,000 kilometres, estimated maintenance costs would be $8,000 fixed and $49,500 variable (90,000 × $0.55) for a total of $57,500.

The high-low method generally produces a reasonable estimate for analysis. However, it does not produce a precise measurement of the fixed and variable elements in a mixed cost, because other activity levels are ignored in the calculation.

BUSINESS INSIGHT   *Oil Prices Affect Shipping Costs*

Is globalization reversible? Until quite recently, this question wouldn't have been taken seriously. However, global energy costs have been increasing at an unprecedented rate. These rising energy costs come at a time when manufacturing activities have been relocated from the developed to the less developed world.

In a world where just-in-time practices have become widely accepted, there has been a pronounced trend to use container ships, and these ships have been increasingly designed to run faster. In fact the increase in ship speed over the past two decades has doubled fuel consumption per unit of freight. In 2000 when oil was $20 per barrel, it cost $3,000 to ship a 40-foot (12-metre) container from Shanghai to North America. In the first half of 2008, the same shipment would have cost $8,000 and if the price of oil were to reach $200 per barrel, then it would cost $15,000 to transport the same amount to North America. However, some shipping companies have slowed down their ship speed to try to save on fuel costs, though that can jeopardize just-in-time delivery systems.

In industries that produce heavy, bulky products, these increased freight costs are shifting trade patterns. For example, Chinese exports of steel to North America were falling in 2008 and U.S. production of steel was increasing. U.S. steelworkers still make a lot more than their Chinese counterparts, but the shift in freight rates was enough to encourage purchasers of some steel products to shop at home.

Source: Jeff Rubin and Benjamin Tal, "Will Soaring Transport Costs Reverse Globalization?", Strategic Economics, CIBC World Markets, May 27, 2008; Jeff Rubin, "How Sustainable Is Growth with Triple-Digit Oil?", *Globe and Mail*, January 19, 2011; Alaric Nightingale and Kyunghee Park, "Container Ship Rates Rally as Fuel Prices Rise: Freight Markets," Bloomberg, January 19, 2011.

What happens to trade patterns when transport costs fall?

Importance of Identifying Variable and Fixed Costs

Why is it important to segregate mixed costs into variable and fixed elements? The answer may become clear if we look at the following four business decisions:

1. If Air Canada is to make a profit when it reduces all domestic fares by 30%, what reduction in costs or increase in passengers will be required? Answer: To make a profit when it cuts domestic

fares by 30%, Air Canada will have to increase the number of passengers or cut its variable costs for those flights. Its fixed costs will not change.

2. If Ford Motor Company of Canada meets the Canadian Auto Workers' demands for higher wages, what increase in sales revenue will be needed to maintain current profit levels? Answer: Higher wages to CAW members at Ford Motor Company will increase the variable costs of manufacturing automobiles. To keep present profit levels, Ford will have to cut other variable costs or increase the price of its automobiles.

3. If Dofasco's program to modernize plant facilities through significant equipment purchases reduces the workforce by 50%, what will the effect be on the cost of producing one tonne of steel? Answer: The modernizing of plant facilities changes the proportion of fixed and variable costs of producing one tonne of steel. Fixed costs increase because of higher depreciation charges, whereas variable costs decrease due to the reduction in the number of steelworkers.

4. What happens if Saputo Inc., Canada's largest dairy products producer, increases its advertising expenses but cannot increase prices because of competitive pressure? Answer: Its sales volume must increase to cover three items: (1) the increase in fixed advertising costs, (2) the variable cost of the increased sales volume, and (3) the desired additional net income.

BEFORE YOU GO ON...

▶Do It! High-Low Method

Byrnes Company accumulates the following data concerning a mixed cost, using units produced as the activity level.

	Units Produced	Total Cost
March	9,800	$14,740
April	8,500	13,250
May	7,000	11,100
June	7,600	12,000
July	8,100	12,460

(a) Calculate the variable and fixed cost elements using the high-low method.

(b) Estimate the total cost if the company produces 6,000 units.

Action Plan

- Determine the highest and lowest levels of activity.
- Calculate variable cost per unit as: Change in total costs ÷ (High − low activity level) = Variable cost per unit.
- Calculate fixed cost as: Total cost − (Variable cost per unit × Units produced) = Fixed cost.

Solution

(a) Variable cost: ($14,740 − $11,100) ÷ (9,800 − 7,000) = $1.30 per unit

Fixed cost: $14,740 − ($1.30 × 9,800 units) = $2,000 or $11,100 − ($1.30 × 7,000) = $2,000

Fixed cost: $14,740 − $12,740 = $2,000 or $11,100 − $9,100 = $2,000

(b) Total estimated cost cannot be determined because 6,000 units are out of the relevant range (9,800 − 7,000) units.

Related exercise material: **BE2-7, BE2-8, E2-25, E2-27,** and **Do It! D2-16.**

the navigator

Manufacturing Costs in Financial Statements

The financial statements of a manufacturer are very similar to those of a merchandiser. For example, you will find many of the same sections and same accounts in the financial statements of Procter & Gamble that you find in the financial statements of Reitmans (Canada) Limited. The principal differences between their financial statements occur in two places: the cost of goods sold section in the income statement and the current assets section in the balance sheet.

INCOME STATEMENT

Under a periodic inventory system, the income statements of a merchandiser and a manufacturer differ in the cost of goods sold section. For a merchandiser, the cost of goods sold is calculated by adding the beginning merchandise inventory to the **cost of goods purchased** and subtracting the ending merchandise inventory. For a manufacturer, the cost of goods sold is calculated by adding the beginning finished goods inventory to the **cost of goods manufactured** and subtracting the ending finished goods inventory, as shown in Illustration 2-14.

▸Illustration 2-14

Cost of goods sold components

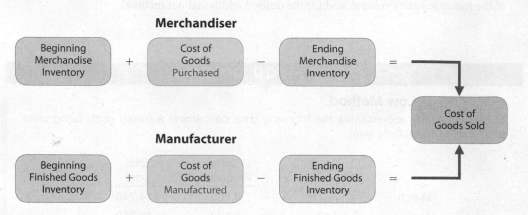

Illustration 2-15 shows the different presentations of the cost of goods sold sections for merchandising and manufacturing companies. The other sections of an income statement are similar for merchandisers and manufacturers.

▸Illustration 2-15

Cost of goods sold sections of merchandising and manufacturing income statements

MERCHANDISING COMPANY Income Statement (partial) Year Ended December 31, 2016		MANUFACTURING COMPANY Income Statement (partial) Year Ended December 31, 2016	
Cost of goods sold		Cost of goods sold	
Merchandise inventory, January 1	$ 70,000	Finished goods inventory, January 1	$ 90,000
Cost of goods purchased	650,000	Cost of goods manufactured	
Cost of goods available for sale	720,000	(see Illustration 2-17)	370,000
Merchandise inventory, December 31	400,000	Cost of goods available for sale	460,000
Cost of goods sold	$320,000	Finished goods inventory,	
		December 31	80,000
		Cost of goods sold	$380,000

Several accounts are involved in determining the cost of goods manufactured. To eliminate excessive detail, income statements typically show only the total cost of goods manufactured. The details are presented in a cost of goods manufactured schedule. Illustration 2-17 shows the form and content of this schedule.

Determining the Cost of Goods Manufactured

An example may help show how the cost of goods manufactured is determined. Assume that ATI Technologies Inc. has graphics cards in various stages of production on January 1. In total, these partially completed units are called **beginning work in process inventory**.

The costs the company assigns to beginning work in process inventory are based on the **manufacturing costs incurred in the prior period**.

ATI Technologies Inc. uses the manufacturing costs incurred in the current year to complete the work in process on January 1. These costs then are used to start the production of other graphics cards. The sum of the direct materials costs, direct labour costs, and manufacturing overhead incurred in the current year is the **total manufacturing cost** for the current period.

We now have two cost amounts: (1) the cost of the beginning work in process and (2) the total manufacturing cost for the current period. The sum of these costs is the **total cost of work in process** for the year.

At the end of the year, some graphics cards may again be only partially completed. The costs of these units become the cost of the **ending work in process inventory**. To find the **cost of goods manufactured**, we subtract this cost from the total cost of work in process. Illustration 2-16 shows how to determine cost of goods manufactured.

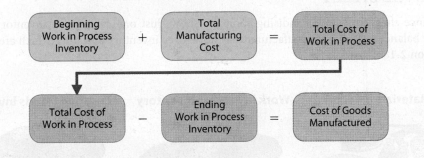

▶Illustration 2-16
Cost of goods manufactured formula

Cost of Goods Manufactured Schedule

An internal report shows each of the cost elements described in Illustration 2-16. This report is called the **cost of goods manufactured schedule**. Illustration 2-17 shows the schedule for Olsen Manufacturing Company (using assumed data). Note that the schedule presents detailed data for direct materials and for manufacturing overhead.

Helpful Hint
Does the amount of "total manufacturing costs for the current year" include the amount of "beginning work in process inventory"?
Answer: No.

▶Illustration 2-17
Cost of goods manufactured schedule

OLSEN MANUFACTURING COMPANY Cost of Goods Manufactured Schedule Year Ended December 31, 2016			
Work in process, January 1			$ 18,400
Direct materials			
Raw materials inventory, January 1	$ 16,700		
Raw materials purchased	152,500		
Total raw materials available for use	169,200		
Less: Raw materials inventory, December 31	22,800		
Direct materials used		$146,400	
Direct labour		175,600	
Manufacturing overhead			
Indirect labour	14,300		
Factory repairs	12,600		
Factory utilities	10,100		
Factory depreciation	9,440		
Factory insurance	8,360		
Total manufacturing overhead		54,800	
Total manufacturing cost			376,800
Total cost of work in process			395,200
Less: Work in process, December 31			25,200
Cost of goods manufactured			$370,000

Numbers or categories in the financial statements are often highlighted in red type to draw your attention to key information.

Review Illustration 2-16 and then examine the cost of goods manufactured schedule in Illustration 2-17. You should be able to distinguish between the total manufacturing cost and the cost of goods manufactured. The difference is the effect of the change in work in process during the period.

DECISION TOOLKIT

Decision Checkpoints	Info Needed for Decision	Tools to Use for Decision	How to Evaluate Results
Is the company maintaining control over the costs of production?	Cost of material, labour, and overhead	Cost of goods manufactured schedule	Compare the cost of goods manufactured with the revenue expected from product sales.

Each chapter presents useful information about how decision makers analyze and solve business problems. **Decision Toolkits** summarize the key features of a decision tool and review why and how to use it.

BALANCE SHEET

The balance sheet for a merchandising company shows just one category of inventory. In contrast, the balance sheet for a manufacturer may have three inventory accounts, which are shown in Illustration 2-18.

►Illustration 2-18

Inventory accounts for a manufacturer

Raw Materials Inventory	**Work in Process Inventory**	**Finished Goods Inventory**

Shows the cost of raw materials on hand.	Shows the cost applicable to units that have gone into production but are only partially completed.	Shows the cost of completed goods on hand.

Finished goods inventory is to a manufacturer what merchandise inventory is to a merchandiser. It represents the goods that are available for sale.

The current assets sections presented in Illustration 2-19 contrast the presentations of inventories for merchandising and manufacturing companies. Manufacturing inventories are generally listed in the order of their liquidity—the order in which they are expected to be realized in cash. Thus, finished goods inventory is listed first. The remainder of the balance sheet is similar for the two types of companies.

►Illustration 2-19

Current assets sections of merchandising and manufacturing balance sheets

MERCHANDISING COMPANY Balance Sheet December 31, 2016		MANUFACTURING COMPANY Balance Sheet December 31, 2016		
Current assets		Current assets		
Cash	$100,000	Cash		$180,000
Receivables (net)	210,000	Receivables (net)		210,000
Merchandise inventory	400,000	Inventories		
Prepaid expenses	22,000	Finished goods	$80,000	
Total current assets	$732,000	Work in process	25,200	
		Raw materials	22,800	128,000
		Prepaid expenses		18,000
		Total current assets		$536,000

Each step in the accounting cycle for a merchandiser applies to a manufacturer. For example, before preparing financial statements, adjusting entries are required. The adjusting entries for a manufacturer are essentially the same as those of a merchandiser. The closing entries are also similar for manufacturers and merchandisers.

DECISION TOOLKIT

Decision Checkpoints	Info Needed for Decision	Tools to Use for Decision	How to Evaluate Results
What is the composition of a manufacturing company's inventory?	Amount of raw materials, work in process, and finished goods inventories	Balance sheet	Determine whether there is sufficient finished goods inventory, raw materials, and work in process to meet expected demand.

BEFORE YOU GO ON...

▶Do It! Cost of Goods Manufactured

The following information is available for Keystone Manufacturing Company.

		March 1	March 31
Raw materials inventory		$12,000	$10,000
Work in process inventory		2,500	4,000
Materials purchased in March	$ 90,000		
Direct labour in March	75,000		
Manufacturing overhead in March	220,000		

Prepare the cost of goods manufactured schedule for the month of March.

Action Plan

- Start with beginning work in process as the first item in the cost of goods manufactured schedule.
- Sum direct materials used, direct labour, and total manufacturing overhead to determine total manufacturing costs.
- Sum beginning work in process and total manufacturing costs to determine total cost of work in process.
- Cost of goods manufactured is the total cost of work in process less ending work in process.

Solution

KEYSTONE MANUFACTURING COMPANY Cost of Goods Manufactured Schedule For the Month Ended March 31		
Work in process, March 1		$ 2,500
Direct materials		
Raw materials, March 1	$ 12,000	
Raw material purchases	90,000	
Total raw materials available for use	102,000	
Less: Raw materials, March 31	10,000	
Direct materials used	$ 92,000	
Direct labour	75,000	
Manufacturing overhead	220,000	
Total manufacturing costs		387,000
Total cost of work in process		389,500
Less: Work in process, March 31		4,000
Cost of goods manufactured		$385,500

Related exercise material: **BE2-12, BE2-13, E2-30, E2-31, E2-32, E2-33, E2-34, E2-35, E2-36, E2-37, E2-38, E2-39,** and **Do It! D2-17.**

ALL ABOUT YOU   *Outsourcing and Offshoring*

To reduce costs and remain competitive, many Canadian companies are turning to outsourcing—using an outside supplier to provide goods or services—and offshoring—purchasing foreign-produced goods or services. Both these practices raise concerns about Canadian job losses, particularly in manufacturing and in service industries, such as IT, engineering, and accounting. Between 2007 and 2009, about 1.9% of all Canadian companies and 5.2% of manufacturers offshored a business activity. In 2012, Canadian companies outsourced an estimated $15 billion of IT services.

What Do You Think?

Suppose you are the managing partner in a public accounting firm with 30 full-time staff. You've heard that some of your competitors have begun to outsource basic tax return preparation work to India. Should you do the same? If you did, you estimate you would have to lay off six staff members.

YES—Indian accountants earn much less than Canadian accountants. You will not be able to compete unless you outsource.

NO—Many customers will be upset to learn that their tax return information is being sent around the world. Also, you are still responsible for the quality of the Indian accountants' work.

Sources: Dana Flavelle, "iGate: Offshore Firms Capture More IT Work, Study Shows," *Toronto Star*, April 10, 2013; Foreign Affairs, Trade and Development Canada, "Canada's State of Trade: Trade and Investment Update 2011"; Erica Alini, "The Future of Manufacturing in Canada," *Macleans*, September 21, 2011.

USING THE DECISION TOOLKIT

Gigantic Manufacturing Co. Ltd. specializes in manufacturing many different models of bicycles. Assume that a new model, the Jaguar, has been well accepted. As a result, the company has established a separate manufacturing facility to produce these bicycles. The company produces 1,000 bicycles per month. Gigantic's monthly manufacturing costs and other expense data related to these bicycles are as follows:

1. Rent on manufacturing equipment (lease cost)	$2,000/month
2. Insurance on manufacturing building	$750/month
3. Raw materials (frames, tires, etc.)	$80/bicycle
4. Utility costs for manufacturing facility	$1,000/month
5. Supplies for general office	$800/month
6. Wages for assembly-line workers in manufacturing facility	$30/bicycle
7. Depreciation on office equipment	$650/month
8. Miscellaneous materials (lubricants, solders, etc.)	$1.20/bicycle
9. Property taxes on manufacturing building	$2,400/year
10. Manufacturing supervisor's salary	$3,000/month
11. Advertising for bicycles	$30,000/year
12. Sales commissions	$10/bicycle
13. Depreciation on manufacturing building	$1,500/month

Instructions

(a) Prepare an answer sheet with the following column headings:

	Product Costs			
Cost Item	Direct Materials	Direct Labour	Manufacturing Overhead	Period Costs

Enter each cost item on your answer sheet, placing an "X" under the appropriate headings.

(b) Calculate the total manufacturing cost for the month.

Solution

(a)

Cost Item	Product Costs			
	Direct Materials	Direct Labour	Manufacturing Overhead	Period Costs
1. Rent on manufacturing equipment ($2,000/month)			X	
2. Insurance on manufacturing building ($750/month)			X	
3. Raw materials ($80/bicycle)	X			
4. Manufacturing utilities ($1,000/month)			X	
5. Office supplies ($800/month)				X
6. Wages for assembly-line workers ($30/bicycle)		X		
7. Depreciation on office equipment ($650/month)				X
8. Miscellaneous materials ($1.20/bicycle)			X	
9. Property taxes on manufacturing building ($2,400/year)			X	
10. Manufacturing supervisor's salary ($3,000/month)			X	
11. Advertising costs ($30,000/year)				X
12. Sales commissions ($10/bicycle)				X
13. Depreciation on manufacturing building ($1,500/month)			X	

(b)

Cost Item	Manufacturing Cost
Rent on manufacturing equipment	$ 2,000
Insurance on manufacturing building	750
Raw materials ($80 × 1,000)	80,000
Manufacturing utilities	1,000
Labour ($30 × 1,000)	30,000
Miscellaneous materials ($1.20 × 1,000)	1,200
Property taxes on manufacturing building ($2,400 ÷ 12)	200
Manufacturing supervisor's salary	3,000
Depreciation on building	1,500
Total manufacturing cost	$119,650

> The **Using the Decision Toolkit** exercises ask you to use business information and the decision tools presented in the chapter. We encourage you to think through the questions related to the decision before you study the Solution.

Summary of Study Objectives

1. **Define the three classes of manufacturing costs and differentiate between product costs and period costs.** Manufacturing costs are typically classified as either (1) direct materials, (2) direct labour, or (3) manufacturing overhead. Raw materials that can be physically and directly associated with the finished product during the manufacturing process are called direct materials. The work of factory employees that can be physically and directly associated with converting raw materials into finished goods is considered direct labour. Manufacturing overhead consists of costs that are indirectly associated with the manufacture of the finished product.

Product costs are costs that are a necessary and integral part of producing the finished product. Product costs are also called inventoriable costs. Under the matching principle, these costs do not become expenses until the inventory to which they attach is sold. Period costs are costs that are identified with a specific time period rather than with a saleable product. These costs relate to non-manufacturing costs and therefore are not inventoriable costs. Prime costs and conversion costs are two other terms that manufacturing accounting systems use. Prime costs are the sum of all direct materials costs and direct labour costs. These are all direct manufacturing costs. Conversion costs are the sum of all direct manufacturing labour costs and the manufacturing overhead costs, which are the costs of converting raw materials into a final product in a manufacturing firm.

2. **Explain variable, fixed, and mixed costs and the relevant range.** Variable costs are costs that vary in total directly and proportionately with changes in the activity index. Fixed costs are costs that remain the same in total regardless of changes in the activity index.

The relevant range is the range of activity in which a company expects to operate during a year.

Mixed costs increase in total but not proportionately with changes in the activity level. One method that management may use is the high-low method.

3. *Apply the high-low method to determine the components of mixed costs.* Determine the variable costs per unit by dividing the change in total costs at the highest and lowest levels of activity by the difference in activity at those levels. Then, determine fixed costs by subtracting total variable costs from the amount of total costs at either the highest or lowest level of activity.

4. *Demonstrate how to calculate cost of goods manufactured and prepare financial statements for a manufacturer.* The cost of the beginning work in process is added to the total manufacturing costs for the current year to arrive at the total

cost of work in process for the year. The ending work in process is then subtracted from the total cost of work in process to arrive at the cost of goods manufactured.

The difference between merchandising and manufacturing income statements is in the cost of goods sold section. A manufacturing cost of goods sold section shows the beginning and ending finished goods inventories and the cost of goods manufactured.

The difference between merchandising and manufacturing balance sheets is in the current assets section. In the current assets section of a merchandising company's balance sheet, one merchandise inventory account is presented. However, in the current assets section of a manufacturing company's balance sheet, three inventory accounts are presented: finished goods inventory, work in process inventory, and raw materials inventory.

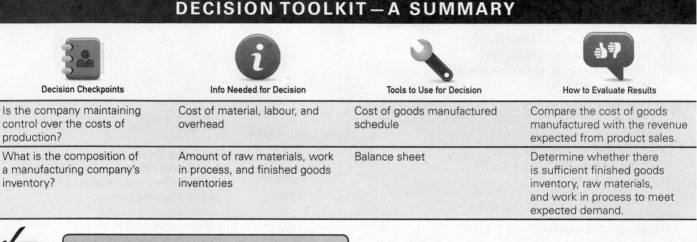

DECISION TOOLKIT—A SUMMARY

Decision Checkpoints	Info Needed for Decision	Tools to Use for Decision	How to Evaluate Results
Is the company maintaining control over the costs of production?	Cost of material, labour, and overhead	Cost of goods manufactured schedule	Compare the cost of goods manufactured with the revenue expected from product sales.
What is the composition of a manufacturing company's inventory?	Amount of raw materials, work in process, and finished goods inventories	Balance sheet	Determine whether there is sufficient finished goods inventory, raw materials, and work in process to meet expected demand.

The **Decision Toolkit—A Summary** reviews the contexts and techniques useful for decision-making that were covered in the chapter.

Glossary

Activity index   The activity that causes changes in the behaviour of costs. (p. 33)

Conversion costs   The sum of direct manufacturing labour costs and manufacturing overhead costs. (p. 29)

Cost   An economic resource given up or foregone to accomplish a particular objective. (p. 28)

Cost behaviour analysis   The study of how specific costs respond to changes in the level of business activity. (p. 32)

Cost object   Anything for which cost information is measured and accumulated. (p. 28)

Cost of goods manufactured   Total cost of work in process less the cost of the ending work in process inventory. (p. 40)

Cost of goods purchased   The net cost of merchandise purchased (after deducting purchase returns, purchase allowances, and purchase discounts) plus the cost of freight-in. (p. 40)

Direct labour   The work of factory employees that can be physically and directly associated with converting raw materials into finished goods. (p. 28)

Direct materials   Raw materials that can be physically and directly associated with manufacturing the finished product. (p. 28)

Ending work in process inventory   Units that were partially completed at the end of the accounting period. (p. 41)

Fixed costs   Costs that remain the same in total regardless of changes in the activity level. (p. 33)

High-low method   A mathematical method to separate mixed costs into their variable and fixed components that uses the total costs incurred at the high and low levels of activity. (p. 37)

Indirect labour   Work of factory employees that has no physical association with the finished product, or for which it is impractical to trace the costs to the goods produced. (p. 28)

Indirect materials Raw materials that do not physically become part of the finished product or cannot be traced because their physical association with the finished product is insignificant. (p. 28)

Manufacturing overhead Manufacturing costs that are indirectly associated with the manufacture of the finished product. (p. 29)

Mixed costs Costs that contain both a variable and a fixed cost element. They change in total but not proportionately with changes in the activity level. (p. 36)

Period costs Costs that are matched with the revenue of a specific time period and charged to expenses as incurred. (p. 29)

Prime costs The sum of direct materials costs and direct manufacturing labour costs. (p. 29)

Product costs Costs that are a necessary and integral part of producing the finished product. (p. 29)

Relevant range The range of the activity index over which the company expects to operate during the year. (p. 35)

Total cost of work in process Cost of the beginning work in process plus the total manufacturing costs for the current period. (p. 41)

Total manufacturing cost The sum of direct materials, direct labour, and manufacturing overhead incurred in the current period. (p. 41)

Variable costs Costs that vary in total directly and proportionately with changes in the activity level. (p. 33)

> Comprehensive Do It! exercises are a final review before you begin homework. Action Plans that appear in the margins give you tips on how to approach the problem, and the Solution provided demonstrates both the form and content of complete answers.

Comprehensive Do It!

Superior Manufacturing Company has the following cost and expense data for the year ending December 31, 2016:

> The **Excel icon** indicates there is an Excel spreadsheet template for this problem on the text companion website.

Raw materials, January 1	$ 30,000	Insurance—factory	$ 14,000
Raw materials, December 31	20,000	Property taxes—factory building	6,000
Raw materials purchased	205,000	Sales (net)	1,500,000
Indirect materials	15,000	Delivery expenses	100,000
Work in process, January 1	80,000	Sales commissions	150,000
Work in process, December 31	50,000	Indirect labour	90,000
Finished goods, January 1	110,000	Factory machinery rent	40,000
Finished goods, December 31	120,000	Factory utilities	65,000
Direct labour	350,000	Depreciation—factory building	24,000
Factory manager's salary	35,000	Administrative expenses	300,000

Instructions

(a) Prepare a cost of goods manufactured schedule for Superior Manufacturing Company for 2016.

(b) Prepare an income statement for Superior Manufacturing Company for 2016.

(c) Assume that Superior Manufacturing Company's ledgers show the following balances in its current asset accounts: Cash $17,000, Accounts Receivable (net) $120,000, Prepaid Expenses $13,000, and Short-Term Investments $26,000. Prepare the current assets section of the balance sheet for Superior Manufacturing Company as at December 31, 2016.

(*continued*)

(continued)

Solution to Comprehensive Do It!

(a)

SUPERIOR MANUFACTURING COMPANY
Cost of Goods Manufactured Schedule
Year Ended December 31, 2016

Work in process, January 1			$ 80,000
Direct materials			
Raw materials inventory, January 1	$ 30,000		
Raw materials purchased	205,000		
Total raw materials available for use	235,000		
Less: Raw materials inventory, December 31	20,000		
Direct materials used		$215,000	
Direct labour		350,000	
Manufacturing overhead			
Indirect labour	90,000		
Factory utilities	65,000		
Factory machinery rent	40,000		
Factory manager's salary	35,000		
Depreciation on building	24,000		
Indirect materials	15,000		
Factory insurance	14,000		
Property taxes	6,000		
Total manufacturing overhead		289,000	
Total manufacturing cost			854,000
Total cost of work in process			934,000
Less: Work in process, December 31			50,000
Cost of goods manufactured			$884,000

(b)

SUPERIOR MANUFACTURING COMPANY
Income Statement
Year Ended December 31, 2016

Sales (net)		$1,500,000
Cost of goods sold		
Finished goods inventory, January 1	$110,000	
Cost of goods manufactured	884,000	
Cost of goods available for sale	994,000	
Less: Finished goods inventory, December 31	120,000	
Cost of goods sold		874,000
Gross profit		626,000
Operating expenses		
Administrative expenses	300,000	
Sales commissions	150,000	
Delivery expenses	100,000	
Total operating expenses		550,000
Net income		$ 76,000

(c)

	SUPERIOR MANUFACTURING COMPANY		
	Balance Sheet (partial)		
	As at December 31, 2016		
Current assets			
Cash			$ 17,000
Short-term investments			26,000
Accounts receivable (net)			120,000
Inventories			
Finished goods		$120,000	
Work in process		50,000	
Raw materials		20,000	190,000
Prepaid expenses			13,000
Total current assets			$366,000

the navigator

WileyPLUS

Self-Test, Brief Exercises, Exercises, Problems—Set A, and many more components are available for practice in WileyPlus.

Self-Study Questions

Answers are at the end of the chapter.

(SO 2) 1. Variable costs are costs that
(a) vary in total directly and proportionately with changes in the activity level.
(b) remain the same per unit at every activity level.
(c) Neither of the above
(d) Both (a) and (b) above

(SO 2) 2. The relevant range is
(a) the range of activity in which variable costs will be curvilinear.
(b) the range of activity in which fixed costs will be curvilinear.
(c) the range that the company expects to operate in during a year.
(d) usually from zero to 100% of operating capacity.

(SO 3) 3. Mixed costs consist of
(a) a variable cost element and a fixed cost element.
(b) a fixed cost element and a controllable cost element.
(c) a relevant cost element and a controllable cost element.
(d) a variable cost element and a relevant cost element.

(SO 3) 4. Kendra Corporation's total utility costs during the past year were $1,200 during its highest month and $600 during its lowest month. These costs corresponded to 10,000 units of production during the high month and 2,000 units during the low month. What are the fixed and variable components of its utility costs using the high-low method?
(a) $0.075 variable and $450 fixed
(b) $0.120 variable and $0 fixed
(c) $0.300 variable and $0 fixed
(d) $0.060 variable and $600 fixed

(SO 1) 5. Direct materials are a

	Product Cost	Manufacturing Overhead	Period Cost
(a)	Yes	Yes	No
(b)	Yes	No	No
(c)	Yes	Yes	Yes
(d)	No	No	No

(SO 1) 6. Indirect labour is a
(a) non-manufacturing cost.
(b) raw materials cost.
(c) product cost.
(d) period cost.

(SO 1)   7. Which of the following costs would be included in the manufacturing overhead of a computer manufacturer?
(a) The cost of the disk drives
(b) The wages earned by computer assemblers
(c) The cost of the memory chips
(d) Depreciation on testing equipment

(SO 1)   8. Which of the following is *not* an element of manufacturing overhead?
(a) The sales manager's salary
(b) The plant manager's salary
(c) The factory maintenance workers' wages
(d) The product inspector's salary

(SO 4)   9. For the year, Redder Company has a cost of goods manufactured of $600,000, beginning finished

goods inventory of $200,000, and ending finished goods inventory of $250,000. The cost of goods sold is
(a) $450,000.
(b) $500,000.
(c) $550,000.
(d) $600,000.

(SO 4)   10. A cost of goods manufactured schedule shows beginning and ending inventories for
(a) raw materials and work in process only.
(b) work in process only.
(c) raw materials only.
(d) raw materials, work in process, and finished goods.

Brief Exercises

(SO 1)
Classify manufacturing costs.

BE2-1   Determine whether each of the following costs should be classified as direct materials (DM), direct labour (DL), or manufacturing overhead (MO):
(a) _____ Frames and tires used in manufacturing bicycles
(b) _____ Wages paid to production workers
(c) _____ Insurance on factory equipment and machinery
(d) _____ Depreciation on factory equipment

(SO 1)
Classify manufacturing costs.

BE2-2   Indicate whether each of the following costs of an automobile manufacturer would be classified as direct materials, direct labour, or manufacturing overhead:
(a) _____ Windshield
(b) _____ Engine
(c) _____ Wages of assembly-line workers
(d) _____ Depreciation of factory machinery
(e) _____ Factory machinery lubricants
(f) _____ Tires
(g) _____ Steering wheel
(h) _____ Salary of painting supervisor

(SO 1)
Identify product and period costs.

BE2-3   Identify whether each of the following costs should be classified as product costs or period costs.
(a) _____ Manufacturing overhead
(b) _____ Selling expenses
(c) _____ Administrative expenses
(d) _____ Direct labour
(e) _____ Advertising expenses
(f) _____ Direct material

(SO 2, 3)
Classify costs as variable, fixed, or mixed

BE2-4   The monthly production costs of Pesavento Company for two levels of production are as follows. Indicate which costs are variable, fixed, and mixed, and give the reason for each answer.

Cost	2,000 units	4,000 units
Indirect labour	$10,000	$20,000
Supervisory salaries	5,000	5,000
Maintenance	4,000	7,000

(SO 2)
Diagram the behaviour of costs within the relevant range.

BE2-5   For Loder Company, the relevant range of production is 40–80% of capacity. At 40% of capacity, a variable cost is $4,000 and a fixed cost is $6,000. Diagram the behaviour of each cost within the relevant range assuming the behaviour is linear.

(SO 3)
Diagram the behaviour of a mixed cost.

BE2-6   For Qiu Company, a mixed cost is $15,000 plus $18 per direct labour hour. Diagram the behaviour of the cost using increments of 500 hours up to 2,500 hours on the horizontal axis and increments of $15,000 up to $60,000 on the vertical axis.

(SO 3)
Determine variable and fixed cost elements using the high-low method.

BE2-7   Deines Company accumulates the following data concerning a mixed cost, using kilometres as the activity level:

	Kilometres Driven	Total Cost		Kilometres Driven	Total Cost
January	8,000	$14,150	March	5,000	$12,330
February	7,500	13,600	April	8,200	16,490

Calculate the variable and fixed cost elements using the high-low method.

BE2-8 Westerville Corp. has collected the following data concerning its maintenance costs for the past six months:

(SO 3)
Determine variable and fixed cost elements using the high-low method.

	Units Produced	Total Cost
July	18,000	$32,000
August	32,000	$48,000
September	36,000	$55,000
October	22,000	$38,000
November	40,000	$65,000
December	38,000	$62,000

Calculate the variable and fixed cost elements using the high-low method.

BE2-9 Presented below are Lang Company's monthly manufacturing cost data related to its personal computer products.
(a) Utilities for manufacturing equipment, $116,000
(b) Raw material (CPU, chips, etc.), $85,000
(c) Depreciation on manufacturing building, $880,000
(d) Wages for production workers, $191,000

(SO 1)
Classify manufacturing costs.

Enter each cost item in the following table, placing an "X" under the appropriate headings.

	Product Costs		
	Direct Materials	Direct Labour	Factory Overhead
(a)			
(b)			
(c)			
(d)			

BE2-10 Presented in alphabetical order below are current asset items for Dieker Company's balance sheet at December 31, 2016. Prepare the current assets section (including a complete heading).

(SO 4)
Prepare current assets section.

Accounts receivable	$200,000
Cash	62,000
Finished goods	71,000
Prepaid expenses	38,000
Raw materials	73,000
Work in process	87,000

BE2-11 Marvel Manufacturing Inc. provides you with the following data for the month of June:
Prime costs were $195,000, conversion costs were $140,000, and total manufacturing costs incurred were $270,000. Beginning and ending work in process inventories were equal. Selling and administrative costs were $200,000.
Calculate the following:
(a) What were the total costs of direct material used, direct labour, and manufacturing overhead?
(b) What were the total costs of production?
(c) What were the total period costs?

(SO 1)
Calculate production and period costs, manufacturing overhead, and the cost of material and labour.

BE2-12 Presented below are incomplete manufacturing cost data. Determine the missing amounts for three different situations.

(SO 4)
Determine missing amounts in calculating total manufacturing costs.

	Direct Materials Used	Direct Labour Used	Factory Overhead	Total Manufacturing Costs
1.	$25,000	$61,000	$ 50,000	?
2.	?	$75,000	$140,000	$296,000
3.	$55,000	?	$111,000	$310,000

BE2-13 Use the same data from BE2-12 above and the data below to determine the missing amounts.

(SO 4)
Determine missing amounts in calculating cost of goods manufactured.

	Total Manufacturing Costs	Work in Process (1/1)	Work in Process (12/31)	Cost of Goods Manufactured
1.	?	$120,000	$82,000	?
2.	$296,000	?	$98,000	$321,000
3.	$310,000	$463,000	?	$715,000

Do It! Review

(SO 1)
Distinguish between product and period costs.

D2-14 A music company has these costs:

Advertising	Paper inserts for CD cases
Blank CDs	CD plastic cases
Depreciation of CD image burner	Salaries of sales representatives
Salary of factory manager	Salaries of factory maintenance employees
Factory supplies used	Salaries of employees who burn music onto CDs

Classify each cost as a period or a product cost. Within the product cost category, indicate if the cost is part of direct materials (DM), direct labour (DL), or manufacturing overhead (MO).

(SO 2)
Classify types of costs.

D2-15 Montana Company reports the following total costs at two levels of production.

	5,000 Units	10,000 Units
Indirect labour	$ 3,000	$ 6,000
Property taxes	7,000	7,000
Direct labour	27,000	54,000
Direct materials	22,000	44,000
Depreciation	4,000	4,000
Utilities	3,000	5,000
Maintenance	9,000	11,000

Classify each cost as variable, fixed, or mixed.

(SO 3)
Calculate costs using high-low method and estimate total cost.

D2-16 Amanda Company accumulates the following data concerning a mixed cost, using units produced as the activity level.

	Units Produced	Total Cost
March	10,000	$18,000
April	9,000	16,650
May	10,500	18,750
June	8,800	16,200
July	9,500	17,100

(a) Calculate the variable and fixed cost elements using the high-low method.
(b) Estimate the total cost if the company produces 8,500 units.

(SO 4)
Prepare cost of goods manufactured schedule.

D2-17 The following information is available for Rolen Manufacturing Company.

	April 1	April 30
Raw materials inventory	$10,000	$14,000
Work in process inventory	5,000	3,500
Materials purchased in April	$ 98,000	
Direct labour in April	60,000	
Manufacturing overhead in April	180,000	

Prepare the cost of goods manufactured schedule for the month of April.

Exercises

(SO 1)
Classify costs into three classes of manufacturing costs.

E2-18 Presented below is a list of costs and expenses usually incurred by Burrand Corporation, a manufacturer of furniture, in its factory:

1. _____ Salaries for assembly-line inspectors
2. _____ Insurance on factory machines
3. _____ Property taxes on the factory building
4. _____ Factory repairs
5. _____ Upholstery used in manufacturing furniture
6. _____ Wages paid to assembly-line workers
7. _____ Factory machinery depreciation
8. _____ Glue, nails, paint, and other small parts used in production
9. _____ Factory supervisors' salaries
10. _____ Wood used in manufacturing furniture

Instructions

Classify the above items into the following categories: (a) direct materials, (b) direct labour, and (c) manufacturing overhead.

E2-19 Wu-Li Corporation incurred the following costs while manufacturing its product:

Materials used in product	$100,000	Advertising expense	$45,000
Depreciation on plant	60,000	Property taxes on plant	14,000
Property taxes on store	7,500	Delivery expense	21,000
Labour costs of assembly-line workers	110,000	Sales commissions	35,000
Factory supplies used	13,000	Salaries paid to sales clerks	50,000

(SO 1)
Identify types of cost and explain their accounting.

Instructions

(a) Identify each of the above costs as direct materials, direct labour, manufacturing overhead, or period costs.

(b) Explain the basic difference in accounting for product costs and period costs.

E2-20 Caroline Company reported the following costs and expenses in May:

Factory utilities	$ 15,500	Direct labour	$69,100
Depreciation on factory equipment	12,650	Sales salaries	46,400
Depreciation on delivery trucks	3,800	Property taxes on factory building	2,500
Indirect factory labour	48,900	Repairs to office equipment	1,300
Indirect materials	80,800	Factory repairs	2,000
Direct materials used	137,600	Advertising	15,000
Factory manager's salary	8,000	Office supplies used	2,640

(SO 1)
Determine the total amount of various types of costs.

Instructions

From the information above, determine the total amount of

(a) manufacturing overhead.

(b) product costs.

(c) period costs.

E2-21 Sota Company is a manufacturer of personal computers. Various costs and expenses associated with its operations are as follows:

1. _____ Property taxes on the factory building
2. _____ Production superintendents' salaries
3. _____ Memory boards and chips used in assembling computers
4. _____ Depreciation on the factory equipment
5. _____ Salaries for assembly-line quality control inspectors
6. _____ Sales commissions paid to sell personal computers
7. _____ Electrical components used in assembling computers
8. _____ Wages of workers assembling personal computers
9. _____ Soldering materials used on factory assembly lines
10. _____ Salaries for the night security guards for the factory building

(SO 1)
Classify various costs into different cost categories.

The company intends to classify these costs and expenses into the following categories: (a) direct materials, (b) direct labour, (c) manufacturing overhead, and (d) period costs.

Instructions

List the items (1) through (10). For each item, indicate its cost category.

E2-22 The administrators of the local hospital are interested in identifying the various costs and expenses that are incurred in producing a patient's X-ray. A list of such costs and expenses is presented below:

1. Salaries for the X-ray machine technicians
2. Wages for the hospital janitorial personnel
3. Film costs for the X-ray machines
4. Property taxes on the hospital building
5. The salary of the X-ray technicians' supervisor
6. Electricity costs for the X-ray department
7. Maintenance and repairs on the X-ray machines
8. X-ray department supplies
9. Depreciation on the X-ray department equipment
10. Depreciation on the hospital building

(SO 1)
Classify various costs into different cost categories.

The administrators want these costs and expenses classified as (a) direct materials, (b) direct labour, or (c) service overhead.

Instructions

List the items (1) through (10). For each item, indicate its cost category.

(SO 2)
Determine fixed, vari-
able, and mixed costs.

E2-23 Dye Company manufactures a single product. Annual production costs incurred in the manufacturing process are shown below for two levels of production:

		Costs Incurred		
Production in Units	5,000		10,000	
Production Costs	Total Cost	Cost/Unit	Total Cost	Cost/Unit
Direct materials	$8,250	$1.65	$16,500	$1.65
Direct labour	9,500	1.90	19,000	1.90
Utilities	1,500	0.30	2,500	0.25
Rent	4,000	0.80	4,000	0.40
Maintenance	800	0.16	1,100	0.11
Supervisory salaries	1,000	0.20	1,000	0.10

Instructions
(a) Define the terms *variable costs*, *fixed costs*, and *mixed costs*.
(b) Classify each cost above as either variable, fixed, or mixed.

(SO 2)
Diagram cost behaviour
to determine relevant
range and classify
costs.

E2-24 Kozy Enterprises is considering manufacturing a new product. It projects the cost of direct materials and rent for a range of output as shown below:

Output in Units	Rent Expense	Direct Materials
1,000	$ 5,000	$ 4,000
2,000	5,000	6,000
3,000	5,000	7,800
4,000	7,000	8,000
5,000	7,000	10,000
6,000	7,000	12,000
7,000	7,000	14,000
8,000	7,000	16,000
9,000	7,000	18,000
10,000	10,000	23,000
11,000	10,000	28,000
12,000	10,000	36,000

Instructions
(a) Diagram the behaviour of each cost for output ranging from 1,000 to 12,000 units.
(b) Determine the relevant range of activity for this product.
(c) Calculate the variable cost per unit within the relevant range.
(d) Indicate the fixed cost within the relevant range.

(SO 3)
Determine fixed and
variable costs using the
high-low method and
prepare graph.

E2-25 The controller of Furgee Industries has collected the following monthly expense data for use in analyzing the cost behaviour of maintenance costs.

Month	Total Maintenance Costs	Total Machine Hours
January	$2,500	300
February	3,000	350
March	3,600	500
April	4,500	690
May	3,200	400
June	4,900	700

Instructions
(a) Determine the fixed- and variable-cost components using the high-low method.
(b) Prepare a graph showing the behavior of maintenance costs, and identify the fixed- and variable-cost elements. Use 100-hour increments and $1,000 cost increments.

(SO 2)
Classify variable, fixed,
and mixed costs.

E2-26 Black Brothers Furniture Corporation incurred the following costs:

1. Wood used in the production of furniture
2. Fuel used in delivery trucks
3. Straight-line depreciation on factory building
4. Screws used in the production of furniture
5. Sales staff salaries
6. Sales commissions

7. Property taxes
8. Insurance on buildings
9. Hourly wages of furniture craftspeople
10. Salaries of factory supervisors
11. Utilities expense
12. Telephone bill

Instructions

Identify the costs above as variable, fixed, or mixed.

E2-27 The controller of Gutierrez Industries has collected the following monthly expense data for use in analyzing the cost behaviour of maintenance costs:

(SO 3)
Determine fixed and variable costs and calculate overheads.

Month	Total Maintenance Costs	Total Machine Hours
January	$2,750	3,500
February	3,000	4,000
March	3,600	6,000
April	4,500	7,900
May	3,200	5,000
June	5,000	8,000

Instructions

(a) Determine the fixed and variable cost components using the high-low method.
(b) Prepare a graph showing the behaviour of maintenance costs, and identify the fixed and variable cost elements. Use 2,000-hour increments and $1,000 cost increments.

E2-28 Mozena Corporation manufactures a single product. Monthly production costs incurred in the manufacturing process are shown below for the production of 3,000 units. The utilities and maintenance costs are mixed costs. The fixed portions of these costs are $300 and $200, respectively.

(SO 2)
Define and classify variable, fixed, and mixed costs.

Production in Units	3,000
Production Costs	
Direct materials	$ 7,500
Direct labour	15,000
Utilities	1,800
Property taxes	1,000
Indirect labour	4,500
Supervisory salaries	1,800
Maintenance	1,100
Depreciation	2,400

Instructions

(a) Identify the above costs as variable, fixed, or mixed.
(b) Calculate the expected costs when production is 5,000 units.

E2-29 Rapid Delivery Service reports the following costs and expenses in June 2016:

(SO 1)
Classify various costs into different cost categories.

Indirect materials	$ 8,400	Drivers' salaries	$15,000
Depreciation on delivery equipment	11,200	Advertising	1,600
Dispatcher's salary	7,000	Delivery equipment repairs	300
Property taxes on office building	2,870	Office supplies	650
CEO's salary	22,000	Office utilities	990
Gas and oil for delivery trucks	2,200	Repairs on office equipment	680

Instructions

Determine the total amount of (a) delivery service (product) costs and (b) period costs.

E2-30 Sinjay Corporation incurred the following costs while manufacturing its product:

(SO 4)
Calculate cost of goods manufactured and sold.

Materials used in product	$120,000	Advertising expense	$45,000
Depreciation on plant	60,000	Property taxes on plant	19,000
Property taxes on warehouse	7,500	Delivery expense	21,000
Labour costs of assembly-line workers	110,000	Sales commissions	35,000
Factory supplies used	25,000	Salaries paid to sales clerks	50,000

Work in process inventory was $10,000 at January 1 and $14,000 at December 31. Finished goods inventory was $60,000 at January 1 and $50,600 at December 31.

Instructions
(a) Calculate cost of goods manufactured.
(b) Calculate cost of goods sold.

(SO 4)
Determine missing amounts in cost of goods manufactured schedule.

E2-31 An incomplete cost of goods manufactured schedule is presented below for Cepeda Manufacturing Company for the year ended December 2016:

Work in process (1/1)			$210,000
Direct materials			
Raw materials inventory (1/1)	?		
Add: Raw materials purchases	$165,000		
Total raw materials available for use	?		
Less: Raw materials inventory (12/31)	17,500		
Direct materials used		$190,000	
Direct labour		?	
Manufacturing overhead			
Indirect labour	15,000		
Factory depreciation	36,000		
Factory utilities	68,000		
Total overhead		119,000	
Total manufacturing costs			?
Total cost of work in process			?
Less: Work in process (12/31)			80,000
Cost of goods manufactured			$550,000

Instructions
Complete the cost of goods manufactured schedule for Cepeda Manufacturing Company.

(SO 4)
Determine the missing amount of different cost items.

E2-32 Manufacturing cost data for Criqui Company are presented below:

	Case A	Case B	Case C
Direct materials used	(a)	$68,400	$130,000
Direct labour	$ 57,400	86,500	(g)
Manufacturing overhead	46,500	81,600	102,000
Total manufacturing costs	175,650	(d)	273,700
Work in process (1/1/16)	(b)	15,600	(h)
Total cost of work in process	221,500	(e)	335,000
Work in process (12/31/16)	(c)	11,000	90,000
Cost of goods manufactured	180,725	(f)	(i)

Instructions
Provide the missing amount for each letter (a) through (i).

(SO 4)
Determine the missing amount of different cost items, and prepare a condensed cost of goods manufactured schedule.

E2-33 Incomplete manufacturing cost data for Ikerd Company for 2016 are presented as follows for four different situations:

	Direct Materials Used	Labour Used	Manufacturing Overhead	Total Manufacturing Costs	Work in Process (1/1)	Work in Process (12/31)	Cost of Goods Manufactured
1.	$127,000	$140,000	$ 89,000	(a)	$33,000	(b)	$360,000
2.	(c)	200,000	123,000	$430,000	(d)	$40,000	470,000
3.	80,000	100,000	(e)	257,000	60,000	80,000	(f)
4.	67,000	(g)	75,000	308,000	45,000	(h)	270,000

Instructions
(a) Indicate the missing amount for each letter.
(b) Prepare a condensed cost of goods manufactured schedule for situation (1) for the year ended December 31, 2016.

E2-34 Aikman Corporation has the following cost records for June 2016:

Indirect factory labour	$ 4,500	Factory utilities	$ 400
Direct materials used	25,000	Depreciation, factory equipment	1,400
Work in process (6/1/16)	3,000	Direct labour	30,000
Work in process (6/30/16)	2,800	Maintenance, factory equipment	1,800
Finished goods (6/1/16)	5,000	Indirect materials	2,200
Finished goods (6/30/16)	9,500	Factory manager's salary	3,000

Instructions
(a) Prepare a cost of goods manufactured schedule for June 2016.
(b) Prepare an income statement through gross profit for June 2016, assuming net sales are $87,100.

(SO 4)
Prepare a cost of goods manufactured schedule and a partial income statement.

E2-35 Suraya Collier, the bookkeeper for Danner, Letourneau, and Majewski, a political consulting firm, has recently completed a managerial accounting course at her local community college. One of the topics covered in the course was the cost of goods manufactured schedule. Suraya wondered if such a schedule could be prepared for her firm. She realized that, as a service-oriented company, it would have no work in process inventory to consider.
   Listed below are the costs her firm incurred for the month ended August 31, 2016:

(SO 1, 4)
Classify various costs into different categories and prepare cost of services provided schedule.

Supplies used on consulting contracts	$ 2,500
Supplies used in the administrative offices	1,500
Depreciation on equipment used for contract work	900
Depreciation used on administrative office equipment	1,050
Salaries of professionals working on contracts	15,600
Salaries of administrative office personnel	7,700
Janitorial services for professional offices	300
Janitorial services for administrative offices	500
Insurance on contract operations	800
Insurance on administrative operations	900
Utilities for contract operations	1,900
Utilities for administrative offices	1,300

Instructions
(a) Prepare a cost of contract services provided schedule (similar to a cost of goods manufactured schedule) for the month.
(b) For those costs not included in part (a), explain how they would be classified and reported in the financial statements.

E2-36 The following information is available for Sassafras Company:

(SO 4)
Prepare a cost of goods manufactured schedule and a partial income statement.

	January 1, 2016	2016	December 31, 2016
Raw materials inventory	$21,000		$30,000
Work in process inventory	13,500		17,200
Finished goods inventory	27,000		21,000
Materials purchased		$150,000	
Direct labour		220,000	
Manufacturing overhead		180,000	
Sales		910,000	

Instructions
(a) Calculate cost of goods manufactured.
(b) Prepare an income statement through gross profit.
(c) Show the presentation of the ending inventories on the December 31, 2016, balance sheet.
(d) How would the income statement and balance sheet of a merchandising company be different from Sassafras's financial statements?

E2-37 Corbin Manufacturing Company produces blankets. From its accounting records it prepares the following schedule and financial statements on a yearly basis:
(a) Cost of goods manufactured schedule.
(b) Income statement.
(c) Balance sheet.

(SO 4)
Indicate in which schedule or financial statement(s) different cost items will appear.

The following items are found in its ledger and accompanying data:

1. Direct labour
2. Raw materials inventory (1/1)
3. Work in process inventory (12/31)
4. Finished goods inventory (1/1)
5. Indirect labour
6. Depreciation on factory machinery
7. Work in process (1/1)
8. Finished goods inventory (12/31)

9. Factory maintenance salaries
10. Cost of goods manufactured
11. Depreciation on delivery equipment
12. Cost of goods available for sale
13. Direct materials used
14. Heat and electricity for factory
15. Repairs to roof of factory building
16. Cost of raw materials purchases

Instructions

List the items (1) through (16). For each item, indicate by using the appropriate letter or letters (a, b, or c), the schedule and/or financial statement(s) in which the item will appear.

(SO 4)
Prepare a cost of goods manufactured schedule, and present the ending inventories of the balance sheet.

E2-38   An analysis of the accounts of Kananaskis Manufacturing reveals the following manufacturing cost data for the month ended June 30, 2016:

Inventories	Beginning	Ending
Raw materials	$10,000	$13,100
Work in process	5,000	13,000
Finished goods	10,000	6,000

Costs incurred: Raw materials purchases $64,000, direct labour $57,000, manufacturing overhead $22,900. The specific overhead costs were as follows: indirect labour $7,500, factory insurance $4,000, machinery depreciation $5,000, machinery repairs $1,800, factory utilities $3,100, miscellaneous factory costs $1,500. Assume that all raw materials used were direct materials.

Instructions

(a) Prepare the cost of goods manufactured schedule for the month ended June 30, 2016.
(b) Show the presentation of the ending inventories on the June 30, 2016, balance sheet.

(SO 4)
Determine the amount of cost to appear in various accounts, and indicate in which financial statements these accounts would appear.

E2-39   Todd Motor Company manufactures automobiles. During September 2016, the company purchased 5,000 head lamps at a cost of $8 per lamp. There was no beginning inventory of lamps. Todd withdrew 4,650 lamps from the warehouse during the month of September. Fifty of these lamps were used to replace the head lamps in automobiles used by travelling sales staff. The remaining 4,600 lamps were put in automobiles manufactured during the month.

Of the autos put into production during September 2016, 90% were completed and transferred to the company's storage lot. Of the cars completed during the month, 75% were sold by September 30.

Instructions

(a) Determine the cost of head lamps that would appear in each of the following accounts at September 30, 2016: Raw Materials, Work in Process, Finished Goods, Cost of Goods Sold, and Selling Expenses.
(b) ▭▭▭▷ Write a short memo to the chief accountant, indicating whether and where each of the accounts in part (a) would appear on the income statement or on the balance sheet at September 30, 2016.

Problems: Set A

(SO 1)
Classify manufacturing costs into different categories and calculate the unit cost.

P2-40A   Mina Company specializes in manufacturing motorcycle helmets. The company has enough orders to keep the factory production at 1,000 motorcycle helmets per month. Mina's monthly manufacturing cost and other expense data are as follows.

Maintenance costs on factory building	$ 1,300
Factory manager's salary	4,000
Advertising for helmets	8,000
Sales commissions	5,000
Depreciation on factory building	700
Rent on factory equipment	6,000
Insurance on factory building	3,000
Raw materials (plastic, polystyrene, etc.)	20,000
Utility costs for factory	800
Supplies for general office	200
Wages for assembly-line workers	55,000
Depreciation on office equipment	500
Miscellaneous materials (glue, thread, etc.)	2,000

Instructions

(a) Prepare an answer sheet with the following column headings.

Product Costs

Cost Item	Direct Materials	Direct Labour	Manufacturing Overhead	Period Costs

Enter each cost item on your answer sheet, placing the dollar amount under the appropriate heading. Total the dollar amounts in each of the columns.

(b) Calculate the cost to produce one helmet.

P2-41A Par Play Company, a manufacturer of driver golf clubs, started production in November 2016. For the preceding five years, Par Play had been a retailer of sports equipment. After a thorough survey of driver golf club markets, Par Play decided to turn its retail store into a driver golf club factory.

Raw materials costs for a driver will total $24 per driver. Workers on the production lines are paid on average $13 per hour. A driver usually takes two hours to complete. In addition, the rent on the equipment used to produce drivers amounts to $1,500 per month. Indirect materials cost $3 per driver. A supervisor was hired to oversee production; her monthly salary is $3,500.

Janitorial costs are $1,400 monthly. Advertising costs for the drivers will be $6,000 per month. The factory building depreciation expense is $9,600 per year. Property taxes on the factory building will be $7,200 per year.

(SO 1)
Classify manufacturing costs into different categories and calculate the unit cost.

Instructions

Prepare an answer sheet with the following column headings.

Product Costs

Cost Item	Direct Materials	Direct Labour	Manufacturing Overhead	Period Costs

(a) Assuming that Par Play manufactures, on average, 2,500 drivers per month, enter each cost item on your answer sheet, placing the dollar amount per month under the appropriate headings. Total the dollar amounts in each of the columns.

(b) Calculate the cost to produce one driver.

P2-42A Incomplete manufacturing costs, expenses, and selling data for two different cases are as follows:

(SO 4)
Indicate the missing amount of different cost items, and prepare a condensed cost of goods manufactured schedule, an income statement, and a partial balance sheet.

	Case 1	Case 2
Direct Materials Used	$ 6,300	$ (g)
Direct Labour	3,000	8,000
Manufacturing Overhead	6,000	4,000
Total Manufacturing Costs	(a)	18,000
Beginning Work in Process Inventory	1,000	(h)
Ending Work in Process Inventory	(b)	3,000
Sales	22,500	(i)
Sales Discounts	1,500	1,400
Cost of Goods Manufactured	14,600	22,000
Beginning Finished Goods Inventory	(c)	3,300
Goods Available for Sale	18,300	(j)
Cost of Goods Sold	(d)	(k)
Ending Finished Goods Inventory	1,500	2,500
Gross Profit	(e)	6,000
Operating Expenses	2,700	(l)
Net Income	(f)	2,200

Instructions

(a) Indicate the missing amount for each letter.

(b) Prepare a condensed cost of goods manufactured schedule for Case 1.

(c) Prepare an income statement and the current assets section of the balance sheet for Case 1.

Assume that in Case 1 the other items in the current assets section are as follows: cash $3,000, receivables (net) $10,000, raw materials $700, and prepaid expenses $200.

(SO 4)
Prepare a cost of goods manufactured schedule, a partial income statement, and a partial balance sheet.

P2-43A The following data were taken from the records of Stellar Manufacturing Company for the fiscal year ended December 31, 2016:

Raw Materials Inventory (1/1/16)	$ 47,000	Factory Machinery Depreciation	$ 7,700
Raw Materials Inventory (12/31/16)	44,800	Factory Utilities	12,900
Finished Goods Inventory (1/1/16)	85,000	Office Utilities Expense	8,600
Finished Goods Inventory (12/31/16)	77,800	Sales	465,000
Work in Process Inventory (1/1/16)	9,500	Sales Discounts	2,500
Work in Process Inventory (12/31/16)	7,500	Plant Manager's Salary	40,000
Direct Labour	145,100	Factory Property Taxes	6,900
Indirect Labour	18,100	Factory Repairs	800
Accounts Receivable	27,000	Raw Materials Purchases	62,500
Factory Insurance	7,400	Cash	28,000

(a) CGM $305,600
(b) Gross profit
    $149,700
(c) Current assets
    $185,100

Instructions
(a) Prepare a cost of goods manufactured schedule. (Assume all raw materials used were direct materials.)
(b) Prepare an income statement through gross profit.
(c) Prepare the current assets section of the balance sheet at December 31, 2016.

(SO 4)
Prepare a cost of goods manufactured schedule and a correct income statement.

P2-44A Tombert Company is a manufacturer of computers. Its controller resigned in October 2016. An inexperienced assistant accountant has prepared the following income statement for the month of October 2016.

TOMBERT COMPANY
Income Statement
For the Month Ended October 31, 2016

Sales (net)		$780,000
Less: Operating expenses		
Raw materials purchases	$264,000	
Direct labour cost	190,000	
Advertising expense	90,000	
Selling and administrative salaries	75,000	
Rent on factory facilities	60,000	
Depreciation on sales equipment	45,000	
Depreciation on factory equipment	31,000	
Indirect labour cost	28,000	
Utilities expense	12,000	
Insurance expense	8,000	803,000
Net loss		$ (23,000)

Prior to October 2016, the company had been profitable every month. The company's president is concerned about the accuracy of the income statement. As his friend, he has asked you to review the income statement and make necessary corrections. After examining other manufacturing cost data, you have acquired the following additional information.

1. Inventory balances at the beginning and end of October were as follows:

	October 1	October 31
Raw materials	$18,000	$29,000
Work in process	16,000	14,000
Finished goods	30,000	45,000

2. Only 75% of the utilities expense and 60% of the insurance expense apply to factory operations. The remaining amounts should be charged to selling and administrative activities.

Instructions
Calculate the following:

(a) CGM $577,800
(b) NI $1,000

(a) Prepare a schedule of the cost of goods manufactured for October 2016.
(b) Prepare a correct income statement for October 2016.

P2-45A Nova Chemicals Corp. incurred the following manufacturing costs for the year 2016:

Raw materials used in production	$ 28,000	Inventories:	
Total manufacturing cost added	160,000	Raw materials, January 1	$ 9,600
Factory overhead	66,000	Raw materials, December 31	10,400
Selling and administration expenses	43,000	Work in process, January 1	14,600
		Work in process, December 31	13,000
		Finished goods, January 1	9,600
		Finished goods, December 31	9,200

Instructions

Calculate the following:

(a) For 2016, what was the cost of raw materials purchased?

(b) For 2016, what was the cost of goods manufactured?

(c) For 2016, what was the cost of goods sold?

(SO 1, 4)
Calculate raw materials purchased, cost of goods manufactured, and cost of goods sold.

(a) $28,800

(b) $161,600

P2-46A The following information is for Montreal Gloves Inc. for the year 2016:

Manufacturing costs	$3,000,000
Number of gloves manufactured	300,000 pairs
Beginning inventory	0 pairs

Sales in 2016 were 298,500 pairs of gloves for $18 per pair.

Instructions

Calculate the following:

(a) What is the cost of goods sold for 2016?

(b) What is the amount of the gross profit for 2016?

(c) What is the cost of the finished goods ending inventory for 2016?

(SO 4)
Calculate cost of goods manufactured, and cost of goods sold.

(b) $2,388,000

P2-47A Rexfield Company recorded the following transactions for the month of February:

	Materials	Work in Process	Finished Goods
Purchases	$100,000		
Beginning Inventory	18,000	$ 8,000	(e)
Ending Inventory	(a)	20,000	$20,000
Direct Materials Used		90,000	
Direct Labour		(b)	
Manufacturing Overhead (including indirect materials of $10,000)		115,000	
Transferred to Finished Goods		(c)	
Cost of Goods Sold			(d)

Sales were $420,000 for the month. Sales prices are determined by a markup on manufacturing cost of 40%. The costs of new inputs to the manufacturing process during the month were $285,000.

Instructions

1. Calculate the missing values in the above schedule.

2. Compare and contrast the behaviour of fixed and variable costs in total and per unit.

(SO 2)
Determine missing amounts in the cost of goods manufactured and sold schedule and compare fixed and variable costs.

(1) (a) 18,000

(e) 43,000

P2-48A Last night, the sprinkler system at Plant A was accidentally set off. The ensuing deluge destroyed most of the cost records in Plant A for the month just completed (May). The plant manager has come to you in a panic—he has to complete his report for head office by the end of today. He wants you to give him the numbers he needs for his report. He can provide you with some fragments of information he has been able to salvage:

Raw materials:	Beginning	$ 25,000
	Ending	55,000
Work in process:	Beginning	15,000
Finished goods:	sold in May	400,000
	Ending	50,000
Manufacturing overhead:	Beginning	0
Accrued wages payable:	Beginning	10,000
	Ending	20,000

(SO 1, 4)
Determine missing amounts and calculate selected costs for schedules of cost of goods manufactured and sold.

Other information:
1. Total direct materials requisitions for the month were $180,000.
2. A total of 10,000 direct labour hours were worked during the month at an average wage of $15/hour.
3. Manufacturing overheads of $100,000 were incurred during the period.
4. On May 31, the ending inventory of work in process is $4,500.

Instructions
Calculate the following:

(a) $210,000

(a) The material purchased during May
(b) The amount paid to the labour force in May

(c) $440,500

(c) The cost of goods transferred from work in process inventory to finished goods inventory in May
(d) The cost of finished goods inventory at the beginning of May

(adapted from CGA-Canada materials, now CPA Canada)

Problems: Set B

(SO 1)
Classify manufacturing costs into different categories and calculate the unit cost.

P2-49B Hite Company specializes in manufacturing motorcycle helmets. The company has enough orders to keep the factory production at 1,000 motorcycle helmets per month. Hite's monthly manufacturing cost and other expense data are as follows:

Maintenance costs on factory building	$ 1,500
Factory manager's salary	4,000
Advertising for helmets	8,000
Sales commissions	5,000
Depreciation on factory building	700
Rent on factory equipment	6,000
Insurance on factory building	3,000
Raw materials (plastic, polystyrene, etc.)	20,000
Utility costs for factory	800
Supplies for general office	200
Wages for assembly-line workers	54,000
Depreciation on office equipment	500
Miscellaneous materials (glue, thread, etc.)	2,000

Instructions

(a) DM $20,000
DL $54,000
MO $18,000
PC $13,700

(a) Prepare an answer sheet with the following column headings.

	Product Costs			
Cost Item	Direct Materials	Direct Labour	Manufacturing Overhead	Period Costs

(b) Enter each cost item on your answer sheet, placing the dollar amount under the appropriate headings. Total the dollar amounts in each of the columns.
(c) Calculate the cost to produce one motorcycle helmet.

(SO 1)
Classify manufacturing costs into different categories and calculate the unit cost.

P2-50B Ladoca Company, a manufacturer of tennis racquets, started production in November 2016. For the preceding five years Ladoca had been a retailer of sports equipment. After a thorough survey of tennis racquet markets, Ladoca decided to turn its retail store into a tennis racquet factory.

Raw materials cost for a tennis racquet will total $23 per racquet. Workers on the production lines are paid on average $13 per hour. A racquet usually takes two hours to complete. In addition, the rent on the equipment used to produce racquets amounts to $1,300 per month. Indirect materials cost $3 per racquet. A supervisor was hired to oversee production; her monthly salary is $3,500.

Factory janitorial costs are $1,400 monthly. Advertising costs for the racquets will be $6,000 per month. The factory building depreciation expense is $8,400 per year. Property taxes on the factory building will be $7,200 per year.

Instructions

(a) DM $57,500
DL $65,000
MO $15,000
PC $6,000

(a) Prepare an answer sheet with the following column headings.

	Product Costs			
Cost Item	Direct Materials	Direct Labour	Manufacturing Overhead	Period Costs

Assuming that Ladoca manufactures, on average, 2,500 tennis racquets per month, enter each cost item on your answer sheet, placing the dollar amount per month under the appropriate headings. Total the dollar amounts in each of the columns.

(b) Calculate the cost to produce one racquet.

P2-51B Incomplete manufacturing costs, expenses, and selling data for two different cases are as follows:

(SO 4)
Indicate the missing amount of different cost items, and prepare a condensed cost of goods manufactured schedule, an income statement, and a partial balance sheet.

	Case	
	1	2
Direct Materials Used	$ 6,300	$ (g)
Direct Labour	3,000	4,000
Manufacturing Overhead	6,000	5,000
Total Manufacturing Costs	(a)	16,000
Beginning Work in Process Inventory	1,000	(h)
Ending Work in Process Inventory	(b)	2,000
Sales	22,500	(i)
Sales Discounts	1,500	1,200
Cost of Goods Manufactured	15,800	20,000
Beginning Finished Goods Inventory	(c)	5,000
Goods Available for Sale	18,300	(j)
Cost of Goods Sold	(d)	(k)
Ending Finished Goods Inventory	1,200	2,500
Gross Profit	(e)	6,000
Operating Expenses	2,700	(l)
Net Income	(f)	2,200

Instructions

(a) Indicate the missing amount for each letter.

(b) Prepare a condensed cost of goods manufactured schedule for Case 1.

(c) Prepare an income statement and the current assets section of the balance sheet for Case 1.

Assume that in Case 1 the other items in the current assets section are as follows: cash $3,000, receivables (net) $10,000, raw materials $700, and prepaid expenses $200.

(c) Current assets
$15,600

P2-52B The following data were taken from the records of Ruiz Manufacturing Company for the year ended December 31, 2016:

(SO 4)
Prepare a cost of goods manufactured schedule, a partial income statement, and a partial balance sheet.

Raw Materials Inventory (1/1/16)	$ 47,000	Factory Machinery Depreciation	$ 7,700
Raw Materials Inventory (12/31/16)	44,200	Factory Utilities	12,900
Finished Goods Inventory (1/1/16)	85,000	Office Utilities Expense	8,600
Finished Goods Inventory (12/31/16)	67,800	Sales	465,000
Work in Process Inventory (1/1/16)	9,500	Sales Discounts	2,500
Work in Process Inventory (12/31/16)	8,000	Plant Manager's Salary	40,000
Direct Labour	145,100	Factory Property Taxes	6,100
Indirect Labour	18,100	Factory Repairs	800
Accounts Receivable	27,000	Raw Materials Purchases	62,500
Factory Insurance	7,400	Cash	28,000

Instructions

(a) Prepare a cost of goods manufactured schedule. (Assume all raw materials used were direct materials.)

(b) Prepare an income statement through gross profit.

(c) Prepare the current assets section of the balance sheet at December 31.

(a) CGM $304,900
(b) Gross profit
$140,400
(c) Current assets
$175,000

P2-53B The following incomplete data are for Atlantic Pride Manufacturing:

(SO 1, 4)
Calculate prime cost, conversion cost, and cost of goods manufactured.

	January 1, 2016	December 31, 2016
Direct materials	$40,000	$60,000
Work in process	80,000	50,000
Finished goods	56,000	70,000

Additional information for 2016:

Direct materials	$200,000
Direct manufacturing labour payroll	160,000
Direct manufacturing labour rate per hour	10
Factory overhead rate per direct manufacturing labour hour	8

Instructions

(c) $518,000

Calculate the following manufacturing costs for 2016: (a) prime cost, (b) conversion cost, and (c) cost of goods manufactured.

(SO 4)

Prepare income statement schedules for cost of goods sold and cost of goods manufactured.

P2-54B   The following incomplete income statement information is available for Sawchule Ltd. for 2016:

Sales	$560,000
Beginning inventory of finished goods	270,000
Cost of goods manufactured	260,000
Net income	50,000
Non-manufacturing costs	170,000

The beginning inventory of work in process was $110,000 and there was no ending inventory of work in process.

Instructions

(a) Calculate the gross profit in 2016.

(b) $340,000
(c) $190,000

(b) Calculate the cost of goods sold in 2016.

(c) Calculate the cost of the ending inventory of finished goods in 2016.

(d) Calculate the total manufacturing cost in 2016.

(SO 2)

Determine missing amounts in the cost of goods manufactured and sold schedule and compare fixed and variable costs.

P2-55B   Incomplete manufacturing costs for the month of June are as follows:

	Materials	Work in Process	Finished Goods
Purchases	$150,000		
Beginning Inventory	28,000	$ 38,000	(e)
Ending Inventory	(a)	30,000	$25,000
Direct Materials Used		125,000	
Direct Labour		(b)	
Manufacturing Overhead (including indirect materials of $20,000)		145,000	
Transferred to Finished Goods		(c)	
Cost of Goods Sold		(d)	

Sales were $780,000 for the month. Sales prices are determined by a markup on manufacturing cost of 30%. The costs of new inputs to the manufacturing process during the month were $498,000.

Instructions

(1) (b) $228,000
(d) $600,000

1. Calculate the missing values in the above schedule.

2. Compare and contrast the behaviour of fixed and variable costs in total and per unit.

(SO 4)

Prepare a cost of goods manufactured schedule and a correct income statement.

P2-56B   Agler Company is a manufacturer of toys. Its controller, Joyce Rotzen, resigned in August 2016. An inexperienced assistant accountant has prepared the following income statement for the month of August 2016.

AGLER COMPANY
Income Statement
For the Month Ended August 31, 2016

Sales (net)			$675,000
Less:	Operating expenses		
	Raw materials purchases	$200,000	
	Direct labour cost	160,000	
	Advertising expense	75,000	
	Selling and administrative salaries	70,000	
	Rent on factory facilities	60,000	
	Depreciation on sales equipment	50,000	
	Depreciation on factory equipment	35,000	
	Indirect labour cost	20,000	
	Utilities expense	10,000	
	Insurance expense	5,000	685,000
Net loss			$ (10,000)

Prior to August 2016, the company had been profitable every month. The company's president is concerned about the accuracy of the income statement. As her friend, she has asked you to review the income statement and make necessary corrections. After examining other manufacturing cost data, you have acquired the following additional information.

1. Inventory balances at the beginning and end of August were as follows:

	August 1	August 31
Raw materials	$19,500	$30,000
Work in process	25,000	21,000
Finished goods	40,000	59,000

2. Only 50% of the utilities expense and 70% of the insurance expense apply to factory operations; the remaining amounts should be charged to selling and administrative activities.

Instructions

(a) Prepare a cost of goods manufactured schedule for August 2016.

(b) Prepare a correct income statement for August 2016.

(a) CGM $477,000

(b) NL $15,500

P2-57B The following data are given for X Firm (in millions of dollars):

Beginning and ending inventories	0
Sales	$390
Direct materials used	80
Direct labour cost	180
Factory overhead	?
Selling and administrative expenses	?
Gross profit	70
Net income (no income taxes)	22

(SO 4)
Calculate selected costs for the income statement and schedules of cost of goods manufactured and sold.

Instructions

Calculate the following amounts:

(a) Cost of goods sold

(b) Total factory overhead cost

(c) Selling and administrative expenses

(d) Total product costs

(e) Total period costs

(f) Prime cost

(g) Conversion cost

(h) Cost of goods manufactured

(a) $320 million

(d) $320 million

(h) $320 million

P2-58B On January 31, 2016, the manufacturing facility of a medium-sized company was severely damaged by an accidental fire. As a result, the company's direct materials, work in process, and finished goods inventories were destroyed. The company did have access to certain incomplete accounting records, which revealed the following:

(SO 4)
Determine missing amounts, prepare cost of goods manufactured, and calculate inventory values.

1. Beginning inventories, January 1, 2016:

Direct materials	$32,000
Finished goods	$30,000
Work in process	$68,000

2. Key ratios for the month of January 2016:

Gross profit = 20% of sales
Prime costs = 70% of manufacturing costs
Factory overhead = 40% of conversion costs
Ending work in process is always 10% of the monthly manufacturing costs.

3. All costs are incurred evenly in the manufacturing process.

4. Actual operations data for the month of January 2016:

Sales	$900,000
Direct labour incurred	$360,000
Direct materials purchases	$320,000

Instructions

(a) From the above data, reconstruct a cost of goods manufactured schedule.

(b) Calculate the total cost of inventory lost, and identify each category where possible (direct materials, work in process, and finished goods), at January 31, 2016.

(a) COGM $788,000

(b) Total $330,000

(adapted from CMA Canada, now CPA Canada)

Cases

C2-59   A fire on the premises of Bydo Inc. destroyed most of its records. Below is an incomplete set of data for operations in 2016:

Sales	?
Raw materials, beginning inventory	$13,000
Purchases	13,000
Raw materials, ending inventory	?
Direct materials	20,000
Direct labour	25,000
Factory overhead	8,000
Manufacturing costs added during the year	?
Work in process, beginning inventory	8,000
Work in process, ending inventory	7,000

Cost of goods manufactured	?
Finished goods, beginning inventory	$ 6,000
Finished goods, ending inventory	?
Cost of goods sold	55,000
Gross profit	9,000
Operating expenses	?
Operating income (loss)	(4,000)

Instructions

Prepare an income statement for 2016. Include separate schedules for the cost of goods sold and cost of goods manufactured.

(adapted from CGA-Canada, now CPA Canada)

C2-60   On January 31, a snowstorm damaged the office of a small business, and some of the accounting information stored in the computer's memory was lost. The following information pertaining to January activities was retrieved from other sources:

Direct materials purchased	$18,000
Work in process—beginning inventory	2,000
Direct materials—beginning inventory	6,000
Direct materials—ending inventory	10,000
Finished goods—beginning inventory	12,000
Finished goods—ending inventory	2,500
Sales	60,000
Manufacturing overhead and direct labour incurred	22,000
Gross profit percentage based on net sales	40%

Instructions

Calculate the following:
(a) What was the cost of direct materials used in January?
(b) What amount of work in process inventory was transferred out to finished goods during January?
(c) Assume that $20,000 of direct materials was used in January and that the cost of goods available for sale in January amounted to $40,000. What did the ending work in process inventory amount to?

C2-61   In January 2016, Sayers Manufacturing incurred the following costs in manufacturing Detecto, its only product:

Direct materials purchased	$900,000
Direct labour incurred	710,000
Benefits	75,000
Overtime premium	50,000
Supervisory salaries	125,000
Utility expenses	92,500
Depreciation (equipment)	2,800
Supplies (factory)	10,000
Factory rent	31,300

An analysis of the accounting records showed the following balances in the inventory accounts at the beginning and end of January:

	January 1	January 31
Direct materials	$ 80,000	$ 90,000
Work in process	110,000	74,600
Finished goods	95,000	108,000

Sayers treats overtime premiums and benefits as indirect costs.

Instructions

(a) Determine the cost of goods manufactured for January 2016.
(b) Calculate the cost of goods sold for January 2016.

(adapted from CMA Canada, now CPA Canada)

C2-62   XYZ Company reports the following inventory data for the month of June:

	June 1	June 30
Direct materials	$ 50	$ 80
Work in process	140	180
Finished goods	240	250

1. Direct materials purchases were $140.
2. Direct costs of production were $220.
3. Variable costs of production were $280.
4. Indirect costs of production were $180.
5. Selling and administrative costs were $210.

Instructions

Caculate the following:
(a) What were the total costs of production?
(b) What was the cost of materials used?
(c) What was the cost of direct labour?
(d) What was the cost of variable overhead?
(e) What was fixed manufacturing overhead?
(f) What was the cost of goods manufactured?
(g) What was the cost of goods sold?
(h) What were the conversion costs?
(i) What were the prime costs?
(j) What were the period costs?

C2-63 Match Manufacturing Company specializes in producing fashion outfits. On July 31, 2016, a tornado touched down at its factory and general office. The inventories in the warehouse and the factory were completely destroyed, as was the general office nearby. However, the next morning, through a careful search of the disaster site, Ross Siggurson, the company's controller, and Catherine Longboat, the cost accountant, were able to recover a small amount of manufacturing cost data for the current month.

"What a horrible experience," sighed Ross. "And the worst part is that we may not have enough records to use in filing an insurance claim."

"It was terrible," replied Catherine. "However, I managed to recover some of the manufacturing cost data that I was working on yesterday afternoon. The data indicate that our direct labour cost in July totalled $240,000 and that we had purchased $345,000 of raw materials. Also, I recall that the amount of raw materials used for July was $350,000. But I'm not sure this information will help. The rest of our records were blown away."

"Well, not exactly," said Ross. "I was working on the year-to-date income statement when the tornado warning was announced. My recollection is that our sales in July were $1.26 million and our gross profit ratio has been 40% of sales. Also, I can remember that our cost of goods available for sale was $770,000 for July."

"Maybe we can work something out from this information!" exclaimed Catherine. "My experience tells me that our manufacturing overhead is usually 60% of direct labour."

"Hey, look what I just found," cried Ross. "It's a copy of this June's balance sheet, and it shows that our inventories as at June 30 were finished goods $38,000, work in process $25,000, and raw materials $19,000."

"Super!" yelled Catherine. "Let's go work something out."

In order to file an insurance claim, Match Manufacturing must determine the amount of its inventories as at July 31, 2016, the date of the tornado touchdown.

Instructions

With the class divided into groups, determine the amount of costs in the Raw Materials, Work in Process, and Finished Goods inventory accounts as at the date of the tornado.

C2-64 Wayne Terrago, controller for Robbin Industries, was reviewing production cost reports for the year. One amount in these reports continued to bother him—advertising. During the year, the company had instituted an expensive advertising campaign to sell some of its slower-moving products. It was still too early to tell whether the advertising campaign was successful.

There had been much internal debate about how to report the advertising cost. The vice-president of finance argued that advertising costs should be reported as a cost of production, just like direct materials and direct labour. He therefore recommended that this cost be identified as manufacturing overhead and reported as part of inventory costs until sold. Others disagreed. Terrago believed that this cost should be reported as an expense of the current period, based on the conservatism principle. Others argued that it should be reported as prepaid advertising and reported as a current asset.

The president finally had to decide the issue. He argued that these costs should be reported as inventory. His arguments were practical ones. He noted that the company was experiencing financial difficulty and expensing this amount in the current period might jeopardize a planned bond offering. Also, reporting the advertising costs as inventory rather than as prepaid advertising would attract less attention from the financial community.

Instructions

Answer the following questions:
(a) Who are the stakeholders in this situation?
(b) What are the ethical issues involved in this situation?
(c) What would you do if you were Wayne Terrago?

"All About You" Activity

C2-65 You work for the controller at Green Partxs Inc., a small specialized supplier to the auto parts industry. Currently, it produces 20,000 units per month, using two shifts, with each shift producing 10,000 units. However, the bankruptcy of one of its major customers means that production must be cut to 11,000 units within the next six months. The company does not expect to regain the lost business for at least another two years, but it is confident that it can still make a profit at this lower production level.

Instructions
(a) Determine the impact on variable costs of the reduction in production.
(b) Determine the impact on fixed costs of the reduction in production and how the Green Partxs management might reduce them.
(c) What else could the company do to increase profits and offset the impact of the reduced production level?

Decision-Making at Current Designs

DM2-1   Diane Buswell, controller for Current Designs, reviewed the accounting records for a recent period, she noted the following items.

Instructions

Classify each item as a product cost or a period cost. If an item is a product cost, note if it is a direct materials, direct labour, or manufacturing overhead item.

| | | Product Costs | | | |
| | | | | Manufacturing | |
Payee	Purpose	Direct Materials	Direct Labour	Overhead	Period Costs
Winona Agency	Property insurance for the manufacturing plant				
Bill Johnson (sales manager)	Payroll cheque—payment to sales manager				
Xcel Energy	Electricity for manufacturing plant				
Winona Printing	Price lists for salespeople				
Jim Kaiser (sales representative)	Sales commissions				
Dave Thill (plant manager)	Payroll cheque—payment to plant manager				
Dana Schultz (kayak assembler)	Payroll cheque—payment to kayak assembler				
Composite One	Bagging film used when kayaks are assembled; it is discarded after use				
Fastenal	Shop supplies—brooms, paper towels, etc.				
Ravago	Polyethylene powder, which is the main ingredient for the rotational moulded kayaks				
Winona County	Property taxes on manufacturing plant				
North American Composites	Kevlar* fabric for composite kayaks				
Waste Management	Garbage disposal for the company office building				
None	Journal entry to record depreciation of manufacturing equipment				

Waterways Continuing Problem

(This is a continuation of the Waterways Problem from Chapter 1.)

WCP-2   Recently Ryan Smith, the plant manager of the manufacturing division of Waterways Corporation, has been focusing on changes to overhead costs. He realizes that Ben Clark's new designs call for more automation in the plant, but he is also investigating if there are any opportunities for cost savings.

Ryan thought it might be helpful to his cost-cutting measures if he could predict what manufacturing overhead would be in the following months. But first he needed to determine the appropriate activity base. He thought there could be two possibilities: direct labour or the number of hours of operation.

From historical data he retrieved the following information:

	Direct Labour	Hours of Operation	Manufacturing Overhead
January	$25,000	500	$145,000
February	24,000	520	148,000
March	30,000	700	170,000
April	32,000	690	176,000
May	27,000	575	150,000
June	25,000	550	140,000

Ryan then asked CFO Jordan Leigh for information available to determine the cost of goods manufactured. Ryan was provided with the following information.

1. The balances in the applicable inventory accounts at the beginning of the month were: Raw materials inventory $35,000; Work in process inventory $52,000.
2. Raw material purchases for the month were $191,000.
3. Of the raw materials used in production, 75% could be traced to the actual production, and the rest was indirect materials.
4. Ending raw materials inventory was $50,000.
5. Actual costs for wages and salaries were $70,000. 60% was considered overhead; the balance was direct labour.
6. Hours of operation for the month were 600.
7. Total manufacturing costs for the month were $315,000.
8. Costs transferred into finished goods inventory for the month were $325,000.

Instructions

(a) Using the high-low method, and based on the historical data provided, determine two possible cost formulas for manufacturing overhead.
(b) Using the cost formulas developed in (a), determine which activity base would be better for predicting manufacturing overhead.
(c) Prepare a condensed cost of goods manufactured schedule.

Answers to Self-Study Questions

1. d   **2.** c   **3.** a   **4.** a   **5.** b   **6.** c   **7.** d   **8.** a   **9.** c   **10.** a

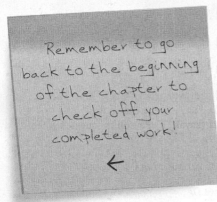

Remember to go back to the beginning of the chapter to check off your completed work!

Job-Order Cost Accounting

study objectives

the navigator

After studying this chapter, you should be able to do the following:

1. Explain the characteristics and purposes of cost accounting.

2. Describe the flow of costs in a job-order cost accounting system.

3. Use a job cost sheet to assign costs to work in process.

4. Demonstrate how to determine and use the predetermined overhead rate.

5. Prepare entries for manufacturing and service jobs completed and sold.

6. Distinguish between under- and over-applied manufacturing overhead.

A PRESSING NEED TO CALCULATE COSTS

You might think that the cost to print a magazine or store flyer would be constant as it's a mass-produced item. But the amount of labour and materials that go into each print job can vary substantially. That's why printing companies use job-order costing; they calculate the cost of each job and charge the customer accordingly.

The printing division of Transcontinental Inc., a corporation with more than 9,000 employees across Canada and the United States and revenues of $2.1 billion in 2013, is Canada's largest printer. It prints flyers for retailers like Best Buy and Future Shop, newspapers such as *The Globe and Mail* and *Vancouver Sun*, and more than 450 magazines, such as *Canadian Living* and *Elle Canada*. It has 27 printing presses across Canada and the United States, equipped with the latest digital, web, sheetfed, coldset, and heatset presses.

Transcontinental has to estimate and invoice for each particular job. Specifications can vary based on page size, paper type, the amount of colour, and what press will be used. Transcontinental can handle special projects such as book covers with a 3D effect and magazine covers that fold out.

Printers such as Transcontinental have to track the cost of every stage of production, from prepress, printing, laminating, binding and finishing, to mailing and distribution. Typically, printers will assign each job a code. Employees enter the job code into the machines and punch it into their time clock, so that labour and machine time is then charged to that job. The accounting department will also factor general overhead and administration costs into the standard rates.

The same happens when purchasing materials. When a printer buys material, such as paper, for a specific job, the purchasing department will code it accordingly, linking it to that job. If an employee takes material out of inventory, they are responsible for charging it to the job.

Print products are increasingly competing with digital media, so printers are trying to reduce their costs. "The printers who will be able to profit from this evolving market are those who use state-of-the art technology to lower their production costs," Transcontinental said in its 2013 annual report. For example, the company recently bought an inkjet web press that shaves several weeks off the printing time for promotional materials.

Many printing contracts are awarded competitively, based mainly on price. Printers need to have an accurate estimate of each project's cost so they can make a reasonable profit if they win the bid. Companies like Transcontinental can print many things, but money isn't one of them.

Sources: The Canadian Press, "Transcontinental Profit, Dividend Up," MSN Money, March 11, 2014; "TC Transcontinental Printing Accelerates Speed to Market with HP T400 Inkjet Web Press," Hewlett-Packard news release, January 30, 2014; Transcontinental Inc. 2013 Annual Report; "Growth by Developing Retailers' Value Chain," Transcontinental investor presentation, September 18, 2013; Transcontinental website, www.tctranscontinental.com/en/home.

Preview of Chapter 3

The feature story about the printing division of Transcontinental Inc. described the job-order costing system used in printing a variety of jobs. It demonstrated that accurate costing is critical to the company's success. For example, in order to submit accurate bids on new jobs and to know whether it profited from past jobs, the company needs a good costing system. This chapter shows how these printing costs would be assigned to specific jobs, such as the printing of an individual magazine. We begin the discussion in this chapter with an overview of the flow of costs in a job-order cost accounting system. We then use a case study to explain and illustrate the documents, entries, and accounts in this type of cost accounting system.

This chapter is organized as follows:

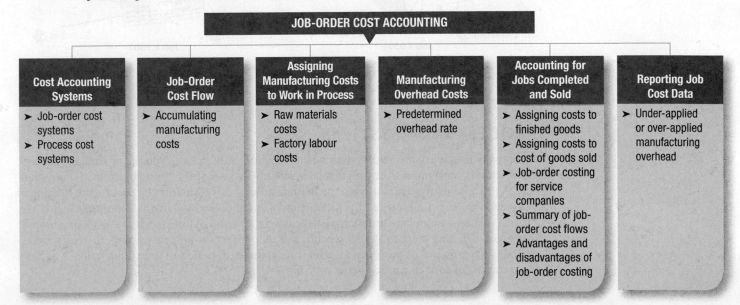

JOB-ORDER COST ACCOUNTING

Cost Accounting Systems	Job-Order Cost Flow	Assigning Manufacturing Costs to Work in Process	Manufacturing Overhead Costs	Accounting for Jobs Completed and Sold	Reporting Job Cost Data
➤ Job-order cost systems ➤ Process cost systems	➤ Accumulating manufacturing costs	➤ Raw materials costs ➤ Factory labour costs	➤ Predetermined overhead rate	➤ Assigning costs to finished goods ➤ Assigning costs to cost of goods sold ➤ Job-order costing for service companies ➤ Summary of job-order cost flows ➤ Advantages and disadvantages of job-order costing	➤ Under-applied or over-applied manufacturing overhead

Cost Accounting Systems

STUDY OBJECTIVE 1

Explain the characteristics and purposes of cost accounting.

Cost accounting involves the measuring, recording, and reporting of product costs. From the data that are collected, companies determine both the total cost and the unit cost of each product. The accuracy of the product cost information produced by the cost accounting system is critical to the company's success. Companies use this information to determine which products to produce, what price to charge, and the amounts to produce. Accurate product cost information is also vital for effective evaluation of employee performance.

A **cost accounting system** consists of accounts for the various manufacturing costs. These accounts are fully integrated into the general ledger of a company. An important feature of a cost accounting system is the use of a **perpetual inventory system**. Such a system provides immediate, up-to-date information on the cost of a product.

There are two basic types of cost accounting systems: (1) a job-order cost system and (2) a process cost system. Although cost accounting systems differ greatly from company to company, most of them are based on one of these two traditional product costing systems.

JOB-ORDER COST SYSTEMS

Under a **job-order cost system**, the company assigns costs to each job or to each batch of goods. Examples of a job would be the manufacture of a private aircraft by Bombardier or the production of a movie by the Canadian Broadcasting Corporation. An example of a batch would be the printing of 225 wedding invitations by a local print shop, or the printing of a weekly issue of *Maclean's* magazine by a high-tech printer. Jobs or batches may be completed to fill a specific customer order or to replenish inventory.

An important feature of job-order costing is that each job (or batch) has its own distinguishing characteristics. For example, each house is custom-built, each consulting engagement is unique, and each printing job is different. The objective is to calculate the cost per job. At each point in the manufacture of a product or the provision of a service, the job and its associated costs can be identified. A job-order cost system measures costs for each completed job, rather than for set time periods. Illustration 3-1 shows the recording of costs in a job-order cost system.

▶Illustration 3-1

Job-order cost system

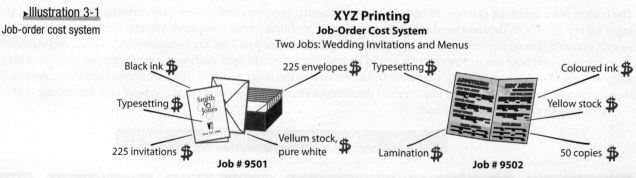

XYZ Printing
Job-Order Cost System
Two Jobs: Wedding Invitations and Menus

Black ink   Typesetting   225 invitations   225 envelopes   Vellum stock, pure white   Typesetting   Lamination   Coloured ink   Yellow stock   50 copies

Job # 9501   **Job # 9502**

Each job has distinguishing characteristics and related costs.

PROCESS COST SYSTEMS

A company uses a **process cost system** when it manufactures a large volume of similar products. Production is continuous to ensure that adequate inventories of the finished product(s) are available. A process cost system is used in the manufacture of dairy products by Saputo, the refining of petroleum by Petro-Canada, and the production of automobiles by General Motors of Canada Ltd. Process costing accumulates product-related costs for a period of time (such as a week or a month) instead of assigning costs to specific products or job orders. In process costing, the costs are assigned to departments or processes for a set (predetermined) period of time. Illustration 3-2 shows the recording of costs in a process cost system.

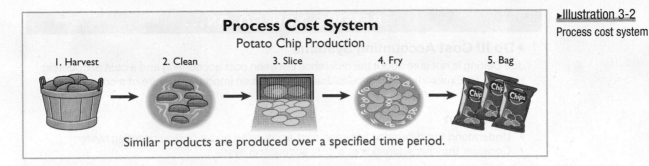

Process Cost System
Potato Chip Production

1. Harvest → 2. Clean → 3. Slice → 4. Fry → 5. Bag

Similar products are produced over a specified time period.

►Illustration 3-2
Process cost system

The process cost system will be discussed further in Chapter 4. Illustration 3-3 summarizes the main features of the job-order and process cost systems.

►Illustration 3-3
Main features of job-order and process cost systems

Job-Order Costing	Process Costing
1. Distinct products with low volumes: home building, shipbuilding, film production, aircraft manufacture, custom machining, furniture manufacture, printing, consulting	1. Homogeneous products with high volumes: chemicals, gasoline, microchips, soft drinks, processed food, electricity
2. Cost totalled by job or batch	2. Costs added by process or department
3. Unit cost calculated by dividing total job costs by units produced	3. Unit cost calculated by dividing total process costs during the period by units produced during that period

A company may use both types of cost systems. For example, General Motors of Canada would use process cost accounting for its standard model cars, such as Aveos and Impalas, and job-order cost accounting for a custom-made limousine for Canada's prime minister. The objective of both systems is to provide unit cost information for product pricing, cost control, inventory valuation, and financial statement presentation.

 BUSINESS INSIGHT *Complex Conditions, Complex Costs*

Visits to emergency rooms and acute care services are the most costly part of Canada's hospital system. Knowing that, many hospitals are focusing their cost-cutting moves on those areas. About 6 in every 10 people who enter a hospital go through the emergency room—a visit that can cost the system more than $150 in Ontario. One hospital is trying to change that. Bridgepoint Active Healthcare in Toronto has created a "model for complexity management." It focuses on people with complex health issues who are in the minority but account for the majority of health care costs. An overnight hospital stay costs about three times more for someone with a complex condition. Someone with a chronic illness, such as diabetes, who has a health problem at night goes to the emergency room, is seen by a health care practitioner who doesn't know them, does expensive tests, prescribes expensive drugs, and sends the patient home, only to have them repeat the process with their own doctor—or the emergency room again—at a later time when the drug they were prescribed interacts with something else they're taking. Bridgepoint is using "complexity teams" of specialists from different disciplines who, through virtual technology, can see a patient at the same time and have access to the patient's complete medical history, to prescribe the best course of action that will help the patient and reduce hospital visits, duplication, and other medical services. Bridgepoint also created short-stay beds to allow family doctors to directly admit chronic patients without the need for an expensive acute admission. Bridgepoint hopes that if all Ontario hospitals adopted the complexity management model, it could shave up to $6 billion in annual health care costs.

Sources: Marian Walsh, "Introducing Bridgepoint Active Healthcare," *Hospital News*, September 3, 2013; Samson Okalow, "Hunting Health Care: Bridgepoint's Plan to Tame Costs," *Canadian Business*, July 17, 2013; "Why Changing How We Treat Our Most Complex Patients Can Make Our Healthcare System More Sustainable," speech by Marian Walsh, President and CEO, Bridgepoint Hospital, to the Economic Club of Canada, June 5, 2013.

What could the health care system do to reduce costs by preventing people from going to the emergency room in the first place?

Job-Order Cost Flow

STUDY OBJECTIVE 2

Describe the flow of costs in a job-order cost accounting system.

The flow of costs (direct materials, direct labour, and manufacturing overhead) in job-order cost accounting parallels the physical flow of the materials as they are converted into finished goods. As shown in Illustration 3-4, manufacturing costs are assigned to the Work in Process Inventory account. When a job is completed, the cost of the job is transferred to the Finished Goods Inventory account. Later, when the goods are sold, their cost is transferred to Cost of Goods Sold.

Illustration 3-4 provides a basic overview of the flow of costs in a manufacturing setting. Illustration 3-5 shows a more detailed presentation of the flow of costs. It indicates that there are two major steps in the flow of costs: (1) *accumulating* the manufacturing costs incurred and (2) *assigning* the accumulated costs to the work done. As shown, manufacturing costs incurred are accumulated in entries 1 to 3 by debits to Raw Materials Inventory, Factory Labour, and Manufacturing Overhead. When these costs are incurred, no attempt is made to associate them with specific jobs. The remaining entries (entries 4 to 8) assign the manufacturing costs incurred. In the remainder of this chapter, we will use a case study to explain how a job-order system operates.

▶Illustration 3-4

Flow of costs in job-order cost accounting

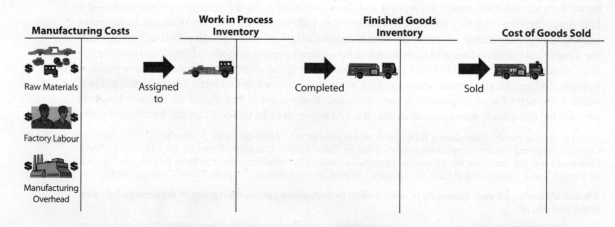

Job-Order Cost Accounting

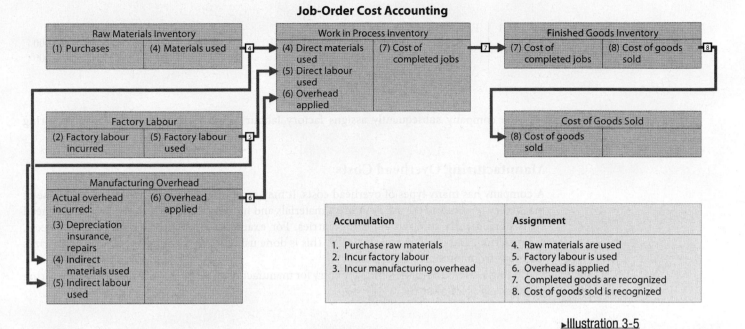

►Illustration 3-5
Job-order cost accounting system

ACCUMULATING MANUFACTURING COSTS

In a job-order cost system, manufacturing costs are recorded in the period when they are incurred. To illustrate, we will use the January transactions of Wallace Manufacturing Company, which makes machine tools.

Raw Materials Costs

When Wallace receives the raw materials that it has purchased, it debits the cost of the materials to Raw Materials Inventory. The company would debit this account for the invoice cost and freight costs that are chargeable to the purchaser. It would credit the account for purchase discounts that are taken and purchase returns and allowances. At this point there is no attempt to associate the cost of materials with specific jobs or orders. To illustrate, assume that Wallace Manufacturing purchases 2,000 handles (Stock No. AA2746) at $5 per unit ($10,000) and 800 modules (Stock No. AA2850) at $40 per unit ($32,000) for a total cost of $42,000 ($10,000 + $32,000). The entry to record this purchase on January 4 is:

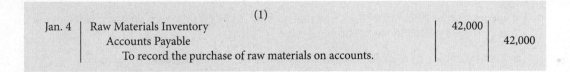

	(1)		
Jan. 4	Raw Materials Inventory	42,000	
	Accounts Payable		42,000
	To record the purchase of raw materials on accounts.		

As we will explain later in the chapter, the company subsequently assigns raw materials inventory to work in process and manufacturing overhead.

Factory Labour Costs

In a manufacturing company, the cost of factory labour consists of (1) the gross earnings of factory workers, (2) employer payroll taxes on these earnings, and (3) fringe benefits incurred by the employer (such as sick pay, group insurance, and vacation pay). Companies debit labour costs to Factory Labour as they incur those costs.

To illustrate, assume that Wallace Manufacturing incurs $32,000 of factory labour costs. Of that amount, $27,000 is for wages payable and $5,000 is for payroll taxes payable in January. The entry is as follows:

	(2)		
Jan. 31	Factory Labour	32,000	
	Factory Wages Payable		27,000
	Employer Payroll Taxes Payable		5,000
	To record factory labour costs.		

The company subsequently assigns factory labour to work in process and manufacturing overhead.

Manufacturing Overhead Costs

A company has many types of overhead costs. It may recognize these costs **daily**, as in the case of machinery repairs and the use of indirect materials and indirect labour. Or, it may record overhead costs **periodically** through adjusting entries. For example, companies record property taxes, depreciation, and insurance periodically. This is done using a **summary entry**, which summarizes the totals from multiple transactions.

Using assumed data, the summary entry for manufacturing overhead in Wallace Manufacturing Company is as follows:

	(3)		
Jan. 31	Manufacturing Overhead	13,800	
	Utilities Payable		4,800
	Prepaid Insurance		2,000
	Accounts Payable (for repairs)		2,600
	Accumulated Depreciation		3,000
	Property Taxes Payable		1,400
	To record overhead costs.		

The company subsequently assigns manufacturing overhead to work in process.

BEFORE YOU GO ON...

▶Do It! Accumulating Manufacturing Costs

During the current month, Laksha Company incurs the following manufacturing costs:

(a) Makes raw material purchases of $4,200 on account.

(b) Incurs factory labour of $18,000. Of that amount, $15,000 relates to wages payable and $3,000 relates to payroll taxes payable.

(c) Factory utilities of $2,200 are payable, prepaid factory insurance of $1,800 has expired, and depreciation on the factory building is $3,500.

Prepare journal entries for each type of manufacturing cost.

Action Plan

- In accumulating manufacturing costs, debit at least one of three accounts: Raw Materials Inventory, Factory Labour, and Manufacturing Overhead.
- Manufacturing overhead costs may be recognized daily. Or manufacturing overhead may be recorded periodically through a summary entry.

Solution

(a)	Raw Materials Inventory	4,200	
	Accounts Payable		4,200
	To record purchases of raw materials on account.		

(b) Factory Labour	18,000	
Factory Wages Payable		15,000
Employer Payroll Taxes Payable		3,000
To record factory labour costs.		
(c) Manufacturing Overhead	7,500	
Utilities Payable		2,200
Prepaid Insurance		1,800
Accumulated Depreciation		3,500
To record overhead costs.		

Related exercise material: **BE3-2, BE3-3, E3-24, E3-27,** and **Do It! D3-13**.

the navigator

Assigning Manufacturing Costs to Work in Process

As shown in Illustration 3-5, assigning manufacturing costs to work in process results in the following entries:

1. Debits are made to Work in Process Inventory.
2. Credits are made to Raw Materials Inventory, Factory Labour, and Manufacturing Overhead. The journal entries to assign costs to work in process are usually made and posted monthly.

An essential accounting record in assigning costs to jobs is the job cost sheet, shown in Illustration 3-6. A **job cost sheet** is a form that is used to record the costs that are chargeable to a specific job and to determine the total and unit costs of the completed job.

Companies keep a separate job cost sheet for each job. The job cost sheets constitute the subsidiary ledger for the Work in Process Inventory account. A subsidiary ledger consists of individual records for each individual item—in this case, each job. The Work in Process account is referred to as a control account because it summarizes the detailed data regarding specific jobs contained in the job cost sheets. Each entry to Work in Process Inventory must be accompanied by a corresponding posting to one or more job cost sheets.

STUDY OBJECTIVE 3
Use a job cost sheet to assign costs to work in process.

Wallace Manufacturing Company
Job Cost Sheet

Job No. _____   Quantity _____
Item _____   Date Requested _____
For _____   Date Completed _____

Date	Direct Materials	Direct Labour	Manufacturing Overhead

Cost of completed job
    Direct materials $ _____
    Direct labour _____
    Manufacturing overhead _____
Total cost $ _____
Unit cost (total dollars ÷ quantity) $ _____

▶Illustration 3-6
Job cost sheet

Helpful Hint
In today's electronic environment, job cost sheets are maintained as computer files.

RAW MATERIALS COSTS

Companies assign raw materials costs when their materials storeroom issues the materials. Requests for issuing raw materials are made on a prenumbered **materials requisition slip**. The materials issued may be used directly on a job, or they may be considered indirect materials. As Illustration 3-7 shows, the requisition slip should indicate the quantity and type of materials withdrawn and the account to be charged. The company will charge direct materials to Work in Process Inventory, and indirect materials to Manufacturing Overhead.

Wallace Manufacturing Company					
Materials Requisition Slip					
Deliver to: Assembly Department			Req. No.: R247		
Charge to: Work in Process–Job No. 101			Date: Jan. 6, 2016		
Quantity	Description	Stock No.	Cost per Unit	Total	
200	Handles	AA2746	$5.00	$1,000	
Requested by: _____			Received by: _____		
Approved by: _____			Costed by: _____		

The company may use any of the inventory costing methods (first in first out [FIFO] or average cost) in costing the requisitions **to the individual job cost sheets**. FIFO assumes that the costs of the earliest goods acquired are the first to be recognized as the cost of goods sold. In the average cost method, however, the cost of goods sold and ending inventory are determined using an average cost, calculated by dividing the cost of goods available for sale by the units available for sale.

Periodically, the requisitions are sorted, totalled, and journalized. For example, if $24,000 of direct materials and $6,000 of indirect materials are used by Wallace Manufacturing in January, the entry is as follows:

		(4)		
Jan. 31	Work in Process Inventory		24,000	
	Manufacturing Overhead		6,000	
	Raw Materials Inventory			30,000
	To assign materials to jobs and overhead.			

This entry reduces Raw Materials Inventory by $30,000, increases Work in Process Inventory by $24,000, and increases Manufacturing Overhead by $6,000, as shown below.

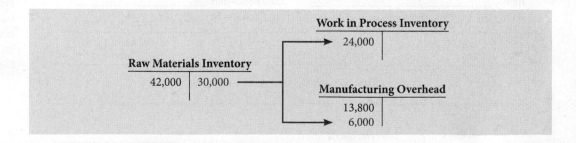

Illustration 3-8 shows the posting of requisition slip R247 (see Illustration 3-7) to Job No. 101 and other assumed postings to the job cost sheets for materials. The requisition slips provide the basis for total direct materials costs of $12,000 for Job No. 101, $7,000 for Job No. 102, and $5,000

for Job No. 103. After the company has completed all postings, the sum of the direct materials columns of the job cost sheets (the subsidiary accounts) should equal the direct materials debited to Work in Process Inventory (the control account).

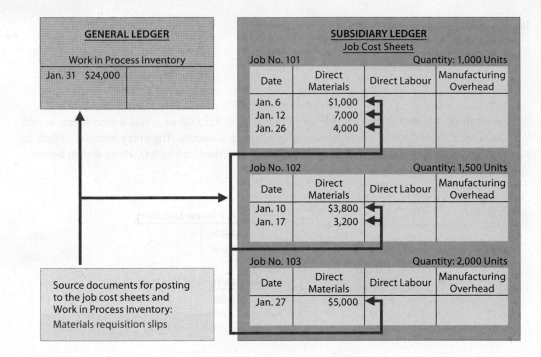

► Illustration 3-8
Job cost sheets—direct materials

Helpful Hint
Companies post to control accounts monthly, and post to job cost sheets daily.

FACTORY LABOUR COSTS

Companies assign factory labour costs to jobs on the basis of time tickets prepared when the work is performed. The **time ticket** indicates the employee, the hours worked, the account and job to be charged, and the total labour cost. Many companies accumulate these data through the use of bar coding and scanning devices. When they start and end work, employees scan bar codes on their identification badges and bar codes associated with each job they work on. When direct labour is involved, the time ticket must indicate the job number, as shown in Illustration 3-9. The employee's supervisor should approve all time tickets.

► Illustration 3-9
Time ticket

Wallace Manufacturing Company
Time Ticket

Date: January 6, 2016

Employee: René Hébert   Employee No.: 124

Charge to: Work in Process   Job No.: 101

Time			Hourly Rate	Total cost
Start	Stop	Total Hours		
0800	1200	4	10.00	40.00

Approved by: _____   Costed by: _____

The time tickets are later sent to the payroll department, which applies the employee's hourly wage rate and calculates the total labour cost. Finally, the company journalizes the time tickets. It debits the account Work in Process Inventory for direct labour and debits Manufacturing Overhead for indirect labour. For example, if the $32,000 total factory labour cost consists of $28,000 of direct labour and $4,000 of indirect labour, the entry is:

	(5)		
Jan. 31	Work in Process Inventory	28,000	
	Manufacturing Overhead	4,000	
	Factory Labour		32,000
	To assign labour to jobs and overhead.		

As a result of this entry, Factory Labour is reduced by $32,000 so it has a zero balance, and labour costs are assigned to the appropriate manufacturing accounts. The entry increases Work in Process Inventory by $28,000 and increases Manufacturing Overhead by $4,000, as shown below.

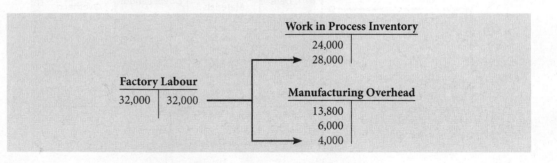

Let's assume that the total labour costs chargeable to Wallace's three jobs are $15,000, $9,000, and $4,000. Illustration 3-10 shows the Work in Process Inventory and job cost sheets after posting. As in the case of direct materials, the postings to the direct labour columns of the job cost sheets should equal the posting of direct labour to Work in Process Inventory.

▶Illustration 3-10
Job cost sheets—direct labour

Helpful Hint
Prove the $28,000 direct labour charge to Work in Process Inventory by totalling the charges by jobs.

101	$15,000
102	9,000
103	4,000
	$28,000

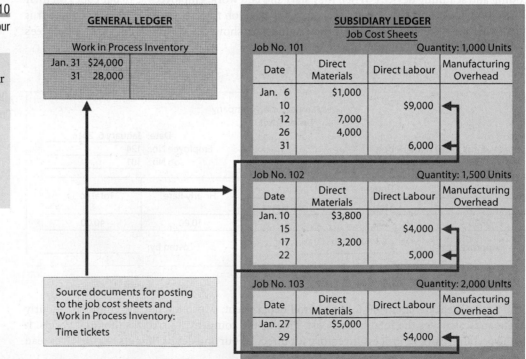

BEFORE YOU GO ON...

►Do It! Work in Process

Danielle Company is working on two job orders. The job cost sheets show the following:

> Direct materials—Job No. 120, $6,000; Job No. 121, $3,600
> Direct labour—Job No. 120, $4,000; Job No. 121, $2,000
> Manufacturing overhead—Job No. 120, $5,000; Job No. 121, $2,500

Prepare the three summary entries to record the assignment of costs to Work in Process Inventory from the data on the job cost sheets.

Action Plan

- Recognize that Work in Process Inventory is the control account for all unfinished job cost sheets.
- Debit Work in Process Inventory for the materials, labour, and overhead charged to the job cost sheets.
- Credit the accounts that were debited when the manufacturing costs were accumulated.

Solution

The three summary entries are as follows:

Work in Process Inventory ($6,000 + $3,600)	9,600	
Raw Materials Inventory		9,600
To assign materials to jobs.		
Work in Process Inventory ($4,000 + $2,000)	6,000	
Factory Labour		6,000
To assign labour to jobs.		
Work in Process Inventory ($5,000 + $2,500)	7,500	
Manufacturing Overhead		7,500
To assign overhead to Jobs.		

Related exercise material: **BE3-6, E3-18, E3-22,** and **Do It! D3-14.**

Manufacturing Overhead Costs

Companies charge the actual costs of direct materials and direct labour to specific jobs. In contrast to this, manufacturing overhead involves production operations as a whole. As a result, overhead costs cannot be assigned to specific jobs on the basis of the actual costs incurred. Instead, manufacturing overhead is assigned to work in process and to specific Jobs on an estimated basis by using a predetermined overhead rate.

PREDETERMINED OVERHEAD RATE

The **predetermined overhead rate** is based on the relationship between the estimated annual overhead costs and the expected annual operating activity. This relationship is expressed through a common **activity base**. The activity may be stated in terms of direct labour costs, direct labour hours, machine hours, or any other measure that will provide a fair basis for applying overhead costs to jobs. The predetermined overhead rate is established at the beginning of the year. Small companies will often have a single, company-wide predetermined overhead rate. Large companies, however, often have rates that vary from department to department. Illustration 3-11 shows the formula for calculating the predetermined overhead rate.

STUDY OBJECTIVE 4

Demonstrate how to determine and use the predetermined overhead rate.

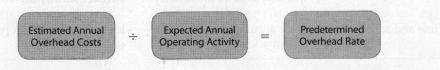

►Illustration 3-11
Formula for predetermined overhead rate

Helpful Hint
In contrast to overhead, the actual costs for direct materials and direct labour are used to assign costs to Work in Process.

We stated earlier that overhead involves a company's production operations as a whole. In order to know what "the whole" is, the logical thing to do would be to wait until the end of the year's operations, when all factory overhead costs for the period would be available. This way, the costs for jobs could be allocated based on the actual factory overhead rate(s) times the actual quantity of the activity base(s) that each job used. This method of costing is called the **actual costing system**. In this method, the direct and indirect costs are assigned to a cost object by using the actual costs incurred during the accounting period. Practically, however, this method is unworkable. Managers cannot wait that long for information about the costs of specific jobs that were completed during the year. They need to be able to price products accurately more quickly as they need to invoice customers for products and services on a timely basis using estimated amounts rather than waiting until the actual results are available at the end of the year. This problem is solved by using a predetermined overhead rate, which makes it possible to determine the costs of a job immediately. Illustration 3-12 shows how manufacturing overhead is assigned to work in process.

▶Illustration 3-12
Using predetermined overhead rates

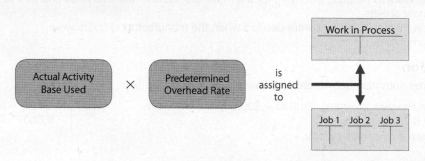

Wallace Manufacturing uses direct labour cost as the activity base. Assuming that annual overhead costs are expected to be $280,000 and that $350,000 of direct labour costs are anticipated for the year, the overhead rate is 80%, calculated as follows:

$$\$280,000 \div \$350,000 = 80\%$$

This means that for every dollar of direct labour that a job requires, 80 cents of manufacturing overhead will be assigned to the job. The use of a predetermined overhead rate enables the company to determine the approximate total cost of each job when the job is completed. The use of a predetermined overhead rate is referred to as the normal costing system.

The **normal costing system** is a costing system that traces direct costs (direct material and direct labour) to a cost object by using the actual cost data used during the accounting period; it allocates indirect costs (factory overhead) based on the predetermined rate(s) times the actual quantity of the activity base(s) used. The major differences between the actual job-order and normal job-order costing systems are summarized in Illustration 3-13.

▶Illustration 3-13
Actual costing system compared with normal costing system

Costs	Actual Costing System	Normal Costing System
Direct cost		
Direct material	• actual direct raw material cost rate times the actual quantity of direct material used	• actual direct raw material cost rate times the actual quantity of direct material used
Direct labour	• actual direct labour cost rate times the actual hours used	• actual direct labour cost rate times the actual hours used
Indirect cost		
Factory overhead	• actual factory overhead rate(s) times the actual quantity used of the activity base(s)	• predetermined factory overhead rate(s) times the actual quantity used of the activity base(s)
Time and accuracy	• more accurate, but untimely information	• less accurate, but more timely information

Historically, direct labour costs or direct labour hours have often been used as the activity base. The reason was the relatively high correlation between direct labour and manufacturing overhead. In recent years, there has been a trend toward using machine hours as the activity base, due to the increased reliance on automation in manufacturing operations. Or, as mentioned in Chapter 1, many companies have instead implemented activity-based costing in order to more accurately allocate overhead costs based on the activities that give rise to these costs.

For Wallace Manufacturing, the total amount of manufacturing overhead is assigned to work in process. It is then applied to specific jobs when the direct labour costs are assigned. The overhead applied for January is $22,400 ($28,000 × 80%), recorded as follows:

	(6)		
Jan. 31	Work in Process Inventory	22,400	
	Manufacturing Overhead		22,400
	To assign overhead to jobs.		

This entry reduces the balance in Manufacturing Overhead and increases Work in Process Inventory by $22,400, as shown below.

Manufacturing Overhead		Work in Process Inventory	
13,800	22,400	24,000	
6,000		28,000	
4,000		22,400	

The overhead applied to each job will be 80% of the direct labour cost of the job for the month. After posting, the Work in Process Inventory account and the job cost sheets will appear as shown in Illustration 3-14. Note that the debit of $22,400 to Work in Process Inventory equals the sum of the overhead applied to jobs: $12,000 (Job No. 101) + $7,200 (Job No. 102) + $3,200 (Job No. 103).

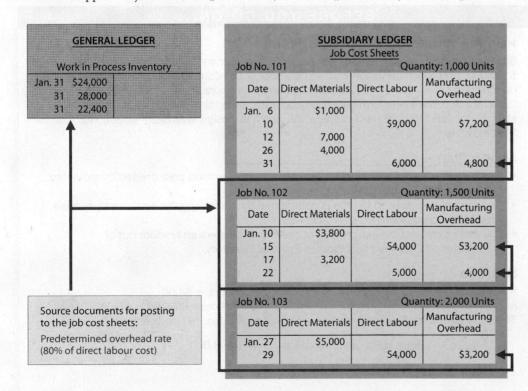

▶Illustration 3-14
Job cost sheets—manufacturing overhead applied

At the end of each month, the balance in Work in Process Inventory should equal the sum of the costs shown on the job cost sheets of unfinished jobs. Assuming that all jobs are unfinished,

Illustration 3-15 shows proof of the agreement of the control and subsidiary accounts for Wallace Manufacturing.

▶Illustration 3-15
Proof of job cost sheets to Work in Process Inventory

Work in Process Inventory		Job Cost Sheets	
Jan. 31	$24,000	No. 101	$39,000
31	28,000	102	23,200
31	22,400	103	12,200
	74,400 ◀——		74,400

DECISION TOOLKIT

Decision Checkpoints

Info Needed for Decision

Tools to Use for Decision

How to Evaluate Results

Decision Checkpoints	Info Needed for Decision	Tools to Use for Decision	How to Evaluate Results
What is the cost of a job?	Cost of material, labour, and overhead assigned to a specific job	Job cost sheet	Compare the costs with those of previous periods and with those of competitors to ensure that costs are reasonable. Compare costs with the expected selling price or service fees that are charged to determine the overall profitability.

the navigator

BEFORE YOU GO ON...

▶Do It! Predetermined Overhead Rate

Stanley Company produces earbuds. During the year, manufacturing overhead costs were $160,000, and machine usage was 40,000 hours. The company assigns overhead based on machine hours. Job No. 302 used 2,000 machine hours.

Calculate the predetermined overhead rate, determine the amount of overhead to allocate to Job No. 302, and prepare the entry to assign overhead to Job No. 302 on March 31.

Action Plan

- Predetermined overhead rate is estimated annual overhead cost divided by expected annual operating activity.
- Assignment of overhead to jobs is determined by multiplying the actual activity base used by the predetermined overhead rate.
- The entry to record the assignment of overhead transfers an amount out of Manufacturing Overhead into Work in Process Inventory.

Solution

Predetermined overhead rate = $160,000 ÷ 40,000 hours = $4.00
Amount of overhead assigned to Job No. 302 = 2,000 hours × $4.00 = $8,000
The entry to record the assignment of overhead to Job No. 302 on March 31 is:

Work in Process Inventory	8,000	
Manufacturing Overhead		8,000
To assign overhead to jobs.		

Related exercise material: **BE3-8, E3-21,** and **E3-22**.

the navigator

Accounting for Jobs Completed and Sold

STUDY OBJECTIVE 5
Prepare entries for manufacturing and service jobs completed and sold.

When a job is completed, the costs are summarized and the lower section of the job cost sheet is completed. For example, if we assume that Wallace Manufacturing completes Job No. 101 on January 31, the job cost sheet will be as in Illustration 3-16.

▸Illustration 3-16
Completed job cost sheet

Wallace Manufacturing Company
Job Cost Sheet

Job No: 101 — Quantity: 1,000
Item: Magnetic Sensors — Date Requested: January 5
For: Tanner Company — Date Completed: January 31

Date	Direct Materials	Direct Labour	Manufacturing Overhead
Jan. 6	$ 1,000		
10		$ 9,000	$ 7,200
12	7,000		
26	4,000		
31		6,000	4,800
	$12,000	$15,000	$12,000

Cost of completed job		
Direct materials	$	12,000
Direct labour		15,000
Manufacturing overhead		12,000
Total cost	$	39,000
Unit cost ($39,000 ÷ 1,000)	$	39.00

ASSIGNING COSTS TO FINISHED GOODS

When a job is finished, an entry is made to transfer its total cost to Finished Goods Inventory. The entry for Wallace Manufacturing is as follows:

	(7)		
Jan. 31	Finished Goods Inventory	39,000	
	Work in Process Inventory		39,000
	To record completion of Job No. 101.		

This entry increases Finished Goods Inventory and reduces Work in Process Inventory by $39,000, as shown in the T accounts below.

Work in Process Inventory		Finished Goods Inventory	
24,000	39,000 →	39,000	
28,000			
22,400			

Finished Goods Inventory is a control account. It controls individual finished goods records in a finished goods subsidiary ledger. Postings to the receipts columns are made directly from completed job cost sheets. Illustration 3-17 shows the finished goods inventory record for Job No. 101.

▸Illustration 3-17
Finished goods record

Item: Magnetic sensors — Job No: 101

	Receipts			Issues			Balance		
Date	Units	Cost	Total	Units	Cost	Total	Units	Cost	Total
Jan. 31	1,000	$39	$39,000	1,000	$39	$39,000	1,000	$39	$39,000

ASSIGNING COSTS TO COST OF GOODS SOLD

The cost of goods sold is recognized when each sale occurs. To illustrate the entries when a completed job is sold, assume that on January 31 Wallace Manufacturing sells for $50,000 on account Job No. 101, which cost $39,000. The entries to record the sale and recognize the cost of goods sold are as follows:

Jan. 31	Accounts receivable	50,000	
	Sales		50,000
	To record sale of Job No. 101.		

		(8)		
Jan. 31	Cost of Goods Sold		39,000	
	Finished Goods Inventory			39,000
	To record cost of Job No. 101.			

The units sold, the cost per unit, and the total cost of goods sold for each job that has been sold are recorded in the issues section of the finished goods record, as shown in Illustration 3-17 above.

JOB-ORDER COSTING FOR SERVICE COMPANIES

Our extended job-order costing example focuses on a manufacturer so that you see the flow of costs through the inventory accounts. It is important to understand, however, that job-order costing is also commonly used by service companies. While service companies do not have inventory, the techniques of job-order costing are still quite useful in many service-industry environments. Consider, for example, the Statcare Clinic (health care), PricewaterhouseCoopers (accounting firm), and CIBC (financial services firm). These companies need to keep track of the cost of jobs performed for specific customers to evaluate the profitability of medical treatments, audits, or consulting engagements.

Many service organizations bill their customers using cost-plus contracts (discussed more fully in Chapter 9). Cost-plus contracts mean that the customer's bill is the sum of the costs incurred on the job, plus a profit amount that is calculated as a percentage of the costs incurred. In order to minimize conflict with customers and reduce potential contract disputes, service companies that use cost-plus contracts must maintain accurate and up-to-date costing records. Up-to-date cost records enable a service company to immediately notify a customer of cost overruns due to customer requests for changes to the original plan or unexpected complications. Timely record keeping allows the contractor and customer to consider alternatives before it is too late.

A service company that uses a job order cost system does not have inventory accounts. It does, however, use an account similar to Work in Process Inventory, referred to here as Service Contracts in Process, to record job costs prior to completion. To illustrate the journal entries for a service company under a job order cost system, consider the following transactions for Fine Interiors, an interior design company. The entry to record the assignment of $9,000 of supplies to projects ($7,000 direct and $2,000 indirect) is:

Service Contracts in Process	7,000	
Operating Overhead	2,000	
Supplies		9,000
To assign supplies to projects.		

The entry to record the assignment of service salaries and wages of $100,000 ($84,000 direct and $16,000 indirect) is:

Service Contracts in Process	84,000	
Operating Overhead	16,000	
Service Salaries and Wages		100,000
To assign personnel costs to project.		

Fine Interiors applies operating overhead at a rate of 50% of direct labour costs. The entry to record the application of overhead ($84,000 × 50%) based on the direct labour cost is:

Service Contracts in Process	42,000	
Operating Overhead		42,000
To assign operating overhead to project.		

Finally, upon completion, the job cost sheet of a design project for Sampson Corporation shows a total cost of $34,000. The entry for Fine Interiors to record completion of this project is:

Cost of Completed Service Contracts	34,000	
Service Contracts in Process		34,000
To record completion of Sampson project.		

Job cost sheets for a service company keep track of materials, labour, and overhead used on a particular job similar to a manufacturer. A number of exercises at the end of this chapter apply job order costing to service companies.

BUSINESS INSIGHT *Track Your Engines*

The aviation division of General Electric (GE), which makes and services jet engines, among other things, accounts for roughly 15% of the multinational company's revenue. It's predicted that worldwide jet engine sales will total $500 billion over a 10-year period. At prices as high as $30 million per engine, you can bet that GE does its best to keep track of costs. It might surprise you that GE doesn't make much profit on the sale of each engine. So why does it bother making them? Of the service revenue during one recent year, about 75% of the division's revenues came from conducting repairs and maintenance on its own products. About 25,000 jet engines from GE and its partner companies are in airline service worldwide. One estimate is that the $13 billion in aircraft engines sold during a recent three-year period will generate about $90 billion in service revenue over the 30-year life of the engines. Because of the high product costs, both the engines themselves and the subsequent service are most likely accounted for using job-order costing. Accurate service cost records are important because GE needs to generate high profit margins on its service jobs to make up for the low margins on the original sale. It also needs good cost records for its service jobs in order to control its costs. Otherwise, a competitor, such as Pratt and Whitney, might submit lower bids for service contracts and take lucrative service jobs away from GE.

Sources: Lewis Krauskopf, "Pratt, GE Battle Over Billions in Jet Engine Orders," Reuters, February 18, 2014; Paul Glader, "GE's Focus on Services Faces Test," Wall Street Journal Online, March 3, 2009; GE Aviation website, "About GE Aviation," www.ge.com/news/company-information/ge-aviation.

Why might GE use job-order costing to keep track of the cost of repairing a malfunctioning engine for a major airline?

SUMMARY OF JOB-ORDER COST FLOWS

Illustration 3-18 shows a completed flow chart for a job-order cost accounting system. All postings are keyed to entries 1–8 in Wallace Manufacturing's accounts presented in the cost flow graphic in Illustration 3-5.

The cost flows in the diagram can be categorized as one of four types:

- **Accumulation:** The company first accumulates costs by (1) purchasing raw materials, (2) incurring labour costs, and (3) incurring manufacturing overhead costs.
- **Assignment to Jobs:** Once the company has incurred manufacturing costs, it must assign them to specific jobs. For example, as it uses raw materials on specific jobs (4), it assigns them to work in process, or treats them as manufacturing overhead if the raw materials cannot be associated with a specific job. Similarly, it either assigns factory labour (5) to work in process, or treats it as manufacturing overhead if the factory labour cannot be associated with a specific job. Finally it assigns manufacturing overhead (6) to work in process using *a predetermined overhead rate.* This deserves emphasis: **Do not assign overhead using actual overhead costs, but instead use a predetermined rate.**
- **Completed Jobs:** As jobs are completed (7), the company transfers the cost of the completed job out of work in process inventory into finished goods inventory.
- **When Goods Are Sold:** As specific items are sold (8), the company transfers their cost out of finished goods inventory into cost of goods sold.

►Illustration 3-18
Flow of costs in a job-order
cost system

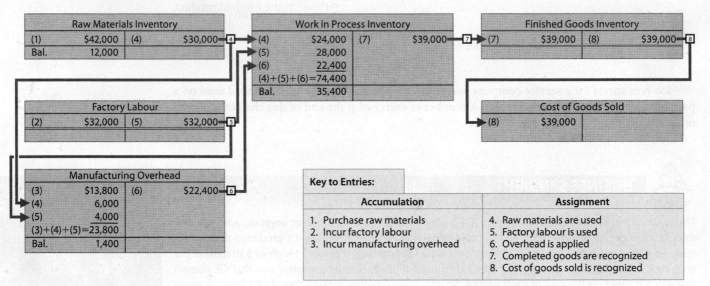

Illustration 3-19 summarizes the flow of documents in a job-order cost system.

►Illustration 3-19
Flow of documents in a job-order
cost system

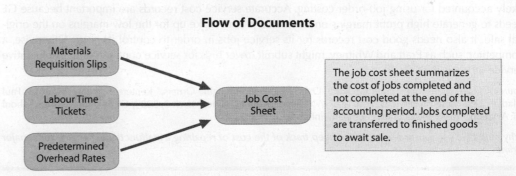

Flow of Documents

The job cost sheet summarizes the cost of jobs completed and not completed at the end of the accounting period. Jobs completed are transferred to finished goods to await sale.

ADVANTAGES AND DISADVANTAGES OF JOB-ORDER COSTING

An advantage of job-order costing is it is more precise in assignment of costs to projects than process costing. For example, assume that home manufacturer Juan Company builds 10 custom homes a year at a total cost of $2 million. One way to determine the cost of the homes is to divide the total construction cost incurred during the year by the number of homes produced during the year. For Juan Company, an average cost of $200,000 ($2,000,000 ÷ 10) is calculated. If the homes are identical, then this approach is adequate for purposes of determining profit per home. But if the homes vary in terms of size, style, and material types, using the average cost of $200,000 to determine profit per home is inappropriate. Instead, Juan Company should use a job-order costing system to determine the specific cost incurred to build each home and the amount of profit made on each. Thus, job-order costing provides more useful information for determining the profitability of particular projects and for estimating costs when preparing bids on future jobs.

One disadvantage of job-order costing is that it requires a significant amount of data entry. For Juan Company, it is much easier to simply keep track of total costs incurred during the year than it is to keep track of the costs incurred on each job (each home built). Recording this information is time-consuming, and if the data are not entered accurately, then the product costs are not accurate. In recent years, technological advances, such as bar-coding devices for both labour costs and materials, have increased the accuracy and reduced the effort needed to record costs on specific jobs. These innovations expand the opportunities to apply job-order costing in a wider variety of business settings, thus improving management's ability to control costs and make better-informed decisions.

A common problem of all costing systems is how to allocate overhead to the finished product. Overhead often represents more than 50% of a product's cost, and this cost is often difficult to allocate meaningfully to the product. How, for example, is the salary of Juan Company's president allocated to the various homes that may differ in size, style, and materials used? The accuracy of the job-order costing system is largely dependent on the accuracy of the overhead allocation process. Even if the company does a good job of keeping track of the specific amounts of materials and labour used on each job, if the overhead costs are not allocated to individual jobs in a meaningful way, the product costing information is not useful. This issue will be addressed in more detail in Chapter 5.

BEFORE YOU GO ON...

▶Do It! Completion and Sale of Jobs

During the current month, Onyx Corporation completed Job 109 and Job 112. Job 109 cost $19,000 and Job 112 cost $27,000. Job 112 was sold on account for $42,000. Journalize the entries for the completion of the two jobs and the sale of Job 112.

Action Plan

- Debit Finished Goods for the cost of completed jobs.
- Debit Cost of Goods Sold for the cost of jobs sold.

Solution

Finished Goods Inventory	46,000	
Work in Process Inventory		46,000
To record completion of Job 109, costing $19,000, and		
Job 112, costing $27,000.		
Accounts Receivable	42,000	
Sales		42,000
To record sale of Job 112.		
Cost of Goods Sold	27,000	
Finished Goods Inventory		27,000
To record cost of goods sold for Job 112.		

Related exercise material: **E3-18, E3-19, E3-22, E3-26,** and **Do It! D3-15.**

the navigator

Reporting Job Cost Data

STUDY OBJECTIVE 6
Distinguish between under- and over-applied manufacturing overhead.

At the end of a period, financial statements are prepared that present summarized data for all the jobs manufactured and sold. The cost of goods manufactured schedule in job-order costing is the same as in Chapter 2, with one exception: the schedule shows manufacturing overhead applied, rather than actual overhead costs. This amount is added to direct materials and direct labour to determine the total manufacturing cost.

Companies prepare the cost of goods manufactured schedule directly from the Work in Process Inventory account. Illustration 3-20 shows a condensed schedule for Wallace Manufacturing Company for January.

▸Illustration 3-20
Cost of goods manufactured schedule

WALLACE MANUFACTURING COMPANY		
Cost of Goods Manufactured Schedule		
Month Ended January 31, 2016		
Work in process, January 1		$ 0
Direct material used	$24,000	
Direct labour	28,000	
Manufacturing overhead applied	22,400	
Total manufacturing cost		74,400
Total cost of work in process		74,400
Less: Work in process, January 31		35,400
Cost of goods manufactured		$39,000

Helpful Hint
Monthly financial statements are usually prepared for management use only.

Note that the cost of goods manufactured ($39,000) is the same as the amount transferred from Work in Process Inventory to Finished Goods Inventory in journal entry no. 7 in Illustration 3-18. The income statement and balance sheet are the same as those illustrated in Chapter 2. For example, Illustration 3-21 shows the partial income statement for Wallace Manufacturing for the month of January.

▸Illustration 3-21
Partial income statement

WALLACE MANUFACTURING COMPANY		
Income Statement (partial)		
Month Ended January 31, 2016		
Sales		$50,000
Cost of goods sold		
Finished goods inventory, January 1	$ 0	
Cost of goods manufactured (see Illustration 3-20)	39,000	
Cost of goods available for sale	39,000	
Less: Finished goods inventory, January 31	0	
Cost of goods sold		39,000
Gross profit		$11,000

UNDER-APPLIED OR OVER-APPLIED MANUFACTURING OVERHEAD

When Manufacturing Overhead has a debit balance, overhead is said to be under-applied. Under-applied overhead means that the overhead assigned to Work in Process is less than the overhead incurred. Conversely, when Manufacturing Overhead has a credit balance, overhead is over-applied. Over-applied overhead means that the overhead assigned to Work in Process is greater than the overhead incurred. Illustration 3-22 shows these concepts.

▸Illustration 3-22
Under-applied and over-applied overhead

Manufacturing Overhead	
Actual (costs incurred)	Applied (costs assigned)

If actual is greater than applied, manufacturing overhead is under-applied.
If actual is less than applied, manufacturing overhead is over-applied.

Cost of Goods Sold Method

At the end of the year, all manufacturing overhead transactions are complete. Accordingly, any balance in Manufacturing Overhead is eliminated by an adjusting entry. Generally the end-of-period under-applied or over-applied overhead costs are treated in one of two methods. The more common method is to make an adjustment to Cost of Goods Sold. Here, the under-applied or over-applied overhead costs are closed into Cost of Goods Sold. Thus, under-applied overhead is debited to Cost of Goods Sold. Over-applied overhead is credited to Cost of Goods Sold. To illustrate, assume that Wallace Manufacturing has a $2,500 credit balance in Manufacturing Overhead at December 31. The adjusting entry for the over-applied overhead is as follows:

Dec. 31	Manufacturing Overhead	2,500	
	Cost of Goods Sold		2,500
	To close over-applied Manufacturing Overhead (that is, to transfer over-applied overhead to cost of goods sold).		

After this entry is posted, Manufacturing Overhead will have a zero balance. In preparing an income statement for the year, the amount reported for cost of goods sold will be the account balance after the adjustment for either under- or over-applied overhead.

Proration Method

The second method of adjusting manufacturing overhead balance is called the proration method. It can be argued that, when under-applied or over-applied overhead is material in amount at the end of the year, the amount should be allocated among Work in Process Inventory, Finished Goods Inventory, and Cost of Goods Sold. In this method, therefore, the under- or over-applied overhead is prorated among these three accounts. This is done by first determining the ratio of each account's balance to the total of the three account balances together, and then applying this ratio to the under- or over-applied overhead amount. The result of this method is that the total of these ending account balances equals the actual costs incurred. To illustrate, assume that Wallace Manufacturing has $10,000 of under-applied overhead in Manufacturing Overhead at December 31 and the following account balances at year end:

Work in Process Inventory	$ 10,000
Finished Goods Inventory	20,000
Cost of Goods Sold	70,000
Total costs	$100,000

If we considered that the $10,000 of under-applied overhead in Manufacturing Overhead at December 31 is material, the adjusting journal entry to close the under-applied overhead would be as follows:

Dec. 31	Work in Process Inventory ($10,000 ÷ $100,000) × $10,000	1,000	
	Finished Goods Inventory ($20,000 ÷ $100,000) × $10,000	2,000	
	Cost of Goods Sold ($70,000 ÷ $100,000) × $10,000	7,000	
	Manufacturing Overhead		10,000
	To close under-applied Manufacturing Overhead.		

However, most firms do not believe this type of allocation is worth the cost and effort. The under- or over-applied overhead is usually adjusted to Cost of Goods Sold because most of the jobs will be completed and sold during the year.

DECISION TOOLKIT

Decision Checkpoints	Info Needed for Decision	Tools to Use for Decision	How to Evaluate Results
Has the company over- or under-applied overhead for the period?	Actual overhead costs and overhead applied	Manufacturing Overhead account	If the account balance is a credit, the overhead applied exceeded the actual overhead cost (the over-applied manufacturing overhead). If the account balance is a debit, the overhead applied was less than the actual overhead cost (the under-applied manufacturing overhead).

BEFORE YOU GO ON...

▶Do It! Applied Manufacturing Overhead

For Karr Company, the predetermined overhead rate is 140% of direct labour cost. During the month, Karr incurred $90,000 of factory labour costs, of which $80,000 is direct labour and $10,000 is indirect labour. Actual overhead incurred was $119,000.

Calculate the amount of manufacturing overhead applied during the month. Determine the amount of under- or over-applied manufacturing overhead.

Action Plan

- Calculate the amount of overhead applied by multiplying the predetermined overhead rate by actual activity.
- If actual manufacturing overhead is greater than applied, manufacturing overhead is under-applied.
- If actual manufacturing overhead is less than applied, manufacturing overhead is over-applied.

Solution

Manufacturing overhead applied = (140% × $80,000) = $112,000
Under-applied manufacturing overhead = ($119,000 − $112,000) = $7,000

Related exercise material: **BE3-11, E3-21, E3-28, E3-29**, and **Do It! D3-16**.

 **ALL ABOUT YOU** *Minding Your Own Business*

After graduating, you might start a small business. As discussed in this chapter, owners of any business need to know how to calculate the cost of their products, because failure to cover costs is one reason why many small businesses fail. Industry Canada reports that 21% of micro-enterprises (those with one to four employees) that began in 2008 didn't make it past their first year.

What Do You Think?

You have decided to start a personal training business. Your cousin has set up your website and will run it for free for the next two years. You will meet your clients at a local gym, which will charge you a 40% commission, or you will go to the client's premises, or eventually meet clients in your parents' basement, which they will not charge you for in the first year. You already own some exercise equipment and a car, which is fully paid for. In pricing your services, should you include the cost of the exercise equipment, your car, the website, or the basement room?

(continued)

ALL ABOUT YOU   *Minding Your Own Business (continued)*

YES—If you don't charge for these costs, your costs are understated and your profitability is overstated.

NO—At this point you are not incurring costs related to these activities; therefore, you shouldn't record charges.

Sources: Industry Canada, "Key Small Business Statistics," August 2013; Matt Lundy, "10 Reasons Why Businesses Fail," *Canadian Business*, October 18, 2012; Government of Canada, "Small Business Survival," Canada Business Network, www.canadabusiness.ca/eng/page/2716/.

USING THE DECISION TOOLKIT

Doctor Garage Inc. is a large manufacturer and marketer of unique, custom-made residential garage doors, as well as a major supplier of industrial and commercial doors, grilles, and counter shutters for new construction, repair, and remodel markets. Doctor Garage Inc. has developed plans for continued expansion of a network of service operations that sell, install, and service manufactured fireplaces, garage doors, and related products.

Doctor Garage Inc. uses a job cost system and applies overhead to production on the basis of direct labour cost. In calculating a predetermined overhead rate for the year 2016, the company estimated manufacturing overhead to be $24 million and direct labour costs to be $20 million. In addition, the following information is available:

Actual costs incurred during 2016	
Direct materials used	$30,000,000
Direct labour cost incurred	21,000,000

Manufacturing costs incurred during 2016	
Insurance—factory	$ 500,000
Indirect labour	7,500,000
Maintenance	1,000,000
Rent on building	11,000,000
Depreciation—equipment	2,000,000

Instructions

Answer each of the following questions:

(a) Why is Doctor Garage Inc. using a job-order costing system?

(b) On what basis does Doctor Garage Inc. allocate its manufacturing overhead? Calculate the predetermined overhead rate for the current year.

(c) Calculate the amount of the under- or over-applied overhead for 2016.

(d) Doctor Garage Inc. had beginning and ending balances in its work in process and finished goods accounts as follows:

	January 1, 2016	December 31, 2016
Work in process	$ 5,000,000	$ 4,000,000
Finished goods	13,000,000	11,000,000

Determine the (1) cost of goods manufactured and (2) cost of goods sold for Doctor Garage Inc. during 2015. Assume that any under- or over-applied overhead should be included in the cost of goods sold.

(e) During 2016, Job G408 was started and completed. Its cost sheet showed a total cost of $100,000, and the company prices its product at 50% above its cost. What is the price to the customer if the company follows this pricing strategy?

(continued)

(*continued*)

Solution

(a) The company is using a job-order system because each job (or batch) has its own distinguishing characteristics. For example, each type of garage door would be different, and therefore a different cost per garage door should be assigned.

(b) The company allocates its overhead on the basis of direct labour cost. The predetermined overhead rate is 120%, calculated as follows:

$$\$24,000,000 \div \$20,000,000 = 120\%$$

(c)

Actual manufacturing overhead	$22,000,000
Applied overhead cost ($21,000,000 × 120%)	25,200,000
Over-applied overhead	$ 3,200,000

(d) 1.

Work in process, January 1, 2016		$ 5,000,000
Direct materials used	$30,000,000	
Direct labour	21,000,000	
Manufacturing overhead applied	25,200,000	
Total manufacturing cost		76,200,000
Total cost of work in process		81,200,000
Less: Work in process, December 31, 2016		4,000,000
Cost of goods manufactured		$77,200,000

2.

Finished goods inventory, January 1, 2016	$13,000,000
Cost of goods manufactured	77,200,000
Cost of goods available for sale	90,200,000
Finished goods inventory, December 31, 2016	11,000,000
Cost of goods sold (unadjusted)	79,200,000
Less: Over-applied overhead	3,200,000
Cost of goods sold	$76,000,000

(e)

Job G408 cost	$ 100,000
Markup percentage	× 50%
Profit	$ 50,000

Price to customer: $150,000 ($100,000 + $50,000)

Summary of Study Objectives

1. *Explain the characteristics and purposes of cost accounting.* Cost accounting involves the procedures for measuring, recording, and reporting product costs. From the data accumulated, the total cost and the unit cost of each product are determined. The two basic types of cost accounting systems are job-order cost and process cost.

2. *Describe the flow of costs in a job-order cost accounting system.* In job-order cost accounting, manufacturing costs are first accumulated in three accounts: Raw Materials Inventory, Factory Labour, and Manufacturing Overhead. The accumulated costs are then assigned to Work in Process Inventory and eventually to Finished Goods Inventory and Cost of Goods Sold.

3. *Use a job cost sheet to assign costs to work in process.* A job cost sheet is a form used to record the costs that are chargeable to a specific job and to determine the total and unit costs

of the completed job. Job cost sheets make up the subsidiary ledger for the Work in Process Inventory control account.

4. *Demonstrate how to determine and use the predetermined overhead rate.* The predetermined overhead rate is based on the relationship between estimated annual overhead costs and expected annual operating activity.

This is expressed in terms of a common activity base, such as direct labour cost. The rate is used in assigning overhead costs to work in process and to specific jobs.

5. *Prepare entries for manufacturing and service jobs completed and sold.* When jobs are completed, the cost is debited to Finished Goods Inventory and credited to Work in Process Inventory. When a job is sold, the entries are as follows: (a) debit Cash or Accounts Receivable and credit Sales for the selling price, and (b) debit Cost of Goods Sold and credit Finished Goods Inventory for the cost of the goods.

6. *Distinguish between under- and over-applied manufacturing overhead.* Under-applied manufacturing overhead means that the over-head assigned to work in process is less than the overhead incurred. Over-applied overhead means that the overhead assigned to work in process is greater than the overhead incurred.

DECISION TOOLKIT—A SUMMARY

Decision Checkpoints	Info Needed for Decision	Tools to Use for Decision	How to Evaluate Results
What is the cost of a job?	Cost of material, labour, and overhead assigned to a specific job	Job cost sheet	Compare the costs with those of previous periods and with those of competitors to ensure that costs are reasonable. Compare costs with the expected selling price or service fees that are charged to determine the overall profitability.
Has the company under- or over-applied overhead for the period?	Actual overhead costs and overhead applied	Manufacturing Overhead account	If the account balance is a credit, the overhead applied exceeded the actual overhead cost. If the account balance is a debit, the overhead applied was less than the actual overhead cost.

Glossary

Activity base A predetermined overhead rate that is based on the relationship between the estimated annual overhead costs and the expected annual operating activity. It is expressed in terms of direct labour costs, direct labour hours, machine hours, or any other measure that will provide a fair basis for applying overhead costs to jobs. (p. 81)

Actual costing system A cost accounting system in which costs are assigned to a cost object by using data on actual costs incurred during the accounting period. (p. 82)

Cost accounting An area of accounting that involves measuring, recording, and reporting product costs. (p. 72)

Cost accounting system Manufacturing cost accounts that are fully integrated into the general ledger of a company. (p. 72)

Job cost sheet A form used to record the costs that are chargeable to a job and to determine the total and unit costs of the completed job. (p. 77)

Job-order cost system A cost accounting system in which costs are assigned to each job or batch. (p. 72)

Materials requisition slip A document authorizing the issue of raw materials from the storeroom to production. (p. 78)

Normal costing system A cost accounting system that traces direct costs to a cost object by using the actual cost data incurred

during the accounting period and that allocates indirect costs based on the predetermined rate(s) times the actual quantity of the cost-allocation base(s). (p. 82)

Over-applied overhead A situation in which overhead assigned to work in process is greater than the overhead incurred. (p. 90)

Predetermined overhead rate A rate based on the relationship between the estimated annual overhead costs and the expected annual operating activity, expressed in terms of a common activity base. (p. 81)

Process cost system A system of accounting that is used when a large volume of similar products are manufactured. (p. 72)

Proration The process of assigning under- and over-applied overhead costs to the inventory accounts Work in Process and Finished Goods, and to Cost of Goods Sold. (p. 91)

Summary entry A journal entry that summarizes the totals from multiple transactions. (p. 76)

Time ticket A document that indicates the employee, the hours worked, the account, the job to be charged, and the total labour cost. (p. 79)

Under-applied overhead A situation in which the overhead assigned to work in process is less than the overhead incurred. (p. 90)

Comprehensive Do It!

During February, Cardella Manufacturing works on two jobs: A16 and B17. Summary data for these jobs are as follows:

Manufacturing Costs Incurred
Raw materials purchased on account: $54,000
Factory labour: $76,000, plus $4,000 of employer payroll taxes
Manufacturing overhead exclusive of indirect materials and indirect labour: $59,800

Assignment of Costs
Direct materials: Job No. A16, $27,000; Job No. B17, $21,000
Indirect materials: $3,000
Direct labour: Job No. A16, $52,000; Job No. B17, $26,000
Indirect labour: $2,000
Manufacturing overhead rate: 80% of direct labour costs
Job A16 was completed and sold on account for $150,000. Job B17 was only partially completed.

Instructions

(a) Journalize the February transactions in the sequence used in the chapter.
(b) What was the amount of under- or over-applied manufacturing overhead?
(c) Assuming the under- or over-applied overhead for the year is not allocated to inventory accounts, prepare the adjusting entry to assign the amount to Cost of Goods Sold.

Solution to Comprehensive Do It!

(a)

(1)

Feb. 28	Raw Materials Inventory	54,000	
	Accounts Payable		54,000
	To record purchase of raw materials on account.		

(2)

28	Factory Labour	80,000	
	Factory Wages Payable		76,000
	Employer Payroll Taxes Payable		4,000
	To record factory labour costs.		

(3)

28	Manufacturing Overhead	59,800	
	Accounts Payable, Accumulated Depreciation, and		59,800
	Prepaid Insurance		
	To record overhead costs.		

(4)

28	Work in Process Inventory	48,000	
	Manufacturing Overhead	3,000	
	Raw Materials Inventory		51,000
	To assign raw materials to production.		

(5)

28	Work in Process Inventory	78,000	
	Manufacturing Overhead	2,000	
	Factory Labour		80,000
	To assign factory labour to production.		

(6)

28	Work in Process Inventory	62,400	
	Manufacturing Overhead (80% × $78,000)		62,400
	To assign overhead to jobs.		

(continued)

Action Plan

- In accumulating costs, debit three accounts: Raw Materials Inventory, Factory Labour, and Manufacturing Overhead.
- When Work in Process Inventory is debited, credit one of the three accounts listed above.
- Debit Finished Goods Inventory for the cost of completed jobs. Debit Cost of Goods Sold for the cost of jobs sold.
- Overhead is under-applied when Manufacturing Overhead has a debit balance.

(*continued*)

		(7)		
28	Finished Goods Inventory		120,600	
	Work in Process Inventory			120,600
	To record completion of Job A16: direct materials $27,000, direct labour $52,000, and manufacturing overhead $41,600.			

		(8)		
28	Accounts Receivable		150,000	
	Sales			150,000
	To record sale of Job A16.			
28	Cost of Goods Sold		120,600	
	Finished Goods Inventory			120,600
	To record cost of sale for Job A16.			

(b) Manufacturing Overhead has a debit balance of $2,400 as shown below:

Manufacturing Overhead

(3) 59,800	(6) 62,400
(4) 3,000	
(5) 2,000	
Bal. 2,400	

Thus, manufacturing overhead is under-applied for the month.

(c) The adjusting entry for the under-applied overhead is as follows:

Cost of Goods Sold	2,400	
Manufacturing Overhead		2,400
To close under-applied overhead to cost of goods sold.		

After this entry is posted, Manufacturing Overhead will have a zero balance. In preparing an income statement for the year, the amount reported for cost of goods sold will be the account balance after the adjustment for under-applied overhead.

the navigator ✓

WileyPLUS   Self-Test, Brief Exercises, Exercises, Problems—Set A, and many more components are available for practice in WileyPlus.

Self-Study Questions

Answers are at the end of the chapter.

(SO 1) 1. Cost accounting involves the measuring, recording, and reporting of
(a) product costs.
(b) future costs.
(c) manufacturing processes.
(d) managerial accounting decisions.

(SO 2) 2. In accumulating raw materials costs, companies debit the cost of raw materials purchased in a perpetual system to
(a) Raw Materials Purchases.
(b) Raw Materials Inventory.
(c) Purchases.
(d) Work in Process.

(SO 2) 3. When incurred, factory labour costs are debited to
(a) Work in Process.
(b) Factory Wages Expense.

(c) Factory Labour.
(d) Factory Wages Payable.

(SO 3) 4. The source documents for assigning costs to job cost sheets are
(a) invoices, time tickets, and the predetermined overhead rate.
(b) materials requisition slips, time tickets, and the actual overhead costs.
(c) materials requisition slips, payroll register, and the predetermined overhead rate.
(d) materials requisition slips, time tickets, and the predetermined overhead rate.

(SO 3) 5. In recording the issuance of raw materials in a job-order cost system, it would be incorrect to
(a) debit Work in Process Inventory.
(b) debit Finished Goods Inventory.

(c) debit Manufacturing Overhead.
(d) credit Raw Materials Inventory.

(SO 3)   6. The entry when direct factory labour is assigned to jobs is a debit to
(a) Work in Process Inventory and a credit to Factory Labour.
(b) Manufacturing Overhead and a credit to Factory Labour.
(c) Factory Labour and a credit to Manufacturing Overhead.
(d) Factory Labour and a credit to Work in Process Inventory.

(SO 4)   7. The formula for calculating the predetermined manufacturing overhead rate is the estimated annual overhead costs divided by an expected annual operating activity, expressed as
(a) direct labour cost.
(b) direct labour hours.
(c) machine hours.
(d) any of the above.

(SO 4)   8. In Crawford Company, the predetermined overhead rate is 80% of the direct labour cost. During the month, Crawford incurs $210,000 of factory labour costs, of which $180,000 is direct labour and $30,000 is indirect labour. Actual overhead incurred was $200,000. The amount of overhead debited to Work in Process Inventory should be
(a) $200,000.
(b) $144,000.
(c) $168,000.
(d) $160,000.

(SO 4)   9. Mynex Company completes Job No. 26 at a cost of $4,500 and later sells it for $7,000 cash. A correct entry is
(a) Debit Finished Goods Inventory $7,000 and credit Work in Process Inventory $7,000.
(b) Debit Cost of Goods Sold $7,000 and credit Finished Goods Inventory $7,000.
(c) Debit Finished Goods Inventory $4,500 and credit Work in Process Inventory $4,500.
(d) Debit Accounts Receivable $7,000 and credit Sales $7,000.

(SO 6)   10. Manufacturing overhead is under-applied if
(a) actual overhead is less than applied.
(b) actual overhead is greater than applied.
(c) the predetermined rate equals the actual rate.
(d) actual overhead equals applied overhead.

Brief Exercises

(SO 1)
Differentiate between the two cost accounting systems.

BE3-1   Your roommate asks for your help in understanding the two types of cost accounting systems. (a) Distinguish between the two types of cost accounting systems for your roommate. (b) Explain to your roommate why a company can use both types of cost accounting systems.

(SO 2)
Prepare a flowchart of a job-order system, and identify transactions.

BE3-2   Reyes Tool & Die begins operations on January 1. Because it does all the work to customer specifications, the company decides to use a job-order costing system. Prepare a flow chart of a typical job-order cost accounting system with arrows showing the flow of costs. Identify the eight transactions.

(SO 2)
Prepare entries in accumulating manufacturing costs.

BE3-3   During January, its first month of operations, Reyes Tool & Die accumulated the following manufacturing costs: raw materials $4,000 on account; factory labour $6,000, of which $5,200 relates to factory wages payable and $800 relates to payroll taxes payable; and utilities payable $2,000. Prepare separate journal entries for each type of manufacturing cost.

(SO 3)
Prepare an entry for the assignment of raw materials costs.

BE3-4   In January, Reyes Tool & Die requisitions raw materials for production as follows: Job 1 $900, Job 2 $1,400, Job 3 $700, and general factory use $800. Prepare a summary journal entry to record raw materials used.

(SO 3)
Prepare an entry for the assignment of factory labour costs.

BE3-5   Factory labour data for Reyes Tool & Die are given in BE3-3. During January, time tickets show that the factory labour of $6,000 was used as follows: Job 1 $2,200, Job 2 $1,600, Job 3 $1,400, and general factory use $800. Prepare a summary journal entry to record factory labour used.

(SO 3)
Prepare job cost sheets.

BE3-6   Data pertaining to job cost sheets for Reyes Tool & Die are given in BE3-4 and BE3-5. Prepare the job cost sheets for each of the three jobs. (*Note:* You may omit the column for Manufacturing Overhead.)

(SO 4)
Calculate predetermined overhead rates.

BE3-7   Marquis Company estimates that annual manufacturing overhead costs will be $900,000. Estimated annual operating activity bases are direct labour cost $500,000, direct labour hours 50,000, and machine hours 100,000. Calculate the predetermined overhead rate for each activity base.

(SO 4)
Using predetermined overhead rates.

BE3-8   During the first quarter, Phuong Company incurs the following direct labour costs: January $40,000, February $30,000, and March $50,000. For each month, prepare the entry to assign overhead to production using a predetermined rate of 90% of direct labour costs.

BE3-9 In March, Stinson Company completes Jobs 10 and 11. Job 10 cost $20,000 and Job 11 cost $30,000. On March 31, Job 10 is sold to the customer for $35,000 in cash. Journalize the entries for the completion of the two jobs and the sale of Job 10.

(SO 5)
Prepare entries for completion and sale of completed jobs.

BE3-10 Jamasji Engineering Contractors incurred service salaries and wages of $32,000 ($24,000 direct and $8,000 indirect) on an engineering project. The company applies overhead at a rate of 25% of direct labour. Record the entries to assign service salaries and wages and to apply overhead.

(SO 5)
Prepare entries for service salaries and operating overheads.

BE3-11 In its first year of operation, Montreal Printing Shop estimated manufacturing overhead costs and activity in order to determine a predetermined overhead rate. At year end, overhead was over-applied by $3,500. It has been decided this over-applied overhead is material at the end of the year and the amount should be allocated among 10% work-in-process, 25% finished goods, and the rest to the cost of goods sold. Prepare the adjusting entry to close out the over-applied overhead.

(SO 6)
Prepare adjusting entries for under- and over-applied overhead.

BE3-12 At December 31, balances in Manufacturing Overhead are Diaz Company—debit $1,200, Garcia Company—credit $900. Prepare the adjusting entry for each company at December 31, assuming the adjustment is made to cost of goods sold.

(SO 6)
Prepare adjusting entries for under- and over-applied overhead.

Do It! Review

D3-13 During the current month, Dalmar Company incurs the following manufacturing costs:

1. Purchased raw materials of $16,000 on account.
2. Incurred factory labour of $40,000. Of that amount, $31,000 relates to wages payable and $9,000 relates to payroll taxes payable.
3. Factory utilities of $3,100 are payable, prepaid factory property taxes of $2,400 have expired, and depreciation on the factory building is $9,500.

Prepare journal entries for each type of manufacturing cost. (Use a summary entry to record manufacturing overhead.)

(SO 2)
Prepare journal entries for manufacturing costs.

D3-14 Fishel Company is working on two job orders. The job cost sheets show the following:

	Job 201	Job 202
Direct materials	$7,200	$9,000
Direct labour	4,000	6,000
Manufacturing overhead	5,200	9,800

Prepare the three summary entries to record the assignment of costs to Work in Process from the data on the job cost sheets.

(SO 3)
Assign costs to work in process.

D3-15 During the current month, Seeza Corporation completed Job 310 and Job 312. Job 310 cost $60,000 and Job 312 cost $40,000. Job 312 was sold on account for $90,000. Journalize the entries for the completion of the two jobs and the sale of Job 312.

(SO 5)
Prepare entries for completion and sale of jobs.

D3-16 For Dene Company, the predetermined overhead rate is 150% of direct labour cost. During the month, Dene incurred $100,000 of factory labour costs, of which $85,000 is direct labour and $15,000 is indirect labour. Actual overhead incurred was $120,000.

Calculate the amount of manufacturing overhead applied during the month. Determine the amount of under- or over-applied manufacturing overhead.

(SO 6)
Apply manufacturing overhead and determine under- or over-application.

Exercises

E3-17 The gross earnings of the factory workers for Vargas Company during the month of January are $66,000. The employer's payroll taxes for the factory payroll are $8,000. The fringe benefits to be paid by the employer on this payroll are $6,000. Of the total accumulated cost of factory labour, 85% is related to direct labour and 15% is attributable to indirect labour.

(SO 2, 3)
Prepare entries for factory labour.

Instructions
(a) Prepare the entry to record the factory labour costs for the month of January.
(b) Prepare the entry to assign factory labour to production.

(SO 2, 3, 4, 5)
Prepare journal entries for manufacturing costs.

E3-18 Milner Manufacturing uses a job-order costing system. On May 1, the company has a balance in Work in Process Inventory of $3,500 and two jobs in process: Job No. 429 $2,000, and Job No. 430 $1,500. During May, a summary of source documents reveals the following:

Job Number	Materials Requisition Slips		Labour Time Tickets	
429	$2,500		$1,900	
430	3,500		3,000	
431	4,400	$10,400	7,600	$12,500
General use		800		1,200
		$11,200		$13,700

Milner Manufacturing applies manufacturing overhead to jobs at an overhead rate of 60% of direct labour cost. Job No. 429 is completed during the month.

Instructions
(a) Prepare summary journal entries to record the:
   1. requisition slips
   2. time tickets
   3. assignment of manufacturing overhead to jobs
   4. completion of Job No. 429
(b) Post the entries to Work in Process Inventory, and prove the agreement of the control account with the job cost sheets.

(SO 2, 3, 4, 5)
Analyze a job cost sheet and prepare entries for manufacturing costs.

E3-19 A job-order cost sheet for Rolen Company is shown below.

Job No. 92   **For 2,000 Units**

Date	Direct Materials	Direct Labour	Manufacturing Overhead
Beginning Balance			
January 1	$ 3,925	$ 6,000	$ 4,200
8	6,000		
12		8,500	6,375
25	2,000		
27		4,000	3,000
	11,925	18,500	13,575

Cost of completed job:	
Direct materials	$11,925
Direct labour	18,500
Manufacturing overhead	13,575
Total cost	$44,000
Unit cost ($44,000/2,000)	$ 22.00

Instructions
(a) On the basis of the foregoing data, answer the following questions:
   1. What was the balance in Work in Process Inventory on January 1 if this was the only unfinished job?
   2. If manufacturing overhead is applied on the basis of direct labour cost, what overhead rate was used in each year?
(b) Prepare summary entries at January 31 to record the current year's transactions pertaining to Job No. 92.

(SO 2, 6)
Analyze costs of manufacturing and determine missing amounts.

E3-20 Manufacturing cost data for Pena Company, which uses a job-order cost system, are presented below.

	Case A	Case B	Case C
Direct materials used	(a)	$ 78,000	$ 72,600
Direct labour	$ 50,000	120,000	(h)
Manufacturing overhead applied	37,500	(d)	(i)
Total manufacturing costs	135,650	(e)	212,600
Work in process 1/1/16	(b)	15,500	23,000
Total cost of work in process	211,500	(f)	(j)
Work in process 12/31/16	(c)	11,800	(k)
Cost of goods manufactured	193,200	(g)	222,000

Instructions
Indicate the missing amount for each letter. Assume that in all cases manufacturing overhead is applied on the basis of direct labour cost and the rate is the same.

E3-21 Millefeuille Company applies operating overhead to photocopying jobs on the basis of machine hours used. It expects overhead costs to total $290,000 for the year and estimates machine usage at 125,000 hours.

 For the year, the company incurs $295,000 of overhead costs and uses 130,000 hours.

(SO 4, 6)
Calculate the manufacturing overhead rate and under- or over-applied overhead.

Instructions

(a) Calculate the service overhead rate for the year.

(b) Calculate the amount of under- or over-applied overhead at December 31.

(c) Assuming the under- or over-applied overhead for the year is not allocated to inventory accounts, prepare the adjusting entry to assign the amount to cost of jobs finished.

E3-22 A job cost sheet of Nilson Company is given below.

(SO 2, 3, 4, 5)
Analyze a job cost sheet and prepare an entry for the completed job.

Job Cost Sheet

Job No. 469   **Quantity:** 2,000

Item: White Lion Cages   **Date Requested:** 7/2

For: Tesla Company   **Date Completed:** 7/31

Date	Direct Materials	Direct Labour	Manufacturing Overhead
7/10	$ 825		
12	900		
15		$400	$560
22		350	490
24	1,600		
27	1,500		
31		500	700

Cost of completed job:

  Direct materials _____

  Direct labour _____

  Manufacturing overhead _____

Total cost _____

Unit cost _____

Instructions

(a) Determine the source documents for direct materials, direct labour, and manufacturing overhead costs assigned to this job.

(b) Calculate predetermined manufacturing overhead rate.

(c) Calculate the total cost and the unit cost of the completed job. (Round the unit cost to the nearest cent.)

(d) Prepare the entry to record the completion of the job.

E3-23 Torre Corporation incurred the following transactions.

(SO 3, 4, 5)
Prepare entries for manufacturing and nonmanufacturing costs.

1. Purchased raw materials on account $46,300.

2. Raw materials of $36,000 were requisitioned to the factory. An analysis of the materials requisition slips indicated that $6,800 was classified as indirect materials.

3. Factory labour costs incurred were $55,900, of which $51,000 pertained to factory wages payable and $4,900 pertained to employer payroll taxes payable.

4. Time tickets indicated that $50,000 was direct labour and $5,900 was indirect labour.

5. Manufacturing overhead costs incurred on account were $80,500.

6. Depreciation on the company's office building was $8,100.

7. Manufacturing overhead was applied at the rate of 150% of direct labour cost.

8. Goods costing $88,000 were completed and transferred to finished goods.

9. Finished goods costing $75,000 to manufacture were sold on account for $103,000.

Instructions

Journalize the transactions. (Omit explanations.)

E3-24 Garnett Printing Corp. uses a job-order cost system. The following data summarize the operations related to the first quarter's production:

(SO 2, 3, 4)
Prepare entries for manufacturing costs.

1. Materials purchased on account were $192,000, and factory wages incurred were $91,500.

2. Materials requisitioned and factory labour used by job were as follows:

Job Number	Materials	Factory Labour
A20	$ 33,240	$18,000
A21	42,920	24,000
A22	36,100	17,000
A23	41,270	25,000
General factory use	4,470	7,500
	$158,000	$91,500

3. Manufacturing overhead costs incurred on account were $59,500.
4. Depreciation on machinery and equipment was $14,550.
5. The manufacturing overhead rate is 80% of the direct labour cost.
6. Jobs completed during the quarter were A20, A21, and A23.

Instructions

Prepare entries to record the operations summarized above. (Prepare a schedule showing the individual cost elements and total cost for each job in item 6.)

(SO 2, 5)
Prepare a cost of goods manufactured schedule and partial financial statements.

E3-25   At May 31, 2016, the accounts of Hannifan Manufacturing Company show the following:

1. May 1 inventories—Finished Goods $12,600, Work in Process $17,400, and Raw Materials $8,200.
2. May 31 inventories—Finished Goods $15,400, Work in Process $17,900, and Raw Materials $7,100.
3. Debit postings to Work in Process were direct materials $54,200, direct labour $32,000, and manufacturing overhead applied $40,000.
4. Sales totalled $200,000.

Instructions

(a) Prepare a condensed cost of goods manufactured schedule.
(b) Prepare an income statement for May through gross profit.
(c) Provide the balance sheet presentation of the manufacturing inventories at May 31, 2016.

(SO 3, 5)
Calculate work in process and finished goods from job cost sheets.

E3-26   Laubitz Company begins operations on April 1. Information from job cost sheets shows the following:

| Job Number | Manufacturing Costs Assigned | | | Month Completed |
	April	May	June	
10	$6,500	$4,400		May
11	4,100	3,900	$3,000	June
12	1,200			April
13		4,700	3,400	June
14		5,400	3,600	Not complete

Each job was sold for 25% above its cost in the month following completion.

Instructions

(a) Calculate the balance in Work in Process Inventory at the end of each month.
(b) Calculate the balance in Finished Goods Inventory at the end of each month.
(c) Calculate the gross profit for May, June, and July.

(SO 2, 4, 5)
Prepare entries for costs of services provided.

E3-27   Shown below are the job cost-related accounts for the law firm of De Witte, Ozols, and Morton and their manufacturing equivalents:

Law Firm Accounts	Manufacturing Firm Accounts
Supplies	Raw Materials
Salaries Payable	Factory Wages Payable
Operating Overhead	Manufacturing Overhead
Work in Process	Work in Process
Cost of Completed Work	Cost of Goods Sold

Cost data for the month of March follow.

1. Purchased supplies on account $1,500.
2. Issued supplies of $1,200 (60% direct and 40% indirect).
3. Time cards for the month indicated labour costs of $60,000 (80% direct and 20% indirect).
4. Operating overhead costs incurred for cash totalled $40,000.
5. Operating overhead is applied at a rate of 90% of direct labour cost.
6. Work completed totalled $75,000.

Instructions

(a) Journalize the transactions for March. Omit explanations.
(b) Determine the balance of the Work in Process account. Use a T account.

(SO 3, 4, 6)
Determine cost of jobs and ending balance in Work in Process and Overhead accounts.

E3-28   Pedro Morales and Associates, a CPA firm, uses job-order costing to capture the costs of its audit jobs. There were no audit jobs in process at the beginning of November. Listed below are data concerning the three audit jobs conducted during November:

	Koppel	Dupont	Rojas
Direct materials	$ 700	$ 400	$ 250
Auditor labour costs	$5,400	$6,600	$3,375
Auditor hours	72	90	40

Overhead costs are applied to jobs on the basis of auditor hours, and the predetermined overhead rate is $60 per auditor hour. The Koppel job is the only incomplete job at the end of November. Actual overhead for the month was $12,000.

Instructions
(a) Determine the cost of each job.
(b) Indicate the balance of the Work in Process account at the end of November.
(c) Calculate the ending balance of the Overhead account for November.

E3-29 Easy Decorating uses a job-order costing system to collect the costs of its interior decorating business. Each client's consultation is treated as a separate job. Overhead is applied to each job based on the number of decorator hours incurred. Listed below are data for the current year:

Estimated overhead	$920,000
Actual overhead	$942,800
Estimated decorator hours	40,000
Actual decorator hours	40,500

The company uses Operating Overhead in place of Manufacturing Overhead.

Instructions
(a) Calculate the predetermined overhead rate.
(b) Prepare the entry to apply the overhead for the year.
(c) Determine whether the overhead was under- or over-applied and by how much.

(SO 4, 6)
Determine the pre-determined overhead rate, apply overhead, and determine whether the overhead was under- or over-applied.

Problems: Set A

P3-30A The consulting firm CMA Financial employs 40 full-time staff. The estimated compensation per employee is $105,000 for 1,750 hours. It charges all direct labour costs to clients. It includes any other costs in a single indirect cost pool and allocates them based on labour hours. Actual indirect costs were $850,000. Estimated indirect costs for the coming year are $1.4 million. The firm expects to have 60 clients in the coming year.

Instructions
(a) Determine overhead rate per direct labour hour.
(b) Determine the direct labour rate per hour.
(c) Calculate the total cost of a job that will take 270 direct labour hours, using a normal cost system.

(SO 4)
Calculate the prede-termined overhead rate and job costs for a service organization.

(a) $20.00
(b) $60.00
(c) $21,600

P3-31A Bertrand Manufacturing uses a job-order cost system and applies overhead to production on the basis of direct labour costs. On January 1, 2016, Job No. 50 was the only job in process. The costs incurred prior to January 1 on this job were as follows: direct materials $30,000, direct labour $15,000, and manufacturing overhead $20,000. As of January 1, Job No. 49 had been completed at a cost of $120,000 and was part of finished goods inventory. There was a $25,000 balance in the Raw Materials Inventory account.

During the month of January, Bertrand Manufacturing began production on Jobs 51 and 52, and completed Jobs 50 and 51. Jobs 49 and 50 were also sold on account during the month for $152,000 and $198,000, respectively. The following additional events occurred during the month:

1. Bertrand purchased additional raw materials of $100,000 on account.
2. It incurred factory labour costs of $75,000. Of this amount, $18,000 related to employer payroll taxes.
3. It incurred manufacturing overhead costs as follows: indirect materials $18,000, indirect labour $17,000, depreciation expense $14,000, and various other manufacturing overhead costs on account $22,000.
4. It assigned direct materials and direct labour to jobs as follows:

Job No.	Direct Materials	Direct Labour
50	$12,000	$ 7,000
51	42,000	28,000
52	35,000	22,000

Instructions
(a) Calculate the predetermined overhead rate for 2016, assuming Bertrand Manufacturing estimates total manufacturing overhead costs of $1.5 million, direct labour costs of $750,000, and direct labour hours of 20,000 for the year.
(b) Open job cost sheets for Jobs 50, 51, and 52. Enter the January 1 balances on the job cost sheet for Job No. 50.
(c) Prepare the journal entries to record the purchase of raw materials, the factory labour costs incurred, and the manu-facturing overhead costs incurred during the month of January.
(d) Prepare the journal entries to record the assignment of direct materials, direct labour, and manufacturing overhead costs to production. In assigning manufacturing overhead costs, use the overhead rate calculated in part (a). Post all costs to the job cost sheets as necessary.
(e) Total the job cost sheets for any job(s) completed during the month. Prepare the journal entry (or entries) to record the completion of any job(s) during the month.

(SO 2, 3, 4, 5, 6)
Prepare entries in a job-order cost system and job cost sheets.

(e) Job 50: $98,000
Job 51: $126,000

(f) Prepare the journal entry (or entries) to record the sale of any job(s) during the month.

(g) Calculate the balance in the Finished Goods Inventory account at the end of the month. What does this balance consist of?

(h) Calculate the amount of under- or over-applied overhead.

(SO 2, 3, 4, 5)
Prepare entries in a job-order cost system and partial income statement.

P3-32A For the year ended December 31, 2016, the job cost sheets of DeVoe Company contained the following data:

Job Number	Explanation	Direct Materials	Direct Labour	Manufacturing Overhead	Total Costs
7640	Balance 1/1	$25,000	$24,000	$28,800	$ 77,800
	Current year's costs	30,000	36,000	43,200	109,200
7641	Balance 1/1	11,000	18,000	21,600	50,600
	Current year's costs	43,000	48,000	57,600	148,600
7642	Current year's costs	58,000	55,000	66,000	179,000

Other data:

1. Raw materials inventory totalled $15,000 on January 1. During the year, $140,000 of raw materials were purchased on account.
2. Finished goods on January 1 consisted of Job No. 7638 for $87,000 and Job No. 7639 for $92,000.
3. Job No. 7640 and Job No. 7641 were completed during the year.
4. Job Nos. 7638, 7639, and 7641 were sold on account for $530,000.
5. Manufacturing overhead incurred on account totalled $120,000.
6. Other manufacturing overhead consisted of indirect materials $14,000, indirect labour $18,000, and depreciation on factory machinery $8,000.

Instructions

(a) $179,000; Job 7642: $179,000

(b) Amount = $6,800

(c) $158,600

(a) Prove the agreement of Work in Process Inventory with job cost sheets pertaining to unfinished work. (*Hint:* Use a single T account for Work in Process Inventory.) Calculate each of the following, then post each to the T account: (1) beginning balance, (2) direct materials, (3) direct labour, (4) manufacturing overhead, and (5) completed jobs.

(b) Prepare the adjusting entry for manufacturing overhead, assuming the balance is allocated entirely to Cost of Goods Sold.

(c) Determine the gross profit to be reported for 2016.

(SO 2, 3, 4, 5)
Prepare entries in a job-order cost system and a cost of goods manufactured schedule.

P3-33A Enos Inc. is a construction company specializing in custom patios. The patios are constructed of concrete, brick, fibreglass, and lumber, depending on customer preference. On June 1, 2016, the general ledger for Enos Inc. contains the following data:

Raw Materials Inventory	$ 4,200	Work in Process Inventory	5,540
Manufacturing Overhead Applied	32,640	Manufacturing Overhead Incurred	31,650

Subsidiary data for Work in Process Inventory on June 1 are as follows:

Job Cost Sheets

	Customer		
Cost Element	Fowler	Haines	Krantz
Direct materials	$ 600	$ 800	$ 900
Direct labour	320	540	580
Manufacturing overhead	400	675	725
	$1,320	$2,015	$2,205

During June, raw materials purchased on account were $3,900, and all wages were paid. Additional overhead costs consisted of depreciation on equipment of $700 and miscellaneous costs of $400 incurred on account.

A summary of materials requisition slips and time tickets for June shows the following:

Customer Job	Materials Requisition Slips	Time Tickets
Fowler	$ 800	$ 450
Farkas	2,000	800
Haines	500	360
Krantz	1,300	1,600
Fowler	300	390
	4,900	3,600
General use	1,500	1,200
	$6,400	$4,800

Overhead was charged to jobs at the same rate of $1.25 per dollar of direct labour cost. The patios for customers Fowler, Haines, and Krantz were completed during June and sold for a total of $18,900. Each customer paid in full.

Instructions

(a) Journalize the June transactions for the following:
  1. purchase of raw materials, factory labour costs incurred, and manufacturing overhead costs incurred
  2. assignment of direct materials, labour, and overhead to production
  3. completion of jobs and sale of goods
(b) Post the entries to Work in Process Inventory.
(c) Reconcile the balance in Work in Process Inventory with the costs of unfinished jobs.
(d) Prepare a cost of goods manufactured schedule for June.

(d) Cost of goods manufactured $14,740

P3-34A   Nicole Limited is a company that produces machinery to customer orders, using a normal job-order cost system. It applies manufacturing overhead to production using a predetermined rate. This overhead rate is set at the beginning of each fiscal year by forecasting the year's overhead and relating it to direct labour costs. The budget for 2016 was as follows:

(SO 6)
Calculate the predetermined overhead rate and proration of overhead.

Direct labour	$1,800,000
Manufacturing overhead	900,000

As at the end of the year, two jobs were incomplete. These were 1768B, with total direct labour charges of $110,000, and 1819C, with total direct labour charges of $390,000. On these jobs, machine hours were 287 hours for 1768B and 647 hours for 1819C. Direct materials issued for 1768B amounted to $220,000, and for 1819C they amounted to $420,000.

Total charges to the Manufacturing Overhead Control account for the year were $897,000, and direct labour charges made to all jobs amounted to $1,583,600, representing 247,216 direct labour hours.

There were no beginning inventories. In addition to the ending work in process just described, the ending finished goods inventory account showed a balance of $720,000.

Sales for the year amounted to $6,201,355; cost of goods sold totalled $3,935,000; and sales, general, and administrative expenses were $1,857,870.

The above amounts for inventories and the cost of goods sold have not been adjusted for any over- or under-application of manufacturing overhead to production. It is the company's practice to allocate any over- or under-applied overhead to inventories and the cost of goods sold.

Instructions

(a) Calculate the under- or over-applied manufacturing overhead for 2016.
(b) Prorate the amount calculated in part (a) based on the ending balances (before prorating) of Work in Process, Finished Goods, and Cost of Goods Sold.
(c) Prepare an income statement for the company for the year. The income tax rate is 40%.

(adapted from CMA Canada, now CPA Canada)

(a) $105,200 under-applied
(b) Allocation to Cost of Goods Sold, $68,485
(c) Net income, $204,000

P3-35A   On November 30, 2016, there was a fire in the factory of Able Manufacturing Limited, where you work as the controller. The work in process inventory was completely destroyed, but both the materials and finished goods inventory were undamaged.

Able uses normal job-order costing and its fiscal year end is December 31. Selected information for the periods ended October 31, 2016, and November 30, 2016, follows:

(SO 3)
Analyze a job-order cost system and calculate work in process.

	October 31, 2016	November 30, 2016
Supplies (including both direct and indirect materials)	$ 79,250	$ 73,250
Work in process inventory	58,875	?
Finished goods inventory	60,000	63,000
Cost of goods sold (year to date)	576,000	656,000
Accounts payable (relates to materials purchased only)	17,960	53,540
Manufacturing overhead incurred (year to date)	129,500	163,300
Manufacturing overhead applied	128,700	?

Other information for November 2016:

Cash payments to suppliers	$ 60,000
Payroll (including $15,375 indirect)	83,500
Indirect materials used	5,848
Over-applied overhead (during November only)	2,750

Instructions

Calculate the normal cost of the work in process inventory lost during the fire.

(adapted from CGA-Canada, now CPA Canada)

Direct materials used: $95,732
Manufacturing overhead applied: $36,550

(SO 4, 6)
Calculate predetermined overhead rates, apply overhead, and calculate under- or over-applied overhead.

P3-36A   Agassi Company uses a job order cost system in each of its three manufacturing departments. Manufacturing overhead is applied to jobs on the basis of direct labour cost in Department D, direct labour hours in Department E, and machine hours in Department K.

In establishing the predetermined overhead rates for 2016, the following estimates were made for the year.

	Department		
	D	E	K
Manufacturing overhead	$1,200,000	$1,500,000	$900,000
Direct labour costs	$1,500,000	$1,250,000	$450,000
Direct labour hours	100,000	125,000	40,000
Machine hours	400,000	500,000	120,000

During January, the job cost sheets showed the following costs and production data.

	Department		
	D	E	K
Direct materials used	$140,000	$126,000	$78,000
Direct labour costs	$120,000	$110,000	$37,500
Manufacturing overhead incurred	$ 99,000	$124,000	$79,000
Direct labour hours	8,000	11,000	3,500
Machine hours	34,000	45,000	10,400

Instructions

(a) E: $12/DLH
(b) K: $193,500

(a) Calculate the predetermined overhead rate for each department.
(b) Calculate the total manufacturing costs assigned to jobs in January in each department.
(c) Calculate the under- or over-applied overhead for each department at January 31.

(SO 6)
Prepare entries and close out under- or over-applied overhead.

P3-37A   Red Fire Inc. produces fire trucks. The company uses a normal job-order costing system to calculate its cost of goods manufactured. The company's policy is to price its job at cost plus 30% markup. On January 1, 2016, there was only one job in process, with the following costs:

	Job 200
Direct materials	$13,500
Direct labour	18,000
Applied overhead	27,000
Total	$58,500

The following balances were taken from the general ledger of the company as of January 1, 2016:

Direct materials inventory	$45,000
Finished goods inventory (for Job 100)	$85,000

During the year 2016, the following events occurred:
Direct materials were purchased on account for $375,000.
Two more jobs were started: Job 300 and Job 400. Direct materials and direct labour costs incurred by each job in process during the year 2016 were as follows:

	Job 200	Job 300	Job 400
Direct materials	$150,000	$45,000	$35,000
Direct labour	$130,000	$45,000	$25,000

The company incurred the following actual factory overhead during the year:

Factory rent	$135,000
Factory supplies	$ 55,500
Indirect labour	$ 85,750

Jobs 200 and 300 were completed.
Jobs 100 and 200 were sold.

Instructions ·

(c) Over-applied overhead: $23,750

(e) Job 200: $693,550

(a) Calculate the total applied overhead for the year 2016. The factory overhead costs are applied to each job on the basis of direct labour dollars.
(b) Prepare simple job-order cost sheets for jobs 200, 300, and 400 for the year ended December 31, 2016.
(c) Determine whether the overhead is over-applied or under-applied. By how much?
(d) Prepare a schedule of cost of goods sold, identifying both normal and adjusted cost of goods sold, for the year ended December 31, 2016.
(e) Calculate the selling price of Job 200.
(f) Calculate the ending balances as of December 31, 2016, for the following accounts: Direct Materials and Work in Process.

P3-38A Vargas Corporation's fiscal year ends on June 30. The following accounts are found in its job-order cost accounting system for the first month of the new fiscal year:

(SO 2, 3, 4, 5, 6)
Analyze manufacturing accounts and determine missing amounts.

Raw Materials Inventory

July 1	Beginning balance	15,000	July 31 Requisitions	(a)
31	Purchases	90,400		
July 31	Ending balance	(b)		

Work in Process Inventory

July 1	Beginning balance	(c)	July 31 Jobs completed	(f)
31	Direct materials	75,000		
31	Direct labour	(d)		
31	Overhead	(e)		
July 31	Ending balance	(g)		

Finished Goods Inventory

July 1	Beginning balance	(h)	July 31 Cost of goods sold	(j)
31	Completed jobs	(i)		
July 31	Ending balance	(k)		

Factory Labour

July 31	Factory wages	(l)	July 31 Wages assigned	(m)

Manufacturing Overhead

July 31	Indirect materials	9,000	July 31 Overhead applied	114,000
31	Indirect labour	16,000		
31	Other overhead	(n)		

Other data:

1. On July 1, two jobs were in process: Job No. 4085 and Job No. 4086, with costs of $19,000 and $13,200, respectively.
2. During July, Job Nos. 4087, 4088, and 4089 were started. On July 31, only Job No. 4089 was unfinished. This job had charges for direct materials of $2,000 and direct labour of $1,500, plus manufacturing overhead. Manufacturing overhead was applied at the rate of 125% of direct labour cost.
3. On July 1, Job No. 4084, costing $145,000, was in the finished goods warehouse. On July 31, Job No. 4088, costing $138,000, was in finished goods.
4. Overhead was $3,000 under-applied in July.

Instructions

List the letters (a) through (n) and indicate the amount pertaining to each letter. Show calculations.

(c) $32,200
(f) $307,025
(i) $307,025

Problems: Set B

P3-39B Lowry Manufacturing uses a job-order cost system and applies overhead to production on the basis of direct labour hours. On January 1, 2016, Job No. 25 was the only job in process. The costs incurred prior to January 1 on this job were as follows: direct materials $10,000, direct labour $6,000, and manufacturing overhead $9,000. Job No. 23 had been completed at a cost of $45,000 and was part of finished goods inventory. There was a $5,000 balance in the Raw Materials Inventory account.

(SO 2, 3, 4, 5, 6)
Prepare entries in a job-order cost system and job cost sheets.

During the month of January, the company began production on Jobs 26 and 27, and completed Jobs 25 and 26. Jobs 23 and 25 were sold on account during the month for $65,000 and $74,000, respectively. The following additional events occurred during the month:

1. The company purchased additional raw materials for $40,000 on account.
2. It incurred factory labour costs of $31,500. Of this amount, $7,000 related to employer payroll taxes.
3. It incurred the following manufacturing overhead costs: indirect materials $10,000, indirect labour $7,500, depreciation expense $12,000, and various other manufacturing overhead costs on account $11,000.
4. It assigned direct materials and direct labour to jobs as follows:

Job No.	Direct Materials	Direct Labour
25	$ 5,000	$ 3,000
26	15,000	12,000
27	13,000	9,900

5. The company uses direct labour hours as the activity base to assign overhead. Direct labour hours incurred on each job were as follows: Job No. 25, 200; Job No. 26, 800; and Job No. 27, 600.

Instructions

(a) Calculate the predetermined overhead rate for 2016, assuming Lowry Manufacturing estimates total manufacturing overhead costs of $500,000, direct labour costs of $300,000, and direct labour hours of 20,000 for the year.

(b) Open job cost sheets for Jobs 25, 26, and 27. Enter the January 1 balances on the job cost sheet for Job No. 25.

(c) Prepare the journal entries to record the purchase of raw materials, the factory labour costs incurred, and the manufacturing overhead costs incurred during the month of January.

(d) Prepare the journal entries to record the assignment of direct materials, direct labour, and manufacturing overhead costs to production. In assigning manufacturing overhead costs, use the overhead rate calculated in part (a). Post all costs to the job cost sheets as necessary.

(e) Job 25: $38,000
Job 26: $47,000

(e) Total the job cost sheets for any job(s) completed during the month. Prepare the journal entry (or entries) to record the completion of any job(s) during the month.

(f) Prepare the journal entry (or entries) to record the sale of any job(s) during the month.

(g) Calculate the balance in the Work in Process Inventory account at the end of the month. What does this balance consist of?

(h) Calculate the amount of under- or over-applied overhead.

(SO 2, 3, 4, 5, 6)
Prepare entries in a job-order cost system and partial income statement.

P3-40B For the year ended December 31, 2016, the job cost sheets of Mazzone Company contained the following data:

Job Number	Explanation	Direct Materials	Direct Labour	Manufacturing Overhead	Total Costs
7650	Balance 1/1	$18,000	$20,000	$25,000	$ 63,000
	Current year's costs	32,000	36,000	45,000	113,000
7651	Balance 1/1	12,000	16,000	20,000	48,000
	Current year's costs	30,000	40,000	50,000	120,000
7652	Current year's costs	35,000	68,000	85,000	188,000

Other data:

1. Raw materials inventory totalled $20,000 on January 1. During the year, $100,000 of raw materials were purchased on account.

2. Finished goods on January 1 consisted of Job No. 7648 for $93,000 and Job No. 7649 for $62,000.

3. Job No. 7650 and Job No. 7651 were completed during the year.

4. Job Nos. 7648, 7649, and 7650 were sold on account for $490,000.

5. Manufacturing overhead incurred on account totalled $135,000.

6. Other manufacturing overhead consisted of indirect materials of $12,000, indirect labour of $16,000, and depreciation on factory machinery of $19,500.

Instructions

(a) Prove the agreement of Work in Process Inventory with job cost sheets pertaining to unfinished work. (*Hint:* Use a single T account for Work in Process Inventory.) Calculate each of the following, then post each to the T account:

(a) (1) $111,000
(4) $180,000
Unfinished Job No. 7652, $188,000

1. beginning balance
2. direct materials
3. direct labour
4. manufacturing overhead
5. completed jobs

(b) Amount = $2,500

(b) Prepare the adjusting entry for Manufacturing Overhead, assuming the balance is allocated entirely to Cost of Goods Sold.

(c) $156,500

(c) Determine the gross profit to be reported for 2016.

(SO 4)
Calculate the predetermined overhead rate and a job cost.

P3-41B Tel Corp. has the following estimated costs for 2016:

Direct materials	$ 160,000
Direct labour	2,000,000
Rent on factory building	150,000
Sales salaries	250,000
Depreciation on factory equipment	80,000
Indirect labour	120,000
Production supervisor's salary	150,000
Machine hours	40,000

Other data:

Tel Corp. estimates that 20,000 direct labour hours will be worked during the year. Assume that manufacturing overhead is applied on the basis of machine hours and Job XY120 is completed during the year.

Instructions

(a) $12.50 per machine hour
(b) $100
(c) $22,500

(a) Calculate the overhead rate per machine hour.

(b) Calculate the rate of direct labour per hour.

(c) Calculate the total cost of a job that will take 200 machine hours, $15,000 in direct material, and 50 direct labour hours using a normal cost system.

P3-42B Giovanni Lofaro is a contractor specializing in custom-built Jacuzzis. On May 1, 2016, his ledger contains the following data:

(SO 2, 3, 4, 5)
Prepare entries in a job-order cost system and cost of goods manufactured schedule.

Raw Materials Inventory	$30,000
Work in Process Inventory	12,200
Manufacturing Overhead	2,500 (dr.)

The Manufacturing Overhead account has debit totals of $12,500 and credit totals of $10,000. Subsidiary data for Work in Process Inventory on May 1 include the following:

Job by Customer	Direct Materials	Direct Labour	Manufacturing Overhead
Looper	$2,500	$2,000	$1,400
Zammit	2,000	1,200	840
Ingle	900	800	560
	$5,400	$4,000	$2,800

During May, the following costs were incurred: (1) raw materials purchased on account $4,000, (2) labour paid $7,600, and (3) manufacturing overhead paid $1,400.

A summary of materials requisition slips and time tickets for the month of May reveals the following:

	Job Cost Sheets	
Job by Customer	Materials Requisition Slips	Time Tickets
Looper	$ 500	$ 400
Zammit	600	1,000
Ingle	2,300	1,300
Gao	1,900	2,900
	5,300	5,600
General use	1,500	2,000
	$6,800	$7,600

Overhead was charged to jobs on the basis of $0.70 per dollar of direct labour cost. The Jacuzzis for customers Looper, Zammit, and Ingle were completed during May. Each Jacuzzi was sold for $12,000 cash.

Instructions

(a) Prepare journal entries for the May transactions:
  1. the purchase of raw materials, factory labour costs incurred, and manufacturing overhead costs incurred
  2. assignment of direct materials, labour, and overhead to production
  3. completion of jobs and sale of goods
(b) Post the entries to Work in Process Inventory.
(c) Reconcile the balance in Work in Process Inventory with the costs of unfinished jobs.
(d) Prepare a cost of goods manufactured schedule for May.

(d) Cost of goods manufactured: $20,190

P3-43B SNC produces fire trucks. The company uses a normal job-order costing system to calculate its cost of goods manufactured. The company's policy is to price its Job at cost plus 40% markup. On January 1, 2016, there was only one job in process with the following costs:

(SO 6)
Prepare entries and close out under- or over-applied overhead.

	Job A-1
Direct materials	$ 3,500
Direct labour	15,000
Applied overhead	18,000
Total	$36,500

The following balances were taken from the general ledger of the company as of January 1, 2016:

Direct materials inventory	$35,000
Finished goods inventory (for Job D-1)	$65,000

During the year 2016, the following events occurred:
  Direct materials were purchased on account for $275,000.
  Two more jobs were started: Job B-1 and Job C-1. Direct materials and direct labour costs incurred by each job in process during the year 2016 are as follows:

	Job A-1	Job B-1	Job C-1
Direct materials	$150,000	$30,000	$10,000
Direct labour	$150,000	$35,000	$15,000

The company incurred the following actual factory overhead during the year:

Factory rent	$120,000
Factory supplies	$ 45,500
Indirect labour	$ 75,750

Jobs A-1 and B-1 were completed and Jobs D-1 and A-1 were sold.

Instructions

(a) $240,000

(a) Calculate the total applied overhead for the year 2016 if the factory overhead costs are applied to each job on the basis of direct labour dollars.

(b) Prepare simple job-order cost sheets for jobs A-1, B-1, and C-1 for the year ended December 31, 2016.

(c) Under-applied: $1,250

(c) Determine whether overhead is over-applied or under-applied. By how much?

(d) Prepare a schedule of cost of goods sold, identifying both normal and adjusted cost of goods sold, for the year ended December 31, 2016.

(f) Direct Materials: $120,000

(e) Calculate the selling price of Job A-1.

(f) Calculate the ending balances as of December 31, 2016, for the following accounts: Direct Materials and Work in Process.

(SO 3, 4, 5, 6)
Prepare entries and close out under- or overapplied overheads.

P3-44B Laramie Ltd. uses a normal job-order cost system. At the beginning of the month of June, two orders were in process as follows:

	Order 8A	Order 10A
Raw materials	$2,000	$1,900
Direct labour	1,200	200
Manufacturing overhead absorbed	1,800	300

There was no inventory of finished goods on June 1. During the month of June, orders 11A and 12A were put into process.

Raw materials requirements amounted to $13,000, direct labour expenses for the month were $20,000, and actual manufacturing overhead recorded during the month amounted to $28,000.

The only order in process at the end of June was order 12A, and the costs incurred for this order were $1,150 of raw materials and $1,000 of direct labour. In addition, order 11A, which was 100% complete, was still on hand as of June 30. Total costs allocated to this order were $3,300. The firm's overhead allocation rate in June was the same as the rate used in May and is based on labour cost.

Instructions

Cost of goods sold: $63,450

Prepare journal entries, with supporting calculations, to record the cost of goods manufactured, the cost of goods sold, and the closing of the over- or under-applied manufacturing overhead to Cost of Goods Sold.

(adapted from CMA Canada, now CPA Canada)

(SO 4, 6)
Calculate predetermined overhead rates, apply overhead, and calculate under- or over-applied overhead.

P3-45B Net Play Company uses a job order cost system in each of its three manufacturing departments. Manufacturing overhead is applied to jobs on the basis of direct labour cost in Department A, direct labour hours in Department B, and machine hours in Department C.

In establishing the predetermined overhead rates for 2014, the following estimates were made for the year.

	Department		
	A	B	C
Manufacturing overhead	$720,000	$640,000	$900,000
Direct labour cost	$600,000	$100,000	$600,000
Direct labour hours	50,000	40,000	40,000
Machine hours	100,000	120,000	150,000

During January, the job cost sheets showed the following costs and production data.

	Department		
	A	B	C
Direct materials used	$92,000	$86,000	$64,000
Direct labour cost	$48,000	$35,000	$50,400
Manufacturing overhead incurred	$60,000	$60,000	$72,100
Direct labour hours	4,000	3,500	4,200
Machine hours	8,000	10,500	12,600

Instructions

(a) B: $16/DLH

(a) Calculate the predetermined overhead rate for each department.

(b) Calculate the total manufacturing costs assigned to jobs in January in each department.

(c) Calculate the under- or over-applied overhead for each department at January 31.

P3-46B Spivey Company's fiscal year ends on June 30. The following accounts are found in its job-order cost accounting system for the first month of the new fiscal year:

(SO 2, 3, 4, 5, 6)
Analyze manufacturing accounts and determine missing amounts.

Raw Materials Inventory

July 1	Beginning balance	19,000	July 31	Requisitions	(a)
31	Purchases	90,400			
July 31	Ending balance	(b)			

Work in Process Inventory

July 1	Beginning balance	(c)	July 31	Jobs completed	(f)
31	Direct materials	70,000			
31	Direct labour	(d)			
31	Overhead	(e)			
July 31	Ending balance	(g)			

Finished Goods Inventory

July 1	Beginning balance	(h)	July 31	Cost of goods sold	(j)
31	Completed jobs	(i)			
July 31	Ending balance	(k)			

Factory Labour

July 31	Factory wages	(l)	July 31	Wages assigned	(m)

Manufacturing Overhead

July 31	Indirect materials	8,900	July 31	Overhead applied	$104,000
31	Indirect labour	16,000			
31	Other overhead	(n)			

Other data:
1. On July 1, two jobs were in process: Job No. 4085 and Job No. 4086, with costs of $19,000 and $8,200, respectively.
2. During July, Job Nos. 4087, 4088, and 4089 were started. On July 31, only Job No. 4089 was unfinished. This job had charges for direct materials of $2,000 and direct labour of $1,500, plus manufacturing overhead. Manufacturing overhead was applied at the rate of 130% of direct labour cost.
3. On July 1, Job No. 4084, costing $135,000, was in the finished goods warehouse. On July 31, Job No. 4088, costing $143,000, was in finished goods.
4. Overhead was $3,000 under-applied in July.

Instructions
List the letters (a) through (n) and indicate the amount pertaining to each letter. Show calculations.

(d) $80,000
(f) $275,750
(l) $ 96,000

P3-47B Price-Gordon Architectural Consultants Ltd. uses a modified job-order costing system to keep track of project costs. During October 2016, the firm worked on four projects. The following table provides a summary of the cost of materials used and the number of consulting hours worked on each of the four projects in October:

(SO 3, 5, 6)
Calculate job costs and inventories, and prepare an income statement for a service organization.

Project Number	Cost of Materials	Consulting Hours Worked
80	$120	138
84	85	145
85	100	160
86	150	187

The records for September showed that 40 hours had been worked and $80 worth of materials had been used on Project 80. Projects 80 and 86 were completed in October, and bills were sent to the clients.

Consultants at Price-Gordon billed clients at $120 per consulting hour. The actual labour cost to the firm (based on salary cost) was $60 per hour. Overhead is charged to projects based on the consultants' time spent on the project. Total overhead for the current fiscal year, based on expected activity of 10,000 consulting hours, was estimated to be $267,000. This total overhead cost included a fixed portion of $84,000, which covered rent, depreciation, and so on. Actual overhead for October was $21,455. Price-Gordon closes under- and over-applied overhead to Cost of Services at month end.

Instructions
(a) Determine the product costs for Project 80.
(b) Determine the balance in Work in Process as at October 31.
(c) Prepare the income statement for October 2016, including the appropriate amount of under- or over-applied overhead. Other expenses for October were $2,340.94.

(a) $15,632.60
(b) $26,628.50
(c) Net Income $4,829.56

(adapted from CMA Canada, now CPA Canada)

Cases

C3-48   Pine Products Company uses a job-order cost system. For a number of months there has been an ongoing rift between the sales department and the production department concerning a special-order product, TC-1. TC-1 is a seasonal product that is manufactured in batches of 2,000 units. It is sold at cost plus a markup of 30%.

The sales department is unhappy because fluctuating unit production costs significantly affect selling prices. Sales personnel complain that this has caused excessive customer complaints and the loss of considerable orders for TC-1.

The production department maintains that each job order must be fully costed on the basis of the costs incurred during the period in which the goods are produced. Production personnel maintain that the only real solution to the problem is for the sales department to increase sales in the slack periods.

Harita Sharma, president of the company, asks you as the company accountant to collect quarterly data for the past year on TC-1.

From the cost accounting system, you accumulate the following production quantity and cost data:

| | Quarter | | | |
Costs	1	2	3	4
Direct materials	$100,000	$220,000	$ 80,000	$200,000
Direct labour	60,000	132,000	48,000	120,000
Manufacturing overhead	105,000	153,000	97,000	125,000
Total	$265,000	$505,000	$225,000	$445,000
Production in batches	5	11	4	10
Unit cost (per batch)	$ 53,000	$ 45,909	$ 56,250	$ 44,500

Instructions

(a) Determine what manufacturing cost element is responsible for the fluctuating unit costs. Why?

(b) Provide a recommended solution to the problem of fluctuating unit cost.

(c) Restate the quarterly data on the basis of your recommended solution.

C3-49   Avid Assemblers uses normal job-order costing to assign costs to products. The company assembles and packages 25 different products according to customer specifications. Products are worked on in batches of 20 to 40 units. Each batch is given a job number. On October 1, the company had the following balances:

Raw materials	$ 9,800
Work in process	65,847
Finished goods	30,640

Work in process consisted of the following jobs:

	Job 22	Job 24	Job 25
Direct materials	$ 6,200	$ 5,190	$ 4,800
Direct labour	10,500	9,210	9,500
Applied overhead	7,350	6,447	6,650
Total	$24,050	$20,847	$20,950
Number of units	20	40	30

Finished goods consisted of Job 23, with the following costs:

Direct materials	$ 8,200
Direct labour	13,200
Applied overhead	9,240
Total	$30,640
Number of units	50

Shown below are the direct cost data related to jobs started in October:

	Job 26	Job 27	Job 28	Total
Direct materials	$ 5,180	$5,600	$4,200	$14,980
Direct labour	11,200	9,340	5,910	26,450
Number of units	20	30	20	

Other information:

1. Direct materials and direct labour added to beginning work in process in October were as follows:

	Job 22	Job 24	Job 25	Total
Direct materials	$1,150	$ 610	$1,500	$ 3,260
Direct labour	3,000	4,500	5,500	$13,000

2. Overhead is applied at a predetermined rate based on the direct labour cost.

3. Actual expenses for October were as follows:

Supervisory salaries	$6,000	Supplies (factory)	$2,100
Factory rent	5,000	Selling expenses	8,500
Depreciation (machines)	5,000	Property tax and insurance	2,250
Indirect labour	4,000	CPP, EI, and other benefits*	4,200

* 80% of employer contributions and benefits relate to factory personnel.

4. Purchases of direct materials (raw materials) during October amounted to $28,500. Indirect materials (supplies) are handled in a separate account.

5. Only Job Nos. 27 and 28 are still in process at closing on October 31. Finished goods consisted only of Job No. 25 at month end.

6. Avid writes off any under- and over-applied overhead to Cost of Goods Sold in the month in which it is incurred.

Instructions

(a) Calculate the predetermined overhead rate used by Avid to apply overhead to jobs.

(b) Calculate the unit cost of Job No. 24 in October.

(c) Calculate the October 31 balances for the following inventory accounts.
    1. Raw Materials   2. Work in Process   3. Finished Goods

(d) What is the cost of goods manufactured in October? (You do not have to prepare a statement.)

(e) Determine the under- or over-applied overhead for October and prepare the journal entry to dispose of this amount.

(adapted from CMA Canada, now CPA Canada)

C3-50 The following data were taken from the records of Cougar Enterprises, a Canadian manufacturer that uses a normal job-order costing system:

Work in Process, December 1

Job Number	70	75	80
Direct materials	$1,800	$2,400	$1,500
Direct labour	1,200	2,400	600
Applied overhead	600	1,350	450
Total	$3,600	$6,150	$2,550

During December, the company worked on jobs numbered 70 through 90 and incurred the following costs:

Job Number	70	75	80	85	90	Total
Direct materials	$600	$ 900	$1,200	$1,350	$1,500	$ 5,550
Direct labour	$750	$1,500	$3,000	$2,250	$6,000	$13,500
Direct labour hours	50	100	200	150	400	900

Additional information:
1. Total overhead costs are applied to jobs on the basis of direct labour hours worked. At the beginning of the year, the company estimated that total overhead costs for the year would be $150,000, and the total labour hours worked would be 12,500.
2. The balance in the Departmental Overhead Control account on December 1 was $160,010. Actual direct labour hours for the previous 11 months (January through November) were 11,250.
3. There were no jobs in finished goods on December 1.
4. Expenses for December were as follows (not yet recorded in the books of account):

Direct materials purchased	$ 7,500
Salaries	
Production clerk	1,500
Supervisor	2,200
Depreciation (plant and equipment)	2,490
Factory supplies	1,500
Sales staff salaries	9,200
Utilities (factory)	1,800
Administrative expenses	9,500
	$35,690

5. The company writes off all under- or over-applied overhead to Cost of Goods Sold at the end of the year.
6. Jobs numbered 70, 80, 85, and 90 were completed during December. Only Job 90 remained in finished goods on December 31.
7. The company charges its customers 250% of total manufacturing cost.
8. Cost of goods sold to December 1 was $358,750.

Instructions
(a) Using the information given, calculate the following amounts:
    1. the predetermined overhead rate used to apply overhead to products
    2. the cost of ending work in process inventory
    3. the cost of goods manufactured in December
    4. the unadjusted gross margin for December
(b) Prepare the summary journal entries to the control accounts required to record all the transactions for December that relate to production. (*Note*: You should not make entries for individual jobs.)
(c) Calculate the under- or over-applied overhead for the year. What effect would this amount have on net income?

(adapted from CMA Canada, now CPA Canada)

C3-51 Baehr Company is a manufacturer with a fiscal year that runs from July 1 to June 30. The company uses a normal job-order cost accounting system for its production costs.

It uses a predetermined overhead rate based on direct labour hours to apply overhead to individual jobs. It prepared three budgets of overhead costs for the 2016 fiscal year as follows:

Direct labour hours	100,000	120,000	140,000
Variable overhead costs	$325,000	$390,000	$455,000
Fixed overhead costs	216,000	216,000	216,000
Total overhead	$541,000	$606,000	$671,000

Although the annual ideal capacity is 150,000 direct labour hours, company officials have determined that 120,000 direct labour hours are the normal capacity for the year.

The following information is for November 2016 when Jobs X-50 and X-51 were completed:

Inventories, November 1

Raw materials and supplies	$ 10,500
Work in process (Job X-50)	54,000
Finished goods	112,500

Purchases of raw materials and supplies

Raw materials	$135,000
Supplies	15,000

Materials and supplies requisitioned for production

Job X-50	$ 45,000
Job X-51	37,500
Job X-52	25,500
Supplies	12,000
	$120,000

Factory direct labour hours (DLH)

Job X-50	3,500 DLH
Job X-51	3,000 DLH
Job X-52	2,000 DLH

Labour costs

Direct labour wages	$ 51,000
Indirect labour wages (4,000 hours)	15,000
Supervisory salaries	6,000
	$ 72,000

Building occupancy costs (heat, light, depreciation)

Factory facilities	$ 6,500
Sales offices	1,500
Administration offices	1,000
	$ 9,000

Factory equipment costs

Power	$ 4,000
Repairs and maintenance	1,500
Depreciation	1,500
Other	1,000
	$ 8,000

Instructions

(a) Calculate the predetermined rate to be used to apply overhead to individual jobs during the fiscal year.
(b) Prepare a schedule showing the costs assigned to each of Jobs X-50, X-51, and X-52.
(c) Calculate the cost of goods manufactured for November.
(d) Calculate the cost assigned to work in process on November 30.
(e) Determine whether overhead for November is under-applied or over-applied, and by what amount.

(adapted from CMA Canada, now CPA Canada)

C3-52   Triple C Ltd. is in the business of manufacturing cabinets, computer stands, and countertops. Most of its jobs are contracts for home builders. The following information is available for the month of July:

	Costs Incurred to July 1		Added in July		
Job Number	Direct Materials	Direct Labour	Direct Materials	Direct Labour	Status at July 31
101	$9,000	$2,000	$ 0	$1,000	Completed but not sold
103	2,500	1,500	?	?	Not completed
111	600	100	500	3,000	Completed but not sold
115			$800	200	Not completed

Activity in accounts:

Opening Account	Balance July 1	Purchased in July	Issued/Used in July	Ending Balance July 31
Direct Materials	$3,000	$6,000	$4,900	$?
Direct Labour			8,000	

On July 1, finished goods inventory consisted of one job, 105, with a total cost of $18,000. This job was sold during July.

(*Note*: Manufacturing overhead is applied at 120% of the direct labour cost.)

Instructions
Calculate the following as at July 31:
(a) The costs of completed jobs 101 and 111
(b) The account balances in Direct Materials Inventory
(c) Work in Process Inventory
(d) Finished Goods Inventory

(adapted from CGA-Canada, now CPA Canada)

C3-53   ESU Printing provides printing services to many different corporate clients. Although ESU bids on most jobs, some jobs, particularly new ones, are negotiated on a cost-plus basis. Cost-plus means that the buyer is willing to pay the actual cost plus a return (profit) on these costs to ESU.

Clara Biggio, controller for ESU, has recently returned from a meeting where ESU's president stated that he wanted her to find a way to charge most of the company's costs to projects that are on a cost-plus basis. The president noted that the company needed more profits to meet its stated goals this period. By charging more costs to the cost-plus projects and therefore fewer costs to the jobs that it bid on, the company should be able to increase its profits for the current year.

Clara knew why the president wanted to take this action. Rumours were that he was looking for a new position and if the company reported strong profits, the president's opportunities would be better. Clara also recognized that she could probably increase the cost of certain jobs by changing the basis used to allocate the manufacturing overhead.

Instructions
Answer the following questions:
(a) Who are the stakeholders in this situation?
(b) What are the ethical issues in this situation?
(c) What would you do if you were Clara Biggio?

"All About You" Activity

C3-54   You are a talented seamstress and designer. After you graduate with a degree in fashion design, you start a small business with some financial help from your parents. Your business has been quite successful and you are now faced with some accounting decisions. Shrtz for Me makes customized embroidered sweatshirts and T-shirts. The shirts are made on the premises and can be customized to suit. Customers can select the colour, fabric, style, and type of decoration for each shirt order. The minimum

order is 20 shirts. Production is located in one rental building that has a small retail store at the front and a workshop in the rear. In a typical year, Shrtz for Me will sell about 10,000 shirts at an average selling price of $50. About 50% of its sales revenue comes from on-line sales.

Instructions
(a) What are the likely fixed overhead costs for a business of this type?
(b) How would you allocate your chosen overhead costs to each shirt order?

Decision-Making at Current Designs

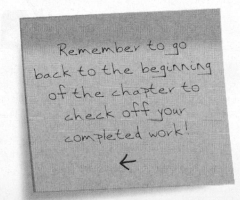

DM3-1 Huegel Hollow Resort has ordered 20 rotomoulded kayaks from Current Designs. Each kayak will be formed in the rotomoulded oven, cooled, and then the excess plastic trimmed away. Then, the hatches, seat, ropes, and bungees will be attached to the kayak.

Dave Thill, the kayak plant manager, knows that manufacturing each kayak requires 54 kg of polyethylene powder and a finishing kit (rope, seat, hardware, etc.). The polyethylene powder used in these kayaks costs $1.50 per kg, and the finishing kits cost $170 each. Each kayak will use two kinds of labour: 2 hours of more skilled type I labour from people who run the oven and trim the plastic, and 3 hours of less-skilled type II labour from people who attach the hatches and seat and other hardware. The type I employees are paid $15 per hour, and the type II employees are paid $12 per hour. For purposes of this problem, assume that overhead is allocated to all jobs at a rate of 150% of direct labour costs.

Instructions

Determine the total cost of the Huegel Hollow order and the cost of each individual kayak in the order. Identify costs as direct materials, direct labour, or manufacturing overhead.

Waterways Continuing Problem

(This is a continuation of the Waterways Problem from Chapters 1 and 2.)

WCP-3 Based on the compatibility and efficiency of its newly designed sprinkler systems, Waterways was successful in its bid to upgrade the irrigation systems for 10 soccer fields owned by the local municipality. Three of the local installation operators were assigned to work on the upgrades as these employees all were familiar with the new systems. At the end of the first month of work the following information was pulled from the work in process inventory records for the jobs that had been started by the three groups.

	Direct Materials	Direct Labour	Manufacturing Overhead	WIP Total
Job SOC-01				
May 10	$ 5,000			
May 15	7,500	$ 7,000	$ 8,400	
May 31	–	6,000	7,200	
	$12,500	$13,000	$15,600	$41,100
Job SOC-02				
May 3	$3,000			
May 15	–	$4,300	$5,160	
May 31	1,200	3,000	3,600	
	$4,200	$7,300	$8,760	$20,260
Job SOC-03				
May 15	$ –	$ 2,000	$ 2,400	
May 18	6,000	6,000	7,200	
May 31	4,500	4,500	5,400	
	$10,500	$12,500	$15,000	$38,000

During the month of June the following transactions related to the three active upgrades took place:

June 1 Requisitioned site supplies from raw materials inventory— Job SOC-01, $1,325; Job SOC-02, $860.

June 1 Annual construction liability insurance premium paid for three site crews, $18,000.

June 2 Monthly rental of small equipment for all three sites, $910.

June 3 Requisitioned site supplies from raw materials inventory— Job SOC-03, $891.

June 5 Requisitioned direct materials from raw materials inventory—Job SOC-01, $2,100; Job SOC-02, $6,000; Job SOC-03, $500.

June 10 Transferred completed raw materials from the factory, $28,000.

June 15 Paid direct labour costs: Job SOC-01, $5,000; Job SOC-02, $8,000; Job SOC-03, $1,500, and employee benefits totalling $2,900.

June 16 Job SOC-01 completed.

June 21 Requisitioned direct materials from raw materials inventory—Job SOC-03, $3,000.

June 21 Requisitioned site supplies from raw materials inventory— Job SOC-03, $756.

June 23 Job SOC-03 completed.

June 30 Monthly depreciation on large equipment for three sites, $6,000.

June 30 Paid direct labour costs: Job SOC-02, $3,200; Job SOC-03, $7,200; and employee benefits of $2,080.

June 30 Paid salary for site supervisors, delivery driver, and site cleaners, $8,000.

June 30 Paid rent for on-site portable toilets and garbage containers for the month, $2,100.

Instructions

(a) Using just the information provided from the work in process balances for May 31, calculate the predetermined overhead rate that Waterways has been using for its installations.

(b) Waterways writes off any balance in the manufacturing overhead account to Cost of Goods Sold at the end of every month. Assuming that all the transactions listed above relate to the three upgrades, calculate the balance in the manufacturing overhead account at the end of June, and indicate if it is over- or under-applied.

(c) Prepare summary journal entries to record all the transactions for the month of June. Dates and explanations are not required.

(d) Determine the balance in the Work in Process account at the end of the month, and reconcile this balance to the jobs not completed at the end of the month.

(e) Waterways received a contract price of $75,000 for each upgrade completed. Determine the gross profit on the completed jobs during the month of June.

Remember to go back to the beginning of the chapter to check off your completed work! ←

Answers to Self-Study Questions

1. a **2.** b **3.** c **4.** d **5.** b **6.** a **7.** d **8.** b **9.** c **10.** b

CHAPTER

4

Process Cost Accounting

The Navigator
Chapter 4

- ☐ Scan *Study Objectives*
- ☐ Read *Feature Story*
- ☐ Read *Chapter Preview*
- ☐ Read text and answer *Before You Go On* p. 121, p. 124, p. 127, p. 134, p. 140
- ☐ Work *Using the Decision Toolkit*
- ☐ Review *Summary of Study Objectives*
- ☐ Review *Decision Toolkit—A Summary*
- ☐ Work *Comprehensive Do It!*
- ☐ Answer *Self-Study Questions*
- ☐ Complete assignments

study objectives

the
navigator

After studying this chapter, you should be able to do the following:

1. Understand who uses process cost systems and explain the similarities and differences between job-order cost and process cost systems.

2. Explain the flow and assignment of manufacturing costs in a process cost system.

3. Calculate equivalent units using the weighted-average method.

4. Explain the four necessary steps to prepare a production cost report.

5. Calculate equivalent units using the FIFO method (Appendix 4A).

BUSINESS IN A BOTTLE

You might not have heard of Canadian-based Cott Corporation, but you might have bought one of its many private-label soft drinks, which are available in stores like Walmart. Though it may not be a household name, Cott had sales of U.S. $2 billion in 2013.

In addition to soft drinks, including RC Cola, Cott makes a variety of beverages, including juice; clear, still, and sparkling flavoured waters; energy drinks; sports products; new-age beverages; and ready-to-drink teas. It owns or leases 34 facilities in Canada, the United States, Mexico, and the United Kingdom and has nearly 4,000 employees worldwide.

To calculate production costs, beverage manufacturers typically use process costing, because making beverages is a continuous process. In the case of soft drinks, that process begins with treating water, which makes up about 94% of soft drinks. The water is clarified, filtered, sterilized, and dechlorinated, to remove impurities, bacteria, and chlorine.

Next, the water is blended with other ingredients in batch tanks. First, sweetener is added. Cott uses mainly high-fructose corn syrup and/or sugar. The syrup must be sterilized, such as with ultraviolet radiation, and fruit-based syrups are usually pasteurized, which requires quickly heating and cooling the syrup. Small quantities of acids, such as citric acid, are added to give a sharp taste. Natural and artificial flavours and preservatives are added. Emulsifiers are added to help keep the ingredients mixed together. Saponins are added to create the foam in soft drinks like cream soda and ginger ale. Finally, most soft drinks become carbonated—that is, carbon dioxide gas is added to give them fizz.

The beverage is then put into bottles (usually PET plastic bottles) or aluminum cans on automated machines that fill containers at extremely high rates—up to 100,000 per hour or more. Next comes labelling. The soft drink containers are often sprayed with warm water to bring them up to room temperature so that condensation won't ruin the labels. A paper or plastic label is usually affixed to bottles; cans generally already contain the product information, such as nutrition information and shelf life, on them. Cott has dozens of labels for the many custom products it makes.

Lastly, the soft drink bottles or cans are put into cartons or trays, then onto pallets or crates, and sent to the warehouses of Cott, distributors, or customers.

Tracking these production costs for each beverage process is crucial for Cott, since it makes so many custom products. "Manufacturing flexibility is one of our core competencies and is critical to our success, as our products will typically feature customized packaging, design and graphics for our key customers," the company said in its 2013 annual report.

Sources: Andrew Kaplan, "Making Waves," *Beverage World*, January 15, 2014; Jennifer Cirillo, "Getting a Handle on Sensitive Drinks," *Beverage World*, April 4, 2013; "The Canadian Soft Drink Industry," Agriculture and Agri-Food Canada, last modified February 28, 2014; "How Products Are Made: Volume 2: Soft Drink," accessed from www.madehow.com/Volume-2/Soft-Drink.html#b; Cott Corporation 2013 annual report.

the navigator

Preview of Chapter 4

The cost accounting system used by companies such as Cott Corporation is called a process cost accounting system. In contrast to job-order cost accounting, which focuses on the individual job, process cost accounting focuses on the processes involved in mass-producing products that are identical or very similar in nature. The purpose of this chapter is to explain and illustrate process cost accounting.

the navigator

The chapter is organized as follows:

PROCESS COST ACCOUNTING

The Nature of Process Cost Systems	Flow and Assignment of Manufacturing Costs	Equivalent Units	The Production Cost Report	FIFO Method—Appendix 4A
➤ Process costing for manufacturing companies ➤ Process costing for service companies ➤ Similarities and differences between job-order cost and process cost systems ➤ Operations costing	➤ Process cost flow ➤ Assignment of manufacturing costs—journal entries	➤ Weighted-average method ➤ Refinements on the weighted-average method	➤ Physical unit flow ➤ Equivalent units of production ➤ Unit production costs ➤ Cost reconciliation schedule ➤ Production cost report ➤ Equivalent units and production cost report—sequential process setting	➤ Equivalent units under FIFO ➤ FIFO and weighted average

The Nature of Process Cost Systems

PROCESS COSTING FOR MANUFACTURING COMPANIES

Companies use **process cost systems** to apply costs to similar products that are mass-produced in a continuous way. Cott Corporation uses a process cost system: production of the beverage, once it begins, continues until the beverage is fully made, and the processing is the same for the entire run—with precisely the same amount of materials, labour, and overhead. Each finished can or bottle of the beverage is like all the others.

A company such as Apotex uses process costing in the manufacturing of pharmaceuticals. Saputo and Agropur use process costing for the production of dairy products, Petro-Canada uses process costing for its oil refining, and Quebec-based Sico Inc. uses process costing for its paint products. At a bottling company like Cott, the manufacturing process begins with the blending of the beverages. Next the beverage is dispensed into bottles that are moved into position by automated machinery. The bottles are then capped, packaged, and forwarded to the finished goods warehouse. Illustration 4-1 shows this process.

▶Illustration 4-1

Manufacturing processes

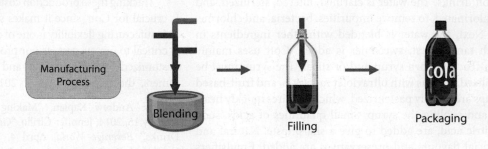

For Cott, as well as the other companies just mentioned, once production begins, it continues until the finished product emerges, and each unit of finished product is like every other unit.

In comparison, costs in a job-order cost system are assigned to a specific job. Examples are the construction of a customized home, the making of a motion picture, or the manufacturing of a specialized machine. Illustration 4-2 provides examples of companies that mostly use either a process cost system or a job-order cost system.

▶Illustration 4-2

Process cost and job-order cost companies and products

Process Cost System		Job-Order Cost System	
Company	Product	Company	Product
Cott Corp., Coca-Cola, Pepsi	Soft drinks	Cossette Communications, J. Walter Thompson, Quebecor Inc.	Advertising and printing
Shell Canada, Petro-Canada, Imperial Oil	Oil	CBC, Walt Disney, Warner Brothers	Television and motion pictures
ATI Technologies Inc., Intel, Advanced Micro Devices	Computer chips	CGI Group Inc.	Service
Dow Chemical Canada Inc., DuPont	Chemicals	TLC the Laser Center Inc., MDS, Extendicare	Patient health care

PROCESS COSTING FOR SERVICE COMPANIES

Frequently, when we think of service companies, we think of specific, nonroutine tasks, such as rebuilding an automobile engine, providing consulting services on a business acquisition, or working on a major lawsuit. However, many service companies specialize in performing repetitive, routine aspects of a particular business. For example, auto-care vendors such as Mr. Lube focus on the routine aspects of car care. H&R Block focuses on the routine aspects of basic tax practice, and many large law firms focus on routine legal services, such as uncomplicated divorces. Service companies that provide specific, nonroutine services will probably benefit from using a job-order cost system. Those that perform routine, repetitive services will probably be better off with a process cost system.

SIMILARITIES AND DIFFERENCES BETWEEN JOB-ORDER COST AND PROCESS COST SYSTEMS

In a job-order cost system, costs are assigned to each job. In a process cost system, costs are tracked through a series of connected manufacturing processes or departments, rather than by individual jobs. Thus, process cost systems are used when a large volume of uniform or relatively homogeneous products is produced. Illustration 4-3 shows the basic flow of costs in these two systems.

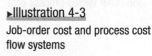
▶Illustration 4-3
Job-order cost and process cost flow systems

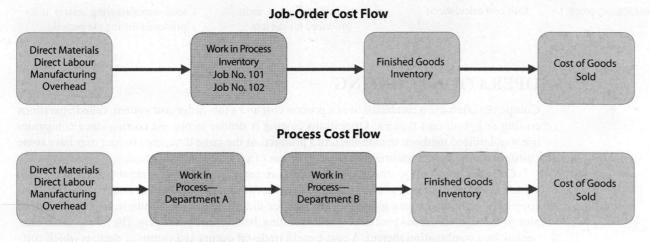

The following analysis highlights the basic similarities and differences between these two systems.

Similarities

Job-order cost and process cost systems are similar in three ways:

1. **The manufacturing cost elements.** Both costing systems track three manufacturing cost elements—direct materials, direct labour, and manufacturing overhead.
2. **The accumulation of the costs of materials, labour, and overhead.** In both costing systems, raw materials are debited to Raw Materials Inventory, factory labour is debited to Factory Labour, and manufacturing overhead costs are debited to Manufacturing Overhead.
3. **The flow of costs.** As noted above, all manufacturing costs are accumulated by debits to Raw Materials Inventory, Factory Labour, and Manufacturing Overhead. These costs are then assigned to the same accounts in both costing systems—Work in Process, Finished Goods Inventory, and Cost of Goods Sold. **The methods of assigning costs, however, differ significantly.** These differences are explained and illustrated later in the chapter.

Differences

The differences between a job-order cost and a process cost system are as follows:

1. **The number of work in process accounts used.** In a job-order cost system, only one work in process account is used. In a process cost system, several work in process accounts are used.

2. **Documents used to track costs.** In a job-order cost system, costs are charged to individual jobs and summarized in a job cost sheet. In a process cost system, costs are summarized in a production cost report for each department.

3. **The point at which costs are totalled.** In a job-order cost system, the total cost is determined when the job is completed. In a process cost system, the total cost is determined at the end of a period of time.

4. **Unit cost calculations.** In a job-order cost system, the unit cost is the total cost per job divided by the units produced. In a process cost system, the unit cost is total manufacturing cost for the period divided by the units produced during the period.

Illustration 4-4 summarizes the major differences between a job-order cost and a process cost system.

▶Illustration 4-4
Job-order versus process cost systems

Features	Job-Order Cost System	Process Cost System
Work in process accounts	• one for each job	• one for each process
Documents used	• job cost sheets	• production cost reports
Determination of total manufacturing costs	• each job	• each period
Unit cost calculations	• cost of each job ÷ units produced for the job	• total manufacturing costs ÷ units produced during the period

OPERATIONS COSTING

Companies often use a combination of a process cost and a job-order cost system, called operations costing or hybrid cost systems. **Operations costing** is similar to process costing since companies use standardized methods to manufacture a product. At the same time, the product may have some customized, individual features that require the use of a job-order cost system.

Consider, for example, the automobile manufacturer Ford Motor Company of Canada. Each vehicle at a particular plant goes through the same assembly line, but different materials (such as seat coverings, paint, and tinted glass) may be used for different vehicles. Similarly, Saputo's Rondeau pies go through numerous processes—mixing, filling, baking, and packaging. The fillings are cream, pecans, or a combination thereof. A cost-benefit trade-off occurs as a company decides which costing system to use. A job-order system, for example, provides detailed information about the cost of the product. Because each job has its own distinguishing characteristics, an accurate cost per job can be provided. This information is useful in controlling costs and pricing products. However, the cost of implementing a job-order cost system is often high because of the accounting costs involved.

On the other hand, for a company like Celestica, which makes computer chips, is there a benefit in knowing whether the cost of the one-hundredth chip produced is different from that of the one-thousandth chip produced? Probably not. An average cost of the product will be good enough for control and pricing purposes. In summary, when it decides to use one of these systems, or a combination system, a company must weigh the costs of implementing the system against the benefits of having the additional information.

BUSINESS INSIGHT   *Squeezing Profits from Wine*

Wineries are a good example of an industry that typically uses a process cost system. It would be almost impossible, and not worthwhile, to determine the cost of producing the first batch of sauvignon blanc compared with the twentieth. Since a winery sells all its bottles from one harvest, or vintage, for the same price, it determines and allocates costs based on the production process for the entire harvest. Most wineries grow several varieties of grapes, but allocate an equal portion of direct labour (such as the winemaker's salary) and manufacturing overhead (such as insurance) to the process cost for each variety. One exception in Canada is icewine, a premium product representing more than $40 million in exports in 2012. Process costs are closely tracked for that particular product, especially labour, since the delicate grapes are picked by hand. The raw materials are expensive because once the grapes freeze, they must be picked during only a few cold days in the fall when temperatures are exactly right or else they spoil. That is why some Canadian wineries charge up to $300 for a single bottle of icewine.

Sources: Martin Patriquin, "Quebec's Ice Wine Industry Prepares for Battle," *Maclean's*, January 11, 2014; "Canadian Vintners Association website, www.canadianvintners.com; Geoff McIntyre, "Operating Lean in the Wine Industry," www.mnp.ca; "Chinese Company Buys Ontario Icewine Maker as Fakes Flourish," *National Post*, August 30, 2007.

What would be some of the variable costs involved in producing wine?

BEFORE YOU GO ON...

▶Do It! Compare Job-Order and Process Cost Systems

Indicate whether each of the following statements is true or false.

1. A law firm is likely to use process costing for major lawsuits.

2. A manufacturer of paintballs is likely to use process costing.

3. Both job-order and process costing determine total costs at the end of a period of time.

4. Process costing does not keep track of manufacturing overhead.

Action Plan

- Use job-order costing in situations where unit costs are high, unit volume is low, and products are unique.
- Use process costing when there is a large volume of relatively homogeneous products.

Solution

1. False.

2. True.

3. False.

4. False.

Related exercise material: **E4-17** and **Do It! D4-12**.

DECISION TOOLKIT

Decision Checkpoints	Info Needed for Decision	Tools to Use for Decision	How to Evaluate Results
What costing method should be used?	Type of product produced	Cost of accounting system; benefits of additional information	The benefits of providing the additional information should exceed the costs of the accounting system that is needed to develop the information.

The Flow and Assignment of Manufacturing Costs

PROCESS COST FLOW

Illustration 4-5 shows the flow of costs in the process cost system for Tyler Company. Tyler Company manufactures automatic can openers that are sold to retail outlets. Manufacturing consists of two processes: machining and assembly. In the machining department, the raw materials are shaped, honed, and drilled. In the assembly department, the parts are assembled and packaged.

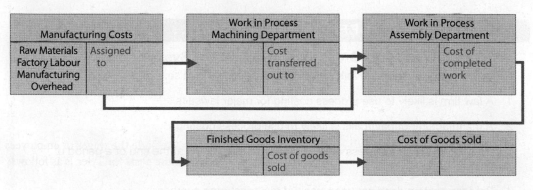

▶Illustration 4-5

Flow of costs in a process cost system

As the flow of costs indicates, materials, labour, and manufacturing overhead can be added in both the machining and assembly departments. When the machining department finishes its work, it transfers the partially completed units to the assembly department. The assembly department finishes the goods and then transfers them to the finished goods inventory. Upon sale, the goods are removed from the finished goods inventory. Each department performs a similar set of activities on each unit that it processes.

ASSIGNMENT OF MANUFACTURING COSTS—JOURNAL ENTRIES

As indicated earlier, the accumulation of the costs of materials, labour, and manufacturing overhead is the same in a process cost system as in a job-order cost system. That is, both systems follow these procedures:

- Companies debit all raw materials to Raw Materials Inventory when the materials are purchased.
- They debit all factory labour to Factory Labour when the labour costs are incurred.
- They debit overhead costs to Manufacturing Overhead as they are incurred.

However, the assignment of the three manufacturing cost elements to Work in Process in a process cost system is different from in a job-order cost system. We will now look at how to assign these manufacturing cost elements in a process cost system.

Materials Costs

Direct Materials

All raw materials that are issued for production are materials costs for the production department. Materials requisition slips may be used in a process cost system, **but fewer requisitions are generally used than in a job-order cost system, because the materials are used for processes rather than for specific jobs.** Requisitions are issued less often in a process cost system because the requisitions are for larger quantities of material.

At the beginning of the first process, a company usually adds most of the materials needed for production. However, in subsequent processes, other materials may be added at various points. For example, in the manufacture of Cott beverages, the sweeteners are added at the beginning of the first process, and the bottles and labels are added at the end of the packaging process. The materials would be entered at the beginning of each process. The journal entry to record the materials used is as follows:

Work in Process Machining	XXXX	
Work in Process Assembly	XXXX	
Raw Materials Inventory		XXXX
To record materials used.		

At Vancouver Island ice cream maker Island Farms, materials are added in three departments: milk and flavouring in the mixing department; extras, such as cherries and walnuts, in the prepping department; and cardboard or plastic containers in the packaging department.

Factory Labour Costs

In a process cost system, as in a job-order cost system, time tickets can be used to determine the cost of labour that should be assigned to production departments. Since labour costs are assigned to a process rather than a job, the labour cost that is chargeable to a process can be obtained from the payroll register or a department's payroll summaries.

Labour costs for Tyler Company's machining department will include the wages of employees who shape, hone, and drill the raw materials. The entry to assign these costs for Tyler is as follows:

Direct Labour

Work in Process—Machining	XXXX	
Work in Process—Assembly	XXXX	
Factory Labour		XXXX
To assign factory labour to production.		

Manufacturing Overhead Costs

The objective in assigning overhead in a process cost system is to allocate the overhead costs to the production departments on an objective and equitable basis. That basis is the activity that "drives" or causes the costs. A major driver of overhead costs in continuous manufacturing operations is **machine time used**, not direct labour. Thus, **machine hours are widely used** to allocate manufacturing overhead costs. The entry to allocate overhead to the two processes Tyler uses is as follows:

Manufacturing Overhead

Work in Process—Machining	XXXX	
Work in Process—Assembly	XXXX	
Manufacturing Overhead		XXXX
To assign overhead to production.		

Transfer to Next Department

At the end of the month, an entry is needed to record the cost of the goods transferred out of the department. For Tyler, the transfer is from the machining department to the assembly department, and the following entry is made:

Work in Process—Assembly	XXXX	
Work in Process—Machining		XXXX
To record transfer of units to the assembly department.		

Transfer to Finished Goods

The units completed in the assembly department are transferred to the finished goods warehouse. The entry for this transfer is as follows:

Finished Goods Inventory	XXXX	
Work in Process—Assembly		XXXX
To record transfer of units to finished goods.		

Transfer to Cost of Goods Sold

Finally, when finished goods are sold, the entry to record the cost of goods sold is as follows:

Cost of Goods Sold	XXXX	
Finished Goods Inventory		XXXX
To record cost of units sold.		

BEFORE YOU GO ON...

▶Do It! Manufacturing Costs in Process Costing

Ruth Company manufactures Zebo Cola through two processes: blending and bottling. In June, raw materials used cost $18,000 for blending and $4,000 for bottling; factory labour costs were $12,000 for blending and $5,000 for bottling; manufacturing overhead costs were $6,000 for blending and $2,500 for bottling. Units completed at a cost of $19,000 in the blending department were transferred to the bottling department. Units completed at a cost of $11,000 in the bottling department were transferred to the finished goods inventory. Journalize the assignment of these costs to the two processes and the transfers of the units.

Action Plan

- In process cost accounting, keep separate work in process accounts for each process.
- When the costs are assigned to production, debit the separate work in process accounts.
- Transfer the cost of completed units to the next process or to Finished Goods Inventory.

Solution

The entries are as follows:

Work in Process—Blending	18,000	
Work in Process—Bottling	4,000	
Raw Materials Inventory		22,000
To record materials used.		
Work in Process—Blending	12,000	
Work in Process—Bottling	5,000	
Factory Labour		17,000
To assign factory labour to production.		
Work in Process—Blending	6,000	
Work in Process—Bottling	2,500	
Manufacturing Overhead		8,500
To assign overhead to production.		

Work in Process—Bottling	19,000	
Work in Process—Blending		19,000
To record transfer of units to the bottling department.		
Finished Goods Inventory	11,000	
Work in Process—Bottling		11,000
To record transfer of units to finished goods.		

Related exercise material: **BE4-1, BE4-2, BE4-3, E4-18, E4-20,** and **Do It! D4-13**.

Equivalent Units

Suppose you were asked to calculate the cost of instruction at your university or college for each full-time equivalent student. You are provided with the following information:

STUDY OBJECTIVE 3
Calculate equivalent units using the weighted-average method.

Costs:	
Total cost of instruction	$9,000,000
Student Population:	
Full-time students	900
Part-time students	1,000

Part-time students take 60% of the classes of a full-time student during the year. To calculate the number of full-time equivalent students per year, you would make the following calculation:

Full-Time Students	+	Equivalent Units of Part-Time Students	=	Full-Time Equivalent Students
900	+	(60% × 1,000)	=	1,500

The cost of instruction per full-time equivalent student is therefore the total cost of instruction ($9,000,000) divided by the number of full-time equivalent students (1,500), which is $6,000 ($9,000,000 ÷ 1,500).

A process cost system uses the same idea—called equivalent units (e.u.) of production. **Equivalent units of production** measure the work done during the period, expressed in fully completed units. This concept is used to determine the cost per unit of completed product.

WEIGHTED-AVERAGE METHOD

Illustration 4-6 shows the formula to calculate equivalent units of production.

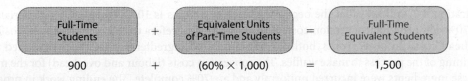

Units Completed and Transferred Out	+	Equivalent Units of Ending Work in Process	=	Equivalent Units of Production

►Illustration 4-6
Equivalent units of production formula

To better understand this concept of equivalent units, consider the following two examples:

Example 1: In a specific period the entire output of Cott Corporation's blending department consists of an ending work in process of 4,000 units, which account for 60% of the materials, labour, and overhead. The equivalent units of production for the blending department are therefore 2,400 units (4,000 × 60%).

IFRS Notes
For inventory items that are interchangeable, IFRS allows the cost of inventories to be assigned by using the first-in, first-out (FIFO) or weighted-average cost formula.

Although both cost formulas are permitted, the same cost formula should be used for inventories that are similar in nature. However, for groups of inventories that have different characteristics, different cost formulas may be used (IAS 2.25 and SIC 1).

Note that the last-in, first-out (LIFO) cost formula is not permitted.

Example 2: Cott's packaging department's output during the period consists of 10,000 units completed and transferred out, and 5,000 units in ending work in process that are 70% completed. The equivalent units of production are therefore 13,500 [10,000 + (5,000 × 70%)].

This method of calculating equivalent units is referred to as the **weighted-average method**. It considers the degree of completion (weighting) of the units completed and transferred out and the ending work in process. An alternative method, called the FIFO method, is discussed in the appendix to this chapter.

REFINEMENTS ON THE WEIGHTED-AVERAGE METHOD

Williams Waffle Company has produced frozen waffles since 1970. Three departments are used to produce these waffles: mixing, baking, and freezing/packaging. In the mixing department, dry ingredients, including flour, salt, and baking powder, are mixed with liquid ingredients, including eggs and vegetable oil, to make waffle batter. Illustration 4-7 provides information for the mixing department at the end of June.

▶Illustration 4-7
Information for mixing department

MIXING DEPARTMENT		Percentage Complete	
	Physical Units	Materials	Conversion Costs
Work in process, June 1	100,000	100%	70%
Started into production	800,000		
Total units	900,000		
Units transferred out	700,000		
Work in process, June 30	200,000	100%	60%
Total units	900,000		

Illustration 4-7 indicates that the beginning work in process is 100% complete for materials cost and 70% complete for conversion costs. **Conversion costs refers to the sum of labour costs and overhead costs.** In other words, both the dry and liquid ingredients (materials) are added at the beginning of the process to make waffles. The conversion costs (labour and overhead) for the mixing of these ingredients were incurred uniformly and are 70% complete. The ending work in process is 100% complete for materials cost and 60% complete for conversion costs.

We then use the mixing department information to determine the equivalent units. **In calculating equivalent units, the beginning work in process is not part of the equivalent units of production formula.** The units transferred out to the baking department are fully complete for both materials and conversion costs. The ending work in process is fully complete for materials, but only 60% complete for conversion costs. **Two equivalent unit calculations are therefore necessary:** one for materials and the other for conversion costs. Illustration 4-8 shows these calculations.

▶Illustration 4-8
Calculation of equivalent units—mixing department

MIXING DEPARTMENT	Equivalent Units	
	Materials	Conversion Costs
Units transferred out	700,000	700,000
Work in process, June 30		
200,000 × 100%	200,000	
200,000 × 60%		120,000
Total equivalent units	900,000	820,000

The earlier formula that we used to calculate equivalent units of production can be refined to show the calculations for materials and conversion costs, as Illustration 4-9 shows.

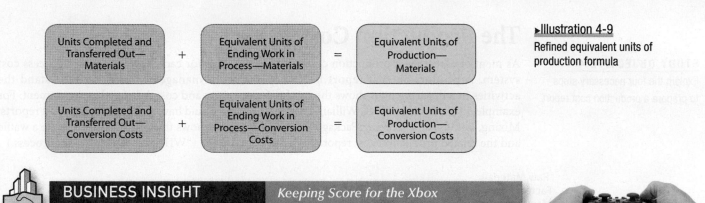

Illustration 4-9
Refined equivalent units of production formula

BUSINESS INSIGHT   *Keeping Score for the Xbox*

When you are as big and as profitable as Microsoft, you get to a point where continued rapid growth is very difficult. For example, many believe it is unlikely that Microsoft will see much growth in software sales. As a result, the company has branched into other markets, such as the video game market with its Xbox player.

Profitability in the video-game hardware market has been elusive. For one thing, Microsoft has manufacturing and distribution costs to contend with that software sales typically don't. When it first launched the Xbox, Microsoft made very high volumes, driving up supply chain costs that initially reduced the company's overall profitability. Also, competition is intense with rival Sony, whose PlayStation console had higher sales than Xbox in 2013, forcing both companies to cut costs and keep console prices down. Given these challenges, rumours circulated in early 2014 that Microsoft would sell its Xbox division and go back to its software roots, which one Microsoft executive dispelled.

Sources: Eddie Makuch, "Microsoft Execs 'Extremely Committed' to Xbox Amid Spinoff Rumors," GameSpot, March 10, 2014; Nick Wingfield, "Microsoft Pins Xbox One Hopes on Titanfall, a Sci-Fi Shooting Game," *New York Times*, March 9, 2014; Robert A. Guth, "Microsoft Net Rises 16%, but Costs Damp Results," *Wall Street Journal*, April 28, 2006.

In what ways has cost accounting probably become more critical for Microsoft in recent years?

BEFORE YOU GO ON...

▶Do It! Equivalent Units

The fabricating department has the following production and cost data for the current month.

Beginning Work in Process	Units Transferred Out	Ending Work in Process
–0–	15,000	10,000

Materials are entered at the beginning of the process. The ending work in process units are 30% complete as to conversion costs. Calculate the equivalent units of production for (a) materials and (b) conversion costs.

Action Plan

- To measure the work done during the period, expressed in fully completed units, calculate equivalent units of production.
- Use the appropriate formula: Units completed and transferred out + Equivalent units of ending work in process = Equivalent units of production.

Solution

(a) Since materials are entered at the beginning of the process, the equivalent units of ending work in process are 10,000. Thus, 15,000 units + 10,000 units = 25,000 equivalent units of production for materials.

(b) Since ending work in process is only 30% complete as to conversion costs, the equivalent units of ending work in process are 3,000 (30% × 10,000 units). Thus, 15,000 units + 3,000 units = 18,000 equivalent units of production for conversion costs.

Related exercise material: **BE4-5, BE4-10, E4-21, E4-22, E4-23, E4-26, E4-28, and Do It! D4-14.**

the navigator

The Production Cost Report

As mentioned earlier, a production cost report is prepared for each department in a process cost system. A **production cost report** is the key document management uses to understand the activities in a department; it shows the production quantity and cost data for that department. For example, in producing waffles, Williams Waffle Company would have three production cost reports: Mixing, Baking, and Freezing/Packaging. Illustration 4-10 shows the flow of costs to make a waffle and the related production cost reports for each department. ("WIP" stands for work in process.)

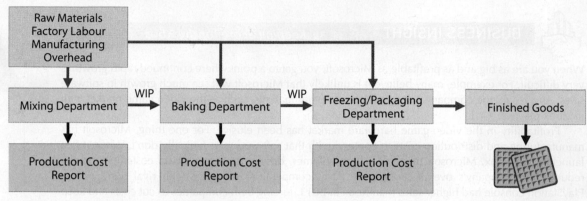

►Illustration 4-10

Flow of costs in making waffles

To be ready to complete a production cost report, the company must perform four steps:

1. Calculate the physical unit flow.
2. Calculate the equivalent units of production.
3. Calculate the unit production costs.
4. Prepare a cost reconciliation schedule.

The next section explores these steps in an extended example.

Illustration 4-11 shows assumed data for the mixing department at Williams Waffle Company for the month of June. We will use this information to complete a production cost report for this department.

►Illustration 4-11

Unit and cost data—mixing department

MIXING DEPARTMENT	
Units	
Work in process, June 1	100,000
Direct materials: 100% complete	
Conversion costs: 70% complete	
Units started into production during June	800,000
Units completed and transferred out to the baking department	700,000
Work in process, June 30	200,000
Direct materials: 100% complete	
Conversion costs: 60% complete	
Costs	
Work in process, June 1	
Direct materials: 100% complete	$ 50,000
Conversion costs: 70% complete	35,000
Cost of work in process, June 1	$ 85,000
Costs incurred during production in June	
Direct materials	$400,000
Conversion costs	170,000
Costs incurred in June	$570,000

CALCULATE THE PHYSICAL UNIT FLOW (STEP 1)

Physical units are the actual units to be accounted for during a period, regardless of any work performed. To keep track of these units, it is necessary to add the units started (or transferred) into production during the period to the units in process at the beginning of the period. This amount is referred to as the **total units to be accounted for**.

The total units are then accounted for by the output of the period. The output consists of units transferred out during the period and any units in process at the end of the period. This amount is referred to as the **total units accounted for**. Illustration 4-12 shows the flow of physical units for Williams Waffle Company for the month of June for the mixing department.

MIXING DEPARTMENT	
	Physical Units
Units to be accounted for	
Work in process, June 1	100,000
Started (transferred) into production	800,000
Total units	900,000
Units accounted for	
Completed and transferred out	700,000
Work in process, June 30	200,000
Total units	900,000

▶Illustration 4-12
Physical unit flow—mixing department

The records indicate that 900,000 units must be accounted for in the mixing department. Of this sum, 700,000 units were transferred to the baking department and 200,000 units were still in process.

CALCULATE THE EQUIVALENT UNITS OF PRODUCTION (STEP 2)

Once the physical flow of the units is determined, it is necessary to measure the mixing department's productivity in equivalent units of production. In the mixing department, materials are added at the beginning of the process, and conversion costs are incurred evenly during the process. Thus, two calculations of equivalent units are required: one for materials, and one for conversion costs. Illustration 4-13 shows the equivalent unit calculation.

> **Helpful Hint**
> Materials are not always added at the beginning of the process. For example, materials are sometimes added uniformly during the process.

	Equivalent Units	
	Materials	Conversion Costs
Units transferred out	700,000	700,000
Work in process, June 30		
200,000 × 100%	200,000	
200,000 × 60%		120,000
Total equivalent units	900,000	820,000

▶Illustration 4-13
Calculation of equivalent units—mixing department

Remember that the beginning work in process is ignored in this calculation.

CALCULATE THE UNIT PRODUCTION COSTS (STEP 3)

Now that we know the equivalent units of production, we can calculate the unit production costs. **Unit production costs** are costs expressed in terms of equivalent units of production. When equivalent units of production are different for materials and for conversion costs, three unit costs are calculated: (1) materials cost, (2) conversion cost, and (3) total manufacturing cost.

Illustration 4-14 shows the calculation of the total materials cost for waffles.

Work in process, June 1	
Direct materials cost	$ 50,000
Costs added to production during June	
Direct materials cost	400,000
Total materials cost	$450,000

▶Illustration 4-14
Materials cost calculation

Illustration 4-15 shows the calculation of the unit materials cost.

▶Illustration 4-15
Unit materials cost calculation

Total Materials Cost	÷	Equivalent Units of Materials	=	Unit Materials Cost
$450,000	÷	900,000	=	$0.50

Illustration 4-16 shows the calculation of the total conversion cost.

▶Illustration 4-16
Total conversion cost calculation

Work in process, June 1	
Conversion cost	$ 35,000
Costs added to production during June	
Conversion cost	170,000
Total conversion cost	$205,000

Illustration 4-17 shows the calculation of the unit conversion cost.

▶Illustration 4-17
Unit conversion cost calculation

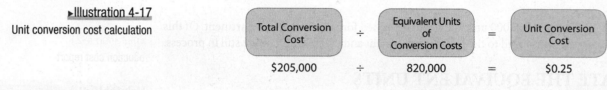

Total Conversion Cost	÷	Equivalent Units of Conversion Costs	=	Unit Conversion Cost
$205,000	÷	820,000	=	$0.25

The total manufacturing cost per unit is therefore calculated as done in Illustration 4-18.

▶Illustration 4-18
Total manufacturing cost per unit

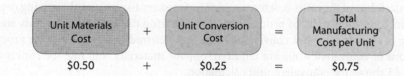

Unit Materials Cost	+	Unit Conversion Cost	=	Total Manufacturing Cost per Unit
$0.50	+	$0.25	=	$0.75

PREPARE A COST RECONCILIATION SCHEDULE (STEP 4)

We are now ready to determine the cost of goods transferred out of the mixing department to the baking department and the costs in ending work in process. Illustration 4-19 shows the total cost that was charged to the mixing department in June.

▶Illustration 4-19
Costs charged to mixing department

Costs to be accounted for	
Work in process, June 1	$ 85,000
Started into production	570,000
Total cost	$655,000

The total costs charged to the mixing department in June are therefore $655,000.

Illustration 4-20 shows a cost reconciliation schedule, which is then prepared to assign these costs to (1) the units transferred out to the baking department and (2) the ending work in process.

▶Illustration 4-20
Cost reconciliation schedule—mixing department

MIXING DEPARTMENT Cost Reconciliation Schedule		
Costs accounted for		
Transferred out (700,000 × $0.75)		$525,000
Work in process, June 30		
Materials (200,000 × $0.50)	$100,000	
Conversion cost (120,000 × $0.25)	30,000	130,000
Total cost		$655,000

The total manufacturing cost per unit, $0.75, is used in costing the units that were completed and transferred to the baking department. In contrast, the unit cost of materials and the unit cost of conversion are needed in costing the units that are still in process. The **cost reconciliation schedule** shows that the total costs accounted for (Illustration 4-20) equal the total costs to be accounted for (Illustration 4-19).

PREPARING THE PRODUCTION COST REPORT

At this point, we are ready to prepare the production cost report for the mixing department. As indicated earlier, this report is an internal document for management that shows the production quantity and cost data for a production department.

There are four steps in preparing a production cost report:

1. Prepare a physical unit schedule.
2. Calculate the equivalent units.
3. Calculate the unit costs.
4. Prepare a cost reconciliation schedule.

Illustration 4-21 shows the production cost report for the mixing department. The report identifies the four steps.

▶Illustration 4-21
Production cost report

MIXING DEPARTMENT
Production Cost Report
Month Ended June 30, 2016

	Physical Units	Equivalent Units Materials	Conversion Costs	
Quantities	**Step 1**	**Step 2**		
Units to be accounted for				
Work in process, June 1	100,000			
Started into production	800,000			
Total units	900,000			
Units accounted for				
Transferred out	700,000	700,000	700,000	
Work in process, June 30	200,000	200,000	120,000	(200,000 × 60%)
Total units	900,000	900,000	820,000	

Costs		Materials Costs	Conversion	Total
Unit costs **Step 3**				
Costs in June	(a)	$450,000	$205,000	$655,000
Equivalent units	(b)	900,000	820,000	
Unit costs [(a) ÷ (b)]		$ 0.50	$ 0.25	$ 0.75
Costs to be accounted for				
Work in process, June 1				$ 85,000
Started into production				570,000
Total costs				$655,000
Cost Reconciliation Schedule **Step 4**				
Costs accounted for				
Transferred out (700,000 × $0.75)				$525,000
Work in process, June 30				
Materials (200,000 × $0.50)			$100,000	
Conversion costs (120,000 × $0.25)			30,000	130,000
Total costs				$655,000

Helpful Hint
What are the two self-checks in the report? Answer: (1) Total physical units accounted for must equal the total units to be accounted for. (2) Total costs accounted for must equal the total costs to be accounted for.

Helpful Hint
Because production cost reports are used as the basis for evaluating department productivity and efficiency, the units, costs, and calculations reported therein should be independently accumulated and analyzed to prevent misstatements by department managers.

Production cost reports give a basis for evaluating a department's productivity. In addition, the cost data can be used to judge whether unit costs and total costs are reasonable. By comparing the quantity and cost data with goals, top management can also judge whether current performance is meeting planned objectives.

CALCULATE EQUIVALENT UNITS AND CREATE A PRODUCTION COST REPORT FOR A SEQUENTIAL PROCESS SETTING

Most manufacturing firms have sequential processing facilities. In this setting, goods are transferred from one department to another in a sequence. For example, the production of waffles at Williams Waffle Company occurs in three departments: mixing, baking, and freezing/packaging.

Manufacturing costs always follow the physical flow of goods. The costs of completed units from the mixing department are treated as input material costs in the baking department. Such a sequential process requires the use of an additional cost component called "transferred in." This cost component has a percentage of completion factor of 100%. The **transferred-in cost** component is treated the same as any other cost component in the calculations of the equivalent units of production and the cost per equivalent unit of production.

The next department may also add more raw material to the units that have been transferred in or it may add labour and overhead costs. Any costs added in by the next department require their own cost component for calculating the equivalent units of production and cost per equivalent unit. In this setting, the final cost of the product is added up cumulatively as the product moves through the production sequence.

Illustration 4-22 shows assumed data for the freezing/packaging department at Williams Waffle for the month of June. The freezing/packaging department uses the weighted-average process costing method.

▶Illustration 4-22

Unit and cost data—freezing/packaging department

FREEZING/PACKAGING DEPARTMENT	
Units	
Work in process, June 1	200,000
Transferred in, 100% complete	
Direct materials, 0% complete	
Conversion, 90% complete	
Units transferred in from baking department during June	700,000
Units completed during June and transferred out to finished goods inventory	800,000
Work in process, June 30	100,000
Transferred in, 100% complete	
Direct material, 0% complete	
Conversion, 75% complete	
Costs	
Work in process, June 1	
Transferred in, 100% complete	$170,000
Direct material, 0% complete	0
Conversion, 90% complete	36,000
Cost of work in process, June 1	$206,000
Costs incurred during production in June	
Transferred in from baking department	$595,000
Direct materials	120,000
Conversion costs	139,000
Total costs during June	$854,000

Illustration 4-23 shows a completed production cost report for the freezing/packaging department. Calculations to support the amounts reported follow the report.

FREEZING/PACKAGING DEPARTMENT
Production Cost Report
Month Ended June 30, 2016

►Illustration 4-23
Production cost report

Quantities	Physical Units	Transferred In	Direct Materials	Conversion Costs	
	Step 1		**Step 2**		
Units to be accounted for					
Work in process	200,000				
Units transferred in	700,000				
Total units	900,000				
Units accounted for					
Transferred out		800,000	800,000	800,000	
Work in process, June 30		100,000	0	75,000	(100,000 × 75%)
Total units		900,000	800,000	875,000	

Costs Step 3

				Total
Unit costs				
Costs in June	(a) $765,000	$120,000	$175,000	$1,060,000
Equivalent units	(b) 900,000	800,000	875,000	
Unit costs [(a) ÷ (b)]	$ 0.85	$ 0.15	$ 0.20	$ 1.20
Costs to be accounted for				
Work in process, June 1				$ 206,000
Started into production				854,000
Total costs				$1,060,000

Cost Reconciliation Schedule: Step 4

Costs accounted for		
Transferred out (800,000 × $1.20)		$ 960,000
Work in process, June 30		
Transferred in (100,000 × $0.85)	$ 85,000	
Direct materials (0 × $0. 15)	0	
Conversion costs (75,000 × $0.20)	15,000	100,000
Total costs		$1,060,000

Additional calculations to support the production cost report data:

Transferred in	$170,000 + $595,000 = $ 765,000
Direct materials	$0 + $120,000 = $ 120,000
Conversion costs	$36,000 + $139,000 = $ 175,000
Total cost	$1,060,000

DECISION TOOLKIT—A SUMMARY

Decision Checkpoints	Info Needed for Decision	Tools to Use for Decision	How to Evaluate Results
What is the cost of a product?	Cost of materials, labour, and overhead assigned to processes used to make the product	Production cost report	Compare costs with previous periods and with competitors to ensure that costs are reasonable. Compare costs with the expected selling price to determine overall profitability.

the navigator ✔

BEFORE YOU GO ON...

▶Do It! Cost Reconciliation Schedule

In March, Rodayo Manufacturing had the following unit production costs: materials $6 and conversion costs $9. On March 1, it had no work in process. During March, 12,000 units were transferred out. At March 31, 800 units, which were 25% complete for conversion costs and 100% complete for materials, were in ending work in process. Assign the costs to the units transferred out and the units in process.

Action Plan

- Assign the total manufacturing cost of $15 per unit to the 12,000 units transferred out.
- Assign the materials cost and conversion costs based on equivalent units of production to the units in process.

Solution

The assignment of costs is as follows:

Costs accounted for		
Transferred out (12,000 × $15)		$180,000
Work in process, March 31		
Materials (800 × $6)	$4,800	
Conversion costs (200* × $9)	1,800	6,600
Total costs		$186,600

*800 × 25%

Related exercise material: **BE4-6, BE4-7, BE4-9, BE4-11, E4-21, E4-22, E4-24, E4-25, E4-26,** and **Do It! D4-15**.

✔ the navigator

⊕ ALL ABOUT YOU   *Walmart Is on the Phone*

If Walmart, the world's largest retailer, called you to do business, would you jump at the chance? Walmart demands extremely low prices of its suppliers, especially after Target entered Canada. Suppliers must exist on razor-thin margins and have accurate cost accounting systems, or they may soon be broke. At its more than 370 stores and supercentres, Walmart Canada carries nearly 100,000 products ranging from clothing to groceries.

What Do You Think?

Suppose that Walmart offered a 30-day trial period to carry the AquaMin save-water gardening tool range at 300 stores. In one month, if Walmart sells 85% of 50,000 tools, it will order more for a much wider distribution. If it doesn't, the deal is off. AquaMin gets between $7 and $12 from other retailers for the tool, but Walmart is willing to pay only $5. Last year, AquaMin's sales were $5 million. If you were Cynthia Wang, AquaMin's owner, would you accept Walmart's offer?

    YES—If only a tiny fraction of Walmart customers buy tools, the company's sales will go through the roof.

    NO—AquaMin has to dramatically increase operations to meet the order, and would be stuck with excess capacity if the deal falls through.

Sources: Hollie Shaw, "Walmart Canada's 'Bricks-and-Mortar Growth Tear' Has its Price," *National Post*, July 26, 2013; Martinne Geller and Jessica Wohl, "Analysis: Wal-Mart's Price Push Tests Manufacturers' Prowess," Reuters, March 6, 2012; Walmart Canada corporate website, www.walmartcanada.ca.

APPENDIX 4A—FIFO METHOD

In Chapter 4, we demonstrated the weighted-average method of calculating equivalent units. Some companies use a different method to calculate equivalent units, called the **first-in, first-out (FIFO) method**. This appendix shows how the FIFO method is used.

Equivalent Units Under FIFO

Under the FIFO method, the calculation of equivalent units is done on a first-in, first-out basis. Some companies prefer the FIFO method because the FIFO cost assumption usually matches the actual physical flow of the goods. Under the FIFO method, it is assumed therefore that the beginning work in process is completed before new work is started.

> **STUDY OBJECTIVE 5**
> Calculate equivalent units using the FIFO method.

Using the FIFO method, equivalent units are the sum of the following work:

1. Work done to finish the units from the beginning work in process inventory.
2. Work done to complete the units started into production during the period (referred to as the units started and completed).
3. Work done to start, but only partially complete, the units in ending work in process inventory.

Normally, in a process costing system, some units will always be in process at both the beginning and the end of the period.

ILLUSTRATION

Illustration 4A-1 shows the physical flow of units for the assembly department of Shutters Inc. In addition, the illustration indicates the degree of completion of the work in process in relation to conversion costs.

> **Helpful Hint**
> The calculation of unit production costs and the assignment of costs to units transferred out and in process also are done on the same basis.

> ▶Illustration 4A-1
> Physical unit flow—assembly department

	Physical Units
Units to be accounted for	
Work in process, June 1 (40% complete)	500
Started (transferred) into production	8,000
Total units	8,500
Units accounted for	
Completed and transferred out	8,100
Work in process, June 30 (75% complete)	400
Total units	8,500

In this case, the units completed and transferred out (8,100) plus the units in ending work in process (400) equals the total units to be accounted for (8,500). We then calculate the equivalent units using FIFO as follows:

1. The 500 units of beginning work in process were 40% complete. Thus, 300 equivalent units (60% × 500 units) were required to complete the beginning inventory.
2. The units started and completed during the current month are the units transferred out minus the units in beginning work in process. For the assembly department, the number of units started and completed is 7,600 (8,100 − 500).
3. The 400 units of ending work in process were 75% complete. Thus, the number of equivalent units is 300 (400 × 75%).

Thus, the number of equivalent units for the assembly department is 8,200, as shown in Illustration 4A-2.

►Illustration 4A-2
Calculation of equivalent
units—FIFO method

ASSEMBLY DEPARTMENT			
Production Data	Physical Units	Work Added This Period	Equivalent Units
Work in process, June 1	500	60%	300
Started and completed	7,600	100%	7,600
Work in process, June 30	400	75%	300
Total	8,500		8,200

COMPREHENSIVE EXAMPLE

To provide a complete illustration of the FIFO method, we will use the data for the mixing department at Williams Waffle Company for the month of June, as shown in Illustration 4A-3.

►Illustration 4A-3
Unit and cost data—mixing
department

MIXING DEPARTMENT	
Units	
Work in process, June 1	100,000
Direct materials: 100% complete	
Conversion costs: 70% complete	
Units started into production during June	800,000
Units completed and transferred out to baking department	700,000
Work in process, June 30	200,000
Direct materials: 100% complete	
Conversion costs: 60% complete	
Costs	
Work in process, June 1	
Direct materials: 100% complete	$ 50,000
Conversion costs: 70% complete	35,000
Cost of work in process, June 1	$ 85,000
Costs incurred during production in June	
Direct materials	$400,000
Conversion costs	170,000
Costs incurred in June	$570,000

Calculate the Physical Unit Flow (Step 1)

Illustration 4A-4 shows the physical flow of units for the month of June for the mixing department of Williams Waffle Company.

►Illustration 4A-4
Physical unit flow—mixing
department

MIXING DEPARTMENT	
	Physical Units
Units to be accounted for	
Work in process, June 1	100,000
Started (transferred) into production	800,000
Total units	900,000
Units accounted for	
Completed and transferred out	700,000
Work in process, June 30	200,000
Total units	900,000

Under the FIFO method, the physical units schedule is often expanded to explain the transferred-out section. As a result, in this section the beginning work in process and the units started and completed are reported. These two items further explain the completed and transferred-out section, as shown in Illustration 4A-5.

MIXING DEPARTMENT	
	Physical Units
Units to be accounted for	
Work in process, June 1	100,000
Started (transferred) into production	800,000
Total units	900,000
Units accounted for	
Completed and transferred out	
Work in process, June 1	100,000
Started and completed	600,000
	700,000
Work in process, June 30	200,000
Total units	900,000

►Illustration 4A-5
Physical unit flow (FIFO)—mixing department

The records indicate that 900,000 units must be accounted for in the mixing department. Of this sum, 700,000 units were transferred to the baking department and 200,000 units were still in process.

Calculate the Equivalent Units of Production (Step 2)

As with the method presented in the chapter, once the physical flow of the units is determined, it is necessary to determine the equivalent units of production. In the mixing department, materials are added at the beginning of the process, and conversion costs are incurred evenly during the process. Thus, two calculations of equivalent units are required: one for materials and one for conversion costs.

Equivalent Units for Materials. Since materials are entered at the beginning of the process, no additional materials costs are required to complete the beginning work in process. In addition, 100% of the materials costs have been incurred on the ending work in process. Thus, the calculation of equivalent units for materials is as shown in Illustration 4A-6.

Helpful Hint
Materials are not always added at the beginning of the process. For example, materials are sometimes added evenly during the process.

MIXING DEPARTMENT—MATERIALS			
Production Data	Physical Units	Materials Added This Period	Equivalent Units
Work in process, June 1	100,000	0%	0
Started and finished	600,000	100%	600,000
Work in process, June 30	200,000	100%	200,000
Total	900,000		800,000

►Illustration 4A-6
Calculation of equivalent units—materials

Equivalent Units for Conversion Costs. The 100,000 units of beginning work in process were 70% complete in terms of conversion costs. Thus, 30,000 equivalent units (30% × 100,000 units) of conversion costs were required to complete the beginning inventory. In addition, the 200,000 units of ending work in process were 60% complete for conversion costs. Thus, the number of equivalent units for conversion costs is 750,000, as calculated in Illustration 4A-7. Normally, in a process costing system, some units will always be in process at both the beginning and the end of the period.

▶Illustration 4A-7
Calculation of equivalent units—
conversion costs

MIXING DEPARTMENT—CONVERSION COSTS			
Production Data	Physical Units	Work Added This Period	Equivalent Units
Work in process, June 1	100,000	30%	30,000
Started and finished	600,000	100%	600,000
Work in process, June 30	200,000	60%	120,000
Total	900,000		750,000

Calculate the Unit Production Costs (Step 3)

Now that we know the equivalent units of production, we can calculate the unit production costs. Unit production costs are costs expressed in terms of equivalent units of production. When equivalent units of production are different for materials and conversion costs, three unit costs are calculated: (1) materials costs, (2) conversion costs, and (3) the total manufacturing cost.

Under the FIFO method, the unit costs of production are based entirely on the production costs incurred during the month. Thus, the costs in beginning work in process are not relevant, because they were incurred on work done in the previous month. As Illustration 4A-3 indicated, the costs incurred during production in June were:

Direct materials	$400,000
Conversion costs	170,000
Total cost	$570,000

Illustration 4A-8 shows the calculation of the unit materials cost, unit conversion cost, and total unit cost for waffles.

▶Illustration 4A-8
Unit cost formulas and calculations—
mixing department

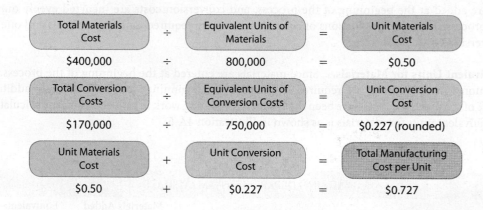

As shown, the unit costs are $0.50 for materials, $0.227 for conversion costs, and $0.727 for the total manufacturing cost.

Prepare a Cost Reconciliation Schedule (Step 4)

We are now ready to determine the cost of goods transferred out of the mixing department into the baking department, and the costs in ending work in process. Illustration 4A-9 shows the total costs that were charged to the mixing department in June.

▶Illustration 4A-9
Costs charged to mixing
department

Costs to be accounted for	
Work in process, June 1	$ 85,000
Started into production	570,000
Total costs	$655,000

The total costs charged to the mixing department in June are $655,000. A cost reconciliation is then prepared to assign these costs to (1) the units transferred out to the baking department and (2) the ending work in process. Under the FIFO method, the first goods to be completed during the period are the units in beginning work in process. Thus, the cost of the beginning work in process is always assigned to the goods transferred to finished goods (or the next department). The FIFO method also means that ending work in process will be assigned only production costs that are incurred in the current period. Illustration 4A-10 shows a cost reconciliation schedule for the mixing department.

MIXING DEPARTMENT Cost Reconciliation Schedule		
Costs accounted for		
Transferred out		
Work in process, June 1		$ 85,000
Costs to complete beginning work in process		
Conversion costs (30,000 × $0.227)		6,810
Total costs		91,810
Units started and completed (600,000 × $0.727)		435,950*
Total costs transferred out		527,760
Work in process, June 30		
Materials (200,000 × $0.50)	$100,000	
Conversion costs (120,000 × $0.227)	27,240	127,240
Total cost		$655,000

*Any rounding errors should be adjusted in the "Units started and completed" section.

▶Illustration 4A-10
Cost reconciliation schedule—mixing department

As you can see, the total costs accounted for ($655,000) equal the total costs to be accounted for ($655,000).

Preparing the Production Cost Report

At this point, we are ready to prepare the production cost report for the mixing department. This report is an internal document for management that shows the production quantity and cost data for a production department.

As mentioned earlier in this chapter, there are four steps in preparing a production cost report.

1. Prepare a physical unit schedule.
2. Calculate the equivalent units.
3. Calculate the unit costs.
4. Prepare a cost reconciliation schedule.

Production cost reports give a basis for evaluating a department's productivity. In addition, the cost data can be used to judge whether unit costs and total costs are reasonable. By comparing the quantity and cost data with goals, top management can also judge whether current performance is meeting planned objectives.

Illustration 4A-11 shows the production cost report for the mixing department, with the four steps identified in the report.

▶Illustration 4A-11
Production cost report

MIXING DEPARTMENT Production Cost Report Month Ended June 30, 2016				
		Equivalent Units		
	Physical Units	Materials	Conversion Costs	Total
Quantities	**Step 1**	**Step 2**		
Units to be accounted for				
Work in process, June 1	100,000			
Started into production	800,000			
Total units	900,000			

(continued)

►Illustration 4A-11
Production cost report (continued)

Units accounted for			
Completed and transferred out			
Work in process, June 1	100,000	0	30,000
Started and completed	600,000	600,000	600,000
Work in process, June 30	200,000	200,000	120,000
Total units	900,000	800,000	750,000

Costs Step 3

Unit costs				
Costs in June (excluding beginning work in process)	(a)	$400,000	$170,000	$570,000
Equivalent units	(b)	800,000	750,000	
Unit costs [(a) ÷ (b)]		$ 0.50	$ 0.227	$ 0.727

Costs to be accounted for	
Work in process, June 1	$ 85,000
Started into production	570,000
Total costs	$655,000

Cost Reconciliation Schedule Step 4

Cost accounted for		
Transferred out		
Work in process, June 1		$ 85,000
Cost to complete beginning work in process		
Conversion costs (30,000 × $0.227)		6,810
		91,810
Units started and completed (600,000 × $0.727)		435,950*
Total costs transferred out		527,760
Work in process, June 30		
Materials (200,000 × $0.50)	$100,000	
Conversion costs (120,000 × $0.227)	27,240	127,240
Total cost		$655,000

*Any rounding errors should be adjusted in the "Units started and completed" section.

Helpful Hint
What are the two self-checks in the report? Answer: (1) Total physical units accounted for must equal the total units to be accounted for. (2) Total costs accounted for must equal the total costs to be accounted for.

FIFO and Weighted Average

The weighted-average method of calculating equivalent units has one major advantage: it is simple to understand and apply. In cases where prices do not fluctuate significantly from period to period, the weighted-average method will be very similar to the FIFO method. In addition, companies that have been using just-in-time procedures effectively for inventory control will have minimal inventory balances, and therefore differences between the weighted-average and the FIFO methods will not be significant.

Conceptually, the FIFO method is better than the weighted-average method because **current performance is measured** using only costs incurred in the current period. Managers are therefore not held responsible for costs from prior periods that they may have had no control over. In addition, the FIFO method **provides current cost information**, which can be used to establish **more accurate pricing strategies** for goods that are manufactured and sold in the current period.

BEFORE YOU GO ON...

►Do It! Equivalent Units Under FIFO

Production costs chargeable to the finishing department in May at Boechler Company are $8,000 for materials, $20,000 for labour, $18,000 for overhead, and $62,000 in transferred-in costs.

Equivalent units of production are 20,000 for materials and 19,000 for conversion costs. Boechler uses the FIFO method to calculate equivalent units. Calculate the unit costs for materials (transferred-in + materials) and conversion costs.

Transferred-in costs are considered materials costs.

Action Plan

- To measure the work done during the period, expressed in fully completed units, calculate equivalent units of production.
- Use the appropriate formula: Equivalent units of production = Equivalent units to complete beginning inventory* + Units started and completed during the period + Equivalent units in ending work in process inventory

*Equivalent units to complete beginning inventory = Units in beginning inventory × (100% − Percentage completion of beginning inventory)

Solution

Total materials costs	÷	Equivalent units of materials	=	Unit materials cost
$70,000[1]		20,000		$3.50

[1]$8,000 + $62,000 = $70,000

Total conversion costs	÷	Equivalent units of conversion costs	=	Unit conversion cost
$38,000[2]		19,000		$2.00

[2]$20,000 + $18,000 = $38,000

Related exercise material: **BE4-11, E4-24, E4-31, E4-32, E4-33, E4-34, E4-35,** and **Do It! D4-16**.

the navigator

USING THE DECISION TOOLKIT

Essence Company manufactures a high-end aftershave lotion called Infinity, in 300-ml shaped glass bottles. Because the market for aftershave lotion is highly competitive, the company is very concerned about keeping its costs under control. Infinity is manufactured through three processes: mixing, filling, and corking. Materials are added at the beginning of the process, and labour and overhead are incurred uniformly throughout each process. The company uses a weighted-average method to cost its product.

A partially completed production cost report for the month of May for the mixing department follows.

			Equivalent Units	
ESSENCE COMPANY Mixing Department Production Cost Report Month Ended May 31, 2016				
	Physical Units			Conversion
			Materials	Costs
Quantities	Step 1		Step 2	
Units to be accounted for				
Work in process, May 1	1,000			
Started into production	2,000			
Total units	3,000			

(continued)

(continued)

Units accounted for			
Transferred out	2,200	?	?
Work in process, May 31	800	?	?
Total units	3,000	?	?

Costs		Materials	Conversion Costs	Total
Unit costs **Step 3**				
Costs in May	(a)	?	?	?
Equivalent units	(b)	?	?	
Unit costs [(a) ÷ (b)]		?	?	?
Costs to be accounted for				
Work in process, May 1				$ 56,300
Started into production				119,320
Total costs				$175,620

Cost Reconciliation Schedule **Step 4**		
Costs accounted for		
Transferred out		?
Work in process, May 31		
Materials	?	
Conversion costs	?	?
Total cost		?

Additional information:
1. Work in process, May 1: 1,000 units

Materials cost (100% complete)	$49,100	
Conversion costs (70% complete)	7,200	$ 56,300
Materials cost for May: 2,000 units		100,000
Conversion costs for May		19,320

2. Work in process, May 31: 800 units, 100% complete for materials and 50% complete for conversion costs

Instructions

(a) Prepare a production cost report for the mixing department for May.
(b) Prepare the journal entry to record the transfer of goods from the mixing department to the filling department.
(c) Explain why Essence Company is using a process cost system to account for its costs.

Solution

(a) A completed production cost report for the mixing department is shown below. Calculations to support the amounts reported are shown after the report.

ESSENCE COMPANY
Mixing Department
Production Cost Report
Month Ended May 31, 2016

	Physical Units	Equivalent Units	
		Materials	Conversion Costs
Quantities	**Step 1**	**Step 2**	
Units to be accounted for			
Work in process, May 1	1,000		
Started into production	2,000		
Total units	3,000		
Units accounted for			
Transferred out	2,200	2,200	2,200
Work in process, May 31	800	800	400 (800 × 50%)
Total units	3,000	3,000	2,600

Costs		Materials	Conversion Costs	Total
Unit costs **Step 3**				
Costs in May	(a)	$149,100	$26,520	$175,620
Equivalent units	(b)	3,000	2,600	
Unit costs [(a) ÷ (b)]		$ 49.70	$ 10.20	$ 59.90
Costs to be accounted for				
Work in process, May 1				$ 56,300
Started into production				119,320
Total costs				$175,620
Cost Reconciliation Schedule **Step 4**				
Costs accounted for				
Transferred out (2,200 × $59.90)				$131,780
Work in process, May 31				
Materials (800 × $49.70)			$39,760	
Conversion costs (400 × $10.20)			4,080	43,840
Total costs				$175,620

Additional calculations to support production cost report data:
Materials cost—$49,100 + $100,000
Conversion costs—$7,200 + 19,320

(b) Work in Process—Filling 131,780
    Work in Process—Mixing 131,780

(c) Process cost systems are used to apply costs to similar products that are mass-produced in a continuous way. Essence Company uses a process cost system: once production of the aftershave lotion begins, it continues until the aftershave lotion emerges. The processing is the same for the entire run—with precisely the same amount of materials, labour, and overhead. Every bottle of Infinity aftershave lotion is identical.

Summary of Study Objectives

1. *Understand who uses process cost systems and explain the similarities and differences between job-order cost and process cost systems.* Process cost systems are used by companies that mass-produce similar products in a continuous way. Once production begins, it continues until the finished product emerges. Each unit of finished product is identical to every other unit.

   Job-order cost systems are similar to process cost systems in three ways: (1) Both systems track the same cost elements—direct materials, direct labour, and manufacturing overhead. (2) Costs are accumulated in the same accounts—Raw Materials Inventory, Factory Labour, and Manufacturing Overhead. (3) Accumulated costs are assigned to the same accounts—Work in Process, Finished Goods Inventory, and Cost of Goods Sold. However, the method of assigning costs differs significantly.

   There are four main differences between the two cost systems: (1) A process cost system uses separate accounts for each production department or manufacturing process, rather than the single work in process account used in a job-order cost system. (2) In a process cost system, costs are summarized in a production cost report for each department; in a job-order cost system, costs are charged to individual jobs and summarized in a job cost sheet. (3) Costs are totalled at the end of a time period in a process cost system and at the completion of a job in a job-order cost system. (4) In a process cost system, the unit cost is calculated as follows: total manufacturing costs for the period divided by the units produced during the period. In a job-order cost system, the calculation of the unit cost is as follows: total cost per job divided by the number of units produced.

2. *Explain the flow and assignment of manufacturing costs in a process cost system.* Manufacturing costs for raw materials, labour, and overhead are assigned to work in process accounts for various departments or manufacturing processes, and the costs of units completed in a department are transferred from one department to another as those units move through the manufacturing process. The costs of completed work are transferred to Finished Goods Inventory. When inventory is sold, costs are transferred to Cost of Goods Sold.

   Entries to assign the costs of raw materials, labour, and overhead consist of a credit to Raw Materials Inventory, Factory Labour, and Manufacturing Overhead, and a debit to Work in Process for each of the departments that are doing the processing.

Entries to record the cost of goods transferred to another department are a credit to Work in Process for the department whose work is finished and a debit for the department that the goods are transferred to.

The entry to record the units completed and transferred to the warehouse is a credit for the department whose work is finished and a debit to Finished Goods Inventory.

Finally, the entry to record the sale of goods is a credit to Finished Goods Inventory and a debit to Cost of Goods Sold.

3. **Calculate equivalent units using the weighted-average method.** Equivalent units of production measure the work done during a period, expressed in fully completed units. This concept is used to determine the cost per unit of completed product. Equivalent units are the sum of units completed and transferred out plus equivalent units of ending work in process.

4. **Explain the four necessary steps to prepare a production cost report.** The four steps to complete a production cost report are as follows: (1) Calculate the physical unit flow; that is, the total units to be accounted for. (2) Calculate the equivalent units of production. (3) Calculate the unit production costs, expressed in equivalent units of production.

(4) Prepare a cost reconciliation schedule, which shows that the total costs accounted for equal the total costs to be accounted for.

The production cost report contains both quantity and cost data for a production department. There are four sections in the report: (1) the number of physical units, (2) the equivalent units determination, (3) the unit costs, and (4) the cost reconciliation schedule.

In this setting, goods are transferred from one department to another. Such a sequential process requires the use of an additional cost component called "transferred in." This cost component has a percentage of completion factor of 100%. The transferred-in cost component is treated the same way as any other cost component in the calculations of the equivalent units of production and the cost per equivalent unit of production.

5. **Calculate equivalent units using the FIFO method (Appendix 4A).** Equivalent units under the FIFO method are the sum of the work performed to (1) finish the units from the beginning work in process inventory, if any; (2) complete the units started into production during the period; and (3) start, but only partially complete, the units in ending work in process inventory.

DECISION TOOLKIT — A SUMMARY

Decision Checkpoints	Info Needed for Decision	Tools to Use for Decision	How to Evaluate Results
What costing method should be used?	Type of product produced	Cost of accounting system; benefits of additional information	The benefits of providing the additional information should exceed the costs of the accounting system that is needed to develop the information.
What is the cost of a product?	Costs of materials, labour, and overhead assigned to processes used to make the product	Production cost report	Compare costs with previous periods and with competitors to ensure that costs are reasonable. Compare costs with the expected selling price to determine overall profitability.

Glossary

Conversion costs The sum of labour costs and overhead costs. (p. 126)

Cost reconciliation schedule A schedule that shows that the total costs accounted for equal the total costs to be accounted for. (p. 131)

Equivalent units of production A measure of the work done during the period, expressed in fully completed units. (p. 125)

First-in, first-out (FIFO) method A process costing method in which the cost assigned to the beginning work in process inventory is separated from current-period production costs. The cost per equivalent unit is related to the current period only. (p. 135)

Operations costing A combination of a process cost and a job-order cost system, in which products are manufactured mainly by standardized methods, with some customization. (p. 120)

Physical units Actual units to be accounted for during a period, regardless of any work performed. (p. 128)

Process cost system   An accounting system used to apply costs to similar products that are mass-produced in a continuous way. (p. 118)

Production cost report   An internal report for management that shows both the production quantity and cost data for a production department. (p. 128)

Total units (costs) accounted for   The sum of the units (costs) transferred out during the period plus the units (costs) in process at the end of the period. (p. 129)

Total units (costs) to be accounted for   The sum of the units (costs) started (or transferred) into production during the period plus the units (costs) in process at the beginning of the period. (p. 129)

Transferred-in cost   A cost component that is used in a sequential (or multiple-department) process setting. It has a percentage of completion factor of 100% and is treated the same as any other cost component in the calculations of the equivalent units of production and the cost per equivalent unit of production. (p. 132)

Unit production costs   Costs expressed in terms of equivalent units of production. (p. 129)

Weighted-average method   A method used to calculate equivalent units of production, which considers the degree of completion (weighting) of the units completed and transferred out and the ending work in process. (p. 126)

Comprehensive Do It!

Karlene Industries produces plastic ice cube trays in two processes: heating and stamping. All materials are added at the beginning in the heating department. Karlene uses the weighted-average method to calculate equivalent units.

On November 1, 2016, 1,000 trays that were 70% complete were in process in the heating department. During November, 12,000 trays were started into production. On November 30, 2,000 trays that were 60% complete were in process.

The following cost information for the heating department is also available:

Work in process, November 1:		Costs incurred in November:	
Materials	$ 640	Materials	$3,000
Conversion costs	360	Labour	2,300
Cost of work in process, Nov. 1	$1,000	Overhead	4,050

Instructions

(a) Prepare a production cost report for the heating department for the month of November, using the weighted-average method.

(b) Journalize the transfer of costs to the stamping department.

Solution to Comprehensive Do It!

(a)

KARLENE INDUSTRIES
Heating Department
Production Cost Report
Month Ended November 30, 2016

		Equivalent Units		
	Physical Units	Materials	Conversion Costs	Total
Quantities	**Step 1**		**Step 2**	
Units to be accounted for				
Work in process, November 1	1,000			
Started in production	12,000			
Total units	13,000			
Units accounted for				
Transferred out	11,000	11,000	11,000	
Work in process, November 30	2,000	2,000	1,200	
Total units	13,000	13,000	12,200	

(continued)

Action Plan

- Calculate the physical unit flow; that is, the total units to be accounted for.
- Calculate the equivalent units of production.
- Calculate the unit production costs, expressed in terms of equivalent units of production.
- Prepare a cost reconciliation schedule, which shows that the total costs accounted for equal the total costs to be accounted for.

(continued)

Costs **Step 3**

Unit costs

Costs in November	(a)	$ 3,640	$ 6,710	$10,350
Equivalent units	(b)	13,000	12,200	
Unit costs [(a) ÷ (b)]		$ 0.28	$ 0.55	$ 0.83

Costs to be accounted for

Work in process, November 1	$ 1,000
Started into production	9,350
Total costs	$10,350

Cost Reconciliation Schedule **Step 4**

Costs accounted for

Transferred out (11,000 × $0.83)		$ 9,130
Work in process, November 30		
Materials (2,000 × $0.28)	$ 560	
Conversion costs (1,200 × $0.55)	660	1,220
Total cost		$10,350

(b)

Work in Process—Stamping	9,130	
Work in Process—Heating		9,130
To record transfer of units to the stamping department.		

✔ the navigator

WileyPLUS

Self-Test, Brief Exercises, Exercises, Problems—Set A, and many more components are available for practice in WileyPlus.

Self-Study Questions

Answers are at the end of the chapter. (The asterisk * indicates material discussed in the chapter appendix.)

(SO 1)   1. Which of the following items is *not* characteristic of a process cost system?
   (a) Once production begins, it continues until the finished product emerges.
   (b) The products produced are heterogeneous in nature.
   (c) The focus is on continually producing relatively uniform products.
   (d) When the finished product emerges, all units have precisely the same amount of materials, labour, and overhead.

(SO 1)   2. Indicate which of the following statements is *not* correct.
   (a) Both a job-order and a process cost system track the same three manufacturing cost elements—direct materials, direct labour, and manufacturing overhead.
   (b) A job-order cost system uses only one work in process account, whereas a process cost system uses multiple work in process accounts.

   (c) Manufacturing costs are accumulated the same way in a job-order and in a process cost system.
   (d) Manufacturing costs are assigned the same way in a job-order and in a process cost system.

(SO 2)   3. In a process cost system, the flow of costs is
   (a) work in process, cost of goods sold, finished goods.
   (b) finished goods, work in process, cost of goods sold.
   (c) finished goods, cost of goods sold, work in process.
   (d) work in process, finished goods, cost of goods sold.

(SO 2)   4. In making the journal entry to assign raw materials costs, a company
   (a) debits Finished Goods Inventory.
   (b) often debits two or more work in process accounts.
   (c) generally credits two or more work in process accounts.
   (d) credits Finished Goods Inventory.

(SO 3)   5. The mixing department's output during the period consists of 20,000 units that are completed and transferred out, and 5,000 units in ending work in process that are 60% complete in terms of materials and conversion costs. Beginning inventory is 1,000 units, 40% complete in terms of materials and conversion costs. The equivalent units of production are
(a) 22,600.
(b) 23,000.
(c) 24,000.
(d) 25,000.

(SO 3)   6. In RYZ Company, there are zero units in beginning work in process, 7,000 units started into production, and 500 units in ending work in process 20% completed. The physical units to be accounted for are
(a) 7,000.
(b) 7,360.
(c) 7,500.
(d) 7,340.

(SO 3)   7. Mora Company has 2,000 units in beginning work in process, 20% complete in terms of conversion costs, 23,000 units transferred out to finished goods, and 3,000 units in ending work in process $33^1/_3$% complete in terms of conversion costs. The beginning and ending inventory is fully complete in terms of materials costs. Equivalent units for materials and conversion costs are, respectively,
(a) 22,000 and 24,000.
(b) 24,000 and 26,000.
(c) 26,000 and 24,000.
(d) 26,000 and 26,000.

(SO 4)   8. Fortner Company has no beginning work in process; 9,000 units are transferred out and 3,000 units in ending work in process are one-third finished in terms of conversion costs and fully complete in terms of materials costs. If the total materials cost is $60,000, the unit materials cost is
(a) $5.00.
(b) $5.45 rounded.
(c) $6.00.
(d) No correct answer is given.

(SO 4)   9. Largo Company has unit costs of $10 for materials and $30 for conversion costs. If there are 2,500 units in ending work in process, 40% complete in terms of conversion costs, and fully complete in

terms of materials cost, the total cost assignable to the ending work in process inventory is
(a) $45,000.
(b) $55,000.
(c) $75,000.
(d) $100,000.

(SO 4)   10. A production cost report
(a) is an external report.
(b) shows both the production quantity and cost data related to a department.
(c) shows equivalent units of production but not physical units.
(d) contains six sections.

(SO 5)   *11. Hollins Company uses the FIFO method to calculate equivalent units. It has 2,000 units in beginning work in process, 20% complete in terms of conversion costs, 25,000 units started and completed, and 3,000 units in ending work in process, 30% complete in terms of conversion costs. All units are 100% complete in terms of materials. Equivalent units for materials and conversion costs are, respectively,
(a) 28,000 and 26,600.
(b) 28,000 and 27,500.
(c) 27,000 and 26,200.
(d) 27,000 and 29,600.

(SO 5)   *12. MLK Company uses the FIFO method to calculate equivalent units. It has no beginning work in process; 9,000 units are started and completed and 3,000 units in ending work in process are one-third completed. All material is added at the beginning of the process. If the total materials cost is $60,000, the unit materials cost is
(a) $5.00.
(b) $6.00.
(c) $6.67 (rounded).
(d) No correct answer given.

(SO 5)   *13. Toney Company uses the FIFO method to calculate equivalent units. It has unit costs of $10 for materials and $30 for conversion costs. If there are 2,500 units in ending work in process, 100% complete in terms of materials and 40% complete in terms of conversion costs, the total cost assignable to the ending work in process inventory is
(a) $45,000.
(b) $55,000.
(c) $75,000.
(d) $100,000.

Brief Exercises

BE4-1   Sargunaraj Manufacturing purchases $75,000 of raw materials on account, and it incurs $80,000 of factory labour costs. Journalize the two transactions on March 31 assuming the labour costs are not paid until April.

(SO 2)
Journalize entries for accumulating costs.

BE4-2   Data for Sargunaraj Manufacturing are given in BE4-1. Supporting records show that (a) the assembly department used $64,000 of raw materials and $45,000 of the factory labour, and (b) the finishing department used the remainder. Journalize the assignment of the costs to the processing departments on March 31.

(SO 2)
Journalize the assignment of materials and labour costs.

(SO 2)
Journalize the assign-
ment of overhead costs.

BE4-3   Factory labour data for Sargunaraj Manufacturing are given in BE4-2. Manufacturing overhead is assigned to departments on the basis of 200% of labour costs. Journalize the assignment of overhead to the assembly and finishing departments.

(SO 4)
Calculate physical units
of production.

BE4-4   Bowyer Manufacturing Company has the following production data for selected months.

			Ending Work in Process	
Month	Beginning Work in Process	Units Transferred Out	Units	% Complete in Terms of Conversion Costs
January	0	30,000	10,000	40%
March	0	40,000	8,000	75%
July	0	40,000	16,000	25%

Calculate the physical units for each month.

(SO 3)
Calculate equivalent
units of production.

BE4-5   Using the data in BE4-4, calculate equivalent units of production for materials and conversion costs, assuming materials are entered at the beginning of the process.

(SO 4)
Calculate unit costs of
production.

BE4-6   Blue-Red Company started 9,000 units during the month of March. There were 2,000 units in the beginning work in process inventory and 3,000 units in the ending work in process inventory. Calculate units completed and transferred out during March.

(SO 4)
Assign costs to units
transferred out and in
process.

BE4-7   Hindi Company has the following production data for April: 40,000 units transferred out, and 5,000 units in ending work in process that are 100% complete for materials and 40% complete for conversion costs. If unit materials cost is $4 and unit conversion cost is $7, determine the costs to be assigned to the units transferred out and the units in ending work in process.

(SO 4, 5)
Calculate unit costs.

*BE4-8   On September 1, Delta Company had 30,000 units in process, which were 30% completed. Materials are added at the beginning of the process. During the month 170,000 units were started and 180,000 completed. Ending work in process was 50% complete.

Calculate (a) the equivalent units of production for materials if weighted average were used and (b) the equivalent units of production for materials if FIFO were used.

(SO 4)
Prepare a cost recon-
ciliation schedule.

BE4-9   Production costs chargeable to the Finishing Department in June at Yeun Company are materials $15,000, labour $29,500, and overhead $18,000. Equivalent units of production are 20,000 for materials and 19,000 for conversion costs. Production records indicate that 18,000 units were transferred out, and 2,000 units in ending work in process were 60% complete in terms of conversion costs and 100% complete in terms of materials. Prepare a cost reconciliation schedule.

(SO 3)
Calculate equivalent
units of production.

BE4-10   The smelting department of Massaro Manufacturing Company has the following production and cost data for November.

Production: 2,000 units in beginning work in process that are 100% complete in terms of materials and 20% complete in terms of conversion costs; 8,000 units transferred out; and 7,000 units in ending work in process that are 100% complete in terms of materials and 40% complete in terms of conversion costs.

Calculate the equivalent units of production for (a) materials and (b) conversion costs for the month of November.

(SO 4, 5)
Assign costs to units
transferred out and in
process and prepare a
partial production cost
report.

*BE4-11   Mora Company has the following production data for March: no beginning work in process, 30,000 units started and completed, and 5,000 units in ending work in process that are 100% complete for materials and 40% complete for conversion costs. Mora uses the FIFO method to calculate equivalent units. Unit materials cost is $8 and unit conversion cost is $12. The total costs to be assigned are $664,000. Calculate (a) the costs to be assigned to the units transferred out and the units in ending work in process and (b) prepare the cost section of the production cost report for Mora Company.

Do It! Review

(SO 1)
Compare job-order
and process cost
systems.

D4-12

Instructions

Indicate whether each of the following statements is true or false.

(a) Many hospitals use job-order costing for small, routine medical procedures.

(b) A manufacturer of computer flash drives would use a job-order cost system.

(c) A process cost system uses multiple work in process accounts.

(d) A process cost system keeps track of costs on job cost sheets.

D4-13   Yussuff Company manufactures CH-21 through two processes: mixing and packaging. In July, the following costs were incurred.

	Mixing	Packaging
Raw materials used	$10,000	$24,000
Factory labour costs	8,000	36,000
Manufacturing overhead costs	12,000	54,000

Units completed at a cost of $21,000 in the mixing department are transferred to the packaging department. Units completed at a cost of $102,000 in the packaging department are transferred to Finished Goods.

Instructions

Journalize the assignment of these costs to the two processes and the transfer of units as appropriate.

D4-14   The assembly department has the following production and cost data for the current month.

Beginning Work in Process	Units Transferred Out	Ending Work in Process
–0–	20,000	16,000

Materials are entered at the beginning of the process. The ending work in process units are 70% complete as to conversion costs.

Instructions

Calculate the equivalent units of production for (a) materials and (b) conversion costs.

D4-15   In March, Lasso Manufacturing had the following unit production costs: materials $10 and conversion costs $8. On March 1, it had zero work in process. During March, Lasso transferred out 22,000 units. As of March 31, 2,000 units that were 40% complete as to conversion costs and 100% complete as to materials were in ending work in process.

Instructions

(a)   Calculate the total units to be accounted for.
(b)   Calculate the equivalent units of production.
(c)   Prepare a cost reconciliation schedule, including the costs of materials transferred out and the costs of materials in process.

***D4-16**   Production costs chargeable to the Finishing Department in May at Kim Company are materials $8,000, labour $20,000, overhead $18,000, and transferred-in costs $67,000. Equivalent units of production are materials 20,000 and conversion costs 19,000. Kim uses the FIFO method to calculate equivalent units.

Instructions

Calculate the unit costs for materials and conversion costs. Transferred-in costs are considered materials costs.

Exercises

E4-17   Wojtek Nakowski has prepared the following list of statements about process cost accounting.

1.   Process cost systems are used to apply costs to similar products that are mass-produced in a continuous fashion.
2.   A process cost system is used when each finished unit is indistinguishable from another.
3.   Companies that produce soft drinks, motion pictures, and computer chips would all use process cost accounting.
4.   In a process cost system, costs are tracked by individual jobs.
5.   Job-order costing and process costing track different manufacturing cost elements.
6.   Both job-order costing and process costing account for direct materials, direct labour, and manufacturing overhead.
7.   Costs flow through the accounts in the same basic way for both job-order costing and process costing.
8.   In a process cost system, only one work in process account is used.
9.   In a process cost system, costs are summarized in a job cost sheet.
10.   In a process cost system, the unit cost is total manufacturing costs for the period divided by the units produced during the period.

Instructions

Identify each statement as true or false. If false, indicate how to correct the statement.

(SO 2)
Journalize transactions.

E4-18 Fernando Company manufactures pizza sauce through two production departments: cooking and canning. In each process, materials and conversion costs are incurred evenly throughout the process. For the month of April, the work in process accounts show the following debits:

	Cooking	Canning
Beginning work in process	$ 0	$ 4,000
Materials	21,000	9,000
Labour	8,500	7,000
Overhead	31,500	25,800
Costs transferred in		53,000

Instructions
Journalize the April transactions.

(SO 2, 3, 4)
Answer questions on costs and production.

E4-19 The ledger of Magdy Company has the following work in process account:

Work in Process—Painting					
5/1	Balance	$3,570	5/31	Transferred out	$?
5/31	Materials	6,460			
5/31	Labour	2,400			
5/31	Overhead	1,626			
5/31	Balance	$?			

Production records show that there were 400 units in the beginning inventory, 30% complete, 1,200 units started, and 1,200 units transferred out. The beginning work in process had materials cost of $2,020 and conversion costs of $1,550.The units in ending inventory were 40% complete. Materials are entered at the beginning of the painting process.

Instructions
Answer the following questions:
(a) How many units are in process at May 31?
(b) What is the unit materials cost for May?
(c) What is the unit conversion cost for May?
(d) What is the total cost of units transferred out in May?
(e) What is the cost of the May 31 inventory?

(SO 2)
Journalize transactions for two processes.

E4-20 Douglas Manufacturing Company has two production departments: cutting and assembly. July 1 inventories are Raw Materials $6,200, Work in Process—Cutting $4,900, Work in Process—Assembly $12,600, and Finished Goods $35,000. During July, the following transactions occurred:
1. Purchased $65,500 of raw materials on account.
2. Incurred $47,000 of factory labour (credit Wages Payable).
3. Incurred $75,000 of manufacturing overhead; $55,000 was paid and the remainder is unpaid.
4. Requisitioned $14,700 in materials for cutting and $11,900 in materials for assembly.
5. Used factory labour of $27,000 for cutting and $19,000 for assembly.
6. Applied overhead at the rate of $22 per machine hour. Machine hours were 1,700 in cutting and 1,650 in assembly.
7. Transferred goods costing $70,700 from the cutting department to the assembly department.
8. Transferred goods costing $140,000 from Assembly to Finished Goods.
9. Sold goods costing $165,000 for $210,000 on account.

Instructions
Journalize the transactions. (Omit explanations.)

(SO 3, 4)
Calculate physical units and equivalent units of production.

E4-21 In Lee Wen Company, materials are entered at the beginning of each process. Work in process inventories, with the percentage of work done on conversion costs, and production data for its sterilizing department in selected months during 2016 are as follows:

	Beginning Work in Process			Ending Work in Process	
		Conversion	Units		Conversion
Month	Units	Cost %	Transferred Out	Units	Cost %
January	0	—	9,000	2,000	60
March	0	—	12,000	4,000	30
May	0	—	14,000	6,000	80
July	0	—	10,000	1,500	20

Instructions
(a) Calculate the physical units for January and May.
(b) Calculate the equivalent units of production for (1) materials and (2) conversion costs for each month.

E4-22 The cutting department of Groneman Manufacturing has the following production and cost data for July.

(SO 3, 4)
Determine equivalent units, unit costs, and assignment of costs.

Production	Costs	
1. Transferred out 12,000 units.	Beginning work in process	$ 0
2. Started 3,000 units that are 60%	Materials	45,000
complete in terms of conversion	Labour	16,200
costs and 100% complete in terms	Manufacturing overhead	18,300
of materials at July 31.		

Materials are entered at the beginning of the process. Conversion costs are incurred uniformly during the process.

Instructions
(a) Determine the equivalent units of production for (1) materials and (2) conversion costs.
(b) Calculate unit costs and prepare a cost reconciliation schedule.

E4-23 The sanding department of Hanninen Furniture Company has the following production and manufacturing cost data for March 2016, the first month of operation.

(SO 3, 4)
Prepare a production cost report.

Production: 11,000 units finished and transferred out; 4,000 units started that are 100% complete in terms of materials and 25% complete in terms of conversion costs. Manufacturing costs: materials $48,000; labour $42,000; overhead $36,000.

Instructions
Prepare a production cost report.

*E4-24 Montreal Manufacturing Inc. has the following cost and production data for the month of April.

(SO 3, 4, 5)
Determine equivalent units using FIFO, unit costs, and assignment of costs.

Beginning WIP	18,000 units
Started in production	100,000
Completed production	94,000
Ending WIP	24,000

The beginning inventory was 60% complete for conversion costs. The ending inventory was 40% complete for conversion costs. Materials are added at the beginning of process.

Costs pertaining to the month of April are as follows:

Beginning inventory costs are:

Materials	$ 65,000
Direct labour	20,000
Factory overhead	15,000

Costs incurred during April include:

Materials	$550,000
Direct labour	195,000
Factory overhead	380,000

Instructions
(a) Calculate the equivalent units of production for (1) materials and (2) conversion costs for the month of April using the first-in, first-out (FIFO) method.
(b) Calculate the unit costs for the month.
(c) Determine the costs to be assigned to the units transferred out and in ending work in process.

E4-25 Toronto Manufacturing Inc. has the following cost and production data for the month of November.

(SO 3, 4)
Determine equivalent units, unit costs, and assignment of costs.

Beginning WIP	18,000 units
Started in production	100,000
Completed production	94,000
Ending WIP	24,000

The ending inventory was 40% complete for conversion costs. Materials are added at the beginning of process.

Costs pertaining to the month of November are as follows:

Beginning inventory costs are:

Materials	$ 65,000
Direct labour	20,000
Factory overhead	15,000

Costs incurred during November include:

Materials	$550,000
Direct labour	195,000
Factory overhead	380,000

Instructions

(a) Calculate equivalent units of production for materials and for conversion costs.

(b) Determine the unit costs of production.

(c) Show the assignment of costs to units transferred out and in process.

(SO 3, 4)
Calculate equivalent
units, unit costs, and
costs assigned.

E4-26   The polishing department of Lacroix Manufacturing Company has the following production and manufacturing cost data for September. Materials are entered at the beginning of the process.

Production: Beginning inventory of 2,500 units that are 100% complete in terms of materials and 30% complete in terms of conversion costs; units started during the period are 12,000; ending inventory of 3,000 units 10% complete in terms of conversion costs.

Manufacturing costs: Beginning inventory costs, comprising $25,000 of materials and $28,080 of conversion costs; materials costs added in polishing during the month, $120,725; labour and overhead applied in polishing during the month, $100,020 and $300,240, respectively.

Instructions

(a) Calculate the equivalent units of production for materials and conversion costs for the month of September.

(b) Calculate the unit costs for materials and conversion costs for the month.

(c) Determine the costs to be assigned to the units transferred out and in process.

(SO 4)
Explain the production
cost report.

E4-27   Wilbur Kumar has recently been promoted to production manager and has just started to receive various managerial reports. One of the reports he has received is the production cost report that you prepared. It showed that his department had 2,000 equivalent units in ending inventory. His department has had a history of not keeping enough inventory on hand to meet demand. He has come to you, very angry, and wants to know why you credited him with only 2,000 units when he knows he had at least twice that many on hand.

Instructions

Explain to Wilbur why his production cost report showed only 2,000 equivalent units in ending inventory. Write an informal memo. Be kind and explain very clearly why he is mistaken.

(SO 3, 4)
Prepare a production
cost report.

E4-28   The welding department of Balogh Manufacturing Company has the following production and manufacturing cost data for February 2016. All materials are added at the beginning of the process.

Manufacturing Costs			Production Data	
Beginning work in process			Beginning work in process	15,000 units
Materials	$18,000			1/10 complete
Conversion costs	14,175	$ 32,175	Units transferred out	49,000
Materials		180,000	Units started	45,000
Labour		52,380	Ending work in process	11,000 units
Overhead		61,445		1/5 complete

Instructions

Prepare a production cost report for the welding department for the month of February.

(SO 3)
Calculate physical units
and equivalent units
of production.

E4-29   Container Shipping, Inc. is contemplating the use of process costing to track the costs of its operations. The operation consists of three segments (departments): receiving, shipping, and delivery. Containers are received at Container Shipping's docks and sorted according to the ship they will be carried on. The containers are loaded onto a ship, which carries them to the appropriate port of destination. The containers are then off-loaded and delivered to the receiving company.

Container Shipping wants to begin using process costing in the shipping department. Direct materials represent the fuel costs to run the ship, and "Containers in transit" represents work in process. Listed below is information about the shipping department's first month of activity.

Containers in transit, April 1	0
Containers loaded	900
Containers in transit, April 30	400 (40% of direct materials and 30% of conversion costs)

Instructions

(a) Determine the physical flow of containers for the month.

(b) Calculate the equivalent units for direct materials and conversion costs.

E4-30 Hi-Tech Mortgage Company uses a process costing system to accumulate costs in its loan application department. When an application is completed, it is forwarded to the loan department for final processing. The following processing and cost data pertain to September:

1. Applications in process on September 1,100
2. Applications started in September, 1,000
3. Completed applications during September, 900
4. Applications still in process at September 30 were 100% complete in terms of materials (forms) and 60% complete in terms of conversion costs.

Beginning work in process:	
Direct materials	$ 1,000
Conversion costs	4,000
September costs:	
Direct materials	$ 4,500
Direct labour	12,000
Overhead	8,480

(SO 3, 4)
Determine equivalent units, unit costs, and assignment of costs.

Materials are the forms used in the application process, and these costs are incurred at the beginning of the process. Conversion costs are incurred uniformly during the process.

Instructions
(a) Determine the equivalent units of service (production) for materials and conversion costs.
(b) Calculate the unit costs and prepare a cost reconciliation schedule.

*E4-31 Using the data in E4-30, assume Hi-Tech Mortgage Company uses the FIFO method. Also assume that the applications in process on September 1 were 100% complete in terms of materials (forms) and 40% complete in terms of conversion costs.

(SO 4, 5)
Calculate equivalent units, unit costs, and costs assigned.

Instructions
(a) Determine the equivalent units of service (production) for materials and conversion costs.
(b) Calculate the unit costs and prepare a cost reconciliation schedule.

*E4-32 The cutting department of Chan Manufacturing has the following production and cost data for August.

(SO 4, 5)
Determine equivalent units, unit costs, and assignment of costs.

Production	Costs	
1. Started and completed 8,000 units.	Beginning work in process	$ 0
2. Started 2,000 units that are 40% completed at August 31.		
	Materials	45,000
	Labour	14,700
	Manufacturing overhead	16,100

Materials are entered at the beginning of the process. Conversion costs are incurred uniformly during the process. Chan Manufacturing uses the FIFO method to calculate equivalent units.

Instructions
(a) Determine the equivalent units of production for (1) materials and (2) conversion costs.
(b) Calculate unit costs and show the assignment of manufacturing costs to units transferred out and in work in process.

*E4-33 The smelting department of Amber Manufacturing Company has the following production and cost data for September.

(SO 4, 5)
Calculate equivalent units, unit costs, and costs assigned.

Production: Beginning work in process of 2,000 units that are 100% complete in terms of materials and 20% complete in terms of conversion costs; 8,000 units started and finished; and 1,000 units in ending work in process that are 100% complete in terms of materials and 40% complete in terms of conversion costs.

Manufacturing costs: Work in process, September 1, $15,200; materials added, $63,000; labour and overhead, $143,000.

Amber uses the FIFO method to calculate equivalent units.

Instructions
(a) Calculate the equivalent units of production for (1) materials and (2) conversion costs for the month of September.
(b) Calculate the unit costs for the month.
(c) Determine the costs to be assigned to the units transferred out and in process.

*E4-34 The ledger of Platt Company has the following work in process account:

(SO 4, 5)
Answer questions on costs and production.

Work in Process—Painting					
3/1	Balance	$3,080	3/31	Transferred out	$?
3/31	Materials	6,600			
3/31	Labour	2,230			
3/31	Overhead	1,280			
3/31	Balance	?			

Production records show that there were 900 units in the beginning inventory, 30% complete, 1,200 units started, and 1,300 units transferred out. The units in ending inventory were 40% complete. Materials are entered at the beginning of the painting process. Platt uses the FIFO method to calculate equivalent units.

Instructions

Answer the following questions:

(a) How many units are in process at March 31?

(b) What is the unit materials cost for March?

(c) What is the unit conversion cost for March?

(d) What is the total cost of units started in February and completed in March?

(e) What is the total cost of units started and finished in March?

(f) What is the cost of the March 31 inventory?

(SO 4, 5)
Prepare a production cost report for a second process.

*E4-35 The welding department of Hirohama Manufacturing Company has the following production and manufacturing cost data for February 2016. All materials are added at the beginning of the process. Hirohama uses the FIFO method to calculate equivalent units.

Manufacturing Costs		Production Data	
Beginning work in process	$ 23,600	Beginning work in process	10,000 units, 10% complete
Costs transferred in	135,000		
Materials	57,000	Units transferred out	65,000
Labour	35,100	Units transferred in	80,000
Overhead	68,400	Ending work in process	25,000, 20% complete

Instructions

Prepare a production cost report for the welding department for the month of February. Transferred-in costs are considered materials costs.

Problems: Set A

(SO 3, 4)
Calculate equivalent units, unit costs, and costs assigned.

P4-36A Toronto Timers Inc.'s costing system uses two cost categories: direct materials and conversion costs. Each of its products must go through the assembly department and the testing department. Direct materials are added at the beginning of production. Conversion costs are allocated evenly throughout production. Data for the assembly department for June 2016 are as follows:

Production Data—Units	
Work in process, beginning inventory	
(60% complete in terms of conversion costs)	850 units
Units started during June	1,300 units
Work in process, ending inventory	450 units
Cost Data	
Work in process, beginning inventory costs	
Direct materials	382,500
Conversion costs	255,000
Direct materials costs added during June	2,500,000
Conversion costs added during June	2,800,000

Instructions

(a) Determine what unit cost can be calculated from the information provided for work in process beginning inventory.

(b) 1,700 units

(b) Calculate how many units were completed and transferred out of the assembly department during June 2016.

(SO 3, 4)
Complete the four steps necessary to prepare a production cost report.

P4-37A Kasten Company manufactures bowling balls through two processes: moulding and packaging. In the moulding department, urethane, rubber, plastic, and other materials are moulded into bowling balls. In the packaging department, the balls are placed in cartons and sent to the finished goods warehouse. All materials are entered at the beginning of each process.

Labour and manufacturing overhead are incurred uniformly throughout each process. Production and cost data for the moulding department during June 2016 are presented below:

Production Data	June
Beginning work in process units	0
Units started into production	22,000
Ending work in process units	2,000
Percent complete—ending inventory	40%

Cost Data	
Materials	$198,000
Labour	53,600
Overhead	112,800
Total	$364,400

Instructions

(a) Prepare a schedule showing physical units of production.
(b) Determine the equivalent units of production for materials and conversion costs.
(c) Calculate the unit costs of production.
(d) Determine the costs to be assigned to the units transferred and in process for June.
(e) Prepare a production cost report for the moulding department for the month of June.

(c) Materials: $9.00
Conversion costs: $8.00
(d) Transferred out: $340,000
Work in process: $24,400

P4-38A Sweet Corporation is in the dairy manufacturing business. Products go through two production departments (A first, then B). Data from those departments for October 2016 are presented below.

(SO 3, 4)
Complete the four steps necessary to prepare a production cost report.

	Department A	Department B
	Beginning work in process	Beginning work in process
Number of units	1,000	200
% complete for materials	100%	
% complete for transferred-in		100%
% complete for conversion	60%	30%
Total materials cost	$24,000	-0-
Total conversion cost	$30,000	$40,000
Total transferred-in costs		15,000

	Department A	Department B
	Ending work in process	Ending work in process
Number of units	600	300
% complete for materials	100%	
% complete for transferred-in		100%
% complete for conversion	30%	40%

Sweet Corporation started 2,600 units of product during the month in department A. Costs incurred in department A for October 2016 totalled $64,000 for material and $132,000 for conversion. Additionally, department B incurred conversion costs in September 2016 of $600,000. Department B adds no materials to the product.

Instructions

(a) Journalize the transfer of goods from department A to department B during October 2016. Sweet Corporation accounts for its costs using the weighted-average method.
(b) Prepare a production cost report for department B for October 2016.

(a) $281,625
(b) Transferred out: $826,292

P4-39A Fiedel Company manufactures its product, Vitadrink, through two manufacturing processes: mixing and packaging. All materials are entered at the beginning of each process. On October 1, 2016, inventories consisted of $26,000 in Raw Materials, $0 in Work in Process—Mixing, $250,000 in Work in Process—Packaging, and $289,000 in Finished Goods. The beginning inventory for Packaging consisted of 10,000 units that were 50% complete in terms of conversion costs and fully complete in terms of materials. During October, 50,000 units were started into production in the mixing department and the following transactions were completed:

(SO 2)
Journalize transactions.

1. Purchased $300,000 of raw materials on account.
2. Issued raw materials for production: mixing $210,000 and packaging $45,000.
3. Incurred labour costs of $258,900.
4. Used factory labour: mixing $182,500 and packaging $76,400.
5. Incurred $810,000 of manufacturing overhead on account.

6. Applied manufacturing overhead on the basis of $24 per machine hour. Machine hours were 28,000 in mixing and 6,000 in packaging.
7. Transferred 45,000 units from mixing to packaging at a cost of $979,000.
8. Transferred 53,000 units from packaging to Finished Goods at a cost of $1,315,000.
9. Sold goods costing $1,604,000 for $2,500,000 on account.

Instructions
Journalize the October transactions.

(SO 2, 3, 4)
Determine assignment
of costs.

P4-40A   The following is partial information for the month of March for Macmillan International Inc., a two-department manufacturer that uses process costing:

Work in process, beginning (67% converted)	15,000 units
Costs of beginning work in process:	
Transferred in from department A	$ 9,500
Materials	0
Conversion	11,200
Units completed and transferred out during March	45,000 units
Units transferred in during March from department A	? units
Work in process, ending (37.5% converted)	16,000 units
Materials costs added during March	$13,000
Conversion costs added during March	$63,000

Other information:

1. Material is introduced at the beginning in department A and more material is added at the very end in department B.
2. Conversion costs are incurred evenly throughout both processes.
3. As the process in department A is completed, goods are immediately transferred to department B; as goods are completed in department B, they are transferred to finished goods.
4. Unit costs of production in department A in March were

Materials	$0.55
Conversion	0.40
Total	$0.95

5. The company uses the weighted-average method.

Instructions

(a) $117,720
(b) $22,682

(a) Calculate the cost of goods transferred out of department B in March.
(b) Calculate the cost of the March ending work in process inventory in department B.

(adapted from CGA-Canada, now CPA Canada)

(SO 3, 4)
Assign costs and
prepare a production
cost report.

P4-41A   Cavalier Company has several processing departments. Costs charged to the assembly department for November 2016 totalled $2,229,000 as follows:

Work in process, November 1		
Materials	$69,000	
Conversion costs	48,150	$ 117,150
Materials added		1,548,000
Labour		225,920
Overhead		337,930

Production records show that 35,000 units were in beginning work in process, 30% complete in terms of conversion costs, 700,000 units were started into production, and 25,000 units were in ending work in process, 40% complete in terms of conversion costs. Materials are entered at the beginning of each process.

(b) Transferred out
$2,165,500
Work in process
$63,500

Instructions

(a) Determine the equivalent units of production and the unit production costs for the assembly department.
(b) Determine the assignment of costs to goods transferred out and in process.
(c) Prepare a production cost report for the assembly department.

(SO 3, 4)
Determine equivalent
units and unit costs
and assign costs.

P4-42A   Chen Company manufactures basketballs. Materials are added at the beginning of the production process and conversion costs are incurred uniformly. Production and cost data for the month of July 2016 are as follows:

Production Data—Basketballs	Units	Percent Complete
Work in process units, July 1	500	60%
Units started into production	1,000	
Work in process units, July 31	600	30%

Cost Data—Basketballs

Work in process, July 1
Materials	$ 750	
Conversion costs	600	$1,350
Direct materials		2,400
Direct labour		1,580
Manufacturing overhead		1,060

Instructions

(a) Calculate the following:
 1. The equivalent units of production for materials and conversion costs
 2. The unit costs of production for materials and conversion costs
 3. The assignment of costs to units transferred out and in process at the end of the accounting period
(b) Prepare a production cost report for the month of July for the basketballs.

(a) Materials:
 (1) 1,500 e.u.
     materials
 (2) $2.10 materials
 (3) Transferred out
     $4,590
     Work in process
     $1,800

P4-43A Luther Processing Company uses a weighted-average process costing system and manufactures a single product—a premium rug shampoo and cleaner. The company has just completed the manufacturing activity for the month of October. A partially completed production cost report for the month of October for the mixing department is shown below.

(SO 3, 4)
Calculate equivalent units and complete a production cost report.

		Equivalent Units	
Quantities	Physical Units	Materials	Conversion Costs
Units to be accounted for			
Work in process, October 1 (all materials, 70% conversion costs)	20,000		
Started into production	160,000		
Total units	180,000		
Units accounted for			
Transferred out	130,000	?	?
Work in process, October 31 (60% materials, 40% conversion costs)	50,000	?	?
Total units accounted for	180,000	?	?

Costs	Materials	Conversion Costs	Total
Unit costs			
Costs in October	$240,000	$105,000	$345,000
Equivalent units	?	?	
Unit costs	$? +	$? =	$?
Costs to be accounted for			
Work in process, October 1			$ 30,000
Started into production			315,000
Total costs			$345,000
Cost Reconciliation Schedule			
Costs accounted for			
Transferred out			$?
Work in process, October 31			
Materials		?	
Conversion costs		?	
Total costs		?	$?

Instructions

(a) Prepare a schedule that shows how the equivalent units were calculated so that you can complete the "Quantities: Units accounted for" equivalent units section of the production cost report, and calculate October unit costs.
(b) Complete the "Cost Reconciliation Schedule" part of the production cost report above.

(a) Materials $1.50
(b) Transferred out
    $286,000
    Work in process
    $59,000

P4-44A Alberta Instrument Company uses a process costing system. A unit of product passes through three departments—moulding, assembly, and finishing—before it is completed.
 The following activity took place in the finishing department during May:

(SO 3, 4)
Determine assignment of costs.

	Units
Work in process inventory, May 1	1,900
Transferred in from the assembly department	14,000
Transferred out to finished goods inventory	11,900

Raw material is added at the beginning of processing in the finishing department. The work in process inventory was 70% complete in terms of conversion costs on May 1 and 40% complete in terms of conversion costs on May 31. Alberta Instrument Company uses the weighted-average method of process costing. The equivalent units and current period costs per equivalent unit of production for each cost factor are as follows for the finishing department:

	Equivalent Units	Current Period Costs per Equivalent Unit
Transferred-in costs	15,400	$ 6.00
Raw materials	15,400	2.00
Conversion costs	13,300	4.00
Total		$12.00

Instructions

Calculate the following amounts:

(a) $142,800

(b) $38,400

(a) The cost of units transferred to finished goods inventory during May

(b) The cost of the finishing department's work in process inventory on May 31

(adapted from CMA Canada, now CPA Canada)

(SO 4, 5)
Determine equivalent units using FIFO.

*P4-45A   Below is information about ABC Ltd., a chemical producer, for the month of June:

Work in process, beginning inventory	25,000 units
Transferred-in units—100% complete	
Direct materials—0% complete	
Conversion costs—80% complete	
Transferred in during June	175,000 units
Completed and transferred out during June	170,000 units
Work in process, ending inventory	? units
Transferred-in units—100% complete	
Direct materials—0% complete	
Conversion costs—40% complete	

Instructions

(a) 30,000

(b) 170,000

(c) 162,000

(a) How many units are in ending work in process inventory?

(b) Under FIFO, what are the equivalent units of production for the month of June for materials?

(c) Under FIFO, what are the equivalent units of production for the month of June for conversion costs?

(SO 4, 5)
Determine assignment of costs using FIFO.

*P4-46A   The Allbright BrickWorks, in Winnipeg, manufactures high-quality bricks used in residential and commercial construction. The firm is small but highly automated and typically produces about 300,000 bricks per month. A brick is created in a continuous production operation. In the initial step, the raw material, a mixture of soils and water, is forced into a brick mould moving along a conveyer belt. No other materials are required in the manufacture of a brick. Each brick takes about three days to complete. They spend the last 36 hours or so on the conveyer belt in an oven that removes moisture from the product. The conveyer belt speed is monitored and controlled by computer. The firm uses a process costing system based on actual costs in three cost pools—direct materials, direct labour, and factory overhead—to assign production costs to output. Cost and production data for October 2016 follow:

Production Data

Beginning work in process inventory (100% complete in terms of direct materials; 60% complete in terms of direct labour; 36% complete in terms of factory overhead)	35,000 bricks
Started this period	295,000 bricks
Ending work in process inventory (100% complete in terms of direct materials; 50% complete in terms of direct labour; 40% complete in terms of factory overhead)	30,000 bricks

Cost Data

	Materials	Direct Labour	Overhead
Beginning inventory	$ 1,330	$ 435	$ 852
Cost in October	12,200	15,000	18,180

Transferred to finished goods $45,262

Ending work in process $2,735

Instructions

Determine the cost of bricks transferred to finished goods inventory and the cost of bricks in ending work in process inventory for October 2016. Assume the company uses the FIFO method.

(adapted from CGA-Canada, now CPA Canada)

*P4-47A   Jessica Company manufactures hockey pucks and soccer balls. For both products, materials are added at the beginning of the production process and conversion costs are incurred evenly. Jessica uses the FIFO method to calculate equivalent units. Production and cost data for the month of August are as follows:

Production Data—Hockey pucks	Units	Percent Complete
Work in process units, August 1	500	70%
Units started into production	1,600	
Work in process units, August 31	600	30%

Cost Data—Hockey pucks	
Work in process, August 1	$1,125
Direct materials	1,600
Direct labour	1,160
Manufacturing overhead	1,000

Production Data—Soccer balls	Units	Percent Complete
Work in process units, August 1	200	90%
Units started into production	2,000	
Work in process units, August 31	150	60%

Cost Data—Soccer balls	
Work in process, August 1	$ 450
Direct materials	2,500
Direct labour	1,000
Manufacturing overhead	995

Instructions
(a) Calculate the following for both the hockey pucks and the soccer balls:
   1. The equivalent units of production for materials and conversion costs
   2. The unit costs of production for materials and conversion costs
   3. The assignment of costs to units transferred out and to work in process at the end of the accounting period
(b) Prepare a production cost report for the month of August for the hockey pucks only.

(SO 4, 5)
Determine equivalent units and unit cost, and prepare a production cost report using FIFO.

Hockey pucks:
(a) 1. Materials: 1,600
   Conversion: 1,330
   2. $1.00; $1.624
   3. Transferred out: $3,993
   Ending WIP: $892

Problems: Set B

*P4-48B   United Dominion Manufacturing Co. produces a wood refinishing kit that sells for $17.95. The final processing of the kits occurs in the packaging department. A quilted wrap is applied at the beginning of the packaging process. A compartmented outside box printed with instructions and the company's name and logo is added when units are 70% through the process. Conversion costs, consisting of direct labour and applied overhead, occur evenly throughout the packaging process. Conversion activities after the completion of the box include package sealing, testing for leakage, and final inspection. The following data are for the packaging department's activities during the month of October:

1. Beginning work in process inventory was 10,000 units, 60% complete in terms of conversion costs.
2. During the month, 40,000 units were transferred to packaging.
3. There were 10,000 units in ending work in process, 70% complete in terms of conversion costs.

The packaging department's October costs were as follows:

Quilted wrap	$80,000
Outside boxes	50,000
Direct labour	22,000
Applied overhead ($3.00/per direct-labour dollar)	66,000

The costs transferred in from prior processing were $3.00 per unit. The cost of goods sold for the month was $240,000, and the ending finished goods inventory was $84,000. United Dominion Manufacturing Co. uses the FIFO method for process costing.

Instructions
(a) Prepare a schedule of equivalent units for the October activity in the packaging department.
(b) Determine the cost per equivalent unit for the October production.

(adapted from CMA Canada, now CPA Canada)

(SO 4, 5)
Analyze a process costing system and calculate equivalent units and unit costs.

(a) Materials 1   40,000
   Materials 2   50,000
   Conversion   41,000
(b) $5.15

P4-49B   Montreal Leather Company manufactures high-quality leather goods. One of the company's main products is a fine leather belt. The belts are produced in a single, continuous process in its Quebec plant. During the process, leather strips are sewn, punched, and dyed. The belts then enter a final finishing stage to conclude the process. Labour and overhead are applied continuously during the manufacturing process. All materials, leather strips, and buckles are introduced at the beginning of the process. The firm uses the weighted-average method to calculate its unit costs.

(SO 3, 4)
Calculate equivalent units, unit costs, and costs assigned.

The leather belts produced at the Quebec plant are sold wholesale for $9.85 each. Management wants to compare the current manufacturing cost per unit with the market prices for leather belts. Top management has asked the Quebec plant controller to submit data on the cost of manufacturing the leather belts for the month of October. These cost data will be used to determine whether modifications in the production process should be initiated or whether an increase in the belts' selling price is justified. The cost per belt used for planning and control is $4.85.

The work in process inventory consisted of 12,200 partially completed units on October 1. The belts were 45% complete in terms of conversion costs. The costs included in the inventory on October 1 were as follows:

Leather strips	$3,000
Buckles	750
Conversion costs	900
Total	$4,650

During October, 22,800 leather strips were placed into production. A total of 21,000 leather belts were completed. The work in process inventory on October 31 consisted of 14,000 belts, which were 50% complete in terms of conversion costs. The costs charged to production during October were as follows:

Leather strips	$ 61,800
Buckles	13,650
Conversion costs	62,100
Total	$137,550

(a) Strips   35,000
    Buckles   35,000   **Instructions**
    Conversion 28,000   In order to provide cost data on the manufacture of leather belts in the Quebec plant to the top management of Montreal
(b) Goods transferred   Leather Company, calculate the following amounts for the month of October:
    out $94,769   (a) The equivalent units for materials and conversion costs
    Ending work in   (b) The assignment of production costs to the October 31 work in process inventory and to goods transferred out
    process $47,430   (c) The weighted-average unit cost of the leather belts completed and transferred to finished goods. Comment on the cost
(c) $4.5128   per belt that the company uses for planning and control.

(adapted from CMA Canada, now CPA Canada)

(SO 4, 5)   ***P4-50B** The following information is for production activities in the refining department of Petro Pure Corporation. All
Calculate equivalent   units in work in process (WIP) were costed using the FIFO cost system.
units, unit costs, and
costs assigned with
FIFO.

Refining Department	Units	Percentage of Completion	Conversion Costs
WIP, February 1	25,000	70%	$ 22,000
Units started and costs incurred during February	135,000		143,000
Units completed and transferred to the mixing department	100,000		
WIP, February 28	?	60%	?

Instructions

(a) Last period $1.257   (a) Calculate the conversion costs per equivalent unit of production during the last period and this period.
    This period $1.2067   (b) Calculate the conversion cost in the work in process inventory account at February 28.
(c) $1.24   (c) Calculate the per-unit conversion cost of the units started last period and completed this period.

(SO 4, 5)   ***P4-51B** Petro Pure Corporation manufactures chemical additives for industrial applications. As the new cost accountant,
Prepare a production   you have been assigned the task of completing the production cost report for the most recent period. The company uses the
cost report using FIFO.   FIFO method of process costing. The following information is for the most recent period:

Production Data—Units	
Beginning WIP inventory (75% complete in terms of materials; 70% complete in terms of conversion costs)	18,000
Units started into production this period	27,000
Units completed and transferred out	33,000
Ending WIP inventory (60% complete in terms of materials; 50% complete in terms of conversion costs)	12,000

Cost Data	
Beginning inventory:	
Materials	$ 32,000
Conversion costs	64,000
Current period:	
Materials	252,000
Conversion costs	440,000

Instructions

Prepare a complete production report for the period using the FIFO method. (Round the cost per equivalent unit to three decimal places; round the costs in the cost report to the nearest dollar.)

(adapted from CGA-Canada, now CPA Canada)

*P4-52B   National Company manufactures bicycles and tricycles. For both products, materials are added at the beginning of the production process, and conversion costs are incurred uniformly. National Company uses the FIFO method to calculate equivalent units. Production and cost data for the month of May are as follows:

Production Data—Bicycles	Units	Percent Complete
Work in process units, May 1	300	70%
Units started into production	1,200	
Work in process units, May 31	500	30%

Cost Data—Bicycles	
Work in process, May 1	$17,400
Direct materials	48,000
Direct labour	19,400
Manufacturing overhead	30,420

Production Data—Tricycles	Units	Percent Complete
Work in process units, May 1	100	75%
Units started into production	900	
Work in process units, May 31	200	40%

Cost Data—Tricycles	
Work in process, May 1	$ 8,000
Direct materials	63,000
Direct labour	31,060
Manufacturing overhead	45,415

Instructions

(a) Calculate the following for both the bicycles and the tricycles:
   1. The equivalent units of production for materials and conversion costs
   2. The unit costs of production for materials and conversion costs
   3. The assignment of costs to units transferred out and in process at the end of the accounting period
(b) Prepare a production cost report for the month of May for the bicycles only.

P4-53B   Bicnell Corporation manufactures water skis through two processes: moulding and packaging. In the moulding department, fibreglass is heated and shaped into the form of a ski. In the packaging department, the skis are placed in cartons and sent to the finished goods warehouse. Materials are entered at the beginning of both processes. Labour and manufacturing overhead are incurred uniformly throughout each process. Production and cost data for the moulding department for January 2016 are presented below:

Production Data	January
Beginning work in process units	0
Units started into production	42,500
Ending work in process units	2,500
Percent complete—ending inventory	40%

Cost Data	
Materials	$510,000
Labour	96,000
Overhead	150,000
Total	$756,000

Instructions

(a) Calculate the physical units of production.
(b) Determine the equivalent units of production for materials and conversion costs.
(c) Calculate the unit costs of production.
(d) Determine the costs to be assigned to the units transferred out and in process.
(e) Prepare a production cost report for the moulding department for the month of January.

Margin notes:

Equivalent units:
materials   26,700
conversion   26,400
Cost per equivalent
unit (total) $26.105
Ending WIP $167,954

(SO 4, 5)
Determine equivalent units and unit costs and assign costs for processes; prepare a production cost report.

(a) Bicycles
   (1) Materials
       1,200 e. u.
   (2) Materials $40
   (3) Transferred
       out $87,270
       Work in
       process $27,950

(SO 3, 4)
Complete the four steps necessary to prepare a production cost report.

(c) Materials $12.00
   Conversion
     costs $6.00
(d) Transferred
     out $720,000
   Work in
     process $36,000

(SO 3, 4, 5)
Complete the four
steps necessary to
prepare a production
cost report.

*P4-54B   Meetha Corporation is in the candy manufacturing business. Products go through two production departments (A first, then B). Data from those departments for September 2016 are presented below.

	Department A	Department B
	Beginning work in process	Beginning work in process
Number of units	1,000	200
% complete for materials	100%	
% complete for transferred-in	100%	
% complete for conversion	60%	30%
Total materials cost	$24,000	
Total conversion cost	$30,000	$40,000
Total transferred-in costs		$15,000
	Ending work in process	Ending work in process
Number of units	600	300
% complete for materials	100%	
% complete for transferred-in	100%	
% complete for conversion	30%	40%

Meetha Corporation started 2,600 units of product during the month in department A. Costs incurred in department A for September 2016 totalled $64,000 for material and $132,000 for conversion. Additionally, department B incurred conversion costs in September 2016 of $600,000. Department B adds no materials to the product.

Instructions

(a) $226,022
(b) Transferred out:
     $834,096

(a) Journalize the transfer of goods from department A to department B during September 2016. Meetha Corporation accounts for its costs using the FIFO method.

(b) Prepare a production cost report for department B for September 2016.

(SO 2)
Journalize transactions.

P4-55B   McNally Company manufactures a nutrient, Everlife, through two manufacturing processes: blending and packaging. All materials are entered at the beginning of each process. On August 1, 2016, inventories consisted of $5,000 in Raw Materials, $0 in Work in Process—Blending, $3,945 in Work in Process—Packaging, and $7,500 in Finished Goods. The beginning inventory for packaging consisted of 500 units, two-fifths complete in terms of conversion costs and fully complete in terms of materials. During August, 9,000 units were started into production in blending, and the following transactions were completed:

1. Purchased $25,000 of raw materials on account.
2. Issued raw materials for production: blending $18,930 and packaging $9,140.
3. Incurred labour costs of $23,770.
4. Used factory labour: blending $13,320 and packaging $10,450.
5. Incurred $41,500 of manufacturing overhead on account.
6. Applied manufacturing overhead at the rate of $25 per machine hour. Machine hours were 900 for blending and 300 for packaging.
7. Transferred 8,200 units from blending to packaging at a cost of $44,940.
8. Transferred 8,600 units from packaging to Finished Goods at a cost of $67,490.
9. Sold goods costing $62,000 for $90,000 on account.

Instructions
Journalize the August transactions.

(SO 3, 4)
Assign costs and
prepare a production
cost report.

P4-56B   Crosby Company has several processing departments. Costs charged to the assembly department for October 2016 totalled $1,249,500, as follows:

Work in process, October 1		
Materials	$29,000	
Conversion costs	16,500	$ 45,500
Materials added		1,006,000
Labour		90,000
Overhead		108,000

Production records show that 25,000 units were in beginning work in process, 40% complete in terms of conversion costs; 425,000 units were started into production; and 35,000 units were in ending work in process, 40% complete in terms of conversion costs. Materials are entered at the beginning of each process.

(b) Transferred
     out $1,162,000
Work in
     process $87,500

Instructions

(a) Determine the equivalent units of production and the unit production costs for the assembly department.

(b) Determine the assignment of costs to goods transferred out and in process.

(c) Prepare a production cost report for the assembly department.

P4-57B Sarku Company manufactures bicycles. Materials are added at the beginning of the production process, and conversion costs are incurred uniformly. Production and cost data for the month of May are as follows:

(SO 3, 4)
Determine equivalent units and unit costs, and assign costs.

Production Data—Bicycles	Units	Percent Complete
Work in process units, May 1	500	80%
Units started into production	2,000	
Work in process units, May 31	800	40%

Cost Data—Bicycles		
Work in process, May 1		
Materials	$15,000	
Conversion costs	18,000	$33,000
Direct materials		50,000
Direct labour		19,020
Manufacturing overhead		33,680

Instructions

(a) Calculate the following:
1. The equivalent units of production for materials and conversion costs
2. The unit costs of production for materials and conversion costs
3. The assignment of costs to units transferred out and in process at the end of the accounting period

(b) Prepare a production cost report for the month of May for the bicycles.

(a) (2) Materials $26
   Conversion
      costs $35
(3) Transferred
      out $103,700
   Work in
      process $32,000

P4-58B Windsor Cleaner Company uses a weighted-average process costing system and manufactures a single product—an all-purpose liquid cleaner. The company has just completed the manufacturing activity for the month of March. A partially completed production cost report for the month of March for the mixing and blending department is shown below.

(SO 3, 4)
Calculate equivalent units and complete a production cost report.

WINDSOR CLEANER COMPANY
Mixing and Blending Department
Production Cost Report
For the Month Ended March 31

		Equivalent Units	
Quantities	Physical Units	Materials	Conversion Costs
Units to be accounted for			
Work in process, March 1 (40% materials, 20% conversion costs)	10,000		
Started into production	100,000		
Total units	110,000		
Units accounted for			
Transferred out	95,000	?	?
Work in process, March 31 (²/₃ materials, ¹/₃ conversion costs)	15,000	?	?
Total units accounted for	110,000	?	?

Costs	Materials	Conversion Costs	Total
Unit costs			
Costs in March	$156,000	$98,000	$254,000
Equivalent units	?	?	
Unit costs	$? +	$?	$?
Costs to be accounted for			
Work in process, March 1			$ 8,700
Started into production			245,300
Total costs			$254,000
Cost Reconciliation Schedule			
Costs accounted for			
Transferred out			$?
Work in process, March 31			
Materials		?	
Conversion costs		?	?
Total costs			$?

(a) Materials $1.4857
(b) Transferred
    out $234,242
  Work in
  process $19,757

(SO 4, 5)
Determine equivalent
units and unit costs
and assign costs for
processes using FIFO;
prepare a production
cost report.

Instructions

(a) Prepare a schedule that shows how the equivalent units were calculated so that you can complete the "Quantities: Units accounted for" equivalent units section in the production cost report above, and calculate March unit costs.
(b) Complete the "Cost Reconciliation Schedule" part of the production cost report above.

*P4-59B Maloney Company manufactures hockey pucks and soccer balls. For both products, materials are added at the beginning of the production process and conversion costs are incurred uniformly. Maloney uses the FIFO method to calculate equivalent units. Production and cost data for the month of August are as shown below.

Production Data—Hockey pucks	Units	Percent Complete
Work in process units, August 1	500	60%
Units started into production	1,600	
Work in process units, August 31	600	50%

Cost Data—Hockey pucks	
Work in process, August 1	$1,125
Direct materials	1,600
Direct labour	1,175
Manufacturing overhead	1,000

Production Data—Soccer balls	Units	Percent Complete
Work in process units, August 1	200	80%
Units started into production	2,000	
Work in process units, August 31	150	70%

Cost Data—Soccer balls	
Work in process, August 1	$ 450
Direct materials	2,600
Direct labour	1,000
Manufacturing overhead	995

(a) Hockey pucks:
  (1) Materials 1,600
  (2) Materials $1
  (3) Transferred
    out $3,865
  Work in
  process $1,035

Instructions

(a) Calculate the following for both the hockey pucks and the soccer balls:
    1. The equivalent units of production for materials and conversion costs
    2. The unit costs of production for materials and conversion costs
    3. The assignment of costs to units transferred out and in process at the end of the accounting period
(b) Prepare a production cost report for the month of August for the hockey pucks only.

Cases

C4-60 Sunshine Beach Company manufactures a suntan lotion, called Surtan, in 350-ml plastic bottles. Surtan is sold in a competitive market. As a result, management is very cost-conscious. Surtan is manufactured through two processes: mixing and filling. Materials are entered at the beginning of each process, and labour and manufacturing overhead occur uniformly throughout each process. Unit costs are based on the cost per litre of Surtan using the weighted-average costing approach.

On June 30, 2016, Jill Ritzman, the chief accountant for the past 20 years, opted to take early retirement. Her replacement, Sid Benili, had extensive accounting experience with motels in the area but only limited contact with manufacturing accounting. During July, Sid correctly accumulated the following production quantity and cost data for the mixing department.

Production quantities: Work in process, July 1, 8,000 litres, 75% complete; started into production 91,000 litres; work in process, July 31,

5,000 litres, 20% complete. Materials are added at the beginning of the process.

Production costs: Beginning work in process $88,000, comprising $21,000 of materials costs and $67,000 of conversion costs; incurred in July—materials $573,000, conversion costs $769,000. Sid then prepared a production cost report on the basis of physical units started into production. His report showed a production cost of $15.71 per litre of Surtan. The management of Sunshine Beach was surprised at the high unit cost. The president comes to you, as Jill's top assistant, to review Sid's report and prepare a correct report if necessary.

Instructions

(a) Show how Sid arrived at the unit cost of $15.71 per litre of Surtan.
(b) Explain what error(s) Sid made in preparing his production cost report.
(c) Prepare a correct production cost report for July.

C4-61 Guion Furniture Company manufactures living room furniture through two departments: framing and upholstering. Materials are entered at the beginning of each process. For May, the following cost data are obtained from the two work in process accounts:

	Framing	Upholstering
Work in process, May 1	$ 0	$?
Materials	450,000	?
Conversion costs	261,000	350,000
Costs transferred in	0	600,000
Costs transferred out	600,000	?
Work in process, May 31	111,000	?

Instructions

(a) If 3,000 sofas were started into production on May 1 and 2,500 sofas were transferred to Upholstering, what was the unit cost of materials for May in the framing department?

(b) Using the data in part (a) above, what was the per-unit conversion cost of the sofas transferred to upholstering?

(c) Continuing the assumptions in part (a) above, what is the percentage of completion of the units in process at May 31 in the framing department?

C4-62 You have recently been appointed as the cost accountant for Silky Hair Co. Ltd., a manufacturer of hair shampoo. Your first task is to clear up the production records of the mixing department for November 2016.

You learn that the mixing department is the last stage of the shampoo production process. Units transferred from the previous department use direct labour and overhead inputs evenly in mixing. A secret ingredient is also added to each unit at the 40% point in processing.

You also find out that the beginning inventory for the month of November was 4,000 units with the following costs:

Transferred-in costs	$16,000
Direct materials	3,600
Conversion costs	24,000

In addition, during November, 16,000 units were transferred to mixing at a $4 unit cost. The ending inventory consisted of 5,000 units that were 60% complete. During the month, direct materials of $26,400 were added and 8,500 hours of direct labour were used at a wage rate of $12.00 per hour.

The overhead rate for 2016, applied on a basis of direct labour hours, was based on a predicted annual usage of 120,000 hours and a cost function derived from the following overhead equation: $Y = 60,000 + 2X$, where Y is the total overhead costs and X is the direct labour hours.

Instructions

Using weighted-average process costing techniques, calculate the following for the mixing department for November 2016:

(a) The predetermined overhead rate for 2016
(b) The number of equivalent units in ending inventory
(c) The unit cost of items transferred to finished goods
(d) The value assigned to ending inventory

(adapted from CGA-Canada, now CPA Canada)

C4-63 Passera Inc. manufactures a single product in a continuous processing environment. All materials are added at the beginning of the process, and conversion costs are applied evenly throughout the process. To assign costs to inventories, the company uses weighted-average process costing.

The following information was available for 2016:

Sales (selling price per unit, $40)	$4,080,000
Actual manufacturing overhead	660,000
Selling and administrative expenses	328,000
Unit costs of production:	
Direct materials (1 kilogram)	$ 6.00
Direct labour (1/2 hour)	8.00
Overhead	9.00
Total	$23.00
Units transferred to finished goods	140,000 units
Materials purchased	125,000 kilograms
Materials used in process	136,000 kilograms

An inventory count at year end (December 31, 2016) revealed that the inventories had the following balances:

Raw materials	8,000 kilograms
Work in process (45% complete)	22,000 units
Finished goods	45,000 units

The January 1, 2016, work in process units are 70% complete. The unit cost of production was the same in 2016 as it was in 2015.

Instructions

Calculate the following amounts for Passera Inc.:

(a) The opening (January 1, 2016) balance in units and costs of (1) raw materials, (2) work in process, and (3) finished goods
(b) The equivalent units for 2016 for (1) materials and (2) conversion costs
(c) The total cost for 2016 for (1) materials used and (2) conversion applied
(d) The cost of ending work in process for 2016
(e) The cost of units completed and transferred to finished goods

(adapted from CMA Canada, now CPA Canada)

---

*C4-64 Icy Delight Company, which manufactures quality ice cream sold at premium prices, uses a single production department. Production begins with the blending of various ingredients, which are added at the beginning of the process, and ends with the packaging of the ice cream. Packaging occurs when the mixture reaches the 90% stage of completion. The two-litre cartons are then transferred to the shipping department for shipment. Labour and overhead are added continuously throughout the process. Manufacturing overhead is applied on the basis of direct-labour hours at the rate of $3.00 per hour.

The company has always used the weighted-average method to determine equivalent units of production and unit costs. Now, production management is considering changing from the weighted-average method to the first-in, first-out method. The following data relate to actual production during the month of May:

Costs	
Work in process inventory, May 1 (16,000 litres; 15% complete)	
Direct materials (ingredients)	$ 45,600
Direct labour ($10 per hour)	6,250
Manufacturing overhead	1,875

Costs Incurred	
Direct materials (ingredients)	$228,400
Direct materials (cartons)	7,000
Direct labour ($10 per hour)	35,000
Manufacturing overhead	10,500

Production Units	Litres
Work in process inventory, May 1 (15% complete)	16,000
Started in May	84,000
Sent to shipping department	80,000
Work in process inventory, May 31 (95% complete)	20,000

Instructions

(a) Prepare a schedule of equivalent units for each cost element for the month of May using (1) the weighted-average method, and (2) the first-in, first-out method.

(b) Calculate the cost (to the nearest cent) per equivalent unit for each cost element for the month of May using (1) the weighted-average method, and (2) the first-in, first-out method.

(c) Discuss the advantages and disadvantages of the weighted-average method versus the first-in, first-out method.

(adapted from CMA Canada, now CPA Canada)

*C4-65   The Saunders Paint Co. uses a process costing system. You have been given the following selected information for July 2016:

	Units	Percent Complete
Beginning work in process	6,000	70%
Units started	24,000	
Ending work in process	10,000	60%

The total cost of the beginning work in process was $37,000, of which $7,000 was for direct labour costs. Overhead is applied on the basis of direct labour costs.

During July, the company added $69,400 of direct materials, $50,500 of direct labour, and $60,600 of overhead to work in process.

All direct materials are added at the beginning of the process, and the conversion costs are incurred evenly throughout the process.

Instructions

(a) Calculate the overhead rate.

(b) Calculate the direct materials, the direct labour, and the overhead cost components of the beginning work in process.

(c) Calculate the number of equivalent units that would be used to establish the weighted-average costs for direct materials, direct labour, and overhead.

(d) Calculate the number of equivalent units that would be used to establish the FIFO costs for direct materials, direct labour, and overhead.

(e) Assuming weighted-average is used, calculate the cost of goods completed and transferred out.

(f) Assuming FIFO is used, calculate the cost of ending work in process inventory for direct materials, direct labour, and overhead. Show each component separately.

(adapted from CGA-Canada, now CPA Canada)

C4-66   R. B. Patrick Company manufactures a high-tech component that passes through two production processing departments: moulding and assembly. Department managers are partially compensated on the basis of units of products completed and transferred out relative to units of product put into production. This was intended as encouragement to be efficient and to minimize waste.

Sue Wooten is the department head in the moulding department, and Fred Baranski is her quality control inspector. During the month of June, Sue had three new employees who were not yet technically skilled. As a result, many of the units produced in June had minor moulding defects. In order to maintain the department's normal high rate of completion, Sue told Fred to pass through inspection and on to the assembly

department all units that had defects not detectable to the human eye. "Company and industry tolerances on this product are too high anyway," says Sue. "Less than 2% of the units we produce are subjected in the market to the stress tolerance we've designed into them. The odds of those 2% being any of this month's units are even less. Anyway, we're saving the company money."

Instructions

Answer the following questions:

(a) Who are the potential stakeholders involved in this situation?

(b) What alternatives does Fred have in this situation? What might the company do to prevent this situation from occurring?

"All About You" Activity

C4-67   You are an accounting intern at Mooz4yoo, a company that produces a range of gourmet organic yogurts that are sold to high-end grocery stores and restaurants. Production of the yogurts occurs in a single building, with offices for management and sales staff upstairs and the plant on the first floor. Production is made up of three processes: raw milk processing, where the milk, which is the major ingredient for the yogurts, is pasteurized; yogurt manufacture, where fruit and flavourings are added to

the milk and the yogurt is made in bulk; and packaging, where the product is put into specially designed containers (with a foil insert).

Instructions

What costs would you expect to be included in the process cost for each of the three processing departments? Differentiate between variable costs, direct overhead costs, and indirect overhead costs.

Decision-Making at Current Designs

DM4-1   Building a kayak using the composite method is a very labour-intensive process. In the fabrication department, the kayaks go through several steps as employees carefully place layers of Kevlar® in a mould and then use resin to fuse together the layers. The excess resin is removed

with a vacuum process, and the upper shell and lower shell are removed from the moulds and assembled.

The seat, hatch, and other components are added in the finishing department.

At the beginning of April, Current Designs had 30 kayaks in process in the fabrication department. Rick Thrune, the production manager, estimated that about 80% of the material costs had been added to these boats, which were about 50% complete with respect to the conversion costs. The cost of this inventory had been calculated to be $8,400 in materials and $9,000 in conversion costs.

During April, 72 boats were started. At the end of the month, the 35 kayaks in the ending inventory had 20% of the materials and 40% of the conversion costs already added to them.

A review of the accounting records for April showed that materials with a cost of $17,500 had been requisitioned by this department and that the conversion costs for the month were $39,600.

Instructions

Complete a production cost report for April 2016 for the fabrication department using the weighted average method.

Waterways Continuing Problem

(This is a continuation of the Waterways Problem from Chapters 1 through 3.)

WCP-4 Because most of the parts for Waterways' drainage and irrigation systems are standard, the company uses a process cost system for most of its manufacturing. Its recent contract to upgrade the city-owned soccer fields has increased the demand for a specific type of maintenance-free piping and the new joints and coupling units that make the systems so flexible.

The parts go through three separate processes: moulding, cutting, and welding. They are then transferred to Raw Materials Inventory where they are available to the installation units for use in the field.

The following information is available for the processing of the piping in the moulding department for the month of July. One metre of piping is considered to be one unit.

Beginning work in process:		
Units in process		40,000
Stage of completion for materials		100%
Stage of completion for labour and overhead		70%
Costs in work in process inventory		
Materials	$138,360	
Labour	27,564	
Overhead	13,782	$179,706
Units started into production in July		62,000
Units completed and transferred out in July		60,000
Costs added to production during July:		
Materials	$216,690	
Labour	48,312	
Overhead	24,156	$289,158
Ending work in process:		
Units in process		42,000
Stage of completion for materials		100%
Stage of completion for labour and overhead		40%

Instructions

(a) Using the weighted-average method, prepare a production cost report for Waterways for the moulding department for the month of July.

(b) Show the equivalent units for materials and conversion costs if Waterways used the FIFO method instead of weighted-average.

Answers to Self-Study Questions

1. b   **2.** d   **3.** d   **4.** b   **5.** b   **6.** a   **7.** c   **8.** a   **9.** b   **10.** b   *11. b   *12. a   *13. b

Remember to go back to the beginning of the chapter to check off your completed work!
←

CHAPTER 5

Activity-Based Costing

© Pratt & Whitney Canada Corp. Reproduced with Permission.

study objectives

![the navigator]

After studying this chapter, you should be able to do the following:

1. Recognize the difference between traditional costing and activity-based costing (ABC) and understand the nature of ABC.

2. Apply activity-based costing to a manufacturer.

3. Understand the benefits and limitations of activity-based costing.

4. Apply activity-based costing to service industries.

THE "ABCs" OF TRACKING COSTS

When a company makes engines that can sell for millions of dollars each, getting a handle on costs is crucial. Yet the traditional way of determining manufacturing costs, by allocating a generic portion of overhead to each product, can end up burying the true cost, resulting in more difficult decision-making.

Pratt & Whitney Canada Corp. makes more than $600 million worth of aerospace and industrial engines at five plants across the country every year, and receives millions of dollars in contracts to maintain these engines. But the company was struggling under its traditional costing method. "Our manufacturing costs were killing us," said Claude Lévesque, former manager of costing operations at Pratt & Whitney Canada. "We knew that we had to reduce them, but first we had to determine what they actually were. We needed to develop far more cost wisdom than was enabled by our traditional standard cost system." Under that system, overhead was allocated to each manufactured part based on time spent in each machine, so a tiny, low-cost washer spending five minutes in an inexpensive machine would be assigned the same amount of overhead as a large, high-cost engine spending five minutes in an expensive machine.

To more accurately determine manufacturing costs, Pratt & Whitney Canada switched to an activity-based costing (ABC) system, which allocates actual overhead costs based on the activities that happen when making a product. To do this, the company's accounting department worked to determine the cost of each process that an engine part undergoes when being produced—starting with materials, proceeding through the machining process, and ending with product inspection and documentation. "It's far more than an accounting exercise," said Mr. Lévesque. "We had to thoroughly understand each manufacturing process, in order to properly accumulate its actual costs as accurately and rationally as possible." Using sophisticated software, the accountants entered costs for hundreds of materials and processes.

Under ABC, Pratt & Whitney Canada assigns overhead based on material usage per activity and not just time spent in a machine. For example, the company discovered that in the sandblasting activity, the cost of the grains of sand was greater than the cost of the time spent in the sandblasting machine, so it adjusted its overhead allocation accordingly. It also can more accurately determine research and development costs and depreciation for each part.

With its previous costing method, Pratt & Whitney Canada determined costs by department, but ABC allows it to know costs per machine. This helps managers understand which machines are underused, which parts cost more to produce, and which plants have higher costs—all important information for decision-making.

Sources: "Pratt & Whitney Canada Signs $75M, 15-Year Helicopter Engine Maintenance Program," *Canadian Manufacturing*, February 27, 2014; "Object Technology Opens New Costing Horizons for Pratt & Whitney Canada," 3C Software case study, www.3csoftware.com; Pratt & Whitney Canada corporate website, www.pwc.ca.

the navigator

Preview of Chapter 5

As indicated in our feature story about Pratt & Whitney Canada Corporation, the traditional costing systems described in earlier chapters are not the best answer for every company. Because Pratt & Whitney suspected that the traditional system was hiding significant differences in its real cost structure, it looked for a new method to assign costs. Similar searches by other companies for ways to improve operations and gather more accurate data for decision-making have resulted in the development of powerful new management tools, including **activity-based costing (ABC)**, which this chapter explains and illustrates.

The chapter is organized as follows:

the navigator

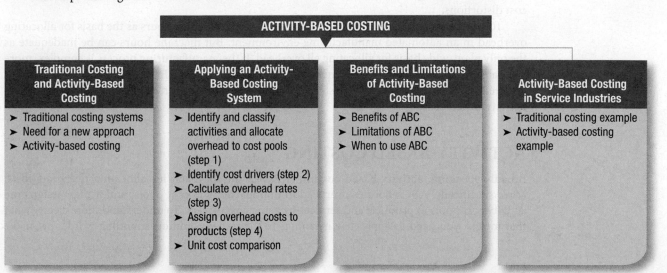

ACTIVITY-BASED COSTING

Traditional Costing and Activity-Based Costing	Applying an Activity-Based Costing System	Benefits and Limitations of Activity-Based Costing	Activity-Based Costing in Service Industries
➤ Traditional costing systems ➤ Need for a new approach ➤ Activity-based costing	➤ Identify and classify activities and allocate overhead to cost pools (step 1) ➤ Identify cost drivers (step 2) ➤ Calculate overhead rates (step 3) ➤ Assign overhead costs to products (step 4) ➤ Unit cost comparison	➤ Benefits of ABC ➤ Limitations of ABC ➤ When to use ABC	➤ Traditional costing example ➤ Activity-based costing example

Traditional Costing and Activity-Based Costing

TRADITIONAL COSTING SYSTEMS

It is probably impossible to determine the **exact** cost of a product or service, However, for managers to make better decisions, they must have the most accurate cost estimates possible. A product's cost can be estimated most accurately when this cost can be traced directly to the product produced or the service provided. Direct material and direct labour costs are the easiest to determine, because these can be traced directly to the product by examining material requisition forms and payroll time sheets. Overhead costs, on the other hand, are an indirect or common cost that generally cannot be easily or directly traced to individual products or services. Instead, we use estimates to assign overhead costs to products and services.

Often the most difficult part of calculating accurate unit costs is determining the proper amount of **overhead cost** to assign to each product, service, or job. In our coverage of job-order costing in Chapter 3 and of process costing in Chapter 4, we used a single or plant-wide overhead rate throughout the year for the entire factory operation. This rate was called the **predetermined overhead rate**. For job-order costing, we assumed that **direct labour cost** was the relevant activity base for assigning all overhead costs to jobs. For process costing, we assumed that **machine hours** were the relevant activity base for assigning all overhead costs to the process or department.

Using direct labour as the activity base made sense when overhead cost allocation systems were first developed. At that time, direct labour made up a large portion of the total manufacturing cost. Therefore, it was widely accepted that there was a high correlation between direct labour and overhead costs. As a result, direct labour became the most popular basis for allocating overhead.

Even in today's increasingly automated environment, direct labour is sometimes the appropriate basis for assigning overhead costs to products. It is appropriate to use direct labour when (a) direct labour is a significant part of the total product cost, and (b) there is a high correlation between direct labour and changes in the amount of overhead costs. Illustration 5-1 shows a simplified (one-stage) traditional costing system that uses direct labour to assign overhead costs.

▶Illustration 5-1

Traditional one-stage costing system

THE NEED FOR A NEW APPROACH

In recent years manufacturers and service providers have experienced tremendous change. Advances in computerized systems, technological innovation, global competition, and automation have changed the manufacturing environment dramatically. As a result, the amount of direct labour that is used in many industries has greatly decreased, and total overhead costs from depreciation on expensive equipment and machinery and from utilities, repairs, and maintenance have significantly increased. When there is no correlation between direct labour and overhead, it is inappropriate to use plant-wide, predetermined overhead rates that are based on direct labour. When this correlation does not exist, companies that use overhead rates based on direct labour have significant product cost distortions.

To avoid these distortions, many companies now use machine hours as the basis for allocating overhead in an automated manufacturing environment. But machine hours can be inadequate as the only plant-wide basis for allocating all overhead. If the manufacturing process is complex, more accurate product cost calculations require multiple allocation bases. In situations like these, managers need to consider an overhead cost-allocation method that uses multiple bases. That method is **activity-based costing**.

ACTIVITY-BASED COSTING

Broadly speaking, **activity-based costing** (ABC) is an approach for allocating overhead costs. More specifically, ABC allocates overhead to multiple activity cost pools, and it then assigns the activity cost pools to products and services by using cost drivers. To understand more clearly what that means, you need to apply new meanings to the rather common-sounding words that make up the definition. In activity-based costing, an **activity** is any event, action, transaction, or work sequence that incurs a cost when producing a product or providing a service. An **activity cost pool** is a distinct type of activity (such as ordering materials or setting up machines). A **cost driver** is any factor or activity that has a direct cause–effect relationship with the resources consumed. The reasoning behind ABC cost allocation is simple: **products consume activities, and activities consume resources**.

Activity-based costing involves the four steps shown in Illustration 5-2:

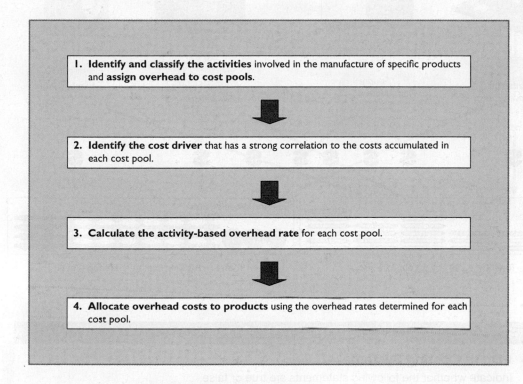

1. **Identify and classify the activities** involved in the manufacture of specific products and **assign overhead to cost pools**.

2. **Identify the cost driver** that has a strong correlation to the costs accumulated in each cost pool.

3. **Calculate the activity-based overhead rate** for each cost pool.

4. **Allocate overhead costs to products** using the overhead rates determined for each cost pool.

▶Illustration 5-2
The four steps of activity-based costing

These definitions will become clearer as we look more closely at how ABC works. ABC allocates overhead in a two-stage process. In the first stage (Step 1), it allocates overhead costs to activity cost pools. (Traditional costing systems, in contrast, allocate these costs to departments or jobs.) Examples of overhead activity cost pools are ordering materials, setting machines, assembling products, and inspecting products.

In the second stage (Steps 2–4), ABC uses cost drivers to assign the overhead allocated to the activity cost pools to specific products using cost drivers. The cost drivers measure the number of individual activities that are performed to produce products or provide services. Examples are the number of purchase orders, number of set-ups, labour hours, or number of inspections. Illustration 5-3 shows examples of activities, and the possible cost drivers that measure them, for a company that manufactures two products: axles and steering wheels.

In the first step (as shown at the top of the illustration), the company allocates its overhead costs to activity cost pools. In this simplified example, it has identified four activity cost pools: purchasing, storing, machining, and supervising. After allocating the costs to the activity cost pools, the company uses cost drivers to measure the costs to be assigned to the individual products (either axles or steering wheels) based on each product's use of each activity. For example, if axles require more activity by the purchasing department, as measured by the number of required purchase orders, then the company will allocate more of the overhead cost from the purchasing pool to the axles.

Not all products or services share equally in these activities. When a product's manufacturing operation is more complex, it is likely to have more activities and cost drivers. If there is little or no correlation between changes in the cost driver and the consumption of the overhead cost, inaccurate **product costs** will result.

Alternative Terminology
Product costs are also called *inventory costs*.

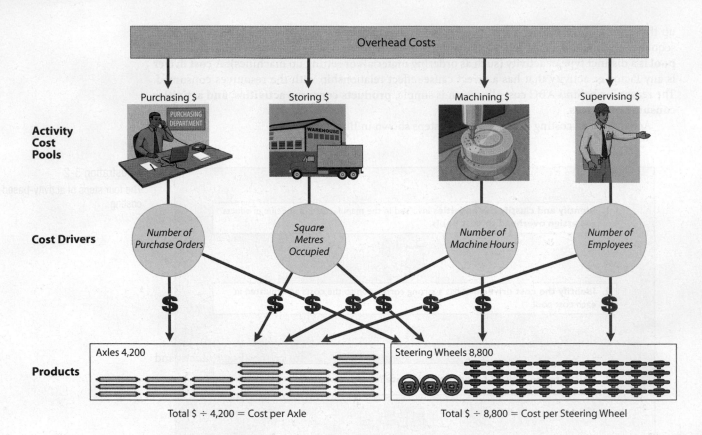

Overhead Costs

Activity Cost Pools

Purchasing $ Storing $ Machining $ Supervising $

Cost Drivers

Number of Purchase Orders   *Square Metres Occupied*   *Number of Machine Hours*   *Number of Employees*

$ $ $ $ $ $ $ $

Products

Axles 4,200

Steering Wheels 8,800

Total $ ÷ 4,200 = Cost per Axle   Total $ ÷ 8,800 = Cost per Steering Wheel

▶Illustration 5-3
Activities and related cost drivers

BEFORE YOU GO ON...

▶Do It! Costing Systems

Indicate whether the following statements are true or false.

(a) A traditional costing system allocates overhead by means of multiple overhead rates in each department.

(b) Activity-based costing allocates overhead costs in a two-stage process.

(c) Direct material and direct labour costs are easier to trace to products than overhead.

(d) As manufacturing processes have become more automated, more companies have chosen to allocate overhead on the basis of direct labour costs.

(e) In activity-based costing, an activity is any event, action, transaction, or work sequence that incurs cost by consuming resources when producing a product.

Action Plan

• Understand that a traditional costing system allocates overhead on the basis of a single predetermined overhead rate in each department.

• Understand that an ABC system allocates overhead to identified activity cost pools, and then assigns costs to products using related cost drivers that measure the resources consumed.

Solution

(a) False. (b) True. (c) True. (d) False. (e) True.

Related exercise material: **BE5-1, BE5-2, E5-17,** and **Do It! D5-13**.

the navigator

Applying an Activity-Based Costing System

STUDY OBJECTIVE 2
Apply activity-based costing to a manufacturer.

You should understand that ABC generally does not replace an existing job-order or process costing system. ABC simply segregates overhead into various cost pools in an effort to provide more accurate cost information. Thus, ABC supplements the traditional cost systems; it does not replace them. We now present a simple case that compares traditional costing and activity-based costing.

Assume that Atlas Company produces two automobile antitheft devices: The Boot and The Club. The Boot is a high-volume item totalling 25,000 units annually. The Club is a low-volume item totalling only 5,000 units per year. Each product requires one hour of direct labour to complete. Total annual direct labour hours are therefore 30,000 (25,000 + 5,000). Expected annual manufacturing overhead costs are $900,000.

Thus, the predetermined overhead rate under traditional costing, using direct labour hours, is $30 ($900,000 ÷ 30,000) per direct labour hour. Since both products require one direct labour hour per unit, both products are allocated overhead costs of **$30 per unit under traditional costing**.

Let's now continue the example of Atlas Company to show how ABC eliminates the distortion that can occur in traditional overhead cost allocation.

We will calculate unit costs under ABC. Activity-based costing involves the following four steps.

1. Identify and classify the major activities involved in the manufacture of specific products, and allocate manufacturing overhead costs to cost pools.
2. Identify the cost driver that has a strong correlation to the costs accumulated in the cost pool.
3. Calculate the overhead rate for each cost driver.
4. Assign manufacturing overhead costs for each cost pool to products, using the overhead rates (cost per driver).

Recall that both products manufactured by the Atlas Company are allocated overhead costs of $30 per unit under traditional costing.

IDENTIFY AND CLASSIFY ACTIVITIES AND ALLOCATE OVERHEAD TO COST POOLS (STEP 1)

A well-designed activity-based costing system starts with an analysis of the activities performed to manufacture a product or provide a service. This analysis should identify all resource-consuming activities. It requires documenting every activity undertaken to accomplish a task. Atlas Company identified three activity-cost pools: setting up machines, machining, and inspecting.

Next, the system assigns overhead costs directly to the appropriate activity cost pool. For example, all overhead costs directly associated with Atlas Company's machine set-ups (such as salaries, supplies, and depreciation) would be assigned to the machine set-up cost pool. Illustration 5-4 shows the three cost pools, along with the estimated overhead allocated to each cost pool.

Activity Cost Pools	Estimated Overhead
Setting up machines	$300,000
Machining	500,000
Inspecting	100,000
Total	$900,000

►Illustration 5-4
Activity cost pools and estimated overhead

IDENTIFY COST DRIVERS (STEP 2)

After costs are allocated to the activity cost pools, the company must identify the cost drivers for each cost pool. The cost driver must accurately measure the actual consumption of the activity by the various products. To achieve accurate costing, a **high degree of correlation** must exist between the cost driver and the actual consumption of the overhead costs in the cost pool.

Illustration 5-5 shows the cost drivers identified by Atlas and their total expected use per activity cost pool.

►Illustration 5-5
Cost drivers and their
expected use

Activity Cost Pools	Cost Drivers	Expected Use of Cost Drivers per Activity
Setting up machines	Number of set-ups	1,500 set-ups
Machining	Machine hours	50,000 machine hours
Inspecting	Number of inspections	2,000 inspections

Availability and ease of obtaining data relating to the cost driver is an important factor that must be considered in its selection.

CALCULATE OVERHEAD RATES (STEP 3)

Next, the company calculates an **activity-based overhead rate** per cost driver by dividing the estimated overhead per activity by the number of cost drivers expected to be used per activity. Illustration 5-6 shows the formula for this calculation.

►Illustration 5-6
Formula for calculating activity-based
overhead rate

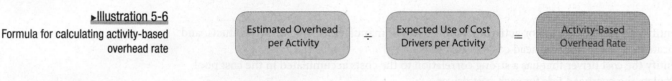

Atlas Company calculates its activity-based overhead rates by using estimated overhead per activity cost pool, shown in Illustration 5-4, and the expected use of cost drivers per activity, shown in Illustration 5-5. These calculations are presented in Illustration 5-7.

►Illustration 5-7
Calculation of activity-based
overhead rates

Activity Cost Pools	Estimated Overhead	÷	Expected Use of Cost Drivers per Activity	=	Activity-Based Overhead Rates
Setting up machines	$300,000		1,500 set-ups		$200 per set-up
Machining	500,000		50,000 machine hours		$ 10 per machine hour
Inspecting	100,000		2,000 inspections		$ 50 per inspection
Total	$900,000				

ASSIGN OVERHEAD COSTS TO PRODUCTS (STEP 4)

In assigning overhead costs, it is necessary to know the expected use of cost drivers **for each product**. Because of its low volume, The Club requires more set-ups and inspections than The Boot. Illustration 5-8 shows the expected use of cost drivers per product for each of Atlas's products.

►Illustration 5-8
Expected use of cost drivers
per product

			Expected Use of Cost Drivers per Product	
Activity Cost Pools	Cost Drivers	Expected Use of Cost Drivers per Activity	The Boot	The Club
Setting up machines	Number of set-ups	1,500 set-ups	500	1,000
Machining	Machine hours	50,000 machine hours	30,000	20,000
Inspecting	Number of inspections	2,000 inspections	500	1,500

To assign overhead costs to each product, Atlas multiplies the activity-based overhead rates per cost driver (Illustration 5-7) by the number of cost drivers expected to be used per product (Illustration 5-8). Illustration 5-9 shows the overhead cost assigned to each product.

Activity Cost Pools	Expected Use of Cost Drivers per Product	×	Activity-Based Overhead Rates	=	Cost Assigned	Expected Use of Cost Drivers per Product	×	Activity-Based Overhead Rates	=	Cost Assigned
ATLAS COMPANY										
The Boot						**The Club**				
Setting up machines	500		$200		$100,000	1,000		$200		$200,000
Machining	30,000		$10		300,000	20,000		$10		200,000
Inspecting	500		$50		25,000	1,500		$50		75,000
Total costs assigned [(a)]					$425,000					$475,000
Units produced [(b)]					25,000					5,000
Overhead cost per unit [(a) ÷ (b)]					$17					$95

►Illustration 5-9

Assignment of activity cost pools to products

Under ABC, the overhead cost per unit is $17 for The Boot and $95 for The Club. When compared with the $30 per unit overhead charge under traditional costing, ABC shifts costs from the high-volume product (The Boot) to the low-volume product (The Club). This shift occurs because low-volume products often require more special handling, such as machine set-ups and inspections. This is true for Atlas Company. Thus, the low-volume product frequently is responsible for more overhead costs per unit than is a high-volume product.[1] Assigning overhead using ABC will usually increase the cost per unit for low-volume products as compared with a traditional overhead allocation. Therefore, traditional cost drivers such as direct labour hours are usually not appropriate for assigning overhead costs to low-volume products.

UNIT COST COMPARISON

Illustration 5-10 shows the unit cost for each product under traditional costing.

Manufacturing Costs	Products The Boot	The Club
Direct materials	$40	$30
Direct labour	12	12
Overhead	30*	30*
Total unit cost	$82	$72

*Predetermined overhead rate × Direct labour hours = $30 × 1 hr. = $30

►Illustration 5-10

Calculation of unit costs—traditional costing

In Illustration 5-11, a comparison of unit manufacturing costs under traditional costing and ABC shows the following significant differences.

Manufacturing Costs	The Boot Traditional Costing	ABC	The Club Traditional Costing	ABC
Direct materials	$40	$40	$30	$ 30
Direct labour	12	12	12	12
Overhead	30	17	30	95
Total cost per unit	$82	$69	$72	$137
	Overstated $13		Understated $65	

►Illustration 5-11

Comparison of unit product costs

The comparison shows that unit costs under traditional costing are significantly distorted. The cost of producing The Boot is overstated by $13 per unit ($82 − $69), and the cost of producing The

[1]Robin Cooper and Robert S. Kaplan, "How Cost Accounting Distorts Product Costs," *Management Accounting 69*, No. 10 (April 1988), pp. 20–27.

Club is understated by $65 per unit ($137 − $72). These differences are entirely due to how manufacturing overhead is assigned. A likely consequence of the differences in assigning overhead is that Atlas Company has been overpricing The Boot and possibly losing market share to competitors. Moreover, it has been sacrificing profitability by underpricing The Club.

BUSINESS INSIGHT   *Handling Baggage Costs*

Have you been on a flight where the airline charged to check the first bag? Did you pay the money to check it or did you just bring a carry-on bag? Either way, the airlines are hoping to reduce their costs or increase their revenues. Baggage handling is extremely labour intensive. When airlines first started charging for checked bags in 2008, it was estimated that the cost of all that tagging, sorting, loading on carts, loading in planes, unloading, and sorting again added up to about $9 per bag. Carriers also have equipment costs: sorters, carts, conveyors, tractors, and storage facilities, for about another $4 per bag. Finally, there is additional fuel cost of an 18-kilogram item—about $2 in fuel for a 3-hour flight. Costs have gone up since then, and many North American airlines are charging $25 to check the first bag, including Air Canada and Porter Airlines on flights to and from the United States. WestJet was also considering implementing baggage fees. Not only does this save the airlines money, it brings in additional passenger fees and increases the amount of space available for hauling cargo. An airline can charge at least $80 for hauling a small parcel for same-day delivery service. The largest U.S. airlines collected a record U.S. $3.5 billion in baggage fees in 2012.

Sources: Tamara Elliott, "WestJet Looks at Adding Baggage Fees," Global News, February 4, 2014; "Porter Airlines Checked Baggage Fee for U.S. Flights Coming in August," The Huffington Post Canada, July 4, 2013; Scott Mayerowitz, The Associated Press, "Airlines Collected Record Baggage Fees in 2012," Global News, May 14, 2013; Vanessa Lu, "Air Canada to Charge for Checked Bags," *Toronto Star*, September 2, 2011; Scott McCartney, "What It Costs an Airline to Fly Your Luggage," Wall Street Journal Online, November 25, 2008.

Why do airlines charge even higher rates for heavier bags, bags that are odd shapes (such as ski bags), and bags with hazardous materials in them?

BEFORE YOU GO ON...

▶Do It! Apply ABC

Using the data on the next page, do the following:

(a) Prepare a schedule that shows the calculations of the activity-based overhead rates per cost driver.

(b) Prepare a schedule for assigning each activity's overhead cost to the two products.

(c) Calculate the overhead cost per unit for each product.

(d) Comment on the comparative overhead cost per unit.

Lift Jack Company, as shown in Illustration 5-12, has seven activity cost pools and two products. It expects to produce 200,000 units of its automobile scissors jack, and 80,000 units of its truck hydraulic jack. Having identified its activity cost pools and the cost drivers for each cost pool, Lift Jack Company accumulated the following data on the activity cost pools and cost drivers.

Annual Overhead Data				Expected Use of Cost Drivers per Product	
Activity Cost Pools	Cost Drivers	Estimated Overhead	Expected Use of Cost Drivers per Activity	Scissors Jacks	Hydraulic Jacks
Ordering and receiving	Purchase orders	$ 200,000	2,500 orders	1,000	1,500
Machine set-up	Set-ups	600,000	1,200 set-ups	500	700
Machining	Machine hours	2,000,000	800,000 hours	300,000	500,000
Assembling	Parts	1,800,000	3,000,000 parts	1,800,000	1,200,000
Inspecting and testing	Tests	700,000	35,000 tests	20,000	15,000
		$5,300,000			

Action Plan

- Determine the activity-based overhead rate by dividing the estimated overhead per activity by the expected use of cost drivers per activity.
- Assign the overhead of each activity cost pool to the individual products by multiplying the expected use of the cost drivers per product by the activity-based overhead rate.
- Determine the overhead cost per unit by dividing the overhead assigned to each product by the number of units of that product.

Solution

(a) Calculations of activity-based overhead rates per cost driver:

Activity Cost Pools	Estimated Overhead	÷	Expected Use of Cost Drivers per Activity	=	Activity-Based Overhead Rates
Ordering and receiving	$ 200,000		2,500 purchase orders		$80 per order
Machine set-up	600,000		1,200 set-ups		$500 per set-up
Machining	2,000,000		800,000 machine hours		$2.50 per machine hour
Assembling	1,800,000		3,000,000 parts		$0.60 per part
Inspecting and testing	700,000		35,000 tests		$20 per test
Total	$5,300,000				

(b) Assignment of each activity's overhead cost to products, using ABC:

Activity Cost Pools	Scissors Jacks			Hydraulic Jacks		
	Expected Use of Cost Drivers per Product ×	Activity-Based Overhead Rates	= Cost Assigned	Expected Use of Cost Drivers per Product ×	Activity-Based Overhead Rates	= Cost Assigned
Ordering and receiving	1,000	$80	$ 80,000	1,500	$80	$ 120,000
Machine set-up	500	$500	250,000	700	$500	350,000
Machining	300,000	$2.50	750,000	500,000	$2.50	1,250,000
Assembling	1,800,000	$0.60	1,080,000	1,200,000	$0.60	720,000
Inspecting and testing	20,000	$20	400,000	15,000	$20	300,000
Total assigned costs			$2,560,000			$2,740,000

(c) Calculation of overhead cost per unit:

	Total costs assigned	Total units produced	Overhead cost per unit
Scissors Jack	$2,560,000	200,000	$12.80
Hydraulic Jack	$2,740,000	80,000	$34.25

(d) These data show that the total overhead assigned to 80,000 hydraulic jacks is nearly as great as the overhead assigned to 200,000 scissors jacks. However, the overhead cost per hydraulic jack is $34.25. It is only $12.80 per scissors jack.

Related exercise material: **BE5-6, BE5-7, E5-17, E5-19, E5-20, E5-21, E5-23,** and **Do It! D5-14**.

Benefits and Limitations of Activity-Based Costing

BENEFITS OF ABC

ABC has three primary benefits:

1. ABC leads to more cost pools and therefore more accurate product costing.
2. ABC leads to enhanced control over overhead costs.
3. ABC leads to better management decisions.

STUDY OBJECTIVE 3
Understand the benefits and limitations of activity-based costing.

The Advantage of Multiple Cost Pools

The main mechanism by which ABC increases product cost accuracy is the use of multiple cost pools. Instead of one plantwide pool (or even several departmental pools) and a single cost driver, companies use numerous activity cost pools with more relevant cost drivers. Thus, costs are allocated more directly on the basis of the cost drivers used to produce each product.

Note that in the Lift Jack Company example, the *manufacturing* cost pool reflected multiple manufacturing activities, including machining, assembling, and painting. These activities were included in a single pool for simplicity. In many companies, the number of activities—and thus the number of pools—can be substantial. For example, Clark-Hurth (a division of Clark Equipment Company), a manufacturer of axles and transmissions, identified over 170 activities. Compumotor (a division of Parker Hannifin) identified over 80 activities in just the procurement function of its Material Control Department. Illustration 5-12 shows the design of a more complex activity-based costing system with seven activity cost pools for Lift Jack Company. Lift Jack Company manufactures two automotive jacks: an automobile scissors jack and a truck hydraulic jack.

▶Illustration 5-12
ABC system design—Lift Jack Company

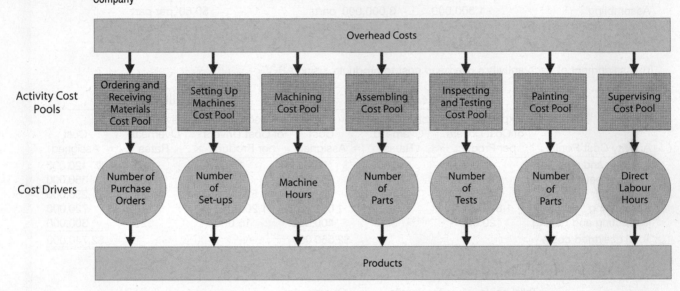

To gain the full advantage of having multiple cost pools, the costs within the pool must be correlated with the driver. To achieve this, a company's managers often characterize activities as belonging to one of the following four activity-level groups when designing an ABC system.

1. **Unit-level activities** are performed for each unit of production. For example, the assembly of cell phones is a unit-level activity because the amount of assembly the company performs increases with each additional cell phone assembled.
2. **Batch-level activities** are performed every time a company produces another batch of a product. For example, suppose that to start processing a new batch of ice cream, an ice cream producer needs to set up its machines. The amount of time spent setting up machines increases with the number of batches produced, not with the number of units produced.
3. **Product-level activities** are performed every time a company produces a new type of product. For example, before a pharmaceutical company can produce and sell a new type of medicine, it must undergo very substantial product tests to ensure the product is effective and safe. The amount of time spent on testing activities increases with the number of products the company produces.
4. **Facility-level activities** are required to support or sustain an entire production process. Consider, for example, a hospital. The hospital building must be insured and heated, and the property taxes must be paid, no matter how many patients the hospital treats. These costs do not vary as a function of the number of units, batches, or products.

Companies may achieve greater accuracy in overhead cost allocation by recognizing these four different levels of activities and, from them, developing specific activity cost pools and their related cost drivers. Illustration 5-13 graphically displays this four-level activity hierarchy, along with the types of activities and examples of cost drivers for those activities at each level.

Four Levels	Types of Activities	Examples of Cost Drivers
Unit-Level Activities	<u>Machine-related</u> Drilling, cutting, milling, trimming, pressing	Machine hours
	<u>Labour-related</u> Assembling, painting, sanding, sewing	Direct labour hours or cost
Batch-Level Activities	Equipment set-ups	Number of set-ups or set-up time
	Purchase ordering	Number of purchase orders
	Inspection	Number of inspections or inspection time
	Materials handling	Number of material moves
Product-Level Activities	Product design	Number of product designs
	Engineering changes	Number of changes
Facility-Level Activities	Plant management salaries	Number of employees managed
	Plant depreciation	Square footage
	Property taxes	Square footage
	Utilities	Square footage

►Illustration 5-13
Hierarchy of activity levels

The Advantage of Enhanced Cost Control

ABC leads to enhanced control over overhead costs. Under ABC, companies can trace many overhead costs directly to activities—allowing some costs previously considered to be indirect costs to be identified as direct costs. In developing an ABC system, managers increase their awareness of the activities performed by the company in its production and supporting processes. This awareness helps managers classify activities as value-added or non–valued-added.

Value-added activities are those activities of **a company's operations** that increase the perceived value of a product or service to customers. Examples of value-added activities in a manufacturing operation include engineering design, machining, assembly, and painting. Examples of value-added activities in a service company include performing surgery at a hospital, providing legal research at a law firm, or delivering packages by a freight company.

Non–value-added activities are those activities that, if eliminated, would not reduce the perceived value of a company's product or service. These activities simply **add cost to, or increase the time spent on, a product or service without increasing its perceived value**. One example is inventory storage. If a company eliminated the need to store inventory, it would not reduce the value of its product, but it would decrease its product costs. Other examples include moving materials, work in process, or finished goods from one location to another in the plant during the production process; waiting for manufacturing equipment to become available; inspecting goods; and fixing defective goods under warranty.

Companies often use **activity flowcharts** to help identify the ABC activities, such as the one shown in Illustration 5-14. The top part of this flowchart identifies activities as value-added (highlighted in red) or non–value-added. Two rows in the lower part of the flowchart show the number of days spent on each activity. The first row shows the number of days spent on each activity under the current manufacturing process. The second row shows the number of days expected to be spent on each activity under management's proposed reengineered manufacturing process.

►Illustration 5-14

Flowchart showing value-added and non–value-added activities

HEARTLAND MANUFACTURING COMPANY
Activity Flowchart

Activities

	NVA	NVA	NVA	NVA	VA		NVA	NVA	VA	NVA	NVA	NVA	VA
	Receive and Inspect Materials	Move and Store Materials	Move Materials to Production and Wait	Set Up Machines	Machining: Drill	Lathe	Inspect	Move and Wait	Assembly	Inspect and Test	Move to Storage	Store Finished Goods	Package and Ship
Current Days	1	12	2.5	1.5	2	1	0.2	6	2	0.3	0.5	14	1

◄———————————— *Total Current Average Time = 44 days* ————————————►

Proposed Days	1	4	1.5	1.5	2	1	0.2	2	2	0.3	0.5	10	1

◄———————————— *Total Proposed Average Time = 27 days* ————————————►

Proposed reduction in non–value-added time = 17 days

VA = value-added   NVA = non–value-added

The proposed changes would reduce time spent on non–value-added activities by 17 days. This 17-day improvement is due entirely to moving inventory more quickly through the non–value-added processes—that is, by reducing inventory time in moving, storage, and waiting.

Not all activities labelled non–value-added are totally wasteful, nor can they be totally eliminated. For example, although inspection time is a non–value-added activity from a customer's perspective, few companies would eliminate their quality control functions. Similarly, moving and waiting time is non–value-added, but it would be impossible to completely eliminate. Nevertheless, when managers recognize the non–value-added characteristic of these activities, they are motivated to minimize them as much as possible. Attention to such matters is part of the growing practice of activity-based management, which helps managers concentrate on **continuous improvement** of operations and activities.

the navigator

DECISION TOOLKIT

Decision Checkpoints	Info Needed for Decision	Tools to Use for Decision	How to Evaluate Results
How can ABC help managers manage the business?	Activities classified as value-added and non–value-added	The activity analysis flowchart extended to identify each activity as value-added or non–value-added	The flowchart should motivate managers to minimize non–value-added activities. Managers should better understand the relationship between activities and the resources they consume.

BUSINESS INSIGHT   *Paper Billing*

Processing customer transactions is a non–value-added activity. Several Canadian companies are trying to reduce transaction costs by charging customers for receiving a paper bill, up to $4 per month, because on-line billing is less costly. These companies are in industries such as banking, telecommunications, and public utilities. They argue that on-line billing is better for the environment and is more convenient for customers, and that customers who have moved to on-line billing shouldn't subsidize the transaction costs of those who receive a paper bill. The move to charge for paper bills is unpopular with consumers, many of whom feel that issuing paper bills is a cost of doing business and that those without Internet access should not be penalized. A survey of members of the Canadian Association of Retired Persons found that two thirds of them said they would move their business to another company that didn't charge for paper statements. The federal government announced in its fall 2013 Throne Speech that it intended to end the practice for telecommunications companies.

Sources: Ellen Roseman, "$2 Paper Phone Bill Fee in CRTC Crosshairs: Roseman," *Toronto Star*, October 27, 2013; Althia Raj, "Charging for Paper Bills: There Oughta Be A Law, Opposition Says," The Huffington Post Canada, October 1, 2013; Leslie MacKinnon, "Fees for Paper Billing Hurt Most Vulnerable, Says NDP," CBC News, November 7, 2012.

What are some ethical issues involved when companies pass on transaction costs to consumers?

The Advantage of Better Management Decisions

Some companies experiencing the benefits of activity-based costing have applied it to a broader range of management activities. **Activity-based management (ABM)** extends the use of ABC from product costing to a comprehensive management tool that focuses on reducing costs and improving processes and decision-making.

Managers extend the use of ABC via ABM for both strategic and operational decisions or perspectives. For example, returning to Atlas Company, its managers might use ABC information about The Boot and The Club to improve the efficiency of its operations. For example, after realizing that both products require a high volume of set-up hours—as well as the costs of these hours—they might want to reduce the hours required to set up production runs. Such information may lead managers to increase the number of units produced with each set-up or to optimize production schedules for the two products.

ABC also helps managers evaluate employees, departments, and business units. Atlas, for example, might use ABC information about salespeople's activities related to customer visits, number of orders, and post-sales customer service. Such information informs managers about how much effort salespeople are exerting, as well as how efficient they are in dealing with customers. Similarly, Atlas might use ABC information about each department's use of shared resources, like inventory space. Such information lets managers know which departments are the most efficient, which in turn leads to sharing best-practices information within the company. ABC information also helps Atlas to establish **performance standards** within the company, as well as **benchmark** its performance against other companies.

The implications of ABC are not limited to operational decisions. The differences in profitability between the The Boot and The Club may suggest a need to change the company's product mix. Such considerations, in turn, have implications for Atlas's marketing strategy. ABM may guide managers in considering different target customer markets for the two products. As another, more extreme, example, managers might consider outsourcing production for one of the products or dropping one of the product lines altogether.

It is often the case that ABM for one perspective has implications for another perspective. For instance, the strategic decision to drop a product line is usually followed by operational decisions regarding what to do with employees' time or the machinery and equipment originally used to manufacture the dropped product. Similarly, increases in employees' efficiency following

IFRS Notes
Depending on how the ABC system is designed, it may not conform to IFRS.

For instance, in ABC, nonmanufacturing costs may be included in overhead cost pools and allocated to products. However, under external reporting and IFRS, only manufacturing costs are inventoriable costs, and nonmanufacturing costs cannot be allocated to products. As a result, many organizations use ABC as a supplement to, rather than a replacement for, their existing cost system.

However, maintaining two cost systems is costlier than maintaining just one system and may cause confusion about which set of numbers to rely on.

A modified form of activity-based costing can be used to develop product costs for external financial reports compliant with IFRS if:

- fixed manufacturing costs are allocated to inventory based on normal capacity, and
- all nonmanufacturing costs are excluded.

from operational decisions often lead to changes in employee hiring and compensation strategy. The interrelated nature of the strategic and operational perspectives often means that a decision is not made until the cascading implications of that decision are also identified and considered.

LIMITATIONS OF ABC

ABC can be very beneficial, but it is not without its limitations. **ABC can be expensive to use**. The increased cost of identifying multiple activities and applying numerous cost drivers discourages many companies from using ABC. ABC systems are also more complex than traditional systems. So companies must ask, is the cost of implementation greater than the benefit of greater accuracy? For some companies, there may be no need to consider ABC at all because their existing system is sufficient.

Further, ABC does not offer complete accuracy because **some arbitrary allocations remain**. Even though more overhead costs can be assigned directly to products through ABC, some overhead costs still need to be allocated by arbitrary cost drivers, such as labour or machine hours.

In light of these limitations, how does a company know when to use ABC? The presence of one or more of the following factors would point to possible use:

1. Product lines differ greatly in volume and manufacturing complexity.
2. Product lines are numerous and diverse, requiring various degrees of support services.
3. Overhead costs constitute a significant portion of total costs.
4. The manufacturing process or the number of products has changed significantly; for example, from labour-intensive to capital-intensive due to automation.
5. Production or marketing managers are ignoring data provided by the existing system and are instead using "bootleg" costing data or other alternative data when pricing or making other product decisions.

Ultimately, it is important to realize that the redesign and installation of a product costing system is a significant decision that requires considerable costs and a major effort to accomplish. Therefore, financial managers need to be cautious and deliberate when initiating changes in costing systems. A key factor in implementing a successful ABC system is the support of top management, especially given that the benefits of ABC are not completely visible until *after* it has been implemented.

the navigator

DECISION TOOLKIT

Decision Checkpoints	Info Needed for Decision	Tools to Use for Decision	How to Evaluate Results
When should we use ABC?	Knowledge of the products or product lines, the manufacturing process, overhead costs, and managers' needs for accurate cost information	A detailed and accurate cost accounting system; co-operation between accountants and operating managers	Compare the results under both costing systems. If managers are better able to understand and control their operations using ABC, and the costs are not prohibitive, use of ABC would be beneficial.

BEFORE YOU GO ON...

▶Do It! Classify Activity Levels

Morgan Toy Company manufactures six primary product lines of toys in its Morganville plant. As a result of an activity analysis, the accounting department has identified eight activity cost pools. Each of the toy products is produced in large batches, with the whole plant devoted to one product at a time. Classify each of the following activities as either unit-level, batch-level, product-level, or facility-level: (a) engineering design, (b) machine set-up, (c) toy design, (d) interviews of prospective employees, (e) inspections after each set-up, (f) polishing parts, (g) assembling parts, and (h) health and safety.

Action Plan

- You should use **unit-level** activities for each unit of product, **batch-level** activities for each batch of product, **product-level** activities for an entire product line, and **facility-level** activities for across the entire range of products.

Solution

(a) Product-level. (b) Batch-level. (c) Product-level. (d) Facility-level. (e) Batch-level. (f) Unit-level. (g) Unit-level. (h) Facility-level.

Related exercise material: **BE5-10, BE5-11, BE5-12, E5-33, E5-34,** and **Do It! D5-15**.

the navigator

Activity-Based Costing in Service Industries

STUDY OBJECTIVE 4
Apply activity-based costing to service industries.

Although initially developed and implemented by manufacturers, activity-based costing is also widely used in service industries. ABC is used by airlines, railroads, hotels, hospitals, banks, insurance companies, telephone companies, and financial services firms. The overall objective of ABC in service firms is no different than it is in a manufacturing company. That objective is to identify the key activities that generate costs and to keep track of how many of those activities are completed for each service performed (by job, service, contract, or customer).

The general approach to identifying activities, activity cost pools, and cost drivers is the same for service companies and for manufacturers. Also, the labelling of activities as value-added and non–value-added, and the attempt to reduce or eliminate non–value-added activities as much as possible, is just as valid in service industries as in manufacturing operations. What sometimes makes implementation of activity-based costing difficult in service industries is that, compared with manufacturers, **a larger proportion of overhead costs are company-wide costs** that cannot be directly traced to specific services performed by the company.

To illustrate how activity-based costing is used in a service company contrasted to traditional costing, we use a public accounting firm. This illustration applies to any service firm that performs numerous services for a client as part of a job, such as a law firm, consulting firm, or architect.

TRADITIONAL COSTING EXAMPLE

Assume that the public accounting firm of Check and Doublecheck prepares the condensed annual budget shown in Illustration 5-15. The firm engages in a number of services, including audit, tax, and computer consulting.

Direct labour is often the professional service performed. Under traditional costing, direct labour is the basis for overhead application to each job. As shown in Illustration 5-15, the predetermined overhead rate of 50% is calculated by dividing the total estimated overhead cost by the total direct labour cost. To determine the operating income earned on any job, Check and Doublecheck applies overhead at the rate of 50% of actual direct professional labour costs incurred. For example, assume that Check and Doublecheck records $140,000 of actual direct professional labour cost during its audit of Plano Moulding Company, which was billed an audit fee of $260,000. Under traditional costing, using 50% as the rate for applying overhead to the job, Check and Doublecheck

►Illustration 5-15
Condensed annual budget of a service firm under traditional costing

CHECK AND DOUBLECHECK, CPAs
Annual Budget

Revenue		$4,000,000
Direct labour	$1,200,000	
Overhead (expected)	600,000	
Total costs		1,800,000
Operating income		$2,200,000

$$\frac{\text{Estimated overhead}}{\text{Direct labour cost}} = \text{Predetermined overhead rate}$$

$$\frac{\$600,000}{\$1,200,000} = 50\%$$

would calculate applied overhead and operating income related to the Plano Moulding Company audit as shown in Illustration 5-16.

►Illustration 5-16
Overhead applied under traditional costing system

CHECK AND DOUBLECHECK, CPAs
Plano Moulding Company Audit

Revenue		$260,000
Less: Direct professional labour	$140,000	
Applied overhead (50% × $140,000)	70,000	210,000
Operating income		$ 50,000

This example, under traditional costing, uses only one cost driver (direct labour cost) to determine the overhead application rate.

ACTIVITY-BASED COSTING EXAMPLE

Under *activity-based costing*, Check and Doublecheck distributes its estimated annual overhead costs of $600,000 to three activity cost pools. The firm calculates activity-based overhead rates per cost driver by dividing each activity overhead cost pool by the expected number of cost drivers used per activity. Illustration 5-17 shows an annual overhead budget using an ABC system.

CHECK AND DOUBLECHECK, CPAs
Annual Overhead Budget

Activity Cost Pools	Cost Drivers	Estimated Overhead	÷	Expected Use of Cost Drivers per Activity	=	Activity-Based Overhead Rates
Administration	Number of partner-hours	$335,000		3,350		$100 per partner-hour
Customer development	Revenue billed	160,000		$4,000,000		$0.04 per $1 of revenue
Recruiting and training	Direct professional hours	105,000		30,000		$3.50 per hour
		$600,000				

►Illustration 5-17
Condensed annual budget of a service firm under activity-based costing

The assignment of the individual overhead activity rates to the actual number of activities used in the performance of the Plano Moulding Company audit results in total overhead assigned of $57,200, as shown in Illustration 5-18.

▶Illustration 5-18
Assigning overhead in a service company

	A	B	C	D	E
1	**CHECK AND DOUBLECHECK, CPAs**				
2	Plano Moulding Company Audit				
3				Activity-	
4			Actual	Based	
5	Activity Cost Pools	Cost Drivers	Use of Drivers	Overhead Rates	Cost Assigned
6	Administration	Number of partner-hours	335	$100.00	$33,500
7	Customer development	Revenue billed	$260,000	$0.04	10,400
8	Recruiting and training	Direct professional hours	3,800	$3.50	13,300
9					$57,200
10					

Under activity-based costing, Check and Doublecheck assigns overhead costs of $57,200 to the Plano Moulding Company audit, as compared with $70,000 under traditional costing. Illustration 5-19 compares total costs and operating margins under the two costing systems.

▶Illustration 5-19
Comparison of traditional costing with ABC in a service company

CHECK AND DOUBLECHECK, CPAs
Plano Moulding Company Audit

	Traditional Costing		ABC	
Revenue		$260,000		$260,000
Expenses				
Direct professional labour	$140,000		$140,000	
Applied overhead	70,000		57,200	
Total expenses		210,000		197,200
Operating income		$ 50,000		$ 62,800
Profit margin		19.2%		24.2%

Illustration 5-19 shows that the assignment of overhead costs under traditional costing and ABC costing is different. The total cost assigned to performing the audit of Plano Moulding Company is greater under traditional costing by $12,800, and the profit margin is significantly lower. Traditional costing understates the profitability of the audit.

BEFORE YOU GO ON...

▶Do It! Apply ABC to Service Company

We Carry It, Inc. is a trucking company. It provides local, short-haul, and long-haul services. The company has developed the following thee cost pools.

Activity Cost Pools	Cost Drivers	Estimated Overhead	Expected Use of Cost Drivers per Activity
Loading and unloading	Number of pieces	$ 70,000	100,000 pieces
Travel	Kilometres driven	250,000	500,000 km
Logistics	Hours	60,000	2,000 hours

(a) Calculate the activity-based overhead rates for each pool.

(b) Determine the overhead allocated to Job A1027, which has 150 pieces and requires 200 km of driving and 0.75 hours of logistics.

(continued)

(continued)

Action Plan

- Divide the estimated overhead by the expected use of cost driver per activity to determine activity-based overhead rate.
- Apply the activity-based overhead rate to jobs based on actual use of drivers.

Solution

(a) The activity-based overhead rates are as follows.

Activity Cost Pools	Estimated Overhead	÷	Expected Use of Cost Drivers per Activity	=	Activity-Based Overhead Rate
Loading and unloading	$ 70,000		100,000 pieces		$0.70 per piece
Travel	250,000		500,000 km		$0.50 per km
Logistics	60,000		2,000 hours		$30 per hour

(b) The overhead applied to Job A1027 is (150 × $0.70) + (200 × $0.50) + (0.75 × $30) = $227.50

Related exercise material: **BE5-9, E5-21, E5-23,** and **Do It! D5-16.**

ALL ABOUT YOU   *Where Does the Time Go?*

A common practice of activity-based management is to try to reduce or eliminate time spent on non–value-added activities. One study found that knowledge workers spend an average of 41% of their time on discretionary activities. How much of your day is spent on activities that do not add value? In 2010, Canadians involved in these leisure activities spent an average of the following amounts per day doing this: 2 hours and 52 minutes watching TV, 1 hour and 23 minutes using a computer, or 2 hours and 20 minutes playing video games.

What Do You Think?

If you don't know where your time is going, try keeping track of everything you do for three to seven days and make notes every hour or so. Note the time; activity; whether it was scheduled, interrupted, or urgent; and the people involved. You may be surprised at how much time is wasted. Would this help you to manage time better?

> YES—There are a limited number of hours in a day. You should try to maximize your chances of achieving your goals by eliminating wasted time.

> NO—Being an efficiency expert doesn't guarantee that you will be happy. Schedules and daily planners are too constraining.

Sources: Julian Birkinshaw and Jordan Cohen, "Make Time for the Work that Matters," *Harvard Business Review,* September 2013; Statistics Canada, "General Social Survey: Time Use," *The Daily,* July 12, 2011; "Time Log Techniques," www.time-management-guide.com/time-log.html.

USING THE DECISION TOOLKIT

Preece Company manufactures a line of high-end exercise equipment of commercial quality. Assume that the controller has proposed changing from a traditional costing system to an activity-based costing system. The vice-president finance is not convinced, so she requests that the next large order for equipment be costed under both systems to compare and analyze. The company receives an order from Slim-Way Salons, Inc., for 150 low-impact treadmills, which the controller identifies as the order to use for dual costing. The following cost data relate to the Slim-Way order.

(continued)

(continued)

Data relevant to both costing systems:

Direct materials	$55,500
Direct labour hours	820
Direct labour rate per hour	$18.00

Data relevant to the traditional costing system:
   The predetermined overhead rate is 300% of direct labour cost.

Data relevant to the activity-based costing system:

Activity Cost Pools	Cost Drivers	Activity-Based Overhead Rate	Expected Use of Cost Drivers for the Order
Engineering design	Engineering hours	$30 per hour	330
Machine set-up	Set-ups	$200 per set-up	22
Machining	Machine hours	$25 per hour	732
Assembly	Number of sub-assemblies	$8 per sub-assembly	1,500
Packaging and shipping	Packaging/shipping hours	$15 per hour	152
Building occupancy	Machine hours	$6 per hour	732

Instructions
Calculate the total cost of the Slim-Way Salons, Inc., order under (a) the traditional costing system and (b) the activity-based costing system. (c) As a result of this comparison, which costing system is Preece likely to adopt? Why?

Solution

(a) Traditional costing system:

Direct materials		$ 55,500
Direct labour (820 × $18)		14,760
Overhead assigned ($14,760 × 300%)		44,280
Total costs assigned to Slim-Way order		$114,540
Number of low-impact treadmills		150
Cost per unit		$ 763.60

(b) Activity-based costing system:

Direct materials		$ 55,500
Direct labour (820 × $18)		14,760
Overhead activity costs:		
Engineering design (330 hours × $30)	$ 9,900	
Machine set-up (22 set-ups × $200)	4,400	
Machining (732 machine hours × $25)	18,300	
Assembly (1,500 sub-assemblies × $8)	12,000	
Packaging and shipping (152 hours × $15)	2,280	
Building occupancy (732 hours × $6)	4,392	51,272
Total costs assigned to Slim-Way order		$121,532
Number of low-impact treadmills		150
Cost per unit		$ 810.21

(c) Preece Company will likely adopt ABC because of the difference in the cost per unit (which ABC found to be higher). More importantly, ABC provides greater insight into the sources and causes of the cost per unit. Managers have a better understanding of which activities to control in order to reduce costs. ABC will provide better product costing and may improve profitability for the company.

the navigator

Summary of Study Objectives

1. *Recognize the difference between traditional costing and activity-based costing (ABC) and understand the nature of ABC.* A traditional costing system allocates overhead to products based on a predetermined plant-wide or department-wide volume of unit-based output rates, such as direct labour or machine hours. An ABC system allocates overhead to identify activity cost pools, and then assigns costs to products using related cost drivers that measure the activities (resources) consumed.

2. *Apply activity-based costing to a manufacturer.* The development of an activity-based costing system for a manufacturer involves four steps: (1) Identify and classify the major activities that pertain to the manufacture of specific products, and allocate manufacturing overhead costs to the appropriate cost pools. To identify activity cost pools, a company must perform an analysis of each operation or process, documenting and timing every task, action, or transaction. (2) Identify the cost driver that has a strong correlation to the costs accumulated in each activity cost pool. Cost drivers that companies identify for activity cost pools must (a) accurately measure the actual consumption of the activity by the various products, and (b) have data on them that are easily available. (3) Calculate the activity-based overhead rate per cost driver. (4) Use the cost drivers to assign overhead costs for each activity cost pool to products or services.

3. *Understand the benefits and limitations of activity-based costing.* What makes ABC a more accurate product costing system is (1) the increased number of cost pools used

to assign overhead, (2) the enhanced control over overhead costs, and (3) the better management decisions it makes possible. The limitations of ABC are (1) the higher analysis and measurement costs that accompany multiple activity centres and cost drivers, and (2) the need to still allocate some costs arbitrarily.

Value-added activities increase the worth of a product or service. Non–value-added activities simply add cost to, or increase the time spent on, a product or service without increasing its market value. Being aware of these classifications helps managers reduce or eliminate the time spent on the non–value-added activities.

Activities may be classified as unit-level, batch-level, product-level, and facility-level. A company controls overhead costs at unit, batch, product, and facility levels by modifying unit-, batch-, product-, and facility-level activities, respectively. Failure to recognize this classification of levels can result in distorted product costing.

4. *Apply activity-based costing to service industries.* The overall objective of using ABC in service industries is the same as in manufacturing industries; that is, improved costing of the services provided (by job, service, contract, or customer). The general approach to costing is the same: analyze operations, identify activities, accumulate overhead costs by activity cost pools, and identify and use cost drivers to assign the cost pools to the services.

DECISION TOOLKIT—A SUMMARY

Decision Checkpoints	Info Needed for Decision	Tools to Use for Decision	How to Evaluate Results
When should we use ABC?	Knowledge of the products or product lines, the manufacturing process, overhead costs, and managers' needs for accurate cost information	A detailed and accurate cost accounting system; co-operation between accountants and operating managers	Compare the results under both costing systems. If managers are better able to understand and control their operations using ABC, and the costs are not prohibitive, the use of ABC would be beneficial.
How can ABC help managers manage the business?	Activities classified as value-added or non–value-added	The activity analysis flowchart extended to identify each activity as value-added or non–value-added	The flowchart should motivate managers to minimize non–value-added activities. Managers should better understand the relationship between activities and the resources they consume.

Glossary

Activity Any event, action, transaction, or work sequence that causes a cost to be incurred in producing a product or providing a service. (p. 171)

Activity-based costing (ABC) An overhead cost allocation system that allocates overhead to multiple activity cost pools and assigns the activity cost pools to products or services by using cost drivers that represent the activities used. (p. 170)

Activity-based management (ABM) An extension of ABC from a product costing system to a management function that focuses on reducing costs and improving processes and decision-making. (p. 181)

Activity cost pool The overhead cost allocated to a distinct type of activity or related activities. (p. 171)

Batch-level activities Activities performed for each batch of products. (p. 178)

Cost driver Any factor or activity that has a direct cause–effect relationship with the resources consumed. In ABC, companies

use cost drivers to assign activity cost pools to products or services. (p. 171)

Facility-level activities Activities required to support or sustain an entire production process that are not dependent on the number of products, batches, or units produced. (p. 178)

Non–value-added activity An activity that adds cost to, or increases the time spent on, a product or service without increasing its market value. (p. 179)

Product-level activities Activities performed for and identifiable with an entire product line. (p. 178)

Unit-level activities Activities performed for each unit of production. (p. 178)

Value-added activity An activity that increases the worth of a product or service. (p. 179)

Comprehensive Do It!

Spreadwell Paint Company manufactures two high-quality base paints: an oil-based paint and a latex paint. Both paints are house paints and are manufactured in a neutral white colour only. The white base paints are sold to franchised retail paint and decorating stores, which add pigments to tint (colour) the paint as desired by the customer. The oil-based paint is made from petroleum products, and is thinned and cleaned with organic solvents such as mineral spirits or turpentine. The latex paint is made from water, and thinned and cleaned with it; synthetic resin particles that are suspended in the water dry and harden when exposed to the air.

Spreadwell uses the same processing equipment to produce both paints in different production runs. Between batches, the vats and other processing equipment must be washed and cleaned.

After analyzing the company's entire operations, Spreadwell's accountants and production managers have identified activity cost pools and have accumulated annual budgeted overhead costs for each pool as follows:

Activity Cost Pools	Estimated Overhead
Purchasing	$ 240,000
Processing (weighing and mixing, grinding, thinning and drying, straining)	1,400,000
Packaging (1-litre and 5-litre containers)	580,000
Testing	240,000
Storage and inventory control	180,000
Washing and cleaning equipment	560,000
Total annual budgeted overhead	$3,200,000

(continued)

(continued)

With further analysis, the company identified activity cost drivers and scheduled their expected use by product and activity as follows:

Activity Cost Pools	Cost Drivers	Expected Use of Cost Drivers per Activity	Expected Use of Cost Drivers per Product	
			Oil-Based	Latex
Purchasing	Purchase orders	1,500 orders	800	700
Processing	Litres processed	1,000,000 litres	400,000	600,000
Packaging	Containers filled	400,000 containers	180,000	220,000
Testing	Number of tests	4,000 tests	2,100	1,900
Storing	Average number of litres on hand	18,000 litres	10,400	7,600
Washing	Number of batches	800 batches	350	450

Spreadwell has budgeted 400,000 litres of oil-based paint and 600,000 litres of latex paint for processing during the year.

Instructions

(a) Prepare a schedule showing the calculations of the activity-based overhead rates.
(b) Prepare a schedule that assigns each activity's overhead cost pool to each product.
(c) Calculate the overhead cost per unit for each product.
(d) Classify each activity cost pool as value-added or non–value-added.

Action Plan

- Identify the major activities that pertain to the manufacture of specific products and allocate manufacturing overhead costs to activity cost pools.
- Identify the cost drivers that accurately measure each activity's contribution to the finished product.
- Calculate the activity-based overhead rates.
- Assign manufacturing overhead costs for each activity cost pool to products, using the activity-based overhead rates.

Solution to Comprehensive Do It!

(a) Calculations of activity-based overhead rates:

Activity Cost Pools	Estimated Overhead	Expected Use of Cost Drivers	Activity-Based Overhead Rates
Purchasing	$ 240,000	1,500 orders	$160 per order
Processing	1,400,000	1,000,000 litres	$1.40 per litre
Packaging	580,000	400,000 containers	$1.45 per container
Testing	240,000	4,000 tests	$60 per test
Storing	180,000	18,000 litres	$10 per litre
Washing	560,000	800 batches	$700 per batch
	$3,200,000		

(b) Assignment of activity cost pools to products: oil-based paint and latex paint

	Oil-Based Paint			Latex Paint		
Activity Cost Pools	Expected Use of Drivers	Overhead Rates	Cost Assigned	Expected Use of Drivers	Overhead Rates	Cost Assigned
Purchasing	800	$160	$ 128,000	700	$160	$ 112,000
Processing	400,000	$1.40	560,000	600,000	$1.40	840,000
Packaging	180,000	$1.45	261,000	220,000	$1.45	319,000
Testing	2,100	$60	126,000	1,900	$60	114,000
Storing	10,400	$10	104,000	7,600	$10	76,000
Washing	350	$700	245,000	450	$700	315,000
Total overhead assigned			$1,424,000			$1,776,000

(c) Calculation of overhead cost assigned per unit:

	Oil-Based Paint	Latex Paint
Total overhead cost assigned	$1,424,000	$1,776,000
Total litres produced	400,000	600,000
Overhead cost per litre	$3.56	$2.96

(d) Value-added activities: processing and packaging; Non–value-added activities: purchasing, testing, storing, and washing

the navigator

WileyPLUS Self-Test, Brief Exercises, Exercises, Problems—Set A, and many more components are available for practice in WileyPlus.

Self-Study Questions

Answers are at the end of the chapter.

(SO 1)   1. Activity-based costing (ABC)
   (a) can be used only in a process cost system.
   (b) focuses on units of production.
   (c) focuses on activities performed to produce a product.
   (d) uses only a single basis of allocation.

(SO 1)   2. Activity-based costing
   (a) is the initial phase of converting to a just-in-time operating environment.
   (b) can be used only in a job-order costing system.
   (c) is a two-stage overhead cost allocation system that identifies activity cost pools and cost drivers.
   (d) uses direct labour as its primary cost driver.

(SO 1, 2) 3. Any activity that causes resources to be consumed is called a
   (a) just-in-time activity.
   (b) facility-level activity.
   (c) cost driver.
   (d) non–value-added activity.

(SO 2)   4. The overhead rate for Machine Set-ups is $100 per set-up. Products A and B have 80 and 60 set-ups, respectively. The overhead assigned to each product is
   (a) Product A $8,000, Product B $8,000.
   (b) Product A $8,000, Product B $6,000.
   (c) Product A $6,000, Product B $6,000.
   (d) Product A $6,000, Product B $8,000.

(SO 2)   5. Donna Crawford Co. has identified an activity cost pool to which it has allocated estimated overhead of $1,920,000. It has determined the expected use of cost drivers for that activity to be 160,000 inspections. Widgets require 40,000 inspections, Gadgets 30,000 inspections, and Targets, 90,000 inspections. The overhead assigned to each product is
   (a) Widgets $40,000, Gadgets $30,000, Targets $90,000.
   (b) Widgets $480,000, Gadgets $360,000, Targets $108,000.
   (c) Widgets $360,000, Gadgets $480,000, Targets $1,080,000.
   (d) Widgets $480,000, Gadgets $360,000, Targets $1,080,000.

(SO 3)   6. An activity that adds costs to the product but does not increase its market value is a
   (a) value-added activity.
   (b) cost driver.
   (c) cost-benefit activity.
   (d) non–value-added activity.

(SO 3)   7. The following activity is value-added:
   (a) Storage of raw materials
   (b) Moving parts from machine to machine
   (c) Shaping a piece of metal on a lathe
   (d) All of the above.

(SO 3)   8. A relevant facility-level cost driver for heating costs is
   (a) machine hours.
   (b) direct material.
   (c) floor space.
   (d) direct labour costs.

(SO 1, 2) 9. An activity that has a direct cause–effect relationship with the resources consumed is a(n)
   (a) cost driver.
   (b) overhead rate.
   (c) cost pool.
   (d) product activity.

(SO 1, 2)10. The first step in activity-based costing is to
   (a) assign manufacturing overhead costs for each activity cost pool to products.
   (b) calculate the activity-based overhead rate per cost driver.
   (c) identify and classify the major activities involved in the manufacture of specific products.
   (d) identify the cost driver that has a strong correlation to the activity cost pool.

the navigator

Brief Exercises

BE5-1 Infotrac Inc. sells a high-speed retrieval system for information. It provides the following information for the year.

(SO 1)
Identify differences between costing systems.

	Budgeted	Actual
Overhead cost	$1,000,000	$950,000
Machine hours	50,000	45,000
Direct labour hours	100,000	92,000

Overhead is applied on the basis of machine hours.

(a) Calculate the predetermined overhead rate.

(b) Determine the amount of overhead applied for the year.

(c) Explain how an activity-based costing system might differ in terms of calculating a predetermined overhead rate.

(SO 1)
Identify differences between costing systems.

BE5-2   Sassafras Inc. has conducted an analysis of overhead costs related to one of its product lines using a traditional costing system (volume-based) and an activity-based costing system. Following are its results:

	Traditional Costing	ABC
Sales revenues	$600,000	$600,000
Overhead costs:		
Product RX3	$ 34,000	$ 50,000
Product Y12	36,000	20,000
	$ 70,000	$ 70,000

Explain how a difference in the overhead costs between the two systems may have occurred.

(SO 2)
Identify cost drivers.

BE5-3   Altex Co. identifies the following activities that pertain to manufacturing overhead: materials handling, machine set-ups, factory machine maintenance, factory supervision, and quality control. For each activity, identify an appropriate cost driver.

(SO 2)
Identify cost drivers.

BE5-4   Ayala Company manufactures four products in a single production facility. The company uses activity-based costing. The company has identified the following activities through its activity analysis: (a) inventory control, (b) machine set-ups, (c) employee training, (d) quality inspections, (e) material ordering, (f) drilling operations, and (g) building maintenance.

For each activity, name a cost driver that might be used to assign overhead costs to products.

(SO 2)
Calculate activity-based overhead activities.

BE5-5   Mordica Company identifies three activities in its manufacturing process: machine set-ups, machining, and inspections. Estimated annual overhead cost for each activity is $150,000, $325,000, and $87,500, respectively. The cost driver for each activity and the expected annual usage are: number of set-ups 2,500, machine hours 25,000, and number of inspections 1,750. Calculate the overhead rate for each activity.

(SO 2)
Calculate activity-based overhead rates.

BE5-6   Coats Galore, Inc. uses activity-based costing as the basis for information to set prices for its six lines of seasonal coats. Calculate the activity-based overhead rates using the following budgeted data for each of the activity cost pools.

Activity Cost Pools	Estimated Overhead	Expected Use of Cost Drivers per Activity
Designing	$ 450,000	10,000 designer hours
Sizing and cutting	4,000,000	160,000 machine hours
Stitching and trimming	1,440,000	80,000 labour hours
Wrapping and packing	336,000	32,000 finished units

(SO 2)
Calculate activity-based overhead rates.

BE5-7   Computer Parts, Inc., a manufacturer of computer chips, employs activity-based costing. The following budgeted data for each of the activity cost pools are provided below for the year 2016.

Activity Cost Pools	Estimated Overhead	Expected Use of Cost Drivers per Activity
Ordering and receiving	$ 90,000	12,000 orders
Etching	480,000	60,000 machine hours
Soldering	1,760,000	440,000 labour hours

For 2016, the company had 11,000 orders and used 50,000 machine hours, and labour hours totalled 500,000. What is the total overhead applied?

(SO 3)
Classify activities as value-added or non–value-added.

BE5-8   Hirani Novelty Company identified the following activities in its production and support operations. Classify each of these activities as either value-added or non–value-added.

(a) Purchasing
(b) Receiving
(c) Design engineering
(d) Storing inventory

(e) Cost accounting
(f) Moving work in process
(g) Inspecting and testing
(h) Painting and packing

BE5-9 Wu and Martin is an architectural firm that is contemplating the installation of activity-based costing. The following activities are performed daily by staff architects. Classify these activities as value-added or non–value-added: (a) designing and drafting, 3 hours; (b) staff meetings, 1 hour; (c) on-site supervision, 2 hours; (d) lunch, 1 hour; (e) consultation with client on specifications, 1.5 hours; (f) entertaining a prospective client for dinner, 2 hours.

(SO 3, 4)
Classify service company activities as value-added or non–value-added.

BE5-10 Quick Pix is a large digital processing centre that serves 130 outlets in grocery stores, service stations, camera and photo shops, and drug stores in 16 nearby towns. Quick Pix operates 24 hours a day, six days a week. Classify each of the following activity costs of Quick Pix as either unit-level, batch-level, product-level, or facility-level.

(a) Colour printing materials
(b) Photocopy paper
(c) Depreciation of machinery
(d) Set-ups for enlargements
(e) Supervisor's salary
(f) Ordering materials
(g) Pickup and delivery
(h) Commission to dealers
(i) Insurance on the building
(j) Loading developing machines

(SO 3, 4)
Classify activities according to level.

BE5-11 Tool Time, Inc. operates 20 injection moulding machines in the production of tool boxes of four different sizes, named the Apprentice, the Handyman, the Journeyman, and the Professional. Classify each of the following costs as unit-level, batch-level, product-level, or facility-level.

(a) First-shift supervisor's salary
(b) Powdered raw plastic
(c) Dies for casting plastic components
(d) Depreciation on injection moulding machines
(e) Changing dies on machines
(f) Moving components to the assembly department
(g) Engineering design
(h) Employee health and medical insurance coverage

(SO 3)
Classify activities according to level.

BE5-12 Spin Cycle Company uses three activity pools to apply overhead to its products. Each activity has a cost driver used to allocate the overhead costs to the product. The activities and related overhead costs are as follows: product design $40,000; machining $300,000; and material handling $100,000. The cost drivers and expected use are as follows.

(SO 2, 3)
Calculate rates and activity levels.

Expected Use of Cost Drivers	Activities	Cost Drivers per Activity
Product design	Number of product changes	10
Machining	Machine hours	150,000
Material handling	Number of set-ups	100

(a) Calculate the predetermined overhead rate for each activity.
(b) Classify each of these activities as unit-level, batch-level, product-level, or facility-level.

Do It! Review

D5-13

Instructions
Indicate whether the following statements are true or false.
(a) The reasoning behind ABC cost allocation is that products consume activities and activities consume resources.
(b) Activity-based costing is an approach for allocating direct labour to products.
(c) In today's increasingly automated environment, direct labour is never an appropriate basis for allocating costs to products.
(d) A cost driver is any factor or activity that has a direct cause–effect relationship with resources consumed.
(e) Activity-based costing segregates overhead into various cost pools in an effort to provide more accurate cost information.

(SO 1)
Identify characteristics of traditional and ABC costing systems.

D5-14 Weber Industries has three activity cost pools and two products. It expects to produce 3,000 units of Product BC113 and 1,400 of Product AD908. Having identified its activity cost pools and the cost drivers for each pool, Weber accumulated the following data relative to those activity cost pools and cost drivers.

(SO 2)
Calculate activity-based overhead rates and assign overhead using ABC.

Annual Overhead Data				Expected Use of Cost Drivers per Product	
Activity Cost Pool	Cost Drivers	Estimated Overhead	Expected Use of Cost Drivers per Activity	Product BC113	Product AD908
Machine set-up	Set-ups	$ 16,000	40	25	15
Machining	Machine hours	110,000	5,000	1,000	4,000
Packing	Orders	30,000	500	150	350

Instructions
(a) Prepare a schedule showing the calculations of the activity-based overhead rates per cost driver.
(b) Prepare a schedule assigning each activity's overhead cost to the two products.
(c) Calculate the overhead cost per unit for each product. (Round to nearest cent.)
(d) Comment on the comparative overhead cost per product.

(SO 3)
Classify activities according to level.

D5-15   Good Harvest Company manufactures four lines of garden tools. As a result of an activity analysis, the accounting department has identified eight activity cost pools. Each of the product lines is produced in large batches, with the whole plant devoted to one product at a time.

Instructions
Classify each of the following activities or costs as unit-level, batch-level, product-level, or facility-level.

(a) Machining parts
(b) Product design
(c) Plant maintenance
(d) Machine set-up

(e) Assembling parts
(f) Purchasing raw materials
(g) Property taxes
(h) Painting

(SO 4)
Apply ABC to a service company.

D5-16   Ready Ride is a trucking company. It provides local, short-haul, and long-haul services. It has developed the following three cost pools.

Activity Cost Pools	Cost Drivers	Estimated Overhead	Expected Use of Cost Driver per Activity
Loading and unloading	Number of pieces	$ 90,000	90,000
Travel	Kilometres driven	450,000	600,000
Logistics	Hours	75,000	3,000

Instructions
(a) Calculate the activity-based overhead rates for each pool.
(b) Determine the overhead allocated to Job XZ3275, which has 150 pieces, requires 200 km of driving, and 0.75 hours of logistics.

Exercises

(SO 1, 2)
Assign overhead using traditional costing and ABC.

E5-17   Elle Inc. has two types of handbags: standard and custom. The controller has decided to use a plant-wide overhead rate based on direct labour costs. The president has heard of activity-based costing and wants to see how the results would differ if this system were used. Two activity cost pools were developed: machining and machine set-up. Presented below is information related to the company's operations.

	Standard	Custom
Direct labour costs	$50,000	$100,000
Machine hours	500	1,000
Set-up hours	100	400

Total estimated overhead costs are $277,500. The overhead cost allocated to the machining activity cost pool is $177,000, and $100,500 is allocated to the machine set-up activity cost pool.

Instructions
(a) Calculate the overhead rate using the traditional (plant-wide) approach.
(b) Calculate the overhead rate using the activity-based costing approach.
(c) ▭▭▭▶ Determine the difference in allocation between the two approaches.

(SO 1)
Explain the difference between traditional and activity-based costing.

E5-18   Khan Inc. has conducted the following analysis related to its product lines using a traditional costing system (volume-based) and an activity-based costing system. Both the traditional and the activity-based costing systems include direct materials and direct labour costs.

Products	Sales Revenue	Total Costs Traditional	Total Costs ABC
Product 440X	$180,000	$55,000	$50,000
Product 137Y	160,000	50,000	35,000
Product 249S	70,000	15,000	35,000

Instructions
(a) For each product line, calculate operating income using the traditional costing system.
(b) For each product line, calculate operating income using the activity-based costing system.

(c) Using the following formula, calculate the percentage difference in operating income for each of Khan's product lines:
[Operating Income (ABC) − Operating Income (traditional cost)] ÷ Operating Income (traditional cost). (Round the percentage to two decimals.)

(d) Provide a rationale for why the costs for Product 440X are approximately the same using either the traditional or activity-based costing system.

E5-19 International Fabrics has budgeted overhead costs of $955,000. It has allocated overhead on a plant-wide basis to its two products (wool and cotton) using direct labour hours, which are estimated to be 477,500 for the current year. The company has decided to experiment with activity-based costing and has created two activity cost pools and related activity cost drivers. These two cost pools are cutting (the cost driver is machine hours) and design (the cost driver is the number of set-ups). Overhead allocated to the cutting cost pool is $400,000 and $555,000 is allocated to the design cost pool. Additional information related to these pools is as follows:

(SO 1, 2)
Assign overhead using traditional costing and ABC.

	Wool	Cotton	Total
Machine hours	100,000	100,000	200,000
Number of set-ups	1,000	500	1,500

Instructions

(a) Determine the amount of overhead allocated to the wool product line and the cotton product line using activity-based costing.

(b) What is the difference between the allocation of overhead to the wool and cotton product lines using activity-based costing versus the traditional approach, assuming direct labour hours were incurred evenly between the wool and cotton?

E5-20 Alonzo Inc. manufactures two products: car wheels and truck wheels. To determine the amount of overhead to assign to each product line, the controller, YuYu Ortega, has developed the following information:

(SO 1, 2)
Assign overhead using traditional costing and ABC.

	Car	Truck
Estimated wheels produced	40,000	10,000
Direct labour hours per wheel	2	6

Total estimated overhead costs for the two product lines are $840,000.

Instructions

(a) Calculate the overhead cost assigned to the car wheels and truck wheels, assuming that direct labour hours is used to allocate overhead costs.

(b) YuYu is not satisfied with the traditional method of allocating overhead because he believes that most of the overhead costs relate to the truck wheel product line because of its complexity. He therefore develops the following three activity cost pools and related cost drivers to better understand these costs:

Activity Cost Pools	Expected Use of Cost Drivers	Estimated Overhead Costs
Setting up machines	500 set-ups	$260,000
Assembling	35,000 labour hours	280,000
Inspection	600 inspections	300,000

Calculate the activity-based overhead rates for these three cost pools.

(c) Calculate the cost that is assigned to the car and truck product lines using an activity-based costing system, given the following information:

	Expected Use of Cost Drivers per Product	
	Car	Truck
Number of set-ups	100	400
Direct labour hours	20,000	15,000
Number of inspections	50	550

(d) What do you believe YuYu should do?

E5-21 Shady Lady sells window coverings to both commercial and residential customers. The following information relates to its budgeted operations for the current year:

(SO 1, 2, 4)
Assign overhead using traditional costing and ABC.

	Commercial		Residential	
Revenues		$300,000		$480,000
Direct material costs	$ 30,000		$ 70,000	
Direct labour costs	100,000		300,000	
Overhead costs	55,000	185,000	162,000	532,000
Operating income (loss)		$115,000		$ (52,000)

The controller, Susan Chan, is concerned about the residential product line. She cannot understand why this line is not more profitable given that window coverings are less complex to install for residential customers. In addition, the residential client base resides close to the company office, so travel costs are not as expensive on a per-client visit for residential customers. As a result, she has decided to take a closer look at the overhead costs assigned to the two product lines to determine whether a more accurate product costing model can be developed. Following are the three activity cost pools and related information she developed:

Activity Cost Pools	Estimated Overhead	Cost Drivers
Scheduling and travel	$84,000	Hours of travel
Set-up time	77,000	Number of set-ups
Supervision	56,000	Direct labour cost

	Expected Use of Cost Drivers per Product	
	Commercial	Residential
Scheduling and travel	1,000	680
Set-up time	450	250

Instructions

(a) Calculate the activity-based overhead rates for each of the three cost pools, and determine the overhead cost assigned to each product line.
(b) Calculate the operating income for each product line, using the activity-based overhead rates.
(c) What do you believe Susan Chan should do?

(SO 1, 2)
Assign overhead using traditional costing and ABC.

E5-22   Perdon Corporation manufactures safe—large mobile safes and large walk-in stationary bank safes. As part of its annual budgeting process, Perdon is analyzing the profitability of its two products. Part of this analysis involves estimating the amount of overhead to be allocated to each product line. The information shown below relates to overhead.

	Mobile Safes	Walk-In Safes
Units planned for production	200	50
Material moves per product line	300	200
Purchase orders per product line	450	350
Direct labour hours per product line	800	1,700

Instructions

(a) The total estimated manufacturing overhead was $260,000. Under traditional costing (which assigns overhead on the basis of direct labour hours), what amount of manufacturing overhead costs are assigned to:
1. One mobile safe?
2. One walk-in safe?
(b) The total estimated manufacturing overhead of $260,000 was composed of $160,000 for material handling costs and $100,000 for purchasing activity costs. Under activity-based costing (ABC):
1. What amount of material handling costs are assigned to:
   a. One mobile safe?
   b. One walk-in safe?
2. What amount of purchasing activity costs are assigned to:
   a. One mobile safe?
   b. One walk-in safe?
(c) Compare the amount of overhead allocated to one mobile safe and to one walk-in safe under the traditional costing approach versus under ABC.

(SO 2, 4)
Identify activity cost pools.

E5-23   Quik Prints Company is a small printing and copying firm with three high-speed offset printing presses, five copiers (two colour and three black and white), one collator, one cutting and folding machine, and one fax machine. To improve its pricing practices, owner-manager Damon Whitebone is installing activity-based accounting. Damon employs five employees: two printers/designers, one receptionist/bookkeeper, one salesperson/copy-machine operator, and one janitor/delivery clerk. Damon can operate any of the machines and, in addition to managing the entire operation, performs the training, designing, selling, and marketing functions.

Instructions

As Quik Prints' independent accountant who prepares tax forms and quarterly financial statements, you have been asked to identify the activities that would be used to accumulate overhead costs for assignment to jobs and customers. Using your knowledge of a small printing and copying firm (and some imagination), identify at least 12 activity cost pools as the start of an activity-based costing system for Quik Prints Company.

(SO 2)
Identify activity cost pools and cost drivers.

E5-24   Galavic Corporation manufactures snowmobiles in its Blue Mountain plant. It has budgeted the following costs for the first quarter's operations.

Machine set-up, indirect materials	$ 4,000	Property taxes	$ 29,000
Inspections	16,000	Oil, heating	19,000
Tests	4,000	Electricity, plant lighting	21,000
Insurance, plant	110,000	Engineering prototypes	60,000
Engineering design	140,000	Depreciation, plant	210,000
Depreciation, machinery	520,000	Electricity, machinery	36,000
Machine set-up, indirect labour	20,000	Custodial (machine maintenance) wages	19,000

Instructions

Classify the above costs of Galavic Corporation into activity cost pools using the following: engineering, machinery, machine set-up, quality control, factory utilities, and maintenance. Then identify a cost driver that may be used to assign each cost pool to each line of snowmobiles.

E5-25 Peter Catalano's Verde Vineyards, in the Niagara Peninsula, produces three varieties of wine: merlot, viognier, and pinot noir. His winemaster, Kyle Pohle, has identified the following activities as cost pools for accumulating overhead and assigning it to products.

(SO 2)
Identify activity cost drivers.

1. Culling and replanting: Dead or overcrowded vines are culled, and new vines are planted or relocated. (Each variety has a separate vineyard.)
2. Tying: The posts and wires are reset, and vines are tied to the wires for the dormant season.
3. Trimming: At the end of the harvest, the vines are cut and trimmed back in preparation for the next season.
4. Spraying: The vines are sprayed with chemicals for protection against insects and fungi.
5. Harvesting: The grapes are hand-picked, placed in carts, and transported to the crushers.
6. Stemming and crushing: Cartfuls of bunches of grapes of each variety are separately loaded into machines, which remove stems and gently crush the grapes.
7. Pressing and filtering: The crushed grapes are transferred to presses, which mechanically remove the juices and filter out bulk and impurities.
8. Fermentation: The grape juice, by variety, is fermented in either stainless-steel tanks or oak barrels.
9. Aging: The wines are aged in either stainless-steel tanks or oak barrels for one to three years, depending on the variety.
10. Bottling and corking: Bottles are machine-filled and corked.
11. Labelling and boxing: Each bottle is labelled, as is each nine-bottle case, with the name of the vintner, vintage, and variety.
12. Storing: Packaged and boxed bottles are stored awaiting shipment.
13. Shipping: The wine is shipped to distributors and private retailers.
14. Heating and air-conditioning of plant and offices.
15. Maintenance of buildings and equipment: Printing, repairs, replacements, and general maintenance are performed in the off-season.

Instructions

For each of Verde's 15 activity cost pools, identify a probable cost driver that might be used to assign overhead costs to its three wine varieties.

E5-26 Fontillas Instrument, Inc. manufactures two products: missile range instruments and space pressure gauges. During April, it produced 50 range instruments and 300 pressure gauges and incurred estimated overhead costs of $94,500. An analysis of estimated overhead costs reveals the following activities:

(SO 2, 3)
Calculate overhead rates, assign overhead using ABC, and discuss the advantages of ABC.

Activities	Cost Drivers	Total Cost
1. Materials handling	Number of requisitions	$40,000
2. Machine set-ups	Number of set-ups	27,500
3. Quality inspections	Number of inspections	27,000
		$94,500

The cost driver volume for each product was as follows:

Cost Drivers	Instruments	Gauges	Total
Number of requisitions	400	600	1,000
Number of set-ups	200	300	450
Number of inspections	200	400	600

Instructions

(a) Determine the overhead rate for each activity.
(b) Assign the manufacturing overhead costs for April to the two products using activity-based costing.
(c) ▭▭▭▭▷ Write a memorandum to the president of Fontillas Instrument explaining the benefits of activity-based costing.

(SO 2, 3)
Calculate overhead
rates and assign
overhead using ABC.

E5-27 H&Y Company uses four activity pools to apply overhead to its products. Each activity has a cost driver used to allocate the overhead costs to the product. The activities and related overhead costs are as follows:

Activity	Total Costs	Volume of Cost Driver
Material handling	$ 200,000	100,000 parts
Purchase orders	210,000	35 orders
Set-up hours	300,000	150 hours
Machining	480,000	3,000 machine hours
Total costs	$1,190,000	

The above activities are used by the two different products as follows:

	PC-21	WX-34
Material handling	75,000 parts	25,000 parts
Purchase orders per product	15	20
Set-up hours	100 hours	50 hours
Number of machine hours	2,000 machine hours	1,000 machine hours

Instructions
(a) Calculate how much of the material handling cost will be allocated to PC-21.
(b) Determine the ABC allocation rate for Purchase orders.
(c) Calculate how much of the Set-up costs will be allocated to WX-34.
(d) Calculate how much of the total activity costs will be allocated to PC-21.

(SO 1, 2, 3)
Assign overhead using
traditional costing
and ABC; classify
activities as
value-added or
non–value-added.

E5-28 Lim Clothing Company manufactures its own designed and labelled sports attire and sells its products through catalogue sales and retail outlets. While Lim has used activity-based costing in its manufacturing activities for years, it has always used traditional costing in assigning its selling costs to its product lines. Selling costs have traditionally been assigned to Lim's product lines at a rate of 80% of direct material costs. Its direct material costs for the month of March for Lim's "high-intensity" line of attire are $400,000. The company has decided to extend activity-based costing to its selling costs. Data relating to the high-intensity line of products for the month of March are as follows:

Activity Cost Pools	Cost Drivers	Overhead Rate	Number of Cost Drivers Used per Activity
Sales commissions	Dollar sales	$0.06 per dollar sales	$950,000
Advertising—TV/Radio	Minutes	$300 per minute	250
Advertising—Newspaper	Column inches	$10 per column inch	2,000
Catalogues	Catalogues mailed	$2.50 per catalogue	6,000
Cost of catalogue sales	Catalogue orders	$1 per catalogue order	9,000
Credit and collection	Dollar sales	$0.04 per dollar sales	$950,000

Instructions
(a) Calculate the selling costs to be assigned to the high-intensity line of attire for the month of March using
  1. the traditional product costing system (direct material cost is the cost driver), and
  2. activity-based costing.
(b) By what amount does the traditional product costing system under-cost or over-cost the high-intensity product line?
(c) Classify each of the activities as value-added or non–value-added.

(SO 1, 2, 3)
Assign overhead using
traditional costing and
ABC; classify activi-
ties as value-added or
non–value-added.

E5-29 Healthy Products, Inc. uses a traditional product costing system to assign overhead costs uniformly to all products. To meet Canadian Food Inspection Agency (CFIA) requirements and to assure its customers of safe, sanitary, and nutritious food, Healthy Products engages in a high level of quality control. It assigns its quality-control overhead costs to all products at a rate of 17% of direct labour costs. Its direct labour cost for the month of June for its low-calorie dessert line is $65,000. In response to repeated requests from its vice-president, finance, Healthy's management agrees to adopt activity-based costing. Data relating to the low-calorie dessert line for the month of June are as follows:

Activity Cost Pools	Cost Drivers	Rate	Number of Cost Drivers Used per Activity
Inspections of material received	Number of kilograms	$0.80 per kilogram	6,000 kilograms
In-process inspections	Number of servings	$0.33 per serving	10,000 servings
CFIA certification	Customer orders	$12.00 per order	420 orders

Instructions

(a) Calculate the quality-control overhead cost to be assigned to the low-calorie dessert product line for the month of June using
   1. the traditional product costing system (direct labour cost is the cost driver), and
   2. activity-based costing.
(b) By what amount does the traditional product costing system under-cost or over-cost the low-calorie dessert line?
(c) Classify each of the activities as value-added or non–value-added.

E5-30 In an effort to expand the usefulness of its activity-based costing system, Peter Catalano's Verde Vineyards decides to adopt activity-based management techniques (ABM). One of these ABM techniques is classifying its activities as either value-added or non–value-added.

(SO 3)
Classify activities as value-added or non–value-added.

Instructions

Using Verde's list of 15 activity cost pools in E5-25, classify each of the activities as either value-added or non–value-added.

E5-31 Anna Bellatorre, Inc. is interested in using its activity-based costing system to improve its operating efficiency and its profit margins by applying activity-based management techniques. As part of this undertaking, you have been asked to classify its plant activities as value-added or non–value-added.

(SO 3)
Classify activities as value-added or non–value-added.

Instructions

Using the list of activities below, classify each activity as either value-added or non–value-added.

(a) Designing new models
(b) Purchasing raw materials and parts
(c) Storing and managing inventory
(d) Receiving and inspecting raw materials and parts
(e) Interviewing and hiring new personnel
(f) Machine forming sheet steel into appliance parts

(g) Manually assembling parts into appliances
(h) Training all employees of the company
(i) Insuring all tangible fixed assets
(j) Supervising production
(k) Maintaining and repairing machinery and equipment
(l) Painting and packaging finished appliances

E5-32 Duplessis and Najarali is a law firm that is initiating an activity-based costing system. Réjean Duplessis, the senior partner and a strong supporter of ABC, has prepared the following list of activities performed by a typical lawyer in a day at the firm:

(SO 3, 4)
Classify service company activities as value-added or non–value-added.

Activities	Hours
Writing contracts and letters	1.0
Attending staff meetings	0.5
Taking depositions	1.0
Doing research	1.0
Travelling to/from court	1.0
Contemplating legal strategy	1.0
Eating lunch	1.0
Litigating a case in court	2.5
Entertaining a prospective client	2.0

Instructions

Classify each of the activities listed by Réjean Duplessis as value-added or non–value-added and defend your classification. How much time was value-added and how much was non–value-added?

E5-33 Having itemized its costs for the first quarter of next year's budget, Galavic Corporation wants to install an activity-based costing system. First, it identified the activity cost pools in which to accumulate factory overhead; second, it identified the relevant cost drivers. (This was done in E5-24.)

(SO 3)
Classify activities by level.

Instructions

Using the activity cost pools identified in E5-24, classify each of those cost pools as either unit-level, batch-level, product-level, or facility-level.

E5-34 Otto Dieffenbach & Sons, Inc. is a small manufacturing company that uses activity-based costing. Dieffenbach & Sons accumulates overhead in the following activity cost pools.

(SO 3)
Classify activities by level.

1. Hiring personnel
2. Managing parts inventory
3. Purchasing
4. Testing prototypes
5. Designing products

6. Setting up equipment
7. Training employees
8. Inspecting machine parts
9. Machining
10. Assembling

Instructions

For each activity cost pool, indicate whether the activity cost pool would be unit-level, batch-level, product-level, or facility-level.

Problems: Set A

(SO 1, 2, 3)
Assign overhead using traditional costing and ABC; calculate unit costs; classify activities as value-added or non–value-added.

P5-35A FireOut, Inc. manufactures steel cylinders and nozzles for two models of fire extinguishers: (1) a home fire extinguisher and (2) a commercial fire extinguisher. The home model is a high-volume (54,000 units), half-litre cylinder that holds 2.5 kilograms of multi-purpose dry chemical at 480 PSI (pounds per square inch). The commercial model is a low-volume (10,200 units), two-litre cylinder that holds 10 kilograms of multi-purpose dry chemical at 390 PSI. Both products require 1.5 hours of direct labour for completion. Therefore, total annual direct labour hours are 96,300 or [1.5 hrs. × (54,000 + 10,200)]. Expected annual manufacturing overhead is $1,502,280. Thus, the predetermined overhead rate is $15.60 or ($1,502,280 ÷ 96,300) per direct labour hour. The direct materials cost per unit is $18.50 for the home model and $26.50 for the commercial model. The direct labour cost is $19 per unit for both the home and the commercial models.

The company's managers identified six activity cost pools and related cost drivers, and accumulated overhead by cost pool as follows:

Activity Cost Pools	Cost Drivers	Estimated Overhead	Expected Use of Cost Drivers	Expected Use of Drivers by Product	
				Home	Commercial
Receiving	Kilograms	$ 70,350	335,000	215,000	120,000
Forming	Machine hours	150,500	35,000	27,000	8,000
Assembling	Number of parts	390,600	217,000	165,000	52,000
Testing	Number of tests	51,000	25,500	15,500	10,000
Painting	Litres	52,580	5,258	3,680	1,578
Packing and shipping	Kilograms	787,250	335,000	215,000	120,000
		$1,502,280			

Instructions

(a) Unit cost—Home model $60.90

(c) Cost assigned—Home model $1,031,300

(d) Cost/unit—Home model $56.60

(a) Under traditional product costing, calculate the total unit cost of each product. Prepare a simple comparative schedule of the individual costs by product (similar to Illustration 5-4).

(b) Under ABC, prepare a schedule showing the calculations of the activity-based overhead rates (per cost driver).

(c) Prepare a schedule assigning each activity's overhead cost pool to each product based on the use of cost drivers. (Include a calculation of overhead cost per unit, rounding to the nearest cent.)

(d) Calculate the total cost per unit for each product under ABC.

(e) Classify each of the activities as a value-added activity or a non–value-added activity.

(f) Comment on

1. the comparative overhead cost per unit for the two products under ABC, and

2. the comparative total costs per unit under traditional costing and ABC.

(SO 1, 2)
Assign overhead costs using traditional costing and ABC; compare results.

P5-36A Allen Inc. is a manufacturer of quality shoes. The company has always used a plant-wide allocation rate for allocating manufacturing overhead to its products. The plant manager believes it is time to change to a better method of cost allocation. The accounting department has established the following relationships between production activities and manufacturing overhead costs:

Activities	Cost Drivers	Allocation Rate
Material handling	Number of parts	$ 8 per part
Assembly	Labour hours	80 per hour
Inspection	Time spent by item at inspection station	12 per minute

The previous plant-wide allocation rate method was based on direct manufacturing labour hours, and if that method is used, the allocation rate is $800 per labour hour.

Instructions

(a) $40 per pair

(b) $36.72 per pair

(a) Assume that a batch of 1,000 pairs of shoes requires 4,000 parts, 50 direct manufacturing labour hours, and 60 minutes of inspection time. What are the indirect manufacturing costs per pair of shoes to produce a batch of 1,000 pairs of shoes, assuming the previous plant-wide allocation rate method is used?

(b) What are the indirect manufacturing costs per pair of shoes to produce a batch of 1,000 pairs of shoes, assuming the activity-based method of allocation is used?

(c) Comment on the results.

(adapted from CMA Canada, now CPA Canada)

(SO 2)
Assign overhead to products using ABC and evaluate the decision.

P5-37A Jacobson Electronics manufactures two HD television models: the Royale, which sells for $1,400, and a new model, the Majestic, which sells for $1,100. The production costs calculated per unit under traditional costing for each model in 2016 were as follows:

Traditional Costing	Royale	Majestic
Direct materials	$600	$320
Direct labour ($20 per hour)	100	80
Manufacturing overhead ($35 per direct labour hour)	175	140
Total per unit cost	$875	$540

In 2016, Jacobson manufactured 20,000 units of the Royale and 10,000 units of the Majestic. The overhead rate of $35 per direct labour hour was determined by dividing total expected manufacturing overhead of $4.9 million by the total direct labour hours (140,000) for the two models.

Under traditional costing, the gross profit on the models was $525 for the Royale or ($1,400 − $875), and $560 for the Majestic or ($1,100 − $540). Because of this difference, management is considering phasing out the Royale model and increasing the production of the Majestic model.

Before finalizing its decision, management asks Jacobson's controller to prepare an analysis using activity-based costing (ABC). The controller accumulates the following information about overhead for the year ended December 31, 2016:

Activity Cost Pools	Cost Drivers	Estimated Overhead	Expected Use of Cost Drivers	Activity-Based Overhead Rate
Purchasing	Number of orders	$ 750,000	25,000	$30 per order
Machine set-ups	Number of set-ups	600,000	20,000	30 per set-up
Machining	Machine hours	3,100,000	100,000	31 per hour
Quality control	Number of inspections	450,000	5,000	90 per inspection

The cost drivers used for each product were as follows:

Cost Drivers	Royale	Majestic	Total
Purchase orders	11,250	13,750	25,000
Machine set-ups	10,000	10,000	20,000
Machine hours	40,000	60,000	100,000
Inspections	2,250	2,750	5,000

Instructions

(a) Assign the total 2016 manufacturing overhead costs to the two products using activity-based costing (ABC).
(b) What was the cost per unit and gross profit of each model using ABC costing?
(c) ✏️⟹ Are management's future plans for the two models sound? Explain.

(a) Royale $2,080,000
(b) Cost/unit—Royale $804

P5-38A Kiddy Company manufactures bicycles. It recently received a request to manufacture 10 units of a mountain bike at a price lower than it normally accepts. Bruce, the sales manager, indicated that if the order were accepted at that price, the company could expect additional orders from the same client. Bruce believes that if Kiddy could offer this price in the market generally, sales of this bike would increase by 30%. Melany, president of Kiddy, is skeptical about accepting the order. The company has a policy of not accepting any order that does not provide a markup of 20% on full manufacturing costs. The price offered is $575 per bike.

(SO 1, 2)
Assign overhead costs using traditional costing and ABC; compare results.

The controller, Sanjay, has recently researched the possibility of using activity-based multiple overhead rates instead of the single rate currently in use. He has promised more accurate estimated overhead product costing, and Melany is curious about how this approach would affect product costing and pricing of the mountain bike.

The plant-wide overhead rate is based on an expected volume of 10,000 direct labour hours and the following budgeted overhead:

Machine operating costs	$ 75,000
Rework labour	45,000
Inspection	25,000
Scrap costs	35,000
General factory overhead	120,000
Total	$300,000

Expected activities for selected cost drivers for 2016:

Machine hours	25,000
Units reworked	600
Inspection hours	500
Units scrapped	140
Direct labour hours	12,000

Estimated data for the production of one mountain bike:

Direct materials	$ 160
Direct labour (7.5 hours/unit)	$ 180
Number of machine hours	6
Number of units reworked	0.25
Number of inspection hours	0.10
Number of units scrapped	0.05

Instructions

(a) Price of bicycle: $678

(a) Using the single-rate method to assign overhead on a plant-wide basis, determine whether or not Kiddy should accept the order for the 10 mountain bikes. Explain your decision.

(b) Price using ABC: $563.10

(b) Using activity-based costing to assign overhead, determine whether or not Kiddy should accept the order for the 10 mountain bikes. Explain your decision.

(adapted from CGA-Canada, now CPA Canada)

(SO 1, 2)
Assign overhead costs using traditional costing and ABC; compare results

P5-39A   Stellar Stairs Co. designs and builds factory-made premium wooden stairs for homes. The manufactured stair components (spindles, risers, hangers, hand rails) permit installation of stairs of varying lengths and widths. All are made of white oak wood. The company's budgeted manufacturing overhead costs for 2016 are as follows:

Overhead Cost Pools	Amount
Purchasing	$ 69,000
Handling materials	82,000
Production (cutting, milling, finishing)	210,000
Setting up machines	95,000
Inspecting	90,000
Inventory control (raw materials and finished goods)	126,000
Utilities	180,000
Total budget overhead costs	$852,000

For the last four years, Stellar Stairs Co. has been charging overhead to products on the basis of machine hours. For 2016, it has budgeted 100,000 machine hours.

Heather Fujar, owner-manager of Stellar Stairs Co., recently directed her accountant, Kiko Nishikawa, to implement the activity-based costing system that she has repeatedly proposed. At Heather Fujar's request, Kiko and the production foreperson identify the following cost drivers and their usage for the previously budgeted overhead cost pools.

Activity Cost Pools	Cost Drivers	Expected Use of Cost Drivers
Purchasing	Number of orders	600
Handling materials	Number of moves	8,000
Production		
(cutting, milling, finishing)	Direct labour hours	100,000
Setting up machines	Number of set-ups	1,250
Inspecting	Number of inspections	6,000
Inventory control		
(raw materials and finished goods)	Number of components	168,000
Utilities	Square metres occupied	9,000

Jason Dion, sales manager, has received an order for 280 stairs from Community Builders, Inc., a large housing development contractor. At Jason's request, Kiko prepares cost estimates for producing components for 280 stairways so Jason can submit a contract price per stair to Community Builders. She accumulates the following data for the production of 280 stairways:

Direct materials	$103,600
Direct labour	112,000
Machine hours	14,500
Direct labour hours	5,000
Number of purchase orders	60
Number of material moves	800
Number of machine set-ups	100
Number of inspections	450
Number of components	16,000
Number of square metres occupied	800

Instructions

(b) Cost/stairway $1,211.21

(c) Cost/stairway $1,012.68

(a) Calculate the predetermined overhead rate using traditional costing with machine hours as the basis.

(b) What is the manufacturing cost per stairway under traditional costing? (Round to the nearest cent.)

(c) What is the manufacturing cost per stairway under the proposed activity-based costing? (Round to the nearest cent. Prepare all of the necessary schedules.)

(d) ▭▭▭▭▷ Which of the two costing systems is preferable in pricing decisions and why?

P5-40A International Steel Company has budgeted manufacturing overhead costs of $1,930,000. It has allocated overhead on a plant-wide basis to its two products (soft steel and hard steel) using machine hours, which are estimated to be 90,000 for the current year. The company has decided to experiment with activity-based costing and has created five activity cost pools and related activity cost drivers as follows:

(SO 1, 2)
Assign overhead costs using traditional costing and ABC; compare results.

Activity Centre	Cost Driver	Estimated Overhead	Expected Activity
Material handling	Number of moves	$280,000	40,000 moves
Purchase orders	Number of orders	$100,000	1,200 orders
Product testing	Number of tests	$420,000	3,500 tests
Machine set-up	Number of set-ups	$320,000	5,000 set-ups
Machining	Machine hours	$810,000	90,000 machine hours

Each unit of the products requires the following:

	Soft Steel	Hard Steel
Direct materials costs	$300	$200
Direct labour costs	$120	$60
Purchase orders	2	3
Machine set-up	5	10
Product testing	3	4
Machining	50	50
Material handling	4	6

Instructions

(a) Under traditional product costing using machine hours, calculate the total manufacturing cost per unit of both products.
(b) Under ABC, prepare a schedule showing the calculation of the activity-based overhead rates (per cost driver).
(c) Calculate the total manufacturing cost per unit for both products under ABC.
(d) ✏️▶ Write a memo to the president of the company discussing the implications of your analysis for the company's plans. In this memo, provide a brief description of ABC, as well as an explanation of how the traditional approach can result in distortions.

(a) Hard Steel: $1,332
(b) Soft Steel: $1,325
(c) Hard Steel: $2,122

P5-41A Hy and van Lamsweerde is a public accounting firm that offers two primary services, auditing and tax return preparation. A controversy has developed between the partners of the two service lines regarding who is contributing the greater amount to the bottom line. The area of contention is the assignment of overhead. The tax partners argue for assigning overhead on the basis of 40% of direct labour dollars, while the audit partners argue for implementing activity-based costing. The partners agree to use next year's budgeted data for analysis and comparison. The following overhead data are collected:

(SO 1, 2, 3, 4)
Assign overhead costs to services using traditional costing and ABC; calculate overhead rates and unit costs; compare results.

Activity Cost Pools	Cost Drivers	Estimated Overhead	Expected Use of Cost Drivers	Expected Use of Cost Drivers per Service Audit	Expected Use of Cost Drivers per Service Tax
Employee training	Direct labour dollars	$216,000	$1,800,000	$1,050,000	$750,000
Typing and secretarial	Number of reports and forms	76,200	2,500	800	1,700
Computing	Number of minutes	204,000	60,000	25,000	35,000
Facility rental	Number of employees	142,500	40	22	18
Travel	Per expense reports	81,300	Direct	56,000	25,300
		$720,000			

Instructions

(a) Using traditional product costing as proposed by the tax partners, calculate the total overhead cost assigned to both services (audit and tax) of Hy and van Lamsweerde.
(b) 1. Using activity-based costing, prepare a schedule showing the calculations of the activity-based overhead rates (per cost driver).
    2. Prepare a schedule assigning each activity's overhead cost pool to each service based on the use of the cost drivers.
(c) Classify each of the activities as a value-added activity or a non–value-added activity.
(d) Comment on the comparative overhead cost for the two services under both traditional costing and ABC.

(b) (2) Cost assigned—
Tax $350,241

(d) Difference—Audit
$50,241

P5-42A GoGo Ltd. manufactures three models of children's swing sets: Standard, Deluxe, and Super. The Standard set is made of steel, the Deluxe set is made of aluminum, and the Super set is made of a titanium-aluminum alloy. Because of the different materials used, production requirements differ significantly across models in terms of machine types and time requirements. However, once the parts are produced, assembly time per set is similar for the three models. For this reason, GoGo has adopted the practice of allocating overhead costs on the basis of machine hours. Last year, the company

(SO 1, 2)
Assign overhead costs using traditional costing and ABC; compare results.

produced 5,000 Standard sets, 500 Deluxe sets, and 2,000 Super sets. The company had the following revenues and expenses for the year:

GOGO LTD.
Income Statement
Year Ended December 31, 2016

	Standard	Deluxe	Super	Total
Sales	$475,000	$380,000	$560,000	$1,415,000
Direct costs:				
Direct materials	200,000	150,000	240,000	590,000
Direct labour	54,000	14,000	24,000	92,000
Variable overhead costs:				
Machine set-ups	?	?	?	25,000
Order processing	?	?	?	60,000
Warehouse	?	?	?	90,000
Shipping	?	?	?	35,000
Contribution margin	?	?	?	523,000
Fixed overhead costs:				
Plant administration				88,000
Other				182,000
Gross profit				$ 253,000

The chief financial officer of GoGo has hired a consultant to recommend cost allocation bases. The consultant has recommended the following:

		Activity Level			
Activities	Cost Drivers	Standard	Deluxe	Super	Total
Machine set-ups	No. of production runs	22	11	17	50
Sales order processing	No. of sales orders received	300	200	300	800
Warehouse costs	No. of units held in inventory	200	100	100	400
Shipping	No. of units shipped	5,000	500	2,000	7,500

The consultant found no basis for allocating the plant administration and other fixed overhead costs, and recommended that they not be applied to products.

Instructions

(a) CM for Super: $233,166

(a) Complete the income statement using the bases recommended by the consultant. Do not allocate any fixed overhead costs.

(b) Explain how activity-based costing might result in better decisions by GoGo's management.

(adapted from CGA-Canada, now CPA Canada)

Problems: Set B

(SO 1, 2, 3)
Assign overhead using traditional costing and ABC; calculate unit costs; classify activities as value-added or non–value-added.

P5-43B VidPlayers, Inc. manufactures two types of DVD players, a deluxe model and a standard model. The deluxe model is a multi-format progressive-scan DVD player with networking capability, Dolby digital, and DTS decoder. The standard model's primary feature is progressive-scan. Annual production is 20,000 units for the deluxe and 50,000 units for the standard.

Both products require two hours of direct labour for completion. Therefore, total annual direct labour hours are 140,000 or 2 hrs. × (20,000 + 50,000). Expected annual manufacturing overhead is $980,000. Thus, the predetermined overhead rate is $7 or ($980,000 ÷ 140,000) per direct labour hour. The direct materials cost per unit is $11 for the deluxe model and $42 for the standard model. The direct labour cost is $18 per unit for both the deluxe and the standard models.

The company's managers identified six activity cost pools and related cost drivers and accumulated overhead by cost pool as follows.

				Expected Use of Drivers by Product	
Activity Cost Pool	Cost Driver	Estimated Overhead	Expected Use of Cost Drivers	Deluxe	Standard
Purchasing	Orders	$130,000	500	150	350
Receiving	Kilograms	30,000	20,000	4,000	16,000
Assembling	Number of parts	370,000	74,000	20,000	54,000
Testing	Number of tests	115,000	23,000	10,000	13,000
Finishing	Units	140,000	70,000	20,000	50,000
Packing and shipping	Kilograms	195,000	78,000	17,000	61,000
		$980,000			

Instructions

(a) Under traditional product costing, calculate the total unit cost of both products. Prepare a simple comparative schedule of the individual costs by product.

(b) Under ABC, prepare a schedule showing the calculations of the activity-based overhead rates (per cost driver).

(c) Prepare a schedule assigning each activity's overhead cost pool to each product based on the use of cost drivers. (Include a calculation of overhead cost per unit, rounding to the nearest cent.)

(d) Calculate the total cost per unit for each product under ABC.

(e) Classify each of the activities as a value-added activity or a non–value-added activity.

(f) Comment on

1. the comparative overhead cost per unit for the two products under ABC, and

2. the comparative total costs per unit under traditional costing and ABC.

(a) Unit cost—Deluxe $43

(c) Cost assigned—
    Deluxe $277,500

(d) Cost/unit—Deluxe
    $42.88

P5-44B Tough Thermos, Inc. manufactures two plastic thermos containers at its plastic moulding facility in Lethbridge, Alberta. Its large container, called the Ice House, has a volume of five litres, side carrying handles, a snap-down lid, and a side drain and plug. Its smaller container, called the Cool Chest, has a volume of two litres, an over-the-top carrying handle, which is part of a tilting lid, and a removable shelf. Both containers and their parts are made entirely of hard-moulded plastic. The Ice House sells for $35 and the Cool Chest sells for $24. The production costs calculated per unit under traditional costing for each model in 2016 were as follows:

(SO 2)
Assign overhead to products using ABC and evaluate decision.

Traditional Costing	Ice House	Cool Chest
Direct materials	$ 9.50	$ 6.00
Direct labour ($10 per hour)	8.00	5.00
Manufacturing overhead ($17.08 per direct labour hour)	13.66	8.54
Total per unit cost	$31.16	$19.54

In 2016, Tough Thermos manufactured 50,000 units of the Ice House and 20,000 units of the Cool Chest. The overhead rate of $17.08 per direct labour hour was determined by dividing total expected manufacturing overhead of $854,000 by the total direct labour hours (50,000) for the two models.

Under traditional costing, the gross profit on the two containers was $3.84 for the Ice House or $35 − $31.16, and $4.46 for the Cool Chest or $24 − $19.54. The gross margin rates on cost are 12% for the Ice House or $3.84 ÷ $31.16, and 23% for the Cool Chest or $4.46 ÷ $19.54. Because Tough Thermos can earn a gross margin rate on the Cool Chest that is nearly twice as great as that earned on the Ice House, with less investment in inventory and labour costs, its management is urging its sales staff to put its efforts into selling the Cool Chest over the Ice House.

Before finalizing its decision, management asks the controller Sven Meza to prepare a product costing analysis using activity-based costing (ABC). Meza accumulates the following information about overhead for the year ended December 31, 2016:

Activities	Cost Drivers	Estimated Overhead	Expected Use of Cost Drivers	Activity-Based Overhead Rate
Purchasing	Number of orders	$179,000	4,475	$40 per order
Machine set-ups	Number of set-ups	195,000	780	$250 per set-up
Extruding	Machine hours	320,000	80,000	$4 per machine hour
Quality control	Tests and inspections	160,000	8,000	$20 per test

The cost drivers used for each product were the following:

Cost Drivers	Ice House	Cool Chest	Total
Purchase orders	2,500	1,975	4,475
Machine set-ups	480	300	780
Machine hours	60,000	20,000	80,000
Tests and inspections	5,000	3,000	8,000

Instructions

(a) Assign the total 2016 manufacturing overhead costs to the two products using activity-based costing (ABC).

(b) What was the cost per unit and gross profit of each model using ABC costing?

(c) ▭▭▭▷ Are management's future plans for the two models sound?

(a) Ice House $560,000

(b) Ice House cost/unit:
    $28.70

P5-45B Mars Company has four categories of overhead: purchasing and receiving materials, machine operating costs, materials handling, and shipping. The costs expected for these categories for the coming year are as follows:

(SO 1, 2)
Assign overhead costs using traditional costing and ABC; compare results.

Purchasing and receiving materials	$ 300,000
Machine operating costs	900,000
Materials handling	160,000
Shipping	140,000
Total	$1,500,000

The plant currently applies overhead using machine hours and expected annual capacity. Expected capacity is 300,000 machine hours. Pragya Jahangir, the financial controller, has been asked to submit a bid on job #287, on which she has assembled the following data:

Direct materials per unit	$1.35
Direct labour per unit	$1.85
Applied overhead	$?
Number of units produced	6,000
Number of purchases and receipts	3
Number of machine hours	3,000
Number of material moves	300
Number of kilometres to ship to the customer	2,300

Pragya has been told that Arrow Company, a major competitor, is using activity-based costing and will bid on job #287 with a price of $6.75 per unit. Before submitting her bid, Pragya wants to assess the effects of this alternative costing approach. She estimates that 850,000 units will be produced next year, 3,000 purchases and receipts will be made, 400,000 moves will be performed plant-wide, and the delivery of finished goods will require 280,000 kilometres. The bid price policy is full manufacturing cost plus 25%.

Instructions

(a) Markup: $1.425

(b) Overhead cost per unit: $1.762

(a) Calculate the bid price per unit of job #287 using machine hours to assign overhead.

(b) Using an activity-based approach, determine whether Mars or Arrow will produce the most competitive bid and obtain the contract. Show all your calculations.

(adapted from CGA-Canada, now CPA Canada)

(SO 1, 2)
Assign overhead costs using traditional costing and ABC; compare results.

P5-46B Prime Furniture designs and builds factory-made, premium, wood armoires for homes. All are made of white oak. Its budgeted manufacturing overhead costs for the year 2016 are as follows.

Overhead Cost Pools	Amount
Purchasing	$ 45,000
Handling materials	50,000
Production (cutting, milling, finishing)	130,000
Setting up machines	85,000
Inspecting	60,000
Inventory control (raw materials and finished goods)	80,000
Utilities	100,000
Total budget overhead costs	$550,000

For the last four years, Prime Furniture has been charging overhead to products on the basis of materials cost. For the year 2016, materials cost of $500,000 were budgeted.

Wei Huang, owner-manager of Prime Furniture, recently directed her accountant, Tom Turkel, to implement the activity-based costing system that he has repeatedly proposed.

At Wei Huang's request, Tom and the production manager identify the following cost drivers and their usage for the previously budgeted overhead cost pools.

Overhead Cost Pools	Activity Cost Drivers	Expected Use of Cost Drivers
Purchasing	Number of orders	500
Handling materials	Number of moves	5,000
Production (cutting, milling, finishing)	Direct labour hours	65,000
Setting up machines	Number of set-ups	1,000
Inspecting	Number of inspections	4,000
Inventory control (raw materials and finished goods)	Number of components	40,000
Utilities	Square metres occupied	5,000

Maria Carvalho, sales manager, has received an order for 10 luxury armoires from Cohn's Interior Design. At Maria's request, Tom prepares cost estimates for producing components for 10 armoires so Maria can submit a contract price per armoire to Cohn's. He accumulates the following data for the production of 10 armoires.

Direct materials	$5,200
Direct labour	$3,500
Direct labour hours	200
Number of purchase orders	3
Number of material moves	32
Number of machine set-ups	4
Number of inspections	20
Number of components	640
Number of square metres occupied	32

Instructions

(a) Calculate the predetermined overhead rate using traditional costing with materials cost as the basis.

(b) What is the manufacturing cost per armoire under traditional costing?

(c) What is the manufacturing cost per armoire under the proposed activity-based costing? (Prepare all of the necessary schedules.)

(d) Determine which of the two costing systems is preferable in pricing decisions and why.

(b) Cost/armoire
$1,442.00

(c) Cost/armoire
$1,225.00

P5-47B Quality Paints Inc. uses a traditional cost accounting system to apply quality-control costs uniformly to all its products at a rate of 30% of the direct labour cost. The monthly direct labour cost for the varnish paint line is $100,000. The company is considering activity-based costing to apply quality-control costs. The monthly data for the varnish paint line have been gathered as follows:

(SO 1, 2)
Assign overhead costs using traditional costing and ABC; compare results.

Activity Cost Pools	Cost Drivers	Unit Rates	Use of Drivers for Varnish Paint
Incoming material inspection	Type of material	$ 25.00 per type	50 types
In-process inspection	Number of units	0.30 per unit	30,000 units
Product certification	Per order	150.00 per order	80 orders

Instructions

(a) Calculate the monthly quality-control cost to be assigned to the varnish paint line using a traditional costing system that allocates overhead based on the direct labour cost.

(b) Calculate the monthly quality-control cost to be assigned to the varnish paint line using an activity-based costing system.

(c) Comment on the results.

(b) Total cost $22,250

(adapted from CMA Canada, now CPA Canada)

P5-48B International Steel Company has budgeted manufacturing overhead costs of $2.5 million. It has allocated overhead on a plant-wide basis to its two products (Standard Steel and Deluxe Steel) using machine hours, which are estimated to be 100,000 for the current year. The company has decided to experiment with activity-based costing and has created five activity cost pools and related activity cost drivers as follows:

(SO 1, 2)
Assign overhead costs using traditional costing and ABC; compare results.

Activity Centre	Cost Driver	Estimated Overhead	Expected Activity
Material handling	Number of moves	$250,000	50,000 moves
Purchase orders	Number of orders	$200,000	4,000 orders
Product testing	Number of tests	$450,000	9,000 tests
Machine set-up	Number of set-ups	$600,000	6,000 set-ups
Machining	Machine hours	$1,000,000	100,000 machine hours

Each unit of the products requires the following:

	Standard Steel	Deluxe Steel
Direct materials costs	$200	$250
Direct labour costs	$100	$120
Purchase orders	2	3
Machine set-up	5	10
Product testing	3	4
Machining	50	50
Materials handling	5	10

Instructions

(a) Under traditional product costing using machine hours, calculate the total manufacturing cost per unit of both products.

(b) Under ABC, prepare a schedule showing the calculation of the activity-based overhead rates (per cost driver).

(c) Calculate the total manufacturing cost per unit for both products under ABC.

(d) ▣▣▣▷ Write a memo to the president of the company discussing the implications of your analysis for the company's plans. In this memo, provide a brief description of ABC, as well as an explanation of how the traditional approach can result in distortions.

(a) Deluxe Steel: $1,620

(b) Standard Steel: $1,275

(c) Deluxe Steel: $2,270

(SO 1, 2)
Assign overhead costs
using traditional
costing and ABC;
compare results.

P5-49B Scalar Manufacturing produces automobile parts in batches in one continuous manufacturing process. The company uses direct labour hours to assign overhead to each part. Magda Malakova, the financial controller, is wondering what the reasons are for the low profits in 2016 and why the gear product line did not attain Scalar's 20% net profit margin target (net profit per unit on sale price). She has calculated the 2016 net profit per unit as follows:

	Brake Disk	Gear
Sales price per unit	$35.00	$43.00
Manufacturing costs per unit:		
Direct materials	10.00	7.50
Direct labour		
(0.1 hour × $12/hour)	1.20	
(0.5 hour × $12/hour)		6.00
Overhead		
(0.1 hour × $50/hour)	5.00	
(0.5 hour × $50/hour)		25.00
Total manufacturing cost per unit	$16.20	$38.50
Net profit per unit	$18.80	$ 4.50
Net profit margin percentage	53.7%	10.5%

Magda intends to implement activity-based costing at Scalar. Each part requires engineering design activity. Once the design is completed, the equipment can be set up for batch production. Once the batch is completed, a sample is taken and inspected to see if the parts are within the tolerances allowed. The manufacturing process has five activities: engineering, set-ups, machining, inspection, and processing. Overhead has been assigned to each activity using direct attribution and resource drivers:

Engineering	$ 80,000
Set-ups	45,000
Machining	120,000
Inspection	60,000
Processing	35,000
Total overhead	$340,000

Magda has identified activity drivers for each activity and listed their practical capacities:

Engineering Hours	Number of Set-ups	Machine Hours	Number of Inspections	Direct Labour Hours
4,000	250	20,000	1,500	7,000

Following are the production data in 2016 for brake disks and gears:

	Brake Disk	Gear
Number of units produced	5,000	3,000
Engineering hours per unit	0.05	0.15
Number of set-ups	25	9
Machine hours per unit	2.5	1
Number of inspections	250	125

Instructions

(a) Percentage of profit margin: brake disk, 12.57%

(a) Using the activity-based approach, calculate the activity rates, the net profit per unit, and the net profit margin percentage for both the brake disk and the gear.

(b) Explain why the new profit margin percentages for the brake disk and the gear are different from what they were originally.

(adapted from CGA-Canada, now CPA Canada)

(SO 1, 2, 3, 4)
Assign overhead costs
to services using tradi-
tional costing and ABC;
calculate overhead
rates; compare results.

P5-50B McDonald and O'Toole is a law firm that serves both individuals and corporations. A controversy has developed between the partners of the two service lines as to who is contributing the greater amount to the bottom line. The area of contention is the assignment of overhead. The individual partners argue for assigning overhead on the basis of 28.125% of direct labour dollars, while the corporate partners argue for implementing activity-based costing. The partners agree to use next year's budgeted data for purposes of analysis and comparison. The following overhead data are collected to develop the comparison.

Activity Cost Pool	Cost Driver	Estimated Overhead	Expected Use of Cost Drivers	Expected Use of Cost Drivers per Service	
				Corporate	Individual
Employee training	Direct labour dollars	$120,000	$1,600,000	$900,000	$700,000
Clerical	Number of reports and forms	60,000	2,000	500	1,500
Computing	Number of minutes	100,000	40,000	17,000	23,000
Facility rental	Number of employees	100,000	25	14	11
Travel	Per expense reports	70,000	Direct	48,000	22,000
		$450,000			

Instructions

(a) Using traditional product costing as proposed by the tax partners, calculate the total overhead cost assigned to both services (individual and corporate) of McDonald and O'Toole.

(b) 1. Using activity-based costing, prepare a schedule showing the calculations of the activity-based overhead rates (per cost driver).

    2. Prepare a schedule assigning each activity's overhead cost pool to each service based on the use of the cost drivers.

(c) Classify each of the activities as a value-added activity or a non–value-added activity.

(d) Comment on the comparative overhead cost service line under both traditional costing and ABC.

(b) (2) Cost assigned— Individual $221,000

(d) Difference— Traditional method $24,125

P5-51B ProDriver Inc. (PDI) recently started operations to obtain a share of the growing market for golf equipment. PDI manufactures two models of specialty drivers: the Thunderbolt model and the Earthquake model. Two professional engineers and a professional golfer, none of whom had any accounting background, formed the company as a partnership. The business has been very successful, and to cope with the increased level of activity, the partners have hired a CPA as their controller. One of the first improvements that the controller wants to make is to update the costing system by changing from a single overhead application rate using direct labour hours to activity-based costing. The controller has identified the following three activities as cost drivers, along with the related cost pools:

(SO 2, 3)
Assign overhead costs using ABC.

Model	Number of Material Requisitions	Number of Product Inspections	Number of Orders Shipped
Thunderbolt	46	23	167
Earthquake	62	31	129
Costs per pool	$54,000	$8,200	$103,000

Instructions

(a) Using activity-based costing, prepare a schedule that shows the allocation of the costs of each cost pool to each model. Show your calculations.

(b) Identify three conditions that should be present in PDI in order for the implementation of activity-based costing to be successful.

(a) Overhead assigned: Thunderbolt, $84,604

(adapted from CGA-Canada, now CPA Canada)

Cases

C5-52 For the past five years, Collins Ltd. has been running a consulting practice in which it provides two major services: general management consulting and executive training seminars. The CFO is not quite sure that he is charging accurate fees for the different services he provides. He has recently read an article about activity-based costing that convinced him he could use ABC to improve the accuracy of his costing. He has gathered the following selected information concerning the consulting practice during the previous year:

Overhead Activities	Cost Pools	Activities	Cost Drivers
Planning and review	$ 900,000	120,000 hours	Billable hours
Research	150,000	400 journals	Journals purchased
General administration	1,800,000	600 clients	Number of clients
Building and equipment	360,000	2,400 square metres	Square metres occupied
Clerical	306,000	34 professionals	Professional staff
	$3,516,000		

In addition, the CFO gathered the following statistics for each of the two types of services provided to clients during the year:

	Management Consulting	Executive Training
Direct labour costs	$1,800,000	$900,000
Billable hours	90,000	30,000
Research—journals purchased	280	120
Number of clients	240	360
Square metres	1,600	800
Professional staff	20	14

Instructions

(a) In the past, the CFO took the total overhead costs and divided them by the total billable hours to determine an average rate. To this amount he would then add the direct labour costs per hour and double this total amount to establish his average hourly charge-out rate. What was the CFO's average hourly charge-out rate using this method?

(b) Using ABC, what would the CFO's charge-out rate be? Note that he will continue to add the overhead to the direct labour costs per hour on a service basis and then double this amount to set an average hourly charge-out rate.

(c) Identify and discuss three ways in which ABC leads to more accurate product costs.

(d) Identify and discuss two limitations of ABC.

(e) After reviewing the ABC methodology described in part (b), identify one significant flaw in how the overhead costs will be allocated by the CFO in the ABC system. Discuss how this flaw would affect the average hourly charge-out rates (that is, increase or decrease the rates) for management consulting and executive training. You do not have to calculate the new rates to answer this part of the question.

(adapted from CGA-Canada, now CPA Canada)

C5-53 Aerotech International Inc. of Montreal has supported a research and development (R&D) department that for many years has been the sole contributor to the company's new products. The R&D activity is an overhead cost centre that provides services only to in-house manufacturing departments (four different product lines), all of which produce aerospace-related products.

The department has never sold its services outside, but because of its long history of success, larger manufacturers of aerospace products have approached Aerotech to hire its R&D department for special projects. Because the costs of operating the R&D department have been spiralling uncontrollably, Aerotech's management is considering taking on these outside contracts to absorb the increasing costs. However, managers don't have any cost basis for charging R&D services to outsiders, and they need to gain control of their R&D costs. Management decide to implement an activity-based costing system in order to determine the charges for both outsiders and the in-house users of the department's services.

R&D activities fall into four pools with the following annual costs:

Market analysis	$1,050,000	Product development	3,600,000
Product design	2,350,000	Prototype testing	1,400,000

Analysis determines that the appropriate cost drivers and their usage for the four activities are as follows:

Activities	Cost Drivers	Total Estimated Drivers
Market analysis	Hours of analysis	15,000 hours
Product design	Number of designs	2,500 designs
Product development	Number of products	90 products
Prototype testing	Number of tests	500 tests

Instructions

(a) Calculate the activity-based overhead rate for each activity cost pool.

(b) How much cost would be charged to an in-house manufacturing department that consumed 1,800 hours of market analysis time, was provided with 280 designs relating to 10 products, and requested 92 engineering tests?

(c) How much cost would serve as the basis for pricing an R&D bid with an outside company on a contract that would consume 800 hours of analysis time, require 178 designs relating to three products, and result in 70 engineering tests?

(d) What is the benefit to Aerotech International Inc. of applying activity-based costing to its R&D activity to charge for both in-house and outside services?

C5-54 B & B Electronics Company manufactures two large-screen television models: the Deluxe, which has been produced for many years and sells for $900, and the Flat, a new model, which sells for $1,260.

Based on the following income statement for 2016, the CFO at B & B has decided to concentrate the marketing resources on the Flat model and to begin to phase out the Deluxe model.

B & B ELECTRONICS COMPANY
Income Statement
Year Ended December 31, 2016

	Flat	Deluxe	Total
Sales	$5,040,000	$19,800,000	$24,840,000
Cost of goods sold	3,680,000	14,960,000	18,640,000
Gross margin	1,360,000	4,840,000	6,200,000
Selling and administrative expenses	780,000	2,640,000	3,420,000
Net profit	$ 580,000	$ 2,200,000	$ 2,780,000
Units produced and sold	4,000	22,000	
Net profit per unit sold	$145.00	$100.00	

The standard unit costs for the Flat and Deluxe models are as follows:

	Flat	Deluxe
Direct materials	$650	$250
Direct labour:		
Flat (3.5 hrs. × $20/hr.)	70	
Deluxe (1.5 hrs. × $20/hr.)		30
Machine usage:		
Flat (4 hrs. × $25/hr.)	100	
Deluxe (8 hrs. × $25/hr.)		200
Manufacturing overhead	100	200
Standard cost	$920	$680

Manufacturing overhead was applied on the basis of machine hours at a predetermined rate of $25 per hour. B & B Electronics Company's CFO is in favour of the use of an activity-based costing system and has gathered the following information about the company's manufacturing overhead costs for 2016:

Activity Centres and Cost Drivers	Activity Costs	Units of the Cost Driver		
		Flat	Deluxe	Total
Soldering (number of solder joints)	$ 900,000	300,000	1,200,000	1,500,000
Shipments (number of shipments)	800,000	4,800	15,200	20,000
Quality control (number of inspections)	1,200,000	21,000	59,000	80,000
Purchase orders (number of orders)	800,000	110,000	50,000	160,000
Machine power (machine hours)	100,000	16,000	176,000	192,000
Machine set-ups (number of set-ups)	1,000,000	4,000	6,000	10,000
Total traceable costs	$4,800,000			

Instructions

Using activity-based costing, determine whether B & B Electronics should continue to emphasize the Flat model and phase out the Deluxe model.

(adapted from CMA Canada, now CPA Canada)

C5-55 Wet Ride Inc. manufactures and distributes three types of water skis: beginner, intermediate, and advanced. Production is highly automated for the beginner model, whereas the intermediate and advanced models require increasing degrees of labour, depending on the shaping and finishing processes. Wet Ride applies all indirect costs to production using a single predetermined overhead (OH) rate based on direct labour hours (DLH).

Management estimates that 30,000 direct labour hours will be used in the upcoming year, at a rate of $14 per hour.

Assume that the following activity took place in the first month of the new year:

	Beginner	Intermediate	Advanced
Number of units produced	20,000	8,000	3,000
Direct material costs	$20,800	$13,000	$8,000
Direct labour hours	500	1,000	2,000
Number of orders	6	4	3
Number of production runs	2	2	3
Kilograms of material used	8,000	3,200	1,500
Machine hours	1,200	300	200
Number of inspections	3	3	3
Number of units shipped	18,000	7,500	2,500

A consultant recently suggested that Wet Ride switch to an activity-based costing system, and assembled the following information:

Activities	Recommended Cost Drivers	Estimated OH Cost	Cost Drivers
Order processing	Number of orders	$ 60,000	100 orders
Materials handling	Kilograms of materials used	600,000	120,000 kilograms
Machine depreciation and maintenance	Machine hours	420,000	20,000 hours
Quality control	Number of inspections	120,000	40 inspections
		$1,200,000	

Instructions

(a) Calculate the production costs for each product in the first month of the upcoming year, using direct labour hours as the allocation base. (Round calculations to the nearest cent.)

(b) Calculate the production costs for each product in the first month of the upcoming year, using activity-based costing. (Round calculations to the nearest cent.)

(c) Compare your answers in parts (a) and (b). Is the overhead charged to each product the same under each method? Explain.

(adapted from CGA-Canada, now CPA Canada)

C5-56 The CEO of Walker Ltd. is currently investigating ways to modernize the company's manufacturing process. At the first staff meeting, the chief engineer presented a proposal for automating the assembly department, and recommended that the company purchase two robots that would be able to replace the eight direct labour employees in the department. The cost savings outlined in the chief engineer's proposal include the elimination of the direct labour cost in the assembly department and a reduction of the manufacturing overhead cost in the department to zero, since the company charges manufacturing overhead on the basis of direct labour dollars using a plant-wide rate. The CEO of Walker Ltd. is puzzled by the chief engineer's explanation: "This just doesn't make any sense. How can a department's overhead rate drop to zero by adding expensive, high-tech manufacturing equipment? If anything, it seems like the rate ought to go up."

The chief engineer responds by saying, "I'm an engineer, not an accountant. But if we're charging overhead on the basis of direct labour, and we eliminate the labour, then we eliminate the overhead."

The CFO explains that as firms become more automated, they should rethink their product costing systems. The CEO asks the CFO to look into the matter and prepare a report for the next staff meeting. The CFO gathers the following data on the manufacturing overhead rates experienced by Walker Ltd. over the last five years. The CFO also estimates the following annual averages for each manufacturing department over the past several years:

Historical Plant-Wide Data

Year	Average Annual Direct Labour Cost	Average Annual Manufacturing Overhead Cost	Average Manufacturing Overhead Application Rate
2012	$ 500,000	$ 1,000,000	200%
2013	600,000	3,000,000	500%
2014	1,000,000	7,000,000	700%
2015	1,500,000	12,000,000	800%
2016	2,000,000	20,000,000	1,000%

Annual Averages during a Recent Year

	Moulding Department	Component Department	Assembly Department
Direct labour costs	$ 1,000,000	$ 875,000	$ 125,000
Manufacturing overhead costs	11,000,000	7,000,000	2,000,000

Instructions

(a) Evaluate Walker Ltd.'s current product costing system of charging manufacturing overhead on the basis of direct labour dollars using a plant-wide rate.

(b) Comment on the chief engineer's statement that the manufacturing overhead cost in the assembly department would be reduced to zero if the automation proposal were implemented.

(c) How might Walker Ltd. find the ABC information useful in applying manufacturing overhead and revising its product-costing system to accommodate automation in the assembly department?

(adapted from CMA Canada, now CPA Canada)

C5-57 The Canadian Motorcycle Company (CMC) produces two models of motorcycles: Faster and Slower. The company has five categories of overhead costs: purchasing, receiving, machine operating costs, handling, and shipping. Each category represents the following percentages of total overhead costs, which amount to $4 million:

Purchasing	25.0%	Handling	10.0%
Receiving	12.5%	Shipping	15.0%
Machine operating	37.5%		

Current capacity is 200,000 machine hours, and the current production uses 100% of the available hours. The sales mix is 45% Faster and 55% Slower. The overhead costs are applied to each model based on machine hours.

The production costs for each model of motorcycle and other relevant information are as follows:

	Faster	Slower
Direct materials per unit	$8,000	$6,500
Direct labour per unit	$1,750	$1,850
Applied overhead	?	?
Number of units produced	400	500
Number of purchases	5	4
Number of shipments received	3	3
Percentage of machine hours consumed by each product	50%	50%
Number of moves in handling	75	100
Number of kilometres to ship to customers	4,000	4,250

Instructions

(a) CMC determines its prices by adding 40% to the cost of direct materials and direct labour. Determine if this pricing policy is appropriate. Show all calculations to support your answer.

(b) Use an activity-based approach to determine whether CMC can make a profit if it sells the Faster model for $15,000. Show all supporting calculations. (Round all answers to the nearest dollar.)

(adapted from CGA-Canada, now CPA Canada)

C5-58 Java Inc. is a distributor and processor of a variety of different blends of coffee. The company buys coffee beans from around the world and roasts, blends, and packages them for resale. Java Inc. currently offers 10 different coffees in 500-gram bags to gourmet shops. The major cost is raw materials; however, there is a substantial amount of manufacturing overhead in the mostly automated roasting and packing process. The company uses relatively little direct labour.

Some of the coffees are very popular and sell in large volumes, while a few of the newer blends have very low volumes. Java Inc. prices its coffee at total product costs, including allocated overhead, plus a markup of 25%. If prices for certain coffees are significantly higher than market, the prices are adjusted lower.

Data for the 2016 budget include manufacturing overhead of $3.5 million, which has been allocated in the existing costing system based on each product's budgeted direct labour cost. The budgeted direct labour cost for 2016 totals $700,000. Purchases and use of materials (mostly coffee beans) are budgeted to total $6 million.

The budgeted prime costs for 500-gram bags of two of the company's products are as follows:

	Mocha	Vanilla
Direct materials	$3.20	$2.80
Direct labour	$0.25	$0.25

Data for the 2016 production of Mocha and Vanilla coffee are as follows. There will be no beginning or ending materials inventory for either of these coffees.

	Mocha	Vanilla
Expected sales	50,000 kilograms	1,000 kilograms
Batch size	50,000 kilograms	250 kilograms
Set-ups	3 per batch	3 per batch
Purchase order size	12,500 kilograms	250 kilograms
Roasting time	1 hour/50 kg	1 hour/50 kg
Blending time	0.5 hour/50 kg	0.5 hour/50 kg
Packaging time	0.1 hour/50 kg	0.1 hour/50 kg

Java's controller believes the traditional costing system may be providing misleading cost information. He has developed an activity-based analysis of the 2016 budgeted manufacturing overhead costs shown in the following table:

Activity Pools	Cost Drivers	Budgeted Units	Budgeted Cost
Purchasing	Purchase orders	1,150	$ 575,000
Materials handling	Set-ups	1,750	612,500
Quality control	Batches	500	150,000
Roasting	Roasting hours	100,000	950,000
Blending	Blending hours	23,125	462,500
Packaging	Packaging hours	30,000	750,000
Total manufacturing overhead cost			$3,500,000

Instructions

(a) Calculate the company's 2016 budgeted manufacturing overhead rate using direct labour costs as the single rate and the 2016 budgeted costs and selling prices of 500 grams of Mocha coffee and 500 grams of Vanilla coffee.

(b) Use the controller's activity-based approach to estimate the 2016 budgeted cost for one kilogram of Mocha coffee and one kilogram of Vanilla coffee.

(c) Comment on the results.

(adapted from CMA Canada, now CPA Canada)

C5-59 Marcus Lim, the cost accountant for Hi-Power Mower Company, recently installed activity-based costing at the company's western lawn tractor (riding mower) plant, where three models are manufactured: the 8-horsepower Bladerunner, the 12-horsepower Quickcut, and the 18-horsepower Supercut. Marcus's new product costs for these three models show that the company's traditional costing system had been significantly undercosting the 18-horsepower Supercut, due primarily to the lower sales volume of the Supercut compared with the Bladerunner and the Quickcut.

Before completing his analysis and reporting these results to management, Marcus is approached by his friend Ray Pon, who is the production manager for the 18-horsepower Supercut model. Ray has heard from one of Marcus's staff about the new product costs and is upset and worried for his job because the new costs show the Supercut to be losing, rather than making, money.

At first Ray condemns the new cost system, so Marcus explains the practice of activity-based costing and why it is more accurate than the company's present system. Even more worried now, Ray begs Marcus, "Massage the figures just enough to save the line from being discontinued. You don't want me to lose my job, do you? Anyway, nobody will know." Marcus holds firm but agrees to review all his calculations for accuracy before submitting his costs to management.

Instructions

Answer the following questions:

(a) Who are the stakeholders in this situation?

(b) What, if any, are the ethical considerations in this situation?

(c) What are Marcus's ethical obligations to the company?

"All About You" Activity

C5-60 Look on the Internet for time management resources that are designed specifically for students. If you cannot find one, look at the University of Guelph library web page.

Instructions

Use the resources to answer the following questions.

(a) Why is it important to set time management goals?

(b) How can a task list, a master plan, and a calendar help you with time management?

(c) Procrastination is a very common problem for students. What are some tips for dealing with it?

Decision-Making at Current Designs

DM5-1   As you learned in the previous chapters, Current Designs has two main product lines—composite kayaks, which are handmade and very labour-intensive, and rotomoulded kayaks, which require less labour but employ more expensive equipment. Current Designs' controller, Diane Buswell, is now evaluating several different methods of assigning overhead to these products. It is important to ensure that costs are appropriately assigned to the company's products. At the same time, the system that is used must not be so complex that its costs are greater than its benefits.

Diane has decided to use the following activities and costs to evaluate the methods of assigning overhead.

Activity	Cost
Designing new models	$121,100
Creating and testing prototypes	152,000
Creating moulds for kayaks	188,500
Operating oven for the rotomoulded kayaks	40,000
Operating the vacuum line for the composite kayaks	28,000
Supervising production employees	180,000
Curing (the time that is needed for the chemical processes to finish before the next step in the production process; many of these costs are related to the space required in the building)	190,400
Total	$900,000

As Diane examines the data, she decides that the cost of operating the oven for the rotomoulded kayaks and the cost of operating the vacuum line for the composite kayaks can be directly assigned to each of these product lines and do not need to be allocated with the other costs.

Instructions

For purposes of this analysis, assume that Current Designs uses $234,000 in direct labour costs to produce 1,000 composite kayaks and $286,000 in direct labour costs to produce 4,000 rotomoulded kayaks each year.

(a)   One method of allocating overhead would allocate the common costs to each product line by using an allocation basis such as the number of employees working on each type of kayak or the amount of factory space used for the production of each type of kayak. Diane knows that about 50% of the area of the plant and 50% of the employees work on the composite kayaks, and the remaining space and other employees work on the rotomoulded kayaks. Using this information, and remembering that the cost of operating the oven and vacuum line have been directly assigned, determine the total amount to be assigned to the composite kayak line and the rotomoulded kayak line, and the amount to be assigned to each of the units in each line.

(b)   Another method of allocating overhead is to use direct labour dollars as an allocation basis. Remembering that the costs of the oven and the vacuum line have been assigned directly to the product lines, allocate the remaining costs using direct labour dollars as the allocation basis. Then, determine the amount of overhead that should be assigned to each unit of each product line using this method.

(c)   Activity-based costing requires a cost driver for each cost pool. Use the following information to assign the costs to the product lines using the activity-based costing approach.

Activity	Cost Driver	Driver Amount for Composite Kayaks	Driver Amount for Rotomoulded Kayaks
Designing new models	Number of models	3	1
Creating and testing prototypes	Number of prototypes	6	2
Creating moulds for kayaks	Number of moulds	12	1
Supervising production employees	Number of employees	12	12
Curing	Number of days of curing time	15,000	2,000

What amount of overhead should be assigned to each composite kayak using this method? What amount of overhead should be assigned to each rotomoulded kayak using this method?

(d)   Which of the three methods do you think Current Designs should use? Why?

Waterways Continuing Problem

(This is a continuation of the Waterways Problem from Chapters 1 through 4.)

WCP-5   Spirits were high at the monthly meeting of the top management of Waterways. Installation was proceeding nicely on the 10 jobs for the city, and the company had just received confirmation that the local school board had accepted its bid to install irrigation systems in 25 school playgrounds. Unfortunately, not everyone was celebrating. Lee Williams, the vice-president of the installation and training division, was troubled. He has been supervising the city jobs and he believes the current system of assigning overhead costs to the jobs does not reflect accurately the actual cost of overhead.

"Several major things have changed since we set our overhead rate at 120% of direct labour cost," Lee explained. "I've noticed that the new systems are requiring a lot of the more expensive glue and they were designed to accommodate only titanium fasteners. We are using special packaging to transport the systems to the sites, not to mention the new heavy equipment we had to purchase to prepare the ground for the install."

Madison Tremblay, vice-president of sales and marketing, was quick to respond. "I can't believe that you're suggesting there's something wrong with our bids," he retorted. He was visibly annoyed. "This is the first time in several years that our sales group has been successful in increasing our market share," he continued, "and now you want to mess with the pricing! I want you to explain that to the salespeople who have just received their first bonus commission cheques in a very long time."

Ben Clark, who designed the new system, agreed with Madison, suggesting that maybe the problem was not with the cost, but was more likely cost *control*.

Their accountant, Jordan Leigh, did not like conflict. "I have an idea," he said. "We have been investigating using a new costing system in our manufacturing plant called activity-based costing, or ABC. ABC is supposed to lead to more accurate overhead costing and it provides a better way to control overhead costs. With a little work I think we could adapt it to our installation services." When he offered to do an analysis and bring his recommendations back to the next management meeting, the rest of the group agreed to wait for the results before making any changes.

Jordan's first action was to identify and classify all the activities that consume resources during this specific type of installation into a number of cost pools, and then determine the overhead costs that should be assigned to each cost pool. At the same time he determined a cost driver for each pool. The following table shows these cost pools along with the estimated overhead allocation to each one.

Activity Cost Pools	Cost Drivers	Estimated Overhead	Expected Use per Activity
Supervision, security, maintenance	Number of workdays	$ 450,000	1,500
Liability insurance	Number of employees	100,000	800
Equipment costs	Hours of operation	90,000	12,000
Indirect supplies and delivery	Length in metres	250,000	250,000
Employee benefits	Direct labour cost	150,000	600,000
		$1,040,000	

Then, based on the information used to prepare the bids, Jordan determined that each of the 25 projects for the school board would require the following overhead activities.

Activity Cost Pools	Cost Drivers	Expected Use per Job
Supervision, security, maintenance	Number of workdays	30
Liability insurance	Number of employees	4
Equipment costs	Hours of operation	240
Indirect supplies and delivery	Length in metres	3,000
Employee benefits	Direct labour cost	$12,000

The material costs for each project were expected to be $13,000.

Instructions

(a) Calculate the expected cost of this type of installation using both the traditional method and activity-based costing.

(b) Given the information calculated in part (a), make a recommendation to the management of Waterways as to what action they should take.

(c) Explain why you think Waterways' current bidding process would lead to increased market share.

Answers to Self-Study Questions

1. c   2. c   3. c   4. b   5. d   6. d   7. c   8. c   9. a   10. c

Remember to go back to the beginning of the chapter to check off your completed work!
←

study objectives

After studying this chapter, you should be able to do the following:

1. Prepare a cost-volume-profit income statement to determine contribution margin.

2. Calculate the break-even point using three approaches.

3. Determine the sales required to earn the target operating income and define the margin of safety.

4. Understand how to apply basic cost-volume-profit concepts in a changing business environment.

5. Explain the term *sales mix* and its effect on break-even sales.

6. Understand how cost structure and operating leverage affect profitability (Appendix 6A).

the navigator

NOT MUCH ROOM TO MOVE ON PRICE

Because an empty hotel room can't generate revenue yet still incurs fixed costs, many hotels would rather sell off available rooms last-minute at a discount than earn nothing. But many luxury brands, like Four Seasons Hotels and Resorts, typically don't offer discounts, partly because it doesn't increase their profit.

Hotels are a good example of how companies use cost-volume-profit analysis, trying to determine the optimal volume of sales and costs to maximize profit. Hotels have fixed costs, no matter how many guests are staying. These fixed costs include full-time managers and employees, and overhead such as a mortgage or rent, insurance, and property taxes. In addition, Four Seasons has fixed costs such as high-quality soundproofing and plumbing. Hotels also have variable costs, which vary based on the number of rooms occupied, including the number of housekeeping and food and beverage staff scheduled. As occupancy rates rise, revenues increase along with variable costs.

This cost-volume-profit relationship is important to Four Seasons, the Toronto-based chain of 92 luxury properties in 38 countries. The privately held company owns only one hotel, in Vancouver, and manages the rest, including setting room rates. During the recent recession, some owners of Four Seasons properties considered cutting costs such as fresh flowers in the rooms to bring down room rates, but head office kept amenities and rates the same. In fact, the company was planning on upping its amenities, which help contribute to its five-star ratings. "We're in the process of introducing a new bed that allows guests to specify the level of firmness they want," said Four Seasons CEO Allen Smith as an example. Because Four Seasons pioneered so many of the luxuries that many chains have adopted, such as rain showerheads and brand-name toiletries, it feels it has to keep innovating in order to meet customer expectations.

One study found that discounting a hotel room by 10% resulted in only a 1.3% rise in occupancy. Many hotels have found that discounting attracts a different type of client, one who is more likely to be more demanding of staff and want more free things, and is less likely to be brand loyal, to pay full price the next time, and to use hotel facilities like spas and restaurants (which can be quite profitable). In fact, Four Seasons' highly trained staff are taught to turn away potential guests whose behaviour is not in line with the chain's standards. In addition, because the costs per room for cleaning, laundry, toiletries, and so on remain the same, the minimal profit from a discounted room is not always worth the potential cost of eroding a luxury brand's image of exclusivity.

Sources: Craig Offman, "Five-Star General: Four Seasons' New CEO and the Era of Peak Hotel Luxury," *The Globe and Mail*, February 21, 2014; Enzo Baglieri, Elena Zambolin, Barbara Resta, Uday Karmarkar, "Positioning Service Industrialization Strategies in the Accommodation Industry," in E. Gummesson, C. Mele, and F. Polese (Eds.), *Service Dominant Logic, Network & Systems Theory and Service Science: The 2011 Naples Forum on Service*, Naples: Giannini, 2011; Ron Adner, "Lifestyles of the Rich and Almost Famous: The Boutique Hotel Phenomenon in the United States," High Tech Entrepreneurship and Strategy Group Project, 2011; Gabor Forgacs, "The Room Rate Conundrum: The Leap From Tactical to Strategic," *Hotel Business Review*, HotelExecutive.com, April 5, 2011; Jeff Higley, "Four Seasons' Global Expansion Moves Forward," HotelNewsNow.com, December 5, 2011; Four Seasons' corporate website, www.fourseasons.com.

the navigator

Preview of Chapter 6

As the feature story about Four Seasons Hotels and Resorts indicates, to manage any business, whatever its size, you must understand how changes in sales volume affect costs, and how costs and revenues affect profits. In this chapter, we discuss and illustrate cost-volume-profit (CVP) analysis and contribution margin analysis.

The chapter is organized as follows:

the navigator

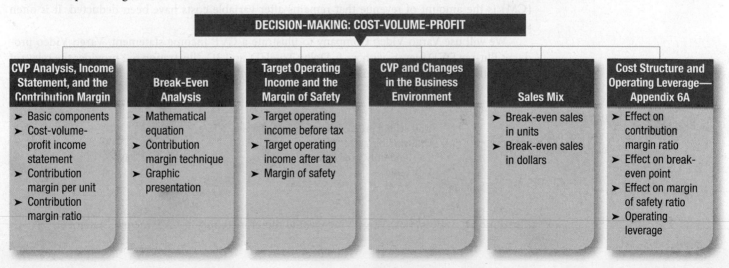

DECISION-MAKING: COST-VOLUME-PROFIT					
CVP Analysis, Income Statement, and the Contribution Margin	**Break-Even Analysis**	**Target Operating Income and the Margin of Safety**	**CVP and Changes in the Business Environment**	**Sales Mix**	**Cost Structure and Operating Leverage— Appendix 6A**
➤ Basic components ➤ Cost-volume-profit income statement ➤ Contribution margin per unit ➤ Contribution margin ratio	➤ Mathematical equation ➤ Contribution margin technique ➤ Graphic presentation	➤ Target operating income before tax ➤ Target operating income after tax ➤ Margin of safety		➤ Break-even sales in units ➤ Break-even sales in dollars	➤ Effect on contribution margin ratio ➤ Effect on break-even point ➤ Effect on margin of safety ratio ➤ Operating leverage

Cost-Volume-Profit Analysis, Income Statement, and the Contribution Margin

Cost-volume-profit (CVP) analysis is the study of the effects that changes in costs and volume have on a company's profits. CVP analysis is important in profit planning. It is also a critical factor in such management decisions as setting selling prices, determining product mix, and maximizing the use of production facilities.

BASIC COMPONENTS

CVP analysis considers the interrelationships among the components shown in Illustration 6-1.

▶Illustration 6-1

Components of CVP analysis

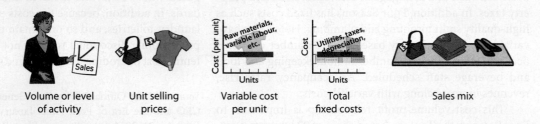

| Volume or level of activity | Unit selling prices | Variable cost per unit | Total fixed costs | Sales mix |

The following assumptions underlie each CVP analysis:

1. The behaviour of both costs and revenues is linear throughout the relevant range of the activity index.
2. All costs can be classified with reasonable accuracy as either variable or fixed.
3. Changes in activity are the only factors that affect costs.
4. Inventory levels remain constant—all units that are produced are sold.
5. When more than one type of product is sold, the sales mix will remain constant. That is, the percentage of total sales that each product represents will stay the same. The sales mix complicates CVP analysis because different products will have different cost relationships. In this chapter, we assume first a single product is being sold. Study objective 5 addresses sales mix issues.

When these five assumptions are not valid, the results of CVP analysis may be inaccurate.

COST-VOLUME-PROFIT INCOME STATEMENT

Because CVP is so important for decision-making, management often wants this information reported in a CVP income statement format. The cost-volume-profit (CVP) income statement classifies costs as variable or fixed and calculates a contribution margin. Contribution margin (CM) is the amount of revenue that remains after variable costs have been deducted. It is often stated both as a total amount and on a per-unit basis.

We will use Vargo Video Company to illustrate a CVP income statement. Vargo Video produces Blu-ray DVD players with wi-fi, Dolby TrueHD, and 3D. Illustration 6-2 provides the relevant data for the Blu-ray DVD players made by this company.

▶Illustration 6-2

Assumed selling and cost data for Vargo Video

Unit selling price of Blu-ray DVD player	$ 500
Unit variable costs	$ 300
Total monthly fixed costs	$200,000
Units sold	1,600

Illustration 6-3 shows how Vargo Video would therefore report its CVP income statement.

VARGO VIDEO COMPANY
CVP Income Statement
Month Ended June 30, 2016

	Total	Per Unit
Sales (1,600 Blu-ray DVD players)	$800,000	$500
Variable costs	480,000	300
Contribution margin	320,000	$200
Fixed costs	200,000	
Operating income	$120,000	

> ▶Illustration 6-3
> CVP income statement, with operating income

Companies often prepare detailed CVP income statements. To illustrate, we use the same base information in Illustration 6-4 as that presented in Illustration 6-3.

VARGO VIDEO COMPANY
CVP Income Statement
For the Month Ended June 30, 2016

	Total	Per Unit
Sales		$800,000	$500
Variable expenses		
Cost of goods sold	$400,000	
Selling expenses	60,000	
Administrative expenses	20,000	
Total variable expenses	480,000	300
Contribution margin	320,000	$200
Fixed expenses		
Cost of goods sold	120,000	
Selling expenses	40,000	
Administrative expenses	40,000	
Total fixed expenses	200,000	
Operating income	$120,000	

> ▶Illustration 6-4
> Detailed CVP income statement

A traditional income statement and a CVP income statement both report the same bottom-line operating income of $120,000. However, a traditional income statement does not classify costs as variable or fixed, and therefore would not report a contribution margin. In addition, a CVP income statement often shows both a total and a per-unit amount to help CVP analysis.

In the examples of CVP analysis that follow, we will assume that the term *cost* includes all costs and expenses for the production and sale of the product. That is, cost includes manufacturing costs, plus selling and administrative expenses.

BUSINESS INSIGHT   *Music to Broadcasters' Ears*

Despite the increase in Internet radio and music downloading, conventional radio continued to be profitable in 2012, Statistics Canada reported. Sales for airtime for private radio broadcasters increased only slightly, by 0.6% from 2011 to $1.59 billion. However, radio stations still earned 19.7 cents of profits before interest and taxes for every dollar of revenue in 2012. Advertising revenues account for nearly 98% of private broadcasters' operating revenues. In 2012, Canadians spent an average of 17.5 hours a week listening to the radio, compared with 17.7 hours the year before.

Sources: Statistics Canada, *Radio Broadcasting Industry 2012*, Cat. No. 56-208X; Canadian Radio-television and Telecommunications Commission, "CRTC Issues Annual Report on the State of the Canadian Communication System," news release, September 26, 2013; Steve Ladurantaye, "Five Things About the Canadian Radio Market," *The Globe and Mail*, June 19, 2013.

Since airtime is limited, how can radio stations determine their per-unit costs for selling advertising?

CONTRIBUTION MARGIN PER UNIT

From Vargo Video's CVP income statement, we can see that the contribution margin is $320,000, and the contribution margin per unit is $200 ($500 − $300). Illustration 6-5 shows the formula for calculating the **contribution margin per unit** using data for Vargo Video.

▶Illustration 6-5

Formula for contribution margin per unit

Unit Selling Price	−	Unit Variable Costs	=	Contribution Margin per Unit
$500	−	$300	=	$200

The contribution margin per unit indicates that for every Blu-ray DVD player sold, Vargo will have $200 to cover its fixed costs and contribute to operating income. Because Vargo Video has fixed costs of $200,000, it must sell 1,000 Blu-ray DVD players ($200,000 ÷ $200) before it earns any operating income. Illustration 6-6 shows Vargo's CVP income statement, assuming a zero operating income.

▶Illustration 6-6

CVP income statement, with zero operating income

VARGO VIDEO COMPANY		
CVP Income Statement		
Month Ended June 30, 2016		
	Total	Per Unit
Sales (1,000 Blu-ray DVD players)	$500,000	$500
Variable costs	300,000	300
Contribution margin	200,000	$200
Fixed costs	200,000	
Operating income	$ 0	

It follows that for every DVD player sold above 1,000 units, operating income increases by $200. For example, assume that Vargo sold one more Blu-ray DVD player, for a total of 1,001 Blu-ray DVD players sold. In this case, it would report operating income of $200, as shown in Illustration 6-7.

▶Illustration 6-7

CVP income statement, with operating income

VARGO VIDEO COMPANY		
CVP Income Statement		
Month Ended June 30, 2016		
	Total	Per Unit
Sales (1,001 Blu-ray DVD players)	$500,500	$500
Variable costs	300,300	300
Contribution margin	200,200	$200
Fixed costs	200,000	
Operating income	$ 200	

CONTRIBUTION MARGIN RATIO

Some managers prefer to use a contribution margin ratio in CVP analysis. The **contribution margin ratio** is the contribution margin per unit divided by the unit selling price. It is generally expressed as a percentage. Illustration 6-8 shows the ratio for Vargo Video.

$200   ÷ $500   =   40%

The contribution margin ratio of 40% means that $0.40 of each sales dollar ($1 × 40%) can be applied to fixed costs and contribute to operating income.

This expression of the contribution margin is very helpful in determining the effect of changes in sales on operating income. For example, if sales increase by $100,000, operating income will increase by $40,000 (40% × $100,000). Thus, by using the contribution margin ratio, managers can quickly determine what increases in operating income will result from any increase in sales.

We can also see this effect through a CVP income statement. Assume that Vargo Video's current sales are $500,000 and it wants to know the effect of a $100,000 increase in sales. It could prepare the comparative CVP income statement shown in Illustration 6-9.

VARGO VIDEO COMPANY
CVP Income Statement
Month Ended June 30, 2016

	No Change		With Change	
	Total	Per Unit	Total	Per Unit
Sales	$500,000	$500	$600,000	$500
Variable costs	300,000	300	360,000	300
Contribution margin	200,000	$200	240,000	$200
Fixed costs	200,000		200,000	
Operating income	$ 0		$ 40,000	

Study these CVP income statements carefully. The concepts used in these statements will be used often in this and later chapters.

BEFORE YOU GO ON...

▶Do It! CVP Income Statement and Contribution Margin

Garner Manufacturing Inc. sold 20,000 units and recorded sales of $800,000 for the first quarter of 2016. In making the sales, the company incurred the following costs and expenses.

	Variable	Fixed
Cost of goods sold	$250,000	$110,000
Selling expenses	100,000	25,000
Administrative expenses	82,000	73,000

(a) Prepare a CVP income statement for the quarter ended March 31, 2016.

(b) Calculate the contribution margin per unit.

(c) Calculate the contribution margin ratio.

Action Plan
• Use the CVP income statement format.
• Use the formula for contribution margin per unit.
• Use the formula for the contribution margin ratio.

(continued)

(continued)

Solution

(a)

GARNER MANUFACTURING INC.
Income Statement
For the Quarter Ended March 31, 2016

Sales (20,000 units)		$800,000
Variable expenses		
Cost of goods sold	$250,000	
Selling expenses	100,000	
Administrative expenses	82,000	
Total variable expenses		432,000
Contribution margin		368,000
Fixed expenses		
Cost of goods sold	110,000	
Selling expenses	25,000	
Administrative expenses	73,000	
Total fixed expenses		208,000
Operating income		$160,000

(b) Contribution margin per unit:
    $40 ($800,000 ÷ 20,000 units) − $21.60 ($432,000 ÷ 20,000 units) = $18.40 per unit.

(c) Contribution margin ratio:
    $368,000 ÷ $800,000 = 46% (or $18.40 ÷ $40 = 46%).

Related exercise material: **BE6-1, BE6-2, E6-24,** and **Do It! D6-16.**

the navigator ✔

DECISION TOOLKIT

Decision Checkpoints	Info Needed for Decision	Tools to Use for Decision			How to Evaluate Results
What was the contribution toward fixed costs and income from each unit sold?	Selling price per unit and variable cost per unit	Contribution margin per unit	= Unit selling price	− Unit variable cost	Every unit sold will increase income by the contribution margin.
What was the increase in income as a result of an increase in sales?	Contribution margin per unit and unit selling price	Contribution margin ratio	= Contribution margin per unit	÷ Unit selling price	Every dollar of sales will increase income by the contribution margin ratio.

Break-Even Analysis

STUDY OBJECTIVE 2

Calculate the break-even point using three approaches.

A key relationship in CVP analysis is the level of activity at which total revenues equal total costs (both fixed and variable). This level of activity is called the **break-even point**. At this volume of sales, the company will realize no income and will suffer no loss. The process of finding the break-even point is called **break-even analysis.** Knowledge of the break-even point is useful to management when it decides whether to introduce new product lines, change sales prices on established products, or enter new market areas.

The break-even point can be

1. calculated with a mathematical equation,
2. calculated by using contribution margin, or
3. derived from a cost-volume-profit (CVP) graph.

The break-even point can be expressed **in either sales units or sales dollars.**

MATHEMATICAL EQUATION

Illustration 6-10 shows a common equation used for CVP analysis.

▶Illustration 6-10
Basic CVP equation

Identifying the break-even point is a type of CVP analysis. Because operating income is zero at the break-even point, **break-even occurs when total sales equal variable costs plus fixed costs.**

The break-even point in units can be calculated directly from the equation by **using unit selling prices** and **unit variable costs.** Illustration 6-11 shows the calculation for Vargo Video.

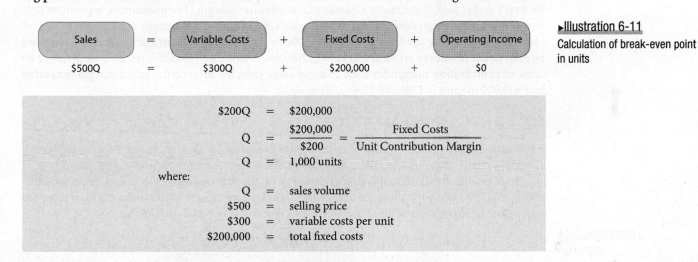

▶Illustration 6-11
Calculation of break-even point in units

Thus, Vargo Video must sell 1,000 units to break even.

To find the **sales dollars** required to break even, we multiply the units sold at the break-even point by the selling price per unit, as shown below:

$$1,000 \times \$500 = \$500,000 \text{ (break-even sales in dollars)}$$

CONTRIBUTION MARGIN TECHNIQUE

Many managers employ the contribution margin to calculate the break-even point.

Contribution Margin in Units

The final step in Illustration 6-11 divides fixed costs by the unit contribution margin (highlighted in red). Thus, rather than walk through all of the steps of the equation approach, we can simply employ this formula shown in Illustration 6-12.

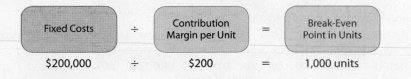

▶Illustration 6-12
Formula for break-even point in units using contribution margin

Why does this formula work? The unit contribution margin is the net amount by which each sale exceeds the variable costs per unit. Every sale generates this much money to pay off fixed costs. Consequently, if we divide fixed costs by the unit contribution margin, we know how many units we need to sell to break even.

Contribution Margin Ratio

As we will see in the next chapter, when a company has numerous products, it is not practical to determine the unit contribution margin for each product. In this case, using the contribution margin ratio is very useful for determining the break-even point in total dollars (rather than units). Recall that the contribution margin ratio is the amount of contribution margin that is generated from each dollar of sales. Therefore, to determine the sales dollars needed to cover fixed costs, we divide fixed costs by the contribution margin ratio, as shown in Illustration 6-13.

▶Illustration 6-13

Formula for break-even point in sales dollars using contribution margin ratio

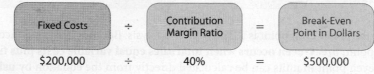

To apply this formula to Vargo Video, consider that its 40% contribution margin ratio means that for every dollar sold, it generates 40 cents of contribution margin. The question is, how many dollars of sales does Vargo need in order to generate total contribution margin of $200,000 to pay off fixed costs? We divide the fixed costs of $200,000 by the 40 cents of contribution margin generated by each dollar of sales to arrive at $500,000 ($200,000 ÷ 40%). To prove this result, if we generate 40 cents of contribution margin for each dollar of sales, then the total contribution margin generated by $500,000 in sales is $200,000 ($500,000 × 40%).

GRAPHIC PRESENTATION

An effective way to find the break-even point is to prepare a break-even graph. Because this graph also shows costs, volume, and profits, it is referred to as a **cost-volume-profit (CVP) graph**.

As shown in the CVP graph in Illustration 6-14, the sales volume is recorded along the horizontal axis. This axis should extend to the maximum level of expected sales. Both the total revenues (sales) and total costs (fixed plus variable) are recorded on the vertical axis.

▶Illustration 6-14
CVP graph

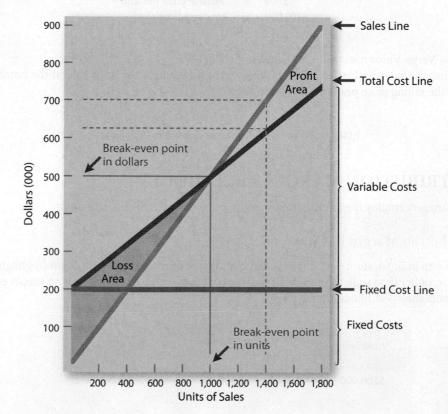

Using the data for Vargo Video, the steps to construct the graph are as follows:

1. Plot the total sales line, starting at the zero activity level. For every DVD player sold, total revenue increases by $500. For example, at 200 units, sales are $100,000. At the upper level of activity (1,800 units), sales are $900,000. Note that the revenue line is assumed to be linear throughout the relevant range of activity.

2. Plot the total fixed cost using a horizontal line. For the Blu-ray DVD players, this line is plotted at $200,000. The fixed cost is the same at every level of activity.

3. Plot the total cost line. This starts at the fixed-cost line at zero activity. It increases by the variable cost at each level of activity. For each DVD player, variable costs are $300. Thus, at 200 units, the total variable cost is $60,000, and the total cost is $260,000. At 1,800 units the total variable cost is $540,000, and the total cost is $740,000. On the graph, the amount of the variable cost can be derived from the difference between the total cost and fixed cost lines at each level of activity.

4. Determine the break-even point from the intersection of the total cost line and the total revenue line. The break-even point in dollars is found by drawing a horizontal line from the break-even point to the vertical axis. The break-even point in units is found by drawing a vertical line from the break-even point to the horizontal axis. For the Blu-ray DVD players, the break-even point is $500,000 of sales, or 1,000 units. At this sales level, Vargo Video will cover costs but make no profit.

The CVP graph also shows both the operating income and net loss areas. Thus, the company can derive the amount of income or loss at each sales level from the total sales and total cost lines.

A CVP graph is useful because a company can quickly see the effects of a change in any element in the CVP analysis. For example, a 10% increase in the selling price will change the location of the total revenue line. Likewise, wage increases will affect total costs.

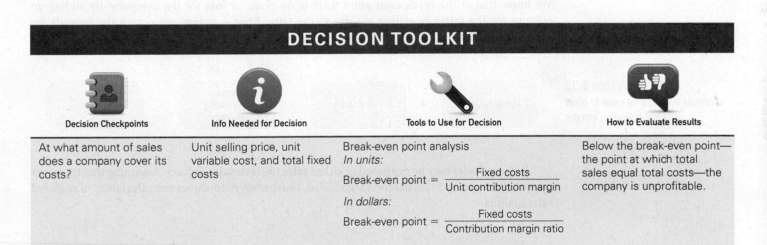

DECISION TOOLKIT

Decision Checkpoints	Info Needed for Decision	Tools to Use for Decision	How to Evaluate Results
At what amount of sales does a company cover its costs?	Unit selling price, unit variable cost, and total fixed costs	Break-even point analysis *In units:* $$\text{Break-even point} = \frac{\text{Fixed costs}}{\text{Unit contribution margin}}$$ *In dollars:* $$\text{Break-even point} = \frac{\text{Fixed costs}}{\text{Contribution margin ratio}}$$	Below the break-even point—the point at which total sales equal total costs—the company is unprofitable.

BEFORE YOU GO ON...

▶Do It! Break-even Analysis

Lombardi Company has a unit selling price of $400, variable costs per unit of $240, and fixed costs of $160,000. Calculate the break-even point in units using (a) a mathematical equation and (b) the contribution margin per unit.

Action Plan

- Apply the formula: sales = variable costs + fixed costs + operating income.
- Apply the formula: fixed costs ÷ contribution margin per unit = break-even point in units.

(continued)

(continued)

Solution

(a) The formula is 400Q = 240Q + $160,000. The break-even point in units is 1,000 = ($160,000 ÷ $160).

(b) The contribution margin per unit is $160 = ($400 − $240). The formula is $160,000 ÷ $160, and the break-even point in units is 1,000.

Related exercise material: **BE6-3, BE6-4, E6-25, E6-28,** and **Do It! D6-14.**

Target Operating Income and the Margin of Safety

TARGET OPERATING INCOME BEFORE TAX

STUDY OBJECTIVE 3
Determine the sales required to earn the target operating income and determine the margin of safety.

Rather than simply "breaking even," management usually sets an income objective for individual product lines. This objective is called the **target operating income**. It indicates the sales the company needs in order to achieve a specified level of income. The sales necessary to achieve the target operating income can be determined from each of the approaches used to determine the break-even sales.

Mathematical Equation

We know that at the break-even point there is no profit or loss for the company. By adding an amount for the target operating income to the same basic equation, we obtain the formula for determining required sales that is shown in Illustration 6-15.

►Illustration 6-15
Formula for required sales to meet target operating income

| Variable Costs | + | Fixed Costs | + | Target Operating Income | = | Required Sales |

Required sales may be expressed in **either sales units or sales dollars.** Assuming that the target operating income is $120,000 for Vargo Video, Illustration 6-16 shows the calculation of required sales in units.

►Illustration 6-16
Calculation of required sales

$$\$500Q = \$300Q + \$200,000 + \$120,000$$
$$\$200Q = \$320,000$$
$$Q = 1,600$$

where:

Q	=	sales volume
$500	=	selling price
$300	=	variable costs per unit
$200,000	=	total fixed costs
$120,000	=	target operating income

The sales dollars required to achieve the target operating income is found by multiplying the units sold by the unit selling price [(1,600 × $500) = $800,000].

Contribution Margin Technique

As in the case of break-even sales, the sales required to meet the target operating income can be calculated in either units or dollars. Illustration 6-17 shows the formula to calculate the required sales in units for Vargo Video using the contribution margin per unit.

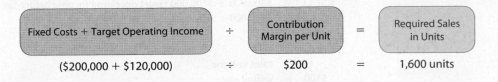

▶Illustration 6-17
Formula for required sales in units using contribution margin per unit

This calculation tells us that to achieve its desired target operating income of $120,000, the company must sell 1,600 Blu-ray DVD players.

Illustration 6-18 shows the formula to calculate the required sales in dollars for Vargo Video using the contribution margin ratio.

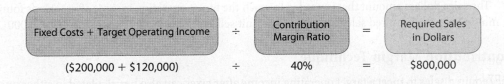

▶Illustration 6-18
Formula for required sales in dollars using contribution margin ratio

This calculation tells us that to achieve its desired target operating income of $120,000, the company must generate sales of $800,000.

Graphic Presentation

The CVP graph in Illustration 6-14 can also be used to find the sales required to meet target operating income. In the profit area of the graph, the distance between the sales line and the total cost line at any point equals operating income. The company can find the required sales amount by analyzing the differences between the two lines until it finds its desired operating income.

For example, suppose Vargo Video sells 1,400 Blu-ray DVD players. Illustration 6-14 shows that a vertical line drawn at 1,400 units intersects the sales line at $700,000 and the total cost line at $620,000. The difference between the two amounts represents the operating income (profit) of $80,000.

TARGET OPERATING INCOME AFTER TAX

So far, we have ignored the effect of income taxes in our CVP analysis.

However, management may want to know the effect of taxes on operating income and to set targets for operating income after taxes. In general, income taxes can be calculated by multiplying the tax rate by operating income before taxes. While management can then calculate the operating income after taxes by subtracting the tax amount from income before taxes, it may also use another calculation: operating income after taxes is equal to operating income before taxes multiplied by the difference between 1 and the tax rate (1 – tax rate):

Operating income after taxes = operating income before taxes × (1 − tax rate)

To figure out what the operating income before taxes needs to be in order to reach a specific target operating income after taxes, we divide the desired operating income after taxes by the difference between 1 and the tax rate (1– tax rate):

Operating income before taxes = operating income after taxes ÷ (1 − tax rate)

Using the previous example, assume that the tax rate is 40% and Vargo Video's target operating income is $120,000 after taxes. The calculation of the required sales in units is as follows:

$$\$500Q = \$300Q + \$200,000 + \frac{\$120,000}{(1-0.4)}$$

$$\$200Q = \$200,000 + \$200,000 \text{ target operating income before tax}$$
$$Q = \$400,000 \div \$200$$
$$Q = 2,000$$

where:

Q	=	sales volume
$500	=	selling price
$300	=	variable costs per unit
$200,000	=	total fixed costs
$120,000	=	target operating income
40%	=	tax rate

The sales dollars amount that is needed to reach the target operating income after taxes is found by multiplying the required sales in units by the unit selling price [(2,000 × $500) = $1,000,000].

Contribution Margin Technique

The required sales to meet a target operating income after taxes can also be calculated in either units or dollars using the contribution margin per unit, as shown in Illustration 6-19.

▶Illustration 6-19
Formula for required sales in units using contribution margin per unit

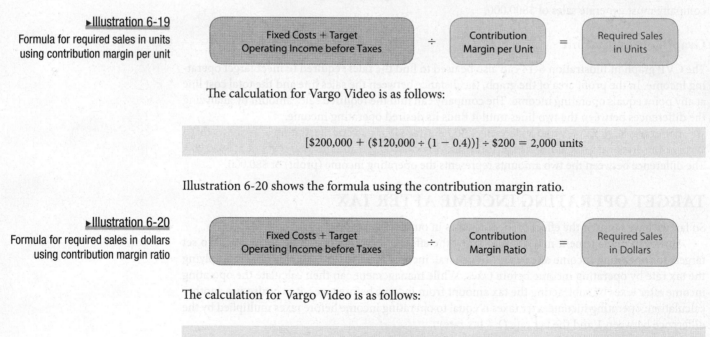

The calculation for Vargo Video is as follows:

$$[\$200,000 + (\$120,000 \div (1 - 0.4))] \div \$200 = 2,000 \text{ units}$$

Illustration 6-20 shows the formula using the contribution margin ratio.

▶Illustration 6-20
Formula for required sales in dollars using contribution margin ratio

The calculation for Vargo Video is as follows:

$$\$400,000 \div 40\% = \$1,000,000$$

MARGIN OF SAFETY

The margin of safety is another relationship that may be calculated in CVP analysis. **Margin of safety** is the difference between actual or expected sales and sales at the break-even point. This relationship measures the "cushion" that management has, allowing it to still break even if expected sales fail to be reached. The margin of safety may be expressed in dollars, units, or as a ratio.

The formula for stating the **margin of safety in dollars** is actual (or expected) sales minus break-even sales. Assuming that actual (expected) sales for Vargo Video are $750,000, Illustration 6-21 provides the calculation.

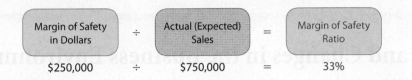

$750,000 — $500,000 = $250,000

►Illustration 6-21
Formula for margin of safety in dollars

This means that the company's sales would have to fall more than $250,000 or over 500 units before it would be operating at a loss.

The margin of safety ratio is calculated by dividing the margin of safety in dollars or in units by actual (or expected) sales in dollars or units. Illustration 6-22 provides the formula and calculation for determining the **margin of safety ratio.**

Margin of Safety in Dollars ÷ Actual (Expected) Sales = Margin of Safety Ratio

$250,000 ÷ $750,000 = 33%

►Illustration 6-22
Formula for margin of safety ratio

This means that the company's sales would have to decline by more than 33% before it would be operating at a loss.

The higher the dollars or the percentage, the greater the margin of safety will be. Based on such factors as how vulnerable the product is to competitive pressures and to downturns in the economy, management should evaluate whether or not the margin of safety is adequate.

BUSINESS INSIGHT   *Rolling in Revenues*

Calculation of break-even and margin of safety is important for service companies. Consider how the promoter for a Rolling Stones' tour would use the break-even point and margin of safety. For example, let's say that one outdoor show brings in 70,000 individuals for a gross of more than $2.4 million. The promoter guarantees $1.2 million to the Rolling Stones. In addition, 20% of gross goes to the stadium in which the performance is staged. Add another $400,000 for other expenses such as ticket takers, parking attendants, advertising, and so on. The promoter also shares in sales of T-shirts and memorabilia for which the promoter will net over $7 million during the tour. At these rates, from a successful Rolling Stones' tour, the promoter could make $35 million! In actuality, the Stones' 2013 world tour earned U.S. $126 million from 23 shows, playing to more than 325,000 people.

Sources: Robert Rheubottom, "Rolling Stones Rank Among Top 5 Highest Paid Musicians in 2014," Examiner.com, March 10, 2014; "Bon Jovi Tops List of Biggest Tours of 2013," NME.com, December 16, 2013; Sean Michaels, "Bon Jovi's World Tour Named Highest-Grossing of 2013," *The Guardian*, December 16, 2013.

What amount of sales dollars is required for the promoter to break even in this hypothetical concert tour?

BEFORE YOU GO ON...

►Do It! Break-Even, Margin of Safety, Target Operating Income

Zootsuit Inc. makes travel bags that sell for $56 each. For the coming year, management expects fixed costs to total $320,000 and variable costs to be $42 per unit. Calculate the following: (a) break-even point in dollars using the contribution margin ratio, (b) the margin of safety assuming actual sales are $1,382,400, and (c) the sales dollars required to earn operating income of $410,000.

Action Plan

- Apply the formula for the break-even point in dollars.
- Apply the formulas for the margin of safety in dollars and the margin of safety ratio.
- Apply the formula for the required sales in dollars.

(continued)

(continued)

Solution

Contribution margin ratio = [($56 − $42) ÷ $56] = 25%
Break-even sales in dollars = $320,000 ÷ 25% = $1,280,000
Margin of safety = $1,382,400 − $1,280,000 = $102,400
Margin of safety ratio = $102,400 ÷ $1,382,400 = 7.4%
Required sales in dollars = ($320,000 + $410,000) ÷ 25% = $2,920,000

Related exercise material: **BE6-5, BE6-6, BE6-7, E6-21, E6-23, E6-26, E6-29, E6-30,** and **Do It! D6-15.**

CVP and Changes in the Business Environment

STUDY OBJECTIVE 4

Understand how to apply basic cost-volume-profit concepts in a changing business environment.

When the IBM personal computer (PC) was introduced in the early 1980s, it sold for around $3,000. Today a computer with much greater functionality sells for much less. Recently, when oil prices rose, the break-even point for airline companies rose dramatically. The point should be clear: business conditions change rapidly, and management must respond intelligently to these changes. CVP analysis can help.

To show how CVP analysis can be used in responding to change, we will look at three independent situations that might occur at Vargo Video. Each case is based on the original DVD player sales and cost data, shown here again in Illustration 6-23.

▸Illustration 6-23
Original DVD player sales and cost data

Unit selling price	$500
Unit variable cost	$300
Total fixed costs	$200,000
Break-even sales	$500,000 or 1,000 units

CASE 1.   A competitor is offering a 10% discount on the selling price of its Blu-ray DVD players. Vargo Video's management must decide whether to offer a similar discount. Question: What effect will a 10% discount on the selling price have on the break-even point for Blu-ray DVD players? Answer: A 10% discount on the selling price reduces the selling price per unit to $450 [$500 − ($500 × 10%)]. Variable costs per unit remain unchanged at $300. Thus, the contribution margin per unit is $150. Assuming no change in fixed costs, break-even sales are 1,333 units, as calculated in Illustration 6-24.

▸Illustration 6-24
Calculation of break-even sales in units

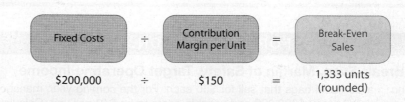

Fixed Costs	÷	Contribution Margin per Unit	=	Break-Even Sales
$200,000	÷	$150	=	1,333 units (rounded)

For Vargo Video, this change would thus require monthly sales to increase by 333 units, or 33.3%, in order to break even. In reaching a conclusion about offering a 10% discount to customers, management must determine how likely it is to achieve the increased sales. Also, management should estimate the possible loss of sales if it doesn't match the competitor's discount price.

CASE 2.   To meet the threat of foreign competition, management invests in new robotic equipment that will lower the amount of direct labour required to make Blu-ray DVD players. It is estimated that total fixed costs will increase by 30% and that the variable cost per unit will decrease by 30%.

Question: What effect will the new equipment have on the sales volume required to break even? Answer: Total fixed costs become $260,000 [$200,000 + (30% × $200,000)]. The variable cost per unit becomes $210 [$300 − (30% × $300)]. The new break-even point is approximately 900 units, as calculated in Illustration 6-25.

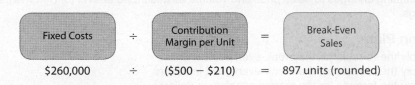

Fixed Costs	÷	Contribution Margin per Unit	=	Break-Even Sales
$260,000	÷	($500 − $210)	=	897 units (rounded)

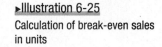
▶Illustration 6-25
Calculation of break-even sales in units

These changes appear to be advantageous for Vargo Video. The break-even point is reduced by 10%, or 100 units.

CASE 3. Vargo Video's principal supplier of raw materials has just announced a price increase. The higher cost is expected to increase the variable cost of Blu-ray DVD players by $25 per unit. Management would like to keep the same selling price for the Blu-ray DVD players. It plans a cost-cutting program that will save $17,500 in fixed costs per month. Vargo Video is currently realizing monthly operating income before taxes of $80,000 on sales of 1,400 Blu-ray DVD players. Question: What increase in units sold will Vargo need to maintain the same level of operating income? Answer: The variable cost per unit increases to $325 ($300 + $25). Fixed costs are reduced to $182,500 ($200,000 − $17,500). Because of the change in variable cost, the contribution margin per unit becomes $175 ($500 − $325). The required number of units sold to achieve the target operating income is as calculated in Illustration 6-26.

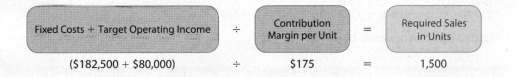

Fixed Costs + Target Operating Income	÷	Contribution Margin per Unit	=	Required Sales in Units
($182,500 + $80,000)	÷	$175	=	1,500

▶Illustration 6-26
Calculation of required sales

To achieve the required sales, 1,500 Blu-ray DVD players will have to be sold, an increase of 100 units. If this does not seem to be a reasonable expectation, management will either have to make further cost reductions or accept less operating income if the selling price remains unchanged.

BEFORE YOU GO ON...

▶Do It! CVP Analysis

Krisanne Company reports the following operating results for the month of June.

KRISANNE COMPANY
CVP Income Statement
For the Month Ended June 30, 2016

	Total	Per Unit
Sales (5,000 units)	$300,000	$60
Variable costs	180,000	36
Contribution margin	120,000	$24
Fixed expenses	100,000	
Operating income	$ 20,000	

To increase operating income, management is considering reducing the selling price by 10%, with no changes to unit variable costs or fixed costs. Management is confident that this change will increase unit sales by 25%.

(continued)

(continued)

Using the contribution margin technique, calculate the break-even point in units and dollars and margin of safety in dollars, (a) assuming no changes to sales price or costs, and (b) assuming changes to sales price and volume as described above. (c) Comment on your findings.

Action Plan
- Apply the formula for the break-even point in units.
- Apply the formula for the break-even point in dollars.
- Apply the formula for the margin of safety in dollars.

Solution
(a) Assuming no changes to sales price or costs: Break-even point in units = 4,167 units (rounded) ($100,000 ÷ $24). Break-even point in sales dollars = $250,000 = ($100,000 ÷ 0.40[a]). Margin of safety in dollars = $50,000 = ($300,000 − $250,000).

(b) Assuming changes to sales price and volume:
Break-even point in units = 5,556 units (rounded) ($100,000 ÷ $18[b]).
Break-even point in sales dollars = $300,000 = ($100,000 ÷ ($18 ÷ $54)).
Margin of safety in dollars = $37,500 = ($337,500[c] − $300,000).

(c) The increase in the break-even point and the decrease in the margin of safety indicate that management should not implement the proposed change. The increase in sales volume will result in a contribution margin of $112,500 (6,250 × $18), which is $7,500 less than the current amount.

[a] $24 ÷ $60
[b] [$60 − (0.10 × $60) − 36] = $18
[c] [5,000 + (0.25 × 5,000)] = 6,250 units, 6,250 units × $54 = $337,500

Related exercise material: **Do It! D6-17.**

DECISION TOOLKIT

Decision Checkpoints	Info Needed for Decision	Tools to Use for Decision	How to Evaluate Results
How can a company use CVP analysis to improve profitability?	Data on what the effect on volume and costs would be of a price change, a fixed-cost change, or a trade-off between fixed and variable costs	Measurement of income at new volume levels	If profitability increases under the proposed change, adopt the change.

Sales Mix

STUDY OBJECTIVE 5

Explain the term *sales mix* and its effect on break-even sales.

To this point, our discussion of CVP analysis has assumed that a company sells only one product. However, most companies sell multiple products. When a company sells many products, it is important that management understand its sales mix.

The **sales mix** is the relative proportion in which each product is sold when a company sells more than one product. For example, if 80% of Hewlett Packard's unit sales are printers and the other 20% are PCs, its sales mix is 80% to 20%.

Sales mix is important to managers because different products often have substantially different contribution margins. For example, Ford's SUVs and F-150 pickup trucks have higher contribution margins compared with its economy cars. Similarly, first-class tickets sold by Air Canada provide substantially higher contribution margins than economy-class tickets.

BREAK-EVEN SALES IN UNITS

Companies can calculate break-even sales for a mix of two or more products by determining the **weighted-average unit contribution margin of all the products.** To illustrate, assume that Vargo Video sells not only Blu-ray DVD players but high-definition TV sets as well. Vargo sells its two products in the following amounts: 1,500 Blu-ray DVD players and 500 TVs. Illustration 6-27 shows the sales mix, expressed as a function of total units sold.

Blu-ray DVD players	TVs
1,500 units ÷ 2,000 units = 75%	500 units ÷ 2,000 units = 25%

▶Illustration 6-27
Sales mix as a function of units sold

That is, 75% of the units sold are Blu-ray DVD players and 25% of the units sold are TVs.

Illustration 6-28 shows additional information related to Vargo Video. The unit contribution margin for Blu-ray DVD players is $200, and for TVs it is $500. Vargo's fixed costs total $275,000.

Unit Data	Blu-ray DVD Players	TVs
Selling price	$500	$1,000
Variable costs	300	500
Contribution margin	$200	$ 500
Sales mix—units	75%	25%
Fixed costs = $275,000		

▶Illustration 6-28
Per-unit data—sales mix

To calculate break-even for Vargo, we then determine the weighted-average unit contribution margin for the two products. We use the weighted-average contribution margin because Vargo sells three times as many Blu-ray DVD players as TV sets, and therefore the Blu-ray DVD players must be counted three times for every TV set sold. The weighted-average contribution margin for a sales mix of 75% Blu-ray DVD players and 25% TVs is $275, which is calculated as shown in Illustration 6-29.

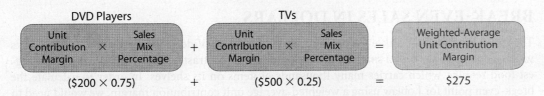

▶Illustration 6-29
Weighted-average unit contribution margin

We then use the weighted-average unit contribution margin of $275 to calculate the break-even point in unit sales. The calculation of break-even sales in units for Vargo Video, assuming $275,000 of fixed costs, is shown in Illustration 6-30.

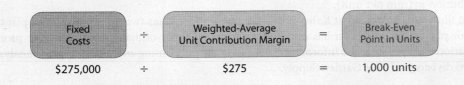

▶Illustration 6-30
Break-even point in units

As shown in Illustration 6-30, the break-even point in units for Vargo Video is 1,000 units. Therefore, in order to break even, Vargo must sell 750 Blu-ray DVD players (0.75 × 1,000 units) and 250 TVs (0.25 × 1,000). This can be verified by the calculations in Illustration 6-31, which shows that the total contribution margin is $275,000 when 1,000 units are sold, which equals the fixed costs of $275,000.

▶Illustration 6-31
Break-even proof—sales units

Product	Unit Sales	×	Unit Contribution Margin	=	Total Contribution Margin
Blu-ray DVD players	750	×	$200	=	$150,000
TVs	250	×	500	=	125,000
	1,000				$275,000

Management should continually review the company's sales mix. At any level of units sold, **operating income will be greater if higher contribution margin units are sold, rather than lower contribution margin units.** For Vargo Video, the television sets produce the higher contribution margin. Consequently, if Vargo sells 300 TVs and 700 Blu-ray DVD players, operating income would be higher than in the current sales mix, even though total units sold are the same.

An analysis of these relationships shows that a shift from low-margin sales to high-margin sales may increase operating income, even though there is a decline in total units sold. Likewise, a shift from high- to low-margin sales may result in a decrease in operating income, even though there is an increase in total units sold.

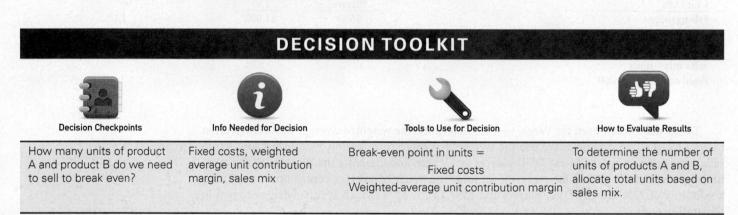

DECISION TOOLKIT

Decision Checkpoints	Info Needed for Decision	Tools to Use for Decision	How to Evaluate Results
How many units of product A and product B do we need to sell to break even?	Fixed costs, weighted average unit contribution margin, sales mix	Break-even point in units = $\dfrac{\text{Fixed costs}}{\text{Weighted-average unit contribution margin}}$	To determine the number of units of products A and B, allocate total units based on sales mix.

BREAK-EVEN SALES IN DOLLARS

The calculation of the break-even point presented for Vargo Video in the previous section works well if a company has only a *small number* of products. In contrast, consider Loblaw, Canada's largest food retailer, which carries many thousands of items on its shelves. In order to calculate the break-even point for Loblaw using a weighted-average unit contribution margin, we would need to calculate thousands of different unit contribution margins. That is not realistic.

Therefore, for a company like Loblaw, we calculate the break-even point in terms of sales dollars (rather than units sold), using sales information for divisions or product lines (rather than individual products). This approach requires that we calculate sales mix as a percentage of total sales dollars (rather than units sold) and that we calculate the contribution margin ratio (rather than contribution margin per unit).

To illustrate, suppose that Kale Garden Supply Company has two divisions: indoor plants and outdoor plants. Each division has hundreds of different types of plants and plant-care products. Illustration 6-32 provides the information necessary for performing cost-volume-profit analysis for the two divisions of Kale Garden Supply.

	Indoor Plant Division	Outdoor Plant Division	Total
Sales	$ 200,000	$ 800,000	$1,000,000
Variable costs	120,000	560,000	680,000
Contribution margin	$ 80,000	$ 240,000	$ 320,000
Sales-mix percentage			
(Division sales ÷ Total sales)	$\frac{\$200,000}{\$1,000,000} = 0.20$	$\frac{\$800,000}{\$1,000,000} = 0.80$	
Contribution margin ratio (Contribution margin ÷ Sales)	$\frac{\$80,000}{\$200,000} = 0.40$	$\frac{\$240,000}{\$800,000} = 0.30$	$\frac{\$320,000}{\$1,000,000} = 0.32$
Total fixed costs = $300,000			

►Illustration 6-32
Cost-volume-profit data for Kale Garden Supply

As shown in Illustration 6-32, the contribution margin ratio for the combined company is 32%, which is calculated by dividing the total contribution margin by total sales. It is useful to note that the contribution margin ratio of 32% is a weighted average of the individual contribution margin ratios of the two divisions (40% and 30%). To illustrate, in Illustration 6-33 we multiply each division's contribution margin ratio by its sales-mix percentage, based on dollar sales, and then add these amounts. As shown later, the calculation in Illustration 6-33 is useful because it enables us to determine how the break-even point changes when the sales mix changes.

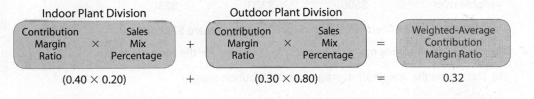

►Illustration 6-33
Calculation of weighted-average contribution margin

Kale Garden Supply's break-even point in dollars is then calculated by dividing fixed costs by the weighted-average contribution margin ratio of 32%, as shown in Illustration 6-34.

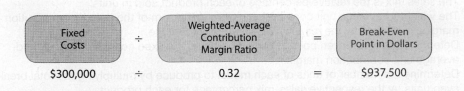

►Illustration 6-34
Calculation of break-even point in dollars

The break-even point is based on the sales mix of 20% to 80%. Of the company's total break-even sales of $937,500, a total of $187,500 (0.20 × $937,500) will come from the Indoor Plant division, and $750,000 (0.80 × $937,500) will come from the outdoor plant division.

What would be the impact on the break-even point if a higher percentage of Kale Garden Supply's sales were to come from the indoor plant division? Because the indoor plant division enjoys a higher contribution margin ratio, this change in the sales mix would result in a higher weighted-average contribution margin ratio, and consequently a lower break-even point in dollars. For example, if the sales mix changes to 50% for the indoor plant division and 50% for the outdoor plant division, the weighted-average contribution margin ratio would be 35% [(0.40 × 0.50) + (0.30 × 0.50)]. The new, lower, break-even point is $857,143 ($300,000 ÷ 0.35). The opposite would occur if a higher percentage of sales were expected from the outdoor plant division. As you can see, the information provided using CVP analysis can help managers better understand the impact of sales mix on profitability.

DECISION TOOLKIT

Decision Checkpoints	Info Needed for Decision	Tools to Use for Decision	How to Evaluate Results
How many dollars of sales are required from each division in order to break even?	Fixed costs, weighted-average contribution margin, sales mix	Break-even point in dollars = $\dfrac{\text{Fixed costs}}{\text{Weighted-average contribution margin ratio}}$	To determine the sales dollars required from each division, allocate the total break-even sales using the sales mix.

BEFORE YOU GO ON...

▶Do It! Sales Mix Break-Even

Manzeck Bicycles International produces and sells three different types of mountain bikes. Information regarding the three models is shown below.

	Pro	Intermediate	Standard	Total
Units sold	5,000	10,000	25,000	40,000
Selling price	$800	$500	$350	
Variable cost	$500	$300	$250	

The company's total fixed costs to produce the bicycles are $7.5 million.

(a) Determine the sales mix as a function of units sold for the three products.

(b) Determine the weighted-average unit contribution margin.

(c) Determine the total number of units that the company must produce to break even.

(d) Determine the number of units of each model that the company must produce to break even.

Action Plan

• The sales mix is the relative percentage of each product sold in units.
• The weighted-average unit contribution margin is the sum of the per-unit contribution margins multiplied by the respective sales-mix percentage.
• Determine the break-even point in units by dividing the fixed costs by the weighted-average unit contribution margin.
• Determine the number of units of each model to produce by multiplying the total break-even units by the respective sales-mix percentage for each product.

Solution

(a) The sales-mix percentages as a function of units sold are as follows:

Pro	Intermediate	Standard
5,000 ÷ 40,000 = 12.5%	10,000 ÷ 40,000 = 25%	25,000 ÷ 40,000 = 62.5%

(b) The weighted-average unit contribution margin is as follows:

[0.125 × ($800 − $500)] + [0.25 × ($500 − $300)] + [0.625 × ($350 − $250)] = $150

(c) The break-even point in units is as follows:

$7,500,000 ÷ $150 = 50,000 units

(continued)

(continued)

(d) The break-even units to produce for each product are the following:

Pro:	50,000 units × 12.5% =	6,250 units
Intermediate:	50,000 units × 25% =	12,500 units
Standard:	50,000 units × 62.5% =	31,250 units
		50,000 units

Related exercise material: **BE6-12, BE6-13, E6-22, E6-32, E6-33, E6-34, E6-35, E6-36,** and **Do It! D6-18.**

✔ the navigator

USING THE DECISION TOOLKIT

B. T. Hernandez Company, maker of high-quality flashlights, has experienced steady growth over the last six years. However, increased competition has led Mr. Hernandez, the president, to believe that an aggressive campaign is needed next year to maintain the company's present growth. The company's accountant has presented Mr. Hernandez with the following data for the current year, 2016, for use in preparing next year's advertising campaign.

COST SCHEDULES

Variable costs		
Direct labour per flashlight	$	8.00
Direct materials		4.00
Variable overhead		3.00
Variable cost per flashlight	$	15.00
Fixed costs		
Manufacturing	$	25,000
Selling		40,000
Administrative		70,000
Total fixed costs		$135,000
Selling price per flashlight	$	25.00
Expected sales, 2017 (20,000 flashlights)		$500,000

Mr. Hernandez has set the sales target for the year 2017 at $550,000 (22,000 flashlights).

Instructions

(Ignore any income tax considerations.)

(a) What is the projected operating income for 2017?

(b) What is the contribution margin per unit for 2017?

(c) What is the break-even point in units for 2017?

(d) Mr. Hernandez believes that to attain the sales target in the year 2017, the company must incur an additional selling expense of $10,000 for advertising in 2017, with all other costs remaining constant. What will be the break-even point in sales dollars for 2017 if the company spends the additional $10,000?

(e) If the company spends the additional $10,000 for advertising in 2017, what is the sales level in dollars required to equal 2016 operating income?

Solution

(a) Expected sales		$500,000
Less:		
Variable cost (20,000 flashlights × $15)		300,000
Fixed costs		135,000
Projected operating income		$ 65,000

(continued)

(continued)

(b) Selling price per flashlight $25
      Variable cost per flashlight   15
      Contribution margin per unit $10

(c) Fixed costs ÷ Contribution margin per unit = Break-even point in units
      $135,000 ÷ $10 = 13,500 units

(d) Fixed costs ÷ Contribution margin ratio = Break-even point in dollars
      $145,000* ÷ 40%** = $362,500

*Fixed costs (from 2016)	$135,000
Additional advertising expense	10,000
Fixed costs (2017)	$145,000

      **Contribution margin ratio = Contribution margin per unit ÷ Unit selling price
      $10 ÷ $25 = 40%

(e) Required sales (Fixed costs + Target operating income) ÷ Contribution margin ratio
      $525,000 = ($145,000 + $65,000) ÷ 40%

the
navigator

APPENDIX 6A—COST STRUCTURE AND OPERATING LEVERAGE

STUDY OBJECTIVE 6
Understand how cost structure and operating leverage affect profitability.

Cost structure refers to the relative proportion of fixed versus variable costs that a company incurs. Cost structure can have a significant effect on profitability. For example, a telecom systems company can substantially reduce its fixed costs by choosing to outsource all of its production. While this makes a company less susceptible to economic swings, it also reduces its ability to experience very high levels of profitability during good times.

Companies must carefully consider their choice of cost structure. Companies can influence their cost structure in many ways. For example, by acquiring sophisticated robotic equipment, many companies have reduced their use of manual labour. Similarly, discount brokerage firms, such as TD Waterhouse, have reduced their reliance on human brokers and have instead invested heavily in computers and on-line technology. In doing so, they have increased their reliance on fixed costs (through depreciation on the computer equipment) and reduced their reliance on variable costs (the variable employee labour cost).

Alternatively, some companies have reduced their fixed costs and increased their variable costs by outsourcing their production. Nike, for example, does very little manufacturing, but instead outsources the manufacture of nearly all of its shoes. It has consequently converted many of its fixed costs into variable costs and therefore changed its cost structure.

Consider the following example of Vargo Video and one of its competitors, New Wave Company. Both make Blu-ray DVD players. Vargo Video uses a traditional, labour-intensive manufacturing process. New Wave Company has invested in a completely automated system. The factory employees are involved only in setting up, adjusting, and maintaining the machinery. Illustration 6A-1 shows CVP income statements for each company.

▶Illustration 6A-1
CVP income statements for two companies

	Vargo Video	New Wave Company
Sales	$800,000	$800,000
Variable costs	480,000	160,000
Contribution margin	320,000	640,000
Fixed costs	200,000	520,000
Operating income	$120,000	$120,000

Both companies have the same sales and the same operating income. However, because of the differences in their cost structures, they differ greatly in the risks and rewards related to increasing or decreasing sales. Let's evaluate the impact of cost structure on the profitability of the two companies.

EFFECT ON CONTRIBUTION MARGIN RATIO

First let's look at the contribution margin ratio. Illustration 6A-2 shows the calculation of the contribution margin ratio for each company.

	Contribution Margin	÷	Sales	=	Contribution Margin Ratio
Vargo Video	$320,000	÷	$800,000	=	0.40
New Wave	$640,000	÷	$800,000	=	0.80

►Illustration 6A-2
Contribution margin ratio for two companies

New Wave has a contribution margin ratio of 80% versus only 40% for Vargo. That means that with every dollar of sales, New Wave generates 80 cents of contribution margin (and thus an 80-cent increase in operating income), versus only 40 cents for Vargo. However, it also means that for every dollar that sales decline, New Wave loses 80 cents in operating income, whereas Vargo will lose only 40 cents. New Wave's cost structure, which relies more heavily on fixed costs, makes it more sensitive to changes in sales revenue.

EFFECT ON BREAK-EVEN POINT

The difference in cost structure also affects the break-even point. Illustration 6A-3 shows the calculation for the break-even point for each company.

	Fixed Costs	÷	Contribution Margin Ratio	=	Break-even Point in Dollars
Vargo Video	$200,000	÷	0.40	=	$500,000
New Wave	$520,000	÷	0.80	=	$650,000

►Illustration 6A-3
Calculation of break-even point for two companies

New Wave needs to generate $150,000 ($650,000 − $500,000) more in sales than Vargo before it breaks even. This makes New Wave riskier than Vargo because a company cannot survive for very long unless it at least breaks even.

EFFECT ON MARGIN OF SAFETY RATIO

We can also evaluate the relative impact that changes in sales would have on the two companies by calculating the margin of safety ratio. Illustration 6A-4 shows the calculation of the **margin of safety ratio** for the two companies.

	(Actual Sales	−	Break-Even Sales)	÷	Actual Sales	=	Margin of Safety Ratio
Vargo Video	($800,000	−	$500,000)	÷	$800,000	=	0.38
New Wave	($800,000	−	$650,000)	÷	$800,000	=	0.19

►Illustration 6A-4
Calculation of margin of safety ratio for two companies

The difference in the margin of safety ratio also reflects the difference in risk between the two companies. Vargo could sustain a 38% decline in sales before it would be operating at a loss. New Wave could sustain only a 19% decline in sales before it would be "in the red."

OPERATING LEVERAGE

Operating leverage is the extent to which a company's operating income reacts to a given change in sales. Companies that have higher fixed costs relative to variable costs have higher operating leverage. When a company's sales revenue is increasing, high operating leverage is a good thing because it means that profits will increase rapidly. But when sales are declining, too much operating leverage can have devastating consequences.

How can we compare operating leverage between two companies? The **degree of operating leverage** provides a measure of a company's earnings volatility and can be used to compare companies. The degree of operating leverage is calculated by dividing contribution margin by operating income. Illustration 6A-5 presents this formula and applies it to our two manufacturers of Blu-ray DVD players.

▶Illustration 6A-5
Calculation of degree of operating leverage

	Contribution Margin	÷	Operating Income	=	Degree of Operating Leverage
Vargo Video	$320,000	÷	$120,000	=	2.67
New Wave	$640,000	÷	$120,000	=	5.33

New Wave's earnings would go up (or down) by about two times (5.33 ÷ 2.67 = 2.00) as much as Vargo's with an equal increase (or decrease) in sales. For example, suppose both companies experience a 10% decrease in sales. Vargo's operating income will decrease by 26.7% (2.67 × 10%), while New Wave's will decrease by 53.3% (5.33 × 10%). Thus, New Wave's higher operating leverage exposes it to greater earnings volatility risk.

You should be careful not to conclude from this analysis that a cost structure that relies on higher fixed costs, and consequently has higher operating leverage, is necessarily bad. When used carefully, operating leverage can add considerably to a company's profitability. For example, computer equipment manufacturer Komag enjoyed a 66% increase in operating income when its sales increased by only 8%. A commentator noted that, "Komag's fourth quarter illustrated the company's significant operating leverage; and that a small increase in sales leads to a big profit rise." However, as our illustration demonstrates, increased reliance on fixed costs increases a company's risk.

BEFORE YOU GO ON...

▶Do It! Operating Leverage

Rexfield Corp., a company specializing in crime scene investigations (CSIs), is contemplating an investment in automated mass-spectrometers. Its current process relies on a high number of lab technicians. The new equipment would employ a computerized expert system. The company's CEO has requested a comparison of the old technology versus the new technology. The accounting department has prepared the following CVP income statements for use in your analysis.

	CSI Equipment	
	Old	New
Sales	$2,000,000	$2,000,000
Variable costs	1,400,000	600,000
Contribution margin	600,000	1,400,000
Fixed costs	400,000	1,200,000
Net income	$ 200,000	$ 200,000

Use the information provided above to do the following.

(a) Calculate the degree of operating leverage for the company under each scenario.

(b) Discuss your results.

(continued)

(continued)

Action Plan

- Divide contribution margin by net income to determine degree of operating leverage.
- A higher degree of operating leverage will result in a higher change in net income with a given change in sales.

Solution

(a)

	Contribution Margin	÷	Net Income	=	Degree of Operating Leverage
Old	$ 600,000	÷	$200,000	=	3
New	$1,400,000	÷	$200,000	=	7

(b) The degree of operating leverage measures the company's sensitivity to changes in sales. By switching to a cost structure dominated by fixed costs, the company would significantly increase its operating leverage. As a result, with a percentage change in sales, its percentage change in net income would be 2.33 (7 ÷ 3) times as much with the new technology as it would under the old.

Related exercise material: **BE6-8, BE6-9, E6-31, E6-37, E6-38,** and **Do It! D6-19.**

 ALL ABOUT YOU *A Hybrid Dilemma*

Have you been tempted to buy a hybrid or all-electric vehicle? They use less gas and don't pollute as much. The most fuel-efficient hybrids, such as the Toyota Prius, can save about $770 per year in fuel (driving 20,000 km, roughly half-city and half-highway, at $1.29 per litre) compared with a similar gas-powered car. But some hybrids cost as much as $6,000 more than conventional models, meaning it may take several years to make your money back in fuel savings. Fuel savings for hybrids are greater in the city. So if you mainly drive on the highway, and don't drive that many kilometres in a year, a hybrid may end up costing more to operate over the long term.

What Do You Think?

Gas prices are eating into your wallet. Does it make sense to buy a hybrid vehicle?

YES—With some hybrids using only around four litres of gas to drive 100 km in the city, I can drive forever before filling up.

NO—Most of my driving is on the highway; I don't think that the extra cost of the vehicle is worth it.

Sources: Jeremy Cato and Michael Vaughan, "What Should He Buy—Diesel or Hybrid?," *The Globe and Mail,* May 2, 2014; Natural Resources Canada, "Fuel Consumption Guide 2013;" "Hybrids & Diesels: Do They Save Money?," *Consumer Reports,* February 2012.

DECISION TOOLKIT

Decision Checkpoints	Info Needed for Decision	Tools to Use for Decision	How to Evaluate Results
How sensitive is the company's operating income to changes in sales?	Contribution margin and operating income	Degree of operating leverage = $\dfrac{\text{Contribution margin}}{\text{Net income}}$	Operating leverage reports the change in operating income that will occur with a given change in sales. A high degree of operating leverage means that the company's operating income is very sensitive to changes in sales.

USING THE DECISION TOOLKIT

Rexfield Corp. is contemplating a huge investment in automated mass-spectrometers for its medical laboratory testing services. Its current process relies heavily on the expertise of a high number of lab technicians. The new equipment would employ a computer expert system that integrates much of the decision-making process and knowledge base that a skilled lab technician currently provides.

Rex Field, the company's CEO, has requested that an analysis of projected results using the old technology versus the new technology be done for the coming year. The accounting department has prepared the following CVP income statements for use in your analysis:

	Old	New
Sales revenue	$2,000,000	$2,000,000
Variable costs	1,400,000	600,000
Contribution margin	600,000	1,400,000
Fixed costs	400,000	1,200,000
Operating income	$ 200,000	$ 200,000

Instructions

Use the information provided above to calculate the break-even point in dollars and the margin of safety ratio for the company under each scenario, and discuss your results.

Solution

(a) To calculate the break-even point in sales dollars, we first need to calculate the contribution margin ratio under each scenario. Under the old structure, the contribution margin ratio would be 0.30 ($600,000 ÷ $2,000,000), and under the new, it would be 0.70 ($1,400,000 ÷ $2,000,000).

	Fixed Costs	÷	Contribution Margin Ratio	=	Break-Even Point in Dollars
Old	$ 400,000	÷	0.30	=	$1,333,333
New	$1,200,000	÷	0.70	=	$1,714,286

Because the company's fixed costs would be substantially higher under the new cost structure, its break-even point would increase significantly, from $1,333,333 to $1,714,286. A higher break-even point is riskier because it means that the company must generate higher sales to be profitable.

The margin of safety ratio tells how far sales can fall before the company is operating at a loss.

	(Actual Sales	−	Break-Even Sales)	÷	Actual Sales	=	Margin of Safety Ratio
Old	($2,000,000	−	$1,333,333)	÷	$2,000,000	=	0.33
New	($2,000,000	−	$1,714,286)	÷	$2,000,000	=	0.14

Under the old structure, sales could fall by 33% before the company would be operating at a loss. Under the new structure, sales could fall by only 14%.

the navigator

Summary of Study Objectives

1. *Prepare a cost-volume-profit income statement to determine contribution margin.* The five components of CVP analysis are (1) volume or level of activity, (2) unit selling prices, (3) variable cost per unit, (4) total fixed costs, and (5) sales mix. The CVP income statement classifies costs as variable or fixed and calculates a contribution margin.

   Contribution margin is the amount of revenue remaining after deducting variable costs. It is identified in a CVP income statement, which classifies costs as variable or fixed. It can be expressed as a per-unit amount or as a ratio.

2. *Calculate the break-even point using three approaches.* The break-even point can be (1) calculated with a mathematical equation, (2) calculated by using a contribution margin technique, or (3) derived from a CVP graph.

3. *Determine the sales required to earn the target operating income and define the margin of safety.*
   Target NI before tax: One formula is required sales = variable costs + fixed costs + target operating income. Another formula is fixed costs + target operating income ÷ contribution margin ratio = required sales.

   Target NI after tax: One formula is required sales = variable costs + fixed costs + target operating income before tax. Another formula is fixed costs + target operating income before tax ÷ contribution margin ratio = required sales.

   Margin of safety is the difference between actual or expected sales and sales at the break-even point. The formulas for margin of safety are actual (expected) sales − break-even sales = margin of safety in dollars, and margin of safety in dollars ÷ actual (expected) sales = margin of safety ratio.

4. *Understand how to apply basic cost-volume-profit concepts in a changing business environment.* CVP can be used to respond to business changes by calculating the break-even sales point, such as when deciding whether to match a competitor's discount, whether to invest in new equipment, and when determining how many units must be sold in order to achieve a target operating income.

5. *Explain the term* **sales mix** *and its effect on break-even sales.* The sales mix is the relative proportion in which each product is sold when a company sells more than one product. For a multi-product company, break-even sales in units is determined by using the weighted-average unit contribution margin of all the products. If the company sells many different products, calculating the break-even point using unit information is not practical. Instead, the company calculates the break-even sales in dollars using the weighted-average contribution margin ratio.

6. *Understand how cost structure and operating leverage affect profitability (Appendix 6A).* Operating leverage is how much a company's operating income reacts to a change in sales. Operating leverage is determined by a company's relative use of fixed versus variable costs. Companies with high fixed costs relative to variable costs have a high operating leverage. A company with a high operating leverage will experience a sharp increase (decrease) in operating income with an increase (decrease) in sales. A company can measure the degree of operating leverage by dividing the contribution margin by operating income.

DECISION TOOLKIT—A SUMMARY

Decision Checkpoints	Info Needed for Decision	Tools to Use for Decision			How to Evaluate Results
What was the contribution toward fixed costs and income from each unit sold?	Selling price per unit and variable cost per unit	Contribution margin per unit	Unit selling = price	Unit − variable cost	Every unit sold will increase income by the contribution margin.
What was the increase in income as a result of an increase in sales?	Contribution margin per unit and unit selling price	Contribution margin ratio	Contribution = margin per unit	Unit selling ÷ price	Every dollar of sales will increase income by the contribution margin ratio.
At what amount of sales does a company cover its costs?	Unit selling price, unit variable cost, and total fixed costs	Break-even point analysis *In units:* $$\text{Break-even point} = \frac{\text{Fixed costs}}{\text{Unit contribution margin}}$$ *In dollars:* $$\text{Break-even point} = \frac{\text{Fixed costs}}{\text{Contribution margin ratio}}$$			Below the break-even point—the point at which total sales equal total costs—the company is unprofitable.

(continued)

(continued)

DECISION TOOLKIT—A SUMMARY

Decision Checkpoints	Info Needed for Decision	Tools to Use for Decision	How to Evaluate Results
How can a company use CVP analysis to improve profitability?	Data on what the effect on volume and costs would be of a price change, a fixed-cost change, or a trade-off between fixed and variable costs	Measurement of income at new volume levels	If profitability increases under the proposed change, adopt the change.
How many units of product A and product B do we need to sell to break even?	Fixed costs, weighted-average unit contribution margin, sales mix	Break-even point in units = $\dfrac{\text{Fixed costs}}{\text{Weighted-average unit contribution margin}}$	To determine the number of units of products A and B, allocate total units based on sales mix.
How many dollars of sales are required from each division in order to break even?	Fixed costs, weighted-average contribution margin ratio, sales mix	Break-even point in dollars = $\dfrac{\text{Fixed costs}}{\text{Weighted-average contribution margin ratio}}$	To determine the sales dollars required from each division, allocate the total break-even sales using the sales mix.
How sensitive is the company's operating income to changes in sales?	Contribution margin and operating income	Degree of operating leverage = $\dfrac{\text{Contribution margin}}{\text{Net income}}$	Operating leverage reports the change in operating income that will occur with a given change in sales. A high degree of operating leverage means that the company's operating income is very sensitive to changes in sales.

Glossary

Break-even point The level of activity at which total revenues equal total costs. (p. 222)

Contribution margin (CM) The amount of revenue remaining after deducting variable costs. (p. 218)

Contribution margin per unit The amount of revenue remaining per unit after deducting variable costs; calculated as the unit selling price minus the unit variable cost. (p. 220)

Contribution margin ratio The percentage of each dollar of sales that is available to contribute to operating income; calculated as the contribution margin per unit divided by the unit selling price. (p. 220)

Cost structure The proportion of fixed costs versus variable costs that a company incurs. (p. 238)

Cost-volume-profit (CVP) analysis The study of the effects of changes in costs and volume on a company's profits. (p. 218)

Cost-volume-profit (CVP) graph A graph showing the relationship between costs, volume, and profits. (p. 224)

Cost-volume-profit (CVP) income statement A statement for internal use that classifies costs and expenses as fixed or variable, and reports contribution margin in the body of the statement. (p. 218)

Degree of operating leverage The percentage effect on profits of a specific percentage increase in sales volume; calculated by dividing the total contribution margin by net profit. (p. 240)

Margin of safety The difference between actual or expected sales and sales at the break-even point. (p. 228)

Operating leverage The effect that fixed costs have on operating profit as a result of a specific percentage change in the sales volume. (p. 239)

Sales mix The relative percentage in which each product is sold when a company sells more than one product. (p. 232)

Target operating income The income objective for individual product lines. (p. 226)

Comprehensive Do It!

Mabo Company makes calculators that sell for $20 each. For the coming year, management expects fixed costs to total $220,000 and variable costs to be $9 per unit.

Instructions
(a) Calculate the break-even point in units using the mathematical equation.
(b) Calculate the break-even point in dollars using the contribution margin ratio.
(c) Calculate the margin of safety percentage, assuming actual sales are $500,000.
(d) Calculate the sales required in dollars to earn an operating income of $165,000.

Solution to Comprehensive Do It!

(a)

Sales	=	variable costs + fixed costs + operating income
$20Q	=	$9Q + $220,000 + $0
$11Q	=	$220,000
Q	=	20,000 units

(b)

Contribution margin per unit	=	unit selling price – unit variable costs
$11	=	$20 – $9
Contribution margin ratio	=	contribution margin per unit ÷ selling price
55%	=	$11 ÷ $20
Break-even point in dollars	=	fixed cost contribution margin ratio
	=	$220,000 ÷ 55%
	=	$400,000

(c)

$$\text{Margin of safety} = \frac{\text{actual sales – break-even sales}}{\text{actual sales}}$$

$$= \frac{\$500,000 - \$400,000}{\$500,000}$$

$$= 20\%$$

(d)

Required sales	=	variable costs + fixed costs + operating income
$20Q	=	$9Q + $220,000 + $165,000
$11Q	=	$385,000
Q	=	35,000 units
35,000 units × $20	=	$700,000 required sales

Action Plan
- Know the formulas.
- Recognize that variable costs change with the sales volume; fixed costs do not.
- Avoid calculation errors.
- Prove your answers.

the navigator

WileyPLUS   Self-Test, Brief Exercises, Exercises, Problems—Set A, and many more components are available for practice in WileyPlus.

Self-Study Questions

Answers are at the end of the chapter.
(The asterisk * indicates material discussed in the chapter appendix.)

(SO 1) 1. Which one of the following is the format of a CVP income statement?
(a) Sales − Variable costs = Fixed costs + Operating income
(b) Sales − Fixed costs − Variable costs − Operating expenses = Operating income
(c) Sales − Cost of goods sold − Operating expenses = Operating income
(d) Sales − Variable costs − Fixed costs = Operating income

(SO 1)   2. Croc Catchers calculates its contribution margin to be less than zero. Which statement is true?
(a) Its fixed costs are less than the variable cost per unit.
(b) Its profits are greater than its total costs.
(c) The company should sell more units.
(d) Its selling price is less than its variable costs.

(SO 1)   3. The following information is available for Chap Company:

Sales	$350,000
Cost of goods sold	$120,000
Total fixed expenses	$ 60,000
Total variable expenses	$100,000

Which amount would you find on Chap's CVP income statement?
(a) Contribution margin of $250,000
(b) Contribution margin of $190,000
(c) Gross profit of $230,000
(d) Gross profit of $190,000

(SO 1)   4. Cournot Company sells 100,000 wrenches for $12 a unit. Fixed costs are $300,000, and operating income is $200,000. What should it report as variable expenses in the CVP income statement?
(a) $700,000
(b) $900,000
(c) $500,000
(d) $1,000,000

(SO 2)   5. Which one of the following describes the break-even point?
(a) It is the point where total sales equals total variable costs plus total fixed costs.
(b) It is the point where the contribution margin equals zero.
(c) It is the point where total variable costs equal total fixed costs.
(d) It is the point where total sales equals total fixed costs.

(SO 3)   6. Operating income will be
(a) greater if more higher-contribution-margin units are sold than lower-contribution-margin units.

(b) greater if more lower-contribution-margin units are sold than higher-contribution-margin units.
(c) equal as long as total sales remain equal, regardless of which products are sold.
(d) unaffected by changes in the mix of products sold.

(SO 3)   7. Marshall Company had actual sales of $600,000 when break-even sales were $420,000.What is the margin of safety ratio?'
(a) 25%
(b) 30%
(c) 35$^{1/3}$%
(d) 45%

(SO 5)   8. Sales mix is
(a) important to sales managers but not to accountants.
(b) easier to analyze on traditional income statements.
(c) a measure of the relative percentage of a company's variable costs to its fixed costs.
(d) a measure of the relative percentage in which a company's products are sold.

(SO 6)   *9. A high degree of operating leverage
(a) indicates that a company has a larger percentage of variable costs relative to its fixed costs.
(b) is calculated by dividing fixed costs by contribution margin.
(c) exposes a company to greater earnings volatility risk.
(d) exposes a company to less earnings volatility risk.

(SO 6) *10. The degree of operating leverage
(a) can be calculated by dividing total contribution margin by operating income.
(b) provides a measure of the company's earnings volatility.
(c) affects a company's break-even point.
(d) All of the above.

✓
the navigator

Brief Exercises

(SO 1)
Determine missing amounts for the contribution margin.

BE6-1   Determine the missing amounts:

Unit Selling Price	Unit Variable Costs	Contribution Margin per Unit	Contribution Margin Ratio
1. $640	$352	(a)	(b)
2. $300	(c)	$ 93	(d)
3. (e)	(f)	$325	25%

(SO 1)
Prepare a CVP income statement.

BE6-2   Fontillas Manufacturing Inc. had sales of $2.4 million for the first quarter of 2016. In making the sales, the company incurred the following costs and expenses:

	Variable	Fixed
Cost of goods sold	$920,000	$440,000
Selling expenses	70,000	45,000
Administrative expenses	86,000	98,000

Prepare a CVP income statement for the quarter ended March 31, 2016.

BE6-3 Panciuk Company has a unit selling price of $520, variable costs per unit of $286, and fixed costs of $163,800. Calculate the break-even point in units using (a) the mathematical equation and (b) the contribution margin per unit.

(SO 2)
Calculate the break-even point.

BE6-4 A firm sells its product for $30 per unit. Its direct material costs are $6 per unit and direct labour costs are $4. Manufacturing overhead costs are $40,000 per period and $8 per unit. Calculate the required sales in dollars to break even.

(SO 2)
Calculate the break-even point.

BE6-5 For Biswell Company, variable costs are 70% of sales and fixed costs are $195,000. Calculate the required sales in dollars that are needed to achieve management's target operating income of $75,000. (Use the contribution margin approach.)

(SO 3)
Calculate sales for target operating income.

BE6-6 For Korb Company, actual sales are $1 million and break-even sales are $840,000. Calculate (a) the margin of safety in dollars and (b) the margin of safety ratio.

(SO 3)
Calculate margin of safety and ratio.

BE6-7 NYX Inc. sells its product for $24 per unit and variable costs are $14 per unit. Its fixed costs are $130,000. Calculate the required sales in units to achieve its target operating income of 10% of total costs.

(SO 3)
Calculate required sales for target operating income.

*BE6-8 The degrees of operating leverage for Delta Corp. and Epsilon Co. are 1.4 and 5.6, respectively. Both have operating incomes of $50,000. Determine their respective contribution margins.

(SO 6)
Determine the contribution margin.

*BE6-9 Sanjay's Shingle Corporation is considering the purchase of a new automated shingle-cutting machine. The new machine will reduce variable labour costs but will increase depreciation expense. The contribution margin is expected to increase from $160,000 to $240,000. Operating income is expected to be the same at $40,000. Calculate the degree of operating leverage before and after the purchase of the new equipment. Interpret your results.

(SO 6)
Calculate the degree of operating leverage.

*BE6-10 Presented below are the CVP income statements for Finch Company and Sparrow Company. They are in the same industry, with the same operating incomes, but different cost structures.

(SO 2, 6)
Calculate the break-even point with a change in operating leverage.

	Finch Co.	Sparrow Co.
Sales	$200,000	$200,000
Variable costs	80,000	50,000
Contribution margin	120,000	150,000
Fixed costs	60,000	90,000
Operating income	$ 60,000	$ 60,000

Calculate the break-even point in dollars for each company and comment on your findings.

BE6-11 Family Furniture Co. has two divisions: bedroom division and dining room division. The results of operations for the most recent quarter are as follows:

(SO 1)
Determine the weighted-average contribution margin.

	Bedroom Division	Dining Room Division
Sales	$500,000	$750,000
Variable costs	250,000	450,000
Contribution margin	$250,000	$300,000

Determine the company's weighted-average contribution margin ratio.

BE6-12 Russell Corporation sells three different models of mosquito "zapper." Model A12 sells for $50 and has variable costs of $40. Model B22 sells for $100 and has variable costs of $70. Model C124 sells for $400 and has variable costs of $300. The sales mix of the three models is as follows: A12, 60%; B22, 25%; and C124, 15%.

(SO 2, 5)
Calculate weighted-average unit contribution margin and the break-even point in units for a company with multiple products.

(a) What is the weighted-average unit contribution margin?
(b) If the company's fixed costs are $199,500, how many units of each model must the company sell in order to break even?

BE6-13 Presto Candle Supply makes candles. The sales mix (as a percentage of total dollar sales) of its three product lines is birthday candles 30%, standard tapered candles 50%, and large scented candles 20%. The contribution margin ratio of each candle type is as follows:

(SO 2, 5)
Calculate the break-even point in dollars for a company with multiple product lines.

Candle Type	Contribution Margin Ratio
Birthday	20%
Standard tapered	20%
Large scented	45%

If the company's fixed costs are $440,000 per year, what is the dollar amount of each type of candle that must be sold to break even?

Do It! Review

(SO 1, 2)
Calculate break-even
point in units.

D6-14   Vince Company has a unit selling price of $250, variable cost per unit of $160, and fixed costs of $135,000.

Instructions

Calculate the break-even point in units using (a) the mathematical equation and (b) contribution margin per unit.

(SO 1, 2, 3)
Calculate break-even
point, margin of safety
ratio, and sales for
target operating
income.

D6-15   Queensland Company makes radios that sell for $30 each. For the coming year, management expects fixed costs to total $200,000 and variable costs to be $20 per unit.

Instructions

(a) Calculate the break-even point in dollars using the contribution margin (CM) ratio.
(b) Calculate the margin of safety ratio assuming actual sales are $750,000.
(c) Calculate the sales dollars required to earn operating income of $120,000.

(SO 1)
Prepare CVP income
statement and calculate
contribution margin.

D6-16   Naylor Manufacturing Inc. sold 8,000 units and recorded sales of $400,000 for the first month of 2016. In making the sales, the company incurred the following costs and expenses.

	Variable	Fixed
Cost of goods sold	$184,000	$70,000
Selling expenses	40,000	30,000
Administrative expenses	16,000	40,000

Instructions

(a) Prepare a CVP income statement for the month ended January 31, 2016.
(b) Calculate the contribution margin per unit.
(c) Calculate the contribution margin ratio.

(SO 2, 3, 4)
Calculate the break-
even point and margin
of safety under
different alternatives.

D6-17   Cottonwood Company reports the following operating results for the month of April.

COTTONWOOD COMPANY
CVP Income Statement
For the Month Ended April 30, 2016

	Total	Per Unit
Sales (9,000 units)	$450,000	$50.00
Variable costs	247,500	27.50
Contribution margin	202,500	$22.50
Fixed expenses	150,000	
Operating income	$ 52,500	

Management is considering the following course of action to increase operating income: Reduce the selling price by 10%, with no changes to unit variable costs or fixed costs. Management is confident that this change will increase unit sales by 30%.

Instructions

Using the contribution margin technique, calculate the break-even point in units and dollars and margin of safety in dollars,

(a) assuming no changes to selling price or costs, and
(b) assuming changes to sales price and volume as described above.

Comment on your findings.

(SO 1, 2, 3, 5)
Calculate sales mix,
weighted-average
contribution margin,
and break-even point.

D6-18   Glacial Springs produces and sells water filtration systems for homeowners. Information regarding its three models is shown below.

	Basic	Basic Plus	Premium	Total
Units sold	840	350	210	1,400
Selling price	$250	$400	$800	
Variable cost	$195	$288	$416	

The company's total fixed costs to produce the filtration systems are $140,000.

Instructions
(a) Determine the sales mix as a function of units sold for the three products.
(b) Determine the weighted-average unit contribution margin.
(c) Determine the total number of units that the company must produce to break even.
(d) Determine the number of units of each model that the company must produce to break even.

*D6-19   Bergen Hospital is contemplating an investment in an automated surgical system. Its current process relies on the number of skilled physicians. The new equipment would employ a computer robotic system operated by a technician. The company requested an analysis of the old technology versus the new technology. The accounting department has prepared the following CVP income statements for use in your analysis.

(SO 6)
Determine operating leverage.

	Old	New
Sales	$3,000,000	$3,000,000
Variable costs	1,600,000	700,000
Contribution margin	1,400,000	2,300,000
Fixed costs	1,000,000	1,900,000
Operating income	$ 400,000	$ 400,000

Instructions
(a) Calculate the degree of operating leverage for the company under each scenario.
(b) Discuss your results.

Exercises

E6-20   Kirkland Video Games Inc has spent $450,000 to develop a new video game. It is the most sophisticated game in the market. It sells the video game for $250 per copy. Variable costs to produce and sell the video game amount to $50 per copy. The company anticipates selling 300 copies of the game per month. The company's policy is to stop producing the video game as soon as a competitor comes out with a more sophisticated version of the video game.

(SO 2, 3)
Calculate break-even point and sales required to earn target operating income in dollars.

Instructions
(a) Calculate the amount of operating income the company will earn if it takes 10 months for a competitor to produce a more sophisticated version of the video game.
(b) Calculate how many units of the video game the company will have to sell in order to break even.
(c) If the company wishes to earn $30,000 over the product's life, calculate the selling price of the video game if a competitor introduces a more sophisticated version of the video game in six months. Assume that unit sales are 300 copies per month.

E6-21   Jagswear, Inc. earned operating income of $100,000 during 2016. The company wants to earn operating income of $140,000 during 2016. Its fixed costs are expected to be $56,000, and variable costs are expected to be 30% of sales.

(SO 3)
Calculate the sales required to earn target operating income in dollars.

Instructions
(a) Determine the required sales to meet the target operating income during 2016.
(b) Fill in the dollar amounts for the summary income statement for 2016 below based on your answer to part A.

Sales revenue	$
Variable costs	
Contribution margin	
Fixed costs	
Operating income	$

E6-22   Trail King manufactures mountain bikes. Its sales mix and contribution margin information per unit are as follows:

(SO 5)
Calculate the break-even point in units for a company with more than one product.

	Sales mix	Contribution margin
Destroyer	15%	$120
Voyager	60%	$ 60
Rebel	25%	$ 40

It has fixed costs of $5,440,000.

Instructions
Calculate the number of each type of bike that the company would need to sell in order to break even under this product mix.

(SO 2, 3)
Calculate the break-even point and margin of safety.

E6-23   The Richibouctou Inn is trying to determine its break-even point. The inn has 75 rooms available that are rented at $50 a night. Operating costs are as follows:

Salaries	$10,000 per month	Maintenance	$500 per month
Utilities	2,000 per month	Housekeeping service	5 per room
Depreciation	1,000 per month	Other costs	25 per room

Instructions
(a) Determine the inn's break-even point in (1) the number of rented rooms per month and (2) dollars.
(b) If the inn plans on renting 30 rooms per day (assuming a 30-day month), what is (1) the monthly margin of safety in dollars and (2) the margin of safety ratio?

(SO 1)
Calculate the variable cost per unit, contribution margin ratio, and increase in fixed costs.

E6-24   In 2015, Demuth Company had a break-even point of $350,000 based on a selling price of $5 per unit and fixed costs of $112,000. In 2016, the selling price and the variable cost per unit did not change, but the break-even point increased to $420,000.

Instructions
(a) Calculate the variable cost per unit and the contribution margin ratio for 2015.
(b) Calculate the increase in fixed costs for 2016.

(SO 1, 2)
Calculate the contribution margin and break-even point.

E6-25   In the month of June, New Day Spa served 560 clients at an average price of $120. During the month, fixed costs were $21,024 and variable costs were 60% of sales.

Instructions
(a) Determine the contribution margin in dollars, per unit, and as a ratio.
(b) Using the contribution margin technique, calculate the break-even point in dollars and in units.

(SO 1, 3)
Calculate various components to derive target operating income under different assumptions.

E6-26   Johansen Company had $210,000 of operating income in 2016 when the selling price per unit was $150, the variable costs per unit were $90, and the fixed costs were $570,000. Management expects per-unit data and total fixed costs to remain the same in 2017. The president of Johansen Company is under pressure from shareholders to increase operating income by $52,000 in 2017.

Instructions
(a) Calculate the number of units sold in 2016.
(b) Calculate the number of units that would have to be sold in 2017 to reach the shareholders' desired profit level.
(c) Assume that Johansen Company sells the same number of units in 2017 as it did in 2016. What would the selling price have to be in order to reach the shareholders' desired profit level?

(SO 1)
Calculate operating income under different alternatives.

E6-27   Moran Company reports the following operating results for the month of August: sales $310,000 (units 5,000); variable costs $217,000; and fixed costs $70,000. Management is considering the following independent courses of action to increase operating income:

1. Increase the selling price by 10% with no change in total variable costs.
2. Reduce variable costs to 65% of sales.
3. Reduce fixed costs by $10,000.

Instructions
Calculate the operating income to be earned under each alternative. Which course of action will produce the highest operating income?

(SO 2)
Calculate break-even point and contribution margin.

E6-28   Friendly Airways, Inc., a small two-plane passenger airline, has asked for your assistance in some basic analysis of its operations. Both planes seat 10 passengers each, and they fly commuters from Friendly's base airport to the major city in the province, Metropolis. Each month 40 round-trip flights are made. Shown below is a recent month's activity in the form of a cost-volume-profit income statement.

Fare revenues (400 fares)		$50,000
Variable costs		
Fuel	$17,900	
Snacks and drinks	1,400	
Landing fees	2,000	
Supplies and forms	1,200	22,500
Contribution margin		27,500
Fixed costs		
Depreciation	3,000	
Salaries	15,000	
Advertising	2,250	
Airport hangar fees	1,750	22,000
Operating income		$ 5,500

Instructions

(a) Calculate the break-even point in (1) dollars and (2) number of fares.

(b) Without calculations, determine the contribution margin at the break-even point.

(c) If fares were decreased by 10%, an additional 80 fares could be generated. However, total variable costs would increase by 20%. Should the fare decrease be adopted?

E6-29 Embleton Company estimates that variable costs will be 60% of sales, and fixed costs will total $800,000. The selling price of the product is $4.

Instructions

(a) Prepare a CVP graph, assuming maximum sales of $3.2 million. (*Note*: Use $400,000 increments for sales and costs, and 100,000 increments for units.)

(b) Calculate the break-even point in (1) units and (2) dollars.

(c) Assuming actual sales are $2.5 million, calculate the margin of safety in (1) dollars and (2) as a ratio.

(SO 2, 3)
Prepare a CVP graph and calculate the break-even point and margin of safety.

E6-30 Volmar Company had sales in 2016 of $1,250,000 on 50,000 units. Variable costs totalled $600,000, and fixed costs totalled $500,000.

A new raw material is available that will decrease the variable costs per unit by 20% (or $2.40). However, to process the new raw material, fixed operating costs will increase by $50,000. Management feel that one half of the decline in the variable costs per unit should be passed on to customers in the form of a sales price reduction. The marketing department expects that this sales price reduction will result in a 10% increase in the number of units sold.

Instructions

Prepare a CVP income statement for 2016, (a) assuming the changes have not been made, and (b) assuming that changes are made as described.

(SO 1, 3)
Prepare a CVP income statement before and after changes in the business environment.

*E6-31 An investment banker is analyzing two companies that specialize in the production and sale of candied apples. Old-Fashion Apples uses a labour-intensive approach, and Mech-Apple uses a mechanized system. Variable costing income statements for the two companies are shown below:

	Old-Fashion Apples	Mech-Apple
Sales	$400,000	$400,000
Variable costs	320,000	160,000
Contribution margin	80,000	240,000
Fixed costs	30,000	190,000
Operating income	$ 50,000	$ 50,000

(SO 6)
Calculate the degree of operating leverage and the impact on the operating income of alternative cost structures.

The investment banker wants to acquire one of these companies. However, she is concerned about the impact that each company's cost structure might have on its profitability.

Instructions

(a) Calculate each company's degree of operating leverage. Determine which company's cost structure makes it more sensitive to changes in its sales volume. Present your answer in terms of the contribution margin ratio.

(b) Determine the effect on each company's operating income (1) if sales decrease by 15% and (2) if sales increase by 10%. Do not prepare income statements.

(c) Determine which company the investment banker should acquire. Explain.

E6-32 Grass King manufactures lawn mowers, weed trimmers, and chainsaws. Grass King has fixed costs of $4.2 million. Its sales mix and contribution margin per unit are as follows:

	Sales Mix	Contribution Margin per Unit
Lawn mowers	20%	$30
Weed trimmers	50%	$20
Chainsaws	30%	$40

(SO 5)
Calculate the break-even point in units for a company with more than one product.

Instructions

Calculate the number of units of each product that Grass King must sell in order to break even under this product mix.

E6-33 Rapid Auto has over 200 auto-maintenance service outlets nationwide. It provides two main lines of service: oil changes and brake repair. Oil changes and related services represent 70% of its sales and provide a contribution margin ratio of 20%. Brake repair represents 30% of its sales and provides a 60% contribution margin ratio. The company's fixed costs are $16 million (that is, $80,000 per service outlet).

(SO 2, 3, 5)
Calculate the product line break-even point and target operating income in dollars for a company with more than one product.

Instructions

(a) Calculate the dollar amount of each type of service that the company must provide in order to break even.

(b) The company has a desired operating income of $60,000 per service outlet. Calculate the dollar amount of each type of service that must be provided by each service outlet to meet the company's target operating income per outlet.

(SO 2, 5)
Calculate the product line break-even point in dollars for a company with more than one product.

E6-34 Blazer Delivery is a rapidly growing delivery service. Last year, 80% of its revenue came from the delivery of mailing "pouches" and small, standardized delivery boxes (which provides a 20% contribution margin). The other 20% of its revenue came from delivering non-standardized boxes (which provides a 70% contribution margin). With the rapid growth of Internet retail sales, Blazer believes that there are great opportunities for growth in the delivery of non-standardized boxes. The company has fixed costs of $12 million.

Instructions

(a) Calculate the company's break-even point in total sales dollars. At the break-even point, how much of the company's sales are provided by each type of service?

(b) The company's management would like to keep its fixed costs constant, but shift its sales mix so that 60% of its revenue comes from the delivery of non-standardized boxes and the remainder from pouches and small boxes. Determine what the company's break-even sales would be, and what amount of sales would be provided by each service if this were to occur.

(SO 2, 5)
Calculate the break-even point in units for a company with multiple products.

E6-35 Veejay Golf Accessories sells golf shoes, gloves, and a laser-guided range-finder that measures distance. Shown below are unit cost and sales data:

	Pairs of Shoes	Pairs of Gloves	Range-Finder
Unit sales price	$100	$30	$270
Unit variable costs	60	10	200
Unit contribution margin	$ 40	$20	$ 70
Sales mix	40%	50%	10%

Fixed costs are $660,000.

Instructions

(a) Calculate the break-even point in units for the company.

(b) Determine the number of units to be sold at the break-even point for each product line.

(c) Verify that the mix of sales units determined in part (b) will generate a zero operating income.

(SO 1, 2, 5)
Determine the break-even point in dollars for two divisions.

E6-36 Mega Electronix sells television sets and Blu-ray DVD players. The business is divided into two divisions along product lines. A variable cost income statement for a recent quarter's activity is presented below:

	TV Division	Blu-ray DVD Player Division	Total
Sales	$800,000	$200,000	$1,000,000
Variable costs	560,000	160,000	720,000
Contribution margin	$240,000	$ 40,000	280,000
Fixed costs			140,000
Operating income			$ 140,000

Instructions

(a) Determine the percentage of sales and contribution margin for each division.

(b) Calculate the company's weighted-average contribution margin ratio.

(c) Calculate the company's break-even point in dollars.

(d) Determine the sales level in dollars for each division at the break-even point.

(SO 6)
Calculate the degree of operating leverage and evaluate the impact of alternative cost structures on operating income.

*E6-37 The CVP income statements shown below are available for Billings Company and Bozeman Company.

	Billings Co.	Bozeman Co.
Sales revenue	$600,000	$600,000
Variable costs	320,000	120,000
Contribution margin	280,000	480,000
Fixed costs	180,000	380,000
Operating income	$100,000	$100,000

Instructions

(a) Calculate the degree of operating leverage for each company and interpret your results.

(b) Assuming that sales revenue increases by 10%, prepare a variable costing income statement for each company.

(c) Discuss how the cost structure of these two companies affects their operating leverage and profitability.

*E6-38   Imagen Arquitectónica of Tijuana, Mexico is contemplating a major change in its cost structure. Currently, all of its drafting work is performed by skilled draftspersons. Alfredo Ayala, Imagen's owner, is considering replacing the draftspersons with a computerized drafting system.

However, before making the change, Alfredo would like to know its consequences, since the volume of business varies significantly from year to year. Shown below are CVP income statements for each alternative:

	Manual System	Computerized System
Sales	$1,500,000	$1,500,000
Variable costs	$1,200,000	900,000
Contribution margin	300,000	600,000
Fixed costs	200,000	500,000
Operating income	$ 100,000	$ 100,000

(SO 3, 6)
Calculate the degree of operating leverage and evaluate the impact of alternative cost structures on operating income and margin of safety.

Instructions
(a) Determine the degree of operating leverage for each alternative.
(b) Calculate which alternative would produce the higher operating income if sales increased by $100,000.
(c) Using the margin of safety ratio, determine which alternative could sustain the greater decline in sales before operating at a loss.

Problems: Set A

P6-39A   Ronald Enterprises, Ltd. has estimated the following costs for producing and selling 15,000 units of its product:

Direct materials	$75,000
Direct labour	90,000
Variable overhead	45,000
Fixed overhead	30,000
Variable selling and administrative expenses	60,000
Fixed selling and administrative expenses	40,000

Ronald Enterprises' income tax rate is 40%.

(SO 2)
Calculate the break-even point in units and target income after tax.

Instructions
(a) Given that the selling price of one unit is $38, calculate how many units Ronald Enterprises would have to sell in order to break even.
(b) Assume the selling price is $43 per unit. Calculate how many units Ronald Enterprises would have to sell in order to produce a profit of $25,000 before taxes.
(c) Calculate what price Ronald Enterprises would have to charge in order to produce a profit of $30,000 after taxes if 7,500 units were produced and sold.
(d) Calculate what price Ronald Enterprises would have to charge in order to produce a before-tax profit equal to 30% of sales if 9,000 units were produced and sold.

(adapted from CGA-Canada, now CPA Canada)

(a) variable cost per unit, $18

P6-40A   The Peace Barber Shop employs four barbers. One barber, who also serves as the manager, is paid a salary of $3,900 per month. The other barbers are paid $1,900 per month. In addition, each barber is paid a commission of $2 per haircut. Other monthly costs are as follows: store rent $700 plus 60 cents per haircut; depreciation on equipment $500; barber supplies 40 cents per haircut; utilities $300; and advertising $100. The price of a haircut is $11.

(SO 1, 2, 3)
Determine variable and fixed costs, calculate the break-even point, prepare a CVP graph, and determine operating income.

Instructions
(a) Determine the variable cost per haircut and the total monthly fixed costs.
(b) Calculate the break-even point in units and dollars.
(c) Prepare a CVP graph, assuming a maximum of 1,800 haircuts in a month. Use increments of 300 haircuts on the horizontal axis and $3,000 increments on the vertical axis.
(d) Determine the operating income, assuming 1,700 haircuts are given in a month.

(b) break-even in units, 1,400

P6-41A   Montreal Seating Co., a manufacturer of chairs, had the following data for 2016:

Sales	2,800 units
Sales price	$50 per unit
Variable costs	$30 per unit
Fixed costs	$30,000

(SO 1, 2, 3)
Determine the contribution margin ratio, break-even point in dollars, and margin of safety.

(a) CM ratio = 40%

Instructions

(a) Calculate the contribution margin ratio.

(b) Calculate the break-even point in dollars.

(c) Calculate the margin of safety in dollars.

(d) The company wishes to increase its total dollar contribution margin by 60% in 2017. Determine by how much it will need to increase its sales if all other factors remain constant.

(adapted from CGA-Canada, now CPA Canada)

(SO 1, 2, 3)
Determine the contribution margin ratio, break-even point in dollars, margin of safety, and sales required to earn target operating income under alternative scenarios.

P6-42A   YUX Corporation sells a single product for $50. Its management estimates the following revenues and costs for the year 2016:

Net sales	$500,000	Selling expenses—variable	$20,000
Direct materials	90,000	Selling expenses—fixed	20,000
Direct labour	60,000	Administrative expenses—variable	10,000
Manufacturing overhead—variable	20,000	Administrative expenses—fixed	10,000
Manufacturing overhead—fixed	30,000		

Instructions

(a) Assuming fixed costs and net sales are spread evenly throughout the year, determine YUX's monthly break-even point in (1) units and (2) dollars.

(b) CM ratio = 60%

(b) Calculate the contribution margin ratio, the annual margin of safety ratio, and the annual profit.

(c) Determine the percentage increase of annual profits if YUX Corporation increases its selling price by 20% and all other factors (including demand) remain constant.

(d) Assume the price remains at $50 per unit and variable costs remain the same per unit, but fixed costs increase by 20% annually. Calculate the percentage increase in unit sales required to achieve the same level of annual profit calculated in part (b).

(e) Determine the sales required to earn an operating income of $360,000 after tax. YUX Corporation's income tax is 40%.

(SO 1, 2, 4)
Calculate the break-even point under alternative courses of action.

P6-43A   Gorham Manufacturing's sales slumped badly in 2016. For the first time in its history, it operated at a loss. The company's income statement showed the following results from selling 60,000 units of product: net sales $1.8 million; total costs and expenses $2,010,000; and net loss $210,000. Costs and expenses consisted of the amounts shown below:

	Total	Variable	Fixed
Cost of goods sold	$1,350,000	$ 930,000	$420,000
Selling expenses	480,000	125,000	355,000
Administrative expenses	180,000	115,000	65,000
	$2,010,000	$1,170,000	$840,000

Management is considering the following independent alternatives for 2017:

1. Increase the unit selling price by 25% with no change in costs, expenses, and sales volume.

2. Change the compensation of salespersons from fixed annual salaries totalling $200,000 to total salaries of $20,000 plus a 5% commission on net sales.

3. Purchase new high-tech factory machinery that will change the proportion between variable and fixed cost of goods sold to 50:50.

Instructions

(a) Calculate the break-even point in dollars for 2016.

(b) Alternative 1, $1,750,000

(b) Calculate the break-even point in dollars under each of the alternative courses of action. (Round all ratios to nearest full percent.)

(SO 1, 2)
Determine the break-even point in dollars and units, and target income.

(a) OI = $390,000

P6-44A   The vice-president of marketing, Carol Chow, thinks that her firm can increase sales by 15,000 units for each $5-per-unit reduction in its selling price. The company's current selling price is $90 per unit and variable expenses are $60 per unit. Fixed expenses are $810,000 per year. The current sales volume is 40,000 units.

Instructions

Answer the following questions:

(a) What is the current yearly operating income?

(b) What is the current break-even point in units and in dollar sales?

(SO 1, 2, 3, 4)
Calculate the break-even point and margin of safety ratio, and prepare a CVP income statement before and after changes in the business environment.

(c) Assuming that Carol is correct, what is the maximum profit that the firm could generate yearly? At how many units and at what selling price(s) per unit would this profit be generated? Assume that capacity is not a problem and total fixed expenses will be the same regardless of volume.

(d) What would be the break-even point(s) in units and in dollar sales using the selling price(s) you have determined?

(adapted from CGA-Canada, now CPA Canada)

P6-45A   Alice Oritz is the advertising manager for Value Shoe Store. She is currently working on a major promotional campaign. Her ideas include the installation of a new lighting system and increased display space that will add $18,000 in fixed costs to the $216,000 currently spent. In addition, Alice is proposing that a 10% price decrease ($30 to $27) will produce a 20% increase in sales volume (20,000 to 24,000). Variable costs will remain at $12 per pair of shoes. Management are impressed with Alice's ideas but are concerned about the effects that these changes will have on the break-even point and the margin of safety.

Instructions

(a) Calculate the current break-even point in units, and compare it with the break-even point in units if Alice's ideas are used.

(b) Calculate the margin of safety ratio for current operations and for after Alice's changes are introduced. (Round to nearest full percent.)

(c) Prepare a CVP income statement for current operations and for after Alice's changes are introduced. (Show column for total amounts only.) Would you make the changes suggested?

(b) Current margin of safety ratio = 40%

P6-46A Poole Corporation has collected the following information after its first year of sales. Net sales were $1.6 million on 100,000 units, selling expenses were $240,000 (40% variable and 60% fixed), direct materials were $511,000, direct labour was $285,000, administrative expenses were $280,000 (20% variable and 80% fixed), and manufacturing overhead was $360,000 (70% variable and 30% fixed). Top management has asked you to do a CVP analysis so that it can make plans for the coming year. Management has projected that unit sales will increase by 10% next year.

(SO 1, 2, 3, 4)
Calculate the contribution margin, fixed costs, break-even point, sales for target net income, and margin of safety ratio, and prepare a CVP income statement before and after changes in the business environment.

Instructions

(a) Calculate (1) the contribution margin for the current year and the projected year, and (2) the fixed costs for the current year. (Assume that fixed costs will remain the same in the projected year.)

(b) Calculate the break-even point in units and sales dollars for the first year.

(c) The company has a target operating income of $310,000. Calculate the required sales amount in dollars for the company to meet its target.

(d) Assuming the company meets its target operating income number, calculate by what percentage its sales could fall before the company operates at a loss. That is, what is its margin of safety ratio?

(e) The company is considering a purchase of equipment that would reduce its direct labour costs by $104,000 and would change its manufacturing overhead costs to 30% variable and 70% fixed (assume the total manufacturing overhead cost is $360,000, as above). It is also considering switching to a pure commission basis for its sales staff. This would change selling expenses to 90% variable and 10% fixed (assume the total selling expense is $240,000, as above). Calculate (1) the contribution margin and (2) the contribution margin ratio, and (3) recalculate the break-even point in sales dollars. Comment on the effect each of management's proposed changes has on the break-even point.

(a) Contribution margin (current year) = $400,000

P6-47A Kosinksi Manufacturing carries no inventories. Its product is manufactured only when a customer's order is received. It is then shipped immediately after it is made. For its fiscal year ended October 31, 2016, Kosinksi's break-even point was $1,350,000. On sales of $1.3 million, its full-cost income statement showed a gross profit of $200,000, direct materials cost of $400,000, and direct labour costs of $500,000. The contribution margin was $117,000, and variable manufacturing overhead was $100,000.

(SO 1)
Determine the contribution margin ratio.

Instructions

(a) Calculate the following:
1. Variable selling and administrative expenses
2. Fixed manufacturing overhead
3. Fixed selling and administrative expenses

(b) Ignoring your answer to part (a), assume that fixed manufacturing overhead was $100,000 and the fixed selling and administrative expenses were $80,000. The marketing vice-president feels that if the company increased its advertising, sales could be increased by 15%. Determine the maximum increased advertising cost the company can incur and still report the same income as before the advertising expenditure.

(a) 1. Variable S&A = $183,000

(adapted from CGA-Canada, now CPA Canada)

P6-48A Newton Cellular Ltd. manufactures and sells the TopLine cell phone. For its 2016 business plan, Newton Cellular estimated the following:

(SO 1, 2, 3)
Determine the contribution margin, break-even point, and target operating income.

Selling price	$750
Variable cost per cell phone	$450
Annual fixed costs	$180,000
Net (after-tax) income	$360,000
Tax rate	25%

The March financial statements reported that sales were not meeting expectations. For the first three months of the year, only 400 units had been sold at the established price. With variable costs staying as planned, it was clear that the 2016 after-tax profit projection would not be reached unless some action was taken. A management committee presented the following mutually exclusive alternatives to the president:

1. Reduce the selling price by $60. The sales team forecasts that, with the significantly reduced selling price, 3,000 units can be sold during the remainder of the year. Total fixed and variable unit costs will stay as budgeted.

2. Lower variable costs per unit by $20 through the use of less expensive direct materials and slightly modified manufacturing techniques. The selling price will also be reduced by $40, and sales of 2,800 units for the remainder of the year are forecast.

3. Cut fixed costs by $20,000 and lower the selling price by 5%. Variable costs per unit will be unchanged. Sales of 2,500 units are expected for the remainder of the year.

Instructions

(a) units to break even, 600

(a) Under the current production policy, determine the number of units that the company must sell to break even and achieve its desired operating income.

(b) Determine which alternative the company should select to achieve its desired operating income.

(adapted from CMA Canada, now CPA Canada)

(SO 2, 3, 6)
Determine the contribution margin, break-even point, target sales, and degree of operating leverage.

*P6-49A   Olin Beauty Corporation manufactures cosmetic products that are sold through a network of sales agents. The agents are paid a commission of 18% of sales. The income statement for the year ending December 31, 2016, is as follows:

OLIN BEAUTY CORPORATION
Income Statement
Year Ending December 31, 2016

Sales		$78,000,000
Cost of goods sold		
Variable	$36,660,000	
Fixed	7,940,000	44,600,000
Gross margin		33,400,000
Selling and marketing expenses		
Commissions	$14,040,000	
Fixed costs	10,260,000	24,300,000
Operating income		$ 9,100,000

The company is considering hiring its own sales staff to replace the network of agents. It will pay its salespeople a commission of 10% and incur fixed costs of $6,240,000.

Instructions

(a) CM ratio = 35%

(a) Under the current policy of using a network of sales agents, calculate the Olin Beauty Corporation's break-even point in sales dollars for the year 2016.

(b) Calculate the company's break-even point in sales dollars for the year 2016 if it hires its own sales force to replace the network of agents.

(c) Calculate the degree of operating leverage at sales of $78 million if Olin Beauty (1) uses sales agents, and (2) employs its own sales staff. Describe the advantages and disadvantages of each alternative.

(d) Calculate the estimated sales volume in sales dollars that would generate an identical operating income for the year ending December 31, 2016, regardless of whether Olin Beauty Corporation employs its own sales staff and pays them a 10% commission or continues to use the independent network of agents.

(adapted from CMA Canada, now CPA Canada)

(SO 1, 2)
Determine the contribution margin, break-even point in units, and target income.

P6-50A   Martin Footwear Co. produces high-quality shoes. To prepare for next year's marketing campaign, the company's controller has prepared the following information for the current year, 2016:

Variable costs (per pair of shoes)	
Direct materials	$40.00
Direct manufacturing labour	19.00
Variable overhead (manufacturing, marketing, distribution, customer service, and administration)	21.00
Total variable costs	$80.00
Fixed costs	
Manufacturing	$2,750,000
Marketing, distribution, and customer service	500,000
Administrative	750,000
Total fixed costs	$4,000,000
Selling price per pair of shoes	$ 180
Expected revenues, 2016 (50,000 units)	$9,000,000
Income tax rate	40%

Instructions

(a) $1.0 million

(a) Calculate the projected operating income before tax for 2016.

(b) Calculate the break-even point in units for 2016.

(c) The company controller has set the revenue target for 2017 at $9.9 million (or 55,000 pairs). He believes an additional marketing cost of $400,000 for advertising in 2017, with all other costs remaining constant, will be necessary to attain the revenue target. Calculate the operating income for 2017 if the additional $400,000 is spent and the revenue target is met.

(adapted from CMA Canada, now CPA Canada)

*P6-51A   The following CVP income statements are available for Old Company and New Company:

	Old Company	New Company
Sales revenue	$400,000	$400,000
Variable costs	180,000	80,000
Contribution margin	220,000	320,000
Fixed costs	170,000	270,000
Operating income	$ 50,000	$ 50,000

Instructions
(a) Calculate the break-even point in dollars and the margin of safety ratio for each company.
(b) Calculate the degree of operating leverage for each company and interpret your results.
(c) Assuming that sales revenue increases by 20%, prepare a variable cost income statement for each company.
(d) Assuming that sales revenue decreases by 20%, prepare a variable cost income statement for each company.
(e) Discuss how the cost structure of these two companies affects their operating leverage and profitability.

P6-52A   The Creekside Inn is a restaurant that specializes in southwestern style meals in a moderate price range. Terry Ducasse, the manager of Creekside, has determined that during the last two years the sales mix and contribution margin ratio of its offerings have been as follows:

	Percent of Total Sales	Contribution Margin Ratio
Appetizers	10%	60%
Main entrees	60%	30%
Desserts	10%	50%
Beverages	20%	80%

Terry is considering a variety of options to try to improve the restaurant's profitability. Her goal is to generate a target operating income of $150,000. The company has fixed costs of $1.2 million per year.

Instructions
(a) Calculate the total restaurant sales and the sales of each product line that would be necessary in order to achieve the desired target operating income.
(b) Terry believes the restaurant could greatly improve its profitability by reducing the complexity and selling prices of its entrees to increase the number of clients that it serves, and by more heavily marketing its appetizers and beverages. She is proposing to drop the contribution margin ratio on the main entrees to 10% by reducing the average selling price. She envisions an expansion of the restaurant that would increase fixed costs by 50%. At the same time, she is proposing to change the sales mix to the following:

	Percent of Total Sales	Contribution Margin Ratio
Appetizers	20%	60%
Main entrees	30%	10%
Desserts	10%	50%
Beverages	40%	80%

Calculate the total restaurant sales and the sales of each product line that would be necessary in order to achieve the desired target operating income if Terry's changes are implemented.
(c) Suppose that Terry drops the selling price on entrees and increases fixed costs as proposed in part (b), but customers are not swayed by the marketing efforts and the product mix remains what it was in part (a). Calculate the total restaurant sales and the sales of each product line that would be necessary in order to achieve the desired target operating income. Comment on the potential risks and benefits of this strategy.

Problems: Set B

P6-53B   Seaton Ltd. manufactures and sells computer laptops. For its 2016 business plan, Seaton estimated the following:

Selling price	$600
Variable cost per laptop	$300
Annual fixed costs	$150,000
Net (after-tax) income	$360,000
Tax rate	25%

The March financial statements reported that sales were not meeting expectations. For the first three months of the year, only 400 units had been sold at the established price. With variable costs staying as planned, it was clear that the 2016

Sidebar (right margin):

(SO 1, 2, 3, 6)
Calculate the break-even point, margin of safety, and the degree of operating leverage and evaluate its impact on financial results.

(a) Margin of safety ratio: Old, 22.73%

(SO 1, 5)
Determine the sales mix under different scenarios.

(a) Weighted average CM ratio = 45%

(SO 1, 2, 3)
Determine the contribution margin, break-even point, and target sales after taxes.

after-tax profit projection would not be reached unless some action was taken. A management committee presented the following mutually exclusive alternatives to the president:

1. Reduce the selling price by $60. The sales team forecasts that, with the significantly reduced selling price, 2,700 units can be sold during the remainder of the year. Total fixed and variable unit costs will stay as budgeted.
2. Lower variable costs per unit by $20 through the use of less expensive direct materials and slightly modified manufacturing techniques. The selling price will also be reduced by $40, and sales of 2,500 units for the remainder of the year are forecast.
3. Cut fixed costs by $20,000 and lower the selling price by 5%. Variable costs per unit will be unchanged. Sales of 2,200 units are expected for the remainder of the year.

Instructions

(a) Break-even point: 500 units

(a) Under the current production policy, determine the number of units that the company must sell to break even and to achieve its desired operating income.
(b) Determine which alternative the company should select to achieve its desired operating income.

(adapted from CMA Canada, now CPA Canada)

(SO 1, 2)
Determine variable and fixed costs, calculate the break-even point, prepare a CVP graph, and determine operating income.

P6-54B Richard Casper owns the Fredonia Barber Shop. He employs five barbers and pays each a base rate of $1,000 per month. One of the barbers serves as the manager and receives an extra $500 per month. In addition to the base rate, each barber also receives a commission of $5.50 per haircut. The price of a haircut is $10.

Other costs are as follows:

Advertising	$200 per month
Rent	$900 per month
Barber supplies	$0.30 per haircut
Utilities	$175 per month plus $0.20 per haircut
Magazines	$25 per month

Instructions

(a) Variable cost per unit = $6

(a) Determine the variable cost per haircut and the total monthly fixed costs.
(b) Calculate the break-even point in units and dollars.
(c) Prepare a CVP graph, assuming a maximum of 1,800 haircuts in a month. Use increments of 300 haircuts on the horizontal axis and $3,000 on the vertical axis.
(d) Determine net income, assuming 1,900 haircuts are given in a month.

(SO 1, 2)
Determine variable and fixed costs and operating income.

P6-55B Maritime Manufacturing Company produces and sells a high-quality handbag. During 2016, handbag sales were $600,000, the contribution margin ratio was 40%, and the margin of safety was $300,000.

Instructions

(b) Variable costs = $360,000

(a) Calculate the break-even sales.
(b) Calculate the variable costs.
(c) Calculate the fixed costs.
(d) Calculate the profits at $500,000 of sales.

(adapted from CGA-Canada, now CPA Canada)

(SO 1, 2, 3)
Determine the contribution margin ratio, break-even point in dollars, margin of safety, and sales required to earn target operating income under alternative scenarios.

P6-56B YUX Corporation sells a single product for $40. Its management estimates the following revenues and costs for the year 2016:

Net sales	$500,000	Selling expenses—variable	$20,000
Direct materials	150,000	Selling expenses—fixed	30,000
Direct labour	90,000	Administrative expenses—variable	10,000
Manufacturing overhead—variable	30,000	Administrative expenses—fixed	20,000
Manufacturing overhead—fixed	40,000		

Instructions

(a) Assuming fixed costs and net sales are spread evenly throughout the year, calculate YUX's monthly break-even point in (1) units and (2) dollars.

(b) CM ratio = 40%

(b) Calculate the contribution margin ratio, the annual margin of safety ratio, and the annual profit.
(c) Assuming YUX Corporation increases its selling price by 30% and all other factors (including demand) remain constant, determine by what percentage annual profits will increase.
(d) Assume the price remains at $40 per unit and variable costs remain the same per unit, but fixed costs increase by 30% annually. Calculate the percentage increase in unit sales required to achieve the same level of annual profit calculated in part (b).
(e) Determine the sales required to earn an operating income of $360,000 after tax. YUX Corporation's income tax is 40%.

(SO 2, 4)
Calculate the break-even point under alternative courses of action.

P6-57B Delgado Manufacturing's sales slumped badly in 2016. For the first time in its history, it operated at a loss. The company's income statement showed the following results from selling 500,000 units of product: net sales $2.5 million, total costs and expenses $2.6 million, and net loss $100,000. Costs and expenses were as follows:

	Total	Variable	Fixed
Cost of goods sold	$2,140,000	$1,540,000	$600,000
Selling expenses	250,000	92,000	158,000
Administrative expenses	210,000	68,000	142,000
	$2,600,000	$1,700,000	$900,000

Management is considering the following independent alternatives for 2017:

1. Increase the unit selling price by 40% with no change in costs and expenses.
2. Change the compensation of salespersons from fixed annual salaries totalling $150,000 to total salaries of $60,000 plus a 5% commission on net sales.

Instructions
(a) Calculate the break-even point in dollars for 2016.
(b) Calculate the break-even point in dollars under each of the alternative courses of action. (Round to nearest full percent.) Which course of action do you recommend?

(b) Alternative 1, $1,764,709

P6-58B John, now retired, owns the Campus Cutter Barber Shop. He employs five barbers and pays each a base salary of $1,500 per month. One of the barbers serves as the manager and receives an extra $500 per month. In addition to the base salary, each barber receives a commission of $6 per haircut. Each barber can do as many as 20 haircuts a day, but the average is 14 haircuts each day. The Campus Cutter Barber Shop is open an average of 24 days per month and charges $15 per haircut.

(SO 1, 2, 3) Determine the break-even point in dollars and target income.

Other costs are incurred as follows:

Advertising	$500 per month
Rent	$1,000 per month
Supplies	$1.50 per haircut
Utilities	$300 per month, plus $0.50 per haircut
Magazines	$50 per month
Cleaning supplies	$0.25 per haircut

Instructions
(a) Calculate the monthly break-even point for the following:
   1. Number of haircuts
   2. Total sales dollars
   3. As a percentage of maximum capacity
(b) In February, 1,500 haircuts were given. Calculate the operating income for February.
(c) If John would like a $4,000 monthly profit, calculate the number of haircuts that must be given per month to achieve this profit.
(d) In March, 1,600 haircuts were given. Assuming demand is sufficient, would it be possible to give enough haircuts in April to bring the total for the two months combined to the target profit of $4,000 for each month?

(a) CM per unit = $6.75

(adapted from CGA-Canada, now CPA Canada)

P6-59B Barb Tsai is the advertising manager for Thrifty Shoe Store. She is currently working on a major promotional campaign. Her ideas include the installation of a new lighting system and increased display space that will add $24,000 in fixed costs to the $270,000 currently spent. In addition, Barb is proposing that a 5% price decrease (from $40 to $38) will produce an increase in sales volume from 20,000 to 24,000 units. Variable costs will remain at $24 per pair of shoes. Management is impressed with Barb's ideas but is concerned about the effects that these changes will have on the break-even point and the margin of safety.

(SO 1, 2, 3, 4) Calculate the break-even point and margin of safety ratio, and prepare a CVP income statement before and after changes in the business environment.

Instructions
(a) Calculate the current break-even point in units, and compare it with the break-even point in units if Barb's ideas are used.
(b) Calculate the margin of safety ratio for current operations and after Barb's changes are introduced. (Round to nearest full percent.)
(c) Prepare a CVP income statement for current operations and after Barb's changes are introduced. Would you make the changes suggested?

(b) Current margin of safety ratio = 15.6%

P6-60B Regina Enterprises, Ltd. has estimated the following costs for producing and selling 8,000 units of its product:

(SO 2, 3) Determine the break-even point and target income.

Direct materials	$32,000
Direct labour	40,000
Variable overhead	20,000

	Fixed overhead	$30,000
	Variable selling and administrative expenses	24,000
	Fixed selling and administrative expenses	33,000

Regina Enterprises' income tax rate is 30%.

Instructions

Answer the following questions:

(a) Per-unit variable
cost = $14.50

(a) Given that the selling price of one unit is $35, how many units would Regina Enterprises have to sell in order to break even?

(b) At a selling price of $37.50 per unit, how many units would Regina Enterprises have to sell in order to produce a profit of $22,000 before taxes?

(c) If 7,500 units were produced and sold, what price would Regina Enterprises have to charge in order to produce a profit of $28,000 after taxes?

(d) If 9,000 units were produced and sold, what price would Regina Enterprises have to charge in order to produce a before-tax profit equal to 30% of sales?

(adapted from CGA-Canada, now CPA Canada)

(SO 1, 2, 3, 4)
Calculate the break-even point and margin of safety ratio, and prepare a CVP income statement before and after changes in the business environment.

(a) (1) CM ratio = 34.7%

P6-61B   Axelle Corporation has collected the following information after its first year of sales. Net sales were $2 million on 100,000 units, selling expenses were $400,000 (30% variable and 70% fixed), direct materials were $600,000, direct labour was $340,000, administrative expenses were $500,000 (30% variable and 70% fixed), and manufacturing overhead was $480,000 (20% variable and 80% fixed). Top managers have asked you to do a CVP analysis so that they can make plans for the coming year. They have projected that unit sales will increase by 20% next year.

Instructions

(a) Calculate (1) the contribution margin for the current year and the projected year, and (2) the fixed costs for the current year. (Assume that fixed costs will remain the same in the projected year.)

(b) Calculate the break-even point in units and sales dollars.

(c) The company has a target operating income of $374,000. Calculate the required sales amount in dollars for the company to meet its target.

(d) Assume the company meets its target operating income number. Calculate by what percentage its sales could fall before it operates at a loss. That is, what is its margin of safety ratio?

(e) The company is considering a purchase of equipment that would reduce its direct labour costs by $140,000 and would change its manufacturing overhead costs to 10% variable and 90% fixed. (Assume the total manufacturing overhead cost is $480,000, as above.) It is also considering switching to a pure commission basis for its sales staff. This would change selling expenses to 80% variable and 20% fixed. (Assume the total selling expense is $400,000, as above.) Calculate (1) the contribution margin and (2) the contribution margin ratio, and (3) recalculate the break-even point in sales dollars. Comment on the effect each of management's proposed changes has on the break-even point.

(SO 1, 2, 3)
Determine the contribution margin ratio, break-even point in dollars, and target sales.

P6-62B   The company that you work for as a managerial accountant uses independent agents to sell its products. These agents are currently being paid a commission of 15% of the sales price but are asking for an increase to 20% of sales made during the coming year. You had already prepared the following income statement for the company based on the 15% commission:

Income Statement
Year Ending April 30, 2016

Sales		$1,000,000
Cost of goods sold (all variable)		600,000
Gross profit		400,000
Selling and administrative expenses		
(variable—commission only)	$150,000	
Fixed costs	10,000	160,000
Income before taxes		240,000
Income tax expense (25%)		60,000
Operating income		$ 180,000

Management wants to examine the possibility of employing the company's own salespeople. The company would need a sales manager at an annual salary of $60,000 and three salespeople at an annual salary of $30,000 each, plus a commission of 5% of sales. All other fixed costs as well as the variable cost percentages would remain the same as in the above pro forma income statement.

Instructions

(a) CM ratio = 25%

(a) Based on the pro forma income statement you have already prepared, calculate the break-even point in sales dollars for the company for the year ending April 30, 2016.

(b) Calculate the break-even point in sales dollars for the year ending April 30, 2016, if the company uses its own salespeople.

(c) Calculate the volume of sales dollars required for the year ending April 30, 2016, to have the same operating income as projected in the pro forma income statement if the company continues to use the independent sales agents and agrees to their demand for a 20% sales commission.

(d) Calculate the estimated sales volume in sales dollars that would generate an identical operating income for the year ending April 30, 2016, regardless of whether the company employs its own salespeople or continues to use the independent sales agents and pays them a 20% commission.

(adapted from CGA-Canada, now CPA Canada)

P6-63B High Quality Toy's projected operating income for 2016 is $1 million, based on a sales volume of 90,000 units. High Quality sells The Toy for $35 per unit. Variable costs consist of the $14 purchase price and a $1 shipping and handling cost. High Quality's annual fixed costs are $800,000.

(SO 1, 2, 3)
Determine the contribution margin, break-even point in dollars, and sales.

Instructions

(a) Calculate the company's break-even point in units.

(b) Calculate the company's operating income in 2016 if there is a 10% increase in projected unit sales.

(c) For 2017, management expects that the unit purchase price of The Toy will increase by 30%. Calculate the sales revenue the company must generate in 2017 to maintain the current year's operating income if the selling price remains unchanged.

(a) CM ratio = 57%

(adapted from CMA Canada, now CPA Canada)

*P6-64B The following CVP income statements are available for Retro Company and Modern Company:

(SO 1, 2, 3, 6)
Calculate the break-even point, the margin of safety, and the degree of operating leverage under various scenarios.

	Retro Company	Modern Company
Sales revenue	$500,000	$500,000
Variable costs	300,000	100,000
Contribution margin	200,000	400,000
Fixed costs	140,000	340,000
Operating income	$ 60,000	$ 60,000

Instructions

(a) Calculate the break-even point in dollars and the margin of safety ratio for each company.

(b) Calculate the degree of operating leverage for each company and interpret your results.

(c) Assuming that sales revenue increases by 25%, prepare a variable cost income statement for each company.

(d) Assuming that sales revenue decreases by 25%, prepare a variable cost income statement for each company.

(e) Discuss how the cost structure of these two companies affects their operating leverage and profitability.

(b) OL for Retro: 3.33;
OL for Modern: 6.67

*P6-65B ComfortCraft manufactures swivel seats for customized vans. It currently manufactures 10,000 seats per year, which it sells for $480 per seat. It incurs variable costs of $180 per seat and fixed costs of $2.2 million. It is considering automating the upholstery process, which is now largely manual. It estimates that if it does so, its fixed costs will be $3.2 million, and its variable costs will decline to $80 per seat.

(SO 1, 2, 3, 6)
Calculate the break-even point, the margin of safety, and the degree of operating leverage under various scenarios.

Instructions

(a) Prepare a CVP income statement based on current activity.

(b) Calculate the contribution margin ratio, break-even point in dollars, margin of safety ratio, and degree of operating leverage based on current activity.

(c) Prepare a CVP income statement assuming that the company invests in the automated upholstery system.

(d) Calculate the contribution margin ratio, break-even point in dollars, margin of safety ratio, and degree of operating leverage assuming the new upholstery system is implemented.

(e) Discuss the implications of adopting the new system.

(b) OL = 3.75

(d) OL = 5.0

P6-66B The Bricktown Pub is a restaurant that specializes in classic east coast fare in a moderate price range. Debbie MacNeil, the manager of Bricktown, has determined that during the last two years the sales mix and contribution margin of its offerings are as follows:

(SO 1, 5)
Determine the sales mix under alternative strategies and evaluate.

	Percent of Total Sales	Contribution Margin Ratio
Appetizers	10%	50%
Main entrees	55%	30%
Desserts	10%	60%
Beverages	25%	75%

Debbie is considering a variety of options to try to improve the restaurant's profitability. Her goal is to generate a target operating income of $155,000. The company has fixed costs of $400,000 per year.

Instructions

(a) Calculate the total restaurant sales and the sales of each product line that would be necessary in order to achieve the desired target operating income.

(b) CM ratio = 51%

(b) Debbie believes the restaurant could greatly improve its profitability by reducing the complexity and selling prices of its entrees to increase the number of clients that it serves, and by more heavily marketing its appetizers and beverages. She is proposing to reduce the contribution margin on the main entrees to 15% by dropping the average selling price. She envisions an expansion of the restaurant that would increase fixed costs by 50%. At the same time, she is proposing to change the sales mix to the following:

	Percent of Total Sales	Contribution Margin Ratio
Appetizers	15%	50%
Main entrees	30%	15%
Desserts	15%	60%
Beverages	40%	75%

Calculate the total restaurant sales, and the sales of each product line that would be necessary in order to achieve the desired target operating income.

(c) Suppose that Debbie drops the selling price on entrees, and increases fixed costs as proposed in part (b), but customers are not swayed by her marketing efforts, and the product mix remains what it was in part (a). Calculate the total restaurant sales and the sales of each product line that would be necessary to achieve the desired target operating income. Comment on the potential risks and benefits of this strategy.

Cases

*C6-67   Clay Company has decided to introduce a new product that can be manufactured by either a capital-intensive method or a labour-intensive method. The manufacturing method will not affect the quality of the product. The estimated manufacturing costs under the two methods are as follows:

	Capital-Intensive	Labour-Intensive
Direct materials	$5 per unit	$5.50 per unit
Direct labour	$6 per unit	$8.00 per unit
Variable overhead	$3 per unit	$4.50 per unit
Fixed manufacturing costs	$2,524,000	$1,550,000

Clay's market research department has recommended an introductory unit sales price of $32. The incremental selling expenses are estimated to be $502,000 annually, plus $2 for each unit sold, regardless of the manufacturing method.

Instructions

(a) Calculate the estimated break-even point in annual unit sales of the new product if Clay Company uses (1) the capital-intensive manufacturing method, or (2) the labour-intensive manufacturing method.

(b) Determine the annual unit sales volume at which there would be no difference between methods.

(c) Explain the circumstances under which Clay should use each of the two manufacturing methods.

(adapted from CMA Canada, now CPA Canada)

C6-68   Production cost and price data for Kempinski Company are as follows:

Maximum capacity per year	300,000 units
Variable manufacturing costs	$18/unit
Fixed factory overhead costs	$500,000/year
Variable selling and administrative costs	$6/unit
Fixed selling and administrative costs	$200,000/year
Current sales price	$28/unit

The company's sales for the year just ended totalled 260,000 units. However, a strike at a major supplier has caused a shortage in raw materials and, as a result, the current year's sales will reach only 240,000 units. Top management are planning to reduce fixed costs this year by $60,000 compared with last year.

Management are also thinking of either increasing the selling price or reducing the variable costs, or both, in order to earn a target operating income that will be the same dollar amount as last year's. The company has already sold 60,000 units this year at $28 per unit, with the variable costs remaining unchanged from last year.

Instructions

(a) Calculate the contribution margin per unit that is required on the remaining 180,000 units in order to reach the target operating income.

(b) The company president is considering a significant change in the manufacturing process for next year. This change would increase the capacity to 450,000 units. The change would increase fixed factory overhead to $3.0 million, while reducing the variable manufacturing cost per unit to $5. All other costs and revenues would remain unchanged. Draft a brief memo to the president explaining the potential benefits and risks of a move to this cost structure. Support your explanation with an analysis of the numbers. (*Hint*: Use the previous year's sales and costs as a point of reference to compare the effects on operating income of a 10% increase or a 20% decrease in sales volume under the current and proposed cost structures.)

(adapted from CGA-Canada, now CPA Canada)

C6-69 The condensed income statement for the Phan and Nguyen partnership for 2016 is as follows:

PHAN AND NGUYEN LLP
Income Statement
Year Ending December 31, 2016

Sales (240,000 units)		$1,200,000
Cost of goods sold		800,000
Gross profit		400,000
Operating expenses		
Selling	$280,000	
Administrative	150,000	430,000
Net loss		$ (30,000)

A cost behaviour analysis indicates that 75% of the cost of goods sold is variable, 42% of the selling expenses are variable, and 40% of the administrative expenses are variable.

Instructions

(Round to nearest unit, dollar, and percentage, where necessary. Use the CVP income statement format in calculating profits.)

(a) Calculate the break-even point in total sales dollars and in units for 2016.

(b) Phan has proposed a plan to get the partnership "out of the red" and improve its profitability. She feels that the quality of the product could be substantially improved by spending $0.25 more per unit on better raw materials. The selling price per unit could be increased to only $5.25 because of competitive pressures. Phan estimates that sales volume will increase by 25%. What effect would Phan's plan have on the partnership's profits and its break-even point in dollars?

(c) Nguyen was a marketing major in university. He believes that the sales volume can be increased only by intensive advertising and promotional campaigns. He therefore proposed the following plan as an alternative to Phan's: (1) increase variable selling expenses to $0.59 per unit, (2) lower the selling price per unit by $0.25, and (3) increase fixed selling expenses by $40,000. Nguyen quoted an old marketing research report that said that sales volume would increase by 60% if these changes were made. What effect would Nguyen's plan have on the partnership's profits and its break-even point in dollars?

(d) Determine which plan should be accepted. Explain your answer.

---

*C6-70 For nearly 20 years, Custom Coatings has provided painting and galvanizing services for manufacturers in its region. Manufacturers of various metal products have relied on the quality and quick turnaround time provided by Custom Coatings and its 20 skilled employees. During the last year, as a result of a sharp upturn in the economy, the company's sales have increased by 30% relative to the previous year. The company has not been able to increase its capacity fast enough, so Custom Coatings has had to turn work away because it cannot keep up with customer requests.

Top management is considering the purchase of a sophisticated robotic painting booth. The booth would represent a considerable move in the direction of automation versus manual labour. If Custom Coatings purchases the booth, it would most likely lay off 15 of its skilled painters. To analyze the decision, the company compiled production information from the most recent year and then prepared a parallel compilation assuming that the company would purchase the new equipment and lay off the workers. The data are shown at right. As you can see, the company projects that during the last year it would have been far more profitable if it had used the automated approach.

	Current Approach	Automated Approach
Sales	$2,000,000	$2,000,000
Variable costs	1,200,000	400,000
Contribution margin	800,000	1,600,000
Fixed costs	200,000	600,000
Operating income	$ 600,000	$1,000,000

Instructions

(a) Calculate and interpret the contribution margin ratio under each approach.

(b) Calculate the break-even point in sales dollars under each approach. Discuss the implications of your findings.

(c) Using the current level of sales, calculate the margin of safety ratio under each approach and interpret your findings.

(d) Determine the degree of operating leverage for each approach at current sales levels. Calculate how much the company's operating income would decline under each approach with a 10% decline in sales.

(e) Determine at what level of sales the company's operating income would be the same under either approach.

(f) Discuss the issues that the company must consider in making this decision.

C6-71 All-Day Candy Company is a wholesale distributor of candy. The company services grocery, convenience, and drug stores in a large metropolitan area.

All-Day Candy Company has achieved small but steady growth in sales over the past few years, but prices have also been increasing. The company is formulating its plans for the coming fiscal year. The following data were used to project the current year's after-tax operating income of $969,600:

Average selling price	$8.00	per box
Average variable costs		
Cost of candy	$4.00	per box
Selling expenses	0.80	per box
Total	$4.80	per box
Annual fixed costs		
Selling	$320,000	
Administrative	560,000	
Total	$880,000	

The expected annual sales volume (780,000 boxes) is $6,240,000 and the tax rate is 40%.

Candy manufacturers have announced that they will increase the prices of their products by an average of 15% in the coming year because of increases in raw material (sugar, cocoa, peanuts, and so on) and labour costs. All-Day Candy Company expects that all other costs will remain at the same rates or levels as during the current year.

Instructions

(a) Calculate All-Day Candy Company's break-even point in boxes of candy for the current year.

(b) Calculate the selling price per box that All-Day Candy Company must charge to cover the 15% increase in the variable cost of candy and still maintain the current contribution margin ratio.

(c) Calculate the volume of sales in dollars All-Day Candy Company must achieve in the coming year to keep the same operating income after taxes that was projected for the current year if the selling price of candy remains at $8 per box and the cost of candy increases by 15%.

(adapted from CMA Canada, now CPA Canada)

C6-72   Labrador Company produces a single product. It sold 75,000 units last year with the following results:

Sales		$1,875,000
Variable costs	$750,000	
Fixed costs	300,000	1,050,000
Operating income before taxes		825,000
Income taxes (45%)		371,250
Operating income		$ 453,750

In an attempt to improve its product, Labrador is considering replacing a component part in its product that has a cost of $5 per unit with a new and better part costing $10 per unit during the coming year. A new machine would also be needed to increase plant capacity. The machine would cost $90,000, with a useful life of six years and no salvage value. The company uses straight-line depreciation on all plant assets.

Instructions

Answer the following questions:

(a) What was Labrador's break-even point in units last year?

(b) How many units of product would Labrador have had to sell in the past year to earn $247,500 in operating income after taxes?

(c) If it holds the sales price constant and makes the suggested changes, how many units of product must the company sell in the coming year to break even?

(d) If it holds the sales price constant and makes the suggested changes, how many units of product will Labrador have to sell to make the same operating income before taxes as last year?

(e) If Labrador wishes to maintain the same contribution margin ratio, what selling price per unit of product must it charge next year to cover the increased materials costs?

(adapted from CMA Canada, now CPA Canada)

C6-73   Ronnie Fraenze is an accountant for Korol Company. Early this year, Ronnie made a highly favourable projection of sales and profits over the next three years for Korol's hot-selling computer PLEX. As a result of the projections Ronnie presented to senior management, management decided to expand production in this area. This decision led to relocations of some plant personnel, who were reassigned to one of the company's newer plants in another province. However, no one was fired, and in fact the company expanded its workforce slightly.

Unfortunately, Ronnie rechecked his calculations on the projections a few months later and found that he had made an error. His projections should have been substantially less. Luckily, sales of PLEX have exceeded projections so far, and management is satisfied with its

decision. Ronnie, however, is not sure what to do. Should he confess his honest mistake and jeopardize his possible promotion? He suspects that no one will catch the error because sales of PLEX have exceeded his projections, and it appears that profits will materialize close to his projections.

Instructions

(a) Name the stakeholders in this situation.

(b) Identify the ethical issues involved in this situation.

(c) Consider the possible alternative actions for Ronnie. What would you do in Ronnie's position?

"All About You" Activity

C6-74   You have been asked to help the local commercial radio station prepare its business plan for the upcoming year. The radio station operates for 18 hours a day (6 a.m. to midnight) seven days a week, all year. It broadcasts on average 15 minutes of on-air advertising per hour. To sell the advertising time, the station uses commissioned sales staff who are paid a base salary plus commission that varies according to the volume of sales. The

station manager asks you to calculate how many hours of advertising it would need to sell in order to break even.

Instructions

(a) Calculate the fixed costs and the variable costs.

(b) Determine how many hours of advertising the station must sell in order to cover its costs. Explain how you calculated the break-even point.

Decision-Making at Current Designs

DM6-1   Current Designs manufactures two different types of kayaks, rotomoulded kayaks and composite kayaks. The following information is available for each product line.

	Rotomoulded	Composite
Sales price/unit	$950	$2,000
Variable costs/unit	$570	$1,340

The company's fixed costs are $820,000. An analysis of the sales mix identifies that rotomoulded kayaks make up 80% of the total units sold.

Instructions

(a) Determine the weighted-average unit contribution margin for Current Designs.

(b) Determine the break-even point in units for Current Designs and identify how many units of each type of kayak will be sold at the break-even point. (Round to the nearest whole number.)

(c) Assume that the sales mix changes, and rotomoulded kayaks now make up 70% of total units sold. Calculate the total number of units that would need to be sold to earn a net income of $2 million and identify how many units of each type of kayak will be sold at this level of income. (Round to the nearest whole number.)

(d) Assume that Current Designs will have sales of $3 million with two-thirds of the sales dollars in rotomoulded kayaks and one third of the sales dollars in composite kayaks. Assuming $660,000 of fixed costs are allocated to the rotomoulded kayaks and $160,000 to the composite kayaks, prepare a CVP income statement for each product line.

(e) Using the information in part (d), calculate the degree of operating leverage for each product line and interpret your findings. (Round to two decimal places.)

Waterways Continuing Problem

(This is a continuation of the Waterways Problem from Chapters 1 through 5.)

WCP-6

Part 1

The vice-president of sales and marketing, Madison Tremblay, is trying to plan for the coming year in terms of production needs to meet the forecasted sales. The board of directors is very supportive of any initiatives that will lead to increased profits for the company in the upcoming year.

Instructions

(a) Waterways markets a simple water controller and timer that it mass produces. During 2016, the company sold 350,000 units at an average selling price of $8.00 per unit. The variable expenses were $1,575,000, and the fixed expenses were $800,000.
   1. What is the product's contribution margin ratio?
   2. What is the company's break-even point in units and in dollars for this product?
   3. What is the margin of safety, both in dollars and as a ratio?
   4. If management wanted to increase income from this product by 10%, how many additional units would the company have to sell to reach this income level?
   5. If sales increase by 71,000 units and the cost behaviours do not change, how much will income increase on this product?

(b) Waterways is considering mass producing one of its special-order screens. This would increase variable costs for all screens by an average of $0.71 per unit. The company also estimates that this change could increase the overall number of screens sold by 10%, and the average sales price would increase by $0.25 per unit. Waterways currently sells 491,740 screen units at an average selling price of $26.50. The manufacturing costs are $6,863,512 variable and $2,050,140 fixed. Selling and administrative costs are $2,661,352 variable and $794,950 fixed.
   1. If Waterways begins mass producing its special-order screens, how would this affect the company?
   2. If the average sales price per screen unit did not increase when the company began mass producing the screen units, what would be the effect on the company?

Part 2

Waterways has a sales mix of sprinklers, valves, and controllers as follows:

Annual expected sales:

Sale of sprinklers	450,000 units at $26.50
Sale of valves	1,500,000 units at $11.20
Sale of controllers	50,000 units at $42.50

Variable manufacturing cost per unit:

Sprinklers	$13.96
Valves	$ 7.95
Controllers	$29.75

Fixed manufacturing overhead cost (total)	$760,000
Variable selling and administrative expenses per unit:	
Sprinklers	$1.30
Valves	$0.50
Controllers	$3.41
Fixed selling and administrative expenses (total)	$1,600,000

Instructions

(a) Determine the sales mix based on unit sales for each product.
(b) Using the annual expected sales for these products, determine the weighted-average unit contribution margin for these three products. (Round to two decimal places.)
(c) Assuming the sales mix remains the same, what is the break-even point in units for these products?

Part 3

The section of Waterways that produces controllers for the company provided the following information:

Sales (in units) for month of February	4,000
Variable manufacturing cost per unit	$9.75
Sales price per unit	$42.50
Fixed manufacturing overhead cost (per month for controllers)	$81,000
Variable selling and administrative expenses per unit	$3.41
Fixed selling and administrative expenses (per month for controllers)	$13,122

Instructions

(a) Using this information for the controllers, determine the contribution margin ratio, the degree of operating leverage, the break-even point in dollars, and the margin of safety ratio for Waterways Corporation on this product.
(b) What does this information suggest if Waterways' cost structure is the same for the company as a whole?

Answers to Self-Study Questions

1. d   2. d   3. a   4. a   5. a   6. a   7. b   8. d   9. c   10. d

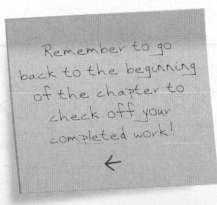

Remember to go
back to the beginning
of the chapter to
check off your
completed work!

study objectives

the
navigator

After studying this chapter, you should be able to do the following:

1. Describe management's decision-making process and the concept of incremental analysis.

2. Identify the relevant costs in accepting an order at a special price.

3. Identify the relevant costs in a make-or-buy decision.

4. Identify the relevant costs in deciding whether to sell or process materials further.

5. Identify the relevant costs in deciding whether to retain or replace equipment.

6. Identify the relevant costs in deciding whether to eliminate an unprofitable segment.

7. Determine the sales mix when a company has limited resources.

OUTSOURCING CAN BE OUTSTANDING

Running a large organization requires expertise, not only in providing services, but also in performing basic functions—making sure the information technology (IT) and administrative support is in place and running efficiently. Often it makes more sense to hire other companies to do this—that is, to outsource. Companies deciding whether to outsource or to perform work internally can benefit from the use of incremental analysis, the process of analyzing the costs of various alternatives.

Montreal-based CGI Group Inc. provides business support services to companies that outsource this function, including systems integration and consulting on business and technology solutions (such as cyber security), day-to-day maintenance and improvement of business applications, and management of business processes.

Serge Godin founded CGI in Saguenay, Quebec, in 1976, when he was just 26 years old. He continues to serve as executive chairman of the board of directors. CGI has continued to grow, through both organic growth and acquisitions. Now headquartered in Montreal, the firm employs 68,000 people worldwide, has offices in 40 countries, and earned $10.1 billion in revenue in 2013. CGI is the world's fifth-largest IT and business process services firm that is independent of any software or hardware vendor.

CGI takes care of "back-office" functions. "Every business or government has a front office and a back office, the front office being everything that's strategic in a business and the back office being everything that's required to run it," said Lorne Gorber, CGI's senior vice-president, global communications and investor relations. "For most companies, you spend 80% of your time in the front office thinking about strategy and clients and sales, and 20% of your investment and time in the back office. We spend 100% of our time and investment in the back office and therefore can bring you scale and efficiency improvement, and ultimately savings that you otherwise wouldn't be able to get on your own."

For a bank, back-office functions may be looking after collections or screening loan applications; for a telecommunications company, streamlining billing and human resources; and for a government department, providing and running the budgeting software. CGI's clients include Bell Canada, Bombardier, Canada Post, Cirque du Soleil, National Bank of Canada, Canadian Payments Association, and several government departments in Canada and the United States.

Several clients have a long-term contract with CGI worth hundreds of millions of dollars each—an investment that frees them up to concentrate on their front end. "It allows them to focus on their core business," said Mr. Gorber. CGI can offer efficiencies through scale by combining its many clients, providing purchasing power for IT equipment or increased data centre storage capacity.

Sources: CGI Fiscal 2013 Results; "CGI Renews and Signs New Contracts with National Bank of Canada for a Total Value of More than $100 Million," CGI news release, February 19, 2014; "CGI Establishes Ottawa Centre Focused on Cyber Security for Businesses," *The Guardian* (Charlottetown, PEI), April 2, 2013; "Interview with the Senior VP - Global Communications and Investor Relations: CGI Group Inc. (GIB) - Lorne Gorber," The Wall Street Transcript, Yahoo! Finance, January 24, 2012.

the navigator

Preview of Chapter 7

the navigator

An important purpose of management accounting is to provide managers with relevant information for decision-making. Companies of all sorts must make product decisions. For instance, aircraft manufacturer Bombardier Inc., in Quebec, discontinued making snowmobiles and eliminated that segment from its business. As our feature story indicated, many companies decide to outsource the marketing and sales of their products to CGI.

This chapter explains management's decision-making process and a decision-making approach called incremental analysis. The use of incremental analysis is demonstrated in a variety of situations. The chapter is organized as follows:

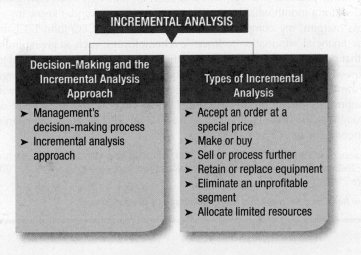

INCREMENTAL ANALYSIS

Decision-Making and the Incremental Analysis Approach
➤ Management's decision-making process
➤ Incremental analysis approach

Types of Incremental Analysis
➤ Accept an order at a special price
➤ Make or buy
➤ Sell or process further
➤ Retain or replace equipment
➤ Eliminate an unprofitable segment
➤ Allocate limited resources

Decision-Making and the Incremental Analysis Approach

MANAGEMENT'S DECISION-MAKING PROCESS

Making decisions is an important management function. However, management's decision-making process does not always follow the same pattern, because decisions vary significantly in their scope, urgency, and importance. It is possible, though, to identify some steps that management frequently uses in the process. Illustration 7-1 shows these steps.

Accounting's contribution to the decision-making process occurs mostly in Steps 2 and 4—evaluating the possible courses of action and reviewing results. In Step 2, for each possible course of action, accounting provides relevant revenue and cost data. These show the expected overall effect on net income. In Step 4, accounting prepares internal reports that review the actual impact of the decision.

▶Illustration 7-1
Management's decision-making process

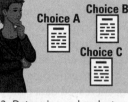
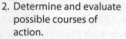
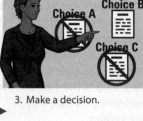

1. Identify the problem and assign responsibility.

2. Determine and evaluate possible courses of action.

3. Make a decision.

4. Review the results of the decision.

In making business decisions, management ordinarily considers both financial and non-financial information. *Financial* information is about revenues and costs and their effect on the company's overall profitability. *Non-financial* information is about such factors as the effect of the decision on employee turnover, the environment, or the company's overall image in the community. Although non-financial information can be as important as financial information, we will focus mainly on financial information that is relevant to the decision.

BUSINESS INSIGHT   *Faster Information, Faster Decisions*

Reliable, timely information is key to decision-making, and the Internet has made that increasingly easier. Not surprisingly, one of the pioneers of the Internet, Cisco Systems Inc., has embraced technology for its financial management and decision-making. "I can now close my books in 24 hours. I've known for a month what my earnings are for this weekend. I know my expenses, my profitability, my gross margins, my components," said Chairman and CEO John T. Chambers. Providing almost real-time financial information to lower-level employees, such as giving individual product gross margins to that product line's manager, allows them to make decisions that used to have to go to Chambers. It's allowed Cisco to spread decision-making responsibilities across the organization, to working groups of some 500 executives. "Quicker decision-making at lower levels will translate into higher profit margins. So instead of the CEO and CFO making 50 to 100 different decisions a quarter, managers throughout the organization can make millions of decisions. Companies that don't do that will be noncompetitive," Chambers said.

Sources: Ellen McGirt, "How Cisco's CEO John Chambers Is Turning the Tech Giant Socialist," *Fast Company*, December/January 2009; "Visionary Vs. Visionary," *Businessweek*, August 27, 2000; Cisco Systems Inc. website, www.cisco.com.

How has Cisco Systems Inc. taken advantage of the digital age?

INCREMENTAL ANALYSIS APPROACH

Decisions involve a choice among alternative courses of action. Suppose that you were deciding whether to buy or lease a car. The financial data would be the cost of leasing versus the cost of purchasing. For example, leasing would involve periodic lease payments; purchasing would require "up-front" payment of the purchase price. In other words, the financial data that are relevant to the decision relate to the expense that would vary in the future among the possible alternatives. The process used to identify the financial expenses that change under alternative courses of action is called **incremental analysis**. In some cases, you will find that when you use incremental analysis, both costs *and* revenues will vary. In other cases, only costs *or* revenues will vary.

Just as your decision to buy or lease a car will affect your future, similar decisions on a larger scale will affect a company's future. Incremental analysis identifies the probable effects of those decisions on future earnings. This type of analysis always involves estimates and uncertainty. Data for incremental analyses may be gathered from market analysts, engineers, and accountants. In quantifying the data, the accountant is expected to produce the most reliable information available at the time the decision must be made.

Illustration 7-2 shows an example of the basic approach in incremental analysis.

Alternative Terminology
Incremental analysis is also called *differential analysis* because the analysis focuses on differences.

	A	B	C	D
1		**Alternative A**	**Alternative B**	**Net Income Increase (Decrease)**
2	Revenues	$125,000	$110,000	$(15,000)
3	Costs	100,000	80,000	20,000
4	Net income	$ 25,000	$ 30,000	$ 5,000
5				

▶Illustration 7-2
Basic approach in incremental analysis

In this example, alternative B is being compared with alternative A. The net income column shows the differences between the alternatives. In this case, incremental revenue will be $15,000 less under alternative B than under alternative A. However, the company will realize a $20,000 incremental cost savings under alternative B.[1] Thus, alternative B will produce $5,000 more net income than alternative A.

In the following pages, you will learn about three important cost concepts that are used in incremental analysis. Illustration 7-3 defines and discusses them.

- **Relevant cost** In incremental analysis, the only factors to be considered are (1) those costs and revenues that are different for each alternative, and (2) those costs and revenues that will occur in the future. These factors are called **relevant costs**. Costs and revenues that do not differ across alternatives and will not occur in the future can be ignored when trying to choose between alternatives.

- **Opportunity cost** In choosing to take one action, the company must often give up the opportunity to benefit from some other action. For example, if a machine is used to make one type of product, the benefit of making another type of product with that machine may be lost. This lost benefit is called an **opportunity cost**.

- **Sunk cost** Costs that have already been incurred and will not be changed or avoided by any future decision are called **sunk costs**. For example, if you have already purchased a machine, and now a new, more efficient machine is available, the book value of the original machine is a sunk cost. It should not affect your decision about whether to buy the new machine. Sunk costs are not relevant costs.

▶Illustration 7-3
Key cost concepts in incremental analysis

Incremental analysis sometimes involves changes that might at first go against your intuition. For example, sometimes variable costs do not change under the alternative courses of action. Also, sometimes fixed costs do change. For example, direct labour, normally a variable cost, is not an incremental cost in deciding between two new factory machines if each asset requires the same

---

[1] Although income taxes are sometimes important in incremental analysis, they are ignored in this chapter in order to keep things simple.

amount of direct labour. In contrast, rent expense, normally a fixed cost, is an incremental cost in a decision about whether to stay in the current building or to purchase or lease a new building.

BEFORE YOU GO ON...

▶Do It! Incremental Analysis

Owen T Corporation is comparing two different options. The company currently follows Option 1, with revenues of $80,000 per year, maintenance expenses of $5,000 per year, and operating expenses of $38,000 per year. Option 2 provides revenues of $80,000 per year, maintenance expenses of $12,000 per year, and operating expenses of $32,000 per year. Option 1 employs a piece of equipment that was upgraded two years ago at a cost of $22,000. If Option 2 is chosen, it will free up resources that will increase revenues by $3,000.

Complete the following table to show the change in income from choosing Option 2 versus Option 1. Designate any sunk costs with an "S."

	Option 1	Option 2	Net Income Increase (Decrease)	Sunk (S)
Revenues				
Maintenance expenses				
Operating expenses				
Equipment upgrade				
Opportunity cost				

Action Plan

- Past costs that cannot be changed are sunk costs.
- Benefits lost by choosing one option over another are opportunity costs.

Solution

	Option 1	Option 2	Net Income Increase (Decrease)	Sunk (S)
Revenues	$80,000	$80,000	$ 0	
Maintenance expenses	5,000	12,000	(7,000)	
Operating expenses	38,000	32,000	6,000	
Equipment upgrade	22,000	0	0	S
Opportunity cost	3,000	0	3,000	
			$ 2,000	

Related exercise material: **BE7-1**, **BE7-2**, and **E7-17**.

Types of Incremental Analysis

Several types of decisions involve incremental analysis. The more common ones are to decide whether to do the following.

1. Accept an order at a special price.
2. Make or buy component parts or finished products.
3. Sell products or process them further.
4. Retain or replace equipment.
5. Eliminate or retain an unprofitable business segment.
6. Allocate limited resources.

We will consider each of these types of incremental analysis in the following pages.

ACCEPT AN ORDER AT A SPECIAL PRICE

Sometimes a company may have an opportunity to obtain additional business if it is willing to make a major price concession to a specific customer (that is, lower its price for the customer). To illustrate, assume that Sunbelt Company produces 100,000 automatic blenders per month, which is 80% of plant capacity. Variable manufacturing costs are $8 per unit. Fixed manufacturing costs are $400,000, or $4 per unit. The blenders are normally sold directly to retailers at $20 each. Sunbelt has an offer from Mexico Co. (a foreign wholesaler) to purchase an additional 2,000 blenders at $11 per unit. Accepting the offer would not affect normal sales of the product, and the additional units can be manufactured without increasing plant capacity. What should management do?

If management makes its decision based on the total cost per unit of $12 ($8 + $4), the order would be rejected, because costs ($12) would exceed revenues ($11) by $1 per unit. However, since the units can be produced within existing plant capacity, the special order *will not increase fixed costs.* Let's identify the relevant data for the decision. First, the variable manufacturing costs will increase by $16,000 ($8 × 2,000). Second, the expected revenue will increase by $22,000 ($11 × 2,000). Thus, as shown in Illustration 7-4, Sunbelt will increase its net income by $6,000 by accepting this special order.

STUDY OBJECTIVE 2
Identify the relevant costs in accepting an order at a special price.

Helpful Hint
This is a good example of different costs for different purposes. In the long run, all costs are relevant, but for this decision only costs that change are relevant.

	A	B	C	D
1		**Reject Order**	**Accept Order**	**Net Income Increase (Decrease)**
2	Revenues	$0	$22,000	$ 22,000
3	Costs	0	16,000	(16,000)
4	Net income	$0	$ 6,000	$ 6,000
5				

►Illustration 7-4
Incremental analysis—accepting an order at a special price

Two points should be emphasized: First, it is assumed that sales of the product in other markets **would not be affected by this special order**. If other sales will be lost, then Sunbelt would have to consider the lost sales in making the decision. Second, if Sunbelt was operating *at full capacity*, it is likely that the special order would be rejected. Under such circumstances, the company would have to expand plant capacity. In that case, the special order would have to absorb these additional fixed manufacturing costs, as well as the variable manufacturing costs.

BEFORE YOU GO ON...

►Do It! Special Orders

Cobb Company incurs a cost of $28 per unit, of which $18 is variable, to make a product that normally sells for $42. A foreign wholesaler offers to buy 5,000 units at $25 each. Cobb will incur shipping costs of $1 per unit. Calculate the increase or decrease in net income Cobb will realize by accepting the special order, assuming Cobb has excess operating capacity. Should Cobb Company accept the special order?

Action Plan
• Identify all revenues that will change as a result of accepting the order.
• Identify all costs that will change as a result of accepting the order, and net this amount against the change in revenues.

Solution

	Reject	Accept	Net Income Increase (Decrease)
Revenue	$0	$125,000	$125,000
Costs	0	95,000*	(95,000)
Net income	$0	$ 30,000	$ 30,000

*(5,000 × $18) + (5,000 × $1)

Given the result of the analysis, Cobb Company should accept the special order.

Related exercise material: **BE7-3, BE7-4, E7-18, E7-19,** and **Do It! D7-11.**

the navigator

MAKE OR BUY

STUDY OBJECTIVE 3

Identify the relevant costs in a make-or-buy decision.

When a manufacturer assembles component parts in producing a finished product, management must decide whether to make or buy the components. The decision to buy parts or services is often called outsourcing. For example, pharmaceutical manufacturer Apotex may either make or buy gelatin capsules used in producing medications. Similarly, Hewlett-Packard Corporation may make or buy the electronic circuitry, cases, and printer heads for its printers. The decision to make or buy components should be made on the basis of incremental analysis.

To illustrate the analysis, assume that Baron Company incurs the annual costs in Illustration 7-5 in producing 25,000 ignition switches for motor scooters.

▶Illustration 7-5

Annual product cost data

Direct materials	$ 50,000
Direct labour	75,000
Variable manufacturing overhead	40,000
Fixed manufacturing overhead	60,000
Total manufacturing costs	$225,000
Total cost per unit ($225,000 ÷ 25,000)	**$9.00**

Instead of making its own switches, Baron Company could purchase the ignition switches from Ignition, Inc. at a price of $8 per unit. The question again is, "What should management do?"

At first glance, it appears that management should purchase the ignition switches for $8, rather than make them at a cost of $9. However, a review of operations indicates that if the ignition switches are purchased from Ignition, Inc., *all* of Baron's variable costs but only $10,000 of its fixed manufacturing costs will be eliminated. Thus, $50,000 of the fixed manufacturing costs will remain if the ignition switches are purchased. The relevant costs for incremental analysis, therefore, are as shown in Illustration 7-6 using a three-column format. The first two columns present the costs of the two alternatives, whereas the third column presents the incremental costs.

▶Illustration 7-6

Incremental analysis—make or buy

	A	B	C	D
1		**Make**	**Buy**	**Net Income Increase (Decrease)**
2	Direct materials	$ 50,000	$ 0	$ 50,000
3	Direct labour	75,000	0	75,000
4	Variable manufacturing costs	40,000	0	40,000
5	Fixed manufacturing costs	60,000	50,000	10,000
6	Purchase price (25,000 × $8)	0	200,000	(200,000)
7	Total annual cost	$225,000	$250,000	$ (25,000)
8				

IFRS Note

IFRS requires that the cost of inventory reported on the external financial statements include all the direct costs of purchase and/or manufacture and the costs of conversion (including both fixed and variable manufacturing overheads). However, this particular definition of cost, which includes fixed manufacturing overhead as an inventoriable cost, must sometimes be analyzed further when making internal management decisions, as demonstrated in these incremental analysis decision-making approaches.

This analysis shows that Baron Company will eliminate $165,000 of variable manufacturing costs and $10,000 of avoidable fixed manufacturing costs if the ignition switches are purchased outside the company. Thus, this is an incremental cost savings of $25,000 by not buying the ignition switches. Therefore, Baron should continue to make the ignition switches even though the total manufacturing cost is $1 higher than the purchase price. The reason is that if the company purchases the ignition switches, it will still have fixed costs of $50,000 to absorb.

Illustration 7-7 presents the relevant costs for incremental analysis in the decision to make or buy using a single-column format that concentrates only on the incremental costs and savings. This analysis shows that $165,000 of variable manufacturing costs and $10,000 of avoidable fixed manufacturing costs can be eliminated if the ignition switches are purchased from Ignition, Inc. for a total cost savings of $175,000. However, the cost of purchasing the ignition switches from Ignition, Inc. is $200,000 (25,000 units × $8). The difference is $25,000 ($200,000 purchase price − $175,000 cost savings). Thus, Baron Company will incur $25,000 by buying the ignition switches from Ignition Inc. Therefore, Baron should continue to make the ignition switches.

	Incremental Cost Analysis
Cost savings (avoidable if ignition switches are purchased externally):	
Direct materials	$ 50,000
Direct labour	75,000
Variable manufacturing costs	40,000
Avoidable fixed manufacturing costs	10,000
Total cost savings	$175,000
Cost of buying ignition switches externally:	
(25,000 units @ $8)	$200,000
Cost savings	175,000
Excess cost of buying ignition switches externally	$ 25,000

▶Illustration 7-7

Single-column format for incremental analysis—make or buy

Opportunity Cost

The make-or-buy analysis we just did is complete only if it is assumed that Baron Company cannot use the production capacity that it uses to make the ignition switches for another purpose. If there is an opportunity to use this productive capacity in some other manner, then the company must consider this opportunity. As indicated earlier, an **opportunity cost** is the potential benefit that a company may lose by following an alternative course of action.

To illustrate, assume that if it buys the switches, Baron Company can use the released productive capacity to generate additional income of $38,000 by producing a different product. This lost income is an additional cost of continuing to make the switches in the make-or-buy decision. The company therefore adds this opportunity cost to the "Make" column, for comparison. As Illustration 7-8 and Illustration 7-9 show, it is now advantageous to buy the ignition switches.

Helpful Hint
In the make-or-buy decision, it is important for management to take into account the social impact of the choice. For instance, buying may be the most economically feasible solution, but it could result in the closure of a manufacturing plant that employs many good workers.

	A	B	C	D
		Make	**Buy**	**Net Income Increase (Decrease)**
1				
2	Total annual cost	$225,000*	$250,000*	$(25,000)
3	**Opportunity cost**	**38,000**	**0**	**38,000**
4	Total cost	$263,000	$250,000	$ 13,000
5				
	* From Illustration 7-6			

▶Illustration 7-8

Incremental analysis—make or buy, with opportunity cost

	Incremental Cost Analysis
Cost of buying ignition switches externally	
(25,000 units @ $8)	$200,000
Cost savings (avoidable if ignition switches purchased externally)	175,000*
Opportunity cost of using the released productive capacity to	
generate additional income of	38,000
	$(13,000)
Net savings from buying ignition switches externally: $13,000	
* From Illustration 7-7	

▶Illustration 7-9

Single-column format for incremental analysis—make or buy, with opportunity cost

The qualitative factors in this decision include the possible loss of jobs for employees who produce the ignition switches. In addition, management must assess how long the supplier will be able to satisfy the company's quality control standards at the quoted price per unit.

BUSINESS INSIGHT   *Outsourcing an Icon*

When Tim Hortons decided in 2001 to close its in-store baking facilities and outsource its doughnut production to a centralized bakery, it was banking on a qualitative factor that no spreadsheet could predict: it was hoping that customers would still love the taste. That apparently is the case, since the Canadian icon reported revenues of $3.1 billion in 2012, up 9.4% from the year before. The company initially invested about U.S. $35 million for a 50% stake in Maidstone Bakeries, a 37,000 square-metre facility in Brantford, Ontario. Not only did outsourcing the baking to Maidstone lower baking costs, but Maidstone became so successful that Tim Hortons sold its share in 2010 for a whopping $475 million. The doughnut chain was to maintain its supply contract with Maidstone until at least 2016 and in the meantime was free to search for other suppliers.

Sources: Eric Lam, "Tim Hortons Cashes in After Bakery Sale," *Financial Post*, August 12, 2010; Sunny Freeman, The Canadian Press, "Tim Hortons Plans to Return $475 Million from Maidstone Sale to Shareholders," *Toronto Star*, August 12, 2010; Tim Hortons 2012 annual report.

What are the advantages of outsourcing baking services?

BEFORE YOU GO ON...

▶Do It! Make or Buy

Juanita Company must decide whether to make or buy some of its components. The costs of producing 166,000 electrical cords for its floor lamps are as follows.

Direct materials	$90,000	Variable overhead	$32,000
Direct labour	$20,000	Fixed overhead	$24,000

Instead of making the electrical cords at an average cost per unit of $1.00 ($166,000 ÷ 166,000), the company has an opportunity to buy the cords at $0.90 per unit. If the company purchases the cords, all variable costs and one quarter of the fixed costs will be eliminated.

(a) Prepare an incremental analysis showing whether the company should make or buy the electrical cords.

(b) Will your answer be different if the released productive capacity will generate additional income of $5,000?

Action Plan

- Look for the costs that change.
- Ignore the costs that do not change.
- Use the format in the chapter for your answer.
- Recognize that opportunity cost can make a difference.

Solution

(a)

	Make	Buy	Net Income Increase (Decrease)
Direct materials	$ 90,000	$ 0	$ 90,000
Direct labour	20,000	0	20,000
Variable manufacturing costs	32,000	0	32,000
Fixed manufacturing costs	24,000	18,000[a]	6,000
Purchase price	0	149,400[b]	(149,400)
Total cost	$166,000	$167,400	$ (1,400)

[a]0.75 × $24,000

[b]166,000 × $0.90

This analysis indicates that Juanita Company will incur $1,400 of additional costs if it buys the electrical cords.

(b)

	Make	Buy	Net Income Increase (Decrease)
Total cost	$166,000	$167,400	$(1,400)
Opportunity cost	5,000	0	5,000
Total cost	$171,000	$167,400	$ 3,600

Yes, the answer is different: The analysis shows that net income increases by $3,600 if Juanita Company purchases the electrical cords.

Related exercise material: **BE7-5, E7-20, E7-21,** and **Do It! D7-12.**

✔
the navigator

SELL OR PROCESS FURTHER

Many manufacturers have the option of selling products at a particular point in the production cycle or continuing to process the products in order to sell them later at a higher price. For example, a bicycle manufacturer such as Rocky Mountain could sell its bicycles to retailers either unassembled or assembled. A furniture manufacturer such as Durham Furniture could sell its dining room sets to furniture stores either unfinished or finished. A company should make the sell-or-process-further decision on the basis of incremental analysis. The basic decision rule is as follows: **Process further as long as the incremental revenue from the processing is more than the incremental processing costs.**

STUDY OBJECTIVE 4
Identify the relevant costs in deciding whether to sell or process materials further.

Single-Product Case

Assume, for example, that Woodmasters Inc. makes tables. The cost to manufacture an unfinished table is $35, as calculated in Illustration 7-10.

Direct material	$15
Direct labour	10
Variable manufacturing overhead	6
Fixed manufacturing overhead	4
Manufacturing cost per unit	$35

▶Illustration 7-10
Per-unit cost of unfinished table

The selling price per unfinished unit is $50. Woodmasters currently has unused productive capacity that is expected to continue indefinitely. What are the relevant costs? Management concludes that it can use some of this capacity to finish the tables and sell them at $60 per unit. For a finished table, direct materials will increase by $2 and direct labour costs will increase by $4. Variable manufacturing overhead costs will increase by $2.40 (60% of direct labour). Management doesn't anticipate any increase in fixed manufacturing overhead. Illustration 7-11 shows the incremental analysis on a per-unit basis.

	A	B	C	D
1		Sell	Process Further	Net Income Increase (Decrease)
2	Sales per unit	$50.00	$60.00	$10.00
3	Cost per unit			
4	Direct materials	15.00	17.00	(2.00)
5	Direct labour	10.00	14.00	(4.00)
6	Variable manufacturing overhead	6.00	8.40	(2.40)
7	Fixed manufacturing overhead	4.00	4.00	0.00
8	Total	35.00	43.40	(8.40)
9	Net income per unit	$15.00	$16.60	$ 1.60
10				

▶Illustration 7-11
Incremental analysis—sell or process further

Helpful Hint
Current net income is known. Net income from processing further is an estimate. In making its decision, management could add a "risk" factor for the estimate.

It would be advantageous for Woodmasters to process the tables further. The incremental revenue of $10.00 from the additional processing is $1.60 higher than the incremental processing costs of $8.40.

Multiple-Product Case

Sell-or-process-further decisions are especially relevant to production processes that produce multiple products simultaneously. In many industries, several end products are produced from a single raw material and a common production process. These multiple end products are commonly called **joint products**. For example, in the meat-packing industry, a single sheep produces meat, internal organs, hides, wool, bones, and fat. In the petroleum industry, crude oil is refined to produce gasoline, lubricating oil, kerosene, paraffin, and ethylene.

Illustration 7-12 presents a joint product situation for Marais Creamery, which must decide whether *to sell or process further cream and skim milk*. Both of these products result from the processing of raw milk.

▶Illustration 7-12

Joint production process—Marais Creamery

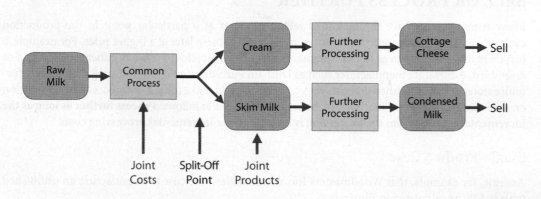

Marais Creamery incurs many costs before it manufactures cream and skim milk. All costs that are incurred before the point at which the two products are separately identifiable (the *split-off point*) are called **joint costs**. To determine the cost of each product, joint product costs must be allocated to the individual products. This is frequently done based on the relative sales value of the joint products. Although this allocation is important for determining the product cost, it is irrelevant in sell-or-process-further decisions. This is because these joint product costs are **sunk costs**. That is, the company has already incurred them and cannot change or avoid them with any later decision.

Illustration 7-13 shows the daily cost and revenue data for Marais Creamery.

▶Illustration 7-13

Cost and revenue data per day

Costs (per day)	
Joint cost allocated to cream	$ 9,000
Joint cost allocated to skim milk	5,000
Processing cream into cottage cheese	10,000
Processing skim milk into condensed milk	8,000
Expected Revenues from Products (per day)	
Cream	$19,000
Skim milk	11,000
Cottage cheese	27,000
Condensed milk	26,000

From this information, we can determine whether the company should simply sell the cream and skim milk, or process them further into cottage cheese and condensed milk. Illustration 7-14 shows the analysis the company needs to do to decide whether to sell the cream or process it further into cottage cheese.

	A	B	C	D
				Net Income
1		**Sell**	**Process Further**	**Increase (Decrease)**
2	Sales per day	$19,000	$27,000	$ 8,000
3	Cost per day			
4	Processing cream into cottage cheese	0	10,000	(10,000)
5		$19,000	$17,000	$ (2,000)
6				

▶Illustration 7-14
Analysis of whether to sell cream or make cottage cheese

From this analysis, we can see that Marais Creamery should not process the cream further, because it will sustain an incremental loss of $2,000. Illustration 7-15, however, shows that Marais Creamery should process the skim milk into condensed milk, as it will increase net income by $7,000.

	A	B	C	D
				Net Income
1		**Sell**	**Process Further**	**Increase (Decrease)**
2	Sales per day	$11,000	$26,000	$15,000
3	Cost per day			
4	Processing skim milk into condensed milk	0	8,000	(8,000)
5		$11,000	$18,000	$ 7,000
6				

▶Illustration 7-15
Analysis of whether to sell skim milk or process into condensed milk

Note that the amount of joint costs allocated to each product ($9,000 to the cream and $5,000 to the skim milk) is irrelevant in deciding whether to sell or process further. Why? The joint costs remain the same whether or not there is further processing.

It is important to understand that these decisions need to be reevaluated as market conditions change. For example, if the price of skim milk increases relative to the price of condensed milk, it may become more profitable to sell the skim milk rather than process it into condensed milk. Consider also oil refineries. As market conditions change, they must constantly re-assess which products to produce from the oil they receive at their plants.

BEFORE YOU GO ON...

▶Do It! Sell or Process Further

Easy Does It manufactures unpainted furniture for the do-it-yourself (DIY) market. It currently sells a child's rocking chair for $25. Production costs are $12 variable and $8 fixed. Easy Does It is considering painting the rocking chair and selling it for $35. Variable costs to paint each chair are expected to be $9, and fixed costs are expected to be $2.

Prepare an analysis showing whether Easy Does It should sell unpainted or painted chairs.

Action Plan

- Identify the revenues that will change as a result of painting the rocking chair.
- Identify all costs that will change as a result of painting the rocking chair, and net the amount against the revenues.

Solution

	Sell	Process Further	Net Income Increase (Decrease)
Revenues	$25	$35	$10
Variable costs	12	21	(9)
Fixed costs	8	10	(2)
Net income	$ 5	$ 4	$ (1)

The analysis indicates that the rocking chair should be sold unpainted because net income per chair will be $1 greater.

Related exercise material: **BE7-6, BE7-7, E7-22, E7-23, E7-24**, and **Do It! D7-13.**

the navigator

RETAIN OR REPLACE EQUIPMENT

STUDY OBJECTIVE 5
Identify the relevant costs in deciding whether to retain or replace equipment.

Management often has to decide whether to continue using an asset or replace it. To illustrate, assume that Jeffcoat Company has a factory machine that originally cost $110,000. It has a balance in Accumulated Depreciation of $70,000, so its book value is $40,000. It has a remaining useful life of four years. The company is considering replacing this machine with a new machine. A new machine is available that costs $120,000. It is expected to have zero salvage value at the end of its four-year useful life. If the new machine is acquired, variable manufacturing costs are expected to decrease from $160,000 to $125,000 annually, and the old unit could be sold for $5,000. Illustration 7-16 shows the incremental analysis for the four-year period.

▶Illustration 7-16
Incremental analysis—Retain or replace equipment

	A	B	C	D
1		Retain Equipment	Replace Equipment	Net Income Increase (Decrease)
2	Variable manufacturing costs	$640,000ᵃ	$500,000ᵇ	**$140,000**
3	New machine cost		120,000	**(120,000)**
4	Sale of old machine		(5,000)	**5,000**
5	Total	$640,000	$615,000	**$ 25,000**
6				
7	ᵃ(4 years × $160,000)			
8	ᵇ(4 years × $125,000)			
9				

In this case, it would be to the company's advantage to replace the equipment. The lower variable manufacturing costs due to replacement more than offset the cost of the new equipment. Note that the $5,000 received from the sale of the old machine is relevant to the decision because it will only be received if the company chooses to replace its equipment. In general, any trade-in allowance or cash disposal value of existing assets is relevant to the decision to retain or replace equipment.

One other point should be mentioned regarding Jeffcoat's decision: **the book value of the old machine does not affect the decision.** Book value is a **sunk cost**—a cost that cannot be changed by any present or future decision. **Sunk costs are not relevant in incremental analysis.** In this example, if the company retains the asset, the book value will be depreciated over its remaining useful life. Or, if it acquires the new unit, it will recognize the book value as a loss in the current period. Thus, the effect of book value on current and future earnings is the same regardless of the replacement decision.

Sometimes, decisions regarding whether to replace equipment are clouded by behavioural decision-making errors. For example, suppose a manager spent $90,000 repairing a machine two months ago. Now, suppose that the machine breaks down again today. The manager might be inclined to think that, because the company recently spent a large amount of money to repair the machine, the machine should now be repaired rather than replaced. However, the amount spent in the past to repair the machine is irrelevant to the current decision. It is a sunk cost.

Similarly, suppose a manager spent $5 million to purchase a new machine. Six months later, a new machine comes on the market that is significantly more efficient than the one recently purchased. The manager might be inclined to think that he or she should not buy the new machine because of the recent purchase. In fact, the manager might fear that buying a different machine so quickly might call into question the merit of the previous decision. Again, the fact that the company recently bought a new machine is not relevant. Instead, the manager should use incremental analysis to determine whether the savings generated by the efficiencies of the new machine would justify its purchase.

BEFORE YOU GO ON...

▶Do It! Retain or Replace Equipment

Evett Corporation uses a machine that winds twine onto spools. The machine is unreliable and results in a significant amount of downtime and excessive labour costs. The management is considering replacing the machine with a more efficient one that will minimize downtime and excessive labour costs. Data are presented below for the two machines:

	Old Machine	New Machine
Original purchase cost	$160,000	$240,000
Accumulated depreciation	120,000	—
Estimated life	4 years	4 years

It is estimated that the new machine will produce annual cost savings of $55,000. The old machine can be sold to a scrap dealer for $24,000. Both machines will have a salvage value of zero if operated for the remainder of their useful lives.

Determine whether the company should purchase the new machine.

Action Plan

- Identify the costs that will change as a result of replacing equipment.
- Identify all cost savings that will result from replacing equipment, and net the amount against the cost of the new equipment.
- Ignore the book value of the old equipment.

Solution

	Retain Equipment	Replace Equipment	Net Income Increase (Decrease)
Cost savings	$0	$220,000*	$ 220,000
New machine cost	0	(240,000)	(240,000)
Proceeds from sale of old machine	0	24,000	24,000
Net incremental savings	$0	$ 4,000	$ 4,000

*$55,000 × 4 = $220,000

The company should purchase the new machine because there will be an increase in net income of $4,000 over the four-year life of the new machine.

Related exercise material: **BE7-8, E7-25,** and **Do It! D7-14.**

the navigator

ELIMINATE AN UNPROFITABLE SEGMENT

Management must sometimes decide whether to eliminate an unprofitable business segment or product. For example, in recent years, many airlines quit servicing certain cities or cut back on the number of flights. Goodyear quit producing several brands in the low-end tire market. Again, the key is to **focus on the relevant costs—the data that change under the alternative courses of action**. To illustrate, assume that Martina Company manufactures tennis racquets in three models: Pro, Master, and Champ. Pro and Master are profitable lines. Champ (highlighted in colour in the table below) operates at a loss. Illustration 7-17 provides condensed income statement data.

STUDY OBJECTIVE 6
Identify the relevant costs in deciding whether to eliminate an unprofitable segment.

Helpful Hint
A decision to discontinue a segment based solely on the bottom line—net loss—is inappropriate.

	Pro	Master	Champ	Total
Sales	$800,000	$300,000	$100,000	$1,200,000
Variable expenses	520,000	210,000	90,000	820,000
Contribution margin	280,000	90,000	10,000	380,000
Fixed expenses	80,000	50,000	30,000	160,000
Net income	$200,000	$ 40,000	$(20,000)	$ 220,000

▶Illustration 7-17
Segment income data

Some might expect total net income to increase by $20,000, to $240,000, if the company eliminates the unprofitable Champ line of racquets. However, **net income may actually decrease if the Champ line is discontinued**. This is because the other products will have to absorb the fixed expenses allocated to the Champ racquets. To illustrate, assume that of the $30,000 of fixed costs applicable to the unprofitable segment, the company allocates two thirds to the Pro model and one third to the Master model after eliminating the Champ model. Fixed expenses will increase to $100,000 ($80,000 + $20,000) in the Pro line and to $60,000 ($50,000 + $10,000) in the Master line. Illustration 7-18 presents the revised income statement.

▶Illustration 7-18

Income data after eliminating the unprofitable product line

	Pro	Master	Total
Sales	$800,000	$300,000	$1,100,000
Variable expenses	520,000	210,000	730,000
Contribution margin	280,000	90,000	370,000
Fixed expenses	100,000	60,000	160,000
Net income	$180,000	$ 30,000	$ 210,000

Total net income has decreased by $10,000 ($220,000 − $210,000). The incremental analysis of the Champ racquets in Illustration 7-19 also obtains this result.

▶Illustration 7-19

Incremental analysis—eliminating an unprofitable segment

	A	B	C	D
1		**Continue**	**Eliminate**	**Net Income Increase(Decrease)**
2	Sales	$100,000	$ 0	$(100,000)
3	Variable costs	90,000	0	90,000
4	Contribution margin	10,000	0	(10,000)
5	Fixed costs	30,000	30,000	0
6	Net income	$ (20,000)	$(30,000)	$ (10,000)
7				

The loss in net income is attributable to the Champ line's contribution margin ($10,000), which the company will not realize if it discontinues the segment.

Assume the same facts as above, except now assume that $22,000 of the fixed costs attributed to the Champ line can be eliminated if the line is discontinued. Illustration 7-20 presents the incremental analysis based on this revised assumption.

▶Illustration 7-20

Incremental analysis—eliminating unprofitable segment with reduction in fixed costs

	A	B	C	D
1		**Continue**	**Eliminate**	**Net Income Increase (Decrease)**
2	Sales	$100,000	$ 0	$(100,000)
3	Variable costs	90,000	0	90,000
4	Contribution margin	10,000	0	(10,000)
5	Fixed costs	30,000	8,000	22,000
6	Net income	$ (20,000)	$(8,000)	$ 12,000
7				

In this case, because the company is able to eliminate some of its fixed costs by eliminating the division, it can increase its net income by $12,000. **This occurs because the $22,000 savings that result from the eliminated fixed costs exceed the $10,000 in lost contribution margin by $12,000 ($22,000 − $10,000).**

In deciding on the future status of an unprofitable segment, management should consider the effect of elimination on related product lines. Product lines that continue may be able to get some or all of the sales lost by the discontinued product line. In some businesses, services or products may be linked—for example, free chequing accounts at a bank, or coffee at a doughnut shop. In addition, management should consider the effect of eliminating the product line on employees who may have to be laid off or retrained.

BEFORE YOU GO ON...

▶Do It! Unprofitable Segments

Lambert, Inc. manufactures several types of accessories. For the year, the knit hats and scarves line had sales of $400,000, variable expenses of $310,000, and fixed expenses of $120,000. Therefore, the knit hats and scarves line had a net loss of $30,000. If Lambert eliminates the knit hats and scarves line, $20,000 of fixed costs will remain. Prepare an analysis showing whether the company should eliminate the knit hats and scarves line.

Action Plan

- Identify the revenues that will change as a result of eliminating a product line.
- Identify all costs that will change as a result of eliminating a product line, and net the amount against the revenues.

Solution

	Continue	Eliminate	Net Income Increase (Decrease)
Sales	$400,000	$ 0	$(400,000)
Variable costs	310,000	0	310,000
Contribution margin	90,000	0	(90,000)
Fixed costs	120,000	20,000	100,000
Net income	$ (30,000)	$(20,000)	$ 10,000

The analysis indicates that Lambert should eliminate the knit hats and scarves line because net income will increase $10,000.

Related exercise material: **BE7-9, E7-27, E7-32,** and **Do It! D7-15.**

the navigator

DECISION TOOLKIT

Decision Checkpoints	Info Needed for Decision	Tools to Use for Decision	How to Evaluate Results
Which alternative should the company choose?	All relevant costs including opportunity costs	Compare the relevant cost of each alternative.	Choose the alternative that maximizes net income.

ALLOCATE LIMITED RESOURCES

In our break-even analysis in Chapter 6, we assumed a certain sales mix. But management must constantly evaluate its sales mix to determine whether it is as good as it can be. One factor that affects the sales mix decision is how much of the available resources each product uses.

Everyone's resources are limited. For a company, the limited resource may be floor space in a retail department store, or raw materials, direct labour hours, or machine capacity in a manufacturing company. When a company has limited resources, management must decide which products to make and sell in order to maximize net income.

STUDY OBJECTIVE 7
Determine the sales mix when a company has limited resources.

To illustrate, assume that Bilodeau Company manufactures deluxe and standard pen-and-pencil sets. The limiting resource is machine capacity, which is 3,600 hours per month. Relevant data appear in Illustration 7-21.

▶**Illustration 7-21**

Contribution margin and machine hours

	Deluxe Sets	Standard Sets
Contribution margin per unit	$8	$6
Machine hours required per unit	0.4	0.2

Helpful Hint
Contribution margin (CM) alone is not enough to make this decision. The key factor is CM per limited resource.

The deluxe sets may appear to be more profitable since they have a higher contribution margin ($8) than the standard sets ($6). However, note that the standard sets take fewer machine hours to produce than the deluxe sets. Therefore, it is necessary to find the **contribution margin per unit of the limited resource**; in this case, the contribution margin per machine hour. This is obtained by dividing the contribution margin per unit of each product by the number of units of the limited resource required for each product, as shown in Illustration 7-22.

▶**Illustration 7-22**

Contribution margin per unit of limited resource

	Deluxe Sets	Standard Sets
Contribution margin per unit (a)	$ 8	$ 6
Machine hours required (b)	÷ 0.4	÷ 0.2
Contribution margin per unit of limited resource [(a) ÷ (b)]	**$20**	**$30**

The calculation shows that the standard sets have a higher contribution margin per unit of the limited resource. This would suggest that, if there is enough demand for standard sets, the company should shift the sales mix to standard sets or increase its machine capacity.

If Bilodeau Company is able to increase machine capacity from 3,600 hours to 4,200 hours, it could use the additional 600 hours to produce either the standard or deluxe pen-and-pencil sets. The total contribution margin under each alternative is found by multiplying the machine hours by the contribution margin per unit of the limited resource, as shown in Illustration 7-23.

▶**Illustration 7-23**

Incremental analysis—calculation of total contribution margin

	Produce Deluxe Sets	Produce Standard Sets
Machine hours (a)	600	600
Contribution margin per unit of limited resource (b)	× $20	× $30
Contribution margin [(a) × (b)]	$12,000	$18,000

From this analysis, we can see that to maximize net income, all of the increased capacity should be used to make and sell the standard sets. When there are multiple limited resources, solving the product mix requires the use of a specialized mathematical technique called linear programming, which is covered in production management or operation research courses.

As indicated in Illustration 7-22, the constraint on the production of the deluxe sets is the larger number of machine hours needed to produce these items. In addressing this problem, we have not questioned the limited number of machine hours, and have simply tried to maximize the contribution margin under this constraint. One question that Bilodeau should ask, however, is whether it can minimize this constraint. For example, the constraint might be due to a bottleneck in production or to poorly trained machine operators. In addition, the company should consider other possible solutions, such as outsourcing part of the production, acquiring additional new equipment (discussed in Chapter 13), or striving to eliminate any non–value-added activities.

As discussed in Chapter 1, this approach to evaluating constraints is referred to as the theory of constraints. The **theory of constraints** is a specific approach to constraints in which the company manages them to improve its overall results. According to this theory, a company must continually identify its constraints and find ways to reduce or eliminate them, where appropriate.

Qualitative Factors

In this chapter, we have focused mainly on the quantitative factors that affect a decision—those attributes that can be easily expressed in numbers or dollars. However, many of the decisions that use incremental analysis have important qualitative features. Although they are not easy to measure, these factors should not be ignored.

Consider, for example, the potential effects of the make-or-buy decision or of the decision to eliminate a line of business on existing employees and the community in which the plant is located. The cost savings that may result from outsourcing or from eliminating a plant should be weighed against these qualitative factors. One factor would be the cost of lost morale that might result. Albert "Chainsaw" Dunlap was a so-called "turnaround" artist who went into many companies, identified inefficiencies (using incremental analysis techniques), and tried to correct these problems to improve corporate profitability. Along the way, he laid off thousands of employees at many companies. As head of Sunbeam, it was Dunlap who lost his job because his draconian approach failed to improve Sunbeam's profitability. It was widely reported that Sunbeam's employees openly rejoiced for days after his departure. Clearly, qualitative factors can matter.

Relationship of Incremental Analysis and Activity-Based Costing

In Chapter 5, we noted that many companies have shifted to activity-based costing to allocate overhead costs to products. The main reason for using activity-based costing is that it results in a more accurate allocation of overhead. That is, activity-based costing better associates the actual increase in overhead costs that results from the manufacture of each product. The concepts presented in this chapter are completely consistent with the use of activity-based costing. In fact, activity-based costing will result in a better identification of relevant costs and, therefore, a better incremental analysis.

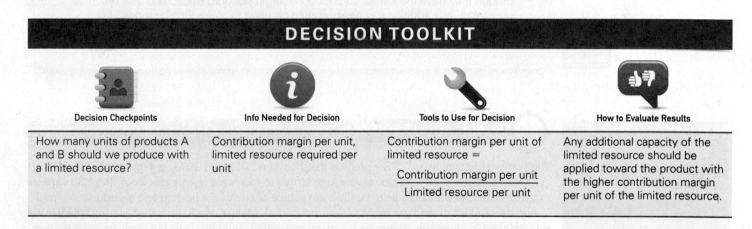

DECISION TOOLKIT

Decision Checkpoints	Info Needed for Decision	Tools to Use for Decision	How to Evaluate Results
How many units of products A and B should we produce with a limited resource?	Contribution margin per unit, limited resource required per unit	Contribution margin per unit of limited resource = $\dfrac{\text{Contribution margin per unit}}{\text{Limited resource per unit}}$	Any additional capacity of the limited resource should be applied toward the product with the higher contribution margin per unit of the limited resource.

BEFORE YOU GO ON...

▶Do It! Sales Mix with Limited Resources

Canada Bearings Corporation manufactures and sells three different types of high-quality sealed ball bearings, which vary in their quality specifications—mainly in terms of their smoothness and roundness. They are referred to as Fine, Extra-Fine, and Super-Fine bearings. Machine time is limited. The company requires more machine time to manufacture the Extra-Fine and Super-Fine bearings. Additional information follows:

	Product		
	Fine	Extra-Fine	Super-Fine
Selling price	$6.00	$10.00	$16.00
Variable costs and expenses	4.00	6.50	11.00
Contribution margin	$2.00	$ 3.50	$ 5.00
Machine hours required	0.02	0.04	0.08

Total fixed costs: $234,000

(continued)

(continued)

(a) Ignoring the machine-time constraint, determine what strategy would be the best.

(b) Calculate the contribution margin per unit of the limited resource for each type of bearing.

(c) Assuming the company could obtain additional machine time, determine how it should use the additional capacity.

Action Plan

- To determine how best to use a limited resource, calculate the contribution margin per unit of the limited resource for each product type.

Solution

(a) The Super-Fine bearings have the highest contribution margin per unit. Thus, ignoring any manufacturing constraints, it would appear that the company should shift toward production of more Super-Fine units.

(b) The contribution margin per unit of the limited resource is calculated as follows:

	Fine	Extra-Fine	Super-Fine
Contribution margin per unit	$ 2	$ 3.5	$ 5
÷ Limited resource consumed per unit	÷ 0.02	÷ 0.04	÷ 0.08
Contribution margin	$100.00	$87.50	$62.50

(c) The Fine bearings have the highest contribution margin per limited resource, even though they have the lowest contribution margin per unit. Because of this resource constraint, any additional capacity should be used to make Fine bearings.

Related exercise material: **BE7-10, E7-28, E7-29, E7-30,** and **Do It! D7-16.**

the navigator

ALL ABOUT YOU   *Big Decisions for Your Energy Future*

The National Energy Board (NEB) predicts that between 2012 and 2035, energy use in Canada will continue to increase, but at a slower rate, largely due to increased energy efficiency. The NEB expects that hydrocarbons will continue to be the main source of energy for heating and transportation, pushing up demand for oil and gas by 28% over that period. Many Canadians are wondering whether we should invest in renewable energy such as wind power that could be costly but might help the environment. Meanwhile, oil and gas extraction accounts for about 3% of Canada's GDP and directly employs over 280,000 Canadians.

What Do You Think?

Imagine that you work for a government department that is preparing a request for proposal for private companies to bid on building either a conventional or renewable energy-producing facility. Should you require bidders to show the environmental costs of conventional energy, such as increased greenhouse gases?

YES—As long as environmental costs are ignored, renewable energy will seem more expensive than conventional energy.

NO—Environmental costs are too difficult to estimate, so government decision-makers can't accurately compare financial bids for conventional and alternative facilities.

Sources: National Energy Board, "Canada's Energy Future 2013: Energy Supply and Demand Projections to 2035," November 2013; Natural Resources Canada, "Additional Statistics on Energy," www.nrcan.gc.ca/publications/statistics-facts/1239; Canadian Centre for Energy Information, "Canada: Statistics," www.centreforenergy.com/FactsStats/Statistics.asp?Template=5,0.

USING THE DECISION TOOLKIT

Suppose Canadian Communications Company must decide whether to make some of its components or buy them from Xenia Corp. The cost of producing 50,000 electrical connectors for its network is $110,000, broken down as follows:

Direct materials	$60,000	Variable overhead	$12,000
Direct labour	30,000	Fixed overhead	8,000

Instead of making the electrical connectors at an average cost per unit of $2.20 ($110,000 ÷ 50,000), the company has an opportunity to buy the connectors at $2.15 per unit. If it purchases the connectors, it will eliminate all variable costs and one half of the fixed costs.

Instructions

(a) Prepare an incremental analysis showing whether the company should make or buy the electrical connectors.
(b) Will your answer be different if the productive capacity that becomes available because of the purchase of the connectors will generate additional income of $25,000?

Solution

(a)

	Make	Buy	Net Income Increase (Decrease)
Direct materials	$ 60,000	$ 0	$ 60,000
Direct labour	30,000	0	30,000
Variable manufacturing costs	12,000	0	12,000
Fixed manufacturing costs	8,000	4,000[a]	4,000
Purchase price	0	107,500[b]	(107,500)
Total cost	$110,000	$111,500	$ (1,500)

[a]$8,000 × 0.50; [b]$2.15 × 50,000

This analysis indicates that Canadian Communications Company will incur $1,500 of additional costs if it buys the electrical connectors. Canadian Communications would therefore choose to make the connectors.

(b)

	Make	Buy	Net Income Increase (Decrease)
Total cost	$110,000	$111,500	$ (1,500)
Opportunity cost	25,000	0	25,000
Total cost	$135,000	$111,500	$23,500

Yes, the answer is different. The analysis shows that if additional capacity is released by purchasing the electrical connectors, net income will increase by $23,500. In this case, Canadian Communications would choose to purchase the connectors.

Summary of Study Objectives

1. **Describe management's decision-making process and the concept of incremental analysis.** Management's decision-making process consists of (a) identifying the problem and assigning responsibility for the decision, (b) determining and evaluating possible courses of action, (c) making the decision, and (d) reviewing the results of the decision.

   Incremental analysis is the process companies use to identify financial data that change under alternative courses of action. These data are relevant to the decision because they will vary in the future among the possible alternatives.

2. **Identify the relevant costs in accepting an order at a special price.** The relevant information in accepting an order at a special price is the difference between the variable manufacturing costs to produce the special order and expected revenues.

3. **Identify the relevant costs in a make-or-buy decision.** In a make-or-buy decision, the relevant costs are (a) the variable manufacturing costs that the company will save, (b) the purchase price, and (c) opportunity costs.

4. Identify the relevant costs in deciding whether to sell or process materials further. The decision rule for whether to sell or process materials further is as follows: process further as long as the incremental revenue from processing is more than the incremental processing costs.

5. Identify the relevant costs in deciding whether to retain or replace equipment. The relevant costs a company needs to consider in determining whether it should retain or replace equipment are the effects on variable costs and the cost of the new equipment. Also, it must consider any disposal value of the existing asset.

6. Identify the relevant costs in deciding whether to eliminate an unprofitable segment. In deciding whether to eliminate an unprofitable segment, the relevant information is the contribution margin, if any, produced by the segment and the disposition of the segment's fixed expenses.

7. Determine the sales mix when a company has limited resources. When a company has limited resources, it is necessary to find the contribution margin per unit of the limited resource. This amount is then multiplied by the units of limited resource to determine which product maximizes net income.

DECISION TOOLKIT—A SUMMARY

Decision Checkpoints	Info Needed for Decision	Tools to Use for Decision	How to Evaluate Results
Which alternative should the company choose?	All relevant costs including opportunity costs	Compare the relevant cost of each alternative	Choose the alternative that maximizes net income.
How many units of products A and B should we produce with a limited resource?	Contribution margin per unit, limited resource required per unit	Contribution margin per unit of limited resource = $$\frac{\text{Contribution margin per unit}}{\text{Limited resource per unit}}$$	Any additional capacity of the limited resource should be applied toward the product with the higher contribution margin per unit of the limited resource.

Glossary

Incremental analysis   The process of identifying the financial data that change under alternative courses of action. (p. 269)

Joint costs   For joint products, all costs incurred before the point at which the two products are separately identifiable. This point is known as the split-off point. (p. 276)

Joint products   Multiple end products produced from a single raw material and a common process. (p. 276)

Opportunity cost   The potential benefit that may be lost from following an alternative course of action. (p. 269)

Relevant costs   Those costs and revenues that differ across alternatives. (p. 269)

Sunk costs   Costs that cannot be changed by any present or future decision. (p. 269)

Theory of constraints   A specific approach that a company uses to identify and manage constraints in order to achieve its goals. (p. 282)

Comprehensive Do It!

Walston Company produces kitchen cabinets for homebuilders across western Canada. The cost of producing 5,000 cabinets is as follows.

Materials	$ 500,000
Labour	250,000
Variable overhead	100,000
Fixed overhead	400,000
Total	$1,250,000

Walston also incurs selling expenses of $20 per cabinet. Wellington Corp. has offered Walston $165 per cabinet for a special order of 1,000 cabinets. The cabinets would be sold to homebuilders in eastern Canada and thus would not conflict with Walston's current sales. Selling expenses per cabinet would be only $5 per cabinet. Walston has available capacity to do the work.

Instructions

(a) Prepare an incremental analysis for the special order.

(b) Should Walston accept the special order? Why or why not?

Solution to Comprehensive Do It!

(a) Relevant costs per unit would be:

Materials	$500,000 ÷ 5,000 =	$100
Labour	250,000 ÷ 5,000 =	50
Variable overhead	100,000 ÷ 5,000 =	20
Selling expenses		5
Total relevant cost per unit		$175

	Reject Order	Accept Order	Net Income Increase (Decrease)
Revenues	$0	$165,000	$165,000
Costs	0	175,000	(175,000)
Net income	$0	$(10,000)	$(10,000)

(b) Walston should reject the offer. The incremental benefit of $165 per cabinet is less than the incremental cost of $175. By accepting the order, Walston's net income would actually decline by $10,000.

> **Action Plan**
> - Determine the relevant cost per unit of the special order.
> - Identify the relevant costs and revenues for the units to be produced.
> - Compare the results related to accepting the special order versus rejecting the special order.

✔ the navigator

WileyPLUS

Self-Test, Brief Exercises, Exercises, Problems—Set A, and many more components are available for practice in WileyPlus.

Self-Study Questions

Answers are at the end of the chapter.

(SO 1) 1. Three of the steps in management's decision-making process are to (1) review the results of the decision, (2) determine and evaluate possible courses of action, and (3) make the decision. The steps are done in the following order:
(a) 1, 2, 3.
(b) 3, 2, 1.
(c) 2, 1, 3.
(d) 2, 3, 1.

(SO 1) 2. Incremental analysis is the process of identifying the financial data that
(a) do not change under alternative courses of action.
(b) change under alternative courses of action.
(c) are mixed under alternative courses of action.
(d) No correct answer is given.

(SO 2) 3. A company incurs $14 of variable costs and $6 of fixed costs to produce product A, which sells for $30. A foreign buyer offers to purchase 3,000 units at $18 each. If the company accepts and produces the special order with unused capacity, its net income will
(a) decrease by $6,000.
(b) increase by $6,000.
(c) increase by $12,000.
(d) increase by $9,000.

(SO 2) 4. A company incurs $14 of variable costs and $6 of fixed costs to produce product A, which sells for $30. A foreign buyer offers to purchase 3,000 units at $18 each. If the company accepts and produces the special order when capacity is already fully used, its net income will
(a) increase by $6,000.
(b) increase by $36,000.
(c) decrease by $6,000.
(d) decrease by $36,000.

(SO 3)　5. In a make-or-buy decision, the relevant costs are
(a) the manufacturing costs that will be saved.
(b) the purchase price of the units.
(c) opportunity costs.
(d) All of the above.

(SO 4)　6. The decision rule in a sell-or-process-further decision is to process further as long as the incremental revenue from processing is more than the
(a) incremental processing costs.
(b) variable processing costs.
(c) fixed processing costs.
(d) No correct answer is given.

(SO 5)　7. In a decision to retain or replace equipment, the book value of the old equipment is a(n)
(a) opportunity cost.
(b) sunk cost.
(c) incremental cost.
(d) marginal cost.

(SO 6)　8. If an unprofitable segment is eliminated,
(a) net income will always increase.
(b) the variable expenses of the eliminated segment will have to be absorbed by other segments.

(c) fixed expenses allocated to the eliminated segment will have to be absorbed by other segments.
(d) net income will always decrease.

(SO 7)　9. If the contribution margin per unit is $15 and it takes three machine hours to produce the unit, the contribution margin per unit of the limited resource is
(a) $25.
(b) $5.
(c) $4.
(d) No correct answer is given.

(SO 6)　10. A segment of Hazard Inc. has the following data:

Sales	$200,000
Variable expenses	140,000
Fixed expenses	100,000

If this segment is eliminated, what will be the effect on the company's net income? Assume that 50% of the fixed expenses will be eliminated and the rest will be allocated to the company's remaining segments.
(a) $120,000 increase
(b) $10,000 decrease
(c) $50,000 increase
(d) $10,000 increase

Brief Exercises

(SO 1)
Identify the steps in management's decision-making process.

BE7-1　The steps in management's decision-making process are listed in random order below. Indicate the order in which the steps should be executed.
_____ Make decision.
_____ Identify the problem and assign responsibility.
_____ Review the results of the decision.
_____ Determine and evaluate possible courses of action.

(SO 1)
Determine incremental changes.

BE7-2　Bogart Company is considering two alternatives. Alternative A will have sales of $160,000 and costs of $100,000. Alternative B will have sales of $180,000 and costs of $125,000. Compare alternative A with alternative B showing incremental revenues, costs, and net income.

(SO 2)
Determine whether to accept a special order.

BE7-3　Waterloo Co. sells product P-14 at a price of $48 a unit. The per-unit cost data are direct materials $15, direct labour $10, and overheads $12 (75% variable). Waterloo Co. has sufficient capacity to accept a special order for 40,000 units, but at a discount of 25% from the regular price. Selling costs associated with this order would be $3 per unit. Determine whether Waterloo Co. should accept the special order.

(SO 2)
Determine whether to accept a special order.

BE7-4　Assume the same information as in BE7-3, except that Waterloo has no excess capacity. Indicate the net income (loss) that Waterloo would realize by accepting the special order.

(SO 3)
Determine whether to make or buy a part.

BE7-5　Emil Manufacturing incurs unit costs of $7.50 ($4.50 variable and $3 fixed) in making a sub-assembly part for its finished product. A supplier offers to make 10,000 of the parts for $5 per unit. If it accepts the offer, Emil will save all variable costs and $1 fixed cost. Prepare an analysis showing the total cost savings, if any, that Emil will realize by buying the part.

(SO 4)
Determine whether to sell or process.

BE7-6　Green Inc. makes unfinished bookcases that it sells for $62. Production costs are $36 variable and $10 fixed. Because it has unused capacity, Green is considering finishing the bookcases and selling them for $70. Variable finishing costs are expected to be $7 per unit with no increase in fixed costs. Prepare an analysis on a per-unit basis that shows whether Green should sell unfinished or finished bookcases.

(SO 4)
Determine whether to sell or process further—joint products.

BE7-7　Each day, Iwaniuk Corporation processes one tonne of a secret raw material into two resulting products, AB1 and XY1. When it processes one tonne of the raw material, the company incurs joint processing costs of $60,000. It allocates $25,000 of these costs to AB1 and $35,000 to XY1. The resulting AB1 can be sold for $90,000. Alternatively, it can be processed further to make AB2 at an additional processing cost of $50,000, and sold for $150,000. Each day's batch of XY1 can be sold for $90,000. Alternatively, it can be processed further to create XY2, at an additional processing cost of $50,000, and sold for $130,000. Discuss what products Iwaniuk Corporation should make.

BE7-8 Chudzick Company has a factory machine with a book value of $180,000 and a remaining useful life of five years. A new machine is available at a cost of $300,000. This machine will have a five-year useful life with no salvage value. The new machine will lower annual variable manufacturing costs from $700,000 to $550,000. Prepare an analysis that shows whether Chudzick should retain or replace the old machine.

(SO 5)
Determine whether to retain or replace equipment.

BE7-9 Lisah Inc. manufactures golf clubs in three models. For the year, the Big Bart line has a net loss of $10,000 from sales $200,000, variable costs $180,000, and fixed costs $30,000. If the Big Bart line is eliminated, $20,000 of fixed costs will remain. Prepare an analysis showing whether the Big Bart line should be eliminated.

(SO 6)
Determine whether to eliminate an unprofitable segment.

BE7-10 In Lebeau Company, data for the contribution margin per unit and machine hours per unit for two products are as follows: product A, $10 and two hours; product B, $12 and three hours. Calculate the contribution margin per unit of the limited resource for each product.

(SO 7)
Determine the allocation of limited resources.

Do It! Review

D7-11 Corn Company incurs a cost of $35 per unit, of which $20 is variable, to make a product that normally sells for $58. A foreign wholesaler offers to buy 6,000 units at $31 each. Corn will incur additional costs of $2 per unit to imprint a logo and to pay for shipping.

(SO 2)
Evaluate a special order.

Instructions
(a) Calculate the increase or decrease in net income Corn will realize by accepting the special order, assuming Corn has sufficient excess operating capacity.
(b) Should Corn Company accept the special order?

D7-12 Maplewood Company must decide whether to make or buy some of its components. The costs of producing 60,000 switches for its generators are as follows.

(SO 3)
Evaluate make-or-buy opportunity.

Direct materials	$30,000	Variable overhead	$45,000
Direct labour	$42,000	Fixed overhead	$60,000

Instead of making the switches at an average cost of $2.95 ($177,000 ÷ 60,000), the company has an opportunity to buy the switches at $2.75 per unit. If the company purchases the switches, all the variable costs and one third of the fixed costs will be eliminated.

Instructions
(a) Prepare an incremental analysis showing whether the company should make or buy the switches.
(b) Would your answer be different if the released productive capacity will generate additional income of $30,000?

D7-13 La Mesa manufactures unpainted furniture for the do-it-yourself (DIY) market. It currently sells a table for $75. Production costs are $39 variable and $10 fixed. La Mesa is considering staining and sealing the table to sell it for $99. Variable costs to finish each table are expected to be $18, and fixed costs are expected to be $3.

(SO 4)
Sell or process further.

Instructions
Prepare an analysis showing whether La Mesa should sell unpainted or finished tables.

D7-14 The law firm of Matadin and Howe relies heavily on a colour laser printer to process the paperwork. Recently the printer has not functioned well and print jobs were not being processed. Management is considering updating the printer with a faster model.

(SO 5)
Prepare incremental analysis for the decision to retain or replace equipment.

	Current Printer	New Model
Original purchase cost	$30,000	$24,000
Accumulated depreciation	17,000	—
Estimated operating costs (annual)	3,000	2,000
Useful life	4 years	4 years

If sold now, the current printer would have a salvage value of $4,000. If operated for the remainder of its useful life, the current printer would have zero salvage value. The new printer is expected to have zero salvage value after four years.

Instructions
Prepare an analysis to show whether the company should retain or replace the printer.

(SO 6)
Analyze whether to
eliminate an unprofit-
able segment.

D7-15 Lion Corporation manufactures several types of accessories. For the year, the gloves and mittens line had sales of $500,000, variable expenses of $375,000, and fixed expenses of $150,000. Therefore, the gloves and mittens line had a net loss of $25,000. If Lion eliminates the line, $40,000 of fixed costs will remain.

Instructions
Prepare an analysis showing whether the company should eliminate the gloves and mittens line.

(SO 7)
Determine sales mix
with limited resources.

D7-16 Capital Corporation manufactures and sells three different types of binoculars. They are referred to as Good, Better, and Best binoculars. Grinding and polishing time is limited. More time is required to grind and polish the lenses used in the Better and Best binoculars. Additional information is provided below.

	Product		
	Good	Better	Best
Selling price	$80.00	$300.00	$900.00
Variable costs and expenses	50.00	180.00	450.00
Contribution margin	$30.00	$120.00	$450.00
Grinding and polishing time required	0.5 hrs	1.5 hrs	6 hrs

Instructions
(a) Determine what strategy would appear to be optimal if time constraints are ignored.
(b) Calculate the contribution margin per unit of limited resource for each type of binocular.
(c) If additional grinding and polishing time could be obtained, how should the additional capacity be used?

Exercises

(SO 1)
Analyze statements
about decision-making
and incremental
analysis.

E7-17 Pender has prepared the following list of statements about decision-making and incremental analysis:

1. The first step in management's decision-making process is to determine and evaluate possible courses of action.
2. The final step in management's decision-making process is to actually make the decision.
3. Accounting's contribution to management's decision-making process occurs primarily in evaluating possible courses of action and in reviewing the results.
4. In making business decisions, management ordinarily considers only financial information because it is objectively determined.
5. Decisions involve a choice among alternative courses of action.
6. The process used to identify the financial data that change under alternative courses of action is called incremental analysis.
7. Costs that are the same under all alternative courses of action sometimes affect the decision.
8. When using incremental analysis, some costs will always change under alternative courses of action, but revenues will not.
9. Variable costs will change under alternative courses of action, but fixed costs will not.

Instructions
Identify each statement as true or false. If false, indicate how to correct the statement.

(SO 2)
Use incremental
analysis for special-
order decision.

E7-18 Gruden Company produces golf discs, which it normally sells to retailers for $7 each. The cost of manufacturing 20,000 golf discs is:

Materials	$ 10,000
Labour	30,000
Variable overhead	20,000
Fixed overhead	40,000
Total	$100,000

Gruden also incurs 5% sales commission ($0.35) on each disc sold.

McGee Corporation offers Gruden $4.80 per disc for 5,000 discs. McGee would sell the discs under its own brand name in foreign markets not yet served by Gruden. If Gruden accepts the offer, its fixed overhead will increase from $40,000 to $46,000 due to the purchase of a new imprinting machine. No sales commission will result from the special order.

Instructions
(a) Prepare an incremental analysis for the special order.
(b) Should Gruden accept the special order? Why or why not?
(c) What assumptions underlie the decision made in part (b)?

(SO 2)
Prepare incremental
analysis for a special-
order decision.

E7-19 Hardy Fibre is the creator of Y-Go, a technology that weaves silver into fabrics to kill bacteria and odour on clothing while managing heat. Y-Go has become very popular in undergarments for sports activities. Operating at capacity, the company can produce one million Y-Go undergarments each year. The per-unit and total costs for the undergarment are as follows:

	Per Undergarment	Total
Direct materials	$2.00	$2,000,000
Direct labour	0.50	500,000
Variable manufacturing overhead	1.00	1,000,000
Fixed manufacturing overhead	1.25	1,250,000
Variable selling expenses	0.25	250,000
Totals	$5.00	$5,000,000

The Canadian Armed Forces (CAF) has approached Hardy Fibre and expressed an interest in purchasing 200,000 Y-Go undergarments for soldiers stationed in extremely warm climates. The CAF would pay the unit cost for direct materials, direct labour, and variable manufacturing overhead costs. In addition, the CAF has agreed to pay an additional $1 per undergarment to cover all other costs and provide a profit. Presently, Hardy Fibre is operating at 70% capacity and does not have any other potential buyers for Y-Go. If Hardy Fibre accepts the CAF's offer, it will not incur any variable selling expenses for this order.

Instructions

(a) Using incremental analysis, determine whether Hardy Fibre should accept the CAF's offer.

(b) Assume Hardy Fibre can now sell one million undergarments in the open market at $8 per unit. Using incremental analysis, determine whether Hardy Fibre should accept the CAF's offer for the 200,000 garments.

E7-20 Young Mi Inc. has been manufacturing its own shades for its table lamps. The company is currently operating at 100% of capacity, and variable manufacturing overhead is charged to production at the rate of 50% of direct labour costs. The direct materials and direct labour costs per unit to make the lampshades are $4 and $6, respectively. Normal production is 50,000 table lamps per year.

A supplier offers to make the lampshades at a price of $13.50 per unit. If Young Mi Inc. accepts the supplier's offer, all variable manufacturing costs will be eliminated, but the $50,000 of fixed manufacturing overhead currently being charged to the lampshades will have to be absorbed by other products.

(SO 3)
Prepare incremental analysis for the make-or-buy decision.

Instructions

(a) Prepare the incremental analysis for the decision to make or buy the lampshades.

(b) ▭▭▶ Should Young Mi Inc. buy the lampshades?

(c) ▭▭▶ Would your answer be different in part (b) if the productive capacity released by not making the lampshades could be used to produce income of $40,000?

E7-21 SY Telc has recently started to manufacture RecRobo, a three-wheeled robot that can scan a home for fires and gas leaks and then transmit this information to a mobile phone. The cost structure to manufacture 20,000 RecRobos is as follows:

(SO 3)
Prepare an incremental analysis for the make-or-buy decision.

	Cost
Direct materials ($35 per robot)	$ 700,000
Direct labour ($30 per robot)	600,000
Variable overhead ($10 per robot)	200,000
Allocated fixed overhead ($25 per robot)	500,000
Total	$2,000,000

SY Telc is approached by Chen Inc., which offers to make RecRobo for $80 per unit or $1.6 million.

Instructions

(a) Using incremental analysis, determine whether SY Telc should accept this offer under each of the following independent assumptions:

1. Assume that $400,000 of the fixed overhead cost is avoidable.

2. Assume that none of the fixed overhead is avoidable. However, if the robots are purchased from Chen Inc., SY Telc can use the released productive resources to generate additional income of $200,000.

(b) Describe the qualitative factors that might affect the decision to buy the robots from an outside supplier.

E7-22 Josée Chabot recently opened her own basket-weaving studio. She sells finished baskets in addition to the raw materials needed by customers to weave baskets of their own. Josée has put together a variety of raw material kits, with each kit including materials at various stages of completion. Unfortunately, because of space limitations, Josée is unable to carry all the varieties of kits she originally assembled and must choose between two basic packages.

The basic introductory kit includes undyed, uncut reeds (with dye included) for weaving one basket. This basic package costs Josée $14 and sells for $30. The second kit, called Stage 2, includes cut reeds that have already been dyed. With this kit, the customer only has to soak the reeds and weave the basket. Josée is able to produce the second kit by using the basic materials included in the first kit and adding one-half hour of her own time, which she values at $18 per hour. The kit of dyed and cut reeds sells for $35.

(SO 4)
Prepare an incremental analysis for the decision to process material further.

Instructions

Determine whether Josée's basket-weaving shop should carry the basic introductory kit with undyed and uncut reeds or the Stage 2 kit with reeds already dyed and cut. Prepare an incremental analysis to support your answer.

(SO 4)
Determine whether to
sell or process
further—joint
products.

E7-23   Bahrat, Inc. produces three separate products from a common process costing $100,000. Each of the products can be sold at the split-off point or can be processed further and then sold for a higher price. The cost and selling price data for a recent period are as follows:

	Sales Value at Split-Off Point	Cost to Process Further	Sales Value after Further Processing
Product 12	$50,000	$100,000	$190,000
Product 14	10,000	30,000	35,000
Product 16	60,000	150,000	220,000

Instructions
(a) Determine the total net income if all products are sold at the split-off point.
(b) Determine the total net income if all products are sold after further processing.
(c) Using incremental analysis, determine which products should be sold at the split-off point and which should be processed further.
(d) Determine the total net income using the results from part (c) and explain why the net income is different from that determined in part (b).

(SO 4)
Determine whether to
sell or process
further—joint
products.

E7-24   Shynee Minerals processes materials extracted from mines. The most common raw material that it processes results in three joint products: Sarco, Barco, and Larco. Each of these products can be sold as is, or they can be processed further and sold for a higher price. The company incurs joint costs of $180,000 to process one batch of the raw material that produces the three joint products. The following cost and selling price information is available for one batch of each product:

	Selling Price at Split-Off Point	Allocated Joint Costs	Cost to Process Further	Selling Price of Processed Product
Sarco	$200,000	$40,000	$100,000	$310,000
Barco	300,000	60,000	89,000	380,000
Larco	500,000	80,000	250,000	800,000

Instructions
Determine whether each of the three joint products should be sold as is, or processed further.

(SO 5)
Prepare incremental
analysis for the
decision to retain or
replace equipment.

E7-25   On January 2, 2015, Riverside Hospital purchased a $100,000 special radiology scanner from Faital Inc. The scanner has a useful life of five years and will have no disposal value at the end of its useful life. The straight-line method of depreciation is used on this scanner. Annual operating costs with this scanner are $105,000.

Approximately one year later, the hospital is approached by Alliant Technology salesperson Jinsil Soon, who indicates that purchasing the scanner in 2015 from Faital was a mistake. She points out that Alliant has a scanner that will save Riverside Hospital $30,000 a year in operating expenses over its three-year useful life. She notes that the new scanner will cost $110,000 and has the same capabilities as the scanner purchased last year. The hospital agrees that both scanners are of equal quality. The new scanner will have no disposal value. Alliant agrees to buy the old scanner from Riverside Hospital for $40,000.

Instructions
(a) Assume Riverside Hospital sells its old scanner on January 2, 2016. Calculate the gain or loss on the sale.
(b) Using incremental analysis, determine whether Riverside Hospital should purchase the new scanner on January 2, 2016.
(c) Explain why the hospital might be reluctant to purchase the new scanner, regardless of the results indicated by the incremental analysis in part (b).

(SO 5)
Prepare incremental
analysis for the
decision to retain or
replace equipment.

E7-26   Twyla Enterprises uses a computer to handle its sales invoices. Lately, business has been so good that it takes an extra three hours per night, plus every third Saturday, to keep up with the volume of sales invoices. Management is considering updating its computer with a faster model that would eliminate all of the overtime processing. Data for the two computers are as follows:

	Current Computer	New Computer
Original purchase cost	$15,000	$25,000
Accumulated depreciation	$ 6,000	$ 0
Estimated operating costs	$25,000	$20,000
Useful life	5 years	5 years

If sold now, the current computer would have a salvage value of $6,000. If it is used for the remainder of its useful life, the current computer would have zero salvage value. The new computer is expected to have zero salvage value after five years.

Instructions
Determine whether the current computer should be replaced. (Ignore the time value of money.)

E7-27 Nicole Filippas, a recent graduate of Rollings University's accounting program, evaluated the operating performance of Poway Company's six divisions. Nicole made the following presentation to Poway's board of directors and suggested the Erie division be eliminated. "If the Erie division is eliminated," she said, "our total profits would increase by $23,870."

(SO 6)
Prepare incremental analysis concerning the elimination of divisions.

	The Other Five Divisions	Erie Division	Total
Sales	$1,664,200	$ 96,200	$1,760,400
Cost of goods sold	978,520	76,470	1,054,990
Gross profit	685,680	19,730	705,410
Operating expenses	527,940	43,600	571,540
Net income	$ 157,740	$ (23,870)	$ 133,870

In the Erie division, the cost of goods sold is $70,000 variable and $6,470 fixed, and operating expenses are $15,000 variable and $28,600 fixed. None of the Erie division's fixed costs will be eliminated if the division is discontinued.

Instructions

▷ Is Nicole right about eliminating the Erie Division? Prepare a schedule to support your answer.

E7-28 Spencer Company manufactures and sells three products. Relevant per-unit data for each product follow:

(SO 7)
Calculate the contribution margin and determine product to be manufactured.

	Product		
	A	B	C
Selling price	$9	$ 12	$14
Variable costs and expenses	$3	$9.50	$12
Machine hours to produce	2	1	2

Instructions

(a) Calculate the contribution margin per unit of the limited resource (machine hours) for each product.
(b) Assuming 1,500 additional machine hours are available, determine which product should be manufactured.
(c) Prepare an analysis that shows the total contribution margin if the additional hours are (1) divided equally among the products, and (2) allocated entirely to the product identified in part (b) above.

E7-29 Dalton Company manufactures and sells two products. Relevant per-unit data concerning each product follow:

(SO 7)
Calculate the contribution margin and determine the products to be manufactured.

	Product	
	Basic	Deluxe
Selling price	$40	$52
Variable costs	$18	$24
Machine hours	0.5	0.7

Instructions

(a) Calculate the contribution margin per machine hour for each product.
(b) If 1,000 additional machine hours are available, which product should Dalton manufacture?
(c) Prepare an analysis showing the total contribution margin if the additional hours are
 1. divided equally between the products.
 2. allocated entirely to the product identified in part (b).

E7-30 Metropole Inc. can produce three different products interchangeably on two machines. The accounting department provides the following information on these products:

(SO 7)
Calculate the contribution margin and determine the products to be manufactured.

	A	B	C
Selling price per unit	$ 25	$35	$ 45
Variable costs per unit	$ 15	$27	$ 37
Units produced per machine hour	10	12	14
Minimum units produced	100	none	140
Maximum units produced	200	none	200

The total machine hours available are 100.

Instructions

(a) Determine the number of machine hours per unit.
(b) Determine the contribution margin per machine hour.
(c) Determine how many units of each product should be produced and the total contribution margin.

(SO 6)
Prepare an incremental analysis for the decision on whether to outsource or manufacture a component.

E7-31 Montel Firm is considering whether to outsource the manufacture of subcomponent JXY. The accounting department provides the following cost information for manufacturing 10,000 units of the subcomponent JXY per month.

Direct materials costs	$40,000
Direct labour costs	30,000
Variable overhead	15,000
Fixed overhead*	14,000

*Fixed overhead includes $5,000 supervisor's salary.

International Firm agrees to supply Montel with 10,000 units per month for a total cost of $120,000. If the subcomponent JXY is outsourced, Montel will be able to increase the production and sales of its final product by 1,000 units per month, which is sold for $100 per unit and its average variable costs per unit are $75. The supervisor's salary will be eliminated if subcomponent JXY is outsourced.

Instructions

(a) Prepare an incremental analysis for the subcomponent JXY. Your analysis should have columns for (1) Make the subcomponent JXY, (2) Buy the subcomponent JXY, and (3) Incremental Costs (Savings).
(b) Based on your analysis, what decision should management make?
(c) Would the decision be different if Montel has the opportunity to produce 2,000 units with the facilities currently being used to manufacture the subcomponent JXY? Show calculations.

(SO 6)
Prepare an incremental analysis for the decision to eliminate a product line.

E7-32 Clarington Company makes three models of phasers. Information on the three products is given below:

	Stunner	Double-Set	Mega-Power
Sales	$320,000	$480,000	$ 200,000
Variable expenses	160,000	200,000	130,000
Contribution margin	160,000	280,000	70,000
Fixed expenses	120,000	225,000	100,000
Net income	$ 40,000	$ 55,000	$ (30,000)

Fixed expenses consist of $300,000 of common costs allocated to the three products based on relative sales, and additional fixed expenses of $35,000 (Stunner), $70,000 (Double-Set), and $40,000 (Mega-Power). The common costs will be incurred regardless of how many models are produced. The other fixed expenses would be eliminated if a model is phased out.

John Liu, an executive with the company, feels the Mega-Power line should be discontinued to increase the company's net income.

Instructions

(a) Calculate current net income for Clarington Company.
(b) Calculate net income by product line and in total for Clarington Company if the company discontinues the Mega-Power product line. (*Hint*: Allocate the $300,000 common costs to the two remaining product lines based on their relative sales.)
(c) Should Clarington eliminate the Mega-Power product line? Why or why not?

(SO 2, 3, 4, 5, 6)
Identify relevant costs for different decisions.

E7-33 The costs listed below relate to a variety of different decision situations.

Cost	Decision
1. Unavoidable fixed overhead	Eliminate an unprofitable segment.
2. Direct labour	Make or buy.
3. Original cost of old equipment	Replace equipment.
4. Joint production costs	Sell or process further.
5. Opportunity cost	Accept a special order.
6. Segment manager's salary	Eliminate an unprofitable segment. (The manager will be terminated.)
7. Cost of new equipment	Replace equipment.
8. Incremental production costs	Sell or process further.
9. Direct materials	Replace equipment. (The amount of materials required does not change.)
10. Rent expense	Purchase or lease a building.

Instructions

For each cost listed above, indicate if it is relevant or not to the related decision. For those costs determined to be irrelevant, briefly explain why.

Problems: Set A

P7-34A Pro Sports Inc. manufactures basketballs for professional basketball associations. For the first six months of 2016, the company reported the following operating results while operating at 90% of plant capacity:

(SO 2)
Prepare an incremental analysis for a special-order decision and identify non-financial factors in the decision.

	Amount	Per Unit
Sales	$4,500,000	$50.00
Cost of goods sold	3,150,000	35.00
Selling and administrative expenses	360,000	4.00
Net income	$ 990,000	$11.00

Fixed costs for the period were cost of goods sold of $900,000, and selling and administrative expenses of $162,000.

In July, normally a slack manufacturing month, Pro Sports receives a special order for 9,000 basketballs at $30 each from the Italian Basketball Association. Accepting the order would increase variable selling and administrative expenses by $0.50 per unit because of shipping costs, but it would not increase fixed costs and expenses.

Instructions
(a) Prepare an incremental analysis for the special order.
(b) Should Pro Sports Inc. accept the special order?
(c) What is the minimum selling price on the special order to produce net income of $5.00 per ball?
(d) ✏️➤ What non-financial factors should management consider in making its decision?

(a) $20,700

(c) $32.70

P7-35A The management of Borealis Manufacturing Company is trying to decide whether to continue manufacturing a part or to buy it from an outside supplier. The part, called WISCO, is a component of the company's finished product.

The following information was collected from the accounting records and production data for the year ending December 31, 2016:

(SO 3)
Prepare an incremental analysis related to a make-or-buy decision, consider opportunity cost, and identify non-financial factors.

1. The machining department produced 8,000 units of WISCO during the year.
2. Variable manufacturing costs applicable to the production of each WISCO unit were direct materials $4.80, direct labour $4.30, indirect labour $0.43, and utilities $0.40.
3. Fixed manufacturing costs applicable to the production of WISCO were as follows:

Cost Item	Direct	Allocated
Depreciation	$2,100	$ 900
Property taxes	500	200
Insurance	900	600
	$3,500	$1,700

The company will eliminate all variable manufacturing and direct fixed costs if it purchases WISCO. Allocated costs will have to be absorbed by other production departments.
4. The lowest quotation for 8,000 WISCO units from a supplier is $80,000.
5. If WISCO units are purchased, freight and inspection costs would be $0.35 per unit, and the machining department would incur receiving costs totalling $1,300 per year.

Instructions
(a) Prepare an incremental analysis for WISCO. Your analysis should have columns for (1) Make WISCO, (2) Buy WISCO, and (3) Net income increase (decrease).
(b) Based on your analysis, what decision should management make?
(c) Would the decision be different if Borealis had the opportunity to produce $3,000 of net income with the facilities currently being used to manufacture WISCO? Show calculations.
(d) ✏️➤ What non-financial factors should management consider in making its decision?

(a) NI (decrease) ($1,160)

(c) NI increase $1,840

P7-36A Jenson College provides its own housekeeping services. The College director would like to outsource this service, and has found a company that will provide the service for $48 per hour. The following information has been collected about the cost per hour to the college for performing its own housekeeping services:

(SO 3)
Identify the relevant costs in an outsourcing decision.

Cost per hour of service:	
Cleaning supplies	$ 4
Direct labour costs	$ 30
Variable overhead	$ 1
Total hours of housekeeping services per year	3,000
Total fixed overhead	$50,000

Instructions

(a) $(14,000)

(a) Determine whether Jenson College should outsource housekeeping, assuming that 50% of fixed costs can be eliminated if the service is outsourced. Provide calculations to support your answer.

(b) 1,923 hours

(b) At what level of service (in hours) would Jenson generally be indifferent between providing housekeeping services or outsourcing them, assuming that 50% of fixed costs can be eliminated?

(c) ✏️ Describe two qualitative factors that might affect this outsourcing decision.

(SO 3)
Calculate the contribution margin and prepare an incremental analysis concerning a make-or-buy decision.

P7-37A Interdesign uses 1,000 units of the component IMC2 every month to manufacture one of its products. The unit costs incurred to manufacture the component are as follows:

Direct materials	$ 70.00
Direct labour	50.00
Overhead	130.00
Total	$250.00

Overhead costs include variable material handling costs of $8, which are applied to products on the basis of direct material costs. The remainder of the overhead costs are applied on the basis of direct labour dollars and consist of 50% variable costs and 50% fixed costs.

A vendor has offered to supply the IMC2 component at a price of $220 per unit.

Instructions

Answer the following questions:

(a) $(31,000)

(a) Should Interdesign purchase the component from the outside vendor if Interdesign's capacity remains idle?

(b) Should Interdesign purchase the component from the outside vendor if it can use its facilities to manufacture another product? What information will Interdesign need to make an accurate decision? Show your calculations.

(c) What are the qualitative factors that Interdesign will have to consider when making this decision?

(adapted from CGA-Canada, now CPA Canada)

(SO 4)
Determine whether a product should be sold or processed further.

P7-38A Miramichi Industrial Products Co. is a diversified industrial-cleaner processing company. The company's main plant produces two products: a table cleaner and a floor cleaner. They are made from a common set of chemical inputs (called CDG). Each week, the company processes 27,000 litres of chemical input at a cost of $210,000 into 18,000 litres of floor cleaner and 9,000 litres of table cleaner. The floor cleaner has no market value until it is converted into a polish with the trade name FloorShine. The additional processing costs for this conversion total $250,000.

FloorShine sells at $20 per one-litre bottle. The table cleaner can be sold for $25 per one-litre bottle. However, the table cleaner can be converted into two other products by adding 9,000 litres of another compound (TCP) to the 9,000 litres of table cleaner. This joint process will yield 9,000 litres each of table stain remover and table polish. The additional processing costs for this process are $120,000. Both table products can be sold for $20 per one-litre bottle.

The company decided not to process the table cleaner into table stain remover and table polish based on the following analysis:

	Table Cleaner	Process Further		
		Table Stain Remover	Table Polish	Total
Production in litres	(9,000)	9,000	9,000	
Revenue	$225,000	$180,000	$180,000	$360,000
Costs				
CDG costs	70,000ᵃ	52,500	52,500	105,000ᵇ
TCP costs	0	60,000	60,000	120,000
Total costs	70,000	112,500	112,500	225,000
Weekly gross profit	$155,000	$ 67,500	$ 67,500	$135,000

ᵃIf the table cleaner is not processed further, it is allocated one third of the $210,000 of CDG cost, which is equal to one third of the total physical output.

ᵇIf the table cleaner is processed further, the total physical output is 36,000 litres. Table stain remover and table polish combined account for 50% of the total physical output and are each allocated 25% of the CDG cost.

Instructions

(a) Do the following to determine whether management made the correct decision by not processing the table cleaner further.

1. Calculate the company's total weekly gross profit assuming the table cleaner is not processed further.

(2) Gross profit $140,000

2. Calculate the company's total weekly gross profit assuming the table cleaner is processed further.

3. Compare the resulting net incomes and comment on management's decision.

(b) Using incremental analysis, determine whether the table cleaner should be processed further.

(adapted from CMA Canada, now CPA Canada)

P7-39A Last year (2015), Calway Condos installed a mechanized elevator for its tenants. The owner of the company, Cab Calway, recently returned from an industry equipment exhibition where he watched a computerized elevator demonstrated. He was impressed with the elevator's speed, comfortable ride, and cost efficiency. Upon returning from the exhibition, he asked his purchasing agent to collect price and operating cost data on the new elevator. In addition, he asked the company's accountant to provide him with cost data on the company's elevator. The information is presented below:

(SO 5)
Calculate gain or loss, and determine whether equipment should be replaced.

	Old Elevator	New Elevator
Purchase price	$120,000	$180,000
Estimated salvage value	0	0
Estimated useful life	6 years	5 years
Depreciation method	Straight-line	Straight-line
Annual operating expenses other than depreciation:		
Variable	$ 35,000	$ 12,000
Fixed	23,000	8,400

Annual revenues are $240,000 and selling and administrative expenses are $29,000, regardless of which elevator is used. If it replaces the old elevator now, at the beginning of 2016, Calway Condos will be able to sell it for $25,000.

Instructions
(a) Determine any gain or loss if the old elevator is replaced.
(b) Prepare a five-year summarized income statement for each of the following assumptions:
  1. The old elevator is kept.
  2. The old elevator is replaced.
(c) Using incremental analysis, determine whether the old elevator should be replaced.
(d) ▭▭▭▭▷ Write a memo to Cab Calway explaining why any gain or loss should be ignored in the decision to replace the old elevator.

(b) (2) NI $698,000

(c) NI $33,000

P7-40A Ribeiro Manufacturing Company has four operating divisions. During the first quarter of 2016, the company reported aggregate income from operations of $145,000 and the following divisional results:

(SO 6)
Calculate the contribution margin and prepare an incremental analysis for the decision whether to eliminate divisions.

	Division			
	I	II	III	IV
Sales	$510,000	$390,000	$310,000	$180,000
Cost of goods sold	300,000	250,000	270,000	150,000
Selling and administrative expenses	60,000	80,000	65,000	70,000
Income (loss) from operations	$150,000	$ 60,000	$ (25,000)	$ (40,000)

Analysis reveals the following percentages of variable costs in each division:

	I	II	III	IV
Cost of goods sold	70%	90%	75%	90%
Selling and administrative expenses	40	50	65	70

Discontinuance of any division would save 50% of the fixed costs and expenses for that division.

Top management is very concerned about the unprofitable divisions (III and IV). Consensus is that the company should discontinue one or both of these divisions.

Instructions
(a) Calculate the contribution margin for divisions III and IV.
(b) Prepare an incremental analysis for the possible discontinuance of (1) division III and (2) division IV. What course of action do you recommend for each division?
(c) Prepare a condensed income statement in columns for Ribeiro Manufacturing, assuming division IV is eliminated. Use the CVP format. Division IV's unavoidable fixed costs are allocated equally to the continuing divisions.
(d) Reconcile the total income from operations of ($145,000) with the total income from operations without division IV.

(b) 2. $22,000

(c) $167,000

P7-41A A company manufactures three products using the same production process. The costs incurred up to the split-off point are $200,000. These costs are allocated to the products on the basis of their sales value at the split-off point. The number of units produced, the selling prices per unit of the three products at the split-off point and after further processing, and the additional processing costs are as follows:

(SO 4)
Prepare incremental analysis for the decision whether to sell or process materials further.

Product	Number of Units Produced	Selling Price at Split-Off	Selling Price after Processing	Additional Processing Costs
A	3,000	$10.00	$15.00	$14,000
B	6,000	11.60	16.20	16,000
C	2,000	19.40	21.60	9,000

Instructions

(a) Determine which information is relevant to the decision on whether to process the products further. Explain why this information is relevant.

(b) Product C, $(4,600)

(b) Which product(s) should the company process further and which should it sell at the split-off point?

(c) Would your decision be different if the company was using the quantity of output to allocate joint costs? Explain.

(adapted from CGA-Canada, now CPA Canada)

(SO 1, 6)
Calculate the contribution margin and prepare incremental analysis concerning the decision to keep or drop a product to maximize operating income.

P7-42A   Straus Company operates a small factory in which it manufactures two products: A and B. Production and sales results for last year were as follows:

	A	B
Units sold	9,000	20,000
Selling price per unit	$ 95	$ 75
Variable costs per unit	50	40
Fixed costs per unit	22	22

For purposes of simplicity, the firm averages total fixed costs over the total number of units of A and B produced and sold.

The research department has developed a new product (C) as a replacement for product B. Market studies show that Straus Company could sell 10,000 units of C next year at a price of $115; the variable costs per unit of C are $40. The introduction of product C will lead to a 10% increase in demand for product A and discontinuation of product B. If the company does not introduce the new product, it expects next year's results to be the same as last year's.

Instructions

Determine whether Straus Company should introduce product C next year. Explain why or why not. Show calculations to support your decision.

(adapted from CMA Canada, now CPA Canada)

(SO 3)
Calculate the contribution margin and prepare incremental analysis for a make-or-buy decision.

P7-43A   The Kamloops Outdoors Corporation, which produces a highly successful line of summer lotions and insect repellents and sells them to wholesalers, has decided to diversify in order to stabilize its sales throughout the year. A natural area for the company to consider is the production of winter lotions and creams to prevent dry and chapped skin.

After considerable research, the company has developed a winter products line. However, because of the conservative nature of company management, the president has decided to introduce only one of the new products for this coming winter. If the product is a success, there will be further expansion in future years.

The product selected is a lip balm to be sold in a lipstick-type tube. The company will sell the product to wholesalers in boxes of 24 tubes for $16.00 per box. Because of available capacity, the company will incur no additional fixed charges to produce the product. However, to allocate a fair share of the company's present fixed costs to the new product, the product will absorb a $150,000 fixed charge.

Using the estimated sales and production of 100,000 boxes of lip balm as the standard volume, the accounting department has developed the following costs per box of 24 tubes:

Direct labour	$ 4.00
Direct materials	6.00
Total overhead	3.00
Total	$13.00

Kamloops Outdoors has approached a cosmetics manufacturer to discuss the possibility of purchasing the tubes for the new product. The purchase price of the empty tubes from the cosmetics manufacturer would be $1.90 per 24 tubes. If Kamloops Outdoors accepts the purchase proposal, it is estimated that direct labour and variable overhead costs would be reduced by 10% and direct materials costs would be reduced by 20%.

Instructions

Answer the following questions:

(a) Should Kamloops Outdoors make or buy the tubes? Show calculations to support your answer.

(b) $1.75

(b) What would be the maximum purchase price acceptable to Kamloops Outdoors for the tubes? Support your answer with an appropriate explanation.

(c) $8,750

(c) Instead of sales of 100,000 boxes, revised estimates show a sales volume of 125,000 boxes. At this new volume, the company must acquire additional equipment, at an annual rental charge of $10,000, to manufacture the tubes. However, this incremental cost would be the only additional fixed cost, even if sales increased to 300,000 boxes. (The 300,000 level is the goal for the third year of production.) Under these circumstances, should Kamloops Outdoors make or buy the tubes? Show calculations to support your answer.

(d) The company has the option of making and buying at the same time. What would be your answer to part (c) if this alternative was considered? Show calculations to support your answer.

(e) What qualitative factors should Kamloops Outdoors Corporation consider in determining whether it should make or buy the lip balm tubes?

(adapted from CMA Canada, now CPA Canada)

P7-44A Manning Industries manufactures and sells three different models of wet-dry shop vacuum cleaners. Although the shop vacs vary in terms of quality and features, all are good sellers. Manning is currently operating at full capacity with limited machine time. Sales and production information relevant to each model is as follows:

(SO 7)
Determine the sales mix with limited resources.

	Product		
	Economy	Standard	Deluxe
Selling price	$30	$50	$100
Variable costs and expenses	$12	$18	$ 42
Machine hours required	0.5	0.8	1.6

Instructions
Answer the following questions:
(a) Ignoring the machine time constraint, which single product should Manning Industries produce?
(b) What is the contribution margin per unit of limited resource for each product?
(c) If it could obtain additional machine time, how should the company use the additional time?

(b) Economy $36

P7-45A Tandy Teck manufactures an electronic component for a high-end computer. The company currently sells 50,000 units a year at a price of $280 per unit. These units are produced using a machine that was purchased five years ago at a cost of $1.5 million. It currently has a book value of $750,000; however, due to its specialized nature, it has a market value today of only $85,000. The machine, which is expected to last another five years, will have no salvage value. The costs to produce an electronic component are as follows:

(SO 5)
Calculate contribution margin and prepare incremental analysis for maximizing operating income and replacing equipment.

Direct materials	$ 25.00
Direct labour (4 hours × $45.00/hour)	180.00
Variable overhead (4 hours × $4/hour)	16.00
Fixed overhead (4 hours × $5/hour)	20.00
Total cost per unit	$241.00

The company expects the following changes for next year:

- The unit selling price will increase by 5%.
- Direct labour rates will increase by 20%.

Management is currently considering the replacement of the company's old machine with a new one that would cost $3.5 million. The new machine is expected to last five years and to have a salvage value of $75,000. By using the new machine, management expects to cut variable direct labour to three hours per unit, and sales are expected to increase to 52,000 units and remain at that level, but the company will have to hire an operator for the machine at $120,000 per year.

Instructions
(Ignore income taxes.)
Determine whether or not the company should purchase the new machine.

(adapted from CMA Canada, now CPA Canada)

Increase in profit, $11,510,000

P7-46A T&G Co. manufactures three types of computer desks. The income statement for the three products and the whole company is shown below:

(SO 6, 7)
Calculate contribution margin and prepare incremental analysis for elimination of product and special order.

	Product A	Product B	Product C	Total
Sales	$75,000	$95,000	$105,000	$275,000
Variable costs	40,000	60,000	90,000	190,000
Fixed costs	28,000	20,000	20,000	68,000
Total costs	68,000	80,000	110,000	258,000
Operating income	$ 7,000	$15,000	$ (5,000)	$ 17,000

The company produces 1,000 units of each product. The company's capacity is 17,000 machine hours. The machine hours for each product are seven hours for Product A, five hours for Product B, and five hours for Product C. Fixed costs are allocated based on machine hours.

Instructions
Answer the following questions:
(a) If the current production levels are maintained, should the company eliminate Product C? Explain your reasoning.
(b) If the company can sell unlimited quantities of any of the three products, which product should be produced?
(c) Suppose the company can sell unlimited quantities of any of the three products. If a customer wanted to purchase 500 units of Product C, what would the minimum sale price per unit be for this order?
(d) The company has a contract that requires it to supply 500 units of each product to a customer. The total market demand for a single product is limited to 1,500 units. How many units of each product should the company manufacture to maximize its total contribution margin including the contract?

(c) $125

(d) produce 1,000 units of A

(adapted from CGA-Canada, now CPA Canada)

Problems: Set B

(SO 3)
Identify the relevant
costs in an outsourcing
decision.

P7-47B   Vanes College provides its own housekeeping services. The College director would like to outsource this service and has found a company that will provide the service for $54 per hour. The following information has been collected about the cost per hour to the college for performing its own housekeeping services:

Cost per hour of service:	
Cleaning supplies	$ 5
Direct labour costs	$ 32
Variable overhead	$ 2
Total hours of housekeeping services per year	4,000
Total fixed overhead	$40,000

Instructions

(a) $(30,000)

(b) 1,333 hours

(a) Determine whether Vanes College should outsource housekeeping, assuming that 75% of fixed costs can be eliminated if the service is outsourced. Provide calculations to support your answer.
(b) At what level of service (in hours) would Vanes generally be indifferent between providing housekeeping services or outsourcing them, assuming that 50% of fixed costs can be eliminated?
(c) Describe two qualitative factors that might affect this outsourcing decision.

(SO 5)
Calculate the
contribution margin
and prepare an
incremental analysis
for maximizing
operating income and
replacing equipment.

P7-48B   Sharp Aerospace has a five-year contract to supply North Plane with four specific spare parts for its fleet of airplanes. The following table provides information on selling prices, costs, and the number of units of each part that the company needs to produce annually according to the contract with North Plane:

	A10	A20	A30	A40
Sales	$1,500,000	$875,000	$450,000	$2,400,000
Variable costs	1,235,000	425,000	187,000	1,875,000
Contribution margin	$ 265,000	$450,000	$263,000	$ 525,000
Production in units	1,000	250	750	600
Machine hours/unit	2	4	1.5	3

Fixed overhead costs amount to $820,000 and are allocated based on the number of units produced. The company has a maximum annual capacity of 6,000 machine hours.

Instructions

Answer the following questions:
(a) If Sharp Aerospace could manufacture only one of the four parts, which spare part should it produce, based on the contribution margin per limited resource? Explain why.
(b) Polaris Airline wants to buy 200 units of part A10 at 110% of the price currently paid by North Plane. Assume that for any of the four parts, Sharp Aerospace has to supply North Plane with at least 90% of the number of units specified in the contract. Should Sharp Aerospace accept the order for 200 units of part A10?

(c) Produce 393 units
of A20

(c) A new technology is available that costs $2.5 million and would increase Sharp Aerospace's annual capacity by 25%. Should the company purchase the new technology? Assume that the technology has an estimated life of four years and that Sharp Aerospace can sell, at the same prices paid by North Plane, all the units it can produce of any of the four parts. Show all your calculations.

(adapted from CGA-Canada, now CPA Canada)

(SO 2, 3)
Prepare incremental
analysis related to a
make-or-buy decision,
consider opportunity
cost, and identify
non-financial factors.

P7-49B   The management of Dunham Manufacturing Company has asked for your assistance in deciding whether to continue manufacturing a part or to buy it from an outside supplier. The part, called Tropica, is a component of Dunham's finished product.

An analysis of the accounting records and the production data revealed the following information for the year ending December 31, 2016:

1. The machinery department produced 40,000 units of Tropica.
2. Each Tropica unit requires 15 minutes to produce. Three people in the machinery department work full-time (2,500 hours per year each) producing Tropica. Each person is paid $15 per hour.
3. The cost of materials per Tropica unit is $3.
4. Manufacturing costs directly applicable to the production of Tropica are as follows: indirect labour, $6,000; utilities, $1,500; depreciation, $2,000; property taxes and insurance, $2,000. All of the costs will be eliminated if the company purchases Tropica.
5. The lowest price for Tropica from an outside supplier is $6 per unit. Freight charges would be $0.50 per unit, and the company would require a part-time receiving clerk at $10,000 per year.
6. If it purchases Tropica, Dunham will use the excess space that becomes available to store its finished product. Currently, Dunham rents storage space at approximately $1.50 per unit stored per year. It stores approximately 6,000 units per year in the rented space.

Instructions

(a) Prepare an incremental analysis for the make-or-buy decision. Should Dunham make or buy the part? Why?

(b) Prepare an incremental analysis, assuming the released facilities (freed-up space) can be used to produce $15,000 of net income in addition to the savings on the rental of storage space. What decision should the company make now?

(c) What non-financial factors should it consider in the decision?

(a) NI decrease $19,000
(b) NI decrease $4,000

P7-50B Bonita Household Products Co. is a diversified household-cleaner processing company. The company's St. Lawrence plant produces two products from a common set of chemical inputs (TLC): a glass cleaner and a metal cleaner. Each week 30,000 litres of chemical input are processed at a cost of $200,000 into 20,000 litres of metal cleaner and 10,000 litres of glass cleaner. The metal cleaner has no market value until it is converted into a polish with the trade name MetalShine. The additional processing costs for this conversion total $270,000. MetalShine sells for $15 per 750-ml bottle.

The glass cleaner can be sold for $24 per 750-ml bottle. However, the glass cleaner can be converted into two other products by adding 10,000 litres of another compound (MST) to the 10,000 litres of glass cleaner. This joint process will yield 10,000 litres each of plastic cleaner and plastic polish. The additional processing costs for this process total $140,000. Both plastic products can be sold for $20 per 750-ml bottle.

The company decided not to process the glass cleaner into plastic cleaner and plastic polish based on the following analysis:

(SO 4)
Determine whether a product should be sold or processed further.

	Glass Cleaner	Process Further		
		Plastic Cleaner	Plastic Polish	Total
Production in litres	(10,000)	10,000	10,000	
Revenue	$240,000	$200,000	$200,000	$400,000
TLC cost	50,000ᵃ	40,000	40,000	80,000ᵇ
MST cost	0	70,000	70,000	140,000
Total costs	50,000	110,000	110,000	220,000
Weekly gross profit	$190,000	$ 90,000	$ 90,000	$180,000

ᵃIf the glass cleaner is not processed further, it is allocated one quarter of the $200,000 of TLC cost, because it represents one quarter of the total physical output.

ᵇIf the glass cleaner is processed further, the total physical output is 40,000 litres. Plastic cleaner and plastic polish combined account for 40% of the total physical output and are each allocated 20% of the TLC cost.

Instructions

(a) Do the following to determine whether management made the correct decision by not processing the glass cleaner further:

1. Calculate the company's total weekly gross profit assuming the glass cleaner is not processed further.

2. Calculate the company's total weekly gross profit assuming the glass cleaner is processed further.

3. Compare the resulting net incomes and comment on management's decision.

(b) Using incremental analysis, determine whether the glass cleaner should be processed further.

(adapted from CMA Canada, now CPA Canada)

2. Gross profit: $323,333

P7-51B Quik Press Inc. offers one-day dry cleaning. At the beginning of 2015, the company purchased a mechanized pressing machine. The owner of the company, Jill Jabowski, recently returned from an industry equipment exhibition where she saw a computerized pressing machine demonstrated. She was impressed with the machine's speed, efficiency, and quality of output. Upon returning from the exhibition, she asked her purchasing agent to collect price and operating cost data on the new pressing machine. In addition, she asked the company's accountant to provide her with cost data on the company's pressing machine. This information is presented below:

(SO 5)
Calculate the gain or loss, and determine if equipment should be replaced.

	Old Pressing Machine	New Pressing Machine
Purchase price	$120,000	$150,000
Estimated salvage value	0	0
Estimated useful life	6 years	5 years
Depreciation method	Straight-line	Straight-line
Annual operating expenses other than depreciation:		
Variable	$ 30,000	$ 10,000
Fixed	20,000	7,000

Annual revenues are $200,000, and selling and administrative expenses are $24,000, regardless of which pressing machine is used. If it replaces the old machine now, at the beginning of 2016, Quik Press will be able to sell it for $10,000.

Instructions

(a) Determine any gain or loss if the old pressing machine is replaced.

(b) (2) NI $555,000

(b) Prepare a five-year summarized income statement for each of the following assumptions:
   1. The old machine is kept.
   2. The old machine is replaced.

(c) NI increase $25,000

(c) Using incremental analysis, determine whether the company should replace the old pressing machine.

(d) ✏️ Write a memo to Jill Jabowski explaining why any gain or loss should be ignored in the decision to replace the old pressing machine.

(SO 3)
Calculate the
contribution margin
and prepare differential
analysis for a make-or-
buy decision.

P7-52B Y&U Company purchases reading lamps and produces student desks. It currently produces 2,000 student desks per year, operating at normal capacity, which is about 80% of full capacity. Each student desk has a reading lamp as one of its components. Y&U purchases reading lamps at $400 each, but the company is considering using the excess capacity to manufacture the reading lamps instead. The manufacturing cost per reading lamp would be $160 for materials, $130 for direct labour, and $180 for overhead. The $180 overhead is based on $120,000 of annual fixed overhead that is allocated using normal capacity.

The president of Y&U has come to you for advice. "It would cost me $470 to make the reading lamp," she says, "but only $400 to buy them. Should I continue buying them or have I missed something?"

Instructions

(a) Buy, for savings of
$20,000

(a) Prepare a per-unit analysis of the differential costs. Briefly explain whether Y&U should make or buy the reading lamps.

(b) Identify three qualitative factors that should be considered by Y&U in this make-or-buy decision.

(adapted from CGA-Canada, now CPA Canada)

(SO 3, 5)
Calculate the
contribution margin
and prepare an
incremental analysis
for a make-or-buy
decision.

P7-53B Quincy Inc. manufactures and sells bakery products and has decided to put a new product on the market: an ice cream cake. The product will be sold in boxes of 24. The price of each box will be $10. The company will use its excess capacity to manufacture the product. The accounting department has decided that it should allocate $100,000 worth of fixed overhead costs to the product.

The accounting department has budgeted the following costs (based on production of 100,000 boxes):

Direct materials (per box)	$4.00
Direct labour (per box)	2.00
Fixed and variable overhead (per box)	2.00
Total	$8.00

Quincy can purchase ice cream units, one of the ingredients, from a dairy company. The dairy company would sell the ice cream units for $1 for 24 units. If Quincy buys the ice cream units from the dairy company, it would reduce direct labour and variable overhead costs by 10%. The direct materials cost would be 20% lower than the original budgeted amount and would not include the cost of the ice cream units purchased from the dairy company.

Instructions

(a) Determine whether Quincy should make or buy the ice cream units. Explain your decision.

(b) Buy for savings of
$22,500

(b) Suppose that sales projections are revised and that Quincy could sell 125,000 boxes instead of 100,000. In such a case, to produce ice cream, it would need to lease a new machine for $10,000 a year. Under these conditions, should Quincy make the ice cream units or buy them from the dairy company? Explain your decision.

(c) $145,000 annual cost

(c) Suppose that sales projections are revised and that Quincy could sell 125,000 boxes instead of 100,000, and that it would need to lease the machine. Would it be better off if it makes the ice cream for the first 100,000 boxes and buys the remainder from the dairy company? Explain your decision. Assume the $1 price is available for any volume.

(d) List four qualitative factors that Quincy should consider when determining whether it should make or buy the ice cream units.

(adapted from CGA-Canada, now CPA Canada)

(SO 6)
Calculate the
contribution margin
and prepare
incremental analysis
for the decision
whether to eliminate
divisions.

P7-54B Laos Manufacturing Company has four operating divisions. During the first quarter of 2016, the company reported total income from operations of $36,000 and the following results for the divisions:

	Division			
	Kelowna	Brandon	Sherbrooke	Moncton
Sales	$405,000	$730,000	$920,000	$500,000
Cost of goods sold	400,000	480,000	576,000	390,000
Selling and administrative expenses	100,000	207,000	246,000	120,000
Income (loss) from operations	$ (95,000)	$ 43,000	$ 98,000	$ (10,000)

Analysis reveals the following percentages of variable costs in each division.

	Kelowna	Brandon	Sherbrooke	Moncton
Cost of goods sold	90%	80%	90%	95%
Selling and administrative expenses	60	60	70	80

Closing any division would save 70% of the fixed costs and expenses for that division.

Top management are deeply concerned about the unprofitable divisions (Kelowna and Moncton). The consensus is that one or both of them should be eliminated.

Instructions

(a) Calculate the contribution margin for the two unprofitable divisions.

(b) Prepare an incremental analysis for the possible elimination of (1) the Kelowna division and (2) the Moncton division. What course of action do you recommend for each division?

(c) Prepare a condensed income statement in columns using the CVP format for Laos Manufacturing Company, assuming (1) the Kelowna division is eliminated, and (2) the unavoidable fixed costs and expenses of the Kelowna division are allocated 30% to Brandon, 50% to Sherbrooke, and 20% to Moncton.

(d) Compare the total income from operations with the Kelowna division ($36,000) versus total income from operations without this division.

(a) Moncton $33,500

(c) Income Sherbrooke $86,000

P7-55B Benkhadour Co. manufactures four different products. Because the quality of its products is high, the demand for them is more than the company can produce.

Based on the enquiries made by current and potential customers, you have estimated the following for the coming year:

Product	Estimated Demand in Units	Selling Price per Unit	Direct Materials Cost per Unit	Direct Labour Cost per Unit
A	8,000	$ 50	$ 5	$ 5
B	24,000	60	10	9
C	20,000	150	25	30
D	30,000	100	15	20

(SO 7)
Calculate the contribution margin and prepare incremental analysis for maximizing operating income.

The following information is also available:

1. The direct labour rate is $15 per hour and the factory has a capacity of 80,000 hours. For the next year, Benkhadour is unable to expand this capacity.
2. Benkhadour is unwilling to increase its selling prices.
3. Apart from direct materials and direct labour, the only other variable expense is variable overhead. The variable overhead is 50% of the direct labour cost.
4. Fixed manufacturing overhead is estimated to be $1 million for the coming year. Fixed marketing and administrative expenses are estimated to be $750,000 for the coming year.

Instructions

Determine which products and how many units of each Benkhadour should produce in the coming year in order to maximize its operating income.

Produce 11,467.5 units of C

(adapted from CGA-Canada, now CPA Canada)

P7-56B Simon Corporation manufactures and sells three different models of storm doors. Although the doors vary in terms of quality and features, all are good sellers. Simon is currently operating at full capacity with limited machine time. Sales and production information relevant to each model is as follows:

(SO 7)
Determine sales mix with limited resources.

	Product		
	Economy	Standard	Deluxe
Selling price	$180	$250	$430
Variable costs and expenses	$ 99	$150	$280
Machine hours required	0.6	0.9	1.2

Instructions

Answer the following questions:

(a) Ignoring the machine time constraint, which single product should Simon produce?

(b) What is the contribution margin per unit of limited resource for each product?

(c) If it could obtain additional machine time, how should the company use the additional time?

(b) Economy $135

P7-57B The following information is for a company that produces four types of microprocessors using the same production process. The common costs of these products, up to the split-off point, are $550,000. Common costs are allocated based on the quantity of output. The following information includes additional processing costs, the selling price of each product at the split-off point, and the selling price of each product after further processing:

(SO 4)
Prepare incremental analysis for the decision whether to sell or process materials further.

Microprocessor	Number of Units Produced	Selling Price at Split-Off Point	Selling Price after Further Processing	Additional Costs for Further Processing
1	3,000	$10.00	$15.00	$14,800
2	4,000	9.50	12.25	8,500
3	2,500	11.00	15.70	12,000
4	500	7.75	10.25	1,250

(a) Product 2

Instructions
(a) Assuming only one product can be processed further, determine which one the company should choose. Briefly explain why.
(b) Referring to your answer in part (a), identify which information is relevant to the decision to process this product further.
(c) If common costs up to the split-off point were allocated on the basis of the market values at the split-off point, would your decision in part (a) be different? Briefly explain why.

(adapted from CGA-Canada, now CPA Canada)

(SO 5)
Calculate the contribution margin and prepare an incremental analysis for maximizing operating income and replacing equipment.

P7-58B ATI Teck manufactures an electronic component for a high-end computer. The company currently sells 50,000 units a year at a price of $180 per unit. These units are produced using a machine that was purchased five years ago at a cost of $1.2 million. It currently has a book value of $600,000; however, due to its specialized nature, it has a market value today of only $70,000. The machine, which is expected to last another five years, will have no salvage value. The costs to produce an electronic component are as follows:

Direct materials	$ 15.00
Direct labour (4 hours × $30.00/hour)	120.00
Variable overhead (4 hours × $2.40/hour)	9.60
Fixed overhead (4 hours × $3.20/hour)*	12.80
Total cost per unit	$157.40

* Based on an annual activity of 100,000 direct labour hours.

The company expects the following changes for next year:

- The unit selling price will increase by 10%.
- Direct labour rates will increase by 15%.
- Sales are expected to increase to 52,000 units (within the capacity of present facilities) and remain at that level.

Management is currently considering the replacement of the company's old machine with a new one that would cost $2.5 million. The new machine is expected to last five years and to have a salvage value of $60,000 (straight-line depreciation is used). By using the new machine, management expects to cut variable direct labour hours to 3.5 hours per unit, but the company will have to hire an operator for the machine at $90,000 per year.

Instructions
(Ignore income taxes.)
(a) Determine whether or not the company should purchase the new machine.

(b) 25,218 units

(b) How many units would the company have to sell to earn annual profits of $460,000 (before taxes) if it were to purchase the new machine? Ignore any gain or loss on the sale of the old machine.

(adapted from CMA Canada, now CPA Canada)

(SO 1, 6)
Calculate contribution margin and prepare an incremental analysis concerning retaining or dropping a product to maximize operating income.

P7-59B Yars Company operates a small factory in which it manufactures two products: A and B. Production and sales results for last year were as follows:

	A	B
Units sold	15,000	30,000
Selling price per unit	$ 80	$ 60
Variable costs per unit	35	30
Fixed costs per unit	20	20

For purposes of simplicity, the firm averages total fixed costs over the total number of units of A and B produced and sold.

The research department has developed a new product C as a replacement for product B. Market studies show that Yars Company could sell 15,000 units of C next year at a price of $80; the variable costs per unit of C are $45. The introduction of product C will lead to a 10% increase in demand for product A and discontinuation of product B. If the company does not introduce the new product, it expects next year's results to be the same as last year's.

Instructions

Decreases CM by $307,500

Determine whether Yars Company should introduce product C next year. Explain why or why not. Show calculations to support your decision.

(adapted from CMA Canada, now CPA Canada)

(SO 6, 7)
Calculate the contribution margin and prepare an incremental analysis for the elimination of a product and special order.

P7-60B Furniture Shop Co. manufactures three types of computer desks. The income statement for the three products and the whole company is shown below:

	Product A	Product B	Product C	Total
Sales	$50,000	$60,000	$ 65,000	$175,000
Variable costs	25,000	40,000	60,000	125,000
Fixed costs	16,000	12,000	8,000	36,000
Total costs	41,000	52,000	68,000	161,000
Operating income	$ 9,000	$ 8,000	$ (3,000)	$ 14,000

The company produces 1,000 units of each product. The company's capacity is 9,000 labour hours. The labour for each product is four hours for Product A, three hours for Product B, and two hours for Product C. Fixed costs are allocated based on labour hours.

Instructions

Answer the following questions:

(a) If it maintains the current production levels, should the company eliminate Product C? Explain your reasoning.

(b) If the company can sell unlimited quantities of any of the three products, which product should it produce?

(c) Suppose the company can sell unlimited quantities of any of the three products. If a customer wanted to purchase 500 units of Product C, what would the minimum sale price per unit be for this order?

(d) The company has a contract that requires it to supply 500 units of each product to a customer. The total market demand for a single product is limited to 1,500 units. How many units of each product should the company manufacture to maximize its total contribution margin?

(c) $73.34

(d) Produce 875 units of A

(adapted from CGA-Canada, now CPA Canada)

Cases

C7-61   Castle Company is considering the purchase of a new machine. The invoice price of the machine is $150,000, freight charges are estimated to be $6,000, and installation costs are expected to be $4,000. The salvage value of the new equipment is expected to be zero after a useful life of four years. The company could retain the existing equipment and use it for an additional four years if it doesn't purchase the new machine. At that time, the equipment's salvage value would be zero. If Castle purchases the new machine now, it would have to scrap the existing machine. Castle's accountant, Shaida Fang, has accumulated the following data for annual sales and expenses, with and without the new machine:

1. Without the new machine, Castle can sell 15,000 units of product annually at a per-unit selling price of $120. If it purchases the new machine, the number of units produced and sold would increase by 20%, and the selling price would remain the same.
2. The new machine is faster than the old machine, and it is more efficient in its use of materials. With the old machine, the gross profit

rate is 20% of sales, whereas the rate will be 25% of sales with the new machine.

3. Annual selling expenses are $180,000 with the current machine. Because the new machine would produce a greater number of units to be sold, annual selling expenses are expected to increase by 10% if it is purchased.
4. Annual administrative expenses are expected to be $100,000 with the old machine, and $90,000 with the new machine.
5. The current book value of the existing machine is $40,000. Castle uses straight-line depreciation.

Instructions

Prepare an incremental analysis for the four years that shows whether Castle should retain the existing machine or buy the new one. (Ignore income tax effects.)

C7-62   Axia Inc. manufactures two electronic products, widgets and gadgets, and has a capacity of 1,000 machine hours. Prices and costs for each product are as follows:

	Widget	Gadget
Selling price per unit	$250	$330
Variable costs per unit		
Direct materials	30	35
Other direct costs	10	12
Manufacturing overhead costs*	30	44

*Variable manufacturing overhead costs are applied at a rate of $40 per machine hour.

Bromont Industries, a potential client, has offered $250 per unit to Axia for 250 special units. These 250 units would incur the following production costs and time:

Direct materials	$8,000
Other direct costs	$3,000
Machine hours	225

Instructions

(a) Assume that Axia has enough excess capacity to produce the special order. Calculate what the total contribution would be if the special order from Bromont were accepted.

(b) Assume that Axia is currently operating at full capacity. Determine whether Axia should produce the units for the special order instead of widget or gadget units. Show your calculations.

(c) Assume that Axia is actually operating at 95% of full capacity. Calculate what the opportunity cost would be if Bromont's special order were accepted. Show your calculations.

(d) Assume that Axia is actually operating at 95% of full capacity, and additional machines can be rented at a cost of $35,000 to produce Bromont's special order. If the special order is accepted, calculate its effect on Axia's profit. Show your calculations.

(adapted from CGA-Canada, now CPA Canada)

C7-63   Technology Plus manufactures small private-label electronic products, such as alarm clocks, stopwatches, kitchen timers, calculators, and automatic pencil sharpeners. It sells some of the products as sets and others individually. The company studies the products for their

sales potential, and then makes cost estimates. The engineering department develops production plans, and then production begins. The company has generally had very successful product introduction. It has discontinued only two products it has introduced.

One of the products it currently sells is a multi-alarm alarm clock. The clock has four alarms that can be programmed to sound at various times and for varying lengths of time. The company has had a lot of trouble making the circuit boards for the clocks. The production process has never operated smoothly. The product is currently unprofitable, mainly because of warranty repairs and product recalls. Two models of the clocks were recalled, for example, because they sometimes caused an electric shock when the alarms were being shut off. The engineering department is trying to revise the manufacturing process, but the revision will take another six months at least.

The clocks were very popular when they were introduced, and since they are a private label, the company has not suffered much from the recalls. Presently, the company has a very large order for several items from a major retailer with locations across Canada. The order includes 5,000 of the multi-alarm clocks. When the company suggested that the retailer purchase the clocks from another manufacturer, the retailer threatened to cancel the entire order unless the clocks were included.

The company has therefore investigated the possibility of having another company make the clocks for it. Its bid for the retailer's order was based on an estimated $6.90 cost to manufacture the clocks, broken down as follows:

Circuit board, 1 each @ $2.00	$2.00
Plastic case, 1 each @ $0.80	0.80
Alarms, 4 @ $0.15 each	0.60
Labour, 15 minutes @ $12/hour	3.00
Overhead, $2.00 per labour hour	0.50

Technology Plus could purchase clocks to fill the retailer's order for $10 from Silver Star, a Korean manufacturer with a very good quality record. Silver Star has offered to reduce the price to $7.50 after Technology Plus has been a customer for six months and agrees to order at least 1,000 units per month. If Technology Plus becomes a "preferred customer" by purchasing 15,000 units per year, Silver Star would reduce the price still further to $4.50.

Alpha Products, a local manufacturer, has also offered to make clocks for Technology Plus. It has offered to sell 5,000 clocks for $5 each. However, Alpha Products has been in business for only six months. It has had significant turnover in its labour force, and the local press has reported that the owners may face tax evasion charges soon. The owner of Alpha Products is an electronics engineer, however, and the quality of the clocks is likely to be good.

If Technology Plus decides to purchase the clocks from either Silver Star or Alpha, all of its current costs to manufacture the alarm clock could be avoided, except a total of $5,000 in overhead costs for machine depreciation. The machinery is fairly new and has no alternative use.

Instructions

Answer the following questions:

(a) What is the difference in profit under each of the alternatives if the clocks are to be sold for $14.50 each to the retailer?

(b) What are the most important non-financial factors that Technology Plus should consider when making this decision?

(c) What do you think Technology Plus should do about the retailer's order? What should it do with regard to continuing to manufacture the multi-alarm alarm clocks? Be prepared to defend your answer.

C7-64 La Mode Design Inc., a high-fashion women's dress manufacturer, is planning to market a new cocktail dress for the coming season. La Mode Design Inc. supplies retailers in Toronto, Montreal, and the Atlantic provinces.

Four metres of material are laid out for the dress pattern. After cutting, some material remains, which can be sold as remnants. The company could also use the leftover material to manufacture a matching cape and handbag. However, if it uses the leftover material for the cape and handbag, more care will be needed in the cutting, and the cutting costs will therefore increase.

The company expects to sell 1,250 dresses if a matching cape and handbag are not available. La Mode Design's market research reveals, however, that dress sales will be 20% higher if a matching cape and handbag were available. The market research indicates that the cape and/or handbag could not be sold individually but only as accessories with the dress. The various combinations of dresses, capes, and handbags that retailers will sell are as follows:

Complete sets of dress, cape, and handbag	70%
Dress and cape	6%
Dress and handbag	15%
Dress only	9%
Total	100%

The material used in the dress costs $12.50 a metre, or $50.00 for each dress. The cost of cutting the dress if the cape and handbag are not manufactured is estimated at $20.00 a dress, and the resulting remnants can be sold for $5.00 for each dress cut out. If the cape and handbag are to be manufactured, the cutting costs will be increased by $9.00 per dress. There will be no saleable remnants if the capes and handbags are manufactured in the quantities estimated.

The selling prices and the costs to complete the three items once they are cut are as follows:

	Selling Price per Unit	Unit Cost to Complete*
Dress	$200.00	$80.00
Cape	27.50	19.50
Handbag	9.50	6.50

* Excludes cost of material and cutting.

Instructions

(a) Prepare La Mode Design's incremental analysis for manufacturing the capes and handbags with the dresses.

(b) Based on your analysis, what decision should management make?

(c) Identify any qualitative factors that could influence the company's decision to manufacture the capes and handbags that match the dresses.

(adapted from CMA Canada, now CPA Canada)

C7-65 John Bourcier operates a small machine shop. He manufactures one standard product that is also available from many other similar businesses, and he also manufactures deluxe products to order. His accountant prepared the following annual income statement:

	Deluxe Sales	Standard Sales	Total
Sales	$50,000	$25,000	$75,000
Costs			
Material	10,000	8,000	18,000
Labour	20,000	9,000	29,000
Depreciation	6,300	3,600	9,900
Power	700	400	1,100
Rent	6,000	1,000	7,000
Heat and light	600	100	700
Other	400	900	1,300
Total costs	44,000	23,000	67,000
Net income	$ 6,000	$ 2,000	$ 8,000

The depreciation charges are for machines used in the product lines. The power charge is apportioned based on an estimate of the power consumed by each line. The rent is for the building space, which has been leased for 10 years at $7,000 per year. The rent and the heat and light costs are apportioned to the product lines based on the amount of floor space occupied by each line. All other costs are current expenses that are identified with the product line causing them.

A valued customer has asked Mr. Bourcier if he would manufacture 5,000 of the deluxe products for him. Mr. Bourcier is working at capacity and would have to give up some other business in order to take this order. He cannot cancel deluxe orders he has already agreed to, so he would have to reduce the output of his standard product by about one half for a year while producing the requested deluxe product. The customer is willing to pay $7.00 for each unit. The material cost will be about $2.00 per unit and the labour will be $3.60 per unit. Mr. Bourcier will have to spend $2,000 for a special device that will be discarded when the job is done.

Instructions
(a) Calculate the incremental cost of the order.
(b) Calculate the full cost of the order.
(c) Calculate the opportunity cost of taking the order.
(d) Determine the sunk costs related to the order.
(e) Should Mr. Bourcier accept the order? Explain your answer.

(adapted from CMA Canada, now CPA Canada)

C7-66 Robert Buey became chief executive officer of Phelps Manufacturing two years ago. At the time, the company was reporting lagging profits and Robert was brought in to "stir things up." The company has three divisions: electronics, fibre optics, and plumbing supplies. Robert has no interest in plumbing supplies, and one of the first things he did was to put pressure on his accountants to reallocate some of the company's fixed costs away from the other two divisions to the plumbing division. This had the effect of causing the plumbing division to report losses during the last two years. In the past it had always reported low, but acceptable, net income. Robert felt that this reallocation would shine a favourable light on him in front of the board of directors because it meant that the electronics and fibre optics divisions would appear to be improving. Since these are "businesses of the future," he believed that the stock market would react favourably to these increases, and not penalize the poor results of the plumbing division.

Without this shift in the allocation of fixed costs, the profits of the electronics and fibre optics divisions would not have improved. But now the board of directors has suggested that the plumbing division be closed because it is reporting losses. This would mean that nearly 500 employees, many of whom have worked for Phelps their whole lives, would lose their jobs.

Instructions
Answer the following questions:
(a) If a division is reporting losses, does that necessarily mean that it should be closed?
(b) Was the reallocation of fixed costs across divisions unethical?
(c) What should Robert do?

"All About You" Activity

C7-67 After deciding on a mortgage, one of the most difficult decisions for new homeowners is when and how to upgrade their home heating system. There are many different home heating fuels and equipment to consider. The skills you have learned in this chapter and the one before will help you make this tricky decision.

Suppose that you are the new homeowner of a property with a 20-year-old standard-efficiency electric furnace in the basement. You also have an old electric hot water heater. You are considering replacing them with a high-efficiency natural gas furnace and water heater.

You have the following information:

Cost of a new 96% high-efficiency gas furnace (including installation, taxes)	$5,700
Cost of a new hot water tank (including installation, inspection, taxes, and so on)	$1,200
Current total annual heating costs	$2,750
Cost of natural gas (average)	$14.40 per gigajoule
Cost of electricity (average)	$0.11452 per KwH
Efficiency of your current furnace	75%
Number of occupants	2

Instructions

Go to the website of the Office of Energy Efficiency, part of Natural Resources Canada, at https://www.nrcan.gc.ca/energy/offices-labs/office-energy-efficiency. Search for the Home Heating System Cost Calculator. Use the calculator to calculate your revised annual heating costs. Discuss the following:

(a) How long will it take you to recover the cost of the new furnace and hot water heater?

(b) What other factors do you need to consider when deciding whether to replace your current furnace and hot water heater with the newer furnace and hot water tank?

Decision-Making at Current Designs

DM7-1   Current Designs faces a number of important decisions that require incremental analysis. Consider each of the following situations independently.

Situation 1

Recently, Mike Cichanowski, owner and CEO of Current Designs, received a phone call from the president of a brewing company. He was calling to inquire about the possibility of Current Designs producing "floating coolers" for a promotion his company was planning. These coolers resemble a kayak but are about one-third the size. They are used to float food and beverages while paddling down the river on a weekend leisure trip. The company would be interested in purchasing 100 coolers for the upcoming summer. It is willing to pay $250 per cooler. The brewing company would pick up the coolers upon completion of the order.

Mike met with Diane Buswell, controller, to identify how much it would cost Current Designs to produce the coolers. After careful analysis, the following costs were identified.

Direct materials	$80/unit	Variable overhead	$20/unit
Direct labour	$60/unit	Fixed overhead	$1,000

Current Designs would be able to modify an existing mould to produce the coolers. The cost of these modifications would be approximately $2,000.

Instructions

(a) Prepare an incremental analysis to determine whether Current Designs should accept this special order to produce the coolers.

(b) Discuss additional factors that Mike and Diane should consider if Current Designs is currently operating at full capacity.

Situation 2

Current Designs is always working to identify ways to increase efficiency while becoming more environmentally conscious. During a recent brainstorming session, one employee suggested to Diane Buswell, controller, that the company should consider replacing the current rotomould oven as a way to realize savings from reduced energy consumption. The oven operates on natural gas, using 17,000 therms of natural gas for an entire year. A new, energy-efficient rotomould oven would operate on 15,000 therms of natural gas for an entire year. After seeking out price quotes from a few suppliers, Diane determined that it would cost approximately $250,000 to purchase a new, energy-efficient rotomould oven. She determines that the expected useful life of the new oven would be 10 years, and it would have no salvage value at the end

of its useful life. Current Designs would be able to sell the current oven for $10,000.

Instructions

(a) Prepare an incremental analysis to determine if Current Designs should purchase the new rotomould oven, assuming that the average price for natural gas over the next 10 years will be $0.65 per therm.

(b) Diane is concerned that natural gas prices might increase at a faster rate over the next 10 years. If the company projects that the average natural gas price of the next 10 years could be as high as $0.85 per therm, discuss how that might change your conclusion in part (a).

Situation 3

One of Current Designs' competitive advantages is found in the ingenuity of its owner and CEO, Mike Cichanowski. His involvement in the design of kayak moulds and production techniques has led to Current Designs being recognized as an industry leader in the design and production of kayaks. This ingenuity was evident in an improved design of one of the most important components of a kayak, the seat. The "Revolution Seating System" is a one-of-a-kind, rotating axis seat that gives unmatched, full-contact, under-leg support. It is quickly adjustable with a lever-lock system that allows for a customizable seat position that maximizes comfort for the rider.

Having just designed the Revolution Seating System, Current Designs must now decide whether to produce the seats internally or buy them from an outside supplier. The costs for Current Designs to produce the seats are as follows.

Direct materials	$20/unit	Direct labour	$15/unit
Variable overhead	$12/unit	Fixed overhead	$20,000

Current Designs will need to produce 3,000 seats this year; 25% of the fixed overhead will be avoided if the seats are purchased from an outside vendor. After soliciting prices from outside suppliers, the company determined that it will cost $50 to purchase a seat from an outside vendor.

Instructions

(a) Prepare an incremental analysis showing whether Current Designs should make or buy the Revolution Seating System.

(b) Would your answer in part (a) change if the productive capacity released by not making the seats could be used to produce income of $20,000?

Waterways Continuing Problem

(This is a continuation of the Waterways Problem from Chapters 1 through 6.)

WCP-7   Phil Clark Jr., president of Waterways, was very pleased with how adopting a CVP approach to reporting operating income was helping management to make good business decisions with respect to planning, production, and sales for the coming year. He has a feeling

that knowing how fixed and variable costs behave might also help them to find savings in the production department. Further, he is concerned that Waterways' production facility is working near full capacity right now, and he does not know if the company could generate enough new business to make adding another shift viable.

Phil decides to sit down with his brother Ben, vice-president of operations, and Ryan Smith, the plant manager, to see if they could "do more with less," as he put it. Jordan Leigh, CFO, had recently presented them with a number of situations that required decisions that would impact operations in the plant. Phil thought that together the four of them could find some efficient solutions.

Part 1

Waterways packages some of its products into sets for do-it-yourself (DIY) installations. The smaller set that sells for $159 has variable costs of $79, while the larger set sells for $249 with variable costs of $159. Fixed costs are assigned at a rate of $6 per machine hour.

It takes 32 minutes of machining time to produce and package the smaller set. The larger set is more complicated and requires 60 minutes of production time. The machines operate for two shifts of eight hours each day for 20 days per month. Maintenance and set-ups are handled outside of these times.

Analysis of the current market trends reveals that monthly demand for the smaller set would not exceed 500 units, while Waterways could sell as many of the larger ones as it can produce.

Instructions

Given the information above, determine the best use of these machines.

Part 2

As we learned in Chapter 6, Waterways markets a simple water controller and timer that it mass produces. During 2016, the company sold 696,000 units at an average selling price of $4.22 per unit. The variable expenses were $2,053,200, and the fixed expenses were $683,338.

Waterways has determined the full cost to manufacture its timers is $1.02 per unit. Recently it was discovered that a competitor was selling this unit for $0.81 per unit. Ryan immediately suggested that Waterways buy the timer from the other supplier, but Jordan was not convinced. He cautioned Ryan that $153,120 worth of fixed costs would not be eliminated by buying the unit. However, he also knew that if Waterways bought the unit from the competitor, it would free up 120 machine hours that could be used to produce the large DIY installations kits described in Part 1.

Instructions

(a) Assuming Waterways requires 696,000 timers, evaluate whether it should continue to make the timer or if it should purchase it from the outside supplier.
(b) What is the maximum price per unit Waterways should be willing to pay to purchase the timer from an outside supplier?
(c) What non-financial factors might be considered in making this decision?

Part 3

Waterways mass produces a special clip that is used to install the irrigation pipes. Because of a limited supply of the raw material used in the manufacturing process, very few other companies can manufacture this clip. These units normally sell for $3.95 per unit. Waterways sells about 35,000 of the units each year.

A company in British Columbia that has been unable to secure enough material to produce the volume of units demanded by its customers has offered to pay $2.90 each for 15,000 units. This is just $0.30 above the variable cost of the unit. In addition, to complete production it would require temporarily adding another shift to the production line, which in turn would increase variable manufacturing costs by $0.30 per unit. However, because the units are going to one company, selling costs would be reduced by $0.15 per unit.

An Alberta company has also asked for a special order. It is willing to pay $3.20 per unit but only needs 10,000 units. Waterways cannot manufacture this order without adding an extra shift. Special packaging required will cost $0.20 per unit.

Currently Waterways has enough raw materials to produce 50,000 units.

Instructions

(a) Determine the consequences of Waterways agreeing to provide the 15,000 units to the B.C. company. Would this be a wise special order to accept?
(b) Should Waterways accept the special order from the Alberta company?
(c) What would be the consequences of accepting both special orders?
(d) What would be the opportunity cost of accepting the special order from the British Columbia company? The Alberta company?

Part 4

Waterways is considering the replacement of an antiquated machine that has been slowing down production of its special clip because of breakdowns and added maintenance. Ryan Smith, the plant manager, estimates the machine has two years left of use. The undepreciated cost on the old machine is $30,000. He notes that the current machine is capable of producing an average of 1,200 units per month. The new model of the machine could produce twice as many units during the same time and variable costs would go down by $0.10 per unit. The replacement machine would cost $57,000 and has a two-year life expectancy.

Costs are not expected to change over the next two years.

Instructions

Given the original information in Part 3, and assuming an unlimited supply of raw materials, determine if Waterways should replace the old machine.

Answers to Self-Study Questions

1. d 2. b 3. c 4. d 5. d 6. a 7. b 8. c 9. b 10. b

Remember to go back to the beginning of the chapter to check off your completed work!
←

CHAPTER 8

Alternative Inventory Costing Methods: A Decision-Making Perspective

The Navigator
Chapter 8

study objectives

the navigator

After studying this chapter, you should be able to do the following:

1. Explain the difference between absorption costing and variable costing.

2. Discuss the effect that changes in the production level and sales level have on net income measured under absorption costing versus under variable costing.

3. Discuss the advantages of variable costing versus absorption costing for management decision-making.

4. Discuss the effect of a normal-costing method on income reported under absorption costing and variable costing (Appendix 8A).

5. Discuss the effect of the throughput-costing method on income reported under variable costing (Appendix 8A).

NO FISHY BUSINESS IN TRACKING COSTS

Lunenburg, Nova Scotia–based High Liner Foods Incorporated is North America's largest processor and marketer of prepared, value-added frozen seafood. The company's branded products are sold throughout the United States, Canada, and Mexico under several labels, including High Liner®, Fisher Boy®, and Sea Cuisine®, and are available in most grocery and club stores. It also makes products for customers such as fast-food restaurants. Through various acquisitions, the company has five plants—one in Lunenburg and four in the United States—that process raw materials that come from around the world. In 2013, High Liner sold $947 million worth of products.

Like all manufacturers, High Liner must closely track its costs and decide on the best method of allocating them. It can choose from the absorption-costing method, where all variable and fixed manufacturing costs are charged to a particular product. Or it can choose to use the variable-costing method, where only direct materials and labour and variable manufacturing overhead costs are assigned to a certain product. Both methods have advantages in particular situations.

For the most part, High Liner uses absorption costing, said Kelly Nelson, who recently retired as CFO. Costs are classified into three categories: direct costs, including direct labour, packaging, ingredients, seafood, and the energy to run the fryers; manufacturing overhead, including service labour (such as forklift drivers), repair and maintenance, other energy costs such as heat and electricity, and sanitation and garbage removal; and fixed overhead, such as rent, depreciation, insurance, property taxes, administrative expenses, and salaried employees.

"We use full standard costs for tracking our profitability," said Mr. Nelson. "We fully allocate the cost both for inventory and cost of sales purposes."

However, there are occasions when the food processor uses variable costing to assess operations internally, such as when analyzing variances between variable and absorbed costs. High Liner measures a number of individual variances—such as for seafood, breading and batter, packaging, and manufacturing overhead—and does a variance analysis for each component. "Yield is very important on the seafood raw material because we've got expensive raw material, throughput is very important on our labour, and waste is important on the other ingredients," said Mr. Nelson.

Also, on the rare occasions High Liner decides to move a product line from one plant to another, it uses variable costing to make the decision since much of the overhead stays. "Part of the manufacturing overheads, we deem to be variable—about 35% of them—so what we do is take the direct cost plus 35% of the manufacturing overhead and compare that from plant to plant," said Mr. Nelson.

Sources: "High Liner Foods Reports Operating Results for the Fourth Quarter and Full-Year of 2013," company news release, February 19, 2014; The Canadian Press, "High Liner Foods Profit Soars as Overall Sales Rise," Metronews.ca, February 19, 2014; Joan Tupponce, "High Liner Foods Expands in Newport News and Abroad," VirginiaBusiness.com, November 27, 2013; High Liner Foods website, www.highlinerfoods.com.

Preview of Chapter 8

As the opening story about High Liner Foods Incorporated suggests, the relationship between a company's fixed and variable costs can have a huge impact on its profitability. In particular, the trend toward cost structures that have mostly fixed costs has significantly increased the volatility of many companies' net income. In order to better track and understand the impact of the cost structure on corporate profitability, some companies use an approach called *variable costing*. This chapter will show how variable costing can be helpful in making solid business decisions.

The chapter is organized as follows:

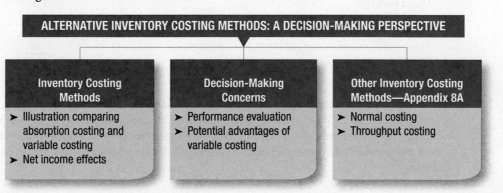

ALTERNATIVE INVENTORY COSTING METHODS: A DECISION-MAKING PERSPECTIVE		
Inventory Costing Methods	**Decision-Making Concerns**	**Other Inventory Costing Methods—Appendix 8A**
➤ Illustration comparing absorption costing and variable costing ➤ Net income effects	➤ Performance evaluation ➤ Potential advantages of variable costing	➤ Normal costing ➤ Throughput costing

Inventory Costing Methods

In the earlier chapters, both variable and fixed manufacturing costs were classified as product costs. In job-order costing, for example, a job is assigned the costs of direct materials, direct labour, and *both* variable and fixed manufacturing overhead. This costing approach is referred to as *full* or **absorption costing** because all manufacturing costs are charged to, or absorbed by, the product. Absorption costing is the approach used for external reporting under generally accepted accounting principles.

An alternative approach is to use variable costing. Under **variable costing**, only direct materials, direct labour, and variable manufacturing overhead costs are considered product costs. Fixed manufacturing overhead costs are recognized as period costs (expenses) when incurred. Illustration 8-1 shows graphically the difference between absorption costing and variable costing.

▶Illustration 8-1
Difference between absorption costing and variable costing

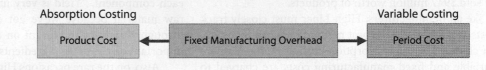

Selling and administrative expenses are period costs under both absorption and variable costing.

ILLUSTRATION COMPARING ABSORPTION COSTING AND VARIABLE COSTING

STUDY OBJECTIVE 1
Explain the difference between absorption costing and variable costing.

To illustrate absorption and variable costing, assume that Premium Products Corporation manufactures a polyurethane sealant called Fix-it for car windshields. Relevant data for Fix-it in January 2016, the first month of production, are shown in Illustration 8-2.

▶Illustration 8-2
Sealant sales and cost data for Premium Products Corporation

Fix-it selling price: $20 per unit
Units: produced 30,000; sold 20,000; beginning inventory zero
Variable unit costs: manufacturing $9 (direct materials $5, direct labour $3, and variable overhead $1);
   selling and administrative expenses $2
Fixed costs: manufacturing overhead $120,000; selling and administrative expenses $15,000

Illustration 8-3 presents the calculation of the per-unit manufacturing cost under each costing approach.

▶Illustration 8-3
Calculation of per-unit manufacturing cost

Type of cost	Absorption costing	Variable costing
Direct materials	$ 5	$5
Direct labour	3	3
Variable manufacturing overhead	1	1
Fixed manufacturing overhead ($120,000 ÷ 30,000 units produced)	4	–
Manufacturing cost per unit	$13	$9

The manufacturing cost per unit is $4 ($13 − $9) higher for absorption costing. This is because fixed manufacturing costs are a product cost under absorption costing. Under variable costing, in contrast, they are a period cost, and are therefore expensed. Based on these data, each unit sold and each unit remaining in inventory is costed at $13 under absorption costing and at $9 under variable costing.

Absorption Costing Illustration

Illustration 8-4 shows the income statement for Premium Products using absorption costing. It shows that the cost of goods manufactured is $390,000, calculated by multiplying the 30,000 units produced by the manufacturing cost of $13 per unit (see Illustration 8-3). Also, both the variable and fixed selling and administrative expenses are treated as period costs and are therefore expensed in 2016. Under absorption costing, $40,000 of the fixed overhead costs (10,000 × $4) is deferred to a future period as part of the cost of ending inventory.

▶Illustration 8-4
Absorption-costing income statement

PREMIUM PRODUCTS CORPORATION Income Statement Month Ended January 31, 2016 Absorption Costing		
Sales (20,000 units × $20)		$400,000
Cost of goods sold		
Inventory, January 1	$ 0	
Cost of goods manufactured (30,000 units × $13)	390,000	
Cost of goods available for sale	390,000	
Inventory, January 31 (10,000 units × $13)	130,000	
Cost of goods sold (20,000 units × $13)		260,000
Gross profit		140,000
Variable selling and administrative expenses		40,000
Fixed selling and administrative expenses		15,000
Net income		$ 85,000

Variable Costing Illustration

As shown in Illustration 8-5, the cost-volume-profit format is used in preparing a variable-costing income statement. The variable manufacturing cost of $270,000 is calculated by multiplying the 30,000 units produced by the variable manufacturing cost of $9 per unit (see Illustration 8-3). As in absorption costing, both variable and fixed selling and administrative expenses are treated as period costs.

There is one primary difference between variable and absorption costing: under variable costing, the fixed manufacturing overhead is charged as an expense in the current period. Fixed overhead costs of the current period, therefore, are not deferred to future periods through the ending inventory. As a result, absorption costing will show a higher net income than variable costing whenever there are more units produced than sold. This difference can be seen in the two income statements for our example (Illustrations 8-4 and 8-5). There is a $40,000 difference in the ending inventories ($130,000 under absorption costing, and $90,000 under variable costing). Under absorption costing, $40,000 of the fixed overhead costs ($10,000 × $4) has been deferred to a future period as a product cost. In contrast, under variable costing, all the fixed manufacturing costs are expensed in the current period.

▶Illustration 8-5
Variable-costing income statement

PREMIUM PRODUCTS CORPORATION Income Statement Month Ended January 31, 2016 Variable Costing		
Sales (20,000 units × $20)		$400,000
Variable costs		
Inventory, January 1	$ 0	
Variable manufacturing costs (30,000 units × $9)	270,000	
Cost of goods available for sale	270,000	
Inventory, January 31 (10,000 units × $9)	90,000	
Variable cost of goods sold	180,000	
Variable selling and administrative expenses		
(20,000 units × $2)	40,000	220,000
Contribution margin		180,000
Fixed manufacturing overhead		120,000
Fixed selling and administrative expenses		15,000
Net income		$ 45,000

In summary, therefore, when there are more units produced than sold, income under absorption costing is higher. When fewer units are produced than sold, income under absorption costing is lower. When units produced and sold are the same, net income will be equal under the two costing approaches. In this case, there is no increase in ending inventory so fixed overhead costs of the current period are not deferred to future periods through the ending inventory.

| BUSINESS INSIGHT | *Saving Costs and the Environment* |

A manufacturer like Granby, Quebec–based Artopex, which makes office furniture, has to rein in its costs to help compete with firms that make their products overseas. Artopex, with more than 400 employees, has variable costs such as the labour and materials required to make different furniture products and fixed costs such as overhead for things like insurance. The company recently spent over $7 million in new, more efficient production equipment, including robotic equipment, that would not only reduce its operating costs, but help the environment by reducing waste and allowing the company to recycle some of the materials wasted in the production process. "The motive was to be more productive and competitive against imports from Asia, but it also helps us to be more sustainable," says Jean Barbeau, an Artopex product specialist. Artopex also helped reduce overhead by changing its factory light bulbs to energy-efficient alternatives, saving 16% annually on energy costs.

Sources: "Artopex—One of Canada's 50 Best Managed Companies for the Fifth Year in a Row!", company news release, February 22, 2012; "Heeding the Call of Customers: Artopex," in *SMEs Set Their Sights on Sustainability*, Canadian Institute of Chartered Accountants, American Institute of CPAs, and Chartered Institute of Management Accountants, September 2011, pp. 13–16; Artopex Corporate Profile 2011, www.artopex.com.

As a private company, Artopex does not publicly report its accounting methods, but do you think it would use the absorption or variable-costing method for inventory?

NET INCOME EFFECTS

STUDY OBJECTIVE 2
Discuss the effect that changes in the production level and sales level have on net income measured under absorption costing versus under variable costing.

To further illustrate the concepts underlying absorption and variable costing, we will now work through an extended example using Overbay Inc., a manufacturer of small airplane drones. We assume that the company's production volume stays the same over the three-year period (at 10 drones per year), but that the number of units sold varies.

2016 Results

As indicated in Illustration 8-6, the manufacturing cost per drone is $300,000, which comprises variable manufacturing costs of $240,000 per drone and fixed manufacturing costs of $60,000 per drone. Overbay also has variable and fixed selling and administrative expenses ($50,000 and $80,000, respectively), which are expensed in 2016. The absorption-costing income statement for Overbay Inc. in Illustration 8-7 shows that the company reports net income of $870,000 under absorption costing.

▶Illustration 8-6
Information for Overbay Inc.

	2016	2017	2018
Volume information			
Drones in beginning inventory	0	0	2
Drones produced	10	10	10
Drones sold	10	8	12
Drones in ending inventory	0	2	0
Financial information			
Selling price per drone	$400,000		
Variable manufacturing costs per drone	240,000		
Fixed manufacturing costs for the year	600,000		
Fixed manufacturing costs per drone	60,000	($600,000 ÷ 10)	
Variable selling and administrative expenses per drone	5,000		
Fixed selling and administrative expenses	80,000		

OVERBAY INC.
Income Statement
Year Ended January 31, 2016
Absorption Costing

Sales (10 drones × $400,000)		$4,000,000
Cost of goods sold (10 drones × $300,000)		3,000,000
Gross profit		1,000,000
Variable selling and administrative expenses		
(10 drones × $5,000)	$50,000	
Fixed selling and administrative expenses	80,000	130,000
Net income		$ 870,000

As indicated earlier, under a variable-costing system, the income statement follows a cost-volume-profit (CVP) format. In this case, the manufacturing cost is composed solely of the variable manufacturing costs of $240,000 per drone. The fixed manufacturing costs of $600,000 for the year are expensed in 2016. As in absorption costing, the fixed and variable selling and administrative expenses are period costs expensed in 2016. Illustration 8-8 shows a variable-costing income statement for Overbay Inc. for 2016.

OVERBAY INC.
Income Statement
Year Ended January 31, 2016
Variable Costing

Sales (10 drones × $400,000)		$4,000,000
Variable cost of goods sold (10 drones × $240,000)	$2,400,000	
Variable selling and administrative expenses		
(10 drones × $5,000)	50,000	2,450,000
Contribution margin		1,550,000
Fixed manufacturing overhead	600,000	
Fixed selling and administrative expenses	80,000	680,000
Net income		$ 870,000

As shown in Illustration 8-8, the variable-costing net income of $870,000 is the same as the absorption-costing net income calculated in Illustration 8-7. **When the number of units produced and sold is the same, net income is equal under the two costing approaches.** Because there is no increase in ending inventory, no fixed manufacturing costs in 2016 are deferred to future periods.

2017 Results

In 2017, Overbay produced 10 drones but sold only eight of them. As a result, there are two drones in ending inventory. Illustration 8-9 shows the absorption-costing income statement for 2017.

OVERBAY INC.
Income Statement
Year Ended January 31, 2017
Absorption Costing

Sales (8 drones × $400,000)		$3,200,000
Cost of goods sold (8 drones × $300,000)		2,400,000
Gross profit		800,000
Variable selling and administrative expenses		
(8 drones × $5,000)	$40,000	
Fixed selling and administrative expenses	80,000	120,000
Net income		$ 680,000

Under absorption costing, the ending inventory of two drones is $600,000 ($300,000 × 2). Each unit of ending inventory includes $60,000 of fixed manufacturing overhead. Therefore, fixed manufacturing costs of $120,000 ($60,000 × 2 drones) are deferred until a future period. Illustration 8-10 shows the variable-costing income statement for 2017.

OVERBAY INC. Income Statement Year Ended January 31, 2017 Variable Costing		
Sales (8 drones × $400,000)		$3,200,000
Variable cost of goods sold (8 drones × $240,000)	$1,920,000	
Variable selling and administrative expenses (8 drones × $5,000)	40,000	1,960,000
Contribution margin		1,240,000
Fixed manufacturing overhead	600,000	
Fixed selling and administrative expenses	80,000	680,000
Net income		$ 560,000

As shown, when more units are produced (10) than sold (8), net income under absorption costing ($680,000) is higher than net income under variable costing ($560,000). This is because the cost of the ending inventory is higher under absorption costing than under variable costing. In 2017, under absorption costing, the fixed manufacturing overhead of $120,000 is deferred and carried to future periods as part of the inventory. Under variable costing, the $120,000 is expensed in the current period and, therefore, the difference in the two net income numbers is $120,000 ($680,000 − $560,000).

2018 Results

In 2018, Overbay produced 10 drones and sold 12 (10 drones from the current year's production and two drones from the beginning inventory). As a result, there are no drones in ending inventory. Illustration 8-11 shows the absorption-costing income statement for 2018.

OVERBAY INC. Income Statement Year Ended January 31, 2018 Absorption Costing		
Sales (12 drones × $400,000)		$4,800,000
Cost of goods sold (12 drones × $300,000)		3,600,000
Gross profit		1,200,000
Variable selling and administrative expenses (12 drones × $5,000)	$60,000	
Fixed selling and administrative expenses	80,000	140,000
Net income		$1,060,000

Fixed manufacturing costs of $720,000 are expensed in 2018—$120,000 of fixed manufacturing costs incurred during 2017 and included in beginning inventory, plus $600,000 of fixed manufacturing costs incurred during 2018. Having now seen the result for the absorption-costing statement, what would you expect the result to be under variable costing? Let's take a look.

Illustration 8-12 shows the variable-costing income statement for 2018.

OVERBAY INC. Income Statement Year Ended January 31, 2018 Variable Costing		
Sales (12 drones × $400,000)		$4,800,000
Variable cost of goods sold (12 drones × $240,000)	$2,880,000	
Variable selling and administrative expenses (12 drones × $5,000)	60,000	2,940,000
Contribution margin		1,860,000
Fixed manufacturing overhead	600,000	
Fixed selling and administrative expenses	80,000	680,000
Net income		$1,180,000

When fewer drones are produced (10) than sold (12), net income under absorption costing ($1,060,000) is less than net income under variable costing ($1,180,000). This difference of $120,000 ($1,180,000 − $1,060,000) occurs because $120,000 of fixed manufacturing overhead costs in the beginning inventory is charged to 2018 under absorption costing. Under variable costing, there is no fixed manufacturing overhead cost in the beginning inventory. Illustration 8-13 summarizes the results for the three years.

Net Income under Both Costing Approaches			
	2016	2017	2018
	Production = Sales	Production > Sales	Production < Sales
Absorption costing	$870,000	$680,000	$1,060,000
Variable costing	870,000	560,000	1,180,000
Difference	$ 0	$120,000	$ (120,000)

►Illustration 8-13
Comparison of net income under both costing approaches

Illustration 8-14 shows graphically this relationship between production and sales and its effect on net income under the two costing approaches.

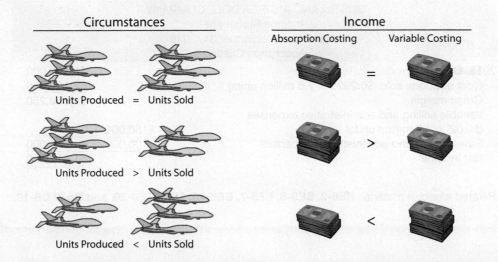

Circumstances	Income	
	Absorption Costing	Variable Costing
Units Produced = Units Sold	=	
Units Produced > Units Sold	>	
Units Produced < Units Sold	<	

►Illustration 8-14
Summary of income effects

BEFORE YOU GO ON...

►Do It! Absorption Costing

Justin and Andrea Doll Company produces and sells tennis balls. The following costs are available for the year ended December 31, 2016. The company has no beginning inventory. In 2016, the company produced 8 million units but sold only 7.5 million units. The unit selling price was $0.50 per ball. Costs and expenses were as follows:

Variable costs per unit	
Direct materials	$0.10
Direct labour	0.05
Variable manufacturing overhead	0.08
Variable selling and administrative expenses	0.02
Annual fixed costs and expenses	
Fixed manufacturing overhead	$500,000
Selling and administrative expenses	$100,000

(a) Calculate the manufacturing cost of one unit of product using absorption costing.

(b) Prepare a 2016 income statement for Justin and Andrea Doll Company using absorption costing.

(continued)

(continued)

Action Plan

• Remember that under absorption costing, fixed manufacturing costs are treated as manufacturing costs.

Solution

(a) The cost of one unit of product under absorption costing would be as follows:

Direct materials	$0.1000
Direct labour	0.0500
Variable manufacturing overhead	0.0800
Fixed manufacturing overhead	0.0625
	$0.2925

(b) The absorption-costing income statement would be as follows:

JUSTIN AND ANDREA DOLL COMPANY Income Statement Year Ended December 31, 2016 Absorption Costing		
Sales		$3,750,000
Cost of goods sold ($0.2925 × 7.5 million units)		2,193,750
Gross margin		$1,556,250
Variable selling and administrative expenses		
($0.02 × 7.5 million units)	$150,000	
Fixed selling and administrative expenses	100,000	250,000
Net income		$1,306,250

Related exercise material: **BE8-2, BE8-5, BE8-7, BE8-10, E8-17, E8-20,** and **Do It! D8-12.**

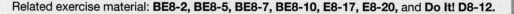

Decision-Making Concerns

STUDY OBJECTIVE 3

Discuss the advantages of variable costing versus absorption costing for management decision-making.

For external reporting purposes, companies must report their financial information using generally accepted accounting principles (GAAP). *GAAP requires companies to use absorption costing for the costing of inventory.* Net income measured under GAAP (absorption costing) is often used internally to evaluate performance, justify cost reductions, or evaluate new projects.

Some companies, however, have recognized that net income calculated using GAAP does not highlight the differences between variable and fixed costs, and may lead to poor business decisions. Consequently, some companies have decided that it is better to use variable costing for their internal reporting. The following discussion and example highlight a significant problem that can happen when companies use absorption costing for decision-making.

IFRS Notes

Accounting standards do not use the managerial terms *variable costing* and *absorption costing*. Instead, IAS 2 *Inventories* provides guidance on the measurement and reporting of inventories by stating, "The cost of inventories shall comprise all costs of purchase, costs of conversion and other costs

PERFORMANCE EVALUATION

When production exceeds sales, absorption costing reports a higher net income than variable costing. As noted earlier, the reason is that some fixed manufacturing costs are not expensed in the current period, but are deferred to future periods as part of the inventory. As a result, management may be tempted to overproduce in a period in order to increase net income. Although net income will increase, this decision to overproduce may not be in the company's best interest.

Suppose, for example, that a division manager's compensation is based on the division's net income. In such a case, the manager may decide to meet the net income targets by increasing production. While this overproduction may increase the manager's compensation, the buildup of inventories will lead to additional costs to the company. The company avoids this situation under variable costing, because net income under variable costing is not affected by changes in production levels. The example that follows shows this point.

Warren Lund, a division manager of Walker Enterprises, is under pressure to boost the performance of the lighting division in 2016. Unfortunately, recent profits have not met expectations. The expected sales for this year are 20,000 units. As he plans for the year, he has to decide whether to produce 20,000 or 30,000 units. Illustration 8-15 provides the facts that are available for the division.

incurred in bringing the inventories to their present location and condition." Integrating your financial and managerial accounting knowledge, you should realize that *costs of purchase* include any non-recoverable taxes, transport, and handling, less trade discounts received, and that *costs of conversion* include both fixed and variable manufacturing overheads. Although managerial accounting finds many methods of costing inventory acceptable, financial accounting following IFRS only accepts one method: absorption costing.

Beginning inventory	0	
Expected sales in units	20,000	
Selling price per unit	$15	
Variable manufacturing costs per unit	$6	
Fixed manufacturing costs (total)	$60,000	
Fixed manufacturing costs per unit		
Based on 20,000 units produced		$3 per unit ($60,000 ÷ 20,000)
Based on 30,000 units produced		$2 per unit ($60,000 ÷ 30,000)
Manufacturing costs per unit		
Based on 20,000 units produced		$9 per unit ($6 variable + $3 fixed)
Based on 30,000 units produced		$8 per unit ($6 variable + $2 fixed)
Variable selling and administrative expenses per unit	$1	
Fixed selling and administrative expenses	$15,000	

►Illustration 8-15
Facts on lighting division—2016

Illustration 8-16 presents the division's results for the two possible levels of output under absorption costing.

If the lighting division produces 20,000 units, its net income is $85,000. If it produces 30,000 units, its net income is $105,000. By producing 30,000 units, the division will have an inventory of 10,000 units. This excess inventory causes net income to increase by $20,000 because $20,000 of fixed costs (10,000 × $2) are not charged to the current year, but are deferred to future periods. What do you think Warren Lund might do in this situation? Given his concern about the profit numbers of the lighting division, he may be tempted to increase production. Although this increased production will increase 2016 net income, it may be costly to the company in the long run.

►Illustration 8-16
Absorption-costing income statement—2016

LIGHTING DIVISION Income Statement Year Ended January 31, 2016 Absorption Costing				
	20,000 Produced		30,000 Produced	
Sales (20,000 units × $15)	$300,000		$300,000	
Cost of goods sold	180,000	(20,000 × $9)	160,000	(20,000 × $8)
Gross profit	120,000		140,000	
Variable selling and administrative expenses				
(20,000 × $1)	20,000		20,000	
Fixed selling and administrative expenses	15,000		15,000	
Net income	$ 85,000		$105,000	

Now let's evaluate the same situation under variable costing. Illustration 8-17 shows the variable-costing income statement for production at both 20,000 and 30,000 units, using the information in Illustration 8-15.

▶Illustration 8-17
Variable-costing income
statement—2016

	20,000 Produced	30,000 Produced
Sales (20,000 × $15)	$300,000	$300,000
Less: Variable cost of goods sold (20,000 × $6)	120,000	120,000
Variable selling and administrative expenses (20,000 × $1)	20,000	20,000
Contribution margin	160,000	160,000
Less: Fixed manufacturing overhead	60,000	60,000
Fixed selling and administrative expenses	15,000	15,000
Net income	$ 85,000	$ 85,000

LIGHTING DIVISION
Income Statement
Year Ended January 31, 2016
Variable Costing

From this example, we see that, under variable costing, net income is not affected by the number of units produced. Net income is $85,000 whether 20,000 or 30,000 units are produced. Why? Because fixed manufacturing overhead is treated as a period expense. Unlike under absorption costing, under variable costing, no fixed manufacturing overhead is deferred through inventory buildup.

POTENTIAL ADVANTAGES OF VARIABLE COSTING

Variable costing has the following potential advantages compared with absorption costing:

1. The use of variable costing is consistent with the cost-volume-profit material presented in Chapter 6 and the incremental analysis material presented in Chapter 7.
2. Net income calculated under variable costing is not affected by changes in production levels. As a result, it is much easier to understand the impact of fixed and variable costs on the calculation of net income when variable costing is used.
3. Net income calculated under variable costing is greatly affected by changes in sales levels (not production levels), and it therefore provides a more realistic assessment of the company's success or failure during a period.
4. Because the fixed and variable cost components are shown in the variable-costing income statement, it is easier to identify these costs and understand their effect on the business. Under absorption costing, the allocation of fixed costs to inventory makes it difficult to evaluate the impact of fixed costs on the company's results.

BUSINESS INSIGHT   *Pedalling to Compete*

Like most North American bike and cycling apparel companies, Montreal-based Dorel Industries has moved all of its manufacturing overseas. In early 2014, Dorel announced that its high-performance Cannondale bikes would no longer be made in Pennsylvania because the product line was no longer competitive. The company used to assemble some bicycle parts in the United States, ship them to Asia for further assembly, then back to the U.S. for completion, which wasn't efficient in terms of time or cost. "We want to significantly reduce development and supply chain lead times, improve cost structures and operating margins, and enhance quality while lowering warranty costs," said Peter Woods, Dorel's global chief financial offer. Dorel expected the closure of its Pennsylvania plant would save at least U.S. $6 million annually.

Sources: John Symon, "Dorel Restructures and Outsources All Production to Asia—Cannondale Assembly in Pennsylvania Affected," *Pedal* magazine, January 31, 2014; Bertrand Marotte, "Dorel to Shutter U.S. Bike Plant, Shift Work to Asia," *The Globe and Mail*, January 23, 2014; "Dorel's Recreational/Leisure Segment Restructures Operations to Enhance Competitiveness," Dorel news release, January 23, 2014.

Based on the fact that Dorel considered its costs of product development, supply chain, and warranty, do you think it uses the absorption or variable-costing method for its bicycle division?

BEFORE YOU GO ON...

▶Do It! Variable Costing

Justin and Andrea Doll Company produces and sells tennis balls. The following costs are available for the year ended December 31, 2016. The company has no beginning inventory. In 2016, the company produced 8 million units but sold only 7.5 million units. The unit selling price was $0.50 per ball. Costs and expenses were as follows:

Variable costs per unit	
Direct materials	$0.10
Direct labour	0.05
Variable manufacturing overhead	0.08
Variable selling and administrative expenses	0.02
Annual fixed costs and expenses	
Manufacturing overhead	$500,000
Selling and administrative expenses	$100,000

(a) Calculate the manufacturing cost of one unit of product using variable costing.

(b) Prepare a 2016 income statement for Justin and Andrea Doll Company using variable costing.

Action Plan

• Remember that under variable costing, only variable manufacturing costs are treated as manufacturing costs.
• Subtract all fixed costs as period costs. This includes both manufacturing overhead and selling and administrative expenses.

Solution

(a) The cost of one unit of product under variable costing would be as follows:

Direct materials	$0.10
Direct labour	0.05
Variable manufacturing overhead	0.08
	$0.23

(b) The variable-costing income statement would be as follows:

JUSTIN AND ANDREA DOLL COMPANY Income Statement Year Ended December 31, 2016 Variable Costing		
Sales		$3,750,000
Variable cost of goods sold	$1,725,000	
Variable selling and administrative expenses	150,000	1,875,000
Contribution margin		1,875,000
Fixed manufacturing overhead	500,000	
Fixed selling and administrative expenses	100,000	600,000
Net income		$1,275,000

Related exercise material: **BE8-1, BE8-4, BE8-7, E8-16, E8-17, E8-19,** and **Do It! D8-13.**

the navigator

ALL ABOUT YOU   *What Is a Degree Worth?*

What do you have a better chance of: Winning a million dollars in the lottery, or finishing university? If you said the latter, you're right, but did you know that Canadian university graduates earn on average $1.3 million more over their careers than high school graduates? Degree holders are also much less likely to be unemployed. On the other hand, if you weren't in school, you could be earning money and wouldn't have the costs of going to school; university undergraduate tuition averaged $5,772 in Canada for the 2013–14 year.

What Do You Think?

Suppose that you are working two jobs and in university full-time. You can't make ends meet and your grades are suffering. Should you drop out of school?

YES—You can always go back to school. If your grades are bad, what good is school doing you anyway?

NO—Once you drop out, it is very hard to get enough momentum to go back. Dropping out will dramatically reduce your long-term opportunities.

Sources: Marc Frenette and René Morissette, "Wages and Full-Time Employment Rates of Young High School Graduates and Bachelor's Degree Holders, 1997 to 2012," Statistics Canada, April 2014; Statistics Canada, "University Tuition Fees, 2013/2014," *The Daily*, September 12, 2013; Association of Universities and Colleges of Canada, "The Value of a University Degree," September 2010.

APPENDIX 8A—OTHER INVENTORY COSTING METHODS

NORMAL COSTING

STUDY OBJECTIVE 4

Discuss the effect of a normal-costing method on income reported under absorption costing and variable costing.

In the previous illustrations of absorption-costing and variable-costing income statements, we assumed fixed manufacturing overhead was allocated to each unit of production based on the actual cost incurred and the actual number of units produced during the month. However, we discussed in Chapter 3 an alternative method to allocate fixed manufacturing overhead using a normal-costing system, which uses actual direct manufacturing costs and actual production units with a predetermined overhead rate. The use of a predetermined overhead rate is more practical for assigning fixed manufacturing overhead costs to production.

To illustrate the effect of normal costing in absorption costing, we assume that Premium Products Corporation used the budgeted relevant data for Fix-it in January 2016, the first month of production. Illustration 8A-1 presents the sealant sales and cost data.

▶Illustration 8A-1

Sealant sales and cost data for Premium Products Corporation

Fix-it selling price:	$20 per unit
Units:	produced 30,000; sold 20,000; beginning inventory zero
Variable unit costs:	manufacturing $9 (direct materials $5, direct labour $3, and variable overhead $1); selling and administrative expenses $2
Fixed costs:	manufacturing overhead $120,000; based on a budgeted volume of 40,000 units, selling and administrative expenses $15,000
Premium Products expenses production volume variance to cost of goods sold in the accounting period in which it occurs.	

Illustration 8A-2 calculates the per-unit manufacturing cost under each costing approach.

Type of cost	Absorption costing	Variable costing
Direct materials	$ 5	$5
Direct labour	3	3
Variable manufacturing overhead	1	1
Fixed manufacturing overhead ($120,000 ÷ 40,000 units produced)	3	—
Manufacturing cost per unit	$12	$9

►Illustration 8A-2
Calculation of per-unit manufacturing cost

The manufacturing cost per unit is $3 ($12 − $9) higher under absorption costing than variable costing. This occurs because fixed manufacturing costs are based on the predetermined rate under absorption costing. Under variable costing, in contrast, fixed manufacturing costs are still a period cost and are therefore expensed. Based on these data, each unit sold and each unit remaining in inventory is costed at $12 under absorption costing and at $9 under variable costing.

Absorption and Normal Costing Illustration

Illustration 8A-3 presents absorption-cost income statements using the same facts as in Illustration 8-4, except we have assumed that Premium Products Corporation's budgeted production volume is 40,000 units. Therefore, its predetermined fixed manufacturing overhead is $3 per unit ($120,000 ÷ 40,000).

PREMIUM PRODUCTS CORPORATION
Income Statement
Month Ended January 31, 2016
Absorption Costing Using Normal-Costing Approach

Sales (20,000 × $20)		$400,000
Cost of goods sold		
Inventory, January 1	$ 0	
Cost of goods manufactured (30,000 units × $12)	360,000	
Cost of goods available for sale	360,000	
Inventory, January 31 (10,000 units × $12)	120,000	
Cost of goods sold (20,000 units × $12)		240,000
Unfavourable volume variance ($120,000 − $90,000)		30,000
Gross profit		130,000
Variable selling and administrative expenses		40,000
Fixed selling and administrative expenses		15,000
Net income		$ 75,000

►Illustration 8A-3
Absorption-costing income statement (using normal-costing approach)—2016

Illustration 8A-3 shows that the cost of goods manufactured is $360,000, calculated by multiplying the 30,000 units produced by the manufacturing cost of $12 per unit. Also, both the variable and fixed selling and administrative expenses are treated as period costs and are therefore expensed in 2016. Under absorption costing, $30,000 of the fixed overhead costs (10,000 × $3) is deferred to a future period as part of the cost of ending inventory. The $3 fixed manufacturing overhead per unit is based on a budgeted production level of 40,000 units per month ($120,000 ÷ 40,000). A production-volume variance occurs whenever actual production deviates from budgeted production level. The $30,000 variance is $3 multiplied by the difference between the actual level of production, 30,000 units, and the budgeted level of production, 40,000 units. The production volume variance is usually expensed to the costs of goods sold. It occurs only under absorption costing and not under variable costing.

We can reconcile the absorption-costing net income to the variable-costing net income by concentrating on the fixed manufacturing overhead in ending inventory:

Absorption-costing net income (Illustration 8A-3)	$75,000
Less: Ending inventory fixed manufacturing overhead (10,000 × $3)	$30,000
Variable-costing net income (Illustration 8-5)	$45,000

BEFORE YOU GO ON...

▶Do It! Normal Costing

Justin and Andrea Doll Company produces and sells tennis balls. The following costs are available for the year ended December 31, 2016. The company has no beginning inventory. In 2016, the company produced 8 million units but sold only 7.5 million units. The unit selling price was $0.50 per ball. Costs and expenses were as follows:

Variable costs per unit	
Direct materials	$0.10
Direct labour	0.05
Variable manufacturing overhead	0.08
Variable selling and administrative expenses	0.02
Annual fixed costs and expenses	
Fixed manufacturing overhead	
based on a budgeted volume of 10 million units	$500,000
Selling and administrative expenses	100,000

Justin and Andrea Doll Company expenses production volume variance to cost of goods sold in the accounting period in which it occurs.

(a) Calculate the manufacturing cost of one unit of product using normal costing.

(b) Prepare a 2016 income statement for Justin and Andrea Doll Company using normal costing.

Action Plan

- Remember that under normal costing, fixed manufacturing costs are treated as manufacturing costs based on a budgeted volume, not on actual production.
- Subtract production volume variance to cost of goods sold in the accounting period in which it occurs when the budget volume is greater than the actual production.

Solution

(a) The cost of one unit of product under normal costing would be as follows:

Direct materials	$0.10
Direct labour	0.05
Variable manufacturing overhead	0.08
Fixed manufacturing overhead based on 10 million budget units	0.05
	$0.28

(b) The normal-costing income statement would be as follows:

JUSTIN AND ANDREA DOLL COMPANY Income Statement Year Ended December 31, 2016 Normal Costing		
Sales		$3,750,000
Cost of goods sold ($0.28 × 7.5 million units)		2,100,000
Unfavourable volume variance ($500,000 − $400,000)		100,000
Gross margin		1,550,000
Variable selling and administrative expenses ($0.02 × 7.5 million units)	$150,000	
Fixed selling and administrative expenses	100,000	250,000
Net income		$1,300,000

Related exercise material: **BE8-9, E8-18, E8-21,** and **Do It! D8-14.**

THROUGHPUT COSTING

Throughput costing, which is also called super-variable costing, treats all costs as period expenses except for direct materials. It is a modified form of a variable-costing system that treats direct labour and variable manufacturing overhead as period expenses. Throughput costing is based on lean manufacturing principles. According to lean manufacturing principles, cost can be reduced and profitability increased by improvements in the manufacturing workflow. It is a process increasingly used by many firms to manage their operations more efficiently and with more control as it eliminates waste and focuses more accurately on the needs of the customer. As such, throughput costing provides some useful tools for understanding and improving flow in a process. A company should probably meet two criteria before it chooses throughput costing. The first criterion relates to the nature of the manufacturing process. Throughput costing is suitable only for companies engaged in a manufacturing process in which conversion costs such as direct labour and manufacturing overhead are fixed costs and do not vary proportionately with the units of production. Assembly-line and continuous processes that are highly automated are most likely to meet this criterion. The second criterion is that management favour cost accounting information that is helpful for short-term, incremental analysis, such as whether the company should accept or reject a special offer at a reduced sales price. In this respect, a company's choice of throughput costing is a logical extension of the company's choice of variable costing over absorption costing.

Under throughput costing, product costs are only direct material costs. Inventory is valued using only direct material costs and all other manufacturing costs are treated as expenses in the accounting period in which they occur.

To illustrate the difference between throughput costing and variable costing, we will use the same Premium Products Corporation data for Fix-it in January 2016, the first month of production, as shown in Illustration 8A-4.

STUDY OBJECTIVE 5
Discuss the effect of the throughput-costing method on income reported under variable costing.

Fix-it selling price:	$20 per unit
Units:	produced 30,000; sold 20,000; beginning inventory zero
Variable unit costs:	manufacturing $9 (direct materials $5, direct labour $3, and variable overhead $1); selling and administrative expenses $2
Fixed costs:	manufacturing overhead $120,000; selling and administrative expenses $15,000

►Illustration 8A-4

Sealant sales and cost data for Premium Products Corporation

Illustration 8A-5 calculates the per-unit manufacturing cost under each costing.

Type of cost	Throughput costing	Variable costing
Direct materials	$5	$5
Direct labour	–	3
Variable manufacturing overhead	–	1
Fixed manufacturing overhead	–	–
Manufacturing cost per unit	$5	$9

►Illustration 8A-5

Calculation of per-unit manufacturing cost

The manufacturing cost per unit is $4 ($9 − $5) lower under throughput costing. This is because all manufacturing costs except direct material costs are treated as period costs and are therefore expensed. Under variable costing, in contrast, direct labour and variable manufacturing overhead costs are treated as product costs. Based on these data, each unit sold and each unit remaining in inventory is costed at $5 under throughput costing and at $9 under variable costing.

Throughput Costing Illustration

As shown in Illustration 8A-6, the throughput-costing format is used in preparing an income statement. The manufacturing cost of $150,000 is calculated by multiplying the 30,000 units produced by the direct material costs of $5 per unit (see Illustration 8A-5). As in absorption costing and variable costing, both variable and fixed selling and administrative expenses are treated as period costs. **Throughput contribution** is the difference between revenues and direct material costs for the units sold. The other operating expenses of $295,000 are direct labour and variable manufacturing overhead for the total production of 30,000 units produced during the accounting period at $4 per unit. They also include variable selling and administrative expenses of $40,000, fixed manufacturing overhead of $120,000, and fixed selling and administrative expenses of $15,000. Ending inventory is valued under throughput costing by the amount of direct materials (10,000 units × $5 per unit = $50,000). Throughput-costing operating income is $40,000 less than variable-costing operating income (see Illustration 8A-7). This difference is the amount of direct labour and variable manufacturing overhead costs (10,000 units × $4 per unit) that are included in the ending inventory under variable costing and expensed as a period cost under throughput costing.

►Illustration 8A-6
Throughput-costing income statement—2016

Helpful Hint
Note the difference in the calculation of the ending inventory: $5 per unit here and $9 per unit under variable costing.

PREMIUM PRODUCTS CORPORATION		
Income Statement		
Month Ended January 31, 2016		
Throughput Costing		
Sales (20,000 × $20)		$400,000
Variable cost of goods sold		
Inventory, January 1	$ 0	
Direct material costs (30,000 units × $5)	150,000	
Cost of goods available for sale	150,000	
Inventory, January 31 (10,000 units × $5)	50,000	
Variable cost of goods sold		100,000
Throughput contribution margin		300,000
Other operating costs		
Direct labour costs (30,000 × $3)	90,000	
Variable overhead costs (30,000 × $1)	30,000	
Variable selling and administrative costs (20,000 × $2)	40,000	
Fixed manufacturing overhead	120,000	
Fixed selling and administrative expenses	15,000	
Total other operating costs		295,000
Net income		$ 5,000

►Illustration 8A-7
Variable-costing income statement—2016

PREMIUM PRODUCTS CORPORATION		
Income Statement		
Month Ended January 31, 2016		
Variable Costing		
Sales (20,000 × $20)		$400,000
Variable cost of goods sold		
Inventory, January 1	$ 0	
Variable manufacturing costs (30,000 units × $9)	270,000	
Cost of goods available for sale	270,000	
Inventory, January 31 (10,000 units × $9)	90,000	
Variable cost of goods sold	180,000	
Variable selling and administrative expenses		
(20,000 units × $2)	40,000	220,000
Contribution margin		180,000
Fixed manufacturing overhead		120,000
Fixed selling and administrative expenses		15,000
Net income		$ 45,000

Conceptually, there is one major difference between throughput costing and variable costing: under throughput costing, the direct labour and variable manufacturing overhead are charged as an expense in the current period. Therefore, they are not deferred to future periods through the ending inventory. As a result, variable costing will show a higher net income than throughput costing whenever there are more units produced than sold. This difference can be seen in the two income statements for our example (Illustrations 8A-6 and 8A-7). There is a $40,000 difference in the ending inventories ($90,000 under variable costing, and $50,000 under throughput costing). Under variable costing, $40,000 of the direct labour and variable overhead costs (10,000 × $4) has been deferred to a future period as a product cost. In contrast, under throughput costing, all the manufacturing costs are expensed in the current period except direct material costs.

In summary, when there are more units produced than sold, income under variable costing is higher. When fewer units are produced than sold, income under variable costing is lower. When the same number of units are produced and sold, net income will be equal under the two costing approaches. In this case, there is no increase in ending inventory. So, direct labour and variable overhead costs of the current period are not deferred to future periods through the ending inventory.

Illustration 8A-8 shows graphically this relationship between production and sales and its effect on net income under the variable-costing and throughput-costing approaches.

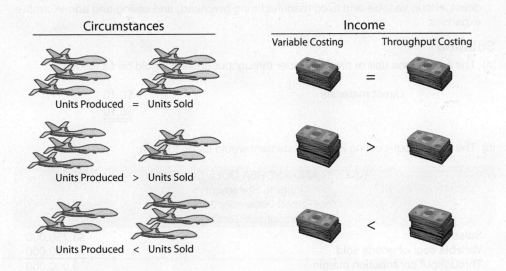

Advantages of Throughput Costing

Advocates of throughput costing state that it reduces the incentive for management to build up excess inventories in order to spread fixed manufacturing costs over a larger number of units produced. The throughput-costing method encourages managers to reduce operating costs such as direct labour and variable overhead, which are treated as period costs, not product costs. On the contrary, under variable costing or absorption costing, many manufacturing costs are initially capitalized as assets (inventory) until goods are sold. Therefore, managers may perceive less need to reduce direct labour and manufacturing overhead.

BEFORE YOU GO ON...

▶Do It! Throughput Costing

Justin and Andrea Doll Company produces and sells tennis balls. The following costs are available for the year ended December 31, 2016. The company has no beginning inventory. In 2016, the company produced 8 million units but sold only 7.5 million units. The unit selling price was $0.50 per ball. Costs and expenses were as follows:

Variable costs per unit	
Direct materials	$0.10
Direct labour	0.05
Variable manufacturing overhead	0.08
Variable selling and administrative expenses	0.02
Annual fixed costs and expenses	
Manufacturing overhead	$500,000
Selling and administrative expenses	100,000

(continued)

(continued)

(a) Calculate the manufacturing cost of one unit of product using throughput costing.

(b) Prepare a 2016 income statement for Justin and Andrea Doll Company using throughput costing.

Action Plan

• Remember that under throughput costing, only direct materials costs are treated as manufacturing costs.
• Subtract all other variable and fixed manufacturing costs as period costs. This includes direct labour, variable and fixed manufacturing overhead, and selling and administrative expenses.

Solution

(a) The cost of one unit of product under throughput costing would be as follows:

Direct materials	$0.10
	$0.10

(b) The throughput-costing income statement would be as follows:

JUSTIN AND ANDREA DOLL COMPANY		
Income Statement		
Year Ended December 31, 2016		
Throughput Costing		
Sales		$3,750,000
Variable cost of goods sold		750,000
Throughput contribution margin		3,000,000
Other operating costs		
Direct labour ($0.05 × 8,000,000)	$400,000	
Variable overhead costs ($0.08 × 8,000,000)	640,000	
Fixed manufacturing overhead	500,000	
Variable selling and administrative expenses	150,000	
Fixed selling and administrative expenses	100,000	1,790,000
Net income		$1,210,000

Related exercise material: **BE8-3, BE8-6, BE8-7, E8-16,** and **Do It! D8-15.**

USING THE DECISION TOOLKIT

T&G Company manufactures and distributes air conditioners. The following data are available for the year ended December 31, 2016. The company had no beginning inventory. In 2016, it produced 3,000 units but sold only 2,800 units. The unit selling price was $6,500. Costs and expenses were as follows:

Variable costs per unit	
Direct materials	$1,200
Direct labour	1,800
Variable manufacturing overhead	500
Variable selling and administrative expenses	100
Annual fixed costs and expenses	
Manufacturing overhead	$1,200,000
Selling and administrative expenses	100,000

(continued)

(continued)

Instructions

(a) Calculate the manufacturing cost of one unit of product using variable costing and throughput costing.

(b) Prepare a 2016 income statement for T&G Company using variable costing and throughput costing.

(c) Show a calculation that explains the difference in net income under variable costing and throughput costing.

Solution

(a)

Type of Cost	Variable Costing Per Unit	Throughput Costing Per Unit
Direct materials	$1,200	$1,200
Direct labour	1,800	–
Variable manufacturing overhead	500	–
Total cost	$3,500	$1,200

(b)

T&G COMPANY
Income Statement
For the Year Ended December 31, 2016
Variable Costing

Sales (2,800 units × $6,500)		$18,200,000
Variable cost of goods sold (2,800 units × $3,500)	$9,800,000	
Variable selling and administrative expenses		
(2,800 units × $100)	280,000	10,080,000
Contribution margin		8,120,000
Fixed manufacturing overhead	1,200,000	
Fixed selling and administrative expenses	100,000	1,300,000
Net income		$ 6,820,000

T&G COMPANY
Income Statement
For the Year Ended December 31, 2016
Throughput Costing

Sales (2,800 units × $6,500)		$18,200,000
Variable cost of goods sold		
Direct material costs (2,800 units × $1,200)		3,360,000
Throughput contribution margin		14,840,000
Other operating costs		
Direct labour costs (3,000 units × $1,800)	$5,400,000	
Variable manufacturing overhead (3,000 units × $500)	1,500,000	
Variable selling and administrative expenses		
(2,800 units × $100)	280,000	
Fixed manufacturing overhead	1,200,000	
Fixed selling and administrative expenses	100,000	8,480,000
Net income		$ 6,360,000

(c) The difference in net income of $460,000 can be explained by the 200-unit difference between the number of units sold (2,800) versus the number of units produced (3,000). Under variable costing, the company defers $1,800 per unit of direct labour and $500 per unit of variable manufacturing overhead costs for the 200 units of ending inventory. This explains the total difference of $460,000 ($2,300 × 200 units) between net income under variable costing ($6,820,000) and net income under throughput costing ($6,360,000).

Summary of Study Objectives

1. *Explain the difference between absorption costing and variable costing.* Under absorption costing, fixed manufacturing costs are product costs. Under variable costing, fixed manufacturing costs are period costs.

2. *Discuss the effect that changes in the production level and sales level have on net income measured under absorption costing versus under variable costing.* If the production volume is greater than the sales volume, net income under absorption costing will be greater than net income under variable costing by the amount of fixed manufacturing costs included in the ending inventory. If the production volume is less than the sales volume, net income under absorption costing will be less than it is under variable costing by the amount of fixed manufacturing costs included in the units sold during the period that were not produced during the period.

3. *Discuss the advantages of variable costing versus absorption costing for management decision-making.* The use of variable costing is consistent with cost-volume-profit analysis and incremental analysis. Net income under variable costing is not affected by changes in production levels. Instead, it is closely tied to changes in sales. The presentation of fixed costs in the variable-costing approach makes it easier to identify fixed costs and to evaluate their impact on the company's profitability.

4. *Discuss the effect of a normal-costing method on income reported under absorption costing and variable costing (Appendix 8A).* Under absorption costing, fixed manufacturing overhead is allocated to the product costs based on a predetermined overhead rate instead of actual overhead costs, and the production volume variance is expensed to the cost of goods sold in the accounting period in which it occurs. Under variable costing, in contrast, the fixed manufacturing cost is still a period cost and is therefore expensed in the accounting period in which it occurs.

5. *Discuss the effect of the throughput-costing method on income reported under variable costing (Appendix 8A).* Under throughput costing, the product cost is only direct material costs, and inventory is valued using only direct material costs. All other manufacturing costs are treated as expenses in the accounting period in which they occur.

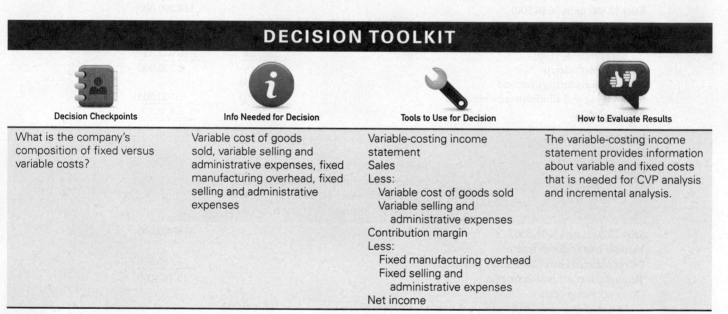

DECISION TOOLKIT

Decision Checkpoints	Info Needed for Decision	Tools to Use for Decision	How to Evaluate Results

What is the company's composition of fixed versus variable costs?	Variable cost of goods sold, variable selling and administrative expenses, fixed manufacturing overhead, fixed selling and administrative expenses	Variable-costing income statement
		Sales
		Less:
		  Variable cost of goods sold
		  Variable selling and
		    administrative expenses
		Contribution margin
		Less:
		  Fixed manufacturing overhead
		  Fixed selling and
		    administrative expenses
		Net income
			The variable-costing income statement provides information about variable and fixed costs that is needed for CVP analysis and incremental analysis.

Glossary

Absorption costing   A costing approach in which all manufacturing costs are charged to the product. (p. 312)

Throughput contribution   The difference between revenues and direct material costs for the units sold. (p. 325)

Throughput costing   A costing approach in which only direct material costs are product costs. Direct labour and variable and fixed manufacturing costs are period costs (expenses). (p. 325)

Variable costing   A costing approach in which only variable manufacturing costs are product costs. Fixed manufacturing costs are period costs (expenses). (p. 312)

Comprehensive Do It!

Taylor Enterprises produces birdhouses. In 2016, it began the year with no beginning inventory. During the year, it produced 10,000 birdhouses and sold 8,000 for $30 per house. Variable manufacturing costs were $9 per house produced (direct material $4, direct labour $3, and variable overhead $2); variable selling and administrative expenses were $4 per unit sold; fixed manufacturing costs were $60,000 in total and $6 per unit ($60,000 ÷ 10,000); and fixed selling and administrative costs were $20,000.

Instructions

(a) Prepare an income statement using absorption costing.
(b) Prepare an income statement using variable costing.
(c) Prepare an income statement using throughput costing.
(d) Show a calculation that explains the difference in net income under absorption costing and variable costing.
(e) Show a calculation that explains the difference in net income under variable costing and throughput costing.
(f) Suppose the accountant for Taylor Enterprises used normal costing rather than actual costing to calculate the cost of goods sold and ending inventory under absorption costing, and fixed manufacturing overhead is $60,000, based on budgeted volume of 12,000 units. Compare the results with those calculated in part (a) after expensing the volume variance to the cost of goods sold.

Solution to Comprehensive Do It!

(a)

TAYLOR ENTERPRISES
Income Statement
Year Ended 2016
Absorption Costing

Sales (8,000 units × $30)	$240,000
Cost of goods sold [8,000 units × ($9 + $6)]	120,000
Gross profit	120,000
Variable selling and administrative expenses (8,000 × $4)	32,000
Fixed selling and administrative expenses	20,000
Net income	$ 68,000

(b)

TAYLOR ENTERPRISES
Income Statement
Year Ended 2016
Variable Costing

Sales (8,000 units × $30)		$240,000
Variable cost of goods sold (8,000 × $9)	$72,000	
Variable selling and administrative expenses (8,000 × $4)	32,000	104,000
Contribution margin		136,000
Fixed manufacturing overhead	60,000	
Fixed selling and administrative expenses	20,000	80,000
Net income		$ 56,000

(*continued*)

Action Plan

- For absorption costing, manufacturing costs include variable materials and labour and overhead, as well as an allocated per-unit charge for the fixed manufacturing overhead.
- Recall that under variable costing, only variable manufacturing costs are treated as manufacturing costs.
- Recall that under throughput costing, only direct material costs are treated as manufacturing costs.
- For variable costing, subtract all fixed costs—both manufacturing overhead and selling and administrative expenses—as period costs.
- For throughput costing, subtract all other variable and fixed manufacturing costs as period costs. This includes direct labour, variable and fixed manufacturing overhead, and selling and administrative expenses.

(continued)

(c)

TAYLOR ENTERPRISES Income Statement Year Ended 2016 Throughput Costing		
Sales (8,000 units × $30)		$240,000
Variable cost of goods sold		
Inventory, January 1	$ 0	
Direct material costs (10,000 units × $4)	40,000	
Cost of goods available for sale	40,000	
Inventory, January 31 (2,000 units × $4)	8,000	
Variable cost of goods sold		32,000
Throughput contribution margin		208,000
Other operating costs		
Direct labour costs (10,000 × $3)	30,000	
Variable overhead costs (10,000 × $2)	20,000	
Variable selling and administrative expenses (8,000 × $4)	32,000	
Fixed manufacturing overhead	60,000	
Fixed selling and administrative expenses	20,000	
Total		162,000
Net income		$ 46,000

(d) The difference in net income of $12,000 can be explained by the 2,000-unit difference between the number of units sold (8,000) versus the number of units produced (10,000). Under absorption costing, the company defers $6 per unit of fixed manufacturing costs in the 2,000 units of ending inventory. This represents the total difference of $12,000 ($6 × 2,000 units) between the net income under variable costing ($56,000) and under absorption costing ($68,000).

(e) The difference in net income of $10,000 can be explained by the 2,000-unit difference between the number of units sold (8,000) versus the number of units produced (10,000). Under variable costing, the company defers $3 per unit of direct labour and $2 variable manufacturing overhead costs in the 2,000 units of ending inventory. This represents the total difference of $10,000 ($5 × 2,000 units) between the net income under variable costing ($56,000) and under throughput costing ($46,000).

(f) The company policy is to use the budgeted volume of 12,000 units to allocate the fixed overhead rate rather than the actual production volume of 10,000 units.

$$\text{Predetermined rate} = \$60,000 \text{ fixed overhead} \div$$
$$12,000 \text{ budgeted production volume} = \$5$$

Based on this rate, the absorption product cost per unit is as follows:

Direct materials	$ 4
Direct labour	3
Variable overhead	2
Fixed overhead predetermined rate	5
Total product cost per unit	$14

(continued)

(continued)

TAYLOR ENTERPRISES	
Income Statement	
Year Ended 2016	
Normal Costing	
Sales (8,000 units × 30)	$240,000
Cost of goods sold [8,000 units ($9 + $5)]	112,000
	128,000
Unfavourable volume variance [$5 × (12,000 units − 10,000 units)]	10,000
Gross profit	118,000
Variable selling and administrative expenses (8,000 × $4)	32,000
Fixed selling and administrative expenses	20,000
Net income	$ 66,000

We can reconcile the absorption-costing net income (see solution to part a) to the normal-costing net income as follows:

Absorption-costing net income	$68,000
Less ending inventory fixed manufacturing overhead (2,000 × $1)	$ 2,000
Normal-costing net income	$66,000

✔ the navigator

WileyPLUS

Self-Test, Brief Exercises, Exercises, Problems—Set A, and many more components are available for practice in WileyPlus.

Self-Study Questions

Answers are at the end of the chapter.

(The asterisk * indicates material discussed in the chapter appendix.)

(SO 1) 1. Fixed manufacturing overhead costs are recognized as
    (a) period costs under absorption costing.
    (b) product costs under absorption costing.
    (c) product costs under variable costing.
    (d) part of the ending inventory costs under both absorption and variable costing.

(SO 1, 2) 2. Net income calculated under absorption costing will be
    (a) higher than net income under variable costing in all cases.
    (b) equal to net income under variable costing in all cases.
    (c) higher than net income under variable costing when more units are produced than sold.
    (d) higher than net income under variable costing when fewer units are produced than sold.

(SO 3) 3. A company will be in compliance with GAAP when it prepares financial statements in accordance with
    (a) cost-volume-profit principles.
    (b) absorption-costing principles.
    (c) variable-costing principles.
    (d) all of the above methods.

(SO 2) 4. A manager can increase reported income by
    (a) producing more units than are sold under absorption costing.
    (b) producing fewer units than are sold under absorption costing.
    (c) producing more units than are sold under variable costing.
    (d) producing fewer units than are sold under variable costing.

(SO 2) 5. Gross profit is disclosed on an income statement prepared using
    (a) CVP analysis.
    (b) absorption costing.
    (c) variable costing.
    (d) all costing methods.

(SO 3) 6. When preparing internal reports, service companies
    (a) cannot benefit from variable costing, because they have no inventory.
    (b) cannot use variable costing.
    (c) can benefit from variable costing, because they have both fixed and variable costs.
    (d) Both (b) and (c) are correct.

(SO 3) 7. Using variable costing rather than absorption costing is an advantage to a company because
    (a) variable costing is consistent with cost-volume-profit and incremental analysis, which managers use for decision-making.
    (b) it agrees with the income information released to external users under GAAP.
    (c) it always produces higher net income.
    (d) it focuses on gross profit, which is the best indicator of a company's ability to meet income goals.

(SO 5) *8. Total manufacturing overhead is treated as a product cost when using
(a) absorption costing.
(b) throughput costing.
(c) variable costing.
(d) throughput costing and absorption costing.

(SO 5) *9. Variable manufacturing overhead is assigned to inventory when using
(a) absorption costing and variable costing.
(b) absorption costing and throughput costing.
(c) variable costing and throughput costing.
(d) absorption costing, variable costing, and throughput costing.

(SO 4) *10. The volume variance under the normal-costing method is calculated as
(a) the difference between budgeted fixed manufacturing overhead costs and assigned fixed manufacturing overhead costs.
(b) the sum of budgeted fixed manufacturing overhead costs and allocated fixed manufacturing overhead costs.
(c) the difference between budgeted fixed manufacturing overhead costs and actual fixed manufacturing overhead costs.
(d) the difference between actual fixed manufacturing overhead costs and assigned fixed manufacturing overhead costs.

Brief Exercises

(SO 1)
Identify costs as product costs or period costs under variable costing.

BE8-1 Determine whether each of the following costs would be classified as product costs or period costs under a variable-costing system:

	Product Cost	Period Cost
Commission fees for salespersons		
Glue for wooden chairs—variable		
Fabric for T-shirts		
Labour costs for producing TVs		
Factory rent expense—fixed		
Factory utility costs—variable		
Car mileage for salespersons		
Administrative expenses—fixed		
Administrative Internet connection fees		
Wages—assembly line		

(SO 1)
Identify costs as product costs or period costs under absorption costing.

BE8-2 Determine whether each of the following costs would be classified as product costs or period costs under an absorption-costing system.

	Product Cost	Period Cost
Commission fees for salespersons		
Glue for wooden chairs—variable		
Fabric for T-shirts		
Labour costs for producing TVs		
Factory rent expense—fixed		
Factory utility costs—variable		
Car mileage for salespersons		
Administrative expenses—fixed		
Administrative Internet connection fees		
Wages—assembly line		

(SO 5)
Identify costs as product costs or period costs under throughput costing.

*BE8-3 Determine whether each of the following costs would be classified as product costs or period costs under a throughput-costing system.

	Product Cost	Period Cost
Commission fees for salespersons		
Glue for wooden chairs—variable		
Fabric for T-shirts		
Labour costs for producing TVs		
Factory rent expense—fixed		
Factory utility costs—variable		
Car mileage for salespersons		
Administrative expenses—fixed		
Administrative Internet connection fees		
Wages—assembly line		

BE8-4 Large Orange Company produces basketballs. It incurred the following costs during the year:

Direct materials	$14,400
Direct labour	25,600
Fixed manufacturing overhead	12,000
Variable manufacturing overhead	29,400
Selling costs	21,000

What is the total product cost for the company under variable costing?

(SO 1) Calculate product costs under variable costing.

BE8-5 Information for Large Orange Company is given in BE8-4. What is the total product cost for the company under absorption costing?

(SO 1) Calculate product costs under absorption costing.

*BE8-6 Information for Large Orange Company is given in BE8-4. What is the total product cost for the company under throughput costing?

(SO 5) Calculate product costs under throughput costing.

*BE8-7 Burns Manufacturing incurred the following costs during the year: direct materials, $20 per unit; direct labour, $14 per unit; variable manufacturing overhead, $15 per unit; variable selling and administrative costs, $8 per unit; fixed manufacturing overhead, $128,000; and fixed selling and administrative costs, $10,000. Burns produced 8,000 units and sold 6,000 units. Determine the manufacturing cost per unit under (a) absorption costing, (b) variable costing, and (c) throughput costing.

(SO 1, 5) Determine the manufacturing cost per unit under the three costing approaches.

BE8-8 During 2016, Rafael Corp. produced 40,000 units and sold 40,000 for $15 per unit. Variable manufacturing costs were $6 per unit. Annual fixed manufacturing overhead was $80,000 ($2 per unit). Variable selling and administrative costs were $2 per unit sold, and fixed selling and administrative expenses were $20,000. Prepare a variable-costing income statement.

(SO 1) Prepare a variable-costing income statement.

*BE8-9 Information for Rafael Corp. is given in BE8-8. Suppose the accountant for Rafael Corp. uses normal costing and uses the budgeted volume of 50,000 units to allocate the fixed overhead rate rather than the actual production volume of 40,000 units. The company expenses production volume variance to cost of goods sold in the accounting period in which it occurs. (a) Calculate the manufacturing cost per unit and prepare a normal-costing income statement for the first year of operation. (b) Reconcile the difference in net income between the variable-costing and normal-costing methods.

(SO 4) Prepare a normal-costing income statement.

BE8-10 Information for Rafael Corp. is given in BE8-8. (a) Prepare an absorption-costing income statement. (b) Reconcile the difference between the net income under variable costing and the net income under absorption costing. That is, show a calculation that explains what causes the difference in net income between the two approaches.

(SO 1, 2) Prepare an absorption-costing income statement and reconcile the difference in net income under the two approaches.

BE8-11 Caspian Company produced 20,000 units and sold 18,000 during the current year. Under absorption costing, net income was $25,000. Fixed overhead was $190,000. Determine the net income under variable costing.

(SO 1, 2) Determine net income under variable costing.

Do It! Review

D8-12 Fresh Air Products manufactures and sells a variety of camping products. Recently the company opened a new plant to manufacture a deluxe portable cooking unit. Cost and sales data for the first month of operations are shown below:

(SO 1, 3) Calculate total product cost and prepare an income statement using absorption costing.

Beginning inventory	0 units
Units produced	12,000
Units sold	10,000
Manufacturing Costs	
Fixed overhead	$108,000
Variable overhead	$3 per unit
Direct labour	$12 per unit
Direct material	$30 per unit
Selling and administrative costs	
Fixed	$200,000
Variable	$4 per unit sold

The portable cooking unit sells for $110. Management is interested in the opening month's results and has asked for an income statement.

Instructions

Assuming the company uses absorption costing:

(a) Calculate the manufacturing cost per unit.

(b) Prepare an absorption-costing income statement for the first month of operation.

(SO 2, 3)
Calculate total product cost and prepare an income statement using variable costing.

D8-13   Information for Fresh Air Products is given in D8-12.

Instructions

(a) Assuming the company uses variable costing:

  1. Calculate the manufacturing cost per unit.

  2. Prepare a variable-costing income statement for the first month of operation.

(b) Reconcile the difference in net income between the absorption-costing and variable-costing methods.

(SO 1, 4)
Calculate total product cost and prepare an income statement using normal costing.

***D8-14**   Information for Fresh Air Products is given in D8-12.

Instructions

(a) Assume the company uses normal costing and uses the budgeted volume of 13,500 units to allocate the fixed overhead rate rather than the actual production volume of 12,000 units. The company expenses production volume variance to cost of goods sold in the accounting period in which it occurs. Do the following:

  1. Calculate the manufacturing cost per unit.

  2. Prepare a normal-costing income statement for the first month of operation.

(b) Reconcile the difference in net income between the absorption-costing and normal-costing methods.

(SO 1, 5)
Calculate total product cost and prepare an income statement using throughput costing.

***D8-15**   Information for Fresh Air Products is given in D8-12.

Instructions

(a) Assuming the company uses throughput costing:

  1. Calculate the manufacturing cost per unit.

  2. Prepare a throughput-costing income statement for the first month of operation.

(b) Reconcile the difference in net income between the variable-costing and throughput-costing methods.

Exercises

(SO 1, 5)
Calculate total product cost and prepare an income statement using variable costing and throughput costing.

***E8-16**   Wu Equipment Company manufactures and distributes industrial air compressors. The following data are available for the year ended December 31, 2016. The company had no beginning inventory. In 2016, it produced 1,500 units but sold only 1,200 units. The unit selling price was $4,500. Costs and expenses were as follows:

Variable costs per unit	
Direct materials	$ 800
Direct labour	1,500
Variable manufacturing overhead	300
Variable selling and administrative expenses	70
Annual fixed costs and expenses	
Manufacturing overhead	$1,200,000
Selling and administrative expenses	100,000

Instructions

(a) Calculate the manufacturing cost of one unit of product using variable costing.

(b) Prepare a 2016 income statement for Wu Company using variable costing.

(c) Calculate the manufacturing cost of one unit of product using throughput costing.

(d) Prepare a 2016 income statement for Wu Company using throughput costing.

(e) Reconcile the difference between variable-costing and throughput-costing net income.

(SO 1)
Prepare income statements under absorption costing and variable costing.

E8-17   Asian Windows manufactures a hand-painted bamboo window shade for standard-size windows. Production and sales data for 2016 are as follows:

Variable manufacturing costs	$40 per shade
Fixed manufacturing costs	$100,000
Variable selling and administrative expenses	$9 per shade
Fixed selling and administrative expenses	$250,000
Selling price	$90 per shade
Units produced	10,000 shades
Units sold	8,500 shades

Instructions

(a) Prepare an income statement using absorption costing.

(b) Prepare an income statement using variable costing.

E8-18 Information for Asian Windows is given in E8-17.

Instructions

(a) Assume the company uses normal costing and uses the budgeted volume of 8,000 units to allocate the fixed overhead rate rather than the actual production volume of 10,000 units. The company expenses production volume variance to cost of goods sold in the accounting period in which it occurs. Do the following:

    1. Calculate the manufacturing cost per unit.

    2. Prepare a normal-costing income statement for 2016.

(b) Reconcile the difference in net income between the absorption-costing and normal-costing methods.

(SO 1, 4)
Calculate total product cost and prepare an income statement using normal costing.

E8-19 Bob's Company builds custom fishing lures for sporting goods stores. In its first year of operations, 2016, the company incurred the following costs:

(SO 1, 3)
Calculate the product cost and prepare an income statement under variable costing.

Variable cost per unit	
Direct materials	$ 6.50
Direct labour	2.75
Variable manufacturing overhead	5.75
Variable selling and administrative expenses	3.90
Fixed costs for year	
Fixed manufacturing overhead	$285,000
Fixed selling and administrative expenses	240,100

Bob's Company sells the fishing lures for $25. During 2016, the company sold 80,000 lures and produced 95,000 lures.

Instructions

(a) Assuming the company uses variable costing, calculate Bob's manufacturing cost per unit for 2016.

(b) Prepare a variable-costing income statement for 2016.

(SO 1)
Calculate the product cost and prepare an income statement under absorption costing.

E8-20 Information for Bob's Company is provided in E8-19.

Instructions

(a) Assuming the company uses absorption costing, calculate Bob's manufacturing cost per unit for 2016.

(b) Prepare an absorption-costing income statement for 2016.

*E8-21** Information for Bob's Company is provided in E8-19.

Instructions

(a) Assume the company uses normal costing and uses the budgeted volume of 93,860 units to allocate the fixed overhead rate rather than the actual production volume of 95,000 units. The company expenses production volume variance to cost of goods sold in the accounting period in which it occurs. Do the following:

    1. Calculate the manufacturing cost per unit.

    2. Prepare a normal-costing income statement for 2016.

(b) Reconcile the difference in net income between the absorption-costing and normal-costing methods.

(SO 4)
Calculate the product cost and prepare an income statement under normal costing.

E8-22 Empey Manufacturing produces towels to be sold as souvenirs at sporting events throughout the world. Assume that units produced equalled units sold in 2016. The company's variable-costing income statement is as follows:

(SO 1, 2, 3)
Calculate the product cost under absorption costing and variable costing, prepare an absorption-costing income statement, and compare the usefulness of the variable-costing format versus the absorption-costing format.

EMPEY MANUFACTURING
Income Statement
Year Ended December 31, 2016
Variable Costing

Sales (260,700 units)		$521,400
Variable cost of goods sold	$255,486	
Variable selling expenses	31,284	
Variable administrative expenses	36,498	323,268
Contribution margin		198,132
Fixed manufacturing overhead	96,459	
Fixed selling expenses	38,500	
Fixed administrative expenses	42,625	177,584
Net income		$ 20,548

Unit selling price	$2.00
Variable costs per unit	
Direct material	$0.26
Direct labour	$0.34
Variable overhead	$0.38
Variable selling expenses	$0.12
Variable administrative expenses	$0.14

Instructions

(a) Calculate the manufacturing cost per towel under variable costing.

(b) Calculate the manufacturing cost per towel under absorption costing.

(c) Prepare an absorption-costing income statement for Empey Manufacturing.

(d) Explain why there is or is not a difference in the net income amounts in the two income statements.

(e) Explain why Empey Manufacturing Company might want to prepare both an absorption-costing income statement and a variable-costing income statement.

(SO 1, 2)

Determine the ending inventory under variable costing; determine whether absorption or variable costing would result in a higher net income.

E8-23 Ortiz Company produced 9,000 units during the past year but sold only 8,200 of the units. The following additional information is also available:

Direct materials used	$79,000
Direct labour incurred	30,000
Variable manufacturing overhead	21,500
Fixed manufacturing overhead	45,000
Fixed selling and administrative expenses	70,000
Variable selling and administrative expenses	10,000

There was no work in process inventory at the beginning of the year. Ortiz did not have any beginning finished goods inventory either.

Instructions

(a) Calculate Ortiz Company's finished goods inventory cost on December 31 under variable costing.

(b) Determine which costing method, absorption or variable, would show a higher net income for the year. By what amount?

(SO 1, 2)

Calculate the manufacturing cost under absorption and variable costing and explain the difference.

E8-24 Hardwood Inc. produces mostly wooden crates used for shipping products by ocean freighter. In 2016, Hardwood incurred the following costs:

Wood used	$54,000
Nails (considered insignificant and a variable expense)	350
Direct labour	43,000
Utilities for the plant: $1,500 each month, plus $0.50 for each kilowatt hour used each month	
Rent expense for plant for year	21,400

Assume Hardwood used an average of 500 kilowatt hours per month over the past year.

Instructions

(a) Calculate Hardwood's total manufacturing cost if it uses a variable-costing approach.

(b) Calculate Hardwood's total manufacturing cost if it uses an absorption-costing approach.

(c) Determine the reason for the difference between manufacturing costs under these two costing approaches.

(SO 1, 2, 5)

Calculate the manufacturing cost under absorption, variable, and throughput costing and explain the differences.

*E8-25 During its second year of operations, TGS Corporation produced 3,000 units and sold 2,800 units at $60 each. The beginning inventory comprised 100 units, and costs were unchanged from the previous year. Costs incurred during the second year were as follows:

Direct materials per unit produced	$ 8
Direct labour per unit produced	9
Variable overhead per unit produced	12
Variable selling and administrative costs per unit sold	3
Total fixed production overhead	18,000
Total fixed selling and administrative costs	6,000

Instructions

(a) Reconcile TGS's income based on absorption costing and variable costing.

(b) Reconcile TGS's income based on variable costing and throughput costing.

Problems: Set A

*P8-26A Blue Mountain Products manufactures and sells a variety of camping products. Recently, the company opened a new plant to manufacture a lightweight, self-standing tent. Cost and sales data for the first month of operations (June 2016) are as follows:

Manufacturing costs	
Fixed overhead	$200,000
Variable overhead	$4 per tent
Direct labour	$16 per tent
Direct material	$40 per tent
Beginning inventory	0 tents
Tents produced	10,000
Tents sold	9,000
Selling and administrative costs	
Fixed	$400,000
Variable	$6 per tent sold

The tent sells for $150. Management is interested in the opening month's results and has asked for an income statement.

Instructions
(a) Assuming the company uses absorption costing:
  1. Calculate the manufacturing cost per unit.
  2. Prepare an absorption-costing income statement for the month of June 2016.
(b) Assuming the company uses variable costing:
  1. Calculate the manufacturing cost per unit.
  2. Prepare a variable-costing income statement for the month of June 2016.
(c) Reconcile the difference in net income between the absorption-costing and variable-costing methods.
(d) Assuming the company uses throughput costing:
  1. Calculate the manufacturing cost per unit.
  2. Prepare a throughput-costing income statement for the month of June 2016.
(e) Reconcile the difference in net income between the variable-costing and throughput-costing methods.

(SO 1, 2, 5)
Calculate the product cost; prepare an income statement under variable costing, absorption costing, and throughput costing; and reconcile the differences.

(a) (1) $80
    (2) NI $176,000

(b) (1) $60
    (2) NI $156,000

P8-27A AFN Company produces plastic that is used for injection-moulding applications such as gears for small motors. In 2016, the first year of operations, AFN Company produced 4,000 tonnes of plastic and sold 3,500 tonnes. In 2017, the production and sales results were exactly reversed. In each year, the selling price per tonne was $2,000; variable manufacturing costs were 15% of the sales price for the units produced; variable selling expenses were 10% of the selling price of the units sold; fixed manufacturing costs were $2.8 million; and fixed administrative expenses were $500,000.

Instructions
(a) Prepare comparative income statements for each year using variable costing. (Use the format from Illustration 8-5.)
(b) Prepare comparative income statements for each year using absorption costing. (Use the format from Illustration 8-4.)
(c) Reconcile the differences in the income from operations each year under the two costing approaches.
(d) ✏️➤ Comment on the effects that the production and sales levels have on net income under the two costing approaches.

(SO 1, 2, 3)
Prepare income statements under absorption costing and variable costing for a company with beginning inventory.

2017 NI:
(a) $2,700,000
(b) $2,350,000

P8-28A Basic Electric Motors is a division of Basic Electric Products Corporation. The division manufactures and sells an electric switch used in a wide variety of applications. During the coming year, it expects to sell 200,000 units for $8 per unit. Ester Madden is the division manager. She is considering producing either 200,000 or 250,000 units during the period. Other information is as follows:

Division Information for 2016	
Beginning inventory	0
Expected sales in units	200,000
Selling price per unit	$8
Variable manufacturing cost per unit	$3
Fixed manufacturing cost (total)	$500,000
Fixed manufacturing overhead costs per unit	
Based on 200,000 units	$2.50 per unit ($500,000 ÷ 200,000)
Based on 250,000 units	$2.00 per unit ($500,000 ÷ 250,000)
Manufacturing cost per unit	
Based on 200,000 units	$5.50 per unit ($3 variable + $2.50 fixed)
Based on 250,000 units	$5.00 per unit ($3 variable + $2 fixed)
Variable selling and administrative expenses	$0.50 per unit
Fixed selling and administrative expenses (total)	$12,000

(SO 1, 2, 3)
Prepare absorption- and variable-costing income statements, reconcile the differences between absorption- and variable-costing income statements when sales and production levels change, and discuss the usefulness of absorption costing versus variable costing.

Instructions

(a) 250,000 produced
NI: $488,000

(b) 250,000 produced
NI: $388,000

(a) Prepare an absorption-costing income statement, with one column showing the results if 200,000 units are produced and one column showing the results if 250,000 units are produced.

(b) Prepare a variable-costing income statement, with one column showing the results if 200,000 units are produced and one column showing the results if 250,000 units are produced.

(c) Reconcile the difference in the net incomes under the two approaches and explain what causes this difference.

(d) ⬤▬▬▶ Discuss the usefulness of the variable-costing income statements versus the absorption-costing income statements for decision-making and for evaluating the manager's performance.

(SO 1, 2, 3, 5)
Prepare an income statement under variable costing, absorption costing, and throughput costing and reconcile the differences; discuss the usefulness of absorption costing versus variable costing.

*P8-29A   Alta Products Ltd. has just created a new division to manufacture and sell DVD players. The facility is highly automated and thus has high monthly fixed costs, as shown in the following schedule of budgeted monthly costs. This schedule was prepared based on an expected monthly production volume of 2,000 units.

Manufacturing costs	
Variable costs per unit	
Direct materials	$ 30
Direct labour	40
Variable overhead	10
Total fixed overhead	70,000
Selling and administrative costs	
Variable	6% of sales
Fixed	$50,000
During August 2016, the following activity was recorded:	
Units produced	2,000
Units sold	1,700
Selling price per unit	$ 175

Instructions

(a) Net income $34,150

(b) Net income $23,650

(a) Prepare an income statement for the month ended August 31, 2016, under absorption costing.

(b) Prepare an income statement for the month ended August 31, 2016, under variable costing.

(c) Reconcile the absorption-costing and variable-costing income figures for the month.

(d) Prepare an income statement for the month ended August 31, 2016, under throughput costing.

(e) Reconcile the variable-costing income and throughput-costing income figures for the month.

(f) What are some of the arguments in favour of using variable costing? What are some of the arguments in favour of using absorption costing?

(adapted from CGA-Canada, now CPA Canada)

(SO 4)
Calculate the product cost and prepare an income statement under normal costing.

(a) 1. Unit cost: $108

*P8-30A   Information for Alta Products Ltd. is provided in P8-29A.

Instructions

(a) Assume the company uses normal costing and uses the budgeted volume of 2,500 units to allocate the fixed overhead rate rather than the actual production volume of 2,000 units. The company expenses production volume variance to cost of goods sold in the accounting period in which it occurs. Do the following:

1. Calculate the manufacturing cost per unit.

2. Prepare a normal-costing income statement for the month ended August 31, 2016.

(b) Reconcile the difference in net income between the absorption-costing and normal-costing methods.

(SO 1, 2, 3)
Calculate product cost, prepare income statements under variable costing and absorption costing, and reconcile the difference when sales and production levels change.

P8-31A   Amanjeet Chinmayi left her job as the production manager of a medium-sized firm two years ago to join a new firm that was manufacturing a revolutionary type of fitness equipment. Amanjeet was made the general manager at the start of operations, and the firm seemed to be doing extremely well. The president was extremely pleased with the company's first-year performance and, at the beginning of the second year, promised Amanjeet a $20,000 bonus if the company's net income were to increase by 25% in year 2.

During year 2, Amanjeet sold 25% more units than she had in year 1 and was so confident that she would receive her bonus that she bought non-refundable airline tickets to Europe for her husband Leo, her three sons, and herself.

At the end of year 2, Amanjeet received the income statement, and it showed that the company's income had decreased from year 1 even though it had sold considerably more units. Amanjeet did not get along very well with the accountant and felt that he had deliberately distorted the financial statements for year 2.

Amanjeet received the following reports:

	Year 1	Year 2
Production (in units)	6,000	3,000
Sales (in units)	4,000	5,000
Unit selling price	$ 500	$ 500
Unit costs		
Variable manufacturing	$ 300	$ 300
Variable selling	20	20
Fixed manufacturing	180,000	210,000
Fixed selling	100,000	140,000
Income Statement—(FIFO)		
Sales	$ 2,000,000	$2,500,000
Cost of goods sold	1,320,000	1,770,000
Gross margin	680,000	730,000
Selling expenses	180,000	240,000
Net income	$ 500,000	$ 490,000

Instructions

(a) Prepare variable-costing income statements for years 1 and 2.

(b) For years 1 and 2, reconcile the differences between the net income as determined by the income statements you have prepared in part (a) and the income statements prepared by the accountant.

(c) Explain to Amanjeet why she lost her $20,000 bonus. Which income statement more accurately measures performance? Why?

(adapted from CGA Canada, now CPA Canada)

(a) Year 1 NI: $440,000;
Year 2 NI: $550,000

*P8-32A   Xantra Corp. is a manufacturer of specialty in-line skates. The operating results for 2016 are as follows:

Units produced	20,000 pairs
Units sold	18,000 pairs
Selling price	$200 per pair

Production information:

Direct materials	$1,000,000
Direct labour	750,000
Variable manufacturing overhead	450,000
Fixed manufacturing overhead	800,000
Variable marketing costs	180,000
Fixed marketing costs	200,000

There was no beginning finished goods inventory.

(SO 1, 2, 3, 5)
Calculate the product cost; prepare income statements under variable costing, absorption costing, and throughput costing; and reconcile the differences.

Instructions

(a) Prepare an absorption-costing income statement.

(b) Prepare a variable-costing income statement.

(c) Reconcile the net incomes under absorption costing and variable costing.

(d) Calculate the break-even point in sales units (pairs of skates) under the current cost structure.

(e) Prepare a throughput-costing income statement.

(f) Reconcile the net incomes under throughput costing and variable costing.

(adapted from CGA Canada, now CPA Canada)

(a) NI: $520,000
(b) NI: $440,000

(d) 12,500 units
(e) NI: $320,000

*P8-33A   Information for Xantra Corp. is provided in P8-32A.

Instructions

(a) Assume the company uses normal costing and uses the budgeted volume of 25,000 pairs to allocate the fixed overhead rate rather than the actual production volume of 20,000 pairs. The company expenses production volume variance to cost of goods sold in the accounting period in which it occurs. Do the following:

1. Calculate the manufacturing cost per unit.

2. Prepare a normal-costing income statement for 2016.

(b) Reconcile the difference in net income between the absorption-costing and normal-costing methods.

(SO 4)
Calculate the product cost and prepare an income statement under normal costing.

(a) 1. Unit cost: $142
2. NI: $504,000

P8-34A   Sun Company, a wholly owned subsidiary of Guardian, Inc., produces and sells three main product lines. At the beginning of 2015, the president of Sun Company presented the budget to the parent company and accepted a commitment to contribute $15,800 to Guardian's consolidated profit in 2016. The president was confident that the year's profit would exceed the budget target, since the monthly sales reports had shown that sales for the year would be 10% more than what had been predicted in the budget. The president is both disturbed and confused when the controller presents an adjusted forecast as at November 30, 2016, indicating that profits will be 11% under budget. The two forecasts are presented below:

(SO 1, 2, 3)
Explain variable costing and absorption costing and reconcile the differences when sales and production levels change.

SUN COMPANY
Forecasts of Operating Results

	January 1, 2016	November 30, 2016
Sales	$268,000	$294,800
Cost of sales	212,000*	233,200
Gross margin	56,000	61,600
Overapplied (underapplied) fixed manufacturing overhead	0	(6,000)
Actual gross margin	56,000	55,600
Selling expenses	13,400	14,740
Administrative expenses	26,800	26,800
Total operating expenses	40,200	41,540
Earnings before tax	$ 15,800	$ 14,060

* Includes fixed manufacturing overhead of $30,000.

There have been no sales price changes or product-mix shifts since the January 1, 2016, forecast. Variable costs have remained constant throughout the year. The only cost that has varied in the income statement is the underapplied manufacturing overhead. This happened because the company worked only 16,000 machine hours during 2016 (budgeted machine hours were 20,000) as a result of a shortage of raw materials when its main supplier was closed by a strike. Fortunately, Sun Company's finished goods inventory was large enough to fill all sales orders received.

Instructions
(a) Analyze and explain why profit has declined in spite of increased sales and control over costs.
(b) What plan, if any, could Sun Company adopt during December to improve the reported profit at year end? Explain your answer.
(c) Explain and illustrate how Sun Company could use a different internal cost reporting procedure that would not result in the confusing effect of the procedure it currently uses.

(adapted from CMA Canada, now CPA Canada)

(SO 1, 2, 3)
Prepare income statements under variable costing and absorption costing and reconcile the differences when sales and production levels change; discuss the usefulness of absorption costing versus variable costing.

P8-35A The Daniels Tool & Die Corporation has been in existence for a little over three years. The company's sales have been increasing each year as it builds a reputation. The company manufactures dies to its customers' specifications and therefore uses a job-order cost system. Factory overhead is applied to the jobs based on direct labour hours—the absorption-costing (full) method. Overapplied or underapplied overhead is treated as an adjustment to cost of goods sold. The company's income statements and other data for the last two years are as follows:

DANIELS TOOL & DIE CORPORATION
2015–2016 Comparative Income Statements

	2015	2016
Sales	$840,000	$1,015,000
Cost of goods sold		
Finished goods, January 1	25,000	18,000
Cost of goods manufactured	548,000	657,600
Total available	573,000	675,600
Finished goods, December 31	18,000	14,000
Cost of goods sold before overhead adjustment	555,000	661,600
Underapplied factory overhead	36,000	14,400
Cost of goods sold	591,000	676,000
Gross profit	249,000	339,000
Selling expenses	82,000	95,000
Administrative expenses	70,000	75,000
Total operating expenses	152,000	170,000
Operating income	$ 97,000	$ 169,000

Daniels Tool & Die Corporation Inventory Balances

	January 1, 2015	December 31, 2016	December 31, 2017
Raw material	$22,000	$30,000	$10,000
Work in process	$40,000	$48,000	$64,000
Direct labour hours (used in WIP)	1,335	1,600	2,100
Finished goods	$25,000	$18,000	$14,000
Direct labour hours (used in FG)	1,450	1,050	820

Daniels used the same predetermined overhead rate in applying overhead to its production orders in both 2015 and 2016. The rate was based on the following estimates:

Fixed factory overhead	$ 25,000
Variable factory overhead	$155,000
Direct labour hours	25,000
Direct labour costs	$150,000

In 2015 and 2016, the actual direct labour hours used were 20,000 and 23,000, respectively. Raw materials put into production were $292,000 in 2015 and $370,000 in 2016. The actual fixed overhead was $42,300 for 2015 and $37,400 for 2016, and the planned direct labour rate was the direct labour achieved.

For both years, all of the administrative costs were fixed. The variable portion of the selling expenses results from a 5% commission that is paid as a percentage of the sales revenue.

Instructions

(a) For the year ended December 31, 2016, prepare a revised income statement for Daniels Tool & Die Corporation using the variable-costing method.

(b) Reconcile the difference in operating income between Daniels Tool & Die Corporation's 2016 absorption-costing income statement and the revised 2016 income statement prepared under variable costing.

(c) Describe both the advantages and disadvantages of using variable costing.

(adapted from CMA Canada, now CPA Canada)

(a) Operating income
$168,730

Problems: Set B

*P8-36B   SpongeFun Products manufactures and sells a variety of swimming products. Recently, the company opened a new plant to manufacture a lightweight, inflatable boat. Cost and sales data for 2016 are shown below:

(SO 1, 2, 5)
Calculate the product cost; prepare income statements under variable costing, absorption costing, and throughput costing; and reconcile the differences.

Manufacturing costs	
Fixed overhead costs	$150,000
Variable overhead	$5 per boat
Direct labour	$10 per boat
Direct materials	$10 per boat
Beginning inventory	0 boats
Boats produced	50,000
Boats sold	46,000
Selling and administrative costs	
Fixed	$300,000
Variable	$8 per boat sold

The boat sells for $60. Management is interested in the first year's results and has asked for an income statement.

Instructions

(a) Assuming the company uses absorption costing:
   1. Calculate the production cost per unit.
   2. Prepare an income statement for 2016.

(a) (1) $28
    (2) NI $804,000

(b) Assuming the company uses variable costing:
   1. Calculate the production cost per unit.
   2. Prepare an income statement for 2016.

(b) (1) $25
    (2) NI $792,000

(c) Reconcile the difference in net income between the absorption-costing and variable-costing methods.

(d) Assuming the company uses throughput costing:
   1. Calculate the manufacturing cost per unit.
   2. Prepare a throughput-costing income statement for 2016.

(d) (1) $10
    (2) NI $732,000

(e) Reconcile the difference in net income between the variable-costing and throughput-costing methods.

*P8-37B   Information for SpongeFun Products is provided in P8-36B.

(SO 4)
Calculate the product cost and prepare an income statement under normal costing.

Instructions

(a) Assume the company uses normal costing and uses the budgeted volume of 60,000 units to allocate the fixed overhead rate rather than the actual production volume of 50,000 units. The company expenses production volume variance to cost of goods sold in the accounting period in which it occurs. Do the following:
   1. Calculate the manufacturing cost per unit.
   2. Prepare a normal-costing income statement for 2016.

(b) Reconcile the difference in net income between the absorption-costing and normal-costing methods.

(b) Difference: $2,000

(SO 1, 2, 3)
Prepare income
statements under
absorption costing and
variable costing for a
company with begin-
ning inventory.

2016 NI:
(a) $2,250,000
(b) $2,500,000
2017 NI:
(a) $3,060,000
(b) $2,810,000

P8-38B Zaki Metal Company produces the steel wire that is used for the production of paper clips. In 2016, the first year of operations, Zaki produced 60,000 km of wire and sold 50,000 km. In 2017, the production and sales results were exactly reversed. In each year, the selling price per kilometre was $120; variable manufacturing costs were 25% of the sales price of the units produced; variable selling expenses were $9 per kilometre sold; fixed manufacturing costs were $1.5 million; and fixed administrative expenses were $300,000.

Instructions
(a) Prepare income statements for each year using variable costing. (Use the format from Illustration 8-5.)
(b) Prepare income statements for each year using absorption costing. (Use the format from Illustration 8-4.)
(c) Reconcile the differences for each year in income from operations under the two costing approaches.
(d) ✏▷ Comment on the effects that the production and sales levels have on net income under the two costing approaches.

(SO 1, 2, 3)
Prepare absorption-
and variable-costing
income statements;
reconcile the differ-
ences between the two
income statements
when sales and pro-
duction levels change;
discuss the usefulness
of the two approaches
to costing.

(a) 90,000 units:
NI $550,000

(b) 90,000 units:
NI $370,000

P8-39B Harrison Pumps is a division of Liverpool Controls Corporation. The division manufactures and sells a pump that is used in a wide variety of applications. During the coming year, it expects to sell 60,000 units for $30 per unit. Imran Qureshi manages the division. He is considering producing either 60,000 or 90,000 units during the period. Other infor-mation is as follows:

Division Information for 2016	
Beginning inventory	0
Expected sales in units	60,000
Selling price per unit	$30
Variable manufacturing cost per unit	$12
Fixed manufacturing overhead cost (total)	$540,000
Fixed manufacturing overhead costs per unit	
Based on 60,000 units	$9 per unit ($540,000 ÷ 60,000)
Based on 90,000 units	$6 per unit ($540,000 ÷ 90,000)
Manufacturing cost per unit	
Based on 60,000 units	$21 per unit ($12 variable + $9 fixed)
Based on 90,000 units	$18 per unit ($12 variable + $6 fixed)
Variable selling and administrative expenses	$2 per unit
Fixed selling and administrative expenses (total)	$50,000

Instructions
(a) Prepare an absorption-costing income statement, with one column showing the results if 60,000 units are produced and one column showing the results if 90,000 units are produced.
(b) Prepare a variable-costing income statement, with one column showing the results if 60,000 units are produced and one column showing the results if 90,000 units are produced.
(c) Reconcile the difference in net incomes under the two approaches and explain what causes this difference.
(d) ✏▷ Discuss the usefulness of the variable-costing income statements versus the absorption-costing income statements for decision-making and for evaluating the manager's performance.

(SO 1, 2, 3, 5)
Calculate the product
cost, prepare income
statements under
variable costing and
absorption costing,
and reconcile the
differences when sales
and production levels
change.

(a) Total NI = $560,000

(b) Total NI = $560,000

*P8-40B Allerdyce Corporation Ltd. (ACL) prepares external financial statements using absorption costing and internal financial statements using variable costing. You have the following information for the operations of ACL for the past two years:

	2015	2016
Sales in units (@ $35 per unit)	25,000	35,000
Production in units	30,000	30,000
Variable production costs per unit	$ 20	$ 20
Fixed production costs	$120,000	$120,000
Fixed marketing costs	$ 50,000	$ 50,000
Beginning inventory	0	

Instructions
(a) Prepare absorption-costing income statements for the years ended December 31, 2015, and 2016. Include a column for totals for the two years.
(b) Prepare variable-costing income statements for the years ended December 31, 2015, and 2016. Include a column for totals for the two years.
(c) Reconcile the year-to-year differences in net income under the absorption-costing and variable-costing methods.

(adapted from CGA-Canada, now CPA Canada)

P8-41B The vice-president of Abscorp Ltd. is not happy. Sales have been rising steadily, but profits have been falling. In September 2016, Abscorp had record sales, but the lowest profits ever. The results for the months of July, August, and September 2016 follow:

(SO 1, 2, 3)
Calculate the product cost, prepare income statements under variable costing and absorption costing, and reconcile the differences when sales and production levels change.

ABSCORP LTD.
Comparative Monthly Income Statements
(in thousands)

	July	August	September
Sales (@ $25 per unit)	$1,750	$1,875	$2,000
Less cost of goods sold			
Opening inventory	80	320	400
Costs applied to production			
Variable manufacturing (@ $9 per unit)	765	720	540
Fixed manufacturing overhead	595	560	420
Cost of goods manufactured	1,360	1,280	960
Goods available for sale	1,440	1,600	1,360
Less ending inventory	320	400	80
Cost of goods sold	1,120	1,200	1,280
Underapplied (overapplied) fixed overhead	(35)	0	140
Adjusted cost of goods sold	1,085	1,200	1,420
Gross margin	665	675	580
Less selling and administrative expenses	620	650	680
Net income (loss)	$ 45	$ 25	$ (100)

You have been asked to explain to the vice-president that the problem is more a matter of appearance than reality by reinterpreting the results in a variable-costing format. You obtain the following information that will help you:

	July	August	September
Production	85,000 units	80,000 units	60,000 units
Sales	70,000	75,000	80,000

Additional information about the company's operations is as follows:

- There were 5,000 units of finished goods in the opening inventory on July 1, 2016.
- Fixed manufacturing overhead costs totalled $1,680,000 per quarter and were incurred evenly throughout the quarter. The fixed manufacturing overhead cost is applied to the units of production based on a budgeted production volume of 80,000 units per month.
- Variable selling and administrative expenses are $6 per unit sold. The remaining selling and administrative expenses on the comparative monthly income statements are fixed.
- The company uses a FIFO cost flow assumption. Work in process inventories are small enough to be ignored.

Instructions
(a) Calculate the monthly break-even point under variable costing.
(b) 1. Calculate the net income for each month under variable costing.
   2. Reconcile the variable-costing and absorption-costing net incomes for each month.
   3. Explain why profits have not been more closely related to changes in the sales volume.

(adapted from CGA-Canada, now CPA Canada)

(a) 76,000 units or
    $1,900,000
(b) 1. July: $(60,000)
       Aug.: $(10,000)
       Sept.: $40,000

P8-42B Boat Refit Inc. produces and sells custom parts for powerboats. The company uses a costing system based on actual costs. Selected accounting and production information for fiscal 2016 is as follows:

(SO 1, 2, 3)
Calculate the product cost contribution margin under variable costing and the gross margin under absorption costing.

Net income (under absorption costing)	$ 400,000
Sales	$3,400,000
Fixed factory overhead	$ 600,000
Fixed selling and administrative costs (all costs are fixed)	$ 400,000
Net income (under variable costing)	$ 310,000
Units produced	2,000
Units sold	?

Boat Refit had no work in process inventory at either the beginning or the end of fiscal 2016. As well, the company did not have any finished goods inventory at the beginning of the fiscal year.

Instructions
(a) Calculate the units sold in fiscal 2016.
(b) Calculate the total contribution margin under variable costing.

(a) 1,700 units
(b) $1,310,000

(c) $800,000
(d) $1,229.41
(e) $1,529.41

(c) Calculate the gross margin under absorption costing.
(d) Calculate the cost per unit sold under variable costing.
(e) Calculate the cost per unit sold under absorption costing.

(adapted from CGA-Canada, now CPA Canada)

(SO 1)
Prepare an income statement under variable costing; discuss the advantages of variable costing over absorption costing.

P8-43B   Wingfoot Co. began operations on July 1, 2015. By the end of its first fiscal year, ended June 30, 2016, Wingfoot had sold 10,000 wingers. Selected data on operations for the year ended June 30, 2016, follow. (Any balance sheet figures are as at June 30, 2016.)

Selling price	$100
Wingers produced	18,000
Ending work in process	0
Total manufacturing overhead	$15,000
Wage rate	$8 per hour
Machine hours used	9,000
Wages payable	$20,000
Direct materials costs	$10 per kilogram
Selling and administrative expenses	$40,000

Additional information:

1. Each winger requires 2 kg of direct materials, 0.5 machine hours, and one direct labour hour.
2. Except for machinery depreciation of $5,000 and a $1,000 miscellaneous fixed cost, all manufacturing overhead is variable.
3. Except for $4,000 in advertising expenses, all selling and administrative expenses are variable.
4. The tax rate is 40%.

Instructions

Net income = $401,400

Assume that the company uses variable costing and prepare a contribution-method income statement in good form for the year ended June 30, 2016.

(adapted from CGA-Canada, now CPA Canada)

(SO 1, 2, 3)
Calculate the product cost; prepare income statements under variable costing and absorption costing, and reconcile the differences when sales and production levels change; discuss the usefulness of absorption costing versus variable costing.

P8-44B   Portland Optics, Inc., specializes in manufacturing lenses for large telescope cameras used in space exploration. Since the specifications for the lenses are determined by the customer and vary considerably, the company uses a job-order costing system. It applies factory overhead to jobs based on direct labour hours using the absorption (full) costing method. Portland's predetermined overhead rates for 2015 and 2016 were based on the following estimates:

	2015	2016
Direct labour hours	32,500	44,000
Direct labour cost	$325,000	$462,000
Fixed factory overhead	$130,000	$176,000
Variable factory overhead	$162,500	$198,000

Marie-Michelle David, Portland's controller, would like to use variable costing for internal reporting since she believes statements prepared using variable costing are more appropriate for making product decisions. In order to explain the benefits of variable costing to the other members of Portland's management team, Marie-Michelle plans to convert the company's income statement from absorption costing to variable costing. She has gathered the following information, along with a copy of Portland's comparative income statement for the years 2015 and 2016.

PORTLAND OPTICS, INC.
Comparative Income Statement
Years 2015–2016

	2015	2016
Net sales	$1,140,000	$1,520,000
Cost of goods sold		
Finished goods, January 1	16,000	25,000
Cost of goods manufactured	720,000	976,000
Total available	736,000	1,001,000
Finished goods, December 31	25,000	14,000
Cost of goods sold before overhead adjustment	711,000	987,000
Overhead adjustment	12,000	7,000
Cost of goods sold	723,000	994,000
Gross profit	417,000	526,000
Selling expenses	150,000	190,000
Administrative expenses	160,000	187,000
Total operating expenses	310,000	377,000
Operating income	$ 107,000	$ 149,000

Portland's actual manufacturing data for the two years are as follows:

	2015	2016
Direct labour hours	30,000	42,000
Direct labour cost	$300,000	$435,000
Raw materials used	$140,000	$210,000
Fixed factory overhead	$132,000	$175,000

The company's actual inventory balances were as follows:

	Dec. 31, 2014	Dec. 31, 2015	Dec. 31, 2016
Raw material	$32,000	$36,000	$18,000
Work in process			
Costs	$44,000	$34,000	$60,000
Direct labour hours	1,800	1,400	2,500
Finished goods			
Costs	$16,000	$25,000	$14,000
Direct labour hours	700	1,080	550

For both years, all administrative costs were fixed. A portion of the selling expenses was variable as it resulted from an 8% commission paid on net sales. Portland reports any over- or underapplied overhead as an adjustment to cost of goods sold.

Instructions

(a) For the year ended December 31, 2016, prepare the revised income statement for Portland Optics, Inc., using the variable-costing method. Be sure to include the contribution margin on the revised income statement.
(b) Describe two advantages of using variable costing rather than absorption costing.

(a) $146,720

(adapted from CMA Canada, now CPA Canada)

Cases

C8-45 ComfortCraft manufactures swivel seats for customized vans. It currently manufactures 20,000 seats per year, which it sells for $680 per seat. It incurs variable costs of $340 per seat and fixed costs of $4,420,000. It is considering automating the upholstery process, which is now largely manual. It estimates that if it does this, its fixed costs will be $5 million, and its variable costs will drop to $280 per seat.

Instructions

(a) Prepare a variable-costing income statement based on current activity.

(b) Calculate the contribution margin ratio, break-even point in dollars, margin of safety ratio, and degree of operating leverage based on current activity.
(c) Prepare a variable-costing income statement assuming that the company invests in the automated upholstery system.
(d) Calculate the contribution margin ratio, break-even point in dollars, margin of safety ratio, and degree of operating leverage assuming the company implements the new upholstery system.
(e) Discuss the implications of adopting the new system.

C8-46 Big Sports Manufacturing produces basketballs used for indoor or outdoor games. The company has had significant troubles over the past few years, as the number of competitors in the basketball market has increased dramatically. Recently, the company was forced to cut back production in order to decrease its rising inventory level. The following is a list of costs for the company in 2016:

Variable costs per unit	
Rubber	$ 2.75
Other materials—indirect	1.40
Ball makers—direct labour	5.60
Factory electricity usage	0.50
Factory water usage	0.15
Other labour—indirect	0.27
Selling and administrative expenses	0.40
Fixed costs per year	
Factory property taxes	$120,000
Factory sewer usage	50,000
Factory electricity usage	40,000
Selling and administrative expenses	83,000

Big Sports Manufacturing had an ending inventory of 85,000 basketballs in 2015. For these units, the fixed manufacturing overhead cost was $4.00 per unit and variable manufacturing costs were $9.67 per unit. In 2016, the company produced 35,000 basketballs, sold 72,500 basketballs, and had an ending inventory of 47,500 units. The basketballs sold for $18 each. Big Sports uses the FIFO method.

Instructions

(a) Calculate Big Sports' manufacturing cost per unit under a variable-costing system.
(b) Prepare a variable-costing income statement for 2016.
(c) Calculate the manufacturing cost per unit under a throughput-costing system.
(d) Prepare a throughput-costing income statement for 2016. Assume that increased costs in 2016 are related to variable costs other than materials.
(e) Calculate Big Sports' manufacturing cost per unit under absorption costing.
(f) Prepare an absorption-costing income statement for 2016.
(g) Big Sports' chief financial officer, Mr. Swetkowski, is contemplating the benefits of using the absorption-costing and

variable-costing approaches. He has asked you to perform a variety of tasks to help him analyze the differences between the two approaches:

1. Reconcile the differences between the income values of the two approaches.
2. Mr. Swetkowski has heard that some basic managerial tasks can be better performed when variable costing is used. Calculate the break-even point in units for the company in 2016 using the variable-costing data.
3. Mr. Swetkowski has been very impressed with the variable-costing techniques that he has seen so far. He has been thinking of eliminating absorption costing for the company. What do you think of this idea?

C8-47 The Wei Nan Company manufactures and sells personal organizers. The following are the operating data for the company for 2015 and 2016:

	2015	2016
Units produced	60,000	50,000
Units sold	54,000	54,000
Selling price per unit	$250	$250
Variable costs per unit		
Direct materials	$80	$80
Direct labour	40	40
Variable overhead	35	35
Selling expenses	30	30
Fixed manufacturing overhead (total)	$2,500,000	$2,500,000
Fixed selling and administrative expenses (total)	$ 300,000	$ 300,000

There was no beginning inventory on January 1, 2015. The company used the FIFO method to calculate the cost of inventories. Ignore income taxes.

Instructions

(a) Prepare income statements for 2015 and 2016 using the absorption-costing method.
(b) Prepare income statements for 2015 and 2016 using the variable-costing method.
(c) Reconcile the absorption-costing and variable-costing net income figures for 2015 and 2016.
(d) Prepare income statements for 2015 and 2016 using the throughput-costing method.
(e) Reconcile the throughput-costing and variable-costing net income figures for 2015 and 2016.

(adapted from CGA-Canada, now CPA Canada)

C8-48 DDD Golf Ltd. produces and sells special golf balls for $20 for a pack of three. In May 2016, the company manufactured 30,000 packs (its normal volume) and sold 28,000 packs. The beginning inventory on May 1, 2016, was 5,000 packs. Production information for May 2016 is as follows:

Direct manufacturing labour per pack	15 minutes
Fixed selling and administrative costs	$40,000
Fixed manufacturing overhead	$132,000
Direct materials costs per pack	$2
Direct labour rate per hour	$24
Variable manufacturing overhead per pack	$4
Variable selling expenses per pack	$2

Instructions

(a) Calculate the total cost per pack under both absorption and variable costing.
(b) Prepare income statements in good form for the month ended May 31, 2016, under absorption and variable costing.
(c) Reconcile the operating income calculated under absorption costing with the operating income calculated under variable costing. Assume that April's costs were the same as those of May.

(adapted from CGA-Canada, now CPA Canada)

C8-49 The vice-president for sales of Huber Corporation has received the following income statement for November, which was prepared on a variable-costing system. The firm has just adopted variable costing for its internal reporting.

HUBER CORPORATION
Income Statement
For the Month of November
(in thousands)

Sales	$2,400
Less variable cost of goods sold	1,200
Contribution margin	1,200
Less fixed manufacturing costs at budget	600
Gross margin	600
Less fixed selling and administrative costs	400
Net income before taxes	$ 200

The controller attached the following notes to the statements:

1. The unit sales price for November averaged $24.
2. The unit manufacturing costs for the month were as follows:

Variable costs	$12
Fixed costs applied	4
Total cost	$16

3. The unit rate for fixed manufacturing costs is a predetermined rate based on a monthly production of 150,000 units.
4. The variable costs per unit have been stable all year.
5. Production for November was 45,000 units in excess of sales.
6. The inventory at November 30 was 80,000 units.

Instructions

(a) The vice-president for sales is not comfortable with the variable-costing system and wonders what the net income would have been under the previous absorption-costing system.

1. Present the November income statement on an absorption-costing basis.
2. Reconcile and explain the difference between the variable-costing and absorption-costing net income figures.

(b) Explain the features of variable-cost income measurement that should be attractive to the vice-president for sales.

(adapted from CMA Canada, now CPA Canada)

C8-50 The following data relate to a year's budgeted activity for Rickuse Limited, a company that manufactures one product:

	Units
Beginning inventory	40,000
Production	140,000
Available for sale	180,000
Sales	130,000
Ending inventory	50,000

	Per unit
Selling price	$8.00
Variable manufacturing costs	2.00
Variable selling, general, and administrative expenses	3.00
Fixed manufacturing costs (based on 100,000 units)	0.50
Fixed selling, general, and administrative expenses (based on 100,000 units)	0.80

Total fixed costs and expenses remain unchanged within the relevant range of 25,000 units to a total capacity of 160,000 units.

Instructions

(a) Calculate the projected annual break-even sales in units.
(b) Calculate the projected net income for the year under variable costing.
(c) Determine the company's projected net income for the year under absorption (full) costing, assuming the fixed overhead adjustment is closed to the cost of goods sold.

(adapted from CMA Canada, now CPA Canada)

C8-51 BBG Corporation manufactures a synthetic element, pixie dust. Management was surprised to learn that income before taxes had dropped even though the sales volume had increased. Steps had been taken during the year to improve profitability. The steps included raising the selling price by 12% because of a 10% increase in production costs, and instructing the selling and administrative departments to spend no more this year than last year. Both changes were implemented at the beginning of the year.

BBG's accounting department prepared and distributed to top management the comparative income statements and related financial information that follow (BBG uses the FIFO inventory method for finished goods):

BBG CORPORATION
Comparative Statements of Operating Income
(in thousands)

	2015	2016
Sales revenue	$9,000	$11,200
Cost of goods sold	7,200	8,320
Manufacturing volume variance	(600)	495
Adjusted cost of goods sold	6,600	8,815
Gross margin	2,400	2,385
Selling and administrative expenses	1,500	1,500
Income before taxes	$ 900	$ 885

BBG CORPORATION
Selected Operating and Financial Data

	2015	2016
Sales price	$ 10.00/kg	$ 11.20/kg
Material costs	$ 1.50/kg	$ 1.65/kg
Direct labour cost	$ 2.50/kg	$ 2.75/kg
Variable overhead costs	$ 1.00/kg	$ 1.10/kg
Fixed overhead costs	$ 3.00/kg	$ 3.30/kg
Total fixed overhead costs	$3,000,000	$3,300,000
Selling and administrative expenses (all fixed)	$1,500,000	$1,500,000
Sales volume	900,000 kg	1,000,000 kg
Beginning inventory	300,000 kg	600,000 kg

Instructions

(a) Explain to management why net income decreased despite the increases in sales price and sales volume.
(b) It has been proposed that the company use variable costing for its internal reporting. Prepare the variable-costing income statement for 2016.
(c) Reconcile the difference in income before taxes using the absorption-costing method currently used by BBG and the variable-costing method proposed for 2016.

(adapted from CMA Canada, now CPA Canada)

C8-52 Scott Wadzicki was hired in January 2016 to manage the home products division of Advanced Techno. As part of his employment contract, he was told that he would get an extra $5,000 bonus for every 1% increase by which the division's profits exceeded the previous year's profits.

Soon after coming on board, Scott met with his plant managers and explained that he wanted the plants to be run at full capacity. Previously, the plant had employed just-in-time inventory practices and had consequently produced units only as they were needed. Scott stated that, under the previous management, the company had missed out on too many sales opportunities because it did not have enough inventory on hand. Because the previous management had employed just-in-time inventory practices, when Scott came on board, there was virtually no beginning inventory. The selling price and variable cost per unit remained the same from 2015 to 2016. Additional information follows:

	2015	2016
Net income	$ 300,00	$ 525,000
Units produced	25,000	30,000
Units sold	25,000	25,000
Fixed manufacturing costs	$1,350,000	$1,350,000
Fixed manufacturing costs per unit	$ 54	$ 45

Instructions

(a) Calculate Scott's bonus based on the net income figures shown.
(b) Recalculate the 2015 and 2016 results using variable costing.
(c) Recalculate Scott's 2016 bonus under variable costing.
(d) Were Scott's actions unethical? Do you think any actions need to be taken by the company?

"All About You" Activity

C8-53 You work for a firm of management consultants that offers assistance to new businesses. One of your clients is Shorttress Manufacturing, a company that manufactures a small, but vital, component for the specialized lighting industry. Shorttress is a new company (and a new client for your employer) and you have been assigned the task of advising them of their options for financing their inventory during the first few months.

The marketing experts have told you that the company should have at least three months of inventory on hand so it can meet all demands from Shorttress's customers.

The annual production of the Shorttress component is projected to be 120,000 units. Annual direct labour and direct material costs together are estimated at $300,000 per year. Variable manufacturing costs are estimated to be $180,000 per year; fixed manufacturing costs are projected to be $500,000 per year. Fixed marketing and administration costs are estimated at $700,000 per year. These projections are all for the company's first year of business.

Instructions

(a) Assuming that Shorttress must hold three months of the component in inventory, what is the cost of the three-month inventory using variable costing? What is the cost of inventory using absorption costing?

(b) Shorttress's bankers have advised their client that bank financing will only cover 50% of the inventory's cost. What alternative strategies can you suggest to Shorttress to help it deal with this funding shortfall?

Decision-Making at Current Designs

DM8-1 Current Designs' CFO retrieved the following information with respect to the top-selling rotomoulded kayaks product line from the income statements for the last two years. During these two years it produced 3,000 units in the first year and 2,400 in the second year, while sales were 2,400 units in the first year and 2,700 in the second year. Variable production costs were $570 per unit during both years (direct materials $200, direct labour $175, and variable overhead $195). The company uses first-in, first-out (FIFO) for inventory costing. The absorption costing comparative income statements for these two years were:

		Year 1		Year 2
Sales		$2,280,000		$2,565,000
Less cost of goods sold:				
Beginning inventory	$ 0		$ 480,000	
Product costs	2,400,000		2,058,000	
Ending inventory	(480,000)	1,920,000	(257,250)	2,280,750
Gross profit		360,000		$ 284,250
Less operating expenses				
(selling and administrative)				
Variable	120,000		135,000	
Fixed	30,000	150,000	30,000	165,000
Operating income		$ 210,000		$ 119,250

Instructions

(a) Using the information provided, prepare condensed, two-year comparative income statements using the variable-costing method. Reconcile the variable-costing income with the absorption-costing income.

(b) Assume that Current Designs uses a normal-costing method. The company had budgeted 3,300 units of production for each of the two

years. Prepare condensed, two-year comparative income statements using the normal-costing method. Reconcile the variable-costing income with the normal-costing income statements.

(c) Using the information provided above, prepare condensed, two-year comparative income statements using the throughput-costing method. Reconcile the normal-costing income statements with the throughput-costing income statements.

Waterways Continuing Problem

(This is a continuation of the Waterways Problem from Chapters 1 through 7.)

WCP-8 When Waterways' management met to review the year-end financial statements, the room was filled with excitement. Sales had been exceptional during the year and every department had exceeded the budget and last year's sales totals. Several years ago Waterways had implemented a bonus system based on percentage of sales over budget, and the managers were expecting healthy cheques at the end of the year.

Yet the plant manager, Ryan Smith, was stunned into silence when he read the bottom line on the income statement for manufacturing operations. It was showing a loss! He immediately approached the CFO asking for an explanation. Ryan wondered, "Why did we go through all that trouble and inconvenience to adopt those cost-cutting measures when they had the opposite effect?" One of those measures was to move toward lean manufacturing.

The CFO retrieved the following information with respect to the top-selling line from the manufacturing operations for the last three years. Production on this line began on January 1, 2014.

	2014	2015	2016
Beginning inventory of finished units	0		
Production in units	80,000	85,000	**60,000**
Sales in units	70,000	75,000	**80,000**
Selling price	$25	$25	**$27**
Direct material	$3	$3	**$4**
Direct labour	2	2	**3**
Variable manufacturing overhead	4	4	**4**
Variable selling and administration	5	5	**5**
Fixed manufacturing overhead	612,000	612,000	**612,000**
Fixed selling and administration	150,000	150,000	**150,000**

Waterways uses the absorption-costing method and accounts for inventory using FIFO.

Instructions

(a) Using the information provided, recreate Waterways' statements for this division using condensed, three-year comparative income statements. Explain why there is a loss in 2016 despite having record sales during the year.

(b) Using the information provided, prepare condensed, three-year comparative income statements using the variable-costing method. Reconcile the variable-costing income with the absorption-costing income calculated in part (a). State at least two advantages of variable costing.

(c) Assume that Waterways uses a normal-costing method. The company had budgeted 80,000 units of production for each of the three years. Calculate the volume variance for each year indicating if it is favourable or unfavourable.

(d) Is Waterways a good candidate for adopting throughput costing? Explain.

Answers to Self-Study Questions

1. b   2. c   3. b   4. a   5. b   6. c   7. a   8. a   9. a   10. a

> Remember to go back to the beginning of the chapter to check off your completed work!
> ←

Pricing

study objectives

the navigator

After studying this chapter, you should be able to do the following:

1. Calculate a target cost when the market determines a product's price.
2. Calculate a target selling price using total cost-plus pricing.
3. Calculate a target selling price using absorption cost-plus pricing.
4. Calculate a target selling price using variable cost-plus pricing.
5. Use time-and-material pricing to determine the cost of services provided.
6. Determine a transfer price using the negotiated, cost-based, and market-based approaches.

A CLEAR PRICING STRATEGY

The traditional way for people to buy glasses or contact lenses was at their eye doctor's office or an optical store. Both charged a certain markup to cover overhead such as a receptionist's salary or store rent. But the Internet radically changed that business model.

In 2000, entrepreneur Roger Hardy launched Coastal Contacts Inc. in his Vancouver home and started selling corrective lenses online. With lower overhead and national sales, the company, through its ClearlyContacts.ca and other websites, competes with bricks-and-mortar eyewear retailers on price. "We try to get our prices as low as we can and win on the scale battle," said Mr. Hardy, Coastal's chief executive officer. "If we sell $160 million worth of contact lenses next year that's more than every optical shop in Canada. On average, those competitors are selling three to five orders a day and we're selling thousands. So we're trying to benefit from economies of scale in our product pricing."

After achieving online success selling contacts, Coastal branched into glasses. The worldwide prescription glasses market is an estimated $50 billion a year, but around the time that Coastal started selling them, only about 1% of that market was online, Mr. Hardy said. Seeing a huge opportunity for growth, Coastal began not only selling eyewear, but manufacturing it as well.

To continue to compete on price, Coastal had to keep manufacturing costs down. It does this by economy of scale. At its Vancouver lab, Coastal spent millions of dollars on machines to make eyeglass frames and lenses, including 12 high-volume machines that produce 1,000 glasses a day, and a $3.5-million machine that makes "progressive" bifocals. It hired about 450 people to run the machinery, which operates 24 hours a day, seven days a week, to maximize productivity. "Progressives retail for between $800 and $1,000, and we're selling them for $199 online," Mr. Hardy said.

Just a decade after launching, Coastal has grown to become the biggest e-tailer of glasses and contacts in the world. It acquired rivals and added distribution centres in Scandinavia and Australia, to further its global economy of scale and keep prices low. And it's opened retail stores in Vancouver and Toronto to help drive people to its website. Sales in its 2013 fiscal year were $218 million, up 11% from the year before. In early 2014, Coastal entered into an agreement for all its common shares to be purchased by French-based Essilor International, the world's leading ophthalmic optics company, for $430 million.

Sources: "Essilor International Agrees to Acquire Coastal.com for $430 Million," Coastal Contacts Inc. news release, February 27, 2014; Jennifer Kwan, "5Q: Roger Hardy, Founder and CEO of Coastal Contacts," Yahoo Finance Canada, December 4, 2013; Daniel Bader, "ClearlyContacts.ca Opens Second Vancouver Retail Store to Push More Customers to its Online Portal," Betakit, August 4, 2013; Jacqueline Nelson, "Business WIthout Borders: Coastal Contacts," *Canadian Business*, March 13, 2012; Coastal Contacts Inc. fourth-quarter management discussion and analysis, 2013.

Preview of Chapter 9

As the feature story about Coastal Contacts Inc. indicates, few management decisions are more important than setting prices. In this chapter, two types of pricing situations are examined. The first part of the chapter explains pricing for goods sold or services provided to external parties. The second part of the chapter examines pricing decisions that need to be made when goods are sold to other divisions within the same company.

The chapter is organized as follows:

PRICING

Pricing Goods for External Sales	Transfer Pricing for Internal Sales
➤ Target costing	➤ Transfer pricing—an explanation
➤ Total cost-plus pricing	➤ Transfer-pricing approaches
➤ Absorption cost-plus pricing	➤ Transfers between divisions in different countries
➤ Variable cost-plus pricing	
➤ Pricing services	

Pricing Goods for External Sales

Establishing the price for any good or service is affected by many factors. Take the pharmaceutical industry as an example. Its approach to profitability has been to spend heavily on research and development in an effort to find and patent a few new drugs, price them high, and market them aggressively. Due to the AIDS crisis in Africa, the drug industry has been under great pressure to lower its prices on drugs that are used to treat AIDS. For example, Merck Co. lowered the price of its AIDS drug Crixivan to $600 per patient in these countries. This compares with the $6,016 it typically charges in the United States.[1] As a consequence, individuals in the United States are questioning whether prices in the U.S. market are too high. The drug companies counter that to cover their substantial financial risks to develop these products, they need to set the prices high. Illustration 9-1 presents the many factors that can affect pricing decisions.

▶Illustration 9-1
Pricing factors

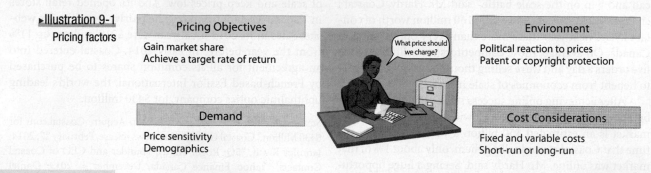

Pricing Objectives

Gain market share
Achieve a target rate of return

Environment

Political reaction to prices
Patent or copyright protection

Demand

Price sensitivity
Demographics

Cost Considerations

Fixed and variable costs
Short-run or long-run

In the long run, a company must price its product to cover the product's costs and eventually earn a reasonable profit. But to price its product appropriately, it must have a good understanding of the market forces at work. In most cases, a company does not set the prices. Instead, the price is set by the competitive market (the laws of supply and demand). For example, gasoline retailers such as Imperial Oil or Petro-Canada cannot set the price of gasoline by themselves. These companies are called **price takers** because the price of gasoline is set by market forces (the supply of oil and the demand from customers). This happens with any product that appears to be identical to competing products, such as farm products (corn or wheat) or minerals (coal or sand).

In other situations, the company sets its own prices. This would be the case where the product is specially made for a customer, as in a one-of-a-kind product, such as a custom designer dress by Chanel or suit by Armani. This also occurs when few or no other producers can manufacture a similar item. An example would be a company that has a patent or copyright on a unique process, such as computer chips by Intel. However, a company also becomes able to set the price when it has been successful at distinguishing its product or service from others. Even in a competitive market like coffee, Starbucks has been able to differentiate its product and charge more for a cup of java.

TARGET COSTING

STUDY OBJECTIVE 1

Calculate a target cost when the market determines a product's price.

Automobile manufacturers like Ford Motor Company of Canada or Toyota Canada face a competitive market. The laws of supply and demand greatly affect the price of an automobile, so no company in this industry can influence the price to a significant degree. Therefore, to earn a profit, companies in the auto industry must focus on controlling their costs. This requires setting a **target cost** that gives a desired profit. Illustration 9-2 shows the relationship between the target cost and the price and desired profit.

▶Illustration 9-2
Target cost as related to price and profit

Market Price − Desired Profit = Target Cost

---

[1] "AIDS Gaffes in Africa Come Back to Haunt Drug Industry at Home," *Wall Street Journal*, April 23, 2001, p. 1.

If General Motors of Canada, for example, can produce its automobiles for the target cost (or less), it will meet its profit goal. If it cannot achieve its target cost, it will fail to produce the desired profit (and will most likely "get hammered" by shareholders and the market). In a competitive market, a company chooses the market segment it wants to compete in; that is, its market niche. For example, it may choose between selling luxury goods or economy goods in order to focus its efforts on one segment or the other.

BUSINESS INSIGHT   *Target Costing at Apple*

Apple Inc., considered the world's most valuable brand, has long been able to charge premium prices for its products, which are often the first on the market in their category. The company counts on consumers to want their iPads and iPhones so badly that they'll pay two or three times what later competitors charge for more generic products. It's believed that Apple uses target costing, aiming for a certain manufacturing cost that will give it a desired profit after selling products for what the company thinks the market will bear. For example, it's estimated that it costs Apple U.S. $213 in materials to manufacture a 16GB iPhone 5S, which had a retail price of U.S. $649. The pricing strategy started to backfire, however, as iPhone sales began to slump compared with smartphones from lower-cost competitors like Samsung. In 2013, Apple responded by launching a cheaper iPhone made of less expensive materials. But companies like Apple that typically market their products as luxury items have to be careful not to lower prices too much and be thought of as "cheap" by consumers who want the cachet of more expensive goods.

Sources: Henry Blodget, "Come On, Apple Fans, It's Time to Admit that the Company Is Blowing It," Businessinsider. com, November 15, 2013; Kurt Badenhausen, "Apple Dominates List of the World's Most Valuable Brands," *Forbes*, November 6, 2013; Ben Rooney, "What Does it Cost to Make an iPhone?", *Wall Street Journal*, September 30, 2013; Brian X. Chen, "Luxury Brands Face Hazards when Testing Lower Costs," *New York Times*, September 9, 2013; Marco Tabini, "How Apple Sets Its Prices," *Macworld*, January 14, 2013.

What other costs does Apple incur with its products besides the materials?

Once the company has identified its segment of the market, it does market research to determine the target price. This target price is the price that the company believes would place it in the best position for its target audience (its customers).

Once the company has determined this target price, it can determine its target cost by setting a desired profit. The difference between the target price and the desired profit is the target cost of the product. (Illustration 9-2 showed this calculation.) After the company determines the target cost, a team of employees with expertise in a variety of areas (production and operations, marketing, and finance) is assembled. The team's task is to design and develop a product that can meet quality specifications without costing more than the target cost. The target cost includes all the product and period costs that are necessary in order to make and market the product or service.

BEFORE YOU GO ON...

Do It! Target Costing

Fine Line Phones is considering introducing a fashion cover for its phones. Market research indicates that 200,000 units can be sold if the price is no more than $20. If Fine Line decides to produce the covers, it will need to invest $1 million in new production equipment. Fine Line requires a minimum rate of return of 25% on all investments.

Determine the target cost per unit for the cover.

Action Plan
- Recall that Market price − Desired profit = Target cost.
- The minimum rate of return is a company's desired profit.

(*continued*)

(continued)

Solution

The desired profit for this new product line is $250,000 ($1,000,000 × 25%).

Each cover must result in $1.25 of profit ($250,000/200,000 units).

Market price	−	Desired profit	=	Target cost per unit
$20	−	$1.25	=	$18.75 per unit

Related exercise material: **BE9-1, E9-16, E9-17,** and **Do It! D9-12.**

DECISION TOOLKIT

Decision Checkpoints	**Info Needed for Decision**	**Tools to Use for Decision**	**How to Evaluate Results**
How does management use target costs to make decisions about manufacturing a product or providing a service?	Target selling price, desired profit, target cost	Target selling price less desired profit equals target cost.	If the target cost is too high, the company will not earn its desired profit. If it does not achieve the desired profit, the company must evaluate whether or not to manufacture the product or provide the service.

TOTAL COST-PLUS PRICING

STUDY OBJECTIVE 2
Calculate a target selling price using total cost-plus pricing.

As discussed, in a competitive product environment, the price of a product is set by the market. In order to achieve its desired profit, the company focuses on achieving a target cost. In a less competitive environment, companies have a greater ability to set the product price. Commonly, when a company sets a product price, it does so as a function of, or relative to, the cost of the product or service. This is referred to as **total cost-plus pricing**. Under total cost-plus pricing, a company first determines a cost base and then adds a **markup** to the cost base to determine the **target selling price**.

If the cost base includes all of the costs required to produce and sell the product, then the markup represents the desired profit. This can be seen in Illustration 9-3, where the markup represents the difference between the selling price and cost—the profit on the product.

▶**Illustration 9-3**
Relation of markup to cost and selling price

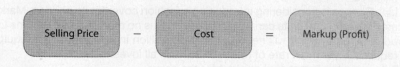

The size of the markup (profit) depends on the return the company hopes to generate on the amount it has invested. In determining the optimal markup, the company must consider competitive and market conditions, political and legal issues, and other relevant factors. Once the company has determined its cost base and its desired markup, it can add the two together to determine the target selling price. The basic cost-plus pricing formula is expressed in Illustration 9-4.

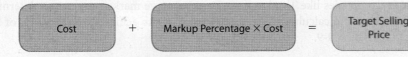

►Illustration 9-4
Total cost-plus pricing formula

To illustrate, assume that Thinkmore Products, Inc. is in the process of setting a selling price on its new video camera pen. It is a functioning pen that will record up to 2 hours of audio and video. The per-unit variable cost estimates for the video camera pen is shown in Illustration 9-5.

	Per Unit
Direct materials	$23
Direct labour	17
Variable manufacturing overhead	12
Variable selling and administrative expenses	8
Variable cost per unit	$60

►Illustration 9-5
Variable cost per unit

To produce and sell its product, Thinkmore incurs fixed manufacturing overhead of $280,000 and fixed selling and administrative expenses of $240,000. To arrive at the cost per unit, we divide total fixed costs by the number of units the company expects to produce. Illustration 9-6 shows the calculation of fixed cost per unit for Thinkmore, assuming the production of 10,000 units.

	Total Costs	÷	Budgeted Volume	=	Cost Per Unit
Fixed manufacturing overhead	$280,000	÷	10,000	=	$28
Fixed selling and administrative expenses	240,000	÷	10,000	=	24
Fixed cost per unit					$52

►Illustration 9-6
Fixed cost per unit, 10,000 units

Management is ultimately evaluated based on its ability to generate a high return on the company's investment. This is frequently expressed as a return on investment (ROI) percentage, calculated as income divided by the average amount invested in a product or service. A higher percentage reflects a greater success in generating profits from the investment in a product or service.

To achieve a desired return on investment percentage, a product's markup should be determined by calculating the desired return on investment (ROI) per unit. This is calculated by multiplying the desired ROI percentage times the amount invested to produce the product, and then dividing this by the number of units produced. Illustration 9-7 shows the calculation used to determine a markup amount based on a desired ROI per unit for Thinkmore, assuming that the company desires a 20% ROI and that it has invested $1 million.

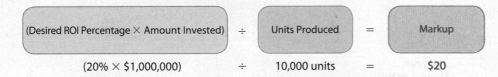

(20% × $1,000,000)   ÷   10,000 units   = $20

►Illustration 9-7
Calculation of markup based on desired ROI per unit

Thinkmore expects to receive income of $200,000 (20% × $1,000,000) on its $1 million investment. On a per-unit basis, the markup based on the desired ROI per unit is $20 ($200,000 ÷ 10,000 units). Given the per-unit costs shown above, Illustration 9-8 calculates the sales price to be $132.

	Per Unit
Variable cost	$ 60
Fixed cost	52
Total cost	112
Desired ROI	20
Selling price per unit	$132

►Illustration 9-8
Calculation of selling price, 10,000 units

In most cases, companies like Thinkmore use a percentage markup on cost to determine the selling price. The formula to calculate the markup percentage to achieve a desired ROI of $20 per unit is shown in Illustration 9-9.

▶Illustration 9-9
Calculation of markup percentage

Desired ROI per Unit	÷	Total Unit Cost	=	Markup Percentage
$20	÷	$112	=	17.86%

Using a 17.86% markup on cost, Thinkmore Products would calculate the target selling price as shown in Illustration 9-10.

▶Illustration 9-10
Calculation of selling price—markup approach

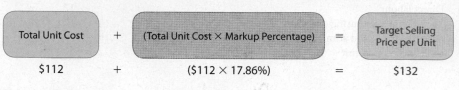

Total Unit Cost	+	(Total Unit Cost × Markup Percentage)	=	Target Selling Price per Unit
$112	+	($112 × 17.86%)	=	$132

Thinkmore should set the price for its video camera pen at $132 per unit.

Limitations of Total Cost-Plus Pricing

The total cost-plus pricing approach has a major advantage: it is simple to calculate. However, this cost model does not consider the demand side. That is, will customers pay the price Thinkmore calculated for its video camera pen? In addition, sales volume plays a large role in determining per-unit costs. The lower the sales volume, for example, the higher the price Thinkmore must charge to meet its desired ROI. To illustrate, if the budgeted sales volume were 8,000 instead of 10,000, Thinkmore's variable cost per unit would remain the same. However, its fixed cost per unit would change, as shown in Illustration 9-11.

▶Illustration 9-11
Fixed cost per unit—8,000 units

	Total Costs	÷	Budgeted Volume	=	Cost per Unit
Fixed manufacturing overhead	$280,000	÷	8,000	=	$35
Fixed selling and administrative expenses	240,000	÷	8,000	=	30
Fixed cost per unit					$65

As indicated in Illustration 9-6, the fixed costs per unit for 10,000 units added up to $52. However, at a lower sales volume of 8,000 units, the fixed cost per unit increases to $65. Thinkmore's desired 20% ROI now results in a $25 ROI per unit [(20% × 1,000,000) ÷ 8,000]. The selling price can be calculated as shown in Illustration 9-12.

▶Illustration 9-12
Selling price per unit—8,000 units

	Per Unit
Variable cost	$ 60
Fixed cost	65
Total cost	125
Desired ROI	25
Selling price per unit	$150

$$20\% = \frac{\$25 \text{ (desired ROI)}}{\$125 \text{ (total unit cost)}}$$

As shown, the lower the budgeted volume, the higher the per-unit price. The reason: fixed costs and ROI are spread over fewer units, and therefore the fixed cost and ROI per unit increase. In this case, at 8,000 units, Thinkmore would have to mark up its total unit costs 20% to earn a desired ROI of $25 per unit, as shown in the margin calculations.

$125 + ($125 × 20%) = $150

The target selling price would then be $150, as indicated earlier, and calculated again as shown in the margin.

The opposite effect will occur if the budgeted volume is higher (for example, at 12,000 units) because the fixed costs and ROI can be spread over more units. As a result, the total cost-plus model of pricing will achieve its desired ROI only when Thinkmore sells the quantity that it budgeted. If the actual sales volume is much less than the budgeted sales volume, Thinkmore will lose money unless it can raise its prices.

In practice, companies use two other cost approaches: (1) absorption cost-plus pricing, and (2) variable cost-plus pricing. Absorption cost-plus pricing is more popular than variable cost-plus pricing.[2] We will illustrate both of them, because both have merit.

ABSORPTION COST-PLUS PRICING

The **absorption cost-plus pricing** approach is consistent with generally accepted accounting principles (GAAP) because it defines the cost base as the manufacturing cost. **Both the variable and fixed selling and administrative costs are excluded from this cost base.** Thus, companies must somehow provide for selling and administrative costs plus the target ROI, which they do through the markup.

The first step in the absorption-cost approach is to calculate the manufacturing cost per unit. For Thinkmore Products, Inc., this amounts to $80 per unit at a volume of 10,000 units, as shown in Illustration 9-13.

STUDY OBJECTIVE 3
Calculate a target selling price using absorption cost-plus pricing.

	Per Unit
Direct materials	$23
Direct labour	17
Variable manufacturing overhead	12
Fixed manufacturing overhead ($280,000 ÷ 10,000)	28
Total manufacturing cost per unit (absorption cost)	$80

►Illustration 9-13
Calculation of manufacturing cost per unit

In addition, Thinkmore provided the information in Illustration 9-14 on selling and administrative expenses per unit and the desired ROI per unit.

Variable selling and administrative expenses	$ 8
Fixed selling and administrative expenses ($240,000 ÷ 10,000)	$24
Desired ROI per unit	20%

►Illustration 9-14
Additional information

The second step in the absorption-cost approach is to calculate the markup percentage using the formula in Illustration 9-15. Note that when using the manufacturing cost per unit as the cost base to calculate the markup percentage, the percentage must cover the desired ROI and also the selling and administrative expenses.

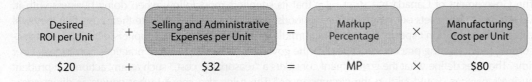

►Illustration 9-15
Markup percentage—absorption-cost approach

Solving the equation we find the following:

Markup percentage = ($20 + $32) ÷ $80 = 65%

The third and final step is to set the target selling price. Using a markup percentage of 65% and the absorption-cost approach, we calculate the target selling price as shown in Illustration 9-16.

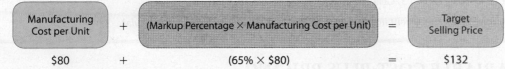

►Illustration 9-16
Calculation of target price—absorption cost-plus approach

---

[2] For a discussion of cost-plus pricing, see Eunsup Shim and Ephraim F. Sudit, "How Manufacturers Price Products," *Management Accounting* (February 1995), pp. 37–39; and V. Govindarajan and R. N. Anthony, "How Firms Use Cost Data in Pricing Decisions," *Management Accounting* (July 1983), pp. 30–36.

Using a target price of $132 will produce the desired 20% return on investment for Thinkmore Products on its video camera pen at a sales volume level of 10,000 units, as proved in Illustration 9-17.

►Illustration 9-17

Proof of 20% ROI—absorption-cost approach

THINKMORE PRODUCTS, INC.	
Budgeted Absorption-Cost Income Statement	
Revenue (10,000 units × $132)	$1,320,000
Less: Cost of goods sold (10,000 units × $80)	800,000
Gross profit	520,000
Less: Selling and administrative expenses [10,000 units × ($8 + $24)]	320,000
Net income	**$ 200,000**

Budgeted ROI

$$\frac{\text{Net income}}{\text{Invested assets}} = \frac{\$200,000}{\$1,000,000} = 20\%$$

Markup Percentage

$$\frac{\text{Net income} + \text{Selling and administrative expenses}}{\text{Cost of goods sold}} = \frac{\$200,000 + \$320,000}{\$800,000} = 65\%$$

Because of the fixed cost element, if more than 10,000 units are sold, the ROI will be greater than 20%. If fewer than 10,000 units are sold, the ROI will be less than 20%. The markup percentage is also verified by adding $200,000 (the net income) and $320,000 (the selling and administrative expenses) and then dividing by $800,000 (the cost of goods sold or the cost base).

Most companies that use cost-plus pricing use either the absorption cost or the total cost as the basis. The reasons are as follows:

1. A company's cost accounting system provides absorption cost information most easily. Because absorption cost data already exist in general ledger accounts, it is cost-effective to use them for pricing.
2. Basing the cost-plus formula on only variable costs could encourage managers to set too low a price in order to boost sales. There is the fear that if only variable costs are used, managers will substitute them for total costs and this can lead to suicidal price-cutting.
3. The absorption cost or total cost is the easiest basis to defend when prices need to be justified to all interested parties—managers, customers, and governments.

IFRS Notes

IAS 2 *Inventories* provides guidance on the measurement and reporting of inventories by stating that capitalized inventory conversion costs "include a systematic allocation of fixed and variable production overheads that are incurred in converting materials into finished goods."

BUSINESS INSIGHT   *The Cost of Doing Government Business*

The Government of Canada has strict rules that its suppliers must follow when doing business with it. Government policy sets out how suppliers of goods and services must calculate their costs that they will charge. The rules don't specify what pricing formula to use, as long as the suppliers determine costs according to accounting practices accepted by the government and apply these practices consistently over time. The rules define what the government considers a "reasonable cost," such as an "action that prudent business persons would take in the circumstances." The rules also specify what counts as direct costs, such as labour, and what counts as indirect costs, such as fixed costs like property taxes and general and administrative expenses. Suppliers are not allowed to charge the government for costs such as losses on investments and bad debts, legal and accounting fees, amortization of unrealized appreciation of assets, and provisions for contingencies. Since most federal government contracts for goods and services are awarded in competitions where price is a factor, suppliers must calculate their prices in their bids carefully.

Sources: Public Works and Government Services Canada, "Your Guide to Doing Business with the Government of Canada," 2011; Public Works and Government Services Canada, "Standard Acquisition Clauses and Conditions (SACC) Manual: Section 3, General Conditions," August 16, 2010.

Why might the government not require suppliers to use a particular pricing formula?

VARIABLE COST-PLUS PRICING

STUDY OBJECTIVE 4

Calculate a target selling price using variable cost-plus pricing.

Under **variable cost-plus pricing**, the cost base consists of all of the variable costs associated with a product, including the variable selling and administrative costs. **Because fixed costs are not included in the base, the markup must cover fixed costs (manufacturing, as well as selling and**

administrative) and the target ROI. Variable cost-plus pricing is more useful for making short-term decisions because it considers variable-cost and fixed-cost behaviour patterns separately.

The **first step** in the variable-cost approach to cost-plus pricing is to calculate the variable cost per unit. For Thinkmore Products, Inc., this amounts to $60 per unit, as shown in Illustration 9-18.

	Per Unit
Direct materials	$23
Direct labour	17
Variable manufacturing overhead	12
Variable selling and administrative expenses	8
Total variable cost per unit	$60

▶Illustration 9-18
Calculation of variable cost per unit

The **second step** in the variable-cost approach is to calculate the markup percentage. Illustration 9-19 shows the formula for the markup percentage. For Thinkmore, the fixed costs include fixed manufacturing overhead of $28 per unit ($280,000 ÷ 10,000) and fixed selling and administrative expenses of $24 per unit ($240,000 ÷ 10,000).

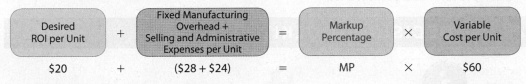

$$\text{Desired ROI per Unit} + \left(\begin{array}{c}\text{Fixed Manufacturing Overhead} + \\ \text{Selling and Administrative} \\ \text{Expenses per Unit}\end{array}\right) = \text{Markup Percentage} \times \text{Variable Cost per Unit}$$

$$\$20 + (\$28 + \$24) = \text{MP} \times \$60$$

▶Illustration 9-19
Calculation of markup percentage—
variable-cost approach

Solving the equation, we find the following:

$$\text{Markup percentage} = \frac{\$20 + (\$28 + \$24)}{\$60} = 120\%$$

The **third step** is to set the target selling price. Using a markup percentage of 120% and the variable-cost approach, the selling price is calculated as shown in Illustration 9-20.

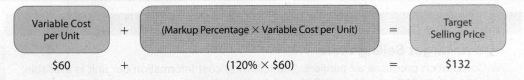

$$\text{Variable Cost per Unit} + (\text{Markup Percentage} \times \text{Variable Cost per Unit}) = \text{Target Selling Price}$$

$$\$60 + (120\% \times \$60) = \$132$$

▶Illustration 9-20
Calculation of target price—
variable-cost approach

Using a target price of $132 will produce the desired 20% return on investment for Thinkmore Products on its video camera pen at a sales volume level of 10,000 units, as proved in Illustration 9-21.

▶Illustration 9-21
Proof of 20% ROI—variable-cost
approach

THINKMORE PRODUCTS, INC.
Budgeted Variable-Cost Income Statement

Revenue (10,000 units × $132)		$1,320,000
Less: Variable costs (10,000 units × $60)		600,000
Contribution margin		720,000
Less: Fixed costs		
Manufacturing (10,000 × $28)	$280,000	
Selling and administrative (10,000 × $24)	240,000	520,000
Net income		$ 200,000

Budgeted ROI

$$\frac{\text{Net income}}{\text{Invested assets}} = \frac{\$200,000}{\$1,000,000} = 20\%$$

Markup Percentage

$$\frac{\text{Net income} + \text{Fixed costs}}{\text{Cost of goods sold}} = \frac{\$200,000 + \$520,000}{\$600,000} = 120\%$$

The major disadvantage of variable-cost pricing is that managers may set the price too low and consequently fail to cover their fixed costs. In the long run, failure to cover fixed costs will lead to losses. As a result, companies that use variable-cost pricing must use higher markups to make sure that the price they set will give a fair return.

Under any of the three approaches we have looked at (total cost, absorption cost, and variable cost), the company will reach its desired ROI only if it reaches the budgeted sales volume for the period. None of these approaches guarantees a profit or a desired ROI. Achieving a desired ROI is the result of many factors, and some of these are beyond the company's control, such as market conditions, political and legal issues, customers' tastes, and competitors' actions.

Because the absorption-cost approach includes allocated fixed costs, it does not clarify how the company's costs will change as the sales volume changes. To avoid blurring the effects of cost behaviour on operating income, some managers therefore prefer the variable-cost approach. The specific reasons for using the variable-cost approach, even though the basic accounting data are less accessible, are as follows:

1. Variable-cost pricing, being based on variable costs, is more consistent with the cost-volume-profit analysis that managers use to measure the profit implications of changes in price and volume.
2. Variable-cost pricing provides the type of data that managers need for pricing special orders. It shows the incremental cost of accepting one more order.
3. Variable-cost pricing avoids an arbitrary allocation of common fixed costs (such as executive salary) to individual product lines.

DECISION TOOLKIT

Decision Checkpoints	Info Needed for Decision	 Tools to Use for Decision	How to Evaluate Results
What factors should management consider in determining the sales price in a less competitive environment?	The total cost per unit and desired profit (cost-plus pricing)	Total cost per unit plus desired profit equals target selling price.	Does the company make its desired profit? If not, is it because of a lower sales volume?

BEFORE YOU GO ON...

▶Do It! Target Selling Price

Air Corporation produces air purifiers. The following cost information per unit is available: direct materials $16; direct labour $18; variable manufacturing overhead $11; fixed manufacturing overhead $10; variable selling and administrative expenses $6; and fixed selling and administrative expenses $10. Using a 45% markup on the total cost per unit, calculate the target selling price.

Action Plan

- Calculate the total cost per unit.
- Multiply the total cost per unit by the markup percentage. Then add this amount to the total cost per unit to determine the target selling price.

Solution

Direct materials	$16
Direct labour	18
Variable manufacturing overhead	11
Fixed manufacturing overhead	10
Variable selling and administrative expenses	6
Fixed selling and administrative expenses	10
Total unit cost	$71

Total unit cost	+	(total unit cost × markup percentage)	=	target selling price
$71	+	($71 × 45%)	=	$102.95

Related exercise material: **BE9-2, BE9-4, E9-19, E9-20, E9-21,** and **Do It! D9-13.**

PRICING SERVICES

Another variation on cost-plus pricing is called **time-and-material pricing**. Under this approach, the company sets two pricing rates: one for the **labour** used on a job and another for the **material**. The labour rate includes direct labour time and other employee costs. The material charge is based on the cost of direct parts and materials used and a material loading charge for related overhead costs. Time-and-material pricing is widely used in service industries, especially professional firms such as public accounting, law, engineering, and consulting firms, as well as construction companies, repair shops, and printers.

To illustrate time-and-material pricing, assume the data in Illustration 9-22 for Lake Holiday Marina, a boat and motor repair shop.

STUDY OBJECTIVE 5
Use time-and-material pricing to determine the cost of services provided.

LAKE HOLIDAY MARINA Budgeted Costs for the Year 2016	Time Charges	Material Loading Charges*
Mechanics' wages and benefits	$103,500	$ –
Parts manager's salary and benefits	–	11,500
Office employee's salary and benefits	20,700	2,300
Other overhead (supplies, amortization, property taxes, advertising, utilities)	26,800	14,400
Total budgeted costs	$151,000	$28,200

*The invoice cost of the materials is not included in the material loading charges.

▶Illustration 9-22
Total annual budgeted time-and-material costs

Using time-and-material pricing involves three steps: (1) calculate the per-hour labour charge, (2) calculate the charge for obtaining and holding materials, and (3) calculate the charges for a particular job.

Step 1: Calculate the labour charge. The first step for time-and-material pricing is to determine a charge for labour time. The charge for labour time is expressed as a rate per hour of labour. This rate includes (1) the direct labour cost of the employee, including the hourly rate or salary and fringe benefits; (2) selling, administrative, and similar overhead costs; and (3) an allowance for a desired profit or ROI per hour of employee time. In some industries, such as auto, boat, and farm equipment repair shops, the same hourly labour rate is charged regardless of which employee performs the work. In other industries, the rate charged depends on the classification or level of the employee. In a public accounting firm, for example, the services of an assistant, senior manager, or partner would be charged at different rates, as would those of a paralegal, associate, or partner in a law firm.

Illustration 9-23 shows the calculation of the hourly charges for Lake Holiday Marina during 2016. The marina budgets 5,000 hours of repair time in 2016, and it desires a profit margin of $8 per hour of labour.

▶Illustration 9-23
Calculation of hourly time-charge rate

	A	B	C	D	E	F
1	Per Hour	Total Cost	÷	Total Hours	=	Per Hour Charge
2	Hourly labour rate for repairs					
3	Mechanics' wages and benefits	$103,500	÷	5,000	=	$20.70
4	Overhead costs					
5	Office employee's salary and benefits	20,700	÷	5,000	=	4.14
6	Other overhead	26,800	+	5,000	=	5.36
7	Total hourly cost	$151,000	÷	5,000	=	30.20
8	Profit margin					8.00
9	Rate charged per hour of labour					$38.20
10						

The marina multiplies this rate of $38.20 by the number of hours of labour used on any particular job to determine the labour charge for that job.

Step 2: Calculate the material loading charge. The charge for materials typically includes the invoice price of any materials used on the job plus a **material loading charge**. The material loading charge covers the costs of purchasing, receiving, handling, and storing materials, plus any desired profit margin on the materials themselves. The material loading charge is expressed as a percentage of the total estimated costs of parts and materials for the year. To determine this percentage, the company does the following: (1) it estimates its total annual costs for purchasing, receiving, handling, and storing materials; (2) it divides this amount by the total estimated cost of parts and materials; and (3) it adds a desired profit margin on the materials themselves.

Illustration 9-24 shows the calculation of the material loading charge Lake Holiday Marina used during 2016. The marina estimates that the total invoice cost of parts and materials used in 2016 will be $120,000. The marina desires a 20% profit margin on the invoice cost of parts and materials.

▶Illustration 9-24

Calculation of material loading charge

	A	B	C	D	E	F
1		Material Loading Charges	÷	Total Invoice Cost, Parts and Materials	=	Material Loading Percentage
2	Overhead costs					
3	Parts manager's salary and benefits	$11,500				
4	Office employee's salary	2,300				
5		13,800	÷	$120,000	=	11.50%
6						
7	Other overhead	14,400	÷	120,000	=	12.00%
8		$28,200	÷	120,000	=	23.50%
9	Profit margin					20.00%
10	Material loading percentage					43.50%
11						

The marina's material loading charge on any particular job is 43.50% multiplied by the cost of materials used on the job. For example, if the marina used $100 in parts, the additional material loading charge would be $43.50.

Step 3: Calculate charges for a particular job. The charges for any particular job are the sum of (1) the labour charge, (2) the charge for the materials, and (3) the material loading charge. For example, suppose that Lake Holiday Marina prepares a price quotation to estimate the cost to refurbish a used 28-foot pontoon boat. Lake Holiday Marina estimates the job will require 50 hours of labour and $3,600 in parts and materials. Illustration 9-25 shows the marina's price quotation.

▶Illustration 9-25

Price quotation for time and material

LAKE HOLIDAY MARINA
Time-and-Material Price Quotation

Job: Marianne Perino, repair of 28-foot pontoon boat		
Labour charge: 50 hours @ $38.20 per hour		$1,910
Material charges		
Cost of parts and materials	$3,600	
Material loading charge (43.5% × $3,600)	1,566	5,166
Total price of labour and material		$7,076

Included in the $7,076 price quotation for the boat repair and refurbishment are charges for labour costs, overhead costs, materials costs, materials handling and storage costs, and a profit margin on both labour and parts. Lake Holiday Marina used labour hours as a basis for calculating the time rate. Other companies—such as machine shops, plastic moulding shops, and printers—might use machine hours.

DECISION TOOLKIT

	Decision Checkpoints	Info Needed for Decision	Tools to Use for Decision	How to Evaluate Results
	How do we set prices when it is difficult to estimate the total cost per unit?	Two pricing rates: one for labour use and another for materials	Calculate the labour rate charge and material rate charge. In each of these calculations, add a profit margin.	Is the company profitable under this pricing approach? Are employees earning reasonable wages?

BEFORE YOU GO ON...

▶Do It! Time and Material Pricing

Presented below are data for Harmon Electrical Repair Shop for next year:

Repair technicians' wages	$130,000
Fringe benefits	30,000
Overhead	20,000

The desired profit margin per labour hour is $10. The material loading charge is 40% of the invoice cost. It is estimated that repair technicians will work 8,000 labour hours next year. If Harmon repairs a TV that takes four hours to repair and uses parts costing $50, calculate the bill for this job.

Action Plan

• Calculate the labour charge.
• Calculate the material loading charge.
• Calculate the bill for the specific repair.

Solution

	Total Cost	÷	Total Hours	=	Per Hour
Repair technicians' wages	$130,000	÷	8,000	=	$16.25
Fringe benefits	30,000	÷	8,000	=	3.75
Overhead	20,000	÷	8,000	=	2.50
	$180,000	÷	8,000	=	22.50
Profit margin					10.00
Rate charged per hour of labour					$32.50
Materials cost	$ 50				
Material loading charge ($50 × 40%)	20				
Total materials cost	$ 70				
Cost of TV repair					
Labour costs ($32.50 × 4)	$130				
Materials cost	70				
Total repair cost	$200				

Related exercise material: **BE9-6, E9-23, E9-24, E9-25,** and **Do It! D9-14.**

the navigator

Transfer Pricing for Internal Sales

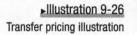

In today's global economy, growth is vital to survival. Frequently, growth is "vertical," which means that the company expands in the direction of either its suppliers or its customers. For example, a manufacturer of bicycles, like Trek, may acquire a chain of bicycle shops. A movie production company like Walt Disney or a broadcaster like Bell Media might acquire a movie theatre chain.

TRANSFER PRICING—AN EXPLANATION

A division within a vertically integrated company normally transfers goods or services to other divisions within the same company, as well as making sales to customers outside the company. When companies transfer goods internally, the price they use to record the transfer between the two divisions is the **transfer price**. Illustration 9-26 highlights these transactions for Aerobic Bicycle Company.

Aerobic Bicycle has two divisions: a bicycle assembly division and a bicycle components manufacturing division. The price charged for intermediate goods is the cost of goods sold to the buying division (assembly division) and revenue to the selling division (manufacturing division). A high transfer price results in high revenue for the selling division and high costs for the buying division. A low transfer price has the reverse outcome and therefore affects the selling division's performance. Thus, transfer prices can be a point of serious disagreement for division managers and can lead to actions that benefit a division but hurt the company as a whole.

▶Illustration 9-26
Transfer pricing illustration

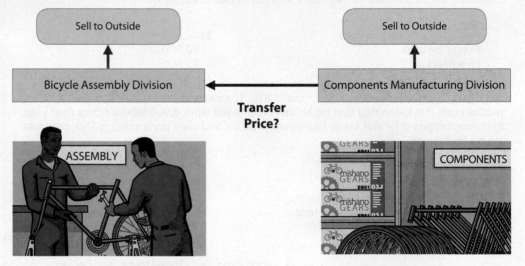

A firm's transfer pricing policy should accomplish three objectives:

1. **Promote goal congruence.** The policy should motivate division managers to choose actions that maximize company earnings as a whole and it should allow each division manager to make decisions that maximize his or her own division's earnings.
2. **Maintain divisional autonomy.** Top management should not interfere with the decision-making process of division managers.
3. **Provide accurate performance evaluation.** The policy should make it possible to accurately evaluate the division managers involved in the transfer.

A general approach to transfer pricing that achieves the above objectives uses the variable costs per unit of product and the opportunity cost for the company as a whole to determine the transfer price. Illustration 9-27 provides the formula.

▶Illustration 9-27
General transfer-pricing formula

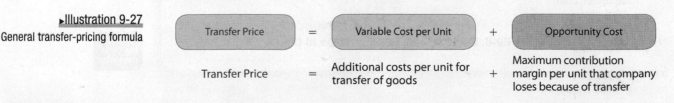

Other key elements in this approach are the minimum price that the selling division is willing to accept and the maximum price that the buying division is willing to pay. For the selling division, the minimum price is the price that it needs to charge the buying division so that the selling division would not be better off if it sold the product to an outside buyer. For the buying division, the maximum price is determined by the outside market. That is, the maximum price is how much the buying division would have to pay an outside seller for the product.

With these minimum and maximum prices known, the division managers can now decide if a transfer should occur. In general, the goods should be transferred internally if the selling division's minimum price is less than or equal to the buying division's maximum price.

To illustrate this general approach to transfer pricing, we will continue with our example of Aerobic Bicycle Company. The manufacturing division transfers some of its products to the company's assembly division, and it sells some of its products under different labels to other companies. As each division manager is compensated based on whether or not his or her division has achieved its target profit amount, the managers are motivated to get the best possible price, from each manager's perspective, for any transfers of goods. Illustration 9-28 provides the data for the two divisions.

Assembly Division		Components Manufacturing Division	
Selling price of Aerobic bicycle	$290	Wholesale selling price of components per bicycle	$130
Variable cost of assembly (not including cost of manufacturing components)	200	Variable cost of manufacturing components per bicycle	95
Contribution margin per unit	$ 90	Contribution margin per unit	$ 35

►Illustration 9-28
Basic data for Aerobic Bicycle Company

The above information indicates that the assembly division has a contribution margin per unit of $90 and the manufacturing division has a contribution margin of $35. The total contribution margin per bicycle is $125 ($90 + $35) for the Aerobic Bicycle Company as a whole. Using these data, we will now apply the general approach to transfer pricing under two different situations: first, when the manufacturing division has no excess capacity and, second, when it has excess capacity.

First Situation: No Excess Capacity

Assume the manufacturing division can sell to outside buyers all the bicycle components it can produce, and that it sells them at the wholesale price of $130 per unit and has no excess capacity remaining. Now let's ask the question, "What would be a fair transfer price if top management wants the company's manufacturing division to transfer all its production to the company's assembly division?"

As indicated in Illustration 9-28, the manufacturing division charges $130 and has a contribution margin of $35 per unit. The division has no excess capacity and produces and sells all its production to outside customers. Therefore, from the division's perspective, it must receive a payment from the assembly division that will at least cover its variable cost per unit plus the contribution margin per unit it would lose (often called the opportunity cost). Otherwise, it makes no sense for the manufacturing division to sell its products to the assembly division. The minimum transfer price that would be acceptable to the manufacturing division, therefore, is $130, as shown in Illustration 9-29.

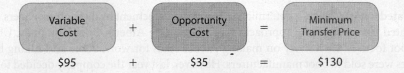

$95 + $35 = $130

►Illustration 9-29
Minimum transfer price—no excess capacity

Goal Congruence.   If the transfer price is charged at $130, according to the general approach, the company achieves goal congruence. The manufacturing division is willing to transfer its products to the assembly division at the price of $130, which is equal to the external market price. The assembly division is willing to buy the bicycle components from the internal division because the assembly division will have a contribution margin of $90 on each bicycle component purchased from the manufacturing division ($290 sales price minus the $70 of variable assembly costs and the transfer price of $130). Thus, the total contribution margin per unit is $125 ($90 + $35) for the Aerobic Bicycle Company.

Second Situation: Excess Capacity

Now assume the manufacturing division has excess capacity. The demand from all sources—internal sales and external market sales—is less than the division's production capacity. In this setting, let's ask the same question as before, "What would be a fair transfer price under the general transfer-price approach?" Because the division has excess capacity and cannot sell all its production to outside customers, from the perspective of the division, it must receive from the assembly division a payment that will at least cover the manufacturing division's variable cost per unit. Otherwise, it makes no sense for the division to sell its products to the assembly division. The minimum transfer price that would be acceptable to the manufacturing division is $95, as shown in Illustration 9-30.

▶Illustration 9-30

Minimum transfer price—excess capacity

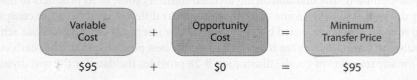

| Variable Cost | + | Opportunity Cost | = | Minimum Transfer Price |
| $95 | + | $0 | = | $95 |

Goal Congruence.   If the transfer price is charged at $95, according to the general approach, Aerobic Bicycle Company achieves goal congruence because the total contribution margin per unit is still $125 ($125 + $0) for the company as a whole. It is in the company's best interest for the bicycle components to be purchased internally from the manufacturing division as long as the variable cost to produce and transfer the bicycle components is less than the outside price of $130. In this situation, it is beneficial for the assembly division to buy the bicycle components from the internal division because it will have a contribution margin that is greater than $90 on the components for each bicycle that it purchases from the internal division ($290 sales price minus the $70 of variable assembly costs and the transfer price up to a maximum market price of $130).

In summary, the pricing issues presented above for transfer pricing are similar to pricing issues for outside buyers. The objective is to maximize the return to the whole company. However, in the transfer-pricing situation, it is also important that divisional performance not decline because of internal transfers. This means that setting a transfer price is often more complicated because of competing interests among divisions within the company. It is not surprising, therefore, that no single transfer-pricing policy will suit every organization's needs.[3] In the following section, we will discuss three possible approaches for determining a transfer price:

1. Negotiated transfer prices
2. Cost-based transfer prices
3. Market-based transfer prices

In theory, a negotiated transfer price should work best; however, due to practical considerations, the other two methods are often used.

TRANSFER-PRICING APPROACHES

Negotiated Transfer Prices

The **negotiated transfer price** is determined through an agreement by division managers. To illustrate the negotiated transfer-pricing approach, we will examine Alberta Boot Company. Until recently, Alberta Boot focused exclusively on making rubber soles for work boots and hiking boots. These rubber soles were sold to boot manufacturers. However, last year the company decided to take advantage of its strong reputation by expanding into the business of making hiking boots. Because of this expansion, the company is now structured as two independent divisions, the boot division and the sole division. The manager of each division is compensated based on how well his or her division achieves its profitability targets.

The sole division continues to make rubber soles for both hiking boots and work boots and to sell these soles to other boot manufacturers. The boot division manufactures leather uppers for

---

[3] Manmohan Rai Kapoor, "Duelling Divisions: A New Dual Transfer Pricing Method," *CMA Magazine*, March 1998, p. 23.

hiking boots and attaches these uppers to rubber soles. During its first year, the boot division purchased its rubber soles from outside suppliers to avoid disrupting the operations of the sole division. However, top management now wants the sole division to provide at least some of the soles used by the boot division. Illustration 9-31 shows the calculation of the contribution margin per unit for each division when the boot division buys soles from an outside supplier.

Boot Division		Sole Division	
Selling price of hiking boots	$90	Selling price of sole	$18
Variable cost of manufacturing boot (not including sole)	35	Variable cost per sole	11
Cost of sole purchased from outside suppliers	17		
Contribution margin per unit	$38	Contribution margin per unit	$ 7
Total contribution margin per unit: $38 + $7 = $45			

Illustration 9-31
Basic data for Alberta Boot Company

This information indicates that the boot division has a contribution margin per unit of $38 and the sole division has one of $7. The total contribution margin per unit for the company is $45 ($38 + $7). Now let's ask the question, "What would be a fair transfer price if the sole division sold 10,000 soles to the boot division?"

No Excess Capacity. As indicated in Illustration 9-31, the sole division charges $18 and gets a contribution margin of $7 per sole. The sole division has no excess capacity and produces and sells 80,000 units (soles) to outside customers. Therefore, the sole division must receive from the boot division a payment that will at least cover its variable cost per sole **plus** its lost contribution margin per sole (the **opportunity cost**). Otherwise, the sole division should not sell its soles to the boot division. The minimum transfer price that would be acceptable to the sole division is $18, as shown in Illustration 9-32.

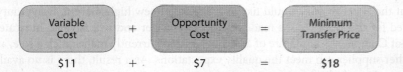

$$\text{Variable Cost} + \text{Opportunity Cost} = \text{Minimum Transfer Price}$$
$$\$11 + \$7 = \$18$$

Illustration 9-32
Minimum transfer price—no excess capacity

From the perspective of the boot division (the buyer), the most it will pay is what the sole would cost from an outside supplier, which in this case is $17. Therefore, an acceptable transfer price is not available in this situation, as shown in Illustration 9-33.

I will pay no more than $17 (the cost from outside suppliers).

I must receive at least $18 to cover my variable cost and my lost contribution margin.

Transfer price of $17

NO DEAL

Boot Division   Sole Division

Illustration 9-33
Transfer-pricing negotiations—no deal

Excess Capacity. What happens if the sole division has excess capacity? For example, assume the sole division can produce 80,000 soles but can sell only 70,000 in the open market. As a result, it has available capacity of 10,000 units. In this situation, the sole division does not lose its contribution margin of $7 per unit and, therefore, the minimum price it would now accept is $11, as shown in Illustration 9-34.

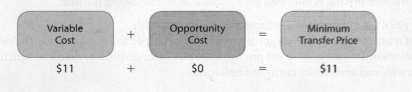

$$\text{Variable Cost} + \text{Opportunity Cost} = \text{Minimum Transfer Price}$$
$$\$11 + \$0 = \$11$$

Illustration 9-34
Minimum transfer price formula—excess capacity

In this case, the boot division and the sole division should negotiate a transfer price within the range of $11 to $17, as shown in Illustration 9-35.

▸Illustration 9-35
Transfer-pricing negotiations—deal

Given excess capacity, Alberta Boot Company will increase its overall net income if it purchases the 10,000 soles internally. This is true as long as the sole division's variable cost is less than the outside price of $17. The sole division will receive a positive contribution margin from any transfer price above its variable cost of $11. The boot division will benefit from any price below $17. At any transfer price above $17, the boot division will go to an outside supplier, a solution that would be undesirable to both divisions, as well as to the company as a whole.

Variable Costs.   In the minimum transfer price formula, **variable cost is defined as the variable cost of units sold** *internally*. In some instances, the variable cost of units sold internally will differ from the variable cost of units sold externally. For example, variable selling expenses are often lower when units are sold internally. In this case, the variable cost of units sold internally will be lower than the cost of units sold externally.

Alternatively, the variable cost of units sold internally could be higher if the internal division requests a special order that requires more expensive materials or additional labour. For example, assume that the boot division would like to make 5,000 new high-margin, heavy-duty boots. The sole required for this boot will be made of a denser rubber and will have an intricate lug design. Alberta Boot Company is not aware of any supplier that currently makes such a sole, and it doubts that any other supplier can meet the quality expectations. As a result, there is no available market price to use as the transfer price.

We can, however, still use the formula for the minimum transfer price to help find a reasonable solution. After evaluating the special sole, the sole division determines that its variable cost would be $19 per sole. The sole division is already at full capacity, however. The sole division's opportunity cost at full capacity is the $7 per sole ($18 − $11) that it earns producing the standard sole and selling it to an outside customer. Therefore, the minimum transfer price that the sole division would be willing to accept for the special-order sole would be as shown in Illustration 9-36.

▸Illustration 9-36
Minimum transfer price formula—
special order

The transfer price of $26 provides the sole division with enough revenue to cover its increased variable cost and its opportunity cost (contribution margin on its standard sole).

Summary of the Negotiated Transfer-Pricing Approach.   Under the negotiated transfer-pricing approach, the selling division establishes a minimum transfer price, and the purchasing division establishes a maximum transfer price. This system provides a sound basis for establishing a transfer price because both divisions are better off if they both use the proper decision rules. However, negotiated transfer pricing is not often used because of the following factors:

- Market price information is sometimes not easily obtainable.
- A lack of trust between the two negotiating divisions may lead to a breakdown in the negotiations.
- Negotiations often lead to different pricing strategies from division to division, which is difficult to work with and sometimes costly to implement.

Many companies, therefore, use more objective and simple systems that are based on cost or market information to develop transfer prices.

Cost-Based Transfer Prices

One method of determining transfer prices is to base the transfer price on the costs of the division that produces the goods or services. If a company uses a **cost-based transfer price**, the transfer price may be based on variable costs alone, or on variable costs plus fixed costs. The selling division may add a markup.

Under a cost-based approach, divisions sometimes use improper transfer prices. This leads to a loss of profitability for the company and unfair evaluations of division performance. To illustrate, assume that Alberta Boot Company requires the divisions to use a transfer price based on the variable cost of the sole. Illustration 9-37 shows what happens to the contribution margin per unit of the two divisions when there is no excess capacity.

►Illustration 9-37
Cost-based transfer price—10,000 units

Boot Division			Sole Division	
Selling price of hiking boots		$90	Selling price of sole	$11
Variable cost of manufacturing boot (not including sole)		35	Variable cost per sole	11
Cost of sole purchased from sole division		11		
Contribution margin per unit		$44	Contribution margin per unit	$ 0
Total contribution margin per unit	$44 ($44 + $0)			

This cost-based transfer system is a bad deal for the sole division, as it reports no profit on the transfer of 10,000 soles to the boot division. If the sole division had sold the 10,000 soles externally, it would have made $70,000 [10,000 × ($18 − $11)]. The boot division, on the other hand, is delighted, as its contribution margin per unit increases from $38 to $44, or $6 more per boot. Overall, Alberta Boot Company loses $10,000 (10,000 units × $1). The sole division lost a contribution margin per unit of $7, and the boot division experienced only a $6 increase in its contribution margin per unit. Illustration 9-38 shows this deficiency.

The overall results change if the sole division **has excess capacity**. In this case, the sole division continues to report a zero profit on these 10,000 units but does not lose the $7 per unit (because it had excess capacity). The boot division gains $6. So overall, the company is better off by $60,000 (10,000 × $6). However, with a cost-based system, the sole division continues to report a zero profit on these 10,000 units.

From this analysis, we can see that a cost-based system does not reflect the division's true profitability. Moreover, it does not even provide enough incentive for the sole division to control costs. Whatever the division's costs are, they are passed on to the next division. One way that some companies try to overcome this problem is to base the transfer price on **standard costs**, rather than actual costs. Although it has these disadvantages, the cost-based system is simple to understand and easy to use because the information is already available in the accounting system. In addition, market information is sometimes not available, so the only alternative is some type of cost-based system. As a result, it is the method that most companies use to establish transfer prices.

Market-Based Transfer Prices

The **market-based transfer price** is based on the actual market prices of competing goods or services. A market-based system is often considered the best approach because it is objective and generally provides the proper economic incentives. For example, if the sole division can charge the market price, it will not care if soles are sold to outside customers or internally to the boot division—it does not lose any contribution margin. Similarly, the boot division will be satisfied because it is paying a price for the goods or services that is at or reasonably close to market prices.

When the sole division has no excess capacity, the market-based system works reasonably well. The sole division receives the market price and the boot division pays the market price.

What happened? We were earning $45 per unit and now it is only $44.

This is great. We now earn $6 more per unit.

Boot Division

Hey, we lost $7 per unit and earned no profit.

Sole Division

►Illustration 9-38
Cost-based transfer price—no excess capacity

If the sole division has excess capacity, however, the market-based system can lead to actions that are not the best ones for the company. For example, the minimum transfer price that the sole division should receive is its variable cost plus opportunity cost. Because the sole division has excess capacity, its opportunity cost is zero. However, under the market-based system, the sole division transfers the goods at the market price of $18, for a contribution margin per unit of $7. The boot division manager then has to accept the $18 sole price. The boot division needs to know, however, that this price is not the cost of the sole when the sole division has excess capacity. If it does not know this, the boot division may overprice its boots in the market by using the market price of the sole plus a markup in setting the price of the boot. This action can lead to losses for Alberta Boot overall.

As indicated earlier, another problem is that in many cases there simply is not a well-defined market for the goods or services being transferred. As a result, a reasonable market value cannot be determined, and companies may therefore use a cost-based system.

Effect of Outsourcing on Transfer Pricing

An increasing number of companies rely on **outsourcing**. Outsourcing involves contracting with an external party to provide goods or services, rather than performing the work internally. Some companies have taken outsourcing to the extreme by outsourcing all of their production. These so-called **virtual companies** have well-established brand names, though they do not manufacture any of their own products. Companies use incremental analysis (Chapter 7) to determine whether outsourcing is profitable. As companies increasingly rely on outsourcing, fewer components are transferred internally between divisions, reducing the need for transfer prices.

TRANSFERS BETWEEN DIVISIONS IN DIFFERENT COUNTRIES

As more companies "globalize" their operations, more transfers are happening between divisions that are in different countries. For example, one estimate suggests that 60% of the trade between countries is simply transfers between divisions. Differences in tax rates in different countries can complicate the determination of the right transfer price.

Companies must pay income tax in the country where income is generated. In order to increase income and pay less income tax, many companies prefer to report more income in countries with low tax rates, and less income in countries with high tax rates. They do this by adjusting the transfer prices they use on internal transfers between divisions located in different countries. The division in the country with the lower tax rate is allocated more contribution margin, and the division in the country with the higher tax rate is allocated less.

To illustrate, suppose that Alberta Boot's boot division is in a country with a corporate tax rate of 10%, and the sole division is in a country with a tax rate of 30%. Illustration 9-39 shows the after-tax contribution margin to the company as a whole assuming, first, that the soles are transferred at a transfer price of $18, and second, that the soles are transferred at a transfer price of $11.

▶Illustration 9-39
After-tax contribution margin per unit under different transfer prices

$18 Transfer Price			
Boot Division		**Sole Division**	
Selling price of hiking boots	$90.00	Selling price of sole	$18.00
Variable cost of manufacturing boot (not including sole)	35.00	Variable cost per sole	11.00
Cost of sole purchased internally	18.00		
Before-tax contribution margin	37.00	Before-tax contribution margin	7.00
Tax at 10%	3.70	Tax at 30%	2.10
After-tax contribution margin	**$33.30**	**After-tax contribution margin**	**$ 4.90**

Before-tax total contribution margin to company: $37 + $7 = **$44**
After-tax total contribution margin to company: $33.30 + $4.90 = **$38.20**

(*continued*)

$11 Transfer Price			
Boot Division		**Sole Division**	
Selling price of hiking boots	$90.00	Selling price of sole	$11.00
Variable cost of manufacturing boot (not including sole)	35.00	Variable cost per sole	11.00
Cost of sole purchased internally	11.00		
Before-tax contribution margin	44.00	Before-tax contribution margin	0.00
Tax at 10%	4.40	Tax at 30%	0.00
After-tax contribution margin	$39.60	After-tax contribution margin	$ 0.00

Before-tax total contribution margin to company: $44 + $0 = $44

After-tax total contribution margin to company: $39.60 + $0 = $39.60

▶Illustration 9-39
After-tax contribution margin per unit under different transfer prices (continued)

Note that the before-tax total contribution margin to Alberta Boot Company is $44 whether the transfer price is $18 or $11. However, the after-tax total contribution margin to Alberta Boot Company is $38.20 using the $18 transfer price, and $39.60 using the $11 transfer price. The reason: when the $11 transfer price is used, more of the contribution margin goes to the division that is in the country with the lower tax rate.

As this analysis shows, Alberta Boot Company would be better off using the $11 transfer price. However, this creates some concerns. First, the sole division manager will not be happy with an $11 transfer price. This price may lead to unfair evaluations of the sole division's manager. Second, the company must ask whether it is legal and ethical to use an $11 transfer price when the market price clearly is higher than that.

Companies will seek to minimize taxes but they have to obey the law. In Canada, transfer prices are subject to CRA scrutiny. The CRA will review transfer prices to ensure they are arm's-length. Consequently there are limits set on a company's ability to minimize its taxes on transactions with foreign subsidiaries. Additional consideration of international transfer pricing is presented further in more advanced accounting courses.

DECISION TOOLKIT

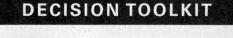

Decision Checkpoints	Info Needed for Decision	Tools to Use for Decision	How to Evaluate Results
What price should a company charge for the transfer of goods between divisions?	Variable costs, opportunity costs, market prices	Variable costs plus opportunity costs should provide a minimum transfer price for the seller.	If the division's income provides for a fair evaluation of managers, then the transfer price is useful. Also, the transfer-pricing approach should not reduce the company's overall income.

BEFORE YOU GO ON...

▶Do It! Transfer Pricing

The clock division of Control Central Corporation manufactures clocks and then sells them to customers for $10 per unit. Its variable cost is $4 per unit, and its fixed cost per unit is $2.50. Management would like the clock division to transfer 8,000 of these clocks to another division within the company at a price of $5. The clock division could avoid $0.50 of variable packaging costs per clock by selling internally.

(continued)

(continued)

(a) Determine the minimum transfer price, assuming the clock division is not operating at full capacity.

(b) Determine the minimum transfer price, assuming the clock division is operating at full capacity.

Action Plan

- Determine whether the division is at full capacity or not.
- Determine variable cost and opportunity cost.
- Apply the minimum transfer price formula.

Solution

(a) If the clock division is not operating at full capacity, the opportunity cost for the clocks is $0. Since internal sales will eliminate $0.50 of packaging costs, the variable cost per clock is $3.50 ($4 − $0.50).

Minimum transfer price	=	Variable cost	+	Opportunity cost
$3.50	=	$3.50	+	$0

(b) If the clock division is already operating at full capacity, the opportunity cost for the clocks is $6 ($10 − $4). Since internal sales will eliminate $0.50 of packaging costs, the variable cost per clock is $3.50 ($4 − $0.50).

Minimum transfer price	=	Variable cost	+	Opportunity cost
$9.50	=	$3.50	+	$6

Related exercise material: **BE9-7, BE9-8, BE9-9, E9-26, E9-27, E9-28, E9-29, E9-30,** and **Do It! D9-15.**

the navigator

ALL ABOUT YOU   *Is the Price Right?*

Since the 1960s, prices in Canada for durable goods such as cars and appliances and semi-durable goods such as clothing constantly rose, but then peaked around 2000 and started to fall. Meanwhile, prices for non-durable goods such as gasoline and food have continued to rise. Prices are affected by things such as commodity supply and demand, rising factory productivity and output, and currency fluctuations. Companies find that pricing their products is tricky because they have to cover variable costs and contribute to fixed overhead and profit, all at a price that consumers like you will bear.

What Do You Think?

There are more than 5,000 products available for sale in this country, ranging from coffee to jewellery, certified by the non-profit Fairtrade Canada. Fair-trade products often cost a bit more because the farmers, artisans, and other producers in developing countries are paid more fairly. Is it worth paying a higher price for fair-trade products?

YES—I want to help those less fortunate than me.

NO—I'm on a tight budget, so I would prefer to donate to a charity that helps producers in developing countries.

Sources: Finn Kelly, "The Price Is Right: Five Factors to Consider when Setting Prices," Smartcompany.com.au, February 27, 2014; "Canadian Businesses Recognized for Commitment to Fair Trade," Fairtrade Canada news release, October 1, 2013; John Baldwin and Ryan Macdonald, "Global Price Movements in Consumer Price Indices," Statistics Canada, May 2013.

USING THE DECISION TOOLKIT

Cedarburg Lumber specializes in building high-end playhouses for kids. It builds the components in its factory, then ships the parts to the customer's home. It has contracted with carpenters across the country to do the final assembly. Each year, it comes out with a new model. This year's model looks like a miniature castle, complete with spires and drawbridge. The following cost estimates for this new product have been provided by the accounting department for a budgeted sales volume of 1,000 units:

	Per Unit	Total
Direct materials	$ 840	
Direct labour	1,600	
Variable manufacturing overhead	400	
Fixed manufacturing overhead		$540,000
Variable selling and administrative expenses	510	
Fixed selling and administrative expenses		320,000

Cedarburg Lumber uses cost-plus pricing to set its selling price. Management also wants the target price to provide a 25% return on investment on invested assets of $4.2 million.

Instructions

(a) Calculate the markup percentage and target selling price on this new playhouse.

(b) Assuming that the sales volume is 1,500 units instead of 1,000 units, calculate the markup percentage and target selling price that will allow Cedarburg Lumber to earn its desired ROI of 25%.

Solution

(a)

Variable cost per unit

	Per Unit
Direct materials	$ 840
Direct labour	1,600
Variable manufacturing overhead	400
Variable selling and administrative expenses	510
Variable cost per unit	$3,350

Fixed cost per unit

	Total Costs	÷	Budgeted Volume	=	Cost per Unit
Fixed manufacturing overhead	$540,000	÷	1,000	=	$540
Fixed selling and administrative expenses	320,000	÷	1,000	=	320
Fixed cost per unit	$860,000				$860

Calculation of selling price (1,000 units)

Variable cost per unit	$3,350
Fixed cost per unit	860
Total cost per unit	4,210
Desired ROI per unit*	1,050
Selling price	$5,260

*($4,200,000 × 0.25) ÷ 1,000

The markup percentage is as follows:

$$\frac{\text{Desired ROI per unit}}{\text{Total unit cost}} = \frac{\$1,050}{\$4,210} = 24.9\%$$

(continued)

(continued)

(b) If the company produces 1,500 units, its selling price and markup percentage would be as follows:

<u>Calculation of selling price (1,500 units)</u>

Variable cost per unit	$3,350
Fixed cost per unit ($860,000 ÷ 1,500)	573
Total cost per unit	3,923
Desired ROI per unit*	700
Selling price	$4,623

*($4,200,000 × 0.25) ÷ 1,500

The markup percentage is:

$$\frac{\text{Desired ROI per unit}}{\text{Total unit cost}} = \frac{\$700}{\$3,923} = 17.8\%$$

Summary of Study Objectives

1. **Calculate a target cost when the market determines a product's price.** To calculate a target cost, the company determines its target selling price. Once the target selling price is set, it determines its target cost by setting a desired profit. The difference between the target price and the desired profit is the target cost of the product.

2. **Calculate a target selling price using total cost-plus pricing.** In cost-plus pricing, the company determines a cost base and adds a markup to it to determine a target selling price. The cost-plus pricing formula is as follows: cost + (markup percentage × cost) = target selling price.

3. **Calculate a target selling price using absorption cost-plus pricing.** The absorption cost-plus approach uses the manufacturing cost as the cost base and covers the selling and administrative costs plus the target ROI through the markup. The target selling price is calculated as follows: manufacturing cost per unit + (markup percentage × manufacturing cost per unit).

4. **Calculate a target selling price using variable cost-plus pricing.** The variable cost-plus approach uses all of the variable costs, including selling and administrative costs, as the cost base

and covers the fixed costs and target ROI through the markup. The target selling price is calculated as follows: variable cost per unit + (markup percentage × variable cost per unit).

5. **Use time-and-material pricing to determine the cost of services provided.** Under time-and-material pricing, the company sets two pricing rates: one for the labour used on a job and another for the material. The labour rate includes direct labour time and other employee costs. The material charge is based on the cost of the direct parts and materials that are used and a material loading charge for related overhead costs.

6. **Determine a transfer price using the negotiated, cost-based, and market-based approaches.** The negotiated price is determined by an agreement between division managers. A cost-based transfer price may be based on total cost, variable cost, or some modification including a markup. The cost-based approach often leads to poor performance evaluations and purchasing decisions. The advantage of the cost-based system is its simplicity. A market-based transfer price is based on actual market prices for products and services. A market-based system is often considered the best approach because it is objective and generally creates good economic incentives.

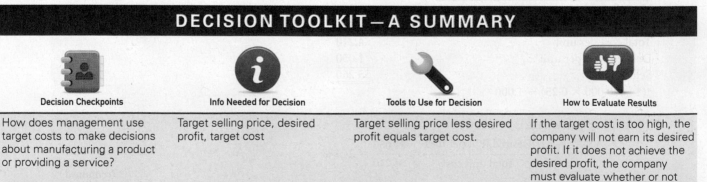

DECISION TOOLKIT—A SUMMARY

Decision Checkpoints	Info Needed for Decision	Tools to Use for Decision	How to Evaluate Results
How does management use target costs to make decisions about manufacturing a product or providing a service?	Target selling price, desired profit, target cost	Target selling price less desired profit equals target cost.	If the target cost is too high, the company will not earn its desired profit. If it does not achieve the desired profit, the company must evaluate whether or not to manufacture the product or provide the service.

(continued)

(continued)

DECISION TOOLKIT—A SUMMARY

Decision Checkpoints	Info Needed for Decision	Tools to Use for Decision	How to Evaluate Results
What factors should management consider in determining the sales price in a less competitive environment?	The total cost per unit and desired profit (cost-plus pricing)	Total cost per unit plus desired profit equals target selling price.	Does the company make its desired profit? If not, is it because of a lower sales volume?
How do we set prices when it is difficult to estimate the total cost per unit?	Two pricing rates: one for labour use and another for materials	Calculate the labour rate charge and material rate charge. In each of these calculations, add a profit margin.	Is the company profitable under this pricing approach? Are employees earning reasonable wages?
What price should a company charge for the transfer of goods between divisions?	Variable costs, opportunity costs, market prices	Variable costs plus opportunity costs should provide a minimum transfer price for the seller.	If the division's income provides for a fair evaluation of managers, then the transfer price is useful. Also, the transfer-pricing approach should not reduce the company's overall income.

Glossary

Absorption cost-plus pricing   An approach to pricing that defines the cost base as the manufacturing cost; it excludes both variable and fixed selling and administrative costs. (p. 359)

Cost-based transfer price   A transfer price that is based on the costs of the division producing the goods. (p. 371)

Market-based transfer price   A transfer price that is based on the actual market prices of products. (p. 371)

Markup   The percentage applied to a product's cost to determine the product's selling price. (p. 356)

Material loading charge   A charge added to cover the cost of purchasing, receiving, handling, and storing materials, plus any desired profit margin on the materials themselves. (p. 364)

Negotiated transfer price   A transfer price that is determined by the agreement of the division managers when no external market price is available. (p. 368)

Outsourcing   Contracting with an external party to provide goods or services rather than performing the work internally. (p. 372)

Target cost   The cost that will provide the desired profit on a product when the seller does not have control over the product's price. (p. 354)

Target selling price   The selling price that will provide the desired profit on a product when the seller can determine the product's price. (p. 356)

Time-and-material pricing   An approach to cost-plus pricing in which the company uses two pricing rates: one for the labour used on a job and another for the material. (p. 363)

Total cost-plus pricing   A process in which a product's selling price is determined by adding a markup to a total cost base. (p. 356)

Transfer price   The price used to record the transfer of goods between two divisions of a company. (p. 366)

Variable cost-plus pricing   An approach to pricing that defines the cost base as all variable costs; it excludes both the fixed manufacturing and fixed selling and administrative costs. (p. 360)

Comprehensive Do It!

Revco Electronics is a division of International Motors, an automobile manufacturer. Revco produces car radio/CD players. Revco sells its products to International Motors and to other car manufacturers and electronics distributors. The following information is for the car radio/CD player:

Selling price of car radio/CD player to external customers	$49
Variable cost per unit	$28
Capacity	200,000 units

(continued)

(continued)

Instructions

Determine whether the goods should be transferred internally or purchased externally and what the appropriate transfer price should be under each of the following independent situations:

(a) Revco Electronics is operating at full capacity. There is a saving of $4 per unit in variable costs if the car radio is made for internal sale. International Motors can purchase a similar car radio from an outside supplier for $47.

(b) Revco Electronics has enough capacity to satisfy the needs of International Motors. International Motors can purchase a similar car radio from an outside supplier for $47.

(c) International Motors wants to purchase a special-order car radio/CD player that also includes an MP3 player. It needs 15,000 units. Revco Electronics has determined that the additional variable cost would be $12 per unit. Revco Electronics has no unused capacity. It will have to lose sales of 15,000 units to external parties in order to provide this special order.

Solution to Comprehensive Do It!

(a) Revco Electronics' opportunity cost (its lost contribution margin) would be $21 ($49 – $28). Using the formula for minimum transfer price, we determine the following:

$$\text{Minimum transfer price} = \text{variable cost} + \text{opportunity cost}$$
$$\$45 = (\$28 - \$4) + \$21$$

Since this minimum transfer price is less than the $47 it would cost if International Motors purchases from an external party, an internal transfer should take place. Revco Electronics and International Motors should negotiate a transfer price between $45 and $47.

(b) Since Revco Electronics has available capacity, its opportunity cost (its lost contribution margin) would be $0. Using the formula for minimum transfer price, we determine the following:

$$\text{Minimum transfer price} = \text{variable cost} + \text{opportunity cost}$$
$$\$28 = \$28 + \$0$$

Since International Motors can purchase the unit for $47 from an external party, the most it would be willing to pay would be $47. It is in the best interest of the company as a whole, as well as the two divisions, for a transfer to take place. The two divisions must reach a negotiated transfer price between $28 and $47 that recognizes the costs and benefits to each party and is acceptable to both.

(c) Revco Electronics' opportunity cost (its lost contribution margin per unit) would be $21 ($49 − $28). Its variable cost would be $40 ($28 + $12). Using the formula for minimum transfer price, we determine the following:

$$\text{Minimum transfer price} = \text{variable cost} + \text{opportunity cost}$$
$$\$61 = \$40 + \$21$$

Note that in this case Revco Electronics has no available capacity. Its management may decide that it does not want to provide this special order because this would force the company to cut off the supply of the standard unit to some of its existing customers. This may anger those customers and result in the company's losing them.

Action Plan

- Determine whether the division is at full capacity or not.
- Find the minimum transfer price, using formulas.
- Compare the maximum price the buyer would pay with the minimum price for the seller.
- Determine if a deal can be made.

the navigator

WileyPLUS

Self-Test, Brief Exercises, Exercises, Problems—Set A, and many more components are available for practice in WileyPlus.

Self-Study Questions

Answers are at the end of the chapter.

(SO 2)   1. Cost-plus pricing means that
   (a) selling price = variable cost + (markup percentage + variable cost).
   (b) selling price = cost + (markup percentage × cost).
   (c) selling price = manufacturing cost + (markup percentage + manufacturing cost).
   (d) selling price = fixed cost + (markup percentage × fixed cost).

(SO 1) 2. Target cost as related to price and profit means that
(a) cost and desired profit must be determined before the selling price is determined.
(b) cost and selling price must be determined before the desired profit is determined.
(c) price and desired profit must be determined before the costs are determined.
(d) costs can be covered only if the company is at full capacity.

(SO 1) 3. Classic Toys has examined the market for toy train locomotives. It believes there is a market niche in which it can sell locomotives at $80 each. It estimates that it could sell 10,000 of these locomotives annually. Variable costs to make a locomotive are expected to be $25. Classic anticipates a profit of $15 per locomotive. What is the target cost for the locomotive?
(a) $80
(b) $65
(c) $40
(d) $25

(SO 2) 4. Adler Company is considering developing a new product. The company has gathered the following information on this product:

Expected total unit cost	$ 25
Estimated investment for new product	$500,000
Desired ROI	10%
Expected number of units to be produced and sold	1,000

The desired markup percentage and selling price are
(a) markup percentage 10%; selling price $55.
(b) markup percentage 200%; selling price $75.
(c) markup percentage 10%; selling price $50.
(d) markup percentage 100%; selling price $55.

(SO 2) 5. Mystique Co. provides the following information for the new product it recently introduced:

Total unit cost	$30
Desired ROI per unit	$10
Target selling price	$40

What would be Mystique Co.'s percentage markup on cost?
(a) 125%
(b) 75%
(c) 33⅓%
(d) 25%

(SO 5) 6. Crescent Electrical Repair has decided to price its work on a time-and-materials basis. It estimates the following costs for the year for labour:

Technician wages and benefits	$100,000
Office employee's salary and benefits	40,000
Other overhead	80,000

Crescent wants a profit margin of $10 per labour hour and budgets 5,000 hours of repair time for the year. The office employee's salary and benefits, and other overhead costs, should be divided evenly between the time charges and material loading charges. What would be Crescent's labour charge per hour?
(a) $42
(b) $34
(c) $32
(d) $30

(SO 6) 7. The plastics division of Zekas Company manufactures plastic moulds and then sells them to customers for $70 per unit. Its variable cost is $30 per unit, and its fixed cost is $10 per unit. Management would like the division to transfer 10,000 of these moulds to another division within the company at a price of $40. The plastics division is operating at full capacity. What is the minimum transfer price that the plastics division should accept?
(a) $10
(b) $30
(c) $40
(d) $70

(SO 6) 8. Assume the same information as question 7, except that the plastics division has available capacity of 10,000 units for plastic mouldings. What is the minimum transfer price that the plastics division should accept?
(a) $10
(b) $30
(c) $40
(d) $70

(SO 3) 9. AST Electrical provides the following cost information for its production of electronic circuit boards:

	Per Unit
Variable manufacturing cost	$40
Fixed manufacturing cost	30
Variable selling and administrative expenses	8
Fixed selling and administrative expenses	12
Desired ROI per unit	15

What is its markup percentage, assuming that AST Electrical uses the absorption-cost approach?
(a) 16.67%
(b) 50%
(c) 54.28%
(d) 118.75%

(SO 4) 10. Assume the same information as in question 9. What is AST Electrical's markup percentage using the variable-cost approach?
(a) 16.67%
(b) 50%
(c) 54.28%
(d) 118.75%

Brief Exercises

(SO 1)
Calculate target cost.

BE9-1 Podrive Company manufactures computer hard drives. The market for hard drives is very competitive. The current market price for a computer hard drive is $45. Podrive would like a profit of $15 per drive. How can Podrive Company accomplish this objective?

(SO 2)
Use cost-plus pricing to determine selling price.

BE9-2 Gruner Corporation produces snowboards. The following cost information per unit is available: direct materials $12; direct labour $8; variable manufacturing overhead $6; fixed manufacturing overhead $14; variable selling and administrative expenses $4; and fixed selling and administrative expenses $12. Using a 30% markup percentage on the total cost per unit, calculate the target selling price.

(SO 2)
Calculate ROI per unit.

BE9-3 Travis Corporation produces high-performance rotors. It expects to produce 50,000 rotors in the coming year. It has invested $10 million to produce the rotors. The company has a required return on investment of 16%. What is its ROI per unit?

(SO 2)
Calculate markup percentage.

BE9-4 Schuman Corporation produces microwave units. The following per-unit cost information is available: direct materials $36; direct labour $24; variable manufacturing overhead $18; fixed manufacturing overhead $40; variable selling and administrative expenses $14; and fixed selling and administrative expenses $28. Its desired ROI per unit is $30. Calculate its markup percentage using a total cost approach.

(SO 2)
Calculate ROI and markup percentage.

BE9-5 During the current year, Bierko Corporation expects to produce 10,000 units and has budgeted the following: net income $300,000; variable costs $1.1 million; and fixed costs $100,000. It has invested assets of $1.5 million. What was the company's budgeted ROI? What was its budgeted markup percentage using a total cost approach?

(SO 5)
Use time-and-material pricing to determine bill.

BE9-6 Swayze Small Engine Repair charges $42 per hour of labour. It has a material loading percentage of 40%. On a recent job to replace the engine of a riding lawnmower, Swayze worked 10.5 hours and used parts with a cost of $700. Calculate Swayze's total bill.

(SO 6)
Determine the minimum transfer price.

BE9-7 The machining division of ITA International has a capacity of 2,000 units. Its sales and cost data are:

Selling price per unit	$ 80
Variable manufacturing costs per unit	25
Variable selling costs per unit	5
Total fixed manufacturing overhead	200,000

(SO 6)
Determine the minimum transfer price with excess capacity.

The machining division is currently selling 1,800 units to outside customers, and the assembly division of ITA International wants to purchase 400 units from machining. If the transaction takes place, the variable selling costs per unit on the units transferred to assembly will be $0/unit, and not $5/unit. What should be the transfer price in order not to affect the machining division's current profit?

(SO 6)
Determine the minimum transfer price for special order.

BE9-8 Use the data from BE9-7. If ITA's assembly division is currently buying from an outside supplier at $75 per unit, what will be the effect on overall company profits if internal sales for 400 units take place at the optimum transfer price?

(SO 3)
Calculate the markup percentage using the absorption-cost approach.

BE9-9 Use the data for ITA International from BE9-7, but assume that the units being requested are special high-performance units, and that the division's variable cost would be $24 per unit. What is the minimum transfer price that the heating division should accept?

BE9-10 Using the data in BE9-4, calculate the markup percentage using the absorption-cost approach.

(SO 4)
Calculate the markup percentage using the variable-cost approach.

BE9-11 Using the data in BE9-4, calculate the markup percentage using variable-cost pricing.

Do It! Review

(SO 1)
Determine target cost.

D9-12 Clear Water is considering introducing a water filtration device for its one-litre water bottles. Market research indicates that 1 million units can be sold if the price is no more than $3. If Clear Water decides to produce the filters, it will need to invest $2 million in new production equipment. Clear Water requires a minimum rate of return of 18% on all investments.

Instructions
Determine the target cost per unit for the filter.

D9-13 Floor Show Corporation produces area rugs. The following per-unit cost information is available: direct materials $18, direct labour $9, variable manufacturing overhead $5, fixed manufacturing overhead $6, variable selling and administrative expenses $3, and fixed selling and administrative expenses $7.

Instructions
Using a 30% markup on total per-unit cost, calculate the target selling price.

(SO 2)
Use cost-plus pricing to determine various amounts.

D9-14 Presented below are data for ProTech Appliance Repair Shop:

Repair technicians' wages	$120,000
Fringe benefits	40,000
Overhead	50,000

The desired profit margin per hour is $18. The material loading charge is 50% of invoice cost. ProTech estimates that 5,000 labour hours will be worked next year.

Instructions
If ProTech repairs a dishwasher that takes 1.5 hours to repair and uses parts that cost $80, calculate the bill for the job.

(SO 5)
Use time-and-material pricing to determine bill.

D9-15 The fastener division of Northern Textile Industries manufactures zippers and then sells them to customers for $8 per unit. Its variable cost is $3 per unit, and its fixed cost per unit is $1.50. Management would like the fastener division to transfer 12,000 of these zippers to another division within the company at a price of $3. The fastener division could avoid $0.25 per zipper of variable packaging costs by selling internally.

Instructions
Determine the minimum transfer price (a) assuming the fastener division is not operating at full capacity, and (b) assuming the fastener division is operating at full capacity.

(SO 6)
Determine transfer prices.

Exercises

E9-16 Culver Cheese Company has developed a new cheese slicer called the Slim Slicer. The company plans to sell this slicer through its monthly catalogue. Given market research, Culver management believes the company can charge $20 for the Slim Slicer. Prototypes of the Slim Slicer, however, are costing $25. By using cheaper materials and gaining efficiencies in mass production, management believes Culver can reduce the Slim Slicer's cost substantially. The company wants to earn a return of 25% of the selling price.

Instructions
(a) Calculate the target cost for the Slim Slicer.
(b) Determine when target costing is particularly helpful in deciding whether to produce a particular product.

(SO 1)
Calculate the target cost.

E9-17 Lasik Look produces and sells high-end golf equipment. The company has recently been involved in developing various types of laser guns to measure distances on the golf course. The potential market for one small laser gun, the LittleLasik, appears to be very large. Because of competition, Lasik Look does not believe that it can charge more than $90 for LittleLasik. At this price, Lasik Look believes it can sell 100,000 laser guns. LittleLasik will cost $8 million to manufacture, and the company wants an ROI of 20%.

Instructions
Determine the target cost for one LittleLasik.

(SO 1)
Calculate the target cost.

E9-18 Mucky Duck makes swimsuits and sells them directly to retailers. Although Mucky Duck has a variety of suits, it does not make the all-body suit used by highly skilled swimmers. The market research department believes that a strong market exists for this type of suit. It says the all-body suit would sell for approximately $110. Given its experience, Mucky Duck believes the all-body suit would have the following manufacturing costs:

Direct materials	$ 25
Direct labour	30
Manufacturing overhead	45
Total costs	$100

(SO 1, 2)
Calculate the target cost using cost-plus pricing.

Instructions
(a) Assume that Mucky Duck uses cost-plus pricing, and sets the price 25% above the product's costs.
1. What would be the price charged for the all-body swimsuit?
2. Under what circumstances might Mucky Duck consider manufacturing the all-body swimsuit given this approach?
3. What is the highest acceptable manufacturing cost Mucky Duck would be willing to incur to produce the all-body swimsuit?
(b) Assume that Mucky Duck uses target costing. What is the price that Mucky Duck would charge the retailer for the all-body swimsuit?

(SO 2)
Use cost-plus pricing to determine the selling price.

E9-19 Select Corporation makes a commercial-grade cooking griddle. The following information is available for Select Corporation's expected annual volume of 30,000 units:

	Per Unit	Total
Direct materials	$17	
Direct labour	8	
Variable manufacturing overhead	11	
Fixed manufacturing overhead		$360,000
Variable selling and administrative expenses	4	
Fixed selling and administrative expenses		150,000

The company uses a 40% markup percentage on total cost.

Instructions
(a) Calculate the total cost per unit.
(b) Calculate the target selling price.

(SO 2)
Use cost-plus pricing to determine various amounts.

E9-20 Ahmed Corporation makes a mechanical stuffed alligator. The following information is available for Ahmed Corporation's expected annual volume of 500,000 units:

	Per Unit	Total
Direct materials	$17	
Direct labour	8	
Variable selling and administrative expenses	11	
Fixed manufacturing overhead		$360,000
Variable selling and administrative expenses	4	
Fixed selling and administrative expenses		150,000

The company has a desired ROI of 25%. It has invested assets of $24 million.

Instructions
(a) Calculate the total cost per unit.
(b) Calculate the desired ROI per unit.
(c) Calculate the markup percentage using the total cost per unit.
(d) Calculate the target selling price.

(SO 2)
Use cost-plus pricing to determine various amounts.

E9-21 Roxy's Recording Studio rents studio time to musicians in two-hour blocks. Each session includes the use of the studio facilities, a digital recording of the performance, and a professional music producer/mixer. Anticipated annual volume is 1,000 sessions. The company has invested $2,352,000 in the studio and expects a return on investment of 20%. Budgeted costs for the coming year are as follows:

	Per Session	Total
Direct materials (tapes, CDs, etc.)	$ 20	
Direct labour	400	
Variable overhead	50	
Fixed overhead		$950,000
Variable selling and administrative expenses	40	
Fixed selling and administrative expenses		500,000

Instructions
(a) Determine the total cost per session.
(b) Determine the desired ROI per session.
(c) Calculate the markup percentage on the total cost per session.
(d) Calculate the target price per session.

(SO 2)
Use cost-plus pricing to determine various amounts.

E9-22 Caan Corporation produces industrial robots for high-precision manufacturing. The following information is given for Caan Corporation:

	Per Unit	Total
Direct materials	$380	
Direct labour	290	
Variable manufacturing overhead	72	
Fixed manufacturing overhead		$1,800,000
Variable selling and administrative expenses	55	
Fixed selling and administrative expenses		324,000

The company has a desired ROI of 20%. It has invested assets of $51 million. It expects to produce 3,000 units each year.

Instructions
(a) Calculate the cost per unit of the fixed manufacturing overhead and the fixed selling and administrative expenses.
(b) Calculate the desired ROI per unit. (Round to the nearest dollar.)
(c) Calculate the target selling price.

E9-23 Padong Remanufacturing rebuilds spot welders for manufacturers. The following budgeted cost data for 2016 are available for Padong:

(SO 5)
Use time-and-material pricing to determine bill.

	Time Charges	Material Loading Charges
Technicians' wages and benefits	$228,000	
Parts manager's salary and benefits		$42,500
Office employee's salary and benefits	38,000	9,000
Other overhead	15,200	24,000
Total budgeted costs	$281,200	$75,500

The company wants a $30 profit margin per hour of labour and a 20% profit margin on parts. It has budgeted for 7,600 hours of repair time in the coming year, and estimates that the total invoice cost of parts and materials in 2016 will be $400,000.

Instructions
(a) Calculate the rate charged per hour of labour.
(b) Calculate the material loading percentage. (Round to three decimal places.)
(c) Lindy Corporation has asked for an estimate on rebuilding its spot welder. Padong estimates that it would require 40 hours of labour and $2,000 in parts. Calculate the total estimated bill.

E9-24 Justin's Custom Electronics (JCE) sells and installs complete security, computer, audio, and video systems for homes. On newly constructed homes, it provides bids using time-and-material pricing. The following budgeted cost data are available:

(SO 5)
Use time-and-material pricing to determine bill.

	Time Charges	Material Loading Charges
Technicians' wages and benefits	$150,000	
Parts manager's salary and benefits		$34,000
Office employee's salary and benefits	28,000	12,000
Other overhead	15,000	42,000
Total budgeted costs	$193,000	$88,000

The company has budgeted for 6,250 hours of technician time during the coming year. It wants a $38 profit margin per hour of labour and a 100% profit on parts. It estimates the total invoice cost of parts and materials in 2016 will be $700,000.

Instructions
(a) Calculate the rate charged per hour of labour. (Round to two decimal places.)
(b) Calculate the material loading percentage. (Round to two decimal places.)
(c) JCE has just received a request for a bid from R. J. Builders on outfitting a $1.2-million new home. The company estimates that it would require 80 hours of labour and $40,000 in parts. Calculate the total estimated bill.

E9-25 Karl's Klassic Kars restores classic automobiles to showroom status. Budgeted data for the current year are as follows:

(SO 5)
Use time-and-material pricing to determine bill.

	Time Charges	Material Loading Charges
Restorers' wages and fringe benefits	$270,000	
Purchasing agent's salary and fringe benefits		$ 67,500
Administrative salaries and fringe benefits	54,000	21,960
Other overhead costs	24,000	77,490
Total budgeted costs	$348,000	$166,950

The company anticipated that the restorers would work a total of 12,000 hours this year and expected that parts and materials would cost $1,260,000.

In late January, the company experienced a fire in its facilities that destroyed most of the accounting records. The accountant remembers that the hourly labour rate was $70.00 and that the material loading charge was 83.25%.

Instructions
(a) Determine the profit margin per hour on labour.
(b) Determine the profit margin on materials.
(c) Determine the total price of labour and materials on a job that was completed after the fire that required 150 hours of labour and $60,000 in parts and materials.

E9-26 Alpha International Corporation has two divisions, beta and gamma. Beta produces an electronic component that sells for $75 per unit, with the following costs based on its capacity of 200,000 units:

(SO 6)
Determine the minimum transfer price.

Direct materials	$25.00
Direct labour	15.00
Variable overhead	5.00
Fixed overhead	10.00

Beta is operating at 75% of normal capacity and gamma is purchasing 15,000 units of the same component from an outside supplier for $70 per unit.

Instructions

(a) Calculate the benefit, if any, to beta in selling to gamma 15,000 at the outside supplier's price.

(b) Calculate the lowest price beta would be willing to accept.

(c) If beta is operating at full capacity what would be the lowest transfer that beta division is willing to accept?

(d) Assume that a transfer price of $75 is used between beta and gamma. Calculate the effect on the profits of beta, gamma, and Alpha International Corporation.

(e) ▭▭▭▭▷ Explain why the level of capacity in the beta division affects the transfer price.

(SO 6)
Determine the minimum transfer price under different situations.

E9-27   The cycle division of TravelFast Company has the following cost data per unit for its most recent cycle, the Roadbuster:

Selling price		$2,200
Variable cost of goods sold		
Body frame	$300	
Other variable costs	900	1,200
Contribution margin		$1,000

The cycle division currently buys its body frames from an outside supplier. However, TravelFast has another division, FrameBody, that makes body frames for other cycle companies. The cycle division believes that FrameBody's product is suitable for its new Roadbuster cycle. FrameBody sells its frames to outside customers for $350 per frame. The variable cost for FrameBody is $250. The cycle division is willing to pay $275 to purchase the frames from FrameBody.

Instructions

(a) Assume that FrameBody has excess capacity and is able to meet all of the cycle division's needs. If the cycle division buys 1,000 frames from FrameBody, determine the following: (1) the effect on the cycle division's income; (2) the effect on FrameBody's income; and (3) the effect on TravelFast's income.

(b) Assume that FrameBody does not have excess capacity and therefore would lose sales if it sold the frames to the cycle division. If the cycle division buys 1,000 frames from FrameBody, determine the following: (1) the effect on the cycle division's income; (2) the effect on FrameBody's income; and (3) the effect on TravelFast's income.

(SO 6)
Determine the minimum transfer price under different situations.

E9-28   The machining division has a capacity of 4,000 units. Its sales and cost data are:

Selling price per unit	$ 160
Variable manufacturing costs per unit	50
Variable selling costs per unit	10
Total fixed manufacturing overhead	100,000

Instructions

(a) The machining division currently sells 1,600 units to outside customers, and the assembly division wants to purchase 800 units from machining. If the transaction takes place, the variable selling costs per unit on the units transferred to assembly will be $0/unit, not $10/unit. What should be the transfer price in order not to affect its current profit?

(b) If the assembly division is currently buying from an outside supplier at $150 per unit, what will be the effect on overall company profits if internal sales for 800 units take place at the optimum transfer price?

(SO 6)
Calculate the minimum transfer price.

E9-29   The national division of Nero International Company is buying 20,000 widgets from an outside supplier at $75 per unit. Nero International's overseas division, which is producing and selling at full capacity (25,000 units), has the following sales and cost structure:

Sales price per unit	$90.00
Variable cost per unit	70.00
Fixed cost (at capacity) per unit	20.00

Instructions

(a) Determine the minimum transfer price if the national division buys 5,000 widgets from the Overseas Division.

(b) Determine the effect on overall company profits if the overseas division meets the outside supplier's price and sells the 5,000 widgets to the national division.

(SO 6)
Determine the minimum transfer price.

E9-30   High Sound Corporation manufactures car stereos. It is a division of Quality Motors, which manufactures vehicles. High Sound sells car stereos to Quality Motors, as well as to other vehicle manufacturers and retail stores. The following information is available for High Sound's standard unit car stereo's costs: variable cost per unit $35; fixed cost per unit $23; and selling price to outside customers $86. Quality Motors currently purchases a standard unit car stereo from an outside supplier for $80. Because of quality concerns and to ensure a reliable supply, the top management of Quality Motors has ordered High Sound to provide 20,000 units per year at a transfer price of $35 per unit. High Sound is already operating at full capacity. High Sound can avoid $5 per unit of variable costs by selling the unit internally.

Instructions

(a) Determine the minimum transfer price that High Sound should accept.

(b) Calculate the potential loss to the corporation as a whole because of this forced transfer price of $35.

(c) How should the company resolve this situation?

E9-31 The information for Ahmed Corporation is given in E9-20.

Instructions

(a) Using absorption-cost pricing, calculate the markup percentage.

(b) Using variable-cost pricing, calculate the markup percentage.

(SO 2, 3, 4)
Calculate the total cost per unit, ROI, and markup percentages.

E9-32 Firefly Corporation produces outdoor portable fireplace units. The following cost information per unit is available: direct materials $21, direct labour $26, variable manufacturing overhead $16, fixed manufacturing overhead $22, variable selling and administrative expenses $9, and fixed selling and administrative expenses $15. The company's ROI per unit is $20.

Instructions

Calculate Firefly Corporation's markup percentage using (a) absorption-cost pricing and (b) variable-cost pricing.

(SO 3, 4)
Calculate markup percentage using absorption-cost pricing and variable-cost pricing.

E9-33 Information for Caan Corporation is given in E9-22.

Instructions

(a) Calculate the markup percentage and target selling price using absorption-cost pricing. (Round to three decimal places.)

(b) Calculate the markup percentage and target selling price using variable-cost pricing. (Round to three decimal places.)

(SO 3, 4)
Calculate various amounts using absorption-cost pricing and variable-cost pricing.

Problems: Set A

P9-34A Auto Glass Company (AGC) manufactures and sells windshield products. AGC entered into a one-time contract to produce an additional 1,000 windshields for the local public transit authority, at a price of "cost plus 20%." The company has a plant with a capacity of 9,000 units per year, but normal production is 4,000 units per year. The annual costs to produce those 4,000 units are as follows:

(SO 2)
Use cost-plus pricing to determine various amounts.

Materials	$200,000
Labour	320,000
Supplies and other variable manufacturing indirect costs	120,000
Fixed indirect costs (allocated based on normal capacity)	160,000
Variable marketing costs	40,000
Administrative costs (all fixed)	80,000

After completing half of the order, the company billed the authority for $138,000. However, the transit authority's purchasing agent then called the president of AGC to dispute the invoice. The purchasing agent stated that the invoice should have been for $96,000.

Instructions

(a) Calculate the components of the "total-cost" unit price charged to the transit authority, as determined by AGC.

(b) Calculate the components of the "variable manufacturing cost" unit price that should have been charged, as determined by the transit authority's purchasing agent.

(c) What price per unit would you recommend? Explain your reasoning. (*Note:* You do not need to limit yourself to the costs selected by the company or by the agent.)

(adapted from CGA-Canada, now CPA Canada)

(a) $230
(b) $160

P9-35A Lafleur Corporation needs to set a target price for its newly designed product, M14-M16. The following data relate to it:

(SO 2)
Use cost-plus pricing to determine various amounts.

	Per Unit	Total
Direct materials	$12	
Direct labour	18	
Variable manufacturing overhead	10	
Fixed manufacturing overhead		$3,000,000
Variable selling and administrative expenses	7	
Fixed selling and administrative expenses		2,000,000

These costs are based on a budgeted volume of 250,000 units produced and sold each year. Lafleur uses cost-plus pricing to set its target selling price. The markup on the total unit cost is 20%.

Instructions

(a) Calculate the total variable cost per unit, total fixed cost per unit, and total cost per unit for M14-M16.

(b) Calculate the desired markup per unit for M14-M16.

(c) Calculate the target selling price for M14-M16.

(d) Assuming that 200,000 M14-M16s are produced during the year, calculate the variable cost per unit, fixed cost per unit, and total cost per unit.

(a) Variable cost per unit = $47

(SO 2, 4)
Use cost-plus pricing to determine various amounts.

P9-36A   Berg and Son Ltd. builds custom-made pleasure boats that range in price from $10,000 to $250,000. For the past 30 years, Mr. Berg Sr. has determined the selling price of each boat by estimating the cost of material, labour, and a prorated portion of overhead, and adding 20% to the estimated costs.

For example, a recent price quotation was determined as follows:

Direct materials	$ 50,000
Direct labour	80,000
Overhead	20,000
	150,000
Plus 20%	30,000
Selling price	$180,000

Estimating total overhead for the year and allocating it at 25% of the direct labour costs determined the overhead costs.

If a customer rejected the price and business was slow, Mr. Berg Sr. might be willing to reduce his markup to as little as 5% over the estimated costs. Thus, average markup for the year was estimated at 15%.

Mr. Berg Jr. has just completed a managerial accounting course that dealt with pricing, and he believes that the firm could use some of the techniques discussed in the course. The course emphasized the variable-cost approach to pricing, and Mr. Berg Jr. feels that such an approach would be helpful in determining an appropriate price for the boats.

Total overhead, which includes selling and administrative expenses for the year, has been estimated at $1.5 million, of which $900,000 is fixed and the remainder is variable in direct proportion to direct labour.

Instructions
(a) Assume the customer rejected the $180,000 quotation and also rejected a $157,500 (5% markup) quotation during a slack period. The customer countered with a $150,000 offer.
   1. What is the minimum selling price Mr. Berg Sr. could have quoted without reducing or increasing the company's net income?

(a) 2. $12,000 increase
   2. What is the difference in company net income for the year between accepting or rejecting the customer's offer?
(b) Identify and briefly explain one advantage and one disadvantage of the variable-cost approach to pricing compared with the approach Berg and Son Ltd. previously used.

(adapted from CGA-Canada, now CPA Canada)

(SO 2)
Use cost-plus pricing to determine various amounts.

P9-37A   Bolus Computer Parts Inc. is setting a selling price on a new component it has just designed and developed. The following cost estimates for this new component have been provided by the accounting department for a budgeted volume of 50,000 units:

	Per Unit	Total
Direct materials	$50	
Direct labour	26	
Variable manufacturing overhead	20	
Fixed manufacturing overhead		$600,000
Variable selling and administrative expenses	19	
Fixed selling and administrative expenses		400,000

Bolus Computer Parts' management requests that the total cost per unit be used in cost-plus pricing of products. On this particular product, management also directs that the target price be set to provide a 25% return on investment on invested assets of $1 million.

Instructions
(Round all calculations to two decimal places.)
(a) Calculate the markup percentage and target selling price that will allow Bolus Computer Parts to earn its desired ROI of 25% on this new component.

(b) Target selling price = $146.25
(b) Assuming that the volume is 40,000 units, calculate the markup percentage and target selling price that will allow Bolus Computer Parts to earn its desired ROI of 25% on this new component.

(SO 5)
Use time-and-material pricing to determine bill.

P9-38A   St-Cyr's Electronic Repair Shop has budgeted the following time and material for 2016:

	Time Charges	Material Charges
Shop employees' wages and benefits	$108,000	$ 0
Parts manager's salary and benefits	0	25,400
Office employee's salary and benefits	20,000	13,600
Invoice cost of parts used	0	100,000
Overhead (supplies, amortization, advertising, utilities)	26,000	18,000
Total budgeted costs	$154,000	$157,000

St-Cyr's budgets 5,000 hours of repair time in 2016 and will bill a profit of $5 per labour hour along with a 30% profit markup on the invoice cost of parts.

On January 5, 2016, St-Cyr's is asked to submit a price estimate to fix a 72-inch big-screen TV. St-Cyr's estimates that this job will consume 20 hours of labour and $500 in parts and materials.

Instructions

(a) Calculate the labour rate for St-Cyr's Electronic Repair Shop for the year 2016.

(b) Calculate the material loading-charge percentage for St-Cyr's Electronic Repair Shop for the year 2016.

(c) Prepare a time-and-material price quotation for fixing the big-screen TV.

(b) 87%

(c) Total = $1,651

P9-39A Ampro Inc. has two divisions. Division A makes and sells student desks. Division B manufactures and sells reading lamps.

Each desk has a reading lamp as one of its components. Division A needs 10,000 lamps for the coming year and can purchase reading lamps at a cost of $10 from an outside vendor.

Division B has the capacity to manufacture 50,000 lamps annually. Sales to outside customers are estimated at 40,000 lamps for the next year. It sells reading lamps for $12 each. Variable costs are $8 per lamp and include $1 of variable sales costs that are not incurred if division B sells lamps internally to division A. The total amount of fixed costs for division B is $80,000.

(SO 6)
Determine the minimum transfer price under different situations.

Instructions

Consider the following independent situations:

(a) What should be the minimum transfer price division B accepts for the 10,000 lamps and the maximum transfer price division A pays? Justify your answer.

(b) Suppose division B could use the excess capacity to produce and sell externally 20,000 units of a new product at a price of $8 per unit. The variable cost for this new product is $6 per unit. What should be the minimum transfer price division B accepts for the 10,000 lamps and the maximum transfer price division A pays? Justify your answer.

(c) If division A needs 15,000 lamps instead of 10,000 during the next year, what should be the minimum transfer price division B accepts and the maximum transfer price division A pays? Justify your answer.

(c) Opportunity cost per unit = $1.33

(adapted from CGA-Canada, now CPA Canada)

P9-40A Wordsmith is a publishing company with several different book lines. Each line has contracts with different authors. The company also owns a printing operation called Pronto Press. The book lines and the printing operation each operate as a separate profit centre. The printing operation earns revenue by printing books by authors under contract with the book lines owned by Wordsmith, as well as authors under contract with other companies. The printing operation bills out at $1 per 100 pages, and a typical book requires 400 pages of print. A manager of Business Books, one of Wordsmith's book lines, has approached the manager of the printing operation and offered to pay $0.007 per page for 1,200 copies of a 400-page book. The book line pays outside printers $0.009 per page. The printing operation's variable cost per page is $0.006.

(SO 6)
Determine the minimum transfer price with no excess capacity and with excess capacity.

Instructions

(a) Determine whether the printing should be done internally or externally, and the appropriate transfer price, under each of the following situations:

   1. Assume that the printing operation is booked solid for the next two years, and it would have to cancel an obligation with an outside customer in order to meet the needs of the internal division.

   2. Assume that the printing operation has available capacity.

(b) ✏️▷ The top management of Wordsmith believes that the printing operation should always do the printing for the company's authors. On several occasions, it has forced the printing operation to cancel jobs with outside customers in order to meet the needs of its own lines. Discuss the pros and cons of this approach.

(c) Calculate the change in contribution margin to each division, and to the company as a whole, if top management forces the printing operation to accept the $0.007 per page transfer price when it has no available capacity.

(c) Loss to company = $480

P9-41A Zapp Manufacturing Company makes various electronic products. The company is divided into autonomous divisions that can either sell to internal units or sell externally. All divisions are located in buildings on the same piece of property. The board division has offered the chip division $20 per unit to supply it with chips for 30,000 boards. It has been purchasing these chips for $22 per unit from outside suppliers. The chip division receives $22.50 per unit for sales made to outside customers on this type of chip. The variable cost of chips sold externally by the chip division is $14.50. It estimates that it will save $4.50 per unit in selling expenses on units sold internally to the board division. The chip division has no excess capacity.

(SO 6)
Determine the minimum transfer price with no excess capacity.

Instructions

(a) Calculate the minimum transfer price that the chip division should accept. Discuss whether it is in the chip division's best interest to accept the offer.

(b) Suppose that the chip division decides to reject the offer. What are the financial consequences for each division, and for the company as a whole, of this decision?

(b) Total loss to company $120,000

P9-42A Wood Inc. manufactures wood poles. Wood has two responsibility centres, harvesting and sawing, which are both evaluated as profit centres. The harvesting division does all the harvesting operations and transfers logs to the sawing division, which converts the wood into poles for external clients. When operating at full capacity, the sawing division can convert 10,000 poles. Management is considering replacing this type of wood pole with another type of wood pole that can be sold at a lower price and could allow the firm to operate at full capacity all the time.

(SO 6)
Determine the minimum transfer price under different situations.

The director of the sawing division suggested that the maximum price the division can pay for each log from harvesting is $29.50. Following is the information that supports this suggestion:

Price per pole that the client would pay	$90.00
Direct labour costs	$35.00
Variable overhead costs	4.50
Fixed overhead costs	8.50
Raw material costs (other than logs)	2.50
	50.50
Profit margin	10.00
Total costs and profit margin	60.50
Maximum price for a log	$29.50

The director of the harvesting division disagrees with selling the logs at a price of $29.50. The division is operating at full capacity and sells logs to external clients for $44.50. Moreover, the director says, "My direct labour costs are $22.50, my variable overhead costs are $4.50, and my fixed overhead costs are $9.00. I can't cut trees for $36.00 and sell them for $29.50."

Instructions

(a) Assuming production is at full capacity, determine whether Wood Inc., as a whole, would make a higher profit if logs were transferred to the sawing division for $29.50 per log. Show your calculations.
(b) Explain the effect of transferring the logs at $29.50 per log on each division's profit performance.
(c) Calculate the minimum and maximum transfer prices that could be used, and recommend an appropriate transfer price. Explain your answer.

(adapted from CGA-Canada, now CPA Canada)

(c) Appropriate transfer price:
$44.50

(SO 6)
Determine the minimum transfer price under different situations.

P9-43A   Next Level (NL) is a division of Global Electronics, Inc. NL produces videogame systems. These systems are sold to retailers. NL recently approached the manager of the personal computer (PC) division regarding a request to buy a special circuit board for a new advanced video game system. NL has requested that the personal computer division produce 200,000 units of this special circuit board. The following facts are available regarding the personal computer division:

Selling price of standard circuit board	$54
Variable cost of standard circuit board	30
Additional variable costs of special circuit board	20

Instructions

For each of the following independent situations, calculate the minimum transfer price, and discuss whether the internal transfer should take place or whether Next Level should purchase the circuit board externally.

(a) Next Level has offered to pay the PC division $62 per circuit board. The PC division has no available capacity. The PC division would have to forgo sales of 200,000 circuit boards to existing customers in order to meet the request of Next Level.

(b) Minimum price $80

(b) Next level has offered to pay the PC division $90 per circuit board. The PC division has no available capacity. The PC division would have to forgo sales of 250,000 circuit boards to existing customers in order to meet the request of Next Level.

(c) Next Level has offered to pay the PC division $62 per circuit board. The PC division has available capacity.

(SO 6)
Determine the minimum transfer price under different situations.

P9-44A   The Atlantic Company is a multidivisional company. Its managers have full responsibility for profits and complete autonomy to accept or reject transfers from other divisions. Division A produces a sub-assembly part, for which there is a competitive market. Division B currently uses this sub-assembly for a final product that is sold outside at $2,400. Division A charges division B market price for the part, which is $1,400 per unit. Variable costs are $1,040 and $1,200 for divisions A and B, respectively.

The manager of division B feels that division A should transfer the part at a lower price than market because, at market, division B is unable to make a profit.

Instructions

(a) Calculate division B's contribution margin if transfers are made at the market price, and calculate the company's total contribution margin.

(b) No transfer

(b) Assume that division A can sell all its production in the open market. Should division A transfer the goods to division B? If so, at what price?

(c) Assume that division A can sell in the open market only 500 of the 1,000 units it can produce every month, at $1,400 per unit. Assume also that a 20% reduction in price is necessary to sell all 1,000 units each month. Should transfers be made? If so, how many units should the division transfer and at what price? To support your decision, submit a schedule that compares the contribution margins under three different alternatives.

(adapted from CMA Canada, now CPA Canada)

(SO 6)
Determine the transfer price for goal congruence.

P9-45A   Lemon Quench manufactures a soft drink. The company is organized into two divisions: glass and filling. The glass division makes bottles and sells them to the filling division. Each division manager receives a bonus based on the division's net income.

In the open market, bottle producers are charging as follows:

Number of Cases per Month	Total Charge	Average Price per Case
11,000	$135,300	$12.30
12,000	144,000	12.00
13,000	152,750	11.75
14,000	158,900	11.35
15,000	165,000	11.00

The costs per case in the glass division are as follows:

Volume per Month	Glass Division Cost per Case
11,000	$10.71
12,000	10.52
13,000	10.35
14,000	10.18

The filling division's costs (excluding bottle purchases) and selling prices are as follows:

Volume per Month	Selling Price	Cost per Case
11,000	$38.00	$24.32
12,000	37.55	24.09
13,000	37.20	23.91
14,000	36.80	23.76
15,000	36.20	23.57

The current capacities are 15,000 cases per month for the filling division and 14,000 cases per month for the glass division.

Instructions

(a) If market prices are used as transfer prices, what is the most profitable volume for each division and for the company as a whole? Show calculations to support your answer. Assume that transfers and sales are made in units of 1,000 and that the glass division is unable to sell its production in the outside market.

(b) Under what conditions should market prices not be used in determining the transfer prices?

(adapted from CMA Canada, now CPA Canada)

(a) Glass division:
    13,000 units

P9-46A Fast Buck Corporation needs to set a target price for its newly designed product EverRun. The following data relate to this new product:

	Per Unit	Total
Direct materials	$20	
Direct labour	40	
Variable manufacturing overhead	10	
Fixed manufacturing overhead		$1,400,000
Variable selling and administrative expenses	5	
Fixed selling and administrative expenses		1,120,000

(SO 3, 4)
Calculate the target price using the absorption-cost and variable-cost approaches.

The costs above are based on a budgeted volume of 80,000 units produced and sold each year. Fast Buck uses cost-plus pricing to set its target selling price. Because some managers prefer the absorption-cost approach and others prefer the variable-cost approach, the accounting department provides information under both approaches, using a markup of 50% on the manufacturing cost per unit and a markup of 75% on the variable cost.

Instructions

(a) Calculate the target price for one unit of EverRun using the absorption-cost approach.

(b) Calculate the target price for one unit of EverRun using the variable-cost approach.

(a) Markup $43.75
(b) Markup $56.25

P9-47A Weather Guard Windows Inc. is setting a target price on its newly designed tinted window. Cost data for the window at a budgeted volume of 4,000 units are as follows:

	Per Unit	Total
Direct materials	$100	
Direct labour	70	
Variable manufacturing overhead	20	
Fixed manufacturing overhead		$120,000
Variable selling and administrative expenses	10	
Fixed selling and administrative expenses		102,000

(SO 3, 4)
Calculate various amounts using the absorption-cost and variable-cost approaches.

Weather Guard Windows uses cost-plus pricing to provide the company with a 25% ROI on its tinted window line. It has committed a total of $1,016,000 in assets to production of the new tinted window.

(a) 45%

Instructions

(a) Calculate the markup percentage under the absorption-cost approach that will allow Weather Guard Windows to realize its desired ROI.

(b) Calculate the target price of the window under the absorption-cost approach, and show proof that the desired ROI is realized.

(c) Calculate the markup percentage under the variable-cost approach that will allow Weather Guard Windows to realize its desired ROI. (Round to three decimal places.)

(d) Calculate the target price of the window under the variable-cost approach, and show proof that the desired ROI is realized.

(e) ✏️➤ Since both the absorption-cost approach and the variable-cost approach produce the same target price and provide the same ROI, why do both methods exist? Isn't one method clearly better than the other?

(SO 6)
Determine the
minimum transfer
price under different
situations.

(a) $280

P9-48A Computech Company operates as a decentralized multidivisional electronics company. Its laptop division buys most of its monitors from the screen division. The screen division's incremental costs for manufacturing the monitors are $280 per unit. The screen division is currently working at 85% of capacity. The monitor's current market price is $310 per unit.

Instructions

(a) Using the general approach to transfer pricing, determine the minimum transfer price for the screen division.

(b) Computech Company's transfer price rules state that whenever divisions with unused capacity sell products internally, they must transfer the products at incremental costs. Discuss how this transfer-price policy will affect goal congruence, division performance, and autonomy.

(c) The screen and laptop divisions have negotiated a transfer price between $280 and $310 per monitor. Discuss the impact of this transfer price on each division in terms of goal congruence, division performance, and division autonomy.

(adapted from CMA Canada, now CPA Canada)

(SO 6)
Determine the
minimum transfer
price with no excess
capacity.

(a) $380

P9-49A Kirkland Metal Corporation has two divisions. The fabrication division transfers partially completed components to the assembly division at a predetermined transfer price. The fabrication division's standard variable production cost per unit is $300. The division has no excess capacity, and it could sell all of its components to outside buyers at $380 per unit.

Instructions

(a) Determine an appropriate transfer price for the fabrication division.

(b) How would the transfer price change if the fabrication division had excess capacity?

(SO 6)
Determine the
minimum transfer
price with excess
capacity.

(a) Loss per unit: $39

P9-50A The data for Kirkland Metal Corporation has been given in P9-49A. Assume that the transfer price for the component has been set at $374, which is the fabrication division's total cost plus a 10% markup. Fabrication division's total cost of a component is $340, which includes fixed overhead applied at the rate of $400,000 of budgeted fixed overhead costs on budgeted annual production of 10,000 units. The assembly division has a special offer for its product of $435. The assembly division incurs variable costs of $100 in addition to the transfer price for the fabrication division's components. Both divisions currently have excess capacity.

Instructions

Answer the following questions:

(a) What is the assembly division's manager likely to do regarding acceptance or rejection of the special offer? Why?

(b) Is this decision in the best interests of the company as a whole? Why?

(c) How could the situation be remedied using the transfer price?

Problems: Set B

(SO 2)
Use cost-plus pricing
to determine various
amounts.

P9-51B Wamser Corporation needs to set a target price for its newly designed product, E2-D2. The following data relate to it:

	Per Unit	Total
Direct materials	$15	
Direct labour	25	
Variable manufacturing overhead	14	
Fixed manufacturing overhead		$4,000,000
Variable selling and administrative expenses	12	
Fixed selling and administrative expenses		2,000,000

These costs are based on a budgeted volume of 1 million units produced and sold each year. Wamser uses cost-plus pricing to set its target selling price. The markup on the total unit cost is 25%.

Instructions

(a) Calculate the total variable cost per unit, total fixed cost per unit, and total cost per unit for E2-D2.

(b) Calculate the desired ROI per unit for E2-D2.

(c) Calculate the target selling price for E2-D2.

(d) Calculate the variable cost per unit, fixed cost per unit, and total cost per unit, assuming that 800,000 E2-D2s are produced during the year. (Round to two decimal places.)

(a) Variable cost per unit = $66

P9-52B Carrier Fabrication Company (CFC) manufactures and sells only one product, a special front-mounting bicycle rack for large vehicles. CFC entered into a one-time contract to produce an additional 1,000 racks for the local public transit authority at a price of "cost plus 20%." The company's plant has a capacity of 9,000 units per year, but normal production is 4,000 units per year. The annual costs to produce those 4,000 units are as follows:

(SO 2)
Use cost-plus pricing to determine various amounts.

Materials	$192,000
Labour	304,000
Supplies and other variable manufacturing indirect costs	128,000
Fixed indirect costs (allocated based on normal capacity)	176,000
Variable marketing costs	32,000
Administrative costs (all fixed)	64,000

After completing half of the order, the company billed the authority for $134,400. However, the transit authority's purchasing agent then called the president of CFC to dispute the invoice. The purchasing agent stated that the invoice should have been for $93,600.

Instructions

(a) Calculate the components of the total cost unit price charged to the transit authority, as determined by CFC.

(b) Calculate the components of the variable manufacturing cost unit price that should have been charged, as determined by the transit authority's purchasing agent.

(c) What price per unit would you recommend? Explain your reasoning. (*Note:* You do not need to limit yourself to the costs selected by the company or by the agent.)

(adapted from CGA-Canada, now CPA Canada)

(b) Unit price = $156

P9-53B Bosworth Electronics Inc. is setting a selling price on a new CDL component it has just developed. The accounting department has provided the following cost estimates for this component for a budgeted volume of 100,000 units:

(SO 2)
Use cost-plus pricing to determine various amounts.

	Per Unit	Total
Direct materials	$30	
Direct labour	20	
Variable manufacturing overhead	17	
Fixed manufacturing overhead		$2,500,000
Variable selling and administrative expenses	8	
Fixed selling and administrative expenses		500,000

Bosworth's management uses cost-plus pricing to set its selling price. Management also requires the target price to be set to provide a 30% return on investment on invested assets of $3 million.

Instructions

(Round all calculations to two decimal places.)

(a) Calculate the markup percentage and target selling price that will allow Bosworth Electronics to earn its desired ROI of 30% on this new CDL component.

(b) Assuming that the volume is 80,000 units, calculate the markup percentage and target selling price that will allow Bosworth Electronics to earn its desired ROI of 30%.

(b) Target selling price $123.75

P9-54B Lemond Bike Repair Shop has budgeted the following time and material for 2016:

(SO 5)
Use time-and-material pricing to determine bill.

	Time Charges	Material Charges
Shop employees' wages and benefits	$36,000	–
Parts manager's salary and benefits	–	$20,000
Office employee's salary and benefits	15,000	10,000
Overhead (supplies, amortization, advertising, utilities)	19,000	15,000
Total budgeted costs	$70,000	$45,000

Lemond budgets 2,500 hours of repair time in 2016. It will bill a profit of $5 per labour hour along with a 15% profit markup on the invoice cost of parts. The estimated invoice cost for parts to be used is $75,000.

On January 5, 2016, Lemond is asked to submit a price estimate to fix an Alpine mountain bike. Lemond estimates that this repair will consume four hours of labour and $200 in parts and materials.

Instructions

(a) Calculate the labour rate for Lemond Bike Repair Shop for 2016.

(b) Calculate the material loading charge percentage for Lemond Bike Repair Shop for 2016. (Round to three decimal places.)

(c) $482

(c) Prepare a time-and-material price quotation for the repair of the Alpine mountain bike.

(SO 6)
Determine the minimum transfer price with no excess capacity.

P9-55B   Pointe Claire Inc. operates as a decentralized multidivisional electronics company. It has two divisions. Division A transfers partially completed components to division B at a predetermined transfer price. The division A's standard variable production cost per unit is $400. Division A is operating at full capacity and it could sell all of its components to outside buyers at $520 per unit.

Instructions

(a) Determine an appropriate transfer price for division A.

(b) How would the transfer price change if division A had excess capacity?

(SO 6)
Determine the minimum transfer price with excess capacity.

P9-56B   The data for Pointe-Claire Inc. are given in P9-55B. Assume that the transfer price has been set at $504, which is division A's total cost plus a 20% markup. Division A's total cost of a component is $420, which includes fixed overhead applied at the rate of $200,000 of budgeted fixed overhead costs on budgeted annual production of 10,000 units. Division B has a special offer for its product of $550. Division B incurs variable costs of $100 in addition to the transfer price for the division A components. Both divisions currently have excess capacity.

Instruction:

(a) What is division B's manager likely to do regarding acceptance or rejection of the special offer? Why?

(b) Income per unit: $50

(b) Is this decision in the best interests of the company as a whole? Why?

(c) How could the situation be remedied using the transfer price?

(SO 6)
Determine the minimum transfer price with no excess capacity and with excess capacity.

P9-57B   Cosmic Sounds is a record company with different labels. Each label has contracts with various recording artists. It also owns a recording studio called Blast Off. The record labels and the recording studio operate as separate profit centres. The studio earns revenue by recording artists under contract with the labels owned by Cosmic Sounds, as well as artists under contract with other companies. The studio bills out at $1,100 per hour, and a typical album requires 80 hours of studio time. A manager from Big Bang, one of Cosmic Sounds' record labels, has approached the recording studio manager offering to pay $800 per hour for an 80-hour session. The record label pays outside studios $1,000 per hour. The recording studio's variable cost per hour is $600.

Instructions

(a) Determine whether the recording should be done internally or externally, and the appropriate transfer price, under each of the following situations:

  1. Assume that the recording studio is booked solid for the next three years, and it would have to cancel a contract with an outside customer in order to meet the needs of the internal division.

  2. Assume that the recording studio has available capacity.

(b) The top management of Cosmic Sounds believes that the recording studio should always do the recording for the company's artists. On several occasions, it has forced the recording studio to cancel jobs with outside customers in order to meet the needs of its own labels. Discuss the pros and cons of this approach.

(c) Loss to company $8,000

(c) ✏️▷ Calculate the change in contribution margin to each division, and to the company as a whole, if top management forces the recording studio to accept the $800 transfer price when it has no available capacity.

(SO 6)
Determine the minimum transfer price under different situations.

(a) $270

P9-58B   Sun Motors Inc. operates as a decentralized multidivisional car company. Its safety division buys most of its airbags from the airbag division. The airbag division's incremental costs for manufacturing the airbags are $270 per unit. The airbag division is currently working at 75% of capacity. The current market price of the airbags is $300 per unit.

Instructions

(a) Using the general approach to transfer pricing, determine the minimum transfer price for the airbag division.

(b) Sun Motors Inc.'s transfer price rules state that whenever divisions with unused capacity sell products internally, they must transfer the products at incremental costs. Discuss how this transfer-price policy will affect goal congruence, division performance, and autonomy.

(c) The safety and airbag divisions have negotiated a transfer price between $270 and $300 per airbag. Discuss the impact of this transfer price on each division in terms of goal congruence, division performance, and division autonomy.

(adapted from CMA Canada, now CPA Canada)

(SO 6)
Determine the minimum transfer price with no excess capacity.

P9-59B   Chula Vista Pump Company makes irrigation pump systems. The company is divided into several autonomous divisions that can either sell to internal units or sell externally. All divisions are located in buildings on the same piece of property. The pump division has offered the washer division $4 per unit to supply it with the washers for 50,000 units. It has been purchasing these washers for $4.30 per unit from outside suppliers. The washer division receives $4.60 per unit for sales of this type of washer to outside customers. The variable cost of units sold externally by the washer division is $3.20. It estimates that it will save 50 cents per unit of selling expenses on units sold internally to the pump division. The washer division has no excess capacity.

Instructions

(a) Calculate the minimum transfer price that the washer division should accept. Discuss whether it is in the washer division's best interest to accept the offer.

(b) Suppose that the washer division decides to reject the offer. What are the financial implications for each division, and the company as a whole, of the decision to reject the offer?

(b) Contribution margin to company: $55,000

P9-60B Heartland Engines is a division of EverGreen Lawn Equipment Company. Heartland makes engines for lawn mowers, snow blowers, and other types of lawn and garden equipment. It sells its engines to the company's lawn mower division and snow blower division, as well as to other lawn equipment companies. It was recently approached by the manager of the lawn mower division with a request to make a special high-performance engine for a lawn mower designed to mow heavy brush. The lawn mower division has asked Heartland to produce 8,500 units of this special engine. The following facts relate to Heartland Engines:

(SO 6)
Determine the minimum transfer price under different situations.

Selling price of standard lawn mower engine	$88
Variable cost of standard lawn mower engine	55
Additional variable costs of special engine	41

Instructions

For each of the following independent situations, calculate the minimum transfer price, and discuss whether the internal transfer should take place or whether the lawn mower division should purchase its goods externally:

(a) The lawn mower division has offered to pay Heartland Engines $110 per engine. Heartland Engines has no available capacity. Heartland Engines would have to cancel sales of 8,500 units to existing customers in order to meet the lawn mower division's request.

(a) $129

(b) The lawn mower division has offered to pay Heartland Engines $170 per engine. Heartland Engines has no available capacity. It would have to cancel sales of 12,000 units to existing customers in order to meet the lawn mower division's request.

(b) $142.59

(c) The lawn mower division has offered to pay Heartland Engines $110 per engine. Heartland Engines has available capacity.

(c) $96

P9-61B Comput Industries is a high-tech company in the United States with several subsidiaries, including Cancomput, which is located in Canada, and Heavencomput, which is located in another country with very favourable tax laws. Both subsidiaries are considered profit centres. Cancomput manufactures components used by Heavencomput and sells all its production to this subsidiary. The controller has established the transfer price at $135 per component, even though Cancomput can sell the same pieces on the external market for $175.

(SO 6)
Discuss the transfer price under different situations.

Instructions

(a) Briefly explain why Comput Industries is fixing a transfer price below the market price. What are the advantages for the company as a whole?

(b) Explain the consequences of the transfer-pricing policy on each subsidiary. Explain what change should be made to improve the situation.

(c) Briefly describe two other transfer-pricing methods that could be used in this situation.

(adapted from CGA-Canada, now CPA Canada)

P9-62B Love, Inc. manufactures a line of men's colognes and aftershave lotions. The manufacturing process is basically a series of mixing operations, with the addition of certain aromatic and colouring ingredients. The finished product is packaged in a company-produced glass bottle and packed in cases of six bottles.

(SO 6)
Determine the transfer price for goal congruence.

Top management feels that the sale of its product is heavily influenced by the appearance and appeal of the bottle and has therefore had managers focus on the bottle-production process. This has resulted in the development of certain unique bottle-production processes that management is quite proud of.

The two areas (perfume production and bottle manufacture) have evolved over the years almost independently; in fact, a rivalry has developed between management personnel as to which division is more important to the company. This attitude is probably intensified because the bottle manufacturing plant was purchased as a whole company 10 years ago and there has been no real exchange of management personnel or ideas (except at the top corporate level).

Since the acquisition, all bottle production has been used by the perfume manufacturing plant. Each area is considered a separate profit centre and evaluated as such. As the new corporate controller, you are responsible for determining a proper transfer value to use in crediting the bottle production profit centre and in debiting the perfume packaging profit centre.

At your request, the bottle division's general manager has asked certain other bottle manufacturers to quote a price for the quantity and sizes of bottles that the perfume division needs. These competitive prices are as follows:

Volume (equivalent cases)*	Total Price	Price per Case
2,000,000	$ 4,000,000	$2.00
4,000,000	7,000,000	1.75
6,000,000	10,020,000	1.67

*An "equivalent case" represents six bottles.

An analysis of the bottle plant indicates that it can produce bottles at the following costs:

Volume (equivalent cases)	Total Price	Price per Case*
2,000,000	$3,200,000	$1.60
4,000,000	5,200,000	1.30
6,000,000	7,200,000	1.20

*The analysis indicates that these costs represent fixed costs of $1.2 million and variable costs of $1.00 per equivalent case.

These figures have resulted in considerable corporate discussion about the proper value to use in the transfer of bottles to the perfume division. Discussions are especially hot because a significant portion of each division manager's income is an incentive bonus that is based on his or her subsidiary's profit. The perfume production division has the following costs in addition to the bottle costs:

Volume (cases)	Total Cost	Cost per Case
2,000,000	$16,400,000	$8.20
4,000,000	32,400,000	8.10
6,000,000	48,420,000	8.07

After considerable analysis, the marketing research department has given you the following price-demand relationship for the finished product:

Sales Volume (cases)	Total Sales Revenue	Sales Price per Case
2,000,000	$25,000,000	$12.50
4,000,000	45,600,000	11.40
6,000,000	63,900,000	10.65

Instructions

(a) 3. Income for company = $8,280,000

(a) Love, Inc. has used market-based transfer prices in the past. Using current market prices and costs, and assuming a volume of 6 million cases, calculate the income for (1) the bottle division, (2) the perfume division, and (3) the company.

(b) Are these production and sales levels the most profitable volumes for (1) the bottle division, (2) the perfume division, and (3) the company? Explain your answer.

(adapted from CMA Canada, now CPA Canada)

(SO 3, 4)
Calculate the target price using absorption-cost pricing and variable-cost pricing.

P9-63B   Refer back to P9-51B, where we learned that Wamser Corporation uses cost-plus pricing methods to set the target selling price of its product E2-D2. Because some managers prefer to work with absorption-cost pricing and other managers prefer variable-cost pricing, the accounting department provides information under both approaches using a markup of 50% on absorption cost and a markup of 80% on variable cost.

Instructions

Using the data provided in P9-51B:

(a) Markup $29.00
(b) Markup $52.80

(a) calculate the target price for one unit of E2-D2 using absorption-cost pricing.
(b) calculate the target price for one unit of E2-D2 using variable-cost pricing.

(SO 3, 4)
Calculate various amounts using absorption-cost pricing and variable-cost pricing.

P9-64B   Santana Furniture Inc. is setting a target price on its newly designed leather recliner sofa. Cost data for the sofa at a budgeted volume of 3,000 units are as follows:

	Per Unit	Total
Direct materials	$140	
Direct labour	80	
Variable manufacturing overhead	40	
Fixed manufacturing overhead		$180,000
Variable selling and administrative expenses	20	
Fixed selling and administrative expenses		90,000

Santana Furniture uses cost-plus pricing to provide a 30% ROI on its stuffed furniture line. A total of $700,000 in assets has been committed to the production of the new leather recliner sofa.

Instructions

(a) 37.5%

(a) Calculate the markup percentage under the absorption-cost approach that will allow Santana Furniture to realize its desired ROI.

(b) Calculate the target price of the sofa under absorption-cost pricing, and show proof that the desired ROI is realized.

(c) 57.143%

(c) Calculate the markup percentage under the variable-cost approach that will allow Santana Furniture to realize its desired ROI.

(d) Calculate the target price of the sofa under variable-cost pricing, and show proof that the desired ROI is realized.

(e) ✏️➤ Since both absorption-cost pricing and variable-cost pricing produce the same target price and provide the same ROI, why do both methods exist? Isn't one method clearly better than the other?

P9-65B Family Inc. has two divisions. Division A makes and sells T-shirts. Division B manufactures and sells ties.

Each T-shirt has a tie as one of its components. Division A needs 10,000 ties for the coming year and can purchase ties at a cost of $30 from an outside vendor.

Division B has the capacity to manufacture 50,000 ties annually. Sales to outside customers are estimated at 40,000 ties for the next year. It sells ties for $35 each. Variable costs are $29 per tie and include $2 of variable sales costs that are not incurred if division B sells ties internally to division A. The total amount of fixed costs for division B is $80,000.

Instructions

Consider the following independent situations:

(a) What should be the minimum transfer price division B accepts for the 10,000 ties and the maximum transfer price division A pays? Justify your answer.

(b) Suppose division B could use the excess capacity to produce and sell externally 20,000 units of a new product at a price of $18 per unit. The variable cost for this new product is $15 per unit. What should be the minimum transfer price division B accepts for the 10,000 ties and the maximum transfer price division A pays? Justify your answer.

(c) If division A needs 15,000 ties instead of 10,000 during the next year, what should be the minimum transfer price division B accepts and the maximum transfer price division A pays? Justify your answer.

(adapted from CGA-Canada, now CPA Canada)

(SO 6)
Determine the minimum transfer price under different situations.

(c) Minimum transfer price: $29

P9-66B The Pacific Company is a multidivisional company. Its managers have full responsibility for profits and complete autonomy to accept or reject transfers from other divisions. Division A produces a sub-assembly part, for which there is a competitive market. Division B currently uses this sub-assembly for a final product that is sold outside at $3,400. Division A charges division B the market price for the part, which is $2,400 per unit. Variable costs are $2,040 and $1,200 for divisions A and B, respectively.

The manager of division B feels that division A should transfer the part at a lower price than market because, at market, division B is unable to make a profit.

Instructions

(a) Calculate division B's contribution margin if transfers are made at the market price, and calculate the company's total contribution margin.

(b) Assume that division A can sell all its production in the open market. Should division A transfer the goods to division B? If so, at what price?

(c) Assume that division A can sell in the open market only 500 of the 1,000 units it can produce every month, at $2,400 per unit. Assume also that it reduces the price to $2,120 as necessary to sell all 1,000 units each month. Should transfers be made? If so, how many units should the division transfer and at what price? To support your decision, submit a schedule that compares the contribution margins under three different alternatives.

(adapted from CMA Canada, now CPA Canada)

(SO 6)
Determine the minimum transfer price under different situations.

(b) $2,400

Cases

C9-67 Aurora Manufacturing has multiple divisions that make a wide variety of products. Recently the bearing division and the wheel division got into an argument over a transfer price. The wheel division needed bearings for garden tractor wheels. It normally buys its bearings from an outside supplier for $25 per set. The company's top management recently started a campaign to persuade the different divisions to buy their materials from each other whenever possible. As a result, Maria Hamblin, the purchasing manager for the wheel division, received a letter from the vice-president of purchasing that instructed her to contact the bearing division to discuss buying bearings from it.

To comply with this request, Maria called Terry Jerabek of the bearing division, and asked the price for 15,000 bearings. Terry responded that the bearings normally sell for $36 per set. However, Terry noted that the bearing division would save $3 on marketing costs by selling internally, and would pass this cost savings on to the wheel division. He further commented that his division was at full capacity, and therefore would not be able to provide any bearings right away. In the future, if he had available capacity, he would be happy to provide bearings.

Maria responded indignantly, "Thanks, but no thanks. We can get all the bearings we need from Falk Manufacturing for $24 per set." Terry snorted back, "Falk makes junk. It costs us $22 per set just to make our bearings. Our bearings can withstand heat of 2,000 degrees Celsius, and

are good to within .00001 centimetres. If you guys are happy buying junk, then go ahead and buy from Falk."

Two weeks later, Maria's boss from the central office stopped in to find out whether she had placed an order with the bearing division. Maria answered that she would rather buy her bearings from her worst enemy than from the bearing division.

Instructions

Answer the following questions:

(a) Why might the company's top management want the divisions to start doing more business with one another?

(b) Under what conditions should management force a buying division to buy from an internal supplier? Under what conditions should management force a selling division to sell to an internal division, rather than to an outside customer?

(c) The vice-president of purchasing thinks that this problem should be resolved by forcing the bearing division to sell to the wheel division at its cost of $22. Is this a good solution for the wheel division? Is this a good solution for the bearing division? Is this a good solution for the company?

(d) Provide at least two other possible solutions to this problem. Discuss the merits and drawbacks of each solution.

C9-68 West-Coast Industries is a decentralized firm. It has two production centres: Vancouver and Kamloops. Each one is evaluated based on its return on investment. Vancouver has the capacity to manufacture 100,000 units of component TR222. Vancouver's variable costs are $150 per unit. Kamloops uses component TR222 in one of its products. Kamloops adds $90 of variable costs to the component and sells the final product for $450.

Instructions

Consider the following independent situations:

(a) Vancouver can sell all 100,000 units of TR222 on the open market at a price of $250 per unit. Kamloops is willing to buy 10,000 of those units. What should the transfer price be? Explain your decision.

(b) Of the 100,000 units of component TR222 it can produce, Vancouver can sell 70,000 units on the open market at a price of $250 per unit. Kamloops is willing to buy an additional 10,000 units. What should the transfer price be? Explain your decision.

(c) Of the 100,000 units of component TR222 it can produce, Vancouver can sell 80,000 units on the open market at a price of $250 per unit. Kamloops is willing to buy an additional 30,000 units. What should the transfer price be? Explain your decision.

(d) The head office of West-Coast has asked the two centres to negotiate a transfer price. List the advantages and disadvantages of negotiated transfer prices.

(adapted from CGA-Canada, now CPA Canada)

C9-69 Solco Industries is a decentralized company with two divisions: mining and processing. They are both evaluated as profit centres. The mining division transfers raw diamonds to the processing division. The processing division is currently operating at 1 million kg below its capacity, while the mining division is operating at full capacity. The mining division can sell raw diamonds externally at $75 per kilogram. The unit cost of 1 kg of polished diamonds produced by the processing division is as follows:

Raw diamonds	$ 75
Direct materials	10
Direct labour ($20/hour)	30
Variable manufacturing overhead	20
Fixed manufacturing overhead*	50
Total unit cost	$185

*Based on a capacity of 5 million kg per year.

The processing division has just received an order from International Diamonds Co. for 300,000 kg of polished diamonds at a price of $175 per kilogram. Solco has a policy that prohibits selling any product below total cost. The total cost of a kilogram of raw diamonds in the mining division is $60, of which 25% is company fixed costs.

Instructions

(a) Would Solco as a whole benefit if the raw diamonds were transferred to the processing division at $60 per kilogram to fill the order from International Diamonds? Show all calculations.

(b) Briefly explain whether anything is wrong with Solco's policy that no product should be sold below total cost.

(c) Calculate the minimum and maximum transfer prices that could be used.

(d) Recommend an appropriate transfer price for raw diamonds sold by the mining division to the processing division. Explain your answer.

(e) If the mining division was not operating at full capacity, would your answer in part (d) be different?

(adapted from CGA-Canada, now CPA Canada)

C9-70 National Industries is a diversified corporation with separate operating divisions. Each division's performance is evaluated based on its total dollar profits and return on division investment.

The WindAir division manufactures and sells air conditioners. The coming year's budgeted income statement, based on a sales volume of 15,000 units, is as follows:

WINDAIR DIVISION Budgeted Income Statement For the Fiscal Year		
	Per Unit	Total (in thousands)
Sales revenue	$400	$6,000
Manufacturing costs		
Compressor	70	1,050
Other raw materials	37	555
Direct labour	30	450
Variable overhead	45	675
Fixed overhead	32	480
Total manufacturing costs	214	3,210
Gross margin	186	2,790
Operating expenses		
Variable selling	18	270
Fixed selling	19	285
Fixed administration	38	570
Total operating expenses	75	1,125
Net income before taxes	$111	$1,665

WindAir's manager believes that sales can be increased if it reduced the unit selling price of the air conditioners. A market research study conducted by an independent firm at the manager's request indicates that a 5% reduction ($20) in the selling price would increase the sales volume by 16%, or 2,400 units. WindAir has enough production capacity to manage this increased volume with no increase in fixed costs.

Currently, WindAir uses a compressor in its units that it purchases from an outside supplier at a cost of $70 per compressor. The manager of WindAir has approached the manager of National Industries' compressor division about the sale of a compressor unit to WindAir. The compressor division currently manufactures and sells to outside firms a unit that is similar to the compressor used by WindAir. The specifications of the WindAir compressor are slightly different and would reduce the compressor division's raw materials cost by $1.50 per unit. In addition, the compressor division would not incur any variable selling costs for the units sold to WindAir. The manager of WindAir wants all of the compressors it uses to come from one supplier and has offered to pay $50 for each compressor unit.

The compressor division has the capacity to produce 75,000 units. The coming year's budgeted income statement for the compressor division, which follows, is based on a sales volume of 64,000 units without considering WindAir's proposal.

COMPRESSOR DIVISION
Budgeted Income Statement
For the Fiscal Year

	Per Unit	Total (in thousands)
Sales revenue	$100	$6,400
Manufacturing costs		
Raw materials	12	768
Direct labour	8	512
Variable overhead	10	640
Fixed overhead	11	704
Total manufacturing costs	41	2,624
Gross margin	59	3,776
Operating expenses		
Variable selling	6	384
Fixed selling	4	256
Fixed administration	7	448
Total operating expenses	17	1,088
Net income before taxes	$ 42	$2,688

Instructions

Answer the following questions:

(a) Should WindAir make the 5% price reduction on its air conditioners even if it cannot acquire the compressors internally for $50 each? Support your conclusion with appropriate calculations.

(b) Ignoring your answer to part (a), assume that WindAir needs 17,400 units. Should the compressor division be willing to supply the compressor units for $50 each? Support your conclusions with appropriate calculations.

(c) Ignoring your answer to part (a), assume that WindAir needs 17,400 units. Would it be in the best interest of National Industries for the compressor division to supply the compressor units at $50 each to the WindAir division? Support your conclusions with appropriate calculations.

(adapted from CMA Canada, now CPA Canada)

C9-71 Future Industries operates as a decentralized, vertically integrated, multidivisional company. One of its divisions, the systems division, manufactures scientific instruments and uses the products of two of the other divisions. The board division manufactures printed circuit boards (PCBs). It makes one PCB model exclusively for the systems division using proprietary designs and sells less complex models to outside markets. The transistor division sells its products in a well-developed competitive market and also to the systems division. The costs per unit of the two products the systems division uses are as follows:

	PCB	Transistor
Direct material	$ 7.50	$1.60
Direct labour	13.50	2.00
Variable overhead	6.00	1.00
Fixed overhead	2.40	1.50
Total cost	$29.40	$6.10

The board division sells its commercial product at total cost plus a 25% markup and believes that the proprietary board it makes for the systems

division would sell for $36.75 per unit on the open market. The market price of the transistor used by the systems division is $7.40 per unit.

Instructions

(a) Using the general approach to transfer pricing, determine the minimum transfer price at which the transistor division would sell the transistor to the systems division.

(b) Determine the maximum transfer price at which the systems division would buy the transistor from the internal division.

(c) Assume the systems division is able to purchase a large quantity of transistors from an outside source at $5.80 per unit and that the transistor division has excess capacity. Evaluate this price using the criteria of goal congruence and division performance.

(d) The board and systems divisions have negotiated a transfer price of $33 per printed circuit board. Evaluate this negotiated transfer price in terms of goal congruence, division performance, and division autonomy.

(adapted from CMA Canada, now CPA Canada)

C9-72 Construction on the Atlantis Full-Service Car Wash is nearing completion. The owner is Jay Giolti, a retired accounting professor. The car wash is strategically located on a busy street that separates an affluent suburban community from a middle-class community. It has two state-of-the-art stalls. Each stall can provide anything from a basic two-stage wash and rinse to a five-stage luxurious bath. It is all "touchless," meaning there are no brushes to potentially damage the car. Outside each stall, there is also a 400-horsepower vacuum. Jay likes to joke that these vacuums are so strong that they will pull the carpet right out of your car if you aren't careful.

Jay has some important decisions to make before he can open the car wash. First, he knows that there is one drive-through car wash attached to a gas station only a 10-minute drive away. It charges $5 for a basic wash, and $4 if you also buy at least 30 litres of gas. It is a brush-type wash with rotating brush heads. There is also a self-serve "stand outside your car and spray until you are soaked" car wash a 15-minute

drive away. He went over and tried this out. He went through $3 in quarters to get the equivalent of a basic wash. He knows that both of these locations always have long lines, which is one reason he decided to build a new car wash.

Jay is planning to offer three levels of wash service: basic, deluxe, and premium. The basic is all automated; it requires no direct intervention by employees. The deluxe is all automated except that, at the end, an employee will wipe down the car and put a window treatment on the windshield that reduces glare and allows rainwater to run off more quickly. The premium level is a "pampered" service. This will include all the services of the deluxe, plus a special wax after the machine wax, and an employee will vacuum the car, wipe down the entire interior, and wash the inside of the windows. To provide the premium service, Jay will have to hire a couple of car wash specialists to do the additional pampering.

Jay has made the following estimates, based on data he received from the local chamber of commerce and information from a trade association:

	Per Unit	Total
Direct materials per basic wash	$0.25	
Direct materials per deluxe wash	0.75	
Direct materials per premium wash	1.05	
Direct labour per basic wash	n/a	
Direct labour per deluxe wash	0.40	
Direct labour per premium wash	2.40	
Variable overhead per basic wash	0.10	
Variable overhead per deluxe or premium wash	0.20	
Fixed overhead		$112,500
Variable selling and administrative expenses—all washes	0.10	
Fixed selling and administrative expenses		121,500

The total estimated number of washes of any type is 45,000 per year. Jay has invested assets of $324,000. He would like a return on investment of 25%.

Instructions

(a) Identify the issues that Jay must consider in deciding on the price of each level of service of his car wash. Also discuss what issues he should consider in deciding on what levels of service to provide.

(b) Jay estimates that of the total 45,000 washes, 20,000 will be basic, 20,000 will be deluxe, and 5,000 will be premium. Using cost-plus pricing, calculate the selling price that Jay should use for each type of wash to achieve his desired ROI of 25%.

(c) During the first year, instead of selling 45,000 washes, Jay sold 43,000 washes. He was quite accurate in his estimate of first-year sales, but he was way off on the types of washes that he sold. He sold 3,000 basic, 31,000 deluxe, and 9,000 premium. His actual total fixed expenses were as he expected, and his variable cost per unit was as estimated. Calculate Jay's net income and his actual ROI.

(d) Jay is using a traditional approach to allocate overhead. As a result, he is allocating overhead equally to all three types of washes, even though the basic wash is considerably less complicated and uses very little of the technical capabilities of the machinery. What should Jay do to determine more accurate costs per unit? How will this affect his pricing and, consequently, his sales?

C9-73 Giant Airlines operates out of three main "hub" airports in the United States. Recently, Mosquito Airlines began operating a flight from Smallville into Giant's Metropolis hub for $360. Giant Airlines offers a price of $595 for the same route. The management of Giant is not happy about Mosquito invading its turf. In fact, Giant has driven off nearly every other competing airline from its hub, so that today 90% of flights into and out of Metropolis are Giant Airline flights. Mosquito is able to offer a lower fare because its pilots are paid less, it uses older planes, and it has lower overhead costs. Mosquito has been in business for only six months, and it services only two other cities. It expects the Metropolis route to be its most profitable.

Giant estimates that it would have to charge $380 just to break even on this flight. It estimates that Mosquito can break even at a price of $320. One day after Mosquito's entry into the market, Giant dropped its price to $300, which Mosquito then matched. Both airlines

maintained this fare for nine months, until Mosquito went out of business. As soon as Mosquito went out of business, Giant raised its fare back to $595.

Instructions

Answer the following questions:

(a) Who are the stakeholders in this case?

(b) What are some of the reasons why Mosquito's break-even point is lower than Giant's?

(c) What are the likely reasons why Giant was able to offer this price for this period of time, while Mosquito could not?

(d) What are some of the possible courses of action that Mosquito could have followed in this situation?

(e) Do you think that this kind of pricing activity is ethical? What are the implications for the stakeholders in this situation?

"All About You" Activity

C9-74 Paying for parking your car is never pleasant, but it hurts a lot when you have to pay to park your vehicle when you go to the hospital, either to visit someone who is ill or as a patient yourself. Many publicly funded hospitals in Canada charge visitors, patients, and staff for parking; parking charges are often vigorously enforced. Even though parking charges are very unpopular with hospital parking users, many hospitals rely on the revenue that is generated to help fund patient services.

Instructions

Consider what factors a Canadian health authority should take into account when setting parking charges. Consider the variable and fixed costs associated with the parking function and other alternatives available to patients and visitors.

Decision-Making at Current Designs

DM9-1 As a service to its customers, Current Designs repairs damaged kayaks. This is especially valuable to customers that have made a significant investment in the composite kayaks. To price the repair jobs, Current Designs uses time-and-material pricing with a desired profit margin of $20 per labour hour and a 50% materials loading charge.

Recently, Bill Johnson, Vice President of Sales and Marketing, received a phone call from a dealer in Brainerd, Minnesota. The dealer has a customer who recently damaged his composite kayak and would like an estimate of the cost to repair it. After the dealer emailed pictures of the damage, Bill reviewed the pictures with the repair technician and determined that the total materials charges for the repair would be

$100. Bill estimates that the job will take 3 labour hours to complete. Following is the budgeted cost data for Current Designs:

Repair technician wages	$30,000
Fringe benefits	$10,000
Overhead	$10,000

Current Designs has allocated 2,000 hours of repair time for the upcoming year. The customer has agreed to transport the kayak to the Winona production facility for the repairs.

Instructions

Determine the price that Current Designs would charge to complete the repairs for the customer.

Waterways Continuing Problem

(This is a continuation of the Waterways Problem from Chapters 1 through 8.)

WCP-9

Part 1

Waterways uses time and material pricing when it bids on drainage projects. Budgeted data for 2016 for installation division 1 are as follows.

Waterways Corporation
Installation Division 1
Budgeted Costs for Drainage Projects for 2016

	Time Charges	Material Loading Charges
Labour wages (5,760 hours)	$241,920	
Supervisor's salary		$ 60,000
Clerical and accountant wages	63,360	4,000
Drainage supplies manager		40,000
Overhead	51,840	21,000
Total	$357,120	$125,000

Waterways desires a $23 profit margin per hour of labour and 25% profit on materials. Materials are transferred in from the manufacturing division. The total estimated invoice cost of materials in 2016 will be $500,000.

Instructions

(a) Calculate the rate per hour of labour.

(b) Calculate the material loading charge.

(c) Waterways has been asked to quote on a project to upgrade the drainage for a large city multi-use park. The drainage manager estimates that it will take about a month to complete the project and require 450 hours of labour and $75,000 of materials. Calculate the total estimated bid price for the park project.

Part 2

Waterways Corporation mass produces a simple water control and timer set. To produce these units, the company incurred variable expenses of $2,053,200 and fixed expenses of $683,338.

During 2016 it sold 696,000 units at an average selling price of $4.22 per unit. This was the combination of selling 346,000 units on the market for $5.50 each, and transferring 350,000 units to the installation divisions at variable cost. Top management had directed the use of this transfer price. Capacity for this unit was 736,000 units.

Recently, Ryan Smith, the plant manager, was approached by a new customer who offered to pay $5.55 per unit for 60,000 units. Ryan, thinking about his bonus that was based on the department's operating income, readily accepted the order. Now he had to break the news to Lee Williams, the service vice-president in charge of installations. In order to fill the new order, Ryan would have to reduce the installation division by 20,000 units because he was not prepared to give up the margin he would receive from the outside sales. He suggested that Lee could purchase what he needed on the outside market.

Instructions

(a) Suppose Ryan accepts the order. Determine what the impact would be on:

1. the plant,
2. the installation division, and
3. the company as a whole.

(b) What do you think would be the best course of action in this situation? Explain.

Answers to Self-Study Questions

1. b **2.** c **3.** b **4.** b **5.** c **6.** a **7.** d **8.** b **9.** b **10.** d

[handwritten note: Remember to go back to the beginning of the chapter to check off your completed work! ←]

study objectives

the navigator

After studying this chapter, you should be able to do the following:

1. State the essentials of effective budgeting and the components of a master budget.

2. Prepare budgets for sales, production, and direct materials.

3. Prepare budgets for direct labour, manufacturing overhead, and selling and administrative expenses, and a budgeted income statement.

4. Prepare the cash budget and the budgeted balance sheet.

5. Explain the applicability of budgeting in non-manufacturing companies.

BUDGETING FOR SMOOTH SKIES

Pilots have long used flight simulators to test their decision-making in certain situations. What if airline managers used a model to simulate complex business conditions and used that for business decision-making? In a way, that's what budgetary planning does. Managers forecast revenues and expenses to predict future profits and take corrective action when the numbers deviate from the budgetary "flight path."

Toronto-based Porter Airlines, which serves 19 destinations in eastern Canada and the United States, used to use spreadsheets for tracking its chart of accounts, budget, and forecasting models. But as the airline grew, it adopted a sophisticated database that improves decision-making. The software generates real-time financial reports for Porter's cost centre managers, who can see when expenses and revenues differ from those in the budget, and take action when necessary. The variance reports show actual versus budget amounts, actual versus prior-year amounts, and current monthly and quarterly amounts versus those from the previous periods.

Porter uses the software to develop two mathematical models. One looks at overall finances. The other examines the profitability of existing and potential routes, which allows managers to allocate and budget resources accordingly. "When we add certain dimensions to the financial model, they add automatically to the route profit model—we just have to select the allocation method," said Scott Murray, Porter's Controller, Financial Reporting and Internal Control. "We're able to observe route by route and choose the level of allocation based on a predetermined method. Right up to the board level, we can easily present the data to identify the profitability of our routes."

Using information in the database regarding key performance indicators (KPIs), Porter can budget more accurately. "This will enable us to focus on additional KPIs—cost per employee, cost per aircraft landing, or available seat miles—because we can pinpoint any and all of the metrics that we hold to be important in the airline industry," Mr. Scott said.

In 2013, readers of the prestigious *Condé Nast Traveler* magazine voted Porter Airlines the best small airline in the world. Among passenger perks are spacious airport waiting areas and free alcohol on board—costs that Porter tracks carefully. The airline carried its 10 millionth passenger in 2013 after just seven years in business. Pending government approval, Porter was hoping to expand its routes by 2016 to serve destinations such as Miami, Los Angeles, and Vancouver with jets instead of its fleet of turboprops. This growth will require careful forecasting and budgetary planning to stay on course.

Sources: Jason McBride, "The End of an Affair," The Grid, January 22, 2014; "Porter Airlines Passes 10 Million Passengers," news release, November 12, 2013; "Porter Is Best Small Airline in World: Condé Nast Traveler," news release, October 30, 2013; "Porter Airlines: Prophix Case Study," Prophix Software, 2012, www.prophix.com.

Preview of Chapter 10

As the feature story about Porter Airlines indicates, budgeting is critical to financial well-being. As a student, you budget your study time and your money. Families budget income and expenses. Our focus in this chapter is budgeting for businesses—how management uses budgeting as a **planning tool**. Through budgeting, management should be able to have enough cash to pay creditors, enough raw materials to meet production requirements, and enough finished goods to meet expected sales. The chapter is organized as follows:

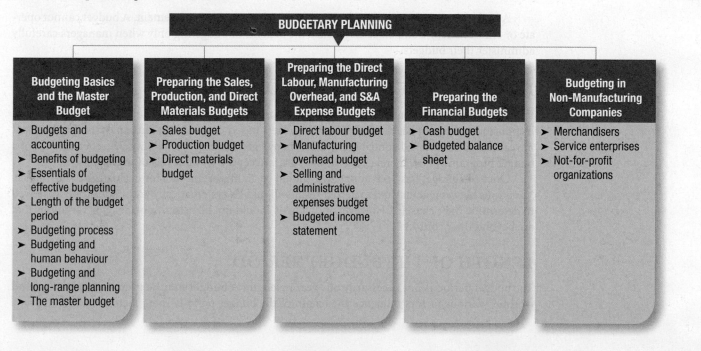

BUDGETARY PLANNING

Budgeting Basics and the Master Budget	Preparing the Sales, Production, and Direct Materials Budgets	Preparing the Direct Labour, Manufacturing Overhead, and S&A Expense Budgets	Preparing the Financial Budgets	Budgeting in Non-Manufacturing Companies
➤ Budgets and accounting ➤ Benefits of budgeting ➤ Essentials of effective budgeting ➤ Length of the budget period ➤ Budgeting process ➤ Budgeting and human behaviour ➤ Budgeting and long-range planning ➤ The master budget	➤ Sales budget ➤ Production budget ➤ Direct materials budget	➤ Direct labour budget ➤ Manufacturing overhead budget ➤ Selling and administrative expenses budget ➤ Budgeted income statement	➤ Cash budget ➤ Budgeted balance sheet	➤ Merchandisers ➤ Service enterprises ➤ Not-for-profit organizations

Budgeting Basics and the Master Budget

STUDY OBJECTIVE 1

State the essentials of effective budgeting and the components of a master budget.

One of management's major responsibilities is planning. As explained in Chapter 1, planning is the process of establishing objectives for the whole company. A successful organization makes both long-term and short-term plans. These plans state the company's objectives and the proposed way of accomplishing them.

A **budget** is a formal written statement in financial terms of management's plans for a specified future time period. It is normally the main way of communicating agreed-upon objectives throughout the organization. Once adopted, a budget becomes an important basis for evaluating performance. It promotes efficiency and discourages waste and inefficiency. Chapter 11 discusses the role of budgeting as a control device.

BUDGETS AND ACCOUNTING

Accounting information makes major contributions to the budgeting process. From the accounting records, management can obtain historical data on revenues, costs, and expenses. These data are helpful in setting future budget goals.

Normally, accountants are responsible for presenting management's budgeting goals in financial terms. In this role, they translate management's plans and communicate the budget to employees throughout the company. Accountants also prepare periodic budget reports that provide the basis for measuring performance and comparing actual results with planned objectives. The budget itself, and the administration of the budget, however, are entirely management's responsibilities.

THE BENEFITS OF BUDGETING

Following are the primary benefits of budgeting:

1. It requires all levels of management to **plan ahead** and to formalize goals on a recurring basis.
2. It provides **definite objectives** for evaluating performance at each level of responsibility.
3. It creates an **early warning system** for potential problems so that management can make changes before things get out of control.
4. It makes it easier to **coordinate activities** within the business. It does this by fitting the goals of each segment with overall company objectives. Thus, production and sales promotion can be integrated with expected sales.
5. It results in greater **management awareness** of the entity's overall operations and the impact on operations of external factors, such as economic trends.
6. It **motivates personnel** throughout the organization to meet planned objectives.

A budget is an aid to management; it is not a substitute for management. A budget cannot operate or enforce itself. Companies can realize the benefits of budgeting only when managers carefully administer their budgets.

ESSENTIALS OF EFFECTIVE BUDGETING

Effective budgeting depends on a **sound organizational structure** that clearly defines authority and responsibility for all phases of operations. Budgets based on **research and analysis** should result in realistic goals that will contribute to a company's growth and profitability. The effectiveness of a budget program is directly related to how well it is **accepted by all levels of management**.

Once the budget has been adopted, it should be an important tool for evaluating performance. Variations between actual and expected results should be systematically and periodically reviewed to determine their cause(s). However, individuals should not be held responsible for variations that are beyond their control.

LENGTH OF THE BUDGET PERIOD

The budget period is not necessarily one year in length. A **budget may be prepared for any period of time**. Various factors influence the length of the budget period. These factors include the type of budget, the type of organization, the need for periodic appraisal, and actual business conditions. For example, cash may be budgeted monthly, whereas a plant expansion budget may cover a 10-year period.

The budget period should be long enough to provide an attainable goal under normal business conditions. Ideally, the time period should be long enough that seasonal or cyclical fluctuations do not have a big impact on it. On the other hand, the budget period should not be so long that reliable estimates are impossible.

The **most common budget period is one year**. The annual budget is then often supplemented by monthly and quarterly budgets. Many companies use **continuous 12-month budgets**. These budgets drop the month just ended and add a future month. One advantage of continuous budgeting is that it keeps management planning a full year ahead.

THE BUDGETING PROCESS

The development of the budget for the coming year generally starts several months before the end of the current year. The budgeting process usually begins with the collection of data from each organizational unit of the company. Past performance is often the starting point for setting future budget goals.

The budget is developed within the framework of a **sales forecast**. This forecast shows potential sales for the industry and the company's expected share of these sales. In sales forecasting, various factors are considered: (1) general economic conditions, (2) industry trends, (3) market research studies, (4) anticipated advertising and promotion, (5) previous market share, (6) changes in prices, and (7) technological developments. The input of sales personnel and top management is essential to the sales forecast.

In small companies, the budgeting process is often informal. In larger companies, responsibility for coordinating the preparation of the budget is assigned to a **budget committee**. The committee ordinarily includes the president, treasurer, chief accountant (controller), and management personnel from each of the major areas of the company, such as sales, production, and research. The budget committee acts as a review board where managers can defend their budget goals and requests. Differences are reviewed, modified if necessary, and reconciled. The budget is then put in its final form by the budget committee, and is approved and distributed.

BUDGETING AND HUMAN BEHAVIOUR

A budget can have a significant impact on human behaviour. It may inspire a manager to higher levels of performance. Or it may discourage additional effort and pull down a manager's morale. Why do these effects occur? The answer is found in how the budget is developed and administered.

In developing the budget, each level of management should be invited to participate. This "bottom-up" approach is called **participative budgeting**. The advantages of participative budgeting are many. First, lower-level managers have more detailed knowledge of their specific area and thus should be able to provide more accurate budgetary estimates. Second, if lower-level managers are invited to participate in the budgeting process, they are more likely to see the resulting budget as fair. The overall goal is to reach agreement on a budget that the managers consider fair and achievable, but that also meets the corporate goals set by top management. When this overall goal is met, the budget will create positive motivation for the managers. In contrast, if the managers view the budget as being unfair and unrealistic, they may feel discouraged and uncommitted to budget goals. The risk of having unrealistic budgets is generally greater when the budget is developed from top management down to lower management than vice versa. Illustration 10-1 graphically displays the flow of budget data from bottom to top under participative budgeting.

For example, at one time, in an effort to revive its plummeting stock, Time Warner's top management determined and publicly announced bold new financial goals for the coming year. Unfortunately, these goals were not reached. The next year, the company got a new CEO who said the company would now actually set reasonable goals that it could meet. The new budgets were developed with each operating unit setting what it felt were optimistic but attainable goals. In the words of one manager, using this approach created a sense of teamwork.

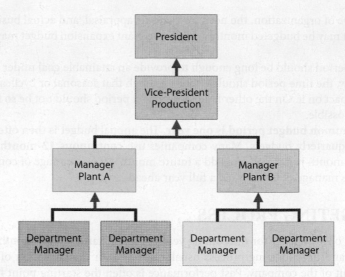

Participative budgeting does, however, have potential disadvantages. First, it can be far more time-consuming (and thus more costly) than a "top-down" approach, in which the budget is simply dictated to lower-level managers. A second disadvantage of participative budgeting is that it can encourage budgetary "gaming" through budgetary slack. **Budgetary slack** occurs when managers intentionally underestimate budgeted revenues or overestimate budgeted expenses in order to make it easier to achieve budgetary goals. To minimize budgetary slack, higher-level managers must carefully review and thoroughly question the budget projections that the employees they supervise provide.

For the budget to be effective, top management must completely support the budget. The budget is an important basis for evaluating performance. It also can be used as a positive aid in achieving projected goals. The effect of an evaluation is positive when top management tempers criticism with advice and assistance. In contrast, a manager is likely to respond negatively if top management uses the budget exclusively to assess blame. A budget should not be used as a pressure device to force improved performance. In sum, a budget can be a manager's friend or a foe.

BUSINESS INSIGHT   *Rolling Forecasts Replace Budgets*

Many organizations use annual budgets to help plan expenses and revenues, and monitor whether the actual amounts vary substantially from the expected amounts and take action if needed. But some observers caution that budgets are not always effective. For one thing, when management bonuses or performance ratings are tied to meeting budget targets, there's an incentive to do things like move money from one account to another, defer expenses to increase profits, or spend money in an account before year end in order not to lose it. A survey of more than 300 certified management accountants at Canadian firms found that a significant number of them said that such "gaming" with budgets sometimes happens in their companies. Another problem with budgeting is the time and resources it takes, only to have the numbers be out of date once the lengthy budgeting process is over. That's why multinational consumer giant Unilever did away with its annual budget in 2010. Instead, it uses an eight-quarter rolling forecast, updated regularly with input from the sales, supply chain, marketing, and finance departments. "Previously, the business units were committed to this arbitrary annual number in the budget and were of the mind-set that they had to stick to it. Now, every division has a target, and it is our job in finance to continually help them reach it," says Neal Vorchheimer, Unilever's senior vice president of finance for North America.

Sources: Theresa Libby and R. Murray Lindsay, "The Effects of Trust and Budget-Based Controls on Budget Gaming and Budget Value," AAA 2013 Management Accounting Section (MAS) Meeting Paper, August 17, 2012; Christopher Hann, "Why You Should Ditch Your Annual Budget," *Entrepreneur*, January 30, 2012; Russ Banham, "Let It Roll: Why More Companies Are Abandoning Budgets in Favor of Rolling Forecasts," *CFO Magazine*, May 1, 2011; Jeff Buckstein, "A Fresh Approach to Budgeting," *CMA Magazine*, September-October 2004.

What are some reasons to continue using a budget?

BUDGETING AND LONG-RANGE PLANNING

Budgeting and long-range planning are not the same. One important difference is the **time period involved**. The maximum length of a budget is usually one year, and budgets are often prepared for shorter periods of time, such as a month or a quarter. In contrast, long-range planning usually covers a period of at least five years.

A second significant difference is in **emphasis**. Budgeting focuses on achieving specific short-term goals, such as meeting annual profit objectives. **Long-range planning,** on the other hand, identifies long-term goals, selects strategies to achieve those goals, and develops policies and plans to implement the strategies. In long-range planning, management also considers anticipated trends in the economic and political environment and how the company should react to them.

The final difference between budgeting and long-range planning pertains to the **amount of detail presented**. Budgets, as you will see in this chapter, can be very detailed. Long-range plans contain much less detail. The data in long-range plans are intended more for a review of progress toward long-term goals than as a basis of control for achieving specific results. The main objective of long-range planning is to develop the best strategy to maximize the company's performance over an extended future period.

THE MASTER BUDGET

The term *budget* is actually a shorthand term to describe several budget documents. All of these documents are combined into a master budget. The **master budget** is a set of interrelated budgets that create a plan of action for a specified time period. Illustration 10-2 shows the individual budgets included in a master budget.

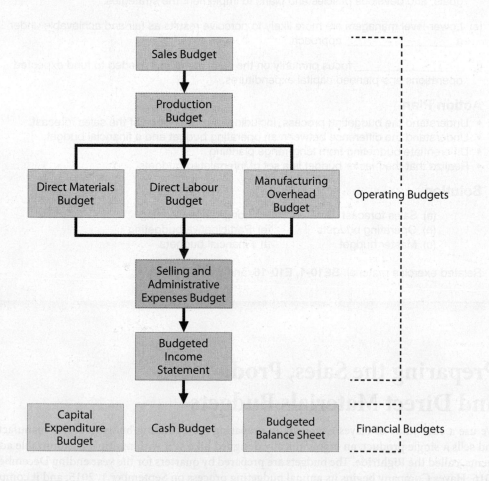

▶Illustration 10-2
Components of the master budget

As the illustration shows, the master budget contains two classes of budgets. **Operating budgets** are the individual budgets that are used to prepare the budgeted income statement. These budgets establish goals for the company's sales and production personnel. In contrast, **financial budgets** are the capital expenditure budget, the cash budget, and the budgeted balance sheet. These budgets focus on the cash resources needed to fund expected operations and planned capital expenditures.

The master budget is prepared in the sequence shown by the arrows in Illustration 10-2. The operating budgets are developed first, beginning with the sales budget. Then the financial budgets are prepared. We will explain and illustrate each budget shown in Illustration 10-2, except the capital expenditure budget, which is discussed under the topic Capital Budgeting in Chapter 13.

BEFORE YOU GO ON...

▶Do It! Budget Terminology

Use this list of terms to complete the sentences that follow.

Long-range planning	Participative budgeting
Sales forecast	Operating budgets
Master budget	Financial budgets

(a) A _____ shows potential sales for the industry and a company's expected share of such sales.

(b) _____ are used as the basis to prepare the budgeted income statement.

(c) The _____ is a set of interrelated budgets that constitutes a plan of action for a specified time period.

(d) _____ identifies long-term goals, selects strategies to achieve these goals, and develops policies and plans to implement the strategies.

(e) Lower-level managers are more likely to perceive results as fair and achievable under a _____ approach.

(f) _____ focus primarily on the cash resources needed to fund expected operations and planned capital expenditures.

Action Plan

- Understand the budgeting process, including the importance of the sales forecast.
- Understand the difference between an operating budget and a financial budget.
- Differentiate budgeting from long-range planning.
- Realize that the master budget is a set of interrelated budgets.

Solution

(a) Sales forecast	(d) Long-range planning
(b) Operating budgets	(e) Participative budgeting
(c) Master budget	(f) Financial budgets

Related exercise material: **BE10-1, E10-16,** and **Do It! D10-11.**

Preparing the Sales, Production, and Direct Materials Budgets

STUDY OBJECTIVE 2

Prepare budgets for sales, production, and direct materials.

We use a case study of Hayes Company in preparing the operating budgets. Hayes manufactures and sells a single product, an ergonomically designed bike seat with multiple customizable adjustments, called the Rightride. The budgets are prepared by quarters for the year ending December 31, 2016. Hayes Company begins its annual budgeting process on September 1, 2015, and it completes the budget for 2016 by December 1, 2015. The company begins by preparing the budgets for sales, production, and direct materials.

SALES BUDGET

As shown in the master budget in Illustration 10-2, **the sales budget is the first budget that is prepared**. Each of the other budgets depends on the sales budget. The **sales budget** is derived from the sales forecast. It represents management's best estimate of sales revenue for the budget period. An inaccurate sales budget may adversely affect net income. For example, an overly optimistic sales budget may result in excessive inventories that may have to be sold at reduced prices. In contrast, an overly conservative budget may result in lost sales revenue due to inventory shortages.

Forecasting sales is challenging. For example, consider Orca Bay Sports & Entertainment, the Vancouver-based entertainment company that owns and operates the Vancouver Canucks National Hockey League franchise and the team's home arena, Rogers Arena. Classified as a small market club under the current NHL economic environment, the Vancouver Canucks must rely on more than just ticket sales and league broadcast rights to generate revenue. Orca Bay is also a retailer, selling an array of Canucks-branded paraphernalia such as jerseys, banners, and posters at several stores at Rogers Arena and in downtown Vancouver. Unlike most retailers, Orca Bay has to drive the vast majority of its sales during a short time and mainly during games, which themselves are dependent on varying attendance, thus adding to the forecasting challenges. Or consider the challenges faced by Hollywood movie producers in predicting the complicated revenue stream produced by a new movie. Movie theatre ticket sales represent only 20% of total revenue. The bulk of revenue comes from global sales, DVDs, video-on-demand, merchandising products, and video games, all of which are difficult to forecast.

The sales budget is prepared by multiplying the expected sales volume in units for each product by its anticipated selling price per unit. For Hayes Company, the sales volume is expected to be 3,000 units in the first quarter, with 500-unit increments in each quarter after that. Illustration 10-3 shows the sales budget for the year, by quarters, based on a sales price of $60 per unit.

▶Illustration 10-3
Sales budget

	A	B	C	D	E	F
1		**HAYES COMPANY**				
2		**Sales Budget**				
3		**For the Year Ending December 31, 2016**				
4		**Quarter**				
5		1	2	3	4	Year
6	Expected unit sales	3,000	3,500	4,000	4,500	15,000
7	Unit selling price	× $60	× $60	× $60	× $60	× $60
8	Total sales	$180,000	$210,000	$240,000	$270,000	$900,000

Some companies classify the expected sales revenue as cash or credit sales, and by geographical region, territory, or salesperson.

PRODUCTION BUDGET

The **production budget** shows the units that must be produced to meet expected sales. Production requirements are determined with the formula in Illustration 10-4.[1]

▶Illustration 10-4
Production requirements formula

A realistic estimate of ending inventory is essential to correctly schedule production requirements. Excessive inventories in one quarter may lead to cutbacks in production and employee layoffs in the next quarter. On the other hand, inadequate inventories may result in either added costs for overtime work or lost sales. Hayes Company believes it can meet its future sales requirements by maintaining an ending inventory that is equal to 20% of the next quarter's budgeted sales volume. For example, the ending finished goods inventory for the first quarter is 700 units (20% × expected second-quarter sales of 3,500 units). Illustration 10-5 shows the production budget.

Units of Finished Goods Inventory	
Beg. Inv.	
Required	Sales
Prod. Units	
End. Inv.	

---

[1]This formula ignores any work in process inventories, which are assumed to be non-existent in Hayes Company.

►Illustration 10-5
Production budget

	A	B	C	D	E	F
1	**HAYES COMPANY**					
2	**Production Budget**					
3	**For the Year Ending December 31, 2016**					
4		Quarter				
5		1	2	3	4	Year
6	Expected unit sales (Illustration 10-3)	3,000	3,500	4,000	4,500	
7	Add: Desired ending finished goods units[a]	700	800	900	1,000[b]	
8	Total required units	3,700	4,300	4,900	5,500	
9	Less: Beginning finished goods units	600[c]	700	800	900	
10	**Required production units**	**3,100**	**3,600**	**4,100**	**4,600**	**15,400**
11						
12	[a]20% of next quarter's sales					
13	[b]Expected 2017 first-quarter sales, 5,000 units × 20%					
14	[c]20% of estimated first-quarter 2016 sales units					

The production budget, in turn, becomes the basis for determining the budgeted costs for each manufacturing cost element, as explained in the following pages.

DIRECT MATERIALS BUDGET

The **direct materials budget** shows both the quantity and cost of direct materials that need to be purchased. The quantities of direct materials to purchase are determined with the formula in Illustration 10-6.

►Illustration 10-6
Formula for direct materials quantities

Direct Materials Units Required for Production + Desired Ending Direct Materials Units − Beginning Direct Materials Units = Required Direct Materials Units to Be Purchased

The budgeted cost of direct materials to be purchased is then calculated by multiplying the required units of direct materials by the expected cost per unit.

The desired ending inventory is again a key component in the budgeting process. For example, inadequate inventories could result in temporary shutdowns of production. Because of its close proximity to suppliers, Hayes Company has found that an ending inventory of raw materials equal to 10% of the next quarter's production requirements is enough. The manufacture of each Rightride requires 2 kg of raw materials, and the expected cost per kilogram is $4. Illustration 10-7 shows the direct materials.

Units of Direct Materials

Beg. Inv. Direct Materials to Purchase	Direct Materials Required for Prod.
End. Inv.	

Units of Direct Materials (1st quarter)

620	
6,300	6,200
720	

►Illustration 10-7
Direct materials budget

	A	B	C	D	E	F
1	**HAYES COMPANY**					
2	**Direct Materials Budget**					
3	**For the Year Ending December 31, 2016**					
4		Quarter				
5		1	2	3	4	Year
6	Units to be produced (Illustration 10-5)	3,100	3,600	4,100	4,600	
7	Direct materials per unit	× 2	× 2	× 2	× 2	
8	Total kilograms needed for production	6,200	7,200	8,200	9,200	
9	Add: Desired ending direct materials (kilograms)[a]	720	820	920	1,020[b]	
10	Total materials required	6,920	8,020	9,120	10,220	
11	Less: Beginning direct materials (kilograms)	620[c]	720	820	920	
12	Direct materials purchases	6,300	7,300	8,300	9,300	
13	Cost per kilogram	× $4	× $4	× $4	× $4	
14	**Total cost of direct materials purchases**	**$25,200**	**$29,200**	**$33,200**	**$37,200**	**$124,800**
15						
16	[a]10% of next quarter's production requirements					
17	[b]Estimated 2017 first-quarter kilograms needed for production, 10,200 × 10%					
18	[c]10% of estimated first-quarter kilograms needed for production					

BEFORE YOU GO ON...

▶Do It! Master Budget

Soriano Company is preparing its master budget for 2016. Relevant data pertaining to its sales, production, and direct materials budgets are as follows:

Sales: Sales for the year are expected to total 1.2 million units. Quarterly sales, as a percentage of total sales, are 20%, 25%, 30%, and 25%, respectively. The sales price is expected to be $50 per unit for the first three quarters and $55 per unit beginning in the fourth quarter. Sales in the first quarter of 2017 are expected to be 10% higher than the budgeted sales for the first quarter of 2016.

Production: Management desires to maintain the ending finished goods inventories at 25% of the next quarter's budgeted sales volume.

Direct materials: Each unit requires 3 kg of raw materials at a cost of $5 per kilogram. Management desires to maintain raw materials inventories at 5% of the next quarter's production requirements. Assume the production requirements for the first quarter of 2017 are 810,000 kg.

Prepare the sales, production, and direct materials budgets by quarters for 2016.

Action Plan

- Know the form and content of the sales budget.
- Prepare the sales budget first, as the basis for the other budgets.
- Determine the units that must be produced to meet anticipated sales.
- Know how to calculate the beginning and ending finished goods units.
- Determine the materials required to meet production needs.
- Know how to calculate the beginning and ending direct materials units.

Solution

	A	B	C	D	E	F
1		SORIANO COMPANY				
2		Sales Budget				
3		For the Year Ending December 31, 2016				
4		Quarter				
5		1	2	3	4	Year
6	Expected unit sales	240,000	300,000	360,000	300,000	1,200,000
7	Unit selling price	× $50	× $50	× $50	× $55	—
8	Total sales	$12,000,000	$15,000,000	$18,000,000	$16,500,000	$61,500,000

	A	B	C	D	E	F
1		SORIANO COMPANY				
2		Production Budget				
3		For the Year Ending December 31, 2016				
4		Quarter				
5		1	2	3	4	Year
6	Expected unit sales	240,000	300,000	360,000	300,000	
7	Add: Desired ending finished goods units[a]	75,000	90,000	75,000	66,000[b]	
8	Total required units	315,000	390,000	435,000	366,000	
9	Less: Beginning finished goods units	60,000[c]	75,000	90,000	75,000	
10	Required production units	255,000	315,000	345,000	291,000	1,206,000
11	[a]25% of next quarter's unit sales					
12	[b]Estimated first-quarter 2017 sales units 240,000 + (240,000 × 10%) = 264,000: 264,000 × 25%					
13	[c]25% of estimated first-quarter 2016 sales units (240,000 × 25%)					
14						

(continued)

(continued)

	A	B	C	D	E	F
1	**SORIANO COMPANY**					
2	Direct Materials Budget					
3	For the Year Ending December 31, 2016					
4		Quarter				
5		1	2	3	4	Year
6	Units to be produced	255,000	315,000	345,000	291,000	
7	Direct materials per unit	× 3	× 3	× 3	× 3	
8	Total kilograms needed for production	765,000	945,000	1,035,000	873,000	
9	Add: Desired ending direct materials (kilograms)	47,250	51,750	43,650	40,500ª	
10	Total materials required	812,250	996,750	1,078,650	913,500	
11	Less: Beginning direct materials (kilograms)	38,250ᵇ	47,250	51,750	43,650	
12	Direct materials purchases	774,000	949,500	1,026,900	869,850	
13	Cost per kilogram	× $5	× $5	× $5	× $5	
14	Total cost of direct materials purchases	$3,870,000	$4,747,500	$5,134,500	$4,349,250	$18,101,250
15						
16	ªEstimated first-quarter 2017 production requirements 810,000 × 5% = 40,500					
17	ᵇ5% of estimated first-quarter kilograms needed for production					
18						

Related exercise material: **BE10-2, BE10-3, BE10-4, E10-17, E10-18, E10-19, E10-20, E10-21,** and **Do It! D10-12.**

Preparing the Direct Labour, Manufacturing Overhead, and S&A Expense Budgets

DIRECT LABOUR BUDGET

STUDY OBJECTIVE 3
Prepare budgets for direct labour, manufacturing overhead, and selling and administrative expenses, and a budgeted income statement.

As shown in Illustration 10-2, the operating budgets culminate with preparation of the budgeted income statement. Before we can do that, we need to prepare budgets for direct labour, manufacturing overhead, and selling and administrative (S&A) expenses.

Like the direct materials budget, the **direct labour budget** contains the quantity (hours) and cost of direct labour that will be needed to meet production requirements. The total direct labour cost is calculated using the formula in Illustration 10-8.

►Illustration 10-8
Formula for direct labour cost

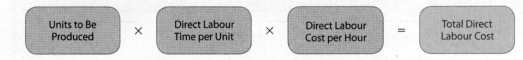

Direct labour hours are determined from the production budget. At Hayes Company, two hours of direct labour are required to produce each unit of finished goods. The expected hourly wage rate is $10. Illustration 10-9 shows these data. The direct labour budget is critical in maintaining a labour force that can meet the expected levels of production.

►Illustration 10-9
Direct labour budget

Helpful Hint
An important assumption in Illustration 10-9 is that the company can add to and subtract from its workforce as needed so that the $10 per hour labour cost applies to a wide range of possible production activity.

	A	B	C	D	E	F
1	**HAYES COMPANY**					
2	Direct Labour Budget					
3	For the Year Ending December 31, 2016					
4		Quarter				
5		1	2	3	4	Year
6	Units to be produced (Illustration 10-5)	3,100	3,600	4,100	4,600	
7	Direct labour time (hours) per unit	× 2	× 2	× 2	× 2	
8	Total required direct labour hours	6,200	7,200	8,200	9,200	
9	Direct labour cost per hour	× $10	× $10	× $10	× $10	
10	**Total direct labour cost**	$62,000	$72,000	$82,000	$92,000	$308,000
11						

MANUFACTURING OVERHEAD BUDGET

The **manufacturing overhead budget** shows the expected manufacturing overhead costs for the budget period. As shown in Illustration 10-10, this budget distinguishes between variable and fixed overhead costs. Hayes Company expects variable costs to fluctuate with the production volume based on the following rates per direct labour hour: indirect materials $1; indirect labour $1.40; utilities $0.40; and maintenance $0.20. Thus, for the 6,200 direct labour hours required to produce 3,100 units, the budgeted indirect materials cost is $6,200 (6,200 × $1), and the budgeted indirect labour cost is $8,680 (6,200 × $1.40). Hayes also recognizes that some maintenance is fixed. The amounts reported for fixed costs are assumed in our example. The accuracy of budgeted fixed overhead cost estimates can be greatly improved by using activity-based costing.

	A	B	C	D	E	F
1		**HAYES COMPANY**				
2		**Manufacturing Overhead Budget**				
3		**For the Year Ending December 31, 2016**				
4				Quarter		
5		1	2	3	4	Year
6	Variable costs					
7	Indirect materials ($1.00/hour)	$ 6,200	$ 7,200	$ 8,200	$ 9,200	$ 30,800
8	Indirect labour ($1.40/hour)	8,680	10,080	11,480	12,880	43,120
9	Utilities ($0.40/hour)	2,480	2,880	3,280	3,680	12,320
10	Maintenance ($0.20/hour)	1,240	1,440	1,640	1,840	6,160
11	Total variable costs	18,600	21,600	24,600	27,600	92,400
12	Fixed costs					
13	Supervisory salaries	20,000	20,000	20,000	20,000	80,000
14	Depreciation	3,800	3,800	3,800	3,800	15,200
15	Property taxes and insurance	9,000	9,000	9,000	9,000	36,000
16	Maintenance	5,700	5,700	5,700	5,700	22,800
17	Total fixed costs	38,500	38,500	38,500	38,500	154,000
18	**Total manufacturing overhead**	**$57,100**	**$60,100**	**$63,100**	**$66,100**	**$246,400**
19	Direct labour hours (Illustration 10-9)	6,200	7,200	8,200	9,200	30,800
20	**Manufacturing overhead rate per direct labour hour ($246,400 ÷ 30,800)**					$8
21						

▶Illustration 10-10
Manufacturing overhead budget

At Hayes Company, overhead is applied to production based on direct labour hours. Thus, as shown in Illustration 10-10, the annual rate is $8 per hour ($246,400 ÷ 30,800).

SELLING AND ADMINISTRATIVE EXPENSES BUDGET

Hayes Company combines its operating expenses into one budget, the **selling and administrative expenses budget**. This budget projects selling and administrative expenses for the budget period. In this budget, as in the preceding one, expenses are classified as either variable or fixed. In this case, the variable expense rates per unit of sales are $3 of sales commissions and $1 of freight out. Variable expenses per quarter are based on the unit sales from the sales budget (Illustration 10-3). For example, sales in the first quarter are expected to be 3,000 units. Thus, the sales commissions expense is $9,000 (3,000 × $3), and freight out is $3,000 (3,000 × $1). Fixed expenses are based on assumed data. Illustration 10-11 shows the selling and administrative expenses budget.

	A	B	C	D	E	F
1	**HAYES COMPANY**					
2	**Selling and Administrative Expenses Budget**					
3	**For the Year Ending December 31, 2016**					
4		Quarter				
5		1	2	3	4	Year
6	Budgeted sales in units (Illustration 10-3)	3,000	3,500	4,000	4,500	15,000
7	Variable expenses					
8	Sales commissions ($3 per unit)	$ 9,000	$10,500	$12,000	$13,500	$ 45,000
9	Freight-out ($1 per unit)	3,000	3,500	4,000	4,500	15,000
10	Total variable expenses	12,000	14,000	16,000	18,000	60,000
11	Fixed expenses					
12	Advertising	5,000	5,000	5,000	5,000	20,000
13	Sales salaries	15,000	15,000	15,000	15,000	60,000
14	Office salaries	7,500	7,500	7,500	7,500	30,000
15	Depreciation	1,000	1,000	1,000	1,000	4,000
16	Property taxes and insurance	1,500	1,500	1,500	1,500	6,000
17	Total fixed expenses	30,000	30,000	30,000	30,000	120,000
18	Total selling and administrative expenses	$42,000	$44,000	$46,000	$48,000	$180,000
19						

BUDGETED INCOME STATEMENT

The **budgeted income statement** is the important end product of the operating budgets. This budget indicates the expected profitability of operations for the budget period. The budgeted income statement provides the basis for evaluating company performance.

As you would expect, this budget is prepared from the various operating budgets. For example, to find the cost of goods sold, it is first necessary to determine the total cost per unit of producing one Rightride. Illustration 10-12 shows this calculation.

Cost of One Rightride

Cost element	Illustration	Quantity	Unit Cost	Total
Direct materials	10-7	2 kg	$ 4.00	$ 8.00
Direct labour	10-9	2 hours	$10.00	20.00
Manufacturing overhead	10-10	2 hours	$ 8.00	16.00
Total unit cost				$44.00

Hayes Company then determines the cost of goods sold by multiplying the units sold by the unit cost. Its budgeted cost of goods sold is $660,000 (15,000 × $44). All data for the statement are obtained from the individual operating budgets except the following: (1) interest expense is expected to be $100, and (2) income taxes are estimated to be $12,000. Illustration 10-13 shows the budgeted income statement.

HAYES COMPANY
Budgeted Income Statement
Year Ending December 31, 2016

Sales (Illustration 10-3)	$900,000
Cost of goods sold (15,000 × $44)	660,000
Gross profit	240,000
Selling and administrative expenses (Illustration 10-11)	180,000
Income from operations	60,000
Interest expense	100
Income before income taxes	59,900
Income tax expense	12,000
Net income	$ 47,900

DECISION TOOLKIT

Decision Checkpoints	**Info Needed for Decision**	**Tools to Use for Decision**	**How to Evaluate Results**
Has the company met its targets for sales, production expenses, selling and administrative expenses, and net income?	Sales forecasts; inventory levels; and projected materials, labour, overhead, and selling and administrative requirements	Master budget—a set of interrelated budgets including the sales, production, materials, labour, overhead, and selling and administrative budgets	The results are favourable if revenues exceed budgeted amounts, or if expenses are less than budgeted amounts.

BEFORE YOU GO ON...

▶Do It! Budgeted Income Statement

Soriano Company is preparing its budgeted income statement for 2016. Relevant data pertaining to its sales, production, and direct materials budgets can be found in the Do It! exercise on page 411.

In addition, Soriano budgets 0.5 hours of direct labour per unit, labour costs at $15 per hour, and manufacturing overhead at $25 per direct labour hour. Its budgeted selling and administrative expenses for 2016 are $12 million.

(a) Calculate the budgeted total unit cost.

(b) Prepare the budgeted income statement for 2016. Ignore income taxes.

Action Plan

- Recall that total unit cost consists of direct materials, direct labour, and manufacturing overhead.
- Recall that direct materials costs are included in the direct materials budget.
- Know the form and content of the income statement.
- Use the total unit sales information from the sales budget to calculate annual sales and cost of goods sold.

Solution

(a)

Cost Element	Quantity	Unit Cost	Total
Direct materials	3.0 kg	$ 5	$15.00
Direct labour	0.5 hours	$15	7.50
Manufacturing overhead	0.5 hours	$25	12.50
Total unit cost			$35.00

(b)

SORIANO COMPANY
Budgeted Income Statement
For the Year Ending December 31, 2016

Sales (1,200,000 units from sales budget, page 411)	$61,500,000
Cost of goods sold (1,200,000 × $35.00/unit)	42,000,000
Gross profit	19,500,000
Selling and administrative expenses	12,000,000
Net income	$ 7,500,000

Related exercise material: **BE10-5, BE10-6, BE10-7, BE10-8, E10-22, E10-23, E10-24, E10-26,** and **Do It! D10-13.**

Preparing the Financial Budgets

As shown in Illustration 10-2, the financial budgets consist of the capital expenditure budget, the cash budget, and the budgeted balance sheet. Chapter 13 discusses the capital expenditure budget, while the following sections explain the other budgets.

CASH BUDGET

The **cash budget** shows expected cash flows. Because cash is so vital, this budget is often considered to be the most important output in preparing financial budgets. To help the treasurer manage the cash well, a cash budget is typically prepared at least once a month, and in some companies, it is prepared daily. The cash budget contains three sections (cash receipts, cash disbursements, and financing) and the beginning and ending cash balances, as shown in Illustration 10-14.

▶Illustration 10-14

Basic form of a cash budget

ANY COMPANY	
Cash Budget	
Beginning cash balance	$X,XXX
Add: Cash receipts (itemized)	X,XXX
Total available cash	X,XXX
Less: Cash disbursements (itemized)	X,XXX
Excess (deficiency) of available cash over cash disbursements	X,XXX
Financing	X,XXX
Ending cash balance	$X,XXX

Helpful Hint
Why is the cash budget prepared after the other budgets are prepared? Answer: Because the information from the other budgets determines the need for inflows and outflows of cash.

The **cash receipts section** includes expected receipts from the company's main source(s) of revenue. These are usually cash sales and collections from customers on credit sales. This section also shows anticipated receipts of interest and dividends, and proceeds from planned sales of investments, plant assets, and the company's capital stock.

The **cash disbursements section** shows expected cash payments. These payments include direct materials, direct labour, manufacturing overhead, and selling and administrative expenses. This section also includes projected payments for income taxes, dividends, investments, and plant assets.

The **financing section** shows expected borrowings and the repayment of the borrowed funds plus interest. This section is needed when there is a cash deficiency or when the cash balance is below management's minimum required balance.

Data in the cash budget must be prepared in sequence. The ending cash balance of one period becomes the beginning cash balance for the next period. Data for preparing the cash budget are obtained from other budgets and from information provided by management. Many companies prepare cash budgets for the year on a monthly basis.

To minimize detail, we will assume that Hayes Company prepares an annual cash budget by quarters. The cash budget for Hayes Company is based on the following assumptions:

1. The January 1, 2016, cash balance is expected to be $38,000. Hayes wishes to maintain a balance of at least $15,000.
2. Sales (Illustration 10-3): 60% are collected in the quarter sold and 40% are collected in the following quarter. Accounts receivable of $60,000 at December 31, 2015, are expected to be collected in full in the first quarter of 2016.
3. Short-term investments are expected to be sold for $2,000 cash in the first quarter.
4. Direct materials (Illustration 10-7): 50% are paid for in the quarter purchased and 50% are paid for in the following quarter. Accounts payable of $10,600 at December 31, 2015, are expected to be paid in full in the first quarter of 2016.

5. Direct labour (Illustration 10-9): 100% is paid in the quarter incurred.
6. Manufacturing overhead (Illustration 10-10) and selling and administrative expenses (Illustration 10-11): All items except depreciation are paid in the quarter incurred.
7. Management plans to purchase a truck in the second quarter for $10,000 cash.
8. Hayes makes equal quarterly payments of its estimated annual income taxes.
9. Loans are repaid in the earliest quarter in which there is sufficient cash (that is, when the cash on hand exceeds the $15,000 minimum required balance).

In preparing the cash budget, it is useful to prepare schedules for collections from customers (assumption No. 2 above) and cash payments for direct materials (assumption No. 4 above). Illustrations 10-15 and 10-16 show the schedules.

	A	B	C	D	E	F
1		**HAYES COMPANY**				
2		**Schedule of Expected Collections from Customers**				
3				Collections by Quarter		
4		Sales[a]	1	2	3	4
5	Accounts receivable, December 31, 2015		$ 60,000			
6	First quarter	$180,000	108,000[b]	$ 72,000[c]		
7	Second quarter	210,000		126,000	$ 84,000	
8	Third quarter	240,000			144,000	$ 96,000
9	Fourth quarter	270,000				162,000
10	Total collections		$168,000	$198,000	$228,000	$258,000
11						
12	[a]Per Illustration 10-3; [b]$180,000 × 0.60; [c]$180,000 × 0.40					
13						

▶Illustration 10-15
Collections from customers

	A	B	C	D	E	F
1		**HAYES COMPANY**				
2		**Schedule of Expected Payments for Direct Materials**				
3				Payments by Quarter		
4		Purchases[a]	1	2	3	4
5	Accounts payable, December 31, 2015		$10,600			
6	First quarter	$25,200	12,600[b]	$12,600[c]		
7	Second quarter	29,200		14,600	$14,600	
8	Third quarter	33,200			16,600	$16,600
9	Fourth quarter	37,200				18,600
10	Total payments		$23,200	$27,200	$31,200	$35,200
11						
12	[a]Per Illustration 10-7; [b]$25,200 × 0.50; [c]$25,200 × 0.50					
13						

▶Illustration 10-16
Payments for direct materials

Illustration 10-17 shows the cash budget for Hayes Company. The budget indicates that $3,000 of financing will be needed in the second quarter to keep a minimum cash balance of $15,000. Since there is an excess of available cash over disbursements of $22,500 at the end of the third quarter, the borrowing, plus $100 interest, is repaid in this quarter.

	A	B	C	D	E	F
1			**HAYES COMPANY**			
2			Cash Budget			
3			For the Year Ending December 31, 2016			
4			Quarter			
5		Assumption	1	2	3	4
6	Beginning cash balance	1	$ 38,000	$ 25,500	$ 15,000	$ 19,400
7	**Add: Receipts**					
8	Collections from customers	2	168,000	198,000	228,000	258,000
9	Sale of securities	3	2,000	0	0	0
10	Total receipts		170,000	198,000	228,000	258,000
11	Total available cash		208,000	223,500	243,000	277,400
12	**Less: Disbursements**					
13	Direct materials	4	23,200	27,200	31,200	35,200
14	Direct labour	5	62,000	72,000	82,000	92,000
15	Manufacturing overhead	6	53,300[a]	56,300	59,300	62,300
16	Selling and administrative expenses	6	41,000[b]	43,000	45,000	47,000
17	Purchase of truck	7	0	10,000	0	0
18	Income tax expense	8	3,000	3,000	3,000	3,000
19	Total disbursements		182,500	211,500	220,500	239,500
20	Excess (deficiency) of available cash over cash disbursements		25,500	12,000	22,500	37,900
21	**Financing**					
22	Borrowings		0	**3,000**	0	0
23	Repayments plus $100 interest	9	0	0	3,100	0
24	Ending cash balance		$ 25,500	$ 15,000	$ 19,400	$ 37,900
25						
26	[a]$57,100 – $3,800 depreciation					
27	[b]$42,000 – $1,000 depreciation					

▶Illustration 10-17

Cash budget

A cash budget contributes to more effective cash management. It can show managers when additional financing will be necessary a long time before the money is needed. And it can indicate when excess cash will be available for investments or other purposes.

DECISION TOOLKIT

Decision Checkpoints	Info Needed for Decision	Tools to Use for Decision	How to Evaluate Results

Is the company going to need to borrow funds in the coming quarter?	Beginning cash balance, cash receipts, cash disbursements, and desired cash balance	Cash budget	The company will need to borrow money if the cash budget indicates that the available cash will be less than the cash disbursements for the quarter.

BUDGETED BALANCE SHEET

The **budgeted balance sheet** is a projection of the company's financial position at the end of the budget period. This budget is developed from the budgeted balance sheet for the preceding year and the budgets for the current year. Relevant data for Hayes from the budgeted balance sheet at December 31, 2015, are as follows:

Buildings and equipment	$182,000	Common shares	$225,000
Accumulated depreciation	28,800	Retained earnings	46,480

Illustration 10-18 shows the budgeted balance sheet at December 31, 2016.

►Illustration 10-18
Budgeted balance sheet

HAYES COMPANY
Budgeted Balance Sheet
December 31, 2016

Assets

Cash		$ 37,900
Accounts receivable		108,000
Finished goods inventory		44,000
Raw materials inventory		4,080
Buildings and equipment	$192,000	
Less: Accumulated depreciation	48,000	144,000
Total assets		$337,980

Liabilities and Shareholders' Equity

Accounts payable	$ 18,600
Common shares	225,000
Retained earnings	94,380
Total liabilities and shareholders' equity	$337,980

The calculations and sources of the amounts are as follows:

Cash: Ending cash balance of $37,900, shown in the cash budget (Illustration 10-17).

Accounts receivable: 40% of fourth-quarter sales of $270,000, shown in the schedule of expected collections from customers (Illustration 10-15).

Finished goods inventory: Desired ending inventory of 1,000 units, shown in the production budget (Illustration 10-5) times the total cost per unit of $44 (shown in Illustration 10-12).

Raw materials inventory: Desired ending inventory of 1,020 kg, times the cost per kilogram of $4, shown in the direct materials budget (Illustration 10-7).

Buildings and equipment: December 31, 2015, balance of $182,000, plus the purchase of a truck for $10,000.

Accumulated depreciation: December 31, 2015, balance of $28,800, plus $15,200 of depreciation shown in the manufacturing overhead budget (Illustration 10-10) and $4,000 of depreciation shown in the selling and administrative expenses budget (Illustration 10-11).

Accounts payable: 50% of fourth-quarter purchases of $37,200, shown in the schedule of expected payments for direct materials (Illustration 10-16).

Common shares: Unchanged from the beginning of the year.

Retained earnings: December 31, 2015, balance of $46,480, plus net income of $47,900, shown in the budgeted income statement (Illustration 10-13).

After the budgeting data are entered into the company's budgeting software, the various budgets (sales, cash, etc.) can be prepared, as well as the budgeted financial statements. Management can also manipulate the budgets in "what if" (sensitivity) analyses based on different hypothetical assumptions. For example, suppose that sales were budgeted to be 10% higher in the coming quarter. What impact would the change have on the rest of the budgeting process and the financing needs of the business? The computer can quickly "play out" the impact on the budgets of the various assumptions. Armed with these analyses, management can make more informed decisions about the impact of various projects. It can also anticipate future problems and business opportunities. Having read this chapter, you may not be surprised to know that budgeting is also one of the top uses of electronic spreadsheets.

BEFORE YOU GO ON...

▶Do It! Cash Budget

Martian Company's management wants to maintain a minimum monthly cash balance of $15,000. At the beginning of March, the cash balance is $16,500, expected cash receipts for March are $210,000, and cash disbursements are expected to be $220,000. How much cash, if any, must be borrowed to keep the desired minimum monthly balance?

Action Plan

• Write down the basic form of the cash budget, starting with the beginning cash balance. Add cash receipts for the period, deduct cash disbursements, and then identify the needed financing to achieve the desired minimum ending cash balance.
• Insert the data into the outlined form of the cash budget.

Solution

MARTIAN COMPANY
Cash Budget
Month Ending March 31, 2016

Beginning cash balance	$ 16,500
Add: Cash receipts for March	210,000
Total available cash	226,500
Less: Cash disbursements for March	220,000
Excess of available cash over cash disbursements	6,500
Financing	8,500
Ending cash balance	$ 15,000

To keep the desired minimum cash balance of $15,000, Martian Company must borrow $8,500 of cash.

Related exercise material: **BE10-9, E10-27, E10-28, E10-29,** and **Do It! D10-14.**

the navigator

Budgeting in Non-Manufacturing Companies

STUDY OBJECTIVE 5

Explain the applicability of budgeting in non-manufacturing companies.

Budgeting is not limited to manufacturers. Budgets may also be used by merchandisers, service enterprises, and not-for-profit organizations.

MERCHANDISERS

As in manufacturing operations, the sales budget for a merchandiser is both the starting point and the key factor in the development of the master budget. There are two major differences between the master budgets of a merchandiser and a manufacturer.

1. A merchandiser **uses a merchandise purchases budget instead of a production budget**.
2. A merchandiser **does not use the manufacturing budgets (direct materials, direct labour, and manufacturing overhead)**.

The **merchandise purchases budget** shows the estimated cost of goods to be purchased to meet expected sales. Illustration 10-19 provides the formula for determining budgeted merchandise purchases.

▶Illustration 10-19
Merchandise purchases formula

Budgeted Cost of Goods Sold	+	Desired Ending Merchandise Inventory	−	Beginning Merchandise Inventory	=	Required Merchandise Purchases

To illustrate, assume that the budget committee of Lima Company is preparing the merchandise purchases budget for July 2016. It estimates that sales will be $300,000 in July and $320,000 in August. The cost of goods sold is expected to be 70% of sales; that is, $210,000 in July (0.70 × $300,000) and $224,000 in August (0.70 × $320,000). The company's desired ending inventory is 30% of the following month's cost of goods sold. The required merchandise purchases for July are therefore $214,200, calculated as shown in Illustration 10-20.

LIMA COMPANY Merchandise Purchases Budget Month Ending July 31, 2016	
Budgeted cost of goods sold ($300,000 × 70%)	$210,000
Plus: Desired ending merchandise inventory ($224,000 × 30%)	67,200
Total	277,200
Less: Beginning merchandise inventory ($210,000 × 30%)	63,000
Budgeted merchandise purchases for July	$214,200

▶Illustration 10-20
Merchandise purchases budget

When a merchandiser is organized by department, separate budgets are prepared for each one. For example, a grocery store may start by preparing sales budgets and purchases budgets for each of its major departments, such as meats, dairy, and produce. It then combines these budgets into a master budget for the store. When a retailer has branch stores, it prepares separate master budgets for each store. Then these budgets are incorporated into master budgets for the company as a whole.

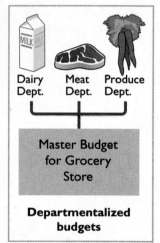

Departmentalized budgets

SERVICE ENTERPRISES

In a service enterprise, such as a public accounting firm, a law office, or a medical practice, the critical factor in budgeting is **coordinating professional staff needs with expected services**. If a firm is overstaffed, several problems may result: (1) Labour costs will be disproportionately high. (2) Profits will be lower because of the additional salaries. (3) Staff turnover may increase because there is not enough challenging work. In contrast, if an enterprise is understaffed, it may lose revenue because it cannot meet the existing and potential needs of clients for services. Also, professional staff may look for other jobs because their workloads are too heavy.

Suppose that Stephan Lawn and Plowing Service estimates that it will service 300 small lawns, 200 medium lawns, and 100 large lawns during the month of July. It estimates its direct labour needs as 1 hour per small lawn, 1.75 hours for a medium lawn, and 2.75 hours for a large lawn. Its average cost for direct labour is $15 per hour. Stephan prepares a direct labour budget as shown in Illustration 10-21.

	A	B	C	D	E
1	STEPHAN LAWN AND PLOWING SERVICE				
2	Direct Labour Budget				
3	For the Month Ending July 31, 2016				
4		Small	Medium	Large	Total
5	Lawns to be serviced	300	200	100	
6	Direct labour time (hours) per lawn	×1	× 1.75	× 2.75	
7	Total required direct labour hours	300	350	275	
8	Direct labour cost per hour	× $15	× $15	× $15	
9	Total direct labour cost	$4,500	$5,250	$4,125	$13,875
10					

▶Illustration 10-21
Direct labour budget for service company

Budget data for service revenue may be obtained from **expected output** or **expected input**. When using output, it is necessary to determine the expected billings of clients for services provided. In a public accounting firm, for example, output would be the sum of the firm's billings in auditing, tax, and consulting services. When using input data, each professional staff member is required to project his or her time that will be billed. Billing rates are then applied to this billable time to calculate the expected service revenue.

| | BUSINESS INSIGHT | *Betting on Good Budgeting* |

The Saskatchewan Gaming Corporation (SaskGaming), which operates casinos in Regina and Moose Jaw, used to set its annual budgets using forecasts based on historical data. It would predict revenue from slot machines in its casinos, for example, by looking at past demand. Recently, it started collecting more data from its operations to monitor changing customer preferences, tracking which games were becoming more popular or less popular, and more accurately predicting the right mix of games and the physical space and budget needed to support them. It can even predict which slot machines will need replacing and when best to replace them to minimize player downtime. This information is all fed into the budget, which helps management plan expenses and revenues, since slot machines accounted for about 83% of SaskGaming's revenue in 2012. "To have the power to reasonably forecast future results and do those 'what if' scenarios at our convenience lets us make decisions about the timing and nature of machine replacements so as to achieve the most desirable business outcomes," said Elliott Daradich, SaskGaming's Director of Slots.

Sources: Craig Crothers, "Analytics and the Modern Casino: A Game Changer," *Canadian Gaming Business,* April 23, 2013; "SaskGaming's Slot Floor Optimization," SAS case study, www.sas.com, 2013; SaskGaming 2012 Annual Report.

Should SaskGaming forecast higher or lower revenues if it thinks the economy will improve in an upcoming budget?

NOT-FOR-PROFIT ORGANIZATIONS

Budgeting is just as important for not-for-profit organizations as for profit-oriented enterprises. The budget process, however, is very different. In most cases, not-for-profit entities budget based **on cash flows (expenditures and receipts), rather than on a revenue and expense basis**. Further, the starting point in the process is usually expenditures, not receipts. For the not-for-profit entity, management's task generally is to find the receipts needed to support the planned expenditures. The activity index is also likely to be quite different. For example, in a university, budgeted faculty positions may be based on full-time equivalent students or credit hours expected to be taught in a department.

For government units such as provincial governments and the federal government, legislative approval is required. After the budget is adopted, it must be strictly followed. Spending on activities not included in the budget is usually illegal. In some municipal government budgets, authorizations tend to be on a line-by-line basis. That is, the budget for a municipality may have a specified authorization for police and fire protection, garbage collection, street paving, and so on. The line-item authorization of municipal governmental budgets significantly limits how much discretion management has. The city manager often cannot use savings from one line item, such as street paving, to cover increased spending in another line item, such as snow removal.

BEFORE YOU GO ON...

▶Do It! Merchandise Purchases Budget

Becker Company estimates that 2016 sales will be $15,000 in quarter 1, $20,000 in quarter 2, and $25,000 in quarter 3. Cost of goods sold is 80% of sales. Management desires to have ending finished goods inventory equal to 15% of the next quarter's expected cost of goods sold. Prepare a merchandise purchases budget by quarter for the first six months of 2016.

Action Plan

- Begin with budgeted cost of goods sold.
- Add desired ending merchandise inventory.
- Subtract beginning merchandise inventory.

Solution

	A	B	C	D
1	**BECKER COMPANY**			
2	Merchandise Purchases Budget			
3	For the Six Months Ending June 30, 2016			
4		Quarter		
5		1	2	Six Months
6	Budgeted cost of goods sold (sales 3 × 0.80)	$12,000	$16,000	
7	Add: Desired ending merchandise inventory			
8	(15% of next quarter's cost of goods sold)	2,400	3,000	
9	Total	14,400	19,000	
10	Less: Beginning merchandise inventory			
11	(15% this quarter's cost of goods sold)	1,800	2,400	
12	**Required merchandise purchases**	**$12,600**	**$16,600**	**$29,200**
13				

Related exercise material: **BE10-10, E10-32,** and **Do It! D10-15.**

the navigator

⊕ ALL ABOUT YOU   *Avoiding Personal Financial Disaster*

Preparing a personal budget is an important step to being able to live within your means and avoid financial disaster, but it's something many Canadians don't do. The real benefit of budgeting comes from comparing your actual results with your personal budget and then making the necessary adjustments before problems set in. In 2012, the average Canadian household's biggest expenditures were on shelter (accounting for 28% of spending), transportation (20%), and food (14%). How do these percentages compare with your spending as a university student? If you don't know, that's even more reason to prepare a personal budget.

What Do You Think?

Many worksheet templates to create personal budgets for postsecondary students treat student loans as an income source. Based on your knowledge of accounting, is this correct?

YES—Student loans provide a source of cash that can be used to pay costs.

NO—Student loans must eventually be repaid; therefore they are not income. As the name suggests, they are loans.

Sources: "Survey of Household Spending, 2012," Statistics Canada, *The Daily*, January 29, 2014; Industry Canada, Office of Consumer Affairs, "Your Budget," www.ic.gc.ca/eic/site/oca-bc.nsf/eng/ca02154.html; Chaya Cooperberg, "The Best of the Free Online Budgeting Tools," *The Globe and Mail*, May 31, 2010.

USING THE DECISION TOOLKIT

The University of Drummondville and its subunits must prepare budgets. One unique subunit of the University of Drummondville is Hilltop Ice Cream, a functioning producer of dairy products associated with the agricultural college (and famous, at least on campus, for its delicious ice cream).

(continued)

(continued)

Assume that Hilltop Ice Cream prepares monthly cash budgets. Relevant data from its assumed operating budgets for 2016 are as follows:

	January	February
Sales	$460,000	$412,000
Direct materials purchases	185,000	210,000
Direct labour	70,000	85,000
Manufacturing overhead	50,000	65,000
Selling and administrative expenses	85,000	95,000

Hilltop sells 50% of its ice cream in its shops on campus and the rest to local stores. Collections from local stores are expected to be 50% in the month of sale, and 50% in the month following sale. Hilltop pays 60% of direct materials purchases in cash in the month of purchase and pays the balance due in the month following the purchase. It pays all other items above in the month incurred. (Depreciation has been excluded from manufacturing overhead and selling and administrative expenses.)

Other data:

1. Sales: November 2015, $370,000; December 2015, $320,000
2. Purchases of direct materials: December 2015, $175,000
3. Other receipts: January—donation received, $2,000
   February—sale of used equipment, $4,000
4. Other disbursements: February—purchased equipment, $10,000
5. Repaid debt: January, $30,000

The company's cash balance on January 1, 2016, is expected to be $50,000. The company wants to keep a minimum cash balance of $45,000.

Instructions

(a) Prepare schedules for (1) the expected collections from customers and (2) the expected payments for direct materials purchases.

(b) Prepare a cash budget, with columns, for January and February.

Solution

(a)

1. Expected Collections from Customers

	January	February
December ($320,000)	$ 80,000	$ 0
January ($460,000)	345,000	115,000
February ($412,000)	0	309,000
Totals	$425,000	$424,000

2. Expected Payments for Direct Materials

	January	February
December ($175,000)	$ 70,000	$ 0
January ($185,000)	111,000	74,000
February ($210,000)	0	126,000
Totals	$181,000	$200,000

(b)

HILLTOP ICE CREAM Cash Budget Two Months Ending February 28, 2016		
	January	February
Beginning cash balance	$ 50,000	$ 61,000
Add: Receipts		
Collections from customers	425,000	424,000
Donations received	2,000	0
Sale of used equipment	0	4,000
Total receipts	427,000	428,000
Total available cash	477,000	489,000
Less: Disbursements		
Direct materials	181,000	200,000
Direct labour	70,000	85,000
Manufacturing overhead	50,000	65,000
Selling and administrative expenses	85,000	95,000
Purchase of equipment	0	10,000
Total disbursements	386,000	455,000
Excess (deficiency) of available cash over disbursements	91,000	34,000
Financing		
Borrowings	0	11,000
Repayments	30,000	0
Ending cash balance	$ 61,000	$ 45,000

Summary of Study Objectives

1. *State the essentials of effective budgeting and the components of the master budget.* The primary benefits of budgeting are that it (a) requires management to plan ahead, (b) provides definite objectives for evaluating performance, (c) creates an early warning system for potential problems, (d) facilitates coordination of activities, (e) results in greater management awareness, and (f) motivates personnel to meet planned objectives. The essentials of effective budgeting are (a) sound organizational structure, (b) research and analysis, and (c) acceptance by all levels of management.

    The master budget consists of the following budgets: (a) sales, (b) production, (c) direct materials, (d) direct labour, (e) manufacturing overhead, (f) selling and administrative expenses, (g) budgeted income statement, (h) capital expenditure budget, (i) cash budget, and (j) budgeted balance sheet.

2. *Prepare budgets for sales, production, and direct materials.* The sales budget is derived from sales forecasts. The production budget starts with budgeted sales units, adds desired ending finished goods inventory, and subtracts beginning finished goods inventory to arrive at the required number of production units. The direct materials budget starts with the direct materials units (such as kilograms) required for budgeted production, adds desired ending direct materials units, and subtracts beginning direct materials units to arrive at required direct materials units to be purchased. This amount is multiplied by the direct materials cost (such as cost per kilogram) to arrive at the total cost of direct materials purchases.

3. *Prepare budgets for direct labour, manufacturing overhead, and selling and administrative expenses, and a budgeted income statement.* The direct labour budget starts with the units to be produced as determined in the production budget. This amount is multiplied by the direct labour hours per unit and the direct labour cost per hour to arrive at the total direct labour cost. The manufacturing overhead budget lists all of the individual types of overhead costs, distinguishing between fixed and variable costs. The selling and administrative expenses budget lists all of the individual types of selling and administrative expense items, distinguishing between fixed and variable costs. The budgeted income statement is prepared from the various operating budgets. Cost of goods sold is determined by calculating the budgeted cost to produce one unit, then multiplying this amount by the number of units sold.

4. *Prepare the cash budget and the budgeted balance sheet.* The cash budget, which shows expected cash flows, contains three sections (cash receipts, cash disbursements, and financing) and the beginning and ending cash balances. The budgeted balance sheet, which is a projection of the company's financial position at the end of the budget period, lists assets and liabilities and shareholders' equity. It is developed from the budgeted balance sheet for the preceding year and the budgets for the current year.

5. *Explain the applicability of budgeting in non-manufacturing companies.* Merchandisers may use budgeting for development of a master budget. In service enterprises, budgeting is a critical factor in coordinating staff needs with anticipated services. In not-for-profit organizations, the starting point in budgeting is usually expenditures, not receipts.

DECISION TOOLKIT—A SUMMARY

Decision Checkpoints	Info Needed for Decision	Tools to Use for Decision	How to Evaluate Results
Has the company met its targets for sales, production expenses, selling and administrative expenses, and net income?	Sales forecasts; inventory levels; and projected materials, labour, overhead, and selling and administrative requirements	Master budget—a set of interrelated budgets including the sales, production, materials, labour, overhead, and selling and administrative budgets	The results are favourable if revenues exceed budgeted amounts, or if expenses are less than budgeted amounts.
Is the company going to need to borrow funds in the coming quarter?	Beginning cash balance, cash receipts, cash disbursements, and desired cash balance	Cash budget	The company will need to borrow money if the cash budget indicates that the available cash will be less than the cash disbursements for the quarter.

Glossary

Budget   A formal written statement, in financial terms, of management's plans for a specified future time period. (p. 402)

Budget committee   A group responsible for coordinating the preparation of the budget. (p. 403)

Budgetary slack   The amount by which a manager intentionally underestimates budgeted revenues or overestimates budgeted expenses in order to make it easier to achieve budgetary goals. (p. 404)

Budgeted balance sheet   A projection of the company's financial position at the end of the budget period. (p. 416)

Budgeted income statement   An estimate of the expected profitability of operations for the budget period. (p. 412)

Cash budget   A projection of expected cash flows. (p. 414)

Direct labour budget   A projection of the quantity and cost of direct labour to be incurred to meet production requirements. (p. 410)

Direct materials budget   An estimate of the quantity and cost of direct materials to be purchased. (p. 408)

Financial budgets   Individual budgets that indicate the cash resources that are needed for expected operations and planned capital expenditures. (p. 405)

Long-range planning   A formalized process of selecting strategies to achieve long-term goals and developing policies and plans to implement the strategies. (p. 405)

Manufacturing overhead budget   An estimate of expected manufacturing overhead costs for the budget period. (p. 411)

Master budget   A set of interrelated budgets that becomes a plan of action for a specific time period. (p. 405)

Merchandise purchases budget   The estimated cost of goods to be purchased by a merchandiser to meet expected sales. (p. 418)

Operating budgets   Individual budgets that result in a budgeted income statement. (p. 405)

Participative budgeting   A budgetary approach that starts with input from lower-level managers and works upward so that managers at all levels participate. (p. 403)

Production budget   A projection of the units that must be produced to meet expected sales. (p. 407)

Sales budget   An estimate of expected sales for the budget period. (p. 407)

Sales forecast   The projection of potential sales for the industry and the company's expected share of these sales. (p. 403)

Selling and administrative expenses budget   A projection of expected selling and administrative expenses for the budget period. (p. 411)

Comprehensive Do It!

Barrett Company has completed all operating budgets other than the income statement for 2016. Selected data from these budgets follow.

Sales: $300,000
Purchases of raw materials: $145,000
Ending inventory of raw materials: $15,000
Direct labour: $40,000
Manufacturing overhead: $73,000, including $3,000 of depreciation expense
Selling and administrative expenses: $36,000 including depreciation expense of $1,000
Interest expense: $1,000
Principal payment on note: $2,000
Dividends declared: $2,000
Income tax rate: 30%

Other information:

Assume that the number of units produced equals the number sold.
Year-end accounts receivable: 4% of 2016 sales.
Year-end accounts payable: 50% of ending inventory of raw materials.
Interest, direct labour, manufacturing overhead, and selling and administrative expenses other than depreciation are paid as incurred.
Dividends declared and income taxes for 2016 will not be paid until 2017.

BARRETT COMPANY		
Balance Sheet		
December 31, 2015		
Assets		
Current assets		
Cash		$20,000
Raw materials inventory		10,000
Total current assets		30,000
Property, plant, and equipment		
Equipment	$40,000	
Less: Accumulated depreciation	4,000	36,000
Total assets		$66,000
Liabilities and Shareholders' Equity		
Liabilities		
Accounts payable	$ 5,000	
Notes payable	22,000	
Total liabilities		$27,000
Shareholders' equity		
Common shares	25,000	
Retained earnings	14,000	
Total shareholders' equity		39,000
Total liabilities and shareholders' equity		$66,000

Instructions

(a) Calculate budgeted cost of goods sold.
(b) Prepare a budgeted multiple-step income statement for the year ending December 31, 2016.
(c) Prepare a budgeted classified balance sheet as at December 31, 2016.

Solution to Comprehensive Do It!

(a) Beginning raw materials + Purchases − Ending raw materials = Cost of direct materials used ($10,000 + $145,000 − $15,000 = $140,000)

Direct materials used + Direct labour + Manufacturing overhead = Cost of goods sold ($140,000 + $40,000 + $73,000 = $253,000)

(continued)

Action Plan

- Recall that beginning raw materials inventory plus purchases less ending raw materials inventory equals direct materials used.
- Prepare the budgeted income statement before the budgeted balance sheet.
- Use the standard form of a cash budget to determine cash on the budgeted balance sheet.
- Add budgeted depreciation expense to accumulated depreciation at the beginning of the year to determine accumulated depreciation on the budgeted balance sheet.
- Add budgeted net income to retained earnings from the beginning of the year and subtract dividends declared to determine retained earnings on the budgeted balance sheet.
- Verify that total assets equal total liabilities and shareholders' equity on the budgeted balance sheet.

(continued)

(b)

BARRETT COMPANY
Budgeted Income Statement
For the Year Ending December 31, 2016

Sales	$300,000
Cost of goods sold	253,000
Gross profit	47,000
Selling and administrative expenses	36,000
Income from operations	11,000
Interest expense	1,000
Income before income tax expense	10,000
Income tax expense (30%)	3,000
Net income	$ 7,000

(c)

BARRETT COMPANY
Budgeted Balance Sheet
December 31, 2016

Assets

Current Assets		
Cash[a]		$ 17,500
Accounts receivable (4% × $300,000)		12,000
Raw materials inventory		15,000
Total current assets		44,500
Property, plant, and equipment		
Equipment	$ 40,000	
Less: Accumulated depreciation	8,000	32,000
Total assets		$ 76,500

Liabilities and Shareholders' Equity

Liabilities		
Accounts payable (50% × $15,000)	$ 7,500	
Income taxes payable	3,000	
Dividends payable	2,000	
Note payable	20,000	
Total liabilities		$ 32,500
Shareholders' equity		
Common shares	25,000	
Retained earnings[b]	19,000	
Total shareholders' equity		44,000
Total liabilities and shareholders' equity		$ 76,500

[a]Beginning cash balance		$ 20,000
Add: Collections from customers (96% × $300,000 sales)		288,000
Total available cash		308,000
Less: Disbursements		
Direct materials ($5,000 + $145,000 − $7,500)	$ 142,500	
Direct labour	40,000	
Manufacturing overhead	70,000	
Selling and administrative expenses	35,000	
Total disbursements		287,500
Excess of available cash over cash disbursements		20,500
Financing		
Less: Repayment of principal and interest		3,000
Ending cash balance		$ 17,500

[b]Beginning retained earnings + Net income − Dividends declared = Ending retained earnings
($14,000 + $7,000 − $2,000 = $19,000)

the
navigator

WileyPLUS
Self-Test, Brief Exercises, Exercises, Problems—Set A, and many more components are available for practice in WileyPlus.

Self-Study Questions

Answers are at the end of the chapter.

(SO 1) 1. Which of the following is not a benefit of budgeting?
   (a) Management can plan ahead.
   (b) An early warning system is provided for potential problems.
   (c) It makes it possible to take disciplinary action at every level of responsibility.
   (d) The coordination of activities is made easier.

(SO 1) 2. The essentials of effective budgeting do not include
   (a) top-down budgeting.
   (b) management acceptance.
   (c) research and analysis.
   (d) sound organizational structure.

(SO 1) 3. Compared with budgeting, long-range planning generally has
   (a) the same amount of detail.
   (b) a longer time period.
   (c) the same emphasis.
   (d) the same time period.

(SO 2) 4. A sales budget is
   (a) derived from the production budget.
   (b) management's best estimate of sales revenue for the year.
   (c) not the starting point for the master budget.
   (d) prepared only for credit sales.

(SO 2) 5. The formula for the production budget is budgeted sales in units plus
   (a) desired ending merchandise inventory less beginning merchandise inventory.
   (b) beginning finished goods units less desired ending finished goods units.
   (c) desired ending direct materials units less beginning direct materials units.
   (d) desired ending finished goods units less beginning finished goods units.

(SO 2) 6. Direct materials inventories are accounted for in kilograms at Byrd Company, and the total kilograms of direct materials needed for production is 9,500. If the beginning inventory is 1,000 kg and the desired ending inventory is 2,200 kg, the total kilograms to be purchased are
   (a) 9,400.
   (b) 9,500.
   (c) 9,700.
   (d) 10,700.

(SO 3) 7. The formula for calculating the direct labour cost budget is to multiply the direct labour cost per hour by the
   (a) total required direct labour hours.
   (b) physical units to be produced.
   (c) equivalent units to be produced.
   (d) No correct answer is given.

(SO 3) 8. Which of the following budgets is not used in preparing the budgeted income statement?
   (a) Sales budget
   (b) Selling and administrative expenses budget
   (c) Capital expenditure budget
   (d) Direct labour budget

(SO 4) 9. Expected direct materials purchases in Read Company are $70,000 in the first quarter and $90,000 in the second quarter. The company pays 40% of the purchases in cash as incurred, and the rest is paid in the following quarter. The budgeted cash payments for purchases in the second quarter are
   (a) $96,000.
   (b) $90,000.
   (c) $78,000.
   (d) $72,000.

(SO 5) 10. The budget for a merchandiser differs from a budget for a manufacturer because
   (a) a merchandise purchases budget replaces the production budget.
   (b) the manufacturing budgets are not applicable.
   (c) None of the above.
   (d) Both (a) and (b) above.

Brief Exercises

BE10-1 Russo Manufacturing Company uses the following budgets: balance sheet, capital expenditures, cash, direct labour, direct materials, income statement, manufacturing overhead, production, sales, and selling and administrative expenses. Prepare a diagram that shows the relationships of the budgets in the master budget. Indicate whether each budget is an operating or a financial budget.   (SO 1) *Prepare diagram of a master budget.*

BE10-2 Maltz Company estimates that unit sales will be 10,000 in quarter 1; 12,000 in quarter 2; 14,000 in quarter 3; and 18,000 in quarter 4. Using a sales price of $80 per unit, prepare the sales budget by quarters for the year ending December 31, 2016.   (SO 2) *Prepare a sales budget.*

(SO 2)
Prepare a production
budget for two quarters.

BE10-3   Sales budget data for Maltz Company are given in BE10-2. Management wants to have an ending finished goods inventory equal to 20% of the next quarter's expected unit sales. Prepare a production budget by quarters for the first six months of 2016.

(SO 2)
Prepare a direct
materials budget for
one month.

BE10-4   Gomez Company has 2,000 kg of raw materials in its December 31, 2016, ending inventory. Required production for January and February is 5,000 and 6,000 units, respectively. Two kilograms of raw materials are needed for each unit, and the estimated cost per kilogram is $6. Management wants an ending inventory equal to 25% of next month's materials requirements. Prepare the direct materials budget for January.

(SO 3)
Prepare a direct labour
budget for two quarters.

BE10-5   For Tracey Company, units to be produced are 5,000 in quarter 1 and 6,000 in quarter 2. It takes 1.6 hours to make a finished unit, and the expected hourly wage rate is $15. Prepare a direct labour budget by quarters for the six months ending June 30, 2016.

(SO 3)
Prepare a manufactur-
ing overhead budget.

BE10-6   Savage Inc. expects variable manufacturing overhead costs to be $20,000 in the first quarter of 2016, with $4,000 increments in each of the remaining three quarters. It estimates fixed overhead costs to be $35,000 in each quarter. Prepare the manufacturing overhead budget by quarters for the year.

(SO 3)
Prepare a selling and
administrative expenses
budget.

BE10-7   Rado Company classifies its selling and administrative expenses budget into variable and fixed components. It expects variable expenses to be $25,000 in the first quarter, and expects $5,000 increments in the remaining quarters of 2016. It expects fixed expenses to be $40,000 in each quarter. Prepare the selling and administrative expenses budget by quarters for 2016.

(SO 3)
Prepare a budgeted
income statement for
year.

BE10-8   Rajiv Company has completed all of its operating budgets. The sales budget for the year shows 50,000 units and total sales of $2,250,000. The total cost of making one unit of sales is $25. It estimates selling and administrative expenses to be $300,000 and income taxes to be $210,000. Prepare a budgeted income statement for the year ending December 31, 2016.

(SO 4)
Prepare data for a cash
budget.

BE10-9   Bruno Industries expects credit sales for January, February, and March to be $200,000, $260,000, and $300,000, respectively. It is expected that 75% of the sales will be collected in the month of sale, and 25% will be collected in the following month. Calculate cash collections from customers for each month.

(SO 5)
Determine required
merchandise purchases
for one month.

BE10-10   Moore Wholesalers is preparing its merchandise purchases budget. Budgeted sales are $400,000 for April and $480,000 for May. Cost of goods sold is expected to be 65% of sales. The company's desired ending inventory is 20% of the following month's cost of goods sold. Calculate the required purchases for April.

Do It! Review

(SO 1)
Identify budget
terminology.

D10-11

Instructions
Use this list of terms to complete the sentences that follow.

| Long-range plans | Master budget | Operating budgets |
| Sales forecast | Participative budgeting | Financial budgets |

(a) _____ establish goals for the company's sales and production personnel.
(b) The _____ is a set of interrelated budgets that constitutes a plan of action for a specified time period.
(c) _____ reduces the risk of having unrealistic budgets.
(d) _____ include the cash budget and the budgeted balance sheet.
(e) The budget is formed within the framework of a _____.
(f) _____ contain considerably less detail than budgets.

(SO 2)
Prepare sales,
production, and direct
materials budgets.

D10-12   Oak Creek Company is preparing its master budget for 2016. Relevant data pertaining to its sales, production, and direct materials budgets are as follows.

Sales: Sales for the year are expected to total 1 million units. Quarterly sales are 20%, 25%, 25%, and 30%, respectively. The sales price is expected to be $40 per unit for the first three quarters and $45 per unit beginning in the fourth quarter. Sales in the first quarter of 2017 are expected to be 10% higher than the budgeted sales for the first quarter of 2016.

Production: Management desires to maintain the ending finished goods inventories at 20% of the next quarter's budgeted sales volume.

Direct materials: Each unit requires 2 kg of raw materials at a cost of $10 per kilogram. Management desires to maintain raw materials inventories at 10% of the next quarter's production requirements. Assume the production requirements for the first quarter of 2017 are 500,000 kg.

Instructions
Prepare the sales, production, and direct materials budgets by quarters for 2016.

D10-13 Oak Creek Company is preparing its budgeted income statement for 2016. Relevant data pertaining to its sales, production, and direct materials budgets are found in D10-12.

In addition, Oak Creek budgets 0.3 hours of direct labour per unit, labour costs at $14 per hour, and manufacturing overhead at $20 per direct labour hour. Its budgeted selling and administrative expenses for 2016 are $7 million.

Instructions
(a) Calculate the budgeted total unit cost.
(b) Prepare the budgeted income statement for 2016.

(SO 3)
Calculate budgeted total unit cost and prepare budgeted income statement.

D10-14 Venetian Company management wants to maintain a minimum monthly cash balance of $20,000. At the beginning of April, the cash balance is $22,000, expected cash receipts for March are $245,000, and cash disbursements are expected to be $256,000.

Instructions
Determine how much cash, if any, must be borrowed to maintain the desired minimum monthly balance.

(SO 4)
Determine amount of financing needed.

D10-15 Zeller Company estimates that 2016 sales will be $40,000 in quarter 1, $48,000 in quarter 2, and $58,000 in quarter 3. Cost of goods sold is 50% of sales. Management desires to have ending finished goods inventory equal to 10% of the next quarter's expected cost of goods sold.

Instructions
Prepare a merchandise purchases budget by quarter for the first six months of 2016.

(SO 5)
Prepare merchandise purchases budget.

Exercises

E10-16 Black Rose Company has always done some planning for the future, but the company has never prepared a formal budget. Now that the company is growing larger, it is considering preparing a budget.

Instructions
✏️ Write a memo to Jack Masad, the president of Black Rose Company, in which you define budgeting, identify the budgets that compose the master budget, identify the benefits of budgeting, and discuss the essentials of effective budgeting.

(SO 1)
Explain the concept of budgeting.

E10-17 Good-Buy Electronics Inc. produces and sells two models of pocket calculators, Deluxe and Standard. The calculators sell for $8 and $5, respectively. Because of the intense competition Good-Buy faces, management budgets sales annually. Its projections for the four quarters of 2016 are as follows:

(SO 2)
Prepare a sales budget for four quarters.

	Unit Sales			
Product	Quarter 1	Quarter 2	Quarter 3	Quarter 4
Deluxe	10,000	15,000	30,000	25,000
Standard	15,000	20,000	25,000	30,000

Instructions
Prepare a sales budget for the four quarters ending December 31, 2016. For each quarter and for the 12 months, indicate the number of units, selling price, and total sales for each product and in total.

E10-18 Roche and Young, CAs, are preparing their service revenue (sales) budget for 2016. Their practice is divided into three departments: auditing, tax, and consulting. Billable hours for each department, by quarter, are as follows:

(SO 2)
Prepare a sales budget for four quarters.

Department	Quarter 1	Quarter 2	Quarter 3	Quarter 4
Auditing	2,200	1,600	2,000	2,400
Tax	3,000	2,400	2,000	2,500
Consulting	1,500	1,500	1,500	1,500

Average hourly billing rates are $60 for auditing, $70 for tax, and $80 for consulting services.

Instructions

Prepare the service revenue (sales) budget for 2016 by listing the departments and showing the billable hours, billable rate, and total revenue for each quarter and the year in total.

(SO 2)
Prepare quarterly
production budgets.

E10-19 Wayans Company produces and sells automobile batteries, including the heavy-duty HD-240. The 2016 sales budget is as follows:

Quarter	Units of HD-240	Quarter	Units of HD-240
1	6,000	3	9,000
2	7,000	4	10,000

The January 1, 2016, inventory of HD-240 is 1,500 units. Management wants an ending inventory each quarter that is equal to 30% of the next quarter's sales. It expects sales in the first quarter of 2017 to be 20% higher than sales in the same quarter in 2016.

Instructions

Prepare quarterly production budgets for each quarter for 2016.

(SO 2)
Prepare a direct
materials purchases
budget.

E10-20 Samano Industries has adopted the following production budget for the four quarters of 2016:

	Quarter 1	Quarter 2	Quarter 3	Quarter 4
Units	6,000	8,000	9,000	10,000

Each unit requires 4 kg of raw materials costing $6 per kilogram. On December 31, 2015, the ending raw materials inventory was 1,800 kg. Management wants to have a raw materials inventory at the beginning of each quarter equal to 30% of the current quarter's production requirements. The production budget for the first quarter of 2017 will be 12,000 units

Instructions

Prepare a direct materials purchases budget by quarters for 2016.

(SO 2)
Prepare production
and direct materials
budgets by quarters for
six months.

E10-21 On January 1, 2017, the Chinlee Company budget committee reached agreement on the following data for the six months ending June 30, 2017:

1. Sales units: First quarter 5,000; second quarter 6,000; third quarter 7,000
2. Ending raw materials inventory: 40% of the next quarter's production requirements
3. Ending finished goods inventory: 25% of the next quarter's expected sales units
4. Third-quarter production: 7,200 units

The ending raw materials and finished goods inventories at December 31, 2016, had the same percentages for production and sales that are budgeted for 2016. Three kilograms of raw materials are needed to make each unit of finished goods. Raw materials purchased are expected to cost $4 per kilogram.

Instructions

(a) Prepare a production budget by quarters for the six-month period ended June 30, 2017.
(b) Prepare a direct materials budget by quarters for the six-month period ended June 30, 2017.

(SO 3)
Prepare a direct labour
budget.

E10-22 Pacer, Inc. is preparing its direct labour budget for 2016 from the following production budget for a full calendar year:

Quarter	Units	Quarter	Units
1	20,000	3	35,000
2	25,000	4	30,000

Each unit requires 1.5 hours of direct labour.

Instructions

Prepare a direct labour budget for 2016. Wage rates are expected to be $16 for the first two quarters and $18 for the remaining two quarters.

(SO 3)
Prepare a manufactur-
ing overhead budget
for the year.

E10-23 Keyser Company is preparing its manufacturing overhead budget for 2016. Relevant data are as follows:

1. Units to be produced (by quarters): 10,000, 12,000, 15,000, 18,000
2. Direct labour: 1.5 hours per unit

3. Variable overhead costs per direct labour hour: indirect materials $0.70; indirect labour $1.20; and maintenance $0.50
4. Fixed overhead costs per quarter: supervisory salaries $35,000; depreciation $16,000; and maintenance $15,000

Instructions
Prepare the manufacturing overhead budget for the year, showing quarterly data.

E10-24 Lockwood Company combines its operating expenses for budget purposes in a selling and administrative expenses budget. For the first six months of 2016, the following data are available:

1. Sales: 20,000 units in quarter 1; 22,000 units in quarter 2
2. Variable costs per dollar of sales: sales commissions 5%; delivery expense 2%; and advertising 4%
3. Fixed costs per quarter: sales salaries $10,000; office salaries $8,000; depreciation $4,200; insurance $1,500; utilities $800; and repairs expense $500
4. Unit selling price: $20

(SO 3)
Prepare a selling and administrative expenses budget for two quarters.

Instructions
Prepare a selling and administrative expenses budget by quarters for the first six months of 2016.

E10-25 Tyson Chandler Company's sales budget projects unit sales of part 198Z of 10,000 units in January, 12,000 units in February, and 13,000 units in March. Each unit of part 198Z requires 2 kg of materials, which cost $3 per kilogram. Tyson Chandler Company wants its ending raw materials inventory to equal 40% of the next month's production requirements, and its ending finished goods inventory to equal 25% of the next month's expected unit sales. These goals were met at December 31, 2015.

(SO 2)
Prepare a production and a direct materials budget.

Instructions
(a) Prepare a production budget for January and February 2016.
(b) Prepare a direct materials budget for January 2016.

E10-26 Haven Company has accumulated the following budget data for the year 2016:

1. Sales: 30,000 units; unit selling price $80
2. Cost of one unit of finished goods: direct materials, 2 kg at $5 per kilogram; direct labour, three hours at $12 per hour; and manufacturing overhead, $6 per direct labour hour
3. Inventories (raw materials only): beginning, 10,000 kg; ending, 15,000 kg
4. Raw materials cost: $5 per kilogram
5. Selling and administrative expenses: $200,000
6. Income taxes: 30% of income before income taxes

(SO 3)
Prepare a budgeted income statement for the year.

Instructions
(a) Prepare a schedule showing the calculation of the cost of goods sold for 2016.
(b) Prepare a budgeted income statement for 2016.

E10-27 Nunez Company expects to have a cash balance of $45,000 on January 1, 2016. Relevant monthly budget data for the first two months of 2016 are as follows:

(SO 4)
Prepare a cash budget for two months.

1. Collections from customers: January $100,000; February $160,000
2. Payments to suppliers: January $60,000; February $80,000
3. Direct labour: January $30,000; February $45,000. Wages are paid in the month they are incurred.
4. Manufacturing overhead: January $26,000; February $31,000. These costs include depreciation of $1,000 per month. All other overhead costs are paid as incurred.
5. Selling and administrative expenses: January $15,000; February $20,000. These costs are exclusive of depreciation. They are paid as incurred.
6. Sales of marketable securities in January are expected to realize $10,000 in cash.

Nunez Company has a line of credit at a local bank. It can borrow up to $25,000. The company wants to keep a minimum monthly cash balance of $25,000.

Instructions
Prepare a cash budget for January and February.

E10-28 Pink Martini Corporation is projecting a cash balance of $30,000 in its December 31, 2016, balance sheet. Pink Martini's schedule of expected collections from customers for the first quarter of 2016 shows total collections of $180,000. The schedule of expected payments for direct materials for the first quarter of 2016 shows total payments of $41,000. Other information gathered for the first quarter of 2016 is as follows: sale of equipment $3,000; direct labour $70,000,

(SO 4)
Prepare a cash budget.

manufacturing overhead $35,000; selling and administrative expenses $45,000; and purchase of securities $14,000. Pink Martini wants to maintain a balance of at least $25,000 cash at the end of each quarter.

Instructions
Prepare a cash budget for the first quarter.

(SO 4)
Prepare schedules of
expected collections
and payments.

E10-29   NIU Company's budgeted sales and direct materials purchases are as follows:

	Budgeted Sales	Budgeted Direct Materials Purchases
January	$190,000	$30,000
February	210,000	35,000
March	300,000	45,000

NIU's sales are 40% cash and 60% credit. It collects credit sales 10% in the month of sale, 50% in the month following sale, and 36% in the second month following sale; 4% are uncollectible. NIU's purchases are 50% cash and 50% on account. It pays purchases on account 60% in the month of purchase, and 40% in the month following purchase.

Instructions
(a) Prepare a schedule of expected collections from customers for March.
(b) Prepare a schedule of expected payments for direct materials for March.

(SO 4, 5)
Prepare schedules
for cash receipts and
cash payments, and
determine the ending
balances for each
balance sheet account.

E10-30   Environmental Landscaping Inc. is preparing its budget for the first quarter of 2016. The next step is to prepare a cash receipts schedule and a cash payments schedule. The following information has been collected:

1. Clients usually pay 50% of their fee in the month when the service is provided, 40% the next month, and 10% in the second month after receiving the service.
2. Actual service revenues for 2015 and expected service revenues for 2016 are as follows: November 2015, $90,000; December 2015, $70,000; January 2016, $110,000; February 2016, $120,000; and March 2016, $130,000.
3. The company pays for purchases of landscaping supplies (direct materials) 60% in the month of purchase and 40% the following month. Actual purchases for 2015 and expected purchases for 2016 are: December 2015, $14,000; January 2016, $13,000; February 2016, $15,000; and March 2016, $20,000.

Instructions
(a) Prepare the following schedules for each month in the first quarter of 2016 and for the quarter in total: (1) expected collections from clients, and (2) expected payments for landscaping supplies.
(b) Determine the following balances at March 31, 2016: (1) accounts receivable, and (2) accounts payable.

(SO 4, 5)
Prepare a cash budget
for two quarters.

E10-31   Pisani Dental Clinic is a medium-sized dental service specializing in family dental care. The clinic is currently preparing the budget for the first two quarters of 2016. It still needs to do only the cash budget. It has collected the following information from parts of the master budget and elsewhere:

Beginning cash balance	$ 30,000
Required minimum cash balance	20,000
Payment of income taxes (2nd quarter)	4,000
Professional salaries:	
1st quarter	140,000
2nd quarter	140,000
Interest from investments (2nd quarter)	7,000
Overhead costs:	
1st quarter	95,000
2nd quarter	120,000
Selling and administrative expenses, including $3,000 of depreciation:	
1st quarter	50,000
2nd quarter	70,000
Purchase of equipment (2nd quarter)	50,000
Sale of equipment (1st quarter)	12,000
Collections from clients:	
1st quarter	245,000
2nd quarter	390,000
Interest on repayments (2nd quarter)	300

Instructions
Prepare a cash budget for each of the first two quarters of 2016.

E10-32 In May 2016, the budget committee of Big Jim Stores assembles the following data for preparing the merchandise purchases budget for the month of June:

1. Expected sales: June $500,000; July $600,000.
2. Cost of goods sold is expected to be 75% of sales.
3. Desired ending merchandise inventory is 30% of the following month's cost of goods sold.
4. The beginning inventory at June 1 will be the desired amount.

Instructions
(a) Calculate the budgeted merchandise purchases for June.
(b) Prepare the budgeted income statement for June through gross profit on sales.

(SO 5)
Prepare a purchases budget and budgeted income statement for a merchandiser.

Problems: Set A

P10-33A Tilger Farm Supply Company manufactures and sells a fertilizer called Snare. The following data are available for preparing budgets for Snare for the first two quarters of 2016.

(SO 2, 3)
Prepare a budgeted income statement and supporting budgets.

1. Sales: Quarter 1, 28,000 bags; quarter 2, 42,000 bags. Selling price is $60 per bag.
2. Direct materials: Each bag of Snare requires 4 kg of Gumm at $4 per kilogram and 6 kg of Tarr at $1.50 per kilogram.
3. Desired inventory levels:

Type of Inventory	January 1	April 1	July 1
Snare (bags)	8,000	12,000	18,000
Gumm (kg)	9,000	10,000	13,000
Tarr (kg)	14,000	20,000	25,000

4. Direct labour: Direct labour time is 15 minutes per bag at an hourly rate of $14 per hour.
5. The company expects selling and administrative expenses to be 15% of sales plus $175,000 per quarter.
6. It expects income taxes to be 30% of income from operations.

Your assistant has prepared two budgets: (1) The manufacturing overhead budget shows expected costs to be 150% of direct labour cost. (2) The direct materials budget for Tarr shows the cost of Tarr purchases to be $297,000 in quarter 1 and $439,500 in quarter 2.

Instructions
Prepare the budgeted income statement for the first six months and all required operating budgets by quarters. (*Note:* Classify items as variable and fixed in the selling and administrative expenses budget). Do not prepare the manufacturing overhead budget or the direct materials budget for Tarr.

Net income $600,250
Cost per bag $33.75

P10-34A Greish Inc. is preparing its annual budgets for the year ending December 31, 2016. Accounting assistants have provided the following data:

(SO 2, 3)
Prepare sales, production, direct materials, direct labour, and income statement budgets.

	Product LN 35	Product LN 40
Sales budget		
Expected volume in units	400,000	240,000
Unit selling price	$30	$35
Production budget		
Desired ending finished good units	30,000	20,000
Beginning finished goods units	20,000	15,000
Direct materials budget:		
Direct materials per unit (kilograms)	2	3
Desired kilograms of ending direct materials	50,000	15,000
Beginning kilograms of direct materials	40,000	10,000
Cost per kilogram	$2	$3
Direct labour budget:		
Direct labour time per unit (hours)	0.5	0.70
Direct labour rate per hour	$12	$12
Budgeted income statement:		
Total unit cost	$11	$20

An accounting assistant has prepared the detailed manufacturing overhead budget and the selling and administrative expenses budget. The latter shows selling expenses of $850,000 for product LN 35 and $390,000 for product LN 40,

(a) Total sales $20,400,000
(b) Required production units: LN 35, 410,000
(c) Total cost of direct materials purchases $3,880,000
(d) Total direct labour cost $4,518,000
(e) Net income $6,482,000

and administrative expenses of $520,000 for product LN 35 and $180,000 for product LN 40. Income taxes are expected to be 30%.

Instructions

Prepare the following budgets for the year. Show data for each product. Quarterly budgets should not be prepared.

(a) Sales
(b) Production
(c) Direct materials

(d) Direct labour
(e) Income statement
(*Note:* Income taxes are not allocated to the products.)

(SO 2, 3)
Prepare production and direct labour budgets.

P10-35A Choo-Foo Company makes and sells artistic frames for pictures. The controller is responsible for preparing the master budget and has accumulated the following information for 2016:

	January	February	March	April	May
Estimated unit sales	10,000	12,000	8,000	9,000	9,000
Sales price per unit	$50.00	$47.50	$47.50	$47.50	$47.50
Direct labour hours per unit	2.0	2.0	1.5	1.5	1.5
Wage per direct labour hour	$ 8.00	$ 8.00	$ 8.00	$ 9.00	$ 9.00

Choo-Foo has a labour contract that calls for a wage increase to $9.00 per hour on April 1. It has installed new labour-saving machinery, which will be fully operational by March 1.

Choo-Foo expects to begin the year with 16,000 frames on hand and has a policy of carrying an end-of-month inventory of 100% of the following month's sales, plus 50% of the next month's sales.

Instructions

(a) Total production = 27,500

(a) Prepare a production budget and a direct labour budget for Choo-Foo by month and for the first quarter of the year. The direct labour budget should include direct labour hours and show the detail for each direct labour cost category.
(b) For each item used in Choo-Foo's production budget and its direct labour budget, identify the other component(s) of the master budget (budget package) that would also use these data.

(adapted from CMA Canada, now CPA Canada)

(SO 2)
Prepare sales and production budgets and calculate the cost per unit under two plans.

P10-36A Colt Industries had sales in 2015 of $5.6 million and gross profit of $1.1 million. Management is considering two alternative budget plans to increase its gross profit in 2016.

Plan A would increase the selling price per unit from $8.00 to $8.40. Sales volume would decrease by 10% from its 2015 level. Plan B would decrease the selling price per unit by $0.50. The marketing department expects that the sales volume would increase by 100,000 units.

At the end of 2015, Colt has 38,000 units of inventory on hand. If Plan A is accepted, the 2016 ending inventory should be equal to 5% of the 2016 sales. If Plan B is accepted, the ending inventory should be equal to 60,000 units. Each unit produced will cost $1.80 in direct labour, $1.30 in direct materials, and $1.20 in variable overhead. The fixed overhead for 2016 should be $1,895,000.

Instructions

(c) Unit cost: Plan A $7.34; Plan B $6.60
(d) Gross profit: Plan A $667,800; Plan B $720,000

(a) Prepare a sales budget for 2016 under each plan.
(b) Prepare a production budget for 2016 under each plan.
(c) Calculate the production cost per unit under each plan. Why is the cost per unit different for each of the two plans? (Round to two decimals.)
(d) Which plan should be accepted? (*Hint:* Calculate the gross profit under each plan.)

(SO 4)
Calculate cash disbursements for one month.

P10-37A Lyon Factory Ltd. manufactures two products: chairs and stools. Each chair requires 3 m of upholstery and 4 kg of steel. Each stool requires 2 m of upholstery and 5 kg of steel. Upholstery costs $2 per metre and steel costs $5 per kilogram.

Lyon Factory expects inventories at January 1, 2016, to be as follows:

Chairs	Stools	Upholstery	Steel
25 units	15 units	75 m	150 kg

Inventories of raw materials should not be allowed to fall below the amounts given as at January 1, 2016. Inventories of finished furniture at the beginning of each month should be enough to cover 25% of the anticipated sales for that month. Upholstery is ordered in units of 100 m and steel in units of 50 kg.

Half of the materials purchased are paid for in the month of purchase and the other half in the following month. The sales budget for the first three months of the year 2016 is as follows:

	January	February	March
Chairs	100 units	120 units	80 units
Stools	60 units	80 units	60 units

Instructions

Calculate the cash disbursements in February for purchases of steel. Show all your supporting calculations.

(adapted from CGA-Canada, now CPA Canada)

Cost for steel in February: $4,250

P10-38A Lorch Company prepares monthly cash budgets. Relevant data from operating budgets for 2017 are as follows:

(SO 4)
Prepare a cash budget for two months.

	January	February
Sales	$350,000	$400,000
Direct materials purchases	120,000	110,000
Direct labour	85,000	112,000
Manufacturing overhead	60,000	75,000
Selling and administrative expenses	75,000	80,000

All sales are on account. Lorch expects collections to be 50% in the month of sale, 40% in the first month following the sale, and 10% in the second month following the sale. It pays 30% of direct materials purchases in cash in the month of purchase and the balance due in the month following the purchase.

Other data are as follows:

1. Credit sales: November 2016, $200,000; December 2016, $280,000
2. Purchases of direct materials: December 2016, $90,000
3. Other receipts: January—collection of December 31, 2016, notes receivable $5,000; February—proceeds from sale of securities $6,000
4. Other disbursements: February—payment of $20,000 for land.

The company expects its cash balance on January 1, 2017, to be $50,000. It wants to maintain a minimum cash balance of $40,000.

Instructions

(a) Prepare schedules for (1) the expected collections from customers and (2) the expected payments for direct materials purchases.

(b) Prepare a cash budget for January and February using columns for each month.

(adapted from CGA-Canada, now CPA Canada)

(a) January: (1) collections $307,000, (2) payments $99,000
(b) Ending cash balance: January $43,000, February $40,000

P10-39A The controller of Harrington Company estimates sales and production for the first four months of 2016 as follows:

(SO 4)
Prepare a cash budget for a quarter.

	January	February	March	April
Sales	$30,000	$40,000	$50,000	$25,000
Production in units	1,000	1,500	2,000	2,500

Sales are 40% cash and 60% on account, and 60% of credit sales are collected in the month of the sale. In the month after the sale, 40% of credit sales are collected. It takes 4 kg of direct material to produce a finished unit, and direct materials cost $5 per kg. All direct materials purchases are on account, and are paid as follows: 40% in the month of the purchase, 60% the following month. Ending direct materials inventory for each month is 40% of the next month's production needs. January's beginning materials inventory is 1,080 kg. Suppose that both accounts receivable and accounts payable are zero at the beginning of January.

Instructions

Answer the following questions:

(a) What are the total cash sales for the January–March quarter?
(b) What is the accounts receivable balance at the end of March?
(c) What is the direct materials inventory balance at the end of March?
(d) What are material purchases costs for February?
(e) What are cash payments on account for February?
(f) What is the ending balance in accounts payable for March?
(g) What is the cash balance for the period January–March?

(adapted from CGA-Canada, now CPA Canada)

(a) $48,000

(d) $34,000

(g) $29,800

(SO 5)
Prepare purchases
and income statement
budgets for a
merchandiser.

P10-40A   The budget committee of Ridder Company collects the following data for its Westwood Store in preparing budgeted income statements for July and August 2016:

1. The store expects sales for July to be $450,000, for August, $500,000, and for September, $550,000.
2. It expects the cost of goods sold to be 60% of sales.
3. Company policy is to maintain ending merchandise inventory at 20% of the following month's cost of goods sold.
4. Operating expenses are estimated as follows:

Sales salaries	$50,000 per month	Rent expense	$3,000 per month
Advertising	4% of monthly sales	Depreciation	$700 per month
Delivery expense	2% of monthly sales	Utilities	$500 per month
Sales commissions	3% of monthly sales	Insurance	$300 per month

(a) Purchases
July: $276,000,
August: $306,000
(b) Net income
July: $59,500,
August: $70,350

5. Income taxes are estimated to be 30% of the income from operations.

Instructions

(a) Prepare the merchandise purchases budget, using columns for each month.
(b) Prepare budgeted income statements, using columns for each month. Show details for the cost of goods sold in the statements.

(SO 2, 4)
Prepare a raw materials
purchase budget in
dollars.

P10-41A   Kirkland Ltd. estimates sales for the second quarter of 2016 will be as follows:

April	2,550 units
May	2,475 units
June	2,390 units

The target ending inventory of finished products is as follows:

March 31	2,000
April 30	2,230
May 31	2,190
June 30	2,310

Two units of material are required for each unit of finished product. Production for July is estimated at 2,700 units to start building inventory for the fall sales period. Kirkland's policy is to have an inventory of raw materials at the end of each month equal to 60% of the following month's production requirements.

Raw materials are expected to cost $4 per unit throughout the period.

Instructions

$19,840

Calculate the May raw materials purchases in dollars.

(adapted from CGA-Canada, now CPA Canada)

(SO 3, 4)
Prepare a budgeted
income statement and
balance sheet.

P10-42A   Kurian Industries' balance sheet at December 31, 2015, follows.

KURIAN INDUSTRIES
Balance Sheet
December 31, 2015
Assets

Current assets		
Cash		$ 7,500
Accounts receivable		82,500
Finished goods inventory (2,000 units)		30,000
Total current assets		120,000
Equipment	$40,000	
Less: Accumulated depreciation	10,000	30,000
Total assets		$150,000

Liabilities and Shareholders' Equity

Liabilities		
Notes payable		$ 25,000
Accounts payable		45,000
Total liabilities		70,000
Shareholders' equity		
Common shares	$50,000	
Retained earnings	30,000	
Total shareholders' equity		80,000
Total liabilities and shareholders' equity		$150,000

Budgeted data for the year 2016 include the following:

	Q4 of 2016	Year 2016 Total
Sales budget (8,000 units at $35)	$84,000	$280,000
Direct materials used	17,000	69,400
Direct labour	12,500	56,600
Manufacturing overhead applied	10,000	54,000
Selling and administrative expenses	18,000	76,000

To meet sales requirements and to have 3,000 units of finished goods on hand at December 31, 2016, the production budget shows 9,000 required units of output. The total unit cost of production is expected to be $18. Kurian Industries uses the first-in, first-out (FIFO) inventory costing method. Selling and administrative expenses include $4,000 for depreciation on equipment. The company expects interest expense to be $3,500 for the year and income taxes to be 30% of the income before income taxes.

All sales and purchases are on account. The company expects to collect 60% of the quarterly sales in cash within the quarter and the remainder in the following quarter. It pays direct materials purchased from suppliers 50% in the quarter incurred and the remainder in the following quarter. Purchases in the fourth quarter were the same as the materials used. In 2016, the company expects to purchase additional equipment costing $19,000. It expects to pay $8,000 on notes payable plus all interest due and payable to December 31 (included in the interest expense of $3,500, above). Accounts payable at December 31, 2016, include amounts due to suppliers (see above) plus other accounts payable of $5,700. In 2016, the company expects to declare and pay a $5,000 cash dividend. Unpaid income taxes at December 31 will be $5,000. The company's cash budget shows an expected cash balance of $9,750 at December 31, 2016.

Instructions

Prepare a budgeted income statement for 2016 and a budgeted balance sheet at December 31, 2016. In preparing the income statement, you will need to calculate the cost of goods manufactured (materials + labour + overhead) and finished goods inventory (December 31, 2016).

Net income: $31,150
Total assets: $142,350

P10-43A The Big Sister Company is in a seasonal business and prepares quarterly budgets. Its fiscal year runs from January 1 through December 31. Production occurs only in the first quarter (January to March), but sales take place throughout the year. The sales forecast for the coming year shows the following:

(SO 4)
Prepare a cash budget for a year.

First quarter	$480,000	Third quarter	$480,000
Second quarter	300,000	Fourth quarter	480,000

There are no cash sales, and the beginning balance of receivables is expected to be collected in the first quarter. Subsequent collections are two thirds in the quarter when sales take place and one third in the following quarter.

The company makes material purchases valued at $400,000 in the first quarter, but makes no purchases in the last three quarters. It makes payment when it purchases the materials.

Direct labour of $350,000 is incurred and paid only in the first quarter. Factory overhead of $340,000 is also incurred and paid in the first quarter, and is at a standby level of $100,000 during the other three quarters. Selling and administrative expenses of $35,000 are paid each quarter throughout the year. Big Sister has an operating line of credit with its bank at an interest rate of 5% per annum. The company plans to keep a cash balance of at least $10,000 at all times, and it will borrow and repay in multiples of $5,000. It makes all borrowings at the beginning of a quarter, and makes all payments at the end of a quarter. It pays interest only on the portion of the loan that it repays in a quarter.

The company plans to purchase equipment in the second and fourth quarters for $70,000 and $150,000, respectively. The cash balance on January 1 is $25,000 and accounts receivable total $150,000.

Instructions

Prepare a cash budget for the year. Show receipts, disbursements, the ending cash balance before borrowing, the amounts borrowed and repaid, interest payments, and the ending cash balance.

Ending cash balance: $11,688

(adapted from CMA Canada, now CPA Canada)

P10-44A Rotech Co. began operations in January 2015. The information below is for Rotech Co.'s operations for the three months from January to March (the first quarter) of 2016:

(SO 4)
Prepare a cash budget.

Expenses for Quarter 1	
Depreciation	$35,000
Factory overhead	15,000
Income taxes	25,000
Payroll	29,000
Selling costs (2% commission on sales)	12,000
Administrative costs	15,000

Costs are assumed to be incurred evenly throughout the year, with the exception of depreciation and income taxes. Depreciation on new assets is first taken in the quarter after the quarter in which they are purchased. Income taxes are payable in semi-annual instalments on the first day of each six-month period, based on last year's actual taxes of $30,000. Other information:

1. Sales (made evenly throughout the quarter)

Quarter 1	(actual)	$600,000
Quarter 2	(forecast)	400,000
Quarter 3	(forecast)	800,000

Collections from sales are as follows: 50% in the quarter of sale; 45% in the following quarter; 5% uncollectible.

2. Purchases (made evenly throughout the quarter)

Quarter 1	(actual)	$300,000

The gross margin ratio is constant at 40%.

Cash payments for purchases are as follows: 50% in the quarter of purchase; 50% in the following quarter. Merchandise purchased during a quarter would include 25% of the next quarter's forecasted sales.

3. The company purchased capital equipment for $150,000 in February 2015. The estimated useful life of this equipment is 10 years; it has no estimated scrap value.
4. Dividends of $20,000 are declared on the last day of each quarter and are paid at the end of the next month.
5. The cash balance in the bank at the end of the first quarter is $45,000.

Instructions

Ending cash balance: $128,000

(a) Prepare a cash budget for Rotech Co. for the second quarter of 2016. Show all your supporting calculations.
(b) List three advantages of budgeting.

(adapted from CGA-Canada, now CPA Canada)

Problems: Set B

(SO 2, 3)
Prepare a budgeted income statement and supporting budgets.

P10-45B Wahlen Farm Supply Company manufactures and sells a pesticide called Basic II. The following data are available for preparing budgets for Basic II for the first two quarters of 2016.

1. Sales: Quarter 1, 40,000 bags; quarter 2, 60,000 bags. Selling price is $60 per bag.
2. Direct materials: Each bag of Basic II requires 6 kg of Crup at $4 per kilogram and 10 kg of Dert at $1.50 per kilogram.
3. Desired inventory levels:

Type of Inventory	January 1	April 1	July 1
Basic II (bags)	10,000	15,000	20,000
Crup (kilograms)	9,000	12,000	15,000
Dert (kilograms)	15,000	20,000	25,000

4. Direct labour: Direct labour time is 15 minutes per bag at an hourly rate of $12 per hour.
5. Selling and administrative expenses are expected to be 10% of sales plus $150,000 per quarter.
6. Income taxes are expected to be 30% of income from operations.

Your assistant has prepared two budgets: (1) The manufacturing overhead budget, which shows expected costs to be 100% of direct labour costs. (2) The direct materials budget for Dert, which shows the cost of Dert purchases to be $682,500 in quarter 1 and $982,500 in quarter 2.

Instructions

Cost per bag: $45

Prepare the budgeted income statement for the first six months of 2016 and all required operating budgets by quarters. (*Note:* Categorize variable and fixed items in the selling and administrative expenses budget.) Do not prepare the manufacturing overhead budget or the direct materials budget for Dert.

P10-46B Quinn Inc. is preparing its annual budgets for the year ending December 31, 2016. Accounting assistants provide the following data:

(SO 2, 3)
Prepare sales, production, direct materials, direct labour, and income statement budgets.

	Product JB 50	Product JB 60
Sales budget		
Anticipated volume in units	300,000	180,000
Unit selling price	$20	$30
Production budget		
Desired ending finished goods units	30,000	25,000
Beginning finished goods units	20,000	15,000
Direct materials budget:		
Direct materials per unit (kilograms)	2	3
Desired kilograms of ending direct materials	50,000	20,000
Beginning kilograms of direct materials	40,000	10,000
Cost per kilogram	$2	$3
Direct labour budget:		
Direct labour time per unit (hours)	0.5	0.75
Direct labour rate per hour	$12	$12
Budgeted income statement:		
Total unit cost	$11	$20

An accounting assistant has prepared the detailed manufacturing overhead budget and the selling and administrative expenses budget. The latter shows selling expenses of $560,000 for product JB 50 and $440,000 for product JB 60, and administrative expenses of $420,000 for product JB 50 and $380,000 for product JB 60. Income taxes are expected to be 30%.

Instructions

Prepare the following budgets for the year. Show data for each product. Do not prepare quarterly budgets.

(a) Sales
(b) Production
(c) Direct materials

(d) Direct labour
(e) Income statement
    (*Note:* Income taxes are not allocated to the products.)

(a) Total sales: $11,400,000
(b) Required production units: JB 50, 310,000

P10-47B Litwin Industries had sales in 2015 of $5.6 million (800,000 units) and a gross profit of $1,344,000. Management is considering two alternative budget plans to increase its gross profit in 2016.

Plan A would increase the selling price per unit from $7 to $7.60. Sales volume would decrease by 5% from its 2015 level. Plan B would decrease the selling price per unit by 5%. The marketing department expects that the sales volume would increase by 150,000 units.

At the end of 2015, Litwin had 70,000 units on hand. If it accepts Plan A, the 2016 ending inventory should be equal to 90,000 units. If it accepts Plan B, the ending inventory should be equal to 100,000 units. Each unit produced will cost $2 in direct materials, $1.50 in direct labour, and $0.50 in variable overhead. The fixed overhead for 2016 should be $980,000.

(SO 2)
Prepare sales and production budgets and calculate the cost per unit under two plans.

Instructions

(a) Prepare a sales budget for 2016 under (1) Plan A and (2) Plan B.
(b) Prepare a production budget for 2016 under (1) Plan A and (2) Plan B.
(c) Calculate the cost per unit under (1) Plan A and (2) Plan B. Explain why the cost per unit is different for each of the two plans. (Round to two decimals.)
(d) Which plan should Litwin Industries accept? (*Hint:* Calculate the gross profit under each plan.)

(c) Unit cost:
Plan A $5.26,
Plan B $5.00
(d) Gross profit:
Plan A $1,778,400
Plan B $1,567,500

P10-48B The following data are for the operations of Zoë's Fashion Footwear Ltd., a retail store:

(SO 3, 5)
Prepare a merchandise purchases budget and a budgeted income statement.

1. Sales Forecast—2016

April	$ 70,000	July	$100,000
May	60,000	August	120,000
June	80,000		

2. The cost of sales is 40% of sales. Other variable costs are 20% of sales.
3. Inventory is maintained at twice the budgeted sales requirements for the following month.
4. Fixed costs are $20,000 per month.
5. The income tax rate is estimated to be 40%.

Instructions

(a) Prepare a merchandise purchases budget in dollars for June 2016.

(b) NI = $7,200

(b) Prepare a budgeted income statement for June 2016.

(adapted from CGA-Canada, now CPA Canada)

(SO 4)
Prepare a cash budget
for a year.

P10-49B   The Big Boy Company is in a seasonal business and prepares quarterly budgets. Its fiscal year runs from July 1 through June 30. Production occurs only in the first quarter (July to September), but sales take place throughout the year. The sales forecast for the coming year shows the following:

First quarter	$390,000	Third quarter	$390,000
Second quarter	750,000	Fourth quarter	390,000

There are no cash sales, and the company expects to collect the beginning balance of receivables in the first quarter. Subsequent collections are two thirds in the quarter when sales take place and one third in the following quarter.

Material purchases valued at $360,000 are made in the first quarter and none are made in the last three quarters. The company pays when it purchases the materials.

Direct labour of $350,000 is incurred and paid only in the first quarter. Factory overhead of $430,000 is also incurred and paid in the first quarter and is at a standby level of $100,000 during the other three quarters. The company pays selling and administrative expenses of $50,000 each quarter throughout the year. Big Boy has an operating line of credit with its bank at an interest rate of 6% per annum. The company plans to keep a cash balance of at least $8,000 at all times, and it will borrow and repay in multiples of $5,000. It makes all borrowings at the beginning of a quarter, and makes all payments at the end of a quarter. It pays interest only on the portion of the loan that it repays in a quarter.

The company plans to purchase equipment in the second and fourth quarters for $150,000 and $50,000, respectively. The cash balance on July 1 is $23,000 and accounts receivable total $130,000.

Instructions

Ending cash balance:
Q1 = $8,000;
Q4 = $70,600

Prepare a cash budget for the year. Show receipts, disbursements, the ending cash balance before borrowing, the amounts borrowed and repaid, interest payments, and the ending cash balance.

(adapted from CMA Canada, now CPA Canada)

(SO 4)
Prepare cash budget for
two months.

P10-50B   Nigh Company prepares monthly cash budgets. Relevant data from operating budgets for 2017 are as follows:

	January	February
Sales	$350,000	$400,000
Direct materials purchases	120,000	110,000
Direct labour	85,000	115,000
Manufacturing overhead	60,000	75,000
Selling and administrative expenses	75,000	80,000

All sales are on account. The company expects collections to be 60% in the month of sale, 30% in the first month following the sale, and 10% in the second month following the sale. It pays 30% of direct materials purchases in cash in the month of purchase and the balance due in the month following the purchase. It pays all other items above in the month incurred. Depreciation has been excluded from manufacturing overhead and selling and administrative expenses. Other data:

1. Credit sales: November 2016, $200,000; December 2016, $280,000
2. Purchases of direct materials: December 2016, $90,000
3. Other receipts: January—collection of December 31, 2016, interest receivable, $3,000; February—proceeds from sale of securities, $5,000
4. Other disbursements: February—payment of $20,000 cash for land

The company's cash balance on January 1, 2017, is expected to be $50,000. The company wants to keep a minimum cash balance of $40,000.

(a) January: (1) collections = $314,000;
(2) payments = $99,000
(b) Ending cash balance: January $48,000

Instructions

(a) Prepare schedules for (1) the expected collections from customers and (2) the expected payments for direct materials purchases.

(b) Prepare a cash budget for January and February, with columns for each month.

P10-51B Raymond Co. began operations in January 2015. The information below is for Raymond Co.'s operations for the three months from January to March (the first quarter) of 2016: (SO 4)

Prepare a cash budget.

Expenses for Quarter 1	
Depreciation	$40,000
Factory overhead	10,000
Income taxes	15,000
Payroll	30,000
Selling costs (2% commission on sales)	8,000
Administrative costs	10,000

Costs are assumed to be incurred evenly throughout the year, with the exception of depreciation and income taxes. Depreciation on new assets is first taken in the quarter after the quarter in which they are purchased. Income taxes are payable in semi-annual instalments, on the first day of each six-month period, based on last year's actual taxes of $30,000. Other information:

1. Sales (made evenly throughout the quarter)

Quarter 1	(actual)	$400,000
Quarter 2	(forecast)	400,000
Quarter 3	(forecast)	800,000

Collections from sales are as follows: 50% in the quarter of sale; 45% in the following quarter; 5% uncollectible.

2. Purchases (made evenly throughout the quarter)

Quarter 1	(actual)	$200,000

The gross margin ratio is constant at 60%.

Cash payments for purchases are as follows: 50% in the quarter of purchase; 50% in the following quarter. Merchandise purchased during a quarter would include 25% of the next quarter's forecasted sales.

3. The company purchased capital equipment for $100,000 in February 2015. The estimated useful life of this equipment is 10 years; it has no estimated scrap value.

4. Dividends of $20,000 are declared on the last day of each quarter, and are paid at the end of the next month.

5. The cash balance in the bank at the end of the first quarter is $25,000.

Instructions

(a) Prepare a cash budget for Raymond Co. for the second quarter of 2016. Show all your supporting calculations.

(b) List three advantages of budgeting.

(adapted from CGA-Canada, now CPA Canada)

Ending balance = $127,000

P10-52B The budget committee of Urbina Company has collected the following data for its Eastwood Store in preparing budgeted income statements for July and August 2016. (SO 5)

Prepare purchases and income statement budgets for a merchandiser.

1. Expected sales: July $400,000, August $450,000, September $500,000.
2. The cost of goods sold is expected to be 60% of sales.
3. Ending merchandise inventory is maintained at 20% of the following month's cost of goods sold.
4. Operating expenses are estimated to be as follows:

Sales salaries	$50,000 per month	Rent expense	$3,000 per month
Advertising	4% of monthly sales	Depreciation	$700 per month
Delivery expense	2% of monthly sales	Utilities	$500 per month
Sales commissions	3% of monthly sales	Insurance	$300 per month

5. Income taxes are estimated to be 30% of the income from operations.

Instructions

(a) Prepare the merchandise purchases budget, using columns for each month.

(b) Prepare budgeted income statements, using columns for each month. Show details in the statements for the cost of goods sold.

(a) Purchases:
July $246,000,
August $276,000
(b) Net income:
July $48,650,
August $59,500

(SO 5)
Calculate purchases and disbursements for a merchandiser.

P10-53B Vergados Brothers is trying to estimate the amount of inventory it needs to purchase next month (April). The controller likes to have twice the number of units he expects to sell on hand at the beginning of the month. He always takes the 3/10, net 30 purchase discount on the inventory purchases. Inventory costs $10 per unit. Actual sales for January and February, and the forecast sales for March to June, are as follows:

	Units			Units
January	11,000		April	14,000
February	10,000		May	15,000
March	13,000		June	13,000

Cash payments for purchases are as follows: two thirds in the month of purchase; one third in the next month. The selling price is $20 per unit, and sales occur evenly throughout the month.

Instructions

(a) 16,000

(b) $151,967

(a) Calculate the number of units to be purchased in April.

(b) Calculate the amount of cash that Vergados Brothers will disburse in April for purchases.

(adapted from CGA-Canada, now CPA Canada)

(SO 2, 3)

Prepare production and direct labour budgets.

P10-54B   Raddington Inc. makes and sells chairs. The controller is responsible for preparing the master budget and has accumulated the following information for 2016:

	January	February	March	April	May
Estimated unit sales	15,000	18,000	13,000	14,000	14,000
Sales price per unit	$85	$75	$75	$75	$75
Direct labour hours per unit	2	2	1.5	1.5	1.5
Wage per direct labour hour	$18	$18	$18	$20	$20

Raddington Inc. has a labour contract that calls for a wage increase to $20 per hour on April 1. It has installed new labour-saving machinery, which will be fully operational by March 1.

Raddington Inc. expects to begin the year with 24,000 chairs on hand and has a policy of carrying an end-of-month inventory of 100% of the following month's sales plus 50% of the next month's sales.

Instructions

(a) Production for Feb: 13,500 units; direct labour total: $1,422,000

(a) Prepare a production budget and a direct labour budget for Raddington Inc. by month and for the first quarter of the year. The direct labour budget should include direct labour hours and show the detail for each direct labour cost category.

(b) For each item used in Raddington Inc.'s production budget and its direct labour budget, identify the other component(s) of the master budget (budget package) that would also use these data.

(adapted from CMA Canada, now CPA Canada)

(SO 4)

Prepare a cash budget for a month.

P10-55B   The controller of Kari Company estimates sales and production for the first four months of 2016 as follows:

	January	February	March	April
Sales	$40,000	$50,000	$60,000	$35,000
Production in units	2,000	2,500	3,000	3,500

Sales are 60% cash and 40% on account, and 40% of credit sales are collected in the month of the sale. In the month after the sale, 60% of credit sales are collected. It takes 5 kg of direct material to produce a finished unit, and direct materials cost $6 per kg. All direct materials purchases are on account, and are paid as follows: 60% in the month of the purchase, 40% the following month. Ending direct materials inventory for each month is 20% of the next month's production needs. January's beginning materials inventory is 2,000 kg. Suppose that both accounts receivable and accounts payable are zero at the beginning of January.

Instructions

(a) What are the total cash sales for the January–March quarter?

(b) $14,400

(b) What is the accounts receivable balance at the end of March?

(c) What is the direct materials inventory balance at the end of March?

(d) What are material purchases costs for February?

(e) $72,000

(f) $37,200

(e) What are cash payments on account for February?

(f) What is the ending balance in accounts payable for March?

(g) What is the cash balance for the period January–March?

(adapted from CGA-Canada, now CPA Canada)

Cases

C10-56   Peters Corporation operates on a calendar-year basis. It begins the annual budgeting process in late August when the president sets targets for the total dollar sales and net income before taxes for the next year.

The sales target is given first to the marketing department. The marketing manager creates a sales budget for each product line in both units and dollars. From this budget, he determines sales quotas by product line in units and dollars for each of the corporation's sales districts. The marketing manager also estimates the cost of the marketing activities that will be needed to support the target sales volume, and he prepares a tentative marketing expense budget.

The executive vice-president uses the sales and profit targets, the sales budget by product line, and the tentative marketing expense budget to determine the dollar amounts that can be used for manufacturing and corporate office expenses. The executive vice-president prepares the budget for corporate expenses. She then forwards to the production department the product-line sales budget in units and the total dollar amount that it can use for manufacturing.

The production manager meets with the factory managers to develop a manufacturing plan that will produce the required units when they are needed, and within the cost set by the executive vice-president. The budgeting process usually falters at this point because the production department does not believe that it has been given enough financial resources.

When this standstill occurs, the vice-president of finance, the executive vice-president, the marketing manager, and the production manager meet to determine the final budgets for each of the areas. This normally results in a modest increase in the total amount that is available for manufacturing costs and cuts to the marketing expense and corporate office expense budgets. The total sales and net income figures proposed by the president are almost never changed. Although the participants are usually unhappy about the compromise, these budgets are final. Each executive then develops a new detailed budget for the operations in his or her area.

None of the areas has achieved its budget in recent years. Sales often run below the target. When budgeted sales are not achieved, each area is expected to cut costs so that the president's profit target can be met. However, the profit target is almost never met because the areas don't cut costs enough. In fact, costs often run above the original budget in all functional areas (marketing, production, and corporate office).

The president is disturbed that Peters Corporation has not been able to meet its sales and profit targets. He therefore hired a consultant with considerable experience with companies in Peters' industry. The consultant reviewed the budgets for the past four years. He concluded that the product-line sales budgets were reasonable and that the cost and expense budgets were enough for the budgeted sales and production levels.

Instructions
(a) Discuss how the budgeting process used by Peters Corporation makes failing to achieve the president's sales and profit targets more likely.
(b) Suggest how Peters Corporation's budgeting process could be revised to correct the problems.
(c) Should the functional areas be expected to cut their costs when the sales volume falls below budget forecast? Explain.

(adapted from CMA Canada, now CPA Canada)

C10-57 Howe Ltd. is trying to decide whether it is going to need to take a loan in January to buy a new microcomputer system. The microcomputer will cost $8,800.

The president, Joan Howe, has collected the following information about her operations as at December 31:

1. Balances of selected general ledger accounts:

Cash	$2,500
Accounts payable	6,667

2. Sales history and forecast (unit selling price, $10):

October	(actual)	$45,000
November	(actual)	33,000
December	(actual)	45,000
January	(forecast)	60,000

3. All sales are on credit and are due 30 days after the sale.

4. Cash payments for purchases are as follows: two thirds in the month of purchase; one third in the month after that.
5. Howe Ltd. collects 50% of a month's sales one month after the sale and 45% two months after the sale; 5% are uncollectible.
6. The company purchases inventory as required under terms of 2/10, net 30. It always takes the 2% discount, but records purchases at gross cost. Accounts payable (shown above) relate solely to inventory purchases. Inventory costs $5 per unit, gross.
7. Other expenses, all paid in cash as required, average about 30% of the sales dollar amount. Depreciation is part of these expenses and costs $3,000 per month.
8. Howe Ltd. keeps a minimum cash balance of $4,000.

Instructions
Prepare a cash budget for January, indicating whether Howe Ltd. will need a loan to finance its computer acquisition.

(adapted from CGA-Canada, now CPA Canada)

C10-58 Solid State sells electronic products. The controller is responsible for preparing the master budget and has accumulated the information below for the months of January, February, and March.

Balances at January 1 are expected to be as follows:

Cash	$ 5,500	Inventories	$309,400
Accounts receivable	416,100	Accounts payable	133,055

The budget is to be based on the following assumptions:

1. Each month's sales are billed on the last day of the month.
2. Customers are allowed a 3% discount if their payment is made within 10 days after the billing date. Receivables are booked at gross.
3. The company collects 60% of the billings within the discount period, 25% by the end of the month after the date of sale, and 9% by the end of the second month after the date of sale; 6% prove uncollectible.
4. It pays 54% of all material purchases and the selling, general, and administrative expenses in the month purchased and the remainder in the following month. Each month's units of ending inventory are equal to 130% of the next month's units of sales.

5. The cost of each unit of inventory is $20.
6. Selling, general, and administrative expenses, of which $2,000 is for depreciation, are equal to 15% of the current month's sales.
7. Actual and projected sales are as follows:

Month	Sales	Units
November	$354,000	11,800
December	363,000	12,100
January	357,000	11,900
February	342,000	11,400
March	360,000	12,000
April	366,000	12,200

Instructions
(a) Calculate the budgeted cash disbursements during the month of February.
(b) Calculate the budgeted cash collections during the month of January.
(c) Calculate the budgeted number of units of inventory to be purchased during the month of March.

(adapted from CMA Canada, now CPA Canada)

C10-59 Sports Fanatic Company is a retail sporting goods store that uses accrual accounting for its records. Information on Sports Fanatic's operations are as follows:

1. The store has budgeted sales at $220,000 for January and $200,000 for February.
2. It expects collections to be 60% in the month of sale and 38% in the month following the sale. It expects 2% of sales to be uncollectible.
3. Gross margin is 25% of sales.

4. It purchases a total of 80% of the merchandise for resale in the month before the month of sale and 20% in the month of sale. It makes payments for merchandise in the month after it purchases it.
5. Other expected monthly expenses to be paid in cash amount to $22,600.
6. Annual depreciation is $216,000.
7. Sports Fanatic's balance sheet at the close of business on December 31 follows.

SPORTS FANATIC COMPANY
Balance Sheet
December 31

Assets	
Cash	$ 22,000
Accounts receivable (net of $4,000 allowance for uncollectible accounts)	76,000
Inventory	132,000
Property, plant, and equipment (net of $680,000 of accumulated depreciation)	870,000
Total assets	$1,100,000
Liabilities and Shareholders' Equity	
Accounts payable	$ 162,000
Common shares	800,000
Retained earnings	138,000
Total liabilities and shareholders' equity	$1,100,000

Instructions

Prepare the budgeted balance sheet and income statement for January.

(adapted from CMA Canada, now CPA Canada)

C10-60 Prasad & Green Inc. manufactures ergonomic devices for computer users. Some of its more popular products include glare screens (for computer monitors), keyboard stands with wrist rests, and laptop stands that allow air to circulate. Over the past five years, it has experienced rapid growth, with sales of all products increasing 20% to 50% each year.

Last year, some of the big manufacturers of computers also began introducing new products with ergonomic designs, such as glare screens and wrist rests, already built in. As a result, sales of Prasad & Green's accessory devices have dropped a bit. The company believes that the laptop stands will probably continue to show growth, but the other products will probably continue to decline. When it prepared the next year's budget, it gave increases to research and development so that the company could develop replacement products or expand into some other product line. Some product lines it is considering are general-purpose ergonomic devices, including back supports, footrests, and sloped writing pads.

The most recent results have shown that sales of the glare screens decreased more than was expected. As a result, the company may have a shortage of funds. Top management has therefore asked that all expenses be reduced by 10% to compensate for these reduced sales. Summary budget information is as follows:

Raw materials	$240,000
Direct labour	110,000
Insurance	50,000
Depreciation	90,000
Machine repairs	30,000
Sales salaries	50,000
Office salaries	80,000
Factory salaries (indirect labour)	50,000
Total	$700,000

Instructions

(a) Determine what the implications are of reducing each of the costs. For example, if the company reduces its raw materials costs, it may have to do this by purchasing lower-quality materials. This may affect sales in the long run.

(b) Based on your analysis in part (a), what do you think is the best way to obtain the $70,000 in cost savings that top management wants? Be specific. Are there any costs that cannot or should not be reduced? Why or why not?

C10-61 Électronique Instruments, a rapidly expanding electronic parts distributor, is formulating its plans for 2016. John Kedrowski, the firm's director of marketing, has completed his 2016 forecast and is confident that the company will meet or exceed sales estimates. The following sales figures show the growth that is expected and are the basis for planning in the other corporate departments:

Month	Forecast Sales	Month	Forecast Sales
January	$2,800,000	July	$4,000,000
February	3,000,000	August	4,000,000
March	2,800,000	September	4,200,000
April	3,200,000	October	4,200,000
May	3,500,000	November	4,000,000
June	3,800,000	December	4,400,000

Tae Hwan, assistant controller, is responsible for the cash flow projection, a critical element during a period of rapid expansion. She will use the following information in preparing her cash analysis:

1. Électronique has experienced an excellent record in accounts receivable collection and expects this trend to continue. The company collects 50% of billings in the month after the sale and 50% in the second month after the sale. Uncollectible accounts are nominal and can be ignored in the analysis.
2. The purchase of electronic parts is Électronique's largest expenditure; the cost of these items is equal to 60% of sales. Électronique receives 40% of the parts one month before it sells them and 60% during the month of sale.
3. Historically, Électronique has cleared 60% of the accounts payable one month after it receives its purchases, and the remaining 40% two months after.
4. Hourly wages, including fringe benefits, depend on the sales volume; they are equal to 20% of the current month's sales. The company pays these wages in the month incurred.
5. General and administrative expenses are projected to be $ 2,750,000 for 2016. The composition of these expenses is given below. The company incurs all of these expenses uniformly throughout the year, except for property taxes. It pays the property taxes in four equal instalments in the last month of each quarter:

Salaries	$ 490,000
Promotion	670,000
Property taxes	250,000
Insurance	370,000
Utilities	350,000
Depreciation	620,000
	$2,750,000

6. Électronique makes income tax payments in the first month of each quarter based on income for the prior quarter. The tax rate is 30%. The net income for the first quarter of 2016 is projected to be $750,000.
7. Électronique has a corporate policy of maintaining an end-of-month cash balance of $200,000. It invests or borrows cash monthly, as necessary, to maintain this balance.
8. Électronique uses a calendar-year reporting period.

Instructions

Prepare a schedule of Cash Receipts and Disbursements for Électronique Instruments, by month, for the second quarter of 2016. Be sure that all receipts, disbursements, borrowing, and investing amounts are presented on a monthly basis. Ignore the interest expense and income from borrowing and investing.

(adapted from CMA Canada, now CPA Canada)

C10-62 You are an accountant in the budgetary, projections, and special projects department of Cross Canada, Inc., a large manufacturing company. The president, Karim Bousalloum, asks you on very short notice to prepare some sales and income projections covering the next two years of the company's much-heralded new product lines. He wants these projections for a series of speeches he is making while on a two-week trip to eight brokerage firms. The president hopes to increase Cross Canada's share sales and price.

You work 23 hours in two days to do the projections and hand deliver them to the president. You are swiftly but graciously thanked as he departs. A week later, you find time to go over some of your calculations and discover a miscalculation that makes the projections grossly overstated. You quickly inquire about the president's itinerary and learn that he has made half of his speeches. You don't know what to do.

Instructions

(a) Determine what the consequences are of telling the president of your gross miscalculation.
(b) Determine what the consequences are of not telling the president of your gross miscalculation.
(c) Determine what the ethical considerations are for you and the president in this situation.

"All About You" Activity

C10-63 In this chapter you learned about the benefits of budgeting for a business. It is also important for individuals, especially students. Jo is an accounting major. Jo's estimate of expenses for the next eight-month academic year (September to May) are given in the chart below. Jo receives $750 per month from family members, $700 from a part-time job, and $1,200 from a bursary.

Tuition and fees	$6,200	Books and supplies	$1,500
Residence and food	9,200	Internet connection	295
Local travel (included with student fees)	0	Travel home	400
Clothing	400	Personal sundries	560
Entertainment and going out	424	Misc.	420

Instructions

(a) Prepare a budget for Jo.
   1. How much is the shortfall?
   2. What suggestions do you have to fund and reduce the shortfall?

(b) Jo has the option of renting a room, with shared kitchen facilities, off campus. For the eight-month period, rent would be $4,800, utilities $800, and cable/Internet charges $640, with food estimated at $2,800. It would take about one and a half hours a day to travel to and from campus. Do you think Jo should take this option?

Decision-Making at Current Designs

DM10-1 Diane Buswell is preparing the 2016 budget for one of Current Designs' rotomoulded kayaks. Extensive meetings with members of the sales department and executive team have resulted in the following unit sales projections for 2016.

Quarter 1	1,000 kayaks
Quarter 2	1,500 kayaks
Quarter 3	750 kayaks
Quarter 4	750 kayaks

Current Designs' policy is to have finished goods ending inventory in a quarter equal to 20% of the next quarter's anticipated sales. Preliminary sales projections for 2017 are 1,100 units for the first quarter and 1,500 units for the second quarter. Ending inventory of finished goods at December 31, 2015, will be 200 rotomoulded kayaks.

Production of each kayak requires 54 kilograms of polyethylene powder and a finishing kit (rope, seat, hardware, etc). Company policy is that the ending inventory of polyethylene powder should be 25% of the amount needed for production in the next quarter. Assume that the ending inventory of polyethylene powder on December 31, 2015, is 19,400 kilograms. The finishing kits can be assembled as they are needed. As a result, Current Designs does not maintain a significant inventory of the finishing kits.

The polyethylene powder used in these kayaks costs $1.50 per kilogram, and the finishing kits cost $170 each. Production of a single kayak requires 2 hours of time by more experienced, type I employees and 3 hours of finishing time by type II employees. The type I employees are paid $15 per hour, and the type II employees are paid $12 per hour.

Selling and administrative expenses for this line are expected to be $45 per unit sold plus $7,500 per quarter. Manufacturing overhead is assigned at 150% of labour costs.

Instructions

Prepare the production budget, direct materials budget, direct labour budget, manufacturing overhead budget, and selling and administrative expenses budget for this product line by quarter and in total for 2016.

Waterways Continuing Problem

(This is a continuation of the Waterways Problem from Chapters 1 through 9.)

WCP-10 Waterways Corporation has recently acquired a small manufacturing operation in British Columbia that produces one of its more popular items. This plant will provide these units for resale in retail hardware stores in British Columbia and Alberta. Because the budget prepared by the plant was incomplete, Jordan Leigh, Waterways' CFO, was sent to B.C. to oversee the plant's budgeting process for the second quarter of 2017.

Jordan asked the various managers to collect the following information for preparing the second-quarter budget.

Sales

Unit sales for February 2017	$ 90,000
Unit sales for March 2017	102,000
Expected unit sales for April 2017	110,000
Expected unit sales for May 2017	115,000
Expected unit sales for June 2017	120,000
Expected unit sales for July 2017	135,000
Expected unit sales for August 2017	160,000
Average unit selling price	$15

Based on the experience from the home plant, Jordan has suggested that the B.C. plant keep 10% of the next month's unit sales in ending inventory. The plant has contracts with some of the major home hardware giants, so all sales are on account; 50% of the accounts receivable is collected in the month of sale, and the balance is collected in the month after sale. This was the same collection pattern from the previous year. The new plant has no bad debts.

Direct Materials

The combined quantity of direct materials (consisting of metal, plastic and rubber) used in each unit is 1.1 kg. Metal, plastic, and rubber together amount to $1.50 per kg. Inventory of combined direct material on March 31 consisted of 12,155 kg.

This plant likes to keep 10% of the materials needed for the next month in its ending inventory. Fifty percent of the payables is paid in the month of purchase, and 50% is paid in the month after purchase.

Accounts Payable on March 31 will total $120,600.

Direct Labour

Labour requires 15 minutes per unit for completion and is paid at an average rate of $18 per hour.

Manufacturing Overhead

Indirect materials	$0.30 per labour hour	Depreciation	$16,800 per month
Indirect labour	$0.50 per labour hour	Property taxes	$2,400 per month
Utilities	$0.45 per labour hour	Insurance	$1,200 per month
Maintenance	$0.25 per labour hour	Janitorial	$2,600 per month
Salaries	$42,065 per month		

Selling and Administrative
Variable selling and administrative expenses per unit is $1.62.

Advertising	$15,000 a month
Depreciation	$2,500 a month
Insurance	$1,400 a month
Other fixed costs	$3,000 a month
Salaries	$72,000 a month

Other Information
The Cash balance on March 31 will be $100,500, but Waterways has decided it would like to maintain a cash balance of at least $500,000 beginning on April 30. The company has an open line of credit with its bank. The terms of the agreement require borrowing to be in $1,000 increments at 3% interest. Borrowing is considered to be on the first day of the month and repayments are on the last day of the month.

In May, $845,000 of new equipment to update operations will be purchased.

Three months' insurance is prepaid on the first day of the first month of the quarter.

Instructions
For the second quarter of 2017:
(a) Prepare a sales budget.
(b) Prepare a schedule for expected cash collections from customers.
(c) Prepare a production budget.
(d) Prepare a direct materials budget.
(e) Prepare a schedule for expected payments for materials purchases.
(f) Prepare a direct labour budget.
(g) Prepare a manufacturing overhead budget.
(h) Prepare a selling and administrative expenses budget.
(i) Prepare a cash budget.

Include supporting calculations.

Answers to Self-Study Questions

1. c **2.** a **3.** b **4.** b **5.** d **6.** d **7.** a **8.** c **9.** c **10.** d

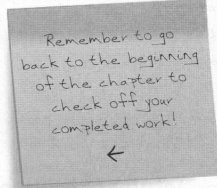

Remember to go back to the beginning of the chapter to check off your completed work!

CHAPTER 11

Budgetary Control and Responsibility Accounting

The Navigator

Chapter 11

- ☐ Scan *Study Objectives*
- ☐ Read *Feature Story*
- ☐ Read *Chapter Preview*
- ☐ Read text and answer *Before You Go On* p. 452, p. 457, p. 458, p. 467, p. 471
- ☐ Work *Using the Decision Toolkit*
- ☐ Review *Summary of Study Objectives*
- ☐ Review *Decision Toolkit—A Summary*
- ☐ Work *Comprehensive Do It!*
- ☐ Answer *Self-Study Questions*
- ☐ Complete assignments

study objectives

the navigator

After studying this chapter, you should be able to do the following:

1. Describe budgetary control and static budget reports.
2. Explain the development of flexible budgets and the usefulness of flexible budget reports.
3. Apply responsibility accounting to cost and profit centres.
4. Explain the basis and formula used for evaluating performance in investment centres.
5. Explain the difference between ROI and residual income (Appendix 11A).

KEEPING THE BUDGET ON TRACK

Budgets are critical to an organization's success. To be useful, they must be accurate, but also flexible to take into account the various changes in an organization's finances.

Montreal-based Bombardier Inc. is the world's only maker of both planes and trains. Its approximately 76,000 employees worldwide design, manufacture, and sell innovative aviation products and provide related services for the commercial and business markets, as well as rolling stock, services, systems, and signalling in rail transportation. In 2013, Bombardier had U.S. $18.2 billion in revenues.

Bombardier ties its annual budget with a strategic plan. "We prepare a budget and strategic plan covering a three-year period, on an annual basis, using a process whereby a detailed one-year budget and two-year strategic plan are prepared by each business unit and then consolidated at the reportable segment and Corporation levels," the company said in its 2013 financial report. "Cash flows and profitability included in the budget and strategic plan are based on existing and future contracts and orders, general market conditions, current cost structures, anticipated cost variations and in-force collective agreements." The budget and strategic plan must then be approved by senior managers and Bombardier's board of directors.

The company said it tracks if actual financial information matches budget projections and adjusts accordingly. "Significant variances in actual performance are a key trigger to assess whether certain estimates used in the preparation of financial information must be revised."

In addition to getting an annual financial view with the budget and a medium-term view with the strategic plan, Bombardier updates its forecasts quarterly to reflect things such as a change in a short-term plan to deliver aircraft in a certain quarter. This occurred in early 2014, when Bombardier announced a delay in its delivery of its new CSeries family of medium-range passenger jets.

Significant investments are needed for aircraft program development, including an estimated U.S. $4.4 billion for the CSeries jets. Bombardier prepares 20-year market forecasts for business and commercial aircraft, presenting the number of aircraft deliveries and potential revenues in the coming years. These forecasts are based on industry trends; market drivers such as the global economy and demand for air travel; and economic forecasts for major commodities like oil, the price of which is a key consideration in planning the size of an aircraft fleet.

Bombardier's budgeting objective is to be not too conservative but not too aggressive. The company maintains this balance with input from managers at all levels and regular review of factors that could influence the numbers.

Sources: Ross Marowits, The Canadian Press, "Bombardier Shares Could Be on the Upswing After Months of Bad News, Say Analysts," Yahoo! Finance, March 14, 2014; Frederic Tomesco, "Bombardier Falls After Cutting 2014 Targets on Costs," Bloomberg, February 13, 2014; Bombardier 2013 Financial Report.

the navigator

Preview of Chapter 11

In Chapter 10, we saw how budgets are developed. It is now time to see how management uses budgets to control operations. In the feature story on Bombardier, we saw that budgeting must consider factors that management cannot control. This chapter focuses on two aspects of management control: (1) budgetary control and (2) responsibility accounting. The chapter is organized as follows:

BUDGETARY CONTROL AND RESPONSIBILITY ACCOUNTING

The Concept of Budgetary Control and Static Budget Reports	Flexible Budgets	Responsibility Accounting for Cost and Profit Centres	Evaluating Performance in Investment Centres	Residual Income—Another Performance Measurement Appendix 11A
➤ Budgetary control ➤ Static budget reports	➤ Why flexible budgets? ➤ Developing the flexible budget ➤ Flexible budget—a case study ➤ Flexible budget reports	➤ The responsibility accounting concept ➤ Controllable versus noncontrollable revenues and costs ➤ Responsibility reporting system ➤ Management by exception ➤ Principles of performance evaluation ➤ Accounting for various responsibility centres	➤ Return on investment (ROI) ➤ Responsibility report ➤ Judgemental factors in ROI ➤ Improving ROI	➤ Residual income compared with ROI ➤ Residual income weakness

The Concept of Budgetary Control and Static Budget Reports

BUDGETARY CONTROL

One of management's major functions is to control company operations. Control consists of the steps that management takes to be sure that the company meets planned objectives. We now ask how management uses budgets to control operations.

The use of budgets in controlling operations is known as **budgetary control**. This control is achieved by using budget reports to compare actual results with planned objectives. Budget reports are used because planned objectives often lose much of their potential value if progress is not monitored along the way. Just as your professors give mid-term exams to evaluate your progress, so do top management require periodic reports on the progress of department managers toward their planned objectives.

Budget reports give management feedback on operations. The feedback for a crucial objective, such as having enough cash on hand to pay bills, may be made daily. For other objectives, such as meeting budgeted annual sales and operating expenses, monthly budget reports may be enough. Budget reports can be prepared as frequently as they are needed. From these reports, management analyzes any differences between actual and planned results and determines their causes. Management then takes corrective action, or it decides to modify future plans.

Budgetary control works best when a company has a formalized reporting system. The system should do the following: (1) identify the name of the budget report, such as the sales budget or the manufacturing overhead budget; (2) state the frequency of the report, such as weekly or monthly; (3) specify the purpose of the report; and (4) indicate who the primary recipient(s) of the report is(are). Budgetary control in a manufacturing company involves the activities shown in Illustration 11-1.

►Illustration 11-1
Budgetary control activities

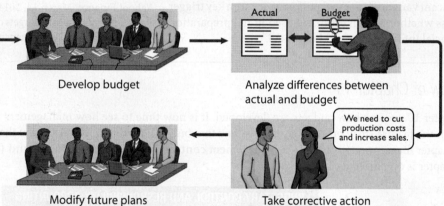

Develop budget

Analyze differences between actual and budget

Modify future plans

Take corrective action

We need to cut production costs and increase sales.

Illustration 11-2 presents a partial budgetary control system for a manufacturing company. Note the frequency of the reports and their emphasis on control. For example, there is a daily report on scrap and a weekly report on labour.

►Illustration 11-2
Budgetary control reporting system

Name of Report	Frequency	Purpose	Primary Recipient(s)
Sales	Weekly	Determine whether sales goals are being met	Top management and sales manager
Labour	Weekly	Control direct and indirect labour costs	Vice-president of production and production department managers
Scrap	Daily	Determine efficient use of materials	Production manager
Departmental overhead costs	Monthly	Control overhead costs	Department manager
Selling expenses	Monthly	Control selling expenses	Sales manager
Income statement	Monthly and quarterly	Determine whether income objectives are being met	Top management

BUSINESS INSIGHT   *Capitalizing on Budgetary Control*

When you spend millions of dollars every year on capital projects, budgetary control is a crucial task for managers. Murphy Oil Corporation's Calgary-based Canadian operation spends about $340 million a year on hundreds of projects: everything from exploring for oil off Canada's east coast to expanding production in Alberta's oil sands. It uses a sophisticated software program to track spending on construction and exploration. Murphy has real-time data on all aspects of a project, including buying land, drilling a well, and purchasing production equipment. Its project managers are responsible for ensuring that cost overruns don't get out of control. They have access to current spending data to compare budget goals against actual spending and take corrective action when necessary.

Sources: Yadullah Hussain, "Canadian Oil Sands Eyes Murphy Oil's Stake in Massive Syncrude Project," *National Post,* January 31, 2013; "Case Study: Murphy Oil Canada; 3esi Offers Petroleum Companies Real-Time Project Management," 3esi case study, 2009; Murphy Oil Corporation company website, www.murphyoilcorp.com.

What might be some corrective action that Murphy Oil would take if a construction project's costs were starting to exceed the budgeted amount?

STATIC BUDGET REPORTS

You learned in Chapter 10 that the master budget formalizes management's planned objectives for the coming year. When it is used in budgetary control, each budget in the master budget is viewed as being static. A **static budget** is a projection of budget data at one level of activity. These budgets do not consider data for different levels of activity. As a result, companies always compare actual results with budget data at the activity level that was used in developing the master budget.

Examples

To illustrate the role of a static budget in budgetary control, we will use selected data that were prepared for Hayes Company in Chapter 10. Illustration 11-3 provides budget and actual sales data for the Rightride product in the first and second quarters of 2016.

Sales	First Quarter	Second Quarter	Total
Budgeted	$180,000	$210,000	$390,000
Actual	179,000	199,500	378,500
Difference	$ 1,000	$ 10,500	$ 11,500

►Illustration 11-3
Budget and actual sales data

Illustration 11-4 presents the sales budget report for Hayes Company's first quarter. The rightmost column reports the difference between the budgeted and actual amounts.

HAYES COMPANY			
Sales Budget Report			
Quarter Ended March 31, 2016			
Product Line	Budget	Actual	Difference: Favourable (F)/ Unfavourable (U)
Rightride*	$180,000	$179,000	$1,000 U

*In practice, each product line would be included in the report.

►Illustration 11-4
Sales budget report—first quarter

The report shows that sales are $1,000 under budget—an unfavourable result. This difference is less than 1% of the budgeted sales ($1,000 ÷ $180,000 = 0.56%). Top management's reaction to unfavourable differences is often influenced by the materiality (significance) of the difference. Since the difference of $1,000 is immaterial in this case, we will assume that Hayes Company's management takes no specific corrective action.

Alternative Terminology
The difference between budgeted numbers and actual results is sometimes called a *budget variance.*

Illustration 11-5 presents the budget report for the second quarter. It has one new feature: cumulative year-to-date information. This report indicates that sales for the second quarter were $10,500 below budget. This is 5% of budgeted sales ($10,500 ÷ $210,000). Top management may now conclude that the difference between budgeted and actual sales requires investigation.

►Illustration 11-5
Sales budget report—second quarter

HAYES COMPANY
Sales Budget Report
Quarter Ended June 30, 2016

	Second Quarter			Year-to-Date		
Product Line	Budget	Actual	Difference: Favourable (F)/ Unfavourable (U)	Budget	Actual	Difference: Favourable (F)/ Unfavourable (U)
Rightride	$210,000	$199,500	$10,500 U	$390,000	$378,500	$11,500 U

Management's analysis should start by asking the sales manager what the cause(s) of the shortfall are. The need for corrective action should be considered. For example, management may decide to help sales by offering sales incentives to customers or by increasing the advertising of Rightrides. Or, if management concludes that a downturn in the economy is responsible for the lower sales, it may modify its planned sales and profit goals for the remainder of the year.

Uses and Limitations

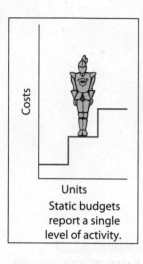

Static budgets report a single level of activity.

From these examples, you can see that a master sales budget is useful in evaluating the performance of a sales manager. We can now ask whether the master budget is appropriate for evaluating a manager's ability to control costs. Recall that in a static budget, data are not modified or adjusted, even if there are changes in activity. It follows, then, that a static budget is appropriate in evaluating how well a manager controls costs when (1) the actual level of activity closely approximates the master budget activity level, and/or (2) the behaviour of the costs in response to changes in activity is fixed.

A static budget report is, therefore, appropriate for fixed manufacturing costs and for fixed selling and administrative expenses. But, as you will see shortly, static budget reports may not be a proper basis for evaluating a manager's performance in controlling variable costs.

BEFORE YOU GO ON...

►Do It! Static Budget Reports

Lawler Company expects to produce 5,000 units of product CV93 during the current month. Budgeted variable manufacturing costs per unit are direct materials $6, direct labour $15, and overhead $24. Monthly budgeted fixed manufacturing overhead costs are $10,000 for depreciation and $5,000 for supervision.

In the current month, Lawler produced 5,500 units and incurred the following costs: direct materials $33,900, direct labour $74,200, variable overhead $120,500, depreciation $10,000, and supervision $5,000.

Prepare a static budget report. (*Hint:* The Budget column is based on estimated production of 5,000 units while the Actual column is the actual costs incurred during the period.) Were costs controlled? Discuss limitations of this budget.

Action Plan

- Classify each cost as variable or fixed.
- Determine the difference as favourable or unfavourable.
- Determine the difference in total variable costs, total fixed costs, and total costs.

(continued)

(continued)

Solution

	A	B	C	D	E
1				Difference	
2				Favourable - F	
3	Units produced	Budget	Actual	Unfavourable - U	
4					
5	Variable costs				
6	Direct materials ($6)	$ 30,000	$ 33,900	$3,900	U
7	Direct labour ($15)	75,000	74,200	800	F
8	Overhead ($24)	120,000	120,500	500	U
9	Total variable costs	225,000	228,600	3,600	U
10					
11	Fixed costs				
12	Depreciation	10,000	10,000	0	
13	Supervision	5,000	5,000	0	
14	Total fixed costs	15,000	15,000	0	
15	Total costs	$240,000	$243,600	$3,600	U
16					

The static budget indicates that actual variable costs exceeded budgeted amounts by $3,600. Fixed costs were exactly as budgeted. The static budget gives the impression that the company did not control its variable costs. However, the static budget does not give consideration to the fact that the company produced 500 more units than planned. As a result, the static budget is not a good tool to evaluate variable costs. It is, however, a good tool to evaluate fixed costs as those should not vary with changes in production volume.

Related exercise material: **BE11-1, BE11-2, E11-17, E11-18,** and **Do It! D11-12.**

the navigator

Flexible Budgets

In contrast to a static budget, which is based on one level of activity, a **flexible budget** projects budget data for various levels of activity. The flexible budget is basically a series of static budgets at different levels of activity. The flexible budget recognizes that the budgetary process is more useful if it can be adapted to changes in operating conditions.

Flexible budgets can be prepared for each of the types of budgets included in the master budget. For example, Choice Hotels Canada can budget revenues and net income on the basis of 60%, 80%, and 100% room occupancy. Similarly, Yanke Expedited Services can budget its operating expenses based on different levels of truck distances driven. Likewise, in the feature story, Bombardier can budget revenue and net income based on estimated revenues and expenses from two core businesses: aerospace and transportation. In the following pages, we will illustrate a flexible budget for manufacturing overhead.

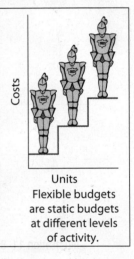

Units

Flexible budgets are static budgets at different levels of activity.

WHY FLEXIBLE BUDGETS?

Assume that you are the manager in charge of manufacturing overhead in the forging department of Barton Steel. In preparing the manufacturing overhead budget for 2016, you prepare the static budget in Illustration 11-6 based on a production volume of 10,000 units of steel ingots.

STUDY OBJECTIVE 2

Explain the development of flexible budgets and the usefulness of flexible budget reports.

BARTON STEEL
Manufacturing Overhead Budget (static)
Forging Department
Year Ended December 31, 2016

Budgeted production in units (steel ingots)	10,000
Budgeted costs	
Indirect materials	$ 250,000
Indirect labour	260,000
Utilities	190,000
Depreciation	280,000
Property taxes	70,000
Supervision	50,000
	$1,100,000

Helpful Hint
The static budget is the master budget of Chapter 10.

▶Illustration 11-6
Static overhead budget

Fortunately for the company, the demand for steel ingots has increased, and it produces and sells 12,000 units during the year, rather than 10,000. You are elated: increased sales mean increased profitability, which should mean a bonus or a raise for you and the employees in your department. Unfortunately, a comparison of the forging department's actual and budgeted costs has complicated matters for you. Illustration 11-7 shows the budget report.

▶Illustration 11-7

Static overhead budget report

Helpful Hint
Which of the following is not likely to help much when costs are variable: the static budget or the flexible budget?
Answer: The static budget.

	A	B	C	D	E
1		**BARTON STEEL**			
2		**Manufacturing Overhead Static Budget Report**			
3		**For the Year Ended December 31, 2016**			
4				Difference	
5		Budget	Actual	Favourable - F Unfavourable - U	
6	Production in units	10,000	12,000		
7					
8	Costs				
9	Indirect materials	$ 250,000	$ 295,000	$ 45,000	U
10	Indirect labour	260,000	312,000	52,000	U
11	Utilities	190,000	225,000	35,000	U
12	Depreciation	280,000	280,000	0	
13	Property taxes	70,000	70,000	0	
14	Supervision	50,000	50,000	0	
15		$1,100,000	$1,232,000	$132,000	U
16					

This comparison uses budget data based on the original activity level (10,000 steel ingots). It indicates that the forging department is significantly over budget for three of the six overhead costs. And, there is a total unfavourable difference of $132,000, which is 12% over budget ($132,000 ÷ $1,100,000). Your supervisor is very unhappy! Instead of sharing in the company's success, you may find yourself looking for another job. What went wrong?

When you calm down and carefully examine the manufacturing overhead budget, you identify the problem: The budget data are not relevant! At the time the budget was developed, the company anticipated that only 10,000 units of steel ingots would be produced, not 12,000 ingots. Comparing actual costs with budgeted variable costs is meaningless. As production increases, the budget allowances for variable costs should increase both directly and proportionately. The variable costs in this example are indirect materials, indirect labour, and utilities.

Analyzing the budget data for these costs at 10,000 units, you arrive at the per-unit results in Illustration 11-8.

▶Illustration 11-8

Variable costs per unit

Item	Total Cost	Per Unit
Indirect materials	$250,000	$25
Indirect labour	260,000	26
Utilities	190,000	19
	$700,000	$70

Illustration 11-9 shows how you can then calculate the budgeted variable costs at 12,000 units.

▶Illustration 11-9

Budgeted variable costs at 12,000 units

Item	Calculation	Total
Indirect materials	$25 × 12,000	$300,000
Indirect labour	$26 × 12,000	312,000
Utilities	$19 × 12,000	228,000
		$840,000

Because fixed costs do not change in total as activity changes, the budgeted amounts for these costs remain the same. Illustration 11-10 shows the budget report based on the flexible budget for 12,000 units of production. (Compare this with Illustration 11-7.)

►Illustration 11-10
Overhead flexible budget report

	A	B	C	D	E
1		**BARTON STEEL**			
2		Manufacturing Overhead Flexible Budget Report			
3		For the Year Ended December 31, 2016			
4				Difference	
5		Budget	Actual	Favourable - F Unfavourable - U	
6	Production in units	12,000	12,000		
7					
8	Variable costs				
9	Indirect materials ($25)	$ 300,000	$ 295,000	**$5,000**	F
10	Indirect labour ($26)	312,000	312,000	**0**	
11	Utilities ($19)	228,000	225,000	**3,000**	F
12	Total variable costs	840,000	832,000	**8,000**	F
13					
14	Fixed costs				
15	Depreciation	280,000	280,000	**0**	
16	Property taxes	70,000	70,000	**0**	
17	Supervision	50,000	50,000	**0**	
18	Total fixed costs	400,000	400,000	**0**	
19	Total costs	$1,240,000	$1,232,000	**$8,000**	F
20					

This report indicates that the forging department is below budget—a favourable difference. Instead of worrying about being fired, you may be in line for a bonus or a raise after all! As this analysis shows, the only appropriate comparison is between actual costs at 12,000 units of production and budgeted costs at 12,000 units. Flexible budget reports provide this comparison.

DEVELOPING THE FLEXIBLE BUDGET

The flexible budget uses the master budget as its basis. To develop the flexible budget, management should take the following steps:

1. Identify the activity index and the relevant range of activity.
2. Identify the variable costs, and determine the budgeted variable cost per unit of activity for each cost.
3. Identify the fixed costs, and determine the budgeted amount for each cost.
4. Prepare the budget for selected increments of activity within the relevant range.

The activity index that management chooses should be something that significantly influences the costs that are being budgeted. For manufacturing overhead costs, for example, the activity index is usually the same as the index used in developing the predetermined overhead rate; that is, direct labour hours or machine hours. For selling and administrative expenses, the activity index is usually sales or net sales.

The choice of the increment of activity is largely a matter of judgement. For example, if the relevant range is 8,000 to 12,000 direct labour hours, increments of 1,000 hours may be selected. The flexible budget is then prepared for each increment within the relevant range.

IFRS Note
Many of the general principles underlying current IFRS and previous Canadian generally accepted accounting principles (GAAP) are the same. However, the application of IFRS principles can result in significant differences from previous GAAP. Therefore, it is important for management to be familiar with the guidance associated with the IFRS standards.

Managers will be accustomed to the way that actual accounting results were recorded under previous Canadian GAAP. Thus, where differences exist between IFRS and previous Canadian GAAP, managers may have some unexpected variances in their budget reports simply due to the change in accounting standards. This change cannot be controlled by the manager, and does not stem from a change in their business practices that they can control.

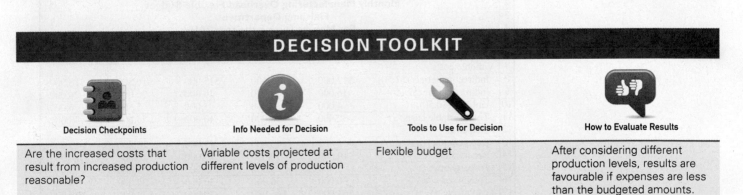

DECISION TOOLKIT

Decision Checkpoints	Info Needed for Decision	Tools to Use for Decision	How to Evaluate Results
Are the increased costs that result from increased production reasonable?	Variable costs projected at different levels of production	Flexible budget	After considering different production levels, results are favourable if expenses are less than the budgeted amounts.

FLEXIBLE BUDGET—A CASE STUDY

To illustrate the flexible budget, we will use Fox Manufacturing Company. Fox's management wants to use a flexible budget for monthly comparisons of its finishing department's actual and budgeted manufacturing overhead costs. The master budget for the year ending December 31, 2016, shows an expected annual operating capacity of 120,000 direct labour hours and the overhead costs shown in Illustration 11-11.

▶Illustration 11-11
Master budget data

Variable Costs		Fixed Costs	
Indirect materials	$180,000	Depreciation	$180,000
Indirect labour	240,000	Supervision	120,000
Utilities	60,000	Property taxes	60,000
Total	$480,000	Total	$360,000

The four steps for developing the flexible budget are applied as follows:

STEP 1: Identify the activity index and the relevant range of activity. The activity index is direct labour hours. Management concludes that the relevant range is 8,000 to 12,000 direct labour hours per month.

STEP 2: Identify the variable costs, and determine the budgeted variable cost per unit of activity for each cost. There are three variable costs. The variable cost per unit is found by dividing each total budgeted cost by the direct labour hours that are used in preparing the master budget (120,000 hours). For Fox Manufacturing, the calculations are as shown in Illustration 11-12.

▶Illustration 11-12
Calculation of variable costs per direct labour hour

Variable Cost	Calculation	Variable Cost per Direct Labour Hour
Indirect materials	$180,000 ÷ 120,000	$1.50
Indirect labour	$240,000 ÷ 120,000	2.00
Utilities	$ 60,000 ÷ 120,000	0.50
Total		$4.00

STEP 3: Identify the fixed costs, and determine the budgeted amount for each cost. There are three fixed costs. Since Fox wants monthly budget data, it finds the budgeted amount by dividing each annual budgeted cost by 12. For Fox, the monthly budgeted fixed costs are depreciation $15,000, supervision $10,000, and property taxes $5,000.

STEP 4: Prepare the budget for selected increments of activity within the relevant range. Management decides to prepare the budget in increments of 1,000 direct labour hours. Illustration 11-13 shows the resulting flexible budget.

▶Illustration 11-13
Flexible monthly overhead budget

	A	B	C	D	E	F
1	**FOX MANUFACTURING COMPANY**					
2	Monthly Manufacturing Overhead Flexible Budget					
3	Finishing Department					
4	For Months During the Year 2016					
5	Activity level					
6	Direct labour hours	8,000	9,000	10,000	11,000	12,000
7	Variable costs					
8	Indirect materials ($1.50)	$12,000	$13,500	$15,000	$16,500	$18,000
9	Indirect labour ($2.00)	16,000	18,000	20,000	22,000	24,000
10	Utilities ($0.50)	4,000	4,500	5,000	5,500	6,000
11	Total variable costs	32,000	36,000	40,000	44,000	48,000
12	Fixed costs					
13	Depreciation	15,000	15,000	15,000	15,000	15,000
14	Supervision	10,000	10,000	10,000	10,000	10,000
15	Property taxes	5,000	5,000	5,000	5,000	5,000
16	Total fixed costs	30,000	30,000	30,000	30,000	30,000
17	Total costs	$62,000	$66,000	$70,000	$74,000	$78,000
18						

Using the budget data, management can use the formula in Illustration 11-14 to determine the total budgeted costs at any level of activity.

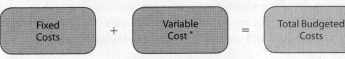

* Total variable cost per unit times the activity level

►Illustration 11-14
Formula for total budgeted costs

Helpful Hint
Using the data given for the Fox Manufacturing Company, what amount of costs would be budgeted for 10,600 direct labour hours? Answer:

Fixed	$30,000
Variable (10,600 × $4)	42,400
Total	$72,400

For Fox Manufacturing, fixed costs are $30,000, and the total variable cost per unit is $4. Thus, at 9,000 direct labour hours, the total budgeted costs are $66,000 [$30,000 + ($4 × 9,000)]. Similarly, at 8,622 direct labour hours, the total budgeted costs are $64,488 [$30,000 + ($4 × 8,622)].

The total budgeted costs can also be shown graphically, as in Illustration 11-15. In the graph, the activity index is shown on the horizontal axis, and costs are indicated on the vertical axis. The graph highlights two activity levels (10,000 and 12,000). As shown, total budgeted costs at these activity levels are $70,000 [$30,000 + ($4 × 10,000)] and $78,000 [$30,000 + ($4 × 12,000)], respectively.

►Illustration 11-15
Flexible budget data graphic—highlighting activity levels of 10,000 and 12,000 hours

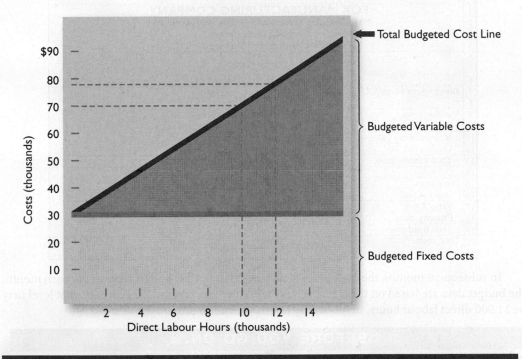

BEFORE YOU GO ON...

►Do It! Flexible Budgets

In Strassel Company's flexible budget graph, the fixed cost line and the total budgeted cost line intersect the vertical axis at $36,000. The total budgeted cost line is $186,000 at an activity level of 50,000 direct labour hours. Calculate total budgeted costs at 30,000 direct labour hours.

Action Plan

- Apply the formula: Fixed costs + Variable costs (Total variable cost per unit × Activity level) = Total budgeted costs.

Solution

Using the graph, fixed costs are $36,000, and variable costs are $3 per direct labour hour [($186,000 − $36,000) ÷ 50,000]. Thus, at 30,000 direct labour hours, total budgeted costs are $126,000 [$36,000 + ($3 × 30,000)].

Related exercise material: **BE11-4, E11-19, E11-21,** and **Do It! D11-13**.

the navigator

FLEXIBLE BUDGET REPORTS

Flexible budget reports are another type of internal report. The flexible budget report has two sections: (1) production data for a selected activity index, such as direct labour hours, and (2) cost data for variable and fixed costs. The report provides a basis for evaluating a manager's performance in two areas: production control and cost control. Flexible budget reports are widely used in production and service departments.

Illustration 11-16 shows a budget report for the finishing department of Fox Company for the month of January. In this month, 9,000 hours were worked. The budget data are therefore based on the flexible budget for 9,000 hours in Illustration 11-13. The actual cost data are assumed.

How appropriate is this report for evaluating the finishing department manager's performance in controlling overhead costs? The report clearly provides a reliable basis. Both the actual and the budget costs are based on the activity level worked during January. Since variable costs are generally incurred directly by the department, the department manager is responsible for the difference between the costs budgeted for those hours and the actual costs.

▸Illustration 11-16
Flexible overhead budget report

	A	B	C	D	E
1	**FOX MANUFACTURING COMPANY**				
2	Manufacturing Overhead Flexible Budget Report				
3	Finishing Department				
4	For the Month Ended January 31, 2016				
5				Difference	
6		Budget at	Actual costs at	Favourable - F Unfavourable - U	
7	Direct labour hours (DLH)	9,000 DLH	9,000 DLH		
8					
9	Variable costs				
10	Indirect materials ($1.50)	$13,500	$14,000	$ 500	U
11	Indirect labour ($2.00)	18,000	17,000	1,000	F
12	Utilities ($0.50)	4,500	4,600	100	U
13	Total variable costs	36,000	35,600	400	F
14					
15	Fixed costs				
16	Depreciation	15,000	15,000	0	
17	Supervision	10,000	10,000	0	
18	Property taxes	5,000	5,000	0	
19	Total fixed costs	30,000	30,000	0	
20	Total costs	$66,000	$65,600	$ 400	F
21					

In subsequent months, the company will prepare other flexible budget reports. For each month, the budget data are based on the actual activity level that was reached. In February, that level may be 11,000 direct labour hours, in July it may be 10,000, and so on.

BEFORE YOU GO ON...

▸Do It! Flexible Budget Reports

Lawler Company expects to produce 40,000 units of product CV93 during the current year. Budgeted variable manufacturing costs per unit are direct materials $6, direct labour $15, and overhead $24. Annual budgeted fixed manufacturing overhead costs are $120,000 for depreciation and $60,000 for supervision.

In the current month, Lawler produced 5,000 units and incurred the following costs: direct materials $33,900, direct labour $74,200, variable overhead $120,500, depreciation $10,000, and supervision $5,000.

Prepare a flexible budget report. (*Note:* You do not have to prepare the heading.) Were costs controlled?

Action Plan

- Use budget for actual units produced.
- Classify each cost as variable or fixed.
- Determine monthly fixed costs by dividing annual amounts by 12.
- Determine the difference as favourable or unfavourable.
- Determine the difference in total variable costs, total fixed costs, and total costs.

(continued)

(continued)

Solution

	A	B	C	D	E
1				Difference	
2		Budget at	Actual costs at	Favourable - F Unfavourable - U	
3	Units produced	5,000 units	5,000 units		
4					
5	Variable costs				
6	Direct materials ($6)	$ 30,000	$ 33,900	$3,900	U
7	Direct labour ($15)	75,000	74,200	800	F
8	Overhead ($24)	120,000	120,500	500	U
9	Total variable costs	225,000	228,600	3,600	U
10					
11	Fixed costs				
12	Depreciation	10,000	10,000	0	
13	Supervision	5,000	5,000	0	
14	Total fixed costs	15,000	15,000	0	
15	Total costs	$240,000	$243,600	$3,600	U
16					
17					

The budget report indicates that actual direct labour was only about 1% different from the budget, and overhead was less than half a percent different. Both appear to have been well controlled.

This was not the case for direct materials. Its 13% unfavourable difference should probably be investigated.

Actual fixed costs had no difference from budget and were well controlled.

Related exercise material: **BE11-5, E11-20, E11-22,** and **Do It! D11-14.**

Responsibility Accounting for Cost and Profit Centres

THE RESPONSIBILITY ACCOUNTING CONCEPT

Like budgeting, responsibility accounting is an important part of management accounting. **Responsibility accounting** involves accumulating and reporting costs (and revenues, where relevant) that involve the manager who has the authority to make the day-to-day decisions about the cost items. Illustration 11-17 shows some examples.

STUDY OBJECTIVE 3
Apply responsibility accounting to cost and profit centres.

►Illustration 11-17
Responsibility for controllable costs at varying levels of management

Department Manager   Division Manager   President

Under responsibility accounting, a manager's performance is evaluated based on matters that are directly under that manager's control. Responsibility accounting can be used at every level of management where the following conditions exist:

1. Costs and revenues can be directly associated with the specific level of management responsibility.
2. The costs and revenues are controllable at the level of responsibility that they are associated with.
3. Budget data can be developed for evaluating the manager's effectiveness in controlling the costs and revenues.

Under responsibility accounting, any individual who has control and is accountable for a specified set of activities can be recognized as a responsibility centre. Thus, responsibility accounting may extend from the lowest level of control to the top layers of management. Once responsibility has been established, the effectiveness of an individual's performance is first measured and reported for the specified activity. It is then reported upward throughout the organization.

Responsibility accounting is especially valuable in a decentralized company. **Decentralization** means that the control of operations is given to many managers throughout the organization. The term **segment** is sometimes used to identify an area of responsibility in decentralized operations. Under responsibility accounting, segment reports are prepared periodically, such as monthly, quarterly, and annually, to evaluate a manager's performance.

Responsibility accounting is an essential part of any effective system of budgetary control. The reporting of costs and revenues under responsibility accounting differs from budgeting in two ways:

1. A distinction is made between controllable and noncontrollable items.
2. Performance reports either emphasize or include only the items that the individual manager can control.

Responsibility accounting applies to both profit and not-for-profit entities. For-profit entities seek to maximize net income. Not-for-profit entities wish to provide services as efficiently as possible.

CONTROLLABLE VERSUS NONCONTROLLABLE REVENUES AND COSTS

All costs and revenues can be controlled at some level of responsibility within a company. This truth emphasizes the adage used by the CEO of any organization that "the buck stops here." Under responsibility accounting, the critical issue is whether or not the cost or revenue can be controlled at the level of responsibility that it is associated with.

A cost is considered to be **controllable** at a particular level of managerial responsibility if the manager has the power to incur it in a specific period of time. From this criterion, the following can be concluded:

1. All costs are controllable by top management because of its broad range of authority.
2. Fewer costs are controllable as one moves down to each lower level of managerial responsibility because the manager's authority decreases at each level.

In general, costs that a level of responsibility directly incurs can be controlled at that level. In contrast, costs that are incurred indirectly and allocated to a responsibility level are considered to be **noncontrollable** at that level.

RESPONSIBILITY REPORTING SYSTEM

In a **responsibility reporting system**, a report is prepared for each level of responsibility in the company's organization chart. To illustrate such a system, we will use the partial organization chart and production departments of Francis Chair Company shown in Illustration 11-18.

The responsibility reporting system begins with the lowest level of responsibility for controlling costs and moves upward to each higher level. Illustration 11-19 shows the connections between levels.

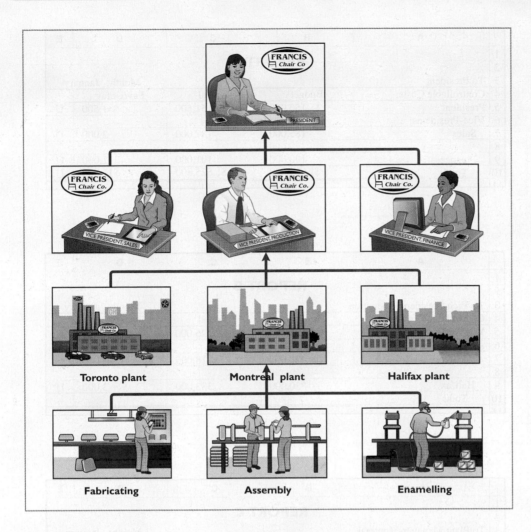

▶Illustration 11-18
Partial organization chart

Report A
President sees summary data of vice-presidents.

Report B
Vice-president sees summary of controllable costs in his/her functional area.

Report C
Plant manager sees summary of controllable costs for each department in the plant.

Report D
Department manager sees controllable costs of his/her department.

Following are brief descriptions of the four reports for Francis Chair Company:

1. **Report D** is typical of reports that go to managers at the lowest level of responsibility shown in the organization chart—department managers. Similar reports are prepared for the managers of the fabricating, assembling, and enamelling departments.
2. **Report C** is an example of reports that are sent to plant managers. It shows the costs of the Montreal plant that are controllable at the second level of responsibility. In addition, Report C shows summary data for each department that the plant manager controls. Similar reports are prepared for the Toronto and Halifax plant managers.
3. **Report B** is a report at the third level of responsibility. It shows the controllable costs of the vice-president of production and summary data on the three assembly plants that this officer is responsible for.
4. **Report A** is typical of the reports that go to the top level of responsibility—the president. This report shows the controllable costs and expenses of this position and summary data on the vice-presidents who are accountable to the president.

A responsibility reporting system makes it possible to use management by exception at each level of responsibility. In addition, each higher level of responsibility can obtain the detailed report for each lower level of responsibility. For example, the vice-president of production at the Francis Chair Company may ask to see the Montreal plant manager's report because this plant is $5,300 over budget (see Illustration 11-19).

This type of reporting system also makes it possible to do comparative evaluations. In Illustration 11-19, the Montreal plant manager can easily rank each department manager's effectiveness in controlling manufacturing costs. Comparative rankings provide further incentive for

►Illustration 11-19
Responsibility reporting system

Report A
President sees summary
data of vice-presidents.

	A	B	C	D	E
1		**REPORT A**			
2					
3	To President			Month: January	
4	Controllable Costs:	Budget	Actual	Fav/Unfav	
5	President	$ 150,000	$ 151,500	$ 1,500	U
6	Vice-Presidents:				
7	Sales	185,000	187,000	2,000	U
8	**Production**	**1,179,000**	**1,186,300**	**7,300**	U
9	Finance	100,000	101,000	1,000	U
10	Total	$1,614,000	$1,625,800	$11,800	U
11					

Report B
Vice-president sees sum-
mary of controllable costs
in his/her functional area.

	A	B	C	D	E
1		**REPORT B**			
2					
3	To Vice-President Production			Month: January	
4	Controllable Costs:	Budget	Actual	Fav/Unfav	
5	V P Production	$ 125,000	$ 126,000	$1,000	U
6	Assembly Plants:				
7	Toronto	420,000	418,000	2,000	F
8	**Montreal**	**304,000**	**309,300**	**5,300**	U
9	Halifax	330,000	333,000	3,000	U
10	Total	**$1,179,000**	**$1,186,300**	**$7,300**	U
11					

Report C
Plant manager sees sum-
mary of controllable costs
for each department in the
plant.

	A	B	C	D	E
1		**REPORT C**			
2					
3	To Plant Manager-Montreal			Month: January	
4	Controllable Costs:	Budget	Actual	Fav/Unfav	
5	Montreal Plant	$110,000	$113,000	$3,000	U
6	Departments:				
7	**Fabricating**	**84,000**	**85,300**	**1,300**	U
8	Enamelling	62,000	64,000	2,000	U
9	Assembly	48,000	47,000	1,000	F
10	Total	**$304,000**	**$309,300**	**$5,300**	U
11					

Report D
Department manager sees
controllable costs of
his/her department.

	A	B	C	D	E
1		**REPORT D**			
2					
3	To Fabricating Department Manager			Month: January	
4	Controllable Costs:	Budget	Actual	Fav/Unfav	
5	Direct Materials	$20,000	$20,500	$ 500	U
6	Direct Labour	40,000	41,000	1,000	U
7	Overhead	24,000	23,800	200	F
8	Total	**$84,000**	**$85,300**	**$1,300**	U
9					

a manager to control costs. For example, the Toronto plant manager will want to continue to be number one in the report to the vice-president of production. The Montreal plant manager will not want to remain number three in future reporting periods.

BUSINESS INSIGHT *Responsibility Accounting in Municipalities*

Managers in government organizations are responsible for their department's spending to elected officials, who are accountable for overall spending to taxpayers. Governments use budgets to forecast and control spending, and financial reports to show taxpayers what was actually spent. But sometimes, those numbers don't add up. A 2014 study by the C. D. Howe Institute examined a decade of municipal budgets and financial reports in major Canadian cities. The study authors found that in some cities, the amounts of actual spending in financial reports at year end varied by up to 20% from the projected spending in the cities' budgets. The study authors say these gaps are not usually due to uncontrolled spending or inaccurate forecasting, but rather are due to the fact that many municipalities use different accounting treatments for budgets than for financial reports. "Most of Canada's senior governments use modern 'accrual' accounting that matches the costs of long-lived assets such as buildings and infrastructure to the period they deliver their services," said Benjamin Dachis, one of the study's authors. "Most municipal budgets, by contrast, show that year's cash outlays on capital, exaggerating the up-front cost of major projects, and understating their later expenses." In other words, "It's treating a 50-year infrastructure project the same as you would a cup of coffee," said William Robson, the other author. The study authors said that municipalities should use the same accounting treatments for budgets and financial reports to improve accountability and transparency to elected officials and taxpayers.

Sources: Alex Ballingall, "C. D. Howe Report Slams City Accounting," *The Toronto Star*, January 15, 2014; "Report Shows Cities with Best and Worst Fiscal Accountability—C. D. Howe Institute," C. D. Howe Institute news release, January 15, 2014; Benjamin Dachis and William B. P. Robson, "Baffling Budgets: Canada's Cities Need Better Financial Reporting," C. D. Howe Institute, Commentary No. 397, January 2014.

Should municipalities adopt the accrual method for both budgets and financial reports? Why or why not?

PRINCIPLES OF PERFORMANCE EVALUATION

Performance evaluation is at the centre of responsibility accounting. **Performance evaluation** is a management function that compares actual results with budget goals. Performance evaluation uses both behavioural and reporting principles.

Management by Exception

Management by exception means that top management's review of a budget report is focused either entirely or mostly on differences between actual results and planned objectives. This approach helps top management focus on problem areas. Management by exception does not mean that top management will investigate every difference. For this approach to be effective, there must be guidelines for identifying an exception. The usual criteria are materiality and controllability.

Materiality

Without quantitative guidelines, management would have to investigate every budget difference no matter how small it was. Materiality is usually expressed as a percentage difference from the budget. For example, management may set the percentage difference at 5% for important items and 10% for other items. The company will investigate all differences that are over or under budget by at least the specified percentage. The company should investigate costs that are over budget to determine why they were not controlled. Likewise, it should investigate costs that are under budget to determine whether costs that are critical to profitability are being cut too much. For example, if maintenance costs are budgeted at $80,000 but only $40,000 is spent, there could be major, unexpected breakdowns in production facilities in the future.

IFRS Note
IAS 1 *Presentation of Financial Statements* defines *materiality* as "Omissions or misstatements of items are material if they could, individually or collectively, influence the economic decisions that users make on the basis of the financial statements. Materiality depends on the size and nature of the omission or misstatement judged in the surrounding circumstances. The size or nature of the item, or a combination of both, could be the determining factor." It also indicates that this assessment may require consideration of the characteristics of those users. Note that this financial accounting definition of materiality can be different than the materiality level chosen for management by exception in order to determine which variances should be investigated further.

Alternatively, a company may specify a single percentage difference from budget for all items and add a minimum dollar limit as well. For example, the exception criterion may be stated at 5% of budget or more than $10,000.

Controllability of the Item

Exception guidelines are usually more for controllable items than for items that the manager cannot control. In fact, there may be no guidelines for noncontrollable items. For example, a large unfavourable difference between the actual and budgeted property tax expense may not be flagged for investigation because the only possible cause is an unexpected increase in the tax rate or in the assessed value of the property. An investigation into the difference will be useless: the manager cannot control the cause.

Behavioural Principles

The human factor is critical in evaluating performance. Behavioural principles include the following:

1. **Managers of responsibility centres should be directly involved in setting budget goals for their areas of responsibility.** Without such involvement, managers may view the goals as unrealistic or arbitrarily set by top management. Such views can decrease the managers' motivation to meet the targeted objectives.
2. **The evaluation of performance should be based entirely on matters that can be controlled by the manager being evaluated.** Criticism of a manager for matters that he or she cannot control reduces the effectiveness of the evaluation process. It leads to negative reactions by the manager and to doubts about the fairness of the company's evaluation policies.
3. **Top management should support the evaluation process.** As explained earlier, the evaluation process begins at the lowest level of responsibility and extends upward to the highest level of management. Managers quickly lose trust in the process when top management ignores, overrules, or bypasses established procedures for evaluating a manager's performance.
4. **The evaluation process must allow managers to respond to their evaluations.** Evaluation is not a one-way street. Managers should have the opportunity to defend their performance. Evaluation without feedback is impersonal and ineffective.
5. **The evaluation should identify both good and poor performance.** Praise for good performance is a powerful motivating factor for a manager. This is especially true when a manager's compensation includes rewards for meeting budget goals.

Reporting Principles

Performance evaluation under responsibility accounting should be based on certain reporting principles. These principles relate mostly to the internal reports that provide the basis for evaluating performance. Performance reports should

1. contain only data that are controllable by the manager of the responsibility centre,
2. provide accurate and reliable budget data to measure performance,
3. highlight significant differences between actual results and budget goals,
4. be tailor-made for the intended evaluation, and
5. be prepared at reasonable intervals.

Helpful Hint
(1) Is the jewellery department of Hudson's Bay a profit centre or a cost centre? (2) Is the props department of a movie studio a profit centre or a cost centre? Answers: (1) Profit centre. (2) Cost centre.

ACCOUNTING FOR VARIOUS RESPONSIBILITY CENTRES

There are three basic types of responsibility centres: cost centres, profit centres, and investment centres. These centres indicate the degree of responsibility the manager has for the performance of the centre.

A **cost centre** incurs costs (and expenses) but does not directly generate revenues. Managers of cost centres have the authority to incur costs. They are evaluated on their ability to control costs. Cost centres are usually either production departments or service departments. The former participate directly in making the product. The latter provide only support services. In a Ford Motor Company of Canada automobile plant, the welding, painting, and assembling departments are production departments; the maintenance, cafeteria, and human resources departments are service departments. All of them are cost centres.

A **profit centre** incurs costs (and expenses) and also generates revenues. Managers of profit centres are judged on the profitability of their centres. Examples of profit centres include the individual departments of a retail store, such as clothing, furniture, and automotive products, and branch offices of banks.

Like a profit centre, an **investment centre** incurs costs (and expenses) and generates revenues. In addition, an investment centre has control over the investment funds that are available for use. Managers of investment centres are evaluated on both the profitability of the centre and the rate of return earned on the funds invested. Investment centres are often associated with product lines and subsidiary companies. For example, General Mills' product lines include cereals, helper dinner mixes, fruit snacks, popcorn, and yogurt. And, in our feature story, Bombardier has two operating segments: aerospace and transportation. The manager of an investment centre (product line) is able to control or significantly influence investment decisions for such matters as plant expansion and entry into new market areas. Illustration 11-20 shows these three types of responsibility centres.

The remainder of this chapter explains the evaluation of a manager's performance in each type of responsibility centre.

Responsibility Accounting for Cost Centres

A manager's performance in a cost centre is evaluated based on his or her ability to meet budgeted goals for controllable costs. Responsibility reports for cost centres compare actual controllable costs with flexible budget data.

Illustration 11-21 shows a responsibility report. The report is adapted from the flexible budget report for Fox Manufacturing Company in Illustration 11-16. It assumes that the finishing department manager is able to control all manufacturing overhead costs except depreciation, property taxes, and his own monthly salary of $6,000. The remaining $4,000 of supervision costs are assumed to be for other supervisory personnel in the finishing department, whose salaries the manager can control.

Types of responsibility centres

Expenses   Revenues
Cost Centre

Expenses + Revenues
Profit Centre

Expenses + Revenues + Return on Investments
Investment Centre

	A	B	C	D	E
1	**FOX MANUFACTURING COMPANY**				
2	Finishing Department				
3	Responsibility Report				
4	For the Month Ended January 31, 2016				
5				Difference	
6	Controllable Cost	Budget	Actual	Favourable - F Unfavourable - U	
7	Indirect materials	$13,500	$14,000	$ 500	U
8	Indirect labour	18,000	17,000	$1,000	F
9	Utilities	4,500	4,600	100	U
10	**Supervision**	**4,000**	**4,000**	**0**	
11		$40,000	$39,600	$ 400	F
12					

Responsibility report for a cost centre

Only controllable costs are included in the report, and no distinction is made between variable and fixed costs. The responsibility report continues the concept of management by exception. In this case, top management may want an explanation for the $1,000 favourable difference in indirect labour and/or the $500 unfavourable difference in indirect materials.

Responsibility Accounting for Profit Centres

To evaluate the performance of a manager of a profit centre, detailed information is needed about both the controllable revenues and the controllable costs. The operating revenues that are earned by a profit centre, such as sales, are controllable by the manager. All variable costs (and expenses) that are incurred by the centre can also be controlled by the manager because they vary with sales. However, to determine the controllability of fixed costs, it is necessary to distinguish between direct and indirect fixed costs.

Direct and Indirect Fixed Costs.   A profit centre may have both direct and indirect fixed costs. **Direct fixed costs** are costs that are specifically for one centre and are incurred for the benefit of that centre alone. Examples of such costs include the salaries established by the profit centre manager for supervisory personnel and the cost of a timekeeping department for the centre's employees. Since these fixed costs can be traced directly to a centre, they are also called **traceable costs. Most direct fixed costs are controllable by the profit centre manager.**

In contrast, **indirect fixed costs** are for a company's overall operating activities and are incurred for the benefit of more than one profit centre. Indirect fixed costs are allocated to profit centres according to some type of equitable basis. For example, property taxes on a building that is occupied by more than one centre may be allocated based on the area of floor space used by each centre. Or, the costs of a company's human resources department may be allocated to profit centres based on the number of employees in each centre. Because these fixed costs apply to more than one centre, they are also called **common costs. Most indirect fixed costs cannot be controlled by the profit centre manager.**

Responsibility Report.   The responsibility report for a profit centre shows the budgeted and actual controllable revenues and costs. The report is prepared using the cost-volume-profit income statement explained in Chapter 6 and has the following features:

1. Controllable fixed costs are deducted from the contribution margin.
2. The amount by which the contribution margin is greater than the controllable fixed costs is identified as the **controllable margin**.
3. Noncontrollable fixed costs are not reported.

Illustration 11-22 shows the responsibility report for the manager of the marine division, a profit centre of Mantle Manufacturing Company. For the year, the marine division also had $60,000 of indirect fixed costs that were not controllable by the profit centre manager.

▶Illustration 11-22

Responsibility report for profit centre

Helpful Hint
Note that we are emphasizing financial measures of performance. These days, companies are also trying to stress non-financial performance measures, such as product quality, labour productivity, market growth, materials' yield, manufacturing flexibility, and technological capability.

Helpful Hint
Responsibility reports are helpful tools for evaluating managerial performance. Too much emphasis on profits or investments, however, can be harmful because it ignores other important performance issues, such as quality and social responsibility.

	A	B	C	D	E
1	**MANTLE MANUFACTURING COMPANY**				
2	Marine Division				
3	Responsibility Report				
4	For the Year Ended December 31, 2016				
5				Difference	
6		Budget	Actual	Favourable - F Unfavourable - U	
7	Sales	$1,200,000	$1,150,000	$50,000	U
8	Variable costs				
9	Cost of goods sold	500,000	490,000	10,000	F
10	Selling and administrative	160,000	156,000	4,000	F
11	Total	660,000	646,000	14,000	F
12	Contribution margin	540,000	504,000	36,000	U
13	**Controllable fixed costs**				
14	Cost of goods sold	100,000	100,000	0	
15	Selling and administrative	80,000	80,000	0	
16	Total	180,000	180,000	0	
17	**Controllable margin**	**$ 360,000**	**$ 324,000**	**$36,000**	**U**
18					

The controllable margin is considered to be the best measure of the manager's performance in controlling revenues and costs. This report shows that the manager's performance was below budgeted expectations by 10% ($36,000 ÷ $360,000). Top management would likely investigate the causes of this unfavourable result. Note that the report does not show the marine division's noncontrollable fixed costs of $60,000. These costs would be included in a report on the profitability of the profit centre.

Responsibility reports for profit centres may also be prepared monthly. In addition, they may include cumulative year-to-date results.

DECISION TOOLKIT

Decision Checkpoints	**Info Needed for Decision**	**Tools to Use for Decision**	**How to Evaluate Results**
Have the individual managers been held accountable for the costs and revenues under their control?	Relevant costs and revenues, where the individual manager has authority to make day-to-day decisions about the items	Responsibility reports focused on cost centres, profit centres, and investment centres, as appropriate	Compare the budget with actual costs and revenues for controllable items.

BEFORE YOU GO ON...

▶Do It! Responsibility Report

Prairie Division operates as a profit centre. It reports the following actual results for the year: sales $1.7 million; variable costs $800,000; controllable fixed costs $400,000; and noncontrollable fixed costs $200,000. The annual budgeted amounts were $1.5 million, $700,000, $400,000, and $200,000, respectively. Prepare a responsibility report for Prairie Division at December 31, 2016.

Action Plan

- Deduct variable costs from sales to show the contribution margin.
- Deduct controllable fixed costs from the contribution margin to show the controllable margin.
- Do not report noncontrollable fixed costs.

Solution

PRAIRIE DIVISION
Responsibility Report
Year Ended December 31, 2016

	Budget	Actual	Difference: Favourable (F)/ Unfavourable (U)
Sales	$1,500,000	$1,700,000	$200,000 F
Variable costs	700,000	800,000	100,000 U
Contribution margin	800,000	900,000	100,000 F
Controllable fixed costs	400,000	400,000	0
Controllable margin	$ 400,000	$ 500,000	$100,000 F

Related exercise material: **BE11-7, E11-29,** and **Do It! D11-15.**

the navigator

Evaluating Performance in Investment Centres

As explained earlier, an investment centre manager can control or significantly influence the investment funds that are available for use. Thus, the main basis for evaluating the performance of a manager of an investment centre is the **return on investment (ROI)**. The return on investment is considered to be a useful performance measurement because it shows **how effectively the manager uses the assets at his or her disposal**.

RETURN ON INVESTMENT (ROI)

Illustration 11-23 shows the formula for calculating the ROI for an investment centre, using assumed data. The investment centre manager can control both factors in the formula. Operating assets consist of the current assets and plant assets that are used in operations by the centre and are controlled by

STUDY OBJECTIVE 4
Explain the basis and formula used for evaluating performance in investment centres.

the manager. Non-operating assets, such as idle plant assets and land held for future use, are excluded. Average operating assets are usually based on the assets' cost or book value at the beginning and end of the year.

▶Illustration 11-23
ROI formula

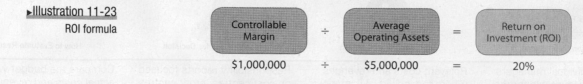

Controllable Margin	÷	Average Operating Assets	=	Return on Investment (ROI)
$1,000,000	÷	$5,000,000	=	20%

RESPONSIBILITY REPORT

The scope of the investment centre manager's responsibility significantly affects the content of the performance report. Since an investment centre is an independent entity for operating purposes, **all fixed costs are controllable by its manager**. This means, for example, that the manager is even responsible for depreciation on the investment centre's assets. This also means that—compared with performance reports for profit centre managers—more fixed costs are classified as controllable in performance reports for investment centre managers. The report also shows the budgeted and actual ROI on a line beneath the controllable margin.

To illustrate this responsibility report, we will now assume that the marine division of Mantle Manufacturing Company is an investment centre. It has budgeted and actual average operating assets of $2 million. We also assume that the manager can control the $60,000 of fixed costs that were not controllable when the division was a profit centre. Illustration 11-24 shows the responsibility report.

▶Illustration 11-24
Responsibility report for investment centre

	A	B	C	D	E
1	**MANTLE MANUFACTURING COMPANY**				
2	Marine Division				
3	Responsibility Report				
4	For the Year Ended December 31, 2016				
5				Difference	
6		Budget	Actual	Favourable - F Unfavourable - U	
7	Sales	$1,200,000	$1,150,000	$ 50,000	U
8	Variable costs				
9	Cost of goods sold	500,000	490,000	10,000	F
10	Selling and administrative	160,000	156,000	4,000	F
11	Total	660,000	646,000	14,000	F
12	Contribution margin	540,000	504,000	36,000	U
13	**Controllable fixed costs**				
14	Cost of goods sold	100,000	100,000	0	
15	Selling and administrative	80,000	80,000	0	
16	**Other fixed costs**	**60,000**	**60,000**	**0**	
17	Total	240,000	240,000	0	
18	**Controllable margin**	**$ 300,000**	**$ 264,000**	**$ 36,000**	U
19	**Return on investment**	**15.0%**	**13.2%**	**1.8%**	U
20		(a)	(b)	(c)	
21					
22		(a) $ 300,000 / $2,000,000	(b) $ 264,000 / $2,000,000	(c) $ 36,000 / $2,000,000	
23					

The report shows that the manager's performance based on the ROI was 12% (1.8% ÷ 15%) below budget expectations. Top management would likely want to know the reasons for this unfavourable result.

JUDGEMENTAL FACTORS IN ROI

The return on investment approach includes two judgemental factors:

1. **Valuation of operating assets**. Operating assets may be valued at their acquisition cost, book value, appraised value, or market value. The first two values are easily found in the accounting records.
2. **Margin (income) measure**. This measure may be the controllable margin, income from operations, or net income.

Each of the alternative values for operating assets can be a reliable basis for evaluating a manager's performance, as long as it is consistently used between reporting periods. However, the use of income measures other than the controllable margin will not result in a valid basis for evaluating the performance of an investment centre manager.[1]

IMPROVING ROI

To determine what factors are driving a division's ROI, managers often restate the ROI formula into its expanded form, as shown in Illustration 11-25.

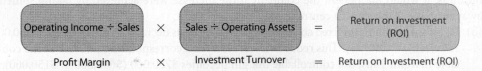

▶Illustration 11-25
ROI expanded form

This expanded formula of ROI helps managers to better understand how to improve the ROI. The first term in the expanded formula is *profit margin*, which focuses on profitability. It shows how the operating margin can be improved by increasing the margin on each dollar of sales. It measures managers' abilities to control the operating expenses that are related to sales during a specific period. The second term of the expanded formula is *investment turnover*, which focuses on efficiency. It shows how investment turnover can be improved by generating more sales for each dollar invested. This expanded formula of ROI is widely known as DuPont profitability analysis. The formula originated at the DuPont Company so that its results from a wider range of business activities could be compared.

The manager of an investment centre can improve the ROI in two ways: (1) increase the controllable margin, and/or (2) reduce the average operating assets. To illustrate, we will use the data in Illustration 11-26 for the marine division of Mantle Manufacturing.

Sales	$2,000,000
Variable costs	1,100,000
Contribution margin (45%)	900,000
Controllable fixed costs	300,000
Controllable margin (a)	$ 600,000
Average operating assets (b)	$5,000,000
Return on investment [(a) ÷ (b)]	12%

▶Illustration 11-26
Assumed data for the marine division

Using the expanded form, the current ROI for the marine division of Mantle Manufacturing can be calculated as shown in Illustration 11-27.

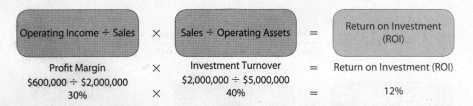

▶Illustration 11-27
Using the expanded form of the ROI formula to calculate the current ROI

Now assume that management adopts a 15% ROI target instead of 12%. This can be achieved by:

1. **Increasing the Controllable Margin.** The controllable margin can be increased by increasing sales or by reducing the variable and controllable fixed costs as follows:
   (a) **Increasing sales by 25%.** Sales increase by $500,000 ($2,000,000 × 0.25). Assuming that there is no change in the contribution margin percentage of 45%, the contribution margin will increase by $225,000 ($500,000 × 0.45). The controllable margin will increase by $150,000 because the controllable fixed costs will increase by 25%. Thus, the controllable margin becomes $750,000 ($1,125,000 − $375,000). The new ROI is 15%, as calculated in Illustration 11-28.

---

[1]Although the ROI approach is often used in evaluating investment performance, it has some disadvantages. The appendix to this chapter illustrates a second method for evaluation, referred to as the residual income approach.

►Illustration 11-28
ROI calculation—increase in sales

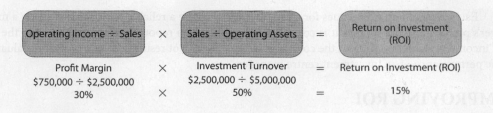

Profit Margin	×	Investment Turnover	=	Return on Investment (ROI)
$750,000 ÷ $2,500,000	×	$2,500,000 ÷ $5,000,000	=	
30%	×	50%	=	15%

An increase in sales benefits both the investment centre and the company if it results in new business. It would not benefit the company if the increase were achieved by taking something away from other investment centres.

(b) **Decrease variable and fixed costs by 10.72%.** Total costs decrease by $150,000[2] [($1,100,000 + $300,000) × 0.10715]. This reduction will result in a corresponding increase in the controllable margin. Thus, the controllable margin becomes $750,000 ($600,000 + $150,000). The new ROI is 15%, as calculated in Illustration 11-29.

►Illustration 11-29
ROI calculation—decrease in costs

$$ \text{ROI} = \frac{\text{Controllable margin}}{\text{Average operating assets}} = \frac{\$750,000}{\$5,000,000} = 15\% $$

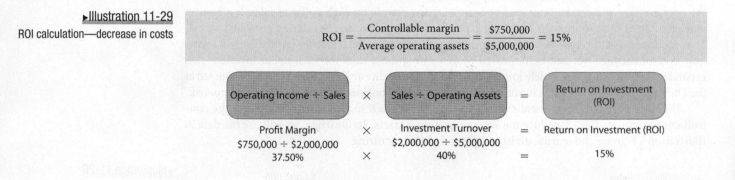

Profit Margin	×	Investment Turnover	=	Return on Investment (ROI)
$750,000 ÷ $2,000,000	×	$2,000,000 ÷ $5,000,000	=	
37.50%	×	40%	=	15%

This type of action is clearly beneficial if it eliminates waste and inefficiencies. But a reduction in such vital costs as required maintenance and inspections is not likely to be acceptable to top management.

2. **Reducing the Average Operating Assets.** Assume that the average operating assets are reduced by 20% or $1 million ($5,000,000 × 0.20). The average operating assets become $4 million ($5,000,000 − $1,000,000). Since the controllable margin remains unchanged at $600,000, the new ROI is 15%, as calculated in Illustration 11-30.

►Illustration 11-30
ROI calculation—decrease in operating assets

$$ \text{ROI} = \frac{\text{Controllable margin}}{\text{Average operating assets}} = \frac{\$600,000}{\$4,000,000} = 15\% $$

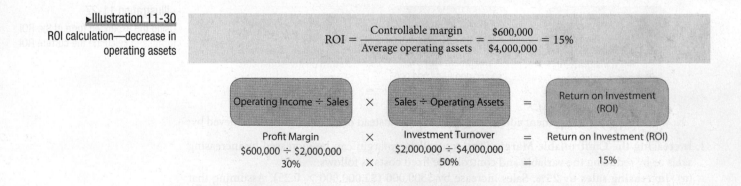

Profit Margin	×	Investment Turnover	=	Return on Investment (ROI)
$600,000 ÷ $2,000,000	×	$2,000,000 ÷ $4,000,000	=	
30%	×	50%	=	15%

Reductions in operating assets may or may not be wise. It is good to eliminate excessive inventories and to dispose of unneeded plant assets. However, it is unwise to reduce inventories below expected needs or to dispose of essential plant assets.

---

[2]Rounding to the nearest $100.

DECISION TOOLKIT

Decision Checkpoints	**Info Needed for Decision**	**Tools to Use for Decision**	**How to Evaluate Results**
Has the investment centre performed up to expectations?	The controllable margin (contribution margin minus controllable fixed costs), and average investment centre operating assets	Return on investment	Compare the actual ROI with the expected ROI.

BEFORE YOU GO ON...

▶Do It! ROI for Investment Centres

The service division of Metro Industries reported the following results for 2016.

Sales	$400,000
Variable costs	320,000
Controllable fixed costs	40,800
Average operating assets	280,000

Management is considering the following independent courses of action in 2017 in order to maximize the return on investment for this division.

1. Reduce average operating assets by $80,000, with no change in controllable margin.

2. Increase sales by $80,000, with no change in the contribution margin percentage.

(a) Calculate the controllable margin and the return on investment for 2016.

(b) Calculate the controllable margin and the expected return on investment for each proposed alternative.

Action Plan

Recall key formulas: Contribution margin = Sales − Variable costs
- Contribution margin percentage = Contribution margin ÷ Sales
- Controllable margin = Contribution margin − Controllable fixed costs
- Return on investment = Controllable margin ÷ Average operating assets
- Return on investment = Profit margin × Investment turnover (expanded form)

Solution

(a) Return on investment for 2016

Sales	$400,000
Variable costs	320,000
Contribution margin	80,000
Controllable fixed costs	40,800
Controllable margin	$ 39,200

$$\text{Return on investment} \quad \frac{\$39,200}{\$280,000} = 14\%$$

(b) Expected return on investment for alternative 1:

$$\frac{\$39,200}{\$280,000 - \$80,000} = 19.6\%$$

OR expanded form

$$(\$39,200 \div \$400,000) \times (\$400,000 \div \$200,000) = 19.6\%$$

(*continued*)

(continued)

Expected return on investment for alternative 2:

Sales ($400,000 + $80,000)	$480,000
Variable costs ([$320,000 ÷ $400,000] × $480,000)	384,000
Contribution margin	96,000
Controllable fixed costs	40,800
Controllable margin	$ 55,200

Return on investment $\dfrac{\$55,200}{\$280,000} = 19.7\%$

OR expanded form

($55,200 ÷ $480,000) × ($480,000 ÷ $280,000) = 19.7%

Related exercise material: **BE11-8, BE11-9, BE11-10, E11-30, E11-31,** and **Do It! D11-16.**

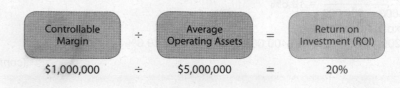

ALL ABOUT YOU   *Budgeting for Housing Costs*

Buying a home is probably the most expensive purchase you will make and it has a huge impact on your budget. Owning has several advantages over renting: it can be a good investment, it forces you to save, and it gives you pride of ownership. Almost 7 in 10 Canadians owned their home in 2011. But house prices in Canada have continued to rise beyond many peoples' means. In 2012, the average prices of homes in Canada rose 0.3% for resales and 2.3% for new homes.

What Do You Think?

Suppose you have just graduated from university and got a good job in a new community. Should you immediately buy a new home?

YES—By purchasing a home soon, I can make my housing cost more like a fixed cost, and reduce future cost increases. Also I will benefit from the appreciation in my home's value.

NO—I just moved to a new town, so I don't know the market. I might be able to afford a better home later when my income increases. In the meantime, I can invest the money that would have been for a down payment.

Sources: Canada Mortgage and Housing Corporation, "Canadian Housing Observer 2013;" Statistics Canada, "2011 National Household Survey: Homeownership and Shelter Costs in Canada," *The Daily*, September 11, 2013; Bill Conerly, "Should You Buy a House or Rent? The Economics of Homeownership," *Forbes*, November 11, 2013.

APPENDIX 11A—RESIDUAL INCOME—ANOTHER PERFORMANCE MEASUREMENT

STUDY OBJECTIVE 5

Explain the difference between ROI and residual income.

Although most companies use the ROI in evaluating their investment performance, the ROI has a significant disadvantage. To illustrate, let's look at the marine division of Mantle Manufacturing Company. It has an ROI of 20%, as calculated in Illustration 11A-1.

▶Illustration 11A-1
ROI formula

Controllable Margin	÷	Average Operating Assets	=	Return on Investment (ROI)
$1,000,000	÷	$5,000,000	=	20%

The marine division is considering producing a new product for its boats, a GPS satellite tracker. To produce the tracker, operating assets will have to increase by $2 million. The tracker is expected to generate an additional $260,000 of controllable margin. Illustration 11A-2 presents a comparison to show how the tracker will affect the ROI.

	Without Tracker	For Tracker	With Tracker
Controllable margin (a)	$1,000,000	$ 260,000	$1,260,000
Average operating assets (b)	$5,000,000	$2,000,000	$7,000,000
Return on investment [(a) ÷ (b)]	20%	13%	18%

►Illustration 11A-2
ROI comparison

The investment in the tracker reduces the ROI from 20% to 18%.

Let's suppose that you are the manager of the marine division and must decide if you should produce the tracker. If you were evaluated using the ROI, you probably would not produce the tracker because your ROI would drop from 20% to 18%. The problem with this ROI analysis is that it ignores an important variable: the **minimum rate of return** on a company's operating assets. The minimum rate of return is the rate at which the marine division can cover its costs and earn a profit. Assuming that the marine division has a minimum rate of return of 10%, it should invest in the tracker because its ROI of 13% is greater than 10%.

RESIDUAL INCOME COMPARED WITH ROI

To evaluate performance using the minimum rate of return, companies use the residual income approach. **Residual income** is the income that remains after subtracting from the controllable margin the minimum rate of return on a company's average operating assets. The residual income for the tracker would be calculated as shown in Illustration 11A-3.

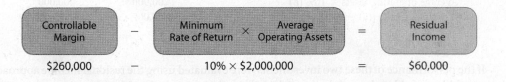

Controllable Margin	−	Minimum Rate of Return × Average Operating Assets	=	Residual Income
$260,000	−	10% × $2,000,000	=	$60,000

►Illustration 11A-3
Residual income formula

As shown, the residual income from the tracker investment is $60,000. Illustration 11A-4 indicates how the residual income changes as the additional investments are made.

	Without Tracker	For Tracker	With Tracker
Controllable margin (a)	$1,000,000	$260,000	$1,260,000
Average operating assets × 10% (b)	500,000	200,000	700,000
Return on investment [(a) − (b)]	$ 500,000	$ 60,000	$ 560,000

►Illustration 11A-4
Residual income comparison

This example shows how performance evaluation that is based on the ROI can be misleading and can even cause managers to reject projects that would actually increase income for the company. As a result, many companies use residual income to evaluate investment alternatives and measure company performance.

The residual income amount can be calculated in several ways, depending on how we define the terms used. The following variant on residual income is often referred to as the **Economic Value Added (EVA)**[3] approach. EVA is similar to residual income since it is a measure of the income created by the investment centre above the cost of invested assets. However, the EVA approach differs from the residual income approach in two ways. First, EVA uses the weighted-average cost of capital instead

---

[3]EVA was established by Stern, Steven & Co. in the United States.

of the minimum rate of return on the invested assets. Second, EVA calculates an investment centre's profit after tax. Basically, the EVA is calculated by deducting the total cost of capital (equity and borrowing) from the net income after tax. Illustration 11A-5 shows how the EVA is calculated.

▶Illustration 11A-5
Economic Value Added (EVA) formula

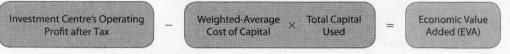

If this EVA result is positive, the company has added economic value. If it is negative, the company has lost capital. Many Canadian corporations have used the EVA approach in evaluating their investment centres, including Equifax Canada, Domtar, and Husky Injection Molding Systems Ltd.

RESIDUAL INCOME WEAKNESS

The goal of the residual income approach is to focus efforts on maximizing the total amount of residual income. This goal, however, ignores the fact that one division might use substantially fewer assets to attain the same level of residual income as another division. For example, we know that to produce the tracker, the marine division of Mantle Manufacturing used $2 million of average operating assets to generate $260,000 of controllable margin. Now let's say a different division produced a product called SeaDog, and it used $4 million to generate $460,000 of controllable margin, as shown in Illustration 11A-6.

▶Illustration 11A-6
Comparison of two products

	Tracker	SeaDog
Controllable margin (a)	$260,000	$460,000
Average operating assets × 10% (b)	200,000	400,000
Residual income [(a) − (b)]	$ 60,000	$ 60,000

If the performance of these two investments were evaluated using the residual income approach, they would be considered equal: both products have the same total residual income amount. This ignores, however, the fact that SeaDog required twice as much in operating assets to achieve the same level of residual income.

USING THE DECISION TOOLKIT

The manufacturing overhead budget for Reebles Company has the following items:

Variable costs	
Indirect materials	$25,000
Indirect labour	12,000
Maintenance	10,000
Manufacturing supplies	6,000
Total variable costs	$53,000
Fixed costs	
Supervision	$17,000
Inspections	1,000
Insurance	2,000
Depreciation	15,000
Total fixed costs	$35,000

(continued)

(continued)

The budget was based on an estimated production of 2,000 units. During November, 1,500 units were produced, and the following costs were incurred:

Variable costs	
Indirect materials	$25,200
Indirect labour	13,500
Maintenance	8,200
Manufacturing supplies	5,100
Total variable costs	$52,000
Fixed costs	
Supervision	$19,300
Inspections	1,200
Insurance	2,200
Depreciation	14,700
Total fixed costs	$37,400

Instructions

(a) Determine which items would be controllable by Ed Lopat, the production manager. (Assume that "supervision" does not include Ed's own salary.)

(b) How much should have been spent during the month for the manufacture of the 1,500 units?

(c) Prepare a flexible manufacturing overhead budget report for Ed.

(d) Prepare a responsibility report. Include only the costs that would have been controllable by Ed. In an attached memo, describe clearly for Ed the areas in which his performance needs to be improved.

Solution

(a) Ed Lopat should be able to control all the variable costs and the fixed costs of supervision and inspection. Insurance and depreciation ordinarily are not the responsibility of the department manager.

(b) The total variable cost per unit is $26.50 ($53,000 ÷ 2,000). The total budgeted cost during the month to manufacture 1,500 units is variable costs $39,750 (1,500 × $26.50) plus fixed costs ($35,000), for a total of $74,750 ($39,750 + $35,000).

(c)

REEBLES COMPANY
Production Department
Manufacturing Overhead Budget Report (flexible)
Month Ended November 30, 2016

	Budget at 1,500 units	Actual at 1,500 units	Difference Favourable (F)/ Unfavourable (U)
Variable costs			
Indirect materials	$18,750	$25,200	$ 6,450 U
Indirect labour	9,000	13,500	4,500 U
Maintenance	7,500	8,200	700 U
Manufacturing supplies	4,500	5,100	600 U
Total variable costs	39,750	52,000	12,250 U
Fixed costs			
Supervision	17,000	19,300	2,300 U
Inspections	1,000	1,200	200 U
Insurance	2,000	2,200	200 U
Depreciation	15,000	14,700	300 F
Total fixed costs	35,000	37,400	2,400 U
Total costs	$74,750	$89,400	$14,650 U

(d) Because a production department is a cost centre, the responsibility report should include only the cost that the production manager can control. In this type of report, no distinction is made between variable and fixed costs. Budget data in the report should be based on the units that are actually produced.

(continued)

(continued)

REEBLES COMPANY
Production Department
Responsibility Report
Month Ended November 30, 2016

Controllable Costs	Budget	Actual	Difference Favourable (F)/ Unfavourable (U)
Indirect materials	$18,750	$25,200	$ 6,450 U
Indirect labour	9,000	13,500	4,500 U
Maintenance	7,500	8,200	700 U
Manufacturing supplies	4,500	5,100	600 U
Supervision	17,000	19,300	2,300 U
Inspections	1,000	1,200	200 U
Total costs	$57,750	$72,500	$14,750 U

To: Mr. Ed Lopat, Production Manager

From: _____, Vice-President of Production

Subject: Performance Evaluation for November

Your performance in controlling costs that are your responsibility was very disappointing in the month of November. As indicated in the accompanying responsibility report, total costs were $14,750 over budget. On a percentage basis, costs were 26% over budget. As you can see, actual costs were over budget for every cost item. In three instances, costs were significantly over budget (indirect materials 34%, indirect labour 50%, and supervision 14%).

Ed, it is imperative that you get costs under control in your department as soon as possible.

I think we need to talk about ways to implement more effective cost-control measures. I would like to meet with you in my office at 9 a.m. on Wednesday to discuss possible alternatives.

Summary of Study Objectives

1. *Describe budgetary control and static budget reports.* Budgetary control consists of (1) preparing periodic budget reports that compare actual results with planned objectives, (2) analyzing the differences to determine their causes, (3) taking appropriate corrective action, and (4) modifying future plans, if necessary.

Static budget reports are useful for evaluating the progress toward planned sales and profit goals. They are also good for assessing a manager's effectiveness in controlling fixed costs and expenses when (1) actual activity closely approximates the master budget activity level, and/or (2) the costs respond to changes in activity in a fixed way.

2. *Explain the development of flexible budgets and the usefulness of flexible budget reports.* To develop a flexible budget, it is necessary to do the following:
1. Identify the activity index and the relevant range of activity.
2. Identify the variable costs, and determine the budgeted variable cost per unit of activity for each cost.
3. Identify the fixed costs, and determine the budgeted amount for each cost.
4. Prepare the budget for selected increments of activity within the relevant range.

Flexible budget reports make it possible to evaluate a manager's performance in controlling production and costs.

3. *Apply responsibility accounting to cost and profit centres.* Responsibility accounting involves accumulating and reporting revenues and costs that involve the individual manager who has the authority to make the day-to-day decisions about the cost items. The evaluation of a manager's performance is based on the matters that are directly under the manager's control. In responsibility accounting, it is necessary to distinguish between controllable and noncontrollable fixed costs and to identify three types of responsibility centres: cost, profit, and investment.

Responsibility reports for cost centres compare actual costs with flexible budget data. The reports show only controllable costs, and no distinction is made between variable and fixed costs.

Responsibility reports show the contribution margin, controllable fixed costs, and controllable margin for each profit centre.

4. *Explain the basis and formula used for evaluating performance in investment centres.* The primary basis for evaluating performance in investment centres is the return on investment (ROI). The formula for calculating the ROI for investment centres is as follows: controllable margin ÷ average operating assets.

5. *Explain the difference between ROI and residual income (Appendix 11A).* ROI is the controllable margin divided by average operating assets. Residual income is the income that remains after subtracting the minimum rate of return on a company's average operating assets. ROI sometimes provides misleading results because profitable investments are often rejected if they would reduce the ROI but increase overall profitability.

DECISION TOOLKIT—A SUMMARY

Decision Checkpoints	Info Needed for Decision	Tools to Use for Decision	How to Evaluate Results
Are the increased costs that result from increased production reasonable?	Variable costs projected at different levels of production	Flexible budget	After considering different production levels, results are favourable if expenses are less than the budgeted amounts.
Have the individual managers been held accountable for the costs and revenues under their control?	Relevant costs and revenues, where the individual manager has authority to make day-to-day decisions about the items	Responsibility reports focused on cost centres, profit centres, and investment centres, as appropriate	Compare the budget with actual costs and revenues for controllable items.
Has the investment centre performed up to expectations?	The controllable margin (contribution margin minus controllable fixed costs), and average investment centre operating assets	Return on investment	Compare the actual ROI with the expected ROI.

Glossary

Budgetary control The use of budgets to control operations. (p. 450)

Controllable costs Costs that a manager has the authority to incur within a specific period of time. (p. 460)

Controllable margin The contribution margin less controllable fixed costs. (p. 466)

Cost centre A responsibility centre that incurs costs but does not directly generate revenues. (p. 464)

Decentralization The situation that exists when control of operations is given to many managers throughout the organization. (p. 460)

Direct fixed costs Costs that relate specifically to a responsibility centre and are incurred for the benefit of that centre alone. (p. 466)

Economic Value Added (EVA) The after-tax controllable margin minus the weighted average cost of the total capital used. (p. 473)

Flexible budget A projection of budget data for various levels of activity. (p. 453)

Indirect fixed costs Costs that are incurred for the benefit of more than one profit centre. (p. 466)

Investment centre A responsibility centre that incurs costs, generates revenues, and has control over the investment funds that are available for use. (p. 465)

Management by exception A review of budget reports by top management that focuses entirely or mostly on differences between actual results and planned objectives. (p. 463)

Noncontrollable costs Costs that are incurred indirectly and are allocated to a responsibility centre that cannot control them. (p. 460)

Profit centre A responsibility centre that incurs costs and also generates revenues. (p. 465)

Residual income The income that remains after subtracting from the controllable margin the minimum rate of return on a company's operating assets. (p. 473)

Responsibility accounting A part of management accounting that involves accumulating and reporting revenues and costs that relate to the manager who has the authority to make the day-to-day decisions about the cost items. (p. 459)

Responsibility reporting system The preparation of reports for each level of responsibility in the company's organization chart. (p. 460)

Return on investment (ROI) A measure of management's effectiveness in using assets at its disposal in an investment centre. (p. 467)

Segment An area of responsibility in decentralized operations. (p. 460)

Static budget A projection of budget data at one level of activity. (p. 451)

Comprehensive Do It!

Glenda Company uses a flexible budget for manufacturing overhead that is based on direct labour hours. For 2016, the master overhead budget for the packaging department at its normal capacity of 300,000 direct labour hours was as follows:

Variable Costs		Fixed Costs	
Indirect labour	$360,000	Supervision	$ 60,000
Supplies and lubricants	150,000	Depreciation	24,000
Maintenance	210,000	Property taxes	18,000
Utilities	120,000	Insurance	12,000
	$840,000		$114,000

During July, 24,000 direct labour hours were worked. The company incurred the following variable costs in July: indirect labour $30,200; supplies and lubricants $11,600; maintenance $17,500; and utilities $9,200. Actual fixed overhead costs were the same as monthly budgeted fixed costs.

Instructions
Prepare a flexible budget report for the packaging department for July.

Solution to Comprehensive Do It!

GLENDA COMPANY
Manufacturing Overhead Budget Report (flexible)
Packaging Department
Month Ended July 31, 2016

	Budget	Actual	Difference: Favourable (F)/ Unfavourable (U)
Direct labour hours	24,000	24,000	
Variable costs			
Indirect labour	$28,800	$30,200	$1,400 U
Supplies and lubricants	12,000	11,600	400 F
Maintenance	16,800	17,500	700 U
Utilities	9,600	9,200	400 F
Total variable costs	67,200	68,500	1,300 U
Fixed costs			
Supervision	5,000	5,000	0
Depreciation	2,000	2,000	0
Property taxes	1,500	1,500	0
Insurance	1,000	1,000	0
Total fixed costs	9,500	9,500	0
Total costs	$76,700	$78,000	$1,300 U

Action Plan

- Use budget data for actual direct labour hours worked.
- Classify each cost as variable or fixed.
- Determine the difference between budgeted and actual costs.
- Identify the difference as favourable or unfavourable.
- Determine the difference in total variable costs, total fixed costs, and total costs.

the navigator

WileyPLUS

Self-Test, Brief Exercises, Exercises, Problems—Set A, and many more components are available for practice in WileyPlus.

Self-Study Questions

Answers are at the end of the chapter.
(The asterisk * indicates material discussed in the chapter appendix.)

(SO 1) 1. Budgetary control involves all of the following except
(a) modifying future plans.
(b) analyzing differences.
(c) using static budgets.
(d) determining differences between actual and planned results.

(SO 1) 2. A static budget is useful in controlling costs when the cost behaviour is
(a) mixed.
(b) fixed.
(c) variable.
(d) linear.

(SO 2)   3. At zero direct labour hours in a flexible budget graph, the total budgeted cost line intersects the vertical axis at $30,000. At 10,000 direct labour hours, a horizontal line drawn from the total budgeted cost line intersects the vertical axis at $90,000. The fixed and variable costs may be expressed as
(a) $30,000 fixed plus $6 per direct labour hour variable.
(b) $30,000 fixed plus $9 per direct labour hour variable.
(c) $60,000 fixed plus $3 per direct labour hour variable.
(d) $60,000 fixed plus $6 per direct labour hour variable.

(SO 2)   4. At 9,000 direct labour hours, the flexible budget for indirect materials is $27,000. If $28,000 of indirect materials costs are incurred at 9,200 direct labour hours, the flexible budget report should show the following difference for indirect materials:
(a) $1,000 unfavourable.
(b) $1,000 favourable.
(c) $400 favourable.
(d) $400 unfavourable.

(SO 3)   5. Under responsibility accounting, the evaluation of a manager's performance is based on matters that the manager
(a) directly controls.
(b) directly and indirectly controls.
(c) indirectly controls.
(d) has shared responsibility for with another manager.

(SO 3)   6. Responsibility centres include
(a) cost centres.
(b) profit centres.
(c) investment centres.
(d) All of the above.

(SO 3)   7. Responsibility reports for cost centres
(a) distinguish between fixed and variable costs.
(b) use static budget data.

(c) include both controllable and noncontrollable costs.
(d) include only controllable costs.

(SO 3)   8. In a responsibility report for a profit centre, controllable fixed costs are deducted from the contribution margin to show the
(a) profit centre margin.
(b) controllable margin.
(c) net income.
(d) income from operations.

(SO 4)   9. In the formula for return on investment (ROI), the factors for the controllable margin and operating assets are, respectively,
(a) the controllable margin percentage and total operating assets.
(b) the controllable margin dollars and average operating assets.
(c) the controllable margin dollars and total assets.
(d) the controllable margin percentage and average operating assets.

(SO 4)   10. A manager of an investment centre can improve the ROI by
(a) increasing average operating assets.
(b) reducing sales.
(c) increasing variable costs.
(d) reducing variable and/or controllable fixed costs.

(SO 5)   *11. In the formula for residual income, the factors for calculating the residual income are
(a) the contribution margin, controllable margin, and average operating assets.
(b) the controllable margin, average operating assets, and ROI.
(c) the controllable margin, average operating assets, and minimum rate of return.
(d) the controllable margin, ROI, and minimum rate of return.

Brief Exercises

BE11-1   For the quarter ended March 31, 2016, Westphal Company accumulates the following sales data for its product, Garden-Tools: $350,000 budgeted; $335,000 actual. Prepare a static budget report for the quarter.

(SO 1)
Prepare static budget reports.

BE11-2   Data for Westphal Company are given in BE11-1. In the second quarter, budgeted sales were $400,000, and actual sales were $405,000. Prepare a static budget report for the second quarter and for the year to date.

(SO 1)
Prepare static budget reports.

BE11-3   In Hinsdale Company, direct labour is $20 per hour. The company expects to operate at 10,000 direct labour hours each month. In January 2016, the company incurs direct labour totalling $204,000 in working 10,400 hours. Prepare (a) a static budget report and (b) a flexible budget report. Evaluate the usefulness of each report.

(SO 1, 2)
Show usefulness of flexible budgets in evaluating performance.

BE11-4   Dukane Company expects to produce 1.2 million units of product XX in 2016. Monthly production is expected to range from 80,000 to 120,000 units. Budgeted variable manufacturing costs per unit are as follows: direct materials $4, direct labour $6, and overhead $8. Budgeted fixed manufacturing costs per unit for depreciation are $2 and for supervision $1. Prepare a flexible manufacturing budget for the relevant range value using increments of 20,000 units.

(SO 2)
Prepare a flexible budget for manufacturing costs.

(SO 2)
Prepare a flexible
budget report.

BE11-5   Data for Dukane Company are given in BE11-4. In March 2016, the company incurs the following costs in producing 100,000 units: direct materials $425,000, direct labour $590,000, and variable overhead $805,000. Prepare a flexible budget report for March. Were costs controlled?

(SO 3)
Prepare a responsibility
report for a cost centre.

BE11-6   In the assembly department of Osaka Company, budgeted and actual manufacturing overhead costs for the month of April 2016 were as follows:

	Budget	Actual
Indirect materials	$16,000	$14,300
Indirect labour	20,000	20,600
Utilities	10,000	10,850
Supervision	5,000	5,000

The department manager can control all costs. Prepare a responsibility report for April for the cost centre.

(SO 3)
Prepare a responsibility
report for a profit centre.

BE11-7   Advent Manufacturing Company accumulates the following summary data for the year ending December 31, 2016, for its water division. The division operates as a profit centre: sales—$2 million budgeted, $2,080,000 actual; variable costs—$1 million budgeted, $1,060,000 actual; and controllable fixed costs—$300,000 budgeted, $305,000 actual. Prepare a responsibility report for the water division.

(SO 4)
Prepare a responsibility
report for an investment
centre.

BE11-8   For the year ending December 31, 2016, Sanjay Company accumulates the following data for the plastics division, which it operates as an investment centre: contribution margin—$700,000 budgeted, $715,000 actual; controllable fixed costs—$300,000 budgeted, $309,000 actual. Average operating assets for the year were $2 million. Prepare a responsibility report for the plastics division, beginning with the contribution margin.

(SO 4)
Calculate the return on
investment using the
ROI formula.

BE11-9   For its three investment centres, Stahl Company accumulates the following data:

	Centre I	Centre II	Centre III
Sales	$2,000,000	$4,000,000	$ 4,000,000
Controllable margin	1,300,000	2,000,000	3,600,000
Average operating assets	5,000,000	8,000,000	12,000,000

Calculate the return on investment (ROI) for each centre.

(SO 4)
Calculate the return
on investment under
changed conditions.

BE11-10   Data for the investment centres for Stahl Company are given in BE11-9. The centres expect the following changes in the next year: Centre I a 15% increase in sales; Centre II a $200,000 decrease in costs; and Centre III a $400,000 decrease in average operating assets. Calculate the expected return on investment for each centre. Assume Centre I has a contribution margin percentage of 75%.

(SO 5)
Calculate the return
on investment and the
residual income.

*BE11-11   Presented below is information related to the Southern Division of Lumber, Inc.

Contribution margin	$1,200,000
Controllable margin	$ 800,000
Average operating assets	$4,000,000
Minimum rate of return	15%

Calculate the Southern Division's return on investment and residual income.

Do It! Review

(SO 1)
Prepare and evaluate a
static budget report.

D11-12   Wade Company expects to produce 5,500 units of product IOA during the current year. Budgeted variable manufacturing costs per unit are direct materials $7, direct labour $13, and overhead $18. Monthly budgeted fixed manufacturing overhead costs are $8,000 for depreciation and $3,800 for supervision.

In the current month, Wade produced 6,000 units and incurred the following costs: direct materials $38,850, direct labour $76,440, variable overhead $116,640, depreciation $8,000, and supervision $4,000.

Instructions
Prepare a static budget report. (*Note:* You do not need to prepare the heading.) Were costs controlled? Discuss limitations of the budget.

(SO 2)
Calculate total
budgeted costs in
flexible budget.

D11-13   In Moore Company's flexible budget graph, the fixed cost line and the total budgeted cost line intersect the vertical axis at $90,000. The total budgeted cost line is $330,000 at an activity level of 60,000 direct labour hours.

Instructions
Calculate total budgeted costs at 70,000 direct labour hours.

D11-14 Chickasaw Company expects to produce 50,000 units of product IOA during the current year. Budgeted variable manufacturing costs per unit are direct materials $7, direct labour $12, and overhead $18. Annual budgeted fixed manufacturing overhead costs are $96,000 for depreciation and $45,000 for supervision.

(SO 2)
Prepare and evaluate a flexible budget report.

In the current month, Chickasaw produced 6,000 units and incurred the following costs: direct materials $38,900, direct labour $70,200, variable overhead $116,500, depreciation $8,000, and supervision $4,000.

Instructions
Prepare a flexible budget report. (*Note:* You do not need to prepare the headings.) Were costs controlled?

D11-15 The Atlantic division operates as a profit centre. It reports the following for the year.

(SO 3)
Prepare a responsibility report.

	Budgeted	Actual
Sales	$2,000,000	$1,800,000
Variable costs	800,000	750,000
Controllable fixed costs	550,000	550,000
Noncontrollable fixed costs	250,000	250,000

Instructions
Prepare a responsibility report for the Atlantic division at December 31, 2016.

D11-16 The service division of Retro Industries reported the following results for 2016.

(SO 4)
Calculate ROI and expected return on investments.

Sales	$500,000	Controllable fixed costs	$ 75,000
Variable costs	300,000	Average operating assets	450,000

Management is considering the following independent courses of action in 2017 in order to maximize the return on investment for this division.

1. Reduce average operating assets by $50,000, with no change in controllable margin.
2. Increase sales by $100,000, with no change in the contribution margin percentage.

Instructions
(a) Calculate the controllable margin and the return on investment for 2016.
(b) Calculate the controllable margin and the expected return on investment for each proposed alternative.

Exercises

E11-17 Jim Thome has prepared the following list of statements about budgetary control.

(SO 1, 2)
Understand the concept of budgetary control.

1. Budget reports compare actual results with planned objectives.
2. All budget reports are prepared on a weekly basis.
3. Management uses budget reports to analyze differences between actual and planned results and determine their causes.
4. As a result of analyzing budget reports, management may either take corrective action or modify future plans.
5. Budgetary control works best when a company has an informal reporting system.
6. The primary recipients of the sales report are the sales manager and the vice-president of production.
7. The primary recipient of the scrap report is the production manager.
8. A static budget is a projection of budget data at one level of activity.
9. Top management's reaction to unfavourable differences is not influenced by the materiality of the difference.
10. A static budget is not appropriate in evaluating a manager's effectiveness in controlling costs unless the actual activity level approximates the static budget activity level or the behaviour of the costs is fixed.

Instructions
Identify each statement as true or false. If false, indicate how to correct the statement.

E11-18 Pargo Company budgeted selling expenses of $30,000 in January, $35,000 in February, and $40,000 in March. Actual selling expenses were $31,200 in January, $34,525 in February, and $46,000 in March.

(SO 1)
Prepare and evaluate a static budget report.

Instructions
(a) Prepare a selling expense report that compares budgeted and actual amounts by month and for the year to date.
(b) Determine the purpose of the report prepared in part (a), and who the primary recipient would be.
(c) Determine the likely result of management's analysis of the report.

(SO 2)
Prepare flexible budget reports for manufacturing overhead costs.

E11-19 Raney Company uses a flexible budget for manufacturing overhead that is based on direct labour hours. The variable manufacturing overhead costs per direct labour hour are as follows:

Indirect labour	$0.70	Indirect materials	$0.50	Utilities	$0.40

Fixed overhead costs per month are as follows: supervision $4,000; depreciation $1,500; and property taxes $800. The company believes it will normally operate in a range of 7,000 to 10,000 direct labour hours per month.

Instructions

Prepare a monthly flexible manufacturing overhead budget for 2016 for the expected range of activity, using increments of 1,000 direct labour hours.

(SO 2)
Prepare flexible budget reports for manufacturing overhead costs, and comment on findings.

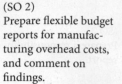

E11-20   Using the information in E11-19, assume that in July 2016, Raney Company incurs the following manufacturing overhead costs:

Variable Costs		Fixed Costs	
Indirect labour	$6,100	Supervision	$4,000
Indirect materials	4,300	Depreciation	3,000
Utilities	3,200	Property taxes	800

Instructions

(a) Prepare a flexible budget performance report, assuming that the company worked 9,000 direct labour hours during the month.

(b) Prepare a flexible budget performance report, assuming that the company worked 8,500 direct labour hours during the month.

(c) ▭▬▭▷ Comment on your findings.

(SO 2)
Prepare a flexible selling expenses budget.

E11-21   Vincent Company uses flexible budgets to control its selling expenses. Monthly sales are expected to range from $170,000 to $200,000. Variable costs and their percentage relationship to sales are as follows: sales commissions 6%; advertising 4%; travelling 3%; and delivery 2%. Fixed selling expenses consist of sales salaries $35,000; depreciation on delivery equipment $7,000; and insurance on delivery equipment $1,000.

Instructions

Prepare a monthly flexible budget for each $10,000 increment of sales within the relevant range for the year ending December 31, 2016.

(SO 2)
Prepare flexible budget reports for selling expenses.

E11-22   The actual selling expenses incurred in March 2016 by Vincent Company are as follows:

Variable Expenses		Fixed Expenses	
Sales commissions	$11,000	Sales salaries	$35,000
Advertising	7,000	Depreciation	7,000
Travel	5,100	Insurance	1,000
Delivery	3,500		

Instructions

(a) Prepare a flexible budget performance report for March using the budget data in E11-21, assuming that March sales were $170,000. Expected and actual sales are the same.

(b) Prepare a flexible budget performance report, assuming that March sales were $180,000. Expected sales and actual sales are the same.

(c) ▭▬▭▷ Comment on the importance of using flexible budgets in evaluating the sales manager's performance.

(SO 2, 3)
Prepare a flexible budget report and a responsibility report for manufacturing overhead.

E11-23   Sublette Company's manufacturing overhead budget for the first quarter of 2016 contained the following data:

Variable Costs		Fixed Costs	
Indirect materials	$12,000	Supervisory salaries	$36,000
Indirect labour	10,000	Depreciation	7,000
Utilities	8,000	Property taxes and insurance	8,000
Maintenance	6,000	Maintenance	5,000

Actual variable costs were as follows: indirect materials $13,900; indirect labour $9,500; utilities $8,700; and maintenance $5,000. Actual fixed costs equalled the budgeted costs except for property taxes and insurance, which were $8,400. The production department manager can control all costs except for depreciation and property taxes and insurance.

Instructions

(a) Prepare a flexible overhead budget report for the first quarter.

(b) Prepare a responsibility report for the first quarter.

E11-24 As sales manager, Kajsa Keyser was given the following static budget report for selling expenses in the clothing department of Dunham Company for the month of October:

(SO 1, 2)
Prepare and discuss a flexible budget report.

DUNHAM COMPANY
Clothing Department
Budget Report
Month Ended October 31, 2016

	Budget	Actual	Difference: Favourable (F)/ Unfavourable (U)
Sales in units	8,000	10,000	2,000 F
Variable costs			
Sales commissions	$ 2,000	$ 2,700	$ 700 U
Advertising expense	800	900	100 U
Travel expense	2,400	2,600	200 U
Free samples given out	1,600	1,500	100 F
Total variable costs	6,800	7,700	900 U
Fixed costs			
Rent	1,500	1,500	0
Sales salaries	1,000	1,000	0
Office salaries	800	800	0
Depreciation—vehicles (sales staff)	500	500	0
Total fixed costs	3,800	3,800	0
Total costs	$10,600	$11,500	$ 900 U

As a result of this budget report, Kajsa was called into the president's office and congratulated on her fine sales performance. She was reprimanded, however, for allowing her costs to get out of control. Kajsa knew something was wrong with the performance report that she had been given. However, she was not sure what to do and has come to you for advice.

Instructions
(a) Prepare a budget report based on flexible budget data to help Kajsa.
(b) Should Kajsa have been reprimanded? Explain.

E11-25 Pronto Plumbing Company is a newly formed company that specializes in plumbing services for home and business. The owner, Paul Pronto, had divided the company into two segments: home plumbing services and business plumbing services. Each segment is run by its own supervisor, while both segments share basic selling and administrative duties.

(SO 2, 3)
Prepare and discuss a responsibility report.

Paul has asked you to help him create a performance reporting system that will allow him to measure each segment's performance in terms of its profitability. The following information has been collected on the home plumbing services segment for the first quarter of 2016:

	Budget	Actual
Service revenue	$30,000	$31,500
Allocated portion of costs		
Building depreciation	11,000	11,000
Advertising	5,000	4,200
Billing	3,500	3,000
Property taxes	1,200	1,000
Materials and supplies	1,500	1,300
Supervisory salaries	10,000	10,500
Insurance	4,000	3,300
Wages	4,000	4,200
Gas and oil	2,700	3,400
Equipment depreciation	1,600	1,300

Instructions
(a) Prepare a responsibility report for the first quarter of 2016 for the home plumbing services segment.
(b) Write a memo to Paul Pronto in which you discuss the principles that he should use when preparing performance reports.

(SO 2)
Calculate costs using total budgeted cost formulas, and prepare a flexible budget graph.

E11-26 Sherrer Company has two production departments: fabricating and assembling. At a department managers' meeting, the controller uses flexible budget graphs to explain the total budgeted costs. Separate graphs based on direct labour hours are used for each department. The graphs show the following:

1. At zero direct labour hours, the total budgeted cost line and the fixed cost line intersect the vertical axis at $50,000 in the fabricating department and at $40,000 in the assembling department.
2. At normal capacity of 50,000 direct labour hours, the line drawn from the total budgeted cost line intersects the vertical axis at $180,000 in the fabricating department, and $135,000 in the assembling department.

Instructions
(a) State the total budgeted cost formula for each department.
(b) Calculate the total budgeted cost for each department, assuming actual direct labour hours worked were 53,000 and 47,000 in the fabricating and assembling departments, respectively.
(c) Prepare the flexible budget graph for the fabricating department, assuming the maximum direct labour hours in the relevant range is 100,000. Use increments of 10,000 direct labour hours on the horizontal axis and increments of $50,000 on the vertical axis.

(SO 3)
Prepare responsibility reports for cost centres.

E11-27 Marcum Company's organization chart includes the president; the vice-president of production; three assembly plants—Vancouver, Hamilton, and Saint John; and two departments within each plant—machining and finishing. Budgeted and actual manufacturing cost data for July 2016 are as follows:

1. Finishing department, Vancouver: direct materials—$51,700 actual, $55,000 budgeted; direct labour—$83,000 actual, $82,000 budgeted; manufacturing overhead—$51,000 actual, $49,200 budgeted.
2. Machining department, Vancouver: total manufacturing costs—$217,000 actual, $216,000 budgeted.
3. Hamilton plant: total manufacturing costs—$424,000 actual, $421,000 budgeted.
4. Saint John plant: total manufacturing costs—$494,000 actual, $496,500 budgeted.

The Vancouver plant manager's office costs were $90,000 actual and $87,500 budgeted. The vice-president of production's office costs were $165,000 actual and $160,000 budgeted. Office costs are not allocated to departments and plants.

Instructions
Using the format shown in Illustration 11-19, prepare the reports in a responsibility system for:
(a) the finishing department in Vancouver,
(b) the plant manager in Vancouver, and
(c) the vice-president of production.

(SO 3)
Prepare a responsibility report for a cost centre.

E11-28 The mixing department manager of Crede Company is able to control all overhead costs except rent, property taxes, and salaries. Budgeted monthly overhead costs for the mixing department, in alphabetical order, are as follows:

Indirect labour	$12,000	Property taxes	$ 1,000
Indirect materials	7,700	Rent	1,800
Lubricants	1,675	Salaries	10,000
Maintenance	3,500	Utilities	5,000

Actual costs incurred for January 2016 are indirect labour $12,250; indirect materials $10,200; lubricants $1,650; maintenance $3,500; property taxes $1,100; rent $1,800; salaries $10,000; and utilities $6,400.

Instructions
(a) Prepare a responsibility report for January 2016.
(b) Determine the likely result of management's analysis of the report.

(SO 3)
Calculate missing amounts in responsibility reports for three profit centres, and prepare a responsibility report.

E11-29 Longhead Manufacturing Inc. has three divisions that are operated as profit centres. Actual operating data for the divisions are as follows:

Operating Data	Women's Shoes	Men's Shoes	Children's Shoes
Contribution margin	$250,000	(c)	$180,000
Controllable fixed costs	100,000	(d)	(e)
Controllable margin	(a)	$ 90,000	95,000
Sales	600,000	450,000	(f)
Variable costs	(b)	320,000	250,000

Instructions
(a) Calculate the missing amounts. Show your calculations.
(b) Prepare a responsibility report for the women's shoe division assuming (1) the data are for the month ended June 30, 2016, and (2) all data match the budgeted amounts, except variable costs, which are $10,000 over budget.

E11-30 The sports equipment division of Brandon McCarthy Company is operated as a profit centre. Sales for the division were budgeted for 2016 at $900,000. The only variable costs budgeted for the division were cost of goods sold ($440,000) and selling and administrative costs ($60,000). Fixed costs were budgeted at $100,000 for cost of goods sold, $90,000 for selling and administrative costs, and $70,000 for noncontrollable fixed costs. Actual results were as follows:

(SO 3, 4)
Prepare a responsibility report for a profit centre and calculate ROI.

Sales	$870,000
Cost of goods sold	
Variable	405,000
Fixed	105,000
Selling and administrative costs	
Variable	62,000
Fixed	78,000
Noncontrollable fixed costs	80,000

Instructions
(a) Prepare a responsibility report for the sports equipment division for 2016.
(b) Assume the division is an investment centre, and average operating assets were $1 million. Calculate ROI.

E11-31 The green division of Campana Company reported the following data for the current year:

(SO 4)
Calculate ROI for the current year and for possible future changes.

Sales	$3,000,000
Variable costs	1,980,000
Controllable fixed costs	600,000
Average operating assets	5,000,000

Top management is unhappy with the investment centre's return on investment. It asks the manager of the green division to submit plans to improve the ROI in the next year. The manager believes it is reasonable to consider each of the following independent courses of action.

1. Increase sales by $320,000 with no change in the contribution margin percentage.
2. Reduce variable costs by $150,000.
3. Reduce average operating assets by 4%.

Instructions
(a) Calculate the return on investment for the current year.
(b) Using the ROI formula, calculate the ROI under each of the proposed courses of action. (Round to one decimal.)

E11-32 The Medina and Haley Dental Clinic provides both preventive and orthodontic dental services. The two owners, Martin Medina and Cybil Haley, operate the clinic as two separate investment centres: preventive services and orthodontic services. Each owner is in charge of one centre: Martin for preventive services and Cybil for orthodontic services. Each month they prepare an income statement on the two centres to evaluate performance and make decisions about how to improve the clinic's operational efficiency and profitability.

(SO 4)
Prepare a responsibility report for an investment centre.

Recently, they have been concerned about the profitability of the preventive services operations. For several months, the centre has been reporting a loss. In addition, the owners know that the investment in operating assets at the beginning of the month was $102,400, and it was $97,600 at the end of the month. They have asked for you to evaluate their current performance reporting system. Shown below is the responsibility report for the month of May 2016:

	Actual	Difference from Budget
Service revenue	$45,000	$2,000 F
Variable costs		
Filling materials	7,000	300 U
Novocaine	4,000	200 U
Supplies	2,000	250 F
Dental assistant wages	2,500	0
Utilities	500	50 U
Total variable costs	16,000	300 U
Fixed costs		
Allocated portion of receptionist's salary	3,000	200 U
Dentist salary	12,000	600 U
Equipment depreciation	6,000	0
Allocated portion of building depreciation	15,000	1,000 U
Total fixed costs	36,000	1,800 U
Operating income (loss)	$ (7,000)	$ 100 U

Instructions

(a) Prepare a responsibility report for an investment centre as illustrated in the chapter.

(b) Write a memo to the owners in which you discuss the weaknesses of their current reporting system.

(SO 4)

Determine missing amounts in responsibility reports for three investment centres.

E11-33   The Transcanadian Transportation Company uses a responsibility reporting system to measure the performance of its three investment centres: planes, taxis, and limos. It measures segment performance using a system of responsibility reports and return on investment calculations. The allocation of resources within the company and the segment managers' bonuses are based in part on the results shown in these reports.

Recently, the company was the victim of a computer virus that deleted portions of its accounting records. This was discovered when the current period's responsibility reports were being prepared. The printout of the actual operating results appeared as follows:

	Planes	Taxis	Limos
Service revenue	$ (a)	$600,000	$ (b)
Variable costs	5,500,000	(c)	320,000
Contribution margin	(d)	200,000	500,000
Controllable fixed costs	2,000,000	(e)	(f)
Controllable margin	(g)	95,000	255,000
Average operating assets	25,000,000	(h)	1,500,000
Return on investment	15%	10%	(i)

Instructions

Determine the missing amounts.

(SO 5)

Calculate and compare ROI and residual income.

*E11-34   Presented below is selected financial information for two divisions of Yono Brewing.

	Lager	Lite Lager
Contribution margin	$500,000	$ 300,000
Controllable margin	$200,000	(c)
Average operating assets	(a)	$1,200,000
Minimum rate of return	(b)	13%
Return on investment	20%	(d)
Residual income	$100,000	$ 204,000

Instructions

Supply the missing information for the lettered items. Fill in information related to ROI and residual income.

(SO 5)

Fill in information related to ROI and residual income.

*E11-35   Point Claire Company had the following results during the most recent year: sales $500,000; residual income $5,000; investment turnover 2.5; and a required rate of return of 15%.

Instructions

(a) Calculate the total assets.

(b) Calculate the operating (pretax) income.

(c) Calculate the return on investment.

(d) Calculate the profit margin.

Problems: Set A

(SO 2, 3)

Prepare a flexible budget and a budget report for manufacturing overhead.

P11-36A   Alcore Company estimates that 240,000 direct labour hours will be worked in the assembly department during 2016. Based on that, the following budgeted manufacturing overhead data are calculated:

Variable Overhead Costs		Fixed Overhead Costs	
Indirect labour	$ 72,000	Supervision	$ 75,000
Indirect materials	48,000	Depreciation	30,000
Repairs	36,000	Insurance	12,000
Utilities	26,400	Rent	9,000
Lubricants	9,600	Property taxes	6,000
	$192,000		$132,000

It is estimated that the direct labour hours worked each month will range from 18,000 to 24,000 hours. During January, 20,000 direct labour hours were worked and the following overhead costs were incurred:

Variable Overhead Costs		Fixed Overhead Costs	
Indirect labour	$ 6,300	Supervision	$ 6,250
Indirect materials	3,800	Depreciation	2,500
Repairs	2,700	Insurance	1,000
Utilities	1,900	Rent	850
Lubricants	830	Property taxes	500
	$15,530		$11,100

Instructions

(a) Prepare a monthly flexible manufacturing overhead budget for each increment of 2,000 direct labour hours (DLH) over the relevant range for the year ending December 31, 2016.

(b) Prepare a manufacturing overhead budget report for January.

(c) 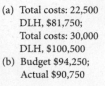 Comment on management's efficiency in controlling the manufacturing overhead costs in January.

(a) Total costs: 18,000 DLH, $25,400
(b) Budget $27,000 Actual $26,630

P11-37A Kitchen Care Inc. (KCI) is a manufacturer of toaster ovens. To improve control over operations, the president of KCI wants to begin using a flexible budgeting system, rather than use only the current master budget. The following data are available for KCI's expected costs at production levels of 90,000, 100,000, and 110,000 units:

(SO 2)
Prepare a flexible budget report for a cost centre.

Variable costs	
Manufacturing	$6 per unit
Administrative	$3 per unit
Selling	$1 per unit
Fixed costs	
Manufacturing	$150,000
Administrative	$ 80,000

Instructions

(a) Prepare a flexible budget for each of the possible production levels: 90,000, 100,000, and 110,000 units.

(b) If KCI sells the toaster ovens for $15 each, how many units will it have to sell to make a profit of $250,000 before taxes?

(adapted from CGA-Canada, now CPA Canada)

(b) 96,000 units

P11-38A High Arctic Manufacturing Company produces one product, Kebo. Because of wide fluctuations in the demand for Kebo, the assembly department has significant variations in its monthly production levels.

The annual master manufacturing overhead budget is based on 300,000 direct labour hours. In July, 27,500 labour hours were worked. The master manufacturing overhead budget for the year and the actual overhead costs incurred in July are as follows:

(SO 2, 3)
Prepare a flexible budget, budget report, and graph for manufacturing overhead.

Overhead Costs	Master Budget (annual)	Actual in July
Variable		
Indirect labour	$ 330,000	$29,000
Indirect materials	180,000	14,000
Utilities	150,000	13,900
Maintenance	90,000	8,350
Fixed		
Supervision	150,000	12,500
Depreciation	96,000	8,000
Insurance and taxes	60,000	5,000
Total	$1,056,000	$90,750

Instructions

(a) Prepare a monthly flexible overhead budget for the year ending December 31, 2016, assuming monthly production levels range from 22,500 to 30,000 direct labour hours. Use increments of 2,500 direct labour hours.

(b) Prepare a budget performance report for the month of July 2016, comparing actual results with budgeted data, based on the flexible budget.

(c) 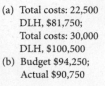 Were costs controlled effectively? Explain.

(d) State the formula for calculating the total monthly budgeted costs for High Arctic Manufacturing Company.

(e) Prepare a flexible budget graph showing total budgeted costs at 25,000 and 27,500 direct labour hours. Use increments of 5,000 on the horizontal axis and increments of $10,000 on the vertical axis.

(a) Total costs: 22,500 DLH, $81,750; Total costs: 30,000 DLH, $100,500
(b) Budget $94,250; Actual $90,750

(SO 1, 2)
Prepare a flexible
budget report; compare
flexible and fixed
budgets.

P11-39A   Doggone Groomers is in the dog-grooming business. Its operating costs are described by these formulas:

Grooming supplies (variable)	$y = \$0 + \$4.00x$
Direct labour (variable)	$y = \$0 + \$12.00x$
Overhead (mixed)	$y = \$8,000 + \$1.00x$

(a) Total cost: 550 units,
$17,350; 600 units,
$18,200; 700 units,
$19,900

(c) Total cost: 550 units,
$31.55; 600 units,
$30.33; 700 units,
$28.43

(d) $51.28

Puli, the owner, has determined that direct labour is the cost driver for all three categories of costs.

Instructions
(a) Prepare a flexible budget for activity levels of 550, 600, and 700 direct labour hours.
(b) Explain why the flexible budget is more informative than the fixed budget.
(c) Calculate the total cost per direct labour hour at each of the activity levels specified in part (a).
(d) The groomers at Doggone normally work a total of 650 direct labour hours during each month. Each grooming job normally takes a groomer 1¼ hours. Puli wants to earn a profit equal to 40% of the costs incurred. Determine what she should charge each pet owner for grooming.

(adapted from CGA-Canada, now CPA Canada)

(SO 1, 2, 3)
State the total budgeted
cost formula, and
prepare flexible budget
reports for two time
periods.

P11-40A   Laesecke Company uses budgets to control costs. The May 2016 budget report for the company's packaging department is as follows:

LAESECKE COMPANY
Budget Report
Packaging Department
Month Ended May 31, 2016

Manufacturing Costs	Budget	Actual	Difference: Favourable (F)/ Unfavourable (U)
Variable costs			
Direct materials	$ 37,500	$ 38,000	$ 500 U
Direct labour	45,000	47,000	2,000 U
Indirect materials	15,000	15,200	200 U
Indirect labour	12,500	13,000	500 U
Utilities	10,000	9,600	400 F
Maintenance	5,000	5,200	200 U
Total variable costs	125,000	128,000	3,000 U
Fixed costs			
Rent	10,000	10,000	0
Supervision	7,000	7,000	0
Depreciation	5,000	5,000	0
Total fixed costs	22,000	22,000	0
Total costs	$147,000	$150,000	$3,000 U

The monthly budget amounts in the report were based on an expected production of 50,000 units per month or 600,000 units per year. The company president was unhappy with the department manager's performance. The department manager could not understand the unfavourable results. In May, 55,000 units were produced.

Instructions
(a) State the total budgeted cost formula.

(b) Budget $159,500

(b) Prepare a budget report for May, using flexible budget data. Why does this report provide a better basis for evaluating performance than the report based on static budget data?

(c) Budget $122,000;
Actual $124,400

(c) In June, 40,000 units were produced. Prepare the budget report using flexible budget data, assuming (1) each variable cost was 20% less in June than its actual cost in May, and (2) fixed costs were the same in the month of June as in May.

(SO 3)
Prepare a responsibility
report for a profit
centre.

P11-41A   Korene Manufacturing Inc. operates the home appliance division as a profit centre. Operating data for this division for the year ended December 31, 2016, are shown in the following table:

	Budget	Difference from Budget
Sales	$2,400,000	$200,000 U
Costs of goods sold		
Variable costs	1,200,000	60,000 U
Controllable fixed costs	200,000	9,000 F
Selling and administrative expenses		
Variable costs	240,000	8,000 F
Controllable fixed costs	60,000	3,000 U
Noncontrollable fixed costs	50,000	2,000 U

In addition, Korene Manufacturing incurred $150,000 of indirect fixed costs that were budgeted at $155,000. It allocates 20% of these costs to the home appliance division. The division manager cannot control any of these costs.

Instructions
(a) Prepare a responsibility report for the home appliance division for the year.
(b) ▭▭▭▷ Comment on the manager's performance in controlling revenues and costs.
(c) Identify any costs that were excluded from the responsibility report and explain why they were excluded.

(a) Gross margin
$251,000 U;
Controllable margin
$246,000 U

P11-42A Chudzik Manufacturing Company makes garden and lawn equipment. The company operates through three divisions. Each division is an investment centre. Operating data for the lawn mower division for the year ended December 31, 2016, and relevant budget data are as follows:

(SO 4)
Prepare a responsibility report for an investment centre, and calculate ROI.

	Actual	Comparison with Budget
Sales	$2,900,000	$150,000 unfavourable
Variable cost of goods sold	1,400,000	100,000 unfavourable
Variable selling and administrative expenses	300,000	40,000 favourable
Controllable fixed cost of goods sold	270,000	On target
Controllable fixed selling and administrative expenses	140,000	On target

Average operating assets for the year for the lawn mower division were $5 million, which was also the budgeted amount.

Instructions
(a) Prepare a responsibility report (in thousands of dollars) for the lawn mower division.
(b) ▭▭▭▷ Evaluate the manager's performance. Which items will likely be investigated by top management?
(c) Calculate the expected ROI in 2016 for the lawn mower division, assuming the following independent changes:
  1. The variable cost of goods sold decreases by 20%.
  2. The average operating assets decrease by 24%.
  3. Sales increase by $700,000 and this increase is expected to increase the contribution margin by $260,000.

(a) Controllable margin:
Budget $1,000,000;
Actual $790,000

*P11-43A Iqaluit Corporation recently announced a bonus plan to be awarded to the manager of the most profitable division. The three managers are to choose whether the ROI or residual income (RI) will be used to measure profitability. In addition, they must decide whether investments will be measured using the gross book value (GBV) or net book value (NBV) of assets. Iqaluit defines income as operating income and investments as total assets. The following information is available for the year just ended:

(SO 5)
Calculate and compare ROI and residual income.

Division	Gross Book Value of Assets	Accumulated Depreciation	Operating Income
A	$800,000	$400,000	$100,000
B	750,000	450,000	85,000
C	250,000	50,000	50,000

NBV ROI	[A]	25.00%
	[B]	28.33%
	[C]	25.00%
GBV RI	[A]	$20,000
	[B]	$10,000
	[C]	$25,000

Iqaluit uses a required rate of return of 10% on investments to calculate residual income (RI).

Instructions
Which method for calculating performance did each vice-president use if each one wanted to show that his or her division had the best performance?

(adapted from CMA Canada, now CPA Canada)

(SO 3)
Prepare reports for cost centres under responsibility accounting, and comment on the performance of managers.

P11-44A Kanjak Company uses a responsibility reporting system. It has divisions in Calgary, Winnipeg, and Sudbury. Each division has three production departments: cutting, shaping, and finishing. Responsibility for each department belongs to a manager who reports to the division production manager. Each division manager reports to the vice-president of production. There are also vice-presidents for marketing and finance. All vice-presidents report to the president.

In January 2016, controllable budgeted and actual manufacturing overhead costs for the departments and divisions were as follows:

Manufacturing Overhead	Actual	Budget
Individual costs—cutting department—Winnipeg		
Indirect labour	$ 95,000	$ 90,000
Indirect materials	62,000	61,000
Maintenance	27,400	25,000
Utilities	25,200	20,000
Supervision	30,000	28,000
	$239,600	$224,000
Total costs		
Shaping department—Winnipeg	$190,000	$177,000
Finishing department—Winnipeg	249,000	246,000
Calgary division	722,000	715,000
Sudbury division	760,000	750,000

Additional overhead costs were incurred as follows: Winnipeg division production manager—actual costs $73,100, budgeted $70,000; vice-president of production—actual costs $73,000, budgeted $70,000; president—actual costs $96,200, budgeted $91,300. These expenses are not allocated.

The vice-presidents, other than the vice-president of production, had the following expenses:

	Actual	Budget
Marketing	$167,200	$160,000
Finance	124,000	120,000

Instructions

(a) Totals:

(a) Using the format in Illustration 11-19, prepare the following responsibility reports:
  1. Manufacturing overhead—cutting department manager—Winnipeg division
  2. Manufacturing overhead—Winnipeg division manager

(3) $54,700U
(4) $70,800U

  3. Manufacturing overhead—vice-president of production
  4. Manufacturing overhead and expenses—president

(b) ✏️▸ Comment on the comparative performances of (1) the department managers in the Winnipeg division, (2) the division managers, and (3) the vice-presidents.

(adapted from CMA Canada, now CPA Canada)

(SO 5)
Calculate ROI and residual income and discuss the impact on manager performance.

*P11-45A Haniwall Industries has manufactured prefabricated houses for over 20 years.

The houses are constructed in sections that are assembled on customers' lots. Haniwall expanded into the precut housing market when it acquired Miramichi Company, one of its suppliers. In this market, various types of lumber are precut into the appropriate lengths, banded into packages, and shipped to customers' lots for assembly. Haniwall designated the Miramichi division as an investment centre.

Haniwall uses the return on investment as a performance measure and defines investment as the average operating assets. Management bonuses are based in part on the ROI. All investments are expected to earn a minimum rate of return of 17%. Miramichi's ROI has ranged from 21.9% to 23.3% since it was acquired. Miramichi had an investment opportunity in 2016 that had an estimated ROI of 19%. Miramichi's management decided against the investment because it believed the investment would decrease the division's overall ROI.

Selected financial information for Miramichi is presented below. The division's average operating assets were $7.5 million for the year 2016.

MIRAMICHI DIVISION
Selected Financial Information
Year Ended December 31, 2016

Sales	$16,000,000
Contribution margin	5,600,000
Controllable margin	1,500,000

Instructions

(a) Totals:
(2) $225,000

(a) Calculate the following performance measures for 2016 for the Miramichi division: (1) return on investment, and (2) residual income.

(b) ✏️▸ Would the management of the division have been more likely to accept the investment opportunity it had in 2016 if residual income had been used as a performance measure instead of the ROI? Explain your answer.

(adapted from CMA Canada, now CPA Canada)

*P11-46A Lawton Homes, founded by a former vice-president of Haniwall Industries in P11-45A, has been manufacturing prefabricated houses for the past five years. To compete with Haniwall, Lawton also expanded into the precut housing market by acquiring one of its suppliers, Presser Company. After designating Presser as an investment centre, Lawton next decided to use the ROI as a performance measure and to give managers bonuses that are partly based on the ROI. Lawton defines investments as average productive assets and expects a minimum return of 15% before income taxes. Presser's ROI has averaged 19.5% since it was acquired.

(SO 4, 5)
Calculate ROI and
residual income and
discuss the impact on
manager performance.

In 2016, Presser found an investment opportunity that would have an estimated ROI of 18%. After analyzing the opportunity, Presser's management finally decided not to make the investment because management did not want the division's overall ROI to decrease.

The 2016 income statement for Presser follows. The division had operating assets of $25.2 million at the end of 2016, which was a 5% increase over the 2016 year-end balance.

PRESSER DIVISION
Income Statement Year Ended June 30, 2016
(in thousands)

Sales revenue		$48,000
Cost of goods sold		31,600
Gross margin		16,400
Operating expenses		
Administrative	$4,280	
Selling	7,200	11,480
Income from operations before income taxes		$ 4,920

Instructions
(a) Calculate the following performance measures for 2016 for the Presser division:
  (1) the return on investment, and (2) the residual income.
(b) Would the management of Presser division have been more likely to accept the investment opportunity it had in 2016 if the company had used residual income as a performance measure instead of the ROI? Explain your answer.
(c) The Presser division is a separate investment centre within Lawton Homes. Identify several items that Presser should control so that it can be evaluated fairly by either the ROI or residual income performance measures.

(adapted from CMA Canada, now CPA Canada)

(a) (1) ROI = 20%

*P11-47A National Motors is a major car manufacturer with a wide variety of models, including its most recent one, the Mountaineer. The new model uses parts and components from external suppliers, as well as some from the following divisions of National Motors:

(SO 3, 4, 5)
Calculate ROI and
residual income,
identify responsibility
centres, and discuss
the impact on manager
performance.

Division S:
This division manufactures stainless steel components for the Mountaineer and other models sold by National Motors. Sales of components for the Mountaineer represent 25% of the division's revenue.

Division F:
This division produces different wipers that fit a wide variety of car models manufactured by National Motors and other major car manufacturers. Sales of wipers for the Mountaineer are negligible. Division F has total assets of $250 million. Last year's revenues were $150 million with operating expenses of $117.5 million.

Division D:
This division uses all its capacity to manufacture engines for the Mountaineer. The division manager is strictly responsible for choosing the inputs used to produce the engines.

National Motors uses the return on investment to evaluate the performance of the division managers. The required rate of return of 14% is the same for all divisions.

At the last meeting of the division managers, Mr. Thiessen, manager of division D, was not happy because he thought that he was not evaluated fairly. The chief executive officer of National Motors did not understand why Mr. Thiessen's evaluation would be unfair as she thought that the ROI was the best measure available to evaluate performance.

Instructions
(a) Calculate the residual income for division F based on last year's results and investment. Show your calculations.
(b) Identify which type of responsibility centre each of the three divisions should be. Briefly explain your reasoning.
(c) Is the ROI appropriate to evaluate the performance of Mr. Thiessen and division D? Briefly explain your answer.

(adapted from CGA-Canada, now CPA Canada)

(a) RI = $(2,500,000)

(SO 4, 5)
Compare ROI and
residual income
with supporting
calculations.

*P11-48A   Colt Division had the following results for the year just ended:

| Sales | $750,000 | Controllable margin | $ 60,000 |
| Contribution margin | 300,000 | Average operating assets | 300,000 |

Colt is considering a new product line that would involve the following:

| Sales | $150,000 | Controllable margin | $12,000 |
| Contribution margin | 60,000 | Average operating assets | 75,000 |

Colt's parent company, North Inc., has a company-wide ROI of 14% and pays bonuses based on divisional ROI.

Instructions

(a) ROI with investment:
19.2%

(a) Determine the effect on Colt's ROI if it introduces the new product line. Would Colt's managers be encouraged to introduce the new product line?

(b) Determine the effect on North Inc's ROI if Colt introduces the new product line. Would the top managers of North Inc. want to introduce the new product line?

(c) Assume a required rate of return of 10% on operational assets invested in each division. Determine the effect on Colt's residual income if it introduces the new product. Would Colt's managers be encouraged to introduce the new product?

(SO 4, 5)
Compare and contrast
performances under
ROI and residual
income.

*P11-49A   Return on investment is often expressed as follows:

$$ROI = \frac{Controllable\ margin}{Average\ operating\ asset} = \frac{Controllable\ margin}{Sales} \times \frac{Sales}{Average\ operating\ assets}$$

Instructions

(a) Explain the advantages of breaking down the ROI calculation into two separate components.

(b) 1. Comparative data on three companies operating in the same industry follow. The minimum required ROI is 10% for all three companies. Determine the missing amounts.

(a) $20,000,000

	Company A	Company B	Company C
Sales	$1,500,000	$750,000	(a)
Net operating income	$ 180,000	$150,000	(b)
Average operating assets	$ 750,000	(c)	$5,000,000
Profit margin	(d)	(e)	0.5%
Assets turnover	(f)	(g)	4
Return on investment	(h)	2%	(i)
Residual income	(j)	(k)	(l)

(h) 24%

2. Compare and contrast the performance of the three companies, with reference to their relative performance as measured by the ROI and residual income.

(adapted from CGA-Canada, now CPA Canada)

Problems: Set B

(SO 2, 3)
Prepare a flexible
budget and budget
report for manufactur-
ing overhead.

P11-50B   Oakley Company estimates that 360,000 direct labour hours will be worked in the packaging department during 2016. Based on that, it has calculated the following budgeted manufacturing overhead cost data for the year.

Fixed Overhead Costs		Variable Overhead Costs	
Supervision	$ 90,000	Indirect labour	$126,000
Depreciation	60,000	Indirect materials	90,000
Insurance	30,000	Repairs	54,000
Rent	24,000	Utilities	72,000
Property taxes	18,000	Lubricants	18,000
	$222,000		$360,000

The company estimates that the direct labour hours worked each month will range from 27,000 to 36,000 hours. During October, 27,000 direct labour hours were worked and the following overhead costs were incurred:

1. Fixed overhead costs—supervision $7,500; depreciation $5,000; insurance $2,470; rent $2,000; and property taxes $1,500.
2. Variable overhead costs—indirect labour $10,360; indirect materials $6,400; repairs $4,000; utilities $5,700; and lubricants $1,640.

Instructions
(a) Prepare a monthly flexible manufacturing overhead budget for each increment of 3,000 direct labour hours over the relevant range for the year ending December 31, 2016.
(b) Prepare a flexible budget report for October.
(c) ✏️▷ Comment on management's efficiency in controlling manufacturing overhead costs in October.

(a) Total costs: 27,000 DLH, $45,500; and 36,000 DLH, $54,500
(b) Total $1,070 U

P11-51B Finesse Company manufactures tablecloths. Sales have grown rapidly over the past two years. As a result, the president has installed a budgetary control system for 2016. The following data were used in developing the master manufacturing overhead budget for the ironing department. The budget is based on an activity index of direct labour hours.

(SO 2, 3)
Prepare a flexible budget, budget report, and graph for manufacturing overhead.

Variable Costs	Rate per Direct Labour Hour	Annual Fixed Costs	
Indirect labour	$0.50	Supervision	$45,000
Indirect materials	0.75	Depreciation	20,000
Factory utilities	0.45	Insurance	15,000
Factory repairs	0.25	Rent	30,000

The company prepared the master overhead budget on the expectation that 600,000 direct labour hours would be worked during the year. In June, 48,000 direct labour hours were worked. At that level of activity, actual costs were as follows:

1. Variable, per direct labour hour—indirect labour $0.53; indirect materials $0.70; factory utilities $0.47; and factory repairs $0.29.
2. Fixed—same as budgeted.

Instructions
(a) Prepare a monthly flexible manufacturing overhead budget for the year ending December 31, 2016, assuming production levels range from 35,000 to 50,000 direct labour hours per month. Use increments of 5,000 direct labour hours.
(b) Prepare a budget performance report for June, comparing actual results with budgeted data based on the flexible budget.
(c) Were costs effectively controlled? Explain.
(d) State the formula for calculating the total budgeted costs for Finesse Company.
(e) Prepare a flexible budget graph, showing total budgeted costs at 35,000 and 45,000 direct labour hours. Use increments of 5,000 direct labour hours on the horizontal axis and increments of $10,000 on the vertical axis.

(a) Total costs:
35,000 DLH, $77,416
50,000 DLH, $106,666
(b) Budget $102,766;
Actual $104,686

P11-52B Yaeger Company uses budgets in controlling costs. The company based the monthly budget amounts in the report on an expected production of 60,000 units per month or 720,000 units per year. The assembling department manager is pleased with the report and expects a raise. The company president, however, is unhappy with the results for August, because only 58,000 units were produced. The August 2016 budget report for the company's assembling department is as follows:

(SO 1, 2, 3)
Prepare flexible budget reports for varying situations using the total budgeted cost formula.

YAEGER COMPANY
Budget Report
Assembling Department
Month Ended August 31, 2016

Manufacturing Costs	Budget	Actual	Difference: Favourable (F)/ Unfavourable (U)
Variable costs			
Direct materials	$ 48,000	$ 47,000	$1,000 F
Direct labour	54,000	51,300	2,700 F
Indirect materials	24,000	24,200	200 U
Indirect labour	18,000	17,500	500 F
Utilities	15,000	14,900	100 F
Maintenance	9,000	9,200	200 U
Total variable costs	168,000	164,100	3,900 F

(continued)

YAEGER COMPANY
Budget Report
Assembling Department
Month Ended August 31, 2016 (*continued*)

Fixed costs			
Rent	12,000	12,000	0
Supervision	17,000	17,000	0
Depreciation	7,000	7,000	0
Total fixed costs	36,000	36,000	0
Total costs	$204,000	$200,100	$3,900 F

Instructions

(a) State the total monthly budgeted cost formula.

(b) Budget $198,400

(b) Prepare a budget report for August using flexible budget data. Why does this report provide a better basis for evaluating performance than the report based on static budget data?

(c) Budget $215,200

(c) In September, 64,000 units were produced. Prepare the budget report using flexible budget data, assuming (1) each variable cost was 10% higher than its actual cost in August, and (2) fixed costs were the same in September as in August.

(SO 3)
Prepare a responsibility report for a profit centre.

P11-53B   Henning Manufacturing Inc. operates its patio furniture division as a profit centre. Operating data for this division for the year ended December 31, 2016, are as follows:

	Budget	Difference from Budget
Sales	$2,500,000	$60,000 F
Costs of goods sold		
Variable costs	1,300,000	41,000 F
Controllable fixed costs	200,000	6,000 U
Selling and administrative expenses		
Variable costs	220,000	7,000 U
Controllable fixed costs	50,000	2,000 U
Noncontrollable fixed costs	70,000	4,000 U

In addition, Henning Manufacturing incurs $180,000 of indirect fixed costs that were budgeted at $175,000. It allocates 20% of these costs to the patio furniture division.

Instructions

(a) Controllable margin $86,000 F

(a) Prepare a responsibility report for the patio furniture division for the year.

(b) ✏️ Comment on the manager's performance in controlling revenues and costs.

(c) Identify any costs that have been excluded from the responsibility report and explain why they were excluded.

(SO 4)
Prepare a responsibility report for an investment centre, and calculate ROI.

P11-54B   Alosio Manufacturing Company manufactures a variety of tools and industrial equipment. The company operates three divisions. Each division is an investment centre. Operating data for the home division for the year ended December 31, 2016, and relevant budget data are as follows:

	Actual	Comparison with Budget
Sales	$1,400,000	$ 100,000 favourable
Variable cost of goods sold	675,000	55,000 unfavourable
Variable selling and administrative expenses	125,000	25,000 unfavourable
Controllable fixed cost of goods sold	170,000	On target
Controllable fixed selling and administrative expenses	80,000	On target

Average operating assets for the year for the home division were $2 million, which was also the budgeted amount.

Instructions

(a) Controllable margin:
Budget $330,000;
Actual $350,000

(a) Prepare a responsibility report (in thousands of dollars) for the home division.

(b) ✏️ Evaluate the manager's performance. Which items will likely be investigated by top management?

(c) Calculate the expected ROI in 2017 for the home division, assuming the following independent changes to actual data:

1. The variable cost of goods sold decrease by 5%.
2. The average operating assets decrease by 10%.
3. Sales increase by $200,000, and this increase is expected to increase the contribution margin by $85,000.

*P11-55B South division had the following results for the year just ended:

(SO 4, 5)
Compare ROI and
residual income
with supporting
calculations.

Sales	$1,500,000	Controllable margin	$120,000
Contribution margin	600,000	Average operating assets	600,000

South is considering a new product line that would involve the following:

Sales	$300,000	Controllable margin	$ 24,000
Contribution margin	120,000	Average operating assets	150,000

South's parent company, Globe Inc., has a company-wide ROI of 14% and pays bonuses based on divisional ROI.

Instructions
(a) Determine the effect on South's ROI if it introduces the new product line. Would South's managers be encouraged to introduce the new product line?
(b) Determine the effect on Globe Inc.'s ROI if South introduces the new product line. Would the top managers of Globe Inc. want to introduce the new product line?
(c) Assume a required rate of return of 10% on operational assets invested in each division. Determine the effect on South's residual income if it introduces the new product. Would South's managers be encouraged to introduce the new product line?

(b) ROI of new product:
16%

*P11-56B Northern Pride Inc., a diversified company, operates four departments. The company has collected the following departmental information for 2016:

(SO 4, 5)
Calculate ROI and
residual income and
rank department
performances.

Department	Sales	Cost of Goods Sold	Operating Expenses	Current Investment
1	$ 200,000	$ 150,000	$ 15,000	$ 175,000
2	90,000	35,000	23,500	210,000
3	1,500,000	1,173,000	195,000	1,100,000
4	1,250,000	750,000	276,000	1,400,000

Instructions
(a) Rank the four departments based on their return on investment.
(b) Rank the four departments based on their residual income. Assume that the company requires a minimum return on the current investment of 10%.
(c) ▱▱▱▱▱▱▷ Explain why the rankings in part (a) and part (b) are similar or different.

(adapted from CGA-Canada, now CPA Canada)

(a) ROI: [1]   20%
        [2]   15%
        [3]   12%
        [4]   16%

*P11-57B Kappa Company has three divisions: A, B, and C. Each year the vice-president in charge of the best-performing division is entitled to a sizeable bonus. The results for the year are now in and each vice-president has claimed that the bonus should be his or hers. They've each used some version of return on investment (ROI) or residual income (RI) and have based their calculations on either the net book value, defined as original/historical cost less accumulated depreciation, or the gross book value (GBV), defined as original/historical cost without any depreciation of the asset base.
    The vice-presidents based their claims on the following information:

(SO 5)
Discuss the impact
of ROI and residual
income on manager
performance.

Division	GBV at Start of Year	Controllable Income
A	$400,000	$47,500
B	380,000	46,000
C	250,000	30,800

All divisions have fixed assets with a 20-year useful life and no disposal value. The fixed assets were purchased 10 years ago. Kappa's cost of capital is 10%. The company's three divisions all use beginning-of-the-year values for invested capital in the ROI or RI calculation. Assume straight-line depreciation.

Instructions
Determine which method for evaluating performance each vice-president used in order to show that his or her division had the best performance.

(adapted from CGA-Canada, now CPA Canada)

[A] NBV RI = $27,500
[B] GBV RI = $8,000
[C] GBV ROI = 12.32%

(SO 4, 5)
Compare and contrast performances under ROI and residual income.

(a) $10,000,000

(c) $5,000,000

*P11-58B   Return on investment is often expressed as follows:

$$ROI = \frac{Controllable\ margin}{Average\ operating\ asset} = \frac{Controllable\ margin}{Sales} \times \frac{Sales}{Average\ operating\ assets}$$

Instructions
(a) Explain the advantages of breaking down the ROI calculation into two separate components.
(b) 1. Comparative data on three companies operating in the same industry follow. The minimum required ROI is 10% for all three companies. Determine the missing amounts.

	Company A	Company B	Company C
Sales	$1,000,000	$500,000	(a)
Net operating income	$ 100,000	$ 50,000	(b)
Average operating assets	$ 500,000	(c)	$5,000,000
Profit margin	(d)	(e)	0.5%
Asset turnover	(f)	(g)	2
Return on investment	(h)	1%	(i)
Residual income	(j)	(k)	(l)

2. Compare and contrast the performance of the three companies, with reference to their relative performance as measured by the ROI and residual income.

(adapted from CGA-Canada, now CPA Canada)

(SO 2)
Prepare a flexible budget report for a cost centre.

(b) 56,250 units

P11-59B   Health Care Inc. (HCI) uses a flexible budgeting system, rather than only the current master budget. The following data are available for HCI's expected costs at production levels of 100,000, 110,000, and 120,000 units:

Variable costs	
Manufacturing	$8 per unit
Administrative	$4 per unit
Selling	$3 per unit
Fixed costs	
Manufacturing	$350,000
Administrative	$150,000

Instructions
(a) Prepare a flexible budget for each of the possible production levels: 100,000, 110,000, and 120,000 units.
(b) If HCI sells its product for $35 each, how many units will it have to sell to make a profit of $500,000 after taxes? The company tax rate is 20%.

(adapted from CGA-Canada, now CPA Canada)

(SO 5)
Calculate ROI and residual income and discuss the impact on manager performance.

*P11-60B   Steelwall Inc. uses the return on investment as a performance measure and defines investment as the average operating assets. The company bases management bonuses in part on the ROI and expects all investments to earn a minimum rate of return of 18%.

Stonewall is a division of Steelwall Inc. Its ROI has ranged from 22% to 25% since it was acquired. Stonewall had an investment opportunity in 2016 that had an estimated ROI of 20%. Stonewall's management decided against the investment because it believed the investment would decrease the division's overall ROI.

Selected financial information for Stonewall are presented below. The division's average operating assets were $25 million for the year 2016.

STONEWALL DIVISION
Selected Financial Information
Year Ended December 31, 2016

Sales	$29,100,000
Contribution margin	9,100,000
Controllable margin	5,000,000

Instructions

(a) Calculate the following performance measures for 2016 for the Stonewall division:
   (1) return on investment, and (2) residual income.
(b) Would the management of the division have been more likely to accept the investment opportunity it had in 2016 if residual income had been used as a performance measure instead of the ROI? Explain your answer.

(a) (1) ROI = 20%
(a) (2) RI = $500,000

(adapted from CMA Canada, now CPA Canada)

Cases

C11-61 Z-Bar Pastures is a 160-hectare farm on the outskirts of Swift Current, Saskatchewan, specializing in the boarding of brood mares and their foals. A recent economic downturn in the thoroughbred industry has led to a decline in breeding activities, and it has made the boarding business extremely competitive. To meet the competition, Z-Bar Pastures planned in 2016 to entertain clients, advertise more extensively, and absorb expenses formerly paid by clients, such as veterinary and blacksmith fees.

The budget report for 2016 is presented below. As shown, the static income statement budget for the year is based on an expected 21,900 boarding days at $25 per mare. The variable expenses per mare per day were budgeted as follows: feed $5; veterinary fees $3; blacksmith fees $0.30; and supplies $0.70. All other expenses were either semi-fixed or fixed.

During the year, management decided not to replace a worker who quit in March, but it did issue a new advertising brochure and entertained clients more.

Z-BAR PASTURES
Static Budget Income Statement
Year Ended December 31, 2016

	Master Budget	Actual	Difference
Number of mares	60	52	8 U
Number of boarding days	21,900	19,000	2,900 U
Sales	$547,500	$380,000	$167,500 U
Less variable expenses			
Feed	109,500	104,390	5,110 F
Veterinary fees	65,700	58,838	6,862 F
Blacksmith fees	5,475	4,984	491 F
Supplies	12,045	10,178	1,867 F
Total variable expenses	192,720	178,390	14,330 F
Contribution margin	354,780	201,610	153,170 U
Less fixed expenses			
Depreciation	40,000	40,000	0
Insurance	11,000	11,000	0
Utilities	14,000	12,000	2,000 F
Repairs and maintenance	11,000	10,000	1,000 F
Labour	95,000	88,000	7,000 F
Advertisement	8,000	12,000	4,000 U
Entertainment	5,000	7,000	2,000 U
Total fixed expenses	184,000	180,000	4,000 F
Net income	$170,780	$ 21,610	$149,170 U

Instructions

(a) Based on the static budget report, answer the following questions:
   1. What was(were) the primary cause(s) of the loss in net income?
   2. Did management do a good, average, or poor job of controlling expenses?
   3. Were management's decisions to stay competitive sound?
(b) Prepare a flexible budget report for the year.

(c) Based on the flexible budget report, answer the three questions in part (a) above.
(d) What course of action do you recommend for the management of Z-Bar Pastures?
(Data for this case are based on Hans Sprohge and John Talbott, "New Applications for Variance Analysis," *Journal of Accountancy* (April 1989), pp. 137–141.)

C11-62 Castle Company manufactures expensive watch cases that are sold as souvenirs. Three of its sales departments are retail sales, wholesale sales, and outlet sales. The retail sales department is a profit centre. The wholesale sales department is a cost centre; its managers merely take orders from customers who purchase through the company's wholesale catalogue. The outlet sales department is an investment centre, because each manager is given full responsibility for an outlet store location. The manager can hire and dismiss employees; purchase, maintain, and sell equipment; and in general is fairly independent of company control.

Sara Sutton is a manager in the retail sales department. Gilbert Kazmierski manages the wholesale sales department. José Lopez manages the Club Cartier outlet store in Montreal. The following are the budget responsibility reports for each of the three departments:

	Budget		
	Retail Sales	Wholesale Sales	Outlet Sales
Sales	$ 750,000	$ 400,000	$200,000
Variable costs			
Cost of goods sold	150,000	100,000	25,000
Advertising	100,000	30,000	5,000
Sales salaries	75,000	15,000	3,000
Printing	10,000	20,000	5,000
Travel	20,000	30,000	2,000
Fixed costs			
Rent	50,000	30,000	10,000
Insurance	5,000	2,000	1,000
Depreciation	75,000	100,000	40,000
Investment in assets	1,000,000	1,200,000	800,000

	Actual Results		
	Retail Sales	Wholesale Sales	Outlet Sales
Sales	$ 750,000	$ 400,000	$200,000
Variable costs			
Cost of goods sold	195,000	120,000	26,250
Advertising	100,000	30,000	5,000
Sales salaries	75,000	15,000	3,000
Printing	10,000	20,000	5,000
Travel	15,000	20,000	1,500
Fixed costs			
Rent	40,000	50,000	12,000
Insurance	5,000	2,000	1,000
Depreciation	80,000	90,000	60,000
Investment in assets	1,000,000	1,200,000	800,000

Instructions

(a) Determine which of the items should be included in the responsibility report for each of the three managers.

(b) Compare the budgeted measures with the actual results. Decide which results should be brought to the attention of each manager.

C11-63 The manufacturing overhead budget for Dillons Company contains the following items:

Variable expenses	
Indirect materials	$24,000
Indirect labour	12,000
Maintenance expenses	10,000
Manufacturing supplies	6,000
Total variable expenses	$52,000

Fixed expenses	
Supervision	$18,000
Inspection costs	1,000
Insurance expenses	2,000
Depreciation	15,000
Total fixed expenses	$36,000

The budget was based on an estimated 2,000 units being produced. During the past month, 1,500 units were produced, and the following costs were incurred:

Variable expenses	
Indirect materials	$24,200
Indirect labour	13,500
Maintenance expenses	8,200
Manufacturing supplies	5,100
Total variable expenses	$51,000
Fixed expenses	
Supervision	$19,300
Inspection costs	1,200
Insurance expenses	2,200
Depreciation	14,700
Total fixed expenses	$37,400

Instructions

(a) Determine which items would be controllable by Hideko Shitaki, the production manager.

(b) How much should have been spent during the month for the manufacture of the 1,500 units?

(c) Prepare a flexible manufacturing overhead budget report for Hideko.

(d) Prepare a responsibility report. Include only the costs that Hideko could have controlled. Assume that the supervision cost above includes the salary of Constantin Farris, the supervisor, of $10,000. In an attached memo, describe clearly for Hideko the areas in which her performance needs to be improved.

C11-64 The Madison Company purchased the Tek Company three years ago. Before the acquisition, Tek manufactured and sold plastic products to various customers. Tek has since become a division of Madison and now manufactures plastic Tek products only for products made by Madison's Macon division. Macon sells its products to hardware wholesalers.

Madison's corporate management gives the Tek division management a considerable amount of authority in running the division's operations. However, corporate management retains authority for decisions about capital investments, price setting on all products, and the quantity of each product to be produced by the Tek division.

Madison has a formal performance evaluation program for the management of all of its divisions. The performance evaluation program relies heavily on each division's return on investment. The income statement below for the Tek division is the basis for evaluating Tek's management.

The financial statements for the divisions are prepared by the corporate accounting staff. Costs for corporate general services are allocated to each division based on their sales dollars. The computer department's actual costs are allocated to the divisions based on usage. The net division investment includes the division's fixed assets at net book value (cost less depreciation), division inventory, and corporate working capital that is allocated to each based on the division's sales dollars.

TEK DIVISION OF MADISON COMPANY
Income Statement
Year Ended March 31, 2016
(in thousands)

Sales		$4,000
Costs and expenses		
Product costs		
Direct materials	$ 500	
Direct labour	1,100	
Factory overhead	1,300	
Total	2,900	
Less: Increase in inventory	350	2,550
Engineering and research		120
Shipping and receiving		240
Division administration		
Manager's office	$ 210	
Cost accounting	40	
Personnel	82	332
Corporate costs		
Computer	$ 48	
General services	230	278
Total costs and expenses		3,520
Divisional operating income		$ 480
Net plant investment		$1,600
Return on investment		30%

Instructions

(a) Discuss Madison Company's financial reporting and performance evaluation program as it relates to the responsibilities of the Tek division.

(b) Based on your answer to part (a), recommend appropriate revisions of the financial information and reports that Madison uses to evaluate

the performance of Tek's management. If revisions are not necessary, explain why they are not needed.

(adapted from CMA Canada, now CPA Canada)

---

*C11-65 Raddington Industries produces tool and die machinery for manufacturers. In 2001, the company acquired one of its suppliers of alloy steel plates, Reigis Steel Company. In order to manage the two separate businesses, the operations of Reigis are reported separately as an investment centre.

Raddington monitors its divisions based on their divisional contribution margin and return on average investment, with investment defined as the average operating assets employed. It bases management bonuses on the ROI. The average cost of capital is 13% of the operating investment.

Reigis's cost of goods sold is considered to be entirely variable, while the division's administrative expenses are not dependent on volume. Selling expenses are a mixed cost, with 40% attributed to the sales volume. Reigis recently contemplated a capital acquisition with an estimated ROI of 13.5%; however, division management decided against the investment because it believed the investment would decrease Reigis's overall ROI. The 2016 operating statement for Reigis follows. The division used operating assets of $25 million at June 30, 2016, a 5% increase over the 2015 year-end balance.

REIGIS STEEL DIVISION
Operating Statement
Year Ended June 30, 2016
(in thousands)

Sales revenue		$27,000
Less expenses:		
Cost of goods sold	$16,500	
Administrative expenses	4,300	
Selling expenses	2,700	23,500
Income from operations before income taxes		$ 3,500

Instructions

(a) Calculate the following performance measures for 2016 for the Reigis Steel division: (1) the ROI before tax, and (2) the residual income.

(b) Explain why management of the Reigis Steel division would have been more likely to accept the capital acquisition if it had used residual income rather than the ROI as a performance measure.

(c) The Reigis Steel division is a separate investment centre within Raddington Industries. Identify several items that Reigis should control if it is to be evaluated fairly by either the ROI or residual income performance measures.

(adapted from CMA Canada, now CPA Canada)

---

*C11-66 The performance of the division manager of Rarewood Furniture is measured by the ROI, defined as divisional segment income divided by the gross book value of total divisional assets. For existing operations, the division's projections for the coming year are as follows:

Sales	$ 25,000,000
Expenses	(22,500,000)
Segment income	$ 2,500,000

The gross book value of the total assets now used in operations is $15 million. Currently, the manager is evaluating an investment in a new product line that would, according to her projections, increase 2016 segment income by $250,000. She has not determined the cost of the investment. The company's cost of capital is 12%.

Instructions

(a) Calculate the ROI for 2016 without the new investment.

(b) Assuming the new product line would require an investment of $1.2 million, calculate the revised projected ROI for the division in 2016 with the new investment. Would the manager likely accept or reject the investment? Explain.

(c) How much would the investment have to cost for the manager to be indifferent about making it?

(d) Create a brief example with numbers to explain and illustrate how the use of residual income as a performance measure may encourage a manager to accept a project that is good for the company, but that he or she might otherwise reject.

(*Hint:* You may use the above situation as an example in your explanation.)

(adapted from CGA-Canada, now CPA Canada)

C11-67 A company operates five different plants, located in Vancouver, Edmonton, Toronto, Montreal, and Halifax. The total company operating income is $1,900,275. The following information was collected for each location:

	Vancouver	Edmonton	Toronto	Montreal	Halifax
Sales	$3,750,000	$4,700,000	$1,800,875	$800,000	$500,250
Materials	1,600,950	1,500,450	500,450	150,450	100,450
Direct labour	800,900	1,590,900	590,900	150,900	280,500
Variable overhead	470,000	170,000	140,000	30,000	40,900
Other operating expenses	600,500	280,000	230,000	352,600	70,000
Current investment	4,550,000	5,500,000	2,000,000	700,000	300,000

Instructions

(a) Determine which plant has the highest return on investment. Show your calculations.

(b) Assume that the company requires a minimum return of 10% on the current investment. Which plant has the highest residual income? Show your calculations.

(c) Compare your answers in parts (a) and (b) and indicate whether they are the same or different. Explain why.

(adapted from CGA-Canada, now CPA Canada)

C11-68 Canadian Products Corporation participates in a highly competitive industry. To compete successfully and reach its profit goals, the company has chosen the decentralized form of organization. The company evaluates each manager of a decentralized investment centre based on the centre's profit contribution, market penetration, and return on investment. When managers fail to meet the objectives set by corporate management, they are either demoted or dismissed.

An anonymous survey of company managers revealed that they feel pressured to compromise their personal ethical standards in order to reach corporate objectives. For example, at certain plant locations there was pressure to reduce quality control to a level that could not ensure that all unsafe products would be rejected. Also, sales personnel were encouraged to use questionable sales tactics to obtain orders, including offering gifts and other incentives to purchasing agents.

The chief executive officer is disturbed by the survey findings. In his opinion, such behaviour cannot be condoned by the company. He concludes that the company should do something about this problem.

Instructions

(a) Determine who the stakeholders are in this situation.

(b) Identify the ethical implications, conflicts, or dilemmas in the situation.

(c) What might the company do to reduce the pressure on managers and eliminate the ethical conflicts?

(adapted from CMA Canada, now CPA Canada)

"All About You" Activity

C11-69 You have received a promotion and are now the manager of the Lakeview Lounge at the hotel where you have been working for some time. The Lakeview Lounge provides alcoholic and non-alcoholic drinks, plus a range of light snacks during the day when the hotel restaurant is not open.

The monthly budget for the Lakeview Lounge profit centre is prepared by head office, in another city. You are responsible for making the lounge profitable for the hotel.

Instructions

(a) Identify the fixed and variable costs for the Lakeview Lounge and indicate if they are controllable by the lounge manager. For overhead costs, indicate if they are direct or indirect.

(b) How much discretion would you expect to receive over selling prices, and why?

Decision-Making at Current Designs

DM11-1 The Current Designs staff has prepared the annual manufacturing budget for the rotomoulded line based on an estimated annual production of 4,000 kayaks during 2016. Each kayak will require 54 kilograms of polyethylene powder and a finishing kit (rope, seat, hardware, etc.). The polyethylene powder used in these kayaks costs $1.50 per kilogram, and the finishing kits cost $170 each. Each kayak will use two kinds of labour—2 hours of type I labour from people who run the oven and trim the plastic, and 3 hours of work from type II workers who attach the hatches and seat and other hardware. The type I employees are paid $15 per hour, and the type II are paid $12 per hour.

Manufacturing overhead is budgeted at $396,000 for 2016, broken down as follows.

Variable costs	
Indirect materials	$ 40,000
Manufacturing supplies	53,800
Maintenance and utilities	88,000
	181,800
Fixed costs	
Supervision	90,000
Insurance	14,400
Depreciation	109,800
	214,200
Total	$396,000

During the first quarter, ended March 31, 2016, 1,050 units were actually produced with the following costs.

Polyethylene powder	$ 87,000
Finishing kits	178,840
Type I labour	31,500
Type II labour	39,060
Indirect materials	10,500
Manufacturing supplies	14,150
Maintenance and utilities	26,000
Supervision	20,000
Insurance	3,600
Depreciation	27,450
Total	$438,100

Instructions

(a) Prepare the annual manufacturing budget for 2016, assuming that 4,000 kayaks will be produced.

(b) Prepare the flexible budget for manufacturing for the quarter ended March 31, 2016. Assume activity levels of 900, 1,000, and 1,050 units.

(c) Assuming the rotomoulded line is treated as a profit centre, prepare a flexible budget report for manufacturing for the quarter ended March 31, 2016, when 1,050 units were produced.

Waterways Continuing Problem

(This is a continuation of the Waterways Problem from Chapters 1 through 10.)

WCP-11 On July 2, 2016, the accounting staff of Waterway's B.C. plant was shocked to discover that their accounting system had been compromised by a brand new computer virus called "badget." While their software supplier was able to provide a fix within hours of the discovery, they were unable to recover any of their budget data.

Now, the accountant was challenged to find a way to determine the budget amounts needed for the flexible budget report that was required for the performance reviews the following week. She thought she would start by looking at what had been reported for the first quarter of the year. The report that printed out was as follows.

	First Quarter 2016		Favourable F	
	Budget	Actual	Unfavourable U Difference	
Units produced	–	78,000	–	
Variable costs				
Indirect materials	–	$106,000	$ 4,600	U
Indirect labour	–	67,750	9,250	U
Utilities	–	49,300	1,400	F
Maintenance	–	76,200	13,800	U
Total variable costs	–	299,250	26,250	U
Fixed costs				
Salaries	–	120,000	1,000	U
Depreciation	–	53,500	–	
Property taxes	–	7,600	–	
Insurance	–	4,100	200	U
Janitorial	–	11,250	750	F
Total fixed costs	–	196,450	450	U
Total overhead	–	$495,700	$26,700	U

The accountant was able to collect a few other bits of information.

1. She knew the first quarter report was developed using the plant's flexible budget for manufacturing costs for 2016.

2. The production supervisor advised her that 73,000 units had been produced during the second quarter.

3. The production accountant provided her with the actual costs for the second quarter.

	Second Quarter 2016 Actual
Variable costs	
Indirect materials	$103,860
Indirect labour	67,750
Utilities	43,700
Maintenance	63,600
Fixed costs	
Salaries	112,000
Depreciation	53,500
Property taxes	7,500
Insurance	3,700
Janitorial	15,500

Instructions

Using the information provided, prepare a flexible manufacturing budget report.

Answers to Self-Study Questions

1. c 2. b 3. a 4. d 5. a 6. d 7. d 8. b 9. b 10. d 11. c

Remember to go back to the beginning of the chapter to check off your completed work!

12

Standard Costs and Balanced Scorecard

study objectives

the navigator

After studying this chapter, you should be able to do the following:

1. Describe standard costs.

2. Determine direct materials variances.

3. Determine direct labour and total manufacturing overhead variances.

4. Prepare variance reports and balanced scorecards.

5. Identify the features of a standard cost accounting system (Appendix 12A).

AN ACADEMIC SCORECARD

Carleton University, located south of Ottawa's city centre, has more than 26,000 full- and part-time undergraduate and graduate students, and 65 programs of study. The university has more than 2,000 employees, including faculty, management, and support staff, along with hundreds of contract instructors and teaching assistants.

A university of this size needs to measure and control both performance and costs. So, over a decade ago, Carleton's Finance and Administration division implemented the balanced scorecard approach to performance measurement. It's part of the university's emphasis on organizational excellence.

Finance and Administration is responsible for several departments—computing and communication services, finance, housing and conference services, human resources, institutional research and planning, pension fund management, facilities management and planning, university safety, and university services. "Although they are all very different in what they do, they all really support students, staff, and faculty," said Cindy Taylor, director of the Office of Quality Initiatives at Carleton University. The division created a vision and mission statement to guide these various departments, and decided to use the balanced scorecard approach to help them meet their objectives.

Carleton adapted the four balanced scorecard perspectives for its own purposes. It renamed the financial perspective "stewardship of resources," the customer perspective became "customer service," internal processes became "the way we work," and learning and growth became "our employees."

Each of the four perspectives contains objectives. For example, one customer service objective is to "foster a culture of service excellence." Finance and Administration measures this through the rating it receives from the Carleton Service Satisfaction Survey it conducts annually with both students and staff. The balanced scorecard provides a long-term and a short-term goal; in the case of service excellence, a satisfaction rating of 8 out of 10 for the long term and a 7.5 rating for the 2013–14 academic year. It also describes initiatives that will ensure that objectives are acted on and identifies who is accountable for them.

A more financially focused objective would be "to provide effective stewardship of university resources," measured by the successful delivery of capital programs, among other things. The level of success is determined by a percentage completed by a target date, such as "90% delivered on time and on budget" within a certain academic year. The division has an over-arching scorecard and one for each department.

The balanced scorecard "gives us a clear picture of what our strategy is . . . and it directs us in what kind of activities we need to do to be successful," said Ms. Taylor. "You can't have customer service without having employees that are totally engaged and processes that work."

Sources: Carleton University Finance and Administration Division, Strategic Planning, Strategic Measures and Initiatives—2013–2014 (balanced scorecard); Susan Hickman, "New Leadership Initiative Puts Carleton on Organizational Excellence Track," *Carleton Now*, December 2013; Kristy Strauss, "Continuous Improvement Alive and Well at Carleton," *Carleton Now*, April 2011; Carleton University website, www.carleton.ca.

Preview of Chapter 12

Standards are a fact of life. You met the admission standards for the school you are attending. The vehicle that you drive had to meet certain governmental emissions standards. The hamburgers and salads you eat in a restaurant have to meet certain health and nutritional standards before they can be sold. And, as described in our feature story, Carleton University develops standards for staff and student satisfaction, website communication, and capital projects. The reason for standards in these cases is very simple: they help to ensure that overall product quality is high while keeping costs under control.

In this chapter, we continue the study of controlling costs. You will learn how to evaluate performance using standard costs and a balanced scorecard.

The chapter is organized as follows:

STANDARD COSTS AND BALANCED SCORECARD

Standards—Needs and Costs	Direct Materials Variances	Direct Labour and Manufacturing Overhead Variances	Variance Reports and the Balanced Scorecard	Standard Cost Accounting System— Appendix 12A
➤ Distinguishing between standards and budgets ➤ Setting standard costs ➤ Analyzing and reporting variances from standards	➤ Causes of materials variances	➤ Direct labour variances ➤ Manufacturing overhead variances	➤ Reporting variances ➤ Statement presentation of variances ➤ Balanced scorecard	➤ Journal entries ➤ Ledger accounts

Standards—Needs and Costs

Standards are common in business. The standards that are imposed by government agencies are often called **regulations**. In Canada, many regulations fall under provincial jurisdiction; for example, in Ontario, the Employment Standards Act and Ontario Human Rights Code. Standards that are established internally by a company may include standards for personnel matters—such as employee absenteeism and ethical codes of conduct—quality control standards for products, and standard costs for goods and services. In managerial accounting, standard costs are predetermined unit costs that are used as measures of performance.

We will focus on manufacturing operations in this chapter. But standard costs also apply to many types of service businesses as well. For example, a fast-food restaurant such as McDonald's knows the price it should pay for pickles, beef, buns, and other ingredients. It also knows how much time it should take an employee to flip hamburgers. If too much is paid for pickles or too much time is taken to prepare Big Macs, the deviations are noticed and corrective action is taken. Standard costs can also be used in not-for-profit enterprises, such as universities, charitable organizations, and government agencies.

Standard costs offer several advantages to an organization, as shown in Illustration 12-1. These advantages are available only when standard costs are carefully established and prudently used. Using standards only as a way of placing blame can have a negative effect on managers and employees. In an effort to minimize this effect, many companies offer money incentives to employees who meet their standards.

▶Illustration 12-1
Advantages of standard costs

Facilitate management planning

Promote greater economy by making employees more "cost-conscious"

Help set selling prices

Contribute to management control by providing basis for evaluation of cost control

Help highlight variances in management by exception

Simplify costing of inventories and reduce clerical costs

BUSINESS INSIGHT *Standardizing Performance Measures*

Similar to international accounting standards, there is a worldwide move to adopt a standard set of performance measures for thousands of business processes. A number of organizations, including corporations, consultants, and governmental agencies, belong to the group, referred to as the Open Standards Benchmarking Collaborative, which was co-founded by APQC, an international organization that researches quality initiatives. Canadian participants include Air Canada, the City of Montreal, Environment Canada, RBC Bank, and Tim Hortons. Organizations that are interested in participating can go to the group's website and enter their business information to compare their performance against the benchmarks established by the collaborative.

Sources: "OSB Participant List," APQC, 2014; Wesley Vestal, "Open Standards Benchmarking Collaborative Research: Making Sense of KM Costs," KMWorld, July 1, 2005; William M. Bulkeley, "Business, Agencies to Standardize Their Benchmarks," *Wall Street Journal*, May 19, 2004.

How do such standards help a business or organization?

DISTINGUISHING BETWEEN STANDARDS AND BUDGETS

In theory, standards and budgets are essentially the same. Both are predetermined costs, and both contribute to management planning and control. There is a difference, however, in the way the terms are expressed. A standard is a unit amount. A budget is a total amount. Thus, it is customary to state, for example, that the standard cost of direct labour for a unit of product is $10. If 5,000 units of the product are produced, the $50,000 of direct labour is the budgeted labour cost. A standard is the budgeted cost per unit of product. A standard is therefore concerned with each individual cost component that makes up the entire budget.

There are important accounting differences between budgets and standards. Except for when manufacturing overhead is applied to jobs and processes, budget data are not journalized in cost accounting systems. In contrast, as will be illustrated in the appendix to this chapter, standard costs are sometimes used in cost accounting systems. Also, a company may report its inventories at standard cost in its financial statements, but it would not report inventories at budgeted costs.

SETTING STANDARD COSTS

Setting standards for the costs to produce a unit of product is a difficult task. It requires input from all individuals who are responsible for costs and quantities. To determine the standard cost of direct materials, management may have to consult purchasing agents, product managers, quality control engineers, and production supervisors. In setting the cost standard for direct labour, the payroll department provides pay rate data, and industrial engineers may determine the labour time requirements. The managerial accountant provides important input for management in the standard-setting process by accumulating historical cost data and by knowing how costs respond to changes in activity levels.

To be effective in controlling costs, standard costs need to be up-to-date at all times. Thus, standards should be reviewed continuously. They should be changed whenever it is determined that the existing standard is not a good measure of performance. Circumstances that could cause the revision of a standard include changed wage rates resulting from a new union contract, a change in product specifications, or the use of a new manufacturing method.

Ideal versus Normal Standards

Companies set standards at one of two levels: ideal or normal. Ideal standards represent optimum levels of performance under perfect operating conditions. Normal standards represent efficient levels of performance that are attainable under expected operating conditions.

Some managers believe ideal standards will stimulate workers to constant improvement. However, most managers believe that ideal standards lower the morale of the entire workforce because they are so difficult, if not impossible, to meet. Very few companies use ideal standards.

Most companies that use standards set them at a normal level. When they are properly set, normal standards are rigorous but attainable. Normal standards allow for rest periods, machine breakdowns, and other "normal" contingencies in the production process. It will be assumed in the remainder of this chapter that standard costs are set at a normal level.

Helpful Hint
When standards are set too high employees sometimes feel pressure to act unethically to meet these standards.

A Case Study

To establish the standard cost of producing a product, it is necessary to establish standards for each manufacturing cost element—direct materials, direct labour, and manufacturing overhead. The standard for each element is determined from the standard price to be paid and the standard quantity to be used.

To illustrate, we use an extended example. Xonic, Inc. uses standard costs to measure performance at the production facility of its caffeinated energy drink, Xonic Tonic. Xonic produces one-litre containers of concentrated syrup that it sells to coffee and smoothie shops, and other retail outlets. The syrup is mixed with ice water or ice "slush" before serving. The potency of the beverage varies depending on the amount of concentrated syrup used.

Direct Materials.   The **direct materials price standard** is the cost per unit of direct materials that should be incurred. This standard should be based on the purchasing department's best estimate of the **cost of raw materials**. This is often based on current purchase prices. The price standard should also include an amount for related costs, such as receiving, storing, and handling the material. Illustration 12-2 shows the calculation of the materials price standard per litre of material for Xonic's tonic.

▶Illustration 12-2

Setting a direct materials price standard

Item	Price
Purchase price, net of discounts	$2.70
Freight	0.20
Receiving and handling	0.10
Standard direct materials price per litre	$3.00

The **direct materials quantity standard** is the quantity of direct materials that should be used per unit of finished goods. This standard is expressed as a physical measure, such as kilograms, barrels, or litres. In setting the standard, management should consider both the quality and quantity of materials that are required to manufacture the product. The standard should include allowances (extra amounts) for unavoidable waste and normal spoilage. The standard quantity per unit for Xonic, Inc., is calculated in Illustration 12-3.

▶Illustration 12-3

Setting a direct materials quantity standard

Item	Quantity (litres)
Required materials	3.5
Allowance for waste	0.4
Allowance for spoilage	0.1
Standard direct materials quantity per unit	4.0

The standard direct materials cost per unit is the standard direct materials price times the standard direct materials quantity. For Xonic, Inc., the standard direct materials cost per litre of tonic is $12.00 ($3.00 × 4 litres).

Direct Labour.   The **direct labour price standard** is the rate per hour that should be incurred for direct labour. This standard is based on current wage rates and is adjusted for expected changes, such as cost of living adjustments (COLAs). The price standard also generally includes employer payroll taxes and benefits, such as paid holidays and vacations. Illustration 12-4 provides the direct labour price standard for Xonic, Inc.

Alternative Terminology
The direct labour price standard is also called the *direct labour rate standard.*

▶Illustration 12-4

Setting a direct labour price standard

Item	Price
Hourly wage rate	$12.50
COLA	0.25
Payroll taxes	0.75
Fringe benefits	1.50
Standard direct labour rate per hour	$15.00

Alternative Terminology
The direct labour quantity standard is also called the *direct labour efficiency standard.*

The **direct labour quantity standard** is the time that should be required to make one unit of the product. This standard is especially critical in labour-intensive companies. Allowances should be made in this standard for rest periods, cleanup, machine set-up, and machine downtime. Illustration 12-5 shows Xonic's direct labour quantity standard.

▶Illustration 12-5

Setting a direct labour quantity standard

Item	Quantity (Hours)
Actual production time	1.5
Rest periods and cleanup	0.2
Set-up and downtime	0.3
Standard direct labour hours per unit	2.0

The **standard direct labour cost per unit is the standard direct labour rate times the standard direct labour hours.** For Xonic, Inc., the standard direct labour cost per litre is $30 ($15.00 × 2 hours).

Manufacturing Overhead. For manufacturing overhead, a **standard predetermined overhead rate** is used in setting the standard. This overhead rate is determined by dividing budgeted overhead costs by an expected standard activity index. Standard direct labour hours and standard machine hours are two examples of standard activity indexes.

As discussed in Chapter 5, many companies use activity-based costing (ABC) to allocate overhead costs. Because ABC uses multiple activity indexes to allocate overhead costs, it results in a better correlation between the activities and costs that are incurred. As a result, the use of ABC can significantly improve the usefulness of a standard cost system for management decision-making.

Xonic, Inc., uses standard direct labour hours as its activity index. The company expects to produce 13,200 litres of Xonic Tonic during the year at normal capacity. **Normal capacity** is the average activity output that a company should experience over the long run. Since it takes two direct labour hours for each litre, the total standard direct labour hours is 26,400 (13,200 × 2). At this level of activity, overhead costs are expected to be $132,000. Of that amount, $79,200 is variable and $52,800 is fixed. The standard predetermined overhead rates are calculated as shown in Illustration 12-6.

Budgeted Overhead Costs	Amount	Standard Direct Labour Hours	Overhead Rate per Direct Labour Hour
Variable	$ 79,200	26,400	$3.00
Fixed	52,800	26,400	2.00
Total	$132,000	26,400	$5.00

►Illustration 12-6
Calculating predetermined overhead rates

The **standard manufacturing overhead rate per unit is the predetermined overhead rate times the activity index quantity standard.** For Xonic, Inc., which uses direct labour hours as its activity index, the standard manufacturing overhead rate per litre of Xonic Tonic is $10 ($5 × 2 hours).

Total Standard Cost Per Unit. Now that the standard quantity and price have been established per unit of product, the total standard cost can be determined. The total standard cost per unit is the sum of the standard costs of direct materials, direct labour, and manufacturing overhead. For Xonic, Inc., the total standard cost per litre of tonic is $42, as shown on the standard cost card in Illustration 12-7.

Product: Xonic Tonic		**Unit Measure: Litre**	
Manufacturing Cost Elements	Standard Quantity	Standard Price	Standard
Direct materials	4 litres	$ 3.00	$12.00
Direct labour	2 hours	15.00	30.00
Manufacturing overhead	2 hours	5.00	10.00
			$52.00

►Illustration 12-7
Standard cost per litre of tonic

A standard cost card is prepared for each product. This card becomes the basis for determining variances from standards.

ANALYZING AND REPORTING VARIANCES FROM STANDARDS

One of the major management uses of standard costs is to identify variances from standards. **Variances** are the differences between total actual costs and total standard costs. To illustrate, we will assume that in producing 1,000 litres of Xonic Tonic in the month of June, Xonic, Inc., incurred the costs shown in Illustration 12-8.

Alternative Terminology
In business, the term *variance* is also used to indicate differences between total budgeted costs and total actual costs.

►Illustration 12-8
Actual production costs

Direct materials	$13,020
Direct labour	31,080
Variable overhead	6,500
Fixed overhead	4,900
Total actual costs	$55,500

Total standard costs are determined by multiplying the units produced by the standard cost per unit. The total standard cost of Xonic Tonic is $52,000 (1,000 litres × $52). Thus, the total variance is $3,500, as shown in Illustration 12-9.

►Illustration 12-9
Calculation of total variance

Actual costs	$55,500
Less: Standard costs	52,000
Total variance	$ 3,500

Note that the variance is expressed in total dollars and not on a per-unit basis.

When actual costs are higher than standard costs, the variance is **unfavourable**. The $3,500 variance in June for Xonic Tonic is unfavourable. An unfavourable variance has a negative connotation. It suggests that too much was paid for one or more of the manufacturing cost elements or that the elements were used inefficiently.

If actual costs are less than standard costs, the variance is **favourable**. A favourable variance has a positive connotation. It suggests there is efficient management of manufacturing costs and efficient use of direct materials, direct labour, and manufacturing overhead. However, be careful: a favourable variance could be obtained by using inferior materials. In printing wedding invitations, for example, a favourable variance could result from using an inferior grade of paper. Or, a favourable variance might be achieved when installing tires on an automobile assembly line by tightening only half of the lug bolts. A variance is not favourable if quality control standards have been sacrificed.

BEFORE YOU GO ON...

►Do It! Standard Costs

Ridette Inc. accumulated the following standard cost data concerning product Cty31.

   Materials per unit: 1.5 kg at $4 per kilogram
   Labour per unit: 0.25 hours at $13 per hour
   Manufacturing overhead: Predetermined rate is 120% of direct labour cost
Calculate the standard cost of one unit of product Cty31.

Action Plan

- Know that standard costs are predetermined unit costs.
- To establish the standard cost of producing a product, establish the standard for each manufacturing cost element: direct materials, direct labour, and manufacturing overhead.
- Calculate the standard cost for each element from the standard price to be paid and the standard quantity to be used.

Solution

Manufacturing Cost Element	Standard Quantity	×	Standard Price	=	Standard Cost
Direct materials	1.5 kg		$ 4.00		$ 6.00
Direct labour	0.25 hours		$13.00		3.25
Manufacturing overhead	120% of direct labour cost		$ 3.25		3.90
Total					$13.15

Related exercise material: **BE12-1, BE12-2, BE12-3, E12-17, E12-18, E12-19,** and **Do It! D12-12.**

the
navigator

To interpret a variance, you must analyze its components. A variance can result from differences related to the cost of materials, labour, or overhead. Illustration 12-10 shows that the total variance is the sum of the materials, labour, and overhead variances.

In the following discussion, you will see that the materials variance and the labour variance are the sum of variances resulting from price differences and quantity differences. Illustration 12-11 shows a format for calculating the price and quantity variances.

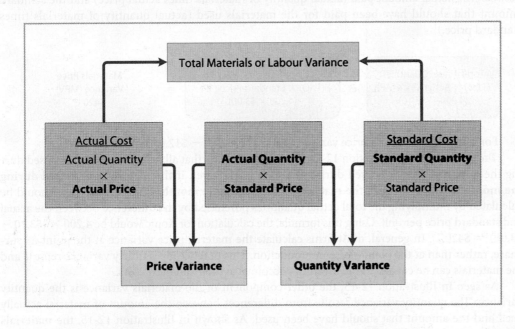

Note that the left side of the matrix is actual cost (actual quantity times actual price). The right hand is standard cost (standard quantity times standard price). The only additional element you need in order to calculate the price and quantity variances is the middle element, the actual quantity at the standard price.

Direct Materials Variances

Part of Xonic's total variance of $3,500 is due to a materials variance. In completing the order for 1,000 litres of Xonic Tonic, the company used 4,200 litres of direct materials. The direct materials were purchased at a price of $3.10 per unit. From Illustration 12-3, we know that Xonic's standards require it to use 4 litres of materials per litre produced, so it should have only used 4,000 (4 × 1,000) litres of direct materials to produce 1,000 litres. Illustration 12-2 shows that the standard cost of each litre of direct materials is $3 instead of the $3.10 actually paid. Illustration 12-12 shows that the **total direct materials budget variance (TDMBV)** is calculated as the difference between the amount paid (actual quantity times actual price) and the amount that should have been paid based on standards (standard quantity times standard price of materials).

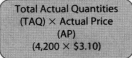

Total Actual Quantities (TAQ) × Actual Price (AP) (4,200 × $3.10) − Total Standard Quantities Allowed (TSQA) × Standard Price (SP) (4,000 × $3.00) = Total Direct Materials Budget Variance (TDMBV) $1,020 U

Thus, for Xonic, the total materials variance is $1,020 ($13,020 − $12,000) unfavourable.

The total materials variance could be caused by differences in the price paid for the materials or by differences in the amount of materials used. Illustration 12-13 shows that the total materials variance is the sum of the materials price variance and the materials quantity variance.

▶Illustration 12-13
Components of total materials variance

The **materials price variance** results from a difference between the actual price and the standard price. Illustration 12-14 shows that the materials price variance is calculated as the difference between the actual amount paid (actual quantity of materials times actual price) and the standard amount that should have been paid for the materials used (actual quantity of materials times standard price.)[1]

▶Illustration 12-14
Formula for materials price variance

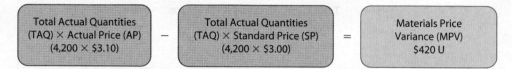

For Xonic, the materials price variance is $420 ($13,020 − $12,600) unfavourable.

Helpful Hint
The alternative formula is as follows: TAQ × (AP − SP) = MPV

The calculation in Illustration 12-14 is based on the fact that all of the material purchased during the month of June was used during the month. However, **if the material purchased during the month is different from the material used during the month,** the price variance should be calculated by multiplying the total actual quantities purchased by the difference between the actual and standard price per unit. Using this formula, the calculation for Xonic would be 4,200 × ($3.10 − $3.00) = $420 U. In general, most firms calculate the material price variance at the point of purchase, rather than at the point of use in production. This practice gives timely variance reports and the materials can be carried in the inventory accounts at their standard costs.

As seen in Illustration 12-13, the other component of the materials variance is the quantity variance. The quantity variance results from differences between the amount of material actually used and the amount that should have been used. As shown in Illustration 12-15, the **materials quantity variance** is calculated as the difference between the standard cost of the actual quantity (actual quantity times standard price) and the standard cost of the amount that should have been used (standard quantity times standard price for materials).

▶Illustration 12-15
Formula for materials quantity variance

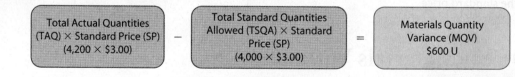

Thus, for Xonic, Inc., the materials quantity variance is $600 ($12,600 − $12,000) unfavourable.

The quantity variance can also be calculated by applying the standard price to the difference between the total actual quantities used and total standard quantities allowed. The calculation in this example is $3.00 × (4,200 − 4,000) = $600 U.

Helpful Hint
The alternative formula is:
SP × (TAQ − TSQ) = MQV

The total materials budget variance of $1,020 (unfavourable), therefore, consists of the amounts shown in Illustration 12-16.

▶Illustration 12-16
Summary of materials variances

Materials price variance	$ 420 U
Materials quantity variance	600 U
Total materials budget variance	$1,020 U

[1] We will assume that all materials purchased during the period are used in production and that no units remain in inventory at the end of the period.

A matrix is sometimes used to analyze a variance. **When a matrix is used, the formulas for each cost element are calculated before the variances are calculated.**

Illustration 12-17 shows the completed matrix for the direct materials variance for Xonic. The matrix provides a convenient structure for determining each variance.

►Illustration 12-17
Matrix for total direct materials budget variances

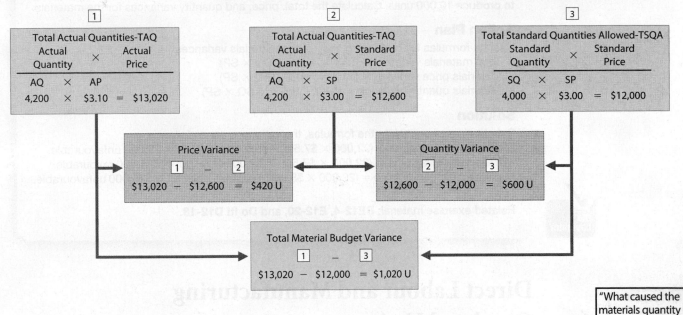

CAUSES OF MATERIALS VARIANCES

What are the causes of a variance? The causes may be both internal and external factors. **The investigation of a materials price variance usually begins in the purchasing department.** Many factors affect the price paid for raw materials. These include the delivery method used, the availability of quantity and cash discounts, and the quality of the materials requested. If these factors have been considered in setting the price standard, the purchasing department should be responsible for any variances.

However, a variance may be beyond the control of the purchasing department. Sometimes, for example, prices may rise faster than expected. Moreover, actions by groups that the company cannot control, such as the OPEC nations' oil price increases, may cause an unfavourable variance. There are also times when a production department may be responsible for the price variance. This can occur when a rush order forces the company to pay a higher price for the materials.

The starting point for determining the cause(s) of an unfavourable **materials quantity variance** is in the **production department**. If the variances are due to inexperienced workers, faulty machinery, or carelessness, the production department would be responsible. However, if the materials obtained by the purchasing department were of inferior quality, then the purchasing department should be responsible.

"What caused the materials quantity variances?"

Production Department

"What caused the materials price variances?"

Purchasing Department

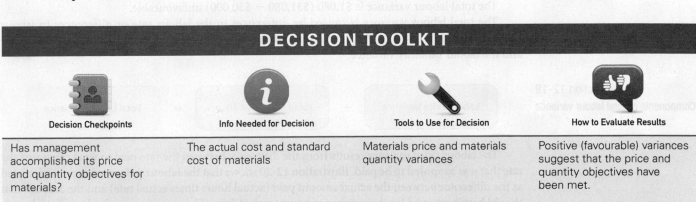

DECISION TOOLKIT

Decision Checkpoints	Info Needed for Decision	Tools to Use for Decision	How to Evaluate Results
Has management accomplished its price and quantity objectives for materials?	The actual cost and standard cost of materials	Materials price and materials quantity variances	Positive (favourable) variances suggest that the price and quantity objectives have been met.

▶Do It! **Direct Materials Variances**

The standard cost of product XX includes two units of direct materials at $8.00 per unit. During July, 22,000 units of direct materials are purchased at $7.50 per unit and are used to produce 10,000 units. Calculate the total, price, and quantity variances for the materials.

Action Plan

Use the formulas for calculating each of the materials variances:
- Total materials variance = (TAQ × AP) − (TSQ × SP)
- Materials price variance = (TAQ × AP) − (TAQ × SP)
- Materials quantity variance = (TAQ × SP) − (TSQ × SP)

Solution

Substituting amounts into the formulas, the variances are as follows:
Total materials variance = (22,000 × $7.50) − (20,000 × $8.00) = $5,000 unfavourable.
Materials price variance = (22,000 × $7.50) − (22,000 × $8.00) = $11,000 favourable.
Materials quantity variance = (22,000 × $8.00) − (20,000 × $8.00) = $16,000 unfavourable.

Related exercise material: **BE12-4, E12-20,** and **Do It! D12-13.**

Direct Labour and Manufacturing Overhead Variances

DIRECT LABOUR VARIANCES

STUDY OBJECTIVE 3
Determine direct labour and total manufacturing overhead variances.

The process of determining direct labour variances is the same as for determining the direct materials variances. In completing the Xonic Tonic order, the company incurred 2,100 direct labour hours at an average hourly rate of $14.80. The standard hours allowed for the units produced were 2,000 hours (1,000 litres × 2 hours). The standard labour rate was $15 per hour.

The total labour variance is the difference between the amount actually paid for labour versus the amount that should have been paid. Illustration 12-18 shows that the total direct labour budget variance (TDLBV) is calculated as the difference between the amount actually paid for labour (actual hours times actual rate) and the amount that should have been paid (standard hours times standard rate for labour).

▶Illustration 12-18
Formula for total labour variance

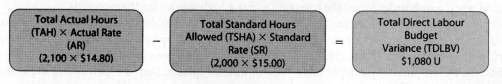

Total Actual Hours (TAH) × Actual Rate (AR) (2,100 × $14.80)	−	Total Standard Hours Allowed (TSHA) × Standard Rate (SR) (2,000 × $15.00)	=	Total Direct Labour Budget Variance (TDLBV) $1,080 U

The total labour variance is $1,080 ($31,080 − $30,000) unfavourable.

The total labour variance is caused by differences in the labour rate or differences in labour hours. Illustration 12-19 shows that the total labour variance is the sum of the labour price variance and the labour quantity variance.

▶Illustration 12-19
Components of total labour variance

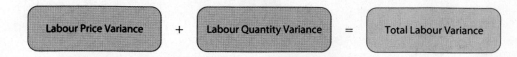

Labour Price Variance	+	Labour Quantity Variance	=	Total Labour Variance

The labour price variance results from the difference between the rate paid to workers versus the rate that was supposed to be paid. Illustration 12-20 shows that the labour price variance is calculated as the difference between the actual amount paid (actual hours times actual rate) and the amount that should have been paid for the number of hours worked (actual hours times standard rate for labour).

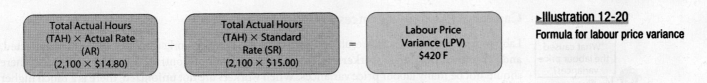

▶Illustration 12-20
Formula for labour price variance

For Xonic, the labour price variance is $420 ($31,080 − $31,500) favourable.

The labour price variance can also be calculated by multiplying actual hours worked by the difference between the actual pay rate and the standard pay rate. The calculation in this example is $2,100 \times (\$15.00 - \$14.80) = \$420$ F.

Helpful Hint
The alternative formula is:
$AH \times (AR - SR) = LPV$

The other component of the total labour variance is the labour quantity variance. The labour quantity variance results from the difference between the actual number of labour hours and the number of hours that should have been worked for the quantity produced. Illustration 12-21 shows that the **labour quantity variance** is calculated as the difference between the amount that should have been paid for the hours worked (actual hours times standard rate) and the amount that should have been paid for the amount of hours that should have been worked (standard hours times standard rate for labour).

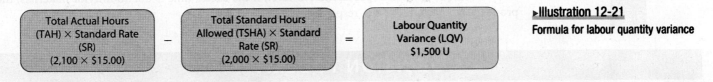

▶Illustration 12-21
Formula for labour quantity variance

For Xonic, the labour quantity variance is $1,500 ($31,500 − $30,000) unfavourable. The same result can be obtained by multiplying the standard rate by the difference between the total actual hours worked and total standard hours allowed. In this case, the calculation is $15.00 \times (2,100 - 2,000) = \$1,500$ U.

The total direct labour budget variance is $1,080 (unfavourable); it consists of the amounts shown in Illustration 12-22.

Helpful Hint
The alternative formula is:
$SR \times (AH - SH) = LQV$

Labour price variance	$ 420 F
Labour quantity variance	1,500 U
Total direct labour budget variance	$1,080 U

▶Illustration 12-22
Summary of labour variances

These results can also be obtained from the matrix in Illustration 12-23.

▶Illustration 12-23
Matrix for total direct labour budget variances

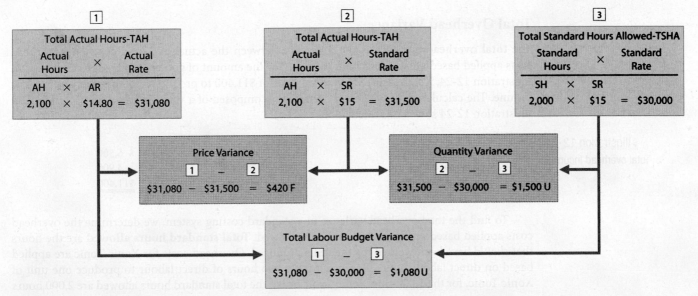

Causes of Labour Variances

"What caused the labour price variances?"

Personnel decisions

"What caused the labour quantity variances?"

Production Department

Labour price variances usually result from two factors: (1) paying workers **higher wages than expected**, and (2) a **misallocation of workers**. In companies where union contracts determine pay rates, there should not be many labour price variances. When workers are not unionized, there is a much higher likelihood of such variances. The manager who authorized the wage increase is responsible for these variances.

Misallocation of the workforce means using skilled workers instead of unskilled workers, and vice versa. The use of an inexperienced worker instead of an experienced one will result in a favourable price variance because of the lower pay rate of the unskilled worker. An unfavourable price variance would result if a skilled worker were substituted for an inexperienced one. The production department is generally responsible for labour price variances that result from misallocation of the workforce.

Labour quantity variances relate to the **efficiency of workers**. The cause of a quantity variance generally can be traced to the production department. The causes of an unfavourable variance may be poor training, worker fatigue, faulty machinery, or carelessness. These causes are the responsibility of the **production department**. However, if the excess time is due to inferior materials, the production department is not responsible.

DECISION TOOLKIT

Decision Checkpoints	Info Needed for Decision	Tools to Use for Decision	How to Evaluate Results
Has management accomplished its price and quantity objectives for labour?	The actual cost and standard cost of labour	Labour price and labour quantity variances	Positive (favourable) variances suggest that the price and quantity objectives have been met.

MANUFACTURING OVERHEAD VARIANCES

The calculation of the manufacturing overhead variances is mostly the same as the calculation of the materials and labour variances. However, the task is more challenging for manufacturing overhead because both variable and fixed overhead costs must be considered.

Total Overhead Variance

The **total overhead variance** is the difference between the actual overhead costs and overhead costs applied based on standard hours allowed for the amount of goods produced. As indicated in Illustration 12-24, Xonic incurred overhead costs of $11,400 to produce 1,000 litres of Xonic Tonic in June. The calculation of the actual overhead is composed of a variable and a fixed component. Illustration 12-24 shows this calculation.

►Illustration 12-24
Total overhead incurred

Variable overhead	$ 6,500
Fixed overhead	4,900
Total actual overhead	$11,400

To find the total overhead variance in a standard costing system, we determine the overhead costs applied based on total standard hours allowed. **Total standard hours allowed** are the hours that *should* have been worked for the units produced. Overhead costs for Xonic Tonic are applied based on direct labour hours. Because it takes two hours of direct labour to produce one unit of Xonic Tonic, for the 1,000-unit Xonic Tonic order, the total standard hours allowed are 2,000 hours

(1,000 units × 2 hours). We then apply the predetermined overhead rate to the 2,000 standard hours allowed. The predetermined rate for Xonic Tonic is $5, composed of a variable overhead rate of $3 and a fixed rate of $2. Recall from Illustration 12-6 that the amount of budgeted overhead costs at normal capacity of $132,000 was divided by normal capacity of 26,400 direct labour hours, to arrive at a predetermined overhead rate of $5 ($132,000 ÷ 26,400). The predetermined rate of $5 is then multiplied by the 2,000 standard hours allowed, to determine the overhead costs applied.

Illustration 12-25 gives the formula for the total overhead variance.

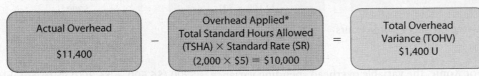

*Based on direct labour hours

▶Illustration 12-25
Formula for total overhead budget variance

Thus, for Xonic, the total overhead variance is $1,400 unfavourable.

The overhead variance is generally analyzed by examining the variable overhead variance and the fixed overhead variance.

Total Variable Overhead Budget Variance (TVOHBV)

The **total variable overhead budget variance (TVOHBV)** shows whether variable overhead costs were effectively controlled. To calculate this variance, the actual variable overhead costs incurred are compared with budgeted costs for the **total standard hours allowed**. The budgeted costs are determined from the flexible manufacturing overhead budget, which was presented in Chapter 11. For Xonic, the budget formula for manufacturing overhead was its variable manufacturing overhead cost of $3 per hour of labour plus its fixed manufacturing overhead costs of $4,400. Illustration 12-26 provides Xonic's budget.

XONIC, INC. Flexible Manufacturing Overhead Budget				
Activity Index				
Standard direct labour hours	1,800	2,000	2,200	2,400
Costs				
Variable costs				
Indirect materials	$1,800	$ 2,000	$ 2,200	$ 2,400
Indirect labour	2,700	3,000	3,300	3,600
Utilities	900	1,000	1,100	1,200
Total variable costs	5,400	6,000	6,600	7,200
Fixed costs				
Supervision	3,000	3,000	3,000	3,000
Depreciation	1,400	1,400	1,400	1,400
Total fixed costs	4,400	4,400	4,400	4,400
Total costs	$9,800	$10,400	$11,000	$11,600

▶Illustration 12-26
Flexible budget using standard direct labour hours

As shown, the budgeted costs for 2,000 standard hours are $10,400 ($6,000 variable and $4,400 fixed).

Illustration 12-27 provides the formula for the variable overhead budget variance.

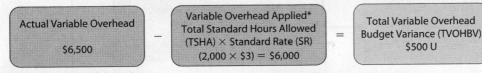

*Based on direct labour hours

▶Illustration 12-27
Formula for the total variable overhead budget variance

The total variable overhead budget variance (TVOHBV) for Xonic is $500 unfavourable.

Xonic can find the reason for the variance by comparing the actual variable overhead costs ($6,500) with the budgeted variable overhead costs ($6,000).

This total variable overhead budget variance (TVOHBV) of $500 (unfavourable) can also be analyzed into a spending (price) variance and an efficiency (quantity) variance. Illustration 12-28 provides the formula for the spending variance.

▶Illustration 12-28

Formula for variable overhead spending (price) variance

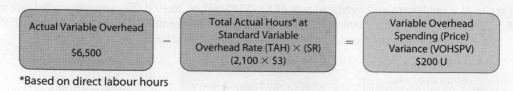

*Based on direct labour hours

For Xonic, the variable overhead spending variance is $200 ($6,500 − $6,300) unfavourable. The variable overhead efficiency variance is derived using the formula in Illustration 12-29.

▶Illustration 12-29

Formula for variable overhead efficiency (quantity) variance

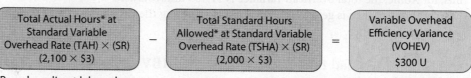

*Based on direct labour hours

Helpful Hint

The alternative formula is:
$SR \times (AH − SH) = VOHEV$

For Xonic, the variable overhead efficiency variance is $300 ($6,300 − $6,000) unfavourable. The same result can be obtained by multiplying the standard rate by the difference between the total actual hours worked and the total standard hours allowed. In this case, the calculation is $3 × (2,100 − 2,000) = $300 U.

The total variable overhead budget variance of $500 (unfavourable), therefore, consists of the amounts shown in Illustration 12-30.

▶Illustration 12-30

Summary of total variable overhead budget variances

Variable overhead spending variance	$200 U
Variable overhead efficiency variance	300 U
Total variable overhead budget variance	$500 U

These results can also be obtained from the matrix in Illustration 12-31.

▶Illustration 12-31

Matrix for variable overhead variances

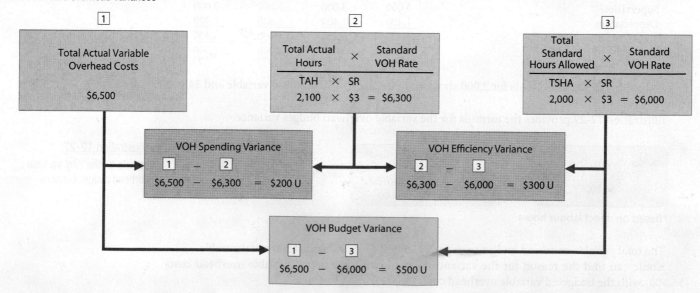

Management can compare the actual and budgeted variable overhead for each manufacturing overhead cost that contributes to the budget variance. In addition, cost and quantity variances can be developed for each overhead cost, such as indirect materials and indirect labour.

Total Fixed Overhead Variance

The **total fixed overhead variance** is the difference between the actual fixed overhead and the total standard hours allowed multiplied by the fixed overhead rate as shown in Illustration 12-32. This fixed overhead (FOH) variance can also be analyzed into a spending (budget) variance and a volume variance. The **fixed overhead spending (budget) variance** shows whether spending on fixed costs was under or over the budgeted fixed costs for the year. To illustrate the fixed overhead rate calculation, recall that Xonic budgeted a fixed overhead cost for the year of $52,800 (Illustration 12-6). At normal capacity, 26,400 standard direct labour hours are required. The fixed overhead rate is therefore $2 ($52,800 ÷ 26,400).

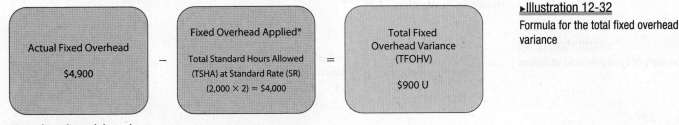

*Based on direct labour hours

►Illustration 12-32
Formula for the total fixed overhead variance

Next, Xonic produced 1,000 units of tonic in June. As indicated earlier, the standard hours allowed for the 1,000 units produced in June is 2,000 (1,000 units × 2 hours). For Xonic, the standard direct labour hours for June at normal capacity (Static Budget) is 2,200 (26,400 annual hours ÷ 12 months). Illustration 12-33 provides the formula for the spending (budget) variance.

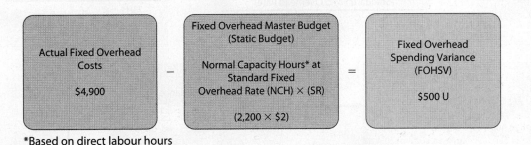

*Based on direct labour hours

►Illustration 12-33
Formula for fixed overhead spending (budget) variance

For Xonic, the fixed overhead spending (budget) variance is $500 ($4,900 − $4,400) unfavourable.

The **fixed overhead volume variance** answers the question of whether Xonic effectively used its fixed capacity. If Xonic produces less than normal capacity would allow, an unfavourable variance results. Conversely, if Xonic produces more tonic than what is considered normal capacity, a favourable variance results.

Illustration 12-34 provides the formula for calculating the fixed overhead volume.

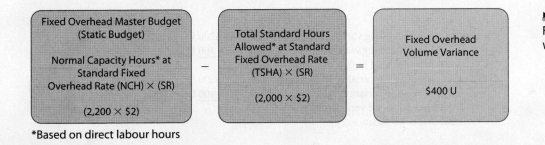

*Based on direct labour hours

►Illustration 12-34
Formula for fixed overhead volume variance

The same result can be obtained by multiplying the standard rate by the difference between the normal capacity hours and the standard hours allowed. The calculation of the fixed overhead volume variance for June is therefore as shown in Illustration 12-35.

►Illustration 12-35
Calculation of fixed overhead volume variance

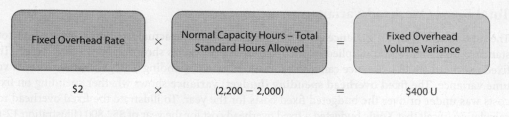

$2 × (2,200 − 2,000) = $400 U

In Xonic's case, a $400 unfavourable volume variance result is unfavourable because Xonic did not produce up to the normal capacity level in the month of June.

The total fixed overhead variance of $900 (unfavourable), therefore, consists of the amounts shown in Illustration 12-36.

►Illustration 12-36
Summary of fixed overhead variances

Fixed overhead spending (budget) variance	$500 U
Fixed overhead volume variance	400 U
Total fixed overhead variance	$900 U

►Illustration 12-37
Matrix for fixed overhead variances

These results can also be obtained from the matrix in Illustration 12-37.

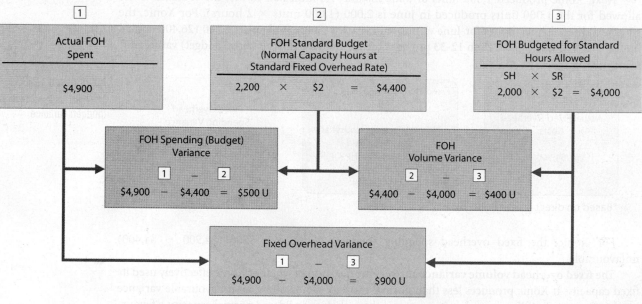

Having investigated these specific variances, we can now see that, in summary, the total overhead variance of $1,400 (unfavourable) consists of the amounts shown in Illustration 12-38.

►Illustration 12-38
Summary of total overhead variances

Variable overhead spending variance	$200 U	
Variable overhead efficiency variance	300 U	
Total variable overhead budget variance		$ 500 U
Fixed overhead spending variance (budget)	$500 U	
Fixed overhead volume variance	400 U	
Total fixed overhead variance		900 U
Total overhead variances		$1,400 U

In calculating the overhead variances, it is important to remember the following:

1. The standard hours allowed are used in each of the variances.
2. The total budget overhead variance generally relates to total variable overhead budget variance and the fixed overhead spending (budget) variance only. In Xonic's case, it is $1,000 unfavourable. (Total variable overhead budget variance (spending + efficiency) of $500 U + Fixed overhead spending (budget) variance of $500 U.)
3. The volume variance relates only to fixed overhead costs and it is also called *production volume variance*.
4. Overapplied or underapplied overhead is the difference between the total actual overhead costs (variable + fixed) and the budget overhead at the standard base* allowed. In Xonic's case, it is $1,400 ($11,400 − $10,000) underapplied.

*Based on direct labour hours

Causes of Manufacturing Overhead Variances

The cause of an unfavourable variance may be (1) a **higher-than-expected use** of indirect materials, indirect labour, and factory supplies, or (2) **increases in indirect manufacturing costs**, such as fuel and maintenance costs.

The **production department** is also responsible for the overhead volume variance if the cause is either inefficient use of direct labour or machine breakdowns. When the cause is a **lack of sales orders**, the production department is not responsible.

"What caused the manufacturing overhead variances?"

Controllable Variance	Overhead Volume Variance
Production Department	Production or Sales Department

DECISION TOOLKIT

Decision Checkpoints	Info Needed for Decision	Tools to Use for Decision	How to Evaluate Results
Has management accomplished its price and quantity objectives for overhead?	The actual cost and standard cost of overhead	The overhead budget variance and fixed overhead volume variance	Positive (favourable) variances suggest that the price and quantity objectives have been met.

BEFORE YOU GO ON...

▶Do It! Labour and Manufacturing Overhead Variances

The standard cost of product YY includes three hours of direct labour at $12.00 per hour. The predetermined overhead rate is $20.00 per direct labour hour. During July, the company incurred 3,500 hours of direct labour at an average rate of $12.40 per hour and $71,300 of manufacturing overhead costs. It produced 1,200 units.

(a) Calculate the total, price, and quantity variances for labour.

(b) Calculate the total overhead variance.

Action Plan

• Use the formulas for calculating each of the variances: Total direct labour budget variance = (TAH × AR) − (TSHA × SR)
Labour price variance = (TAH × AR) − (TAH × SR)
Labour quantity variance = (TAH × SR) − (TSHA × SR)
Total overhead variance = Actual overhead − Overhead applied*

*Based on standard hours allowed.

(*continued*)

(continued)

Solution

Substituting amounts into the formulas, the variances are:

(a) Total labour variance = (3,500 × $12.40) − (3,600 × $12.00) = $200 unfavourable
    Labour price variance = (3,500 × $12.40) − (3,500 × $12.00) = $1,400 unfavourable
    Labour quantity variance = (3,500 × $12.00) − (3,600 × $12.00) = $1,200 favourable

(b) Total overhead variance = $71,300 − $72,000* = $700 favourable

*3,600 hours × $20.00

Related exercise material: **BE12-5, BE12-6, BE12-7, BE12-8, E12-21, E12-22, E12-23,** and **Do It! D12-14.**

Variance Reports and the Balanced Scorecard

REPORTING VARIANCES

STUDY OBJECTIVE 4
Prepare variance reports and balanced scorecards.

All variances should be reported to appropriate levels of management as soon as possible. The sooner management is informed, the sooner problems can be evaluated and corrective actions can be taken, if necessary.

The form, content, and frequency of variance reports vary considerably among companies. One approach is to prepare a weekly report for each department that has primary responsibility for cost control. Under this approach, materials price variances are reported to the purchasing department, and all other variances are reported to the production department that did the work. The report in Illustration 12-39 for Xonic, Inc., with the type of materials for the Xonic Tonic order listed first, shows this approach.

▶Illustration 12-39
Materials price variance report

Type of Materials	Quantity Purchased	Actual Price	Price Standard	Price Variance	Explanation
× 100	4,200 litres	$3.10	$3.00	$420 U	Rush order
× 142	1,200 units	2.75	2.80	60 F	Quantity discount
A 85	600 doz.	5.20	5.10	60 U	Regular supplier on strike
Total price variance				$420 U	

XONIC, INC.
Variance Report—Purchasing Department
Week Ended June 8, 2016

The explanation column is completed after the purchasing department manager has been consulted.

Variance reports make it easier to use the "management by exception" approach explained in Chapter 11. For example, the vice-president of purchasing can use the report shown above to evaluate the effectiveness of the purchasing department manager. Or the vice-president of production can use production department variance reports to determine how well each production manager is controlling costs. In using variance reports, top management normally looks for **significant variances**. These may be judged based on some quantitative measure, such as more than 10% of the standard or more than $1,000.

STATEMENT PRESENTATION OF VARIANCES

In income statements **prepared for management** under a standard cost accounting system, **cost of goods sold is stated at standard cost and the variances are disclosed separately**. Unfavourable variances increase cost of goods sold, while favourable variances decrease cost of goods sold. Illustration 12-40 shows the presentation of variances in an income statement. This income statement is based on the production and sale of 1,000 units of Xonic Tonic at $70 per unit. It also assumes selling and administrative costs of $3,000. Observe that each variance is shown, as well as the total net variance. In this example, variations from standard costs reduced net income by $3,500.

▶Illustration 12-40
Variances in income statement for management

XONIC, INC. Income Statement Month Ended June 30, 2016		
Sales		$60,000
Cost of goods sold (at standard)		42,000
Gross profit (at standard)		18,000
Variances unfavourable		
Materials price	$ 420	
Materials quantity	600	
Labour price	(420)	
Labour quantity	1,500	
Variable overhead budget (spending and efficiency)	500	
Fixed overhead spending (budget) variance	500	
Overhead volume	400	
Total variance unfavourable		3,500
Gross profit (actual)		14,500
Selling and administrative expenses		3,000
Net income		$11,500

IFRS Note
IFRS and ASPE require that a manufacturer's inventory valuation be based on the cost principle. This means that the inventories, the cost of goods sold, and the resulting net income must reflect the manufacturer's actual costs. Standard costing will meet the IFRS and ASPE requirements as long as the results approximate cost, and those included in inventory are based on normal levels of the factors of production, efficiency, and capacity utilization.

In financial statements prepared for shareholders and other external users, standard costs may be used. The costing of inventories at standard costs is in accordance with generally accepted accounting principles when there are no significant differences between actual costs and standard costs. Hewlett-Packard and Jostens, Inc., for example, report their inventories at standard costs. However, if there are significant differences between actual and standard costs, inventories and the cost of goods sold must be reported at actual costs.

Variances can also be shown in an income statement prepared in the contribution margin format. To do so, it is necessary to analyze the overhead variances into variable and fixed components. This type of analysis is explained in cost accounting textbooks.

BALANCED SCORECARD

Financial measures (measurements of dollars), such as variance analysis and the return on investment (ROI), are useful tools for evaluating performance. However, many companies now use non-financial measures as well as financial measures in order to better assess performance and be ready for future results. For example, airlines like Air Canada and WestJet use capacity utilization as an important measure to understand and predict future performance. And publishers of such newspapers as the *National Post* or *La Presse* use circulation figures as another measure for evaluating performance. Illustration 12-41 lists some key non-financial measures that are used in various industries.

►Illustration 12-41
Non-financial measures used in various industries

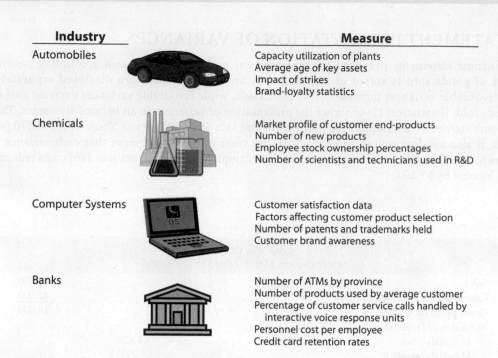

Industry	Measure
Automobiles	Capacity utilization of plants Average age of key assets Impact of strikes Brand-loyalty statistics
Chemicals	Market profile of customer end-products Number of new products Employee stock ownership percentages Number of scientists and technicians used in R&D
Computer Systems	Customer satisfaction data Factors affecting customer product selection Number of patents and trademarks held Customer brand awareness
Banks	Number of ATMs by province Number of products used by average customer Percentage of customer service calls handled by interactive voice response units Personnel cost per employee Credit card retention rates

Most companies recognize that both financial and non-financial measures can provide useful insights into what is happening in the company. As a result, many companies now use a broad-based approach to performance measurement, called the balanced scorecard, to evaluate performance. The **balanced scorecard** uses financial and non-financial measures in an integrated system that links performance measurement and a company's strategic goals. The balanced scorecard concept is very popular: nearly 50% of the largest companies in Canada and the United States, including Bombardier and Walmart, use this approach.

BUSINESS INSIGHT   *Lofty Environmental Goals*

An increasingly important aspect of the balanced scorecard approach is to measure how organizations are performing in terms of environmental sustainability. Aéroports de Montréal (ADM), the non-profit entity that operates Pierre Elliott Trudeau and Dorval airports, has received certification under ISO 14001, the global standard on environmental initiatives from the International Organization for Standardization. In so doing, ADM had to commit to meeting environmental goals every year, through continuous improvement of its operations, which handled more than 14.1 million passengers in 2013. Among the moves to save energy were to install motorized blinds that automatically open and close in the terminal buildings to maintain optimal natural light, and replace sliding doors with revolving ones, to reduce heating and air conditioning. ADM also built a high-performance thermal plant, improving energy efficiency by 70%. The airports planned to buy a fleet of energy-efficient vehicles and convert some vehicles from gasoline to propane. ADM has also helped in the dismantling and recycling of retired aircraft in an environmentally responsible manner. "Sustainable development must be seen not as an expense but as an investment," says Philippe Rainville, Vice-President Finance and Administration at ADM.

Sources: "Aéroports de Montréal Announces Its Results for Fiscal 2013," Aéroports de Montréal news release, March 13, 2014; "In a Canadian First, Air Transat and Aerocycle Lay the Foundations for a Program for Green Dismantling of Commercial Aircraft," Air Transat news release, January 16, 2014; "A Flying Start for Sustainability: Aéroports de Montréal," in *SMEs Set Their Sights on Sustainability*, Canadian Institute of Chartered Accountants, American Institute of CPAs, and Chartered Institute of Management Accountants, September 2011, pp. 33–36.

In what ways could an airport measure whether its expenses to help the environment are providing a return on its investment?

The balanced scorecard evaluates company performance from a series of "perspectives." The four most commonly used perspectives are as follows:

1. The **financial perspective** is the most traditional view of the company. It uses the financial measures of performance that most firms use.
2. The **customer perspective** evaluates how well the company is performing from the viewpoint of those people who buy and use its products or services. This view measures how well the company compares with competitors in terms of price, quality, product innovation, customer service, and other dimensions.
3. The **internal process perspective** evaluates the internal operating processes that are critical to success. All critical aspects of the value chain—including product development, production, delivery, and after-sale service—are evaluated to ensure that the company is operating effectively and efficiently.
4. The **learning and growth perspective** evaluates how well the company develops and retains its employees. This would include an evaluation of such things as employee skills, employee satisfaction, training programs, and the communication of information.

The four perspectives of the balanced scorecard are linked to each other by a flow of influence. The linkage starts with the learning and growth perspective. Corporate success begins with well-trained and happy employees. If employees are well trained, then the company will have good internal processes. If the company's internal processes are functioning well, then customers will be satisfied. If customers are satisfied, then the company should experience financial success. Illustration 12-42 shows this flow.

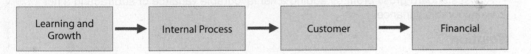

▶Illustration 12-42
Flow of influence across balanced scorecard perspectives

Within each perspective, the balanced scorecard identifies objectives that will contribute to attaining the strategic goals, as is done at Carleton University in our feature story. Illustration 12-43 shows examples of objectives within each perspective.

▶Illustration 12-43
Examples of objectives within the four perspectives of the balanced scorecard

Financial perspective	**Internal process perspective**
Return on assets	Percentage of defect-free products
Net income	Stockouts
Credit rating	Labour use rates
Share price	Waste reduction
Profit per employee	Planning accuracy
Customer perspective	**Learning and growth perspective**
Percentage of customers who would recommend the product to a friend	Percentage of employees leaving in less than one year
Customer retention	Number of cross-trained employees
Response time per customer request	Ethics violations
Brand recognition	Training hours
Customer service expenses per customer	Reportable accidents

The objectives are linked across the perspectives so that performance measurement is tied to company goals. The financial objectives are normally set first, and then objectives are set in the other perspectives that will help accomplish the financial objectives. For example, within the financial perspective, a common goal is to increase the profit per dollar invested as measured by the ROI. In order to increase the ROI, a customer perspective objective might be to increase customer satisfaction, as measured by the percentage of customers who would recommend the product to a friend. In order to increase customer satisfaction, an objective for the internal process perspective might be to increase product quality, as measured by the percentage of defect-free units. Finally, in order to increase the percentage of defect-free units, the objective for the learning and growth perspective might be to reduce factory employee turnover, as measured by the percentage of employees leaving in less than one year. Through this linked process, the company can better understand how to achieve its goals and what measures to use to evaluate performance.

In summary, the balanced scorecard does the following:

1. Employs both financial and non-financial measures (for example, ROI is a financial measure; employee turnover is a non-financial measure).
2. Creates links so that high-level corporate goals can be communicated all the way down to the shop floor.
3. Provides measurable objectives for such non-financial measures as product quality, rather than vague statements such as "We would like to improve quality."
4. Integrates all of the company's goals into a single performance measurement system, so that too much weight will not be placed on any single goal.

BEFORE YOU GO ON...

▶Do It! Reporting Variances

Polar Vortex Corporation experienced the following variances: materials price $250 F, materials quantity $1,100 F, labour price $700 U, labour quantity $300 F, and overhead $800 F. Sales revenue was $102,700, and cost of goods sold (at standard) was $61,900. Determine the actual gross profit.

Action Plan

- Gross profit at standard is sales revenue less cost of goods sold at standard.
- Adjust standard gross profit by adding a net favourable variance or subtracting a net unfavourable variance.

Solution

Sales revenue		$102,700
Cost of goods sold (at standard)		61,900
Standard gross profit		40,800
Variances		
Materials price	$ 250 F	
Materials quantity	1,100 F	
Labour price	700 U	
Labour quantity	300 F	
Overhead	800 F	
Total variance favourable		1,750
Gross profit (actual)		$ 42,550

Related exercise material: **BE12-9, E12-32, E12-33, E12-34,** and **Do It! D12-15.**

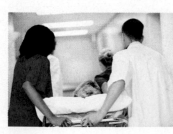

ALL ABOUT YOU   *Balancing Costs and Quality in Health Care*

Have you ever visited a hospital emergency room? If so, how long did you wait? In 2010–11, the average stay in a Canadian emergency department was 4.4 hours—longer than any other country in a survey of 11 developed nations. Numbers like these are tracked by the Canadian Institute for Health Information (CIHI), which sets basic standards for the way the public health system should keep its financial and other records. CIHI also sets performance indicators, including standard treatment costs based on factors such as patient diagnoses and length of hospital stay.

What Do You Think?

Given that personal income taxes fund 49% of health care costs, there is a public tension between quality and costs. Can we use financial performance measures and still meet Canadians' quality expectations?

(continued)

YES—Managerial accounting concepts should be applied to health care so that sound decisions are made about where to spend scarce tax resources.

NO—You can't put a price tag on health. We should spend whatever it costs to keep Canadians healthy.

Sources: André Picard, "Canadians Use Average of $220,000 in Public Health Care over Lifetime," *The Globe and Mail*, May 14, 2013; Canadian Institute for Health Information, "Health Care in Canada, 2012: A Focus on Wait Times," 2013; Joseph Hall, "Canadians Face Longest Emergency Room Waits in Developed World, Survey Finds," *The Toronto Star*, November 29, 2012.

APPENDIX 12A—STANDARD COST ACCOUNTING SYSTEM

A **standard cost accounting system** is a double-entry system of accounting. In this system, standard costs are used in making entries, and variances are formally recognized in the accounts. A standard cost system may be used with either job-order or process costing. At this point, we will explain and illustrate a **standard cost job-order cost accounting system.** The system is based on two important assumptions: (1) Variances from standards are recognized at the earliest opportunity. (2) The Work in Process account is maintained using only standard costs. In practice, there are many variations among standard cost systems. The system described here should prepare you for systems you will see in the workplace.

JOURNAL ENTRIES

We will use the transactions of Xonic, Inc., to illustrate the journal entries. As you study the entries, note that the major difference between the entries here and those for the job-order cost accounting system in Chapter 3 is the **variance accounts**. The transactions and entries are as follows:

1. Purchased raw materials on account for $13,020 when the standard cost is $12,600.

Raw Materials Inventory	12,600	
Materials Price Variance	420	
Accounts Payable		13,020
To record purchase of materials.		

The inventory account is debited for the actual quantities at standard cost. This enables the perpetual materials records to show actual quantities. The price variance, which is unfavourable, is debited to Materials Price Variance.

2. Incurred direct labour costs of $31,080 when the standard labour cost is $31,500.

Factory Labour	31,500	
Labour Price Variance		420
Wages Payable		31,080
To record direct labour costs.		

Like the raw materials inventory account, Factory Labour is debited for the actual hours worked at the standard hourly rate of pay. In this case, the labour variance is favourable. Thus, Labour Price Variance is credited.

STUDY OBJECTIVE 5
Identify the features of a standard cost accounting system.

IFRS Note
IFRS requires that an entity report its actual costs when reporting expenses. This appears to be at odds with standard costing, which is used instead of actual costs because it is considerably easier to compile. The cost accountant should calculate and record the variances between the actual and standard cost of goods sold in every financial reporting period. Any cost variances that relate to a lower than normal level of efficiency or capacity utilization, however, cannot be allocated to ending inventory. They must be recognized in income in the current period.

3. Incurred actual manufacturing overhead costs of $10,900.

Manufacturing Overhead	11,400	
Accounts Payable/Cash/Acc. Depreciation		11,400
To record overhead incurred.		

The budget overhead variance is not recorded at this time. It depends on the standard hours applied to work in process. This amount is not known at the time the overhead is incurred.

4. Issued raw materials for production at a cost of $12,600 when the standard cost is $12,000.

Work in Process Inventory	12,000	
Materials Quantity Variance	600	
Raw Materials Inventory		12,600
To record issue of raw materials.		

Work in Process Inventory is debited for standard materials quantities used at standard prices. The variance account is debited because the variance is unfavourable. Raw Materials Inventory is credited for the actual quantities at standard prices.

5. Assigned factory labour to production at a cost of $31,500 when the standard cost is $30,000.

Work in Process Inventory	30,000	
Labour Quantity Variance	1,500	
Factory Labour		31,500
To assign factory labour to jobs.		

Work in Process Inventory is debited for standard labour hours at standard rates. The unfavourable variance is debited to Labour Quantity Variance. The credit to Factory Labour produces a zero balance in this account.

6. Applied $10,000 of manufacturing overhead to production.

Work in Process Inventory	10,000	
Manufacturing Overhead		10,000
To assign overhead to jobs.		

Work in Process Inventory is debited for the standard hours allowed multiplied by the standard overhead rate.

7. Transferred $52,000 of completed work to finished goods.

Finished Goods Inventory	52,000	
Work in Process Inventory		52,000
To record transfer of completed work to finished goods.		

In this example, both inventory accounts are at standard cost.

8. The 1,000 litres of Xonic Tonic are sold for $70,000.

Accounts Receivable	70,000	
Cost of Goods Sold	52,000	
Sales		70,000
Finished Goods Inventory		52,000
To record sale of finished goods and the cost of goods sold.		

Cost of Goods Sold is debited at standard cost. Gross profit, in turn, is the difference between sales and the standard cost of goods sold.

9. Recognized unfavourable overhead variances: budget, $1000; volume, $400.

Overhead Budget Variance	1000	
Overhead Volume Variance	400	
Manufacturing Overhead		1,400
To recognize overhead variances.		

Before this entry, there was a debit balance of $1,400 in Manufacturing Overhead. This entry therefore produces a zero balance in the account. The information needed for this entry is often not available until the end of the accounting period.

LEDGER ACCOUNTS

The cost accounts for Xonic, after posting the entries, are shown in Illustration 12A-1. Note that six variance accounts are included in the ledger. The remaining accounts are the same as those illustrated for a job-order cost system in Chapter 3, in which only actual costs were used.

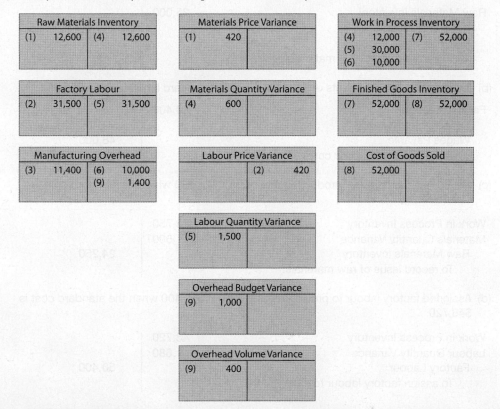

▶Illustration 12A-1
Cost accounts with variances

Helpful Hint
All debit balances in variance accounts indicate unfavourable variances; all credit balances indicate favourable variances.

BEFORE YOU GO ON...

▶Do It! Journalizing Transactions

Journalize the following transactions for B&Y Manufacturing.

(a) Purchased 10,000 units of raw materials on account for $24,000. The standard cost was $25,000.

(b) Incurred direct labour costs of $48,000 for 6,000 hours. The standard labour cost was $50,400.

(c) Issued 9,700 units of raw materials for production. The standard units were 9,500 units of raw materials.

(d) Assigned 6,000 direct labour hours costing $48,000 to production. Standard hours allowed were 5,800.

(continued)

(continued)

Action Plan

The inventory account is recorded for the actual quantities at standard cost. Materials Price Variance is used to record the price variance.

Factory Labour is recorded for the actual hours worked at the standard hourly rate of pay. Labour Price Variance is used to record the labour variance.

Work in Process Inventory is recorded for standard materials quantities used at standard prices. Materials Inventory is recorded for the actual quantities at standard prices.

Work in Process Inventory is recorded for standard labour hours at standard rates.

Solution

(a) Purchased raw materials on account for $24,000 when the standard cost is $25,000.

Raw Materials Inventory	25,000	
Accounts Payable		24,000
Materials Price Variance		1,000
To record purchase of materials.		

(b) Incurred direct labour costs of $48,000 when the standard labour cost is $50,400.

Factory Labour	50,400	
Labour Price Variance		2,400
Wages Payable		48,000
To record direct labour costs.		

(c) Issued raw materials for production at a cost of $24,250 when the standard cost is $23,750.

Work in Process Inventory	23,750	
Materials Quantity Variance	500	
Raw Materials Inventory		24,250
To record issue of raw materials.		

(d) Assigned factory labour to production at a cost of $50,400 when the standard cost is $48,720.

Work in Process Inventory	48,720	
Labour Quantity Variance	1,680	
Factory Labour		50,400
To assign factory labour to jobs.		

Related exercise material: **BE12-10, BE12-11, E12-36, E12-37, E12-38, E12-39,** and **Do It! D12-16.**

USING THE DECISION TOOLKIT

Assume that during the past month, Fineway produced 10,000 cartons of Sharpline highlighters. Sharpline has a translucent barrel and cap with a visible ink supply for see-through colour. The special fluorescent ink is fade- and water-resistant. Each carton contains 100 boxes of markers, and each box contains five markers. The markers come in boxes of one of five fluorescent colours—orange, blue, yellow, green, and pink—and in a five-colour set. The standard cost for one carton of 500 markers is as follows:

(continued)

(continued)

Manufacturing Cost Elements	Standard		
	Quantity	Price	Cost
Direct materials			
Tips (boxes of 500)	500	× $ 0.03 =	$ 15.00
Translucent barrels and caps (boxes of 500)	500	× $ 0.09 =	45.00
Fluorescent ink (5-litre container)	5 litres	× $ 6.40 per litre =	32.00
Total direct materials			92.00
Direct labour	0.25 hours × $ 9.00 =		2.25
Overhead	0.25 hours × $ 48.00 =		12.00
			$106.25

During the month, the following transactions occurred in manufacturing the 10,000 cartons of highlighters:

1. Purchased 10,000 boxes of tips for $148,000 ($14.80 per 500 tips); purchased 10,200 boxes of translucent barrels and caps for $453,900 ($44.50 per 500 barrels and caps); and purchased 9,900 containers of fluorescent ink for $328,185 ($33.15 per five-litre container).
2. All materials purchased during the period were used to make markers during the period.
3. A total of 2,300 direct labour hours were worked at a total labour cost of $20,240 (an average hourly rate of $8.80).
4. The variable manufacturing overhead incurred was $34,600, and the fixed overhead incurred was $84,000.

The manufacturing overhead rate of $48.00 is based on a normal capacity of 2,600 direct labour hours. The total budget at this capacity is $83,980 fixed and $40,820 variable.

Instructions
Determine whether Fineway met its price and quantity objectives for materials, labour, and overhead.

Solution
To determine whether Fineway met its price and quantity objectives, calculate the total variance and the variances for each of the manufacturing cost elements.

Total Variance

Actual cost incurred:		
Direct materials		
Tips	$148,000	
Translucent barrels and caps	453,900	
Fluorescent ink	328,185	
Total direct materials		$ 930,085
Direct labour		20,240
Overhead		118,600
Total actual costs		1,068,925
Standard cost (10,000 × $106.25)		1,062,500
Total variance		$ 6,425 U

Direct Materials Variances

Total	=	$930,085	−	$920,000	= $10,085 U
				(10,000 × $92)	
Price (tips)	=	$148,000	−	$150,000	= $ 2,000 F
	=	(10,000 × $14.80)		(10,000 × $15.00)	
Price (barrels and caps)	=	$453,900	−	$459,000	= $ 5,100 F
	=	(10,200 × $44.50)		(10,200 × $ 45.00)	
Price (ink)	=	$328,185	−	$316,800	= $11,385 U
		(9,900 × 33.15)		(9,900 × $32.00)	
Quantity (tips)	=	$150,000	−	$150,000	= $ 0
		(10,000 × $15.00)		(10,000 × $15.00)	
Quantity (barrels and caps)	=	$459,000	−	$450,000	= $ 9,000 U
		(10,200 × $45.00)		(10,000 × $45.00)	
Quantity (ink)	=	$316,800	−	$320,000	$ 3,200 F
		(9,900 × $32.00)		(10,000 × $32.00)	

(continued)

(continued)

Direct Labour Variances

Total	= $20,240	− $22,500	=	$2,260 F
	(2,300 × $8.80)	(2,500 × $9.00)		
Price	= $20,240	− $20,700	=	$ 460 F
	(2,300 × $8.80)	(2,300 × $9.00)		
Quantity	= $20,700	− $22,500	=	$1,800 F
	(2,300 × $9.00)	(2,500 × $9.00)		

Overhead Variances

Total	= $118,600	− $120,000	=	$1,400 F
	($84,000 + $34,600)	(2,500 × $48)		
Budget overhead	= $118,600	− $123,230	=	$4,630 F
	($84,000 + $34,600)	[(2,500 × $15.70) + $83,980]		
Volume	= $123,230	− $120,000	=	$3,230 U
	[(2,500 × $15.70) + $83,980]	(2,500 × $48)		

The same result for overhead variances can also be obtained by the following analysis:

Overhead Variances

Total	= $118,600	− $120,000	=	$ 1,400 F
	($84,000 + $34,600)	(2,500 × $48)		
Variable overhead spending	= $34,600	− $36,110	=	$ 1,510 F*
	$34,600	(2,300 × $15.70)		
Variable overhead efficiency	= $36,110	− $39,250	=	$ 3,140 F*
	(2,300 × $15.70)	(2,500 × $15.70)		
Fixed overhead spending	= $84,000	− $83,980	=	$ 20 U*
	$84,000	(2,600 × $32.30)		
Fixed overhead volume	= $83,980	− $80,750	=	$ 3,230 U
	(2,600 × $32.30)	(2,500 × $32.30)		

* Overhead budget variance = ($1,510 F + $3,140 F) − $20 U = $4,630 F

Fineway's total variance was $6,425 unfavourable. The unfavourable materials variance outweighed the favourable labour and overhead variances. The main causes were an unfavourable price variance for ink and an unfavourable quantity variance for barrels and caps.

Summary of Study Objectives

1. *Describe standard costs.* Both standards and budgets are predetermined costs. The main difference is that a standard is a unit amount, whereas a budget is a total amount. A standard may be regarded as the budgeted cost per unit of product.

Standard costs offer several advantages. They facilitate management planning, promote greater economy and efficiency, are useful in setting selling prices, contribute to management control, permit "management by exception," simplify the costing of inventories, and reduce clerical costs.

The direct materials price standard should be based on the delivered cost of raw materials plus an allowance for receiving and handling. The direct materials quantity standard should establish the required quantity plus an allowance for waste and spoilage. The direct labour price standard should be based on current wage rates and expected adjustments, such as COLAs. It also generally includes payroll taxes and fringe benefits. Direct labour quantity standards should be based on required production time plus an allowance for rest periods, cleanup, machine set-up, and machine downtime. For manufacturing overhead, a standard predetermined overhead rate is used. It is based on an expected standard activity index, such as standard direct labour hours or standard direct labour cost.

2. *Determine direct materials variances.* The formulas for the direct materials variances are as follows:

(Total actual quantities × Actual price) − (Total standard quantities allowed × Standard price) = Total materials variance

(Total actual quantities × Actual price) − (Total actual quantities × Standard price) = Materials price variance

(Total actual quantities × Standard price) − (Total standard quantities allowed × Standard price) = Materials quantity variance

3. *Determine direct labour and total manufacturing overhead variances.*

The formulas for direct labour are as follows:

(Total actual hours × Actual rate) − (Total standard hours allowed × Standard rate) = Total labour variance

(Total actual hours × Actual rate) − (Total actual hours × Standard rate) = Labour price variance

(Total actual hours × Standard rate) − (Total standard hours allowed × Standard rate) = Labour quantity variance

The formulas for the manufacturing overhead variances are as follows:

Actual overhead − Overhead applied = Total overhead variance

Actual overhead − (Variable overhead applied + Fixed overhead budgeted) = Overhead budget variance

Fixed overhead rate × (Normal capacity hours − Standard hours allowed) = Overhead volume variance

4. *Prepare variance reports and balanced scorecards.* Variances are reported to management in variance reports. The reports aid management by exception by highlighting significant differences.

Under a standard cost system, an income statement prepared for management will report the cost of goods sold at standard cost and then disclose each variance separately.

The balanced scorecard uses financial and non-financial measures in an integrated system that links performance measurement and a company's strategic goals. It uses four perspectives: financial, customer, internal processes, and learning and growth. Objectives are set within each of these perspectives and link to objectives in the other perspectives.

5. *Identify the features of a standard cost accounting system (Appendix 12A).* In a standard cost accounting system, standard costs are journalized and posted, and separate variance accounts are maintained in the ledger. When actual costs and standard costs do not differ significantly, inventories may be reported at standard costs.

DECISION TOOLKIT—A SUMMARY

Decision Checkpoints	Info Needed for Decision	Tools to Use for Decision	How to Evaluate Results
Has management accomplished its price and quantity objectives for materials?	The actual cost and standard cost of materials	Materials price and materials quantity variances	Positive (favourable) variances suggest that the price and quantity objectives have been met.
Has management accomplished its price and quantity objectives for labour?	The actual cost and standard cost of labour	Labour price and labour quantity variances	Positive (favourable) variances suggest that the price and quantity objectives have been met.
Has management accomplished its price and quantity objectives for overhead?	The actual cost and standard cost of overhead	The overhead budget variance and overhead volume variance	Positive (favourable) variances suggest that the price and quantity objectives have been met.

Glossary

Balanced scorecard   An approach that uses financial and non-financial measures in an integrated system that links performance measurement and a company's strategic goals. (p. 524)

Customer perspective   A viewpoint used in the balanced scorecard to evaluate the company from the perspective of those people who buy and use its products or services. (p. 525)

Direct labour price standard   The rate per hour that should be incurred for direct labour. (p. 508)

Direct labour quantity standard   The time that should be required to make one unit of product. (p. 508)

Direct materials price standard   The cost per unit of direct materials that should be incurred. (p. 508)

Direct materials quantity standard   The quantity of direct materials that should be used per unit of finished goods. (p. 508)

Financial perspective   A viewpoint used in the balanced scorecard to evaluate a company's performance using financial measures. (p. 525)

Fixed overhead spending (budget) variance   The difference between the actual fixed overhead and the standard fixed overhead master budget. (p. 519)

Fixed overhead volume variance   The difference between the overhead budgeted for the normal standard hours and the overhead applied. (p. 519)

Ideal standards   Standards based on the optimum level of performance under perfect operating conditions. (p. 507)

Internal process perspective   A viewpoint used in the balanced scorecard to evaluate the effectiveness and efficiency of a company's value chain, including product development, production, delivery, and after-sale service. (p. 525)

Labour price variance The difference between the actual hours of labour multiplied by the actual labour rate, and the actual hours multiplied by the standard rate. (p. 514)

Labour quantity variance The difference between the actual hours of labour multiplied by the standard labour rate, and standard hours multiplied by the standard rate. (p. 515)

Learning and growth perspective A viewpoint used in the balanced scorecard to evaluate how well a company develops and retains its employees. (p. 525)

Materials price variance The difference between the actual quantity of materials multiplied by the actual price of materials, and the actual quantity multiplied by the standard price. (p. 512)

Materials quantity variance The difference between the actual quantity of materials multiplied by the standard price of materials, and the standard quantity multiplied by the standard price. (p. 512)

Normal capacity The average activity output that a company should experience over the long run. (p. 509)

Normal standards Standards based on an efficient level of performance that are attainable under expected operating conditions. (p. 507)

Standard cost accounting system A double-entry system of accounting in which standard costs are used in making entries and variances are recognized in the accounts. (p. 527)

Standard costs Predetermined unit costs that are used as measures of performance. (p. 506)

Standard predetermined overhead rate An overhead rate that is determined by dividing the budgeted overhead costs by an expected standard activity index. (p. 509)

Total direct labour budget variance (TDLBV) The difference between the total actual hours of labour multiplied by the actual labour rate and the total standard hours allowed multiplied by the standard rate. (p. 514)

Total direct materials budget variance (TDMBV) The difference between the total actual quantities of materials multiplied by the actual price of materials and the total standard quantities allowed multiplied by the standard price. (p. 511)

Total fixed overhead variance The difference between the actual fixed overhead and the total standard hours allowed multiplied by the fixed overhead rate. (p. 519)

Total overhead variance The difference between actual overhead costs and the overhead costs applied to work done. (p. 516)

Total standard hours allowed The hours that should have been worked for the units produced. (p. 516)

Total variable overhead budget variance (TVOHBV) The difference between the actual overhead incurred and the overhead budgeted for (the standard hours allowed for variable overhead and normal hours for fixed overhead). (p. 517)

Variances The difference between total actual costs and total standard costs. (p. 509)

Comprehensive Do It!

Manlow Company makes a pasta sauce for the restaurant industry. The standard cost for one tub of sauce is as follows:

	Standard		
Manufacturing Cost Elements	Quantity	Price	Cost
Direct materials	6 litres	$ 0.90	$ 5.40
Direct labour	0.5 hours	$12.00	6.00
Manufacturing overhead	0.5 hours	$ 4.80	2.40
			$13.80

During the month, the following transactions occurred in manufacturing 10,000 tubs of sauce:

1. A total of 58,000 litres of materials were purchased at $1.00 per litre.
2. All the materials purchased were used to produce the 10,000 tubs of sauce.
3. A total of 4,900 direct labour hours were worked at a total labour cost of $56,350.
4. The variable manufacturing overhead incurred was $15,000 and the fixed overhead incurred was $10,400.

The manufacturing overhead rate of $4.80 is based on a normal capacity of 5,200 direct labour hours. The total budget at this capacity is $10,400 fixed and $14,560 variable.

Instructions
Calculate the total variance and the variances for each of the manufacturing cost elements.

(continued)

(continued)

Solution to Comprehensive Do It!

Total Variance

Actual costs incurred	
Direct materials	$ 58,000
Direct labour	56,350
Manufacturing overhead	25,400
	139,750
Standard cost (10,000 × $13.80)	138,000
Total variance	$ 1,750 U

Direct Materials Variances

Total	= $58,000	−	$54,000	= $4,000 U
	(58,000 × $1.00)		(60,000 × $0.90)	
Price	= $58,000	−	$52,200	= $5,800 U
	(58,000 × $1.00)		(58,000 × $0.90)	
Quantity	= $52,200	−	$54,000	= $1,800 F
	(58,000 × $0.90)		(60,000 × $ 0.90)	

Direct Labour Variances

Total	= $56,350	−	$60,000	= $3,650 F
	(4,900 × $11.50)		(5,000 × $12.00)	
Price	= $56,350	−	$58,800	= $2,450 F
	(4,900 × $11.50)		(4,900 × $12.00)	
Quantity	= $58,800	−	$60,000	= $1,200 F
	(4,900 × $12.00)		(5,000 × $12.00)	

Overhead Variances

Total	= $25,400	−	$24,000	= $1,400 U
	($15,000 + $10,400)		(5,000 × $4.80)	
Budget	= $25,400	−	$24,400	= $1,000 U
	($15,000 + $10,400)		($14,000 + 10,400)	
Volume	= $24,400	−	$24,000	= $ 400 U
	($14,000 + $10,400)		(5,000 × $4.80)	

The same result of overhead variances can also be obtained by the following analysis:

Overhead Variances

Total	= $25,400	−	$24,000	= $1,400 U
	($15,000 + $10,400)		(5,000 × $4.80)	
Variable overhead spending	= $15,000	−	$13,720	= $1,280 U*
	$15,000		(4,900 × $2.80)	
Variable overhead efficiency	= $13,720	−	$14,000	= $ 280 F*
	(4,900 × $2.80)		(5,000 × $2.80)	
Fixed overhead spending	= $10,400	−	$10,400	= $ 0*
	$10,400		(5,200 × $2.00)	
Fixed overhead volume	= $10,400	−	$10,000	= $ 400 U
	(5,200 × $2.00)		(5,000 × $2.00)	

* Overhead budget variance = $1,280 U + $280 F + $0 = $1,000 U

Self-Study Questions

Answers are at the end of the chapter.

(The asterisk * indicates material discussed in the chapter appendix.)

(SO 1)   1. Standards differ from budgets in that
   (a) budgets but not standards may be used in valuing inventories.
   (b) budgets but not standards may be journalized and posted.
   (c) budgets are a total amount and standards are a unit amount.
   (d) only budgets contribute to management planning and control.

(SO 1)   2. The advantages of standard costs include all of the following except
   (a) management by exception may be used.
   (b) management planning is made easier.
   (c) the costing of inventories is made simpler.
   (d) management must use a static budget.

(SO 1)   3. The setting of standards is
   (a) a managerial accounting decision.
   (b) a management decision.
   (c) a worker decision.
   (d) preferably set at the ideal level of performance.

(SO 3, 4, 5)   4. Each of the following formulas is correct except
   (a) Labour price variance = (actual hours × actual rate) − (actual hours × standard rate).
   (b) Overhead budget variance = actual overhead − overhead budgeted.
   (c) Materials price variance = (actual quantity × actual cost) − (standard quantity × standard cost).
   (d) Overhead volume variance = overhead budgeted − overhead applied.

(SO 3)   5. In producing product AA, 6,300 kg of direct materials were used at a cost of $1.10 per kilogram. The standard was 6,000 kg at $1 per kilogram. The direct materials quantity variance is
   (a) $330 unfavourable.
   (b) $300 unfavourable.
   (c) $600 unfavourable.
   (d) $630 unfavourable.

(SO 3)   6. In producing product ZZ, 14,800 direct labour hours were used at a rate of $8.20 per hour. The standard was 15,000 hours at $8.00 per hour. Based on these data, the direct labour
   (a) quantity variance is $1,600 favourable.
   (b) quantity variance is $1,600 unfavourable.
   (c) price variance is $2,960 favourable.
   (d) price variance is $3,000 unfavourable.

(SO 3)   7. Which of the following is correct about overhead variances?
   (a) The budget variance generally relates to fixed overhead costs.
   (b) The volume variance relates only to variable overhead costs.
   (c) The standard hours actually worked are used in each variance.
   (d) Budgeted overhead costs are based on the flexible overhead budget.

(SO 3)   8. The formula for calculating the total overhead variance is
   (a) actual overhead less overhead applied.
   (b) overhead budgeted less overhead applied.
   (c) actual overhead less overhead budgeted.
   (d) none of the above.

(SO 4)   9. Which of the following is incorrect about variance reports?
   (a) They aid "management by exception."
   (b) They should be sent only to the top level of management.
   (c) They should be prepared as soon as possible.
   (d) They may vary in form, content, and frequency in different companies.

(SO 4)   10. Which of the following would not be an objective used in the customer perspective of the balanced scorecard approach?
   (a) The percentage of customers who would recommend the product to a friend
   (b) Customer retention
   (c) Brand recognition
   (d) Earnings per share

Brief Exercises

(SO 1)
Distinguish between standard and budget costs.

BE12-1   Valdez Company uses standards and budgets. For the year, estimated production of product X is 500,000 units. The total estimated costs for materials and labour are $1.3 million and $1.7 million, respectively. Calculate the estimates for (a) a standard cost and (b) a budgeted cost.

BE12-2 Hideo Company accumulates the following data concerning raw materials in making one unit of finished product: (1) Price—net purchase price $2.50, freight in $0.40, and receiving and handling $0.25. (2) Quantity—required materials 3 kg, allowance for waste and spoilage 0.5 kg. Calculate the following:
(a) standard direct materials price per unit
(b) standard direct materials quantity per unit
(c) total standard material cost per unit

(SO 1)
Determine the direct materials standard.

BE12-3 Labour data for making one unit of finished product in Hideo Company are as follows: (1) Price—hourly wage rate $15.00, payroll taxes $0.95, and fringe benefits $1.5. (2) Quantity—actual production time 1.5 hours, rest periods and cleanup 0.3 hours, and set-up and downtime 0.20 hours. Calculate the following:
(a) standard direct labour rate per hour
(b) standard direct labour hours per unit
(c) standard labour cost per unit

(SO 1)
Determine the direct labour standard.

BE12-4 Sprague Company's standard materials cost per unit of output is $10 (2 kg × $5.00). During July, the company purchases and uses 3,200 kg of materials costing $16,160 in making 1,500 units of finished product. Calculate the total, price, and quantity materials variances.

(SO 2)
Calculate direct materials variances.

BE12-5 Talbot Company's standard labour cost per unit of output is $22 (2 hours × $11.00 per hour). During August, the company incurs 2,100 hours of direct labour at an hourly cost of $10.80 per hour in making 1,000 units of finished product. Calculate the total, price, and quantity labour variances.

(SO 3)
Calculate direct labour variances.

BE12-6 H&X Co. uses a standard job cost system with a normal capacity of 25,000 direct labour hours. H&X Co. produces 12,000 units, which cost $185,700 for direct labour (23,000 hours), $27,525 for variable overhead, and $136,400 for fixed overhead. The standard variable overhead per unit is $2 (2 hours at $1 per hour), and the standard fixed overhead per unit is $10 (2 hours at $5 per hour).
Calculate the variable overhead spending variance and the variable overhead efficiency variance.

(SO 3)
Calculate the total manufacturing overhead variance.

BE12-7 Using the data in BE12-6, calculate the fixed overhead spending (budget) variance.

(SO 3)
Calculate the overhead budget variance.

BE12-8 Using the data in BE12-6, calculate the fixed overhead production volume variance.

(SO 3)
Calculate overhead volume variance.

BE12-9 The four perspectives in the balanced scorecard are (1) financial, (2) customer, (3) internal process, and (4) learning and growth. Match each of the following objectives with the perspective it is most likely associated with:
(a) Plant capacity utilization
(b) Employee workdays missed due to injury
(c) Return on assets
(d) Brand recognition

(SO 4)
Match balanced scorecard perspectives.

***BE12-10** Journalize the following transactions for Orkin Manufacturing.
(a) Purchased 6,000 units of raw materials on account for $11,500. The standard cost was $12,000.
(b) Issued 5,600 units of raw materials for production. The standard units were 5,800.

(SO 5)
Journalize materials variances.

***BE12-11** Journalize the following transactions for Rogler Manufacturing.
(a) Incurred direct labour costs of $24,000 for 3,000 hours. The standard labour cost was $25,500.
(b) Assigned 3,000 direct labour hours costing $24,000 to production. Standard hours were 3,150.

(SO 5)
Journalize labour variances.

Do It! Review

D12-12 The standard cost of product 999 includes two units of direct materials at $6.00 per unit. During August, the company bought 29,000 units of materials at $6.20 and used those materials to produce 15,000 units.

(SO 1)
Calculate standard cost.

Instructions
Calculate the total, price, and quantity variances for materials.

D12-13 Riuto Company accumulated the following standard cost data concerning product I-Tal.
Materials per unit: 2 kg at $5 per kilogram
Labour per unit: 0.2 hours at $14 per hour
Manufacturing overhead: Predetermined rate is 125% of direct labour cost

(SO 2)
Calculate materials variance.

Instructions
Calculate the standard cost of one unit of product I-Tal.

(SO 2, 3)
Calculate labour and
manufacturing
overhead variances.

D12-14   The standard cost of product 2525 includes 1.9 hours of direct labour at $14.00 per hour. The predetermined overhead rate is $22.00 per direct labour hour. During July, the company incurred 4,100 hours of direct labour at an average rate of $14.30 per hour and $81,300 of manufacturing overhead costs. It produced 2,000 units.

Instructions
(a) Calculate the total, price, and quantity variances for labour.
(b) Calculate the total overhead variance.

(SO 4)
Match balanced
scorecard perspectives
and their objectives.

D12-15   The following are objectives for Whitefeather Corporation:

1. Ethics violations
2. Credit rating
3. Customer retention

4. Stockouts
5. Reportable accidents
6. Brand recognition

Instructions
Indicate which of the four perspectives in the balanced scorecard is most likely associated with the objectives above.

(SO 5)
Journalize transactions.

*D12-16   T&Y Company purchased 12,000 units of raw material on account for $23,400, when the standard cost was $24,000. Later in the month, T&Y Company issued 11,200 units of raw materials for production, when the standard units allowed were 11,600.

T&Y Company incurred direct labour costs of $36,000 for 4,000 hours. The standard labour cost was $36,400. During the month, T&Y Company assigned 4,000 direct labour hours costing $36,000 to production. The standard hours allowed were 4,200.

Instructions
Journalize the transactions for T&Y Company to account for these activities.

Exercises

(SO 1)
Calculate budgeted
amounts and standard
costs.

E12-17   Lovitz Company is planning to produce 2,000 units of product in 2016. Each unit requires 3 kg of materials at $5 per kilogram and a half hour of labour at $15 per hour. The overhead rate is 70% of direct labour.

Instructions
(a) Calculate the budgeted amounts for 2016 for direct materials to be used, direct labour, and applied overhead.
(b) Calculate the standard cost of one unit of product.
(c) What are the potential advantages to a corporation of using standard costs?

(SO 1)
Calculate standard
materials costs.

E12-18   Raul Mondesi manufactures and sells homemade wine, and he wants to develop a standard cost per litre. The following are required for production of a 200-litre batch:

90 litres of grape concentrate at $1.35 per litre
27 kg of granulated sugar at $0.60 per kilogram
60 lemons at $0.60 each
50 yeast tablets at $0.25 each
50 nutrient tablets at $0.20 each
75 litres of water at $0.10 per litre

Raul estimates that 4% of the grape concentrate is wasted, 10% of the sugar is lost, and 20% of the lemons cannot be used.

Instructions
Calculate the standard cost of the ingredients for one litre of drink. (Carry calculations to three decimal places.)

(SO 1)
Calculate the standard
cost per unit.

E12-19   Muhsin Company has gathered the following information about its product:

Direct materials: Each unit of product contains 4.5 kg of materials. The average waste and spoilage per unit produced under normal conditions is 0.5 kg. Materials cost $5 per kilogram, but Muhsin always takes the 2% cash discount that all of its suppliers offer. Freight costs average $0.25 per kilogram.
Direct labour: Each unit requires two hours of labour. Set-up, cleanup, and downtime average 0.3 hours per unit. The average hourly pay rate of Muhsin's employees is $12. Payroll taxes and fringe benefits are an additional $3 per hour.
Manufacturing overhead: Overhead is applied at a rate of $7 per direct labour hour.

Instructions
Calculate Muhsin's total standard cost per unit.

E12-20 The standard cost of product B manufactured by Bhaskara Company includes three units of direct materials at $5.00 per unit. During June, the company purchases 29,000 units of direct materials at a cost of $4.70 per unit and uses 29,000 units of direct materials to produce 9,500 units of product B.

(SO 2)
Calculate materials, price, and quantity variances.

Instructions
(a) Calculate the materials variance, and the price and quantity variances.
(b) Repeat part (a), assuming the purchase price is $5.15 and the quantity purchased and used is 28,000 units.

E12-21 Pagley Company's standard labour cost of producing one unit of product DD is four hours at the rate of $12.00 per hour. During August, 40,800 hours of labour are incurred at a cost of $12.10 per hour to produce 10,000 units of product DD.

(SO 3)
Calculate labour price and quantity variances.

Instructions
(a) Calculate the total labour variance.
(b) Calculate the labour price and quantity variances.
(c) Repeat part (b), assuming the standard is 4.2 hours of direct labour at $12.20 per hour.

E12-22 Rapid Repair Services, Inc. is trying to establish the standard labour cost of a typical oil change. The following data have been collected from time and motion studies conducted over the past month:

(SO 1, 3)
Calculate labour quantity variances.

Actual time spent on the oil change	1.0 hour
Hourly wage rate	$12.00
Payroll taxes	10% of wage rate
Set-up and downtime	20% of actual labour time
Cleanup and rest periods	30% of actual labour time
Fringe benefits	25% of wage rate

Instructions
(a) Determine the standard direct labour hours per oil change.
(b) Determine the direct labour hourly rate.
(c) Determine the direct labour cost per oil change.
(d) If an oil change took 1.6 hours at the standard hourly rate, what was the direct labour quantity variance?

E12-23 Kopecky Inc., which produces a single product, has prepared the following standard cost sheet for one unit of the product:

(SO 2, 3)
Calculate materials and labour variances.

Direct materials (6 kg at $2.50 per kilogram)	$15.00
Direct labour (3.1 hours at $12 per hour)	$37.20

During the month of April, the company manufactures 250 units and incurs the following actual costs:

Direct materials purchased and used (1,600 kg)	$4,192
Direct labour (760 hours)	$8,740

Instructions
Calculate the total, price, and quantity variances for materials and labour.

E12-24 Buerhle Company purchased (at a cost of $12,800) and used 3,300 kg of materials during May. Buerhle's standard cost of materials per unit produced is based on 2 kg per unit at a cost $4 per kilogram. Production in May was 1,540 units.

(SO 2)
Calculate variances for materials.

Instructions
(a) Calculate the total, price, and quantity variances for materials.
(b) Assume Buerhle also had an unfavourable labour quantity variance. What is a possible scenario that would provide one cause for the variances calculated in part (a) and the unfavourable labour quantity variance?

E12-25 During March 2016, Garner Tool & Die Company worked on four jobs. A review of the direct labour costs reveals the following summary data:

(SO 3, 4)
Prepare a variance report for direct labour.

	Actual		Standard		
Job Number	Hours	Costs	Hours	Costs	Total Variance
A257	220	$ 5,500	225	$ 5,625	$ 125 F
A258	450	12,150	430	10,750	1,400 U
A259	240	6,180	240	6,000	180 U
A260	115	2,530	110	2,750	220 F
Total variance					$1,235 U

Analysis reveals that Job A257 was a repeat job. Job A258 was a rush order that required overtime work at premium rates of pay. Job A259 required a more experienced replacement worker on one shift. Work on Job A260 was done for one day by a new trainee when a regular worker was absent.

Instructions

Prepare a report for the plant supervisor on direct labour cost variances for March. The report should have columns for the following headings: (1) Job No., (2) Actual Hours, (3) Standard Hours, (4) Labour Quantity Variance, (5) Actual Rate, (6) Standard Rate, (7) Labour Price Variance, and (8) Explanations.

(SO 2, 3, 4)
Calculate materials and
labour variances and
list reasons for
unfavourable variances.

E12-26 The following direct materials and direct labour data are for the operations of Batista Manufacturing Company for the month of August:

Costs		Quantities	
Actual labour rate	$13.00 per hour	Actual hours incurred and used	3,200 hours
		Actual quantity of materials	
Actual materials price	$89.00 per tonne	purchased and used	910 tonnes
Standard labour rate	$12.00 per hour	Standard hours used	3,240 tonnes
Standard materials price	$90.00 per tonne	Standard quantity of materials used	900 tonnes

Instructions

(a) Calculate the total, price, and quantity variances for materials and labour.

(b) ⬛▬▭⟩ Provide two possible explanations for each of the unfavourable variances calculated in part (a), and suggest which department might be responsible for the unfavourable result.

(SO 3, 4)
Calculate overhead
variances and list
reasons for
unfavourable variances.

E12-27 The following information was taken from the annual manufacturing overhead cost budget of Fernetti Company:

Variable manufacturing overhead costs	$34,650
Fixed manufacturing overhead costs	$19,800
Normal production level in labour hours	16,500
Normal production level in units	4,125
Standard labour hours per unit	4

During the year, 4,000 units were produced, 16,100 hours were worked, and the actual manufacturing overhead was $55,000. Actual fixed manufacturing overhead costs equalled the budgeted fixed manufacturing overhead costs. Overhead is applied based on direct labour hours.

Instructions

(a) Calculate the total, fixed, and variable predetermined manufacturing overhead rates.

(b) Calculate the total, budget, and volume overhead variances.

(c) ⬛▬▭⟩ Briefly interpret the overhead budget and volume variances calculated in part (b).

(SO 3)
Determine missing
amounts for overhead
variances.

E12-28 The loan department of Your Local Bank uses standard costs to determine the overhead cost of processing loan applications. During the current month, a fire occurred, and the accounting records for the department were mostly destroyed. The following data were salvaged from the ashes:

Standard variable overhead rate per hour	$ 9
Standard hours per application	2
Standard hours allowed	2,000
Standard fixed overhead rate per hour	$ 6
Actual fixed overhead cost	$12,600
Variable overhead budget based on standard hours allowed	$18,000
Fixed overhead budget	$12,600
Overhead budget variance	$ 1,200 U

Instructions

(a) Determine the following:
   1. Total actual overhead cost
   2. Actual variable overhead cost
   3. Variable overhead cost applied
   4. Fixed overhead cost applied
   5. Overhead volume variance

(b) Determine how many loans were processed.

(SO 2, 3, 4)
Calculate variances.

E12-29 Jackson Company's overhead rate was based on estimates of $200,000 for overhead costs and 20,000 direct labour hours. Jackson's standards allow two hours of direct labour per unit produced. Production in May was 900 units, and actual overhead incurred in May was $19,000. The overhead budgeted for 1,800 standard direct labour hours is $17,600 ($5,000 fixed and $12,600 variable).

Instructions

(a) Calculate the total, budget, and volume variances for overhead.

(b) What are possible causes of the variances calculated in part (a)?

E12-30 Rondell Company uses a standard cost system. Indirect costs were budgeted at $200,000 plus $15 per direct labour hour. The overhead rate is based on 10,000 hours. Actual results were:

<table>
<tr><td>Standard direct labour hours allowed</td><td>9,000</td></tr>
<tr><td>Actual direct labour hours</td><td>10,000</td></tr>
<tr><td>Fixed overhead</td><td>$190,000</td></tr>
<tr><td>Variable overhead</td><td>$185,000</td></tr>
</table>

(SO 3)
Calculate overhead variances.

Instructions

(a) Calculate the fixed overhead production volume variance.

(b) Calculate the variable overhead spending variance.

(c) Calculate the variable overhead efficiency variance.

(d) Calculate the over- or under-applied overhead.

E12-31 Jay Levitt Company budgeted the following cost standards for the current year:

<table>
<tr><td>Direct materials (2 kg of plastic at $5 per kilogram)</td><td>$10.00</td></tr>
<tr><td>Direct labour (2 hours at $12 per hour)</td><td>24.00</td></tr>
<tr><td>Variable manufacturing overhead</td><td>12.00</td></tr>
<tr><td>Fixed manufacturing overhead</td><td>6.00</td></tr>
<tr><td>Total standard cost per unit</td><td>$52.00</td></tr>
</table>

(SO 2, 3)
Calculate direct materials and direct labour variances.

Actual costs for producing 2,750 units were as follows:

<table>
<tr><td>Direct materials used</td><td>6,050 kg</td></tr>
<tr><td>Direct materials purchased (6,500 kg)</td><td>$31,200</td></tr>
<tr><td>Direct labour (6,875 hours)</td><td>$68,750</td></tr>
<tr><td>Variable manufacturing costs</td><td>$33,000</td></tr>
<tr><td>Fixed manufacturing costs</td><td>$18,000</td></tr>
</table>

Instructions

(a) Calculate the material price variance for materials purchased.

(b) Calculate the material efficiency variance.

(c) Calculate the labour price variance.

(d) Calculate the labour efficiency variance.

E12-32 Imperial Landscaping plants grass seed as basic landscaping for business terrains. During a recent month, the company worked on three projects (Ames, Korman, and Stilles). The company is interested in controlling its material costs—grass seed costs—for these planting projects.

(SO 4)
Prepare variance reports.

In order to provide management with useful cost control information, the company uses standard costs and prepares monthly variance reports. Analysis reveals that the purchasing agent mistakenly purchased poor-quality seeds for the Ames project. The Korman project, however, received seed that was on sale but was higher than standard quality. The Stilles project received standard seeds; however, the price had increased and a new employee had spread the seed. Shown below are quantity and cost data for each project:

Project	Actual Quantity	Actual Costs	Standard Quantity	Standard Costs	Total Variance
Ames	500 kg	$1,400	460 kg	$1,380	$ 20 U
Korman	400	1,160	410	1,230	70 F
Stilles	415	1,328	400	1,200	128 U
Total variance					$ 78 U

Instructions

(a) Prepare a variance report for the purchasing department with the following column headings: (1) Project, (2) Actual Kilograms Purchased, (3) Actual Price, (4) Standard Price, (5) Price Variance, and (6) Explanation.

(b) Prepare a variance report for the production department with the following column headings: (1) Project, (2) Actual Kilograms, (3) Standard Kilograms, (4) Standard Price, (5) Quantity Variance, and (6) Explanation.

(SO 4)
Complete a variance report.

E12-33 Archangel Corporation prepared the following variance report.

ARCHANGEL CORPORATION
Variance Report—Purchasing Department
for Week Ended January 9, 2016

Type of Materials	Quantity Purchased	Actual Price	Standard Price	Price Variance	Explanation
Rogue 11	? kg	$5.20	$5.00	$3,000 ?	Price increase
Storm 17	5,000 mg	?	4.20	1,050 U	Rush order
Beast 29	22,000 units	0.55	?	440 F	Bought larger quantity

Instructions
Fill in the appropriate amounts or letters for the question marks in the report.

(SO 4)
Prepare an income statement for management.

E12-34 Carlos Company uses a standard cost accounting system. During January, the company reported the following manufacturing variances:

Materials price variance	$1,200 U	Labour quantity variance	$ 750 U
Materials quantity variance	800 F	Overhead variance	800 U
Labour price variance	550 U		

In addition, 8,000 units of product were sold at $8 per unit. Each unit sold had a standard cost of $5. Selling and administrative expenses were $8,000 for the month.

Instructions
Prepare an income statement for management for the month ending January 31, 2016.

(SO 1, 4)
Identify performance evaluation terminology.

E12-35 The following is a list of terms related to performance evaluation:

1. Balanced scorecard
2. Variance
3. Learning and growth perspective
4. Non-financial measures
5. Customer perspective
6. Internal process perspective
7. Ideal standards
8. Normal standards

Instructions
Match each of the following descriptions with one of the terms above:
(a) The difference between total actual costs and total standard costs
(b) An efficient level of performance that is attainable under expected operating conditions
(c) An approach that uses financial and non-financial measures in an integrated system that links performance measurement and a company's strategic goals
(d) A viewpoint used in the balanced scorecard to evaluate how well a company develops and retains its employees
(e) An evaluation tool that is not based on dollars
(f) A viewpoint used in the balanced scorecard to evaluate the company from the perspective of those people who buy and use its products or services
(g) An optimum level of performance under perfect operating conditions
(h) A viewpoint used in the balanced scorecard to evaluate the efficiency and effectiveness of the company's value chain

(SO 2, 3, 5)
Determine missing entries and balances for variances.

*E12-36 Tovar Company uses a standard cost accounting system. Some of the ledger accounts have been destroyed in a fire. The controller asks for your help in reconstructing some missing entries and balances.

Instructions
(a) Materials Price Variance shows a $3,000 favourable balance. Accounts Payable shows $148,000 of raw materials purchases. What was the amount debited to Raw Materials Inventory for raw materials purchased?
(b) Materials Quantity Variance shows a $3,000 unfavourable balance. Raw Materials Inventory shows a zero balance. What was the amount debited to Work in Process Inventory for direct materials used?
(c) Labour Price Variance shows a $1,800 unfavourable balance. Factory Labour shows a debit of $170,000 for wages incurred. What was the amount credited to Wages Payable?
(d) Factory Labour shows a credit of $170,000 for direct labour used. Labour Quantity Variance shows a $500 unfavourable balance. What was the amount debited to Work in Process for direct labour used?
(e) Overhead applied to Work in Process totalled $198,000. If the total overhead variance was $1,200 unfavourable, what was the amount of overhead costs debited to Manufacturing Overhead?
(f) Overhead Budget Variance shows a debit balance of $2,700. What was the amount and type of balance (debit or credit) in Overhead Volume Variance?

(SO 5)
Journalize entries for materials and labour variances.

*E12-37 Data for Kopecky Inc. are given in E12-23.

Instructions
Journalize the entries to record the materials and labour variances.

*E12-38   Data for Rondell Company are given in E12-30.

Instructions

(a) Journalize the incurrence of the overhead costs and the application of overhead to the job, assuming a standard cost accounting system is used.

(b) Prepare the adjusting entry for the overhead variances.

*E12-39   Marley Company installed a standard cost system on January 1. Selected transactions for the month of January are as follows:

1. Purchased 24,000 units of raw materials on account at a cost of $4.50 per unit. Standard cost was $4.30 per unit.
2. Issued 24,000 units of raw materials for jobs that required 23,500 standard units of raw materials.
3. Incurred 20,400 actual hours of direct labour at an actual rate of $4.80 per hour. The standard rate is $5.50 per hour. (Note: Credit Wages Payable.)
4. Performed 20,400 hours of direct labour on jobs when standard hours were 20,600.
5. Applied overhead to jobs at 100% of the direct labour cost for the standard hours allowed.

Instructions
Journalize the January transactions.

Problems: Set A

P12-40A   You have been given the following information about the production of Gamma Co., and are asked to provide the plant manager with information for a meeting with the vice-president of operations:

	Standard Cost Card
Direct materials (6 kg at $3 per kilogram)	$18.00
Direct labour (0.8 hours at $5)	4.00
Variable overhead (0.8 hours at $3 per hour)	2.40
Fixed overhead (0.8 hours at $7 per hour)	5.60
	$30.00

The following is a production report for the most recent period of operations:

			Variances		
Costs	Total Standard Cost	Price/ Rate	Spending/ Budget	Quantity/ Efficiency	Volume
Direct materials	$405,000	$6,900 F		$9,000 U	
Direct labour	90,000	4,850 U		7,000 U	
Variable overhead	54,000		$1,300 F	?	
Fixed overhead	126,000		500 F		$14,000 U

Instructions

(a) How many units were produced during the period?
(b) How many kilograms of raw material were purchased and used during the period?
(c) What was the actual cost per kilogram of raw materials?
(d) How many actual direct labour hours were worked during the period?
(e) What was the actual rate paid per direct labour hour?
(f) What was the actual variable overhead cost incurred during the period?
(g) What is the total fixed cost in the company's master budget?
(h) What were the master budget hours for fixed overhead?

(adapted from CGA-Canada, now CPA Canada)

P12-41A   Inman Corporation manufactures a single product. The standard cost per unit of product is as follows:

Direct materials—2 kg of plastic at $5 per kilogram	$10.00
Direct labour—2 hours at $12 per hour	24.00
Variable manufacturing overhead	8.00
Fixed manufacturing overhead	6.00
Total standard cost per unit	$48.00

The master manufacturing overhead budget for the month based on the normal productive capacity of 20,000 direct labour hours (10,000 units) shows total variable costs of $80,000 ($4 per labour hour) and total fixed costs of $60,000 ($3 per labour hour). Normal production capacity is 20,000 direct hours. Overhead is applied based on direct labour hours. Actual costs for producing 9,800 units in November were as follows:

Direct materials (20,500 kg)	$100,450
Direct labour (19,600 hours)	239,120
Variable overhead	78,100
Fixed overhead	59,200
Total manufacturing costs	$476,870

The purchasing department normally buys the quantities of raw materials that are expected to be used in production each month. Raw materials inventories, therefore, can be ignored.

Instructions

(a) MPV = $2,050 F

(b) $100 U

(a) Calculate all of the materials and labour variances.

(b) Calculate the total overhead variance.

(c) Calculate the overhead budget variance and the overhead volume variance.

(SO 2, 3, 4)

Calculate variances and prepare an income statement.

P12-42A   Soriano Manufacturing Company uses a standard cost accounting system to account for the manufacturing of exhaust fans. In July 2016, it accumulates the following data for 1,500 units started and finished:

Cost and Production Data	Actual	Standard
Raw materials		
Units purchased	21,000	
Units used	21,000	22,000
Unit cost	$ 3.40	$ 3.00
Direct labour		
Hours worked	3,450	3,600
Hourly rate	$ 11.80	$ 12.50
Manufacturing overhead		
Incurred	$101,500	
Applied		$108,000

Manufacturing overhead was applied based on direct labour hours. Normal capacity for the month was 3,400 direct labour hours. At normal capacity, budgeted overhead costs were $20 per labour hour variable and $10.00 per labour hour fixed. Total budgeted fixed overhead costs were $34,000.

Jobs finished during the month were sold for $280,000. Selling and administrative expenses were $25,000.

Instructions

(a) LQV = $1,875 F

(b) OHV = $6,500 F

(a) Calculate all of the variances for direct materials and direct labour.

(b) Calculate the total manufacturing overhead variance.

(c) Calculate the overhead budget variance and the overhead volume variance.

(d) Prepare an income statement for management showing the variances. Ignore income taxes.

(SO 1, 2, 3)

Prepare a flexible budget, determine standard costs, and calculate variances.

P12-43A   Under a contract with the provincial government, ChemLabs Inc. analyzes the chemical and bacterial composition of well water in various municipalities in the interior of British Columbia. The contract price is $25.20 per test performed. The normal volume is 10,000 tests per month. Each test requires two testing kits, which have a standard price of $3.80 each. Direct labour to perform the test is 10 minutes at $22.80 per hour. At normal volume, the overhead costs are as follows:

Variable overhead costs		
Indirect labour	$18,000	
Utilities	4,000	
Labour-related costs	15,000	
Laboratory maintenance	11,000	$ 48,000
Fixed overhead costs		
Depreciation	28,000	
Supervisor	30,000	
Base utilities	9,000	
Insurance	2,000	69,000
Total overhead		$117,000

Overhead is allocated based on direct labour hours.

During May 2016, 9,000 tests were performed. The records show the following actual costs and production data:

	Activity	Actual Cost
Number of test kits purchased	19,000	$70,300
Number of test kits used	18,500	
Direct labour	1,623 hours	37,646
Total overhead costs		
Variable		45,200
Fixed		68,500

Test kits are kept in inventory at standard cost. At the end of May, no tests were in process.

Instructions
(a) Prepare a flexible overhead budget based on 80% of the normal volume.
(b) Prepare a standard cost card for a water test.
(c) Calculate the direct materials price and quantity variances and the direct labour rate and efficiency variances for May 2016, indicating whether they are favourable or unfavourable.
(d) Calculate the laboratory variable overhead variances for the month, indicating whether they are favourable or unfavourable.

(a) Total OH costs = $107,400

(adapted from CGA-Canada, now CPA Canada)

P12-44A Kohler Clothiers manufactures women's business suits. The company uses a standard cost accounting system. In March 2016, 15,700 suits were made. The following standard and actual cost data applied to the month of March when normal capacity was 20,000 direct labour hours. All materials purchased were used in production:

(SO 2, 3, 4)
Calculate variances, identify significant variances, and discuss causes.

Cost Element	Standard (per unit)	Actual
Direct materials	5 m at $6.75 per metre	$547,200 for 76,000 m
		($7.20 per metre)
Direct labour	1 hour at $11.45 per hour	$165,760 for 14,800 hours
		($11.20 per hour)
Overhead	1 hour at $9.40 per hour	$120,000 fixed overhead
	(fixed $6.25; variable $3.15)	$ 49,000 variable overhead

Overhead is applied based on direct labour hours. At normal capacity, budgeted fixed overhead costs were $125,000, and budgeted variable overhead costs were $63,000.

Instructions
(a) Calculate the total, price, and quantity variances for materials and labour, and calculate the total, overhead, and volume variances for manufacturing overhead.
(b) ▭▭▭▷ Which of the materials and labour variances should be investigated if management considers a variance of more than 5% from standard to be significant? Discuss the potential causes of this variance.

(a) LQV: $10,305 F

P12-45A You have been given the following information about ALG Co. Ltd., which uses a standard cost system in accounting for its one product:

(SO 2, 3)
Calculate various amounts from standard costs and variances.

1. In the month of November 2016, 5,000 units were produced.
2. The annual overhead budget includes $750,000 for variable and $1,050,000 for fixed overhead items. Budgeted production for the year is 50,000 units. Overhead is applied based on direct labour hours.
3. The materials standard per unit is 20 litres at $1.
4. The direct labour standard per unit is 3 hours at $10.
5. The actual price paid for material was $0.99.
6. The actual direct labour rate was $10.50.
7. Actual fixed overhead costs totalled $88,000.
8. The following variances have already been calculated:

Materials price	600 F
Materials quantity	1,600 U
Labour rate	7,400 U
Variable overhead spending	1,800 U

Instructions
Calculate the following:
(a) The quantity of material purchased
(b) The quantity of material used
(c) The actual direct labour hours worked
(d) The labour efficiency variance

(a) 60,000 litres

(e) The variable overhead efficiency variance

(f) $75,800

(f) The actual variable overhead
(g) The fixed overhead budget variance
(h) The fixed overhead production volume variance

(SO 2, 3)
Answer questions
about variances.

P12-46A   Crede Manufacturing Company uses a standard cost accounting system. In 2016, 28,000 units were produced. Each unit took several kilograms of direct materials and 1.6 standard hours of direct labour at a standard hourly rate of $12. Normal capacity was 50,000 direct labour hours. During the year, 117,000 kg of raw materials were purchased at $0.92 per kilogram. All materials purchased were used during the year.

Instructions

(b) 4.0 kg

(a) If the materials price variance was $3,510 favourable, what was the standard materials price per kilogram?
(b) If the materials quantity variance was $4,750 unfavourable, what was the standard materials quantity per unit?
(c) What were the standard hours allowed for the units produced?
(d) If the labour quantity variance was $7,200 unfavourable, what were the actual direct labour hours worked?
(e) If the labour price variance was $9,080 favourable, what was the actual rate per hour?

(f) $7.20 per DLH

(f) If total budgeted manufacturing overhead was $360,000 at normal capacity, what was the predetermined overhead rate?
(g) What was the standard cost per unit of product?
(h) How much overhead was applied to production during the year?
(i) Using selected answers above, what were the total costs assigned to work in process?

(SO 2, 3, 4)
Calculate variances
and prepare an income
statement.

P12-47A   Hi-Tek Labs performs steroid testing services for colleges and universities. Because the company works only with educational institutions, the price of each test is strictly regulated. Therefore, the costs incurred must be carefully monitored and controlled. Shown below are the standard costs for a typical test:

Direct materials (1 Petri dish at $1.80 per dish)	$ 1.80
Direct labour (0.5 hours at $20.50 per hour)	10.25
Variable overhead (0.5 hours at $8 per hour)	4.00
Fixed overhead (0.5 hours at $5 per hour)	2.50
Total standard cost per test	$18.55

The lab does not maintain an inventory of Petri dishes. Therefore, the dishes purchased each month are used that month. Actual activity for the month of May 2016, when 2,500 tests were conducted, resulted in the following:

Direct materials (2,530 dishes)	$ 5,060
Direct labour (1,240 hours)	26,040
Variable overhead	10,100
Fixed overhead	5,700

Monthly budgeted fixed overhead is $6,000. Revenues for the month were $55,000, and selling and administrative expenses were $2,000.

Instructions

(a) LQV $205 F

(a) Calculate the price and quantity variances for direct materials and direct labour.
(b) Calculate the total overhead variance.
(c) Prepare an income statement for management.
(d) ✎ Provide possible explanations for each unfavourable variance.

(SO 3)
Calculate variances.

P12-48A   Pointe Claire Company applies overhead based on direct labour hours. Two direct labour hours are required for each unit of product. Planned production for the period was set at 9,000 units. Manufacturing overhead is budgeted at $135,000 for the period (20% of this cost is fixed). The 17,200 hours worked during the period resulted in the production of 8,500 units. The variable manufacturing overhead cost incurred was $108,500 and the fixed manufacturing overhead cost was $28,000.

Instructions

(a) $5,300 U

(a) Calculate the variable overhead spending variance for the period.
(b) Calculate the variable overhead efficiency (quantity) variance for the period.
(c) Calculate the fixed overhead budget (spending) variance for the period.

(d) $1,500 U

(d) Calculate the fixed overhead volume variance for the period.

(adapted from CMA Canada, now CPA Canada)

(SO 2, 3, 4, 5)
Journalize and post
standard cost entries,
and prepare an income
statement.

*P12-49A   Fayman Manufacturing Company uses standard costs with its job-order cost accounting system. In January, an order (Job 84) was received for 5,500 units of product D. The standard cost of one unit of product D is as follows:

Direct materials—1.4 kg at $4 per kilogram	$ 5.60
Direct labour—1 hour at $9 per hour	9.00
Overhead—1 hour (variable $7.40; fixed $8.00)	15.40
Standard cost per unit	$30.00

Overhead is applied based on direct labour hours. Normal capacity for the month of January was 6,000 direct labour hours. During January, the following transactions applicable to Job No. 84 occurred:

1. Purchased 8,200 kg of raw materials on account at $3.60 per kilogram.
2. Requisitioned 8,200 kg of raw materials for production.
3. Incurred 5,200 hours of direct labour at $9.25 per hour.
4. Worked 5,200 hours of direct labour on Job No. 84.
5. Incurred $85,760 of manufacturing overhead on account.
6. Applied overhead to Job No. 84 based on the direct labour hours.
7. Transferred Job No. 84 to finished goods.
8. Billed customer for Job No. 84 at a selling price of $280,000.
9. Incurred selling and administrative expenses of $65,000 on account.

Instructions
(a) Journalize the transactions.
(b) Post to the job-order cost accounts.
(c) Prepare the entry to recognize the overhead variances.
(d) Prepare the income statement for management for January 2016.

(d) NI = $51,620

P12-50A   Toronto Manufacturing Company uses a standard cost system. John Robert, a financial analyst for Toronto Manufacturing Company, has been given information with respect to standard cost variances for one of the plants. These variances are given below.

(SO 3)
Calculate overhead variances and discuss their meaning.

Materials quantity variance	$10,500 favourable
Labour rate variance	6,000 favourable
Labour efficiency variance	18,000 unfavourable
Factory overhead spending variance	4,500 favourable
Factory overhead efficiency variance	9,000 unfavourable
Factory overhead volume variance	75,000 favourable

He has determined that the company has manufactured 75,000 units of product with standard costs as follows:

Direct materials	$1,050,000
* Direct labour	450,000
Variable factory overhead	225,000
Fixed factory overhead	375,000
Total standard cost	$2,100,000

* Standard labour time per product unit is 45 minutes.

The actual fixed factory overhead was equal to the master budgeted fixed factory overhead.
    Mr. Robert would like to use the variances to develop some of the cost data for the fiscal period.

Instructions
Answer the following questions:
(a) How many units of product should be manufactured at the master budget capacity?
(b) Determine the total fixed factory overhead for the master budget.
(c) How many direct labour hours should have been used to manufacture 75,000 units of product?
(d) How many direct labour hours were actually used to manufacture 75,000 units of product?
(e) What were the total actual costs of direct labour?
(f) What were the total standard costs of the direct materials used in production?
(g) What was the actual variable factory overhead cost?
(h) What was the budget variable factory overhead for actual time used to manufacture 75,000 units of product?
(i) What was the budget variable factory overhead for the required time to manufacture 75,000 units of product?

(a) 60,000 units

(c) 56,250 hours

P12-51A   Montreal Inc. manufactures garden hoses for large stores. The standard costs for a dozen garden hoses are as follows:

(SO 2, 3)
Calculate variances.

Direct materials	24 m × $2 per metre = $48
Direct labour	3 hours × $12 per hour = $36

During February, Montreal Inc. worked on three separate orders of garden hoses. Job cost records for the month disclose the following:

Lot	Units in Lot	Materials Used	Hours Worked
4503	1,000 dozen	24,100 m	2,980
4504	1,500 dozen	36,150 m	5,130
4505	2,000 dozen	48,200 m	2,890

You have been able to gather the following information:

1. Montreal Inc. purchased 110,000 m of material during February at a cost of $242,000. The material price variance is recorded when goods are purchased, and all inventories are carried at standard cost.

2. The payroll department reported that production employees were paid $12.50 per hour.
3. There was no beginning work in process. During February, lots 4503 and 4504 were completed, and all materials were issued for lot 4505, which was 60% complete in terms of labour.
4. Montreal Inc. applies fixed and variable overhead based on machine hours. Below are the results for Montreal Inc. for the month of February:

The normal activity in machine hours	40,000
Flexible budget variable overhead per machine hour	$ 2.80
Actual variable overhead cost incurred	117,000
Actual fixed overhead cost incurred	302,100
Variable overhead cost applied to production	117,600
Variable overhead efficiency variance (unfavourable)	8,400
Fixed overhead budget variance (unfavourable)	2,100

Instructions

Calculate the following:

(a) MQV = $900 U

(a) The material price, quantity, and total variances
(b) The labour price, efficiency, and total variances
(c) The variable overhead spending, efficiency, and total variances

(d) $12,900 F

(d) The fixed overhead spending, volume, and total variances
(e) Underapplied (overapplied) total overhead

(adapted from CGA-Canada, now CPA Canada)

Problems: Set B

(SO 2, 3)
Calculate variances.

P12-52B Ranier Corporation manufactures a single product. The standard cost per unit of the product is shown below:

Direct materials—1.5 kg of plastic at $8 per kilogram	$12.00
Direct labour—2 hours at $15 per hour	30.00
Variable manufacturing overhead	10.00
Fixed manufacturing overhead	5.00
Total standard cost per unit	$57.00

The predetermined manufacturing overhead rate is $7.50 per direct labour hour ($15.00 ÷ 2). This rate was calculated from a master manufacturing overhead budget based on normal production of 20,000 direct labour hours (10,000 units) for the month. The master budget showed total variable costs of $100,000 ($5.00 per hour) and total fixed costs of $50,000 ($2.50 per hour). Actual costs for October in producing 9,600 units were as follows:

Direct materials (10,200 kg)	$ 74,500
Direct labour (14,000 hours)	175,000
Variable overhead	112,500
Fixed overhead	37,500
Total manufacturing costs	$399,500

The purchasing department normally buys the quantities of raw materials that are expected to be used in production each month. Raw materials inventories can therefore be ignored.

Instructions

(a) MPV = $7,100 F
   LQV = $78,000 F

(a) Calculate all of the materials and labour variances.
(b) Calculate the total overhead variance.
(c) Calculate the overhead budget variance and the overhead volume variance.

(SO 2, 3)
Calculate variances and identify significant variances.

P12-53B Sasha Clothiers is a small company that manufactures oversize suits. The company uses a standard cost accounting system. In May 2016, it produced 11,200 suits.

The following standard and actual cost data applied to the month of May when normal capacity was 14,000 direct labour hours. All materials purchased were used.

Cost Element	Standard (per unit)	Actual
Direct materials	8 m at $4.40 per metre	$375,575 for 90,500 m ($4.15 per metre)
Direct labour	1.2 hours at $13.40 per hour	$200,220 for 14,200 hours ($14.10 per hour)
Overhead	1.2 hours at $6.10 per hour	$49,000 fixed overhead
	(fixed $3.50; variable $2.60)	$37,000 variable overhead

Overhead is applied based on direct labour hours. At normal capacity, the budgeted fixed overhead costs are $49,000, and the budgeted variable overhead is $36,400.

Instructions
(a) Calculate all of the materials and labour variances.
(b) Calculate the total overhead budget and volume variances.
(c) ⬤▬▬▶ Which of the materials and labour variances should be investigated if management considers a variance of more than 4% from standard to be significant?

(a) MPV $22,625 F

P12-54B Milberg Co. uses absorption costing and standard costing to improve cost control.
In 2016, the total budgeted overhead rate was $1.55 per direct labour hour. When preparing the budget, Milberg expected a monthly activity level of 10,000 direct labour hours. The monthly variable overhead cost budgeted for this level of activity was $9,500.
The following data on actual results are provided for the month of November 2016.

(SO 2, 3)
Calculate variances.

Materials purchased	20,000 units
Direct labour costs incurred	$36,000
Total of direct labour rate and efficiency variances	$ 500 F
Actual wage rate ($0.20 less than standard)	$ 4.80
Underapplied variable overhead costs	$ 1,065 U
Total underapplied fixed and variable overhead costs	$ 2,256 U
Materials price variance	$ 200 F
Materials efficiency variance	$ 610 F
Price of purchased materials	$ 0.60 per unit
Materials used	15,000 units

Instructions
Identify and calculate as many different variances as you can for 2016.

(adapted from CGA-Canada, now CPA Canada)

LPV = $1,500 F

P12-55B Harbaugh Manufacturing company uses a standard cost accounting system. In 2016, 45,000 units were produced. Each unit took several kilograms of direct materials and two standard hours of direct labour at a standard hourly rate of $12. Normal capacity was 86,000 direct labour hours. During the year, 200,000 kg of raw materials were purchased at $1.00 per kilogram. All materials purchased were used during the year.

(SO 2, 3)
Answer questions about variances.

Instructions
Answer the following questions:
(a) If the materials price variance was $10,000 unfavourable, what was the standard materials price per kilogram?
(b) If the materials quantity variance was $23,750 favourable, what was the standard materials quantity per unit?
(c) What were the standard hours allowed for the units produced?
(d) If the labour quantity variance was $10,080 unfavourable, what were the actual direct labour hours worked?
(e) If the labour price variance was $18,168 favourable, what was the actual rate per hour?
(f) If total budgeted manufacturing overhead was $713,800 at normal capacity, what was the predetermined overhead rate per direct labour hours?
(g) What was the standard cost per unit of product?
(h) How much overhead was applied to production during the year?
(i) Using one or more answers above, what were the total costs assigned to work in process?

(b) 5.0 kilograms

(f) $8.30 per DLH

P12-56B Ronaldo Manufacturing Company uses a standard cost system in accounting for the cost of one of its products. The budgeted monthly production is 1,750 units per month. The standard direct labour cost is 15 hours per unit at $5 per hour. The budgeted cost for manufacturing overhead is set as follows:

(SO 2, 3)
Calculate variances.

Fixed overhead per month	$183,750
Variable overhead per month	78,750
Total budgeted overhead	$262,500

The manufacturing overhead rate is 200% of the direct labour cost.
During the month of April, the plant produced 1,650 units and the cost of production was as follows:

Direct materials (99,000 litres)	$ 792,000
Direct labour (23,100 hours)	121,275
Fixed manufacturing overhead	195,000
Variable manufacturing overhead	63,525
	$1,171,800

Instructions
Calculate the following:
(a) Labour price and quantity variances
(b) Variable overhead spending and quantity variances
(c) Fixed overhead spending and volume variances

(a) LPV = $5,775 U

(adapted from CMA Canada, now CPA Canada)

(SO 2, 3)
Determine amounts
from the variance
report.

P12-57B   You have been given the following information about the production of Theta Co. and are asked to provide the plant manager with information for a meeting with the vice-president of operations:

	Standard Cost Card
Direct materials (3 kg at $6 per kilogram)	$18.00
Direct labour (2 hours at $5 per hour)	10.00
Variable overhead (2 hours at $3 per hour)	6.00
Fixed overhead (2 hours at $7 per hour)	14.00
	$48.00

The following is a production report for the most recent period of operations:

Costs	Total Standard Cost	Price/ Rate	Spending/ Budget	Quantity/ Efficiency	Volume
Direct materials	$450,000	$6,900 U		$ 9,000 F	
Direct labour	250,000	4,860 F		7,000 F	
Variable overhead	150,000		$1,300 U	?	
Fixed overhead	364,000		500 U	$14,000 U	

Instructions

Answer the following questions:

(a) How many units were produced during the period?
(b) How many kilograms of raw material were purchased and used during the period?
(c) What was the actual cost per kilogram of raw materials?
(d) How many actual direct labour hours were worked during the period?
(e) What was the actual rate paid per direct labour hour?
(f) What was the actual variable overhead cost incurred during the period?
(g) What is the total fixed cost in the company's flexible budget?

(c) AP $6.09

(g) $378,000

(adapted from CGA-Canada, now CPA Canada)

(SO 3)
Calculate variances.

P12-58B   Biotech Inc. applies overhead based on direct labour hours. Three direct labour hours are required for each unit of product. Planned production for the period was set at 8,100 units. Manufacturing overhead is budgeted at $405,000 for the period (30% of this cost is fixed). The 24,500 hours worked during the period resulted in the production of 8,000 units. The variable manufacturing overhead cost incurred was $288,500 and the fixed manufacturing overhead cost was $123,000.

Instructions

(a) Calculate the variable overhead spending variance for the period.
(b) Calculate the variable overhead efficiency (quantity) variance for the period.
(c) Calculate the fixed overhead budget (spending) variance for the period.
(d) Calculate the fixed overhead volume variance for the period.

(a) $2,585 U

(d) $1,500 U

(adapted from CMA Canada, now CPA Canada)

(SO 3)
Calculate overhead
variances and discuss
their meaning.

P12-59B   The Multi-Tool Manufacturing Company uses a standard cost system. Stéphanie Roget, a financial analyst for Multi-Tool Manufacturing Company, has been given information with respect to standard cost variances for one of the plants. These variances are given below.

Materials quantity variance	$ 7,000 favourable
Labour rate variance	4,000 favourable
Labour efficiency variance	12,000 unfavourable
Factory overhead spending variance	3,000 favourable
Factory overhead efficiency variance	6,000 unfavourable
Factory overhead volume variance	50,000 favourable

She has determined that the company has manufactured 50,000 units of product with standard costs as follows:

Direct materials	$ 700,000
* Direct labour	300,000
Variable factory overhead	150,000
Fixed factory overhead	250,000
Total standard cost	$1,400,000

* Standard labour time per product unit is 30 minutes.

The actual fixed factory overhead was equal to the master budgeted fixed factory overhead.
Ms. Roget would like to use the variances to develop some of the cost data for the fiscal period.

Instructions

(a) 40,000 units

(a) How many units of the product should be manufactured at the master budget capacity?
(b) Determine the total fixed factory overhead for the master budget.

(c) How many direct labour hours should have been used to manufacture 50,000 units of product?

(d) How many direct labour hours were used?

(c) 25,000 direct labour hours

(e) What were the total actual costs of direct labour?

(f) What were the total standard costs of the direct materials used in production?

(g) What was the actual variable factory overhead cost?

(h) What was the budget variable factory overhead for actual time used to manufacture the 50,000 units of product?

(i) What was the budget variable factory overhead for the required time to manufacture the 50,000 units of product?

P12-60B Farm Labs, Inc. provides mad cow disease testing for both provincial and federal government agriculture agencies. Because the company's customers are government agencies, prices are strictly regulated. Farm Labs must therefore constantly monitor and control its testing costs. Shown below are the standard costs for a typical test:

(SO 2, 3, 4)
Calculate variances and prepare an income statement.

Direct materials (2 test tubes at $1.46 per tube)	$ 2.92
Direct labour (1 hour at $24 per hour)	24.00
Variable overhead (1 hour at $6 per hour)	6.00
Fixed overhead (1 hour at $10 per hour)	10.00
Total standard cost per test	$42.92

The lab does not maintain an inventory of test tubes. The tubes purchased each month are used that month. Actual activity for the month of November 2016, when 1,475 tests were conducted, resulted in the following:

Direct materials (3,050 test tubes)	$ 4,270
Direct labour (1,500 hours)	35,650
Variable overhead	7,400
Fixed overhead	15,000

Monthly budgeted fixed overhead is $14,000. Revenues for the month were $75,000, and selling and administrative expenses were $5,000.

Instructions

(a) Calculate the price and quantity variances for direct materials and direct labour, and the budget and volume variances for overhead.

(a) LQV, $600U

(b) Prepare an income statement for management.

(c) Provide possible explanations for each unfavourable variance.

P12-61B Finley Manufacturing Corporation accumulates the following data for jobs started and finished during the month of June 2016:

(SO 2, 3, 4)
Calculate variances and prepare an income statement.

Cost and Production Data	Actual	Standard
Raw materials unit cost	$ 2.25	$ 2.00
Raw materials units used	10,600	10,000
Direct labour payroll	$122,400	$120,000
Direct labour hours worked	14,400	15,000
Manufacturing overhead incurred	$184,500	
Manufacturing overhead applied		$189,000
Machine hours expected to be used at normal capacity		42,500
Budgeted fixed overhead for June		$ 51,000
Variable overhead rate per hour		$ 3.00
Fixed overhead rate per hour		$ 1.20

Overhead is applied based on standard machine hours. Three hours of machine time are required for each direct labour hour. The jobs were sold for $400,000. Selling and administrative expenses were $40,000. Assume that the amount of raw materials purchased equalled the amount used.

Instructions

(a) Calculate all of the materials and labour variances.

(a) LQV, $4,800 F

(b) Calculate the total overhead variances.

(c) Calculate the overhead budget variance and the overhead volume variance.

(d) Prepare an income statement for management. Ignore income taxes.

(d) COGS $329,000

*P12-62B** Berman Corporation uses standard costs with its job-order cost accounting system. In January, an order (Job No. 12) for 1,950 units of product B was received. The standard cost of one unit of product B is as follows:

(SO 2, 3, 4, 5)
Journalize and post standard cost entries, and prepare an income statement.

Direct materials	3 kg at $1 per kilogram	$ 3.00
Direct labour	1 hour at $8 per hour	8.00
Overhead	2 hours (variable $4 per machine hour; fixed $2.25 per machine hour)	12.50
Standard cost per unit		$23.50

Normal capacity for the month was 4,200 machine hours. During January, the following transactions applicable to Job No. 12 occurred:

1. Purchased 6,250 kg of raw materials on account at $1.06 per kilogram.
2. Requisitioned 6,250 kg of raw materials for Job No. 12.
3. Incurred 2,100 hours of direct labour at a rate of $7.75 per hour.
4. Worked 2,100 hours of direct labour on Job No. 12.
5. Incurred manufacturing overhead of $25,800 on account.
6. Applied overhead to Job No. 12 based on standard machine hours used.
7. Completed Job No. 12.
8. Billed customer for Job No. 12 at a selling price of $70,000.
9. Incurred selling and administrative expenses of $2,000 on account.

Instructions

(a) Journalize the transactions.
(b) Post to the job-order cost accounts.
(c) Prepare the entry to recognize the overhead variances.

(d) Gross profit $21,300

(d) Prepare the January 2016 income statement for management.

(SO 2, 3, 5)
Calculate variances and prepare journal entries.

*P12-63B Azim Shirts Inc. manufactures sweatshirts for large stores. The standard costs for a dozen sweatshirts are:

Direct materials 24 m × $1.10 per metre = $26.40
Direct labour 3 hours × $7.35 per hour = $22.05

During February, Azim worked on three separate orders of sweatshirts. Job cost records for the month disclose the following:

Lot	Units in Lot	Materials Used	Hours Worked
4503	1,000 dozen	24,100 m	2,980
4504	1,700 dozen	40,440 m	5,130
4505	1,200 dozen	28,825 m	2,890

You have been able to gather the following information:

1. Azim purchased 95,000 m of material during February at a cost of $106,400. The material price variance is recorded when goods are purchased, and all inventories are carried at standard cost.
2. The payroll department reported that production employees were paid $7.50 per hour.
3. There was no beginning work in process. During February, lots 4503 and 4504 were completed, and all materials were issued for lot 4505, which was 80% complete in terms of labour.

Instructions

(a) MPV = $1,900 U
(b) LPV = $1,650 U

(a) Calculate the material price variance and make the appropriate journal entry.
(b) Calculate the remaining relevant variances for total production.
(c) Prepare journal entries to charge materials and labour to production.

(adapted from CGA-Canada, now CPA Canada)

Cases

C12-64 Agmar Professionals, a management consulting firm, specializes in strategic planning for financial institutions. Tim Agler and Padmasree Marlin, partners in the firm, are assembling a new strategic planning model for clients to use. The model is designed to be used on most personal computers and replaces a rather lengthy manual model currently marketed by the firm. To market the new model, Tim and Padmasree will need to provide clients with an estimate of the number of labour hours and the computer time needed to operate the model. The model is currently being test-marketed at five small financial institutions. These financial institutions are listed below, along with the number of combined computer/labour hours used by each institution to run the model once:

Financial Institutions	Computer/Labour Hours Required
Canadian National	25
First Funds	45
Financial Federal	40
Pacific Coast	30
Lakeview Savings	30
Total	170
Average	34

Any company that purchases the new model will need to purchase user manuals to access and operate the system. Also required are specialized computer forms that are sold only by Agmar Professionals. User manuals will be sold to clients in cases of 20, at a cost of $320 per case. One manual must be used each time the model is run because each manual includes a non-reusable computer password for operating the system. The specialized computer forms are sold in packages of 250 at a cost of $60 per package. One application of the model requires the use of 50 forms. This amount includes two forms that are generally wasted in each application due to printer alignment errors. The overall cost of the strategic planning model to user clients is $12,000. Most clients will use the model four times each year.

Agmar Professionals must provide its clients with estimates of on-going costs that are incurred in operating the new strategic planning model. They would like to provide this information in the form of standard costs.

Instructions
(a) Determine what factors should be considered in setting a standard for computer/labour hours.
(b) Determine what alternatives for setting a standard for computer/labour hours might be used.
(c) State what standard for computer/labour hours you would select. Justify your answer.
(d) Determine the standard materials cost associated with the user manuals and computer forms for each application of the strategic planning model.

C12-65 Mo Coughlin and Associates is a medium-sized company located near a large metropolitan area in the Prairies. The company manufactures cabinets of mahogany, oak, and other fine woods for use in expensive homes, restaurants, and hotels. Although some of the work is custom, many of the cabinets are a standard size.

One non-custom model is called the Luxury Base Frame. Normal production is 1,000 units per month. Each unit has a direct labour hour standard of five hours. Overhead is applied to production based on standard direct labour hours. During the most recent month, only 900 units were produced; 4,500 direct labour hours were allowed for standard production, but only 4,000 hours were used. Standard and actual overhead costs were as follows:

	Standard (1,000 units)	Actual (900 units)
Indirect materials	$ 12,000	$ 12,300
Indirect labour	43,000	51,000
Manufacturing supervisors, salaries (fixed)	22,500	22,000
Manufacturing office employees, salaries (fixed)	13,000	12,500
Engineering costs (fixed)	27,000	25,000
Computer costs	10,000	10,000
Electricity	2,500	2,500
Manufacturing building depreciation (fixed)	8,000	8,000
Machinery depreciation (fixed)	3,000	3,000
Trucks and forklift depreciation (fixed)	1,500	1,500
Small tools	700	1,400
Insurance (fixed)	500	500
Property taxes (fixed)	300	300
Total	$144,000	$150,000

Instructions
(a) Determine the overhead application rate.
(b) Determine how much overhead was applied to production.
(c) Calculate the budget overhead variance and the overhead volume variance.
(d) Decide which overhead variances should be investigated.
(e) Discuss the causes of the overhead variances. What can management do to improve its performance next month?

C12-66 You have started working as a cost accountant for a firm that has only been in business for one month. The firm is able to buy a new type of biodegradable plastic at a fixed price of $100 per roll. The plastic is then cut and sealed to make garbage bags. Fixed factory overhead is estimated to be $125,000 per month. During this past month, 8,000 cartons of garbage bags were produced, which represents 80% of the activity volume. You are given the following information:

Rolls of plastic used	40
Variable overhead incurred	$61,000
Overhead efficiency variance	$5,000 U
Standard costs per carton of garbage bags:	
Labour hours	2
Wage rate	$8 per hour
Total overhead	$20
Rolls of plastic	0.004 rolls

Instructions
Calculate the following:
(a) Applied overhead per direct labour hour
(b) Standard direct labour hours allowed for units produced
(c) Activity volume
(d) Predetermined fixed overhead rate
(e) Fixed overhead applied
(f) Variable overhead spending variance
(g) Actual number of direct labour hours incurred
(h) Labour efficiency variance
(i) Materials quantity variance
(j) Fixed overhead budget variance
(k) Fixed overhead volume variance

(adapted from CGA-Canada, now CPA Canada)

C12-67 The Kohler Chemical Manufacturing Company produces two primary chemical products to be used as base ingredients for a variety of products. The 2016 budget for the two products (in thousands) was as follows:

	LX-4	ABC-8	Total
Level of production in litres	1,800	1,800	3,600
Direct materials	$4,500	$5,625	$10,125
Direct labour	2,700	2,700	5,400
Total direct manufacturing cost	$7,200	$8,325	$15,525

The following planning assumptions were used for the budget: (1) a direct materials yield of 96%, and (2) a direct labour rate of $6 per hour. The actual results for 2016 were as follows (in thousands):

	LX-4	ABC-8	Total
Total litres produced	1,710	1,974	3,684
Direct materials	$4,104.00	$6,415.50	$10,519.50
Direct labour	2,808.00	3,276.00	6,084.00
Total direct manufacturing cost	$6,912.00	$9,691.50	$16,603.50

The actual production yield was 95% for LX-4 and 94% for ABC-8. The direct labour cost per hour for both products was $6.50.

Instructions

(a) Calculate for product LX-4: (1) the direct materials price variance, and (2) the direct materials efficiency (yield) variance.

(b) Calculate for product ABC-8: (1) the direct labour rate variance, and (2) the direct labour efficiency variance.

(adapted from CPA Canada)

C12-68 Delta Manufacturing Company uses a standard cost system in accounting for the cost of its main product. The following standards have been established for the direct manufacturing costs per unit:

Direct materials (2 kg at $7.50 per kilogram)	$15.00 per unit
Direct labour (3 hours at $12 per hour)	$36.00 per unit

Budgeted overhead for the month of April (based on expected activity of 9,000 direct labour hours) is as follows:

Variable overhead	$29,250
Fixed overhead	$19,500
Total overhead	$48,750

Overhead is applied based on labour hours. The average activity per month is 9,750 direct labour hours. The company calculates overhead rates based on average activity. Results for the month of April are as follows:

Units produced	3,150
Direct materials used (6,500 kg)	$ 44,850
Direct labour (9,500 hours)	116,375
Variable overhead	28,500
Fixed overhead	20,000
Total costs	$209,725

There was no beginning or ending work in process inventory.

Instructions

Calculate the following:

(a) Direct materials price, usage, and budget variances

(b) Labour price, usage, and budget variances

(c) Variable overhead spending, quantity, and budget variances

(d) Fixed overhead spending and volume variances

C12-69 At Camden Manufacturing Company, production workers in the painting department are paid based on productivity. The labour time standard for a unit of production is established through periodic time studies conducted by Foster Management Inc. In a time study, the actual time a worker requires to complete a specific task is observed. Allowances are then made for preparation time, rest periods, and cleanup time. Dan Renfro is one of several veterans in the painting department. Dan is informed by Foster Management that he will be used in the time study for the painting of a new product. The findings will be the basis for establishing the labour time standard for the next six months. During the test, Dan deliberately slows his normal work pace in an effort to obtain a labour time standard that will be easy to meet. Because it is a new product, the Foster Management representative who conducted the test is unaware that Dan did not give the test his best effort.

Instructions

(a) Who benefited and who was harmed by Dan's actions?

(b) Was Dan ethical in the way he performed the time-study test?

(c) What measure(s) might the company take to obtain valid data for setting the labour time standard?

"All About You" Activity

C12-70 In 2013, CPA Canada was established with the goal of uniting the three accounting designations—CA, CGA, and CMA—into one designation: the CPA, or Chartered Professional Accountant. Each province and territory has the authority to regulate the accounting profession within its own jurisdiction, so the legislated bodies controlling the accounting profession across Canada have been voting to unify the profession under the CPA designation. Once each accounting body votes to unify with CPA Canada, the change requires each provincial legislature to pass legislation, so the process has been taking some time.

Instructions

What are the advantages and disadvantages of a single unified professional accounting designation in Canada? More information about this proposal is available on the CPA Canada website.

Decision-Making at Current Designs

DM12-1 The executive team at Current Designs has gathered to evaluate the company's operations for the last month. One of the topics on the agenda is a special order to produce a batch of 20 kayaks for a client.

Mike Cichanowski asked the others if the special order caused any particular problems in the production process. Dave Thill, the production manager, made the following comments: "Since we wanted to complete this order quickly and make a good first impression on this new customer, we had some of our most experienced type I workers run the rotomould oven and do the trimming. They were very efficient and were able to complete that part of the manufacturing process even more quickly than the regular crew. However, the finishing on these kayaks required a different technique than what we usually use, so our type II workers took a little longer than usual for that part of the process."

Deb Welch, who is in charge of the purchasing function, said, "We had to pay a little more for the polyethylene powder for this order because the customer wanted a colour that we don't usually stock. We also ordered a little extra since we wanted to make sure that we had enough to allow us to calibrate the equipment. The calibration was a little tricky, and we used all of the powder that we had purchased. Since the number of kayaks in the order was fairly small, we were able to use some rope and other parts that were left over from last year's production in the finishing kits. We've seen a price increase for these components in the last year, so using the parts that we already had in inventory cut our costs for the finishing kits."

Instructions

(a) Based on the comments above, predict whether each of the following variances will be favourable or unfavourable. If you don't have enough information to make a prediction, use "NEI" to indicate "Not Enough Information."
   1. Quantity variance for polyethylene powder.
   2. Price variance for polyethylene powder.

   3. Quantity variance for finishing kits.
   4. Price variance for finishing kits.
   5. Quantity variance for type I workers.
   6. Price variance for type I workers.
   7. Quantity variance for type II workers.
   8. Price variance for type II workers.

(b) Diane Buswell examined some of the accounting records and reported that Current Designs purchased 1,200 kg of pellets for this order at a total cost of $2,040. Twenty finishing kits were assembled at a total cost of $3,240. The payroll records showed that the type I employees worked 38 hours on this project at a total cost of $570. The type II finishing employees worked 65 hours at a total cost of $796.25. A total of 20 kayaks were produced for this order.

The standards that had been developed for this model of kayak are as follows for each kayak:
   54 kg of polyethylene powder at $1.50 per kilogram
   1 finishing kit (rope, seat, hardware, etc.) at $170
   2 hours of type I labour from people who run the oven and trim the plastic at a standard wage rate of $15 per hour
   3 hours of type II labour from people who attach the hatches and seat and other hardware at a standard wage rate of $12 per hour.
Calculate the eight variances that are listed in part (a) of this problem.

Waterways Continuing Problem

(This is a continuation of the Waterways Problem from Chapters 1 through 11.)

WCP-12 At the end of June the manager of the B.C. manufacturing plant was provided with the following variance analysis report.

	Budget	Actual	Variance	Favourable (F)/ Unfavourable (U)
Production in units	338,000	357,000	19,000	F
Production costs:				
Direct material	$ 562,009	$ 571,484	$ (9,475)	U
Direct labour	1,521,000	1,572,185	(51,185)	U
Variable overhead costs	126,750	132,488	(5,738)	U
Fixed overhead costs	195,195	192,612	2,583	F
Total production costs	$2,404,954	$2,468,769	$(63,815)	U

The manager immediately called the production supervisor, demanding an explanation for the large unfavourable variance for the quarter. The production supervisor was puzzled. He thought the cost-cutting measures they had incorporated were beginning to work. He certainly wasn't expecting such a large discrepancy.

The budget that was created in Chapter 10 was used to establish the standard rates the plant was using with its normal costing system. They are summarized below.

	Volume	Cost
Direct material	1.10 kg per unit	$1.50 per kg
Direct labour	0.25 hour per unit	$18.00 per hour
Predetermined overhead rate:		
Variable	0.25 hour per unit	$1.50 per hour
Fixed	0.25 hour per unit	$2.31 per hour

Other relevant information:

1. A total of 400,000 kg of direct materials were purchased during the quarter at a cost of $1.55 per kilogram.

2. A total of 380,990 kg of direct materials were used in production to manufacture 357,000 units.

3. Payroll recorded 88,325 direct labour hours at an average cost of $17.80 per hour.

Instructions

Do you agree with the plant manager that the production supervisor performed poorly, as might be indicated by the large unfavourable variance? Explain fully. Include in your response calculations of all production variances.

Remember to go back to the beginning of the chapter to check off your completed work! ←

Answers to Self-Study Questions

study objectives

the navigator

After studying this chapter, you should be able to do the following:

1. Discuss capital budgeting inputs and apply the cash payback technique.
2. Explain the net present value method.
3. Identify capital budgeting challenges and refinements.
4. Explain the internal rate of return method.
5. Describe the annual rate of return method.

PLANNING BIG PROJECTS TAKES ENERGY

Few managerial decision-making tasks in the energy sector are as important as planning for capital projects, which can cost billions of dollars and take years to complete. Companies must explore natural resources, negotiate to buy land, obtain government approval, obtain financing, and complete construction—all while energy prices fluctuate.

Calgary-based Husky Energy Inc., one of Canada's largest integrated energy companies, is involved in oil and natural gas exploration, production, refining, and transportation. It has properties and interests in Western Canada, Atlantic Canada, and the Asia Pacific region, and operates more than 500 Husky and Mohawk retail gas stations across the country.

Husky Energy is continually spending on capital projects to increase production. Its capital expenditures, considered investing activities, were $5.0 billion in 2013 and a budgeted $4.8 billion in 2014.

In 2014, production began at the Liwan natural gas project in the South China Sea, in which Husky has a 49% interest. Husky said that the project, which took seven years and cost an estimated U.S. $6.5 billion, was on time and on budget. Not only is Liwan the largest project ever undertaken by Husky in its 75-year history, but at the time it was the largest investment by a Canadian company in China. The project consists of three underwater fields, about 300 km southeast of Hong Kong, plus an undersea production system and pipeline transportation, and an onshore gas processing facility. Once all three fields are in operation in 2016 or 2017, they were expected to produce between 400 and 500 million cubic feet of natural gas per day, supplying about 4% of China's natural gas.

Among other recent Husky projects are two heavy oil projects in Saskatchewan, expected to generate a total of 20,000 barrels of crude a day when they started producing in 2016. The company also announced a $300-million upgrade to its Ohio refinery that was expected to process up to 40,000 barrels a day of heavy crude from Western Canada.

Husky funds most of its upstream capital programs—exploration and production—with cash from operating activities and issuance of debt and equity. "During times of low oil and gas prices, a portion of capital programs can generally be deferred," Husky said in its 2013 financial statements. However, because projects take so long to plan and complete, many have to go ahead even when energy prices are lower, Husky said. The company tracks commodity prices and financing costs and adjusts its capital planning accordingly. "The Company prepares annual capital expenditure budgets, which are monitored and updated as required."

Sources: Claudia Cattaneo, "Husky Energy Inc's Liwan Natural Gas Project Opens Doors to China," *Financial Post*, March 31, 2014; "Husky Energy Delivers Production at the Liwan Gas Project in the South China Sea," Husky Energy news release, March 30, 2014; "Husky Moves Forward with Heavy Crude Oil Flexibility Project at Lima Refinery," Husky Energy news release, February 3, 2014; The Canadian Press, "Husky Approves Pair of Heavy Oil Projects in Saskatchewan," CanadianManufacturing.com, January 9, 2014; Husky Energy Inc. 2013 financial statements; Husky corporate website, www.huskyenergy.com.

Preview of Chapter 13

Companies like Husky Energy Inc. must constantly determine how to invest their resources. The process of making capital expenditure decisions is called capital budgeting. **Capital budgeting** involves choosing among various capital projects to find the one(s) that will maximize a company's return on its financial investment. This chapter discusses the various techniques that companies use to make effective capital budgeting decisions. This chapter is organized as follows:

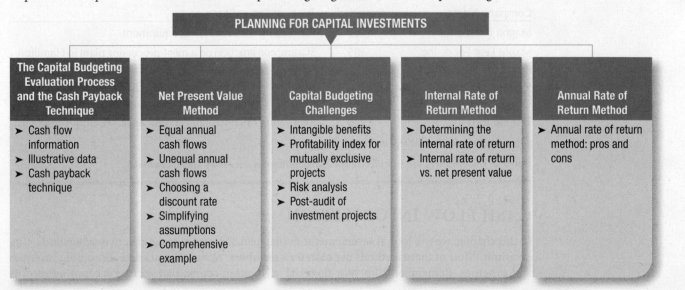

PLANNING FOR CAPITAL INVESTMENTS

The Capital Budgeting Evaluation Process and the Cash Payback Technique	Net Present Value Method	Capital Budgeting Challenges	Internal Rate of Return Method	Annual Rate of Return Method
➤ Cash flow information ➤ Illustrative data ➤ Cash payback technique	➤ Equal annual cash flows ➤ Unequal annual cash flows ➤ Choosing a discount rate ➤ Simplifying assumptions ➤ Comprehensive example	➤ Intangible benefits ➤ Profitability index for mutually exclusive projects ➤ Risk analysis ➤ Post-audit of investment projects	➤ Determining the internal rate of return ➤ Internal rate of return vs. net present value	➤ Annual rate of return method: pros and cons

The Capital Budgeting Evaluation Process and the Cash Payback Technique

Many companies follow a carefully set process in capital budgeting. At least once a year, proposals for projects are requested from each department. A capital budgeting committee examines the proposals and submits its findings to the officers of the company. The officers, in turn, choose the projects that they believe are the most worthy of funding. They submit this list of projects to the board of directors. Ultimately, the directors approve the capital expenditure budget for the year. Illustration 13-1 shows this process.

►Illustration 13-1

Corporate capital budget authorization

1. Project proposals are requested from departments, plants, and authorized personnel.

2. Proposals are examined by a capital budget committee.

3. Officers determine which projects are worthy of funding.

4. The board of directors approves the capital budget.

The involvement of top management and the board of directors in the process shows how important capital budgeting decisions are. These decisions often have a significant impact on a company's future profitability and poor capital budgeting decisions can cost a lot of money. Think of the estimated U.S. $6.5-billion cost of the Liwan natural gas project by our feature story company, Husky Energy Inc. It was completed on time and on budget, but that was not by accident. Projects of this scale require very effective cost controls and good relationships with a wide variety of stakeholders to ensure that spending remains within the budgetary scope.

BUSINESS INSIGHT   *Corporate Canada's Capital Spending*

Monitoring capital expenditure amounts is one way to learn about a company's growth potential. Few companies can grow without making large capital investments. Here are four well-known Canadian companies and the amounts and types of capital expenditures they made in the year 2013:

Company Name	$ million (rounded)	Types of Expenditures
Magna International Inc.	1,169	Purchasing manufacturing equipment.
Maple Leaf Foods Inc.	385	Starting construction on a meat-processing plant in Hamilton, Ontario.
Suncor Energy Inc.	6,380	Maintaining and upgrading infrastructure and equipment in the oil sands operations, including storage tanks and pipelines.
Tim Hortons Inc.	220	Renovating 139 restaurants and enhancing 639 drive-throughs.

Sources: Company annual reports for 2013.

How can shareholders see whether a capital expenditure is necessary and/or desirable?

CASH FLOW INFORMATION

In this chapter, we will look at several methods that help companies make effective capital budgeting decisions. Most of these methods use **cash flow numbers**, rather than accrual accounting revenues and expenses. Remember from your financial accounting course that accrual accounting records revenues and expenses, rather than cash inflows and cash outflows. In fact, revenues and expenses that are measured during a period often differ significantly from their cash flow counterparts. Accrual accounting has advantages over cash accounting in many contexts. **But for the purposes of capital budgeting, estimated cash inflows and outflows are the preferred inputs.** Why? Because ultimately, the value of all financial investments is determined by the value of the cash flows received and paid.

Sometimes cash flow information is not available. In this case, adjustments can be made to accrual accounting numbers to estimate cash flow. Often, net annual cash flow is estimated by adding depreciation expense back to net income. Depreciation expense is added back because it is an expense that does not require an outflow of cash. Accordingly, the depreciation expense that is deducted in determining net income is added back to net income to determine net annual cash flow. Suppose, for example, that Reno Company's net income of $13,000 includes a charge for depreciation expense of $26,000. Its estimated net annual cash flow would be $39,000 ($13,000 + $26,000).

Illustration 13-2 lists some typical cash outflows and inflows related to equipment purchases and replacement.

Cash Outflows	Cash Inflows
Initial investment	Sale of old equipment
Repairs and maintenance	Increased cash received from customers
Increased operating costs	Reduced cash outflows for operating costs
Overhaul of equipment	Salvage value of equipment when project is complete

▶Illustration 13-2
Typical cash flows related to capital budgeting decisions

These cash flows are the inputs that are considered relevant in capital budgeting decisions. The capital budgeting decision, under any technique, depends in part on a variety of considerations:

- **The availability of funds.** Does the company have unlimited funds, or will it have to ration capital investments?
- **Relationships among proposed projects.** Are proposed projects independent of each other, or does the acceptance or rejection of one depend on the acceptance or rejection of another?
- **The company's basic decision-making approach.** Does the company want to produce an accept-reject decision, or a ranking of desirability among possible projects?
- **The risk associated with a particular project.** How certain are the projected returns? The certainty of estimates varies, depending on market considerations or the length of time before returns are expected.

ILLUSTRATIVE DATA

For our discussion of quantitative techniques, we will use an ongoing example, as this will make it easier to compare the results of the various techniques. Assume that Stewart Soup Company is considering an investment of $130,000 in new equipment. The new equipment is expected to last 10 years. It will have zero salvage value at the end of its useful life. The annual cash inflows are $200,000, and the annual cash outflows are $176,000. These data are summarized in Illustration 13-3.

Initial investment	$130,000
Estimated useful life	10 years
Estimated salvage value	0
Estimated annual cash flows	
Cash inflows from customers	$200,000
Cash outflows for operating costs	176,000
Net annual cash flow	$ 24,000

▶Illustration 13-3
Investment information for Stewart Soup Company

In the following two sections, we will examine two popular techniques for evaluating capital investments: the cash payback technique and the net present value method.

CASH PAYBACK TECHNIQUE

The **cash payback technique** identifies the time period required to recover the cost of the capital investment from the net annual cash flow produced by the investment. Illustration 13-4 shows the formula for calculating the cash payback period.

▶Illustration 13-4
Cash payback formula

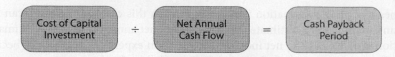

The cash payback period in the Stewart Soup example is 5.42 years, calculated as follows:

$$\$130{,}000 \div \$24{,}000 = 5.42 \text{ years}$$

The evaluation of the payback period is often related to the expected useful life of the asset. For example, assume that at Stewart Soup a project is unacceptable if the payback period is longer than 60% of the asset's expected useful life. The 5.42-year payback period in this case is a bit over 50% of the project's expected useful life. Thus, the project is acceptable.

It follows, therefore, that when a company uses the payback technique to decide among acceptable alternative projects, **the shorter the payback period, the more attractive the investment**. This is true for two reasons: (1) The earlier the company recovers its investment, the sooner it can use the cash funds for other purposes. (2) The risk of loss from obsolescence and changed economic conditions is less in a shorter payback period.

Cash Payback with Unequal Annual Cash Flows

Helpful Hint
Net annual cash flow can also be approximated by "Net cash provided by operating activities" from the statement of cash flows.

The preceding calculation of the cash payback period assumes equal net annual cash flows in each year of the investment's life. In many cases, this assumption is not valid. In the case of **uneven** net annual cash flows, the cash payback period is determined when the cumulative net cash flows from the investment equal the cost of the investment. To illustrate, assume that Chan Company proposes an investment in a new website that is estimated to cost $300,000. Illustration 13-5 shows the proposed investment cost, net annual cash flows, cumulative net cash flows, and cash payback period.

▶Illustration 13-5
Cash inflow schedule

Year	Investment	Net Annual Cash Flow	Cumulative Net Cash Flow
0	$300,000		
1		$ 60,000	$ 60,000
2		90,000	150,000
3		90,000	240,000
4		120,000	360,000
5		100,000	460,000
		Cash payback period = 3.5 years	

As indicated in Illustration 13-5, at the end of year 3, the cumulative cash inflow of $240,000 is less than the investment cost of $300,000, but at the end of year 4, the cumulative cash inflow of $360,000 is higher than the investment cost. The cash inflow needed in year 4 to equal the investment cost is $60,000 ($300,000 − $240,000). Assuming the cash inflow occurred evenly during year 4, this amount is then divided by the net annual cash flow in year 4 ($120,000) to determine the point during the year when the cash payback occurs. Thus, the result is 0.5 ($60,000 ÷ $120,000), or half of the year; thus the cash payback period is 3.5 years.

Cash Payback: Pros and Cons

The cash payback technique may be useful as an initial screening (evaluation) tool for projects. It also may be the most critical factor in the capital budgeting decision for a company that wants a fast turnaround on its investment because of a weak cash position. Finally, it is fairly easy to calculate and understand.

However, the cash payback technique should not ordinarily be the only basis for the capital budgeting decision, because it ignores the project's expected profitability after the payback period. To illustrate, assume that Projects A and B have the same payback period, but Project A's useful life is double the useful life of Project B. Project A's earning power, therefore, is twice as long as Project B's. Another disadvantage of the cash payback technique is that it ignores the time value of money.

BEFORE YOU GO ON...

▶Do It! Cash Payback Period

Watertown Paper Corporation is considering adding another machine for the manufacture of corrugated cardboard. The machine would cost $900,000. It would have an estimated life of six years and no salvage value. The company estimates that annual cash inflows would increase by $400,000 and that annual cash outflows would increase by $190,000. Calculate the cash payback period.

Action Plan

- Annual cash inflows − Annual cash outflows = Net annual cash flow.
- Cash payback period = Cost of capital investment ÷ Net annual cash flow.

Solution

Estimated annual cash inflows	$400,000
Estimated annual cash outflows	190,000
Net annual cash flow	$210,000

Cash payback period = $900,000 ÷ $210,000 = 4.3 years.

Related exercise material: **BE13-1** and **Do It! D13-10**.

Net Present Value Method

Recognizing the time value of money can significantly alter the long-term impact of the capital budgeting decision. For example, cash flows that occur early in the life of an investment will be worth more than those that occur later because of the time value of money. It is therefore useful to recognize the timing of cash flows when evaluating projects.

Capital budgeting techniques that consider both the time value of money and the estimated net cash flow from an investment are called **discounted cash flow techniques**. They are generally recognized as the most informative and best-conceived approaches to making capital budgeting decisions. The expected net cash flow that is used in discounting cash flows consists of the annual net cash flows plus the estimated liquidation proceeds (salvage value) when the asset is sold at the end of its useful life.

The primary discounted cash flow technique is called **net present value**. A second method, discussed later in the chapter, is the **internal rate of return**.

The **net present value (NPV) method** involves discounting net cash flows to their present value and then comparing that present value with the capital outlay required by the investment. The difference between these two amounts is referred to as the **net present value (NPV)**. The interest rate used in discounting the future net cash flows is a rate determined by management. This rate, often called the **discount rate** or required rate of return, is discussed in a later section.

The NPV decision rule is thus the following: **A proposal is acceptable when net present value is zero or positive**. At either of those values, the rate of return on the investment equals or exceeds the required rate of return. When net present value is negative, the project is unacceptable. Illustration 13-6 shows the net present value decision criteria.

STUDY OBJECTIVE 2
Explain the net present value method.

▶Illustration 13-6

Net present value decision criteria

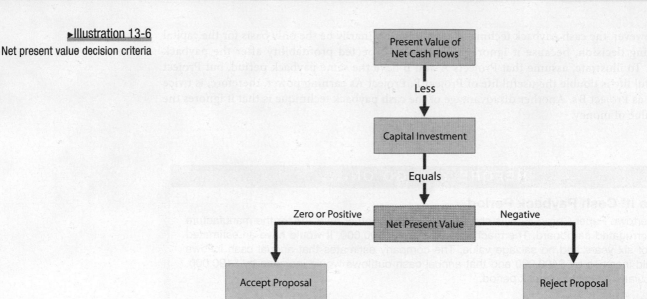

When making a selection among acceptable proposals, **the higher the positive net present value, the more attractive the investment**. The next two sections describe the application of this method to two cases. In each case, we will assume that the investment has no salvage value at the end of its useful life.

EQUAL ANNUAL CASH FLOWS

Stewart Soup's net annual cash flows are $24,000. If we assume this amount **is uniform over the asset's useful life**, we can calculate the present value of the net annual cash flows by using the present value of an ordinary annuity of 1 for 10 periods (from Table 4 in Appendix 13A). Assuming a discount rate of 12%, the present value of net cash flows is calculated as shown in Illustration 13-7 (rounded to the nearest dollar).

▶Illustration 13-7

Calculation of present value of equal net annual cash flows

	Present Value at 12%
Discount factor for 10 periods	5.65022
Present value of net cash flows:	
$24,000 × 5.65022	$135,605

Illustration 13-8 shows the analysis of the proposal by the net present value method.

▶Illustration 13-8

Calculation of net present value— equal net annual cash flows

	12%
Present value of net cash flows	$135,605
Capital investment	130,000
Net present value	$ 5,605

The proposed capital expenditure is acceptable at a required rate of return of 12% because the net present value is positive.

UNEQUAL ANNUAL CASH FLOWS

When net annual cash flows are unequal, we cannot use annuity tables to calculate their present value. Instead, tables showing the **present value of a single future amount must be applied to each annual cash flow**. To illustrate, assume that Stewart Soup management expects the same total net cash flows of $240,000 over the life of the investment. But because of a declining market demand for the new product over the life of the equipment, the net annual cash flows will be higher in the early years and lower in the later years. The present value of the net annual cash flows is calculated as shown in Illustration 13-9, using Table 2 in Appendix 13A.

Helpful Hint

The ABC Co. expects equal cash flows over an asset's five-year useful life. What discount factor should be used in determining present values if management wants (a) a 12% return or (b) a 15% return? Answer: Using Table 4, the factors are (a) 3.60478 and (b) 3.35216.

Year	Assumed Annual Net Cash Flows	Discount Factor 12%	Present Value 12%
	(1)	(2)	(1) × (2)
1	$ 34,000	0.89286	$ 30,357
2	30,000	0.79719	23,916
3	27,000	0.71178	19,218
4	25,000	0.63552	15,888
5	24,000	0.56743	13,618
6	22,000	0.50663	11,146
7	21,000	0.45235	9,499
8	20,000	0.40388	8,078
9	19,000	0.36061	6,852
10	18,000	0.32197	5,795
	$240,000		$144,367

▶Illustration 13-9
Calculation of present value of unequal annual cash flows

Therefore, the analysis of the proposal by the net present value method is as shown in Illustration 13-10.

	12%
Present value of net cash flows	$144,367
Capital investment	130,000
Net present value	$ 14,367

▶Illustration 13-10
Calculation of net present value—unequal annual cash flows

In this example, the present value of the net cash flows is greater than the $130,000 capital investment. Thus, the project is acceptable at a 12% required rate of return (discount rate). The difference between the present values using the 12% rate under equal cash flows ($135,605) and unequal cash flows ($144,367) is due to the pattern of the flows. Since more money is received sooner under this particular uneven cash flow scenario, its present value is greater.

CHOOSING A DISCOUNT RATE

Now that you understand how the net present value method is applied, it is logical to ask a related question: How is a discount rate (required rate of return) chosen in real capital budgeting decisions? In most instances, a company uses a discount rate that is equal to its **cost of capital**; that is, the rate that it must pay to obtain funds from creditors and shareholders.

The cost of capital is a weighted average of the rates paid on borrowed funds as well as on funds that are provided by investors in the company's common and preferred shares. If a project is believed to be of higher risk than the company's usual line of business, the discount rate should be increased. That is, the discount rate has two elements: a cost of capital element and a risk element.

Using an incorrect discount rate can lead to incorrect capital budgeting decisions. Consider again the Stewart Soup example in Illustration 13-8, where we used a discount rate of 12%. Suppose that this discount rate does not take into account the fact that this project is riskier than most of the company's investments. A more appropriate discount rate, given the risk, might be 15%. Illustration 13-11 compares the net present values at the two rates. At the higher, more appropriate discount rate of 15%, the net present value is negative, and the company should reject the project.

Helpful Hint
Cost of capital is the rate that management expects to pay on all borrowed and equity funds. It does not relate to the cost of funding a *specific* project.

	Present Values at Different Discount Rates	
	12%	15%
Discount factor for 10 periods	5.65022	5.01877
Present value of net cash flows:		
$24,000 × 5.65022	$135,605	
$24,000 × 5.01877		$120,450
Capital investment	130,000	130,000
Positive (negative) net present value	$ 5,605	$ (9,550)

▶Illustration 13-11
Comparison of net present values at different discount rates

The discount rate is often given other names, including the **hurdle rate**, the **required rate of return**, and the **cut-off rate**. Determination of the cost of capital varies somewhat, depending on whether the entity is a for-profit or not-for-profit enterprise. Calculation of the cost of capital is discussed more fully in advanced accounting and finance courses.

SIMPLIFYING ASSUMPTIONS

In our examples of the net present value method, we have made a number of simplifying assumptions:

- **All cash flows come at the end of each year.** In reality, cash flows will come at uneven intervals throughout the year. However, it is far simpler to assume that all cash flows come at the end (or in some cases the beginning) of the year. In fact, this assumption is frequently made in practice.
- **All cash flows are immediately reinvested in another project that has a similar return.** In most capital budgeting situations, cash flows are received during each year of a project's life. To determine the return on the investment, some assumption must be made about how the cash flows are reinvested in the year that they are received. It is customary to assume that cash flows received are reinvested in some other project that has a similar return until the end of the project's life.
- **All cash flows can be predicted with certainty.** The outcomes of business investments are full of uncertainty. There is no way of knowing how popular a new product will be, how long a new machine will last, or what competitors' reactions might be to changes in a product. But, in order to make investment decisions, analysts must estimate future outcomes. In this chapter, we have assumed that future amounts are known with certainty. In reality, little is known with certainty. More advanced capital budgeting techniques deal with uncertainty by considering the probability that various outcomes will occur.

A simplifying assumption made by many financial analysts is that projected results are known with certainty. In reality, projected results are only estimates that are based on the forecaster's belief about what is most likely to happen. One approach for dealing with such uncertainty is **sensitivity analysis**. Sensitivity analysis uses several outcome estimates to get a sense of the variability among potential returns. Illustration 13-11 presented an example of sensitivity analysis, where we illustrated the impact on NPV of different discount rate assumptions. A higher-risk project would be evaluated using a higher discount rate. Similarly, to take into account the fact that cash flows that are further away are often more uncertain, a company can use a higher discount rate to discount more distant cash flows. Other techniques to handle uncertainty are discussed in more advanced courses.

COMPREHENSIVE EXAMPLE

Best Taste Foods is considering investing in new equipment to produce fat-free snack foods. Management believes that although demand for these foods has levelled off, fat-free foods are here to stay. Illustration 13-12 shows the estimated cost flows, cost of capital, and cash flows that were determined in consultation with the marketing, production, and finance departments.

▶Illustration 13-12
Investment information for Best Taste Foods

Initial investment	$1,000,000
Cost of equipment overhaul in five years	$ 200,000
Salvage value of equipment in 10 years	$ 20,000
Cost of capital	15%
Estimated annual cash flows	
Cash inflows received from sales	$ 500,000
Cash outflows for cost of goods sold	$ 200,000
Maintenance costs	$ 30,000
Other direct operating costs	$ 40,000

Remember that in our analysis we are using cash flows, not accrual revenues and expenses determined using the accrual method. The direct operating costs, therefore, would not include depreciation expense, since depreciation expense does not use cash. Illustration 13-13 presents the calculation of the net annual cash flows of this project.

Cash inflows received from sales	$500,000
Cash outflows for cost of goods sold	(200,000)
Maintenance costs	(30,000)
Other direct operating costs	(40,000)
Net annual cash flow	$230,000

►Illustration 13-13
Calculation of net annual cash flows

Illustration 13-14 shows the calculation of the net present value for this proposed investment.

Event	Time Period	Cash Flow	× 15% Discount Factor	= Present Value
Equipment purchase	0	$1,000,000	1.00000	$(1,000,000)
Equipment overhaul	5	200,000	0.49719	(99,438)
Net annual cash flow	1–10	230,000	5.01877	1,154,317
Salvage value	10	20,000	0.24718	4,944
Net present value				$ 59,823

►Illustration 13-14
Calculation of net present value for Best Taste Foods investment

Because the project's net present value is positive, the project should be accepted.

BEFORE YOU GO ON...

►Do It! Net Present Value

Watertown Paper Corporation is considering adding another machine for the manufacture of corrugated cardboard. The machine would cost $900,000. It would have an estimated life of six years and no salvage value. The company estimates that annual cash inflows would increase by $400,000 and that annual cash outflows would increase by $190,000. Management has a required rate of return of 9%. Calculate the net present value on this project and discuss whether it should be accepted.

Action Plan

• Estimated annual cash inflows − Estimated annual cash outflows = Net annual cash flow.
• Use the NPV technique to calculate the difference between net cash flows and the initial investment.
• Accept the project if the net present value is positive.

Solution

Estimated annual cash inflows	$400,000
Estimated annual cash outflows	190,000
Net annual cash flow	$210,000

	Cash Flow	9% Discount Factor	Present Value
Present value of net annual cash flows	$210,000	4.48592*	$942,043
Capital investment			900,000
Net present value			$ 42,043

*Table 4, Appendix 13A.

Since the net present value is greater than zero, Watertown should accept the project.

Related exercise material: **BE13-2, BE13-3, E13-15,** and **Do It! D13-11.**

the navigator

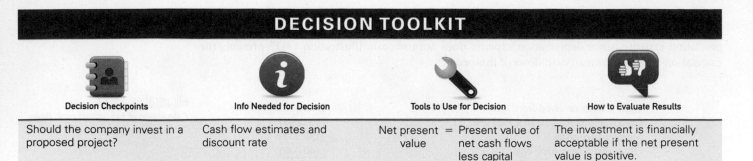

DECISION TOOLKIT

Decision Checkpoints	Info Needed for Decision	Tools to Use for Decision	How to Evaluate Results
Should the company invest in a proposed project?	Cash flow estimates and discount rate	Net present value = Present value of net cash flows less capital investment	The investment is financially acceptable if the net present value is positive.

Capital Budgeting Challenges

Now that you understand how the net present value method works, we can add some "wrinkles." Specifically, these are the impact of intangible benefits, a way to compare mutually exclusive projects, refinements that take risk into account, and the need to conduct post-audits of investment projects.

INTANGIBLE BENEFITS

The NPV evaluation techniques we have used so far rely on tangible costs and benefits that are fairly easy to measure. Some investment projects, especially high-tech projects, fail to make it through initial capital budget screens because only the project's "tangible" benefits are considered. But by ignoring intangible benefits, such as increased quality, improved safety, or greater employee loyalty, capital budgeting techniques might incorrectly eliminate projects that could be financially beneficial to the company.

To avoid rejecting projects that actually should be accepted, two possible approaches are suggested:

1. Calculate net present value ignoring intangible benefits. Then, if the NPV is negative, ask whether the intangible benefits are worth at least the amount of the negative NPV.
2. Make rough, conservative estimates of the value of the intangible benefits, and incorporate these values into the NPV calculation.

Example

Assume that Berg Company is considering the purchase of a new robot for soldering electrical connections. Illustration 13-15 shows the estimates for this proposed purchase.

▶Illustration 13-15
Investment information for Berg Company

	Cash Flows	×	12% Discount Factor	=	Present Value
Initial investment					$200,000
Annual cash inflows					$ 50,000
Annual cash outflows					20,000
Net annual cash flow					$ 30,000
Estimated life of equipment					10 years
Discount rate					12%
Present value of net cash flows	$30,000	×	5.65022	=	$169,507
Initial investment					200,000
Net present value					$ (30,493)

Based on the negative net present value of $30,493, the proposed project is not acceptable. This calculation, however, ignores important information. First, the company's engineers believe that purchasing this machine will dramatically improve the electrical connections in the company's products.

As a result, future warranty costs will be reduced. Also, the company believes that higher quality will translate into higher future sales. Finally, the new machine will be much safer than the previous one.

This new information can be brought into the capital budgeting decision in the two ways mentioned above. First, one might simply ask whether the reduced warranty costs, increased sales, and improved safety benefits have an estimated total present value to the company of at least $30,493. If yes, then the project is acceptable.

Alternatively, the company can make an estimate of the annual cash flows of these benefits. In our initial calculation, each of these benefits was assumed to have a value of zero. It seems likely that their actual values are much higher than zero. Given the difficulty of estimating these benefits, however, conservative values should be assigned to them. If, after using conservative estimates, the net present value is positive, the project should be accepted.

To illustrate, assume that Berg estimates a sales increase of $10,000 annually as a result of an increase in quality from the customer's perspective. Berg also estimates that cost outflows would be reduced by $5,000 as a result of lower warranty claims, reduced injury claims, and fewer worker absences. Consideration of the intangible benefits results in the revised NPV calculation shown in Illustration 13-16.

Initial investment	$200,000
Annual cash inflows (revised)	$ 60,000
Annual cash outflows (revised)	15,000
Net annual cash flow	$ 45,000
Estimated life of equipment	10 years
Discount rate	12%

	Cash Flows	×	12% Discount Factor	=	Present Value
Present value of net cash flows	$45,000	×	5.65022	=	$254,260
Initial investment					200,000
Net present value					$ 54,260

▶Illustration 13-16
Revised investment information for Berg Company, including intangible benefits

Using these conservative estimates of the value of the additional benefits, it appears that Berg should accept the project.

 BUSINESS INSIGHT   *Intangible Benefits in Airplane Acquisition*

The decision of whether to lease or buy aircraft is a big one for airlines, since commercial planes cost millions of dollars, must sometimes be ordered years in advance from the manufacturers, and have very long useful lives. Airlines consider many types of financial information when deciding whether to lease or buy aircraft, including financing costs. But potential intangible benefits come into play as well. For example, Canadian regulations allow airlines to lease planes and crews from foreign carriers under limited conditions, a practice called "wet leasing." A Canadian airline undergoing labour negotiations with pilots may want to buy aircraft for a certain route instead of wet leasing in order to appease its employees that the airline will be using its own crews. Airlines can also lease just airplanes, without crews, from other carriers, known as "dry leasing," which allows carriers to fly to new routes to meet current market demand, rather than waiting years. By expanding operations, airlines would need to hire more employees for its crews, which would also help with labour peace. Some union contracts in the airline industry require membership agreement before big changes like additional routes and aircraft are made.

Sources: Scott Deveau, "WestJet Airlines Ltd Could Start Flying Wide-Body Aircraft Next Year," *National Post*, February 27, 2014; "The Canadian Press, "Air Canada Places a $6.5-billion (U.S.) Order for Up to 109 Boeing Aircraft," *Toronto Star*, December 11, 2013; *Canada's Policy for Wet-Leasing of Aircraft*, Transport Canada, 2013; Robert Fife and Philip Ling, "Critics Say Leasing Foreign Aircraft 'A Question of Standards,'" CTV News, February 27, 2013.

What are some other intangible benefits to an airline that decides not to "wet lease" planes from foreign carriers?

PROFITABILITY INDEX FOR MUTUALLY EXCLUSIVE PROJECTS

In theory, all projects with positive NPVs should be accepted. However, companies rarely are able to adopt all positive-NPV proposals. First, proposals are often **mutually exclusive**. This means that if the company adopts one proposal, it would be impossible also to adopt the other proposal. For example, a company may be considering the purchase of a new packaging machine and is looking at various brands and models. It needs only one packaging machine. Once the company has determined which brand and model to purchase, it will not purchase the others—even though they may also have positive net present values.

Even in instances where projects are not mutually exclusive, managers often must choose between various positive-NPV projects because the company's resources are limited. For example, the company might have ideas for two new lines of business, each of which has a projected positive NPV. However, both of these proposals require skilled personnel, and the company determines that it will not be able to find enough skilled personnel to staff both projects. Management will have to choose the project that it thinks is a better option.

When choosing between alternative proposals, it is tempting simply to choose the project with the higher NPV. Consider the example of two mutually exclusive projects in Illustration 13-17. Each is assumed to have a 10-year life and a 12% discount rate.

▶Illustration 13-17
Investment information for mutually exclusive projects

	Project A	Project B
Initial investment	$40,000	$ 90,000
Net annual cash inflow	10,000	19,000
Salvage value	5,000	10,000
Present value of net cash flows		
($10,000 × 5.65022) + ($5,000 × 0.32197)	58,112	
($19,000 × 5.65022) + ($10,000 × 0.32197)		110,574

From the information in Illustration 13-17, we can calculate the net present values of Project A and Project B as shown in Illustration 13-18.

▶Illustration 13-18
Net present value calculation

	Project A	Project B
Present value of net cash flows	$58,112	$110,574
Initial investment	40,000	90,000
Net present value	$18,112	$ 20,574

Project B has the higher NPV, and so it would seem that the company should adopt B. Note, however, that Project B also requires more than twice the original investment of Project A. In choosing between the two projects, the company should also include in its calculations the amount of the original investment.

One relatively simple method of comparing alternative projects is the **profitability index**. This method considers both the size of the original investment and the discounted cash flows. The profitability index is calculated by dividing the present value of cash flows that occur after the initial investment by the initial investment.

Illustration 13-19 shows the formula.

▶Illustration 13-19
Formula for profitability index

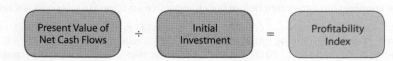

| Present Value of Net Cash Flows | ÷ | Initial Investment | = | Profitability Index |

The profitability index makes it possible to compare the relative desirability of projects that require different initial investments. Note that any project with a positive NPV will have a profitability index above 1. The profitability index for the two projects is calculated in Illustration 13-20.

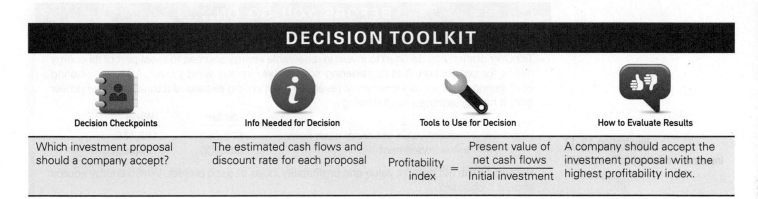

In this case, the profitability index of Project A exceeds that of Project B. Thus, Project A is more desirable. Again, if these were not mutually exclusive projects, and if resources were not limited, then the company should invest in both projects, since both have positive NPVs. Additional matters to consider in preference decisions are discussed in more advanced courses.

DECISION TOOLKIT

Decision Checkpoints	Info Needed for Decision	Tools to Use for Decision	How to Evaluate Results
Which investment proposal should a company accept?	The estimated cash flows and discount rate for each proposal	$\text{Profitability index} = \dfrac{\text{Present value of net cash flows}}{\text{Initial investment}}$	A company should accept the investment proposal with the highest profitability index.

RISK ANALYSIS

A simplifying assumption made by many financial analysts is that projected results are known with certainty. In reality, projected results are only estimates based upon the forecaster's belief as to the most probable outcome. One approach for dealing with such uncertainty is sensitivity analysis. Sensitivity analysis uses a number of outcome estimates to get a sense of the variability among potential returns. An example of sensitivity analysis was presented in Illustration 13-11, where we illustrated the impact on NPV of different discount rate assumptions. A higher-risk project would be evaluated using a higher discount rate.

Similarly, to take into account that more distant cash flows are often more uncertain, a higher discount rate can be used to discount more distant cash flows. Other techniques to address uncertainty are discussed in advanced courses.

POST-AUDIT OF INVESTMENT PROJECTS

Any well-run organization should perform an evaluation, called a **post-audit**, of its investment projects after they are completed. A post-audit is a thorough evaluation of how well a project's actual performance matches the original projections. In a story about Campbell Soup, a decision to invest in a new line of convenient meals called Intelligent Quisine was made based on management's best estimates of future cash flows. During the development phase of the project, the company hired an outside consulting firm to evaluate the project's potential for success. Because actual results during the initial years were far below the estimated results, and because the future did not look promising either, the project was terminated.

Performing a post-audit is important for many reasons. First, if managers know that their estimates will be compared with actual results, they will be more likely to submit reasonable and accurate data when they make investment proposals. This clearly is better for the company than having managers submit overly optimistic estimates in an effort to get their favourite projects approved. Second, a post-audit provides a formal mechanism for deciding whether existing projects should be supported or terminated. Third, post-audits improve future investment proposals because, by evaluating past successes and failures, managers improve their estimation techniques.

A post-audit uses the same evaluation techniques that were used in making the original capital budgeting decision—for example, the NPV method. The difference is that, in the post-audit, actual figures are inserted because they are known, and estimations of future amounts are revised based on new information. The managers responsible for the estimates used in the original proposal must explain the reasons for any significant differences between their estimates and actual results.

Post-audits are not foolproof. When Campbell Soup abandoned its Intelligent Quisine line, some observers suggested that the company was too quick to drop the project. Industry analysts suggested that with more time and more advertising expenditures, the company might have enjoyed success.

BEFORE YOU GO ON...

▶ Do It! Profitability Index

Taz Corporation has decided to invest in renewable energy sources to meet part of its energy needs for production. It is considering solar power versus wind power. After considering cost savings as well as incremental revenues from selling excess electricity into the power grid, it has determined the following.

	Solar	Wind
Present value of annual cash flows	$78,580	$168,450
Initial investment	$45,500	$125,300

Determine the net present value and profitability index of each project. Which energy source should it choose?

Action Plan

• Determine the net present value of annual cash flows of each mutually exclusive project.
• Determine profitability index by dividing the present value of annual cash flows by the amount of the initial investment.
• Choose the project with the highest profitability index.

Solution

	Solar	Wind
Present value of annual cash flows	$78,580	$168,450
Less: Initial investment	45,500	125,300
Net present value	$33,080	$ 43,150
Profitability index	1.73*	1.34**

*$78,580 ÷ $45,500
**168,450 ÷ 125,300

While the investment in wind power generates the higher net present value, it also requires a substantially higher initial investment. The profitability index favours solar power, which suggests that the additional net present value of wind is outweighed by the cost of the initial investment. The company should choose solar power.

Related exercise material: **BE13-4, BE13-5, BE13-6, E13-16,** and **Do It! D13-12.**

the navigator

Internal Rate of Return Method

STUDY OBJECTIVE 4
Explain the internal rate of return method.

The **internal rate of return method** differs from the net present value method since it finds the **interest yield of the potential investment**. The **internal rate of return** is the interest rate that will cause the present value of the proposed capital expenditure to equal the present value of the expected net annual cash flows. This means that it finds the rate that results in an NPV equal to zero. Note that because it recognizes the time value of money, the internal rate of return method is (like the NPV method) a discounted cash flow technique.

DETERMINING THE INTERNAL RATE OF RETURN

How does one determine the internal rate of return? One way is to use a financial (business) calculator or computerized spreadsheet to solve for this rate. If not using a calculator or computer spreadsheet, a trial-and-error procedure is done.

To illustrate, assume that Brock Company is considering the purchase of a new front-end loader at a cost of $244,371. Net annual cash flows from this loader are estimated to be $100,000 a year for three years. To determine the internal rate of return on this front-end loader, we find the discount rate that results in a net present value of zero. As shown in Illustration 13-21, at a rate of return of 10%, Brock has a positive net present value of $4,315. At a rate of return of 12%, it has a negative net present value of $4,188. At 11%, the net present value is zero; therefore, this rate is the internal rate of return for this investment.

Year	Annual Cash Flows	Discount Factor 10%	Present Value 10%	Discount Factor 11%	Present Value 11%	Discount Factor 12%	Present Value 12%
1	$100,000	0.90909	$ 90,909	0.90090	$ 90,090	0.89286	$ 89,286
2	100,000	0.82645	82,645	0.81162	81,162	0.79719	79,719
3	100,000	0.75132	75,132	0.73119	73,119	0.71178	71,178
			248,686		244,371		240,183
Less: Initial investment			244,371		244,371		244,371
Net present value			$ 4,315		$ 0		$ (4,188)

▶Illustration 13-21
Determination of internal rate of return

An easier approach to solving for the internal rate of return can be used if the net annual cash flows are **equal**, as in the Brock Company example. In this special case, we can find the internal rate of return using the following equation:

$$\$244,371 = \$100,000 \times \text{Present value of } \$100,000 \text{ for 3 years at x\%}$$

Solving for the interest rate, we find:

$$\frac{\$244,371}{\$100,000} = 2.44371 = \text{Present value of } \$100,000 \text{ for 3 years at x\%}$$

We then look up the factor 2.44371 in Table 4 of Appendix 13A in the three-period row and find it under 11%. Row 3 is reproduced below for your convenience.

TABLE 4
Present Value of an Ordinary Annuity of 1

(n) Periods	2%	2.5%	3%	4%	5%	6%	8%	9%	10%	11%	12%	15%
3	2.88388	2.85602	2.82861	2.77509	2.72325	2.67301	2.57710	2.53129	2.48685	2.44371	2.40183	2.28323

Recognize that if the cash flows are **uneven**, then a trial-and-error approach or a financial calculator or computerized spreadsheet must be used.

Once managers know the internal rate of return (IRR), they compare it with management's required rate of return (the discount rate). The IRR decision rule is as follows: **Accept the project when the internal rate of return is equal to or greater than the required rate of return. Reject the project when the internal rate of return is less than the required rate of return.** Illustration 13-22 shows these relationships.

Alternative Terminology
The minimum required rate of return is sometimes referred to as the *hurdle rate* or the *cut-off rate*.

►Illustration 13-22
Internal rate of return decision criteria

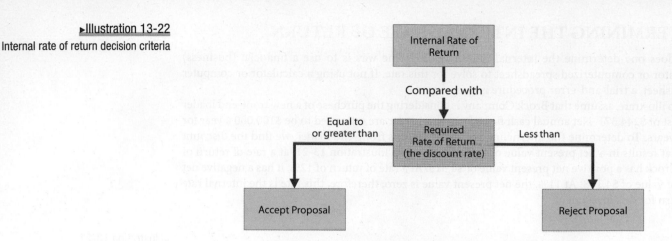

The internal rate of return method is widely used. Most managers find the internal rate of return easy to interpret.

INTERNAL RATE OF RETURN VS. NET PRESENT VALUE

Illustration 13-23 presents a comparison of the two discounted cash flow methods: net present value and internal rate of return. When properly used, either method will provide management with relevant quantitative data for making capital budgeting decisions.

However, the net present value method does have two advantages. First, we can use the NPV method in situations where the discount rate varies over the life of the project because of risk considerations. In the internal rate of return method, we cannot use more than one discount rate to make risk adjustments. The internal rate of return solves for only a single discount rate over the life of the project. Second, in evaluating different combinations of individual projects, we can add the NPVs of the individual projects in each combination to estimate the effect of accepting or rejecting a combination of projects. We can do this because the result of the NPV method is a dollar amount, not a percentage.

►Illustration 13-23
Comparison of discounted cash flow methods

	Net Present Value	Internal Rate of Return
Objective:	Calculate net present value (a dollar amount).	Calculate the internal rate of return (a percentage).
Decision rule:	If the net present value is zero or positive, accept the proposal. If the net present value is negative, reject the proposal.	If the internal rate of return is equal to or greater than the required rate of return, accept the proposal. If the internal rate of return is less than the required rate of return, reject the proposal.

DECISION TOOLKIT

Decision Checkpoints	Info Needed for Decision	Tools to Use for Decision		How to Evaluate Results
Should the company invest in a proposed project?	The estimated cash flows and the required rate of return (hurdle rate)	Internal rate of return =	Interest rate that results in a net present value of zero	If the internal rate of return is higher than the required rate of return for the project, then the project is financially acceptable.

BEFORE YOU GO ON...

▶Do It! Internal Rate of Return

Watertown Paper Corporation is considering adding another machine for the manufacture of corrugated cardboard. The machine would cost $900,000. It would have an estimated life of six years and no salvage value. The company estimates that annual cash inflows would increase by $400,000 and that annual cash outflows would increase by $190,000. Management has a required rate of return of 9%. Calculate the internal rate of return on this project and discuss whether it should be accepted.

Action Plan

• Estimated annual cash inflows − Estimated annual cash outflows = Net annual cash flow.
• Capital investment ÷ Net annual cash flows = Internal rate of return factor.
• Look up the factor in the present value of an annuity table to find the internal rate of return.
• Accept the project if the internal rate of return is equal to or greater than the required rate of return.

Solution

Estimated annual cash inflows	$400,000
Estimated annual cash outflows	190,000
Net annual cash flow	$210,000

$900,000 ÷ 210,000 = 4.285714. Using Table 4 of Appendix 13A and the factors that correspond with the six-period row, 4.285714 is between the factors for 10% and 11%. Since the project has an internal rate that is greater than 10% and the required rate of return is only 9%, the project should be accepted.

Related exercise material: **BE13-7, BE13-8, E13-17, E13-18,** and **Do It! D13-11.**

the navigator

Annual Rate of Return Method

The final capital budgeting technique we will look at is the **annual rate of return method**. It is based directly on accrual accounting data rather than on cash flows. It indicates the **profitability of a capital expenditure** by dividing the expected annual net income by the average investment. This method has many different names, including simple rate of return, accounting rate of return, unadjusted rate of return, and rate of return on assets. The formula for calculating the annual rate of return is shown in Illustration 13-24.

STUDY OBJECTIVE 5
Describe the annual rate of return method.

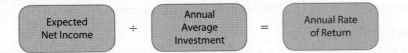

Expected Net Income ÷ Annual Average Investment = Annual Rate of Return

▶Illustration 13-24
Annual rate of return formula

Assume that Reno Company is considering an investment of $130,000 in new equipment. The new equipment is expected to last five years and have zero salvage value at the end of its useful life. The straight-line method of depreciation is used for accounting purposes. Illustration 13-25 shows the expected annual revenues and costs of the new product that will be produced from the investment.

▶Illustration 13-25
Estimated annual net income from Reno Company's capital expenditure

Sales		$200,000
Less: Costs and expenses		
Manufacturing costs (not including depreciation)	$132,000	
Depreciation expense ($130,000 ÷ 5)	26,000	
Selling and administrative expenses	22,000	180,000
Income before income taxes		20,000
Income tax expense		7,000
Net income		$ 13,000

Reno's expected annual net income is $13,000. Illustration 13-26 gives the formula for determining the average investment.

►Illustration 13-26
Formula for calculating average investment

$$\text{Average investment} = \frac{\text{Original investment} + \text{Value at end of useful life}}{2}$$

The value at the end of the useful life is equal to the asset's salvage value, if any.

For Reno, the average investment is $65,000 [($130,000 + $0) ÷ 2]. The expected annual rate of return on Reno's investment in new equipment is therefore 20%, calculated as follows:

$$\$13,000 \div \$65,000 = 20\%$$

Management then compares the annual rate of return with its required rate of return for investments of similar risk. The required rate of return is generally based on the company's cost of capital. The decision rule is this: **A project is acceptable if its rate of return is greater than management's required rate of return.** It is unacceptable when the reverse is true. When companies use the annual rate of return technique in deciding among several acceptable projects, **the higher the rate of return for a particular risk, the more attractive the investment.**

ANNUAL RATE OF RETURN METHOD: PROS AND CONS

The main advantages of this method are the simplicity of its calculation and management's familiarity with the accounting terms used in the calculation. A major limitation of the annual rate of return method is that it does not consider the time value of money. For example, no consideration is given to whether cash inflows will occur early or late in the life of the investment. The time value of money can make a significant difference between the future value and the discounted present value of an investment. A second disadvantage is that this method relies on accrual accounting numbers rather than expected cash flows.

IFRS Notes
Unlike the other capital budgeting methods that we have discussed, the annual rate of return method does not focus on cash flows. Rather, it focuses on accounting for net operating income. As a result, it is the only method discussed that will be affected by the choice of accounting policies under IFRS; for instance, the choice of inventory cost formula (FIFO, average, or specific identification) and the choice of depreciation method (straight-line, declining balance, or an activity-based method).

Helpful Hint
A capital budgeting decision based on only one technique may be misleading. It is often wise to analyze an investment from different perspectives.

BEFORE YOU GO ON...

►Do It! Annual Rate of Return

Watertown Paper Corporation is considering adding another machine for the manufacture of corrugated cardboard. The machine would cost $900,000. It would have an estimated life of six years and no salvage value. The company estimates that annual revenues would increase by $400,000 and that annual expenses excluding depreciation would increase by $190,000. It uses the straight-line method to calculate depreciation expense. Management has a required rate of return of 9%. Calculate the annual rate of return.

Action Plan
- Expected annual net income = Annual revenues − Annual expenses (including depreciation expense).
- Annual rate of return = Expected annual net income ÷ Average investment.
- Average investment = (Original investment + Value at end of useful life) ÷ 2.

Solution

Revenues		$400,000
Less:		
Expenses (excluding depreciation)	$190,000	
Depreciation ($900,000 ÷ 6 years)	150,000	340,000
Annual net income		$ 60,000

Average investment = ($900,000 + 0) ÷ 2 = $450,000.
Annual rate of return = $60,000 ÷ $450,000 = 13.3%.

Since the annual rate of return (13.33%) is greater than Watertown's required rate of return (9%), the proposed project is acceptable.

Related exercise material: **BE13-9, E13-19, E13-20, E13-21,** and **Do It! D13-13.**

the navigator

ALL ABOUT YOU   *More about Mortgages*

Buying a home is likely the biggest single capital expenditure decision you will ever make. Many Canadians are using non-traditional mortgages to try to bring down their mortgage payments. One such mortgage, the variable-rate mortgage, uses an interest rate that rises and falls with Canada's prime lending rate. For homes purchased in 2013, 9% of mortgages were variable-rate mortgages.

What Do You Think?

You've found the perfect home. You will need a mortgage of $200,000, amortized over 25 years. You're considering either a 5-year fixed rate mortgage at 5.44%, with monthly payments of $1,213.81, or a 5-year closed variable interest rate mortgage at 3.8%, with payments starting at $1,033.71 a month and the option of locking in later. Should you go for the cheaper payments?

YES—I am comfortable with interest rate fluctuations and I want to take advantage of the lower interest rate. If interest rates go up, I can always lock in.

NO—I need the certainty of knowing how much my mortgage payments are going to be, so I don't have to worry about interest rates going up.

Sources: Rob Carrick, "Five Things to Know about Canada's Mortgage Market Right Now," *The Globe and Mail*, March 31, 2014; Garry Marr, "How Lower Interest Rates Are Making Variable Mortgages More Tempting," *Financial Post*, March 4, 2014; Will Dunning, "Annual State of the Residential Mortgage Market in Canada," Canadian Association of Accredited Mortgage Professionals, November 2013.

USING THE DECISION TOOLKIT

Stewart Soup is considering expanding its international presence. It sells 38% of the soup consumed in Canada, but only 2% of soup worldwide. Thus the company believes that it has great potential for international sales. Recently, 20% of Stewart's sales were in foreign markets (and nearly all of that was in Europe). Its goal is to have 30% of its sales in foreign markets. In order to accomplish this goal, the company will have to invest heavily.

In recent years, Stewart has spent between $300 million and $400 million on capital expenditures. Suppose that Stewart is interested in expanding its presence in South America by building a new production facility there. After considering tax, marketing, labour, transportation, and political issues, Stewart has determined that the most desirable location is either Buenos Aires or Rio de Janeiro. The following estimates have been provided:

	Buenos Aires	Rio de Janeiro
Initial investment	$2,500,000	$1,400,000
Estimated useful life	20 years	20 years
Annual revenues (accrual)	$ 500,000	$ 380,000
Annual expenses (accrual)	$ 200,000	$ 180,000
Annual cash inflows	$ 550,000	$ 430,000
Annual cash outflows	$ 222,250	$ 206,350
Estimated salvage value	$ 500,000	$ 0
Discount rate	9%	9%

Instructions

Evaluate each of these mutually exclusive proposals using (a) the cash payback technique, (b) the net present value method, (c) the profitability index, (d) the internal rate of return method, and (e) the annual rate of return method. Discuss the implications of your findings.

(continued)

(continued)

Solution

(a) Cash payback

Buenos Aires	Rio de Janeiro
$\dfrac{\$2,500,000}{\$327,750} = 7.63$ years	$\dfrac{\$1,400,000}{\$223,650} = 6.26$ years

(b) Net present value

Buenos Aires	Rio de Janeiro
Present value of net cash flows	
$327,750 × 9.12855 = $2,991,882	$223,650 × 9.12855 = $2,041,600
$500,000 × 0.17843 = 89,215	
3,081,097	
Less: Initial investment 2,500,000	1,400,000
Net present value $ 581,097	$ 641,600

(c) Profitability index

Buenos Aires	Rio de Janeiro
$\dfrac{\$3,081,097}{\$2,500,000} = 1.23$	$\dfrac{\$2,041,600}{\$1,400,000} = 1.46$ years

(d) Internal rate of return: The internal rate of return can be approximated by experimenting with different discount rates to see which one comes the closest to resulting in a net present value of zero. Doing this, we find that the Buenos Aires location has an internal rate of return of approximately 12%, while the internal rate of return of the Rio de Janeiro location is approximately 15%, as shown below. Rio, therefore, is preferable.

Buenos Aires				Rio de Janeiro		
Cash Flows ×	12% Discount Factor	=	Present Value	Cash Flows ×	15% Discount Factor	= Present Value
$327,750 ×	7.46944	=	$2,448,109	$223,650 ×	6.25933	= $1,399,899
$500,000 ×	0.10367	=	51,835			
			2,499,944			
Less: Capital investment			2,500,000			1,400,000
Net present value			$ (56)			$(101)

(e) Annual rate of return

Buenos Aires	Rio de Janeiro
Average investment	
$\dfrac{(\$2,500,000 + \$500,000)}{2} = \$1,500,000$	$\dfrac{(\$1,400,000 + \$0)}{2} = \$700,000$
Annual rate of return	
$\dfrac{\$300,000}{\$1,500,000} = 0.20 = 20\%$	$\dfrac{\$200,000}{\$700,000} = 0.286 = 28.6\%$

Implications: Although the annual rate of return is higher for Rio de Janeiro, this method has the disadvantage of ignoring the time value of money, as well as using accrual numbers rather than cash flows. The cash payback of Rio de Janeiro is shorter, but this method also ignores the time value of money. Thus, while these two methods can be used for a quick assessment, neither should be relied on as the only evaluation tool.

From the net present value calculation, it would appear that the two projects are nearly identical in their acceptability. However, the profitability index indicates that the Rio de Janeiro investment is far more desirable because it generates its cash flows with a much smaller initial investment. A similar result is found by using the internal rate of return. Overall, assuming that the company will invest in only one project, it would appear that it should choose the Rio de Janeiro project.

the navigator

Summary of Study Objectives

1. *Discuss capital budgeting inputs and apply the cash payback technique.* Project proposals are gathered from each department and submitted to a capital budget committee, which screens the proposals and recommends worthy projects. Company officers decide which projects to fund, and the board of directors approves the capital budget. In capital budgeting, estimated cash inflows and outflows, rather than accrual accounting numbers, are the preferred inputs.

   The cash payback technique identifies the time period it will take to recover the cost of the investment. The formula when net annual cash flows are the same is as follows: Cost of capital expenditure ÷ estimated net annual cash inflow = cash payback period. The shorter the payback period, the more attractive the investment.

2. *Explain the net present value method.* Under the net present value method, the present value of future cash inflows is compared with the capital investment to determine the net present value. The decision rule is as follows: Accept the project if the net present value is zero or positive. Reject the project if the net present value is negative.

3. *Identify capital budgeting challenges and refinements.* Intangible benefits are difficult to measure, and thus are often ignored in capital budgeting decisions. This can result in incorrectly rejecting some projects. One method for considering intangible benefits is to calculate the NPV, ignoring intangible benefits. If the resulting NPV is below zero, evaluate whether the benefits are worth at least the amount of the negative net present value. Alternatively, intangible benefits can be included in the NPV calculation, using conservative estimates of their value.

   The profitability index is a tool for comparing the relative merits of two alternative capital investment opportunities. It is calculated by dividing the present value of net cash flows by the initial investment. The higher the index, the more desirable the project.

   A post-audit is an evaluation of a capital investment's actual performance. Post-audits create an incentive for managers to make accurate estimates. Post-audits are also useful for determining whether a project should be continued, expanded, or terminated. Finally, post-audits provide feedback that is useful for improving estimation techniques.

4. *Explain the internal rate of return method.* The objective of the internal rate of return method is to find the interest yield of the potential investment, which is expressed as a percentage rate. The decision rule is this: Accept the project when the internal rate of return is equal to or greater than the required rate of return. Reject the project when the internal rate of return is less than the required rate of return.

5. *Describe the annual rate of return method.* The annual rate of return uses accounting data to indicate the profitability of a capital investment. It is calculated by dividing the expected annual net income by the amount of the average investment. The higher the rate of return, the more attractive the investment.

DECISION TOOLKIT—A SUMMARY

Decision Checkpoints	Info Needed for Decision	Tools to Use for Decision	How to Evaluate Results
Should the company invest in a proposed project?	Cash flow estimates and discount rate	Net present value = Present value of net cash flows less capital investment	The investment is financially acceptable if the net present value is positive.
Which investment proposal should a company accept?	The estimated cash flows and discount rate for each proposal	Profitability index = Present value of net cash flows / Initial investment	A company should accept the investment proposal with the highest profitability index.
Should the company invest in a proposed project?	The estimated cash flows and the required rate of return (hurdle rate)	Internal rate of return = Interest rate that results in a net present value of zero	If the internal rate of return is higher than the required rate of return for the project, then the project is financially acceptable.

Glossary

Annual rate of return method A method for determining how profitable a capital expenditure is, calculated by dividing expected annual net income by the average investment. (p. 573)

Capital budgeting The process of making capital expenditure decisions in business. (p. 557)

Cash payback technique A capital budgeting technique that identifies the time period needed to recover the cost of a capital investment from the annual cash inflow produced by the investment. (p. 560)

Cost of capital The average rate of return that the firm must pay to obtain borrowed and equity funds. (p. 563)

Discount rate The interest rate used in discounting the future net cash flows to determine the present value. (p. 561)

Discounted cash flow technique A capital budgeting technique that considers both the estimated total cash inflows from the investment and the time value of money. (p. 561)

Internal rate of return The rate that will cause the present value of the proposed capital expenditure to equal the present value of the expected annual cash inflows. (p. 570)

Internal rate of return method A method used in capital budgeting that results in finding the interest yield of the potential investment. (p. 570)

Net present value (NPV) The difference that results when the original capital outlay is subtracted from the discounted cash inflows. (p. 561)

Net present value (NPV) method A method used in capital budgeting in which cash inflows are discounted to their present value and then compared with the capital investment. (p. 561)

Post-audit A thorough evaluation of how well a project's actual performance matches the projections made when the project was proposed. (p. 569)

Profitability index A method of comparing alternative projects that considers both the size of the investment and its discounted future cash flows. The index is calculated by dividing the present value of net future cash flows by the initial investment. (p. 568)

Comprehensive Do It!

Action Plan

- Calculate the time it will take to pay back the investment: cost of the investment divided by net annual cash flows.
- When calculating NPV, remember that net annual cash flow equals annual net income plus annual depreciation expense.
- Be careful to use the correct discount factor in using the net present value method.
- Calculate the annual rate of return: expected annual net income divided by average investment.

Cornfield Company is considering a long-term capital investment project in laser equipment. This will require an investment of $280,000, and it will have a useful life of five years. Annual net income is expected to be $16,000 a year. Depreciation is calculated by the straight-line method with no salvage value. The company's cost of capital is 10%. (*Hint:* Assume cash flows can be calculated by adding back depreciation expense.)

Instructions
(Round all calculations to two decimal places.)
  (a) Calculate the cash payback period for the project. (Round to two decimals.)
  (b) Calculate the net present value for the project. (Round to nearest dollar.)
  (c) Calculate the annual rate of return for the project.
  (d) Should the project be accepted? Why or why not?

Solution to Comprehensive Do It!
  (a) $280,000 ÷ $72,000 ($16,000 + $56,000) = 3.89 years
  (b)

	Present Value at 10%
Discount factor for five periods	3.79079
Present value of net cash flows:	
$72,000 × 3.79079	$272,937
Capital investment	280,000
Negative net present value	$ (7,063)

  (c) $16,000 ÷ $140,000 ($280,000 ÷ 2) = 11.4%
  (d) The annual rate of return of 11.4% is good. However, the cash payback period is 78% of the project's useful life, and net present value is negative. The recommendation is to reject the project.

WileyPLUS

Self-Test, Brief Exercises, Exercises, Problems—Set A, and many more components are available for practice in WileyPlus.

Self-Study Questions

Answers are at the end of the chapter.

(SO 1)   1. Which of the following is not an example of a capital budgeting decision?
   (a) The decision to build a new plant
   (b) The decision to renovate an existing facility
   (c) The decision to buy a piece of machinery
   (d) All of these are capital budgeting decisions.

(SO 1)   2. What is the order of involvement of the following parties in the capital budgeting authorization process?
   (a) Plant managers, officers, capital budget committee, board of directors
   (b) Board of directors, plant managers, officers, capital budget committee
   (c) Plant managers, capital budget committee, officers, board of directors
   (d) Officers, plant managers, capital budget committee, board of directors

(SO 1)   3. What is a weakness of the cash payback technique?
   (a) It uses accrual-based accounting numbers.
   (b) It ignores the time value of money.
   (c) It ignores the useful life of alternative projects.
   (d) Both (b) and (c) are true.

(SO 2)   4. Which is a true statement about using a higher discount rate to calculate the net present value of a project?
   (a) It will make it less likely that the project will be accepted.
   (b) It will make it more likely that the project will be accepted.
   (c) It is appropriate to use a higher rate if the project is seen as being less risky than other projects being considered.
   (d) It is appropriate to use a higher rate if the project will have a short useful life compared with other projects being considered.

(SO 2)   5. A positive net present value means that the
   (a) project's rate of return is less than the cut-off rate.
   (b) project's rate of return exceeds the required rate of return.

   (c) project's rate of return equals the required rate of return.
   (d) project is unacceptable.

(SO 2)   6. Which of the following is not an alternative name for the discount rate?
   (a) Hurdle rate
   (b) Required rate of return
   (c) Cut-off rate
   (d) All of these are alternative names for the discount rate.

(SO 3)   7. If a project has intangible benefits with a value that is hard to estimate, the best thing to do is
   (a) ignore these benefits, since any estimate of their value will most likely be wrong.
   (b) include a conservative estimate of their value.
   (c) ignore their value in your initial net present value calculation, but then estimate whether their potential value is worth at least the amount of the net present value deficiency.
   (d) Both (b) and (c) are correct.

(SO 3)   8. A post-audit of an investment project should be performed
   (a) on all significant capital expenditure projects.
   (b) on all projects that management feels might be financial failures.
   (c) on randomly selected projects.
   (d) only on projects that are a tremendous success.

(SO 4)   9. A project should be accepted if its internal rate of return exceeds
   (a) zero.
   (b) the rate of return on a government bond.
   (c) the company's required rate of return.
   (d) the rate the company pays on borrowed funds.

(SO 5)   10. Which of the following is incorrect about the annual rate of return technique?
   (a) The calculation is simple.
   (b) The accounting terms used are familiar to management.
   (c) The timing of the cash inflows is not considered.
   (d) The time value of money is considered.

✔ the navigator

Brief Exercises

BE13-1   Mega Company is considering the purchase of a new machine. The invoice price of the machine is $75,000, freight charges are estimated to be $4,000, and installation costs are expected to be $6,000. The annual cost savings are expected to be $20,000 for 10 years. Calculate the cash payback period.

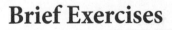

(SO 1)
Calculate the cash payback period for a capital investment.

(SO 2)
Calculate the net present value of an investment.

BE13-2 Nien Company accumulates the following data for a proposed capital investment: cash cost, $215,000; net annual cash flows, $40,000; present value factor of cash inflows for 10 years, 5.65 (rounded). Determine the net present value, and indicate whether the company should make the investment.

(SO 2)
Calculate the net present value of an investment.

BE13-3 Timo Corporation, which operates an amusement park, is considering a capital investment in a new ride. The ride would cost $136,000 and have an estimated useful life of five years. The park will sell it for $65,000 at that time. (Amusement parks need to rotate rides to keep people interested.) The ride will be expected to increase net annual cash flows by $25,000. The company's borrowing rate is 8%. Its cost of capital is 10%. Calculate the net present value of this project to the company.

(SO 2, 3)
Calculate the net present value with intangible benefits.

BE13-4 Michener Bottling Corporation is considering the purchase of a new bottling machine. The machine would cost $200,000 and has an estimated useful life of eight years with zero salvage value. Management estimates that the new bottling machine will provide net annual cash flows of $35,000. Management also believes that the new machine will save the company money because it is expected to be more reliable than other machines, and thus will reduce downtime. How much would the reduction in downtime have to be worth in order for the project to be acceptable? Assume a discount rate of 9%. (*Hint:* Calculate the net present value.)

(SO 2, 3)
Calculate the net present value and profitability index.

BE13-5 Jonczyk Company is considering two different, mutually exclusive capital expenditure proposals. Project A will cost $395,000, has an expected useful life of 10 years, a salvage value of zero, and is expected to increase net annual cash flows by $70,000. Project B will cost $270,000, has an expected useful life of 10 years, a salvage value of zero, and is expected to increase net annual cash flows by $50,000. A discount rate of 9% is appropriate for both projects. Calculate the net present value and profitability index of each project. Which project should be accepted?

(SO 2, 3)
Perform a post-audit.

BE13-6 Martelle Company is performing a post-audit of a project completed one year ago. The initial estimates were that the project would cost $250,000, would have a useful life of nine years and zero salvage value, and would result in net annual cash flows of $45,000 per year. Now that the investment has been in operation for one year, revised figures indicate that it actually cost $260,000, will have a useful life of 11 years, and will produce net annual cash flows of $38,000 per year. Evaluate the project's success. Assume a discount rate of 10%.

(SO 4)
Calculate the internal rate of return.

BE13-7 Frost Company is evaluating the purchase of a rebuilt spot-welding machine to be used in the manufacture of a new product. The machine will cost $176,000, has an estimated useful life of seven years and a salvage value of zero, and will increase net annual cash flows by $33,740. What is its approximate internal rate of return?

(SO 4)
Calculate the internal rate of return.

BE13-8 Viera Corporation is considering investing in a new facility. The estimated cost of the facility is $2,045,000. It will be used for 12 years, then sold for $716,000. The facility will generate annual cash inflows of $400,000 and will need new annual cash outflows of $150,000. The company has a required rate of return of 7%. Calculate the internal rate of return on this project, and discuss whether the project should be accepted.

(SO 5)
Calculate the annual rate of return.

BE13-9 Engles Oil Company is considering investing in a new oil well. It is expected that the oil well will increase annual revenues by $130,000 and will increase annual expenses by $70,000, including depreciation. The oil well will cost $470,000 and will have a $10,000 salvage value at the end of its 10-year useful life. Calculate the annual rate of return.

Do It! Review

(SO 1)
Calculate the cash payback period for an investment.

D13-10 Sierra Company is considering a long-term investment project called ZIP. ZIP will require an investment of $120,000. It will have a useful life of four years and no salvage value. Annual cash inflows would increase by $80,000, and annual cash outflows would increase by $41,000.

Instructions
Calculate the cash payback period.

(SO 2, 4)
Calculate net present value of an investment and its internal rate of return.

D13-11 Information for Sierra Company is given in D13-10. In addition, the company's required rate of return is 12%.

Instructions
(a) Calculate the net present value on this project and discuss whether it should be accepted.
(b) Calculate the internal rate of return on this project and discuss whether it should be accepted.

(SO 3)
Calculate profitability index.

D13-12 Ranger Corporation has decided to invest in renewable energy sources to meet part of its energy needs for production. It is considering solar power versus wind power. After considering cost savings as well as incremental revenues from selling excess electricity into the power grid, it has determined the following.

	Solar	Wind
Present value of annual cash flows	$52,580	$128,450
Initial investment	$39,500	$105,300

Instructions
Determine the net present value and profitability index of each project. Which energy source should it choose?

D13-13 Information for Sierra Company is given in D13-10. Assume that annual revenues would increase by $80,000, and annual expenses (excluding depreciation) would increase by $41,000. Sierra uses the straight-line method to calculate depreciation expense. The company's required rate of return is 12%.   (SO 5)
Calculate annual rate of return.

Instructions
Calculate the annual rate of return.

Exercises

E13-14 Dobbs Corporation is considering purchasing a new delivery truck. The truck has many advantages over the company's current truck (not the least of which is that it runs). The new truck would cost $56,000. Because of the increased capacity, reduced maintenance costs, and increased fuel economy, the new truck is expected to generate cost savings of $7,500. At the end of eight years, the company will sell the truck for an estimated $27,000. Traditionally, the company has used a general rule that it should not accept a proposal unless it has a payback period that is less than 50% of the asset's estimated useful life. Pavel Chepelev, a new manager, has suggested that the company should not rely only on the payback approach, but should also use the net present value method when evaluating new projects. The company's cost of capital is 8%.   (SO 1, 2)
Calculate cash payback and net present value.

Instructions
(a) Calculate the cash payback period and net present value of the proposed investment.
(b) Does the project meet the company's cash payback criteria? Does it meet the net present value criteria for acceptance? Discuss your results.

E13-15 Jack's Custom Manufacturing Company is considering three new projects. Each one requires an equipment investment of $25,000, will last for three years, and will produce the following net annual cash flows: (SO 1, 2)
Calculate cash payback and net present value.

Year	AA	BB	CC
1	$ 7,000	$ 9,600	$13,000
2	9,000	9,600	9,000
3	12,000	9,600	11,000
Total	$28,000	$28,800	$33,000

The equipment's salvage value is zero, and Jack uses straight-line depreciation. Jack will not accept any project with a payback period longer than two and a half years. Jack's required rate of return is 12%.

Instructions
(a) Calculate each project's payback period, indicating the most desirable project and the least desirable project using this method. (Round to two decimals and use average annual cash flows in your calculations.)
(b) Calculate the net present value of each project. Does your evaluation change? (Round to the nearest dollar.)

E13-16 TLC Corp. is considering purchasing one of two new diagnostic machines. Either machine would make it possible for the company to bid on jobs that it currently is not equipped to do. Estimates for each machine are as follows: (SO 2, 3)
Calculate the net present value and profitability index.

	Machine A	Machine B
Original cost	$98,000	$170,000
Estimated life	8 years	8 years
Salvage value	0	0
Estimated annual cash inflows	$25,000	$40,000
Estimated annual cash outflows	$5,000	$12,000

Instructions
Calculate the net present value and profitability index of each machine. Assume a 10% discount rate. Which machine should be purchased?

E13-17 Kendra Corporation is involved in the business of injection moulding of plastics. It is considering the purchase of a new computer-aided design and manufacturing machine for $430,000. The company believes that with this new machine it will improve productivity and increase quality, resulting in a $101,000 increase in net annual cash flows for the next five years. Management requires a 10% rate of return on all new investments.   (SO 4)
Determine the internal rate of return.

Instructions
Calculate the internal rate of return on this new machine. Should management accept the investment?

(SO 4)
Determine the internal
rate of return.

E13-18   Summer Company is considering three capital expenditure projects. Relevant data for the projects are as follows:

Project	Investment	Annual Income	Life of Project
22A	$240,000	$16,700	6 years
23A	270,000	20,600	9 years
24A	280,000	17,500	7 years

Annual income is constant over the life of the project. Each project is expected to have zero salvage value at the end of the project. Summer Company uses the straight-line method of depreciation.

Instructions
(a) Determine the internal rate of return for each project. (Round to three decimals.)
(b) Determine which projects are acceptable if Summer Company's required rate of return is 11%.

(SO 5)
Calculate the annual
rate of return.

E13-19   Mane Event is considering opening a new hair salon in Lethbridge, Alberta. The cost of building a new salon is $300,000. A new salon will normally generate annual revenues of $70,000, with annual expenses (including depreciation) of $41,500. At the end of 15 years, the salon will have a salvage value of $80,000.

Instructions
Calculate the annual rate of return on the project.

(SO 1, 5)
Calculate the cash
payback period and
annual rate of return.

E13-20   Dryden Service Centre just purchased an automobile hoist for $18,600. The hoist has a five-year life and an estimated salvage value of $1,400. Installation costs and freight charges were $3,900 and $900, respectively. Dryden uses straight-line depreciation.

The new hoist will be used to replace mufflers and tires on automobiles. Dryden estimates that the new hoist will enable its mechanics to replace five extra mufflers per week. Each muffler sells for $75, installed. The cost of a muffler is $35, and the labour cost to install a muffler is $15.

Instructions
(a) Calculate the payback period for the new hoist.
(b) Calculate the annual rate of return for the new hoist. (Round to one decimal.)

(SO 1, 2, 5)
Calculate the annual
rate of return, cash
payback period, and
net present value.

E13-21   Morgan Company is considering a capital investment of $210,000 in additional productive facilities. The new machinery is expected to have a useful life of five years with no salvage value. Depreciation is by the straight-line method. During the life of the investment, annual net income and net annual cash flows are expected to be $20,000 and $60,000, respectively. Morgan has a 12% cost of capital rate, which is also the minimum acceptable rate of return on the investment.

Instructions
(Round to two decimals.)
(a) Calculate (1) the cash payback period and (2) the annual rate of return on the proposed capital expenditure.
(b) Using the discounted cash flow technique, calculate the net present value.

Problems: Set A

(SO 1, 2)
Calculate initial invest-
ment, cash payback,
and net present value.

P13-22A   BioFarm Inc. wants to replace its current equipment with new high-tech equipment. The existing equipment was purchased five years ago at a cost of $120,000. At that time, the equipment had an expected life of 10 years, with no expected salvage value. The equipment is being depreciated on a straight-line basis. Currently, the market value of the old equipment is $45,000.

The new equipment can be bought for $175,000, including installation. Over its 10-year life, it will reduce operating expenses from $190,000 to $150,000 for the first six years, and from $200,000 to $190,000 for the last four years. Net working capital requirements will also increase by $20,000 at the time of replacement.

It is estimated that the company can sell the new equipment for $25,000 at the end of its life. Since the new equipment's cash flows are relatively certain, the project's cost of capital is set at 10%, compared with 15% for an average-risk project. The firm's maximum acceptable payback period is five years.

Instructions
(a) Calculate the initial investment amount.

(b) 3.75 years
(c) NPV = $59,453

(b) Calculate the project's cash payback period.
(c) Calculate the project's net present value.
(d) State whether or not the company should replace its current equipment with the new high-tech equipment. Justify your answer.

(adapted from CGA-Canada, now CPA Canada)

P13-23A The Taylor Company Limited reported a cost of goods sold of $640,000 last year, when 20,000 units were produced and sold. The cost of goods sold was 35% materials, 42% direct labour, and 23% overhead.

    The company is considering the purchase of a machine costing $165,000, with an expected useful life of five years and a salvage value at that time of $25,000. The machine would have a maximum capacity of 30,000 units per year and is expected to reduce direct labour costs by 30%; however, it would require an additional supervisor at a cost of $45,000 per year. The machine would be depreciated over the five years using the straight-line method.

    Production and sales for the next five years are expected to be as follows:

Year	Production and Sales
2016	20,000 units
2017	20,000 units
2018	22,000 units
2019	22,000 units
2020	22,000 units

Instructions

(a) Determine whether the company should purchase the machine if the company has a minimum desired rate of return of 12%.

(b) Calculate the payback on this investment.

(c) At 12%, calculate how high the salvage value must be before recommending that the company make the investment.

(adapted from CMA Canada, now CPA Canada)

P13-24A Saskatoon First Company must expand its manufacturing capabilities to meet the growing demand for its products. The first alternative is to expand its current manufacturing facility, which is located next to a vacant lot in the heart of the city. The second alternative is to convert a warehouse the company already owns, which is located 20 km outside the city. Saskatoon First's controller obtains the following information to evaluate both proposals.

    The plant and equipment investment to expand the current manufacturing facility is $19 million, while a $22-million investment is required to convert the warehouse. At either site, Saskatoon First needs to invest $3 million in working capital. Cash revenues from products made in the new facility are expected to equal $13 million each year. If the warehouse is converted, cash operating costs are expected to be $10 million per year. Expanding the current facility will increase efficiency: annual cash operating costs, if the current facility is expanded, will be $1 million less than the cash operating costs if the warehouse is converted. The controller uses a 10-year period and a 14% required rate of return to evaluate manufacturing investments. The estimated disposal price of the new facility (including a recovery of working capital of $3 million) at the end of 10 years is $8 million at both locations. Saskatoon First depreciates the investment in plant and equipment using straight-line depreciation over 10 years on the difference between the initial investment and the disposal price.

Instructions

Calculate the net present value of the proposals to expand the current manufacturing facility and to convert the warehouse. Which project should Saskatoon First choose based on the NPV calculations?

(adapted from CMA Canada, now CPA Canada)

P13-25A Madden Limited is the largest Canadian producer of dairy products. The company needs to replace its equipment. The current equipment was purchased 18 years ago at a cost of $2 million, and it was depreciated over a 20-year period using the straight-line method, assuming no expected salvage value. Management believes that, currently, the equipment could be sold for $150,000.

    The new equipment would cost $2,850,000 and have an expected residual value of $525,000 at the end of its estimated life of 10 years. With the new equipment, the current operating costs of $1.5 million would decrease by 30% in year 1, remain at that level for year 2 and year 3, decrease by another 10% in year 4, and remain at that level for the remaining life of the asset. With the new equipment, the company would have to hire another operator at an annual cost of $30,000. The company's cost of capital is 12%.

Instructions

(a) Assuming that the company decides to buy the new equipment now, calculate the initial investment.

(b) Calculate the total net savings in operating costs over the expected life of the new equipment. Show your calculations.

(c) Calculate the net present value of investing in the new equipment. Show your calculations.

(d) If the maximum acceptable payback period for the company is eight years, should the company replace the equipment now? Explain your rationale and show your calculations.

(adapted from CGA-Canada, now CPA Canada)

P13-26A K&G Company currently sells 1 million units per year of a product to one customer at a price of $3.80 per unit. The customer requires that the product be exclusive and expects no increase in sales during the five-year contract. The company manufactures the product with a machine that it purchased seven years ago at a cost of $700,000. Currently, the machine has a book value of $450,000 but the market value is only $230,000. The machine is expected to last another five years, after which it will have no salvage value. Last year, the production variable costs per unit were as follows:

Direct materials	$1.20
Direct labour	0.70
Variable overhead	0.50
Total variable cost per unit	$2.40

The company president is considering replacing the old machine with a new one that would cost $800,000. The new machine is expected to last five years. At the end of that period, the salvage value will be $350,000. The president expects to save 5% of the company's total variable costs with the new machine.

Instructions

NPV = $61,173

Assume that the company's desired rate of return is 12%. Using the net present value method, determine if the company should replace the old machine with the new one, and briefly explain why or why not. Show your calculations.

(adapted from CGA-Canada, now CPA Canada)

(SO 1, 2, 5)
Calculate the annual rate of return and net present value, and apply decision rules.

P13-27A   The Three Stages partnership is considering three long-term capital investment proposals. Each investment has a useful life of five years. Relevant data on each project are as follows:

	Project Main	Project Odyssey	Project Duo
Capital investment:	$150,000	$160,000	$200,000
Annual net income:			
Year 1	$ 13,000	$ 18,000	$ 27,000
2	13,000	17,000	22,000
3	13,000	16,000	21,000
4	13,000	12,000	13,000
5	13,000	9,000	12,000
Total	$ 65,000	$ 72,000	$ 95,000

Depreciation is calculated by the straight-line method and there is no salvage value. The company's cost of capital is 15%. (Use average net annual cash flows in your calculations.)

Instructions

(a) Calculate the cash payback period for each project. (Round to two decimals.)

(b) Main $(5,857)

(b) Calculate the net present value for each project. (Round to the nearest dollar.)

(c) Calculate the annual rate of return for each project. (Round to two decimals.)

(d) Rank the projects based on each of your answers for parts (a), (b), and (c). Which project do you recommend?

(SO 1, 2, 5)
Calculate the payback period, annual rate of return, and net present value, and apply decision rules.

(a) 3.6875 years

P13-28A   ALGS Inc. wants to purchase a new machine for $30,000, excluding $1,500 in installation costs. The old machine was bought five years ago and had an expected economic life of 10 years without salvage value. This old machine now has a book value of $2,000 and ALGS Inc. expects to sell it for that amount. The new machine would decrease operating costs by $8,000 each year of its economic life. The straight-line depreciation method would be used for the new machine, for a five-year period with no salvage value.

Instructions

(a) Determine the cash payback period. (Ignore income taxes.)

(b) Calculate the annual rate of return.

(c) Calculate the net present value assuming a 10% rate of return. (Ignore income taxes.)

(d) State your conclusion on whether the company should purchase the new machine.

(adapted from CGA-Canada, now CPA Canada)

(SO 1, 2, 5)
Calculate the payback period, annual rate of return, and net present value, and discuss findings.

P13-29A   Magna Inc. is considering modernizing its production facility by investing in new equipment and selling the old equipment. The following information has been collected on this investment:

Old Equipment		New Equipment	
Cost	$80,000	Cost	$38,000
Accumulated depreciation	$40,000	Estimated useful life	8 years
Remaining life	8 years	Salvage value in 8 years	$ 5,000
Current salvage value	$10,000	Annual cash operating costs	$30,000
Salvage value in 8 years	$ 0		
Annual cash operating costs	$36,000		

Depreciation is $10,000 per year for the old equipment. The straight-line depreciation method would be used for the new equipment over an eight-year period with salvage value of $5,000.

Instructions

(a) Determine the cash payback period (ignore income taxes).

(b) Calculate the annual rate of return.

(c) Calculate the net present value assuming a 16% rate of return (ignore income taxes).

(d) ▭▭▭▭▭▭▶ State your conclusion on whether the company should purchase the new equipment.

(b) 8.72%

P13-30A MCA Corporation is reviewing an investment proposal. The schedule below presents the initial cost and estimates of the book value of the investment at the end of each year, the net cash flows for each year, and the net income for
each year. All cash flows are assumed to take place at the end of the year. The investment's salvage value at the end of each
year is equal to its book value. There would be no salvage value at the end of the investment's life.

(SO 1, 2, 5)
Calculate payback,
annual rate of return,
and net present value.

Investment Proposal

Year	Initial Cost and Book Value	Annual Cash Flows	Annual Net Income
0	$105,000		
1	70,000	$45,000	$16,000
2	42,000	40,000	18,000
3	21,000	35,000	20,000
4	7,000	30,000	22,000
5	0	25,000	24,000

MCA Corporation uses a 15% target rate of return for new investment proposals.

Instructions

(a) What is the cash payback period for this proposal?

(b) What is the annual rate of return for the investment?

(c) What is the net present value of the investment?

(adapted from CMA Canada, now CPA Canada)

(b) 38.10%

P13-31A Prestige Auto Care is considering the purchase of a new tow truck. The garage currently has no tow truck, and
the $60,000 price tag for a new truck would be a major expenditure for it. Jenna Lind, owner of the garage, has compiled
the following estimates in trying to determine whether she should purchase the tow truck:

(SO 2, 3)
Calculate the net
present value,
considering intangible
benefits.

Initial cost	$60,000
Estimated useful life	8 years
Net annual cash flows from towing	$ 8,000
Overhaul costs (end of year 4)	$ 5,000
Salvage value	$15,000

Jenna's good friend, Reid Shaw, stopped by. He is trying to convince Jenna that the tow truck will have other benefits that
Jenna has not even considered. First, he says, cars that need towing need to be fixed. Thus, when Jenna tows them to her
facility, her repair revenues will increase. Second, he notes that the tow truck could have a plow mounted on it, thus saving
Jenna the cost of plowing her parking lot. (Reid will give her a used plow blade for free if Jenna will plow Reid's driveway.)
Third, he notes that the truck will generate goodwill; that is, people who are rescued by Jenna and her tow truck will feel
grateful and might be more inclined to use her service station in the future, or buy gas there. Fourth, the tow truck will
have "Prestige Auto Care" on its doors, hood, and back tailgate—a form of free advertising wherever the tow truck goes.
  Reid estimates that, at a minimum, these benefits would be worth the following:

Additional annual net cash flows from repair work	$3,000
Annual savings from plowing	500
Additional annual net cash flows from customer goodwill	1,000
Additional annual net cash flows resulting from free advertising	500

The company's cost of capital is 9%.

Instructions

(a) Calculate the net present value, ignoring the additional benefits described by Reid. Should Jenna purchase the tow
truck?

(a) $(11,735)

(b) Calculate the net present value, including the additional benefits suggested by Reid. Should Jenna purchase the tow
truck?

(b) $15,939

(c) Suppose Reid has been overly optimistic in his assessment of the value of the additional benefits (perhaps because he
wants his driveway plowed). At a minimum, how much would the additional benefits have to be worth in order for
Jenna to purchase the truck?

P13-32A Berens River Clinic is considering investing in new heart monitoring equipment. It has two options: Option A
would have an initial lower cost but would require a significant expenditure for rebuilding after four years. Option B would
require no rebuilding expenditure, but its maintenance costs would be higher. Since the Option B machine is of a higher

(SO 2, 3, 4)
Calculate the net
present value,
profitability index, and
internal rate of return.

initial quality, the clinic expects it to have a salvage value at the end of its useful life. The clinic made the following cash flow estimates:

	Option A	Option B
Initial cost	$160,000	$227,000
Annual cash inflows	70,000	80,000
Annual cash outflows	30,000	26,000
Cost to rebuild (end of year 4)	50,000	0
Salvage value	0	8,000
Estimated useful life	7 years	7 years

The clinic's cost of capital is 8%.

Instructions

(a) (1) NPV A $11,503
(3) IRR B 15%

(a) Calculate the (1) net present value, (2) profitability index, and (3) internal rate of return for each option. (*Hint:* To solve for the internal rate of return, experiment with alternative discount rates to arrive at a net present value of zero.)
(b) Determine which option the clinic should accept.

(SO 2, 4)
Calculate the net present value and internal rate of return with sensitivity analysis.

P13-33A Bonita Corp. is thinking about opening a soccer camp in southern Ontario. In order to start the camp, the company would need to purchase land and build four soccer fields and a dormitory-type sleeping and dining facility to house 150 soccer players. Each year, the camp would be run for eight sessions of one week each. The company would hire university soccer players as coaches. The camp attendees would be male and female soccer players aged 12 to 18. Property values in southern Ontario have enjoyed a steady increase in value. It is expected that after using the facility for 20 years, Bonita can sell the property for more than it was originally purchased for. The company has estimated the following amounts:

Cost of land	$ 300,000
Cost to build dorm and facility	$ 600,000
Annual cash inflows assuming 150 players and eight weeks	$ 940,000
Annual cash outflows	$ 840,000
Estimated useful life	20 years
Salvage value	$1,500,000
Discount rate	8%

Instructions

(a) NPV $403,640

(a) Calculate the project's net present value.
(b) To gauge the sensitivity of the project to these estimates, assume that if only 125 players attend each week, revenues will be $800,000 and expenses will be $750,000. What is the net present value using these alternative estimates? Discuss your findings.
(c) Assuming the original facts, what is the net present value if the project is actually riskier than first assumed, and an 11% discount rate is more appropriate?

(d) IRR 12%

(d) ▬▬▬▶ Assume that during the first five years the annual net cash flows each year were only $40,000. At the end of the fifth year, the company is running low on cash, so management decides to sell the property for $1,332,000. What was the actual internal rate of return on the project? Explain how this return was possible if the camp did not appear to be successful.

Problems: Set B

(SO 1, 2)
Calculate the net present value and payback period.

P13-34B Azim Electronics Inc. reported a cost of goods sold of $900,000 last year, when it produced and sold 25,000 units. The cost of goods sold was 25% materials, 65% direct labour, and 10% overhead.

The company is considering the purchase of a machine costing $400,000, with an expected useful life of five years and a salvage value at that time of $25,000. The machine would have a maximum capacity of 35,000 units per year and is expected to reduce direct labour costs by 30%; however, it would require an additional supervisor at a cost of $50,000 per year. The machine would be depreciated over the five years using the straight-line method.

Production and sales for the next five years are expected to be as follows:

Year	Production and Sales
2016	25,000 units
2017	25,000 units
2018	30,000 units
2019	30,000 units
2020	30,000 units

Instructions

(a) Determine whether the company should purchase the machine if the company has a minimum desired rate of return of 12%.

(b) Calculate the payback on this investment.

(adapted from CMA Canada, now CPA Canada)

(a) NPV $133,794

P13-35B The partnership of Lou and Bud is considering three long-term capital investment proposals. Relevant data on each project are as follows:

(SO 1, 2, 5)
Calculate the annual rate of return, payback period, and net present value, and apply decision rules.

	Project Brown	Project Red	Project Yellow
Capital investment:	$140,000	$170,000	$190,000
Annual net income:			
Year 1	$ 9,000	$ 12,500	$ 19,000
2	9,000	12,000	15,000
3	9,000	11,000	14,000
4	9,000	8,000	9,000
5	9,000	6,000	8,000
Total	$ 45,000	$ 49,500	$ 65,000

The salvage value is expected to be zero at the end of each project. Depreciation is calculated by the straight-line method. The company's required rate of return is the company's cost of capital, which is 12%. (Use average net annual cash flows in your calculations.)

Instructions

(a) Calculate the cash payback period for each project. (Round to two decimals.)

(b) Calculate the net present value for each project. (Round to the nearest dollar.)

(c) Calculate the average annual rate of return for each project. (Round to two decimals.) (*Hint:* Use average annual net income in your calculation.)

(d) Rank the projects on each of your answers in parts (a), (b), and (c). Which project do you recommend?

(a) Project Brown:
3.78 years
Project Red:
3.87 years
Project Yellow:
3.73 years

P13-36B Biotec Inc. wants to replace its R&D equipment with new high-tech equipment. The existing equipment was purchased five years ago at a cost of $150,000. At that time, the equipment had an expected life of 10 years, with no expected salvage value. The equipment is being depreciated on a straight-line basis. Currently, the old equipment's market value is $75,000.

The new equipment can be bought for $200,000, including installation. Over its 10-year life, it will reduce raw material usage and overhead, and as a result R&D costs will decrease from $179,000 to $158,000 for the first six years and from $144,000 to $105,200 for the last four years. Net working capital requirements will also increase by $25,000 at the time of replacement.

It is estimated that the new equipment can be sold for $50,000 at the end of its life. Since the new equipment's cash flows are relatively certain, the project's cost of capital is set at 10%, compared with 15% for an average-risk project. The firm's maximum acceptable payback period is five years.

(SO 1, 2)
Calculate the initial investment, cash payback, and net present value.

Instructions

(a) Calculate the initial investment amount.

(b) Calculate the project's cash payback period.

(c) Calculate the project's net present value.

(d) State whether or not the company should replace the old R&D equipment with the new high-tech equipment. Justify your answer.

(a) $150,000

(adapted from CGA-Canada, now CPA Canada)

P13-37B K&M International is considering modernizing its production facility by investing in new equipment and selling the old equipment. The following information has been collected on this investment:

(SO 1, 2, 5)
Calculate the annual rate of return, cash payback, and net present value.

Old Equipment		New Equipment	
Cost	$160,000	Cost	$80,000
Accumulated depreciation	$ 80,000	Estimated useful life	4 years
Remaining life	4 years	Salvage value in 4 years	$10,000
Current salvage value	$ 30,000	Annual cash operating costs	$25,000
Salvage value in 4 years	$ -0-		
Annual cash operating costs	$ 40,000		

Depreciation is $20,000 per year for the old equipment. The straight-line depreciation method would be used for the new equipment over a four-year period with salvage value of $10,000.

Instructions

(a) Determine the cash payback period (ignore income taxes).

(b) Calculate the annual rate of return.

(c) NPV: $(2,504)

(c) Calculate the net present value assuming a 16% rate of return. (Ignore income taxes.)

(d) ▭▭▭▭▷ State your conclusion on whether the company should purchase the new equipment.

(SO 2)
Calculate the net present value and apply the decision rule.

P13-38B   A company currently sells 850,000 units per year of a product to one customer at a price of $0.80 per unit. The customer requires that the product be exclusive and expects no increase in sales during the next year. The product is manufactured with a machine that was purchased seven years ago at a cost of $500,000. Currently, the machine has a book value of $150,000 but its market value is only $30,000. The machine is expected to last another three years, after which it will have no salvage value. The annual activity is 200,000 machine hours and each product requires 0.20 machine hours. Fixed overhead includes depreciation. Last year, the production costs per unit were as follows:

Direct materials	$0.20
Direct labour	0.12
Variable overhead	0.08
Fixed overhead	0.15
Total cost per unit	$0.55

The company president is considering replacing the old machine with a new one that would cost $400,000. The new machine is expected to last five years. At the end of that period, the salvage value will be $50,000. The president expects to save 10% of the company's total variable costs with the new machine.

Instructions

Investment NPV: $(219,065)

Assume that the company's desired rate of return is 12%. Using the net present value method, determine if the company should replace the old machine with the new one, and briefly explain why or why not. Show your calculations.

(adapted from CGA-Canada, now CPA Canada)

(SO 2)
Calculate the net present value and apply the decision rule.

P13-39B   Vorteck Inc. manufactures snowsuits. Vorteck is considering purchasing a new sewing machine at a cost of $2.5 million. Its existing machine was purchased five years ago at a price of $1.8 million, and six months ago Vorteck spent $55,000 to keep it operational. The existing sewing machine can be sold today for $260,000. The new sewing machine would require a one-time, $85,000 training cost. Operating costs would decrease by the following amounts for years 1 to 7:

Year 1	$390,000
2	400,000
3	411,000
4	426,000
5	434,000
6	435,000
7	436,000

The new sewing machine would be depreciated according to the declining-balance method at a rate of 20%. The salvage value is expected to be $380,000. This new equipment would require maintenance costs of $95,000 at the end of the fifth year. The cost of capital is 9%.

Instructions

Purchase NPV = $(85,293)

Use the net present value method to determine whether Vorteck should purchase the new machine to replace the existing machine, and state the reason for your conclusion.

(adapted from CGA-Canada, now CPA Canada)

(SO 2, 3)
Calculate the net present value considering intangible benefits.

P13-40B   The Fort McMurchy Sanitation Company is considering the purchase of a garbage truck. The $77,000 price tag for a new truck would represent a major expenditure for the company. Kalia Vang, owner of the company, has compiled the following estimates in trying to determine whether she should purchase the garbage truck:

Initial cost	$77,000
Estimated useful life	10 years
Net annual cash flows	$12,000
Overhaul costs (end of year 5)	$ 7,000
Salvage value	$15,000

One of the company's employees is trying to convince Kalia that the truck has other merits that have not been considered in the initial estimates. First, the new truck will be more efficient, with lower maintenance and operating costs. Second, the new truck will be safer. Third, the new truck has the ability to handle recycled materials at the same time as garbage, thus offering a new revenue source. Estimates of the minimum value of these benefits are as follows:

Annual savings from reduced operating costs	$400
Annual savings from reduced maintenance costs	800
Additional annual net cash savings from reduced employee absence	500
Additional annual net cash inflows from recycling	300

The company's cost of capital is 10%.

Instructions

(a) Calculate the net present value, ignoring the additional benefits. Should Kalia purchase the truck?

(b) Calculate the net present value, including the additional benefits. Should Kalia purchase the truck?

(c) Suppose management has been overly optimistic in assessing the value of the additional benefits. At a minimum, how much would the additional benefits have to be worth in order for Kalia to purchase the truck?

(a) NPV $(1,828)

(b) NPV $10,461

P13-41B   Benjamin Corp. is thinking about opening a hockey camp in Barrie, Ontario. In order to start the camp, the company would need to purchase land, and build four ice rinks and a dormitory-type sleeping and dining facility to house 110 players. Each year, the camp would be run for eight sessions of one week each. The company would hire university hockey players as coaches. The camp attendees would be male and female hockey players aged 12 to 18. Property values in this area have enjoyed a steady increase in recent years. Benjamin Corp. expects that after using the facility for 20 years, the rinks will have to be dismantled, but the land and buildings will be worth more than they were originally purchased for. The following amounts have been estimated:

(SO 2)
Calculate the net present value with sensitivity analysis, and discuss findings.

Cost of land	$200,000
Cost to build rinks, dorm, and dining hall	$350,000
Annual cash inflows assuming 110 players and eight weeks	$700,000
Annual cash outflows	$570,000
Estimated useful life	20 years
Salvage value	$700,000
Discount rate	12%

Instructions

(a) Calculate the project's net present value.

(b) To evaluate how sensitive the project is to these estimates, assume that if only 90 players attend each week, revenues will be $570,000 and expenses will be $508,000. What is the net present value using these alternative estimates? Discuss your findings.

(c) Assuming the original facts, what is the net present value if the project is actually riskier than first assumed, and a 15% discount rate is more appropriate?

(d) Assume that during the first five years the annual net cash flows each year were only $65,000. At the end of the fifth year, the company is running low on cash, so management decides to sell the property for $668,000. What was the actual internal rate of return on the project? Explain how this return was possible given that the camp did not appear to be successful.

(a) NPV $348,458

(d) IRR 15%

P13-42B   Aqua Tech Testing is considering investing in a new testing device. It has two options. Option A would have an initial lower cost but would require a significant expenditure for rebuilding after five years. Option B would require no rebuilding expenditure, but its maintenance costs would be higher. Since the Option B machine is of a higher initial quality, the company expects it to have a salvage value at the end of its useful life. The company provided the following estimates:

(SO 2, 3, 4)
Calculate the net present value, profitability index, and internal rate of return.

	Option A	Option B
Initial cost	$ 90,000	$170,000
Annual cash inflows	180,000	140,000
Annual cash outflows	160,000	108,000
Cost to rebuild (end of year 5)	26,500	0
Salvage value	0	27,500
Estimated useful life	8 years	8 years

The company's cost of capital is 9%.

Instructions

(a) Calculate the (1) net present value, (2) profitability index, and (3) internal rate of return for each option. (*Hint:* To solve for the internal rate of return, experiment with alternative discount rates to arrive at a net present value of zero.)

(b) Determine which option the company should accept.

(a) (1) NPV A $3,473
      (3) IRR B 12%

P13-43B   ICA Corporation is reviewing an investment proposal. The schedule below presents the initial cost and estimates of the investment's book value at the end of each year, the net cash flows for each year, and the net income for each year. All cash flows are assumed to take place at the end of the year. The investment's salvage value at the end of each year is equal to its book value. There would be no salvage value at the end of the investment's life.

(SO 1, 2, 5)
Calculate the payback, annual rate of return, and net present value.

		Investment Proposal	
Year	Initial Cost and Book Value	Annual Cash Flows	Annual Net Income
0	$250,000		
1	170,000	$90,000	$25,000
2	140,000	75,000	27,000
3	90,000	60,000	29,000
4	45,000	40,000	31,000
5	0	30,000	33,000

ICA Corporation uses a 15% target rate of return for new investment proposals.

Instructions

(b) ARR 23.2%

(a) Calculate the cash payback period for this proposal.
(b) Calculate the annual rate of return for the investment.
(c) Calculate the net present value of the investment.

(adapted from CMA Canada, now CPA Canada)

(SO 2, 3, 4)
Calculate net present value, profitability index, and internal rate of return.

P13-44B Platteville Eye Clinic is considering investing in new optical-scanning equipment. It has two options: Option A would have an initial lower cost but would require a significant expenditure for rebuilding after 3 years. Option B would require no rebuilding expenditure, but its maintenance costs would be higher. Since the Option B machine is of initial higher quality, it is expected to have a salvage value at the end of its useful life. The following estimates were made of the cash flows. The company's cost of capital is 11%.

	Option A	Option B
Initial cost	$100,000	$160,000
Annual cash inflows	$ 56,000	$ 60,000
Annual cash outflows	$ 24,000	$ 24,000
Cost to rebuild (end of year 3)	$ 53,000	$ 0
Salvage value	$ 0	$ 24,000
Estimated useful life	6 years	6 years

Instructions

(a) (1) NPV A $(3,376)
(3) IRR B 12%

(a) Calculate the (1) net present value, (2) profitability index, and (3) internal rate of return for each option. (*Hint:* To solve for internal rate of return, experiment with alternative discount rates to arrive at a net present value of zero.)
(b) Which option should be accepted?

Cases

C13-45 Migami Company is considering the purchase of a new machine. The invoice price of the machine is $122,000, freight charges are estimated to be $3,000, and installation costs are expected to be $5,000. The salvage value of the new equipment is expected to be zero after a useful life of four years. Existing equipment could be retained and used for an additional four years if the company does not purchase the new machine. At that time, the equipment's salvage value would be zero. If the company purchases the new machine now, it would have to scrap the existing machine. Migami's accountant, Caitlyn Lahr, has accumulated the following data regarding annual sales and expenses with and without the new machine:

1. Without the new machine, Migami can sell 10,000 units of product annually at a per-unit selling price of $100. With the new machine, the number of units produced and sold would increase by 20%, and the selling price would remain the same.
2. The new machine is faster than the old machine, and it is more efficient in its use of materials. With the old machine, the gross profit rate is 28.5% of sales, whereas the rate will be 30% of sales with the new machine.

3. Annual selling expenses are $160,000 with the current equipment. Because the new equipment would produce a greater number of units to be sold, annual selling expenses are expected to increase by 10% if it is purchased.
4. Annual administrative expenses are expected to be $100,000 with the old machine, and $112,000 with the new machine.
5. The current book value of the existing machine is $40,000. Migami uses straight-line depreciation.
6. Migami management has a required rate of return of 15% on its investments and a payback period of no more than three years.

Instructions

(a) Calculate the annual rate of return for the new machine. (Round to two decimals.)
(b) Calculate the payback period for the new machine. (Round to two decimals.)
(c) Calculate the net present value of the new machine. (Round to the nearest dollar.)
(d) Based on your answer above, would you recommend that Migami buy the machine? Why or why not?

C13-46 The City of Craston has recently turned its attention to the apparent problem of a shortage of public transportation. In the last few years, more and more complaints have surfaced regarding inadequate bus services or difficulties in obtaining taxi services in the suburbs.

To operate a taxi in the city requires a special licence, which the city council's Taxi Commission issues. The Commission has issued no new licences since a freeze was instituted in 1995. There are currently only 1,750 licences still in use out of 4,500. The freedom exists, however, to transfer ownership of a licence. Such transactions have been recently quoted at $1,750 on the open market.

The addition of an airport on the outskirts of the city and three hotels in the city has created an apparent shift by taxi drivers to the core of the city and to the airport routes, resulting in poor services in the suburban areas. In contemplating this situation, the City of Craston recognizes two viable alternatives to correct the problem. Either the city can increase the number of buses serving the suburban areas, or it can issue additional taxi licences.

The Commission regulates taxi fares. Tax revenues are currently being collected from taxi drivers at a rate of 3% of gross revenues. The average trip is estimated to be 10 km. This year, the fare consists of a $1.10 flat rate plus $0.50 for every kilometre. It has been determined that each taxi driver collects revenues from 19,200 trips per year. The City estimates that in order to get the desired results, it would have to issue 85 licences at the given open market price. In addition, an incentive of $0.10 per kilometre would have to be placed on the flat rate trips originating in the suburban areas to attract taxi drivers. Accordingly, the ratio of suburban to core city and airport trips would be 1 to 4.

The other alternative cited above is to increase the number of buses serving the suburban areas. Public transit fares are $1 per ride. The City estimates that if it increased the number of buses, at a cost of $1.4 million, the number of single trips would increase by 1.5 million per year. The buses would have an expected life of five years, at which time their combined salvage value would equal $100,000. The buses would be depreciated on a straight-line basis. For the duration of five years, five additional workers would have to be employed, each at an annual salary of $30,000, and maintenance costs would increase by $36,000 per year.

So far, investigation of these alternatives has revealed that if additional taxi licences are issued, the public transit revenues will drop by $350,000 per year.

Instructions

The City of Craston has asked you to evaluate the two proposals and provide a recommendation. In your analysis, assume that the rates charged for public transit and taxi fares will remain constant for the five-year period and that all cash flows occur at year end. The City of Craston currently has a 13% required rate of return.

(adapted from CMA Canada, now CPA Canada)

C13-47 The owners of Les Tigres de Trois-Rivières hockey club are considering a deal with an older, established club whereby they can acquire the services of Pierre Luc, a very high scorer and great gate attraction, in exchange for Robert McCain (currently paid $15,000 annually). The established club would also receive $500,000 cash from Les Tigres. The owners' accountants have assembled the following data:

Estimated useful life of Luc	5 years
Estimated residual value of Luc	$20,000
Estimated useful life of McCain	5 years
Estimated residual value of McCain	None
Current cash offer for McCain received from another club	$50,000
Applicable desired rate of return	10%

Other information:

Year	Luc's Salary	Additional Gate Receipts Because of Luc	Additional Expenses of Handling Higher Volume
1	$60,000	$330,000	$33,000
2	70,000	300,000	30,000
3	80,000	200,000	20,000
4	80,000	100,000	10,000
5	72,000	40,000	4,000

Instructions

Based on your analysis of the data, recommend whether or not the club should acquire the services of Pierre Luc.

(adapted from CMA Canada, now CPA Canada)

C13-48 Lapides Ltd. is a small company that is currently analyzing capital expenditure proposals for the purchase of equipment. The capital budget is limited to $250,000, which Lapides believes is the maximum capital it can raise.

The financial adviser is preparing an analysis of four projects that the company is considering, as follows:

	Project A	Project B	Project C	Project D
Net initial investment:	$200,000	$190,000	$250,000	$210,000
Projected cash inflows:				
Year 1	$50,000	$40,000	$75,000	$75,000
2	50,000	50,000	75,000	75,000
3	50,000	70,000	60,000	60,000
4	50,000	75,000	80,000	40,000
5	50,000	75,000	100,000	20,000

Instructions

(a) Calculate the cash payback period for each of the four projects.

(b) Calculate the net present value for each project at a cost of capital of 12%.

(c) Which projects, if any, would you recommend funding, and why?

(adapted from CMA Canada, now CPA Canada)

C13-49 Ms. Cookie Corporation is a company specializing in selling cookies for fundraising activities. One year ago, the company purchased a special cookie-cutting machine. However, to have more efficient operations, Ms. Cookie is considering the purchase of a more advanced machine. The new machine would be acquired on December 31, 2016, and management expects that it would sell 1 million dozen cookies in each of the next six years. The selling price of the cookies is expected to average $5.15 per dozen.

Ms. Cookie has two options: continue to operate the old machine, or sell the old machine and purchase the new machine. The following information has been collected to help management decide which option is more profitable:

	Old Machine	New Machine
Original cost of machine at acquisition	$360,000	$520,000
Remaining useful life as of December 31, 2016	6 years	6 years
Expected annual cash operating expenses		
Variable cost per dozen	$ 0.80	$ 0.45
Total fixed costs	$ 60,000	$ 50,000
Estimated cash value of machine		
December 31, 2016	$ 80,000	$520,000
December 31, 2022	$ 20,000	$ 20,000

Assume that all operating revenues and expenses occur at the end of the year.

Instructions

Use the net present value method to determine whether Ms. Cookie should keep the old machine or acquire the new one. The company has a 10% required rate of return on its investments.

(adapted from CMA Canada, now CPA Canada)

C13-50 Tony Skateboards is considering building a new plant. Mahmoud Al-Saigh, the company's marketing manager, is an enthusiastic supporter of the new plant. Alyssa Minh, the company's chief financial officer, is not so sure that the plant is a good idea. Currently, the company purchases its skateboards from foreign manufacturers. The following figures were estimated for the construction of a new plant:

Cost of plant	$6,000,000
Annual cash inflows	$6,000,000
Annual cash outflows	$5,550,000
Estimated useful life	15 years
Salvage value	$1,000,000
Discount rate	8%

Mahmoud believes that these figures understate the true potential value of the plant. He suggests that by manufacturing its own skateboards the company will benefit from a "buy Canadian" patriotism. He also notes that the firm has had numerous quality problems with the skateboards manufactured by its suppliers. He suggests that the inconsistent quality has resulted in lost sales, increased warranty claims, and some costly lawsuits. Overall, he believes sales will be $250,000 higher each year than projected above, and that the savings from lower warranty costs and legal costs will be $100,000 per year. He also believes that the project is not as risky as assumed above, and that a 6% discount rate is more reasonable.

Instructions

(a) Calculate the project's net present value based on the original projections.

(b) Calculate the net present value including Mahmoud's estimates of the value of the intangible benefits, but still using the 8% discount rate.

(c) Calculate the net present value using the original estimates, but using the 6% discount rate that Mahmoud suggests is more appropriate.

(d) Comment on your findings.

C13-51 Impro Company operates in a province where corporate taxes and workers' compensation insurance rates have recently doubled. Impro's president has just assigned you the task of preparing an economic analysis and making a recommendation about whether or not to move the company's entire operation to New Brunswick. The president is slightly in favour of such a move because New Brunswick is his boyhood home and he also owns a fishing lodge there. You have just completed building your dream house, moved in, and sodded the lawn. Your children are all doing well in school and sports, and they and your spouse want no part of a move to New Brunswick. If the company does move, you will have to as well because the town where you now live is a one-industry community and you and your spouse will have to move

to have employment. Moving when everyone else does will cause you to take a big loss on the sale of your house. The same hardships will be suffered by your co-workers, and the town will be devastated.

In gathering the costs of moving versus not moving, you have a lot of freedom in the assumptions you make, the estimates you calculate, and the discount rates and time periods you project. You are in a position to influence the decision in a major way.

Instructions
Answer the following questions:
(a) Who are the stakeholders in this situation?
(b) What are the ethical issues in this situation?
(c) What would you do in this situation?

"All About You" Activity

C13-52 You are excited because your employer has offered you a promotion, with an increased salary. But it will mean you must relocate to Vancouver and you are concerned because you have heard a lot about the high cost of housing in that city.

Your employer will pay all your moving costs (including costs associated with the sale of your current home). You and your partner currently live in a two-bedroom condo in your city; if you sell it you will have about $100,000 after paying out the mortgage. Your partner is an accountant and expects to find a job at roughly the same salary as now within a few months of relocating.

After an initial visit to the city and talking to your new colleagues, you have narrowed your choices of accommodation down to two: a one-bed, one-bath loft-style condo in the downtown core in a very new and stylish building that is within walking distance of your new office and close to all the attractions or an older, more spacious two-bed, two-bath condo in a nearby suburb, which is located in a residential neighbourhood quite close to a shopping mall and public transit.

Here are some details about the two properties:

	Downtown condo	Suburban condo
Price	$529,000	$360,000
Condo fees, per month (includes heat and hot water)	$237	$360
Size	668 square feet	1,031 square feet
Annual property taxes	$2,231	$1,766
Cost of a monthly transit pass	$81	$110
Year built	2015	1988

Instructions
Consider what factors, both financial and personal, would help you to decide which property to buy.

Decision-Making at Current Designs

DM13-1 A company that manufactures recreational pedal boats has approached Mike Cichanowski to ask if he would be interested in using Current Designs' rotomould expertise and equipment to produce some of the pedal boat components. Mike is intrigued by the idea and thinks it would be an interesting way of complementing the present product line.

One of Mike's hesitations about the proposal is that the pedal boats are a different shape than the kayaks that Current Designs produces. As a result, the company would need to buy an additional rotomould oven in order to produce the pedal boat components. This project clearly involves risks, and Mike wants to make sure that the returns justify the risks. In this case, since this is a new venture, Mike thinks that a 15% discount rate is appropriate to use to evaluate the project.

As an intern at Current Designs, Mike has asked you to prepare an initial evaluation of this proposal. To aid in your analysis, he has provided the following information and assumptions.

1. The new rotomould oven will have a cost of $256,000, a salvage value of $0, and an 8-year useful life. Straight-line depreciation will be used.
2. The projected revenues, costs, and results for each of the 8 years of this project are as follows.

Sales		$220,000
Less:		
Manufacturing costs	$140,000	
Depreciation	32,000	
Shipping and administrative costs	22,000	194,000
Income before income taxes		26,000
Income tax expense		10,800
Net income		$ 15,200

Instructions

(a) Calculate the annual rate of return. (Round to two decimal places.)

(b) Calculate the payback period. (Round to two decimal places.)

(c) Calculate the NPV using a discount rate of 9%. (Round to nearest dollar.) Should the proposal be accepted using this discount rate?

(d) Calculate the NPV using a discount rate of 15%. (Round to nearest dollar.) Should the proposal be accepted using this discount rate?

Waterways Continuing Problem

(This is a continuation of the Waterways Problem from Chapters 1 through 12.)

WCP-13 Waterways puts much emphasis on cash flow when it plans for capital investments. The company chose its discount rate of 8% based on the rate of return it must pay its owners and creditors. Using that rate, Waterways then uses different methods to determine the best decisions for making capital outlays.

In 2016 Waterways is considering buying five new backhoes to replace the backhoes it now has with its installation and training division.

The new backhoes are faster, cost less to run, provide for more accurate trench digging, have comfort features for the operators, and have associated one-year maintenance agreements. The old backhoes are working well, but they do require considerable maintenance. The operators are very familiar with the old backhoes and would need to learn some new skills to use the new equipment.

The following information is available to use in deciding whether to purchase the new backhoes.

	Old Backhoes	New Backhoes
Purchase cost when new	$90,000	$200,000
Salvage value now	$42,000	None
Investment in major overhaul needed in next year	$55,000	None
Salvage value in 8 years	None	$ 50,000
Remaining life	8 years	8 years
Net cash flow generated each year	$25,250	$ 41,000

Instructions

(a) Using the following methods, evaluate whether to purchase the new equipment or overhaul the old equipment. (*Hint:* For the old machine, the initial investment is the cost of the overhaul. For the new machine, subtract the salvage value of the old machine to determine the initial cost of the investment.) Ignore income taxes in your analysis.

1. Use the net present value method for buying new or keeping the old.

2. Use the payback method for each choice. (*Hint:* For the old machine, evaluate the payback of an overhaul.)

3. Compare the profitability index for each choice.

4. Compare the internal rate of return for each choice to the required 8% discount rate.

(b) Are there any intangible benefits or negatives that would influence this decision?

(c) What decision would you make and why?

Answers to Self-Study Questions

1. d **2.** c **3.** d **4.** a **5.** b **6.** d **7.** d **8.** a **9.** c **10.** d

Remember to go back to the beginning of the chapter to check off your completed work!

←

APPENDIX 13A—TIME VALUE OF MONEY

TABLE 1
Future Value of 1
(Future Value of a Single Sum)

$$FVF_{n,i} = (1 + i)^n$$

(n) Periods	2%	2.5%	3%	4%	5%	6%	8%	9%	10%	11%	12%	15%
1	1.02000	1.02500	1.03000	1.04000	1.05000	1.06000	1.08000	1.09000	1.10000	1.11000	1.12000	1.15000
2	1.04040	1.05063	1.06090	1.08160	1.10250	1.12360	1.16640	1.18810	1.21000	1.23210	1.25440	1.32250
3	1.06121	1.07689	1.09273	1.12486	1.15763	1.19102	1.25971	1.29503	1.33100	1.36763	1.40493	1.52088
4	1.08243	1.10381	1.12551	1.16986	1.21551	1.26248	1.36049	1.41158	1.46410	1.51807	1.57352	1.74901
5	1.10408	1.13141	1.15927	1.21665	1.27628	1.33823	1.46933	1.53862	1.61051	1.68506	1.76234	2.01136
6	1.12616	1.15969	1.19405	1.26532	1.34010	1.41852	1.58687	1.67710	1.77156	1.87041	1.97382	2.31306
7	1.14869	1.18869	1.22987	1.31593	1.40710	1.50363	1.71382	1.82804	1.94872	2.07616	2.21068	2.66002
8	1.17166	1.21840	1.26677	1.36857	1.47746	1.59385	1.85093	1.99256	2.14359	2.30454	2.47596	3.05902
9	1.19509	1.24886	1.30477	1.42331	1.55133	1.68948	1.99900	2.17189	2.35795	2.55803	2.77308	3.51788
10	1.21899	1.28008	1.34392	1.48024	1.62889	1.79085	2.15892	2.36736	2.59374	2.83942	3.10585	4.04556
11	1.24337	1.31209	1.38423	1.53945	1.71034	1.89830	2.33164	2.58043	2.85312	3.15176	3.47855	4.65239
12	1.26824	1.34489	1.42576	1.60103	1.79586	2.01220	2.51817	2.81267	3.13843	3.49845	3.89598	5.35025
13	1.29361	1.37851	1.46853	1.66507	1.88565	2.13293	2.71962	3.06581	3.45227	3.88328	4.36349	6.15279
14	1.31948	1.41297	1.51259	1.73168	1.97993	2.26090	2.93719	3.34173	3.79750	4.31044	4.88711	7.07571
15	1.34587	1.44830	1.55797	1.80094	2.07893	2.39656	3.17217	3.64248	4.17725	4.78459	5.47357	8.13706
16	1.37279	1.48451	1.60471	1.87298	2.18287	2.54035	3.42594	3.97031	4.59497	5.31089	6.13039	9.35762
17	1.40024	1.52162	1.65285	1.94790	2.29202	2.69277	3.70002	4.32763	5.05447	5.89509	6.86604	10.76126
18	1.42825	1.55966	1.70243	2.02582	2.40662	2.85434	3.99602	4.71712	5.55992	6.54355	7.68997	12.37545
19	1.45681	1.59865	1.75351	2.10685	2.52695	3.02560	4.31570	5.14166	6.11591	7.26334	8.61276	14.23177
20	1.48595	1.63862	1.80611	2.19112	2.65330	3.20714	4.66096	5.60441	6.72750	8.06231	9.64629	16.36654
21	1.51567	1.67958	1.86029	2.27877	2.78596	3.39956	5.03383	6.10881	7.40025	8.94917	10.80385	18.82152
22	1.54598	1.72157	1.91610	2.36992	2.92526	3.60354	5.43654	6.65860	8.14028	9.93357	12.10031	21.64475
23	1.57690	1.76461	1.97359	2.46472	3.07152	3.81975	5.87146	7.25787	8.95430	11.02627	13.55235	24.89146
24	1.60844	1.80873	2.03279	2.56330	3.22510	4.04893	6.34118	7.91108	9.84973	12.23916	15.17863	28.62518
25	1.64061	1.85394	2.09378	2.66584	3.38635	4.29187	6.84847	8.62308	10.83471	13.58546	17.00006	32.91895
26	1.67342	1.90029	2.15659	2.77247	3.55567	4.54938	7.39635	9.39916	11.91818	15.07986	19.04007	37.85680
27	1.70689	1.94780	2.22129	2.88337	3.73346	4.82235	7.98806	10.24508	13.10999	16.73865	21.32488	43.53532
28	1.74102	1.99650	2.28793	2.99870	3.92013	5.11169	8.62711	11.16714	14.42099	18.57990	23.88387	50.06561
29	1.77584	2.04641	2.35657	3.11865	4.11614	5.41839	9.31727	12.17218	15.86309	20.62369	26.74993	57.57545
30	1.81136	2.09757	2.42726	3.24340	4.32194	5.74349	10.06266	13.26768	17.44940	22.89230	29.95992	66.21177
31	1.84759	2.15001	2.50008	3.37313	4.53804	6.08810	10.86767	14.46177	19.19434	25.41045	33.55511	76.14354
32	1.88454	2.20376	2.57508	3.50806	4.76494	6.45339	11.73708	15.76333	21.11378	28.20560	37.58173	87.56507
33	1.92223	2.25885	2.65234	3.64838	5.00319	6.84059	12.67605	17.18203	23.22515	31.30821	42.09153	100.69983
34	1.96068	2.31532	2.73191	3.79432	5.25335	7.25103	13.69013	18.72841	25.54767	34.75212	47.14252	115.80480
35	1.99989	2.37321	2.81386	3.94609	5.51602	7.68609	14.78534	20.41397	28.10244	38.57485	52.79962	133.17552
36	2.03989	2.43254	2.89828	4.10393	5.79182	8.14725	15.96817	22.25123	30.91268	42.81808	59.13557	153.15185
37	2.08069	2.49335	2.98523	4.26809	6.08141	8.63609	17.24563	24.25384	34.00395	47.52807	66.23184	176.12463
38	2.12230	2.55568	3.07478	4.43881	6.38548	9.15425	18.62528	26.43668	37.40434	52.75616	74.17966	202.54332
39	2.16474	2.61957	3.16703	4.61637	6.70475	9.70351	20.11530	28.81598	41.14479	58.55934	83.08122	232.92482
40	2.20804	2.68506	3.26204	4.80102	7.03999	10.28572	21.72452	31.40942	45.25926	65.00087	93.05097	267.86355

TABLE 2
Present Value of 1
(Present Value of a Single Sum)

$$PVF_{n,i} = \frac{1}{(1 + i)^n} = (1 + i)^{-n}$$

(n) Periods	2%	2.5%	3%	4%	5%	6%	8%	9%	10%	11%	12%	15%
1	0.98039	0.97561	0.97087	0.96154	0.95238	0.94340	0.92593	0.91743	0.90909	0.90090	0.89286	0.86957
2	0.96117	0.95181	0.94260	0.92456	0.90703	0.89000	0.85734	0.84168	0.82645	0.81162	0.79719	0.75614
3	0.94232	0.92860	0.91514	0.88900	0.86384	0.83962	0.79383	0.77218	0.75132	0.73119	0.71178	0.65752
4	0.92385	0.90595	0.88849	0.85480	0.82270	0.79209	0.73503	0.70843	0.68301	0.65873	0.63552	0.57175
5	0.90573	0.88385	0.86261	0.82193	0.78353	0.74726	0.68058	0.64993	0.62092	0.59345	0.56743	0.49719
6	0.88797	0.86230	0.83748	0.79031	0.74622	0.70496	0.63017	0.59627	0.56447	0.53464	0.50663	0.43233
7	0.87056	0.84127	0.81309	0.75992	0.71068	0.66506	0.58349	0.54703	0.51316	0.48166	0.45235	0.37594
8	0.85349	0.82075	0.78941	0.73069	0.67684	0.62741	0.54027	0.50187	0.46651	0.43393	0.40388	0.32690
9	0.83676	0.80073	0.76642	0.70259	0.64461	0.59190	0.50025	0.46043	0.42410	0.39092	0.36061	0.28426
10	0.82035	0.78120	0.74409	0.67556	0.61391	0.55839	0.46319	0.42241	0.38554	0.35218	0.32197	0.24718
11	0.80426	0.76214	0.72242	0.64958	0.58468	0.52679	0.42888	0.38753	0.35049	0.31728	0.28748	0.21494
12	0.78849	0.74356	0.70138	0.62460	0.55684	0.49697	0.39711	0.35554	0.31863	0.28584	0.25668	0.18691
13	0.77303	0.72542	0.68095	0.60057	0.53032	0.46884	0.36770	0.32618	0.28966	0.25751	0.22917	0.16253
14	0.75788	0.70773	0.66112	0.57748	0.50507	0.44230	0.34046	0.29925	0.26333	0.23199	0.20462	0.14133
15	0.74301	0.69047	0.64186	0.55526	0.48102	0.41727	0.31524	0.27454	0.23939	0.20900	0.18270	0.12289
16	0.72845	0.67362	0.62317	0.53391	0.45811	0.39365	0.29189	0.25187	0.21763	0.18829	0.16312	0.10687
17	0.71416	0.65720	0.60502	0.51337	0.43630	0.37136	0.27027	0.23107	0.19785	0.16963	0.14564	0.09293
18	0.70016	0.64117	0.58739	0.49363	0.41552	0.35034	0.25025	0.21199	0.17986	0.15282	0.13004	0.08081
19	0.68643	0.62553	0.57029	0.47464	0.39573	0.33051	0.23171	0.19449	0.16351	0.13768	0.11611	0.07027
20	0.67297	0.61027	0.55368	0.45639	0.37689	0.31180	0.21455	0.17843	0.14864	0.12403	0.10367	0.06110
21	0.65978	0.59539	0.53755	0.43883	0.35894	0.29416	0.19866	0.16370	0.13513	0.11174	0.09256	0.05313
22	0.64684	0.58086	0.52189	0.42196	0.34185	0.27751	0.18394	0.15018	0.12285	0.10067	0.08264	0.04620
23	0.63416	0.56670	0.50669	0.40573	0.32557	0.26180	0.17032	0.13778	0.11168	0.09069	0.07379	0.04017
24	0.62172	0.55288	0.49193	0.39012	0.31007	0.24698	0.15770	0.12641	0.10153	0.08170	0.06588	0.03493
25	0.60953	0.53939	0.47761	0.37512	0.29530	0.23300	0.14602	0.11597	0.09230	0.07361	0.05882	0.03038
26	0.59758	0.52623	0.46369	0.36069	0.28124	0.21981	0.13520	0.10639	0.08391	0.06631	0.05252	0.02642
27	0.58586	0.51340	0.45019	0.34682	0.26785	0.20737	0.12519	0.09761	0.07628	0.05974	0.04689	0.02297
28	0.57437	0.50088	0.43708	0.33348	0.25509	0.19563	0.11591	0.08955	0.06934	0.05382	0.04187	0.01997
29	0.56311	0.48866	0.42435	0.32065	0.24295	0.18456	0.10733	0.08216	0.06304	0.04849	0.03738	0.01737
30	0.55207	0.47674	0.41199	0.30832	0.23138	0.17411	0.09938	0.07537	0.05731	0.04368	0.03338	0.01510
31	0.54125	0.46511	0.39999	0.29646	0.22036	0.16425	0.09202	0.06915	0.05210	0.03935	0.02980	0.01313
32	0.53063	0.45377	0.38834	0.28506	0.20987	0.15496	0.08520	0.06344	0.04736	0.03545	0.02661	0.01142
33	0.52023	0.44270	0.37703	0.27409	0.19987	0.14619	0.07889	0.05820	0.04306	0.03194	0.02376	0.00993
34	0.51003	0.43191	0.36604	0.26355	0.19035	0.13791	0.07305	0.05340	0.03914	0.02878	0.02121	0.00864
35	0.50003	0.42137	0.35538	0.25342	0.18129	0.13011	0.06763	0.04899	0.03558	0.02592	0.01894	0.00751
36	0.49022	0.41109	0.34503	0.24367	0.17266	0.12274	0.06262	0.04494	0.03235	0.02335	0.01691	0.00653
37	0.48061	0.40107	0.33498	0.23430	0.16444	0.11579	0.05799	0.04123	0.02941	0.02104	0.01510	0.00568
38	0.47119	0.39128	0.32523	0.22529	0.15661	0.10924	0.05369	0.03783	0.02674	0.01896	0.01348	0.00494
39	0.46195	0.38174	0.31575	0.21662	0.14915	0.10306	0.04971	0.03470	0.02430	0.01708	0.01204	0.00429
40	0.45289	0.37243	0.30656	0.20829	0.14205	0.09722	0.04603	0.03184	0.02210	0.01538	0.01075	0.00373

TABLE 3
Future Value of an Ordinary Annuity of 1

$$fVF - OA_{n,i} = \frac{(1 + i)^n - 1}{i}$$

(n) Periods	2%	2.5%	3%	4%	5%	6%	8%	9%	10%	11%	12%	15%
1	1.00000	1.00000	1.00000	1.00000	1.00000	1.00000	1.00000	1.00000	1.00000	1.00000	1.00000	1.00000
2	2.02000	2.02500	2.03000	2.04000	2.05000	2.06000	2.08000	2.09000	2.10000	2.11000	2.12000	2.15000
3	3.06040	3.07563	3.09090	3.12160	3.15250	3.18360	3.24640	3.27810	3.31000	3.34210	3.37440	3.47250
4	4.12161	4.15252	4.18363	4.24646	4.31013	4.37462	4.50611	4.57313	4.64100	4.70973	4.77933	4.99338
5	5.20404	5.25633	5.30914	5.41632	5.52563	5.63709	5.86660	5.98471	6.10510	6.22780	6.35285	6.74238
6	6.30812	6.38774	6.46841	6.63298	6.80191	6.97532	7.33592	7.52334	7.71561	7.91286	8.11519	8.75374
7	7.43428	7.54743	7.66246	7.89829	8.14201	8.39384	8.92280	9.20044	9.48717	9.78327	10.08901	11.06680
8	8.58297	8.73612	8.89234	9.21423	9.54911	9.89747	10.63663	11.02847	11.43589	11.85943	12.29969	13.72682
9	9.75463	9.95452	10.15911	10.58280	11.02656	11.49132	12.48756	13.02104	13.57948	14.16397	14.77566	16.78584
10	10.94972	11.20338	11.46388	12.00611	12.57789	13.18079	14.48656	15.19293	15.93743	16.72201	17.54874	20.30372
11	12.16872	12.48347	12.80780	13.48635	14.20679	14.97164	16.64549	17.56029	18.53117	19.56143	20.65458	24.34928
12	13.41209	13.79555	14.19203	15.02581	15.91713	16.86994	18.97713	20.14072	21.38428	22.71319	24.13313	29.00167
13	14.68033	15.14044	15.61779	16.62684	17.71298	18.88214	21.49530	22.95339	24.52271	26.21164	28.02911	34.35192
14	15.97394	16.51895	17.08632	18.29191	19.59863	21.01507	24.21492	26.01919	27.97498	30.09492	32.39260	40.50471
15	17.29342	17.93193	18.59891	20.02359	21.57856	23.27597	27.15211	29.36092	31.77248	34.40536	37.27971	47.58041
16	18.63929	19.38022	20.15688	21.82453	23.65749	25.67253	30.32428	33.00340	35.94973	39.18995	42.75328	55.71747
17	20.01207	20.86473	21.76159	23.69751	25.84037	28.21288	33.75023	36.97371	40.54470	44.50084	48.88367	65.07509
18	21.41231	22.38635	23.41444	25.64541	28.13238	30.90565	37.45024	41.30134	45.59917	50.39593	55.74971	75.83636
19	22.84056	23.94601	25.11687	27.67123	30.53900	33.75999	41.44626	46.01846	51.15900	56.93949	63.43968	88.21181
20	24.29737	25.54466	26.87037	29.77808	33.06595	36.78559	45.76196	51.16012	57.27500	64.20283	72.05244	102.44358
21	25.78332	27.18327	28.67649	31.96920	35.71925	39.99273	50.42292	56.76453	64.00250	72.26514	81.69874	118.81012
22	27.29898	28.86286	30.53678	34.24797	38.50521	43.39229	55.45676	62.87334	71.40275	81.21431	92.50258	137.63164
23	28.84496	30.58443	32.45288	36.61789	41.43048	46.99583	60.89330	69.53194	79.54302	91.14788	104.60289	159.27638
24	30.42186	32.34904	34.42647	39.08260	44.50200	50.81558	66.76476	76.78981	88.49733	102.17415	118.15524	184.16784
25	32.03030	34.15776	36.45926	41.64591	47.72710	54.86451	73.10594	84.70090	98.34706	114.41331	133.33387	212.79302
26	33.67091	36.01171	38.55304	44.31174	51.11345	59.15638	79.95442	93.32398	109.18177	127.99877	150.33393	245.71197
27	35.34432	37.91200	40.70963	47.08421	54.66913	63.70577	87.35077	102.72314	121.09994	143.07864	169.37401	283.56877
28	37.05121	39.85980	42.93092	49.96758	58.40258	68.52811	95.33883	112.96822	134.20994	159.81729	190.69889	327.10408
29	38.79223	41.85630	45.21885	52.96629	62.32271	73.63980	103.96594	124.13536	148.63093	178.39719	214.58275	377.16969
30	40.56808	43.90270	47.57542	56.08494	66.43885	79.05819	113.28321	136.30754	164.49402	199.02088	241.33268	434.74515
31	42.37944	46.00027	50.00268	59.32834	70.76079	84.80168	123.34587	149.57522	181.94343	221.91317	271.29261	500.95692
32	44.22703	48.15028	52.50276	62.70147	75.29883	90.88978	134.21354	164.03699	201.13777	247.32362	304.84772	577.10046
33	46.11157	50.35403	55.07784	66.20953	80.06377	97.34316	145.95062	179.80032	222.25154	275.52922	342.42945	664.66553
34	48.03380	52.61289	57.73018	69.85791	85.06696	104.18376	158.62667	196.98234	245.47670	306.83744	384.52098	765.36535
35	49.99448	54.92821	60.46208	73.65222	90.32031	111.43478	172.31680	215.71076	271.02437	341.58955	431.66350	881.17016
36	51.99437	57.30141	63.27594	77.59831	95.83632	119.12087	187.10215	236.12472	299.12681	380.16441	484.46312	1,014.34568
37	54.03425	59.73395	66.17422	81.70225	101.62814	127.26812	203.07032	258.37595	330.03949	422.98249	543.59869	1,167.49753
38	56.11494	62.22730	69.15945	85.97034	107.70955	135.90421	220.31595	282.62978	364.04343	470.51056	609.83053	1,343.62216
39	58.23724	64.78298	72.23423	90.40915	114.09502	145.05846	238.94122	309.06646	401.44778	523.26673	684.01020	1,546.16549
40	60.40198	67.40255	75.40126	95.02552	120.79977	154.76197	259.05652	337.88245	442.59256	581.82607	767.09142	1,779.09031

TABLE 4
Present Value of an Ordinary Annuity of 1

$$PVF - OA_{n,i} = \frac{1 = \dfrac{1}{(1+i)^n}}{i}$$

(n) Periods	2%	2.5%	3%	4%	5%	6%	8%	9%	10%	11%	12%	15%
1	0.98039	0.97561	0.97087	0.96154	0.95238	0.94340	0.92593	0.91743	0.90909	0.90090	0.89286	0.86957
2	1.94156	1.92742	1.91347	1.88609	1.85941	1.83339	1.78326	1.75911	1.73554	1.71252	1.69005	1.62571
3	2.88388	2.85602	2.82861	2.77509	2.72325	2.67301	2.57710	2.53129	2.48685	2.44371	2.40183	2.28323
4	3.80773	3.76197	3.71710	3.62990	3.54595	3.46511	3.31213	3.23972	3.16986	3.10245	3.03735	2.85498
5	4.71346	4.64583	4.57971	4.45182	4.32948	4.21236	3.99271	3.88965	3.79079	3.69590	3.60478	3.35216
6	5.60143	5.50813	5.41719	5.24214	5.07569	4.91732	4.62288	4.48592	4.35526	4.23054	4.11141	3.78448
7	6.47199	6.34939	6.23028	6.00205	5.78637	5.58238	5.20637	5.03295	4.86842	4.71220	4.56376	4.16042
8	7.32548	7.17014	7.01969	6.73274	6.46321	6.20979	5.74664	5.53482	5.33493	5.14612	4.96764	4.48732
9	8.16224	7.97087	7.78611	7.43533	7.10782	6.80169	6.24689	5.99525	5.75902	5.53705	5.32825	4.77158
10	8.98259	8.75206	8.53020	8.11090	7.72173	7.36009	6.71008	6.41766	6.14457	5.88923	5.65022	5.01877
11	9.78685	9.51421	9.25262	8.76048	8.30641	7.88687	7.13896	6.80519	6.49506	6.20652	5.93770	5.23371
12	10.57534	10.25776	9.95400	9.38507	8.86325	8.38384	7.53608	7.16073	6.81369	6.49236	6.19437	5.42062
13	11.34837	10.98319	10.63496	9.98565	9.39357	8.85268	7.90378	7.48690	7.10336	6.74987	6.42355	5.58315
14	12.10625	11.69091	11.29607	10.56312	9.89864	9.29498	8.24424	7.78615	7.36669	6.98187	6.62817	5.72448
15	12.84926	12.38138	11.93794	11.11839	10.37966	9.71225	8.55948	8.06069	7.60608	7.19087	6.81086	5.84737
16	13.57771	13.05500	12.56110	11.65230	10.83777	10.10590	8.85137	8.31256	7.82371	7.37916	6.97399	5.95423
17	14.29187	13.71220	13.16612	12.16567	11.27407	10.47726	9.12164	8.54363	8.02155	7.54879	7.11963	6.04716
18	14.99203	14.35336	13.75351	12.65930	11.68959	10.82760	9.37189	8.75563	8.20141	7.70162	7.24967	6.12797
19	15.67846	14.97889	14.32380	13.13394	12.08532	11.15812	9.60360	8.95012	8.36492	7.83929	7.36578	6.19823
20	16.35143	15.58916	14.87747	13.59033	12.46221	11.46992	9.81815	9.12855	8.51356	7.96333	7.46944	6.25933
21	17.01121	16.18455	15.41502	14.02916	12.82115	11.76408	10.01680	9.29224	8.64869	8.07507	7.56200	6.31246
22	17.65805	16.76541	15.93692	14.45112	13.16300	12.04158	10.20074	9.44243	8.77154	8.17574	7.64465	6.35866
23	18.29220	17.33211	16.44361	14.85684	13.48857	12.30338	10.37106	9.58021	8.88322	8.26643	7.71843	6.39884
24	18.91393	17.88499	16.93554	15.24696	13.79864	12.55036	10.52876	9.70661	8.98474	8.34814	7.78432	6.43377
25	19.52346	18.42438	17.41315	15.62208	14.09394	12.78336	10.67478	9.82258	9.07704	8.42174	7.84314	6.46415
26	20.12104	18.95061	17.87684	15.98277	14.37519	13.00317	10.80998	9.92897	9.16095	8.48806	7.89566	6.49056
27	20.70690	19.46401	18.32703	16.32959	14.64303	13.21053	10.93516	10.02658	9.23722	8.54780	7.94255	6.51353
28	21.28127	19.96489	18.76411	16.66306	14.89813	13.40616	11.05108	10.11613	9.30657	8.60162	7.98442	6.53351
29	21.84438	20.45355	19.18845	16.98371	15.14107	13.59072	11.15841	10.19828	9.36961	8.65011	8.02181	6.55088
30	22.39646	20.93029	19.60044	17.29203	15.37245	13.76483	11.25778	10.27365	9.42691	8.69379	8.05518	6.56598
31	22.93770	21.39541	20.00043	17.58849	15.59281	13.92909	11.34980	10.34280	9.47901	8.73315	8.08499	6.57911
32	23.46833	21.84918	20.38877	17.87355	15.80268	14.08404	11.43500	10.40624	9.52638	8.76860	8.11159	6.59053
33	23.98856	22.29188	20.76579	18.14765	16.00255	14.23023	11.51389	10.46444	9.56943	8.80054	8.13535	6.60046
34	24.49859	22.72379	21.13184	18.41120	16.19290	14.36814	11.58693	10.51784	9.60858	8.82932	8.15656	6.60910
35	24.99862	23.14516	21.48722	18.66461	16.37419	14.49825	11.65457	10.56682	9.64416	8.85524	8.17550	6.61661
36	25.48884	23.55625	21.83225	18.90828	16.54685	14.62099	11.71719	10.61176	9.67651	8.87859	8.19241	6.62314
37	25.96945	23.95732	22.16724	19.14258	16.71129	14.73678	11.77518	10.65299	9.70592	8.89963	8.20751	6.62882
38	26.44064	24.34860	22.49246	19.36786	16.86789	14.84602	11.82887	10.69082	9.73265	8.91859	8.22099	6.63375
39	26.90259	24.73034	22.80822	19.58448	17.01704	14.94907	11.87858	10.72552	9.75696	8.93567	8.23303	6.63805
40	27.35548	25.10278	23.11477	19.79277	17.15909	15.04630	11.92461	10.75736	9.77905	8.95105	8.24378	6.64178

Company Index

Subject Index   Boldface indicates key terms and definitions

Photo Credits

RAPID REVIEW
Chapter Content

MANAGERIAL ACCOUNTING (Chapter 1)

Characteristics of Managerial Accounting

Primary Users	Internal users
Reports	Internal reports issued as needed
Purpose	Special purpose for a particular user
Content	Pertains to subunits, may be detailed, use of relevant data
Verification	No independent audits

MANAGERIAL COST CONCEPTS AND COST BEHAVIOUR ANALYSIS (Chapter 2)

Types of Manufacturing Costs

Direct materials	Raw materials directly associated with finished product
Direct labour	Work of employees directly associated with turning raw materials into finished product
Manufacturing overhead	Costs indirectly associated with manufacture of finished product

Types of Cost Behaviours

Variable costs	Vary in total directly and proportionately with changes in activity level
Fixed costs	Remain the same in total regardless of change in activity level
Mixed costs	Contain both a fixed and a variable element

JOB-ORDER AND PROCESS COST ACCOUNTING (Chapters 3 and 4)

Types of Accounting Systems

Job-order	Costs are assigned to each unit or each batch of goods
Process cost	Costs are applied to similar products that are mass-produced in a continuous fashion

Job-Order and Process Cost Flow

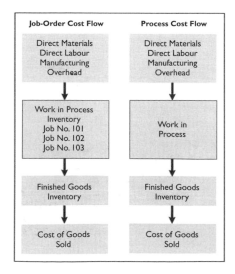

ACTIVITY-BASED COSTING (Chapter 5)

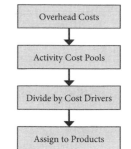

Activity-based costing involves the following four steps:

1. Identify and classify the major activities involved in the manufacture of specific products, and allocate the manufacturing overhead costs to the appropriate cost pools.
2. Identify the cost driver that has a strong correlation to the costs accumulated in the cost pool.
3. Compute the overhead rate for each cost driver.
4. Assign manufacturing overhead costs for each cost pool to products, using the overhead rates (cost per driver).

DECISION-MAKING: COST-VOLUME-PROFIT (Chapter 6)

CVP Income Statement Format

	Total	Per Unit
Sales	$xx	$xx
Variable cost	xx	xx
Contribution margin	xx	$xx
Fixed costs	xx	
Net income	$xx	

Contribution margin per unit	=	Unit selling price	−	Unit variable costs

Break-even point in units	=	Fixed costs	÷	Unit contribution margin*

Break-even point in dollars	=	Fixed costs	÷	Contribution margin ratio*

Required sales in units for target net income	=	(Fixed costs + Target net income)	÷	Contribution margin per unit

Degree of operating leverage	=	Contribution margin	÷	Operating income

*For multiple products, use weighted-average.

INCREMENTAL ANALYSIS (Chapter 7)

1. Identify the relevant costs associated with each alternative. **Relevant costs** are those costs and revenues that differ across alternatives. Choose the alternative that maximizes net cash flow.
2. **Opportunity costs** are those benefits that are given up when one alternative is chosen instead of another one. Opportunity costs are relevant costs.
3. **Sunk costs** have already been incurred and will not be changed or avoided by any future decision. Sunk costs are not relevant costs.

ALTERNATIVE INVENTORY COSTING METHODS (Chapter 8)

Type of cost	Absorption costing	Variable costing	Normal costing	Throughput costing
Direct materials	$x	$x	$x	$x
Direct labour	y	y	y	—
Variable manufacturing overhead	z	z	z	—
Fixed manufacturing overhead (Total FC/ Total units produced)	FC/unit	—	PFOHR*-FC/unit	—
Manufacturing cost per unit	$x+y+z+FC/unit	$x+y+z	$x+y+z+PFOHR-FC/unit	$x

*Predetermined fixed overhead rate.

	Net income
Production = Sales	Absorption = Variable
Production > Sales	Absorption > Variable
Production < Sales	Absorption < Variable